19 EDITION

Basic Marketing

A Marketing Strategy Planning Approach

William D. Perreault, Jr., Ph.D.
UNIVERSITY OF NORTH CAROLINA

Joseph P. Cannon, Ph.D.
COLORADO STATE UNIVERSITY

E. Jerome McCarthy, Ph.D.
MICHIGAN STATE UNIVERSITY

McGraw-Hill Irwin

McGraw-Hill Irwin

BASIC MARKETING: A MARKETING STRATEGY PLANNING APPROACH, NINETEENTH EDITION

Published by McGraw-Hill/Irwin, a business unit of The McGraw-Hill Companies, Inc., 1221 Avenue of the Americas, New York, NY, 10020.

Some ancillaries, including electronic and print components, may not be available to customers outside the United States.

This book is printed on acid-free paper.

1 2 3 4 5 6 7 8 9 0 DOW/DOW 1 0 9 8 7 6 5 4 3

ISBN 978-125-906076-2
MHID 125-906076-4

All credits appearing on page or at the end of the book are considered to be an extension of the copyright page.

The Internet addresses listed in the text were accurate at the time of publication. The inclusion of a website does not indicate an endorsement by the authors or McGraw-Hill, and McGraw-Hill does not guarantee the accuracy of the information presented at these sites.

www.mhhe.com

Authors of Basic Marketing, 19/e

William D. Perreault, Jr.

William D. Perreault, Jr., is Kenan Professor of Business at the University of North Carolina. Dr. Perreault is the recipient of the two most prestigious awards in his field: the American Marketing Association Distinguished Educator Award and the Academy of Marketing Science Outstanding Educator Award. He also was selected for the Churchill Award, which honors career impact on marketing research. He was editor of the *Journal of Marketing Research* and has been on the review board of the *Journal of Marketing* and other journals.

The Decision Sciences Institute has recognized Dr. Perreault for innovations in marketing education, and at UNC he has received several awards for teaching excellence. His books include two other widely used texts: *Basic Marketing* and *The Marketing Game!*

Dr. Perreault is a past president of the American Marketing Association Academic Council and served as chair of an advisory committee to the U.S. Census Bureau and as a trustee of the Marketing Science Institute. He has also worked as a consultant to organizations that range from GE and IBM to the Federal Trade Commission and Venezuelan Ministry of Education.

Joseph P. Cannon

Joseph P. Cannon is professor of marketing at Colorado State University. He has also taught at the University of North Carolina at Chapel Hill, Emory University, Instituto de Empresa (Madrid, Spain), INSEAD (Fontainebleau, France), and Thammasat University (Bangkok, Thailand). He has received several teaching awards and honors.

Dr. Cannon's research has been published in the *Journal of Marketing, Journal of Marketing Research, Journal of the Academy of Marketing Science, Journal of Operations Management, Journal of Personal Selling and Sales Management, Journal of Public Policy and Marketing, Antitrust Bulletin,* and *the Academy of Management Review* among others. He is a two-time recipient of the Louis W. and Rhona L. Stern Award for high-impact research on interorganizational issues. He has also written many teaching cases. He has served on the editorial review boards of the *Journal of Marketing, Journal of the Academy of Marketing Science, Journal of Personal Selling and Sales Management,* and *Journal of Marketing Education.* He has received several distinguished reviewer awards. He served as chair of the American Marketing Association's Interorganizational Special Interest Group (IOSIG). Before entering academics, Dr. Cannon worked for six years in sales and marketing for Eastman Kodak Company.

E. Jerome McCarthy

E. Jerome McCarthy received his Ph.D. from the University of Minnesota and was a Ford Foundation Fellow at the Harvard Business School. He has taught at the Universities of Oregon, Notre Dame, and Michigan State. He was honored with the American Marketing Association's Trailblazer Award in 1987, and he was voted one of the "top five" leaders in marketing thought by marketing educators.

Besides publishing various articles, he is the author of books on data processing and social issues in marketing. He has been a frequent presenter at marketing conferences in the United States and internationally.

In addition to his academic interests, Dr. McCarthy has been involved in guiding the growth of organizations in the United States and overseas—both as a consultant and as a director. He has also been active in executive education. However, throughout his career, his primary interests have been in (1) "converting" students to marketing and effective marketing strategy planning and (2) preparing teaching materials to help others do the same. This is why he has spent a large part of his career developing and improving marketing texts to reflect the most current thinking in the field.

Preface

Basic Marketing Is Designed to Satisfy *Your* Needs

This book is about marketing and marketing strategy planning. And, at its essence, marketing strategy planning is about figuring out how to do a superior job of satisfying customers. We take that point of view seriously and believe in practicing what we preach. So you can trust that this new edition of *Basic Marketing*—and all of the other teaching and learning materials that accompany it—will satisfy your needs. We're excited about this 19th edition of *Basic Marketing* and we hope that you will be as well.

In developing this edition, we've made hundreds of big and small additions, changes, and improvements in the text and all of the supporting materials that accompany it. We'll highlight some of those changes in this preface, but first it's useful to put this newest edition in a longer-term perspective.

Building on Pioneering Strengths

Basic Marketing pioneered an innovative structure—using the "four Ps" with a managerial approach—for the introductory marketing course. It quickly became one of the most widely used business textbooks ever published because it organized the best ideas about marketing so that readers could both understand and apply them. The unifying focus of these ideas is: how does a marketing manager decide which customers to target, and what is the best way to meet their needs?

Over many editions of *Basic Marketing,* there have been constant changes in marketing management and the market environment. As a result, we have made ongoing changes to the text to reflect marketing's best practices and ideas. Throughout all of these changes, *Basic Marketing* and the supporting materials that accompany it have been more widely used than any other teaching materials for introductory marketing. It is gratifying that the four Ps framework has proved to be an organizing structure that has worked well for millions of students and teachers.

The success of *Basic Marketing* is not the result of a single strength—or one long-lasting innovation. Other textbooks have adopted our four Ps framework, and we have continuously improved the book. And the text's four Ps framework, managerial orientation, and strategy planning focus have proved to be foundation pillars that are remarkably robust for supporting new developments in the field and innovations in the text and package. Thus, with each new edition of *Basic Marketing* we have continued to innovate to better meet the needs of students and faculty. In fact, we have made ongoing changes in how we develop the logic of the four Ps and the marketing strategy planning process. As always, though, our objective is to provide a flexible, high-quality text and choices from comprehensive and reliable support materials—so that instructors and students can accomplish their learning objectives.

What's Different about *Basic Marketing*?

The biggest distinguishing factor about *Basic Marketing* is our integrative approach to creating a teaching and learning package for the introductory marketing course. This integration makes it easier to learn about marketing, teach marketing, and apply it in the real world. For many students, the introductory marketing course will be the only marketing class they ever take. They need to come away with a strong understanding of the key concepts in marketing and how marketing operates in practice. So in *Basic Marketing*: (1) we examine *both* what marketing is and how to do it; (2) we integrate special topics like services, international, ethics, and more, across the text with coverage in almost every chapter; and (3) we deliver a supplements package completely developed or closely managed by the authors—so each part links closely with the textbook content. See Exhibit P-1. The integration of these three elements delivers a proven product for instructors and students. Let us show you what we mean—and why and how instructors and students benefit from the *Basic Marketing* teaching and learning package.

Marketing operates in dynamic markets. Fast-changing global markets, environmental challenges and sustainability, and the blurring speed of technological advances—including an explosion in the use of digital tools by both consumers and businesses—are just a few of the current trends confronting today's marketing manager. While some marketing texts merely attempt to describe this market environment, *Basic Marketing* teaches students *analytical abilities* and *how-to-do-it skills* that prepare them for success. To propel

Exhibit P–1
Basic Marketing Integrates Marketing

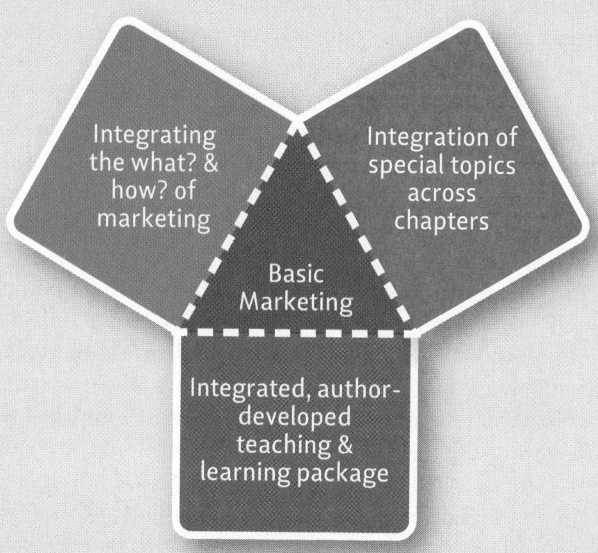

students in this direction, we deliberately include a variety of examples, explanations, frameworks, conceptual organizers, exercises, cases, and how-to-do-it techniques that relate to our overall framework for marketing strategy planning. Taken together, these different learning aids speed the development of "marketing sensibility" and enable students to analyze marketing situations and develop marketing plans in a confident and meaningful way. They are practical and they work. And because they are interesting and understandable, they motivate students to see marketing as the challenging and rewarding area it is. In the end, the *Basic Marketing* teaching and learning package prepares students to analyze marketing situations and develop exceptional marketing strategies—not just recite endless sets of lists.

In contrast to many other marketing textbooks, we emphasize careful *integration of special topics*. Some textbooks treat "special" topics—like marketing relationships, international marketing, services marketing, the Internet, digital lifestyles, nonprofit organizations, marketing ethics, social issues, and business-to-business marketing—in separate chapters (or parts of chapters). We deliberately avoid doing that because we are convinced that treating such topics separately leads to an unfortunate compartmentalization of ideas. We think they are too important to be isolated in that way. For example, to simply tack on a new chapter on e-commerce or marketing applications on the Internet completely ignores the reality that these are not just isolated topics but rather must be considered broadly across the whole fabric of marketing decisions. Conversely, there is virtually no area of marketing decision making where it's safe to ignore the impact of e-commerce, the Internet, or information technology. The same is true with other topics. So they are interwoven and illustrated throughout the text to emphasize that marketing thinking is crucial in all aspects of our society and economy. Exhibit P-2 shows the coverage of some key topics across specific chapters.

Exhibit P–2 Coverage of Special Topics Across Chapters*

Special Topic	Chapter																			
	1	2	3	4	5	6	7	8	9	10	11	12	13	14	15	16	17	18	19	20
Marketing relationships	X	X	X	X	X	X	X	X	X	X	X	X	X	X	X	X	X	X	X	X
International	X	X	X	X	X	X	X	X	X	X	X	X	X	X	X	X		X	X	X
Ethics	X	X	X	X	X	X	X	X	X	X	X	X	X	X	X	X	X	X	X	X
Services	X	X	X	X	X	X	X	X	X	X	X	X	X	X	X	X	X	X	X	X
B2B	X	X	X	X		X	X	X	X	X	X	X	X	X	X	X	X	X	X	X
Technology, Internet, "Big Data" & digital lifestyle	X	X	X	X	X	X	X	X	X	X	X	X	X	X	X	X	X	X	X	X
Environment & sustainability	X	X	X		X	X	X	X	X	X	X		X	X	X	X			X	X
Non-profits	X	X	X	X		X	X	X			X		X		X	X			X	X
Quality	X	X	X	X	X	X	X	X			X		X	X	X	X	X	X	X	X
Customer value	X	X	X	X	X	X	X	X	X	X	X	X	X	X	X	X	X	X	X	X
Marketing's link with other functions	X	X	X	X	X	X	X	X	X	X	X	X	X	X	X	X	X	X	X	X

*"X" indicates coverage in the form of a section of the chapter, example, illustration, or discussion.

The teaching and learning materials—designed and developed by the authors—are integrated to work effectively with *Basic Marketing*. We don't tack on extras that have been outsourced and don't integrate well with our package. Because of this, you (the instructor) have flexible tools that allow you to *teach marketing your way*. Marketing can be studied and used in many ways, and the *Basic Marketing* text material is only the central component of our *P*rofessional *L*earning *U*nits *S*ystem (*P.L.U.S.*) for students and teachers. Instructors and students can select from our units to develop their own personalized teaching and learning systems. Our objective is to offer you a *P.L.U.S.* "menu" so that you can conveniently select units you want—and disregard what you do not want. Many combinations of units are possible depending on course and learning objectives. Later in this Preface we highlight each *P.L.U.S.* element—and the full details can be found in the discussion of the Instructor's Resource CD in the Instructor's Manual.

Students only take the introductory marketing course once. They deserve the benefits of a highly innovative yet *proven* set of integrated learning materials. Our teaching and learning materials—from the textbook to the iPod videos to the test question bank to the online materials—have been constantly updated yet are proven to work for generations of students. Do you want to use an unproven textbook with your students?

What's New in This Edition of *Basic Marketing?*

There are several big changes to this edition of *Basic Marketing* and hundreds of smaller ones. *Basic Marketing* is quick to recognize the many dramatic changes in the market environment and marketing strategy—we are also quick to jump on new pedagogical innovations. So here is a quick overview of what we changed for the 19th edition of *Basic Marketing*.

Shorter and easier to read. Students and instructors appreciate concise coverage. We have had to make some difficult decisions, because one instructor's cut is another's favorite topic. We may have cut one of your pet topics. The biggest change we made was to eliminate a chapter. Our chapter-long treatment of global demographic issues is gone. These topics have not been eliminated, but are now covered in an abbreviated form in chapters 3 and 5. Where appropriate, we have included PowerPoint slides that cover these topics so you can still address them in class if you choose.

Social media and digital lifestyles. A major thrust of the 18th edition of *Basic Marketing* addressed customers' digital lifestyles. The growth in smartphone ownership and overall use of the Internet continues to march on, having an impact on all areas of marketing. We continued to make updates to reflect this market dynamic.

"Big data" and its implications. One of the most profound recent changes in marketing has been the explosion of what is being called "big data"—data sets too large and complex to work with typical database management tools. Organizations are using this to more narrowly target individual customers with tailored marketing mixes. It raises strategic and ethical questions. Almost every chapter in the book has a reference to this trend.

LearnSmart adaptive learning technology. We are excited to add McGraw-Hill's LearnSmart adaptive learning technology to *Basic Marketing*. Students love LearnSmart. It is a great self-assessment tool that helps them know if they are "getting it." Plus, the adaptive technology provides remediation (through additional questions or even points them back to the text) or moves them more quickly through the review if they are demonstrating they get it. We highly recommend you add this feature to your classes.

Up-to-date content, examples, exhibits, and images. We continually update *Basic Marketing* with each new edition. Students and instructors appreciate current, relevant examples that demonstrate important marketing concepts. We update each and every chapter opening case scenario. There are dozens of new examples and specific concepts spread throughout the book. While we don't have space to list all of these changes, we can provide you with some highlights of the more significant changes with this edition of *Basic Marketing:*

Chapter 1. We wrote a new chapter opener that features Nike, one of our students' favorite brands. We added an extended example in the text describing how Chipotle adds value for its customers. *Triple bottom line* is a new concept and key term.

Chapter 2. We significantly modified our coverage of lifetime customer value and customer equity. Customer lifetime value is a new key term. A new boxed teaching note looks more closely at differentiation.

Chapter 3. This has traditionally been one of the longest chapters in the book—so we made an effort to streamline coverage of all topics. The competitor, technology, and cultural and social environment sections were updated and re-written. The chapter now includes some of the demographic information previously covered in the now eliminated demographics chapter. This is where you will now find coverage of GDP/GNI, population, and generational changes like the graying of America, baby boomers, and generations X and Y. Sustainable competitive advantage and gross national income are new key terms.

Chapter 4. A new chapter opener case features LEGO. The boxed teaching note in this chapter is the first extended treatment of "big data"—with a look at how Target stores uses big data to predict what customers will want to buy.

Chapter 5. We now cover income here (previously in the demographics chapter), integrating it with our coverage of economic factors influencing consumer behavior. Drawing on Charles Duhigg's *The Power of Habit,* we adapted our treatment of learning and introduced an extended example on Febreze. We moved coverage of the family life cycle to this chapter. Cloud storage service Dropbox is featured as an extended example of the adoption process.

Chapter 6. The organizational buying chapter includes a number of minor changes, with more current examples and more concise coverage. We further recognize the growing role of social media and online search as key sources of information for organizational buyers.

Chapter 7. Big data provides a natural extension to our traditional coverage of marketing information systems, data warehouses, and decision support systems. Consequently we give students an important foundation on big data in the market research chapter. A new boxed teaching note "Big Data. Big Opportunity" offers context and application. Related topics, including sentiment analysis are covered later in the chapter along with a new Internet exercise on the topic. An extended example describes the marketing research Heinz used to develop new ketchup packages.

Chapter 8. We have increased coverage of goods and service combinations, product lines, and the "battle of the brands." An extended example on Coca-Cola replaces one on Yahoo! New coverage on international trademarks spurred by problems Apple had with "iPad" in China.

Chapter 9. We have been reading a lot about innovation. New thinking abounds; so we beefed up coverage of this critical area. We have new sections on 1) idea generation, 2) "the pivot" as key to new product introduction, 3) stimulating growth in mature markets (featuring the recent story of Philadelphia Cream Cheese), and different types of innovations from the customer's perspective (with some great new examples). A new Internet exercise features innovation consulting firm IDEO. A new boxed teaching note looks more closely at nature as a source of ideas through biomimicry. We also describe how big data is important to product quality. A tradeoff in adding these new topics is a cutback in our treatment of product quality.

Chapter 10. The use of *multiple* channels of distribution continues to grow—and so does our coverage of this trend and related topics here and in Chapter 12. We added discussions of firms using both direct and indirect channels and enhanced coverage of multichannel distribution. There is a new Internet exercise covering franchising.

Chapter 11. There were a few minor changes to this chapter. We describe how transportation companies utilize big data to lower costs.

Chapter 12. A new chapter opening case features Macy's—a retailer leading a renaissance of the department store. Macy's use of big data and effective integration of brick-and-mortar and online retailing fuel its revival. Online retailing continues to evolve—and this section has received major revision including extensive coverage of showrooming and big data. We also discuss the ethics of big data and retailing.

Chapter 13. We refined our coverage of promotion objectives and cut back on direct response promotion. We add a distinction between inbound and outbound promotion. We updated our treatment of budgeting for promotion.

Chapter 14. A new boxed teaching note describes the use of analytics to match customer service reps with customers—a kind of matchmaking that helped Assurant Solutions significantly increase customer retention. We updated our coverage of personal selling and information technology.

Chapter 15. We updated lots of numbers in this chapter. Our revised coverage of media reflects changes being brought on by technology and big data. Online advertising became "Digital Advertising" with greater attention to advertising on both the Internet and cell phones. We also cover how big data is used for social targeting. Our groundbreaking treatment of social media as a form of publicity has been well-received; we built on that to cover new methods of social media.

Chapter 16. We debated swapping out the opening case on Flip because Cisco discontinued the video camera. But this case covers the breadth of pricing issues in a way that students really seem to like, so while it is now "classic," it still works. New topics address the use of big data for dynamic pricing, which is now being used in more product-markets.

Chapter 17. We cut sections on target-return pricing, marginal analysis in oligopoly markets, and price leaders.

Chapter 18. Trends in big data and technology have had a big impact on implementation—especially in the speed of implementation and adaptation of strategy. The latest changes are reflected in the revised chapter.

Chapter 19. Our cross-functional integration chapter now explicitly considers information systems—a major new section to the chapter. While we cover IT throughout the book, in this chapter we demonstrate key IT issues related to developing and implementing marketing plans. Related to this, we examine big data, data security (as related to marketing), and enterprise resource planning (ERP) systems. We also updated the human resources section to reflect new research.

Chapter 20. We add coverage of the role of the Internet in keeping companies honest. Big data has lots of issues around privacy, so we added a new section and a boxed teaching note "Marketers Use Big Data—Creepy or Cool" that helps students understand what this trend means.

Twenty Chapters—with an Emphasis on Marketing Strategy Planning

The emphasis of *Basic Marketing* is on marketing strategy planning. Twenty chapters introduce the important concepts in marketing and help the student see marketing through the eyes of the manager. The organization of the chapters and topics is carefully planned. But we took special care in writing so that

- It is possible to rearrange and use the chapters in many different sequences—to fit different needs.
- All of the topics and chapters fit together into a clear, overall framework for the marketing strategy planning process.

Exhibit P–3 *Basic Marketing* and the Marketing Strategy Planning Process

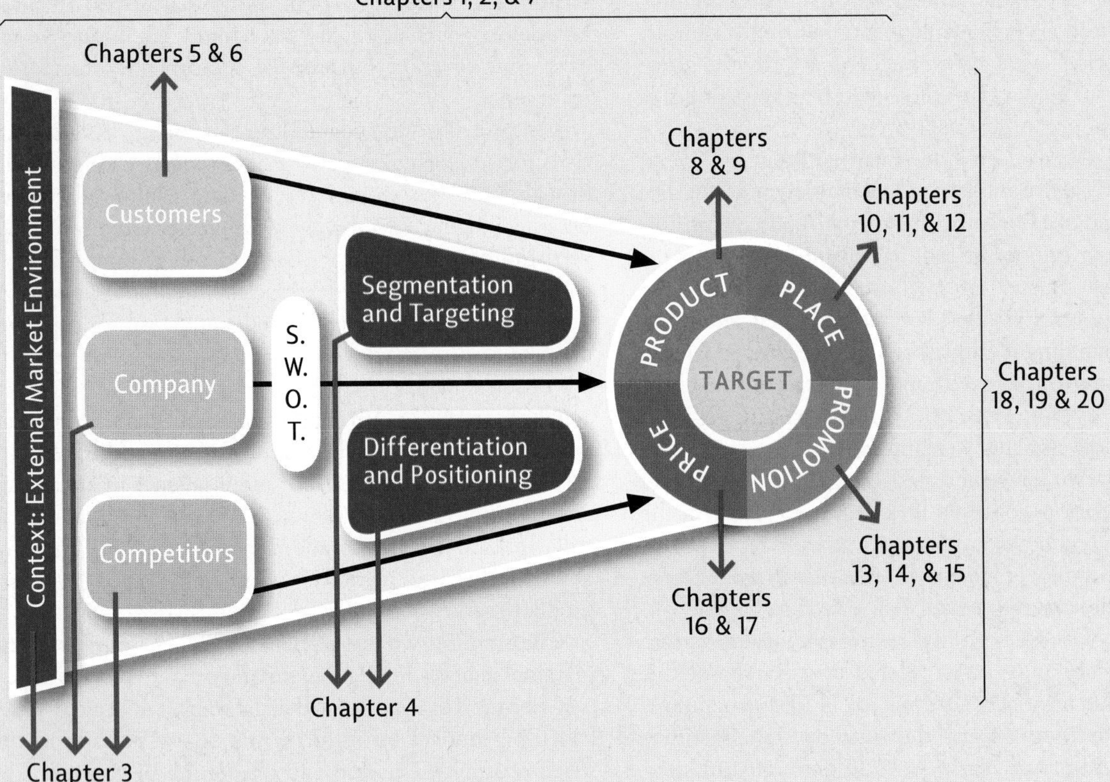

Broadly speaking, the chapters fall into three groupings. The first seven chapters introduce marketing and a broad view of the marketing strategy planning process. We introduce the marketing strategy planning process in Chapter 2 and use this framework as a structure for our coverage of marketing. See Exhibit P-3. Chapters 3–7 cover topics such as the market environment, competition, segmentation, differentiation, and buyer behavior, as well as how marketing information systems and research provide information about these forces to improve marketing decisions. The second part of the text goes into the details of planning the four Ps, with specific attention to the key strategy decisions in each area. Finally, we conclude with an integrative review and an assessment of marketing's challenges and opportunities.

The first chapter deals with the important role of marketing—focusing not only on how a marketing orientation guides a business or nonprofit organization in the process of providing superior value to customers but also on the role of macro-marketing and how a market-directed economy shapes choices and quality of life for consumers. Chapter 2 builds on these ideas with a focus on the marketing strategy planning process and why it involves narrowing down to the selection of a specific target market and blending the four Ps into a marketing mix to meet the needs of those customers. With that foundation in place, the chapter introduces an integrative model of the marketing strategy planning process that serves as an organizing framework for the rest of the text.

Chapter 3 introduces students to the importance of evaluating opportunities in the external environments affecting marketing. This chapter also highlights the critical role of screening criteria for narrowing down from possible opportunities to those that the firm will pursue. Then, Chapter 4 shows how analysis of the market relates to segmentation and differentiation decisions as well as the criteria for narrowing down to a specific target market and marketing mix.

You have to understand customers in order to segment markets and satisfy target market needs. So the next two chapters take a closer look at *customers*. Chapter 5 studies the behavioral aspects of the final consumer market. Chapter 6 looks at how business and organizational customers—like manufacturers, channel members, and government purchasers—are similar to and different from final consumers.

Chapter 7 is a contemporary view of getting information—from marketing information systems and marketing research—for marketing planning. This chapter includes discussion of how information technology—ranging from intranets to speedy collection of market research data—is transforming the marketing job. This sets the stage for discussions in later chapters about how research and marketing information improve each area of marketing strategy planning.

The next group of chapters—Chapters 8 through 17—is concerned with developing a marketing mix out of the four Ps: Product, Place (involving channels of distribution, logistics, and distribution customer service), Promotion, and Price. These chapters are concerned with developing the "right" Product and making it available at the "right" Place with the "right" Promotion and the "right" Price—to satisfy target customers and still meet the objectives of the business. These chapters are presented in an integrated, analytical way—as part of the overall framework for the marketing strategy planning process—so students' thinking about planning marketing strategies develops logically.

Chapters 8 and 9 focus on product planning for goods and services as well as managing product quality, new-product development, and the different strategy decisions that are required at different stages of the product life cycle. We emphasize the value of an organized new-product development process for developing really new products that propel a firm to profitable growth. These chapters also detail how quality management approaches can improve implementation, including implementation of better service quality.

Chapters 10 through 12 focus on Place. Chapter 10 introduces decisions a manager must make about using direct distribution (for example, selling from the firm's own website) or working with other firms in a channel of distribution. We put special emphasis on the need for channel members to cooperate and coordinate to better meet the needs of customers. Chapter 11 focuses on the fast-changing arena of logistics and the strides that firms are making in using e-commerce to reduce the costs of storing, transporting, and handling products while improving the distribution service they provide customers. Chapter 12 provides a clear picture of retailers, wholesalers, and their strategy planning, including exchanges taking place via the Internet. This composite chapter helps students see why the big changes taking place in retailing are reshaping the channel systems for many consumer products.

Chapters 13 through 15 deal with Promotion. These chapters build on the concepts of integrated marketing communications, direct-response promotion, and customer-initiated digital communication, which are introduced in Chapter 13. Chapter 14 deals with the roles of personal selling, customer service, and sales technology in the promotion blend. Chapter 15 covers advertising, publicity, and sales promotion, including the ways that managers are taking advantage of the Internet and other highly targeted media to communicate more effectively and efficiently.

Chapters 16 and 17 deal with Price. Chapter 16 focuses on pricing objectives and policies, including use of information technology to implement flexible pricing; pricing in the channel; and the use of discounts, allowances, and other variations from a list price. Chapter 17 covers cost-oriented and demand-oriented pricing approaches and how they fit in today's competitive environments. The careful coverage of marketing costs helps equip students to deal with the renewed cost-consciousness of the firms they will join.

Chapter 18 examines implementation and control with an emphasis on the role of information technology. Then, Chapter 19 deals with the links between marketing and other functional areas. The marketing concept says that people in an organization should work together to satisfy customers at a profit. No other text has a chapter that explains how to accomplish the "working together" part of that idea. Yet it's increasingly important in the business world today, so that's what this important chapter is designed to do.

The final chapter considers how efficient the marketing process is. Here we evaluate the effectiveness of both micro- and macro-marketing—and we consider the competitive, technological, ethical, and social challenges facing marketing managers now and in the future. Chapter 20 also reinforces the integrative nature of marketing management and reviews the marketing strategy planning process that leads to creative marketing plans.

Three appendices can be used to supplement the main text material. Appendix A provides some traditional economic analysis of supply and demand that can be a useful tool in analyzing markets. Appendix B reviews some quantitative tools—or marketing arithmetic—which help marketing managers who want to use accounting data in analyzing marketing problems. Appendix B also reviews forecasting as a way to predict market potential and sales for a company's product. Finally, many students like to look at Appendix C—which is about career opportunities in marketing.

The following sections include 44 cases. Eight of these written cases supplement video cases available to instructors in their video package and online to students. Almost all of the 36 short written cases have been updated with new information to make sure they reflect the realities of the current marketplace. The focus of these cases is on problem solving. They encourage students to apply, and really get involved with, the concepts developed in the text. At the end of each chapter, we recommend particular cases that best relate to that chapter's content.

Teaching and Learning Your Way—Elements of P.L.U.S.

Basic Marketing can be studied and used in many ways—the *Basic Marketing* text material is only the central component of our *P*rofessional *L*earning *U*nits *S*ystem (*P.L.U.S.*) for students and teachers. Instructors (and students) can select from our units to develop their own personalized systems. Many combinations of units are possible, depending on course objectives. As a quick overview, in addition to the *Basic Marketing* text, the *P.L.U.S.* package includes a variety of new and updated supplements.

Most of the instructor resources can be found on the *Instructor's Resource CD* and the instructor side of the Online Learning Center.

Beyond the *Basic Marketing* textbook, the key components of *P.L. U.S.* include

- ***Connect Marketing* for *Basic Marketing.*** This is one of the most exciting developments—new with this edition of *Basic Marketing. Connect Marketing* for *Basic Marketing* is an online assignment and assessment solution that connects students with the tools and resources they'll need to achieve success. And McGraw-Hill has partnered with Blackboard® to deliver the content and tools directly inside your learning management system. More details are provided in the next section of this preface.
- ***"Teach the 4 Ps" blog for instructors.*** The blog provides links to online articles, blog posts, videos, video clips, and commercials. The site is a great way to stay up-to-date and bring current content into your classroom. Many of these posts will also appear on the "Learn the 4 Ps" website that targets students.
- ***Electronic Presentation Slides.*** Our "best in the business" multimedia lecture support package includes a variety of materials. For each chapter there is a set of PowerPoint presentations for a complete lecture that includes television commercials and short video clip examples, examples of print advertisements that demonstrate important concepts, and questions to use with "clickers" or simply to check if students are getting it. We also have a set of archive slides with a high-quality selection of ads and photos. NEW with this edition, we have added more than 80 slides with embedded YouTube videos. Bring virtual guest speakers, viral videos, case studies, and new ads to your classroom presentations. The archive slides also include slides with material that we may have cut from this edition of the book.
- ***Multimedia Lecture Support Guide.*** This guide supports the presentation slides and includes detailed lecture scripts, outlines, and archives.
- ***Videos and Video Cases.*** The video package has been updated with eight new videos—to give you 31 full-length videos. In addition, we have 138 short (1 to 4 minutes) video clips—many integrated into the PowerPoint presentation slides. See the Video Instructor's Manual for more ideas about how to use the videos in class.
- **Instructor's Manual to Accompany *Basic Marketing.*** This manual includes an overview of all the teaching/learning units, as well as suggested answers to all questions, exercises, and assignments.
- **Test Bank.** Our test bank includes thousands of objective test questions—every question *developed or edited by the authors* to ensure it works seamlessly with the text. McGraw-Hill's EZ-Test program facilitates the creation of tests. We take great pride in having a test bank that works for students and instructors.
- **Online Learning Center: www.mhhe.com/fourps.** The website for the book provides access to a variety of student and instructor resources.
- ***Basic Marketing* Cartridges for Blackboard and WebCT.** Include *Basic Marketing* materials directly in your online course management program.

Another set of resources is designed to be directly accessed by students usually via the web. Students can access the learning resources at www.mhhe.com/fourps or in the Student Library of their class' *Connect Marketing* website. They include

- **Self-Test Quizzes.** These help students prepare for tests.
- **Computer-Aided Problems.** This easy-to-use spreadsheet software program works with exercises at the end of each chapter in the text to help develop analytical skills needed by today's managers.
- ***Marketing Plan Coach.*** This online software tool helps students build marketing plans using materials and concepts directly from the textbook. It was created by the authors specifically for use with *Basic Marketing.*
- ***"Learn the 4 Ps"* Blog, Twitter, and Facebook Page.** These offer links to current online articles, websites, podcasts, and videos—providing motivated students more ways to learn about marketing.
- **Learning with Ads.** These are great for visual learners who can preview or study concepts from each chapter and examine applications in real print ads. About 10 to 15 ads per chapter.
- **Video Cases.** Clips from video cases in the book.

Teaching and Learning Resources

Instructor's Resource CD (IRCD)
ISBN 0077512472

This CD contains the Instructor's Manual, a Test Bank, and PowerPoint® presentations.

Connect Instructor Library and Online Learning Center

www.mhhe.com/fourps Access everything you need to teach a great course through our convenient online resource. A secured Instructor Library/Resource Center stores your essential course materials to save you prep time before class.

- **Instructor's Manual** The Instructor's Manual to accompany this text is an all-inclusive resource designed to support instructors in effectively teaching the principles of marketing. This manual includes an overview of all the teaching/learning units, as well as suggested answers to all questions, exercises, and assignments.
- **Test Bank and EZ Test Online** The Test Bank offers more than 2,000 questions, which are categorized by topic, level of learning (knowledge, comprehension, or application), Learning Objectives, Bloom's Taxonomy, and accreditation standards (AACSB).
- **PowerPoint® Presentations** The PowerPoint presentations feature slides that can be used and personalized by instructors to help present concepts to the students effectively. Each set of slides contains additional figures and tables from the text.
- **Videos and Video Cases** McGraw-Hill provides industry-leading video support to help students understand concepts and see how they apply in the real world. The video package has been updated with eight new videos—to give you 31 full-length videos. In addition, we have 138 short (1 to 4 minutes) video clips—many integrated into the PowerPoint presentation slides. See the Video Instructor's Manual for more ideas about how to use the videos in class.
- ***Marketing Plan Coach*** This online software tool helps students build marketing plans using materials and concepts directly from the textbook. It was created by the authors specifically for use with Basic Marketing.
- **Learning with Ads** These are great for visual learners who can preview or study concepts from each chapter and examine applications in real print ads. About 10 to 15 ads per chapter.

Teaching Options and Solutions

McGraw-Hill Higher Education and Blackboard have teamed up. What does this mean for you?

1. **Your life, simplified. Single Sign-On:** A single login and single environment provide seamless access to all course resources—all McGraw-Hill's resources are available within the Blackboard Learn platform.
2. **Deep integration of content and tools. Deep Integration:** One click access to a wealth of McGraw-Hill content and tools—all from within Blackboard Learn.™
3. **Seamless Gradebooks. One Gradebook:** Automatic grade synchronization with Blackboard gradebook. All grades for McGraw-Hill *Connect* assignments are recorded in the Blackboard gradebook automatically.
4. **A solution for everyone. Openness:** Unique in Higher Education, the partnership of McGraw-Hill Higher Education and Blackboard preserves the spirit of academic freedom and openness. Blackboard remains publisher independent, and McGraw-Hill remains LMS (Learning Management System) independent. The result makes our content, engines and platform more usable and accessible, with fewer barriers to adoption and use.

5. **100% FERPA** -compliant solution protects student privacy.
6. **McGraw-Hill and Blackboard** can now offer you easy access to industry-leading technology and content, whether your campus hosts it, or we do. Be sure to ask your local McGraw-Hill representative for details.

MHCampus™

McGraw-Hill Campus™ is a new one-stop teaching and learning experience available to users of any learning management system. This institutional service allows faculty and students to enjoy single sign-on (SSO) access to all McGraw-Hill Higher Education materials, including the award winning McGraw-Hill *Connect* platform, from directly within the institution's website. McGraw-Hill Campus™ provides faculty with instant access to all McGraw-Hill Higher Education teaching materials (e.g. eTextbooks, test banks, PowerPoint slides, animations and learning objects, etc), allowing them to browse, search, and use any instructor ancillary content in our vast library at no additional cost to instructor or students. Students enjoy SSO access to a variety of free (e.g. quizzes, flash cards, narrated presentations, etc.) and subscription based products (e.g. McGraw-Hill *Connect*). With this program enabled, faculty and students will never need to create another account to access McGraw-Hill products and services. Learn more at **www.mhcampus.com.**

McGraw-Hill *Connect Plus Marketing*

connect plus+

McGraw-Hill reinvents the textbook-learning experience for today's students with *Connect Plus Marketing.* A seamless integration of an eBook and *Connect* provides all of the *Connect* features plus the following:

- An integrated eBook, allowing for anytime, anywhere online access to the textbook.
- Dynamic links between the problems or questions assigned to students and the location in the eBook where that problem or question is covered.
- Powerful search function to pinpoint and connect key concepts in a snap.

For more information about *Connect,* go to **connect.mcgraw-hill.com,** or contact your local McGraw-Hill sales representative.

CourseSmart

Learn Smart. Choose Smart. CourseSmart is a new way for faculty to find and review eTextbooks. It's also a great option for students who are interested in accessing their course materials digitally, and saving money.

CourseSmart offers thousands of the most commonly adopted textbooks across hundreds of courses from a wide variety of higher education publishers. It is the only place for faculty to review and compare the full text of a textbook online, providing immediate access without the environmental impact of requesting a print exam copy.

With the CourseSmart eTextbook, students can save up to 45 percent off the cost of a printed book, reduce their impact on the environment, and access powerful web tools for learning. CourseSmart users access and view their textbook online when connected to the Internet. Students can also print sections of the book for maximum portability. CourseSmart eTextbooks are available in one standard online reader with full text search, notes, and highlighting, and e-mail tools for sharing notes between classmates. For more information on CourseSmart, go to **http://www.coursesmart.com.**

Create

Instructors can now tailor their teaching resources to match the way they teach! With McGraw-Hill Create, **www.mcgrawhillcreate.com,** instructors can easily rearrange chapters, combine material from other content sources, and quickly upload and integrate their own content, like course syllabi or teaching notes. Find the right content in Create by searching through thousands of leading McGraw-Hill textbooks. Arrange the material to fit your teaching style. Order a Create book and receive a complimentary print review copy in 3–5 business days or a complimentary electronic review copy (echo) via e-mail within one hour. Go to **www.mcgrawhillcreate.com** today and register.

Tegrity Campus: Lectures 24/7

Tegrity Campus is a service that makes class time available 24/7 by automatically capturing every lecture in a searchable format for students to review when they study and complete assignments. With a simple one-click start-and-stop process, you capture all computer screens and corresponding audio. Students can replay any part of any class with easy-to-use browser-based viewing on a PC or Mac.

Educators know that the more students can see, hear, and experience class resources, the better they learn. In fact, studies prove it. With patented Tegrity "search anything" technology, students instantly recall key class moments for replay online, or on iPods® and mobile devices. Instructors can help turn all their students' study time into learning moments immediately supported by their lecture. To learn more about Tegrity watch a 2-minute Flash demo at **http://tegritycampus.mhhe.com.**

Assurance of Learning Ready

Many educational institutions today are focused on the notion of *assurance of learning,* an important element of some accreditation standards. *Basic Marketing* is designed specifically to support instructors' assurance of learning initiatives with a simple, yet powerful solution.

Each test bank question for *Basic Marketing* maps to a specific chapter learning outcome/objective listed in the text. Instructors can use our test bank software, EZ Test and EZ Test Online, to easily query for learning outcomes/objectives that directly relate to the learning objectives for their course. Instructors can then use the reporting features of EZ Test to aggregate student results in similar fashion, making the collection and presentation of assurance of learning data simple and easy.

AACSB Statement

The McGraw-Hill Companies is a proud corporate member of AACSB International. Understanding the importance and value of AACSB accreditation, *Basic Marketing* recognizes the curricula guidelines detailed in the AACSB standards for business accreditation by connecting selected questions in the text and the test bank to the six general knowledge and skill guidelines in the AACSB standards.

The statements contained in *Basic Marketing* are provided only as a guide for the users of this textbook. The AACSB leaves content coverage and assessment within the purview of individual schools, the mission of the school, and the faculty. While the *Basic Marketing* teaching package makes no claim of any specific AACSB qualification or evaluation, we have within *Basic Marketing* labeled selected questions according to the six general knowledge and skills areas.

McGraw-Hill Customer Experience Group Contact Information

At McGraw-Hill, we understand that getting the most from new technology can be challenging. That's why our services don't stop after you purchase our products. You can e-mail our Product Specialists 24 hours a day to get product training online. Or you can search our knowledge bank of Frequently Asked Questions on our support website. For Customer Support, call **800-331-5094,** e-mail **hmsupport@mcgraw-hill.com,** or visit **www.mhhe.com/support.** One of our Technical Support Analysts will be able to assist you in a timely fashion.

Responsibilities of Leadership

In closing, we return to a point raised at the beginning of this preface. *Basic Marketing* has been a leading textbook in marketing since its first edition. We take the responsibilities of that leadership seriously. We know that you want and deserve the very best teaching and learning materials possible. It is our commitment to bring you those materials—today with this edition and in the future with subsequent editions.

We recognize that fulfilling this commitment requires a process of continuous improvement. Revisions, updates, and development of new elements must be ongoing—because needs change. You are an important part of this evolution, of this leadership. We encourage your feedback. The most efficient way to get in touch with us is to send an e-mail message to Joe.Cannon@colostate.edu. If you prefer the traditional approach, send a letter to Joe Cannon at Colorado State University, College of Business, Fort Collins, CO 80528-1278, United States of America. Thoughtful criticisms and suggestions from students and teachers alike have helped to make *Basic Marketing* what it is. We hope that you will help make it what it will be in the future.

William D. Perreault, Jr.
Joseph P. Cannon
E. Jerome McCarthy

Let's Walk through Your *Basic Marketing* Textbook . . .

Basic Marketing Helps You Learn about Marketing and Marketing Strategy Planning

At its essence, marketing strategy planning is about figuring out how to do a superior job of satisfying customers. With that in mind, the 19th edition of *Basic Marketing* was developed to satisfy your desire for knowledge and add value to your course experience. Not only will this text teach you about marketing and marketing strategy planning, but its design, pedagogy, and supplements package were developed to work well with the text and a variety of study situations.

Each person has a different approach to studying. Some may focus on reading that is covered during class, others prefer to prepare outside of the classroom and rely heavily on in-class interaction, and still others prefer more independence from the classroom. Some are more visual or more "hands on" in the way they learn, and others just want clear and interesting explanations. To address a variety of needs and course situations, many hours went into creating and designing the *Basic Marketing* textbook and other learning materials. We highlight how you can use these materials in the following section.

Take a moment now to learn more about all of the resources available to help you best prepare for this course and—whether you plan to work in marketing or not—for your future career.

Basic Marketing: An Innovative Marketing Experience

With 20 chapters that introduce the important concepts in marketing management, you will see all aspects of marketing through the eyes of the marketing manager. The first seven chapters introduce marketing and give you a framework for understanding marketing strategy planning in any type of organization, and then the next section of the text takes you into planning the four Ps of marketing (Product, Place, Promotion, and Price) with specific attention to the key strategy decisions in each area. The text concludes with a review and assessment of marketing's challenges and opportunities.

Basic Marketing pioneered the "four Ps" approach to organize and describe managerial marketing for introductory marketing courses. This new edition covers the dynamic changes taking place in marketing management and the market environment. But this new edition helps you understand the changes taking place and reflects today's best marketing practices and ideas.

Start each chapter with an overview

Each chapter begins with an in-depth case study developed specifically to motivate your interest and highlight a real-life example of the learning objectives and specific marketing decision areas covered in that chapter. Each case study is accompanied by a list of learning objectives that will help you understand and identify important terms and concepts covered in the chapter. We recommend you read the opening case and learning objectives and then take just a few minutes to skim through the chapter, check out the exhibits, pictures, and headings before reading the conclusion. This preview gives you a picture of the chapter and how it fits together—and research shows that it helps increase your comprehension of the reading.

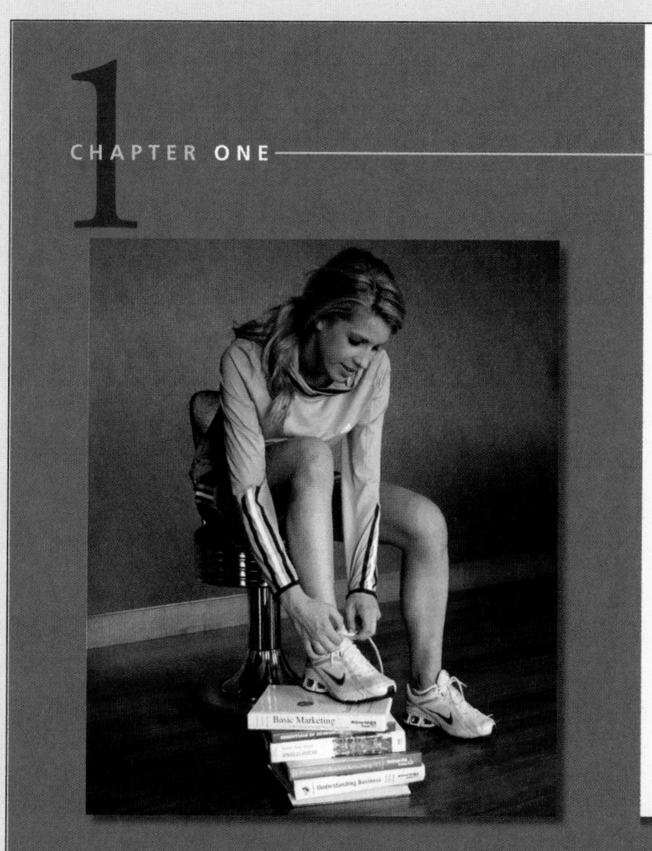

Marketing's Value to Consumers, Firms, and Society

When it's time to roll out of bed in the morning, does the alarm ringtone on your Samsung Galaxy smartphone wake you, or is it your SiriusXM radio playing your favorite satellite station? Is the station playing hip-hop, classical, or country music—or perhaps a Red Cross ad asking you to donate blood? Maybe you'll start your day with a quick run while wearing your Adidas hoodie and running shorts and your favorite Nike running shoes. Then you could meet a friend at Starbucks for coffee and a study session. Oops, you slept in this morning and aren't sure you have time? Well maybe you should just throw on your Levi's jeans, shirt from Abercrombie and Fitch, and your favorite Sperry Top-Sider shoes and grab a quick bite at home. Perhaps you can find a Chiquita banana and a Lender's Bagel with cream cheese—or maybe a bowl of General Mills Cheerios cereal and a glass of calcium-fortified Simply Orange juice to start your day. If you hurry, your roommate can give you a ride to school in her new Nissan Leaf, but you might just have to take the bus that the city bought from Mercedes-Benz.

When you think about it, you can't get very far into a day without bumping into marketing—and what the whole marketing system does for you. It affects every aspect of our lives—often in ways we don't even consider.

In other parts of the world, people wake up each day to different kinds of experiences. A family in rural Africa may have little choice about what food they will eat or where their clothing will come from. In some countries, economic decisions are still made by government officials. But in the world's most developed countries, consumers determine what's on store shelves. If no one buys a particular color, size, or style, then companies no longer produce it. So you may have trouble finding Cheerios in Tokyo, where they are more likely to eat Kokuho Rose Rice for breakfast.

One brand found around the world is Nike. How has Nike become the shoe of choice for so many professional and casual athletes around the world? Is it the endorsements from star athletes like LeBron James and Cristiano Ronaldo? Maybe the constant innovations like the new lightweight Flyknit running shoes? Do you think Nike's 24,000 retailers play a part? What about all that advertising Nike does? And those three-minute videos that Nike posts on YouTube can't hurt—"My Time Is Now" racked up nine million views in its first three days.

Almost 50 years ago Phil Knight and his college track coach Bill Bowerman founded Blue Ribbon Sports (later renamed Nike) to distribute Japanese running shoes. A few years later they were designing, producing, and selling athletic shoes. Today Nike is the 25th most valuable brand in the world, with annual sales of more than $21 billion. Part of its success comes from adapting its marketing strategy to changing market conditions—but Nike hasn't always adapted quickly enough. Back in the early 1980s, Nike was so focused on running shoes that it missed the aerobics shoe craze and fell behind rival Reebok. Nike profits plummeted so quickly that only aggressive cost-cutting saved the company.

After Nike signed Michael Jordan to endorse its basketball shoes in 1984, the Air Jordan line took the market by storm. It didn't hurt when Nike's advertising agency came up with the "Just Do It!" slogan and an advertising campaign that covered television, magazines, and billboards around the world. This helped carry Nike through the 1990s and its profits soared on rising sales aided by low-cost foreign production.

However, in the late 1990s, the company came under attack when it was reported that some of its suppliers used child labor. At first Nike denied responsibility, claiming it couldn't control how its suppliers operated. But public protest showed that society expected more from a large, successful corporation, and Nike began to closely monitor its suppliers' labor practices.

Since then Nike's social responsibility efforts have turned around its reputation. For example, Nike leads a group of 10 partners in the GreenXchange, a web-based marketplace where member firms collaborate and share ideas to foster sustainability. Nike's Reuse-A-Shoe program turns old shoes into Nike Grind, which is used as a surface on playgrounds, gym floors, and running tracks.

These days Nike targets growth in emerging markets like China. Nike's goal is to sell $4 billion there by 2015—almost doubling what it sold there in 2010. Nike has adapted its marketing strategy for the Chinese market.

The exhibits, photos, and ads will help you understand the concepts . . .

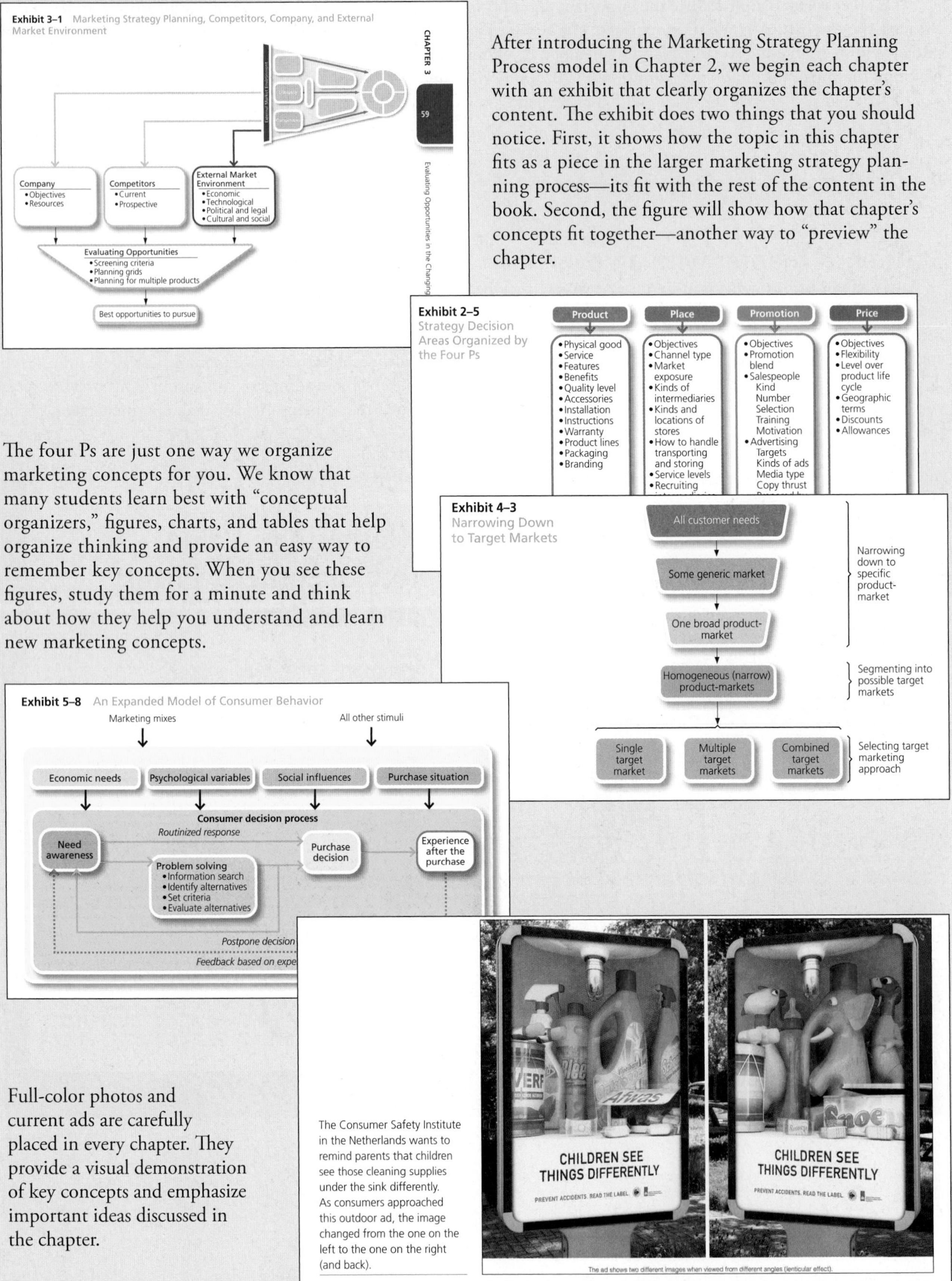

The Consumer Safety Institute in the Netherlands wants to remind parents that children see those cleaning supplies under the sink differently. As consumers approached this outdoor ad, the image changed from the one on the left to the one on the right (and back).

The ad shows two different images when viewed from different angles (lenticular effect).

After introducing the Marketing Strategy Planning Process model in Chapter 2, we begin each chapter with an exhibit that clearly organizes the chapter's content. The exhibit does two things that you should notice. First, it shows how the topic in this chapter fits as a piece in the larger marketing strategy planning process—its fit with the rest of the content in the book. Second, the figure will show how that chapter's concepts fit together—another way to "preview" the chapter.

The four Ps are just one way we organize marketing concepts for you. We know that many students learn best with "conceptual organizers," figures, charts, and tables that help organize thinking and provide an easy way to remember key concepts. When you see these figures, study them for a minute and think about how they help you understand and learn new marketing concepts.

Full-color photos and current ads are carefully placed in every chapter. They provide a visual demonstration of key concepts and emphasize important ideas discussed in the chapter.

Think critically about the issues facing marketing managers . . .

This book includes a variety of different opportunities for you to learn about the types of decisions facing real marketing managers. Stop and think about the Ethics Questions you confront in your reading. Visit the websites we call out in the Internet Exercises and think about the questions posed. At the end of each chapter, we suggest some cases—which are interesting situations faced by real marketers. You can find the cases near the end of the book.

Ethics Question

You are a marketing assistant for Auntie Em's Cookie Company, which makes and distributes packaged cookies through grocery stores. Your company recently ran a test market for a new brand of low-fat cookies called Tastee DeeLites. The new brand meets government standards to be labeled and advertised as "low fat," so the ads and package used in the test market highlighted that benefit. Test-market sales were very promising. However, now a consumer activist group has created a website (www.TasteeDeLIES.com) that claims Tastee DeeLites package and ads are misleading because the product's high calories make it even more fattening than most other cookies. Your boss has asked you to recommend how Auntie Em's should handle this situation. Drawing on what you've learned about consumer behavior, do you think consumers are being misled? Does your company have any responsibility to respond to these charges? Should changes be made to the product, package, or promotion?

SUGGESTED CASES

1. McDonald's "Seniors" Restaurant
3. NOCO United Soccer Academy
8. Besitti's Restaurant
9. Peaceful Rest Motor Lodge
10. Cooper's Ice Center
11. Running Room
12. DrJane.com—Custom Vitamins
30. Walker-Winkle Mills, Ltd.

Explore special topics . . .

Follow a topic online with the Internet Exercises that let you see how firms can use the web to enhance their marketing. And each chapter includes a boxed scenario to help you learn more about a particular marketing topic.

Zipcar—saving money and the environment

Evolving needs, attitudes, and lifestyles are creating opportunities for new transportation services. Many consumers, whether captivated by the green movement or simple economics, want to give up their cars—but some have trouble handing over their keys.

Zipcar offers a solution. It provides a car-sharing service that's now available in dozens of big cities across the United States, Canada, and the U.K. Car-sharing saves both money and time. With monthly payments, insurance, parking, gas, depreciation, and maintenance, the cost of car ownership averages $8,000 a year. City dwellers face the additional hassle of finding parking and worrying about theft. Zipcar's rates vary by city, but average $10 an hour or $70 a day. That's a big difference from car ownership!

Zipcar has worked hard to make car-sharing easy and fun. Signing up is simple—go online, fill out an application, and pay your $50 annual membership fee. Zipcar checks the applicant's driving record—and if he passes, a Zipcard arrives in his mail a few days later. Renting a car is even simpler. A member (called a ... nd cars ... cars are ... in park- ... ate and ... r simply ... quency ... e with a Zipcar app at the car and it automatically unlocks. Grab the keys from beneath the steering wheel, turn the ignition and you're ready to go.

Zipcar has identified different market segments and localized a marketing mix for each group. Some big city neighborhoods appreciate the environmental benefits. Here, most prefer driving a smaller and more economical car like a Toyota Prius or Mini Cooper when they visit a friend, though some want the convenience of a hatchback on a shopping trip. They're proud of the Zipcar logo on the car doors—it shows their green side and fellow Zipsters wave when they drive by.

Zipsters in more upscale neighborhoods are offered a selection of Volvos and BMWs. Zipcar found these customers usually borrow cars for a big night out or to head to the beach for the weekend. And they don't like (so they don't get) the green sign on the car door.

You can also find Zipcars on more than 250 college campuses—where students often don't have a regular need for a car and almost always have difficulty with parking. Spreading a dozen Zipcars—like Scion xBs and Honda Insight hybrids—across campus reduces the need for more than a hundred parking spaces. In tight economic times, campus administrations have responded enthusiastically to a program that reduces traffic and parking problems.

Zipcar is growing quickly by providing an economical and environmentally friendly solution to today's transportation needs. More and more Zipsters are learning a new way to get around—and they're having fun doing it.[11]

GM and Nissan introduced all-electric cars. Malt-O-Meal breakfast cereals, a low-cost brand that has always been packaged in bags, touted the environmental benefits of this packaging. Its "Bag the Box" campaign garnered publicity on a small budget. Many consumers have positive attitudes toward brands that try to make a difference in this area.[9]

Most marketers work with existing attitudes

Because consumer attitudes tend to be enduring, it's usually more economical for marketers to work with them than try to change them. Changing negative attitudes is probably the most difficult job marketers face.[10]

Ethical issues may arise

Part of the marketing job is to inform and persuade consumers about a firm's

Internet Exercise

Climate Counts is a nonprofit organization that provides information to help consumers make choices that have a positive impact on the planet. Go to the Climate Counts website (www.climatecounts.org), click on the "Climate Scores" link, choose a market sector, and compare the different companies. Do you think this information will affect how *consumers* behave? Do you think the information will affect how *companies* behave? What will be the effect on consumer and company behavior if some consumers use Twitter to tweet ratings, or e-mail to share ratings with others?

Beyond the Book—Check out all the online resources for *Basic Marketing* where you will find more interactivity and more ways to . . .

. . . think about the *Basic Marketing* text book as the centerpiece of your learning experience. Through computers and the Internet, there are many additional features to help you learn about marketing. We have designed the *Basic Marketing* learning package to give you a variety of different ways to learn and study. So if you are looking for other pathways to learning, check out what you can find at the Online Learning Center (www.mhhe.com/fourps), *Learn the 4 Ps* website (www.learnthe4ps.com), and through *Connect Marketing* for *Basic Marketing*. See Exhibit W-1.

Exhibit W–1 Online Resources in the *Basic Marketing* Learning Package

	Online Learning Center (OLC)	*Learn the 4 Ps*	*Connect Marketing*
Description	*Basic Marketing* site	Blog, Twitter, and Facebook sites	Available with some book packages.
Availability	www.mhhe.com/fourps	learnthe4ps.com	See your instructor
Student Chapter Quizzes—10 multiple-choice questions per chapter—check if you're ready for your next exam.	x		x
Computer-Aided Problems (CAPs)—easy-to-use spreadsheet software program works with exercises at the end of each chapter to develop analytical skills needed by today's managers.	x		x
Marketing Plan Coach—this online software tool helps students build marketing plans by drawing on concepts from *Basic Marketing*.	x		x
Learn the 4 Ps—Pick your favorite way to stay current with online articles, websites, podcasts, and videos delivered on a blog, Twitter, and Facebook.		x	
***Connect* Quizzes**—20 multiple-choice questions per chapter—check if you're ready for your next exam.			x
Learning with Ads—a great way to preview concepts from each chapter and see how they are applied in real print ads.			x
Video Cases—clips from video cases in the book			x
LearnSmart—An adaptive learning system designed to help students learn faster, study more efficiently, and retain more knowledge.			x
***Connect* Homework**—Homework exercises (available with some book packages—instructor set-up required).			x

Available for free at the *Basic Marketing* website (www.mhhe.com/fourps)

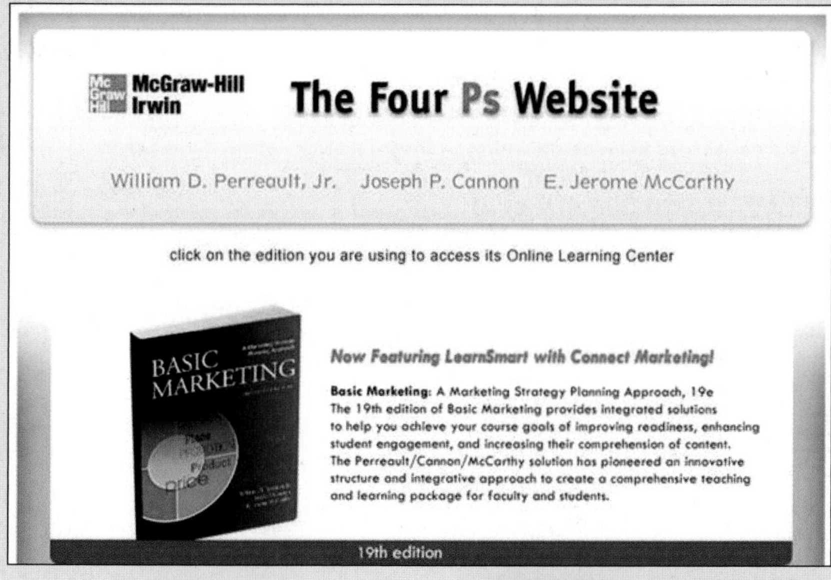

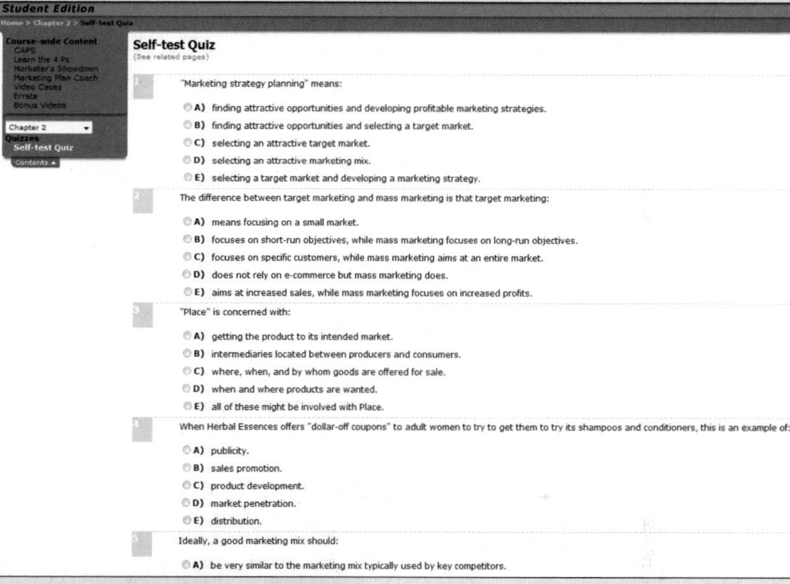

Help me study for my next test!

The *Basic Marketing* website has Student Chapter Quizzes—10 self-test questions for each chapter.

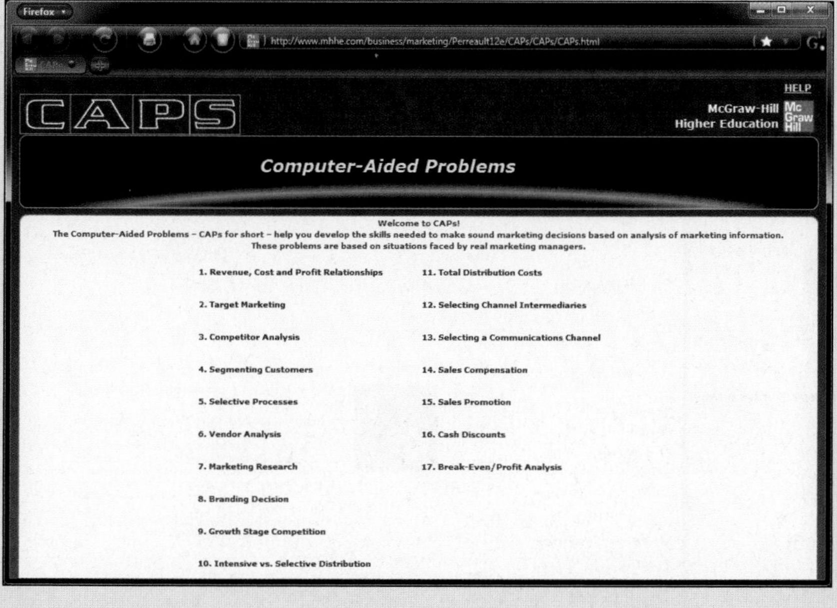

Learn how marketing managers use numbers and spreadsheets to analyze data and make marketing decisions!

Our Computer-Aided Problems (we call them CAPs) allow you to apply concepts from the book while you develop and hone analytical skills needed by today's marketing managers. The CAPs are also available in the student resources area of *Connect Marketing* for *Basic Marketing*.

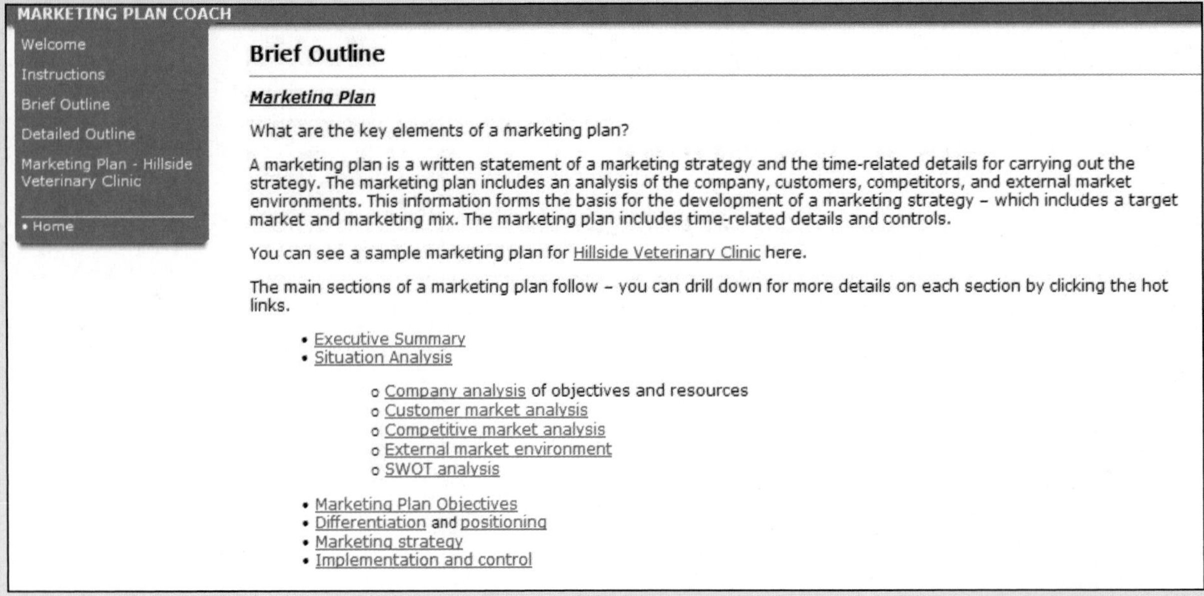

MARKETING PLAN COACH
Welcome
Instructions
Brief Outline
Detailed Outline
Marketing Plan - Hillside Veterinary Clinic
• Home
Brief Outline
Marketing Plan
What are the key elements of a marketing plan?
A marketing plan is a written statement of a marketing strategy and the time-related details for carrying out the strategy. The marketing plan includes an analysis of the company, customers, competitors, and external market environments. This information forms the basis for the development of a marketing strategy – which includes a target market and marketing mix. The marketing plan includes time-related details and controls.
You can see a sample marketing plan for Hillside Veterinary Clinic here.
The main sections of a marketing plan follow – you can drill down for more details on each section by clicking the hot links.
• Executive Summary
• Situation Analysis
o Company analysis of objectives and resources
o Customer market analysis
o Competitive market analysis
o External market environment
o SWOT analysis
• Marketing Plan Objectives
• Differentiation and positioning
• Marketing strategy
• Implementation and control

I want to write a marketing plan!

Check out the *Marketing Plan Coach*—it connects the concepts in your textbook with a real marketing plan. This website was designed by the authors of *Basic Marketing*—so it really works with your book. The *Marketing Plan Coach* is also available in the student resources area of *Connect Marketing* for *Basic Marketing.*

Stay current at *Learn the 4 Ps*—we have a blog (www.learnthe4ps.com), Twitter feed (@learnthe4ps), and Facebook page (www.facebook.com/learnthe4ps.com).

Connect® *Marketing* for *Basic Marketing*—More Interactivity and More Ways to Learn

Connect Marketing is a premium resource—it may be included in the package your instructor chose for your textbook. *Connect Marketing* for *Basic Marketing* includes some of the same materials you can find at the Online Learning Center for Basic Marketing: 1) student chapter quizzes, 2) Computer-Aided Problems (CAPs), and 3) *Marketing Plan Coach*. In addition, in *Connect Marketing*, you can find premium materials: 1) *Connect* quizzes, 2) Learning with Ads, 3) Video Cases, 4) LearnSmart, and 5) *Connect* assignments.

What do I get with *Connect Marketing*?

1. *Connect* Quizzes—study for that next test with 20 multiple-choice questions per chapter.

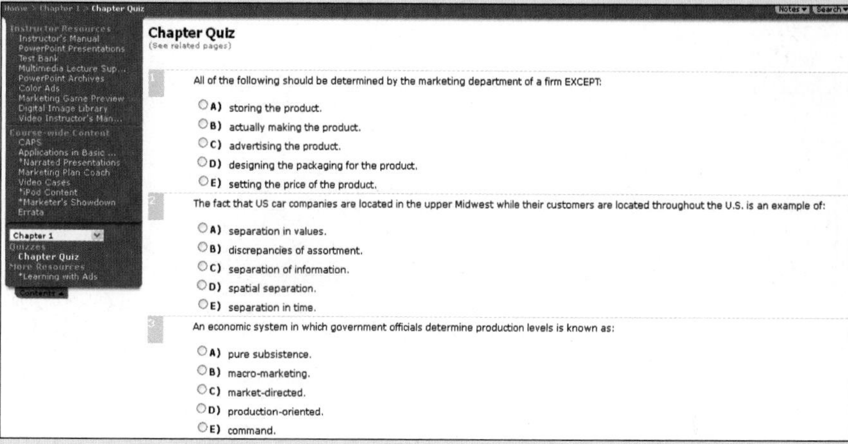

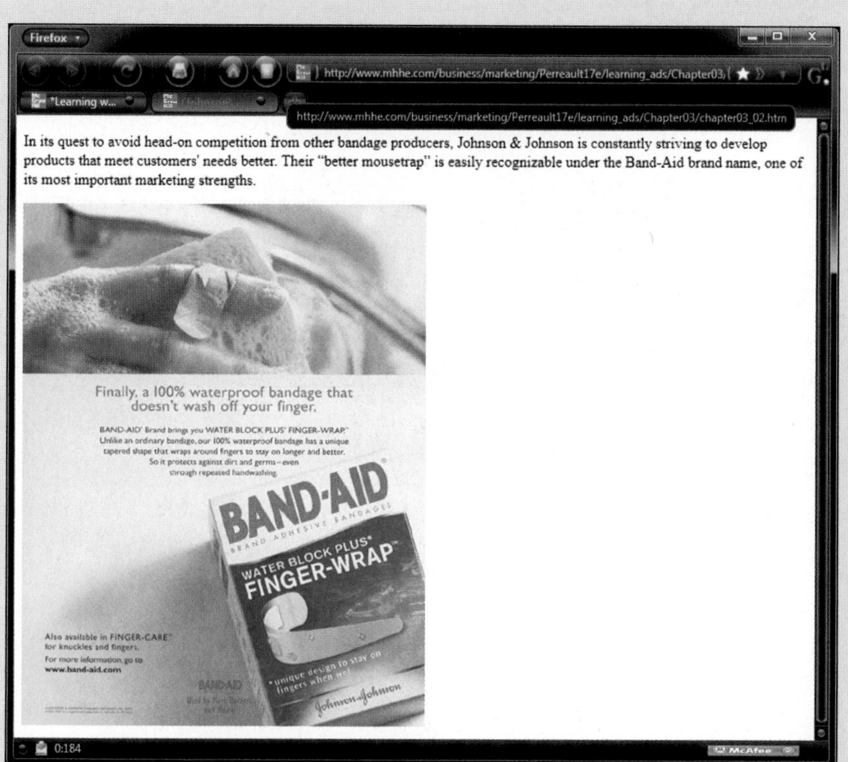

2. Learning with Ads—a great way to preview ideas from each chapter. You can look through print ads and read comments for ideas about how a chapter's concepts are applied by real companies. Great for visual learners.

3. Video Cases—get ready access to video clips from our video cases. Listen to and watch successful marketing in action.

4. LearnSmart™—LearnSmart is an adaptive learning system designed to help you learn faster, study more efficiently, and retain more knowledge for greater success.

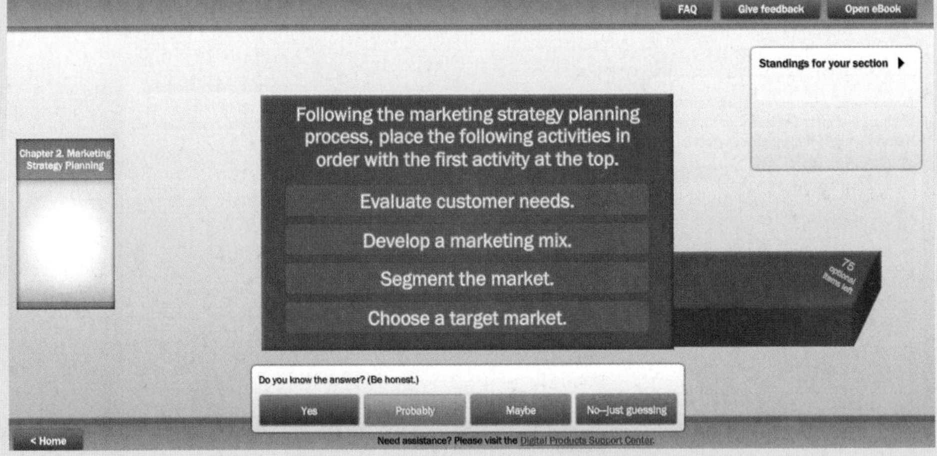

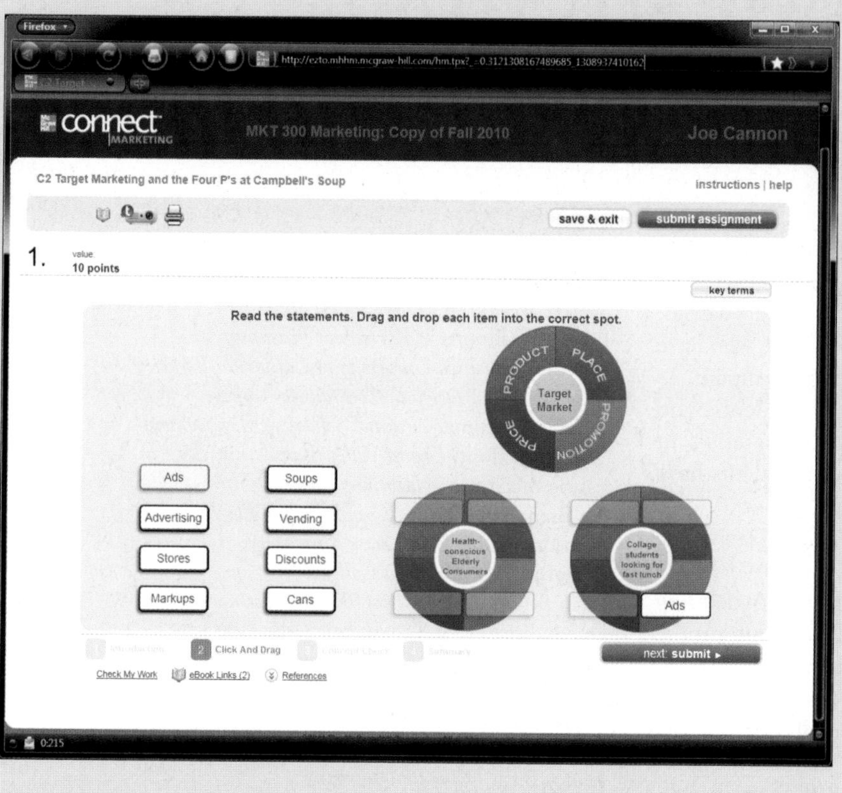

5. *Connect®* Assignments—*Connect Marketing* assignments give you interactive and engaging exercises. You get to apply the concepts you have learned in the book and you get immediate feedback.

Acknowledgments

Basic Marketing has been influenced and improved by the inputs of more people than it is possible to list. We do, however, want to express our appreciation to those who have played the most significant roles, especially in this edition.

We are especially grateful to our many students who have criticized and made comments about materials in *Basic Marketing*. Indeed, in many ways, our students have been our best teachers.

We owe our greatest debt of gratitude to Lin Davis. The book probably wouldn't exist if it weren't for her—because without her help it would have been just too overwhelming and we'd have quit! Lin has been part of this team for more than 25 years. During that time, she has made contributions in every aspect of the text and package. Over the years she spent countless hours researching photos and case histories, and she critiqued thousands of manuscript pages through countless revisions of the text and all the accompanying materials. She has reviewed, edited, and critiqued every word we've written. Her hard work, positive attitude, and dedication to quality throughout the whole process is without match. Lin cut back on the time she put into this edition of Basic Marketing as she moved into semi-retirement. Yet her mark on this project is indelible. We could not have asked for a better friend and colleague.

Many improvements in recent editions were stimulated by feedback from a number of colleagues around the country. Their feedback took many forms. In particular, we would like to recognize the helpful contributions of:

Cliff Ashmead Abdool, *CUNY College of Staten Island*
Roshan (Bob) Ahuja, *Ramapo College of New Jersey*
Thomas Ainscough, *University of South Florida*
Ian Alam, *Ramapo College of New Jersey*
Mary Albrecht, *Maryville University*
David Andrus, *Kansas State University at Manhattan*
Chris Anicich, *Broome Community College*
Maria Aria, *Missouri State University*
April Atwood, *University of Washington*
Ainsworth Bailey, *University of Toledo*
Turina Bakker, *University of Wisconsin*
Jeff Bauer, *University of Cincinnati—Batavia*
Leta Beard, *Washington University*
Amy Beattie, *Nichols College of Champlain*
Cathleen Behan, *Northern VA Community College*
Patty Bellamy, *Black Hills State University*
Suzeanne Benet, *Grand Valley State University*
Shahid Bhuian, *Louisiana Tech University*
John S. Bishop, Jr., *Ohio State University*
David Blackmore, *University of Pittsburgh*
Ross Blankenship, *University of California Berkeley*
Maurice Bode, *Delgado Community College*
Jonathan Bohlman, *Purdue School of Management*
William J. Bont, *Grand Valley State University*
Laurie Brachman, *University of Wisconsin*
Kit Brenan, *Northland Community College*
John Brennan, *Florida State University*
Richard Brien, *De Anza College*
Elten Briggs, *University of Texas—Austin*
Denny Bristow, *St. Cloud State University*
Susan Brudvig, *Ball State University*
Kendrick W. Brunson, *Liberty University*
Derrell Bulls, *Texas Women's University*
Helen Burdenski, *Notre Dame College of Ohio*
Nancy Bush, *Wingate University*
Carmen Calabrese, *University of North Carolina—Pembroke*
Catherine Campbell, *University of Maryland University College*
James Carlson, *Manatee Community College*
Donald Caudill, *Bluefield State College*
Karen Cayo, *Kettering University*
Kenny Chan, *California State University—Chico*
E. Wayne Chandler, *Eastern Illinois University*
Chen Ho Chao, *Baruch College, City University of New York*
Valeri Chukhlomin, *Empire State College*
Margaret Clark, *Cincinnati State Technical and Community College*
Paris Cleanthous, *New York University—Stern School*
Thomas Cline, *St. Vincent College*
Gloria Cockerell, *Collin County Community College*
Linda Jane Coleman, *Salem State College*
Brian Connett, *California State University—Northridge*
Craig Conrad, *Western Illinois University*
Barbara Conte, *Florida Atlantic University*
Sherry Cook, *Southwest Missouri State*
Matt Critcher, *University of Arkansas Community College—Batesville*
Tammy Crutchfield, *Mercer University*
Brent Cunningham, *Jacksonville State University*
Madeline Damkar, *Cabrillo Community College/CSUEB*
Charles Davies, *Hillsdale College*
J. Charlene Davis, *Trinity University*
Scott Davis, *University of California at Davis*
Dwane Dean, *Manhattan College*
Larry Degaris, *California State University*
Nicholas Didow, *University of North Carolina-Chapel Hill*
Susan Higgins DeFago, *John Carroll University*
Oscar W. DeShields, Jr., *California State University—Northridge*
Les Dlabay, *Lake Forest College*

Glenna Dod, *Wesleyan College*
Gary Donnelly, *Casper College*
Paul Dowling, *University of Utah*
Laura Downey, *Purdue University*
Phillip Downs, *Florida State University*
Michael Drafke, *College of DuPage*
John Drea, *Western Illinois University*
Colleen Dunn, *Bucks Community College*
Sean Dwyer, *Louisiana Technical University*
Mary Edrington, *Drake University*
Steven Engel, *University of Colorado*
Keith Fabes, *Berkeley College*
Peter Fader, *University of Pennsylvania*
Ken Fairweather, *LeTourneau University*
Phyllis Fein, *Westchester Community College*
Lori S. Feldman, *Purdue University*
Mark Fenton, *University of Wisconsin—Stout*
Jodie L. Ferguson, *Virginia Commonwealth University*
Richard Kent Fields, *Carthage College*
Lou Firenze, *Northwood University*
Michael Fitzmorris, *Park University*
Richard Fogg, *Kansas State University*
Kim Folkers, *Wartburg College*
Renee Foster, *Delta State University*
Frank Franzak, *Virginia Commonwealth University*
John Gaffney, *Hiram College*
John Gaskins, *Longwood University*
Carol Gaumer, *University of Maryland; Univeristy College*
Karl Giulian, *Fairleigh Dickinson University-Madison*
Thomas Giese, *University of Richmond*
J. Lee Goen, *Oklahoma Baptist University*
Brent G. Goff, *University of Houston—Downtown*
David Good, *Central Missouri State University*
Pradeep Gopalakrishna, *Pace University*
Rahul Govind, *University of Mississippi*
Norman Govoni, *Babson College*
Gary Grandison, *Alabama State University*
Wade Graves, *Grayson County College*
Mitch Griffin, *Bradley University*
Mike Griffith, *Cascade College*
Alice Griswold, *Clarke College*
Barbara Gross, *California State University, Northridge*
Susan Gupta, *University of Wisconsin at Milwaukee*
John Hadjmarcou, *University of Texas at El Paso*
Khalil Hairston, *Indiana Institute of Technology*
Adam Hall, *Western Kentucky University*
Bobby Hall, *Wayland Baptist University*
Joan Hall, *Macomb Community College*
David Hansen, *Schoolcraft College*
Dorothy Harpool, *Wichita State University*
LeaAnna Harrah, *Marion Technical College*
James Harvey, *George Mason University*
John S. Heise, *California State University—Northridge*
Lewis Hershey, *University of North Carolina—Pembroke*
James Hess, *Ivy Tech Community College*
Wolfgang Hinck, *Louisiana State University—Shreveport*
Pamela Homer, *California State University—Long Beach*
Ronald Hoverstad, *University of the Pacific*
John Howard, *Tulane University*
Doug Hughes, *Michigan State University-East Lansing*
Deborah Baker Hulse, *University of Texas at Tyler*
Janet Hunter, *Northland Pioneer College*
Phil Hupfer, *Elmhurst College*
Hector Iweka, *Lasell College*
Annette Jajko, *Triton College/College of DuPage*
Carol Johanek, *Washington University*
Timothy Johnston, *University of Tennessee at Martin*
Keith Jones, *North Carolina A&T State University*
Sungwoo Jung, *Saint Louis University*
Fahri Karakaya, *University of Massachusetts*
Gary Karns, *Seattle Pacific University*
Pat Karush, *Thomas College*
Eileen Kearney, *Montgomery County Community College*
James Kellaris, *University of Cincinnati*
Robin Kelly, *Cuyahoga Community College*
Courtney Kernek, *Texas A&M University—Commerce*
Brian Kinard, *PennState University-University Park*
Rob Kleine, *Ohio Northern University*
Ken Knox, *Ohio State University-Athens*
Kathleen Krentler, *San Diego State University*
Dmitri Kuksov, *Washington University*
Jean Laliberte, *Troy State University*
Tim Landry, *Kutztown University of Pennsylvania*
Geoffrey Lantos, *Oregon State University*
Linda Lamarca, *Tarleton State University*
Kevin Lambert, *Southeast Community College*
Richard LaRosa, *Indiana University of Pennsylvania*
Donald Larson, *The Ohio State University*
Dana-Nicoleta Lascu, *Richmond University*
Debra Laverie, *Texas Tech University*
Marilyn Lavin, *University of Wisconsin—Whitewater*
Freddy Lee, *California State University—Los Angeles*
Steven V. LeShay, *Wilmington University*
David Levy, *Bellevue University*
Doug Livermore, *Morningside College*
Lori Lohman, *Augsburg College*
Paul James Londrigan, *Mott Community College*
Guy Lochiatto, *California State University*
Sylvia Long-Tolbert, *University of Toledo*
Terry Lowe, *Heartland Community College*
Harold Lucius, *Rowan University*
Navneet Luthar, *Madison Area Technical College*
Richard Lutz, *University of Florida*
W. J. Mahony, *Southern Wesleyan University*
Rosalynn Martin, *MidSouth Community College*
Phyllis Mansfield, *Pennsylvania State University—Erie*
James McAloon, *Fitchburg State University*
Lee McCain, *Shaw University*
Christina McCale, *Regis University*
Michele McCarren, *Southern State Community College*
Kevin McEvoy, *University of Connecticut—Stamford*
Rajiv Mehta, *New Jersey Institute of Technology*
Rajiv Mehta, *Truman State University*
Amit Mukherjee, *Providence College*
Sanjay Mehta, *Sam Houston State University*
Matt Meuter, *California State University—Chico*
Michael Mezja, *University of Las Vegas*
Margaret Klayton Mi, *Mary Washington College*
Herbert A. Miller, Jr., *University of Texas—Austin*
Linda Mitchell, *Lindon State College*
Ted Mitchell, *University of Nevada, Reno*
Robert Montgomery, *University of Evansville*

Todd Mooradian, *College of William and Mary*
Kelvyn A. Moore, *Clark Atlanta University*
Marlene Morris, *Georgetown University*
Brenda Moscool, *California State University—Bakersfield*
Ed Mosher, *Laramie Community College*
Reza Motameni, *California State University—Fresno*
Steve Mumsford, *Gwynedd-Mercy College*
Clara Munson, *Albertus Magnus*
Thomas Myers, *University of Richmond*
Cynthia Newman, *Rider University*
Philip S. Nitse, *Idaho State University at Pocatello*
J. R. Ogden, *Kutztown University*
David Oh, *California State University—Los Angeles*
Sam Okoroafo, *University of Toledo*
Jeannie O'Laughlin, *Dakota Wesleyan University*
Louis Osuki, *Chicago State University*
Daniel Padgett, *Auburn University*
Esther S. Page-Wood, *Western Michigan University*
Karen Palumbo, *University of St. Francis*
Terry Paridon, *Cameron University*
Terry Paul, *Ohio State University*
Sheila Petcavage, *Cuyahoga Community College*
Stephen Peters, *Walla Walla Community College*
Man Phan, *Comsumnes River College*
Linda Plank, *Ferris State University*
Lucille Pointer, *University of Houston—Downtown*
Brenda Ponsford, *Clarion University*
Joel Poor, *University of Missouri*
Tracy Proulx, *Park University*
Anthony Racka, *Oakland Community College*
Kathleen Radionoff, *Cardinal Stritch University*
Daniel Rajaratnam, *Baylor University*
Catherine Rich-Duval, *Merrimack College*
Charles W. Richardson, Jr., *Clark Atlanta University*
Lee Richardson, *University of Baltimore*
Daniel Ricica, *Sinclair Community College*
Brent Richard, *Ramapo College of New Jersey*
Darlene Riedemann, *Eastern Illinois University*
Sandra Robertson, *Thomas Nelson Community College*
Kim Rocha, *Barton College*
Amy Rodie, *University of Nebraska—Omaha*
Carlos Rodriguez, *Governors State University*
Robert Roe, *University of Wyoming*
Ann R. Root, *Florida Atlantic University*
Ann R. Root, *Florida Atlantic University-Boca Raton*
Mark Rosenbaum, *Northern Illinois University*
Donald Roy, *Middle Tennessee State University*
Joel Saegert, *University of Texas at San Antonio*
Nate Scharff, *Grossmont College*
Henry Schrader, *Ramapo College of New Jersey*
C. M. Sashi, *Florida Atlantic University*
Erika Schlomer-Fischer, *California Lutheran University*
Lewis Schlossinger, *Community College of Aurora*
Charles Schwepker, *Central Missouri State University*
Murphy Sewell, *University of Connecticut—Storrs*
Kenneth Shamley, *Sinclair College*
Doris Shaw, *Northern Kentucky University*
Donald Shifter, *Fontbonne College*
Jeremy Sierra, *New Mexico State University*
Lisa Simon, *California Polytech—San Luis Obispo*
Rob Simon, *University of Nebraska*
James Simpson, *University of Alabama in Huntsville*
Aditya Singh, *Pennsylvania State University—McKeesport*
Mandeep Singh, *Western Illinois University*
Jill Slomski, *Mercyhurst College*
Robert Smoot, *Lees College*
Don Soucy, *University of North Carolina—Pembroke*
Roland Sparks, *Johnson C. Smith University*
Gene Steidinger, *Loras College*
Jim Stephens, *Emporia State University*
Tom Stevenson, *University of North Carolina*
Geoffrey Stewart, *University of Louisiana at Lafayette*
Karen Stewart, *The Richard Stockton College of New Jersey*
Stephen Strange, *Henderson Community College*
Randy Stuart, *Kennesaw State University*
Rajneesh Suri, *Drexel University*
John Talbott, *Indiana University*
Uday Tate, *Marshall University*
A. J. Taylor, *Austin Peay State University*
Scott Taylor, *McHenry County College*
Janice Taylor, *Miami University*
Kimberly Taylor, *Florida International University*
Steven Taylor, *Illinois State University*
Jeff Thieme, *Syracuse University*
Scott Thompson, *University of Wisconsin—Oshkosh*
Dennis Tootelian, *California State University—Sacramento*
Gary Tschantz, *Walsh University*
Fran Ucci, *Triton College/College of DuPage*
Sue Umashankar, *University of Arizona*
David Urban, *Virginia Commonwealth University*
Kristin Uttech, *Madison Area Technical College*
Peter Vantine, *Georgia Tech*
Steve Vitucci, *Tarleton State University*
Sharon Wagner, *Missouri Western State College*
Suzanne Walchli, *University of the Pacific*
Jane Wayland, *Eastern Illinois University*
Danny "Peter" Weathers, *Louisiana State University*
John Weiss, *Colorado State University*
M. G. M. Wetzeis, *Universiteit Maastrict, The Netherlands*
Fred Whitman, *Mary Washington College*
Judy Wilkinson, *Youngstown State University*
Phillip Wilson, *Midwestern State University*
Robert Witherspoon, *Triton College*
John Withey, *Indiana University—South Bend*
Brent Wren, *Manhattanville College*
Jim Wong, *Shenandoah University*
Joyce H. Wood, *N. Virginia Community College*
Newell Wright, *James Madison University*
Joseph Yasaian, *McIntosh College*
Gary Young, *Worcester State College*

We've always believed that the best way to build consistency and quality into the text and the other P.L.U.S. units is to do as much as possible ourselves. With the growth of multimedia technologies, it's darn hard to be an expert on them all. But we've had spectacular help in that regard.

The lecture-support PowerPoints have been a tremendous effort over many editions. We appreciate the efforts of Jay Carlson, Mandy Noelle Carlson, David Urban, Milt Pressley, and Lewis Hershey for their creative work on the lecture-support PowerPoint presentation slides.

Nick Childers at Shadows and Light Creative Services has been the guru behind the scenes in production work on the video package for many editions. He also worked with us in developing the first versions of our CDs. Nick Childers and Debra Childers continue to play an important role not only in the videos but in multimedia innovations.

For several editions, Judy Wilkinson has played a big role as producer of the video series for the book. In that capacity, she worked closely with us to come up with ideas, and she provided guidance to the talented group of marketing professors and managers who created or revised videos for this edition. Judy also is the author of several outstanding video segments. We express respect for and deep appreciation to Judy for her work on the video series.

Of course, like other aspects of *Basic Marketing,* the video series has evolved and improved over time, and its current strength is partly due to the insights of Phil Niffenegger, who served as producer for our early video efforts. The video series also continues to benefit from the contributions of colleagues who developed videos in earlier editions. They are

Gary R. Brockway
James Burley
David Burns
Debra Childers
Martha O. Cooper
Carolyn Costley
Angie Fenton
W. Davis Folsom
Pam Girardo
Brenda Green
Douglas Hausknecht
Scott Johnson
Bart Kittle
Gene R. Lazniak
Bill Levy
Charles S. Madden
Don McBane
W. Glynn Mangold
Becky Manter
Robert Miller
J. R. Montgomery
Linda Mothersbaugh
Michael R. Mullen
Phillip Niffenegger
Deborah Owens
Thomas G. Ponzurick
George Prough
Peter Rainsford
Jane Reid
Clinton Schertzer
Roger Schoenfeldt
Thomas Sherer
Jeanne M. Simmons
Walter Strange
Jeff Tanner
Ron Tatham
Rollie O. Tillman
Carla Vallone
Robert Welsh
Holt Wilson
Poh-Lin Yeou

Faculty and students at our current and past academic institutions—Michigan State University, University of North Carolina, Colorado State University, Emory, Notre Dame, University of Georgia, Northwestern University, University of Oregon, University of Minnesota, and Stanford University—have significantly shaped the book. Professor Andrew A. Brogowicz of Western Michigan University contributed many fine ideas to early editions of the text and supplements. Neil Morgan, Charlotte Mason, Rich Gooner, Gary Hunter, John Workman, Nicholas Didow, Barry Bayus, Ken Manning, and Ajay Menon have provided a constant flow of helpful suggestions.

We are also grateful to the colleagues with whom we collaborate to produce international adaptations of the text. In particular, Lindsey Meredith, Lynne Ricker, Stan Shapiro, Ken Wong, and Pascale G. Quester have all had a significant impact on *Basic Marketing.*

The designers, artists, editors, and production people at McGraw-Hill/Irwin who worked with us on this edition warrant special recognition. All of them have shared our commitment to excellence and brought their own individual creativity to the project. First, we should salute Christine Vaughan, who has done a great (and patient) job as production manager for the project. Without her adaptive problem solving, we could not have succeeded with a (very) rapid-response production schedule—which is exactly what it takes to be certain that teachers and students get the most current information possible.

Gabriela Gonzalez worked as development editor on this edition; her insight and project management skills are much appreciated. Our executive editor, Sankha Basu, provides a valuable perspective on the *Basic Marketing* franchise. His ideas have had a great impact on the book.

The layout and design of the book included a great team of professionals. Keith McPherson is a long-time creative and valued contributor to *Basic Marketing.* He is a great talent and we sincerely appreciate his past efforts that continue to be reflected in the book's design. We sincerely appreciate the talents of Laurie Entringer who created the interior and cover for this edition of *Basic Marketing.* We also appreciate Mike Hruby, who again tracked down permissions for photos and ads we selected to use to illustrate important ideas. Kendra Miller helped edit this edition of the book and brought new energy and insight along with a sharp eye for detail.

Our marketing manager, Donielle Xu, has brought creativity, energy, and great ideas to the book. Her assistant, Liz Steiner, has also been extremely helpful.

Our families have been patient and consistent supporters through all phases in developing *Basic Marketing.* The support has been direct and substantive. Pam Perreault and Chris Cannon have provided valuable assistance and more encouragement than you could imagine. Our kids—Suzanne, Will, Kelly, Ally, and Mallory—provide valuable suggestions and ideas as well as encouragement and support while their dads are too often consumed with a never-ending set of deadlines.

We are indebted to all the firms that allowed us to reproduce their proprietary materials here. Similarly, we are grateful to associates from our business experiences who have shared their perspectives and feedback and enhanced our sensitivity to the key challenges of marketing management. In that regard, we especially acknowledge Kevin Clancy, Peter Krieg, and their colleagues at Copernicus Marketing Consulting. The combination of pragmatic experience and creative insight they bring to the table is very encouraging. If you want to see great marketing, watch them create it.

A textbook must capsulize existing knowledge while bringing new perspectives and organization to enhance it. Our thinking has been shaped by the writings of literally thousands of marketing scholars and practitioners. In some cases, it is impossible to give unique credit for a particular idea or concept because so many people have played important roles in anticipating, suggesting, shaping, and developing it. We gratefully acknowledge these contributors—from the early thought-leaders to contemporary authors and researchers—who have shared their creative ideas. We respect their impact on the development of marketing and more specifically this book.

To all of these persons—and to the many publishers who graciously granted permission to use their materials—we are deeply grateful. Responsibility for any errors or omissions is certainly ours, but the book would not have been possible without the assistance of many others. Our sincere appreciation goes to all who contributed.

William D. Perreault, Jr.
Joseph P. Cannon
E. Jerome McCarthy

Brief Contents

Contents

1

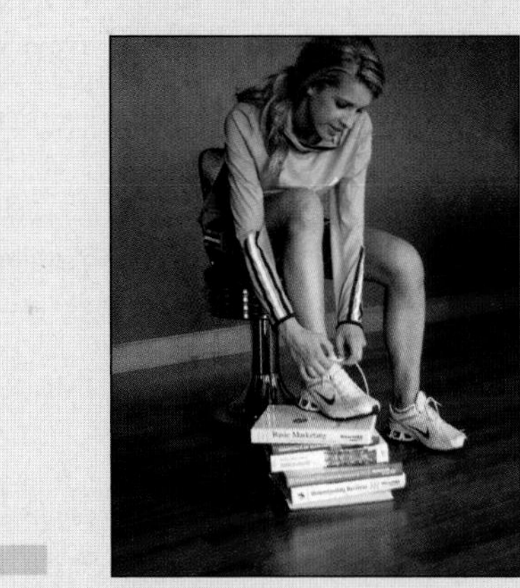

CHAPTER ONE

CHAPTER TWO

Marketing Strategy Planning 30

CHAPTER THREE

Evaluating Opportunities in the Changing Market Environment 56

CHAPTER FOUR

Focusing Marketing Strategy with Segmentation and Positioning 86

CHAPTER FIVE

Final Consumers and Their Buying Behavior 117

CHAPTER SIX

Business and Organizational Customers and Their Buying Behavior 142

CHAPTER SEVEN

Improving Decisions with Marketing Information 168

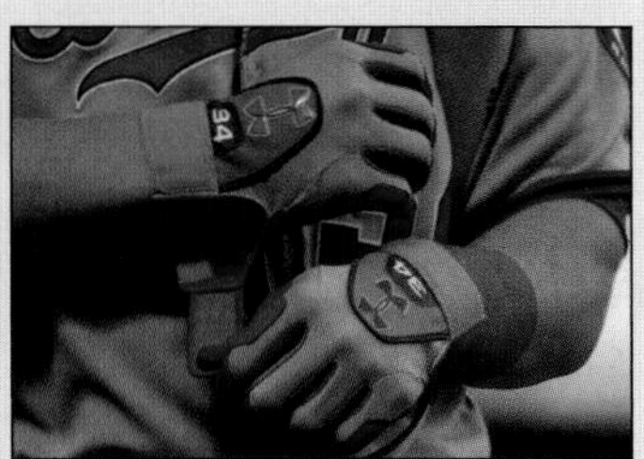

CHAPTER EIGHT

Elements of Product Planning for Goods and Services 196

CHAPTER NINE

Product Management and New-Product Development 234

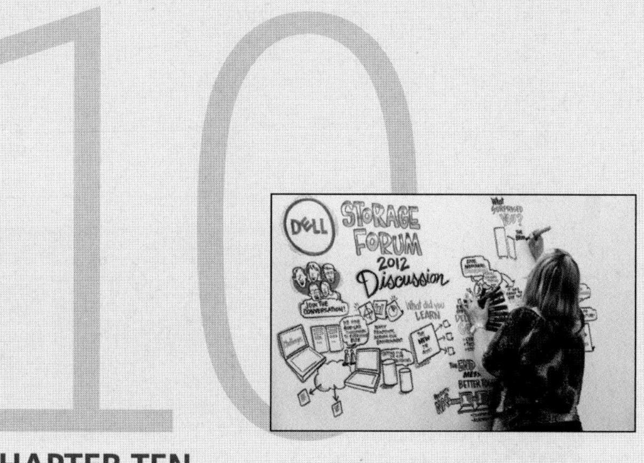

CHAPTER TEN

Place and Development of Channel Systems 253

CHAPTER ELEVEN

Distribution Customer Service and Logistics 278

CHAPTER TWELVE

Retailers, Wholesalers, and Their Strategy Planning 300

CHAPTER THIRTEEN

Promotion—Introduction to Integrated Marketing Communications 328

CHAPTER FOURTEEN

Personal Selling and Customer Service 356

CHAPTER FIFTEEN

Advertising, Publicity, and Sales Promotion 384

CHAPTER SIXTEEN

Pricing Objectives and Policies 418

CHAPTER SEVENTEEN

Price Setting in the Business World 446

CHAPTER EIGHTEEN

Implementing and Controlling Marketing Plans: Evolution and Revolution 474

CHAPTER NINETEEN

Managing Marketing's Link with Other Functional Areas 500

CHAPTER TWENTY

Ethical Marketing in a Consumer-Oriented World: Appraisal and Challenges 524

Basic Marketing

A Marketing Strategy Planning Approach

1

CHAPTER ONE

Marketing's Value to Consumers, Firms, and Society

When it's time to roll out of bed in the morning, does the alarm ringtone on your Samsung Galaxy smartphone wake you, or is it your SiriusXM radio playing your favorite satellite station? Is the station playing hip-hop, classical, or country music—or perhaps a Red Cross ad asking you to donate blood? Maybe you'll start your day with a quick run while wearing your Adidas hoodie and running shorts and your favorite Nike running shoes. Then you could meet a friend at Starbucks for coffee and a study session. Oops, you slept in this morning and aren't sure you have time? Well maybe you should just throw on your Levi's jeans, shirt from Abercrombie and Fitch, and your favorite Sperry Top-Sider shoes and grab a quick bite at home. Perhaps you can find a Chiquita banana and a Lender's Bagel with cream cheese—or maybe a bowl of General Mills Cheerios cereal and a glass of calcium-fortified Simply Orange juice to start your day. If you hurry, your roommate can give you a ride to school in her new Nissan Leaf, but you might just have to take the bus that the city bought from Mercedes-Benz.

When you think about it, you can't get very far into a day without bumping into marketing—and what the whole marketing system does for you. It affects every aspect of our lives—often in ways we don't even consider.

In other parts of the world, people wake up each day to different kinds of experiences. A family in rural Africa may have little choice about what food they will eat or where their clothing will come from. In some countries, economic decisions are still made by government officials. But in the world's most developed countries, consumers determine what's on store shelves. If no one buys a particular color, size, or style, then companies no longer produce it. So you may have trouble finding Cheerios in Tokyo, where they are more likely to eat Kokuho Rose Rice for breakfast.

One brand found around the world is Nike. How has Nike become the shoe of choice for so many professional and casual athletes around the world? Is it the endorsements from star athletes like LeBron James and Cristiano Ronaldo? Maybe the constant innovations like the new lightweight Flyknit running shoes? Do you think Nike's 24,000 retailers play a part? What about all that advertising Nike does? And those three-minute videos that Nike posts on YouTube can't hurt—"My Time Is Now" racked up nine million views in its first three days.

Almost 50 years ago Phil Knight and his college track coach Bill Bowerman founded Blue Ribbon Sports (later renamed Nike) to distribute Japanese running shoes. A few years later they were designing, producing, and selling athletic shoes. Today Nike is the 25th most valuable brand in the world, with annual sales of more than $21 billion. Part of its success comes from adapting its marketing strategy to changing market conditions—but Nike hasn't always adapted quickly enough. Back in the early 1980s, Nike was so focused on running shoes that it missed the aerobics shoe craze and fell behind rival Reebok. Nike profits plummeted so quickly that only aggressive cost-cutting saved the company.

After Nike signed Michael Jordan to endorse its basketball shoes in 1984, the Air Jordan line took the market by storm. It didn't hurt when Nike's advertising agency came up with the "Just Do It!" slogan and an advertising campaign that covered television, magazines, and billboards around the world. This helped carry Nike through the 1990s and its profits soared on rising sales aided by low-cost foreign production.

However, in the late 1990s, the company came under attack when it was reported that some of its suppliers used child labor. At first Nike denied responsibility, claiming it couldn't control how its suppliers operated. But public protest showed that society expected more from a large, successful corporation, and Nike began to closely monitor its suppliers' labor practices.

Since then Nike's social responsibility efforts have turned around its reputation. For example, Nike leads a group of 10 partners in the GreenXchange, a web-based marketplace where member firms collaborate and share ideas to foster sustainability. Nike's Reuse-A-Shoe program turns old shoes into Nike Grind, which is used as a surface on playgrounds, gym floors, and running tracks.

These days Nike targets growth in emerging markets like China. Nike's goal is to sell $4 billion there by 2015—almost doubling what it sold there in 2010. Nike has adapted its marketing strategy for the Chinese market.

Chinese consumers are crazy about basketball and LeBron James, so Nike touts the NBA star in its ads. Nike also relies on local stars like Olympic hurdler Liu Xiang and tennis player Li Na. To appeal to a more price-sensitive Chinese consumer, Nike's product line includes lower-priced shoes than those it sells in the United States. And because China doesn't have many large shopping malls, Nike worked with retail partners to open 5,000 small stores—many focusing on a single sport.

Recognizing the importance of technology, Nike offers its customers online services in addition to sportswear. For runners worldwide, it collaborated with Apple on the Nike+ iPod Sport Kit. The product places a small sensor in a runner's shoe that communicates with the iPod to record distance, pace, time, and calories burned on each run—and then uploads the data to a website. Similarly, the Nike FuelBand fits on users' wrists and tracks activity all day long. Nike needs to continually innovate to stay ahead of strong competitors that include Adidas, Under Armour, and Chinese upstart Li Ning.[1]

Learning Objectives

In this chapter, you'll learn what marketing is all about and why it's important to you as a consumer. We'll also explore why it is so crucial to the success of individual firms and nonprofit organizations and the impact that it has on the quality of life in different societies.

When you finish this chapter, you should be able to:

1 know what marketing is and why you should learn about it.

2 understand the difference between marketing and macro-marketing.

3 know the marketing functions and why marketing specialists—including intermediaries and collaborators—develop to perform them.

4 understand what a market-driven economy is and how it adjusts the macro-marketing system.

5 know what the marketing concept is—and how it should guide a firm or nonprofit organization.

6 understand what customer value is and why it is important to customer satisfaction.

7 know how social responsibility and marketing ethics relate to the marketing concept.

8 understand the important new terms (shown in red).

Marketing—What's It All About?

LO 1.1

Marketing is more than selling or advertising

Many people think that marketing means "selling" or "advertising." It's true that these are parts of marketing. But *marketing is much more than selling and advertising.*

How did all those bicycles get here?

To illustrate some of the other important things that are included in marketing, think about all the bicycles being pedaled with varying degrees of energy by bike riders around the world. Most of us don't make our own bicycles. Instead, they are made by firms like Trek, Schwinn, Mongoose, and Electra.

Most bikes do the same thing—get the rider from one place to another. But a bike rider can choose from a wide assortment of models. They are designed in different sizes and with or without gears. Off-road bikes have large knobby tires. Kids and older people may want more wheels—to make balancing easier. Some bikes need baskets or even trailers for cargo. You can buy a basic bike for less than $50. Or you can spend more than $2,500 for a custom frame.

This variety of styles and features complicates the production and sale of bicycles. The following list shows some of the things a manager should do before and after deciding to produce and sell a bike.

"Life Comes at You Fast." Nationwide's trademarked phrase and "buildingscape" ad really get attention and remind consumers that Nationwide can help when things go awry. Creative advertising like this is an important part of marketing, but modern marketing involves much more. For example, Nationwide conducts research to understand customers' needs and then develops new policies and services to satisfy those needs at a price that represents a good value.

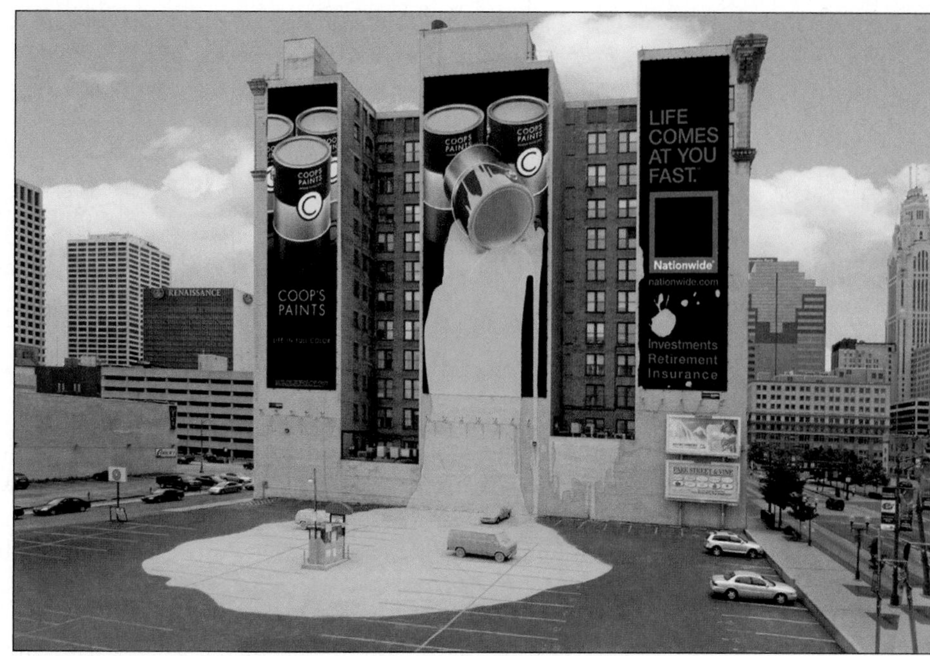

1. Analyze the needs of people who might buy a bike and decide if they want more or different models.
2. Predict what types of bikes—handlebar styles and types of wheels, brakes, and materials—different customers will want and decide which of these people the firm will try to satisfy.
3. Estimate how many of these people will want to buy bicycles, and when.
4. Determine where in the world these bike riders are and how to get the firm's bikes to them.
5. Estimate what price they are willing to pay for their bikes and if the firm can make a profit selling at that price.
6. Decide which kinds of promotion should be used to tell potential customers about the firm's bikes.
7. Estimate how many competing companies will be making bikes, what kind, and at what prices.
8. Figure out how to provide customer service if a customer has a problem after buying a bike.

Marketing helps make sure that customers get the bicycle that best meets their needs.

The above activities are not part of **production**—actually making goods or performing services. Rather, they are part of a larger process—called *marketing*—that provides needed direction for production and helps make sure that the right goods and services are produced and find their way to consumers.

You'll learn much more about marketing activities in Chapter 2. For now, it's enough to see that marketing plays an essential role in providing consumers with need-satisfying goods and services and, more generally, in creating customer satisfaction. Simply put, **customer satisfaction** is the extent to which a firm fulfills a customer's needs, desires, and expectations.

Marketing Is Important to You

Marketing is important to every consumer

Marketing affects almost every aspect of your daily life. The choices you have among the goods and services you buy, the stores where you shop, and the radio and TV programs you tune in to are all possible because of marketing. In the process of providing all these choices, marketing drives organizations to focus on what it takes to satisfy you, the customer. Most of the things you want or need are available conveniently *when* and *where* you want or need them.

Some courses are interesting when you take them but never relevant again once they're over. That's not so with marketing—you'll be a consumer dealing with marketing for the rest of your life regardless of what career you pursue. Moreover, as a consumer, you pay for the cost of marketing activities. In advanced economies, marketing costs about 50 cents of every consumer dollar. For some goods and services, the percentage is much higher. It makes sense to be an educated consumer and to understand what you get and don't get from all that spending.

Marketing will be important to your job

Another reason for studying marketing is that it offers many exciting and rewarding career opportunities. Throughout this book, you will find information about opportunities in different areas of marketing.

If you're aiming for a nonmarketing job, knowing about marketing will help you do your own job better. Throughout the book, we'll discuss ways that marketing relates to other functional areas. Further, marketing is important to the success of every organization. The same basic principles used to sell soap are also used to "sell" ideas, politicians, mass transportation, health care services, conservation, museums, and even colleges. Even your job résumé is part of a marketing campaign to sell yourself to some employer![2]

Use a marketing approach to get your next job

You will probably be seeking a job sometime soon, offering your services—as an accountant, a salesperson, a computer programmer, a financial analyst, or perhaps a store manager. Or maybe you will be looking for an opportunity with more responsibility or higher pay where you currently work. You will have more success getting the job you want when you take a marketing approach and try to figure out how to best satisfy the needs, interests, and desires of a prospective employer the same way a business looks at customers. Much of what you learn about how businesses use marketing can be applied in the job market. See Appendix C for more details on how to write your personal marketing plan.

Marketing affects innovation and standard of living

An even more basic reason for studying marketing is that marketing plays a big part in economic growth and development. One key reason is that marketing encourages research and **innovation**—the development and spread of new ideas, goods, and services. As firms offer new and better ways of satisfying consumer needs, customers have more choices among products and this fosters competition for consumers' money. This competition drives down prices. Moreover, when firms develop products that really satisfy customers, fuller employment and higher incomes can result. The combination of these forces means that marketing has a big impact on consumers' standard of living—and it is important to the future of all nations.[3]

How Should We Define Marketing?

There are micro and macro views of marketing

In our bicycle example, we saw that a producer of bicycles has to perform many customer-related activities besides just making bikes. The same is true for an insurance company or an art museum. This supports the idea of marketing as a set of activities done by an individual organization to satisfy its customers.

On the other hand, people can't survive on bicycles and art museums alone! In advanced economies, it takes goods and services from thousands of organizations to satisfy the many needs of society. Further, a society needs some sort of marketing system to organize the efforts of all the producers, wholesalers, and retailers needed to satisfy the varied needs of all its citizens. So marketing is also an important social process.

We can view marketing in two ways: *from a micro view as a set of activities performed by organizations and also from a macro view as a social process.* Yet, in everyday use when people talk about marketing, they have the micro view in mind. So that is the way we will define marketing here. However, the broader macro view that looks at the whole production-distribution system is also important, so later we will provide a separate definition and discussion of macro-marketing.

Marketing defined

Marketing is the performance of activities that seek to accomplish an organization's objectives by anticipating customer or client needs and directing a flow of need-satisfying goods and services from producer to customer or client.

Let's look at this definition.[4]

Applies to profit and nonprofit organizations

Marketing applies to both profit and nonprofit organizations. Profit is the objective for most business firms. But other types of organizations may seek more members—or acceptance of an idea. Customers or clients may be individual consumers, business firms, nonprofit organizations, government agencies, or even foreign nations. While most customers and clients pay for the goods and services they receive, others may receive them free of charge or at a reduced cost through private or government support.

More than just persuading customers

Marketing isn't just selling and advertising. Unfortunately, some executives still think of it that way. They feel that the job of marketing is to "get rid of" whatever the company happens to produce. In fact, the aim of marketing is to identify customers' needs and meet those needs so well that the product almost "sells itself." This is true whether the product is a physical good, a service, or even an idea. If the whole marketing job has been done well,

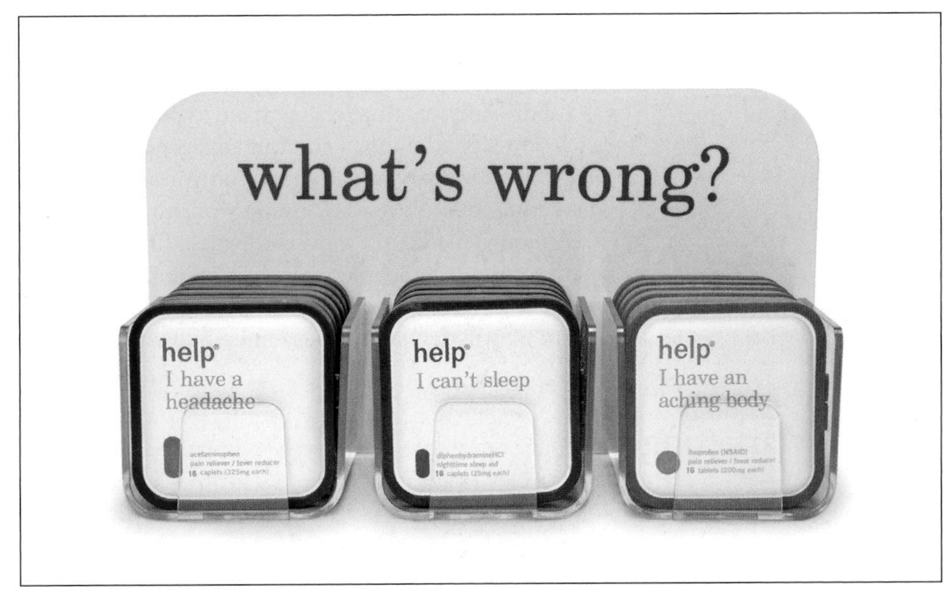

Marketing aims to identify customer needs and meet those needs so well that the product sells itself. Help Remedies found many customers looking for simple solutions to minor health problems.

customers don't need much persuading. They should be ready to buy. And after they buy, they'll be satisfied and ready to buy the same way the next time.

Begins with customer needs

Marketing should begin with potential customer needs—not with the production process. Marketing should try to anticipate needs. And then marketing, rather than production, should determine what goods and services are to be developed—including decisions about product design and packaging; prices or fees; credit and collection policies; transporting and storing policies; advertising and sales policies; and, after the sale, installation, customer service, warranty, and perhaps even disposal and recycling policies.

Does not do it alone

This does not mean that marketing should try to take over production, accounting, and financial activities. Rather, it means that marketing—by interpreting customers' needs—should provide direction for these activities and try to coordinate them.

Marketing involves exchanges

The idea that marketing involves a flow of need-satisfying offerings from a producer to a customer implies that there is an exchange of the need-satisfying offering for something else, such as the customer's money. Marketing focuses on facilitating exchanges. In fact, *marketing doesn't occur unless two or more parties are willing to exchange something for something else.* For example, in a **pure subsistence economy**—when each family unit produces everything it consumes—there is no need to exchange goods and services and no marketing is involved. (Although each producer-consumer unit is totally self-sufficient in such a situation, the standard of living is typically relatively low.)

Builds a relationship with the customer

Keep in mind that a marketing exchange is often part of an ongoing relationship, not just a single transaction. When marketing helps everyone in a firm really meet the needs of a customer before and after a purchase, the firm doesn't just get a single sale. Rather, it has a sale and an ongoing *relationship* with the customer. Then, in the future, when the customer has the same need again—or some other need that the firm can meet—other sales will follow. Often, the marketing *flow* of need-satisfying goods and services is not just for a single transaction but rather is part of building a long-lasting relationship that benefits both the firm and the customer.

The focus of this text—management-oriented micro-marketing

Since you are probably preparing for a career in management, the main focus of this text will be on managerial marketing. We will see marketing through the eyes of the marketing manager.

The marketing ideas we will be discussing throughout this text apply to a wide variety of situations. They are important for new ventures started by one person as well as big corporations, in domestic and international markets, and regardless of whether the focus is on marketing physical goods, services, or an idea or cause. They are equally critical whether the relevant customers or clients are individual consumers, businesses, or some other type of organization. For editorial convenience, we will sometimes use the term *firm* as a shorthand way of referring to any type of organization, whether it is a political party, a religious organization, a government agency, or the like. However, to reinforce the point that the ideas apply to all types of organizations, throughout the book we will illustrate marketing concepts in a wide variety of situations.

Although marketing within individual firms is the primary focus of the text, marketing managers must remember that their organizations are just small parts of a larger macro-marketing system. Therefore, next we will briefly look at the macro view of marketing. Then, we will develop this idea more fully in later chapters.

Macro-Marketing

LO 1.2

Macro-marketing is a social process that directs an economy's flow of goods and services from producers to consumers in a way that effectively matches supply and demand and accomplishes the objectives of society.[5]

Emphasis is on whole system

With macro-marketing we are still concerned with the flow of need-satisfying goods and services from producer to consumer. However, the emphasis with macro-marketing is not on the activities of individual organizations. Instead, the emphasis is on *how the whole marketing system works.* This includes looking at how marketing affects society and vice versa.

Every society needs a macro-marketing system to help match supply and demand. Different producers in a society have different objectives, resources, and skills. Likewise, not all consumers share the same needs, preferences, and wealth. In other words, within every society there are both heterogeneous (highly varied) supply capabilities and heterogeneous demands for goods and services. The role of a macro-marketing system is to effectively match this heterogeneous supply and demand *and* at the same time accomplish society's objectives.

An effective macro-marketing system delivers the goods and services that consumers want and need. It gets products to them at the right time, in the right place, and at a price they're willing to pay. It keeps consumers satisfied after the sale and brings them back to purchase again when they are ready. That's not an easy job—especially if you think about the variety of goods and services a highly developed economy can produce and the many kinds of goods and services consumers want.

Separation between producers and consumers

Effective marketing in an advanced economy is difficult because producers and consumers are often separated in several ways. As Exhibit 1-1 shows, exchange between producers and consumers is hampered by spatial separation, separation in time, separation of

Exhibit 1–1 Marketing Facilitates Production and Consumption

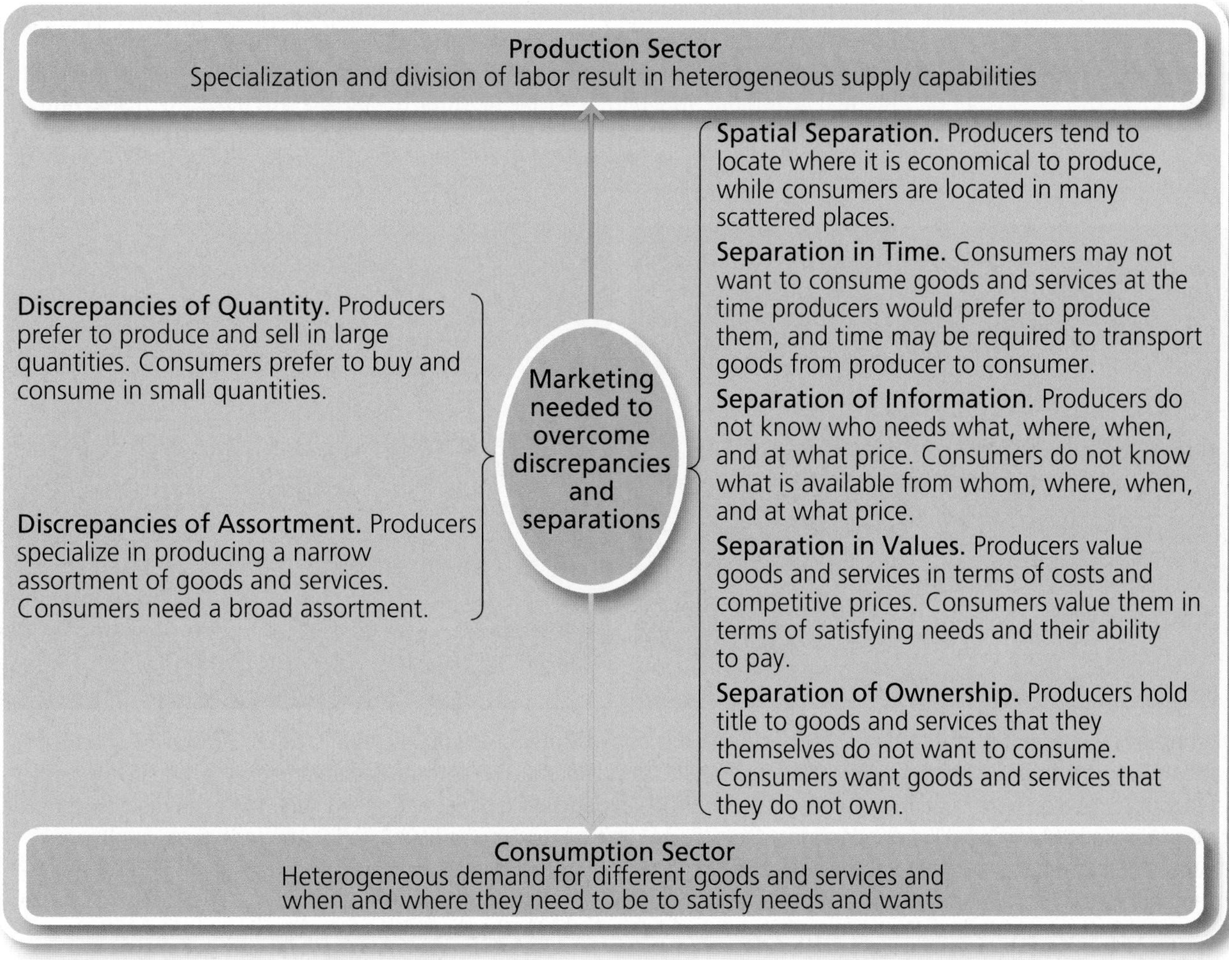

Production Sector
Specialization and division of labor result in heterogeneous supply capabilities

Discrepancies of Quantity. Producers prefer to produce and sell in large quantities. Consumers prefer to buy and consume in small quantities.

Discrepancies of Assortment. Producers specialize in producing a narrow assortment of goods and services. Consumers need a broad assortment.

Marketing needed to overcome discrepancies and separations

Spatial Separation. Producers tend to locate where it is economical to produce, while consumers are located in many scattered places.

Separation in Time. Consumers may not want to consume goods and services at the time producers would prefer to produce them, and time may be required to transport goods from producer to consumer.

Separation of Information. Producers do not know who needs what, where, when, and at what price. Consumers do not know what is available from whom, where, when, and at what price.

Separation in Values. Producers value goods and services in terms of costs and competitive prices. Consumers value them in terms of satisfying needs and their ability to pay.

Separation of Ownership. Producers hold title to goods and services that they themselves do not want to consume. Consumers want goods and services that they do not own.

Consumption Sector
Heterogeneous demand for different goods and services and when and where they need to be to satisfy needs and wants

information and values, and separation of ownership. You may love your cell phone, but you probably don't know when or where it was produced or how it got to you. The people in the factory that produced it don't know about you or how you live.

In addition, most firms specialize in producing and selling large amounts of a narrow assortment of goods and services. This allows them to take advantage of mass production with its **economies of scale**—which means that as a company produces larger numbers of a particular product, the cost of each unit of the product goes down. Yet most consumers only want to buy a small quantity; they also want a wide assortment of different goods and services. These "discrepancies of quantity" and "discrepancies of assortment" further complicate exchange between producers and consumers (Exhibit 1-1). That is, each producer specializes in producing and selling large amounts of a narrow assortment of goods and services, but each consumer wants only small quantities of a wide assortment of goods and services.[6]

Marketing functions help narrow the gap

LO 1.3

The purpose of a macro-marketing system is to overcome these separations and discrepancies. The "universal functions of marketing" help do this.

The **universal functions of marketing** are buying, selling, transporting, storing, standardization and grading, financing, risk taking, and market information. They must be performed in all macro-marketing systems. *How* these functions are performed—and *by whom*—may differ among nations and economic systems. But they are needed in any macro-marketing system. Let's take a closer look at them now.

Any kind of exchange usually involves buying and selling. The **buying function** means looking for and evaluating goods and services. The **selling function** involves promoting the product. It includes the use of personal selling, advertising, customer service, and other direct and mass selling methods. This is probably the most visible function of marketing.

The **transporting function** means the movement of goods from one place to another. The **storing function** involves holding goods until customers need them.

Standardization and grading involve sorting products according to size and quality. This makes buying and selling easier because it reduces the need for inspection and

POM nurtures 90 percent of the pomegranates grown in the United States on 18,000 acres in Central California—and then creates an assortment of products including the raw fruit, POM Wonderful 100 percent Pomegranate Juice, and POMx Iced Coffee. But to overcome the spatial separation between POM's production facilities and consumers, someone must perform a variety of marketing functions, like standardizing and grading the fruit; transporting and storing the fruit, juice, and other products; and buying and selling them. When its products arrive at local supermarkets, consumers are able to find POM's assortment of products alongside a range of other grocery goods.

sampling. **Financing** provides the necessary cash and credit to produce, transport, store, promote, sell, and buy products. **Risk taking** involves bearing the uncertainties that are part of the marketing process. A firm can never be sure that customers will want to buy its products. Products can also be damaged, stolen, or outdated. The **market information function** involves the collection, analysis, and distribution of all the information needed to plan, carry out, and control marketing activities, whether in the firm's own neighborhood or in a market overseas.

Producers, consumers, and marketing specialists perform functions

Producers and consumers sometimes handle some of the marketing functions themselves. However, exchanges are often easier or less expensive when a marketing specialist performs some of the marketing functions. For example, both producers and consumers may benefit when an **intermediary**—someone who specializes in trade rather than production—plays a role in the exchange process. In Chapters 11 and 12 we'll cover the variety of marketing functions performed by the two basic types of intermediaries: retailers and wholesalers. Imagine what it would be like to shop at many different factories and farms for the wide variety of brands of packaged foods that you like rather than at a well-stocked local grocery store. While wholesalers and retailers must charge for services they provide, this charge is usually offset by the savings of time, effort, and expense that would be involved without them. So these intermediaries can help to make the whole macro-marketing system more efficient and effective.

Internet Exercise

Go to the Target home page (**www.target.com**) and click on a tab for one of the product categories. How many different manufacturers' products or brands are shown? Would consumers be better off if each manufacturer just sold directly from its own website?

A wide variety of other marketing specialists may also help smooth exchanges between producers, consumers, or intermediaries. These specialists are **collaborators**—firms that facilitate or provide one or more of the marketing functions other than buying or selling. These collaborators include advertising agencies, marketing research firms, independent product-testing laboratories, Internet service providers, public warehouses, transporting firms, communications companies, and financial institutions (including banks).

New specialists develop to fill market needs

New types of marketing specialists develop or evolve when there are opportunities to make exchanges between producers and consumers more efficient or effective. The growth of the Internet provided one such opportunity and resulted in the rapid growth of e-commerce. **E-commerce** refers to exchanges between individuals or organizations—and activities that facilitate these exchanges—based on applications of information technology. Internet-based intermediaries—like Amazon.com and eBay.com—help cut the costs of many marketing functions. Other marketing specialists have popped up online: Search engines like Google facilitate information search, PayPal reduces consumer risks associated with paying for goods purchased online, and chat-based customer service firms help any company provide 24/7 customer support. Collectively, developments in e-commerce have significantly increased the efficiency and effectiveness of our macro-marketing system. At the same time, many individual firms take advantage of these innovations to improve profitability and customer satisfaction.[7]

Through innovation, specialization, or economies of scale, marketing intermediaries and collaborators are often able to perform the marketing functions better—and at a lower cost—than producers or consumers can. This allows producers and consumers to spend more time on production, consumption, or other activities—including leisure.

Functions can be shifted and shared

From a macro-marketing viewpoint, all of the marketing functions must be performed by someone—an individual producer or consumer, an intermediary, a marketing collaborator, or, in some cases, even a nation's government. No function can be

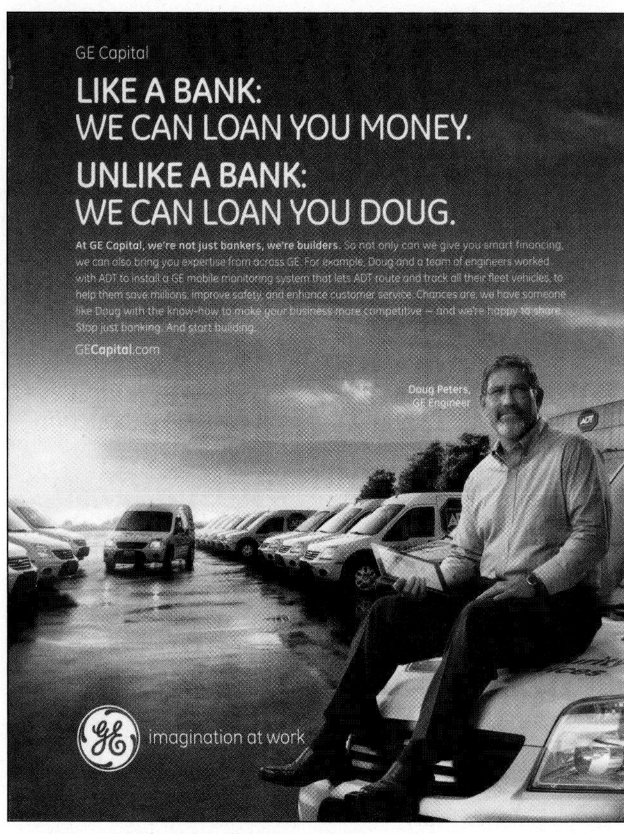

Intermediaries and collaborators develop and offer specialized services that facilitate exchange between producers and customers. An American online retailer can work with Canada Post to make it easier to serve Canadian customers. GE Capital can loan customers money to make buying easier.

completely eliminated. *However, from a micro viewpoint, not every firm must perform all of the functions. Rather, responsibility for performing the marketing functions can be shifted and shared in a variety of ways. Further, not all goods and services require all the functions at every level of their production.* "Pure services"—like a plane ride—don't need storing, for example. But storing is required in the production of the plane and while the plane is not in service.

Regardless of who performs the marketing functions, in general they must be performed effectively and efficiently or the performance of the whole macro-marketing system will suffer. With many different possible ways for marketing functions to be performed in a macro-marketing system, how can a society hope to arrive at a combination that best serves the needs of its citizens? To answer this question, we can look at the role of marketing in different types of economic systems.

The Role of Marketing in Economic Systems

LO 1.4

All societies must provide for the needs of their members. Therefore, every society needs some sort of **economic system**—the way an economy organizes to use scarce resources to produce goods and services and distribute them for consumption by various people and groups in the society.

How an economic system operates depends on a society's objectives and the nature of its political institutions.[8] But regardless of what form these take, all economic

Marketing helps India's rural poor

In recent decades India has experienced rapid economic growth. Many of its citizens have more income and enjoy a higher quality of life. That helps to explain why Unilever's Indian subsidiary, Hindustan Unilever Limited (HUL), has worked hard to build a 40 percent share of the Indian market with its product lines that include soaps, toothpaste, and packaged foods.

Previously, HUL focused primarily on India's urban areas. Yet, almost three-fourths of India's one *billion* plus people still live in rural areas. Only half of these rural villagers have access to electricity—and less than half have basic sanitation. Many of them have an income of less than $2 a day. Conventional wisdom suggests that these poor rural villagers have too little money to be an attractive market. And it's expensive to distribute products to far-flung villages.

But now that is changing. HUL's marketing managers have decided that Indian villagers represent an opportunity for growth—and that villagers might benefit if they could purchase the soaps, toothpaste, and packaged food products that HUL is successfully selling in urban areas of India.

HUL has tailored a new marketing strategy to this target market. Many products have been repackaged in "sachets"—small bags that contain a one- or two-day supply. HUL prices the small sachets so that villagers can afford them—and that in turn gives customers a chance to try quality products that were previously unavailable.

HUL has created its "Shakti Ammas" (women entrepreneurs) program to communicate the benefits of its products and distribute them in remote rural areas. The program sets rural women up as home-based distributors and sales agents. These women stock HUL products at their homes and go door-to-door to sell them. They also organize meetings in local schools and at village fairs to educate their fellow villagers on health and hygiene issues.

HUL will soon have more than 50,000 Shakti Ammas operating in 500,000 villages, reaching 600 million people across India. The Indian success spurred Unilever to adapt the model to developing countries around the globe. These women have a new source of income and are learning about business—while they bring the health benefits of improved hygiene to rural villages. And, of course, HUL hopes to clean up with a new source of growth.[9]

systems must develop some method—along with appropriate economic institutions—to decide what and how much is to be produced and distributed by whom, when, to whom, and why.

There are two basic kinds of economic systems: command economies and market-directed economies. Actually, no economy is entirely command-oriented or market-directed. Most are a mixture of the two extremes.

Government officials may make the decisions

In a **command economy**, government officials decide what and how much is to be produced and distributed by whom, when, to whom, and why. These decisions are usually part of an overall government plan, so command economies are also called "planned" economies. It sounds good for a government to have a plan, but as a practical matter attempts by a government to dictate an economic plan often don't work out as intended.

Producers in a command economy generally have little choice about what goods and services to produce. Their main task is to meet the production quotas assigned in the plan. Prices are also set by government planners and tend to be very rigid—not changing according to supply and demand. Consumers usually have some freedom of choice—it's impossible to control every single detail! But the assortment of goods and services may be quite limited. Activities such as market research, branding, and advertising usually are neglected. Sometimes they aren't done at all.

Government planning in a command economy may work fairly well as long as an economy is simple and the variety of goods and services is small. It may even be necessary under certain conditions—during wartime, drought, or political instability, for example. However, as economies become more complex, government planning

Artists and craftsmen in developing economies often do not have a local market for their products. Ten Thousand Villages operates retail stores and an e-commerce website to help artisans reach customers and promote economic development in their communities. The stores open a market for Loeng Hanh's finely crafted ceramic pieces. Hanh's profits allow her to earn a living and save money for her four-year-old son's education.

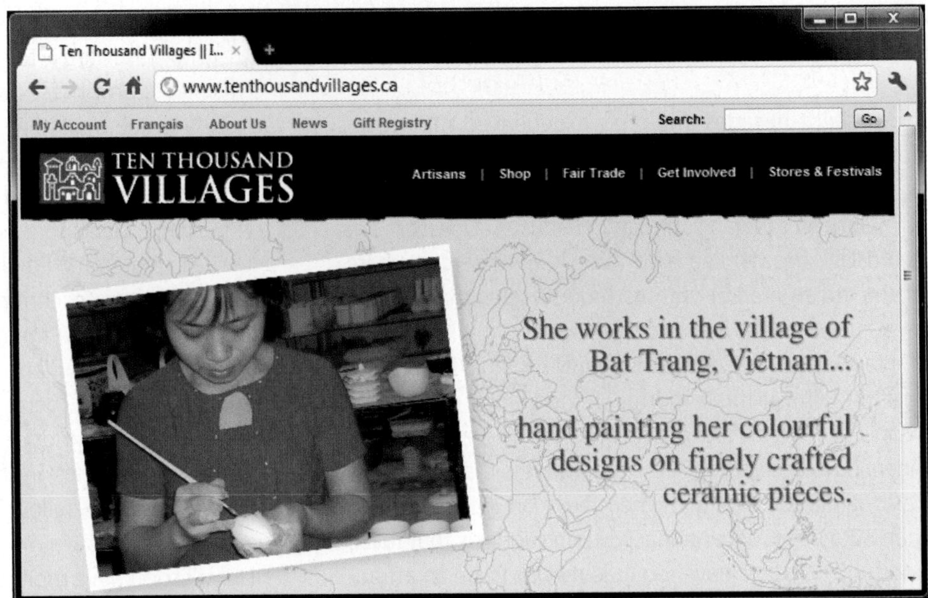

becomes more difficult and tends to break down. That's what happened to the economy in the former Soviet Union. Countries such as North Korea, Cuba, and Iran still rely on command-oriented economic systems. Even so, around the world there is a broad move toward market-directed economic systems—because they are more effective in meeting consumer needs.

A market-directed economy adjusts itself

In a **market-directed economy**, the individual decisions of the many producers and consumers make the macro-level decisions for the whole economy. In a pure market-directed economy, consumers make a society's production decisions when they make their choices in the marketplace. They decide what is to be produced and by whom—through their dollar "votes."

Price is a measure of value

Prices in the marketplace are a rough measure of how society values particular goods and services. If consumers are willing to pay the market prices, then apparently they feel they are getting at least their money's worth. Similarly, the cost of labor and materials is a rough measure of the value of the resources used in the production of goods and services to meet these needs. New consumer needs that can be served profitably—not just the needs of the majority—will probably be met by some profit-minded businesses.

Greatest freedom of choice

Consumers in a market-directed economy enjoy great freedom of choice. They are not forced to buy any goods or services, except those that must be provided for the good of society—things such as national defense, schools, police and fire protection, highway systems, and public-health services. These are provided by the community—and the citizens are taxed to pay for them.

Similarly, producers are free to do whatever they wish—provided that they stay within the rules of the game set by government *and* receive enough dollar "votes" from consumers. If they do their job well, they earn a profit and stay in business. But profit, survival, and growth are not guaranteed.

The role of government

The American economy and most other Western economies are mainly market-directed—but not completely. Society assigns supervision of the system to the government.

For example, besides setting and enforcing the "rules of the game," government agencies control interest rates and the supply of money. They also set import and export rules that affect international competition, regulate radio and TV broadcasting, sometimes control wages and prices, and so on. Government also tries to be sure that property is protected, contracts are enforced, individuals are not exploited, no group unfairly monopolizes markets, and producers deliver the kinds and quality of goods and services they claim to be offering.[10]

Public interest groups and consumers spread the news

In many Western economies, public interest groups and consumers provide an additional check on a market-directed economy. For example, the Center for Science in the Public Interest (CSPI) is a consumer watchdog group that pressures food companies to make healthier products. CSPI regularly issues reports on unhealthy foods like the high fat content in movie theater popcorn and Chinese food. The consulting firm UL TerraChoice regularly points out firms that make false or exaggerated environmental claims about their products. Consumers can also report their satisfaction or dissatisfaction with companies by posting reviews on websites. Because most of this information can easily be found on the Internet by prospective customers, firms have an additional incentive to play by the socially accepted "rules of the game."

Is a macro-marketing system effective and fair?

The effectiveness and fairness of a particular macro-marketing system must be evaluated in terms of that society's objectives. Obviously, all nations don't share the same objectives. For example, Swedish citizens receive many "free" services—like health care and retirement benefits. Goods and services are fairly evenly distributed among the Swedish population. By contrast, North Korea places little emphasis on producing goods and services for individual consumers—and more on military spending. In India the distribution of goods and services is very uneven—with a big gap between the have-nots and the elite haves. Whether each of these systems is judged "fair" or "effective" depends on the objectives of the society.

So far, we have described how a market-directed macro-marketing system adjusts to become more effective and efficient by responding to customer needs. See Exhibit 1-2. As

Exhibit 1–2
Model of a Market-Directed Macro-Marketing System

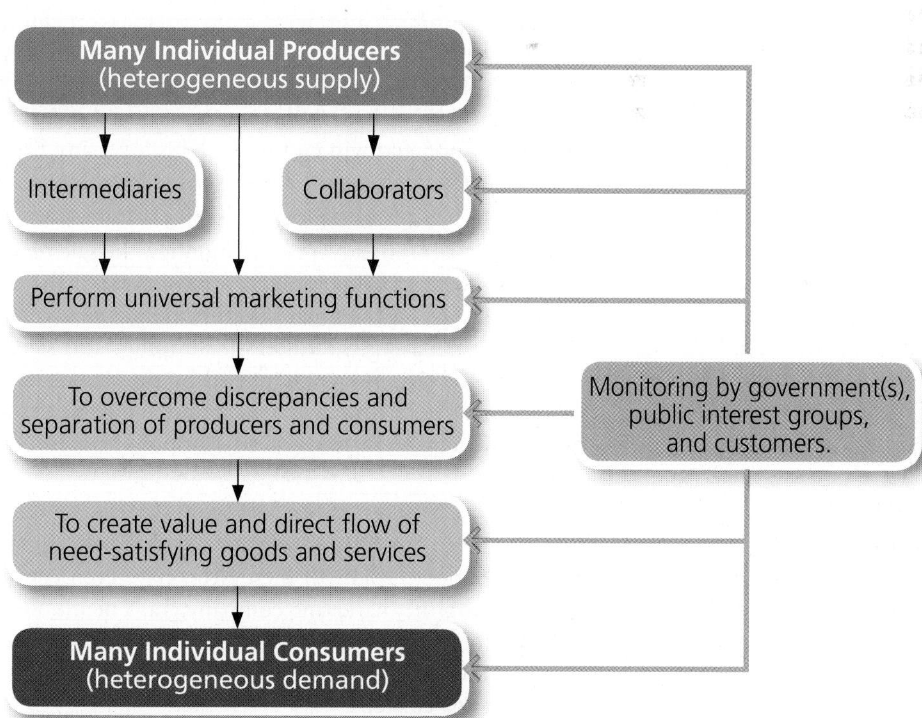

you read this book, you'll learn more about how marketing affects society and vice versa. You'll also learn more about specific marketing activities and be better informed when drawing conclusions about how fair and effective the macro-marketing system is. For now, however, we'll return to our general emphasis on a managerial view of the role of marketing in individual organizations.

Marketing's Role Has Changed a Lot Over the Years

It's clear that marketing decisions are very important to a firm's success. But marketing hasn't always been so complicated. In fact, understanding how marketing thinking has evolved makes the modern view clearer. So we will discuss five stages in marketing evolution: (1) the simple trade era, (2) the production era, (3) the sales era, (4) the marketing department era, and (5) the marketing company era. We'll talk about these eras as if they applied generally to all firms—but keep in mind that *some managers still have not made it to the final stages.* They are stuck in the past with old ways of thinking.

Simple trade era to production era

When societies first moved toward some specialization of production and away from a subsistence economy where each family raised and consumed everything it produced, traders played an important role. Early "producers for the market" made products that were needed by themselves and their neighbors. As bartering became more difficult, societies moved into the **simple trade era**—a time when families traded or sold their "surplus" output to local distributors. These specialists resold the goods to other consumers or other distributors. This was the early role of marketing—and it is still the focus of marketing in many of the less-developed areas of the world. In fact, even in the United States, the United Kingdom, and other more advanced economies, marketing didn't change much until the Industrial Revolution brought larger factories more than a hundred and fifty years ago.

From the production to the sales era

From the Industrial Revolution until the 1920s, most companies were in the production era. The **production era** is a time when a company focuses on production of a few specific products—perhaps because few of these products are available in the market. "If we can make it, it will sell" is management thinking characteristic of the production era. Because of product shortages, many nations—including some of the post-communist republics of Eastern Europe—continue to operate with production era approaches.

By about 1930, most companies in the industrialized Western nations had more production capability than ever before. Now the problem wasn't just to produce—but to beat the competition and win customers. This led many firms to enter the sales era. The **sales era** a time when a company emphasizes selling because of increased competition.

To the marketing department era

For most firms in advanced economies, the sales era continued until at least 1950. By then, sales were growing rapidly in most areas of the economy. The problem was deciding where to put the company's effort. Someone was needed to tie together the efforts of research, purchasing, production, shipping, and sales. As this situation became more common, the sales era was replaced by the marketing department era. The **marketing department era** a time when all marketing activities are brought under the control of one department to improve short-run policy planning and to try to integrate the firm's activities.

To the marketing company era

Since 1960, most firms have developed at least some managers with a marketing management outlook. Many of these firms have even graduated from the marketing department era into the marketing company era. The **marketing company era** is a time when, in addition to short-run marketing planning, marketing people develop long-range plans—sometimes five or more years ahead—and the whole company effort is guided by the marketing concept.

In the past, many banks created products but left it to the marketing department to sell them. In today's more competitive environment, banks are doing research to discover customer needs. A bank that develops products that meet its users' needs will have more satisfied customers. When Bank of the Wichitas added an online branch, it decided to use an untraditional approach and called it Redneck Bank. Redneck Bank offers customers "flat out free checking" and convenience served with a healthy dollop of humor. The approach has been successful as the small bank from Oklahoma quickly added customers from all over the United States.

What Does the Marketing Concept Mean?

LO 1.5

The **marketing concept** means that an organization aims *all* its efforts at satisfying its *customers*—at a *profit*. The marketing concept is a simple but very important idea. See Exhibit 1-3.

The marketing concept is not a new idea—it's been around for a long time. But some managers show little interest in customers' needs. These managers still have a **production orientation**—making whatever products are easy to produce and *then* trying to sell them. They think of customers existing to buy the firm's output rather than of firms existing to serve customers and—more broadly—the needs of society.

Well-managed firms have replaced this production orientation with a marketing orientation. A **marketing orientation** means trying to carry out the marketing concept. Instead of just trying to get customers to buy what the firm has produced, a marketing-oriented firm tries to offer customers what they need.

Three basic ideas are included in the definition of the marketing concept: (1) customer satisfaction, (2) a total company effort, and (3) profit—not just sales—as an objective. These ideas deserve more discussion.

Customer satisfaction guides the whole system

"Give the customers what they need" seems so obvious that it may be hard for you to see why the marketing concept requires special attention. However, people don't always do the logical—especially when it means changing what they've done in the past. In a typical company 50 years ago, production managers thought mainly about getting out the product. Accountants were interested only in balancing the books. Financial people looked after the company's cash position. And salespeople were mainly concerned with getting orders for

Exhibit 1–3
Organizations with a Marketing Orientation Carry Out the Marketing Concept

whatever product was in the warehouse. Each department thought of its own activity as the center of the business. Unfortunately, this is still true in many companies today.

Work together to do a better job

Ideally, all managers should work together as a team. Every department may directly or indirectly impact customer satisfaction. But some managers tend to build "fences" around their own departments. There may be meetings to try to get them to work together—but they come and go from the meetings worried only about protecting their own turf.

We use the term *production orientation* as a shorthand way to refer to this kind of narrow thinking—and lack of a central focus—in a business firm. But keep in mind that this problem may be seen in sales-oriented sales representatives, advertising-oriented agency people, finance-oriented finance people, directors of nonprofit organizations, and so on. It is not a criticism of people who manage production. They aren't necessarily any more guilty of narrow thinking than anyone else.

The fences come down in an organization that has accepted the marketing concept. There may still be departments because specialization often makes sense. But the total system's effort is guided by what customers want—instead of what each department would like to do. In Chapter 19, we'll go into more detail on the relationship between marketing and other functions; here, however, you should see that the marketing concept provides a guiding focus that *all* departments adopt. It should be a philosophy of the whole organization, not just an idea that applies to the marketing department.

Survival and success require a profit

Firms must satisfy customers. But keep in mind that it may cost more to satisfy some needs than any customers are willing to pay. Or it may be much more costly to try to attract new customers than it is to build a strong relationship with—and repeat purchases from—existing customers. So profit—the difference between a firm's revenue and its total costs—is the bottom-line measure of the firm's success and ability to survive. It is the balancing point that helps the firm determine what needs it will try to satisfy with its total (sometimes costly!) effort.

Many organizations go beyond profit

Some organizations explicitly consider a **triple bottom line**—which measures an organization's economic, social, and environmental outcomes—as a measure of long-term success. Profit is the economic outcome. Social refers to how the company's business activities

Exhibit 1–4 Some Differences in Outlook between Adopters of the Marketing Concept and the Typical Production-Oriented Managers

Topic	Marketing Orientation	Production Orientation
Attitudes toward customers	Customer needs determine company plans.	They should be glad we exist, trying to cut costs and bringing out better products.
Product offering	Company makes what it can sell.	Company sells what it can make.
Role of marketing research	To determine customer needs and how well company is satisfying them.	To determine customer reaction, if used at all.
Interest in innovation	Focus is on locating new opportunities.	Focus is on technology and cost cutting.
Customer service	Satisfy customers after the sale and they'll come back again.	An activity required to reduce consumer complaints.
Focus of advertising	Need-satisfying benefits of goods and services.	Product features and how products are made.
Relationship with customer	Customer satisfaction before and after sale leads to a profitable long-run relationship.	Relationship ends when a sale is made.
Costs	Eliminate costs that do not give value to customer.	Keep costs as low as possible.

affect its employees and other people in the communities where it operates. The third bottom line takes into account environmental responsibility, usually seeking to at least not harm the natural environment. Together, these are sometimes referred to as measures of people, planet, and profit.[11]

Adoption of the marketing concept is not universal

The marketing concept may seem obvious, but it is easy to maintain a production-oriented way of thinking. Producers of industrial commodities like steel, coal, and chemicals have tended to remain production–oriented in part because buyers see little difference among competitors. Some industries with limited competition, including electric utilities and cable television providers, have also been slow to adopt the marketing concept. When an industry gets competitive, consumers have choices and flock to those that deliver customer satisfaction. This provides an incentive for more firms to practice the marketing concept.[12]

Take a look at Exhibit 1-4. It shows some differences in outlook between adopters of the marketing concept and typical production-oriented managers. As the exhibit suggests, the marketing concept forces the company to think through what it is doing—and why.

The Marketing Concept and Customer Value

LO 1.6

Take the customer's point of view

A manager who adopts the marketing concept sees customer satisfaction as the path to profits. To better understand what it takes to satisfy a customer, it is useful to take the customer's point of view.

A customer may look at a market offering from two perspectives. One deals with the potential benefits of that offering; the other concerns what the customer has to give up to get those benefits. Consider a student who has just finished an exam and is thinking about getting an iced coffee from Starbucks. Our coffee lover might see this as a great-tasting treat, a quick pick-me-up, a quiet place to relax and meet friends, and even as a way to get to know an attractive classmate. Clearly, different needs are associated with these different benefits. The cost of getting these benefits would include the price of the coffee and any tip to the server, but there might be other nondollar costs. For example, how difficult it will be to park is a convenience cost. Slow service would be an aggravation.

Exhibit 1–5
Costs, Benefits, and Customer Value

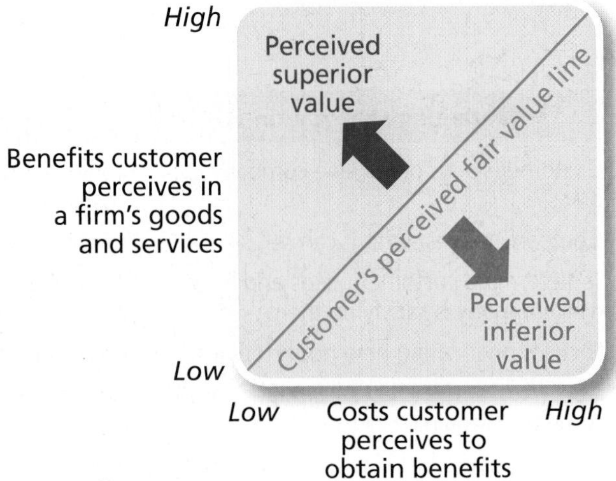

Customer value reflects benefits and costs

As this example suggests, both benefits and costs can take many different forms, perhaps ranging from economic to emotional. They also may vary depending on the situation. However, it is the customer's view of the various benefits and costs that is important. This leads us to the concept of **customer value**—the difference between the benefits a customer sees from a market offering and the costs of obtaining those benefits.

Some people think that higher customer value comes from a low price. But that may not be the case at all. A good or service that doesn't meet a customer's needs results in low customer value, even if the price is very low. A high price may be more than acceptable when it obtains the desired benefits. Think again about our Starbucks example. You can get a cup of coffee for a much lower price, but Starbucks offers more than just a cup of coffee. Customers find superior value when costs are lower and/or benefits are higher. This is indicated in the upper left hand corner of Exhibit 1-5.

Customers may not think about it very much

It is useful for a manager to evaluate ways to improve the benefits, or reduce the costs, of what the firm offers customers. However, this doesn't mean that customers stop and compute some sort of customer value score before making each purchase. If they did, there wouldn't be much time in life for anything else. So a manager's objective and thorough analysis may not accurately reflect the customer's impressions. Yet it is the customer's view that matters—even when the customer has not thought about it.

Where does competition fit?

You can't afford to ignore competition. Consumers usually have choices about how they will meet their needs. So a firm that offers superior customer value is likely to win and keep customers.

Often the best way to improve customer value, and beat the competition, is to be first to satisfy a need that others have not even considered. The competition between Coca-Cola and Pepsi illustrates this. Coca-Cola and Pepsi were spending millions of dollars on promotion—fighting head-to-head for the same cola customers. They put so much emphasis on the cola competition that they missed other opportunities. That gave firms like Snapple the chance to enter the market and steal away customers. For these customers, the desired benefits—and the greatest customer value—came from the variety of a fruit-flavored drink, not from one more cola.

Build relationships with customer value

Firms that embrace the marketing concept seek ways to build a profitable long-term relationship with each customer. Even the most innovative firm faces competition sooner or later. Trying to get new customers by taking them away from a competitor is usually more costly than retaining current customers by really satisfying their needs. Satisfied customers buy again and again while dissatisfied customers often tell others not to buy. With a long-term relationship, the customer's buying job is easier, and it also increases the selling firm's profits.

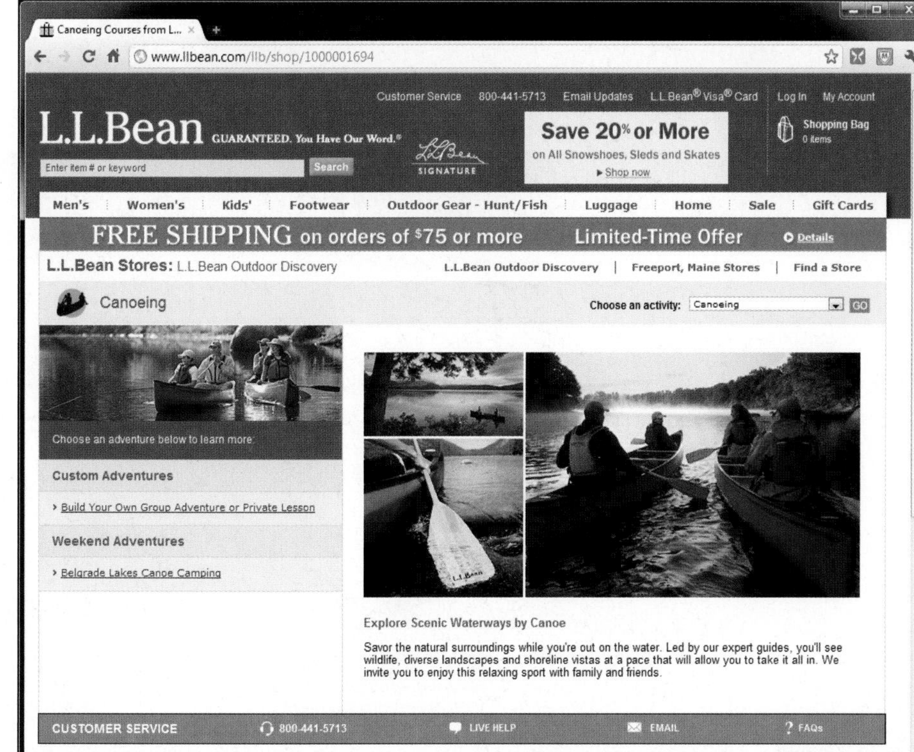

L.L. Bean has always focused on customer satisfaction and customer value as a way to build long-term relationships with customers. At its website (www.llbean.com), the online retailer offers customers a lot more than clothing and equipment. Its "Outdooor Discovery Schools" offer customers an opportunity to learn about and experience the outdoors.

Building relationships with customers requires that everyone in a firm work together to provide customer value before *and after* each purchase. If there is a problem with a customer's bill, the accounting people can't just leave it to the salesperson to straighten it out or, even worse, act like it's "the customer's problem." These hassles raise customers' costs of doing business. The long-term relationship with the customer—and the lifetime value of the customer's future purchases—is threatened unless everyone works together to make things right for the customer. Similarly, the firm's advertising might encourage a customer to buy once, but if the firm doesn't deliver on the benefits promised in its ads, the customer is likely to go elsewhere the next time the need arises. In other words, any time the customer value is reduced—because the benefits to the customer decrease or the costs increase—the relationship is weakened.[13]

Exhibit 1-6 summarizes these ideas. In a firm that has adopted the marketing concept, everyone focuses on customer satisfaction. They look for ways to offer superior customer value. That helps attract customers in the first place—and keeps them satisfied after they buy. So when they are ready to make repeat purchases, the firm is able to keep them as customers. Sales may increase further because satisfied customers are likely to buy other products offered by the firm. In this way, the firm builds profitable relationships with its customers. In other words, when a firm adopts the marketing concept, it wins and so do its customers.

Chipotle's value delivers satisfied customers—again and again

Chipotle Mexican Grill, a restaurant chain that specializes in tacos and burritos, illustrates these ideas. Since opening its first store in 1993, Chipotle has successfully built enduring relationships with customers looking for good food fast. Chipotle does relatively little advertising to acquire new customers. When Chipotle opens a new store, it usually gives away thousands of burritos to build buzz and generate publicity. New customers usually see value from Chipotle's fresh ingredients, great tasting menu, convenient locations, and fast service, even at $8 to $9 for a burrito and drink. Predictably, they tell their friends.

Many customers also get satisfaction knowing they are eating organically grown local produce and meat from animals raised on family farms without the use of antibiotics and

Exhibit 1–6
Satisfying Customers with Superior Customer Value to Build Profitable Relationships

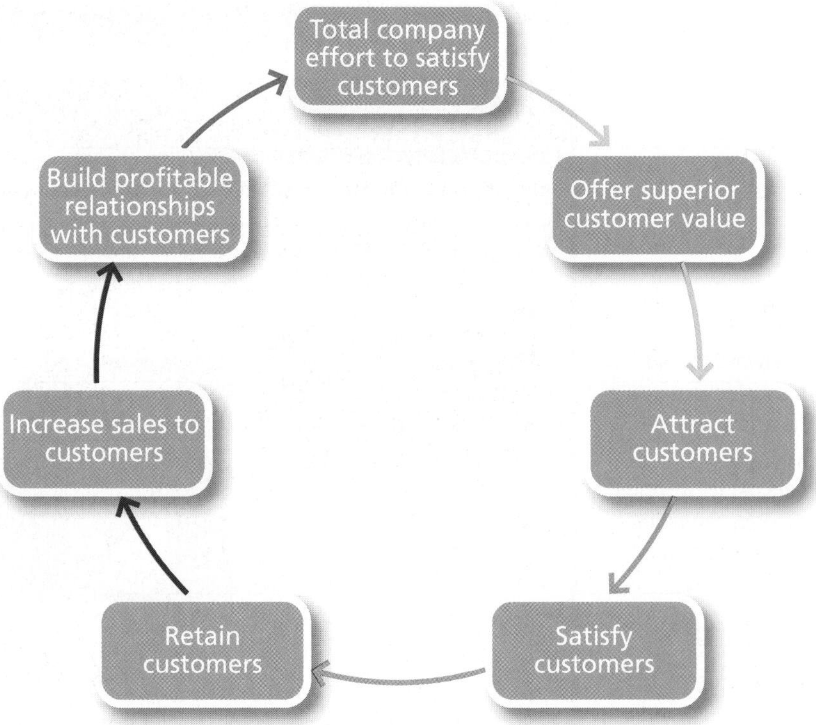

> **Internet Exercise**
>
> What does Chipotle offer customers at its website (**www.chipotle.com**)? How does this increase the value a customer receives from Chipotle? What else could Chipotle do to further enchance relationships with customers?

added hormones. Chipotle lets customers know about its food and its "food with integrity" values through its website, various promotions, advertising, and online videos. Chipotle produced a video on sustainable farming that went viral with millions of views. You can find "Back to the Start" featuring Coldplay's "The Scientist" sung by Willie Nelson on YouTube. Chipotle's friendly staff and great food deliver satisfied customers who come back again and again. That's why Chipotle is one of the fastest-growing restaurant chains in the world.[14]

The Marketing Concept Applies in Nonprofit Organizations

Newcomers to marketing thinking

The marketing concept is as important for nonprofit organizations as it is for business firms. In fact, marketing applies to all sorts of public and private nonprofit organizations—ranging from government agencies, health care organizations, educational institutions, and religious groups to charities, political parties, and fine arts organizations.

Support may not come from satisfied "customers"

As with any business firm, a nonprofit organization needs resources and support to survive and achieve its objectives. Yet support often does not come directly from those who receive the benefits the organization produces. For example, the World Wildlife Fund protects animals. If supporters of the World Wildlife Fund are not satisfied with its efforts—don't think the benefits are worth what it costs to provide them—they will put their time and money elsewhere.

Just as most firms face competition for customers, most nonprofits face competition for the resources and support they need. The Air Force faces a big problem if it can't attract new recruits. A shelter for the homeless may fail if supporters decide to focus on some other cause, such as AIDS education.

What is the "bottom line"?

As with a business, a nonprofit must take in as much money as it spends or it won't survive. However, a nonprofit organization does not measure "profit" in the same way as a firm. And its key measures of long-term success are also different. The YMCA, colleges, symphony orchestras, and the United Way, for example, all seek to achieve different objectives and need different measures of success. When everyone in an organization agrees to *some* measure(s) of long-run success, it helps the organization focus its efforts.

May not be organized for marketing

Some nonprofits face other challenges in organizing to adopt the marketing concept. Often no one has overall responsibility for marketing activities. Even when some leaders do the marketing thinking, they may have trouble getting unpaid volunteers with many different interests to all agree with the marketing strategy. Volunteers tend to do what they feel like doing![15]

The Marketing Concept, Social Responsibility, and Marketing Ethics

LO 1.7

Society's needs must be considered

The marketing concept is so logical that it's hard to find fault with it. Yet when a firm focuses its efforts on satisfying some consumers—to achieve its objectives—there may be negative effects on society. For example, producers and consumers making free choices can cause conflicts and difficulties. This is called the **micro-macro dilemma**. What is "good" for some firms and consumers may not be good for society as a whole.

For instance, many people in New York City buy bottled water because they like the convenience of easy-to-carry disposable bottles with spill-proof caps. On the other hand, the city already provides citizens with good tasting, safe tap water at a fraction of the cost. Is this just a matter of free choice by consumers? It's certainly a popular choice! On the other hand, critics point out that it is an inefficient use of resources to waste oil making and transporting millions of plastic bottles that end up in landfills where they leach chemicals into the soil. That kind of thinking, about the good of society as a whole, explains why New York City has run ads that encourage consumers to "get your fill" of free city water. What do you think? Should future generations pay the environmental price for today's consumer conveniences?[16]

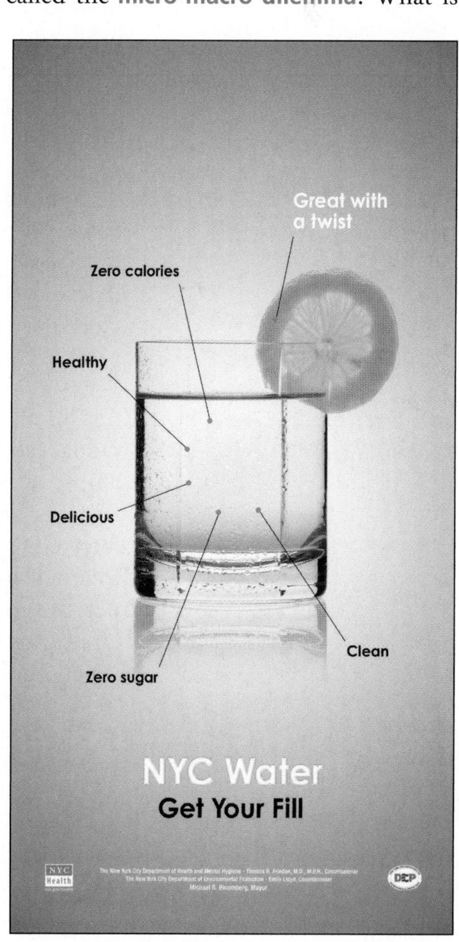

Questions like these are not easy to answer. The basic reason is that many different people may have a stake in the outcomes—and social consequences—of the choices made by individual managers *and* consumers in a market-directed system. This means that marketing managers

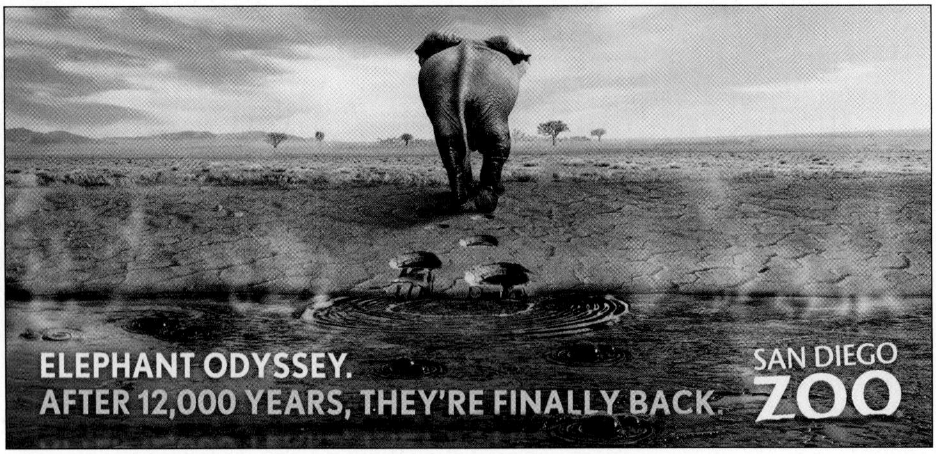

Marketing is now widely accepted by many local, national, and international nonprofit organizations. For example, this ad for the San Diego Zoo announces the addition of elephants to its menagerie of residents.

should be concerned with **social responsibility**—a firm's obligation to improve its positive effects on society and reduce its negative effects. As you read this book and learn more about marketing, you will also learn more about social responsibility in marketing—and why it must be taken seriously. You'll also see that being socially responsible sometimes requires difficult trade-offs.

Consider, for example, the environmental problems created by CFCs, chemicals that were used in hundreds of critical products, including fire extinguishers, cooling systems, and electronic circuit boards. When it was learned that CFCs deplete the earth's ozone layer, it was not possible to immediately stop producing and using all CFCs. For many products critical to society, there was no feasible short-term substitute. Du Pont and other producers of CFCs worked hard to balance these conflicting demands until substitute products could be found. Yet you can see that there are no easy answers for how such conflicts should be resolved.[17]

The issue of social responsibility in marketing also raises other important questions—for which there are no easy answers.

Should all consumer needs be satisfied?

Some consumers want products that may not be safe or good for them in the long run. Some critics argue that businesses should not offer high-heeled shoes, alcoholic beverages, or sugar-coated cereals because they aren't "good" for consumers in the long run. Similarly, bicycles and roller blades are among the most dangerous products identified by the Consumer Product Safety Commission. Who should decide if these products will be offered to consumers?

Do all marketers act responsibly?

Not all marketers act in a socially responsible manner. Sometimes firms or individuals advance their own short-term interests at the expense of customers. For example, during the recent housing boom, some mortgage brokers took advantage of trusting customers and sold them mortgages they could not afford while earning large commissions for themselves. As a result, many homebuyers were unable to pay for their homes, and this contributed to a global economic recession. When products are complicated, consumers may be vulnerable to unscrupulous sellers. In these circumstances we can debate whether it is better to "let the buyer beware" or enact stricter government regulation.

What if it cuts into profits?

There are times when being socially responsible can increase not only a firm's profits, but also its costs. Even though some consumers will pay premium prices to buy "fair trade" coffee, napkins made from recycled paper, hybrid cars that pollute less, or products made in overseas factories that pay a "fair wage," these items may cost more to produce. At the same time, other consumers attach little or no value to these social measures and refuse to pay a higher price for such products. Consequently, many firms selling to this second group are reluctant to be more socially responsible.

TOMS started by selling shoes on a one-for-one model; for each pair of shoes TOMS sells, it gives a pair to a person in need.

When a society feels that the social benefits are important, it may add regulations to create a level playing field for all firms and to assure that these benefits are provided. For example, there are laws that protect rivers from water pollution and that restrict the use of child labor. Still, it is difficult for governments to impose regulations that govern all circumstances where such trade-offs occur. So is the marketing concept really desirable?

Socially conscious marketing managers are trying to answer these questions. Their definition of customer satisfaction includes long-range effects—as well as immediate customer satisfaction. They try to balance consumer, company, and social interests.

The marketing concept guides marketing ethics

A manager cannot be truly consumer-oriented and at the same time intentionally unethical. However, at times, problems and criticism may arise because a manager did not fully consider the ethical implications of a decision. In either case, there is no excuse for sloppiness when it comes to **marketing ethics**—the moral standards that guide marketing decisions and actions. Each individual develops moral standards based on his or her own values. That helps explain why opinions about what is right or wrong often vary from one person to another, from one society to another, and among different groups within a society. It is sometimes difficult to say whose opinions are "correct." Even so, such opinions may have a very real influence on whether an individual's (or a firm's) marketing decisions and actions are accepted or rejected. So marketing ethics are not only a philosophical issue; they are also a pragmatic concern.

Problems may arise when some individual manager does not share the same marketing ethics as others in the organization. One person operating alone can damage a firm's reputation and even survival.

To be certain that standards for marketing ethics are as clear as possible, many organizations have developed their own written codes of ethics. These codes usually state—at least at a general level—the ethical standards that everyone in the firm should follow in dealing with customers and other people. Many professional societies also have such codes. For example, the American Marketing Association's code of ethics—see Exhibit 1-7—sets specific ethical standards for many aspects of marketing.[18]

Throughout the text, we will be discussing the types of ethical issues individual marketing managers face. But we won't be moralizing and trying to tell you how you

Exhibit 1–7 Summary of American Marketing Association Statement of Ethics

Preamble

The American Marketing Association commits itself to promoting the highest standard of professional ethical norms and values for its members (practitioners, academics, and students). Norms are established standards of conduct that are expected and maintained by society and/or professional organizations. Values represent the collective conception of what communities find desirable, important, and morally proper. Values also serve as the criteria for evaluating our own personal actions and the actions of others. As marketers, we recognize that we not only serve our organizations but also act as stewards of society in creating, facilitating, and executing the transactions that are part of the greater economy. In this role, marketers are expected to embrace the highest professional ethical norms and the ethical values implied by our responsibility toward multiple stakeholders (e.g., customers, employees, investors, peers, channel members, regulators, and the host community).

Ethical Norms

As Marketers, we must:

- Do no harm.
- Foster trust in the marketing system.
- Embrace ethical values.

Ethical Values

- Honesty—to be forthright in dealings with customers and stakeholders.
- Responsibility—to accept the consequences of our marketing decisions and strategies.
- Fairness—to balance justly the needs of the buyer with the interests of the seller.
- Respect—to acknowledge the basic human dignity of all stakeholders.
- Transparency—to create a spirit of openness in marketing operations.
- Citizenship—to fulfill the economic, legal, philanthropic, and societal responsibilities that serve stakeholders.

The full document may be found on the American Marketing Association website (www.marketingpower.com).

should think on any given issue. Rather, by the end of the course we hope that *you* will have some firm personal opinions about what is and is not ethical in micro-marketing activities.[19]

Fortunately, the prevailing practice of most businesspeople is to be fair and honest. However, not all criticisms of marketing focus on ethical issues.

Ethics Question

A customer purchases a Sony digital camera that comes with a 90-day manufacturer's warranty on parts and labor. The salesperson suggests that the customer consider the store's three-year extended service to cover any problems with the camera. The customer replies, "I'm getting a Sony because it's a reputable brand—and at $98 the service agreement is one-third the cost of the camera." Four months later, the customer returns to the store and complains that the camera no longer takes pictures and that "the store needs to make it right." If you were the store manager, what would you say? Would your response be any different if you knew that the customer was going to post his complaint on a consumer website?

Marketing has its critics

We must admit that marketing—as it exists in the United States and other developed societies—has many critics. Marketing activity is especially open to criticism because it is the part of business most visible to the public.

A number of typical complaints about marketing are summarized in Exhibit 1-8. Think about these criticisms and whether you agree with them or not. What complaints do you have that are not covered by one of the categories in Exhibit 1-8?

Exhibit 1–8
Sample Criticisms of Marketing

- Advertising is everywhere, and it's often annoying, misleading, or wasteful.
- The quality of products is poor and often they are not even safe.
- There are too many unnecessary products.
- Retailers add too much to the cost of distribution and just raise prices without providing anything in return.
- Marketing serves the rich and exploits the poor.
- Marketers overpromise service, and when a consumer has a problem, nobody cares.
- Marketing creates interest in products that pollute the environment.
- Private information about consumers is collected and used to sell them things they don't need.
- Marketing makes people too materialistic and motivates them toward "things" instead of social needs.
- Easy consumer credit makes people buy things they don't need and can't afford.

Such complaints should not be taken lightly. They show that many people are unhappy with some parts of the marketing system. Certainly, the strong public support for consumer protection laws proves that not all consumers feel they are being treated like royalty.

As you consider the various criticisms of marketing, keep in mind that not all of them deal with the marketing practices of specific firms. Some of the complaints about marketing really focus on the basic idea of a market-directed macro-marketing system—and these criticisms often occur because people don't understand what marketing is—or how it works.[20] As you go through this book, we'll discuss some of these criticisms. Then in our final chapter, we will return to a more complete appraisal of marketing in our consumer-oriented society.

CONCLUSION

The basic purpose of this chapter is to introduce you to marketing and highlight its value for consumers, firms, and society. In Chapter 2, we introduce a marketing strategy planning process that is the framework for ideas developed throughout the rest of the text—and that will guide your marketing thinking in the future. This chapter sets the stage for that by introducing basic principles that guide marketing thinking.

You've learned about two views of marketing, both of which are important. One takes a micro view and focuses on marketing activities by an individual business (or other type of organization). This is what most people (including most business managers) have in mind when they talk about marketing. But it's important to understand that marketing also plays a more macro role. Macro-marketing is concerned with the way the whole marketing system works in a society or economy. It operates to make exchanges and relationships between producers and their customers more effective.

We discussed the functions of marketing and who performs them. This includes not only producers and their customers but also marketing specialists who serve as intermediaries between producers and consumers and other specialists (like product-testing labs and advertising agencies) who are collaborators and facilitate marketing functions.

We explained how a market-directed economy works, through the macro-marketing system, to provide consumers with choices. We introduced macro-marketing in this chapter, and we'll consider macro-marketing issues throughout the text. But the major focus of this book is on marketing by individual organizations. Someone in an organization must plan and manage its activities to make certain that customer needs are satisfied.

That's why understanding the marketing concept is another objective. The marketing concept is the basic philosophy that provides direction to a marketing-oriented firm. It stresses that the company's efforts should focus on satisfying some target customers—at a profit. Production-oriented firms tend to forget this. The various departments within a production-oriented firm let their natural conflicts of interest get in the way of customer satisfaction.

We also introduced the customer value concept. It is marketing's responsibility to make certain that what the firm offers customers really provides them with value that is greater than they can obtain somewhere else. In today's competitive markets, a firm must offer superior customer value if it wants to attract customers, satisfy them, and build beneficial long-term relationships with them.

A final objective was for you to see how social responsibility and marketing ethics relate to the marketing concept. The chapter ends by considering criticisms of marketing—both of the way individual firms work and of the whole macro system. When you have finished reading this book, you will be better able to evaluate these criticisms.

By learning more about marketing-oriented decision making, you will be able to make more efficient and socially responsible decisions. This will help improve the performance of individual firms and organizations (your employers). And eventually it will help our macro-marketing system work better.

KEY TERMS

LO 1.8

production, *6*
customer satisfaction, 6
innovation, *6*
marketing, *7*
pure subsistence economy, *8*
macro-marketing, *8*
economies of scale, *10*
universal functions of marketing, *9*
buying function, *9*
selling function, *9*
transporting function, *9*
storing function, *9*
standardization and grading, *10*
financing, *11*
risk taking, *11*
market information function, *11*
intermediary, *11*
collaborators, *11*
e-commerce, *11*
economic system, *12*
command economy, *13*
market-directed economy, *14*
simple trade era, *16*
production era, *16*
sales era, *16*
marketing department era, *16*
marketing company era, *16*
marketing concept, *17*
production orientation, *17*
marketing orientation, *17*
triple bottom line, *18*
customer value, *20*
micro-macro dilemma, *23*
social responsibility, *24*
marketing ethics, *25*

QUESTIONS AND PROBLEMS

1. List your activities for the first two hours after you woke up this morning. Briefly indicate how marketing affected your activities.
2. If a producer creates a really revolutionary new product and consumers can learn about it and purchase it at a website, is any additional marketing effort really necessary? Explain your thinking.
3. Distinguish between the micro and macro views of marketing. Then explain how they are interrelated, if they are.
4. Refer to Exhibit 1-1, and give an example of a purchase you made recently that involved separation of information and separation in time between you and the producer. Briefly explain how these separations were overcome.
5. Describe a recent purchase you made. Indicate why that particular product was available at a store and, in particular, at the store where you bought it.
6. Define the functions of marketing in your own words. Using an example, explain how they can be shifted and shared.
7. Online computer shopping at websites makes it possible for individual consumers to get direct information from hundreds of companies they would not otherwise know about. Consumers can place an order for a purchase that is then shipped to them directly. Will growth of these services ultimately eliminate the need for retailers and wholesalers? Explain your thinking, giving specific attention to what marketing functions are involved in these "electronic purchases" and who performs them.
8. Explain why a small producer might want a marketing research firm to take over some of its information-gathering activities.
9. Distinguish between how economic decisions are made in a command economy and how they are made in a market-directed economy.
10. Would the functions that must be provided and the development of wholesaling and retailing systems be any different in a command economy from those in a market-directed economy?
11. Explain why a market-directed macro-marketing system encourages innovation. Give an example.
12. Define the marketing concept in your own words, and then explain why the notion of profit is usually included in this definition.

13. Define the marketing concept in your own words, and then suggest how acceptance of this concept might affect the organization and operation of your college.
14. Distinguish between production orientation and marketing orientation, illustrating with local examples.
15. Explain why a firm should view its internal activities as part of a total system. Illustrate your answer for (*a*) a large grocery products producer, (*b*) a plumbing wholesaler, (*c*) a department store chain, and (*d*) a cell phone service.
16. Give examples of some of the benefits and costs that might contribute to the customer value of each of the following products: (*a*) a wristwatch, (*b*) a weight-loss diet supplement, (*c*) a cruise on a luxury liner, and (*d*) a checking account from a bank.
17. What are examples of the benefits that you can provide to a prospective employer in your field? What are examples of the costs that employer would incur if they hired you? How do you think you can increase the value you offer a prospective employer?
18. Give an example of a recent purchase you made where the purchase wasn't just a single transaction but rather part of an ongoing relationship with the seller. Discuss what the seller has done (or could do better) to strengthen the relationship and increase the odds of you being a loyal customer in the future.
19. Discuss how the micro-macro dilemma relates to each of the following products: high-powered engines in cars, nuclear power, bank credit cards, and pesticides that improve farm production.

SUGGESTED CASES

1. McDonald's "Seniors" Restaurant
2. Golden Valley Foods, Inc.
18. Whistler Township Volunteer Fire Department

Video Case 1. Chick-fil-A

COMPUTER-AIDED PROBLEM

1. REVENUE, COST, AND PROFIT RELATIONSHIPS

This problem introduces you to the computer-aided problem (CAP) software—which is at the Online Learning Center for this text—and gets you started with the use of spreadsheet analysis for marketing decision making. This problem is simple. In fact, you could work it without the software. But by starting with a simple problem, you will learn how to use the program more quickly and see how it will help you with more complicated problems. Instructions for the software are available at the end of this text.

Sue Cline, the business manager at Magna University Student Bookstore, is developing plans for the next academic year. The bookstore is one of the university's nonprofit activities, but any "surplus" (profit) it earns is used to support the student activities center.

Two popular products at the bookstore are the student academic calendar and notebooks with the school name. Sue Cline thinks that she can sell calendars to 90 percent of Magna's 3,000 students, so she has had 2,700 printed. The total cost, including artwork and printing, is $11,500. Last year the calendar sold for $5.00, but Sue is considering changing the price this year.

Sue thinks that the bookstore will be able to sell 6,000 notebooks if they are priced right. But she knows that many students will buy similar notebooks (without the school name) from stores in town if the bookstore price is too high.

Sue has entered the information about selling price, quantity, and costs for calendars and notebooks in the spreadsheet program so that it is easy to evaluate the effect of different decisions. The spreadsheet is also set up to calculate revenue and profit, based on

$$\text{Revenue} = (\text{Selling price}) \times (\text{Quantity sold})$$

$$\text{Profit} = (\text{Revenue}) - (\text{Total cost})$$

Use the program to answer the questions that follow. Record your answers on a separate sheet of paper.

a. From the Spreadsheet Screen, how much revenue does Sue expect from calendars? How much revenue from notebooks? How much profit will the store earn from calendars? From notebooks?
b. If Sue increases the price of her calendars to $6.00 and still sells the same quantity, what is the expected revenue? The expected profit? (*Note:* Change the price from $5.00 to $6.00 on the spreadsheet and the program will recompute revenue and profit.) On your sheet of paper, show the calculations that confirm that the program has given you the correct values.
c. Sue is interested in getting an overview of how a change in the price of notebooks would affect revenue and profit, assuming that she sells all 6,000 notebooks she is thinking of ordering. Prepare a table—on your sheet of paper—with column headings for three variables: selling price, revenue, and profit. Show the value for revenue and profit for different possible selling prices for a notebook—starting at a minimum price of $1.60 and adding 8 cents to the price until you reach a maximum of $2.40. At what price will selling 6,000 notebooks contribute $5,400.00 to profit? At what price would notebook sales contribute only $1,080.00? (*Hint:* Use the What If analysis feature to compute the new values. Start by selecting "selling price" for notebooks as the value to change, with a minimum value of $1.60 and a maximum value of $2.40. Select the revenue and profit for notebooks as the values to display.)

2 CHAPTER TWO

Marketing Strategy Planning

There was a time when it didn't seem to be an exaggeration for Barnum & Bailey's ads to tout the circus as "the greatest show on earth." For a hundred years, circuses had brought excitement and family entertainment to towns all over the country. Parents hardly noticed the hard benches that they sat on as they watched their kids cheer for the acrobats, clowns, and animal acts. But by the 1980s the popularity of traditional circuses was in decline; many simply went out of business.

You can imagine why this sad state of affairs would be a concern for Guy Laliberté—a stilt walker, accordion player, and fire eater—and others in his band of performers. But instead of bemoaning the demise of the circus, they saw an opportunity for a new kind of entertainment—and their idea gave birth to "Cirque du Soleil."

Their new style of circus still traveled to the audience and set up a "big top" tent, but costly and controversial animal acts were eliminated. Instead, the entertainment focused on an innovative combination of acrobatics, music, and theater. This more sophisticated offering appealed to adults. Importantly, adults were willing to pay more for tickets when the show was targeted at them and not just kids—especially when the traditional circus benches were replaced with more comfortable seats.

Cirque du Soleil quickly struck a chord with audiences and soon the producers were developing new shows and expanding tours to reach new markets. Now more than 20 different shows appear around the world. At any one time, about a dozen different Cirque du Soleil shows travel across Europe, Asia, Australia, and North and South America. Each show performs in a host city for anywhere from two weeks to three months. Nine other Cirque du Soleil shows have permanent homes and target tourists visiting Las Vegas, New York City, Los Angeles and Orlando, Florida. Each of the shows has a unique theme. For example, KÀ highlights the martial arts, OVO looks at the world of insects, and Iris celebrates Hollywood movies.

When considering new shows, each idea is evaluated on its creativity, uniqueness, and likelihood of becoming a real blockbuster. New shows can take more than five years and $100 million to develop. But these development costs can be recouped over each show's anticipated 10-year run. For example, a series of programs now in development include Arena 2013, which has a theme of extreme sports, and new Cirque du Soleil shows for permanent facilities in Moscow, Russia, and Dubai, United Arab Emirates.

As all of this suggests, Cirque du Soleil's marketing managers constantly evaluate new opportunities. A few years ago the company even considered a plan to diversify into hotels and spas based on the circus theme. This idea was screened out—at least for now—and instead the focus has been on developing new products for current customers. For example, in Las Vegas Cirque du Soleil created lounges with the Cirque du Soleil theme where customers could relax before or after one of their shows.

Cirque du Soleil also reaches new customers through television specials and DVDs. These small screen shows not only generate additional revenue but they also give customers a taste of Cirque du Soleil and whet their appetite for a live show.

Once customers see a live Cirque du Soleil show, they want to see more. So Cirque advertising focuses on motivating customers to see that first show. For example, ads in airline magazines target travelers who are headed to cities with permanent shows and traveling shows are heavily advertised in local media. But publicity and word-of-mouth are also important. Local newspapers and TV shows are often interested in doing stories about touring productions that are coming to town. Cirque du Soleil's website helps reporters in this effort by providing photos, videos, and interviews for easy download. To encourage word-of-mouth, they also rely on exclusive "premieres" where influential people in the community are invited to a gala opening night. Further, the troupe offers free tickets and its members volunteer time to help build close relationships with local art and charitable organizations. After experiencing the troupe's magic, people often tell their friends and look forward to the next opportunity to see Cirque du Soleil in action.

These new fans are likely to visit Cirque du Soleil's website (www.cirquedusoleil.com), where they can buy a t-shirt, umbrella, or coffee mug emblazoned with an image from their favorite Cirque du Soleil show. They can also link to Cirque du Soleil's YouTube channel to watch videos of events like the stilt-walking parade, or click to its Flickr page for behind-the-scenes photos. While online they can "Like" Cirque du Soleil's Facebook page to start receiving regular updates in their Facebook news feed, watch a video interview with a cast member, and post or read comments from other fans. For up-to-the minute news, they can follow Cirque du Soleil on Twitter or download an app for their cell phone.

Cirque du Soleil has been very successful, but it must continue to focus on ways to improve its customers' experiences. Imitators, like the Canadian Cirque Éloize and Le Rêve in Las Vegas, now try to offer similar entertainment fare. The reputation of the powerful Cirque du Soleil brand name gives the troupe a competitive advantage when it introduces new shows. It also allows Cirque to charge a premium price for tickets, which range from $40 to over $200 for the exclusive *Tapis Rouge* (red carpet) tickets. Cirque du Soleil's carefully crafted marketing mix generates ticket sales that exceed half a billion dollars each year.[1]

Learning Objectives

Marketing managers at Cirque du Soleil make many decisions as they develop marketing strategies. Making good marketing strategy decisions is never easy, yet knowing what basic decision areas to consider helps you to plan a more successful strategy. This chapter will get you started by giving you a framework for thinking about marketing strategy planning—which is what the rest of this book is all about.

When you finish this chapter, you should be able to:

1 understand what a marketing manager does.

2 know what marketing strategy planning is—and why it is the focus of this book.

3 understand target marketing.

4 be familiar with the four Ps in a marketing mix.

5 know the difference between a marketing strategy, a marketing plan, and a marketing program.

6 understand what customer lifetime value and customer equity are and why marketing strategy planners seek to increase them.

7 be familiar with the text's framework for marketing strategy planning.

8 know four broad types of marketing opportunities that help in identifying new strategies.

9 understand why strategies for opportunities in international markets should be considered.

10 understand the important new terms (shown in red).

The Management Job in Marketing

LO 2.1

In Chapter 1 you learned about the marketing concept—a philosophy to guide the whole firm toward satisfying customers at a profit. From the Cirque du Soleil case, it's clear that marketing decisions are very important to a firm's success. Let's look more closely at the marketing management process.

The **marketing management process** is the process of (1) *planning* marketing activities, (2) directing the *implementation* of the plans, and (3) *controlling* these plans. Planning, implementation, and control are basic jobs of all managers—but here we will emphasize what they mean to marketing managers.

Exhibit 2-1 shows the relationships among the three jobs in the marketing management process. The jobs are all connected to show that the marketing management process is continuous. In the planning job, managers set guidelines for the implementing job and specify expected results. They use these expected results in the control job to determine if everything has worked out as planned. The link from the control job to the planning job is especially important. This feedback often leads to changes in the plans or to new plans.

Exhibit 2–1
The Marketing Management Process

Managers should seek new opportunities

Smart managers are not satisfied just planning for the present market. Markets are dynamic. Consumers' needs, competitors, and the environment keep changing. Consider Hasbro, a company that seemed to have a "Monopoly" in family games. While it continued selling board games, firms like Sega, Sony, and Nintendo zoomed in with video game competition. Then came online multiplayer games like World of Warcraft and Facebook-based Farmville—and Hasbro fell further behind customer trends. Of course, not every opportunity is good for every company. Really attractive opportunities are those that fit with what the whole company wants to do and is able to do well.

Strategic management planning concerns the whole firm

The job of planning strategies to guide a whole company is called **strategic (management) planning**—the managerial process of developing and maintaining a match between an organization's resources and its market opportunities. This is a top-management job. It includes planning not only for marketing but also for production, finance, human resources, and other areas.

Although marketing strategies are not whole-company plans, company plans should be market-oriented. And the marketing plan often sets the tone and direction for the whole company. So we will use *strategy planning* and *marketing strategy planning* to mean the same thing.[2]

What is a Marketing Strategy?

LO 2.2

Marketing strategy planning means finding attractive opportunities and developing profitable marketing strategies. But what is a "marketing strategy"? We have used these words rather casually so far. Now let's see what they really mean.

What is a marketing strategy?

A **marketing strategy** specifies a target market and a related marketing mix. It is a big picture of what a firm will do in some market. Two interrelated parts are needed:

1. A **target market**—a fairly homogeneous (similar) group of customers to whom a company wishes to appeal.
2. A **marketing mix**—the controllable variables the company puts together to satisfy this target group.

Exhibit 2–2
A Marketing Strategy

The importance of target customers in this process can be seen in Exhibit 2-2, where the target market is at the center of the diagram. The target market is surrounded by the controllable variables that we call the "marketing mix." A typical marketing mix includes some product, offered at a price, with some promotion to tell potential customers about the product, and a way to reach the customer's place.

The marketing strategy for Herbal Essences hair care products aims at a specific group of target customers: young women in their late teens and early 20s. The products include various shampoos, conditioners, gels, and hairspray for different types of hair. The product names and brightly colored packaging grab customers' attention. Long Term Relationship (in bright red bottles) is formulated to add silkiness to long hair, and Body Envy (in orange bottles) adds body to flat hair. The curvy, matched, and nested shampoo and conditioner bottles encourage customers to buy the products together. By seeking eye-level placement at stores like Target and Walmart, Herbal Essences is locating its products where most target customers shop for hair care essentials. The brand's print, television, and online advertising incorporate a mythical quality that supports the products' organic origins. Herbal Essences' homepage (www.herbalessences.com) includes hundreds of customer ratings and reviews, links to a Facebook Fan page (with over 800,000 fans), a Twitter feed, and a YouTube channel. The shampoo and conditioner retail for $6 to $8 a bottle, with occasional dollar-off coupons to encourage new customer trial. Fast-growing sales suggest this marketing mix hits the bulls-eye for this target market.[3]

Selecting a Market-Oriented Strategy is Target Marketing

LO 2.3

Target marketing is not mass marketing

Note that a marketing strategy specifies some *particular* target customers. This approach is called "target marketing" to distinguish it from "mass marketing." **Target marketing** says that a marketing mix is tailored to fit some specific target customers. In contrast, **mass marketing**—the typical production-oriented approach—vaguely aims at "everyone" with the same marketing mix. Mass marketing assumes that everyone is the same—and it considers everyone to be a potential customer. It may help to think of target marketing as the "rifle approach" and mass marketing as the "shotgun approach." See Exhibit 2-3.

Exhibit 2–3
Production-Oriented and Marketing-Oriented Managers Have Different Views of the Market

Production-oriented manager sees everyone as basically similar and practices "mass marketing"

Marketing-oriented manager sees everyone as different and practices "target marketing"

Mass marketers may do target marketing

Commonly used terms can be confusing here. The terms *mass marke**ting*** and *mass marke**ters*** do not mean the same thing. Far from it! *Mass marke**ting*** means trying to sell to "everyone," as we explained earlier. *Mass marke**ters*** like Kraft Foods and Walmart are aiming at clearly defined target markets. The confusion with mass marketing occurs because their target markets usually are large and spread out.

Target marketing can mean big markets and profits

Target marketing is not limited to small market segments—only to fairly homogeneous ones. A very large market—even what is sometimes called the "mass market"—may be fairly homogeneous, and a target marketer will deliberately aim at it. For example, a very large group of parents of young children are homogeneous on many dimensions, including their attitudes about changing baby diapers. In the United States alone, this group spends about $5 billion a year on disposable diapers—so it should be no surprise that it is a major target market for companies like Kimberly-Clark (Huggies) and Procter & Gamble (Pampers). On the other hand, babies and their parents are not the only ones who need disposable diapers. Many elderly people, especially those who are in nursing homes and have mobility problems, use diapers. Needless to say, the marketing mix that's right for babies isn't right for elder care. It's not just the sizes that are different, but also the forms. The elderly don't like the idea of needing "diapers"—so instead they wear disposable "pull ups."

The basic reason to focus on some specific target customers is so that you can develop a marketing mix that satisfies those customers' *specific* needs better than they are satisfied by some other firm. For example, E*trade uses a website (www.etrade.com) to target knowledgeable investors who want a convenient, low-cost way to buy and sell stocks online without a lot of advice (or pressure) from a salesperson.

Ethics Question

You have been working for a major online retailer in the entertainment products category and have responsibility for DVD movie sales. You've been approached by a company that offers a behavioral targeting software program. When a customer visits your website, this program can tell whether that customer has been "shopping around"—it knows if the customer has looked at DVD movies at other online stores. Assuming these customers are looking for a good deal, the new software allows you to charge a lower price only to these "shopping around" customers. Higher, regular prices would be shown to all other customers. The seller claims the software will double your profits in the DVD category. Would you purchase this service? Explain your decision.

Developing Marketing Mixes for Target Markets

LO 2.4

There are many marketing mix decisions

There are many possible ways to satisfy the needs of target customers. A product might have many different features. Customer service levels before or after the sale can be adjusted. The package, brand name, and warranty can be changed. Various advertising media—newspapers, magazines, cable, the Internet—may be used. A company's own sales force or other sales specialists can be used. The price can be changed, discounts can be given, and so on. With so many possible variables, is there any way to help organize all these decisions and simplify the selection of marketing mixes? The answer is yes.

The "four Ps" make up a marketing mix

It is useful to reduce all the variables in the marketing mix to four basic ones:

Product
Place
Promotion
Price

It helps to think of the four major parts of a marketing mix as the "four Ps."

Customer is not part of the marketing mix

The customer—the target market—is shown surrounded by the four Ps in Exhibit 2-4. Some students assume that the customer is part of the marketing mix—but this is not so. The customer should be the *target* of all marketing efforts.

Exhibit 2-5 shows some of the strategy decision variables organized by the four Ps. These will be discussed in later chapters. For now, let's just describe each P briefly.

Exhibit 2–4
A Marketing Strategy—Showing the Four Ps of a Marketing Mix

Product—the good or service for the target's needs

The Product area is concerned with developing the right "product" for the target market. This offering may involve a physical good, a service, or a blend of both. Keep in mind that Product is not limited to physical goods. For example, the Product of H & R Block is a completed tax form. The Product of a political party is the policies it works to achieve. The important thing to remember is that your good or service should satisfy some customers' needs.

Along with other Product-area decisions like branding, packaging, and warranties, we will talk about developing and managing new products, product quality, and whole product lines.

Place—reaching the target

Place is concerned with all the decisions involved in getting the "right" product to the target market's Place. A product isn't much good to a customer if it isn't available when and where it's wanted.

A product reaches customers through a channel of distribution. A **channel of distribution** is any series of firms (or individuals) that participate in the flow of products from producer to final user or consumer.

Sometimes a channel of distribution is short and runs directly from a producer to a final user or consumer. This is common in business markets and in the marketing of services. For example, Geico sells its insurance directly to final consumers. However, as

Exhibit 2–5
Strategy Decision Areas Organized by the Four Ps

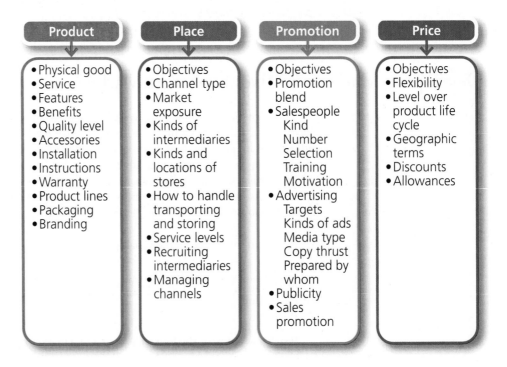

Product	Place	Promotion	Price
• Physical good • Service • Features • Benefits • Quality level • Accessories • Installation • Instructions • Warranty • Product lines • Packaging • Branding	• Objectives • Channel type • Market exposure • Kinds of intermediaries • Kinds and locations of stores • How to handle transporting and storing • Service levels • Recruiting intermediaries • Managing channels	• Objectives • Promotion blend • Salespeople Kind Number Selection Training Motivation • Advertising Targets Kinds of ads Media type Copy thrust Prepared by whom • Publicity • Sales promotion	• Objectives • Flexibility • Level over product life cycle • Geographic terms • Discounts • Allowances

A firm's product may involve a physical good or a service or a combination of both. Chilean airline LAN provides a service but the quality of its equipment, especially the special sleeper seats on its planes, helps the firm do a superior job in meeting the needs of international travelers. German airline Lufthansa supplements its primary service, helping customers travel to a new location, by offering them access to the Internet while on its flights.

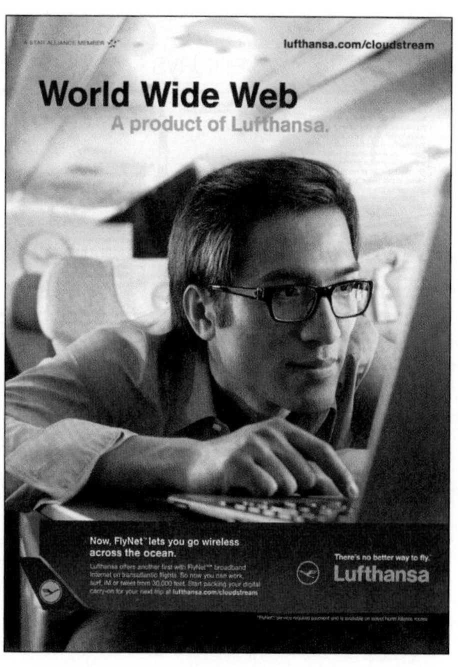

shown in Exhibit 2-6, channels are often more complex—as when Nestlé's food products are handled by wholesalers and retailers before reaching consumers. When a marketing manager has several different target markets, several different channels of distribution may be needed.

We will also see how physical distribution service levels and decisions concerning logistics (transporting, storing, and handling products) relate to the other Place decisions and the rest of the marketing mix.

Promotion—telling and selling the customer

The third P—Promotion—is concerned with telling the target market or others in the channel of distribution about the "right" product. Sometimes promotion is focused on acquiring new customers, and sometimes it's focused on retaining current customers. Promotion includes personal selling, mass selling, and sales promotion. It is the marketing manager's job to blend these methods of communication.

Personal selling involves direct spoken communication between sellers and potential customers. Personal selling may happen face-to-face, over the telephone or even via a

Exhibit 2–6
Four Examples of Basic Channels of Distribution for Consumer Products

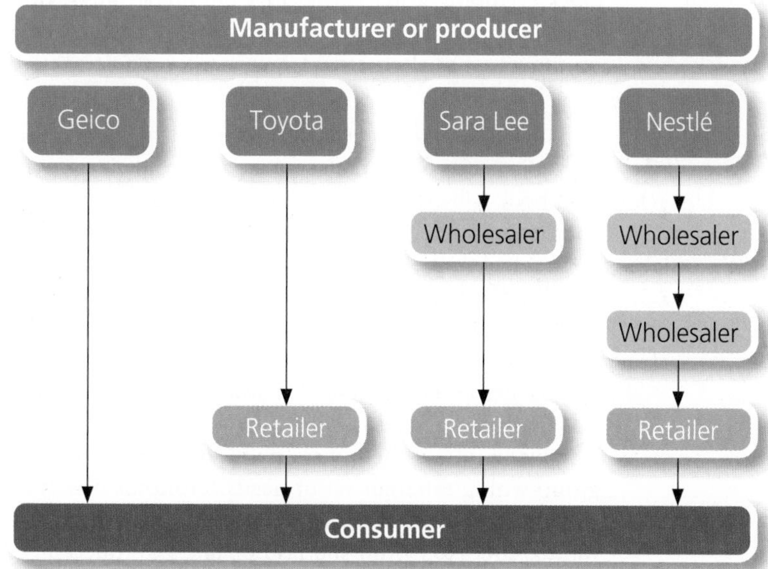

videoconference over the Internet. Sometimes personal attention is required *after the sale.* **Customer service**—a personal communication between a seller and a customer who wants the seller to resolve a problem with a purchase—is often a key to building repeat business. Individual attention comes at a price; personal selling and customer service can be very expensive. Often this personal effort has to be blended with mass selling and sales promotion.

Mass selling is communicating with large numbers of customers at the same time. The main form of mass selling is **advertising**—any *paid* form of nonpersonal presentation of ideas, goods, or services by an identified sponsor. **Publicity**—any *unpaid* form of nonpersonal presentation of ideas, goods, or services—includes getting favorable coverage in newspaper stories or on television as well as creating and placing content on the web for customers to find or pass along to others. Mass selling may involve a wide variety of media, ranging from newspapers and billboards to the Internet.

Sales promotion refers to those promotion activities—other than advertising, publicity, and personal selling—that stimulate interest, trial, or purchase by final customers or others in the channel. This can involve use of coupons, point-of-purchase materials, samples, signs, contests, events, catalogs, novelties, and circulars.

Price—making it right

In addition to developing the right Product, Place, and Promotion, marketing managers must also set the right Price. Price setting must consider the kind of competition in the target market and the cost of the whole marketing mix. A manager must also try to estimate customer reaction to possible prices. Besides this, the manager must know current practices as to markups, discounts, and other terms of sale. And if customers won't accept the Price, all of the planning effort is wasted.

Each of the four Ps contributes to the whole

All four Ps are needed in a marketing mix. In fact, they should all be tied together. But is any one more important than the others? Generally speaking, the answer is no—all contribute to one whole. When a marketing mix is being developed, all (final) decisions about the Ps should be made at the same time. That's why the four Ps are arranged around the target market in a circle—to show that they all are equally important.

Let's sum up our discussion of marketing mix planning thus far. We develop a *Product* to satisfy the target customers. We find a way to reach our target customers' *Place.* We use *Promotion* to tell the target customers (and others in the channel) about the product that has been designed for them. And we set a *Price* after estimating expected customer reaction to the total offering and the costs of getting it to them.

Strategy jobs must be done together

It is important to stress—it cannot be overemphasized—that selecting a target market *and* developing a marketing mix are interrelated. Both parts of a marketing strategy must be decided together. It is *strategies* that must be evaluated against the company's objectives—not alternative target markets or alternative marketing mixes.

Understanding target markets leads to good strategies

The needs of a target market often virtually determine the nature of an appropriate marketing mix. So marketers must analyze their potential target markets with great care. This book will explore ways of identifying attractive market opportunities and developing appropriate strategies.

Let's look at the strategy planning process more closely in the classic case of Jeff Silverman and Toddler University (TU), Inc., a shoe company he started. During high school and college, Silverman worked as a salesperson at local shoe stores. He also gained valuable experience during a year working for Nike. From these jobs he learned a lot about customers' needs and interests. He also realized that some parents were not satisfied when it came to finding shoes for their preschool children.

Silverman saw there were many different types of customers for baby shoes, each group with a different set of needs. From his observations, there was one market that was underserved. These *Attentive Parents* wanted shoes that met a variety of needs. They wanted shoes to be fun and fashionable and functional. They didn't want just a good fit

Toddler University's marketing strategy was successful because it developed a distinctive marketing mix that was precisely relevant to the needs of its target market.

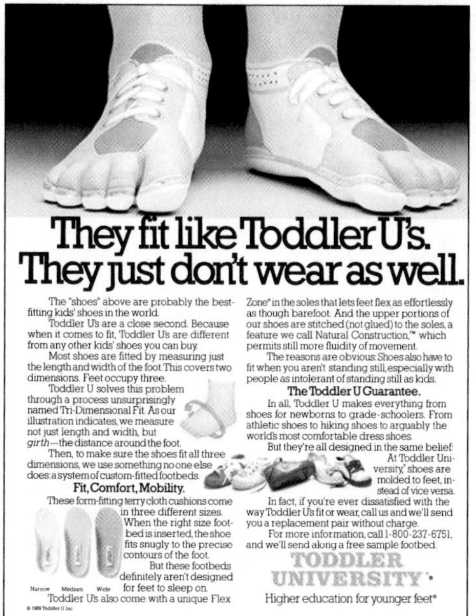

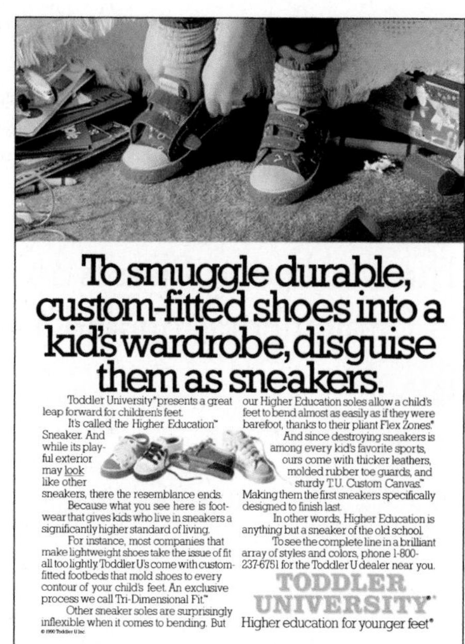

but also design and materials that were really right for baby play and learning to walk. These well-informed, upscale shoppers were likely to buy from a store that specialized in baby items. They were also willing to pay a premium price if they found the right product. Silverman saw an opportunity to serve the Attentive Parents target market with a marketing mix that combined, in his words, "fit and function with fun and fashion." He developed a detailed marketing plan that attracted financial backers, and his company came to life.

Silverman contracted with a producer in Taiwan to make shoes to his specs with his Toddler University brand name. TU's specs were different—they improved the product for this target market. Unlike most rigid high-topped infant shoes, TU's shoes were softer with more comfortable rubber soles. The shoes were stitched rather than glued so they lasted longer and included an extra-wide opening so the shoes slipped easier onto squirming feet. A patented special insert allowed parents to adjust the shoes' width. The insert also helped win support from retailers. With 11 sizes of children's shoes—and five widths—retailers usually stocked 55 pairs of each style. TU's adjustable width reduced the stocking requirements, making the line more profitable than competing shoes. TU's Product and Place decisions worked together to provide customer value and also to give TU a competitive advantage.

For promotion, TU's print ads featured close-up photos of babies wearing the shoes and informative details about their special benefits. Creative packaging promoted the shoe and attracted customers in the store. For example, TU put one athletic-style shoe in a box that looked like a gray gym locker. TU also provided stores with "shoe rides"—electric-powered rocking replicas of its shoes. The rides attracted kids to the shoe department, and because they were coin-operated, they paid for themselves in a year.

TU priced most of its shoes at $35 to $40 a pair. This is a premium price, but the Attentive Parents typically have smaller families and are willing to spend more on each child.

In just four years, TU's sales jumped from $100,000

Internet Exercise

Jeffrey Silverman, the founder of Toddler University, recently started Preschoolians, which specializes in shoes for preschool kids. Go to the Preschoolians website (**www.preschoolians.com**) and review the site to learn about the company. Concisely describe its strategy.

to over $40 million. To keep growth going, Silverman expanded distribution to reach new markets in Europe. To take advantage of TU's relationship with its satisfied target customers, TU expanded its product line to offer shoes for older kids. Then Silverman made his biggest sale of all: He sold his company to Genesco, one of the biggest firms in the footwear business.[4]

The Marketing Plan Is a Guide to Implementation and Control

LO 2.5

Marketing plan fills out marketing strategy

As the Toddler University case illustrates, a marketing strategy sets a target market and a marketing mix. It is a big picture of what a firm will do in some market. A marketing plan goes farther. A **marketing plan** is a written statement of a marketing strategy *and* the time-related details for carrying out the strategy. It should spell out the following in detail: (1) what marketing mix will be offered, to whom (that is, the target market), and for how long; (2) what company resources (shown as costs) will be needed at what rate (month by month perhaps); and (3) what results are expected (sales and profits perhaps monthly or quarterly, customer satisfaction levels, and the like). The plan should also include some control procedures—so that whoever is to carry out the plan will know if things are going wrong. This might be something as simple as comparing actual sales against expected sales—with a warning flag to be raised whenever total sales fall below a certain level.

The website for this text includes a feature called "Marketing Plan Coach," which contains a sample marketing plan for a veterinary clinic. At the end of each chapter, there is a Marketing Plan Coach exercise that introduces you to aspects of a marketing plan that are related to the topics in that chapter. This gives you a step-by-step way to develop your plan-building skills as you progress through the text. In Chapter 18, we will review all of the elements in a marketing plan. At that point, you will have learned about all of the major strategy decision areas (Exhibit 2-5) and how to blend them into an innovative strategy.

Implementation puts plans into operation

After a marketing plan is developed, a marketing manager knows *what* needs to be done. Then the manager is concerned with **implementation**—putting marketing plans into operation. Strategies work out as planned only when they are effectively implemented. Many **operational decisions**—short-run decisions to help implement strategies—may be needed.

Campbell's has developed different soups (and related marketing mixes) that are targeted to the specific needs of different target markets. The marketing plan for each type of soup fits into Campbell's overall marketing program.

Exhibit 2–7 Relation of Strategy Policies to Operational Decisions for Baby Shoe Company

Marketing Mix Decision Area	Strategy Policies	Likely Operational Decisions
Product	Carry as limited a line of colors, styles, and sizes as will satisfy the target market.	Add, change, or drop colors, styles, and/or sizes as customer tastes dictate.
Place	Distribute through selected "baby-products" retailers that will carry the full line and provide good in-store sales support and promotion.	In market areas where sales potential is not achieved, add new retail outlets and/or drop retailers whose performance is poor.
Promotion	Promote the benefits and value of the special design and how it meets customer needs.	When a retailer hires a new salesperson, send current training package with details on product line; increase use of local newspaper print ads during peak demand periods (before holidays, etc.).
Price	Maintain a "premium" price, but encourage retailers to make large-volume orders by offering discounts on quantity purchases.	Offer short-term introductory price "deals" to retailers when a new style is first introduced.

Managers should make operational decisions within the guidelines set down during strategy planning. They develop product policies, place policies, and so on as part of strategy planning. Then operational decisions within these policies probably will be necessary—while carrying out the basic strategy. Note, however, that as long as these operational decisions stay within the policy guidelines, managers are making no change in the basic strategy. If the controls show that operational decisions are not producing the desired results, however, the managers may have to reevaluate the whole strategy—rather than just working harder at implementing it.

It's easier to see the difference between strategy decisions and operational decisions if we illustrate these ideas using our Toddler University example. Possible four Ps or basic strategy policies are shown in the left-hand column in Exhibit 2-7, and examples of operational decisions are shown in the right-hand column.

It should be clear that some operational decisions are made regularly—even daily—and such decisions should not be confused with planning strategy. Certainly, a great deal of effort can be involved in these operational decisions. They might take a good part of the sales or advertising manager's time. But they are not the strategy decisions that will be our primary concern.

Analytical tools provide control

Our focus in this text is on developing marketing strategies. But eventually marketing managers must control the marketing plans that they develop and implement. The control job provides feedback so managers can change marketing strategies to better meet customer needs. To maintain control, a marketing manager uses a number of analytical tools to learn more about customers and their buying habits. That might involve measuring customers' shopping behaviors and purchase decisions. In Chapter 18 we look more closely at how firms control marketing plans and programs. In addition, as we talk about each of the marketing decision areas in Chapters 8 through 17, we will discuss some of the analytical tools used to control each area. For example, we will discuss how companies evaluate the effectiveness of their advertising. At this time it is important for you to understand that marketing strategy is regularly evaluated and changed as feedback identifies what is working and what could work better.[5]

Several plans make a whole marketing program

Most companies implement more than one marketing strategy—and related marketing plan—at the same time. Procter & Gamble targets users of laundry detergent with at least three different strategies. Some consumers want Tide's superior cleaning capabilities; others prefer the color protection of Cheer or the pleasant scents of Gain. Each detergent has a different formulation and a different approach for letting its target market know about

Exhibit 2–8 Elements of a Firm's Marketing Program

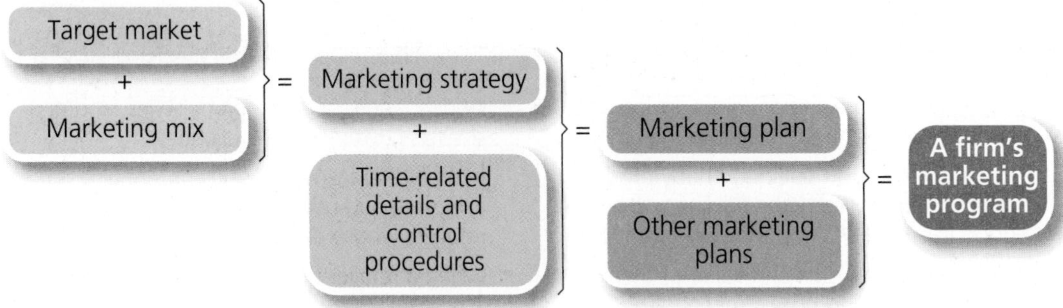

its benefits. Yet P&G must implement each of these marketing strategies at the same time—along with strategies for Bounty, Olay, Charmin, and many other brands.

A **marketing program** blends all of the firm's marketing plans into one "big" plan. See Exhibit 2-8. But the success of the marketing program depends on the care that goes into planning the individual strategies and how well they work together to create value for customers and the firm.

Recognizing Customer Lifetime Value and Customer Equity

LO 2.6

In Chapter 1 we introduced the idea that building customer value attracts customers, and that satisfying those customers builds profitable long-term relationships. Let's take that a step further and understand how marketing strategies and marketing programs that build relationships with customers can create financial value for a marketer.

Relationships increase lifetime customer value

Loyal customers continue to buy brands that satisfy them, often seeking out other products from that same company. Many firms recognize this and measure the **customer lifetime value** or total stream of purchases that a customer could contribute to the company over the length of the relationship. For example, a 22-year-old college graduate might purchase a new Honda Fit for $16,000. A few years later she could be in the market for a small sport utility vehicle, and if she was happy with how the Fit ran and the service she received, she might buy a Honda CR-V for $25,000. Maybe a couple of kids later, a Honda Odyssey starts to look good, followed over a few decades by additional Honda cars and trucks. A Honda lawn mower or two may be purchased along the way. If Honda continues to provide good value to this customer, her customer lifetime value could exceed $400,000.

Financial analysis can demonstrate how important it is for a company to maintain customers over a lifetime. A good marketing program develops multiple strategies to make it easy for satisfied customers to buy more from the company. In this case, Honda has vehicles to satisfy consumers as they move along in life.

Customer equity estimates profitability

We can take the idea of customer lifetime value a step further by taking into account all of a firm's current and future customers and the costs associated with each. **Customer equity** is the expected earnings stream (profitability) of a firm's current and prospective customers over some period of time. By estimating customer equity with different marketing strategies and marketing programs, a firm can make financially informed marketing strategy choices.

Increasing customer equity requires marketing managers to place an emphasis on long-term profits—not just the next quarter or year. This means that marketing strategies can focus on attracting new customers as well as retaining and growing current customers.

Let's look at how a large bank like Wells Fargo develops a marketing program to enhance customer equity. To attract new customers, Wells Fargo can offer customers $100 for opening a new account with a deposit of more than $1,000. This sounds like a high price to pay for a new customer, so how can it be profitable? If Wells Fargo provides the

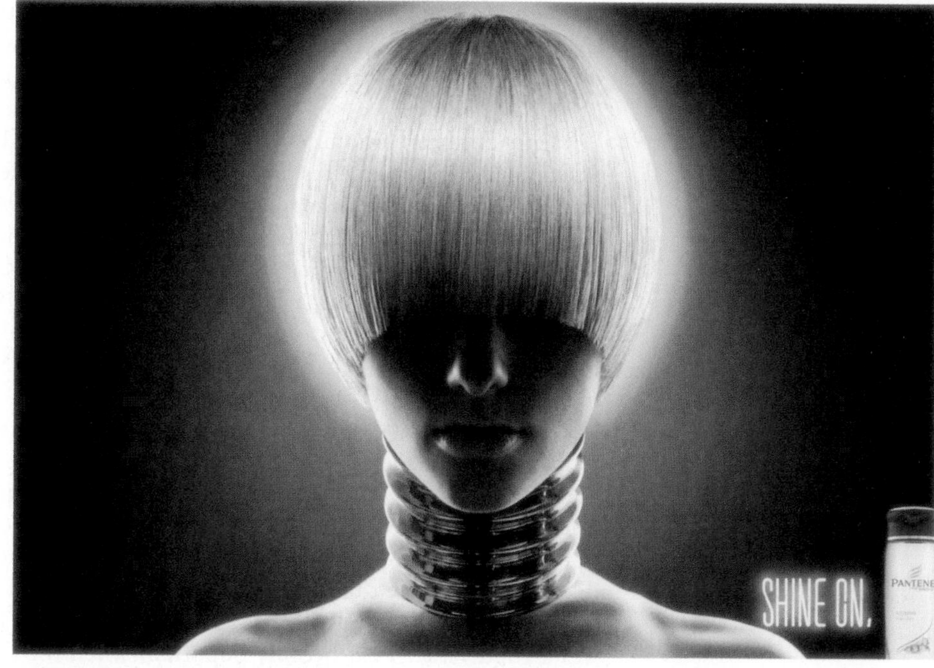

This Pantene Pro-V Ice Shine shampoo ad from China is illustrative of the many personalized products offered by the company in its effort to meet the specific needs of its customers around the world. In the U.S., the Pantene brand wins awards for excellence every year and carries the Good Housekeeping Seal of Approval. Visitors to its website can answer a few quick questions and then get suggestions for products that address their individual needs. Women not only like its products, but its causes. For example, in its Beautiful Lengths Program, Pantene has partnered with the American Cancer Society to give real-hair wigs to women fighting cancer, and, on Facebook, it shares the inspiring stories of women who have donated their hair and those who have been recipients. To attract new customers, the company offers a Total Hair Satisfaction Guarantee or double your money back. Customers worldwide who have tried one of Pantene's risk-free products and were pleased are likely to be attracted to its other products and to its innovative new offerings—no matter where they live. And, to keep its global profits growing, Pantene considers what strategies will increase customer equity when seeking new opportunities—whether at home or abroad.

customer with great service, the customer will be with the bank for many years. Further, a satisfied customer will be more interested in other products, and open to a Wells Fargo Visa card when it is suggested by a bank teller. Over time, the customer becomes even more profitable by taking out a home equity loan and opening a retirement savings account. Wells Fargo managers know that the more products a customer buys, the more likely they are to stay a Wells Fargo customer for a long time—so it encourages its customer service reps to cross-sell new products to customers. A focus on customer equity allows the bank's marketing strategies for each of these products to work together to increase the value the customer receives and enhance customer equity for Wells Fargo.[6]

The Importance of Marketing Strategy Planning

We emphasize the planning part of the marketing manager's job for a good reason. The "onetime" strategy decisions—the decisions that decide what business the company is in and the strategies it will follow—usually determine success, or failure. While firms regularly monitor their market and adapt strategies, most firms find that some strategies work better than others—and some don't work at all. Still, effective strategy planning significantly increases the chances for success. The case history that follows shows the importance of planning and why we emphasize marketing strategy planning throughout this text.

Driving new strategies in the auto industry

Henry Ford revolutionized the automobile industry 100 years ago when he built an assembly line to produce his durable and practical Model T. The line helped him make cars for much less than his competitors. By the early 1920s the Model T sold for just $290 (equivalent to less than $2,500 today). That price helped the car appeal to a larger target market even if available in "any color as long as it is black." Ford benefited from publicity in newspapers, and local car clubs educated customers about the pleasures of driving. Advertising spread the word and a network of local dealers made the cars widely available. Soon Model Ts made up half the cars sold in the United States and 40 percent of the cars sold in England.

By the mid-1920s competitors offered more choice and useful features like electric starters. When General Motors introduced the more powerful and stylish Chevrolet in 1926, sales of the Model T plummeted. Ford realized it had to become more market-oriented. So it closed its plants for six months and retooled to produce the new Model A—which came in more than 20 different styles including a station wagon, convertible, and truck. The Model A also added features like a safety glass windshield and in-cab heat. Priced from $385 for the Roadster to $1,400 for the Town Car, the Model A was a good value. That became important when the Great Depression hit just a few years later.

By the mid-1950s, the company thought it needed a new line of cars positioned between its economical Fords and the more upscale Mercury and Lincoln models it also produced. Extensive customer research led to a new product line. Prerelease advertising ballyhooed the new Edsel as a totally new kind of car with "more YOU ideas." But when it arrived, customers were disappointed to find that the Edsel looked a lot like other Ford models—and cost more than they expected. Just three years later Ford dropped the Edsel.

In 1961 Ford saw an opportunity for a sporty car inspired by Ferrari and Maserati, which would seat four, generate good margins, and sell for less than $2,500. The Mustang was launched in 1964. Advertising, positive reviews from the automotive press, and a prominent placement in the James Bond movie Goldfinger made the car an instant hit. It sold triple its forecast in the first year—and it's still a popular model today.

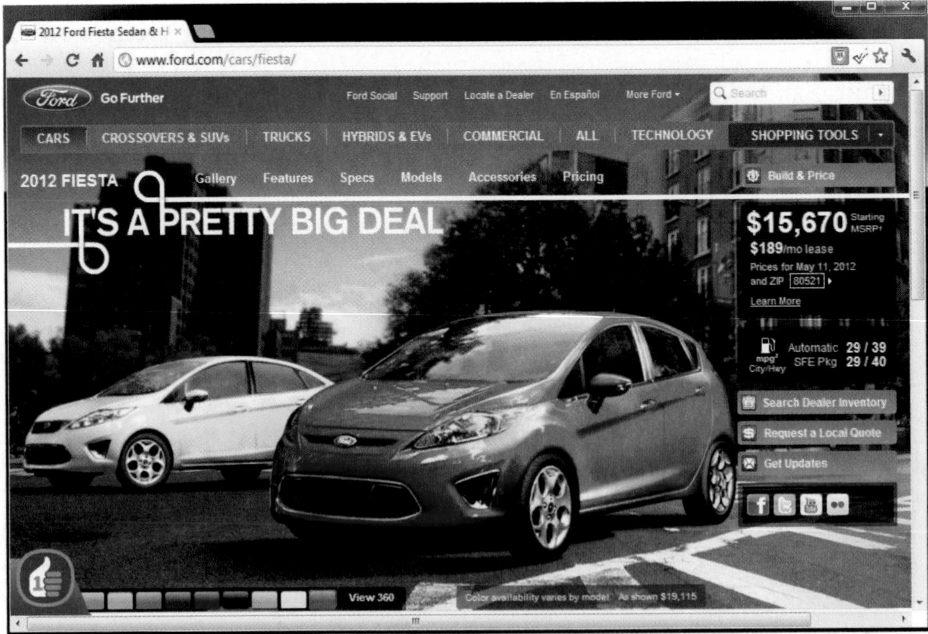

Ford has revised its strategy over the years and found innovative ways to meet consumer needs. The marketing mix for the new Fiesta has been designed to appeal to a younger, more "connected" generation.

The market changed again in the 1970s when gas prices spiked and the U.S. government mandated that cars pollute less. Ford struggled to find a marketing strategy to appeal to customers who now wanted smaller, more fuel-efficient cars. By the 1980s, Ford and other American automakers were ceding significant market share to Japanese competitors like Toyota and Honda that produced the high quality, reliable, and economical cars favored by many.

Ford had more success in the highly profitable truck and sport utility vehicle (SUV) segments. Many families valued safety and hauling capacity, and when gas prices fell in the 1990s, SUV sales took off. The comfortable and stylish Ford Explorer and its upscale "twin," the Mercury Mountaineer, became best sellers. However, concerns about quality and safety, rising gas prices, and a sagging economy soon gouged sales.

Seeing how gas prices affected sales, Ford invested in gas-electric hybrid technology to gain greater fuel economy. In 2004 Ford launched Escape, the first hybrid SUV. Initially, this small SUV appealed to an environmentally conscious target market willing to pay the $3,500 premium. But, by its third year on the market, its buyers were more concerned about economic benefits, including higher gas mileage, a $1,000 rebate, and tax credits of more than $2,000 per vehicle.

More recently, Ford and Microsoft cooperated to develop the SYNC in-car communications and entertainment system. With voice activation, SYNC lets drivers control their phone and iPod, listen to text messages, and tune in to Pandora online radio. SYNC especially appeals to the younger, more digitally savvy customers Ford targets with its small, sporty Fiesta. Fiesta's marketing managers used an aggressive social media campaign to build excitement for the North American launch—knowing this target market was especially suspicious of traditional advertising. Ford loaned Fiestas to 100 "agents"—social trendsetters chosen from over 4,000 who applied online. Agents completed Ford-assigned missions like delivering Meals on Wheels, or their own adventures like eloping, in their Fiestas. Then they shared their experiences honestly on social media including Facebook, YouTube, and Twitter. The campaign generated more than 6 million YouTube views and 50,000 requests for more information.

Internet Exercise

The Scion brand targets a similar group of customers as the Ford Fiesta. Go to the Scion website (**www.scion.com**) and check out the different Scion models and the features each offers. Look at the pricing and the information provided at the website. Then, go to the Fiesta website (**www.ford.com/cars/fiesta**) and check the same information. Based on the websites, which car do you think appeals better to a younger target market? Why?

Ford has been adapting its marketing mixes to address evolving customer needs for more than 100 years. Constant changes in the economy, technology, and competition mean that marketing strategies at Ford must be revised often if it is to continue its success.[7]

What Are Attractive Opportunities?

LO 2.7

Effective marketing strategy planning matches opportunities to the firm's resources (what it can do) and its objectives (what top management wants to do). Successful strategies get their start when a creative manager spots an attractive market opportunity. Yet an opportunity that is attractive for one firm may not be attractive for another. Attractive opportunities for a particular firm are those that the firm has some chance of doing something about—given its resources and objectives.

Breakthrough opportunities are best

Throughout this book, we will emphasize finding **breakthrough opportunities**—opportunities that help innovators develop hard-to-copy marketing strategies that will be very profitable for a long time. That's important because there are always imitators who want to "share" the innovator's profits—if they can. It's hard to continuously provide *superior* value to target customers if competitors can easily copy your marketing mix.

Competitive advantage is needed—at least

Even if a manager can't find a breakthrough opportunity, the firm should try to obtain a competitive advantage to increase its chances for profit or survival. **Competitive advantage** means that a firm has a marketing mix that the target market sees as better

Attractive new opportunities are often fairly close to markets the firm already knows. Kleenex took the decorative packaging for its facial tissues to new heights with this summer collection inspired by the colors and shapes of fruit.

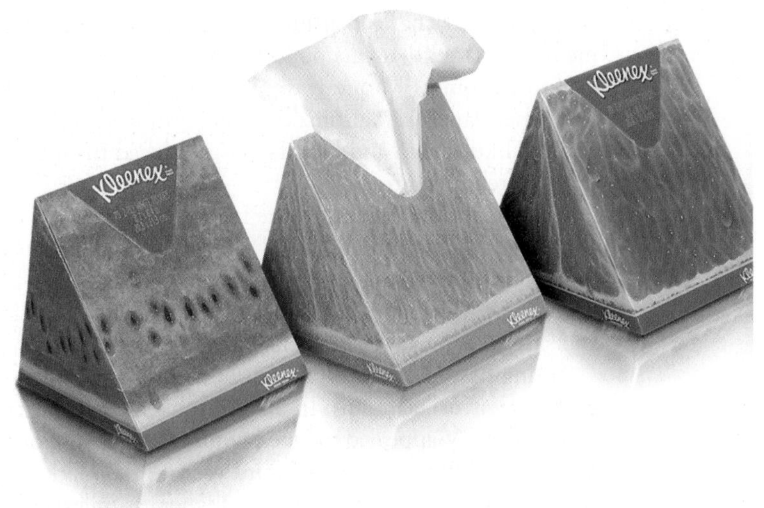

than a competitor's mix. A competitive advantage may result from efforts in different areas of the firm—cost cutting in production, innovative R&D, more effective purchasing of needed components, or financing for a new distribution facility. Similarly, a strong sales force, a well-known brand name, or good dealers may give it a competitive advantage in pursuing an opportunity. Whatever the source, an advantage only succeeds if it allows the firm to provide superior value and satisfy customers better than some competitor.[8]

Avoid hit-or-miss marketing with a logical process

You can see why a manager *should* seek attractive opportunities. But that doesn't mean that everyone does—or that everyone can turn an opportunity into a successful strategy. It's all too easy for a well-intentioned manager to react in a piecemeal way to what appears to be an opportunity. Then by the time the problems are obvious, it's too late.

Developing a successful marketing strategy doesn't need to be a hit-or-miss proposition. And it won't be if you learn the marketing strategy planning process developed in this text. Exhibit 2-9 summarizes the marketing strategy planning process we'll be developing throughout the rest of the chapters.

Exhibit 2–9
Overview of Marketing Strategy Planning Process

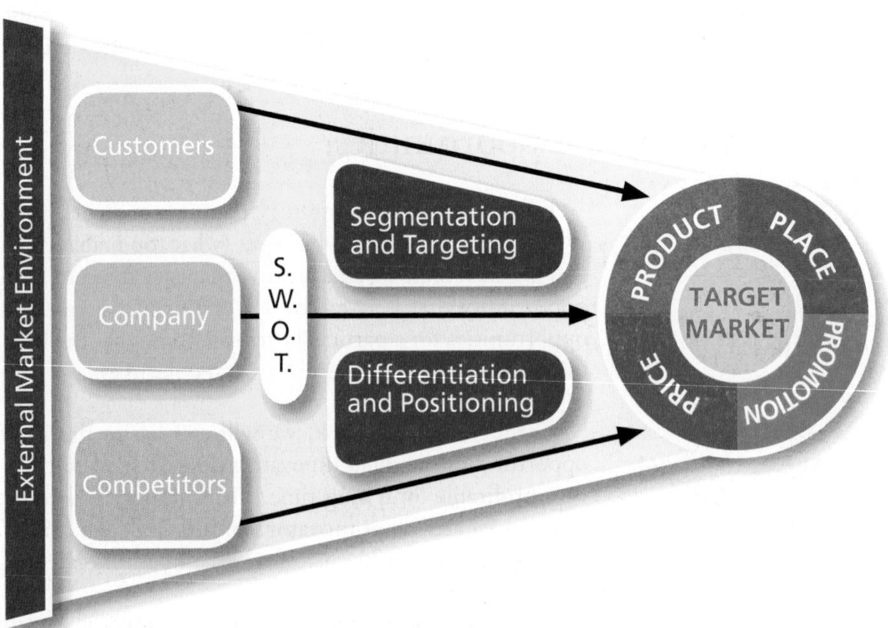

Note: Marketing manager narrows down from screening broad market opportunities to develop a focused marketing strategy. S.W.O.T. denotes Strengths, Weaknesses, Opportunities, and Threats.

Marketing Strategy Planning Process Highlights Opportunities

We've emphasized that a marketing strategy requires decisions about the specific customers the firm will target and the marketing mix the firm will develop to appeal to that target market. We can organize the many marketing mix decisions (review Exhibit 2-5) in terms of the four Ps—Product, Place, Promotion, and Price. Thus, the "final" strategy decisions are represented by the target market surrounded by the four Ps. However, the idea isn't just to come up with *some* strategy. After all, there are hundreds or even thousands of combinations of marketing mix decisions and target markets (i.e., strategies) that a firm might try. Rather, the challenge is to zero in on the best strategy.

Process narrows down from broad opportunities to specific strategy

As Exhibit 2-9 suggests, it is useful to think of the marketing strategy planning process as a narrowing-down process. Later in this chapter and in Chapters 3 and 4 we will go into more detail about strategy decisions relevant to each of the terms in this figure. Then, throughout the rest of the book, we will present a variety of concepts and "how to" frameworks that will help you improve the way you make these strategy decisions. As a preview of what's coming, let's briefly overview the general logic of the process depicted in Exhibit 2-9.

The process starts with a broad look at a market—paying special attention to customer needs, the firm's objectives and resources, and competitors. This helps to identify new and unique opportunities that might be overlooked if the focus is narrowed too quickly.

Screening criteria make it clear why you select a strategy

There are usually more opportunities—and strategy possibilities—than a firm can pursue. Each one has its own advantages and disadvantages. Trends in the external market environment may make a potential opportunity more or less attractive. These complications can make it difficult to zero in on the best target market and marketing mix. However, developing a set of specific qualitative and quantitative screening criteria can

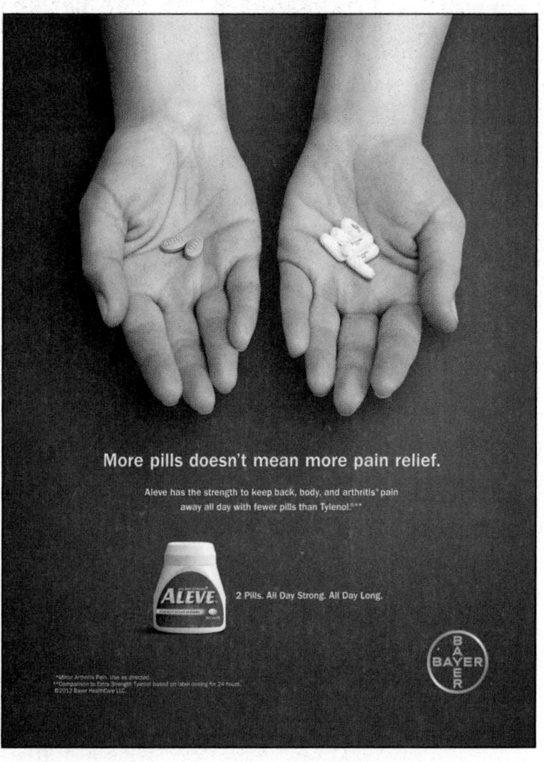

Customers want to buy a product that is somehow different from what competitors offer. The Phillipines tourism office wants vacationers to know that visiting the Phillipine islands can offer similar scenery at a fraction of the price of a trip to Phuket Thailand. Aleve wants customers to know that fewer pills can provide the same results as a multitude of their competitors' pills..

help a manager define what business and markets the firm wants to compete in. We will cover screening criteria in more detail in Chapter 3. For now, you should realize that the criteria you select in a specific situation grow out of an analysis of the company's objectives and resources.

S.W.O.T. analysis highlights advantages and disadvantages

A useful aid for organizing information from the broader market and developing relevant screening criteria is the **S.W.O.T. analysis**—which identifies and lists the firm's strengths, weaknesses, opportunities and threats. The name S.W.O.T. is simply an abbreviation for the first letters in the words *s*trengths, *w*eaknesses, *o*pportunities and *t*hreats. Strengths and weaknesses come from assessing the company's resources and capabilities. For example, a local farmer's market might have a great reputation in its community (strength) but have limited financial resources (weakness).

Opportunities and threats emerge from an examination of customers, competition and the external market environment. The farmer's market might see an opportunity when a growing number of customers in its community show an interest in eating locally produced food, while a threat could be a drought that limits local farmers' production. With a S.W.O.T. analysis, a marketing manager can begin to identify strategies that take advantage of the firm's strengths and opportunities while avoiding weaknesses and threats.

Segmentation helps pinpoint the target

In the early stages of a search for opportunities we're looking for customers with needs that are not being satisfied as well as they might be. Of course, potential customers are not all alike. They don't all have the same needs—nor do they always want to meet needs in the same way. Part of the reason is that there are different possible types of customers with many different characteristics. In spite of the many possible differences, there often are subgroups (segments) of consumers who are similar and could be satisfied with the same marketing mix. Thus, we try to identify and understand these different subgroups—with market segmentation. We will explain approaches for segmenting markets later in Chapter 4. Then, in Chapters 5 and 6, we delve into the many interesting aspects of customer behavior. For now, however, you should know that really understanding customers is at the heart of using market segmentation to narrow down to a specific target market. In other words, segmentation helps a manager decide to serve some segment(s)—subgroup(s) of customers—and not others.

Customers want something different

A marketing mix won't get a competitive advantage if it *just* meets needs in the same way as some other firm. Marketing managers want to identify customer needs that are not being addressed or might be met better than the competition. Combining analyses of customers, competitors, and company help the marketing manager identify possible strategies that differentiate a marketing mix from the competition. **Differentiation** means that the marketing mix is distinct from what is available from a competitor. In Chapter 4 we will discuss differentiation and how it is used to help position a brand in a customer's mind.

Narrowing down to a superior marketing mix

Sometimes difference is based mainly on one important element of the marketing mix—say, an improved product or faster delivery. However, differentiation often requires that the firm fine-tune all of the elements of its marketing mix to the specific needs of a distinctive target market. Target customers are more likely to recognize differentiation when there is a consistent theme integrated across the four Ps decision areas. The theme should emphasize the differences so target customers will think of the firm as being in a unique position to meet their needs.

For example, in northern Europe many auto buyers are particularly concerned about driving safely on snowy roads. So Audi offers a permanent four-wheel-drive system called quattro that helps the car to hold the road. Audi's advertising emphasizes this point of differentiation. Rather than show the car, ads feature things that are very sticky (like bubblegum!) and the only text is the headline "sticks like quattro" along with the Audi brand

Offering more by offering less

Just how much difference do customers think there is between Mobil and Exxon gasoline? Levi's and Lee jeans? Visa and MasterCard? Marriott and Holiday Inn hotels? American, Delta, and United Airlines? While some customers see big differences and have their own favorite, many see little difference and end up buying the lowest-priced option. Marketing managers want to carefully craft a marketing mix that differs from what customers offer and appeals to target customers.

Some brands differentiate by offering less than the competition in most areas—and then add a little something unexpected for the category. Take a look at the airline JetBlue. When JetBlue entered the market in 2000, all the major airlines offered free meals on every flight, the choice of flying in first class, business class, or coach, and a wide range of different fares. JetBlue offered none of these benefits. But JetBlue wasn't a budget carrier either—every plane featured plush leather seats from the front to the back of the plane with satellite television in each seat. JetBlue also promised to never bump anyone from a flight. Over time, competitors followed JetBlue's lead, so its initial differentiation declined—yet many customers see differences and remain loyal.

If you live in the western United States, you might find an In-N-Out Burger nearby. Unlike other fast food joints, In-N-Out doesn't have kids' meals, a children's menu, salads, or desserts. In fact, the menu includes just six items! Yet there is more here than meets the eye. In-N-Out makes everything on the menu from scratch using fresh (not frozen) ingredients. Unless you're an insider, you won't know about the "secret menu" and won't think to ask for your order "Protein Style" or "Animal Style."

When IKEA brought its stores to the United States, selling ready-to-assemble furniture, appliances, and home accessories, there was nothing like it. American furniture shoppers were accustomed to high levels of customer service and wide selections of styles. IKEA arrived with only Danish-style furnishings, little sales help on the showroom floor, and no delivery service—and by the way, you have to put the furniture together yourself when you get home. The furniture was cheap, and not only the prices. IKEA told customers they should plan to replace it in a few years. Yet IKEA stores are not bare bones—each features a restaurant with smoked salmon and Swedish meatballs. Each store features day care centers for kids—and now they are testing play centers called Mänland for husbands and boyfriends.

Some businesses differentiate by offering more than the competition—test drive a 740 horsepower Ferrari or stay at a luxurious Mandarin Oriental Hotel. But JetBlue, In-N-Out, and IKEA went the other direction. When competitors added more, these companies offered less—and something special—and their most loyal customers like the difference.[9]

name. Audi has other strengths, but handling in the snow is an important one that helps position Audi as better than competing brands with this target market. In Chapters 8 to 17 we'll cover many ways in which the four Ps of the marketing mix can be developed to meet a target market's needs.

Exhibit 2-9 focuses on planning each strategy by carefully narrowing down to a specific marketing strategy. Of course this same approach works well when several strategies are to be planned. This may require different managers working together to develop a marketing program that increases customer equity.[10]

Types of Opportunities to Pursue

LO 2.8

Many opportunities seem "obvious" only after someone else identifies them. So early in the marketing strategy planning process it's useful for marketers to have a framework for thinking about the broad kinds of opportunities they may find. Exhibit 2-10 shows four broad possibilities: market penetration, market development, product development, and diversification. We will look at these separately to clarify the ideas. However, some firms pursue more than one type of opportunity at the same time.

Exhibit 2–10
Four Basic Types of Opportunities

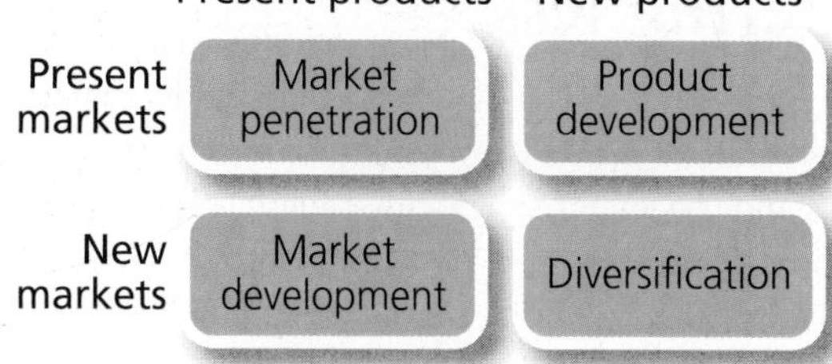

Present products
New products
Present markets
Market penetration
Product development
New markets
Market development
Diversification

Market penetration

Market penetration means trying to increase sales of a firm's present products in its present markets—probably through a more aggressive marketing mix. The firm may try to strengthen its relationship with customers to increase their rate of use or repeat purchases, or try to attract competitors' customers or current nonusers. Coleman got a 50 percent increase in sales of its outdoor equipment, like camping lanterns and coolers, by reaching its target market with special promotional displays at outdoor events like concerts, fishing tournaments, and NASCAR races. For example, about 250,000 auto racing fans camp on-site at NASCAR races each year—so a display at the campground is an effective way to reach customers when they have leisure time to browse through product displays and demos.[11]

New promotion appeals alone may not be effective. A firm may need to make it easier for customers to place repeat orders on the Internet. Or it may need to add more stores in present areas for greater convenience. Short-term price cuts or coupon offers may help.

Many firms try to increase market penetration by developing closer relationships with customers so that they will be loyal. Frequent buyer clubs use this approach. Similarly, firms often analyze customer databases to identify "cross-selling" opportunities. For example, when a customer goes online to register Adobe's Acrobat Reader, the web page promotes other related products, including its popular Photoshop software.

Market development

Market development means trying to increase sales by selling present products in new markets. This may involve searching for new uses for a product. E-Z-Go, a producer of golf carts, has done this. Its carts are now a quiet way for workers to get around malls, airports, and big factories. The large units are popular as utility vehicles on farms, at outdoor sports events, and at resorts. E-Z-Go even fits carts with ice compartments and cash drawers so they can be used for mobile food services.

Firms may also try advertising in different media to reach new target customers. Or they may add channels of distribution or new stores in new areas, including overseas. For example, to reach new customers, Dunkin' Donuts now sells its popular coffee at grocery stores and not just at its own outlets.[12]

Product development

Product development means offering new or improved products for present markets. By knowing the present market's needs, a firm may see new ways to satisfy customers. For example, in 2003 Campbell's came out with a line of soups with 25 percent less sodium than its regular product. That may seem like a minor change, but by 2008 it resulted in $650 million in sales because it was important to Campbell's health-conscious consumers. Ski resorts have developed trails for hiking and biking to bring their winter ski customers back in the summer. Nike moved beyond shoes and sportswear to offer its athletic target market a running watch, digital audio player, and even a portable heart-rate monitor. And of course Intel boosts sales by developing newer and faster chips.[13]

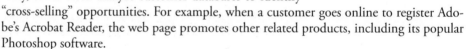

The Heinz ad is a clever visual reminder of the fresh taste of the tomatoes in Heinz Ketchup. The primary purpose of this type of promotion is to increase market penetration, which means increasing sales of a firm's present products in its present markets. Delta is well-known for its faucets. But its new Touch O'Technology faucet is a product development opportunity that it hopes will increase customer equity. Touch anywhere on the spout or handle with your wrist or forearm to start and stop the flow of water.

HEINZ
TOMATO
KETCHUP
No one grows Ketchup like Heinz.

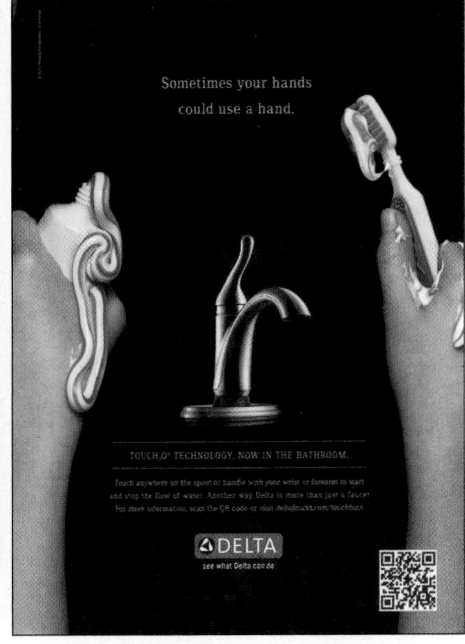

Sometimes your hands
could use a hand.
TOUCH2O® TECHNOLOGY. NOW IN THE BATHROOM.
DELTA

Diversification

Diversification means moving into totally different lines of business—perhaps entirely unfamiliar products, markets, or even levels in the production-marketing system. Products and customers that are very different from a firm's current base may look attractive to the optimists—but these opportunities are usually hard to evaluate. That's why diversification usually involves the biggest risk. McDonald's, for example, opened two hotels in Switzerland. The plan was to serve families on the weekend, but business travelers were the target during the week. Business travelers are not the group that McDonald's usually serves, and an upscale hotel is also very different from a fast-food restaurant. This helps to explain why operation of the Golden Arch hotels was taken over by a hospitality management company after two years. On the other hand, diversification can be successful—especially when the new strategy fits well with the firm's resources and marketing program.[14]

Which opportunities come first?

Usually firms find attractive opportunities fairly close to markets they already know. Most firms think first of greater market penetration. They want to increase profits and grow customer equity where they already have experience and strengths. On the other hand, many firms find that market development—including the move into new international markets—profitably takes advantage of current strengths.

International Opportunities Should be Considered

LO 2.9

It's easy for a marketing manager to fall into the trap of ignoring international markets, especially when the firm's domestic market is prosperous. Yet there are good reasons to go to the trouble of looking elsewhere for opportunities.

The world is getting smaller

Many countries have reduced barriers, like taxes on imports, which made international trade more costly. These moves have increased international trade all over the world. In addition, advances in e-commerce, transportation, and communications are making it easier and cheaper to reach international customers. With a website and e-mail, even the smallest firm can provide international customers with a great deal of information—and easy ways to order—at very little expense.

Levi Strauss & Co. created the dENiZEN™ brand because it saw a strong opportunity for great fitting, quality and affordable jeanswear in markets like China where there is a significant emerging middle class consumer segment. The brand name combines "denim" with the Asian "zen"—which means "meditative state." The dENiZEN™ brand will eventually be available in Latin America and Africa also.

Develop a competitive advantage at home and abroad

If customers in other countries are interested in the products a firm offers—or could offer—serving them may improve economies of scale. Lower costs (and prices) may give a firm a competitive advantage both in its home markets *and* abroad. Black and Decker, for example, uses electric motors in many of its tools and appliances. By selling overseas as well as in the United States, it gets economies of scale and the cost per motor is very low.

Get an early start in a new market

A company facing tough competition, thin profit margins, and slow sales growth at home may get a fresh start in another country where demand for its product is just beginning to grow. A marketing manager may be able to transfer marketing know-how—or some other competitive advantage—the firm has already developed. Consider JLG, a Pennsylvania-based producer of equipment used to lift workers and tools at construction sites. Faced with tough competition, JLG's profits all but evaporated. By cutting costs, the company improved its domestic sales. But it got an even bigger boost from expanding overseas. In the first five years, its international sales were greater than what its total sales had been before. Then, when JLG added distribution in China, international sales grew to be half of its business. Now JLG continues to enjoy growth, in spite of the home construction downturn in the United States, because JLG sales in Europe benefit from new safety rules that require workers to be on an aerial platform if they're working up high.[15]

Find better trends in variables

Unfavorable trends in the market environment at home—or favorable trends in other countries—may make international marketing particularly attractive. For example, population growth in the United States has slowed and income is leveling off. In other places in the world, population and income are increasing rapidly. Many U.S. firms can no longer rely on the constant market growth that once drove increased domestic sales. Growth—and perhaps even survival—will come only by aiming at more distant customers. It doesn't make sense to casually assume that all of the best opportunities exist "at home."[16]

Weigh the risks of going abroad

Marketing managers should consider international opportunities, but risks are often higher in foreign markets. Many firms fail because they don't know the foreign country's culture. Learning foreign regulations can be difficult and costly. Political or social unrest make it difficult to operate in some countries. Venezuela is a striking example. Current Venezuelan leaders have threatened to nationalize some international businesses that have located there. Careful planning can help reduce some of these risks, but ultimately managers must assess both the risks and opportunities that exist in each international market.

CONCLUSION

This chapter introduces you to the basic decision areas involved in marketing strategy planning and explains the logic for the marketing strategy planning process summarized in Exhibit 2-9. In the remainder of this book we'll rely on this exhibit as a way to highlight the organization of the topics we are discussing.

In this chapter, you learned that the marketing manager must constantly study the market environment—seeking attractive opportunities and planning new strategies. A marketing strategy specifies a target market and the marketing mix the firm will offer to provide that target market with superior customer value. A marketing mix has four major decision areas: the four Ps—Product, Place, Promotion, and Price.

There are usually more potential opportunities than a firm can pursue, so possible target markets must be matched with marketing mixes the firm can offer. This is a narrowing-down process. The most attractive strategies—really, marketing plans and whole marketing programs—are chosen for implementation.

Marketing programs should recognize customer lifetime value and customer equity. These ideas can help marketing managers demonstrate the financial value for a firm that not only acquires customers, but satisfies them by offering superior customer value and sees repeat purchases over time.

Controls are needed to be sure that the plans are carried out successfully. If anything goes wrong along the way, continual feedback should cause the process to be started over again—with the marketing manager planning more attractive marketing strategies. Thus, the job of marketing management is one of continuous planning, implementing, and control. Strategies are not permanent; changes should be expected as market conditions change.

Firms need effective strategy planning to survive in our increasingly competitive markets. The challenge isn't just to come up with some strategy, but to zero in on the strategy that is best for the firm given its objectives and resources—and taking into consideration its strengths and weaknesses and the opportunities and threats that it faces. To improve your ability in this area, this chapter introduces a framework for marketing strategy planning. The rest of this text is organized to deepen your understanding of this framework and how to use it to develop profitable marketing mixes for clearly defined target markets. After several chapters on analyzing target markets, we will discuss each of the four Ps in greater detail.

While market-oriented strategy planning is helpful to marketers, it is also needed by financial managers, accountants, production and personnel people, and all other specialists. A market-oriented plan lets everybody in the firm know what ballpark they are playing in and what they are trying to accomplish.

We will use the term *marketing manager* for editorial convenience, but really, when we talk about marketing strategy planning, we are talking about the planning that a market-oriented manager should do when developing a firm's strategic plans. This kind of thinking should be done—or at least understood—by everyone in the organization. And this includes even the entry-level salesperson, production supervisor, retail buyer, or human resources counselor.

KEY TERMS

LO 2.10

marketing management process, *32*
strategic (management) planning, *33*
marketing strategy, *33*
target market, *33*
marketing mix, *33*
target marketing, *34*
mass marketing, *34*
channel of distribution, *36*
personal selling, *37*
customer service, *38*
mass selling, *38*
advertising, *38*
publicity, *38*
sales promotion, *38*
marketing plan, *40*
implementation, *40*
operational decisions, *40*
marketing program, *42*
customer lifetime value, *42*

customer equity, *42*
breakthrough opportunities, *45*
competitive advantage, *45*
S.W.O.T. analysis, *48*
differentiation, *48*
market penetration, *50*
market development, *50*
product development, *50*
diversification, *51*

QUESTIONS AND PROBLEMS

1. Distinguish clearly between a marketing strategy and a marketing mix. Use an example.
2. Distinguish clearly between mass marketing and target marketing. Use an example.
3. Why is the target market placed in the center of the four Ps in the text diagram of a marketing strategy (Exhibit 2-4)? Explain, using a specific example from your own experience.
4. If a company sells its products only from a website, which is accessible over the Internet to customers from all over the world, does it still need to worry about having a specific target market? Explain your thinking.
5. Explain, in your own words, what each of the four Ps involves.
6. Evaluate the text's statement, "A marketing strategy sets the details of implementation."
7. Distinguish between strategy decisions and operational decisions, illustrating for a local retailer.
8. In your own words, explain what customer equity means and why it is important.
9. Distinguish between a strategy, a marketing plan, and a marketing program, illustrating for a local retailer.
10. Outline a marketing strategy for each of the following new products: (*a*) a radically new design for a toothbrush, (*b*) a new fishing reel, (*c*) a new wonder drug, and (*d*) a new industrial stapling machine.
11. Provide a specific illustration of why marketing strategy planning is important for all businesspeople, not just for those in the marketing department.
12. Research has shown that only about three out of every four customers are, on average, satisfied by a firm's marketing programs. Give an example of a purchase you made where you were not satisfied and what the firm could have changed to satisfy you. If customer satisfaction is so important to firms, why don't they score better in this area?
13. Distinguish between an attractive opportunity and a breakthrough opportunity. Give an example.
14. Explain how new opportunities may be seen by defining a firm's markets more precisely. Illustrate for a situation where you feel there is an opportunity—namely, an unsatisfied market segment—even if it is not very large.
15. In your own words, explain why the book suggests that you should think of marketing strategy planning as a narrowing-down process.
16. Explain the major differences among the four basic types of growth opportunities discussed in the text and cite examples for two of these types of opportunities.
17. Explain why a firm may want to pursue a market penetration opportunity before pursuing one involving product development or diversification.
18. In your own words, explain several reasons why a marketing manager should consider international markets when evaluating possible opportunities.
19. Give an example of a foreign-made product (other than an automobile) that you personally have purchased. Give some reasons why you purchased that product. Do you think that there was a good opportunity for a domestic firm to get your business? Explain why or why not.

CREATING MARKETING PLANS

The Marketing Plan Coach software on the text website includes a sample marketing plan for Hillside Veterinary Clinic. Skim through the different sections of the marketing plan. Look more closely at the "Marketing Strategy" section.

a. What is the target market for this marketing plan?
b. What is the strategy Hillside Veterinary Clinic intends to use?
c. What are your initial reactions to this strategy? Do you think it will be successful? Why or why not?

SUGGESTED CASES

3. NOCO United Soccer Academy
4. Hometown Tech
5. Polystyrene Solutions
12. DrJane.com—Custom Vitamins
29. Quality Iron Castings, Inc.

Video Case 1. Chick-fil-A
Video Case 2. Bass Pro Shops
Video Case 3. Potbelly Sandwich
Video Case 6. Big Brothers and Big Sisters of America

COMPUTER-AIDED PROBLEM

2. TARGET MARKETING

Marko, Inc.'s managers are comparing the profitability of a target marketing strategy with a mass marketing "strategy." The spreadsheet gives information about both approaches.

The mass marketing strategy is aiming at a much bigger market. But a smaller percent of the consumers in the market will actually buy this product—because not everyone needs or can afford it. Moreover, because this marketing mix is not tailored to specific needs, Marko will get a smaller share of the business from those who do buy than it would with a more targeted marketing mix.

Just trying to reach the mass market will take more promotion and require more retail outlets in more locations—so promotion costs and distribution costs are higher than with the target marketing strategy. On the other hand, the cost of producing each unit is higher with the target marketing strategy—to build in a more satisfying set of features. But because the more targeted marketing mix is trying to satisfy the needs of a specific target market, those customers will be willing to pay a higher price.

In the spreadsheet, "quantity sold" (by the firm) is equal to the number of people in the market who will actually buy one each of the product—multiplied by the share of those purchases won by the firm's marketing mix. Thus, a change in the size of the market, the percent of people who purchase, or the share captured by the firm will affect quantity sold. And a change in quantity sold will affect total revenue, total cost, and profit.

a. On a piece of paper, show the calculations that prove that the spreadsheet "total profit" value for the target marketing strategy is correct. (*Hint:* Remember to multiply unit production cost and unit distribution cost by the quantity sold.) Which approach seems better—target marketing or mass marketing? Why?

b. If the target marketer could find a way to reduce distribution cost per unit by $.25, how much would profit increase?

c. If Marko, Inc., decided to use the target marketing strategy and better marketing mix decisions increased its share of purchases from 50 to 60 percent—without increasing costs—what would happen to total profit? What does this analysis suggest about the importance of marketing managers knowing enough about their target markets to be effective target marketers?

3 CHAPTER THREE

Evaluating Opportunities in the Changing Market Environment

Back in 1995, when Amazon.com first went online, its founder Jeff Bezos saw a potential breakthrough opportunity by changing the retail shopping experience. Amazon's strategy took advantage of trends Bezos observed, especially rapid consumer adoption of the World Wide Web. Laws didn't require the collection of sales tax, which helped offset charges for shipping and handling. At the time, buoyed by a strong economy, early investors were patient as Amazon lost $3 billion from 1995 to 2003 yet kept acquiring customers.

Amazon wasn't just "lucky" to be in the right place and time. Bezos pushed his firm to be innovative in every aspect of the customer experience online. For example, Amazon pioneered community features like customer reviews to help customers discover new products and make more informed decisions. Its "1-Click" checkout technology made it faster and easier for customers to pay for items and arrange shipping.

In the early days, most consumers thought of Amazon as just another competitor for "brick-and-mortar" bookstores. Bezos soon expanded into new product-markets with offerings that initially included CDs, movies, games, electronics, home and garden, and later others ranging from health and beauty aids to industrial tools and cloud computing services. These moves were consistent with Amazon's mission statement, which states its desire "to be earth's most customer-centric company; to build a place where people can come to find anything they might want to buy online."

Amazon quickly pursued global growth, launching sites in both the United Kingdom and Germany by 1998. These markets were attractive initial targets because, like the United States, each offered a large number of customers with high average incomes and access to the Internet. They later opened sites serving customers in Canada, Italy, France, Japan, and China; now 45 percent of Amazon's sales come from abroad.

Amazon has also become a leader in using customer relationship management (CRM) systems to enhance the shopping experience. CRMs store data on each customer in a large database. For example, Amazon knows what each customer looks at, what they buy, and what they don't buy. This information is combined with data from other customers to tailor messages and even the website for each customer. If Amazon knows a customer buys DVDs and bought *Game of Thrones* books, they can send that customer an e-mail announcing the availability of *Game of Thrones* DVDs. When regular customers arrive at the website, they click to their own personal "store," where Amazon puts products specifically geared to that customer's interests.

The troubled global economy that emerged in 2008 was not all bad news for Amazon.com. The depressed economic environment actually gave Amazon a boost. Amazon's online approach, with wide selections of popular products at low prices, seemed to be exactly what penny-pinching consumers were looking for—and Amazon continued to grow rapidly during the recession.

Amazon offers more than just low prices—it also makes online shopping convenient. Many of its customers pay an annual fee for Amazon Prime and receive free two-day shipping on all their purchases. This move encourages customers to shop at the store more often. Amazon Prime customers also get access to free movies. With Amazon's Subscribe and Save program, customers receive discounts and free shipping when they sign up to receive shipment of a product. For example, they receive 15 percent off to have a case of toilet paper delivered monthly.

As consumers live increasingly digital lifestyles, Amazon continues to respond to this trend. Some of these customers like to use tablet computers and phones for shopping, so Amazon has apps for that. With Amazon's Price Check app, customers can comparison shop with their smartphone. When they scan a barcode (or type or speak the product name into the phone) up pops the Amazon price, and with 1-Click, customers can place an order.

While Amazon's heritage was built on print books, digital e-books are the future. Anticipating this trend, it developed the Kindle line of e-book readers, with screens in sizes from 6–9.7 inches and holding up to 3,500 books. Each Kindle comes with a 3G or Wi-Fi wireless connection to the Kindle store, where any of Amazon's selection of more than a million e-books can be downloaded in less than a minute. Consumers love the selection and Amazon's low price; most e-books sell for $9.99 or less. Kindle owners with an Amazon Prime account can even "borrow" books (one at a time) from the Kindle Owners' Lending Library.

The Kindle Fire tablet comes with a 7-inch color screen that allows users to surf the web, watch videos, play games, run a wide range of apps—and oh yeah, read books, too. That versatility makes it a hit with families. Some people thought Amazon was crazy when it sold the Kindle Fire for just $199—less than it cost to produce. But Amazon understands the lifetime value of its customers; the Kindle Fire helps them build relationships with customers who will purchase more books, movies, and games for their Kindle Fire and be profitable over time.

Amazon faces some mighty strong competitors across its markets. Walmart and its online store have engaged in price wars with Amazon over books, toys, and DVDs. Amazon battles Netflix in video downloads. Apple sells tablet computers and online music and video. But Amazon has never been afraid to tackle markets with strong competitors. To the contrary, it seeks large and growing markets where it can leverage its competitive strengths, including its size, technology skills, efficient operations, and reach. To grow in these competitive and fast-changing market environments, Amazon must continue to successfully adjust its marketing strategies.[1]

Learning Objectives

The Amazon case shows that a marketing manager must analyze customer needs and choose marketing strategy variables within the framework of the market environment and how it is changing. Opportunities need to fit with a firm's objectives and resources, and managers should screen for opportunities where there is a chance for competitive advantage and, if possible, favorable trends in the external environment.

When you finish this chapter, you should be able to:

1 know the variables that shape the environment of marketing strategy planning.

2 understand why company objectives are important in guiding marketing strategy planning.

3 see how the resources of a firm affect the search for opportunities.

4 know how to conduct a competitor analysis and how different types of competition affect strategy planning.

5 understand how the economic and technological environments can affect strategy planning.

6 know how elements of the political and legal environment affect marketing strategy planning.

7 understand the cultural and social environment and how demographic trends affect strategy planning.

8 understand how to screen and evaluate marketing strategy opportunities.

9 understand the important new terms (shown in red).

The Market Environment

LO 3.1

The marketing strategy planning process (see Exhibit 2-9) requires narrowing down to the best opportunities and developing a strategy that gives the firm a competitive advantage and provides target customers with superior customer value. This narrowing-down process should consider the important elements of the market environment and how they are shifting.

A large number of forces shapes the market environment. The direct market environment includes customers, the company, and competitors. The external market environment is broader and includes four major areas:

1. Economic environment
2. Technological environment
3. Political and legal environment
4. Cultural and social environment

Exhibit 3–1 Marketing Strategy Planning, Competitors, Company, and External Market Environment

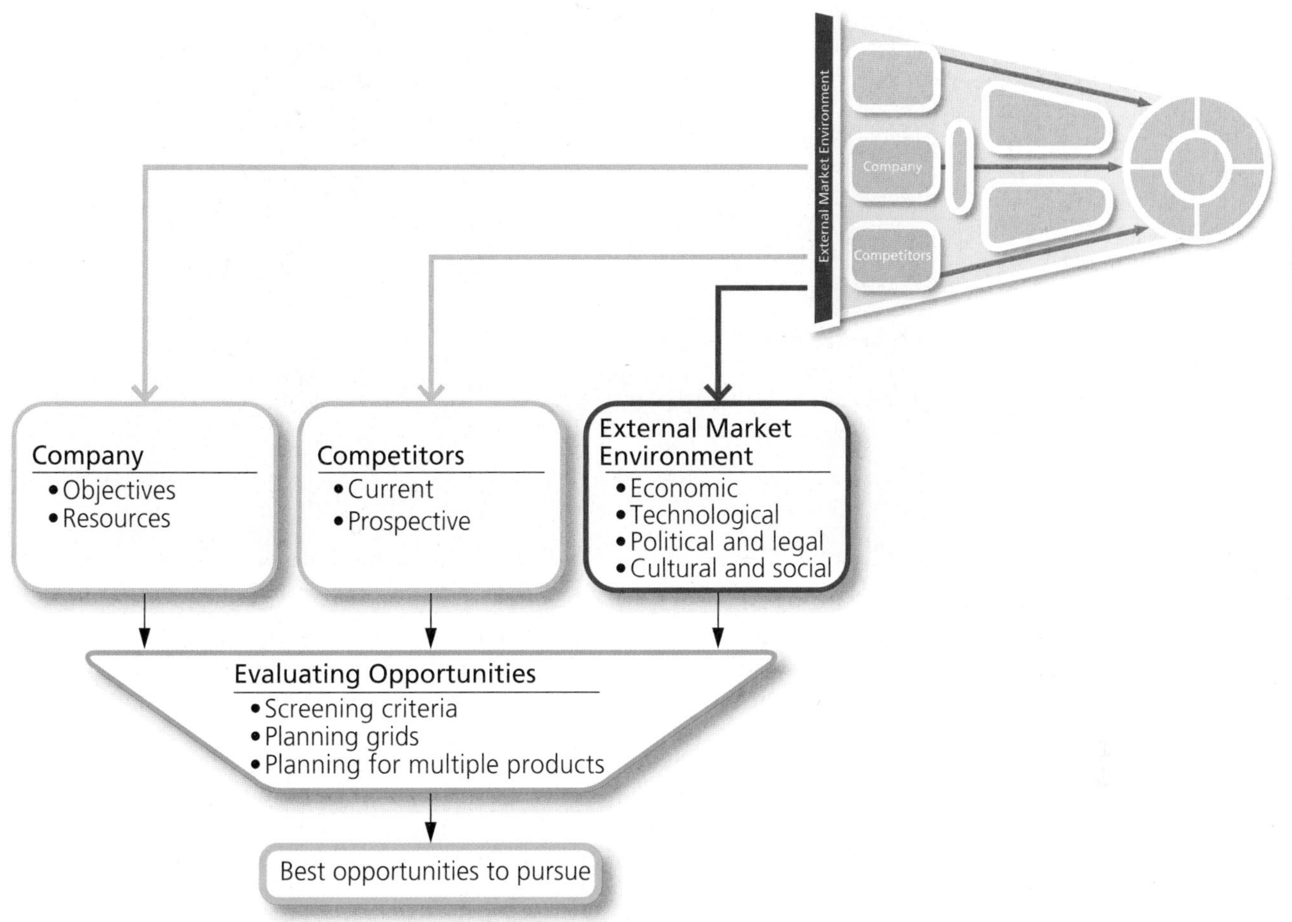

Managers can't alter the variables of the market environment. That's why it's useful to think of them as uncontrollable variables. On the other hand, a manager should analyze the environment when making decisions that can be controlled. For example, a manager can select a strategy that leads the firm into a market where competition is not yet strong or where trends in the external market are likely to support market growth.

In this chapter, we'll look at the key market environment variables shown in Exhibit 3-1 in more detail. We'll see how they shape opportunities—limiting some possibilities but making others more attractive.

Objectives Should Set Firm's Course

LO 3.2

A company must decide where it's going, or it may fall into the trap expressed so well by the quotation: "Having lost sight of our objective, we redoubled our efforts." Company objectives should shape the direction and operation of the whole business.

It is difficult to set objectives that really guide the present and future development of a company. The marketing manager should be heard when the company is setting objectives. But setting whole company objectives—within resource limits—is ultimately the responsibility of top management. Top management must look at the whole business, relate its present objectives and resources to the external environment, and then decide what the firm wants to accomplish in the future.

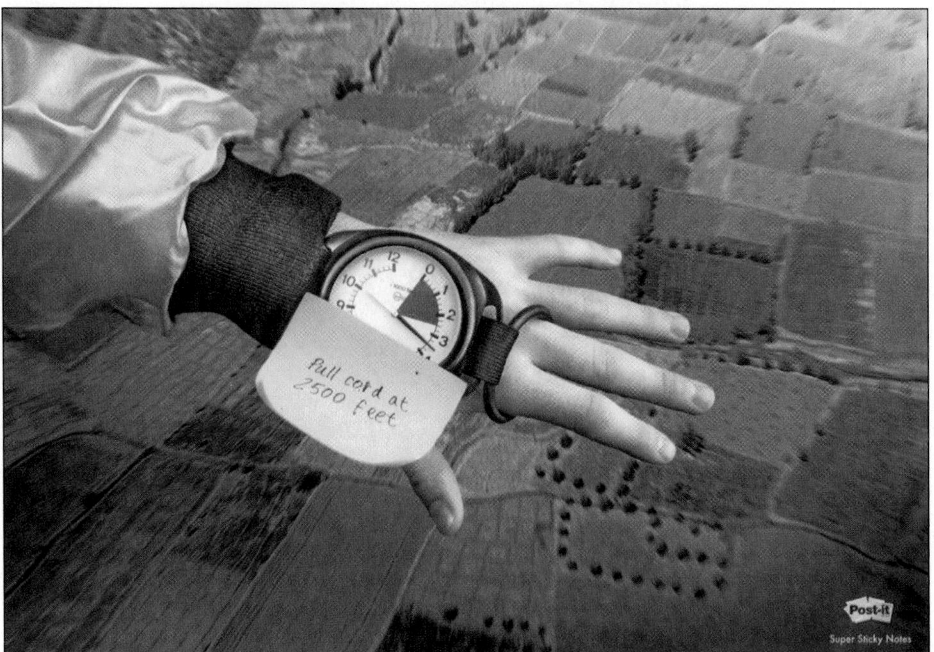

3M has introduced a super sticky version of its popular Post-It notes to stay ahead of competitors who try to imitate its original product.

A mission statement helps set the course

Each firm needs to develop its own objectives based on its own situation. This is important, but top executives often don't state their objectives clearly. If objectives aren't clear from the start, different managers may hold unspoken and conflicting objectives.

Many firms try to avoid this problem by developing a **mission statement**, which sets out the organization's basic purpose for being. For example, the mission statement for the American Red Cross states that it "will provide relief to victims of disaster and help people prevent, prepare for, and respond to emergencies." A good mission statement should focus on a few key goals rather than embracing everything. It should also supply guidelines that help managers determine which opportunities to pursue. For example, a Red Cross employee would not pursue a grant that supports children's literacy—even if it's a good cause. But, when there's an opportunity to develop a program that enables people to donate to Red Cross disaster relief efforts by sending a short text message, it should be clear that this program falls within the charity's stated mission. A mission statement may need to be revised as new market needs arise or as the market environment changes. But this would be a fundamental change and not one that is made casually.[2]

The whole firm must work toward the same objectives

A mission statement is important, but it is not a substitute for more specific objectives that provide guidance in screening possible opportunities. For example, top management might set objectives such as "earn 25 percent annual return on investment" and "introduce at least three innovative and successful products in the next two years."

Of course, when there are a number of specific objectives stated by top management, it is critical that they be compatible. For example, the objective of introducing new products is reasonable. However, if the costs of developing and introducing the new products cannot be recouped within one year, the return on investment objective is impossible.

Company objectives should lead to marketing objectives

To avoid such problems, the marketing manager should at least be involved in setting company objectives. Company objectives guide managers as they search for and evaluate opportunities—and later plan marketing strategies. Particular *marketing* objectives should be set within the framework of larger company objectives. As shown in Exhibit 3-2, firms need a hierarchy of objectives—moving from company objectives to marketing department objectives. For each marketing strategy, firms also need objectives for each of the four Ps—as well as more detailed objectives. For example, in the Promotion area, we need objectives for personal selling, mass selling, *and* sales promotion.

Exhibit 3–2 A Hierarchy of Objectives

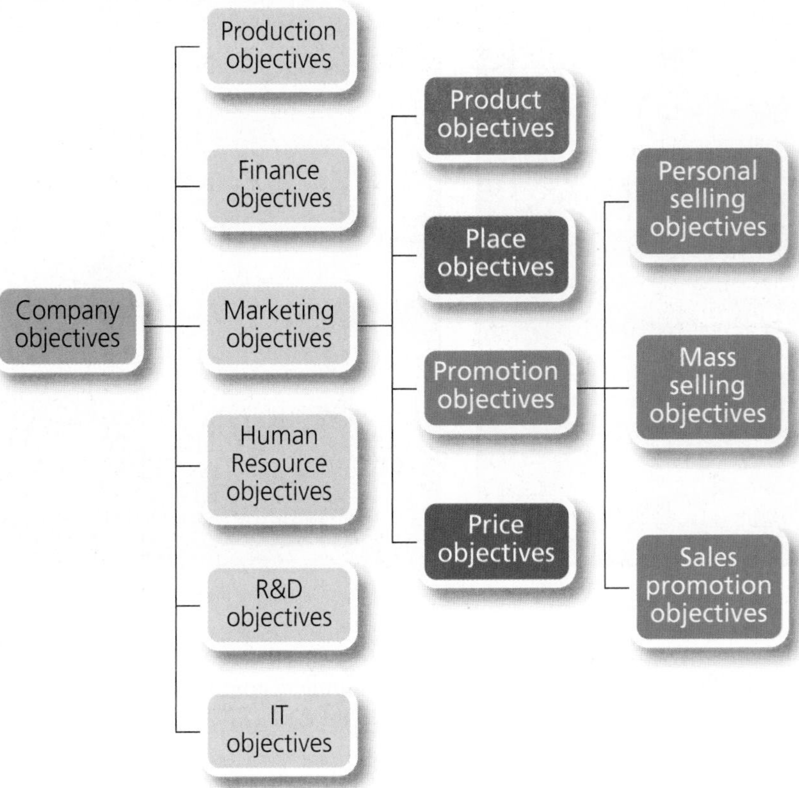

Insurance company USAA provides an example. One of USAA's top objectives is to deliver high levels of customer satisfaction. Because customer service is a key driver of satisfaction, it is critical to have highly qualified and well-trained customer service representatives (CSRs) responding to customers' questions or problems. This leads to human resources objectives that guide the hiring and training of CSRs. Similarly, it's imperative for USAA's information technology group to develop software that increases the effectiveness of CSRs in their dealings with customers. So new software was designed to allow CSRs to view the same online screens as customers see on their PCs at home. With these capabilities, CSRs can solve customer problems more efficiently. USAA expects these efforts to deliver even higher levels of customer satisfaction and customer retention in the competitive insurance market.[3]

Both company objectives and marketing objectives should be realistic and achievable. Overly ambitious objectives are useless if the firm lacks the resources to achieve them.

Company Resources May Limit Search for Opportunities

LO 3.3

Every firm has some resources—hopefully some unique ones—that set it apart. Breakthrough opportunities—or at least some competitive advantage—come from making use of these strengths while avoiding direct competition with firms having similar strengths.

To find its strengths or recognize weaknesses, a firm must evaluate its functional areas (production, research and engineering, marketing, general management, and finance) as well as its present products and markets. The knowledge of people at the firm can also be a unique resource. By analyzing successes or failures in relation to the firm's resources, management can discover why the firm was successful—or why it failed—in the past.

Financial strength

Some opportunities require large amounts of capital just to get started. Money may be required for R&D, production facilities, marketing research, or advertising before a firm makes its first sale. And even a really good opportunity may not be profitable for years. So lack of financial strength is often a barrier to entry into an otherwise attractive market.

Producing capability and flexibility

In many businesses, the cost of producing and selling each unit decreases as the quantity increases. Therefore, smaller firms can be at a great cost disadvantage if they try to win business from larger competitors. On the other hand, new—or smaller—firms sometimes have the advantage of flexibility. They are not handicapped with large, special-purpose facilities that are obsolete or poorly located.

Many firms increase flexibility by not having any "in-house" manufacturing for their brands. Hanes is a good example. At one point, Hanes had U.S. factories for its underwear and T-shirts. But the factories were sold when most textile-related manufacturing moved to other countries with lower labor costs. Top managers for the brand said that

The opportunities a firm decides to pursue may depend on its resources and capabilities. For example, General Mills was already producing a key ingredient for its new Chocolate Chex Mix, so it went ahead and launched Chex Mix Turtle. Similarly, Nucor knows how to produce steel in large mills, but recently it has begun operating smaller steel mills in rural towns. Both General Mills and Nucor are innovative in other ways, which helps them to be flexible and responsive to changes in the market environment.

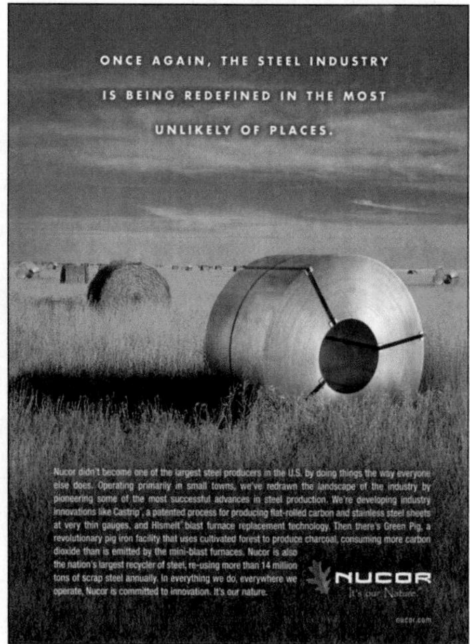

they didn't have a competitive advantage in manufacturing anyway. Now, as Hanes' needs change, it has the flexibility to work with whatever suppliers around the world are best able to meet its specifications.

Marketing strengths

Marketing resources can create opportunities for a firm. In the product area, for example, a familiar brand can be a big strength. Starbucks is famous for its coffee beverages. When Starbucks introduced its Coffee Ice Cream, many people quickly tried it because they knew what Starbucks flavor meant.[4]

A new idea or process may be protected by a *patent*. A patent owner has a 20-year monopoly to develop and use its new product, process, or material. If one firm has a strong patent, competitors may be limited to second-rate offerings—and their efforts may be doomed to failure.[5]

Good relations with wholesalers and retailers can also be an important resource—especially when introducing new products. Marketing managers at Clorox relied on this when they introduced the Green Works line of household cleaners. After years of working with the company on well-established products like Clorox Bleach, retailers trusted Clorox to create an effective marketing strategy for Green Works.

Promotion and price resources must be considered too. Fidelity Investments already has a skilled sales force. Marketing managers know these sales reps can handle new products and customers. And expertise to create an Internet website for online orders may enable a firm to expand into a new target market.

Analyzing Competitors and The Competitive Environment

LO 3.4

Choose opportunities that avoid head-on competition

The **competitive environment** affects the number and types of competitors the marketing manager faces and how they may behave. Although marketing managers usually can't control these factors, they can choose strategies that avoid head-on competition. And where competition is inevitable, they can plan for it.

Economists describe four basic kinds of market (competitive) situations: pure competition, oligopoly, monopolistic competition, and monopoly. Understanding the differences among these market situations is helpful in analyzing the competitive environment, and our discussion assumes some familiarity with these concepts. (For a review, see Exhibit A-11 and the related discussion in Appendix A following Chapter 20.)

LOOK DEEPER.
YOUR COMPANY DESERVES A DEEPER NETWORK.
The Delta Dental system includes three out of every four dentists—which makes our networks the biggest in the nation. Offering your employees access to the deepest networks improves the chance that their preferred dentists participate in one or more of our plans. That, in turn, helps us deliver greater plan savings to you. So if you're not with Delta Dental, shouldn't you be? To learn more about Delta Dental, please contact your broker or visit www.wedodentalbetter.com.
We do dental. Better.
DELTA DENTAL

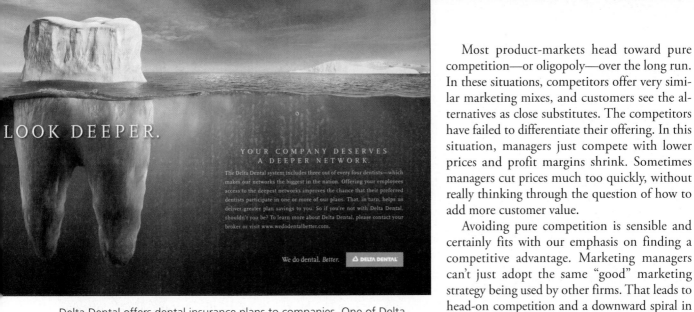

Delta Dental offers dental insurance plans to companies. One of Delta Dental's strengths is its extensive network, which includes three out of every four dentists. The deeper network of dentists provides Delta Dental's customers with more options and greater employee satisfaction.

Most product-markets head toward pure competition—or oligopoly—over the long run. In these situations, competitors offer very similar marketing mixes, and customers see the alternatives as close substitutes. The competitors have failed to differentiate their offering. In this situation, managers just compete with lower prices and profit margins shrink. Sometimes managers cut prices much too quickly, without really thinking through the question of how to add more customer value.

Avoiding pure competition is sensible and certainly fits with our emphasis on finding a competitive advantage. Marketing managers can't just adopt the same "good" marketing strategy being used by other firms. That leads to head-on competition and a downward spiral in prices and profits. So target marketers try to offer a marketing mix better suited to target customers' needs than competitors' offerings.

Competitor-free environments are rare

Monopoly situations, in which one firm completely controls a broad product-market, are rare in market-directed economies. Further, governments commonly regulate monopolies. For example, in many parts of the world prices set by utility companies (electricity and water) must be approved by a government agency. Monopolies can be tempted to ignore customer needs. Yet monopolies often face competition sooner or later—for example, cable television providers now have competition from satellite providers—so it pays to be responsive to customers even when little competition exists.

Monopolistic competition is typical and a challenge

In monopolistic competition, a number of different firms offer marketing mixes that at least some customers see as different. Each competitor tries to get control (a monopoly) in its "own" target market. But competition still exists because some customers see the various alternatives as substitutes. Most marketing managers in developed economies face monopolistic competition.

In monopolistic competition, marketing managers sometimes try to differentiate very similar products by relying on other elements of the marketing mix. For example, many consumers believe that most brands of gasoline are very similar. This makes it difficult for a Texaco station to attract customers by claiming it offers better gas. So a Texaco station might serve Seattle's Best Coffee, offer discounted car washes, maintain longer hours of operation, or keep a well-lit, safe storefront. Yet such approaches may not work for long if they are easily copied by competitors. So marketing managers should actively seek **sustainable competitive advantage**, a marketing mix that customers see as better than a competitor's mix and cannot be quickly or easily copied.

Analyze competitors to find competitive advantage

The best way for a marketing manager to avoid head-on competition is to find new or better ways to satisfy customers' needs and provide value. The search for a breakthrough opportunity—or some sort of competitive advantage—requires an understanding not only of customers but also of competitors. That's why marketing managers turn to **competitor analysis**—an organized approach for evaluating the strengths and weaknesses of current or potential competitors' marketing strategies.

The basic approach to competitor analysis is simple. You compare the strengths and weaknesses of your current (or planned) target market and marketing mix with what competitors are currently doing or are likely to do in response to your strategy.

The initial step in competitor analysis is to identify potential competitors. It's useful to start broadly and from the viewpoint of target customers. Companies may offer quite

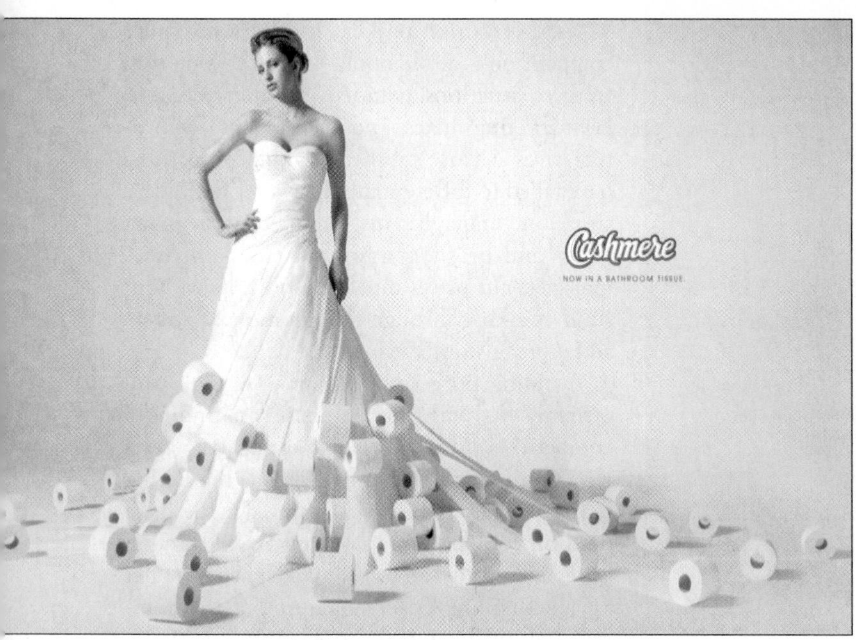

Many consumers think that toilet paper is a commodity—where one brand is about the same as any other. Cashmere's bathroom tissue is softer and its ad campaign encourages consumers to see how special it is. However, consumer attitudes may be difficult to change.

different products to meet the same needs, but they are competitors if customers see them as offering close substitutes. For example, disposable diapers, cloth diapers, and diaper rental services all compete in the same broad market concerned with baby care. Identifying a broad set of potential competitors helps marketing managers understand the different ways customers are currently meeting needs and sometimes points to new opportunities. For example, even parents who usually prefer the economy of cloth diapers may be interested in the convenience of disposables when they travel.

Usually, however, marketing managers quickly narrow the focus of their analysis to the set of **competitive rivals**—firms that will be the closest competitors. Rivals offering similar products are usually easy to identify. However, with a really new and different product concept, the closest competitor may be a firm that is currently serving similar needs with a different type of product. Although such firms may not appear to be close competitors, they are likely to fight back—perhaps with a directly competitive product—if another firm starts to take away customers.

Organize competitor analysis in a competitor matrix

A useful tool for organizing the competitor analysis is a **competitor matrix**, an organized table that compares the strengths and weaknesses of a company with those of its competitive rivals. A competitor matrix helps the marketing manager identify potential opportunities for differentiating the marketing mix.

Exhibit 3-3 provides an example of a competitor matrix that compares P&G's situation with those of two competitors in Japan. P&G was about to replace its original Pampers, which were selling poorly, with a new version that offered improved fit and better absorbency. Kao and Uni-Charm, the two leading Japanese competitors, both had better distribution networks. Kao also had a better computer system to handle reorders. Because many Japanese grocery stores and drugstores are very small, frequent restocking by wholesalers is critical. So getting cooperation in the channel was a challenge for P&G. To overcome this problem, P&G changed its packaging to take up less space and offered wholesalers and retailers better markups.[6]

Internet Exercise

A marketing manager for Netflix may find it helpful to know more about how competitors advertise on search pages (like Google and Yahoo). The website KeywordSpy (**www.keywordspy.com**) offers that information and more. Go to this site and type "dvd rental" into its search bar. What competitors are identified? What information can you learn about Netflix and its competitors at this site? How could this information help Netflix's marketing manager?

Actively seek information about competitors

A marketing manager should actively seek information about current and potential competitors. Although most firms try to keep the specifics of their plans secret, much public information may be available. Sources of competitor information include trade publications, alert sales reps, suppliers, and other industry experts. In business markets, customers may be quick to explain what competing suppliers are offering.

Exhibit 3–3 Competitor Matrix Disposable Diaper Competition in Japan

	P&G's Current and Planned Strategy	Kao's Strengths (+) and Weaknesses (–)	Uni-Charm's Strengths (+) and Weaknesses (–)
Target Market(s)	Upscale, modern parents who can afford disposable diapers	Same as for P&G	Same as for P&G, but also budget-conscious segment that includes cloth diaper users (+)
Product	Improved fit and absorbency (+); brand name imagery weak in Japan (–)	Brand familiarity (+), but no longer the best performance (–)	Two brands—for different market segments—and more convenient package with handles (+)
Place	Distribution through independent wholesalers to both food stores and drugstores (+), but handled by fewer retailers (–)	Close relations with and control over wholesalers who carry only Kao products (+); computerized inventory reorder system (+)	Distribution through 80% of food stores in best locations (+); shelf space for two brands (+)
Promotion	Heaviest spending on daytime TV, heavy sales promotion, including free samples (+); small sales force (–)	Large, efficient sales force (+); lowest advertising spending (–) and out-of-date ad claims (–)	Advertising spending high (+); effective ads that appeal to Japanese mothers (+)
Price	High retail price (–), but lower unit price for larger quantities (+)	Highest retail price (–), but also best margins for wholesalers and retailers (+)	Lowest available retail price (+); price of premium brand comparable to P&G (–)
(Potential) Competitive Barriers	Patent protection (+), limits in access to retail shelf space (–)	Inferior product (–), excellent logistics support system (+)	Economies of scale and lower costs (+); loyal customers (+)
Likely Response(s)	Improve wholesaler and retailer margins; faster deliveries in channel; change package to require less shelf space	Press retailers to increase in-store promotion; change advertising and/or improve product	Increase short-term sales promotions; but if P&G takes customers, cut price on premium brand

Ethical issues may arise

The search for information about competitors can raise ethical issues. For example, people who change jobs and move to competing firms may have a great deal of information, but is it ethical for them to use it? Similarly, some firms have been criticized for going too far—like waiting at a landfill for competitors' trash to find copies of confidential company reports or "hacking" a competitor's computer network.

Beyond the moral issues, spying on competitors to obtain trade secrets is illegal. Damage awards can be huge. The courts ordered competing firms to pay Procter & Gamble about $125 million in damages for stealing secrets about its Duncan Hines soft cookies.[7]

Ethics Questions

You are a salesperson for a company that manufactures industrial lighting used in factories. During a recent sales call, an engineer at your customer firm comments about a new energy-saving lightbulb that his company is testing for a competing supplier. Your company was not aware of the competitor's new product—which you think may make one of your product lines obsolete. Should you pass this competitive intelligence to your sales manager? Should you question the engineer or others at the customer firm to learn more? If you gather more information, should you share that with your company?

The Economic Environment

LO 3.5

The **economic environment** refers to macro-economic factors, including national income, economic growth, and inflation, that affect patterns of consumer and business spending. The rise and fall of the economy in general, within certain industries, or in specific parts of the world can have a big impact on what customers buy.

Economic conditions change rapidly

The economic environment can, and does, change quite rapidly. The effects can be far-reaching and require changes in marketing strategy.

Even a well-planned marketing strategy may fail if a country or region goes through a rapid business decline. You can see how quickly this can occur by considering what happened in the U.S. housing market just a few years ago. Earlier in the decade the economy was growing, household incomes were increasing, and interest rates were low. As a result, the housing market was hot. Manufacturers of building materials, home-builders, real estate firms, and mortgage companies all enjoyed strong profits as they scrambled to keep up with demand. By 2008 the economy was in a recession and the housing market abruptly collapsed. Firms that had done so well a year earlier were suffering huge losses—and many went bankrupt. Worse, millions of people lost their homes when they could not afford rising payments for variable-rate mortgages.

Adapting marketing strategies in an economic downturn

When the economy declines consumers spend less in many categories that are not necessities—like eating out and buying new cars. In a recent downturn, some marketing managers found ways to adapt their marketing strategies and lessen the impact of the recession. For example, Hyundai knew that many potential car buyers didn't buy because they worried about their jobs and their abilities to make car payments in the future. So Hyundai lowered their risk when it promised customers that, if they bought or leased a new Hyundai and later lost their job, they could return the car with no impact on their credit. Hyundai generated lots of positive publicity when it announced its promise in a splashy Super Bowl commercial. The bold move helped Hyundai boost market share by over 25 percent (from a little over 3 percent to more than 4 percent in one year) and a year later less than 100 Hyundais had been returned.[8]

In a down economy, some firms will use coupons or other low price offers to appeal to more price conscious consumers.

Interest rates and inflation affect buying

Changes in the economy are often accompanied by changes in the interest rate—the charge for borrowing money. Interest rates directly affect the total price borrowers must pay for products. So the interest rate affects when, and if, they will buy. This is an especially important factor in some business markets. But it also affects consumer purchases of homes, cars, and other items usually bought on credit.

Interest rates usually increase during periods of inflation, and inflation is a fact of life in many economies. In some Latin American countries, inflation has exceeded 400 percent a year in recent years. In contrast, recent U.S. levels—3 to 20 percent—seem low. Still, inflation must be considered in strategy planning. When costs are rising rapidly and there are no more cost-cutting measures to take, a marketing manager may have to increase prices. For example, airlines and freight carriers can raise prices sharply in response to spiraling fuel costs.

The global economy is connected

The economies of the world are connected—and changes in one economy quickly affect others. One reason for this is that the amount of international trade is increasing—and it is affected by changes in and between economies. For example, economic problems in Greece and Spain made it difficult for Europe to recover from the recent economic downturn. This, in turn, slowed recovery in the rest of the world.

Changes in the *exchange rate*—how much one country's money is worth in another country's money—have an important effect on international trade. When the dollar is strong, it's worth more in foreign countries. This sounds good—but it makes U.S. products more expensive overseas and foreign products cheaper in the United States. New domestic competition arises as foreign products gain a competitive edge with lower prices. A country's whole economic system can change as the balance of imports and exports shifts—affecting jobs, consumer income, and national productivity.

Marketing managers must watch the economic environment carefully. In contrast to the cultural and social environment, economic conditions can move rapidly and require immediate strategy changes.[9]

The Technological Environment

Technology affects opportunities

Technology is the application of science to convert an economy's resources to output. Technology affects marketing in two basic ways; it creates opportunities for new products and for new processes (ways of doing things). Let's look at how that happens.

Technology often leads to breakthrough opportunities

Rapid advances in technology have resulted in new products across a wide range of industries. Digital photography replaced film and foreshadowed the bankruptcy of Eastman Kodak, once the world's largest photography company. Digital photography created opportunities for camera makers like Nikon and Canon and for software like Apple iPhoto and Adobe Photoshop. Vestagen leveraged another technology advance, making anti-microbial, fluid-resistant clothing that helps protect doctors and nurses from infectious diseases. Project Peanut Butter developed and distributes a therapeutic food that treats severely malnourished children in Africa—allowing them to be treated and recover at home. Digitized music allows some musicians to make a living without a record company—they just create a website for fans to download the music and they collect all the revenue. Marketers who spot appropriate applications of new technologies can find breakthrough opportunities.

Technology changes marketing processes

Technology changes how customers and marketers do things. Facebook was founded in 2004 and just eight years later boasted almost a billion users. Now many organizations have Facebook pages or run highly targeted ads on the social network—fans of the Pittsburgh Steelers usually say that right on their Facebook page, opening them to ads for gear with their favorite football team's logo. The Internet has changed the nature of retailing as many consumers shop from their keyboard—or tablet device—and have

Researchers at Coca-Cola developed a new technology for the plastic bottles used for many of its products. PlantBottle packaging looks and functions just like traditional PET plastic bottles—and it is recyclable. But because these bottles are partially made from plant material, they have a much smaller carbon footprint, making them better for the environment. Coke works with Ford, Heinz, Nike, and Procter & Gamble (not Pepsi) to accelerate future development of plant based plastics.

purchases delivered to their home. Computer databases allow sellers to more closely watch supply and demand—and adjust prices accordingly. Hotels and airlines often lower prices when they have extra rooms or seats. Throughout this textbook you will read about how marketing is changing because of new applications of technology.

Technology comes with challenges

Technological change opens up many new opportunities, but it also poses challenges for marketers. For some marketing managers, change can be difficult and they avoid technologies they do not understand. For others it is easy to fall in love with the latest technology—whether from the firm's R&D lab or a consultant selling social media tools—and blindly add it to the firm's marketing strategy. Both approaches can lead to a production-oriented way of thinking. That makes it more important than ever for marketing thinking to guide the process. Finding the best applications of technology still requires that marketing managers begin with customer needs.

Technology can pose ethical dilemmas

Breakthrough products can raise questions—do the benefits outweigh the costs? For example, many genetically modified foods can potentially increase crop yields and provide greater nutrition. Critics are concerned about human safety and other concerns. Aseptic drink boxes are convenient but difficult to recycle.

New technologies give marketers new ways to track consumers and perhaps deliver a more tailored experience—but does that invade consumers' privacy? Website visitors may not be aware that small computer files (called cookies) are often placed on their computers. Cookies allow the company to track what the customer does on the web. This information can be used to give a web-surfer a better online experience, perhaps serving up useful information, advertising, and discounts. On the other hand, users are often tracked without their knowledge and may prefer to retain their privacy.[10]

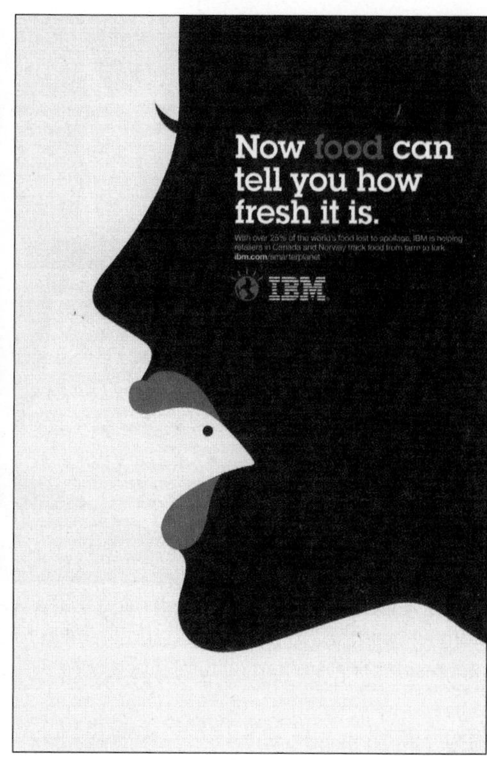

New technology creates opportunities for new products and services. Target stores has created a smartphone app that allows customers to shop on the run, check prices in the store, view the weekly ad, and generally enhance the experience of shopping at Target. IBM technology helps retailers track food from field to store to reduce the amount of food that spoils along the way.

The Political Environment

LO 3.6

The attitudes and reactions of people, social critics, and governments all affect the political environment. Consumers in the same country usually share a common political environment, but the political environment can also affect opportunities at a local or international level.

Nationalism can be limiting in international markets

Strong sentiments of **nationalism**—an emphasis on a country's interests before everything else—affect how macro-marketing systems work. They can affect how marketing managers work as well. Nationalistic feelings can reduce sales—or even block all marketing activity—in some international markets. For many years, China has made it difficult for outside firms to do business there—in spite of the fact that the Chinese economy has experienced explosive growth as its factories have turned out larger and larger portions of the goods sold in the United States, Europe, and other parts of the world.

The "Buy American" policy in many government contracts and business purchases reflects this same attitude in the United States. There is broad consumer support for protecting U.S. producers—and jobs—from foreign competition. Automaker Chrysler draws on this sentiment in its "Imported from Detroit" campaign, which features Detroit rap music artist Eminem and a two-minute Super Bowl commercial "Halftime in America" featuring Clint Eastwood. Both promote Chrysler's ties to Detroit, Michigan, Chrysler's American home, and to the United States.[11]

Regional groupings are becoming more important

Important dimensions of the political environment are likely to be similar among nations that have banded together to have common regional economic boundaries. The move toward the unification of Europe and free trade among the nations of North America are examples of this sort of regional grouping.

The unification of European markets

Twenty years ago, each country in Europe had its own unique trade rules and regulations. These differences made it difficult and expensive to move products from one country to the others. Now, the almost 30 countries of the European Union (EU) are reducing conflicting

オワリダ
THAT'S JAPANESE FOR "YOU'RE TOAST" IF YOUR WEBSITE CAN'T ACCOMMODATE OUR LANGUAGE AND CURRENCY.
THINK YOU'RE READY TO DO E-BUSINESS WITH A COMPLETELY DIFFERENT CULTURE? ARE YOU SPEAKING THE RIGHT LANGUAGE? USING THE RIGHT CURRENCY? BEFORE DIVING INTO ANY FOREIGN MARKET, YOU'VE GOT TO MAKE SURE YOUR BUSINESS APPROACH IS APPROPRIATE AND ON TARGET. ADERO CAN HELP. FROM TOKYO TO PARIS, ADERO'S WORLDWIDE NETWORK ROUTES THE RIGHT WEB CONTENT TO THE RIGHT PEOPLE. THAT WAY, YOU WON'T GET BURNED.
adero›
The world wants your business.
WWW.ADERO.COM

Adero wants marketers to keep in mind that a website that can attract prospects from all over the world won't be successful in turning them into customers if it ignores nationalism and cultural differences.

laws, taxes, and other obstacles to trade within Europe. This, in turn, is reducing costs and the prices European consumers pay and creating new jobs. Many of the member countries use the same currency (the euro), simplifying inter-European commerce and trade yet more.

Although Europe is becoming a large unified market, marketers will still encounter differences among European countries. What happened to Lands' End, the Wisconsin-based Internet and mail-order retailer, illustrates the issues. To better reach European consumers, Lands' End set up shop in England and Germany. As in the United States, its promotion and website touted the unconditional lifetime guarantee that is a key part of its strategy. However, German consumer protection rules prohibited promotion of the guarantee; the Germans argued that the promotion was a misleading gimmick (on the logic that the cost of the guarantee was "hidden" in higher prices that consumers would pay). German officials wanted this ban to apply even if the German consumer purchased the product from a Lands' End website in England. Quirky local rules like this could erode some of the benefits that should come from more European unification.[12]

NAFTA builds trade cooperation in North America

The international competition fostered by the moves to unify Europe provided impetus for the United States, Mexico, and Canada to develop more cooperative trade agreements. The **North American Free Trade Agreement (NAFTA)** lays out a plan to reshape the rules of trade among the United States, Canada, and Mexico. NAFTA basically enlarges the free-trade pact that had already knocked down most barriers to U.S.–Canada trade, and eliminated most such barriers with Mexico. It also established a forum for resolving trade disputes.

The changes that result from NAFTA may ultimately be as significant as those in Europe. Talks are under way to explore the concept of expanding the agreement to create a free-trade zone for 34 countries across North, South, and Central America. While smoothing trade lowers costs, NAFTA has not been without controversy; critics worry about the environmental impact and loss of jobs in higher labor cost countries like the United States.

Of course, removal of some economic and political barriers—whether across all of the Americas or Europe—will not eliminate the need to adjust strategies to reach submarkets of consumers. Centuries of cultural differences will not disappear overnight. Some may never disappear.[13]

The Legal Environment

Changes in the political environment often lead to changes in the legal environment and in the way existing laws are enforced. To illustrate the effects of the legal environment, we will discuss how it has evolved in the United States. However, laws often vary from one country to another.

Trying to encourage competition

American economic and legislative thinking is based on the idea that competition among many small firms helps the economy. Therefore, attempts by business to limit competition are considered contrary to the public interest.

Starting in 1890, Congress passed a series of antimonopoly laws. Exhibit 3-4 shows the names and dates of these laws. Although the specific focus of each law is different, in general they are all intended to encourage competition.

Because of a change in regulations, some non-prescription drugs are no longer available on self-service retail shelves but rather are behind the pharmacy counter. With this change in the legal environment, marketers for Mucinex D want customers to know how to find the product in the store.

Antimonopoly law and marketing mix planning

In later chapters, we will specifically apply antimonopoly law to the four Ps. For now you should know what kind of proof the government must have to get a conviction under each of the major laws. You should also know which of the four Ps are most affected by each law. Exhibit 3-4 provides such a summary—with a phrase following each law to show what the government must prove to get a conviction.

Prosecution is serious—you can go to jail

Businesses and *individual managers* are subject to both criminal and civil laws. Penalties for breaking civil laws are limited to blocking or forcing certain actions—along with fines. Where criminal law applies, jail sentences can be imposed. For example, several managers at Beech-Nut Nutrition Company were fined $100,000 each and sent to jail. In spite of ads claiming that Beech-Nut's apple juice was 100 percent natural, they tried to bolster profits by secretly using low-cost artificial ingredients.[14]

Consumer protection laws are not new

Although antimonopoly laws focus on protecting competition, the wording of the laws in Exhibit 3-4 has, over time, moved toward protecting consumers. Some consumer protections are also built into the English and U.S. common law systems. A seller has to tell the truth (if asked a direct question), meet contracts, and stand behind the firm's product (to some reasonable extent). Beyond this, it is expected that vigorous competition in the marketplace will protect consumers—*so long as they are careful.*

Yet focusing only on competition didn't protect consumers very well in some areas. So the government found it necessary to pass other laws. For example, various laws regulate packaging and labels, telemarketing, credit practices, and environmental claims. Usually, however, the laws focus on specific types of products.

Foods and drugs are controlled

Consumer protection laws in the United States go back to 1906 when Congress passed the Pure Food and Drug Act. Unsanitary meat-packing practices in the Chicago stockyards stirred consumer support for this act. Before the law, it was assumed that common law and the old warning "let the buyer beware" would take care of consumers.

Later acts corrected some loopholes in the law. The law now bans the shipment of unsanitary and poisonous products and requires much testing of drugs. The Food and Drug Administration (FDA) attempts to control manufacturers of these products. It can seize products that violate its rules—including regulations on branding and labeling.

Product safety is controlled

The Consumer Product Safety Act (of 1972), another important consumer protection law, set up the Consumer Product Safety Commission. This group has broad power to set safety standards and can impose penalties for failure to meet these standards. There is some question as to how much safety consumers really want—the commission found the bicycle the most hazardous product under its control!

Exhibit 3–4 Focus (mostly prohibitions) of Federal Antimonopoly Laws on the Four Ps

Law	Product	Place	Promotion	Price
Sherman Act (1890) Monopoly or conspiracy in restraint of trade	Monopoly or conspiracy to control a product	Monopoly or conspiracy to control distribution channels		Monopoly or conspiracy to fix or control prices
Clayton Act (1914) Substantially lessens competition	Forcing sale of some products with others—tying contracts	Exclusive dealing contracts (limiting buyers' sources of supply)		Price discrimination by manufacturers
Federal Trade Commission Act (1914) Unfair methods of competition		Unfair policies	Deceptive ads or selling practices	Deceptive pricing
Robinson-Patman Act (1936) Tends to injure competition			Prohibits "fake" advertising allowances or discrimination in help offered	Prohibits price discrimination on goods of "like grade and quality" without cost justification, and limits quanitity discounts
Wheeler-Lea Amendment (1938) Unfair or deceptive practices	Deceptive packaging or branding		Deceptive ads or selling claims	Deceptive pricing
Antimerger Act (1950) Lessens competition	Buying competitors	Buying producers or distributors		
Magnuson-Moss Act (1975) Unreasonable practices	Product warranties			

But given that the commission has the power to *force* a product off the market—or require expensive recalls to correct problems—it is obvious that safety must be considered in product design. And safety must be treated seriously by marketing managers. There is no more tragic example of this than the recalls of Firestone tires used as original equipment on Ford's Explorer SUV. Hundreds of consumers were killed or seriously injured in accidents.[15]

State and local laws vary

Besides federal legislation—which affects interstate commerce—marketers must be aware of state and local laws. There are state and city laws regulating minimum prices and the setting of prices, regulations for starting up a business (licenses, examinations, and even tax payments), and in some communities, regulations prohibiting certain activities—such as telephone selling or selling on Sundays or during evenings.

The Cultural and Social Environment

LO 3.7

The **cultural and social environment** affects how and why people live and behave as they do—which affects customer buying behavior and eventually the economic, political, and legal environments. Many variables make up the cultural and social environment. Some examples are the languages people speak; the type of education they have; their religious beliefs; what type of food they eat; the style of clothing and housing they have; and how they

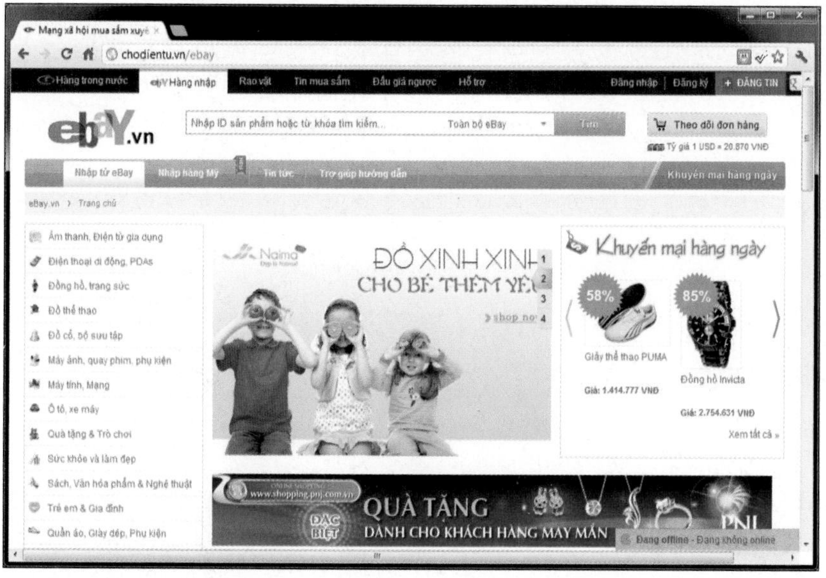

Marketing managers for eBay have found many opportunities for growth fast-growing markets like in Vietnam.

view work, marriage, and family. Because the cultural and social environment has such broad effects, most people don't stop to think about it, how it may be changing, or how it may differ for other people.

For example, over decades, the role of women has changed significantly. Sixty years ago most people in the U.S. thought that a woman's primary role was in the home—as wife and mother. Now more than 70 percent of women age 35–44 work outside the home. Such changes have increased household income, changed shopping habits, and generated a greater need for many products, including child care services and prepared take-out food. It has also changed who does the shopping for the household. Nowadays almost half of all grocery shopping is done by men—and advertisers have been slow to craft ads that effectively speak to men.[16]

Demographic data related to population, income, and technology adoption provide a lot of insight about a society and its culture. Understanding the demographic dimensions is also important to marketing strategy planning, so it's useful to look at some demographic patterns and trends.

Where people are around the world

Exhibit 3-5 summarizes data for a number of representative countries from different regions around the world. Even with a current population of over 310 million, the United States makes up only 4.5 percent of the world's seven-billion-plus people. Marketing managers in any country may seek growth opportunities in other countries.

Although the size of a market is important, the population trend also matters. The world's population is growing fast, but that population growth varies dramatically from country to country. For example, between 2010 and 2025, population is projected to grow 50 percent or more in Ethiopia and Somalia. During this same period, growth will be about 15 percent in the United States and less than 4 percent in China, while Japan, Russia, and many European countries will experience declining populations. These trends have many marketing managers paying increased attention to fast-growing developing countries.[17]

A shift from rural to urban areas

Just 50 years ago, about two-thirds of the world's population lived in rural areas. Today about half live in urban areas, as more people move to cities for better job opportunities. The extent of urbanization varies widely across countries. While about 80 percent of U.S. residents live in urban areas, more than 90 percent do in Singapore, Israel, and Argentina (see Exhibit 3-5). By contrast, in Bangladesh, Ethiopia, and Kenya, 25 percent or less of the population lives in urban areas. The concentration of people in major cities often simplifies Place and Promotion decisions.

There's no market when there's no income

Profitable markets require income—as well as people. The amount of money people can spend affects the products they are likely to buy. When considering international markets, income is often one of the most important demographic dimensions. There are a variety of different measures of national income. One widely used measure is **gross domestic product (GDP)**—the total market value of all goods and services provided in a country's economy in a year by both residents and nonresidents of that country. **Gross national income (GNI)** is a measure that is similar to GDP, but GNI does not include income earned by foreigners who own resources in that nation. By contrast, GDP does include foreign income.

Exhibit 3–5 Demographic Dimensions and Characteristics for Selected Countries

Country	2010 Projected Population (000s)	2025 Projected Population (000s)	2010–2025 Projected Population Change (%)	2009 Population Density per square mile	2009 Percent of Population in Urban Areas	2008 GNI Per Capita ($U.S.)	2008 GDP (billions of $U.S.)	Estimated Literacy Percent	2008 Mobile Phones/ 100 Inhabitants	% Mobile Phone Growth 2003–2008	% of Population Using Internet 2009	% User Growth 2000–2009
Algeria	34,586	40,290	16.5%	37	63	4,260	173.9	69.9	92.72	2203	12.0	8,100
Argentina	41,343	47,165	14.1%	39	91	7,200	328.4	97.2	116.61	593	48.9	700
Australia	21,516	25,054	16.4%	7	83	40,350	1,015.2	99.0	104.96	154	80.1	158
Bangladesh	158,066	192,976	22.1%	3,018	25	520	79.0	47.9	27.90	3270	0.4	456
Brazil	201,103	231,887	15.3%	61	84	7,350	1,612.5	88.6	78.47	325	34.0	1,250
Canada	33,760	37,559	11.3%	10	81	41,730	1,400.1	99.0	66.42	166	74.9	98
China	1,347,563	1,394,639	3.5%	372	46	2,940	4,326.2	90.9	47.95	238	26.9	1,500
Egypt	80,472	103,742	28.9%	205	43	1,800	162.8	71.4	50.62	712	15.9	2,693
Ethiopia	88,013	140,140	59.2%	197	16	280	26.5	42.7	2.42	3810	0.4	3,500
Finland	5,255	5,251	−0.1%	45	63	48,120	271.3	100.0	128.76	144	83.5	127
France	64,768	68,482	5.7%	261	77	42,250	2,853.1	99.0	93.45	139	69.3	407
Germany	82,283	80,637	−2.0%	611	73	42,440	3,652.8	99.0	128.27	163	65.9	126
Haiti	9,203	11,955	29.9%	849	43	660	7.0	52.9	32.40	1000	—	—
India	1,173,108	1,396,046	19.0%	1,008	29	1,070	1,217.5	61.0	29.36	1030	7.0	1,520
Iran	67,038	76,779	14.5%	105	67	3,540	385.1	77.0	58.65	1246	48.5	12,780
Israel	7,354	8,984	22.2%	922	92	24,700	199.5	97.1	127.38	136	72.8	314
Italy	58,091	56,234	−3.2%	512	68	35,240	2,293.0	98.4	151.57	159	51.7	127
Japan	126,804	117,816	−7.1%	878	86	38,210	4,909.8	99.0	86.73	127	75.5	104
Kenya	40,047	51,261	28.0%	177	19	770	34.5	85.1	42.06	1025	8.6	1,580
Libya	6,461	8,342	29.1%	9	77	11,590	99.9	82.6	76.71	3802	5.1	3,130
Mexico	112,469	130,199	15.8%	150	77	9,980	1,086.0	91.0	69.37	250	24.8	918
Nigeria	152,217	197,223	29.6%	424	47	1,160	212.1	68.0	41.66	2000	7.4	5,400
Norway	4,676	4,917	5.2%	39	80	87,070	450.0	100.0	110.16	129	90.9	93
Pakistan	177,277	217,927	22.9%	581	35	980	168.3	49.9	49.74	3661	10.6	13,716
Romania	22,181	21,260	−4.2%	250	55	7,930	200.1	97.3	114.54	348	33.4	829
Russia	139,390	128,180	−8.0%	21	73	9,620	1,607.8	99.4	141.11	552	32.3	1,360
Saudi Arabia	29,207	35,680	22.2%	35	81	15,500	467.6	78.8	142.85	497	26.8	3,750
Singapore	4,701	5,101	8.5%	17,662	100	34,760	181.9	92.5	138.15	178	72.4	181
Somalia	10,112	15,148	49.8%	41	37	—	—	37.8	7.02	314	1.0	50,900
Spain	40,549	39,578	−2.4%	210	77	31,960	1,604.2	97.9	111.67	133	71.8	440
Switzerland	7,623	7,774	2.0%	495	73	65,330	488.5	99.0	117.97	144	75.5	169
Turkey	77,804	90,498	16.3%	258	63	9,340	794.2	87.4	89.05	236	34.5	1,225
United Kingdom	61,285	63,819	4.1%	655	80	45,390	2,645.6	99.0	126.34	143	76.4	203
United States	310,233	357,452	15.2%	87	79	47,580	14,204.3	99.0	86.79	168	74.1	139
Vietnam	89,571	102,459	14.4%	705	28	890	90.7	90.3	80.37	2553	24.8	10,882

Most people would agree that a motorcycle is not a good way for a family of six to get around. But most people in India don't have the money to afford cars that are common in the United States. That's why Tata Motors in India plans to produce a very basic "People's Car" that will sell for about $2,500.

When you compare countries with different patterns of international investment, the income measure you use can make a difference. For example, Ford has a factory in Thailand. The GDP measure for Thailand would include the profits from that factory because they were earned in that country. However, Ford is not a Thai firm, and most of its profit will ultimately flow out of Thailand. The Thai GNI would not include those profits. You should see that using GDP income measures can give the impression that people in less developed countries have more income than they really do. In addition, in a country with a large population, the income of the whole nation must be spread over more people. So *GNI per capita* (per person) is a useful figure because it gives some idea of the income level of people in the country.

Exhibit 3-5 gives an estimate of GNI per capita and GDP for each country listed. You can see that the more developed industrial nations—including the United States, Japan, and Germany—account for the biggest share of the world's GDP. In these countries, the GNI per capita is also quite high. This explains why so much trade takes place between these countries—and why many firms see them as the more important markets. In general, markets like these offer the best potential for products that are targeted at consumers with higher income levels. As a point of comparison, the GNI per capita in the United States is $47,580.[18]

Many managers, however, see great potential—and less competition—where GNI per capita is low. For example, Coca-Cola has made a push in Africa, where it hopes to establish a relationship with consumers now, and then turn that brand loyalty into profitable growth as consumer incomes rise.

Internet Exercise

Michigan State University's Center for International Business Education and Research (CIBER) created globalEDGE—a website with information and tools for learning about global markets. At the home page for the globalEDGE website (**http://globaledge.msu.edu**) select "Countries>Europe>Italy" Then select "Global Insights" then "Insights by Country" and choose "Italy." Then look at "Statistics" for Italy—and look more closely at those under "Economy" and "People." Now check the same statistics for Brazil. How are these countries similar? How are they different? What marketing opportunities might be available in each country?

Reading, writing, and marketing problems

The ability of a country's people to read and write has a direct influence on the development of its economy—and on marketing strategy planning. The degree of literacy affects the way information is delivered, which in marketing means promotion. The United Nations estimates that 16 percent of adults (age 15 or older) in the world cannot read and write. Two-thirds of them are women. You may be surprised by the low literacy rates for some of the countries in Exhibit 3-5. Illiteracy creates challenges for product labels, instructions, and print advertising.[19]

Technology adoption races across continents

Cell phone and Internet usage has increased rapidly around the world. These technologies may have their greatest impact in developing countries where, for example, they've completely skipped the adoption of landline phones and instead moved directly to a reliance on mobile phones.

Let's look at this phenomenon more closely. With the introduction of cell phones to the developing world came an ability to instantly communicate supply and demand to buyers and sellers. This has dramatically increased efficiency in some markets. For example, after fishermen in India began using cell phones, they called ashore to find out which ports had the most demand for their catch. This helped match supply and demand, lowering waste and stabilizing prices.[20]

Adoption of these technologies varies across the globe (see Exhibit 3-5). Take cell phones, for example. Some people in Europe and Russia have separate phones for work and personal use, so the number of cell phones exceeds the population. While penetration is lower in many of the poorest nations, those countries are experiencing very fast adoption rates. In Bangladesh, for instance, the 2008 ownership rate of 28 phones per 100 people is almost 33 times greater than it was just five years earlier. Similar differences can be observed in Internet access. Marketing managers need to recognize how target markets utilize this technology to determine its role in marketing strategy. For example, setting up a website in another language may be more useful in some countries than others.[21]

Population trends in the U.S. consumer market

While the U.S. population is not growing as quickly as in some other countries, Exhibit 3-6 shows that current population and population growth vary a lot in different regions of the country. The states shaded blue and green are growing at the fastest rate. The greatest growth is in the west and southeastern United States. These different rates of growth are important to marketers. Sudden growth in one area may create a demand for new shopping centers—while retailers in declining areas face tougher competition for a smaller number of customers.[22]

Boomers drive the graying of America

Another important dimension of U.S. society is its age distribution. In 1980, the median age of the U.S. population was 30—but by 2010 the median age rose to 37. The median age is growing because the percentage of the population in older age groups has

Exhibit 3–6 2010 Population (in millions) and Percent Change by State, 2000–2010

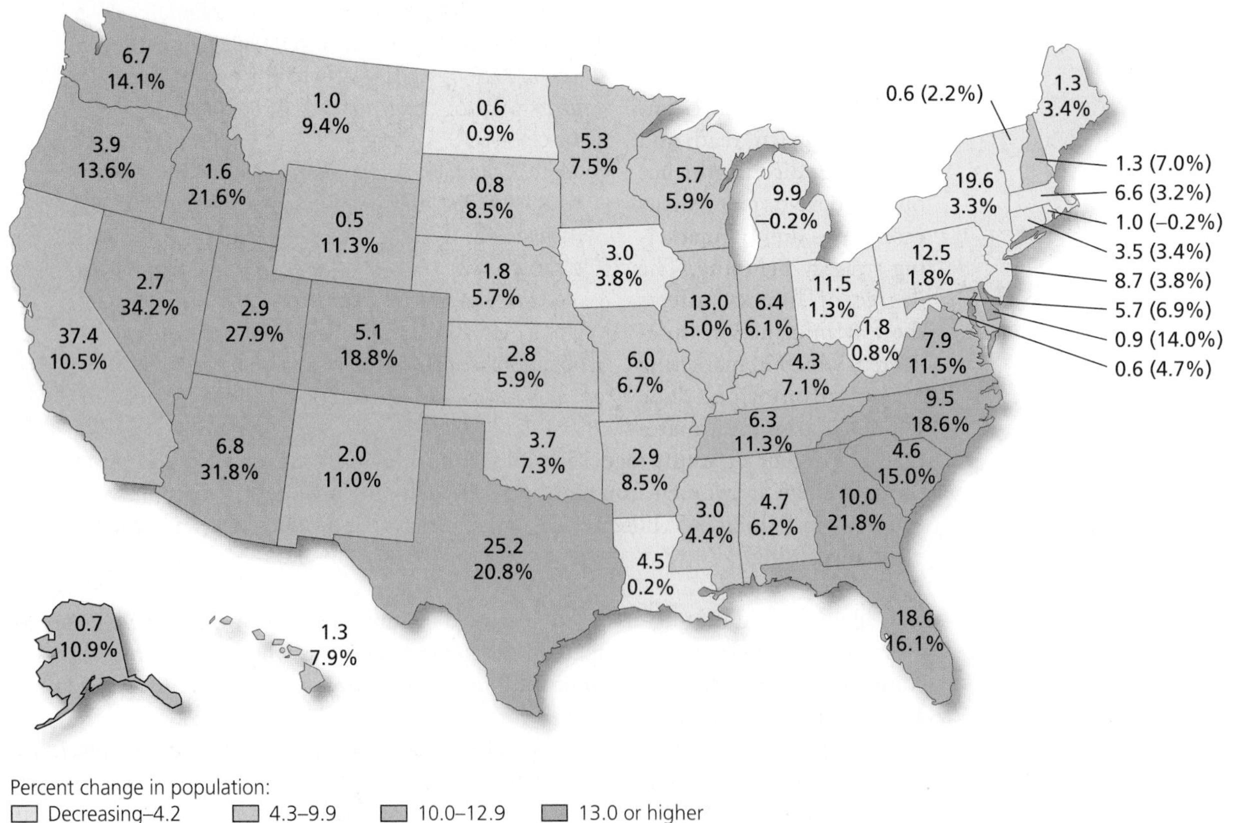

Sales of minivans were in decline as baby boomers perceived them to be "uncool." Toyota responded with an online campaign featuring a couple rapping about life in the suburbs and driving their kids in their "Swagger Wagon." The campaign generated millions of online views and sales of Toyota's Sienna jumped. Watch the videos at toyotaswaggerwagon.com.

increased. Exhibit 3-7 shows population trends by age groups. The graphic shows the number of people in the United States at various age groups in 2005, 2015, and 2025.

In Exhibit 3-7, these changes can be seen most dramatically when looking at the population of those over age 60. The three age bands (60–69, 70–79 and 80+) each show a large increase by 2025. This will significantly increase the number of **senior citizens** (people over 65). This increase is partly due to better healthcare and Americans living longer lives. It is also because of **baby boomers**, those born between 1946 and 1964, reached age 65 in 2011. Baby boomers are a powerful demographic force, as there are large numbers of people in this group. Looking ahead, these shifts create new opportunities in industries such as tourism, healthcare and financial services—all of which are more important to the middle-aged and retired.[23]

Generation X—fewer in number

Generation X, sometimes called Gen X, refers to the generation born immediately following the baby boom—from 1965 to 1977. This group is much smaller in number than the baby boomers it follows—notice the decline in 40–49 year olds from 2005 to 2015 and the decline in 50–59 year olds from 2015 to 2025. Starting in the mid-1980s, when the Gen X group reached college age, colleges were left with excess capacity and lost revenue. To keep their doors open, colleges aggressively recruited these students, which helped make Gen X better educated than previous generations.

Generation Y—techno savvy

Generation Y, sometimes called Millennials, refers to those born from 1978 to 1994. This group emerged from the echo boom—when baby boomers started having kids. In Exhibit 3-7, this is most prominent in the rise of those in their 20s from 2005–2015 and in their 30s from 2015 to 2025. This should make Gen Y an increasingly attractive market for industries like housing, appliances, furniture, and electronics—though the recent recession dampened that opportunity.[24]

Changes come slowly

The demographic data we've been reviewing show that changes in cultural values and social attitudes come slowly. An individual firm should monitor and anticipate such big changes and identify potential constraints and opportunities.

Exhibit 3–7 Population Distribution by Age Group in 2005, 2015, and 2025

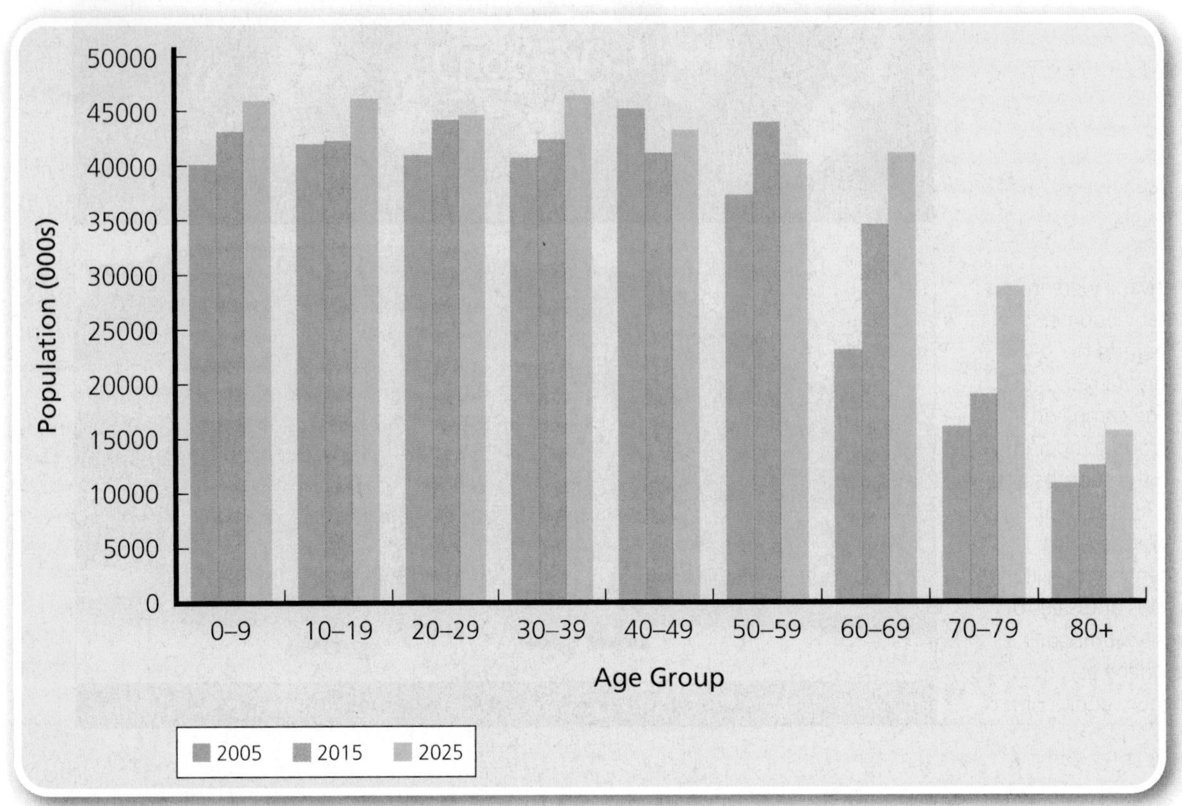

Source: U.S. Census Bureau.

Using Screening Criteria to Narrow Down to Strategies

Developing and applying screening criteria

The Schick Xtreme 3 Eco razor uses 100% recylced materials in both the product and the package. As companies and consumers have become more concerned about the environment, sustainability has become a more important screening criteria used to evaluate opportunities.

After you analyze the firm's resources (for strengths and weaknesses), the environmental trends the firm faces, and the objectives of top management, you merge them all into a set of product-market screening criteria. These criteria should include both quantitative and qualitative components. The quantitative components summarize the firm's objectives: sales, profit, and return on investment (ROI) targets. (Note: ROI analysis is discussed briefly in Appendix B, which follows Chapter 20.) The qualitative components summarize what kinds of businesses the firm wants to be in, what businesses it wants to exclude, what weaknesses it should avoid, and what resources (strengths) and trends it should build on.[25]

Developing screening criteria is difficult but worth the effort. They summarize in one place what the firm wants to accomplish. When a manager can explain the specific criteria that are relevant to selecting (or screening out) an opportunity, others can understand the manager's logic. Thus, marketing decisions are not just made or accepted based on intuition and gut feel.

The criteria should be realistic—that is, they should be achievable. Opportunities that pass the screen should be viable strategies that the firm can implement with the resources it has. For example, Exhibit 3-8 illustrates some product-market screening criteria for a small retail and wholesale distributor.

Sometimes screening criteria can help bring focus to opportunities that fit well with trends in the external market environment. For example, GE operates many types of businesses, from jet aircraft engines and water treatment facilities to medical imaging and lightbulbs. Top management at GE believes that the really crucial needs of society relate to protecting the environment. They believe that efforts in this arena are so critical that they should be supported across all dimensions of the external environment. Thus, they want all GE managers to look for opportunities that fit what GE calls "ecomagination"—applying GE's creativity to solve problems related to ecology. GE is not alone in this kind of thinking. Many organizations now screen opportunities on **sustainability**—the idea that it's important to meet present needs without compromising the ability of future generations to meet their own needs. In many lines of business, that is a tall order. At GE that means lightbulbs that use less energy, medical images with no toxic waste, jets that burn less fuel, and new ways to turn seawater into drinking water.[26]

Exhibit 3–8 An Example of Product-Market Screening Criteria for a Small Retail and Wholesale Distributor ($10 million annual sales)

1. **Quantitative criteria**
   a. Increase sales by $1,500,000 per year for the next five years.
   b. Earn ROI of at least 25 percent before taxes on new ventures.
   c. Break even within one year on new ventures.
   d. Opportunity must be large enough to justify interest (to help meet objectives) but small enough so company can handle with the resources available.
   e. Several opportunities should be pursued to reach the objectives—to spread the risks.
2. **Qualitative criteria**
   a. Nature of business preferred.
      (1) Should take advantage of our Internet order system and website promotion.
      (2) New goods and services for present customers to strengthen relationships and customer equity.
      (3) "Quality" products that do not cannibalize sales of current products.
      (4) Competition should be weak and opportunity should be hard to copy for several years.
      (5) There should be strongly felt (even unsatisfied) needs—to reduce promotion costs and permit "high" prices.
   b. Constraints.
      (1) Nature of businesses to exclude.
         (a) Manufacturing.
         (b) Any requiring large fixed capital investments.
         (c) Any requiring many support people who must be "good" all the time and would require much supervision.
      (2) Geographic.
         (a) United States, Mexico, and Canada only.
      (3) General.
         (a) Make use of current strengths.
         (b) Attractiveness of market should be reinforced by more than one of the following basic trends: technological, demographic, social, economic, political.
         (c) Address environmental problems.

Exhibit 3–9
Expected Sales and Cost Curves of Two Strategies over Five-Year Planning Periods

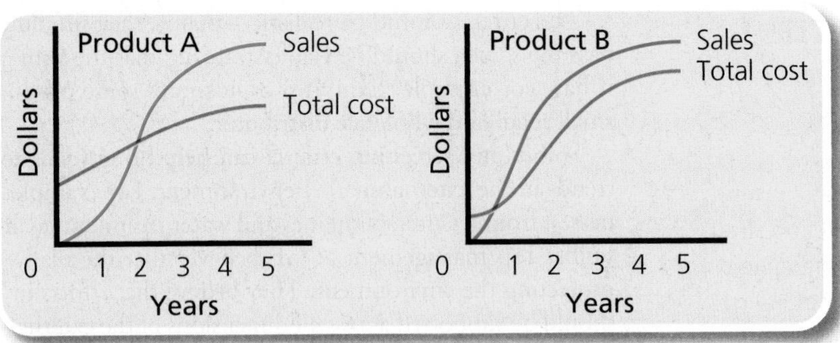

Whole plans should be evaluated

You need to forecast the probable results of implementing a marketing strategy to apply the quantitative part of the screening criteria because only implemented plans generate sales, profits, and return on investment. For a rough screening, you only need to estimate the likely results of implementing each opportunity over a logical planning period. If a product's life is likely to be three years, for example, a good strategy may not produce profitable results for 6 to 12 months. But evaluated over the projected three-year life, the product may look like a winner. When evaluating the potential of possible opportunities (product-market strategies), it is important to evaluate similar things—that is, whole plans.

Total profit approach can help evaluate possible plans

Note that managers can evaluate different marketing plans at the same time. Exhibit 3-9 compares a much improved product and product concept (Product A) with a "me-too" product (Product B) for the same target market. In the short run, the me-too product will make a profit sooner and might look like the better choice—if managers consider only one year's results. The improved product, on the other hand, will take a good deal of pioneering—but over its five-year life will be much more profitable.

Planning Grids Help Evaluate a Portfolio of Opportunities

LO 3.8

When a firm has many scenarios to evaluate, comparisons are best made with graphical approaches—such as the nine-box strategic planning grid developed by General Electric and used by many other companies. Such grids can help evaluate a firm's whole portfolio of strategic plans or businesses.

General Electric looks for green positions

General Electric's (GE) strategic planning grid—see Exhibit 3-10—forces company managers to make three-part judgments (high, medium, and low) about the business strengths and industry attractiveness of all proposed or existing product-market plans. As

Exhibit 3–10
General Electric's Strategic Planning Grid

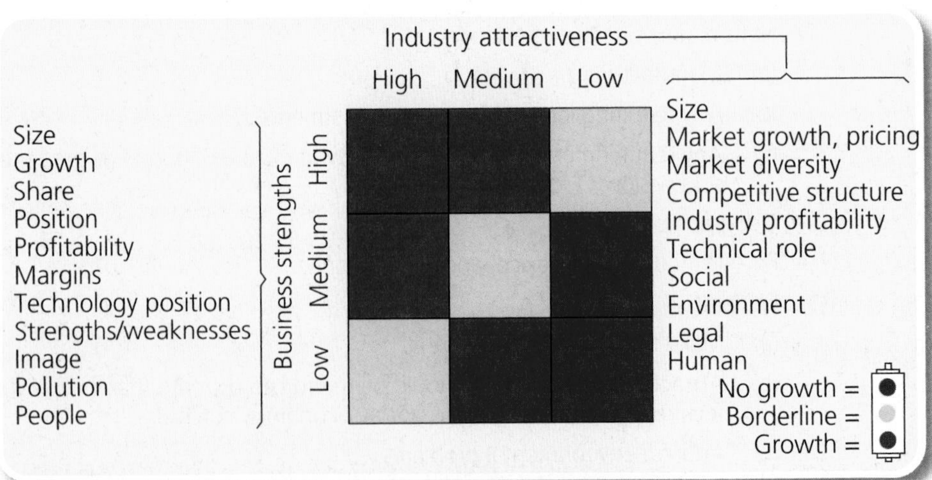

Marketing that meets earthly needs

Twenty years ago, few managers worried about costs to the environment when evaluating market opportunities. And most consumers didn't see increased customer value in marketing strategies that were "planet friendly." Now that is changing. Problems like global warming and depletion of natural resources—even scarcity of drinking water for major urban areas—are receiving much attention. New federal and local laws push for conservation. The economics have changed as well; many firms are proving that it can be lucrative to solve ecological problems. There's also a cultural shift in consumers. Many seek "green" offerings and are even willing to pay a premium to get them.

Companies are finding a host of big and small ways to contribute solutions. For example, Unilever created a more concentrated version of its All liquid detergent and put it in a "small and mighty" bottle. In just two years, this simple change saved 1.3 million gallons of diesel fuel, 10 million pounds of plastic resin, and 80 million square feet of cardboard. Seeing results like that, P&G followed suit and converted all its liquid detergents to double concentration. Staples, the office supply retailer, has eco-modified 3,000 of its store-brand products—everything from sticky notes to cardboard boxes—to include 30 percent recycled paper. This isn't a choice that's left to Staples' customers. The recycled product is the only version available. Competing firms are now copying this approach.

Marketers have usually focused on encouraging people to consume. But now more firms are looking for opportunities that relate to what happens to products when consumers are through with them. Sony, for example, has a new program to recycle all used Sony electronic products—from PlayStation game consoles and Trinitron TVs to Vaio laptops and Walkman tape players. Dell, HP, and others already have recycling programs in place, but Sony plans for its approach to earn profits. This type of thinking is prompting some firms to design new products for easy *dis*assembly. Parts snap together without fasteners or glue, lead-based solder and other biohazards are avoided, and pieces that can't be recycled are biodegradable. Automobile companies are making headway in this area as well.

We are a long way from solving some of our most pressing environmental problems. However, creative marketers know that finding solutions to these problems can be good for their firms as well as their customers, not only in the short term but long into the future.[27]

you can see from Exhibit 3-10, this approach helps a manager organize information about the company's marketing environments (discussed earlier in this chapter) along with information about its strategy and translate it into relevant screening criteria.

The industry attractiveness dimension helps managers answer the question: Does this product-market plan look like a good idea? To answer that question, managers have to judge such factors (screening criteria) as the size of the market and its growth rate, the nature of competition, the plan's potential environmental or social impact, and how laws might affect it. Note that an opportunity may be attractive for *some* company—but not well suited to the strengths (and weaknesses) of a particular firm. That is why the GE grid also considers the business strengths dimension.

The business strengths dimension focuses on the ability of the company to pursue a product-market plan effectively. To make judgments along this dimension, a manager evaluates whether the firm has people with the right talents and skills to implement the plan, whether the plan is consistent with the firm's image and profit objectives, and whether the firm could establish a profitable market share given its technical capability, costs, and size. Here again, these factors suggest screening criteria specific to this firm and market situation.

GE feels opportunities that fall into the green boxes in the upper left-hand corner of the grid are its best growth opportunities. Managers give these opportunities high marks on both industry attractiveness and business strengths. The red boxes in the lower right-hand corner of the grid, on the other hand, suggest a no-growth policy. Existing red businesses may continue to generate earnings, but they no longer deserve much investment. Yellow businesses are borderline cases—they can go either way. GE may continue to support an existing yellow business but will probably reject a proposal for a new one. It simply wouldn't look good enough on the relevant screening criteria.

GE's "stoplight" evaluation method is a subjective, multiple-factor approach. It avoids the traps and possible errors of trying to use oversimplified, single-number criteria—like ROI or market share. Instead, top managers review detailed written summaries of many different screening criteria that help them make summary judgments. This approach helps everyone understand why the company supports some new opportunities and not others.[28]

General Electric considers factors that reflect its objectives. Another firm might modify the evaluation to emphasize other screening criteria—depending on its objectives and the type of product-market plans it is considering.

Evaluating Opportunities in International Markets

Evaluate the risks

The approaches we've discussed so far apply to international markets just as they do to domestic ones. But in international markets it is often harder to fully understand the market environment variables. This may make it more difficult to see the risks involved in particular opportunities. Some countries are politically unstable; their governments and constitutions come and go. An investment safe under one government might become a takeover target under another.

To reduce the risk of missing some basic variable that may help screen out a risky opportunity, marketing managers sometimes need a detailed analysis of the market environment they are considering to enter. Such an analysis can reveal facts about an unfamiliar market that a manager in a distant country might otherwise overlook. Further, a local citizen who knows the market environment may be able to identify an "obvious" problem ignored even in a careful analysis. Thus, it is very useful for the analysis to include inputs from locals—perhaps cooperative distributors.[29]

Risks vary with environmental sensitivity

The farther you go from familiar territory, the greater the risk of making big mistakes. But not all products, or marketing mixes, involve the same risk. Think of the risks as running along a "continuum of environmental sensitivity." See Exhibit 3-11.

Some products are relatively insensitive to the economic and cultural environment into which they're placed. These products may be accepted as is—or they may require just a little

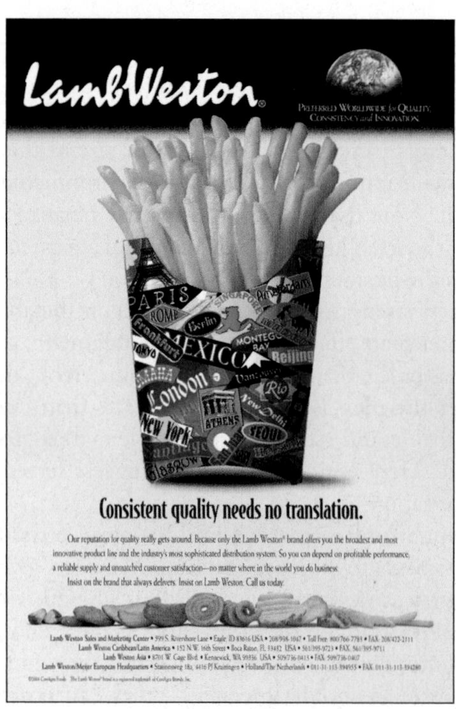

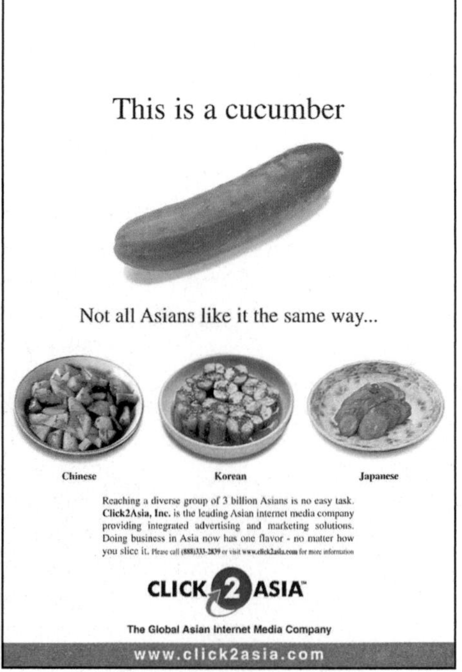

Lamb Weston is successful in international markets because potatoes—in many different forms—are common in the diet of most cultures. Other products are much more sensitive to cultural differences.

Exhibit 3–11
Continuum of Environmental Sensitivity

Insensitive		Sensitive
Industrial products	Basic commodity-type consumer products	Consumer products that are linked to cultural variables

adaptation to make them suitable for local use. Most industrial products are near the insensitive end of this continuum.

At the other end of the continuum, we find highly sensitive products that may be difficult or impossible to adapt to all international situations. Consumer products closely linked to other social or cultural variables are at this end. For example, some cultures view dieting as unhealthy; that explains why products like Diet Pepsi, while popular in the United States, have sometimes done poorly in other countries. Many American quick-serve restaurants succeed in international markets only after adapting their menus to foreign tastes. McDonald's in India sells the Majaraja Mac, which is made from lamb or chicken, and in Japan the Ebi Filit-O, which is a kind of shrimp burger.

This continuum helps explain why many of the early successes in international marketing were basic commodities such as gasoline, soap, transportation vehicles, mining equipment, and agricultural machinery. It also helps explain why some consumer products firms have been successful with basically the same promotion and products in different parts of the globe.

Yet some managers don't understand the reason for these successes. They think they can develop a global marketing mix for just about *any* product. They fail to see that firms producing and/or selling products near the sensitive end of the continuum should carefully analyze how their products will be seen and used in new environments—and plan their strategies accordingly.[30]

What if risks are still hard to judge?

If the risks of an international opportunity are hard to judge, it may be wise to look first for opportunities that involve exporting. This gives managers a chance to build experience, know-how, and confidence over time. Then the firm will be in a better position to judge the prospects and risks of taking further steps.

CONCLUSION

Businesses need innovative strategy planning to survive in our increasingly competitive markets. In this chapter, we discussed the variables that shape the broad environment of marketing strategy planning and how they may affect opportunities. First we looked at how the firm's own resources and objectives may help guide or limit the search for opportunities. Then we went on to look at the need to understand competition and how to do a competitive analysis. Next we shifted our focus to the external market environments. They are important because changes in these environments present new opportunities, as well as problems, that a marketing manager must deal with in marketing strategy planning.

The economic environment—including chances of recession or inflation—also affects the choice of strategies. And the marketer must try to anticipate, understand, and deal with these changes—as well as changes in the technology underlying the economic environment.

The marketing manager must also be aware of legal restrictions and be sensitive to changing political climates. The acceptance of consumerism has already forced many changes.

The cultural and social environment affects how people behave and what marketing strategies will be successful.

Demographic data, including trends in population, income, and technology usage, provide an indicator of social trends. So we looked at these more closely.

Developing good marketing strategies within all these environments isn't easy. You can see that marketing planning is a challenging job that requires integration of information from many disciplines.

Eventually, managers need procedures for screening and evaluating opportunities. We explained an approach for developing qualitative and quantitative screening criteria—from an analysis of the strengths and weaknesses of the company's resources, the environmental trends it faces, and top management's objectives. We also discussed ways for evaluating and managing quite different opportunities—using the GE strategic planning grid and SBUs.

Now we can go on in the rest of the book to discuss how to turn opportunities into profitable marketing plans and programs.

KEY TERMS

LO 3.9

mission statement, *60*
competitive environment, *62*
sustainable competitive advantage, *63*
competitor analysis, *63*
competitive rivals, *64*
competitor matrix, *64*
economic environment, *66*
technology, *67*
nationalism, *69*
North American Free Trade Agreement (NAFTA), *70*
cultural and social environment, *72*
gross domestic product (GDP), *73*
gross national income (GNI), *73*
senior citizens, *77*
baby boomers, *77*
Generation X, *77*
Generation Y, *77*
sustainability, *79*

QUESTIONS AND PROBLEMS

1. Do you think it makes sense for a firm to base its mission statement on the type of product it produces? For example, would it be good for a division that produces electric motors to have as its mission: "We want to make the best (from our customers' point of view) electric motors available anywhere in the world"?
2. Explain how a firm's objectives may affect its search for opportunities.
3. Specifically, how would various company objectives affect the development of a marketing mix for a new type of Internet browser software? If this company were just being formed by a former programmer with limited financial resources, list the objectives the programmer might have. Then discuss how they would affect the development of the programmer's marketing strategy.
4. Explain how a firm's resources may limit its search for opportunities. Cite a specific example for a specific resource.
5. In your own words, explain how a marketing manager might use a competitor analysis to avoid situations that involve head-on competition.
6. The owner of a small hardware store—the only one in a medium-sized town in the mountains—has just learned that a large home improvement chain plans to open a new store nearby. How difficult will it be for the owner to plan for this new competitive threat? Explain your answer.
7. Discuss the probable impact on your hometown if a major breakthrough in air transportation allowed foreign producers to ship into any U.S. market for about the same transportation cost that domestic producers incur.
8. Will the elimination of trade barriers between countries in Europe eliminate the need to consider submarkets of European consumers? Why or why not?
9. What and who is the U.S. government attempting to protect in its effort to preserve and regulate competition?
10. For each of the *major* laws discussed in the text, indicate whether in the long run the law will promote or restrict competition (see Exhibit 3-3). As a consumer without any financial interest in business, what is your reaction to each of these laws?
11. Drawing on data in Exhibit 3-4, do you think that Romania would be an attractive market for a firm that produces home appliances? What about Finland? Discuss your reasons.
12. Discuss the value of gross domestic product and gross national income per capita as measures of market potential in international consumer markets. Refer to specific data in your answer.
13. Discuss how the worldwide trend toward urbanization is affecting opportunities for international marketing.
14. Discuss how slower population growth will affect businesses in your local community.
15. Discuss the impact of changes in the size and use of technology in the 18–29 age group on marketing strategy planning in the United States.
16. Name three specific examples of firms that developed a marketing mix to appeal to senior citizens.
17. Explain the product-market screening criteria that can be used to evaluate opportunities.
18. Explain General Electric's strategic planning grid approach to evaluating opportunities.

CREATING MARKETING PLANS

The Marketing Plan Coach software on the text website includes a sample marketing plan for Hillside Veterinary Clinic. The situation analysis section of the marketing plan includes sections labeled "Competitors" and "External Market Environment." Review those sections and answer the following questions.

a. In the Competitors section, what dimensions were used to analyze competitors? What other dimensions might have been examined?

b. How was competitor information gathered? How else could Hillside have gathered information about its competitors?

c. What aspects of the External Market Environment are included in the marketing plan? What do you think is the most important information in this section?

SUGGESTED CASES

2. Golden Valley Foods
6. Applied Steel
22. Bright Light Innovations
33. Kennedy & Gaffney

Video Case 4. Potbelly Sandwich
Video Case 5. Suburban Regional Shopping Malls

COMPUTER-AIDED PROBLEM

3. COMPETITOR ANALYSIS

Mediquip, Inc., produces medical equipment and uses its own sales force to sell the equipment to hospitals. Recently, several hospitals have asked Mediquip to develop a laser-beam "scalpel" for eye surgery. Mediquip has the needed resources, and 200 hospitals will probably buy the equipment. But Mediquip managers have heard that Laser Technologies—another quality producer—is thinking of competing for the same business. Mediquip has other good opportunities it could pursue—so it wants to see if it would have a competitive advantage over Laser Tech.

Mediquip and Laser Tech are similar in most ways, but there are a few important differences. Laser Technologies already produces key parts that are needed for the new laser product—so its production costs would be lower. It would cost Mediquip more to design the product—and getting parts from outside suppliers would result in higher production costs.

On the other hand, Mediquip has marketing strengths. It already has a good reputation with hospitals—and its sales force calls on only hospitals. Mediquip thinks that each of its current sales reps could spend some time selling the new product and that it could adjust sales territories so only four more sales reps would be needed for good coverage in the market. In contrast, Laser Tech's sales reps call on only industrial customers, so it would have to add 14 reps to cover the hospitals.

Hospitals have budget pressures—so the supplier with the lowest price is likely to get a larger share of the business. But Mediquip knows that both suppliers' prices will be set high enough to cover the added costs of designing, producing, and selling the new product—and leave something for profit.

Mediquip gathers information about its own likely costs and can estimate Laser Tech's costs from industry studies and Laser Tech's annual report. Mediquip has set up a spreadsheet to evaluate the proposed new product.

a. The initial spreadsheet results are based on the assumption that Mediquip and Laser Tech will split the business 50/50. If Mediquip can win at least 50 percent of the market, does Mediquip have a competitive advantage over Laser Tech? Explain.

b. Because of economies of scale, both suppliers' average cost per machine will vary depending on the quantity sold. If Mediquip had only 45 percent of the market and Laser Tech 55 percent, how would their costs (average total cost per machine) compare? What if Mediquip had 55 percent of the market and Laser Tech only 45 percent? What conclusion do you draw from these analyses?

c. It is possible that Laser Tech may not enter the market. If Mediquip has 100 percent of the market, and quantity purchases from its suppliers will reduce the cost of producing one unit to $6,500, what price would cover all its costs and contribute $1,125 to profit for every machine sold? What does this suggest about the desirability of finding your own unsatisfied target markets? Explain.

4 CHAPTER FOUR

Focusing Marketing Strategy with Segmentation and Positioning

In the early 1930s in Billilund, Denmark, carpenter Ole Kirk Christiansen started a company that built wooden toys. He named his company LEGO, combining the first two letters from each word in the Danish phrase *leg godt* which means "play well." Christiansen believed in quality, claiming that for LEGO, "only the best is good enough"—a value that stays with LEGO to this day.

During the 1950s, LEGO articulated its plastic bricks as part of a "system of play," based on learning through imagination, creativity, and problem solving. By 1958 LEGO had refined the design of the classic LEGO brick; those 1958 bricks still click and lock with any of the 40 billion bricks LEGO has made since.

Buoyed by the tail end of the baby boom generation, LEGO grew rapidly in the 1960s and 1970s. That growth slowed when the 1980s brought a recession and the "construction toy market" lost favor to electronic toys and software.

LEGO reacted by broadening its market definition to the "children's market" and a range of new opportunities. So in the 1990s, LEGO opened three new Legoland theme parks, developed video games and electronic toys, produced books and TV shows, and licensed watches and clothing. While the new product lines increased sales, costs rose even more quickly. In 2004, LEGO lost more than $300 million. LEGO needed a strategy to turn things around—and fast!

To address the immediate financial weakness, LEGO sold off Legoland theme parks, outsourced production, and consolidated its product lines. In assessing its strengths, LEGO knew its brand name was widely trusted, and its enduring system of play, based on the widely recognized brick, provided a platform for innovation. To focus its new strategy, LEGO redefined its market around the iconic brick with a vision to equip children for the future through creative, playful learning. LEGO thought it could profitably grow in the "active play market."

LEGO's next step—get to know its customers better. So LEGO set loose teams of researchers that embedded with families to understand how 7–9 year old boys in Germany and the U.S. lived and played. One finding shattered a myth that had guided LEGO's thinking much of the previous decade. LEGO had taken the wrong lessons from the growth of video games when it assumed kids needed immediate gratification. In response, LEGO had dumbed down many of its toys. But the new research found that kids wanted opportunities to demonstrate mastery—evidenced by the scoring, ranking, sharing, and levels common in many computer games. LEGO also found that while kids lived very scheduled lives, they appreciated time to themselves. These findings guided new strategic thinking at LEGO.

For these 7–9 year old boys, LEGO focused on its kits—from LEGO City's fire station and police station to kits with Harry Potter and Star Wars movie themes. As boys get older, they appreciate LEGO products that bridge the virtual world of computers and the physical world. So they developed LEGO Design byME, where anyone can go online and use LEGO's proprietary 3-D software to create an original design. The software then generates a kit with all the pieces, which can be shipped directly to a customer's home. LEGO's Mindstorms programmable robot-building kits also proved popular with this target market of young boys.

LEGO also segments its markets based on country. For example, while many German and American parents seek out toys that combine the values of learning and play, Japanese parents draw a sharper line between the two and don't seek out educational toys as much. These differences affect how products are promoted in each market.

Those Mindstorms robots and Star Wars kits struck a chord with another market segment—adults. Thanks to the Internet, the dispersed adult fans of LEGO (they call themselves AFOLs) found they weren't alone. Here they formed online communities, like the LEGO User Group Network (www.LUGnet.com), where AFOLs meet to share their passion for bricks, along with photos and design specs of their creations.

At first, LEGO made no special efforts to develop a marketing strategy to the AFOL segment. Then it found that many AFOLs spend thousands of dollars a year on LEGO. So LEGO introduced the 3,104-piece, $299 Imperial Star Destroyer kit, and it flew off shelves. The LEGO Ambassadors program enlists 40 AFOLs from around the globe to help LEGO manage relationships with its most ardent AFOL users. At conventions and online, the Ambassadors, who are paid in LEGO pieces, act as important two-way communication channel between LEGO and AFOLs. LEGO even flew four AFOLs to Denmark, where they worked closely with LEGO designers and engineers to create the highly successful second-generation Mindstorms NXT robot kits. AFOLs now account for 5–10 percent of all LEGO sales and influence even more.

Together, these new strategies helped LEGO earn more than $700 million in 2011. But LEGO is not resting on its laurels. LEGO has had limited success with girls. After age five, girls seem to lose interest in LEGO products. While previous efforts to appeal to girls have failed, LEGO still sees a big opportunity.

Once again LEGO sent out teams of researchers to conduct observational research—this time with girls. The findings drove many of the decisions made with the new LEGO Friends line. For example, while boys like to complete a kit before they start playing, girls like to play along the way. So the Friends kits come with bagged parts, allowing the girls to start storytelling and rearranging sooner. Boys play with people (LEGO calls them mini-figs) in the third person, while girls project themselves onto each figure. Girls found the traditional stubby mini-fig ugly—so the mini-figs in Friends look more like real people. Plus, the five main mini-fig characters in LEGO Friends come with names and backstories described in accompanying books.

Can LEGO finally crack the girls market? Only time will tell, but knowing its customers and defining and segmenting the market provides a good start to building a solid marketing strategy. LEGO has seen it work before.[1]

Learning Objectives

As the LEGO case illustrates, a manager who develops an understanding of the needs and characteristics of specific groups of target customers within the broader market may see new, breakthrough opportunities. But it's not always obvious how to identify the real needs of a target market—or the marketing mix that those customers will see as different from, and better than, what is available from a competitor. This chapter covers concepts and approaches that will help you to succeed in the search for those opportunities.

When you finish this chapter, you should be able to:

1 know about defining generic markets and product-markets.

2 know what market segmentation is and how to segment product-markets into submarkets.

3 know three approaches to market-oriented strategy planning.

4 know dimensions that may be useful for segmenting markets.

5 know a seven-step approach to market segmentation that you can do yourself.

6 recognize how some computer-aided methods are used in segmenting.

7 know what positioning is and why it is useful.

8 understand the important new terms (shown in red).

Search For Opportunities Can Begin by Understanding Markets

LO 4.1

Strategy planning is a narrowing-down process

In Chapter 2 we provided a framework for a logical marketing strategy planning process. It involves careful evaluation of the market opportunities available before narrowing down to focus on the most attractive target market and marketing mix. In Chapter 3, we focused on approaches for analyzing how competitors and the external market environment shape the evaluation of opportunities. In this chapter we discuss concepts that can guide the selection of specific target customers. See Exhibit 4-1 for an overview.

In a broad sense, this chapter is about understanding and analyzing customers in a market. In Chapters 5 and 6 we will look more closely at specific influences on the behavior of both final consumers and organizational customers. However, this chapter sets the stage for that by explaining how marketing managers combine different types of information about customers to guide targeting decisions.

Since this chapter is about bringing focus to the search for market opportunities, a good place to start is by discussing what we really mean when we use the term *market.*

Exhibit 4–1
Focusing Marketing Strategy with Segmentation and Positioning

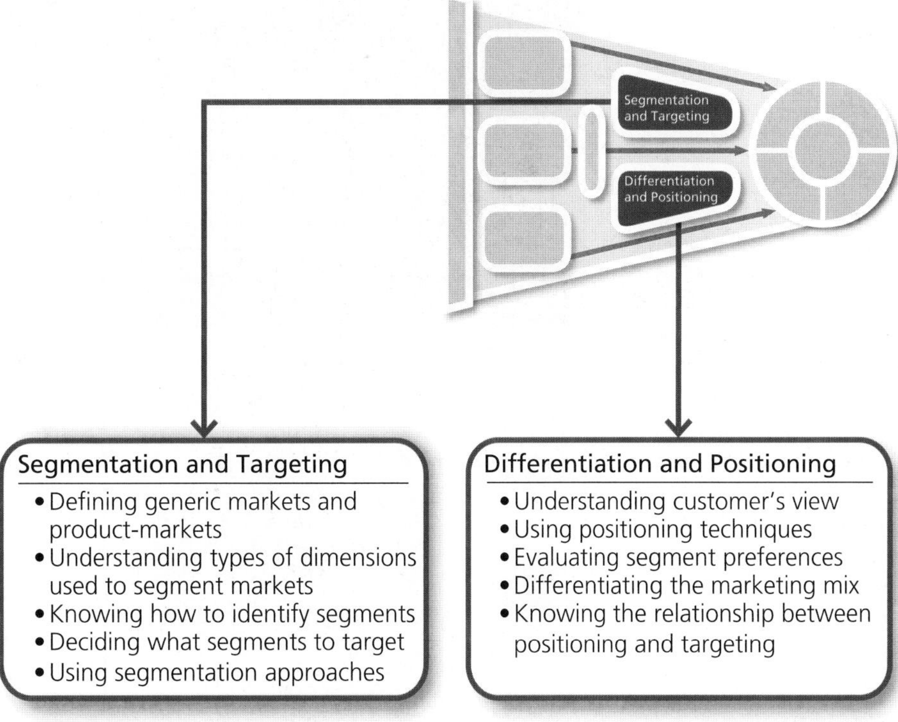

Segmentation and Targeting
Differentiation and Positioning
Segmentation and Targeting
• Defining generic markets and product-markets
• Understanding types of dimensions used to segment markets
• Knowing how to identify segments
• Deciding what segments to target
• Using segmentation approaches
Differentiation and Positioning
• Understanding customer's view
• Using positioning techniques
• Evaluating segment preferences
• Differentiating the marketing mix
• Knowing the relationship between positioning and targeting

What is a company's market?

Identifying a company's market is an important but sticky issue. In general, a **market** is a group of potential customers with similar needs who are willing to exchange something of value with sellers offering various goods or services—that is, ways of satisfying those needs. However, within a general market, marketing-oriented managers develop marketing mixes for *specific* target markets. Getting the firm to focus on specific target markets is vital.

Don't just focus on the product

Some production-oriented managers don't understand this narrowing-down process. They get into trouble because they ignore the tough part of defining markets. To make the narrowing-down process easier, they just describe their markets in terms of *products* they sell. For example, producers and retailers of greeting cards might define their market as the "greeting card" market. But this production-oriented approach ignores customers—and customers make a market! This also leads to missed opportunities. Hallmark isn't missing these opportunities. Instead, Hallmark aims at the "personal-expression" market. Hallmark stores and dealers offer all kinds of products that allow people to express their feelings by capturing and saving memories. As opportunities related to these needs change, Hallmark changes, too. For example, at a Hallmark store you can find Father's Day cards or a picture frame. Hallmark also offers a photo album that allows customers to attach voice recordings to each picture. At Hallmark.com, subscribers will find they can access unlimited e-cards, tips on how to write thank-you notes, and ideas about how to take better baby pictures. There is even a Hallmark iPhone app to help you keep up on the latest offers and newest products at the Hallmark Gold Crown store nearest you.[2]

From generic markets to product-markets

To understand the narrowing-down process, it's useful to think of two basic types of markets. A **generic market** is a market with *broadly* similar needs—and sellers offering various, *often diverse,* ways of satisfying those needs. In contrast, a **product-market** is a market with *very* similar needs and sellers offering various *close substitute* ways of satisfying those needs.[3]

A generic market description looks at markets broadly and from a customer's viewpoint. Entertainment-seekers, for example, have several very different ways to satisfy their needs. An entertainment-seeker might buy a Blu-ray disc player and a high-definition TV (HDTV), sign up for a cruise on the Carnival Line, or reserve season tickets for the symphony. Any one of these *very different* products may satisfy this entertainment need. Sellers

Camera makers try to stand out in a competitive product-market where each addresses customers' needs to capture and record memories. Leica's D-Lux 5 recognizes faces; GoPro's HD Hero2 cameras attach to helmets, skis, and bikes to take action shots during action sports; Lytro allows customers to focus different parts of the picture after the photo is taken; and Fujifilm offers a waterproof model.

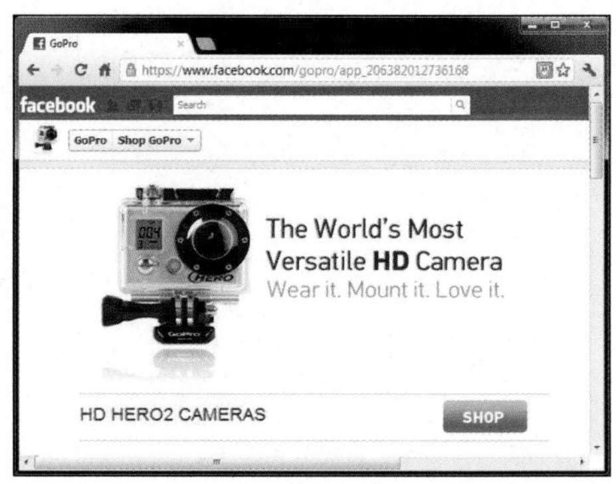

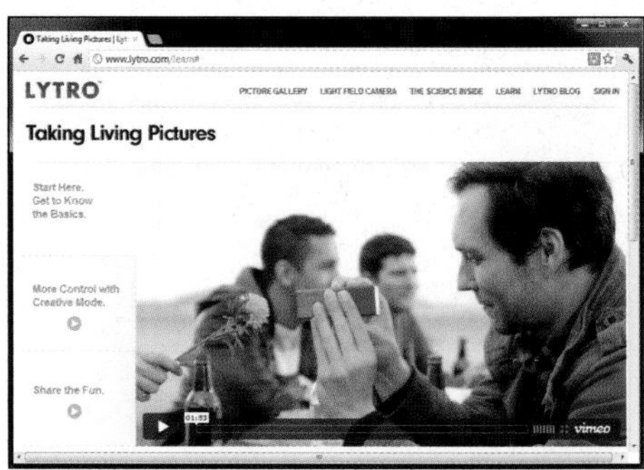

in this generic entertainment-seeker market have to focus on the need(s) the customers want satisfied—not on how one seller's product (HDTV system, vacation, or live music) is better than that of another producer.

It is sometimes hard to understand and define generic markets because *quite different product types may compete with each other.* For example, a person on a business trip to Italy might want a convenient way to record memories of the trip. Minolta's digital camera, a camera in a Samsung cell phone, Sony's video camcorder, and even postcards from local shops may all compete to serve our traveler's needs. If customers see all these products as substitutes—as competitors in the same generic market—then marketers must deal with this complication.

Suppose, however, that our traveler decides to satisfy this need with a digital camera. Then—in this product-market—Canon, Kodak, Fujifilm, Nikon, and many other brands may compete with each other for the customer's dollars. In this *product*-market concerned with digital cameras *and* needs to conveniently record memories, consumers compare similar products to satisfy their imaging needs.

Broaden market definitions to find opportunities

Broader market definitions—including both generic market definitions and product-market definitions—can help firms find opportunities. But deciding *how* broad to go isn't easy. Too narrow a definition limits a firm's opportunities—but too broad a definition makes the company's efforts and resources seem insignificant. Consider, for example, the mighty Coca-Cola Company. It has great success and a huge market share in the U.S. cola-drinkers' market. On the other hand, its share of all beverage drinking worldwide is very small.

Here we try to match opportunities to a firm's resources and objectives. So the *relevant market for finding opportunities* should be bigger than the firm's present product-market—but not so big that the firm couldn't expand and be an important competitor. A small manufacturer of screwdrivers in Mexico, for example, shouldn't define its market as broadly as "the worldwide tool users market" or as narrowly as "our present screwdriver customers." But it may have the capabilities to consider "the handyman's hand-tool market in North America." Carefully naming your product-market can help you see possible opportunities.

Nestlé targets customers in many different geographic markets around the world, but often the product-markets in one country are different than in another. For example, Nestlé created banana-flavored milk ice on a stick to fit the local tastes and preferences of Chinese consumers. The same product would probably not have a following in other places.

Naming Product-Markets and Generic Markets

Some managers think about markets just in terms of the product they already produce and sell. But this approach can lead to missed opportunities. For example, think about how photographic film has been largely replaced with digital pictures, digital video recorders (DVRs) are replacing VCRs, and MP3 players have replaced portable CD players.

As this suggests, when evaluating opportunities, product-related terms do not—by themselves—adequately describe a market. A complete product-market definition includes a four-part description.

What:	**1. Product type (type of good and type of service)**
To meet what:	**2. Customer (user) needs**
For whom:	**3. Customer types**
Where:	**4. Geographic area**

We refer to these four-part descriptions as product-market "names" because most managers label their markets when they think, write, or talk about them. Such a four-part definition can be clumsy, however, so we often use a nickname. And the nickname should refer to people—not products—because, as we emphasize, people make markets!

Product type should meet customer needs

Product type describes the goods and/or services that customers want. Sometimes the product type is strictly a physical good or strictly a service. But marketing managers who ignore the possibility that *both* are important can miss opportunities.

Customer (user) needs refer to the needs the product type satisfies for the customer. At a very basic level, product types usually provide functional benefits such as nourishing, protecting, warming, cooling, transporting, cleaning, holding, and saving time. Although we need to identify such "basic" needs first, in advanced economies, we usually go on to emotional needs—such as needs for fun, excitement, pleasing appearance, or status. Correctly defining the need(s) relevant to a market is crucial and requires a good understanding of customers. We discuss these topics more fully in Chapters 5 and 6.

Customer type refers to the final consumer or user of a product type. Here we want to choose a name that describes all present (possible) types of customers. To define customer type, marketers should identify the final consumer or user of the product type, rather than the buyer—if they are different. For instance, producers should avoid treating intermediaries as a customer type—unless intermediaries actually use the product in their own business.

The *geographic area* is where a firm competes, or plans to compete, for customers. Naming the geographic area may seem trivial, but understanding the geographic boundaries

Exhibit 4–2 Relationship between Generic and Product-Market Definitions

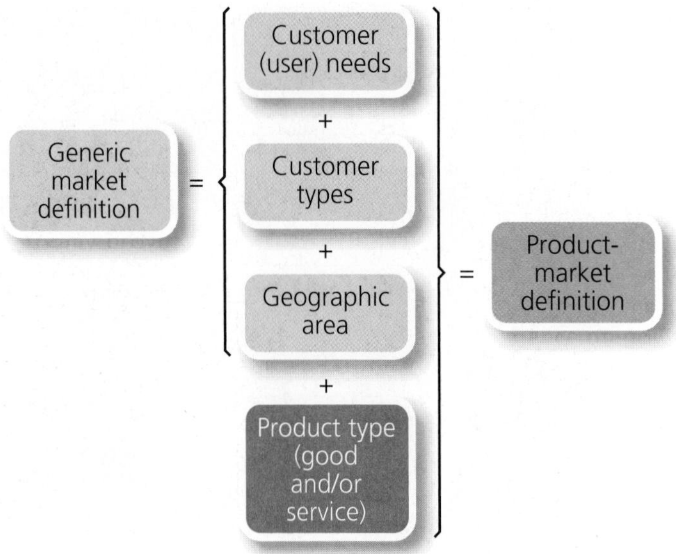

of a market can suggest new opportunities. A firm aiming only at the domestic market, for example, may want to expand to other countries.

Product-market boundaries provide focus

This idea of making a decision about the boundaries of a market applies not just to geographic areas served but also to decisions about customer needs and product and customer types. Thus, naming the market is not simply an exercise in assigning labels. Rather, the manager's market definition sets the limits of the market(s) in which the firm will compete. For example, Canon targets a wide range of photographic needs and might approach a product-market named the "digital photographers market," defined as digital cameras (product type), that are easy to use and take high quality digital photographs (customer needs), for amateur photographers (customer types), in developing countries (geographic area). Canon's product line should appeal to this broad product-market. On the other hand, camera maker GoPro focuses on a more specific set of customer needs and has tighter boundaries on its market definition. GoPro might define the "adventure video market" as digital video cameras (product type), that are rugged, waterproof, and don't need to be operated by hand (customer needs), for adventure sports enthusiasts (customer types), who live anywhere in the world (geographic area). GoPro's video cameras attach to surfboards, handlebars, or helmets so that adventure sport enthusiasts can capture all the action. These product-market definitions give each company a focus that sharpens marketing strategy.

No product type in generic market names

A generic market description *doesn't include any product-type terms.* It consists of only three parts of the product-market definition—without the product type. This emphasizes that any product type that satisfies the customer's needs can compete in a generic market. Exhibit 4-2 shows the relationship between generic market and product-market definitions.

Later we'll study the many possible dimensions for segmenting markets. But for now you should see that defining markets only in terms of current products is not the best way to find new opportunities. Instead, the most effective way to find opportunities is to use market segmentation.

Market Segmentation Defines Possible Target Markets

LO 4.2

Market segmentation is a two-step process

Market segmentation is a two-step process of (1) *naming* broad product-markets and (2) *segmenting* these broad product-markets in order to select target markets and develop suitable marketing mixes.

This two-step process isn't well understood. First-time market segmentation efforts often fail because beginners start with the whole mass market and try to find one or two

Exhibit 4–3
Narrowing Down to Target Markets

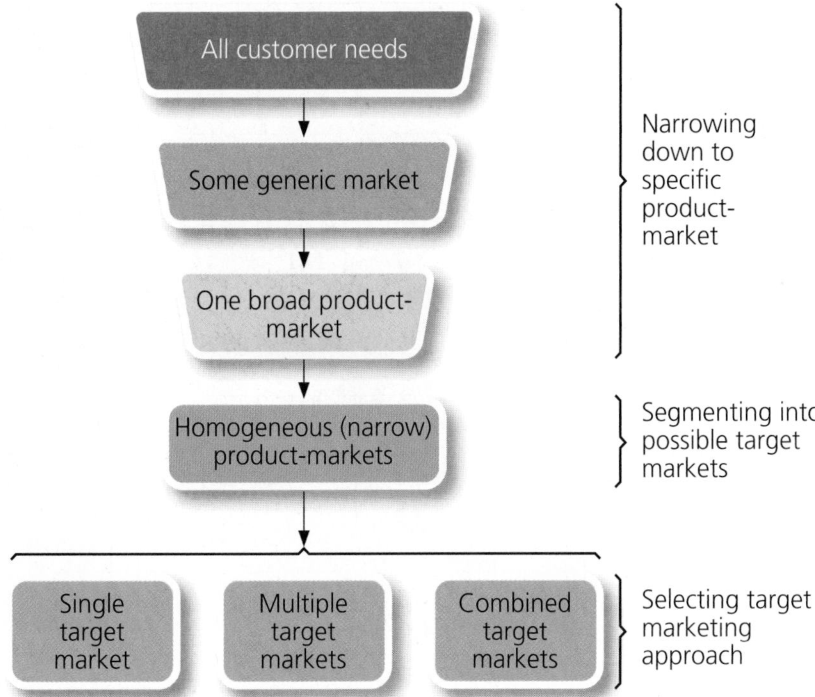

demographic characteristics to divide up (segment) this market. Customer behavior is usually too complex to be explained in terms of just one or two demographic characteristics. For example, a recent study of older adults without kids at home found that while half never visit social networking sites like Facebook, almost one in five visited daily.[4]

Naming broad product-markets is disaggregating

The first step in effective market segmentation involves naming a broad product-market of interest to the firm. Marketers must break apart—disaggregate—all possible needs into some generic markets and broad product-markets in which the firm may be able to operate profitably. See Exhibit 4-3. No one firm can satisfy everyone's needs. So the naming—disaggregating—step involves brainstorming about very different solutions to various generic needs and selecting some broad areas—broad product-markets—where the firm has some resources and experience. This means that a car manufacturer would probably ignore all the possible opportunities in food and clothing markets and focus on the generic market, "transporting people in the world," and probably on the broad product-market, "cars, trucks, and utility vehicles for transporting people in the world."

Market grid is a visual aid to market segmentation

Assuming that any broad product-market (or generic market) may consist of submarkets, picture a market as a rectangle with boxes that represent the smaller, more homogeneous product-markets.

Exhibit 4-4, for example, represents the broad product-market of bicycle riders. The boxes show different submarkets. One submarket might focus on people who want basic

Exhibit 4–4
A Market Grid Diagram with Submarkets

Broad product-market (or generic market) name goes here
(The bicycle-riders product-market)

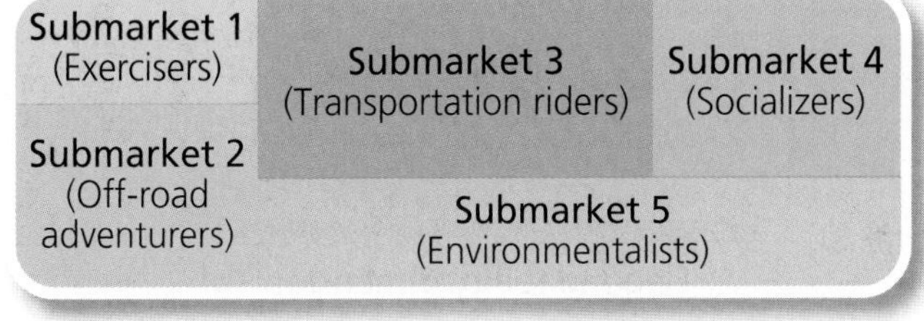

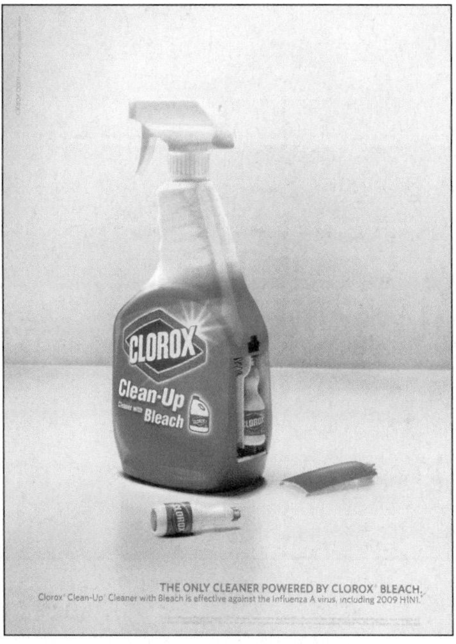

Consumers associate the Clorox brand with strong cleaning power and bleach. Clorox uses the Green Works brand to target customers who want natural cleaning products that don't have harsh chemical fumes or residue.

transportation, another on people who want exercise, and so on. Alternatively, in the generic "transporting market" discussed earlier, we might see different product-markets of customers for bicycles, motorcycles, cars, airplanes, ships, buses, and "others."

Segmenting is an aggregating process

Marketing-oriented managers think of **segmenting** as an aggregating process—clustering people with similar needs into a "market segment." A **market segment** is a (relatively) homogeneous group of customers who will respond to a marketing mix in a similar way.

This part of the market segmentation process takes a different approach from the naming part. Here we look for similarities rather than basic differences in needs. Segmenters start with the idea that each person is one of a kind but that it may be possible to aggregate some similar people into a product-market.

Segmenters see each of these one-of-a-kind people as having a unique set of dimensions. Consider a product-market in which customers' needs differ on two important segmenting dimensions: need for status and need for dependability. In Exhibit 4-5A, each dot shows a person's position on the two dimensions. While each person's position is unique, many of these people are similar in terms of how much status and dependability they want. So a segmenter may aggregate them into three (an arbitrary number) relatively

Exhibit 4–5
Every Individual Has His or Her Own Unique Position in a Market—Those with Similar Positions Can Be Aggregated into Potential Target Markets

A. Product-market showing three segments

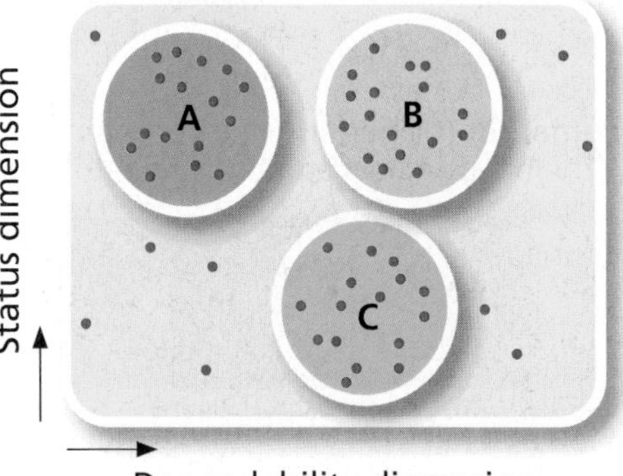

B. Product-market showing six segments

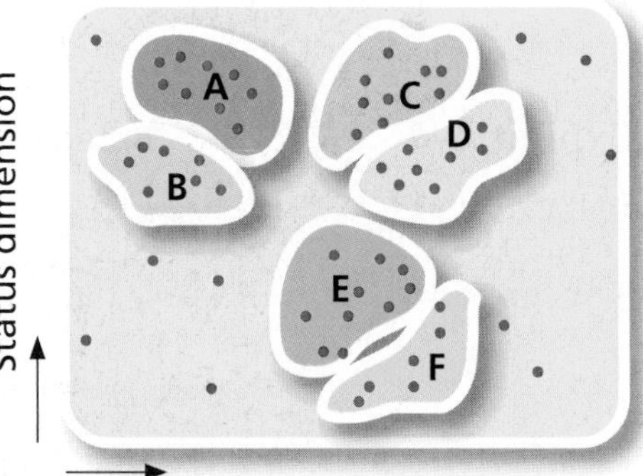

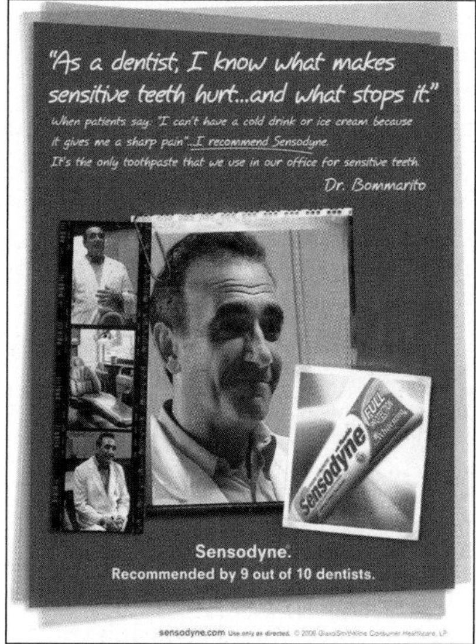

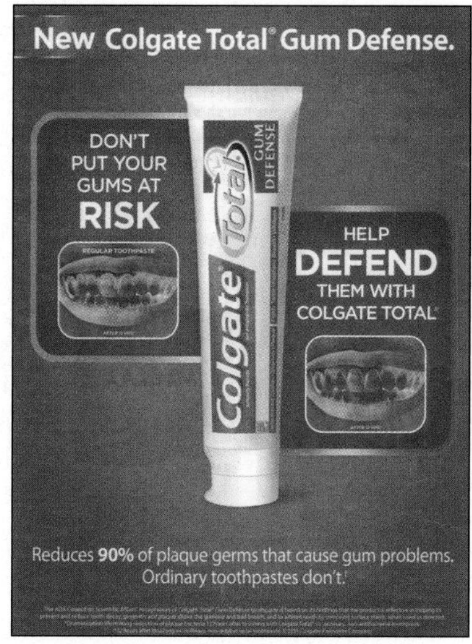

Firms that compete in the oral health care market have developed a variety of products that appeal to the needs of different customer segments. Sensodyne targets consumers with sensitive teeth, Colgate Total Gum Defense aims at those concerned about their gums' health, and Orajel Toddler Training toothpaste addresses concerns of parents with young children.

homogeneous submarkets—A, B, and C. Group A might be called "status-oriented" and Group C "dependability-oriented." Members of Group B want both and might be called the "demanders."

How far should the aggregating go?

The segmenter wants to aggregate individual customers into some workable number of relatively homogeneous target markets and then treat each target market differently.

Look again at Exhibit 4-5A. Remember we talked about three segments. But this was an arbitrary number. As Exhibit 4-5B shows, there may really be six segments. What do you think—does this broad product-market consist of three segments or six?

Another difficulty with segmenting is that some potential customers just don't fit neatly into market segments. For example, not everyone in Exhibit 4-5B was put into one of the groups. Forcing them into one of the groups would have made these segments more heterogeneous and harder to please. Further, forming additional segments for them probably wouldn't be profitable. They are too few and not very similar in terms of the two dimensions. These people are simply too unique to be catered to and may have to be ignored—unless they are willing to pay a high price for special treatment.

The number of segments that should be formed depends more on judgment than on some scientific rule. But the following guidelines can help.

Criteria for segmenting a broad product-market

Ideally, "good" market segments meet the following criteria:

1. *Homogeneous (similar) within*—the customers in a market segment should be as similar as possible with respect to their likely responses to marketing mix variables *and* their segmenting dimensions.
2. *Heterogeneous (different) between*—the customers in different segments should be as different as possible with respect to their likely responses to marketing mix variables *and* their segmenting dimensions.
3. *Substantial*—the segment should be big enough to be profitable.
4. *Operational*—the segmenting dimensions should be useful for identifying customers and deciding on marketing mix variables.

It is especially important that segments be *operational*. This leads marketers to include demographic dimensions such as age, sex, income, location, and family size. In fact, it is difficult to make some Place and Promotion decisions without such information. For example, magazines, websites, and television shows have data on the demographic characteristics of their readers, visitors, and viewers. This makes it easier for a marketing manager to match these qualities with its target market.

Avoid segmenting dimensions that have no practical operational use. For example, you may find a personality trait such as moodiness among the traits of heavy buyers of a product, but how could you use this fact? Salespeople can't give a personality test to each buyer. Similarly, advertising couldn't make much use of this information. So although moodiness might be related in some way to previous purchases, it would not be a useful dimension for segmenting.

Target marketers aim at specific targets

LO 4.3

Once you accept the idea that broad product-markets may have submarkets, you can see that target marketers usually have a choice among many possible target markets.

There are three basic ways to develop market-oriented strategies in a broad product-market.

1. The **single target market approach**—segmenting the market and picking one of the homogeneous segments as the firm's target market.
2. The **multiple target market approach**—segmenting the market and choosing two or more segments, and then treating each as a separate target market needing a different marketing mix.
3. The **combined target market approach**—combining two or more submarkets into one larger target market as a basis for one strategy.

Note that all three approaches involve target marketing. They all aim at specific, clearly defined target markets. See Exhibit 4-6. For convenience, we call people who follow the first two approaches the "segmenters" and people who use the third approach the "combiners."

Combiners try to satisfy "pretty well"

Combiners try to increase the size of their target markets by combining two or more segments. Combiners look at various submarkets for similarities rather than differences. Then they try to extend or modify their basic offering to appeal to these "combined"

Exhibit 4–6
Segmenters and Combiners Aim at Specific Target Markets

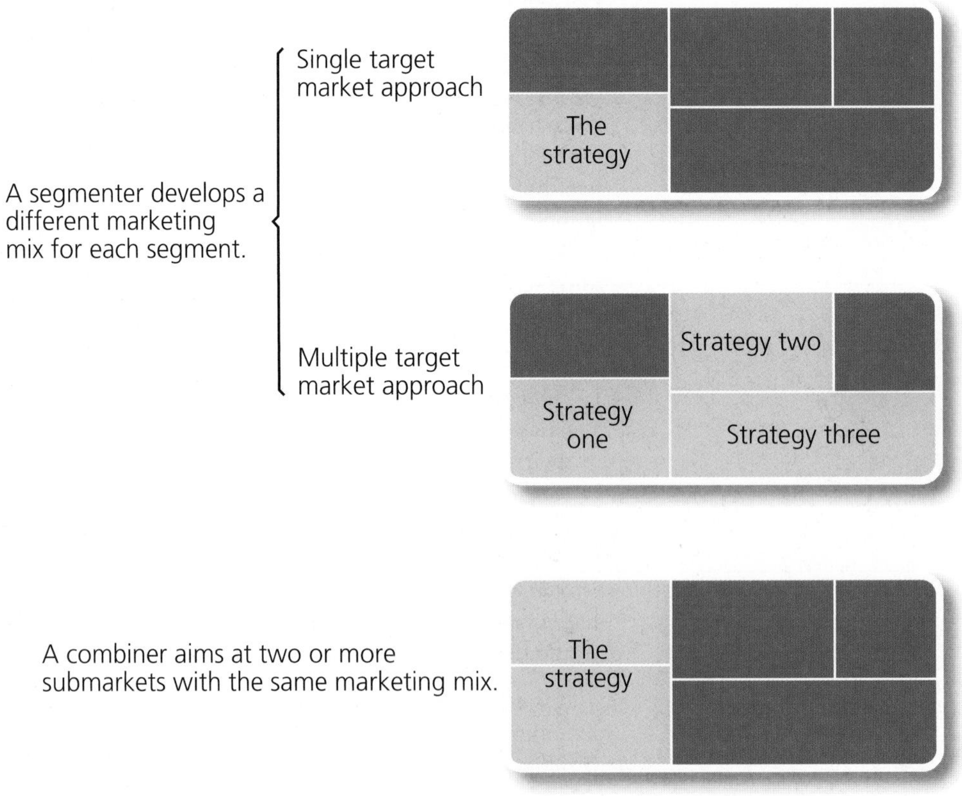

A segmenter develops a different marketing mix for each segment.

Single target market approach

The strategy

Multiple target market approach

Strategy one

Strategy two

Strategy three

A combiner aims at two or more submarkets with the same marketing mix.

The strategy

customers with just one marketing mix. For example, a combiner who faces the broad bicycle-riders product-market shown in Exhibit 4-4 might try to develop a marketing mix that would do a pretty good job of appealing to both the *Exercisers* and the *Off-road adventurers*. The combined market would be bigger than either segment by itself. However, there are some distinct differences between the two submarkets. Thus, our combiner will have to make compromises in developing the marketing mix. The combiner doesn't try to fine-tune each element of the marketing mix to appeal to each of the smaller submarkets. Rather, the marketing mix is selected to work "fairly well" with each segment.

A combined target market approach may help achieve some economies of scale. It may also require less investment than developing different marketing mixes for different segments—making it especially attractive for firms with limited resources.

Segmenters try to satisfy "very well"

Segmenters aim at one or more homogeneous segments and try to develop a different marketing mix for each segment. Segmenters usually fine-tune their marketing mixes for each target market—perhaps making basic changes in the product itself— because they want to satisfy each segment very well.

Instead of assuming that the whole market consists of a fairly similar set of customers (like the mass marketer does) or merging various submarkets together (like the combiner), segmenters believe that aiming at one, or some, of these smaller markets makes it possible to provide superior value and satisfy them better. This then provides greater profit potential for the firm.

Segmenting may produce bigger sales

Note that segmenters are not settling for a smaller sales potential or lower profits. Instead, they hope to increase sales by getting a much larger share of the business in the market(s) they target. A segmenter who really satisfies the target market can often build such a close relationship with customers that he or she faces no real competition. A segmenter who offers a marketing mix precisely matched to the needs of the target market can often charge a higher price, thus producing higher profits. Customers are willing to pay a higher price because the whole marketing mix provides better customer value.

Consider the success of the Aeron desk chair developed by Herman Miller (HM), an 80-year-old company that makes office furniture. Most firms that sell office furniture offered similar lines of executive desk chairs that were padded for comfort and conveyed the look of success. Marketing managers at HM realized that some customers felt that these traditional chairs were boring. Further, in an e-commerce world, even top executives sit at computers and want a chair that provides both good support and good looks. So to satisfy this upscale segment, HM designed a new type of chair from scratch. There's no fabric or padding, but everything about it adjusts to your body. It's so comfortable that HM positions it as "the chair you can wear." With a price tag of $750 or more, the Aeron chair became a status symbol for high-tech managers and has been as profitable as it is popular.[5]

Should you segment or combine?

Which approach should a firm use? This depends on the firm's resources, the nature of competition, and—most important—the similarity of customer needs, attitudes, and buying behavior.

It's usually safer to be a segmenter—that is, to try to satisfy some customers *very* well instead of many just *fairly* well. That's why many firms use the single or multiple target market approach instead of the combined target market approach. For example, Procter & Gamble produces both Tide and Cheer laundry detergents, which have different marketing mixes. Even within the Tide brand, there are different formulas. Tide Free & Gentle is free from dye and perfumes and targets families with newborn babies or individuals with allergies. Tide plus Febreze Sport is designed for washing sports apparel, which might have grass or blood stains. The product, promotion, and place differ between these and other Tide specialty detergents. Though extremely effective, this approach may not be possible for a smaller firm with more limited resources. A smaller firm may have to use the single target market approach—focusing all its efforts at the one submarket niche where it sees the best opportunity.[6]

Kaepa, Inc., is a good example. Sales of its all-purpose sneakers plummeted as larger firms like Nike and Reebok stole customers with a multiple target market approach. They developed innovative products and aimed their promotion at specific needs—like jogging, aerobics, cross-training, and walking. Kaepa turned things around by catering to the needs of cheerleaders. Cheerleading squads can order Kaepa shoes with custom team logos and colors. The soles of the shoes feature finger grooves that make it easier for cheerleaders to build human pyramids. Kaepa also carefully targets its market research and promotion. Kaepa salespeople attend the cheerleading camps that each summer draw 40,000 enthusiasts. Kaepa even arranges for the cheering teams it sponsors to do demos at retail stores. This generates publicity and pulls in buyers, so retailers put more emphasis on the Kaepa line.[7]

Profit is the balancing point

In practice, cost considerations often encourage more aggregating and favor combining submarkets as costs often drop due to economies of scale. On the other hand, many customers prefer to have their needs satisfied more exactly—and will be more satisfied by a segmenter that develops a marketing mix that more closely matches their needs. Profit is the balancing point. It determines how unique a marketing mix the firm can afford to offer to a particular market segment.

What Dimensions Are Used to Segment Markets?

LO 4.4

Segmenting dimensions guide marketing mix planning

Market segmentation forces a marketing manager to decide which product-market dimensions might be useful for planning marketing strategies. The dimensions should help guide marketing mix planning. Exhibit 4-7 shows the basic kinds of dimensions we'll be talking about in Chapters 5 and 6—and their probable effect on the four Ps. Ideally, we want to describe any potential product-market in terms of all three types of customer-related dimensions—plus a product type description—because these dimensions help us develop better marketing mixes.

Exhibit 4–7 Relation of Potential Target Market Dimensions to Marketing Strategy Decision Areas

Potential Target Market Dimensions	Effects on Strategy Decision Areas
1. Behavioral needs, attitudes, and how present and potential goods and services fit into customers' consumption patterns.	Affects *Product* (features, packaging, product line assortment, branding) and *Promotion* (what potential customers need and want to know about the firm's offering, and what appeals should be used).
2. Urgency to get need satisfied and desire and willingness to seek information, compare, and shop.	Affects *Place* (how directly products are distributed from producer to customer, how extensively they are made available, and the level of service needed) and *Price* (how much potential customers are willing to pay).
3. Geographic location and other demographic characteristics of potential customers.	Affects size of *Target Markets* (economic potential), *Place* (where products should be made available), and *Promotion* (where and to whom to target with advertising, publicity, sales promotion and personal selling).

People who are out in the sun should protect their skin. This safety need is a qualifying dimension of consumers in the market for sunblock products. However, parents may especially seek Banana Boat Baby and Kids Sunblock Lotion and Baby Sprays because they are easy on kids' eyes and don't cause tearing. For these parents this is a determining need. There are a variety of ways that Coffee-Mate is different from cream, but this ad focuses on the idea that it does not need to be refrigerated. For some consumers, that determines what they will buy.

Many segmenting dimensions may be considered

Customers can be described by many specific dimensions. Exhibit 4-8 shows some dimensions useful for segmenting consumer markets. A few are behavioral dimensions; others are geographic and demographic. We discuss these final consumer segmenting dimensions in Chapters 3 and 5. Exhibit 4-9 shows some additional dimensions for segmenting markets when the customers are businesses, government agencies, or other types of organizations. These dimensions for segmenting organizational customers are covered in Chapter 6. Regardless of whether customers are final consumers or organizations, segmenting a broad product-market *usually* requires using several different dimensions at the same time.[8]

What are the qualifying and determining dimensions?

To select the important segmenting dimensions, think about two different types of dimensions. **Qualifying dimensions** are those relevant to including a customer type in a product-market. **Determining dimensions** are those that actually affect the customer's purchase of a specific product or brand in a product-market.

A prospective car buyer, for example, has to have enough money—or credit—to buy a car and insure it. Our buyer also needs a driver's license. This still doesn't guarantee a purchase. He or she must have a real need—like a job that requires "wheels" or kids who have to be carpooled. This need may motivate the purchase of *some* car. But these qualifying dimensions don't determine what specific brand or model car the person might buy. That depends on more specific interests—such as the kind of safety, performance, or appearance the customer wants. Determining dimensions related to these needs affect the specific car the customer purchases. If safety is a determining dimension for a customer, a Volvo wagon that offers side impact protection, air bags, and all-wheel drive might be the customer's first choice.

Consider Ford's efforts to sell cars in Vietnam. When it arrived in the country a few years ago, many consumers didn't even know how to drive a car—an important *qualifying* dimension when you are selling cars. To increase the size of its market, Ford created a free driving school for Vietnamese. Ford hoped that training drivers using Ford cars would build brand preference that would become a *determining* dimension for future Vietnamese drivers.[9]

Exhibit 4–8 Possible Segmenting Dimensions and Typical Breakdowns for Consumer Markets

Behavioral	
Needs	Economic, functional, physiological, psychological, social, and more detailed needs.
Benefits sought	Situation specific, but to satisfy specific or general needs.
Thoughts	Favorable or unfavorable attitudes, interests, opinions, beliefs.
Rate of use	Heavy, medium, light, nonusers.
Purchase relationship	Positive and ongoing, intermittent, no relationship, bad relationship.
Brand familiarity	Insistence, preference, recognition, nonrecognition, rejection.
Kind of shopping	Convenience, comparison shopping, specialty, none (unsought product).
Type of problem solving	Routinized response, limited, extensive.
Information required	Low, medium, high.
Geographic	
Region of world, country	North America (United States, Canada), Europe (France, Italy, Germany), and so on.
Region in country	(Examples in United States): Pacific, Mountain, West North Central, West South Central, East North Central, East South Central, South Atlantic, Middle Atlantic, New England.
Size of city	No city; population under 5,000; 5,000–19,999; 20,000–49,999; 50,000–99,999; 100,000–249,999; 250,000–499,999; 500,000–999,999; 1,000,000–3,999,999; 4,000,000 or over.
Demographic	
Income	Under $10,000; $10,000–24,999; $25,000–49,999; $50,000–74,999; $75,000–99,999; $100,000–149,999; 150,000–$249,999; $250,000 or more.
Sex	Male, female.
Age	Infant; under 6; 6–11; 12–17; 18–24; 25–34; 35–49; 50–64; 65 or over.
Family size	1, 2, 3–4, 5 or more.
Family life cycle	Young, single; young, married, no children; young, married, youngest child under 6; young, married, youngest child over 6; older, married, with children; older, married, no children under 18; older, single; other variations for single parents, divorced, etc.
Occupation	Professional and technical; managers, officials, and proprietors; clerical sales; craftspeople; foremen; operatives; farmers; retired; students; housewives; unemployed.
Education	Grade school or less; some high school; high school graduate; some college; college graduate; some graduate school; graduate degree.
Ethnicity	Asian, Black, Hispanic, Native American, White, multiracial.
Social class	Lower-lower, upper-lower, lower-middle, upper-middle, lower-upper, upper-upper.

Note: Terms used in this table are explained in detail later in the text.

Determining dimensions may be very specific

How specific the determining dimensions are depends on whether you are concerned with a general product type or a specific brand. See Exhibit 4-10. The more specific you want to be, the more particular the determining dimensions may be. In a particular case, the determining dimensions may seem minor. But they are important because they *are* the determining dimensions.

Marketers at General Mills know this. Lots of people try to check e-mail or drive a car while eating breakfast or lunch. General Mills has figured out that for many of these target customers the real determining dimension in picking a snack is whether it can be eaten "one-handed."

Exhibit 4–9 Possible Segmenting Dimensions for Business/Organizational Markets

Kind of relationship	Weak loyalty → strong loyalty to vendor Single source → multiple vendors "Arm's length" dealings → close partnership
Type of customer	Manufacturer, service producer, government agency, military, nonprofit, wholesaler or retailer (when end user), and so on
Demographics	Geographic location (region of world, country, region within country, urban → rural); Size (number of employees, sales volume); Primary business or industry (North American Industry Classification System); Number of facilities
How customer will use product	Installations, components, accessories, raw materials, supplies, professional services
Type of buying situation	Decentralized → centralized Buyer → multiple buying influence Straight rebuy → modified rebuy → new-task buying
Purchasing methods	Vendor analysis, purchasing specifications, Internet bids, negotiated contracts, long-term contracts, e-commerce websites

Note: Terms used in this table are explained in detail later in the text.

Qualifying dimensions are important too

The qualifying dimensions help identify the "core benefits" that must be offered to everyone in a product-market. For example, people won't choose General Mills' one-handed snacks unless they qualify as being tasty. Qualifying and determining dimensions work together in marketing strategy planning.

Different dimensions needed for different submarkets

Note that each different submarket within a broad product-market may be motivated by a different set of dimensions. In the snack food market, for example, health food enthusiasts are interested in nutrition, dieters worry about calories, and economical shoppers with lots of kids may want volume to "fill them up."

Ethical issues in selecting segmenting dimensions

Marketing managers sometimes face ethical decisions when selecting segmenting dimensions. Problems may arise if a firm targets customers who are somehow at a disadvantage in dealing with the firm or who are unlikely to see the negative effects of their own choices. For example, some people criticize shoe companies for targeting poor, inner-city kids who see

Exhibit 4–10 Finding the Relevant Segmenting Dimensions

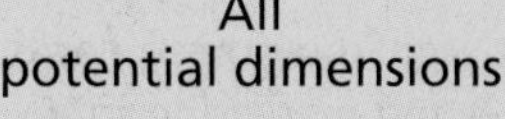

expensive athletic shoes as an important status symbol. Many firms, including producers of infant formula, have been criticized for targeting consumers in less-developed nations. Some nutritionists criticize firms that market soft drinks, candy, and snack foods to children.

Sometimes a marketing manager must decide whether a firm should serve customers it really doesn't want to serve. For example, banks sometimes offer marketing mixes that are attractive to wealthy customers but drive off low-income consumers.

People often disagree about what segmenting dimensions are ethical in a given situation. A marketing manager needs to consider not only his or her own view but also the views of other groups in society. Even when there is no clear "right" answer, negative publicity may be very damaging. This is what Amazon.com encountered when it was revealed that it was charging some regular customers higher prices than new customers at its site.[10]

Ethics Question

My Favorite is a popular cereal brand that makes mostly sugary breakfast cereals aimed at young children. It created a suite of online games that prominently feature cartoon characters associated with its different cereal brands. A consumer group criticized My Favorite for its use of the online advergames—games that contain advertising—because they target children. The group suggests that advergames are worse for kids than TV advertising because 6- to 11-year-olds actively seek out these games and spend an average of 30 minutes per day playing the games. My Favorite countered that the games contain no explicit promotion of its cereal brands; only the characters are featured. Further, the site is closely monitored and offers a free place for kids to have good clean fun. Because My Favorite's internal research indicates that users of its site and their parents have more favorable opinions of its brand than nonusers, it is reluctant to stop. What do you think of this marketing activity? If you were the marketing manager for My Favorite, would you use advergames? Why or why not?[11]

International marketing requires even more segmenting

Success in international marketing requires even more attention to segmenting. There are over 192 nations with their own unique cultures! And they differ greatly in language, customs (including business ethics), beliefs, religions, race, and income distribution patterns. (We discuss some of these differences in Chapters 3 and 5.) These additional differences can complicate the segmenting process. Even worse, critical data is often less available—and less dependable—as firms move into international markets. This is one reason why some firms insist that local operations and decisions be handled by natives. They, at least, have a feel for their markets.

Segmenting international markets may require more dimensions. But one practical method adds just one step to the approach discussed earlier. First, marketers segment by country or region—looking at demographic, cultural, and other characteristics, including stage of economic development. This may help them find regional or national submarkets that are fairly similar. Then—depending on whether the firm is aiming at final consumers or business markets—they apply the same basic approaches presented before.

A Best Practice Approach to Segmenting Product-Markets

LO 4.5

Most marketing managers embrace the idea of using market segmentation to narrow down from a broad set of opportunities to a specific target market and marketing strategy (review Exhibit 2-9). There are also hundreds of books and articles about different approaches and tools for market segmentation that a manager might consider. Yet many managers don't do a good job with market segmentation. One reason is that they are often unclear where to start or how to fit the ideas together. So that *you* don't have this knowledge gap, here we introduce a logical seven-step approach to market segmentation. Later

Exhibit 4–11 A Best Practice Approach for Segmenting Product-Markets

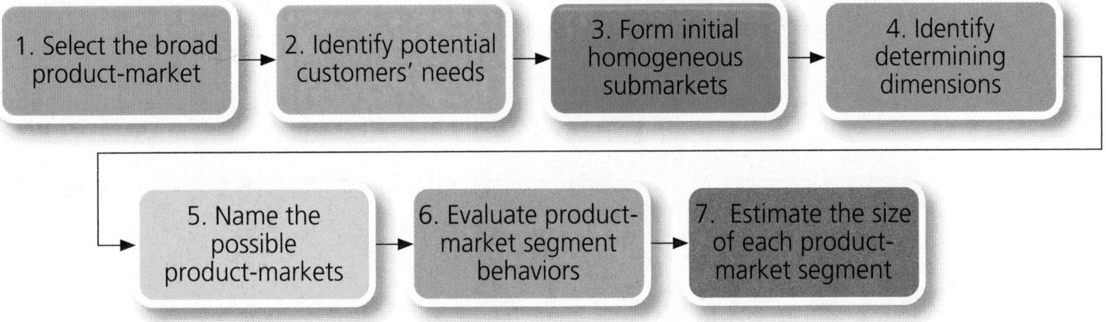

in Chapter 8 you'll learn more about how marketing research can help to fine-tune some of the decisions made with this approach. But even without additional research, *this approach works*—and it has led to successful strategies. It is especially useful for finding the determining dimensions for product types. However, when you want to find dimensions for specific brands— especially when there are several competing brands—you may need more sophisticated techniques.

Exhibit 4-11 provides an overview of the seven-step approach, which ties together the concepts we have been discussing. To be sure you understand this approach, we will review each step separately and use an ongoing example to show how each step works. The example concerns people who need a place to stay—in particular, the market for motel guests in a big urban area.

1: Select the broad product-market

First, decide what broad product-market the firm wants to be in. This may be stated in the firm's objectives. Or if the firm is already successful in some product-market, its current position might be a good starting point. Try to build on the firm's strengths and avoid its weaknesses and competitors' strengths. Available resources, both human and financial, will limit the possibilities—especially if the firm is just getting started.

Example

A firm has been building small motels around the edges of a large city and renting rooms to travelers. A narrow view—considering only the firm's current products and markets—might lead the firm to think only of more small motels. A bigger view might see such motels as only a small part of the larger "overnight lodging needs" market in the firm's geographic area. Taking an even bigger view, the firm could consider expanding to other geographic areas—or moving into other kinds of products (like apartment buildings, retirement centers, or even parks for people who travel in their own recreational vehicles).

There has to be some balance between naming the product-market too narrowly (same old product, same old market) and naming it too broadly (the whole world and all its needs). Here the firm decides on the whole market of motel users in one city—because this is a city where the number of visitors is growing and where the firm has some experience.

2: Identify potential customers' needs

Identify and write down as many relevant needs as you can—considering all of the potential customers in the broad product-market. This is a brainstorming step. The list doesn't have to be complete yet, but it should provide enough input to help stimulate your thinking in the next steps. To see possible needs, think about *why* some people buy the present offerings in this broad product-market. At this point, focus on the basic needs—but begin to consider what a company could offer to meet those needs.

Example

In the broad motel guest market, you can easily list some possible needs: privacy (including a private room and furnishings), safety and security (security guards, lighted parking lots with video coverage), comfort (a good bed and nice furnishings), space for

It is better for promotion to focus on what customer needs are satisfied by products rather than on the product characteristics themselves.

activities (exercise, work, socializing), entertainment (TV, radio, video games), convenience (registration, check-out, reservations, access to highways), economy (costs), communicating (phone, messages, fax, voice mail, wireless Internet), and the like.

3: Form homogeneous submarkets—narrow product-markets

Assuming that some people have (or emphasize) different needs than others, form different submarkets based on each submarket's specific needs. Start by forming one submarket around some typical type of customer (perhaps even yourself), and then aggregate similar people into this segment as long as they can be satisfied by the same marketing mix. Write down the important need dimensions and customer-related characteristics (including demographic characteristics) of each submarket to help you decide whether each new customer type should be included in the first segment. This will also help later—when you name the submarkets.

For example, if the people in one market are young families looking for a good place to stay on vacation, this will help you understand what they want and why—and will help you name the market (perhaps as "family vacationers").

Put people who are not homogeneous—who don't fit in the first segment—in a new submarket. List their different need dimensions on another line. Continue this classifying until three or more submarkets emerge.

Example

A young family on a vacation probably wants a motel to provide a clean room large enough for adults and children, convenient parking, a location near tourist attractions, a pool for recreation with a lifeguard for safety, entertainment in the room (a TV, video games, and movies on demand), and perhaps a refrigerator or vending machine for snacks. A traveling executive, on the other hand, has quite different interests—a room with a desk, but *also* a nice restaurant, fast transportation to and from an airport, more services (room service, dry cleaning, a way to send and receive a fax, and fast check-in)—without distracting noise from children. See Exhibit 4-12.

4: Identify the determining dimensions

Review the list of need dimensions for each possible segment and identify the determining dimensions (perhaps by putting an asterisk beside them). Although the qualifying dimensions are important—perhaps reflecting "core needs" that should be satisfied—they are not the *determining* dimensions we are seeking now.

Exhibit 4–12 Segmenting the Broad Product-Market for Motel Guests in a Large Urban Area

Nickname of Product-Market	Need Dimensions (benefits sought)	Customer-Related Characteristics
1 Family vacationers	Comfort, security, privacy, *family fun, recreation (playground, pool), entertainment (video games, movies), child care, and snacks*	Couples and single parents with children who want a fun family experience: young, active, and energetic.
2 Upscale executives	Comfort, security, privacy, *distinctive furnishings, attentive staff, prestige status, easy access to airport and business meetings, express check-in and check-out, quality dining, business services (copying, fax, Wi-Fi Internet)*	Senior business executives with a big expense account who want to be pampered with "very important person" service and accommodations; often repeat guests.
3 Budget-oriented travelers	Comfort, security, privacy, *economy, (no extras that increase cost), convenience (to low-cost restaurants, highways), free parking*	Young people, retirees, and salespeople who travel by car, pay their own expenses, and want a simple place for one night—before moving on.
4 Long-stay guests	Comfort, security, privacy, *homelike amenities (kitchenette, separate living room), laundry and exercise facilities, pleasant grounds, entertainment, staying "connected" (e-mail, etc.)*	Businesspeople, out-of-town visitors, and others who stay in the same motel for a week or more; want many of the comforts they have at home.
5 Event-centered visitors	Comfort, security, privacy, *socializing (lounges and public areas), conference facilities (including catering of group meals), message and transportation services*	Individuals who are attending events scheduled at the motel (a business meeting or conference, family reunion, wedding, etc.) often for several days.
6 Resort seekers	Comfort, security, privacy, *relaxation (golf, whirlpool bath), pleasure (fine dining, nice views), fun, variety information (arrangements for theater, activities)*	Sophisticated couples with leisure time to relax and have "adult" fun; they want to show their individuality and have discretionary income to spend.

Note: Comfort, security, and privacy are core qualifying needs. Determining dimensions for each segment are in italic.

To help identify the determining dimensions, think carefully about the needs and attitudes of the people in each possible segment. They may not seem very different from market to market, but if they are determining to those people then they *are* determining!

Example

With our motel customers, basic comfort needs (heating and cooling, a good bed, a clean bathroom), a telephone for communicating, and safety and security are probably not determining. Everyone has these qualifying needs. Looking beyond these common needs helps you see the determining dimensions—such as different needs with respect to recreation, restaurant facilities, services, and so on. See the needs highlighted in italic in Exhibit 4-12.

5: Name (nickname) the possible product-markets

Review the determining dimensions—market by market—and name (nickname) each one based on the relative importance of the determining dimensions (and aided by your description of the customer types). A market grid is a good way to help visualize this broad product-market and its narrow product-markets.

Draw the market grid as a rectangle, with boxes inside representing smaller, more homogeneous segments. See Exhibit 4-13. Think of the whole grid as representing the broad product-market and each of the boxes as a different (narrower) product-market. Since the markets within a broad product-market usually require very different segmenting dimensions, don't try to use the same dimensions to name every submarket. Then label each segment with its nickname.

Exhibit 4–13
Market Grid Diagram for Hotel Guest Market with Product Markets

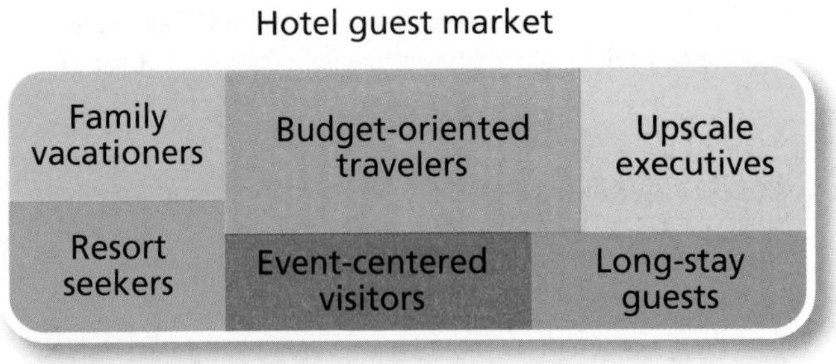

Hotel guest market

Family vacationers	Budget-oriented travelers	Upscale executives
Resort seekers	Event-centered visitors	Long-stay guests

Example

Exhibit 4-13 identifies the following overnight guest submarkets: (1) family vacationers, (2) upscale executives, (3) budget-oriented travelers, (4) long-stay guests, (5) event-centered visitors, and (6) resort seekers. Note that each segment has a different set of determining dimensions (benefits sought) that follow directly from customer type and needs.

6: Evaluate why product-market segments behave as they do

After naming the markets as we did in step 5, think about what else you know about each segment to see how and why these markets behave the way they do. Different segments may have similar, but slightly different, needs. This may explain why some competitive offerings are more successful than others. It can also mean you have to split and rename some segments.

Example

The resort seekers might have been treated as family vacationers in step 5 because the "family" characteristic did not seem important. But with more thought, we see that while some of the resort seekers are interested in the same sort of fun and recreation as the family vacationers, resort seekers focus on adult fun—not activities with children. For them, getting away from the family vacationer's children may be part of the escape they want. Further, although the resort seekers are a higher-income group who are similar to the upscale executives, they have different needs than the executives and probably should be treated as a separate market. The point is that you might discover these market differences only in step 6. At this step you would name the "resort seekers" market—and create a related row in the grid to describe the new segment.

7: Make a rough estimate of the size of each product-market segment

Remember, we are looking for profitable opportunities. So now we must try to tie our product-markets to demographic data—or other customer-related characteristics—to make it easier to estimate the size of these markets. We aren't trying to estimate our likely sales yet. Sales depend on the competition as well as the particulars of the marketing mix. Now we only want to provide a basis for later forecasting and marketing mix planning. The more we know about possible target markets, the easier those jobs are.

Fortunately, we can obtain a lot of data on the size of markets—especially demographic data. And bringing in demographics adds a note of economic reality. Some possible product-markets may have almost no market potential. Without hard facts, we risk aiming at such markets.

To refine the market grid, you might want to change the height of the rows so that they give a better idea of the size of the various segments. This will help highlight the larger, and perhaps more attractive, opportunities. Remember, the relative sizes of the markets might vary depending on what geographic areas you consider. The market sizes might vary from city to city or from one country to another.

Example

We can tie the family vacationers to demographic data. Most of them are between 21 and 45. The U.S. Census Bureau publishes detailed data by age, family size, and related information. Moreover, a state tourist bureau or city Chamber of Commerce might be able to provide estimates of how many families vacation in a specific city during a year and how long they stay. Given this information, it's easy to estimate the total number of nights family vacationers will need motel rooms in a certain city.

Market dimensions suggest a good mix

Once we follow all seven steps, we should be able to outline the kinds of marketing mixes that would appeal to the various markets. For example, based on the determining dimensions (benefits sought) in Exhibit 4-12, a motel designed to appeal to the upscale executives might offer rooms with quality furniture (including a desk and chair for reading and an extra comfortable bed with special luxury sheets and pillows), a high-quality restaurant with all-hours room service, special business services (copying, fax, wireless Internet) on an extra-cost basis, limousine pickup at the airport, someone to help with travel problems, and precleared check-in and check-out. The motel might also provide a quiet bar and exercise room and extras such as thick bath towels and a valet service for free shoe shines. It might also offer a business library for after-hours reading and a free copy of *The Wall Street Journal* delivered every morning. Of course, the price could be high to pay for this special treatment. It's also useful to think about what the executives would *not* want: noisy facilities shared by families with young children!

> **Internet Exercise**
>
> The Intercontinental Hotel Group owns a number of different hotel brands including Holiday Inn, Holiday Inn Express, Crowne Plaza, and Staybridge Suites. Go to the Holiday Inn website (**www.holidayinn.com**) and click on the link for "IHG brands" at the bottom of the screen (or search for "IHG brands" on Google). Click through to each of the hotel brands. In which of the product-markets in Exhibit 4-12 does each brand compete? Why? Why not?

While the discussion above focuses on the upscale executives, profitable marketing mixes can be developed for the other segments as well. For example, Super 8 has done very well by targeting budget-oriented travelers. Similarly, Residence Inns cater to the needs of long-stay guests with kitchens and grocery shopping services, fireplaces, and convenient recreation areas. Courtyard by Marriott has been successful with facilities designed for event-centered visitors. During the week, many of its customers are there for business conferences, but on the weekend the focus often shifts to family events—such as meals and receptions related to a wedding or family reunion.[12]

Improve the marketing mix for current customers

Our motel example highlights an approach to identify new target market and marketing mix opportunities. However, the same approaches provide a basis for identifying new ways to serve existing customers and strengthen the relationship with them. Too often, firms let their strategies get stagnant. For example, special business services related to the determining needs of upscale executives (like voice mail) might initially help a motel win this business with superior customer value. However, the motel loses its competitive edge if other motels start to offer the same benefits. Or the benefit might disappear if customer needs change; executives who carry a cell phone don't need voice mail at the motel. Then the determining dimensions change. To retain the base of customers it has built or attract new ones, the motel needs to find new and better ways to meet the executives' needs. Reevaluating the need dimensions and customer-related characteristics, perhaps in greater detail, may point to new opportunities. For example, our motel might offer more personalized services.

Targeting a segment of one

Many luxury hotel chains, for example, try to appeal to the needs of a "segment of one" by adapting a marketing mix to an individual customer. The first time a new guest reserves a room at the Mandarin Oriental, she's asked about her personal preferences, which are saved in a database for future visits. On her second arrival at the exclusive hotel, this guest finds the room thermostat set to her preferred temperature, the phone's color touch screen shows the weather back home, and the three down feather pillows she enjoys already on the bed. While this guest has many of the same basic needs as the broader segment of "upscale executives" in Exhibit 4-12, the personalized attention she receives ensures a unique experience. From a practical perspective, this extreme segmentation still involves the seven-step process, with fine-tuning operating at the level of individual customers within a larger segment.

More Sophisticated Techniques May Help in Segmenting

LO 4.6

Marketing researchers and managers often turn to computer-aided methods for help with the segmenting job. A detailed review of the possibilities is beyond the scope of this book. But a brief discussion will give you a flavor of how computer-aided methods work. In addition, the computer-aided problem for this chapter (4, Segmenting Customers) on the text website gives you a hands-on feel for how managers use them.

Clustering usually requires a computer

Clustering techniques try to find similar patterns within sets of data. Clustering groups customers who are similar on their segmenting dimensions into homogeneous segments. Clustering approaches use computers to do what previously was done with much intuition and judgment.

The data to be clustered might include such dimensions as demographic characteristics, the importance of different needs, attitudes toward the product, and past buying behavior. The computer searches all the data for homogeneous groups of people. When it finds them, marketers study the dimensions of the people in the groups to see why the computer clustered them together. The results sometimes suggest new, or at least better, marketing strategies.[13]

A cluster analysis of the toothpaste market, for example, might show that some people buy toothpaste because it tastes good (the sensory segment), while others are concerned with the effect of clean teeth and fresh breath on their social image (the sociables). Still others worry about decay or gum disease (the worriers), and some are just interested in the best value for their money (the value seekers). Each of these market segments calls for a different marketing mix—although some of the four Ps may be similar.

Customer database can focus the effort

A variation of the clustering approach is based on customer relationship management methods. With **customer relationship management (CRM)**, the seller fine-tunes the marketing effort with information from a detailed customer database. This usually includes data on a customer's past purchases as well as other segmenting information. For example, an auto-repair garage that keeps a database of customer oil changes can send a reminder postcard when it's time for the next oil change. Similarly, a florist that keeps a database of customers who have ordered flowers for Mother's Day or Valentine's Day can call them in advance with a special offer. Firms that operate over the Internet may have a special advantage with these database-focused approaches. They are able to communicate with customers via a website or e-mail, which means that the whole effort is not only targeted but also very inexpensive. Further, it's fast and easy for a customer to reply.[14]

Amazon.com takes this idea further. When a customer orders a book, the Amazon CRM system at the website recommends related books that have been purchased by other customers who bought that book.

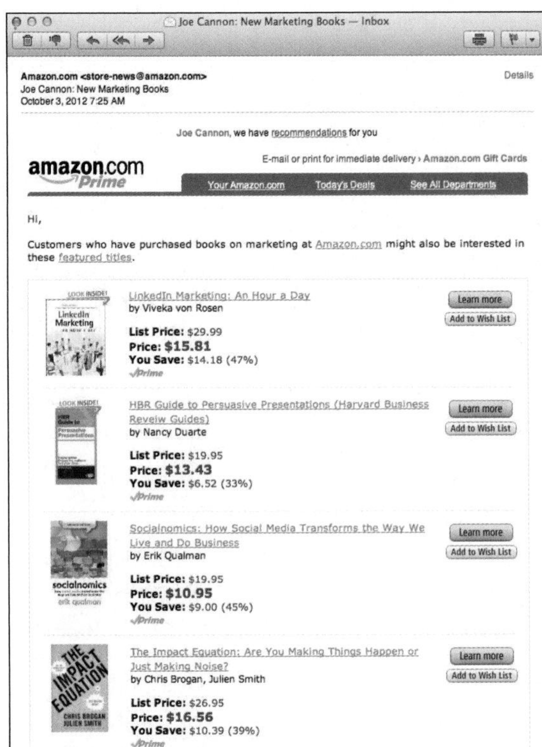

Amazon.com sends e-mails to customers with recommendations based on their past purchases. Many customers find these messages, which inform them of new toys, books, music, or movies that actually match their interests, useful.

Target reads its customers minds?

A few years ago a man walked into a Target store outside Minneapolis demanding to see a manager. The man was upset that Target was sending his teenage daughter coupons for baby clothes and cribs. "Are you trying to encourage her to get pregnant?" he asked the manager. The store manager promised to look into it, but a few days later the father called back and sheepishly admitted that there was more going on in his house than he knew about. His daughter was due in August. How did Target know? Why would Target care?

Consumers' shopping habits are hard to break. Once customers start shopping at a particular store for groceries, DVDs, or greeting cards, they get into a habit and don't even consider shopping at other stores. It turns out that a few major life events—new job, marriage and yes, new baby—significantly weaken those ties, at least for a short time. At those vulnerable moments, a competing store has an opportunity to steal a customer away—perhaps encouraging a switch with some well-timed promotions—and maybe help them develop a new shopping habit.

So how does a retail store like Target segment its market and target pregnant shoppers? Target's marketing managers wondered if their customer relationship management (CRM) database might hold an answer. The database includes information on the shopping behavior of customers who sign up for the store's loyalty card or use a credit card. Along with additional data Target purchases from third parties, the database offers a detailed profile of millions of Target customers.

Some of these customers already told Target they were pregnant by signing up for the store's baby registry; though only a small fraction of Target's pregnant customers make it that easy. Target's statisticians used data from the customers they knew were pregnant and "mined" their CRM data to try to determine how their shopping behavior changed during pregnancy.

The statisticians discovered 25 products that were purchased more frequently during pregnancy. For example, while many people buy lotions, about six months before their due date purchases of unscented lotions bumped up. Around that same time pregnant women stocked up on supplements like calcium, magnesium, and zinc. A few months later there was an uptick in purchases of scent-free soap, extra-large bags of cotton balls, hand sanitizers, and washcloths.

The statisticians used this information to develop a prediction score for each customer in Target's CRM database—predicting if each was pregnant and when they would deliver. Customers with high scores receive customized direct mailings with coupons for a new crib or disposable diapers. Target wants these customers to start buying groceries and other products at Target, too. So they make sure the mailings also include other products these customers didn't yet buy at Target. Many of these customers were soon making Target their primary shopping location. So the next time you open a promotion for something you are thinking about buying, the store may be reading your mind—via their CRM database.[15]

Differentiation and Positioning Take the Customer Point of View

LO 4.7

Differentiate the marketing mix—to serve customers better

As we've emphasized throughout, the reason for focusing on a specific target market—by using marketing segmentation approaches or tools such as cluster analysis or CRM—is so that you can fine-tune the whole marketing mix to provide some group of potential customers with superior value. By *differentiating* the marketing mix to do a better job meeting customers' needs, the firm builds a competitive advantage. When this happens, target customers view the firm's position in the market as uniquely suited to their preferences and needs. Further, because everyone in the firm is clear about what position it wants to achieve with customers, the Product, Promotion, and other marketing mix decisions can be blended better to achieve the desired objectives.

Although the marketing manager may want customers to see the firm's offering as unique, that is not always possible. Me-too imitators may come along and copy the firm's strategy. Further, even if a firm's marketing mix is different, consumers may not know or care. They're busy and, simply put, the firm's product may not be that important in their lives. This is where another important concept, *positioning,* comes in.

Internet Exercise

The Brand Tags website (**www.brandtags.net**) asks visitors to type the first word or phrase (a "tag") that comes to mind when a logo or brand name appears on the screen. Go to this site and tag a few brands. Then, select "Explore Brands" and see how others tagged the brand (this may require registration on the site). Note that the larger the font, the more frequently that word or phrase has been used. How could a marketing manager use this information to better understand her brand? A competitor's brand?

Positioning is based on customers' views

Positioning refers to how customers think about proposed or present brands in a market. Without a realistic view of how customers think about offerings in the market, it's hard for the marketing manager to differentiate. At the same time, the manager should know how he or she *wants* target customers to think about the firm's marketing mix. Positioning issues are especially important when competitors in a market appear to be very similar. For example, many people think that there isn't much difference between one provider of home owner's insurance and another. But State Farm Insurance uses advertising to emphasize the value of the service and personal attention from its agents, who live right in the customer's neighborhood. Low-price insurers who sell from websites or toll-free numbers can't make that claim.

Emailing in London is like emailing in London, KY.
Use your phone like you do at home.
AT&T's new, more affordable international data packages make it easier to use your phone abroad. att.com/global
Rethink Possible

AT&T's cell phones have more coverage around the world as compared with its competition. Its advertising campaign tells customers about this point of differentiation.

Once you know what customers think, then you can decide whether to leave the product (and marketing mix) alone or reposition it. This may mean *physical changes in the product* or simply *image changes based on promotion.* For example, most cola drinkers can't pick out their favorite brand in a blind test—so physical changes might not be necessary (and might not even work) to reposition a cola.

Figuring out what customers really think about competing products isn't easy, but there are approaches that help. Most of them require some formal marketing research. The results are usually plotted on graphs to help show how consumers view the competing products. Usually, the products' positions are related to two or three product features that are important to the target customers.

Managers make the graphs for positioning decisions by asking consumers to make judgments about different brands—including their "ideal" brand—and then use computer programs to summarize the ratings and plot the results. The details of positioning techniques—sometimes called *perceptual mapping*—are beyond the scope of this text. But Exhibit 4-14 shows the possibilities.[16]

Exhibit 4-14 shows the "product space" for different brands of bar soap using two dimensions—the extent to which consumers think the soaps moisturize and deodorize their skin. For example, consumers see Dove as quite high on moisturizing but low on deodorizing. Dove and Tone are close together—implying that consumers think of them as similar on these characteristics. Dial is viewed as different from Dove and Tone and at a distance from them on the graph. Remember that positioning maps are based on *customers' perceptions*—the actual characteristics of the products (as determined by a chemical test) might be different!

Exhibit 4–14
"Product Space" Representing Consumers' Perceptions for Different Brands of Bar Soap

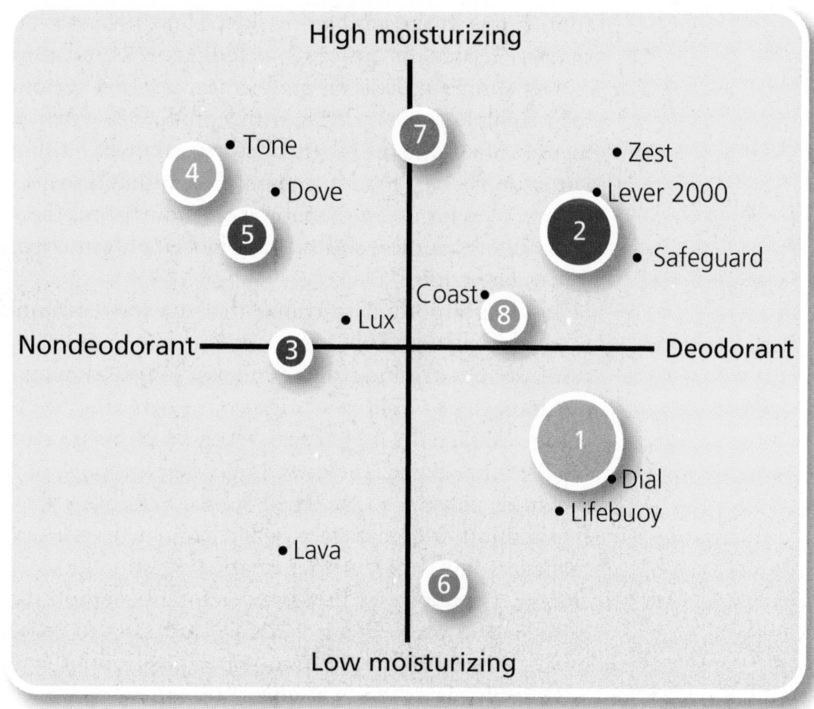

Each segment may have its own preferences

The circles in Exhibit 4-14 show different sets (submarkets) of consumers clustered near their ideal soap preferences. Groups of respondents with a similar ideal product are circled to show apparent customer concentrations. In this graph, the size of the circles suggests the size of the segments for the different ideals.

Ideal clusters 1 and 2 are the largest and are close to two popular brands—Dial and Lever 2000. It appears that customers in cluster 2 want more moisturizing than they see in Dial. However, exactly what this brand should do about this isn't clear. Perhaps Dial should leave its physical product alone—but emphasize moisturizing more in its promotion to make a stronger appeal to those who want moisturizers. A marketing manager talking about this approach might simply refer to it as "positioning the brand as a good moisturizer." Of course, whether the effort is successful depends on whether the whole marketing mix delivers on the promise of the positioning communication.

Note that ideal cluster 7 is not near any of the present brands. This may suggest an opportunity for introducing a new product—a strong moisturizer with some deodorizers. A firm that chooses to follow this approach would be making a segmenting effort.

Combining versus segmenting

Positioning analysis may lead a firm to combining—rather than segmenting—if managers think they can make several general appeals to different parts of a "combined" market. For example, by varying its promotion, Coast might try to appeal to segments 8, 1, and 2 with one product. These segments are all quite similar (close together) in what they want in an ideal brand. On the other hand, there may be clearly defined submarkets—and some parts of the market may be "owned" by one product or brand. In this case, segmenting efforts may be practical—moving the firm's own product into another segment of the general market area where competition is weaker.

Positioning as part of broader analysis

A positioning analysis helps managers understand how customers see their market. It is a visual aid to understanding a product-market. The first time such an analysis is done, managers may be shocked to see how much customers' perceptions of a market differ from their own. For this reason alone, positioning analysis may be crucial. But a positioning analysis usually focuses on specific product features and brands that are close competitors in the product-market. Thus, it is a product-oriented approach. Important *customer*-related dimensions—including needs and attitudes—may be overlooked.

Premature emphasis on product features is dangerous in other ways as well. As our bar soap example shows, starting with a product-oriented definition of a market and how bar soaps compete against other bar soaps can make a firm miss more basic shifts in markets. For example, bars have lost popularity to liquid soaps. Other products, like bath oils or body washes for use in the shower, are now part of the relevant competition also. Managers wouldn't see these shifts if they looked only at alternative bar soap brands—the focus is just too narrow.

It's also important to realize that the way consumers look at a product isn't just a matter of chance. Let's return to our bar soap example. While many consumers do think about soap in terms of moisturizing and deodorizing, other needs shouldn't be overlooked. For example, some consumers are especially concerned about wiping out germs. Marketers for Dial soap recognized this need and developed ads that positioned Dial as "the choice" for these target customers. This helped Dial win new customers, including those who switched from Lifebuoy—which was otherwise similar to Dial (see Exhibit 4-14). In fact, what happened to Lifebuoy highlights what happens if managers don't update their marketing strategy as customer needs and competition change. Lifebuoy was the first deodorant soap on the market; it was a leading brand for over 100 years. But it gradually lost sales to competitors with stronger marketing mixes (clearer differentiation, better positioning, and superior customer value) until sales declined and Lever stopped selling it.

Positioning statement provides direction for marketing strategy

Sometimes marketing managers use a positioning statement to provide focus for a marketing mix. A *positioning statement* concisely identifies the firm's desired target market, product type, primary benefit or point of differentiation, and the main reasons a buyer should believe the firm's claims. The one or two benefits highlighted in the statement should be those most important to the target market—and unique to the brand. It's important that everyone involved in planning the marketing strategy agree with the positioning statement because it helps narrow options and guide the selection of a marketing mix.

Some firms use a template like the following to aid in preparation of a positioning statement:

> For (*our target market*), (*our brand*) of all (*product type*) delivers (*key benefit or point of differentiation*) because (*our brand*) is (*reasons to believe*).

A few years ago, marketing managers for Mountain Dew used this template to develop the following positioning statement:

> For 16 to 24-year-old males, who embrace excitement, adventure, and fun, Mountain Dew of all carbonated soft drinks, delivers great taste that exhilarates like no other because Mountain Dew is energizing, thirst-quenching, and has a one-of-a-kind citrus flavor.

The positioning statement provided Mountain Dew's advertising agency with a direction to follow that lead to a series of television commercials that reinforced this positioning. The statement guided decisions about packaging, point-of-purchase promotion, sponsorships, the look and feel of a website, and new flavors. The marketing strategy based on this positioning helped Mountain Dew gain market share with this target market.[17]

As we emphasize throughout the text, you must understand potential needs and attitudes when planning marketing strategies. If customers treat different products as substitutes, then a firm has to position itself against those products too. Customers won't always be conscious of all of the detailed ways that a firm's marketing mix might be different, but careful positioning can help highlight a unifying theme or benefits that relate to the determining dimensions of the target market. Thus, it's useful to think of positioning as part of the broader strategy planning process—because the purpose is to ensure that the whole marketing mix is positioned for competitive advantage.

CONCLUSION

Chapters 2 and 3 introduced a framework for strategy planning that starts with analysis of the broad market and then narrows down to a specific target market and marketing mix. The basic purpose of this chapter is to show how marketing managers use market segmentation and positioning to guide that narrowing-down process.

Now that you've read this chapter you should understand how to carefully define generic markets and product-markets and how that can help in identifying and evaluating opportunities. We stressed the shortcomings of a too narrow, product-oriented view of markets and explained why it's better to take a broader view that also includes consideration of customer needs, the product type, the customer type, and the geographic area.

We also discussed approaches for market segmentation—the process of naming and then segmenting broad product-markets to find potentially attractive target markets. Some people try to segment markets by starting with the mass market and then dividing it into smaller submarkets based on a few demographic characteristics. But this can lead to poor results. Instead, market segmentation should first focus on a broad product-market and then group similar customers into homogeneous submarkets. The more similar the potential customers are, the larger the submarkets can be. Four criteria for evaluating possible product-market segments were presented.

Once a broad product-market is segmented, marketing managers can use one of three approaches to market-oriented strategy planning: (1) the single target market approach, (2) the multiple target market approach, or (3) the combined target market approach. In general, we encourage marketers to be segmenters rather than combiners.

We also offer a logical seven-step approach for segmentation that will help you understand and apply concepts from this chapter. Then we cover computer-aided approaches such as clustering techniques, CRM, and positioning. We emphasize the role of positioning in providing a focus or theme to the various elements of a differentiated marketing mix that fits the preferences of target customers.

In summary, good marketers should be experts on markets and likely segmenting dimensions. By creatively segmenting markets, they may spot opportunities—even breakthrough opportunities—and help their firms succeed against aggressive competitors offering similar products. Segmenting is basic to target marketing. And the more you practice segmenting, the more meaningful market segments you will see. In Chapters 5 and 6 you'll learn more about the buying behavior of final consumers and organizational customers. As you enrich your understanding of customers and how they behave, you will develop command of a broader set of dimensions that are important for segmentation and positioning.

KEY TERMS

LO 4.8

market, *89*
generic market, *89*
product-market, *89*
market segmentation, *92*
segmenting, *94*
market segment, *94*
single target market approach, *96*
multiple target market approach, *96*
combined target market approach, *96*
combiners, *96*
segmenters, *97*
qualifying dimensions, *99*
determining dimensions, *99*
clustering techniques, *108*
customer relationship management (CRM), *108*
positioning, *110*

QUESTIONS AND PROBLEMS

1. Distinguish between a generic market and a product-market. Illustrate your answer.
2. Explain what market segmentation is.
3. List the types of potential segmenting dimensions, and explain which you would try to apply first, second, and third in a particular situation. If the nature of the situation would affect your answer, explain how.
4. Explain why segmentation efforts based on attempts to divide the mass market using a few demographic dimensions may be very disappointing.
5. Illustrate the concept that segmenting is an aggregating process by referring to the admissions policies of your own college and a nearby college or university.
6. Review the types of segmenting dimensions listed in Exhibits 4-8 and 4-9, and select the ones you think

should be combined to fully explain the market segment you personally would be in if you were planning to buy a new watch today. List several dimensions and try to develop a shorthand name, like "fashion-oriented," to describe your own personal market segment. Then try to estimate what proportion of the total watch market would be in your market segment. Next, explain if there are any offerings that come close to meeting the needs of your market. If not, what sort of a marketing mix is needed? Would it be economically attractive for anyone to try to satisfy your market segment? Why or why not?

7. Identify the determining dimension or dimensions that explain why you bought the specific brand you did in your most recent purchase of a (*a*) soft drink, (*b*) shampoo, (*c*) shirt or blouse, and (*d*) larger, more expensive item, such as a bicycle, camera, or boat. Try to express the determining dimension(*s*) in terms of your own personal characteristics rather than the product's characteristics. Estimate what share of the market would probably be motivated by the same determining dimension(*s*).
8. Consider the market for off-campus apartments in your city. Identify some submarkets that have different needs and determining dimensions. Then evaluate how well the needs in these market segments are being met in your geographic area. Is there an obvious breakthrough opportunity waiting for someone?
9. Explain how positioning analysis can help a marketing manager identify target market opportunities.

CREATING MARKETING PLANS

The Marketing Plan Coach software on the text website includes a sample marketing plan for Hillside Veterinary Clinic. Look through the "Customers" section.

a. How does the marketing plan segment the market?
b. Can you think of other segmentation dimensions that could be used?
c. What do you think of the approach Hillside used to determine target markets? Are they using a single target market, multiple target market, or combined target market approach?
d. How does Hillside plan to differentiate and position its offering?

SUGGESTED CASES

3. NOCO United Soccer Academy
7. Omarama Mountain Lodge
10. Cooper's Ice Center
30. Walker-Winkle Mills, Ltd.

Video Case 2. Bass Pro Shops
Video Case 4. Potbelly Sandwich
Video Case 7. Invacare
Video Case 8. Segway

COMPUTER-AIDED PROBLEM

4. SEGMENTING CUSTOMERS

The marketing manager for Audiotronics Software Company is seeking new market opportunities. He is focusing on the voice recognition market and has narrowed down to three segments: the Fearful Typists, the Power Users, and the Professional Specialists. The Fearful Typists don't know much about computers—they just want a fast way to create e-mail messages, letters, and simple reports without errors. They don't need a lot of special features. They want simple instructions and a program that's easy to learn. The Power Users know a lot about computers, use them often, and want a voice recognition program with many special features. All computer programs seem easy to them—so they aren't worried about learning to use the various features. The Professional Specialists have jobs that require a lot of writing. They don't know much about computers but are willing to learn. They want special features needed for their work—but only if they aren't too hard to learn and use.

The marketing manager prepared a table summarizing the importance of each of three key needs in the three segments (see table that follows).

	Importance of Need (1 = not important; 10 = very important)		
Market Segment	**Features**	**Easy to Use**	**Easy to Learn**
Fearful typists	3	8	9
Power users	9	2	2
Professional specialists	7	5	6

Audiotronics' sales staff conducted interviews with seven potential customers who were asked to rate how important each of these three needs were in their work. The manager prepared a spreadsheet to help him cluster (aggregate) each person into one of the segments—along with other similar people. Each person's ratings are entered in the spreadsheet, and the clustering procedure computes a similarity score that indicates how similar (a low score) or dissimilar (a high score) the person is to the typical person in each of the segments. The manager can then "aggregate" potential customers into the segment that is most similar (that is, the one with the *lowest* similarity score).

a. The ratings for a potential customer appear on the first spreadsheet. Into which segment would you aggregate this person?

b. The responses for seven potential customers who were interviewed are listed in the following table. Enter the ratings for a customer in the spreadsheet and then write down the similarity score for each segment. Repeat the process for each customer. Based on your analysis, indicate the segment into which you would aggregate each customer. Indicate the size (number of customers) of each segment.

c. In the interview, each potential customer was also asked what type of computer he or she would be using. The responses are shown in the table along with the ratings. Group the responses based on the customer's segment. If you were targeting the Fearful Typists segment, what type of computer would you focus on when developing your software?

d. Based on your analysis, which customer would you say is least like any of the segments? Briefly explain the reason for your choice.

	Importance of Need (1 = not important; 10 = very important)			
Potential Customer	**Features**	**Easy to Use**	**Easy to Learn**	**Type of Computer**
A.	8	1	2	Dell laptop
B.	6	6	5	HP desktop
C.	4	9	8	Apple
D.	2	6	7	Apple
E.	5	6	5	HP desktop
F.	8	3	1	Dell laptop
G.	4	6	8	Apple

CHAPTER FIVE

Final Consumers and Their Buying Behavior

When Sony introduced its Walkman in the late 1970s, it quickly became a popular way for on-the-go music lovers to play tapes of their favorite music—anywhere they went. Competing players quickly emerged, but Sony kept its lead by improving its Walkman and then offering models for CDs and digital audiotapes when those media came on the market.

In the late 1990s, the new MP3 format offered quality music from a small digital file that played on a computer or portable player. Diamond Multimedia's Rio was the first MP3 player. The Rio was innovative, but users had to download music from virus-ridden websites like Napster—or use special software to "rip" CDs to MP3 format. Many music buffs liked the idea of having songs at their fingertips, but getting the digital files was just too complicated. Further, music companies filed lawsuits charging some with illegally downloading MP3 music files. All of this slowed down the initial adoption of MP3 players.

Attitudes quickly changed when Apple offered an innovative marketing mix that addressed these customer needs. The online iTunes store offered legal downloads of songs at a reasonable price and without the risk of viruses. Apple's free iTunes software made it easy to organize digital music on a computer and transfer it to Apple's iPod. The iPod was designed to be stylish and easy to use. Apple's ads told customers about the new concept with the promise of "a thousand songs in your pocket." Even skeptics who ignored the ads couldn't help but notice the distinctive white iPod cords dangling from the ears of a friend who was "in" on this cool new product. That prompted a lot of product conversations and on-the-spot iPod demos. Testimonials on blogs, online consumer reviews, and posts on MySpace (there was no Facebook yet) also helped spread the word.

Although most iPod owners were satisfied with their purchases, competitors like Microsoft, Sony, and Creative Labs raised expectations in the market by promoting benefits like longer battery life, capacity for more songs, and lower prices. For some consumers, all of this choice required a more careful purchase decision. For example, some would search for information and reviews on the Internet or talk with salespeople in stores to figure out which model was best.

Cell phones that played music were already on the market when Apple introduced the iPhone, but most consumers couldn't see the benefits. The iPhone changed that. The iPhone's colorful touchscreen display, web-surfing capabilities, and music player wowed consumers. Soon iPhone owners customized their phones with software applications ("apps") from the iTunes store that let them play games like "Angry Birds" and "Words with Friends," watch Netflix movies, or check stock portfolios—right on their iPhones.

Many customers buy Apple's products sight unseen; the first iPad tablet computer had almost a half million pre-orders from customers who had never held one. These customers trust the iPad to live up to expectations based on their previous experiences with other Apple products.

New apps took advantage of the iPad's large screen. For example, the iPad became a popular e-reader for books, magazines, and newspapers. Other apps met the needs of families, and soon kids were pressuring their parents to buy an iPad. Teens like using it to watch Netflix or Hulu and to update their Facebook page. Younger kids love the children's books that have been adapted for the iPad like *PopOut! The Tale of Peter Rabbit,* where characters giggle, speak, wiggle, and move when kids touch them.

Apple mania became a global phenomenon. For example, in Tokyo's Ginza shopping district, more than a thousand people lined up to buy the iPad—counting down the final seconds before the Apple store opened. Apple sees a big opportunity in Asia, especially in China, where the middle class is growing quickly. Apple found Chinese consumer behavior different than in the West. Most Chinese buy iPhones based on word-of-mouth; they especially like to buy what their friends or people they admire own. So Apple's marketing strategy has focused on getting key opinion leaders and celebrities to use the iPhone.

Not everyone is satisfied with Apple's products. When the iPhone 4S was announced, a key feature was Siri, a digital personal assistant. Apple's television ads touted how Siri recognized customers' voice commands and suggested restaurants, took notes, and even made appointments—just by asking Siri to perform the task. Some customers were disappointed when the digital assistant didn't perform as advertised; some even sued Apple. But Apple's biggest fans ignored Siri's flaws; their selective perception had them focused on the iPhone's superior camera, faster processor, and new apps. And subsequent versions of Siri improved.

Other customers' attitudes toward Apple changed with reports of poor working conditions at some of Apple's Chinese suppliers. These issues were particularly distressing to Apple's core customers, who tend to be well-educated and particularly sensitive to social and environmental issues. Apple started monitoring its supply chain more closely and joined the Fair Labor Association, which works to improve working conditions around the world, helping to alleviate customer concerns.

Samsung, Amazon, Microsoft, and Google are just some of the big competitors that want a piece of Apple's pie. All this competition means new features and more choices for consumers, but it also complicates the consumer decision process for buyers of new phones and tablet computers. For Apple to build on its successes, it must continue to identify new and better ways to meet customer needs.[1]

Learning Objectives

Many variables influence consumer buying behavior. As the Apple case highlights, successful marketing strategy planning requires a clear understanding of how target consumers buy—and what factors affect their decisions. The learning objectives for this chapter will help you develop that understanding.

When you finish this chapter, you should be able to:

1 describe how economic needs influence the buyer decision process.

2 understand how psychological variables affect an individual's buying behavior.

3 understand how social influences affect an individual's buying behavior.

4 explain how characteristics of the purchase situation influence consumer behavior.

5 explain the process by which consumers make buying decisions.

6 understand important new terms (shown in red).

Consumer Behavior: Why Do They Buy What They Buy?

The Apple case shows the in-depth customer knowledge needed for effective marketing strategy planning. Without that understanding, it would be difficult to zero in on the right target market, or to develop and adapt a marketing mix that will be the best value for customers.

Understanding consumer behavior can be a challenge. Specific behaviors vary a great deal for different people, products, and purchase situations. In today's global markets the variations are countless. That makes it impractical to catalog all the possibilities. But there are general behavioral principles—frameworks—that marketing managers can apply to better understand their specific target markets. In this chapter our approach focuses on developing your skill in working with these frameworks by exploring thinking from economics, psychology, sociology, and other behavioral disciplines. We'll take a look at the topics overviewed in Exhibit 5-1, which includes a simplified model of consumer behavior.

We will begin with a discussion of influences on the consumer decision process: economic needs, psychological variables, social influences, and the purchase situation. Exhibit 5-2 provides an expanded look at these influences. Following our discussion of these different categories of influences, we will look more closely at the consumer decision process. We conclude the chapter with a discussion of consumer behavior in international markets.

Economic Needs Affect Most Buying Decisions

LO 5.1

Economic buyers seek the best uses of time and money

Most economists assume that consumers are **economic buyers**—people who know all the facts and logically compare choices to get the greatest satisfaction from spending their time and money. The economic-buyer theory says that consumers decide what to buy based on **economic needs**, which are concerned with making the best use of a consumer's

Exhibit 5–1 Consumer Behavior for Marketing Strategy Planning

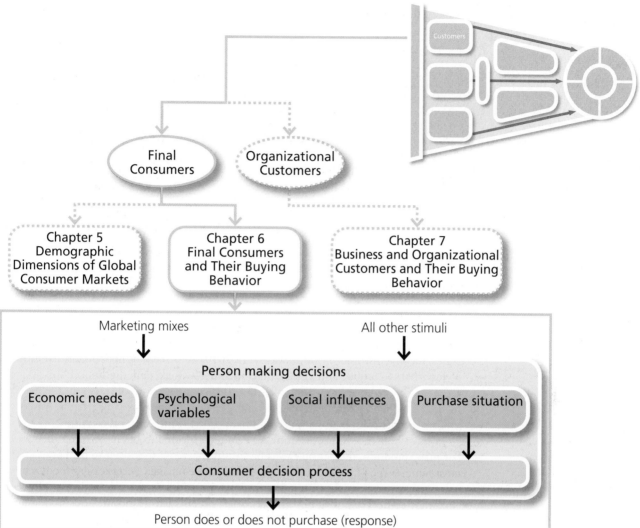

time and money—as the consumer judges it. Some consumers look for the lowest price. Others will pay extra for convenience. And others may weigh price and quality for the best value. Some economic needs are

1. Economy of purchase or use
2. Efficiency in operation or use
3. Dependability in use
4. Improvement of earnings
5. Convenience

Clearly, marketing managers must be alert to new ways to appeal to economic needs. Most consumers appreciate firms that offer them improved economic value for the money they spend. But improved value does not just mean offering lower and lower prices. For example, products can be designed to work better, require less service, or last longer. Promotion can inform consumers about product benefits in terms of measurable factors like operating costs, the length of the guarantee, or the time a product will save. Carefully planned Place decisions can make it easier and faster for customers who face a poverty of time to make a purchase.

Many firms adjust their marketing mixes for target markets that place a high value on convenience. Whole Foods Market sells more takeout food than most restaurants. Tide-to-Go is an instant stain remover that fits easily in a purse or briefcase and requires no water. A growing number of consumers like the convenience of online shopping at Zappos.

Exhibit 5–2 A Model of Influences on Consumer Behavior

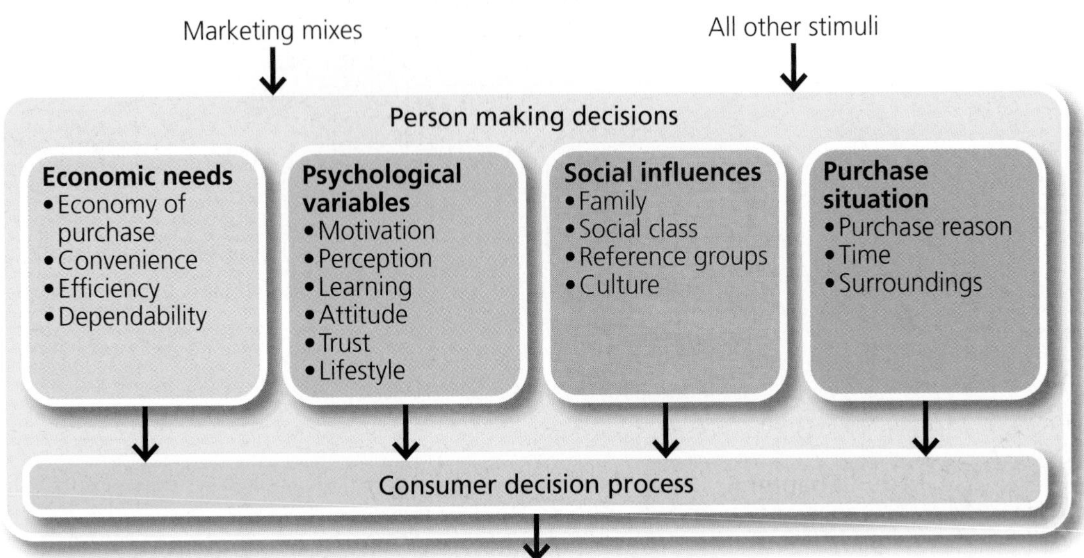

Income affects needs

The ability to satisfy economic needs largely depends on how much money a consumer has available—which in turn depends a great deal on household income. In the United States, income distribution varies widely. In 2010, 20 percent of households had income of less than $20,000, and the median income—where half the households earned more and half earned less—was $49,445. After taking account of inflation, the median income declined 7 percent in the previous decade. During this same period, America's middle-income consumers have been hit hard by the rising costs of necessities.

In most households, people don't have enough income to buy everything they want. For many products, these people can't be customers even if they want to be. For example, most families spend a good portion of their income on such necessities as food, rent or house payments, home furnishings, transportation and insurance. A family's purchase of "luxuries" comes from **discretionary income**—what is left of income after paying taxes and paying for necessities.

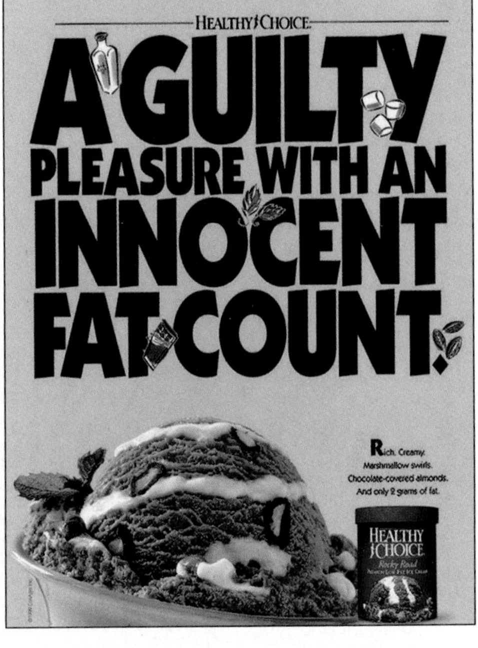

Economic needs affect many buying decisions, but for some purchases the behavioral influences on a consumer are more important.

Discretionary income is an elusive concept because the definition of necessities varies from family to family and over time. It depends on what they think is necessary for their lifestyle. High-speed Internet service purchased out of discretionary income by a lower-income family may be considered a necessity by a higher-income family.[2]

Consumer confidence affects spending

Economic conditions affect consumer confidence and spending. In a strong economy, consumers feel confident and secure in their jobs, so they are more likely to borrow money to buy a larger house, a new car, or vacation in an exotic locale. On the other hand, when consumers worry about job prospects or their retirement savings decline, they are more cautious spenders.

Economic value and income are important factors in many purchase decisions. But most marketing managers think that buyer behavior is not as simple as the economic-buyer model suggests. So let's look more closely at the psychological variables that influence buying behavior. See Exhibit 5-2.

Psychological Influences within an Individual

LO 5.2

Needs motivate consumers

Everybody is motivated by needs and wants. **Needs** are the basic forces that motivate a person to do something. Some needs involve a person's physical well-being, others the individual's self-view and relationship with others. Needs are more basic than wants. **Wants** are "needs" that are learned during a person's life. For example, everyone needs water or some kind of liquid, but some people also have learned to want Clearly Canadian's raspberry-flavored sparkling water on the rocks.

When a need is not satisfied, it may lead to a drive. The need for liquid, for example, leads to a thirst drive. A **drive** is a strong stimulus that encourages action to reduce a need. Drives are internal—they are the reasons behind certain behavior patterns. In marketing, a product purchase results from a drive to satisfy some need.

Some critics imply that marketers can somehow manipulate consumers to buy products against their will. But trying to get consumers to act against their will is a waste of time. Instead, a good marketing manager studies what consumer drives, needs, and wants already exist and how they can be satisfied better.

Whether a product is a want or a need depends on what a consumer has learned during his/her life.

Consumers seek benefits to meet needs

We're all a bundle of needs and wants. Exhibit 5-3 lists some important needs that might motivate a person to some action. This list, of course, is not complete. But thinking about such needs can help you see what *benefits* consumers might seek from a marketing mix.

When a marketing manager defines a product-market, the needs may be quite specific. For example, the food need might be as specific as wanting a Domino's thick-crust pepperoni pizza—delivered to your door hot and ready to eat.

Several needs at the same time

Consumer psychologists often argue that a person may have several reasons for buying—at the same time. Maslow is well known for his five-level hierarchy of needs. We will discuss a similar four-level hierarchy that is easier to apply to consumer behavior.

Exhibit 5–3 Possible Needs Motivating a Person to Some Action

Types of Needs	Specific Examples			
Physiological needs	Food Sex	Rest Liquid	Activity Self-preservation	Sleep Warmth/coolness
Psychological needs	Nurturing Playing-relaxing Self-identification	Curiosity Order Power	Independence Personal fulfillment Pride	Love Playing-competition Self-expression
Desire for . . .	A better world Acceptance Affiliation Esteem Knowledge	Respect Status Achievement Appreciation Sympathy	Beauty Happiness Self-satisfaction Variety Affection	Companionship Distinctiveness Recognition Sociability Fun
Freedom from . . .	Fear Pain	Depression Stress	Loss Sadness	Anxiety Illness

Exhibit 5-4 illustrates the four levels along with an example showing how a company has tried to appeal to each need. The lowest-level needs are physiological. Then come safety, social, and personal needs.[3]

Physiological needs are concerned with biological needs—food, liquid, rest, and sex. **Safety needs** are concerned with protection and physical well-being (perhaps involving health, financial security, medicine, and exercise). Marketers that offer *solutions* to consumer problems build brand loyalty. Charmin addressed such a need for holiday shoppers in New York City. Because it can be difficult to find a public restroom—and coffee shops don't like it when noncustomers use their facilities—Charmin's "holiday gift to the City" was luxury public restrooms located in Times Square. Many users will remember Charmin's gift the next time they buy toilet tissue.

Social needs are concerned with love, friendship, status, and esteem—things that involve a person's interaction with others. Marketers that help people *connect* with others inspire positive feelings about their own brands. Coca-Cola addressed this need with a series of viral videos around the theme of delivering happiness. One featured a bright red Coca-Cola truck that stopped on streets in Brazil. A sign on the back of the truck told consumers to "Push" a large button. When they did, the truck dispensed happiness in the form of Cokes and fun items like t-shirts, soccer balls, and even a surfboard. The truck created on-the-street social connections. The fun video created more social connection when viewers forwarded a link to friends and family.

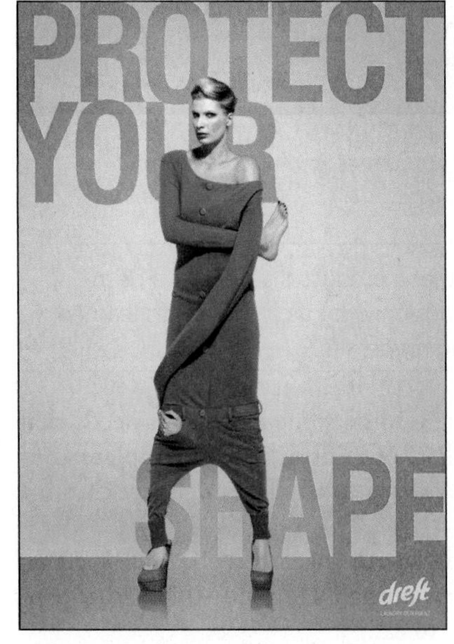

Most products must fill more than one need at the same time. Dreft detergent cleans clothes but also makes sure they don't stretch in the washing process.

Personal needs, on the other hand, are concerned with an individual's need for personal satisfaction—unrelated to what others think or do. Examples include accomplishment, fun, freedom, and relaxation—as well as a desire to make the world a better place. Many people want to make food choices that enable them to achieve a healthier balance in their lives. So ConAgra Foods (maker of healthy foods like SmartPop! Popcorn and Egg Beaters) developed an online tool to help. Members complete a survey at "Start Making Choices" and then receive feedback and advice on nutrition, activity, and well-being based on a calculated "Balanced Life Index." Weekly contact between the company and its customers keeps the relationship alive.

Often marketing managers are able to address multiple needs. Consider the California Milk Processing Board (creators of "Got Milk?") and its online game—"Get the Glass." The game appealed to kids—the group that needs milk the most—and, besides being fun, it educated players on why milk is important (personal needs). It could be played with family—or forwarded to friends (social needs). Of course drinking milk addresses thirst (physiological needs) and promotes strong bones (safety needs). In the online game's first two months, more than 6 million people visited the site with 650,000

Exhibit 5–4 The PSSP Hierarchy of Needs

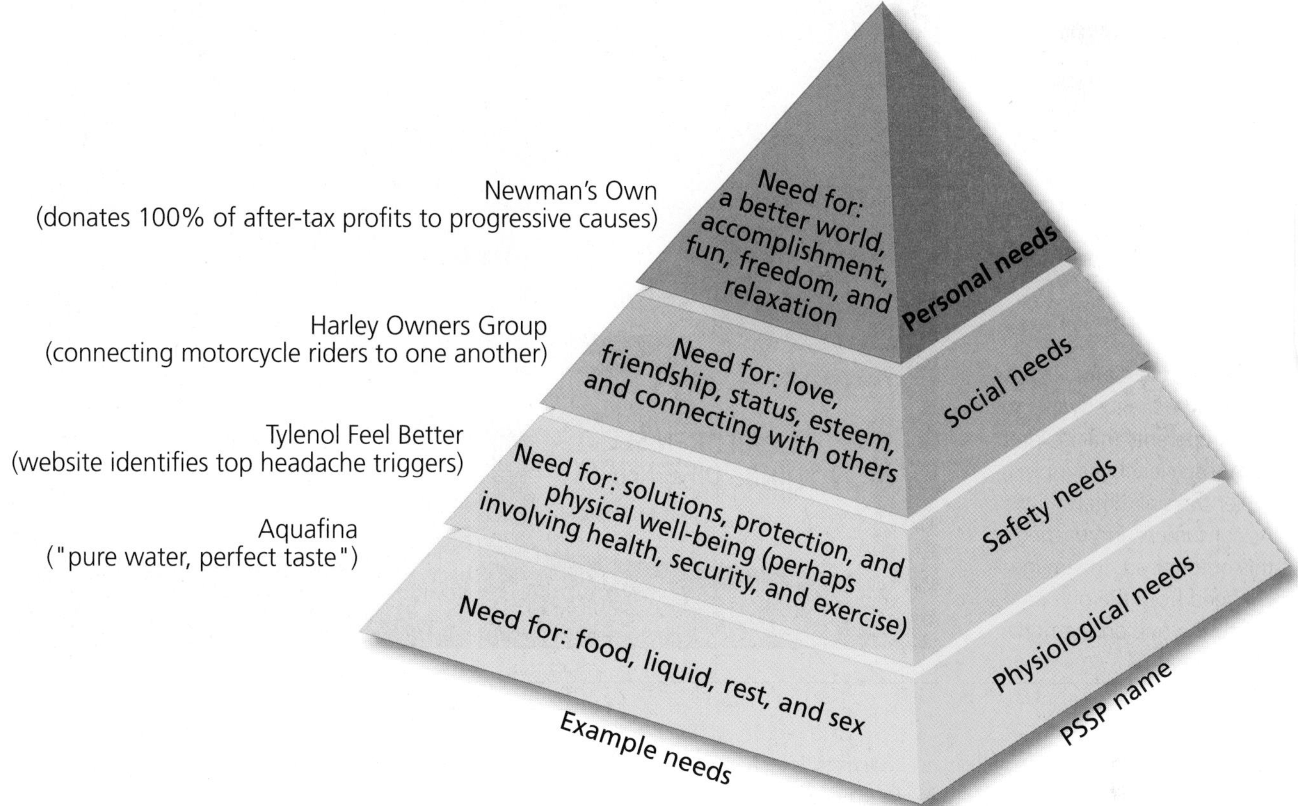

reaching the Glass at Fort Fridge. The game was credited with helping boost sales of milk by more than 10 million gallons compared to the same period a year earlier.[4]

Perception determines what consumers see and feel

Consumers select varying ways to meet their needs sometimes because of differences in **perception**—how we gather and interpret information from the world around us.

We are constantly bombarded by stimuli—ads, products, stores—yet we may not hear or see anything. This is because we apply the following selective processes:

1. **Selective exposure**—our eyes and minds seek out and notice only information that interests us. How often have you closed a pop-up ad at a website without even noticing what it was for?
2. **Selective perception**—we screen out or modify ideas, messages, and information that conflict with previously learned attitudes and beliefs.
3. **Selective retention**—we remember only what we want to remember.

These selective processes help explain why some people are not affected by some advertising—even offensive advertising. They just don't see or remember it! Even if they do, they may dismiss it immediately. Some consumers are skeptical about advertising messages in general.

These selective processes are stronger than many people realize. For example, to make their positioning efforts memorable, many companies use a common slogan ("tag line") on all of their ads. However, when researchers showed consumers the tag lines for 22 of the biggest advertisers (each spending over $100 million a year), 16 were recognized by less than 10 percent of the consumers.[5]

Our needs affect these selective processes. And current needs receive more attention. For example, Goodyear tire retailers advertise some sale in the newspaper almost weekly. Most of the time we don't even notice these ads. Only when we need new tires do we tune in to Goodyear's ads.

The Consumer Safety Institute in the Netherlands wants to remind parents that children see those cleaning supplies under the sink differently. As consumers approached this outdoor ad, the image changed from the one on the left to the one on the right (and back).

CHILDREN SEE THINGS DIFFERENTLY
PREVENT ACCIDENTS. READ THE LABEL.
CHILDREN SEE THINGS DIFFERENTLY
PREVENT ACCIDENTS. READ THE LABEL.
The ad shows two different images when viewed from different angles (lenticular effect).

Learning determines what response is likely

Learning is a change in a person's thought processes caused by prior experience. Learning is often based on direct experience: A little girl tastes her first cone of Ben & Jerry's Cherry Garcia flavor ice cream, and learning occurs! Learning may also be based on indirect experience or associations. If you watch an ad that shows other people enjoying Ben & Jerry's Chocolate Fudge Brownie low-fat frozen yogurt, you might conclude that you'd like it too.

Consumer learning may result from things that marketers do, or it may result from stimuli that have nothing to do with marketing. Either way, almost all consumer behavior is learned.[6]

Experts describe a number of steps in the learning process. We've already discussed the idea of a drive as a strong stimulus that encourages action. Depending on the **cues**—products, signs, ads, and other stimuli in the environment—an individual chooses some specific response. A **response** is an effort to satisfy a drive. The specific response chosen depends on the cues and the person's past experience.

Reinforcement of the learning process occurs when the response is followed by satisfaction—that is, reduction in the drive. Reinforcement strengthens the relationship between the cue and the response. And it may lead to a similar response the next time the drive occurs. Repeated reinforcement leads to development of a habit—making the individual's decision process routine. Exhibit 5-5 shows the relationships of the important variables in the learning process.

Exhibit 5–5
The Learning Process

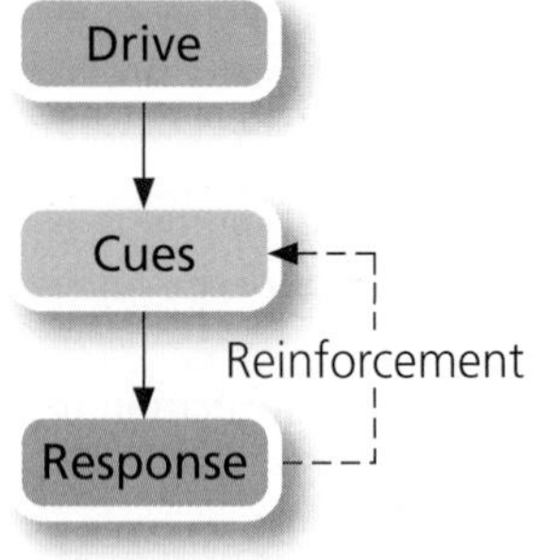
Drive
Cues
Reinforcement
Response

Sales take off after Febreze learns a lesson

Marketing managers for Febreze used the learning process to develop a best-selling product, but first they had to get the drive, cue, response, and reinforcement just right. Febreze contains a chemical very effective at eliminating odors—spray it on clothing, furniture, or carpet and smells magically disappear. Febreze's marketing managers figured that most consumers desired a home free of offensive odors (drive), so the first television ads for Febreze focused on smells around the house. For example, one showed a dog on a couch and a woman saying "Sophie will always smell like Sophie, but now my couch doesn't have to" (cue). In the ad, the woman sprays Febreze on the couch (response), and the dog smell disappears (reinforcement).

In spite of the advertising, when Febreze was first introduced, it sold poorly. To learn why, marketing researchers interviewed customers in their homes. They discovered two problems. First, many people living in the smelliest homes simply didn't realize their homes smelled at all. They had become desensitized to the smells of their pets, cigarette smoke, or other odors, so for them, the desired cue didn't exist. Second, what Febreze provided—lack of a smell—didn't provide positive reinforcement for the customer.

So Febreze's marketing managers went back to the drawing board. They interviewed more customers and reviewed video tape of people cleaning their homes. They identified another market, people who wanted a clean house (drive). When they saw a messy home (cue), they cleaned the house (response) and finished by rewarding themselves with something relaxing or happy—maybe just a smile (reinforcement). Here marketing managers realized that a scented version of Febreze might provide positive reinforcement—something that could signal the cleaning job was done. So Febreze added scents and new advertising that showed homemakers spraying a room with Febreze after cleaning (reinforcement). Sales took off; now Febreze sells more $1 billion a year. And Febreze's marketing managers learned a valuable lesson.[7]

Many needs are culturally learned

Many needs are culturally (or socially) learned. The need for food, for instance, may lead to many specific food wants. Many Japanese enjoy sushi (raw fish), and their children learn to like it. Fewer Americans, however, have learned to enjoy it.

Some critics argue that marketing efforts encourage people to spend money on learned wants totally unrelated to any basic need. For example, Germans are less concerned about perspiration, and many don't buy or use antiperspirants. Yet Americans spend millions of dollars on such products. Advertising says that using Ban deodorant "takes the worry out of being close." But is marketing activity the cause of the difference in the two cultures? Most research says that advertising can't convince buyers of something contrary to their basic attitudes.

Attitudes relate to buying

An **attitude** is a person's point of view toward something. The "something" may be a product, an advertisement, a salesperson, a firm, or an idea. Attitudes are an important topic because they affect the selective processes, learning, and the buying decisions.

Because attitudes are usually thought of as involving liking or disliking, they have some action implications. Beliefs are not so action-oriented. A **belief** is a person's opinion about something. Beliefs may help shape a consumer's attitudes but don't necessarily involve any liking or disliking. It is possible to have a belief—say, that Listerine PocketPak strips have a medicinal taste—without really caring what they taste like. On the other hand, beliefs about a product may have a positive or negative effect in shaping consumers' attitudes. For example, promotion for Splenda, a no-cal sweetener in a yellow packet, informs consumers that it's "made from sugar so it tastes like sugar." A dieter who believes that Splenda will taste better because it is made from sugar might try it instead of just routinely rebuying another brand, like Equal. On the other hand, a person with diabetes might believe that he

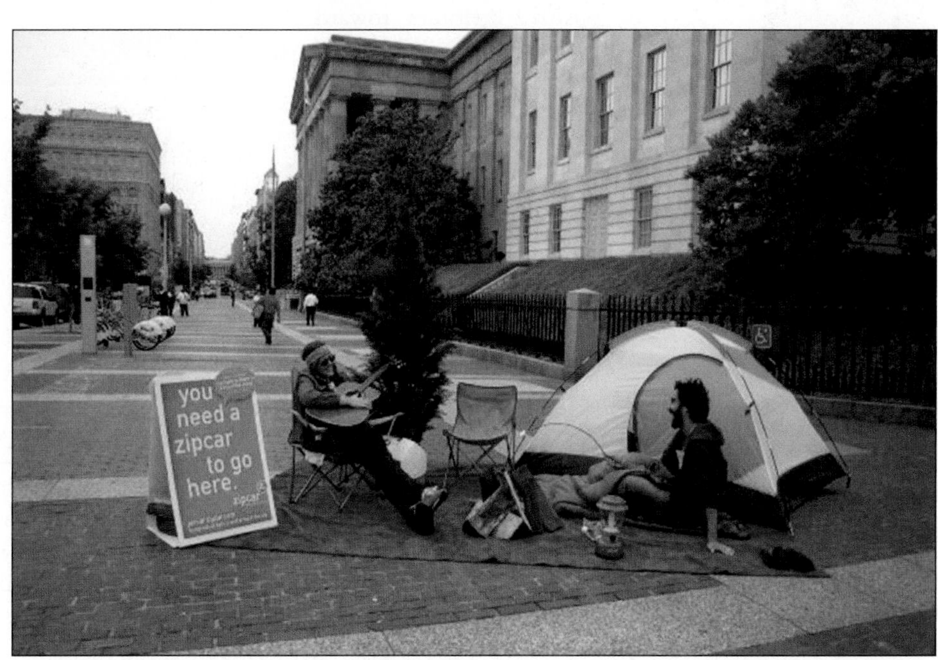

Zipcar appeals to urban consumers who do not have their own car. For three weeks in Washington, DC, Zipcar set up installations (like the one shown here) to change consumer attitudes about renting a car to get out of town.

"WOULD YOU CARE MORE
IF I WAS A PANDA?"
WWF

Consumer attitudes can affect their purchasing (and donating) behavior. The World Wildlife Fund knows consumers have more favorable attitudes toward panda bears as compared to bluefin tuna—but both species are endangered and need support.

should avoid Splenda—like he avoids other products made from sugar—even though Splenda is actually suitable for people with diabetes.[8]

In an attempt to relate attitude more closely to purchase behavior, some marketers stretch the attitude concept to include consumer "preferences" or "intention to buy." Managers who must forecast how much of their brand customers will buy are particularly interested in the intention to buy. Forecasts would be easier if attitudes were good predictors of intentions to buy. Unfortunately, the relationships usually are not that simple. A person may have positive attitudes toward GPS navigation systems for cars, but no intention of buying one.

"Green" attitudes and beliefs change marketing mixes

A growing number of consumers believe that making "greener" purchases has a positive effect on the environment. Marketing managers have responded by developing marketing mixes to address these ecological interests. Subway sandwich shops have added recycling bins. GM and Nissan introduced all-electric cars. Malt-O-Meal breakfast cereals, a low-cost brand that has always been packaged in bags, touted the environmental benefits of this packaging. Its "Bag the Box" campaign garnered publicity on a small budget. Many consumers have positive attitudes toward brands that try to make a difference in this area.[9]

Most marketers work with existing attitudes

Because consumer attitudes tend to be enduring, it's usually more economical for marketers to work with them than try to change them. Changing negative attitudes is probably the most difficult job marketers face.[10]

Ethical issues may arise

Part of the marketing job is to inform and persuade consumers about a firm's offering. An ethical issue sometimes arises, however, if consumers have *inaccurate* beliefs. For example, promotion of a "children's cold formula" may play off parents' fears that adult medicines are too strong—even though the basic ingredients in the children's formula are the same and only the dosage is different.

Internet Exercise

Climate Counts is a nonprofit organization that provides information to help consumers make choices that have a positive impact on the planet. Go to the Climate Counts website (**www.climatecounts.org**), click on the "Climate Scores" link, choose a market sector, and compare the different companies. Do you think this information will affect how *consumers* behave? Do you think the information will affect how *companies* behave? What will be the effect on consumer and company behavior if some consumers use Twitter to tweet ratings, or e-mail to share ratings with others?

Zipcar—saving money and the environment

Evolving needs, attitudes, and lifestyles are creating opportunities for new transportation services. Many consumers, whether captivated by the green movement or simple economics, want to give up their cars—but some have trouble handing over their keys.

Zipcar offers a solution. It provides a car-sharing service that's now available in dozens of big cities across the United States, Canada, and the U.K. Car-sharing saves both money and time. With monthly payments, insurance, parking, gas, depreciation, and maintenance, the cost of car ownership averages $8,000 a year. City dwellers face the additional hassle of finding parking and worrying about theft. Zipcar's rates vary by city, but average $10 an hour or $70 a day. That's a big difference from car ownership!

Zipcar has worked hard to make car-sharing easy and fun. Signing up is simple—go online, fill out an application, and pay your $50 annual membership fee. Zipcar checks the applicant's driving record—and if he passes, a Zipcard arrives in his mail a few days later. Renting a car is even simpler. A member (called a Zipster) simply logs on to Zipcar's website to find cars in his area and make a reservation. Because cars are typically parked on a street, in gas stations, or in parking lots throughout the city, they're easy to locate and usually nearby. At the reserved time, the Zipster simply waves his Zipcard (with embedded radio frequency identification technology) or his smartphone with a Zipcar app at the car and it automatically unlocks. Grab the keys from beneath the steering wheel, turn the ignition and you're ready to go.

Zipcar has identified different market segments and localized a marketing mix for each group. Some big city neighborhoods appreciate the environmental benefits. Here, most prefer driving a smaller and more economical car like a Toyota Prius or Mini Cooper when they visit a friend, though some want the convenience of a hatchback on a shopping trip. They're proud of the Zipcar logo on the car doors—it shows their green side and fellow Zipsters wave when they drive by.

Zipsters in more upscale neighborhoods are offered a selection of Volvos and BMWs. Zipcar found these customers usually borrow cars for a big night out or to head to the beach for the weekend. And they don't like (so they don't get) the green sign on the car door.

You can also find Zipcars on more than 250 college campuses—where students often don't have a regular need for a car and almost always have difficulty with parking. Spreading a dozen Zipcars—like Scion xBs and Honda Insight hybrids—across campus reduces the need for more than a hundred parking spaces. In tight economic times, campus administrations have responded enthusiastically to a program that reduces traffic and parking problems.

Zipcar is growing quickly by providing an economical and environmentally friendly solution to today's transportation needs. More and more Zipsters are learning a new way to get around—and they're having fun doing it.[11]

Marketers must also be careful about promotion that might encourage false beliefs, even if the advertising is not explicitly misleading. For example, ads for Ultra Slim-Fast low-fat beverage don't claim that anyone who buys the product will lose weight and look like the slim models who appear in the ads—but some critics argue that the advertising gives that impression.

Ethics Question

You are a marketing assistant for Auntie Em's Cookie Company, which makes and distributes packaged cookies through grocery stores. Your company recently ran a test market for a new brand of low-fat cookies called Tastee DeeLites. The new brand meets government standards to be labeled and advertised as "low fat," so the ads and package used in the test market highlighted that benefit. Test-market sales were very promising. However, now a consumer activist group has created a website (www.TasteeDeLIES.com) that claims Tastee DeeLites package and ads are misleading because the product's high calories make it even more fattening than most other cookies. Your boss has asked you to recommend how Auntie Em's should handle this situation. Drawing on what you've learned about consumer behavior, do you think consumers are being misled? Does your company have any responsibility to respond to these charges? Should changes be made to the product, package, or promotion?

Meeting expectations is important

Attitudes and beliefs sometimes combine to form an **expectation**—an outcome or event that a person anticipates or looks forward to. Consumer expectations often focus on the benefits or value that the consumer expects from a firm's marketing mix. This is an important issue for marketers because a consumer is likely to be dissatisfied if his or her expectations are not met. Promotion that overpromises can create this problem. Finding the right balance, however, can be difficult. A few years ago Van Heusen came up with a new way to treat its wash-and-wear shirts so that they look better when they come out of the wash. Van Heusen promoted these shirts as "wrinkle-free." The new shirt is an improvement, but consumers who expect it to look as if it had been ironed are disappointed.[12]

Building consumer trust builds sales

Trust is the confidence a person has in the promises or actions of another person, brand, or company. Trust drives expectations, because when people trust, they *expect* the other party to fulfill promises or perform capably.

Customers may come to trust through experience with a company or person. For example, if your dog always happily chows down Purina dog food—and remains healthy and active—you might come to trust the Purina brand. A customer might trust a travel agent who previously planned enjoyable vacations for her family. Trust can also relate to recommenders—for example, many consumers trust *Consumer Reports* magazine and put a lot of stock in its product reviews and ratings.

Highly trusted people, brands, and companies have many advantages in the marketplace. Consumers prefer to buy from and are more loyal to brands they trust. Trusted brands are less susceptible to price-based competition. For example, few people would switch from a trusted hair stylist just to save a few dollars.

Trust can be very important in some purchase situations. For example, when a busy executive needs a package to arrive somewhere in short order, he is more likely to request a shipper he trusts. Because FedEx is usually ranked near the top in surveys of most trusted brands, it's likely that our busy executive will choose it to make that delivery. Similarly, when buying a family car, many shoppers want a very safe and reliable car. While many car companies make this claim, customers must decide which brand they believe will really deliver. For many years Toyota had a strong reputation in this area, but reports of unintended acceleration caused many customers to lose trust in the carmaker. Trust can be fragile and companies must work to maintain the customer trust that has been built—sometimes over many decades.[13]

Psychographics focus on activities, interests, and opinions

Psychographics or **lifestyle analysis** is the analysis of a person's day-to-day pattern of living as expressed in that person's Activities, Interests, and Opinions—sometimes referred to as AIOs. Exhibit 5-6 shows a number of variables for each of the AIO dimensions—along with some demographics used to add detail to the lifestyle profile of a target market.

Understanding the lifestyle of target customers has been especially helpful in providing ideas for advertising themes. Let's see how it adds to a typical demographic description. It may not help Hyundai marketing managers much to know that an average member of the

Exhibit 5–6
Lifestyle Dimensions (and some related demographic dimensions)

Dimension	Examples		
Activities	Work Hobbies Social events	Vacation Entertainment Club membership	Surfing web Shopping Sports
Interests	Family Home Job	Community Recreation Fashion	Food Media Achievements
Opinions	Themselves Social issues Politics	Business Economics Education	Products Future Culture
Demographics	Income Age Family life cycle	Geographic area Ethnicity Dwelling	Occupation Family size Education

Schwann's home delivery of food products and complete meals appeals to dual-career families and professionals who place a high value on their time.

target market for a Veracruz CUV is 34.8 years old, married, lives in a three-bedroom home, and has 2.3 children. Lifestyles help marketers paint a more human portrait of the target market. For example, lifestyle analysis might show that the 34.8-year-old is also a community-oriented consumer with traditional values who especially enjoys spectator sports and spends much time in other family activities. An ad might show the Veracruz being used by a happy family at a ball game so the target market could really identify with the ad. And the ad might be placed on an ESPN show whose viewers match the target lifestyle profile.[14]

Marketing managers for consumer products firms who are interested in learning more about the lifestyle of a target market sometimes turn to outside specialists for help. For example, Strategic Business Insights, a research firm, offers a service called geoVALS (VALS is an abbreviation for values, attitudes, and lifestyles). GeoVALS uses psychographics to show where customers live and why they behave as they do; it is especially useful for targeting direct-mail ad campaigns.[15]

Internet Exercise

The VALS survey described in the text can be taken at the Strategic Business Insights website (**www.strategicbusinessinsights.com/vals/presurvey.shtml**). Read about VALS, and then complete the survey. What is your primary and secondary VALS type? Do you think it accurately describes you?

Social Influences Affect Consumer Behavior

LO 5.3

We've been discussing some of the ways needs, attitudes, and other psychological variables influence the buying process. Now we'll look at how a consumer's family, social class, reference groups, culture, and ethnic groups influence the consumer decision process.

Family life cycle influences needs

Relationships with other family members influence many aspects of consumer behavior. Family members may share many attitudes and values, consider each other's opinions, and divide various buying tasks. Marital status, age, and the age of any children in the family have an especially important effect on how people spend their income. Put together, these dimensions tell us about the life-cycle stage of a family. Exhibit 5-7 shows a summary of stages in the family life cycle. Let's take a closer look at how a few of these stages influence buying behavior.

Young people and families accept new ideas

Singles and young couples seem to be more willing to try new products and brands—and they are careful, price-conscious shoppers. Although many young people are waiting longer to marry, most tie the knot eventually. These younger families—especially those with no children—are still accumulating durable goods, such as automobiles and home furnishings. Only as children arrive and grow does family spending shift to soft goods and services, such as education, medical, and personal care. To meet

Exhibit 5–7 Stages in Modern Family Life Cycles

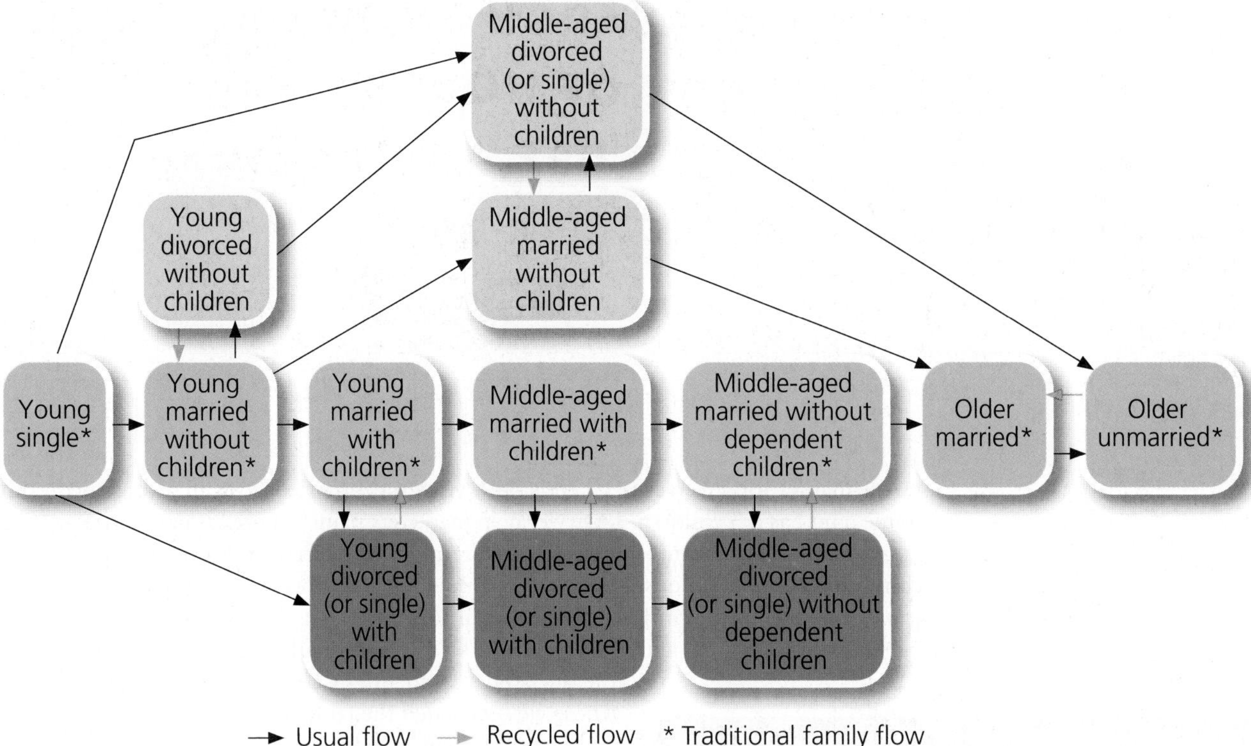

expenses, people in this age group often make more purchases on credit, and they save less of their income.[16]

Divorce—increasingly a fact of American life—disrupts the traditional family life-cycle pattern. The mother usually has custody of the children, and the father may pay child support. The mother and children typically have much less income than two-parent families. Such families spend a larger portion of their income on housing, child care, and other necessities leaving little for discretionary purchases. If a single parent remarries, the family life cycle may start over again.[17]

Growing singles market

The singles market is growing. With more people choosing to remain single and others getting divorced, more Americans and Europeans now live alone. In the U.S., more than a quarter of all households consist of just one person, while in some cities, including Washington D.C., Seattle, and Atlanta, the number is over 40%. This trend creates opportunities for more than just builders of apartment buildings and condominiums. Ikea has seen growth in product lines designed for small space living, Norwegian Cruise Lines now offers studio staterooms for single travelers, and Lowe's has an ad showing a single woman renovating her bathroom.[18]

Reallocation for teenagers

Once children become teenagers, further shifts in spending occur. Teenagers eat more, want to wear expensive clothes, like music, and develop recreation and education needs that are hard on the family budget. American teens currently spend almost $200 billion a year. They are a target for many firms; Bausch & Lomb's contact-lens sales hit record levels when the firm refocused its marketing efforts on teens.[19]

Selling to the empty nesters

Another important category is the **empty nesters**—people whose children are grown and who are now able to spend their money in other ways. This tends to be a high-income period, especially for white-collar workers. Empty nesters are an attractive market for many items. Often they spend more on travel and other things they couldn't afford earlier in life. Much depends on their income, of course.[20]

Who is the real decision maker in family purchases?

In years past, most marketers in the United States targeted the wife as the family purchasing agent. Now, with sex-role stereotypes changed and with night and weekend shopping more popular, men and older children take more responsibility for shopping and decision making. Family roles vary from one culture to another.

Buying responsibility and influence vary greatly depending on the product and the family. Although often only one family member goes to the store for a specific purchase, other family members may influence the decision or really decide what to buy. Still others may use the product. A lot of kids just have to have a Burger King hamburger because they really want the "free" crown.[21]

Social class affects attitudes, values, and buying

Up to now, we've been concerned with individuals and their family relationships. Now let's consider how society looks at an individual and perhaps the family—in terms of social class. A **social class** is a group of people who have approximately equal social position as viewed by others in the society.

Almost every society has some social class structure. In most countries, social class is closely related to a person's occupation, but it may also be influenced by education, community participation, where a person lives, income, possessions, social skills, and other factors—including what family a person is born into.

In most countries—including the United States—there is *some* general relationship between income level and social class. But people with the same income level may be in different social classes. So income by itself is usually not a good measure of social class. And people in different social classes may spend, save, and borrow money in very different ways.

The U.S. class system is far less rigid than those in most countries. Children start out in the same social class as their parents—but they can move to a different social class depending on their education and job. By contrast, India's social structure is much more rigid, and individuals can't easily move up in the class system.

Marketers want to know what buyers in various social classes are like. In the United States, simple approaches for measuring social class groupings are based on a person's *occupation, education,* and *type and location of housing.* By using marketing research surveys or available census data, marketers can get a feel for the social class of a target market.

What do these classes mean?

While many people think of America as a middle-class society, studies suggest that in many marketing situations distinctive social class groups do exist. Various classes shop at different stores. They prefer different treatment from salespeople. They buy different brands of products—even though prices are about the same. And they have different attitudes toward spending and saving—even when they have the same income level.

Reference groups help people form attitudes

A **reference group** is the people to whom an individual looks when forming attitudes about a particular topic. People normally have several reference groups for different topics. Some they meet face-to-face; others they just wish to imitate—for example, performers or

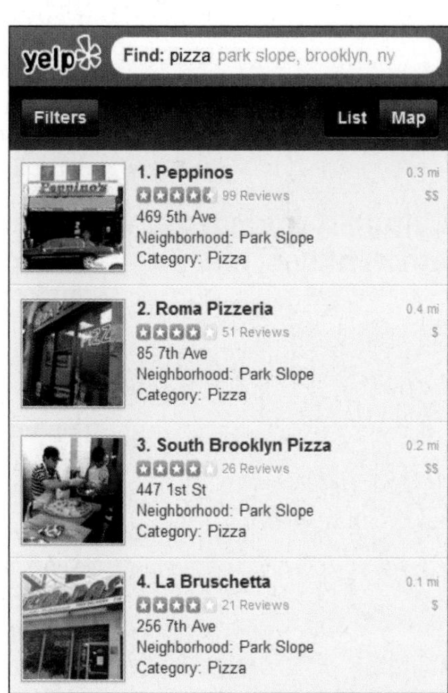

Consumers often look to other consumers for buying advice. Yelp's website and cell phone app allow consumers to rate and read reviews of restaurants, nightlife, auto repair shops and much more.

athletes. In either case, they may take values from these reference groups and make buying decisions based on what the group might accept.

Reference influence is stronger for products that others "see" and which relate to status in the group. For example, while one group might view owning a fur coat as a sign of "having arrived," a group of animal lovers may see the same purchase as bad judgment.[22]

Marketing managers often target opinion leaders because they influence others. The Syfy television network wants advertisers to know that many of its viewers are opinion leaders.

Opinion leaders influence buyers

An **opinion leader** is a person who influences others. Opinion leaders aren't necessarily wealthier or better educated. And opinion leaders on one subject aren't necessarily opinion leaders on another. For example, you may have a friend who is ahead of the curve in knowing about videogames, but you might not want that friend's opinion about new clothing styles and cosmetics.

Some marketing mixes aim especially at opinion leaders, since their opinions affect others and they have many product-related discussions with "followers." The Internet has helped some opinion leaders get more followers and therefore more influence. For example, some moms have had great success writing blogs that attract tens of thousands of readers. They often blog about products they like—and don't like. Kodak identified 10 influential "mommy bloggers" with whom it wanted to work. The bloggers then used their blogs to promote a contest where readers wrote a story about one of their photos. The winner received a new Kodak HD Camera—and Kodak got a lot of positive publicity.

Marketing managers must also be wary of online opinion leaders. They can be quick to let their followers know when they don't like a marketing mix. Motrin had to pull an advertisement after thousands of bloggers and Twitter tweets attacked one of its ads as demeaning to mothers.[23]

Culture surrounds the other influences

Culture is the whole set of beliefs, attitudes, and ways of doing things of a reasonably homogeneous set of people. In this chapter, as well as Chapter 3, we look at the broad impact of culture.

We can think of the American culture, the French culture, or the Chinese culture. People within these cultural groupings tend to be more similar in outlook and behavior. But often it is useful to think of subcultures within such groupings. For example, within the American culture, there are various religious, ethnic, and regional subcultures.

Failure to consider cultural differences, even subtle ones, can result in problems. To promote their product and get people to try it, marketers for Pepto-Bismol often provide free samples at festivals and street fairs. Their idea is that people tend to overindulge at such events. However, when they distributed sample packets at a festival in San Francisco's Chinatown, they insulted many of the people they wanted to influence. Booths with Chinese delicacies lined the streets, and many of the participants interpreted the sample packets (which featured the word "Nauseous" in large letters) as suggesting that Chinese delicacies were nauseating. The possibility of this misinterpretation may seem obvious in hindsight, but if it had been that obvious in advance the whole promotion would have been handled differently.[24]

Do ethnic groups buy differently?

America may be called the melting pot, but ethnic groups deserve special attention when analyzing markets. One basic reason is that people from different ethnic groups may be influenced by very different cultural variables. They may have quite varied needs and their own ways of thinking. Moreover, Americans value diversity and the United States is becoming a multicultural market. As a result, rather than disappearing in a melting pot, some important cultural and ethnic dimensions are being preserved and highlighted. This creates both opportunities and challenges for marketers.

Stereotypes are common—and misleading

A marketer needs to study ethnic dimensions very carefully because they can be subtle and fast-changing. This is also an area where stereotyped thinking is the most common—and misleading. Many firms make the mistake of treating all consumers in a particular ethnic group as homogeneous. For example, some marketing managers treat all 39.9 million African American consumers as "the black market," ignoring the great variability among African American households on other segmenting dimensions.

Ethnic markets are becoming more important

More marketers pay attention to ethnic groups now because the number of ethnic consumers is growing at a much faster rate than the overall society. Much of this growth results from immigration. In addition, however, the median age of Asian Americans, African Americans, and Hispanics is much lower than that of whites—and the birthrate is higher. In combination, these factors have a dramatic effect.

The buying power of ethnic submarkets is also increasing rapidly. Estimates indicate that Hispanics and African Americans each spend more than $1 trillion a year and Asian Americans over $500 billion a year. It's also important to marketers that much of this buying power is concentrated in certain cities and states, which makes targeted promotion and distribution more efficient. For example, over 20 percent of San Francisco residents are Asians.

Hispanic market is growing

Let's take a closer look at Hispanic Americans. Hispanics are the largest and fastest growing ethnic group in the United States. In 2010, the Hispanic population was about 50.5 million and made up 16.3 percent of the total U.S. population—up from 35.3 million and 12.5 percent in 2000. We can expect more growth because in 2010, 23.1 percent of all children under age 18 were Hispanic. Their relative youth and the growth potential suggest the Hispanic market offers marketing opportunities.[25]

Many companies are responding to this trend. For example, Wells Fargo branches in the Southwest have added Latin-style decor, bicultural tellers, and Spanish-language promotion. Efforts such as these have significantly increased Wells Fargo's business. P&G found Hispanic consumers like using fragrances in their homes and developed Febreze Destinations Collections, a line of air fresheners targeting this market. The growth is reflected in media that targets Hispanics, too. ESPN Deportes (Spanish for "ESPN Sports")—a 24-hour cable television channel and companion website—focus on the particular interests of the Hispanic sports fan.

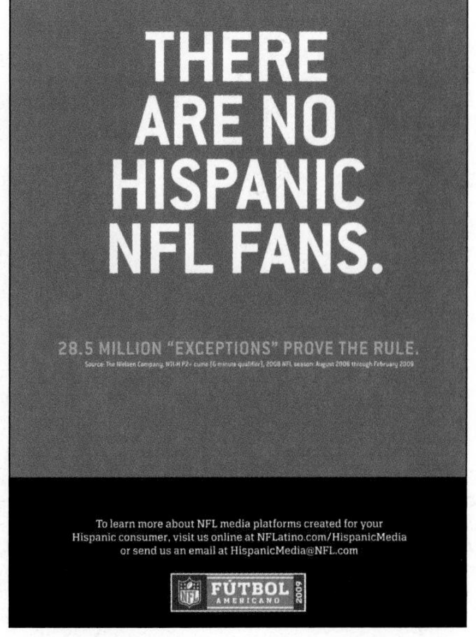

Many firms are developing strategies to appeal to the fast-growing Hispanic market. Goya wants to let grocers know that demand for Coconut Milk spikes during the holidays because it is a vital part of many Hispanic celebrations. The National Football League wants to dispel common wisdom that Hispanics are not fans of "American" football.

Asian American market grows fast, too

While there are fewer Asian Americans (about 14.4 million in 2010 and 4.6 percent of the population), the number has more than tripled since 1980. Asian Americans have the highest median family income ($64,308) of the major ethnic groups. Because of this growth and income, companies as varied as Kraft, Walmart, and Allstate are targeting these consumers, especially in California, New York, and Texas, where half the Asian American population is concentrated.[26]

Culture varies in international markets

Planning strategies that consider cultural differences in international markets can be even harder—and such cultures usually vary more. Each foreign market may need to be treated as a separate market with its own submarkets. Ignoring cultural differences—or assuming that they are not important—almost guarantees failure in international markets.

Consider the situation faced by marketers as they introduced Swiffer, the fast-selling wet mop, in Italy. Research showed that Italian women wash their floors four times more often than Americans. Based on that, you might predict a big success for Swiffer in Italy. Yet many new cleaning products flop there. Fortunately, the research suggested a reason. Many Italians have negative attitudes about ad claims that a product makes cleaning *easier*. This is a popular appeal in the United States, but many Italian women doubt that something that works easily will meet their standards for cleanliness. So for the Italian market Swiffer was modified and beeswax was added to polish floors after they have been mopped. Now Swiffer is a top seller in Italy.[27]

Individuals Are Affected by the Purchase Situation

LO 5.4

Purchase reason can vary

Why a consumer makes a purchase can affect buying behavior. For example, a student buying a pen to take notes might pick up an inexpensive Bic. But the same student might choose a Cross pen as a gift for a friend. And a gadget-lover with some free time on his hands might buy a digital pen that transfers handwritten notes to a tablet computer—just for the fun of trying it.

Consumer behavior varies with situational factors. Buying gifts is one situational factor—BoConcept tries to make gift buying easier with a range of selections. Time pressure can also influence purchasing behavior. Groupon offers its members great deals—but most of the bargains are only available for purchase for one or two days.

Time affects what happens

Time influences a purchase situation. *When* consumers make a purchase—and the time they have available for shopping—will influence their behavior. Socializing with friends at a Starbucks induces different behavior than grabbing a quick cup of 7-Eleven coffee on the way to work.

The urgency of the need is another time-related factor. A sports buff who needs a digital video recorder with an "instant replay" feature in time for the Super Bowl—that evening—might spend an hour driving across town in heavy traffic to get the right unit. In a different circumstance, the same person might order a unit online from a website and figure that the extra time for it to be shipped is well worth the money saved.

Surroundings affect buying too

Surroundings can affect buying behavior. The excitement at an on-site auction may stimulate impulse buying. Checking out an auction online might lead to a different response. Consider how the warehouse-like setting in a Sam's Club store signals low-cost operations and price reductions.[28]

Needs, benefits sought, attitudes, motivation, and even how a consumer selects certain products all vary depending on the purchase situation. So different purchase situations may require different marketing mixes—even when the same target market is involved.

The Consumer Decision Process

LO 5.5

The model in Exhibit 5-2 organizes the many different influences on consumer behavior. It helps explain *why* consumers make the decisions they make. Now, we'll expand that model with a closer look at the steps in the consumer decision process and a focus on *how* consumers make decisions.[29] See Exhibit 5-8.

Recognizing a need creates a problem for the consumer

The consumer decision process begins when a consumer becomes aware of an unmet need. The consumer's problem-solving process then focuses on how best to meet that need. Problem recognition often happens quickly. A student on the way to class, for example, may realize that she's thirsty and wants something to drink. Or problem recognition may

Exhibit 5–8 An Expanded Model of Consumer Behavior

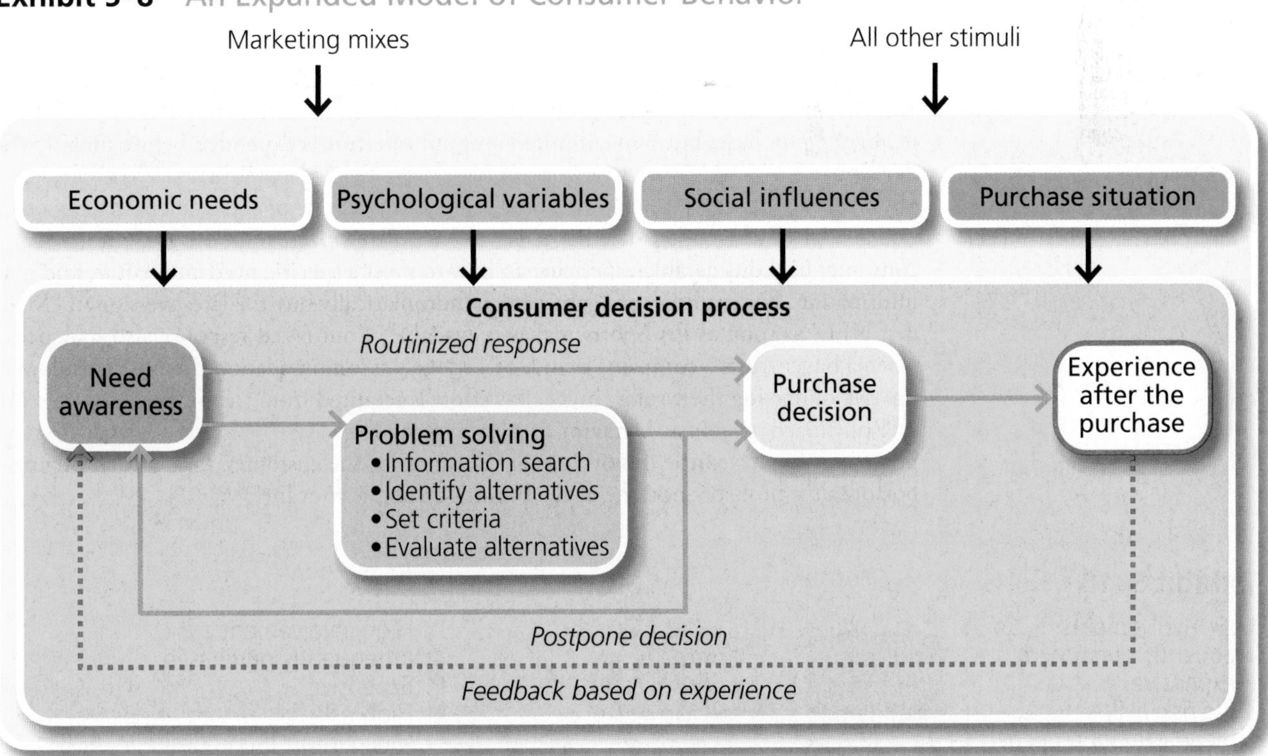

take shape over time. For example, a recent grad with a new apartment might want a comfortable place to sit while watching TV in the evening. These situations present problems that may be solved with a purchase. But what purchase should it be?

Three levels of problem solving are useful

How a consumer solves the problem depends on the situation. Exhibit 5-9 highlights the basic problem-solving steps a consumer may go through to satisfy a need. A consumer may search for information, identify alternatives, decide what factors (criteria) are important, and then evaluate one or more alternative products that meet the need. These activities may require a lot of time and effort on the part of a consumer, very little time, or be skipped altogether.

Exhibit 5–9 Consumer Problem Solving

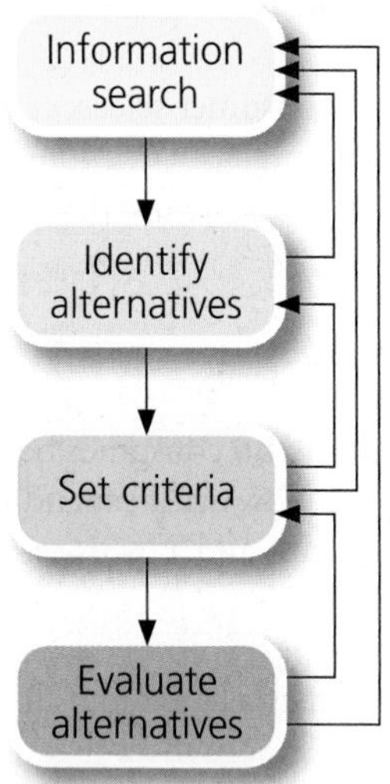

How much effort is put into a buying decision depends in part on the economic needs, psychological variables, social influences, and purchase situation factors discussed earlier in this chapter. It's also tied to the amount of risk a buyer sees in making a wrong choice. For instance, when a buyer has little involvement in the purchase or the expense is small, a poor buying decision will result in little financial or social risk. Under these circumstances the buyer usually puts little effort into the buying decision. On the other hand, when a buyer is highly involved and cares deeply about the choice, or when the price is high, there may be more risk in making a bad decision. So the buyer often extends more effort in order to be more confident. Exhibit 5-10 suggests three levels of problem solving that relate to the amount of effort the buyer puts into the decision.

Consumers use **extensive problem solving** when they put much effort into deciding how to satisfy a need—as is likely for a completely new purchase or to satisfy an important need. For example, an avid computer "gamer" may put a great deal of effort into buying a new gaming computer. Our gamer might solicit friends' opinions about the graphics speed and audio quality for different models before going online to compare options and prices and read technical reviews. Then, the gamer might visit a local store for a hands-on demo of a favorite game on a few computers. To narrow down to a final choice, the gamer could evaluate customer-service support and warranties. This is certainly not an impulse purchase! The decision to buy—and what to buy—comes only after an extensive effort.

Limited problem solving is used by consumers when *some* effort is required in deciding the best way to satisfy a need. This is typical when the consumer has some previous experience with a product but isn't quite sure which choice to make at the moment. A seasoned computer gamer, for instance, may already know that he likes sports games and what store has the newest releases. At the store he might get the salesperson's advice and check out the video quality on a few games before deciding which to buy. This is a deliberate purchase, but only a limited amount of effort is expended before making the decision.

A consumer uses **routinized response behavior** when he or she regularly selects a particular way of satisfying a need when it occurs. Routinized response is typical when a consumer has considerable experience in how to meet a specific need and requires no new information. For example, our gamer might automatically buy the latest version of "Madden NFL" as soon as EA Sports makes it available. Routinized response also may occur when a buyer trusts a company, brand, or a friend's recommendation. Because trust lowers the risk of making the wrong choice, less effort is required from the buyer.

Routinized response behavior is also typical for **low-involvement purchases**—purchases that have little importance or relevance for the customer. Let's face it, buying a box of salt is probably not one of the burning issues in your life.[30]

Exhibit 5–10 Problem-Solving Continuum

Low involvement
Frequently purchased
Inexpensive
Little risk
Little information needed

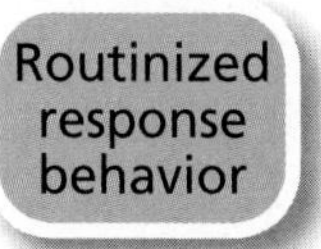

Limited problem solving

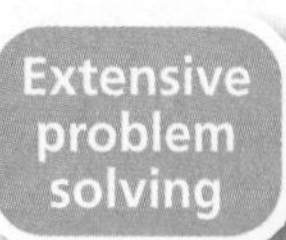

High involvement
Infrequently purchased
Expensive
High risk
Much information desired

Buying isn't always rational

The idea of a decision process does *not* imply that consumers always apply *rational* processes in their buying decisions. To the contrary, consumers don't always seek accurate information or make smart choices that provide the best economic value. This is often because of the influences on consumer behavior that we discussed earlier in the chapter. For example, most sport utility vehicles never leave the paved road, but buyers like the image of driving an SUV and *knowing* they can get off the paved road if they want to. When a tourist spends 1,000 euros on a Loewe leather purse, it may simply be that she loves the style, can afford it, and "has to have it." Needs are operating in such a purchase, but they are higher-level needs and not some sort of functional "requirement."

Consumers can have second thoughts after a purchase

After making a purchase, buyers often have second thoughts and wonder if they made the right choice. The resulting tension is called **dissonance**—a feeling of uncertainty about whether the correct decision was made. (In layman's terms, "buyer's remorse.") This may lead a customer to seek additional information to confirm the wisdom of the purchase.[31]

Post-purchase regret is a bigger problem

Sometimes uncertainty isn't the issue. Rather the consumer is certain about being unhappy with a purchase. When a post-purchase experience fails to live up to expectations, a customer will be disappointed. For example, going out for an expensive dinner—and then getting slow service and cold food—results in considerable dissatisfaction and regret over the choice. The diner is much less likely to visit that restaurant again. A consumer may regret making a purchase for a variety of reasons that the consumer didn't anticipate when making the purchase. But, whatever the reason, regret is not likely to lead to the same decision in the future.

Some consumers spread the word after they buy

Many consumers talk about their purchases and share opinions about their good and bad experiences. Recommendations from friends can have a big influence on whether we try a new restaurant, buy a hybrid car, or choose a different dentist. Consumers are even more likely to share stories about being dissatisfied than satisfied. This is important for a marketer to remember. At times, his or her career might call for countering negative publicity—damage control—to save a product's image.

The Internet gives people a forum to share their opinions with a large audience. Many people rely on such information in making purchase choices. For example, online audiobook retailer Audible.com's customers often use reviews by other listeners to help make selections. A recent study revealed that more than a fourth of Google search results on the top 20 brands link to consumer opinions. However, sometimes information posted by consumers isn't accurate—and that can be a real headache for marketers.[32]

New concepts require an adoption process

When consumers face a really new concept, their previous experience may not be relevant. These situations involve the **adoption process**—the steps individuals go through on the way to accepting or rejecting a new idea. Although the adoption process is similar to the decision-making process, learning plays a clearer role and promotion's contribution to a marketing mix is more visible.

In the adoption process, an individual moves through some fairly definite steps:

1. *Awareness*—the potential customer comes to know about the product but lacks details. The consumer may not even know how it works or what it will do.
2. *Interest—if* the consumer becomes interested, he or she will gather general information and facts about the product.
3. *Evaluation*—a consumer begins to give the product a mental trial, applying it to his or her personal situation.
4. *Trial*—the consumer may buy the product to experiment with it in use. A product that is either too expensive to try or isn't available for trial may never be adopted.
5. *Decision*—the consumer decides on either adoption or rejection. A satisfactory evaluation and trial may lead to adoption of the product and regular use. According to psychological learning theory, reinforcement leads to adoption.
6. *Confirmation*—the adopter continues to rethink the decision and searches for support for the decision—that is, further reinforcement.[33]

Dropbox had to work with the adoption process when it introduced cloud storage—an idea that was not familiar to many computer users. Dropbox lets users create a file folder on their devices—say their laptop, tablet, or smartphone—and share it with the others. For example, if a consumer places a photo, song, or document in the Dropbox folder on their laptop, it would automatically be replicated on their phone and tablet computer. The file is also backed up on the Internet. Furthermore, folders can also be shared with friends or work colleagues.

Dropbox first targeted techies, who are comfortable with technology. The techies quickly downloaded Dropbox because it filled a need, since these users tend to have many digital devices. Dropbox came with 2 GB of online storage. To encourage early customers to spread *awareness* and *generate* interest in Dropbox, they were given additional storage space for each person they referred to Dropbox. Many techies found good value in Dropbox and were happy to spread the word. A video on its website demonstrated how Dropbox works, making it easy for customers to *evaluate* its usefulness to them. The software was easy to install and it was free, making *trial* easy, too. As others used Dropbox, many began to share files with friends, family, and co-workers. This acted as *confirmation* and *reinforced* their decision. Some customers use the service so much they pay for additional storage space.

Consumer Behavior in International Markets

All the influences interact—often in subtle ways

You're a consumer, so you probably have very good intuition about the many influences on consumer behavior that we've been discussing. That's good, but it's also a potential trap—especially when developing marketing mixes for consumers in international markets. The less a marketing manager knows about the *specific* social and intrapersonal variables that shape the behavior of target customers, the more likely it is that relying on intuition or personal experience will be misleading. Many specific influences do not generalize from one culture to another.

Consider the experiences some brands have had in China. Mattel shuttered its Barbie stores in China; they discovered that Chinese parents want studious daughters, an image they don't see in Barbie. Home Depot closed about half of its stores after finding that not enough Chinese were into do-it-yourself projects. When Oreo cookies first came to China, they sold the same round black and white cookies popular in the United States. Sales were modest and the cookies were almost pulled out of the market. After conducting market research, Oreo's flavor and later its shape were changed. Oreo is now the best-selling cookie in China.[34]

Sometimes an understanding of local cultural influences points to new ways to blend the four Ps. For example, Nestlé knew that free samples would be a good way to kick-start the adoption process when it wanted to introduce a new line of food flavorings in Brazil. In the United States, it's common to distribute samples at stores. But local Nestlé managers knew a more effective approach. In Brazil, cooks rely on stoves that run on gas rather than electricity, so local deliverymen regularly bring canisters of gas into consumers' kitchens. Nestlé paid the deliverymen to offer their customers samples of the flavorings and explain how to use them. Consumers showed more interest in the samples when the conversation usually took place with someone they trusted right by the stove where the flavorings would be used.[35]

Watch out for stereotypes, and social changes

Consumers in a foreign culture may be bound by some similar cultural forces, but that doesn't mean that they are all the same. So it's important to watch out for oversimplifying stereotypes. Further, changes in the underlying social forces may make outdated views irrelevant.

In Saudi Arabia, McDonald's modifies its marketing mix to adapt to the local culture. For example, the McDonald's in Riyadh is segregated by sex, with a separate section for women and children.

Developing a marketing mix that really satisfies the needs of a target market takes a real understanding of consumer behavior and the varied forces that shape it. So when planning strategies for international markets, it's best to involve locals who have a better chance of understanding the experiences, attitudes, and interests of your customers.

CONCLUSION

In this chapter, we analyzed the individual consumer as a problem solver who is influenced by economic needs, psychological variables, social influences, and the purchase situation. We showed how these variables influence the consumer decision process, what the steps in that process are, and why it is important to consider these steps when planning a marketing strategy. For example, we discussed three levels of problem solving that you can use to evaluate how consumers approach different types of purchase decisions. We also discussed how the consumer's experience after the purchase impacts what that consumer will do in the future.

From a broader perspective, this chapter makes it clear that each consumer and purchase decision is somewhat unique. So it isn't possible to catalog all of the individual possibilities. Rather, the overall focus of this chapter is to provide you with general frameworks that you can use to analyze consumers regardless of what the particular product or decision may be. This also helps you to identify the dimensions of consumer behavior that are most important for segmenting the market and developing a targeted marketing mix.

By now it should be clear that expensive marketing errors can be made when you assume that other consumers will behave in the same manner as you or your family and friends. That's why we rely on the social and behavior sciences for insight about consumer behavior in general and why marketing research is so important to marketing managers when they are developing a marketing strategy for a particular target market. When managers understand how and why consumers behave the way they do, they are better able to develop effective marketing mixes that really meet the needs of their target market.

KEY TERMS

LO 5.6

economic buyers, 118
economic needs, 118
discretionary income, 120
needs, 121
wants, 121
drive, 121
physiological needs, 122
safety needs, 122
social needs, 122
personal needs, 122
perception, 123
selective exposure, 123
selective perception, 123
selective retention, 123
learning, 124
cues, 124
response, 124
reinforcement, 124
attitude, 125
belief, 125
expectation, 128
trust, 128
psychographics, 128
lifestyle analysis, 128
empty nesters, 130
social class, 131
reference group, 131
opinion leader, 132
culture, 132
extensive problem solving, 136
limited problem solving, 136
routinized response behavior, 136
low-involvement purchases, 136
dissonance, 137
adoption process, 137

QUESTIONS AND PROBLEMS

1. In your own words, explain economic needs and how they relate to the economic-buyer model of consumer behavior. Give an example of a purchase you recently made that is consistent with the economic-buyer model. Give another that is not explained by the economic-buyer model. Explain your thinking.
2. Explain what is meant by a hierarchy of needs and provide examples of one or more products that enable you to satisfy each of the four levels of need.
3. Cut out or photocopy two recent advertisements: one full-page color ad from a magazine and one large display ad from a newspaper. In each case, indicate to which needs the ads appeal.
4. Explain how an understanding of consumers' learning processes might affect marketing strategy planning. Give an example.
5. Briefly describe your own *beliefs* about the potential value of low-energy compact fluorescent lightbulbs, your *attitude* toward them, and your *intention* about buying one the next time you need to replace a bulb.
6. Give an example of a recent purchase experience in which you were dissatisfied because a firm's marketing mix did not meet your expectations. Indicate how the purchase fell short of your expectations—and also explain whether your expectations were formed based on the firm's promotion or on something else. Will it affect how much you trust that firm or brand in the future?
7. Explain psychographics and lifestyle analysis. Explain how they might be useful for planning marketing strategies to reach college students, as opposed to average consumers.
8. A supermarket chain is planning to open a number of new stores to appeal to Hispanics in southern California. Give some examples that indicate how the four Ps might be adjusted to appeal to the Hispanic subculture.
9. How should social class influences affect the planning of a new restaurant in a large city? How might the four Ps be adjusted?
10. Illustrate how the reference group concept may apply in practice by explaining how you personally are influenced by some reference group for some product. What are the implications of such behavior for marketing managers?
11. Give two examples of recent purchases where the specific purchase situation influenced your purchase decision. Briefly explain how your decision was affected.
12. Give an example of a recent purchase in which you used extensive problem solving. What sources of information did you use in making the decision?
13. On the basis of the data and analysis presented in Chapter 5, what kind of buying behavior would you expect to find for the following products: (*a*) a haircut, (*b*) a shampoo, (*c*) a digital camera, (*d*) a tennis racket, (*e*) a dress belt, (*f*) a cell phone, (*g*) life insurance, (*h*) an ice cream cone, and (*i*) a new checking account? Set up a chart for your answer with products along the left-hand margin as the row headings and the following factors as headings for the columns: (*a*) how consumers would shop for these products, (*b*) how far they would travel to buy the product, (*c*) whether they would buy by brand, (*d*) whether they would compare with other products, and (*e*) any other factors they should consider. Insert short answers—words or phrases are satisfactory—in the various boxes. Be prepared to discuss how the answers you put in the chart would affect each product's marketing mix.
14. Review the model in Exhibit 5-2 and then reread the Apple case at the beginning of this chapter. List and briefly describe specific points in the case that illustrate the model.

15. Interview a friend or family member about two recent purchase decisions. One decision should be an important purchase, perhaps the choice of an automobile, a place to live, or a college. The second purchase should be more routine, such as a meal from a fast-food restaurant or a regularly purchased grocery item. For each purchase, ask your friend questions that will help you understand how the decision was made. Use the model in Exhibit 5-8 to guide your questions. Describe the similarities and differences between the two purchase decisions.

CREATING MARKETING PLANS

The Marketing Plan Coach software on the text website includes a sample marketing plan for Hillside Veterinary Clinic. Look through the "Customers" section and consider the following questions.

a. Based on the marketing plan, what do we know about the consumer behavior of the target market?
b. What additional information do you think would be helpful before developing a marketing strategy for Hillside?

SUGGESTED CASES

1. McDonald's "Seniors" Restaurant
3. NOCO United Soccer Academy
8. Besitti's Restaurant
9. Peaceful Rest Motor Lodge
10. Cooper's Ice Center
11. Running Room
12. DrJane.com—Custom Vitamins
30. Walker-Winkle Mills, Ltd.

COMPUTER-AIDED PROBLEM

5. SELECTIVE PROCESSES

Submag, Inc., uses direct-mail promotion to sell magazine subscriptions. Magazine publishers pay Submag $3.12 for each new subscription. Submag's costs include the expenses of printing, addressing, and mailing each direct-mail advertisement plus the cost of using a mailing list. There are many suppliers of mailing lists, and the cost and quality of different lists vary.

Submag's marketing manager, Shandra Debose, is trying to choose between two possible mailing lists. One list has been generated from phone directories. It is less expensive than the other list, but the supplier acknowledges that about 10 percent of the names are out-of-date (addresses where people have moved away.) A competing supplier offers a list of active members of professional associations. This list costs 4 cents per name more than the phone list, but only 8 percent of the addresses are out-of-date.

In addition to concerns about out-of-date names, not every consumer who receives a mailing buys a subscription. For example, *selective exposure* is a problem. Some target customers never see the offer—they just toss out junk mail without even opening the envelope. Industry studies show that this wastes about 10 percent of each mailing—although the precise percentage varies from one mailing list to another.

Selective perception influences some consumers who do open the mailing. Some are simply not interested. Others don't want to deal with a subscription service. Although the price is good, these consumers worry that they'll never get the magazines. Submag's previous experience is that selective perception causes more than half of those who read the offer to reject it.

Of those who perceive the message as intended, many are interested. But *selective retention* can be a problem. Some people set the information aside and then forget to send in the subscription order.

Submag can mail about 25,000 pieces per week. Shandra Debose has set up a spreadsheet to help her study effects of the various relationships discussed earlier and to choose between the two mailing lists.

a. If you were Debose, which of the two lists would you buy based on the initial spreadsheet? Why?
b. For the most profitable list, what is the minimum number of items that Submag will have to mail to earn a profit of at least $3,500?
c. For an additional cost of $.01 per mailing, Submag can include a reply card that will reduce the percent of consumers who forget to send in an order (Percent Lost—Selective Retention) to 45 percent. If Submag mails 25,000 items, is it worth the additional cost to include the reply card? Explain your logic.

CHAPTER SIX

Business and Organizational Customers and Their Buying Behavior

MetoKote Corp. specializes in protective coating applications, like powder-coat and liquid paint, that other manufacturers need for the parts and equipment they make. For example, when you see John Deere agricultural, construction, or lawn- and grounds-care equipment, many of the components have likely been coated (painted) in a MetoKote facility. In fact, Deere and MetoKote have a close buyer–seller relationship. While Deere uses a variety of methods to identify suppliers and get competitive bids for many items it needs, it's different with MetoKote. Deere isn't going to switch to some other supplier just because other options provide cheaper coatings. MetoKote not only provides protective coatings for many Deere products, it has built facilities right next to some Deere plants. When it's time for a component to be coated, a conveyer belt moves the part out of the Deere plant and into the MetoKote facility. A short time later it's back—and it's green or yellow.

Deere favors this type of arrangement. It lets MetoKote's experts keep up with all of the environmental regulations and new technologies for coatings.

For a manufacturer, this type of relationship allows its facilities to be smaller and less costly to build and maintain, as the space isn't required for large spray booths. With MetoKote's facilities located nearby, newly coated parts for Deere do not have to be shipped, resulting in fewer scratches and dents—which produces higher-quality parts with less rework required.

Many people were involved in the decision to purchase coating services in this way. The responsibility for choosing vendors didn't just rest with the purchasing department but involved input from people in finance, quality control, and in some cases even the production employees.

Deere needs high-quality protective finishes because its customers want durable, long-lasting equipment. Like Deere, they want good value—and Deere is known for delivering that.

Deere's reputation follows from its focus on helping customers and dealers earn higher profits. For example, some Deere farm equipment includes a global positioning device that tracks exactly where the equipment goes when it is plowing, seeding, or cutting. The company's GreenStar system, which can easily be moved from machine to machine, uses advanced technology to measure average farm and field yields and to facilitate documentation of tillage practices, planting, spraying, weather, and more. Another innovation in Deere's new cotton harvester inserts a radio frequency ID (RFID) tag as it spools a 4,750 pound bale of cotton fiber and then automatically wraps it in a plastic film. The RFID chip, combined with global positioning system (GPS) data, lets cotton processors trace the precise origin of each bale. They know, for instance, if the cotton was grown without pesticides and qualifies to be sold as organic. The plastic film eliminates the 20 percent drop in the quality of the cotton fiber that can result from water damage. Deere innovations like these can help a farmer make data-driven decisions, increase productivity, and add value to the entire farming operation.

John Deere sees big opportunities in South America where farms are growing food for the world. Brazil, for example, produces more than half of the world's orange juice—almost all for export. Farms in Brazil can be very large; a single farm might stretch over 200,000 acres and purchase millions of dollars in farm equipment each year. So when John Deere managers asked, farmers in Brazil responded that they wanted powerful tractors capable of hauling wider planters and other implements. The new 8R tractor costs more than other tractors on the market, but Brazilian farmers find it helps them get more done with fewer tractors and less labor. Those savings plus the greater reliability and durability of Deere equipment create value; John Deere sales in South America are growing more than 30 percent per year.

Deere's reputation for quality service is equally as important as the company's reputation for quality products. So Deere has streamlined distribution with the goal of giving customers and dealers better service. It's dropping dealers who don't measure up to its goals for customer satisfaction—and encouraging the dealers that remain to consolidate so that they will have economies of scale in purchasing, be able to afford more specialists in important areas like e-commerce, and be able to share inventory among multiple locations. Dealers appreciate that Deere set up the MachineFinder website and Facebook page, which help customers find used Deere equipment being sold by its dealers. Deere even finances used purchases through John Deere Credit.

Deere designs marketing strategies that solve particular customer problems. For example, golf course managers buy Deere equipment to maintain their fairways, greens, and sand traps because they value the reliability and durability of the brand's products. However, they also need a variety of operating supplies—ranging from grass seed and irrigation equipment to ball washers and chemicals. Golf course managers have many responsibilities besides purchasing, so Deere introduced its One Source service, which provides golf course managers with a "one-stop shop" for the things they need—all backed by the trusted Deere name. One Source saves time and strengthens Deere's relationships with both its dealers and their golf course customers. Of course, it creates new challenges for Deere's purchasing department. It must identify, evaluate, monitor, and recommend the suppliers for the products that golf courses need. Deere's dealers and golf course customers rely on Deere's purchasing specialists to make the right decisions, but that's part of the value that Deere provides.

Innovative approaches to delivering customer value make Deere the supplier of choice for many business customers.[1]

Learning Objectives

As the John Deere case illustrates, the buying behavior of organizational customers can be very different from the buying behavior of final consumers. Marketing strategy planning requires a solid understanding of who these organizational customers are and how they buy.

When you finish this chapter, you should be able to:

1. describe who the business and organizational buyers are.
2. see why business and organizational purchase decisions often involve multiple influences.
3. understand the problem-solving behavior of organizational buyers and how they get market information.
4. understand the different types of buyer–seller relationships and their benefits and limitations.
5. know about the number and distribution of manufacturers and why they are an important customer group.
6. know how buying by service firms, retailers, wholesalers, and governments is similar to—and different from—buying by manufacturers.
7. understand important new terms (shown in red).

Business and Organizational Customers—A Big Opportunity

LO 6.1

Most people think about an individual final consumer when they hear the term *customer*. But many marketing managers aim at customers who are not final consumers. In fact, more purchases are made by businesses and other organizations than by final consumers.

Business and organizational customers are any buyers who buy for resale or to produce other goods and services. There are many different types of organizational customers, including the following:

- *Producers of goods and services*—including manufacturers, farmers, real estate developers, hotels, banks, even doctors and lawyers
- *Intermediaries*—wholesalers and retailers
- *Government units*—federal agencies in the United States and other countries as well as state and local governments
- *Nonprofit organizations*—national organizations like the Red Cross and Girl Scouts as well as local organizations like museums and churches

As this suggests, not all organizational customers are business firms. Even so, they are sometimes loosely referred to as *business buyers, intermediate buyers,* or *industrial buyers*—and

Exhibit 6–1 Understanding Business and Organizational Customers for Marketing Strategy Planning

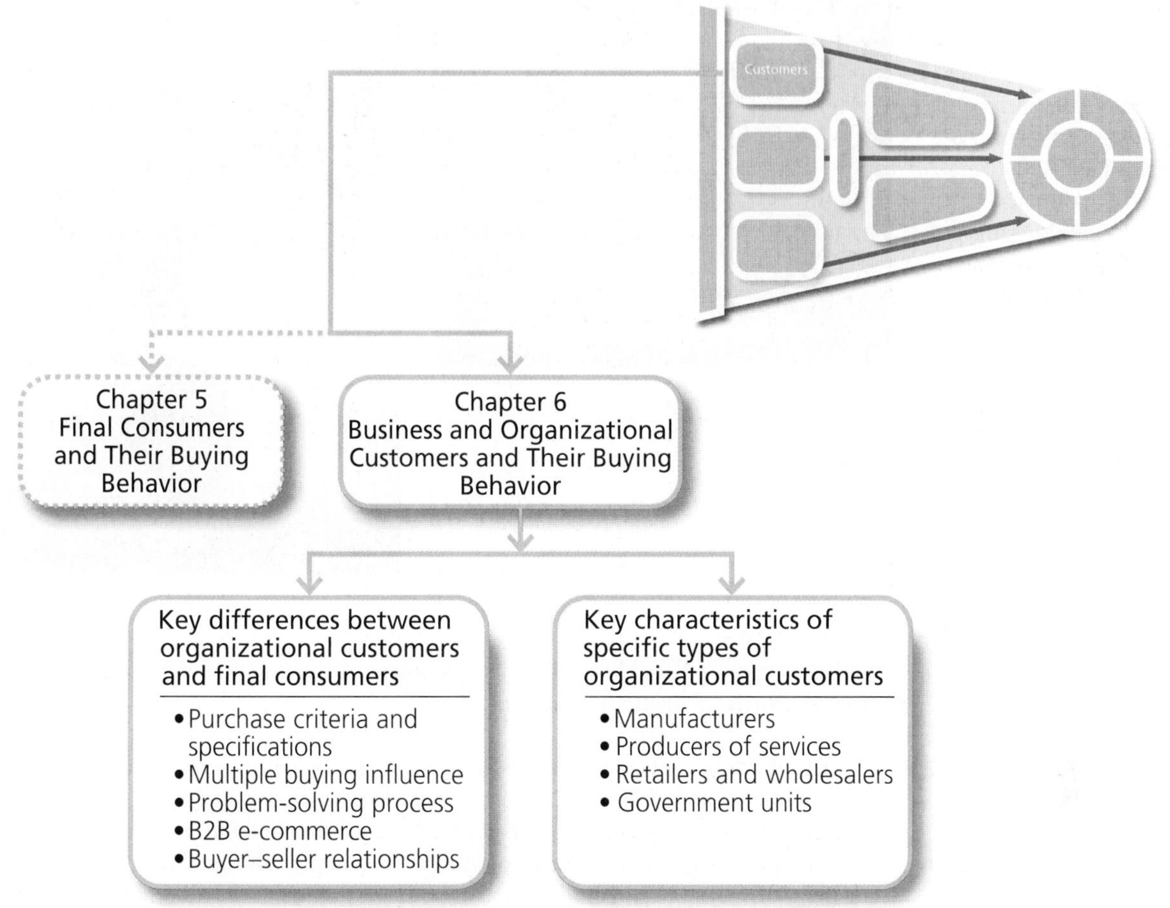

marketing managers often refer to organizational customers collectively as the "business-to-business" market, or simply, the *B2B market.*

In this chapter, we'll focus on organizational customers and their buying behavior. See Exhibit 6-1. In Chapter 5 we focused on buying by final consumers, so here we'll start by covering important ways that organizational buying tends to be different from buying by final consumers. Then, later in the chapter, we'll focus on some key differences among the specific types of organizational customers.

So keep in mind that, for many firms, marketing strategy planning is about meeting the needs of organizational customers, not final consumers. A firm can target both final consumers and organizations, but different marketing mixes may be needed. As you learn about the buying behavior of organizations, think about how a firm's marketing mix may need to be different and how it may be adjusted.

Organizational Customers Are Different

Organizations buy for a basic purpose

Like final consumers, organizations make purchases to satisfy needs. But it's often easier to understand an organization's needs because most organizations make purchases for the same basic reason. They buy goods and services that will help them meet the demand for the goods and services that they in turn supply to their markets. In other words, their basic need is to satisfy their own customers and clients. A producer buys because it wants to earn a profit by making and selling goods or services. A wholesaler or retailer buys

Promotion to organizational buyers often focuses on economic factors. Kyocera's ad, targeted at office and IT managers, promotes the long life, lower operating costs, and environmentally friendly nature of its business printers. As police departments seek ways to lower costs, T3 Motion's vehicles allow officers to cover more ground at much lower costs than if they were driving automobiles.

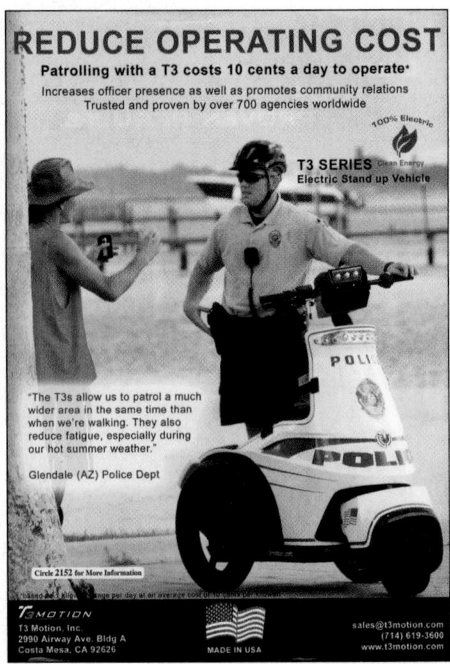

products it can profitably resell to its customers. A town government wants to meet its legal and social obligations to citizens.

Basic purchasing needs are economic

Organizations typically focus on economic factors when they make purchase decisions and are usually less emotional in their buying than final consumers.

Buyers try to consider the total cost of selecting a supplier and its particular marketing mix, not just the initial price of the product. For example, a hospital that needs a new type of digital X-ray equipment might look at both the original cost and ongoing costs, how it would affect doctor productivity, and, of course, the quality of the images it produces. The hospital might also consider the seller's reliability and its ability to provide speedy maintenance and repair.

The matter of dependability deserves further emphasis. An organization may not be able to function if purchases don't arrive when they're expected. For example, a manufacturer forced to shut down a production line because sellers haven't delivered the goods suffers far-reaching repercussions. Dependable product quality is important too. For example, a bug in e-commerce software purchased by a firm might cause the firm's online order system to shut down. The costs of finding and correcting the problem—to say nothing about the cost of the lost business—could be much greater than the original cost of the software.

Even small differences are important

Understanding how the buying behavior of a particular organization differs from others can be very important. Even seemingly trivial differences in buying behavior may be important because success often hinges on fine-tuning the marketing mix.

Sellers often approach each organizational customer directly, usually through a sales representative. This gives the seller more opportunities to tailor the marketing mix to each individual customer. A seller may even develop a unique strategy for each individual customer. This approach carries target marketing to its extreme. But sellers often need unique strategies to compete for large-volume purchases.

Serving customers in international markets

Many marketers discover that there are good opportunities to serve business customers in different countries around the world. Specific business customs do vary from one country to another—and the differences can be important. For example, while Americans often look to humor and small talk to build relationships, Russians expect seriousness in business settings. So when an American businessman visiting Russia to establish a partnership smiled frequently and cracked a few jokes, he was met with a dreary, unhappy response. Both the American and the Russian were trying to impress each other, but they didn't understand how to go about it.[2]

However, the basic approaches marketers use to deal with business customers in different parts of the world are much less varied than those required to reach individual consumers. This is probably why the shift to a global economy has been so rapid for many firms. Their business customers in different countries tend to buy in similar ways and can usually be reached with similar marketing mixes. Moreover, business customers are often willing to work with distant suppliers who have developed superior marketing mixes.

Specifications describe the need

Organizational buyers often buy on the basis of a set of **purchasing specifications**—a written (or electronic) description of what the firm wants to buy. When quality is highly standardized, as is often the case with manufactured items, the specification may simply consist of a brand name or part number. Often, however, the purchase requirements are more complicated; then the specifications may set out detailed information about the performance standards the product must meet. Purchase specifications for services tend to be detailed because services are less standardized and usually are not performed until after they're purchased.

Customers may expect quality certification

Organizational customers considering a new supplier or one from overseas may be concerned about product quality. However, this is becoming less of an obstacle because of ISO 9000. **ISO 9000** is a way for a supplier to document its quality procedures according to internationally recognized standards.

ISO 9000 assures a customer that the supplier has effective quality checks in place, without the customer having to conduct its own costly and time-consuming audit. Some customers won't buy from any supplier who doesn't have it. To get ISO 9000 certified, a company must prove to outside auditors that it documents how the company operates and who is responsible for quality every step of the way.[3]

Many Different People May Influence a Decision

LO 6.2

Purchasing managers are specialists

Many organizations rely on specialists to ensure that purchases are handled sensibly. These specialists have different titles in different firms (such as procurement officer, supply manager, purchasing agent, or buyer), but basically they are all **purchasing managers**—buying specialists for their employers. In large organizations, they usually specialize by product area and are real experts.

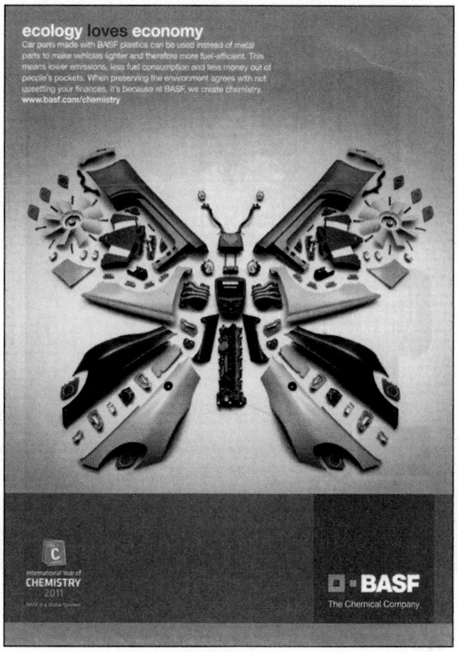

Some people think purchasing is handled by clerks who sit in cubicles and do the paperwork to place orders. That view is out of date. Today, most firms look to their procurement departments to help cut costs and provide competitive advantage. In this environment, purchasing people have a lot of clout. And there are good job opportunities in purchasing for capable business graduates.

Salespeople often have to see a purchasing manager first—before they contact any other employee. These buyers hold important positions and take a dim view of sales reps who try to go around them. Rather

BASF plastics can be used in automobile parts—replacing heavier metal parts. The lower weight can increase fuel efficiency. BASF personnel work with purchasing managers and engineers at automakers to determine where plastic parts offer the greatest benefit to the end user (car buyer).

than being "sold," these buyers want salespeople to provide accurate information that will help them solve problems and buy wisely. They like information on new goods and services, and tips on potential price changes, supply shortages, and other changes in market conditions. Sometimes all it takes for a sales rep to keep a buyer up to date is to send an occasional e-mail. But a buyer can tell when a sales rep has the customer firm's interest at heart.

Although purchasing managers usually coordinate relationships with suppliers, other people may also play important roles in influencing the purchase decision.[4]

Multiple buying influence in a buying center

Multiple buying influence means that several people—perhaps even top management—play a part in making a purchase decision. Possible buying influences include

1. *Users*—perhaps production line workers or their supervisors.
2. *Influencers*—perhaps engineering or R&D people who help write specifications or supply information for evaluating alternatives.
3. *Buyers*—the purchasing managers who have the responsibility for working with suppliers and arranging the terms of the sale.
4. *Deciders*—the people in the organization who have the power to select or approve the supplier—often a purchasing manager but perhaps top management for larger purchases.
5. *Gatekeepers*—people who control the flow of information within the organization—perhaps a purchasing manager who shields users or other deciders. Gatekeepers can also include receptionists, secretaries, research assistants, and others who influence the flow of information about potential purchases.

The following example portrays how different buying influences work. Electrolux, the Swedish firm that produces vacuum cleaners, recognized the environmental problem of plastic trash drifting in our oceans. To call attention to this problem and provide demand for the plastic, Electrolux designed five new vacuum cleaners made out of plastic recycled from the sea.

Suppose that production of these vacuums requires purchasing new equipment to mold the plastic body of the new vacuum cleaners. An assistant to the purchasing manager (a gatekeeper) first reviews current suppliers and searches the Internet to develop a list of

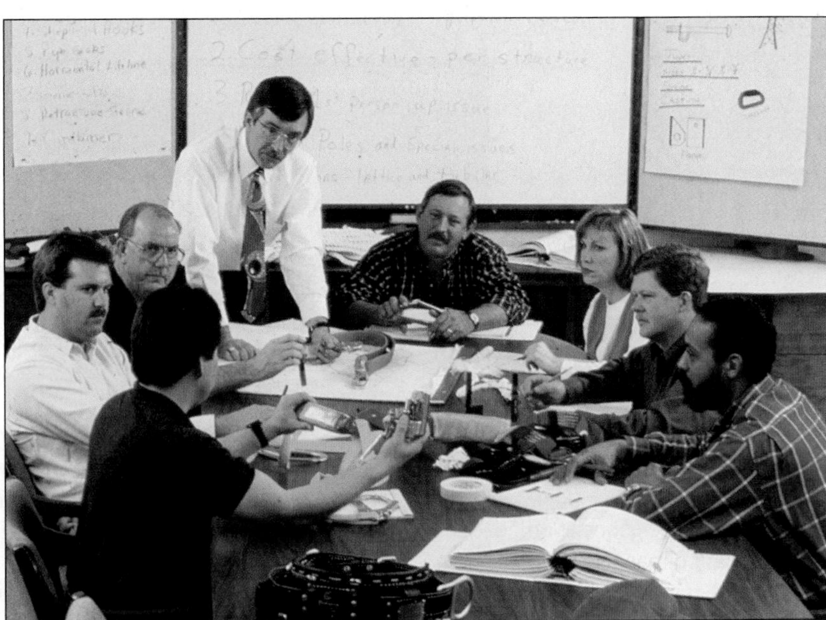

A person who works on a utility firm's high-power wires needs safe, durable climbing gear. Many representatives from different departments influence the decision about which gear the firm should buy.

plastic molding equipment makers that might meet Electrolux's needs. The purchasing manager e-mails a description of the new product and Electrolux's requirements to five vendors on the list. It turns out that each of them is eager to get the business and submits a proposal. Several different people at Electrolux (influencers) help to evaluate the vendors' proposals. A finance manager worries about cash flow and suggests leasing the machine. The design engineer wants to be sure that the molding equipment can meet quality standards and certain specifications. The production manager is interested in speed of operation. The production line workers (users) will be happiest with a machine that is easy to use so they can continue to rotate jobs.

The purchasing manager's assistant schedules visits from salespeople representing the three most promising vendors. The Electrolux head of production (the decider) seeks input from everyone who attends the presentations and reviews the proposals, but retains the power to make the final choice. After all these buying influences are considered and a vendor is selected, one of the purchasing agents for the firm (the buyer) works with the chosen vendor to arrange the terms of the sale, including delivery dates, payment, installation, and after-sale service.

It is helpful to think of a **buying center** as all the people who participate in or influence a purchase. Because different people may make up a buying center from one decision to the next, the salesperson must study each case carefully. Just learning whom to talk with may be hard, but thinking about the various roles in the buying center can help.

The salesperson may have to talk to every member of the buying center—stressing different topics for each. This not only complicates the promotion job but also lengthens it. Approval of a routine order may take anywhere from a day to several months. On very important purchases—a new building, major equipment, or a new information system—the selling period may take a year or more.[5]

Vendor analysis considers all of the influences

Considering all of the factors relevant to a purchase decision can be very complex. A supplier or product that is best in one way may not be best in others. To try to deal with these situations, many firms use **vendor analysis**—a formal rating of suppliers on all relevant areas of performance. The purpose isn't just to get a low price from the supplier on a given part or service. Rather, the goal is to lower the *total costs* associated with purchases. Analysis might show that the best vendor is the one that helps the customer reduce costs of excess inventory, retooling of equipment, or defective parts.[6]

Behavioral needs are relevant too

Vendor analysis tries to focus on economic factors, but organizational buyers are often influenced by non-economic factors. Many of the behavioral dimensions mentioned in Chapter 5 are relevant here, too. Purchasing managers and others involved in buying decisions are human, and they want friendly relationships with suppliers.

The purchasing people in some firms are eager to imitate progressive competitors or even to be the first to try new products. Such "innovators" deserve special attention when new products are being introduced.

Most members of the buying center want to do their jobs well, and good suppliers try to help them accomplish that. A recent survey found that buyers are more motivated to receive and open e-mails from marketers who offer fresh insight and ideas.[7]

Buyers usually want to avoid taking risks that might reflect badly on their decisions. Honda reminds customers that its reputation for reliability is one that buyers can count on.

A seller's marketing mix may need to consider both the needs of the customer company as well as the needs of individuals who influence the purchase decision.

The different people involved in purchase decisions are also human with respect to protecting their own interests and their own position in the company. That's one reason people from different departments may have different priorities in trying to influence what is purchased. For many purchases, buyers know that choosing a supplier who delivers poor quality or late deliveries can be very costly—and the buyer may be blamed. Buyers want to avoid this risk—and a marketer who develops a marketing mix that lowers the buyer's risk puts himself or herself in a stronger position.

A seller's marketing mix should satisfy *both* the needs of the customer company as well as the needs of individuals who influence the purchase. Therefore, sellers need to find an overlapping area where both can be satisfied. See Exhibit 6-2 for a summary of this idea.

Ethical conflicts may arise

Although organizational buyers are influenced by their own needs, most are serious professionals who are careful to avoid a conflict between their own self-interest and company outcomes. Marketers must be careful here. A salesperson who offers one of his company pens to a prospect may view the giveaway as part of the promotion effort—but the customer firm may have a policy against employees accepting *any* gift from a supplier.

While most organizational buyers act in an ethical manner, there have been highly publicized abuses. For example, Omnicare Inc., which provides pharmaceutical drugs to customers that include nursing homes, was charged with soliciting and receiving kickback payments from its nursing home customers and drug maker suppliers, including Johnson & Johnson

Exhibit 6–2
Overlapping Needs of Individual Influencers and the Customer Organization

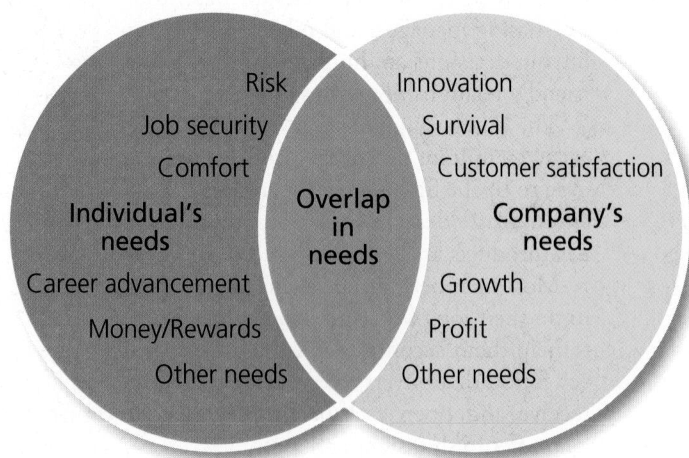

(J&J). J&J and Omnicare apparently sold the drug Risperdal to nursing homes as a treatment for dementia and anxiety, conditions for which it was not approved. The two companies also agreed to downplay risks of diabetes and weight gain when talking to patients and doctors. The case may cost the two firms more than one billion dollars in fines and other charges.

Marketers need to take concerns about conflict of interest very seriously. There can be a lot of pressure on marketing managers to make sales goals. Part of the promotion job is to persuade different individuals who may influence an organization's purchase. Yet the whole marketing effort may be tainted if it even appears that a marketer has encouraged a person who influences a decision to put personal gain ahead of company interest.[8]

Ethics Question

Assume that you are a salesperson in a small company. For months you've been trying to get a big order from a large firm. A purchasing manager at the firm casually mentions that she is trying to help two friends find tickets for a big hockey game. Your boss has season tickets for entertaining customers, but you know that the purchasing manager's company strictly prohibits any gift to employees. When you ask your boss what to do, the reply is, "Well, the tickets would be used by the friends and not the customer firm's employee, so you can offer them if you think you should." What should you do? What are the pros and cons of your decision?

Purchasing may be centralized

If a large organization has facilities at many locations, much of the purchasing work may be done at a central location. With centralized buying, a sales rep may be able to sell to facilities all over a country—or even across several countries—without leaving a base city. Walmart handles most of the purchase decisions for stores in its retail chain from its headquarters in Arkansas. Many purchasing decisions for agencies of the U.S. government are handled in Washington, DC.

Many firms also have centralized controls on who can make purchases. A person who needs to purchase something usually completes a **requisition**—a request to buy something. This is frequently handled online to cut time and paper shuffling. Even so, there may be delays before a supervisor authorizes the requisition and a purchasing manager can select the "best" seller and turn the authorization into a purchase order. The process may take a few hours for a simple purchase—but it may turn into months for a complex purchase.

From innovation blooms innovative design.
Eastman Tritan™ copolyester can empower designers and engineers with a new level of design freedom. It lets you open your mind to shapes, colors, dimensions and functional integrity that weren't possible — or practical — until now. Tritan and an open mind are sure to open new market opportunities for you.
Your challenge: Separate your products from the rest of the bunch.
Tritan is a powerful tool for enhancing existing products — or creating dramatic new solutions. Clarity, toughness, chemical resistance, easy processing, higher heat resistance and much more all help you produce superior products with lasting value.
Whatever shape your innovations take in the future, you can count on Eastman Chemical Company, a world leader in polymer technology, to help apply Tritan in the most creative and effective ways.
To see recent product applications and the latest regulatory approvals for Tritan, visit www.eastman.com/tritan or call (1) 888-321-1021 (U.S.), (31) 10 2402 888 (Europe). How will you use Tritan to transform the future?

Eastman Chemical Co. developed Eastman Tritan, an innovative copolyester (plastic-like) material. Tritan is durable, heat resistant, and offers design flexibility and ease of processing. It is ideal for the molded parts needed by kitchen appliance manufacturers. Yet Eastman still faces a challenge. A customer firm that is making straight rebuys from a supplier it has worked with in the past may not be seeking new materials or suppliers.

Organizational Buyers Are Problem Solvers

LO 6.3

Three kinds of buying processes are useful

In Chapter 5, we discussed problem solving by consumers and how it might vary from extensive problem solving to routine buying. In organizational markets, we can adapt these concepts slightly and work with three similar buying processes: a new-task buying process, a modified rebuy process, or a straight rebuy.[9] See Exhibit 6-3.

New-task buying occurs when a customer organization has a new need and wants a great deal of information. New-task buying can involve setting product specifications, evaluating sources of supply, and establishing an order routine that can be followed in the future if results are satisfactory. Multiple buying influence is most often found in new-task buying.

Exhibit 6–3 Organizational Buying Processes

Characteristics	Type of Process		
	New-Task Buying	Modified Rebuy	Straight Rebuy
Time Required	Much	Medium	Little
Multiple Influence	Much	Some	Little
Review of Suppliers	Much	Some	None
Information Needed	Much	Some	Little

A **straight rebuy** is a routine repurchase that may have been made many times before. Buyers probably don't bother looking for new information or new sources of supply. Most of a company's small or recurring purchases are of this type—but they take only a small part of an organized buyer's time. Important purchases may be made this way too—but only after the firm has decided what procedure will be "routine."

The **modified rebuy** is the in-between process where some review of the buying situation is done—though not as much as in new-task buying. Sometimes a competitor will get lazy enjoying a straight rebuy situation. An alert marketer can turn these situations into opportunities by providing more information or a better marketing mix.

Straight rebuys often use e-commerce order systems

E-commerce computer systems *automatically* handle a large portion of straight rebuys. Buyers program decision rules that tell the computer how to order and leave the details of following through to the computer. For example, when an order comes in that requires certain materials or parts, the computer information system automatically orders them from the appropriate suppliers, sets the delivery date, and schedules production.

If conditions change, buyers modify the computer instructions. When nothing unusual happens, however, the computer system continues to routinely rebuy as needs develop—electronically sending purchase orders to the regular supplier.

New-task buying requires information

While buyers want to stay current on all facets of purchasing, new-task buying situations motivate them to seek specific information. Often a new-task buy starts with a *user* who becomes aware of a need and begins researching solutions. Even though a wide variety of information sources are available (see Exhibit 6-4), business buyers will use the sources they trust. To build trust, a marketer must make sure its information is reliable.

Exhibit 6–4 Major Sources of Information Used by Organizational Buyers

	Marketing sources	Nonmarketing sources
Personal sources	• Salespeople • Others from supplier firms • Trade shows	• Buying center members • Outside business associates • Consultants and outside experts
Impersonal sources	• Online events and virtual trade shows • Sales literature and catalogs • E-mails and newsletters • Website content including blogs, video, case studies, and white papers	• Online searches • Rating services • Trade associations • News publications • Product directories • Online communities

How much information a customer collects depends on the importance of the purchase and the level of uncertainty about what choice might be best. The time and expense of searching for information may not be justified for a minor purchase. But a major purchase often involves real detective work by the buyer.

New-task buying situations provide a good opportunity for a new supplier to make inroads with a customer. With a buyer actively searching for information, the seller's promotion has a much greater chance of being noticed and having an impact. Advertising, trade show exhibits, e-mails, and salespeople can all help build the buyer's attention, but an informative website may be essential for getting attention in the first place.[10]

Search engines—a first step to gathering information

Most purchasing managers start with an Internet search when they need to identify new suppliers, better ways to meet needs, or information to improve decisions. Buyers often rely on highly specialized search engines—like one that finds all types of steel that meet certain technical specifications and then compares delivered prices. But buyers also use general-purpose search engines like Google. A search across the whole web can often locate off-the-shelf products that eliminate the need to buy expensive, custom-made items. For example, a firm in Saudi Arabia ordered $1,000 worth of tiny rubber grommets from Allstates Rubber & Tool, a small firm in the suburbs of Chicago. If the buyer's search hadn't located the Allstates website, the only alternative would have been to pay much more for custom-made grommets—and Allstates wouldn't have picked up a new customer.[11]

Internet Exercise

Go to the Buyer Zone website (**www.buyerzone.com**). Type office chairs into the search box. On this page, look at the Buyer's Guide—there are several links. Look at the Buyer's Guides for other products as well. What other features are available on this site? What can be learned about buying different products from BuyerZone.com? For a marketing manager targeting small businesses, how could this site be useful?

Marketing managers know that it is critical to have a website that buyers can find. That's why suppliers often pay for a sponsored link (an ad) that appears when certain keywords are included in a search. A supplier might also change its website so that it is more likely to appear high on a list of searches.

Buyers want sites with useful content

Having useful content on a website not only moves it higher on the buyer's search results, but also gives buyers a reason to stick around the seller's website. Instead of trying to sell the customer, a supplier needs to educate buyers about their needs and present the advantages and disadvantages of the seller's products. Buyers like to read targeted *white papers* (reports designed to help them make decisions about a particular topic). White papers often advocate a seller's solution; but they also help establish a firm as a thought leader in a particular area. Buyers also like to read *case studies* to learn about how other companies have addressed similar needs. Video content and blogs can also make a seller's website more useful.

Consider the online content that Kadient created for its target customers. Kadient makes software that helps firms improve the performance of their sales force. The firm created eBooks that were distributed freely online—including *Dive Deeper Into Your Sales Metrics*. Kadient also created a funny video, "Confessions of a Sales VP," which showed a sales manager confessing to a priest about how he lies to his CEO about the number of leads he has. The video highlights challenges facing sales managers and shows how Kadient can help solve those problems. This type of information brings interested buyers to the seller's website.

Buyers share experiences in online communities

Buyers especially value recommendations from others who have already dealt with a similar need. Now online social networks are springing up to make connecting with other buyers easier. For example, at Spiceworks Community (www.spiceworks.com), IT professionals ask and answer technical questions, research best practices, and learn what others think about a product or service they are considering. Buyers trust this source of information, and similar online communities have developed around other industries. As buyers rely more on social networks, communications from marketers may have less influence on buyers' attitudes and choices.[12]

Buyers ask for competitive bids to compare offerings

When buyers in B2B markets have identified potential suppliers, they sometimes ask them to submit a **competitive bid**—the terms of sale offered by the supplier in response to the purchase specifications posted by a buyer. If different suppliers' quality, dependability, and delivery schedules all meet the specs, the buyer will select the low-price bid. But a creative marketer needs to look carefully at the buyer's specs—and the need—to see if other elements of the marketing mix could provide a competitive advantage.

Rather than search for suppliers, buyers sometimes post their requirements and invite qualified suppliers to submit a bid. Some firms set up or participate in a procurement website that directs suppliers to companies (or divisions of a company) that need to make purchases. These sites make it easy for suppliers to find out about the purchase needs of the organizations that sponsor the sites. This helps increase the number of suppliers competing for the business and that can drive down prices or provide more beneficial terms of sale. For example, when the California Department of Transportation was planning $4 billion in new construction projects, it established a procurement site so that potential suppliers knew each project's requirements for submitting a competitive bid.

Which buying procedure becomes routine is critical

From our earlier discussion, you can see that buyers make important decisions about how to deal with one or more suppliers. At one extreme, a buyer might want to rely on competition among all available vendors to get the best price on each and every order it places. At the other extreme, it might just routinely buy from one vendor with whom it already has a good relationship. In practice, there are many important and common variations between these extremes. To better understand the variations, let's take a closer look at the benefits and limitations of different types of buyer–seller relationships.

Buyer–Seller Relationships in Business Markets

LO 6.4

Close relationships may produce mutual benefits

There are often significant benefits of a close working relationship between a supplier and a customer firm. And such relationships are becoming common. Many firms are reducing the number of suppliers with whom they work—expecting more in return from the suppliers that remain. The best relationships involve real partnerships where there's mutual trust and a long-term outlook. Closely tied firms often share tasks at lower total cost than would be possible working at arm's length.

The partnership between AlliedSignal and Betz Laboratories, for example, shows the benefits of a good relationship. A while back, Betz was just one of several suppliers that sold Allied chemicals to keep the water in its plants from gunking up pipes and rusting machinery. But Betz didn't stop at selling commodity powders. Teams of Betz experts and Allied engineers studied each plant to find places where water was being wasted. In less than a year, a team in one plant found $2.5 million in potential cost reductions. For example, by adding a few valves to recycle the water in a cooling tower, Betz was able to save 300 gallons of water a minute, which resulted in savings of over $100,000 a year and reduced environmental impact. Because of ideas like this, Allied's overall use of water treatment chemicals decreased. However, Betz sales to Allied doubled because it became Allied's sole supplier.[13]

Relationships can involve many from both sides

As the Allied-Betz Laboratories collaboration shows, some buyer-seller relationships can involve more than just a purchasing agent and a salesperson. To develop effective

Warming up to sustainable purchasing

With increased attention on global warming and the environment, managers in many organizations are wondering what their responsibility should be. It's true that the first focus of most organizational buying decisions is on green—dollars, that is. However, when purchasing managers consider sustainability as part of their vendor analysis, green choices often prove to be winners.

Attention to sustainability often identifies savings that previously were not obvious. Sometimes all that is involved is a simple change from what's routine. For example, when Falconbridge Limited's aluminum smelter changed to more efficient (but more expensive) lightbulbs, it saved almost $100,000 per year in energy bills. When the Fairmont Hotel in Vancouver searched for alternative chemicals to use in its pool, it found new ones that were healthier for guests and cut costs by $2,000. Hotels everywhere cleaned up when they stopped rewashing all of their linens every day. All it took was a card in the bath that says, "If you'd like us to replace a towel with a clean one, put it on the floor." The cards cost pennies, whereas the hot water, detergent, labor, and wear on linens cost millions.

Retailers and wholesalers must be guided by what customers want; putting green products on their shelves will just rack up losses unless there's customer demand. But firms like Walmart and Home Depot advertise their sustainable choices because many consumers do want them. Walmart took note when—in one year—its customers bought 100 million eco-friendly fluorescent lightbulbs. Home Depot has identified more than 4,000 Eco Option products that meet government specifications for water conservation, energy efficiency, clean air, and sustainable forestry. Both retailers are building more energy-efficient stores and prodding their suppliers to think green by using less packaging.

In California, some city governments are cooperating with energy firms to develop generators powered by ocean waves. Across the Atlantic, the mayor of London requires city agencies to buy recycled goods whenever possible. And federal agencies in the United States must buy energy-efficient PCs and monitors made without toxins that could later pollute landfills.

Some progressive firms don't need to see financial benefits; they simply make sustainability an essential buying criterion. New Belgium Brewing Company puts sustainable values in its mission statement; that means its purchasing people select more energy efficient (but higher-priced) brew kettles, use wind-powered electricity, and build facilities that are more costly but use the latest green ideas. Many nonprofit organizations take this altruistic approach. It's hard to imagine an environmental organization like the Sierra Club not having sustainability as a value when it's time to make purchases.[14]

solutions, those closest to the problems should be directly involved. This may mean bringing people together from accounting, finance, production, information systems, and/or other functional areas of both the buyer and seller firms.

Relationships may not make sense

Although close relationships can produce benefits, they are not always best. For buyers, long-term commitments can also reduce flexibility. When competition drives down prices and spurs innovation, customers may be better off letting suppliers compete for their business. It may not be worth the customer's investment to build a relationship for purchases that are not particularly important or made that frequently. Besides that, close relationships take time and attention to build and manage.

Sellers don't usually want closer relationships with all of their customers either. Some customers may place orders that are too small or require so much special attention that the relationship would never be profitable for the seller. Also, in situations where a customer doesn't want a relationship, trying to build one may cost more than it's worth. Buyers and sellers should choose closer relationships where the benefits outweigh the costs.[15]

Relationships have many dimensions

Relationships are not "all or nothing" arrangements. Many firms may have a close relationship in some ways and not in others. Thus, it's useful to think about five key dimensions that help characterize most buyer–seller relationships: cooperation, information sharing, operational linkages, legal bonds, and relationship-specific adaptations. Purchasing managers for the buying firm and salespeople for the supplier usually coordinate the different dimensions of a relationship. However, as shown in Exhibit 6-5, close relationships often involve direct contacts between a number of people from other areas in both firms.[16]

Cooperation treats problems as joint responsibilities

In cooperative relationships, the buyer and seller work together to achieve both mutual and individual objectives. The two firms treat problems that arise as a joint responsibility. National Semiconductor (NS) and Siltec, a supplier of silicon wafers, found clever ways to cooperate and cut costs. Workers at the NS plant used to throw away the expensive plastic cassettes that Siltec uses to ship the silicon wafers. Now Siltec and NS cooperate to recycle the cassettes. This helps the environment and also saves more than $300,000 a year. Siltec passes along most of that to NS as lower prices.[17]

In today's business markets, suppliers of both goods and services are working to build closer relationships with their business customers—to meet needs better and create a competitive advantage. AFLAC provides cost-effective insurance products that help companies attract and retain employees.

Shared information is useful but may be risky

Some relationships involve open sharing of information. This might include the exchange of proprietary cost data or demand forecasts, or through working jointly on new product designs. Information might be shared in discussions between personnel, or through information systems connected via the Internet, a key facet of B2B e-commerce. The electronic approach has a big advantage in that it is fast and easy to update the information. It also saves time. A customer can check detailed product specs or the status of a job on the production line without having to wait for someone to respond.

Information sharing can lead to better decisions and better planning. However, firms don't want to share information if there's a risk that a partner might misuse it. For example, some suppliers claim that a former General Motors' purchasing chief showed blueprints of their secret technology to competing suppliers. Violations of trust in a relationship are an ethical matter and should be taken seriously.

Exhibit 6–5
Key Dimensions of Relationships in Business Markets

Suppliers can be wary to share bad news with an important customer. For example, a supplier may wait to tell a customer of financial problems—and that can cause trouble. When Edscha, a German supplier of sunroofs to BMW, unexpectedly filed for insolvency, BMW had a crisis in the making. BMW was about to launch its new Z4 convertible—and Edscha supplied all the tops. Getting a new supplier up-to-speed would have taken six months, so BMW scrambled to support Edscha and launch the Z4 on schedule. A more trusting and open relationship might have provided more lead time to work out problems.[18]

Marketers who ask for feedback from customers can learn how to improve and increase the value of the relationship. Good buying organizations provide regular feedback to their suppliers without being asked—and smart suppliers listen closely and respond to them. Honda, for example, provides a monthly report card that details the supplier's performance in five areas: quality, delivery, quantity delivered, performance history, and any special incidents. The report fosters an ongoing dialogue between Honda and its suppliers and improves supplier performance.[19]

Operational linkages share functions between firms

Operational linkages are direct ties between the internal operations of the buyer and seller firms. These linkages usually involve ongoing coordination of activities between the firms. Shared activities are especially important when neither firm, working on its own, can perform a function as well as the two firms can working together.

Business customers often require operational linkages to reduce total inventory costs, maintain adequate inventory levels, and keep production lines moving. On the other hand, keeping too much inventory is expensive. Providing a customer with inventory when it's needed may require that a supplier be able to provide **just-in-time delivery**—reliably getting products there *just* before the customer needs them. We'll discuss just-in-time systems in more detail in Chapter 12. For now, it's enough to know that closer relationships between buyers and sellers involve operational linkages that lower costs and increase efficiency.

Contracts spell out obligations

Many purchases in business markets are simple transactions. The seller's responsibility is to transfer title to goods or perform services, and the buyer's responsibility is to pay the agreed price. However, more complex relationships may be spelled out in detailed legal contracts. An agreement may apply only for a short period, but long-term contracts are also common.

For example, a customer might ask a supplier to guarantee a 6 percent price reduction for a particular part for each of the next three years and pledge to virtually eliminate

EmpordAigua believes that no two drops of water are alike—nor are any two customers' water needs. So EmpordAigua develops close buyer-seller relationships based on cooperation, information sharing, and relationship-specific adaptations to develop custom water solutions for each of its client's needs.

defects. In return, the customer might offer to double its orders and help the supplier boost productivity.

Sometimes the buyer and seller know roughly what is needed but can't fix all the details in advance. For example, specifications or total requirements may change over time. Then the relationship may involve **negotiated contract buying**, which means agreeing to contracts that allow for changes in the purchase arrangements. In such cases, the general project and basic price is described but with provision for changes and price adjustments up or down.

Some managers figure that even a detailed contract isn't a good substitute for regular good-faith reviews to make sure that neither party gets hurt by changing business conditions. Harley-Davidson used this approach when it moved toward closer relationships with a smaller number of suppliers. Purchasing executives tossed out detailed contracts and replaced them with a short statement of principles to guide relationships between Harley and its suppliers.

Specific adaptations invest in the relationship

Relationship-specific adaptations involve changes in a firm's product or procedures that are unique to the needs or capabilities of a relationship partner. Industrial suppliers often custom design a new product for just one customer; this may require investments in R&D or new manufacturing technologies. MetoKote, in its relationship with John Deere described at the beginning of this chapter, made a specific adaptation by building its coating plant right next door to Deere's factory.

Buying firms may also adapt to a particular supplier; When Apple designed MacBook computers with an Intel computer chip, it made it difficult later to change to a different chipmaker. However, buyers are often hesitant to make big investments that increase dependence on a specific supplier. Typically, they do it only when there isn't a good alternative—perhaps because only one or a few suppliers are available to meet a need—or if the benefits of the investment are clear before it's made.

Specific adaptations are usually made when the buying organization chooses to **outsource**—contract with an outside firm to produce goods or services rather than to produce them internally. Many firms have turned to outsourcing to cut costs—and that's why much outsourcing is handled by suppliers in countries where labor costs are lower. For example, many American companies are outsourcing production to firms in China and customer service to India.[20]

Powerful customer may control the relationship

Although a marketing manager may want to work in a cooperative partnership, that may be impossible with large customers who have the power to dictate how the relationship will work. Often a powerful customer negotiates lower prices from suppliers. For example, when Hewlett-Packard started selling personal computers through Walmart stores, it knew a rock-bottom price would be required. So it used its large sales volume to demand lower prices from its suppliers and the contract manufacturers that assembled the PCs. This helped H-P offer lower priced computers while maintaining higher profit margins than its competition.[21]

Buyers usually use several sources to spread their risk

Even if a marketing manager develops the best marketing mix possible and cultivates a close relationship with the customer, the customer may not give *all* of its business to one supplier. Buyers often look for several dependable sources of supply to protect themselves from unpredictable events such as strikes, fires, or floods in one of their suppliers' plants. For example, Western Digital, the world's largest provider of hard-disk drives, produces most of its drives in Thailand. When flooding in Thailand closed down many of Western Digital's manufacturing plants, it significantly tightened the world's supply of personal computers.[22]

Even when buyers don't want a single source of supply, a good marketing mix is still likely to win a larger share of the total business—which can prove to be very important. From a buyer's point of view, it may not seem like a big deal to give a particular supplier a 40 percent share of the orders rather than a 20 percent share. But for the seller that doubles their sales with that one customer—a 100 percent increase.

Variations in buying by customer type

We've been discussing aspects of relationships and buying approaches that generally apply with different types of customer organizations—in both the United States and internationally. However, it's also useful to have more detail about specific types of customers. Knowing the size, number, geographic location, and buying procedures of manufacturers, service firms, retailers, wholesalers, and governments help marketing managers to segment markets, identify targets, and create more effective marketing mixes.

Manufacturers Are Important Customers

LO 6.5

There are not many big ones

One of the most striking facts about manufacturers is how few there are compared to final consumers. This is true in every country. In the United States, for example, there are about 330,000 factories. Exhibit 6-6 shows that the majority of these are quite small—over half have less than 10 workers. But output from these small firms accounts for less than 3 percent of manufacturing value. In small plants, the owners often do the buying. And they buy less formally than buyers in the relatively few large manufacturing plants—which employ most of the workers and produce a large share of the value added by manufacturing. For example, only about 3 percent of all plants have 250 or more employees, yet they employ about 44 percent of the production workers and produce about 58 percent of the value added by manufacturers.

Customers cluster in geographic areas

In addition to concentration by company size, industrial markets are concentrated in certain geographic areas. Internationally, industrial customers are concentrated in countries that are at the more advanced stages of economic development. From all the talk in the news about the United States shifting from an industrial economy to a service and information economy, you might conclude that the United States is an exception—that the industrial market in this country is shrinking. It is true that the number of people employed in manufacturing has been shrinking, but U.S. manufacturing output is higher than at any other time in the nation's history. The rate of growth, however, is fastest in countries where labor is cheap.[23]

Within a country, there is often further concentration of manufacturing in specific areas. In the United States, many factories are concentrated in big metropolitan areas—especially in New York, Pennsylvania, Ohio, Illinois, Texas, and California. There is also concentration by industry. In Germany, for example, the steel industry is concentrated in the Ruhr Valley. Similarly, U.S. manufacturers of high-tech electronics are concentrated in California's famous Silicon Valley near San Francisco.

Exhibit 6–6 Size Distribution of Manufacturing Establishments

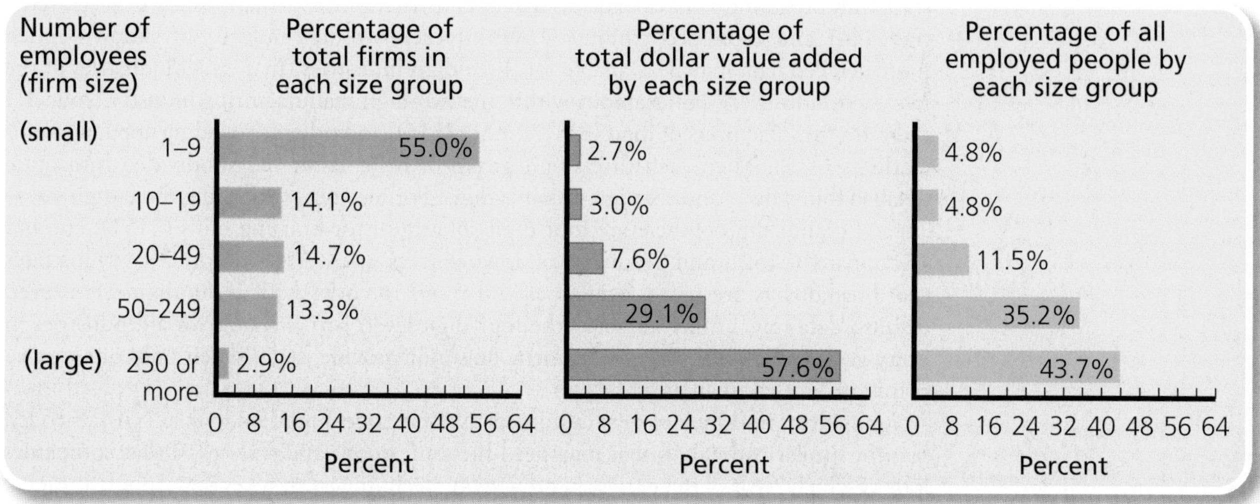

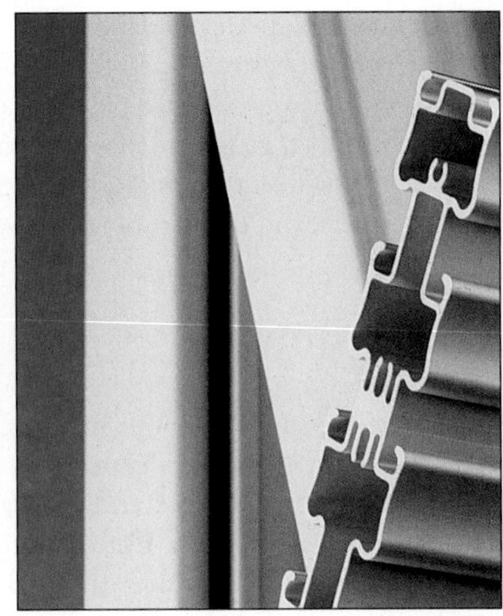

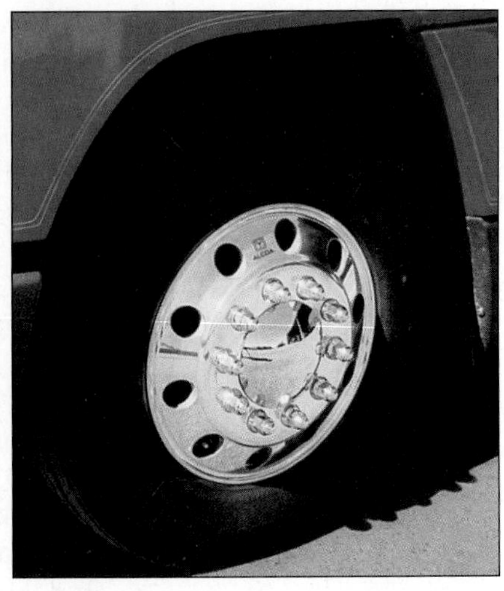

A firm like Alcoa Aluminum is likely to find that the majority of its customers are concentrated within a few industries that it can identify by North American Industry Classification System code number.

Business data often classify industries

The products an industrial customer needs to buy depend on the business it is in. Because of this, sales of a product are often concentrated among customers in similar businesses. For example, apparel manufacturers are the main customers for zippers. Marketing managers must focus their marketing mixes on prospective customers who exhibit characteristics similar to their current customers.

> **Internet Exercise**
>
> Comprehensive information about NAICS codes is available online (**www.naics.com**). At the website, select "Code Search" and when the search page appears submit a query for the keyword "welding." If your firm was interested in selling its lasers to manufacturers of laser welding equipment, what is the NAICS code of the industry for which you would want to get a list of manufacturers?

Detailed information is often available to help a marketing manager learn more about customers in different lines of business. The U.S. government collects and publishes data by the **North American Industry Classification System (NAICS) codes**—groups of firms in similar lines of business. (NAICS is pronounced like "nakes.") The number of establishments, sales volumes, and number of employees—broken down by geographic areas—are given for each NAICS code. A number of other countries collect similar data, and some of them try to coordinate their efforts with an international variation of the NAICS system. However, in many countries data on business customers are incomplete or inaccurate.

So let's take a closer look at how the NAICS codes work. The NAICS code breakdowns start with broad industry categories such as construction (23), manufacturing (31), retail trade (44), and so on. See Exhibit 6-7. Within each two-digit industry breakdown, much more detailed data may be available for three-digit industries (that is, subindustries of the two-digit industries). For example, within the two-digit manufacturing industry (code 31) there are manufacturers of food (311), leather (316), and others, including apparel manufacturers (315). Then each three-digit group of firms is further subdivided into more detailed four-, five-, and six-digit classifications. For instance, within the three-digit (315) apparel manufacturers there are four-digit subgroups for knitting mills (3151), cut and sew apparel (3152), and producers of apparel accessories (3159). Exhibit 6-7 illustrates that breakdowns are more detailed as you move to codes with more digits. However, detailed data (say, broken down at the four-digit level) isn't available for all industries in every geographic area. The government does not provide detail when only one or two plants are located in an area.

Many firms find their *current* customers' NAICS codes and then look at NAICS-coded lists for similar companies that may need the same goods and services. Other companies look at which NAICS categories are growing or declining to discover new opportunities.[24]

Exhibit 6–7 Illustrative NAICS Code Breakdown for Apparel Manufacturers

Producers of Services—Smaller and More Spread Out

LO 6.6

The service side of the U.S. economy is large and has been growing fast. Service operations are also growing in some other countries. There are many good opportunities to provide these service companies with the products they need to support their operations. But there are also challenges.

The United States has almost 6 million service firms—more than 17 times as many as it has manufacturers. Some of these are big companies with international operations. Examples include AT&T, Hilton Hotels, Prudential Insurance, Pricewaterhouse-Coopers, Wells Fargo, and Accenture. These firms have purchasing departments that are like those in large manufacturing organizations. But as you might guess given the large number of service firms, most of them are small. They're also more spread out around the country than manufacturing concerns. Factories often locate where transportation facilities are good, raw materials are available, and it is less costly to produce goods in quantity. Service operations, in contrast, often have to be close to their customers.

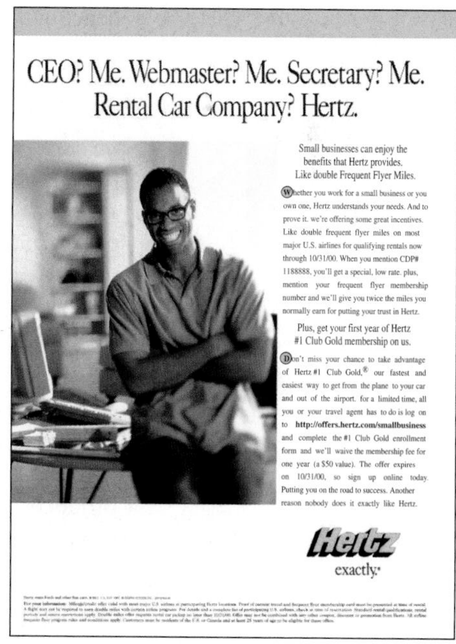

In a smaller service organization, purchases may be made by the person who is in charge rather than a person with full-time responsibility for purchasing.

Buying may not be as formal

Purchases by small service firms are often handled by whoever is in charge or their administrative assistant. This may be a doctor, lawyer, owner of a local insurance agency, hotel manager, or their secretary or office manager. Suppliers who usually deal with purchasing specialists in large organizations may have trouble adjusting to this market. Personal selling is still an important part of promotion, but reaching these customers in the first place often requires more advertising. And small service firms may need much more help in buying than a large corporation.

Small service customers like Internet buying

Small service companies that don't attract much personal attention from salespeople often rely on e-commerce for many of their purchases. Purchases by small customers can add up—so for many suppliers these customers are an important target market. Increasingly suppliers cater to the needs of these customers with specially designed websites. A well-designed website can be efficient for both customers and suppliers. Customers can get information, place orders, or follow up with a call or e-mail for personal attention from a salesperson or customer service rep when it's needed.

Retailers and Wholesalers Buy for Their Customers

Most retail and wholesale buyers see themselves as purchasing agents for their target customers—remembering the old saying that "Goods well bought are half sold." For example, the buying specialist at Walgreens Drugstores who handles products targeted at ethnic consumers is a real expert. He knows what ethnic customers want and won't be persuaded by a sales rep for a manufacturer who can't provide it. Of course, there is a place for collaboration, as when the Walgreens buyer works with people at Soft Sheen Products to develop a new product for the African American target market. That's profitable for both firms.

Committee buying is impersonal

Space in retail stores is limited, and buyers for retail chains simply are not interested in carrying every product that some salesperson wants them to sell. In an average week, 150 to 250 new items are offered to the buying offices of a large chain like Safeway. If the chain accepted all of them, it would add 10,000 new items during a single year! Obviously, these firms need a way to deal with this overload.

The entrepreneurs who started PenAgain, for example, had to have more than a unique product to get shelf space at Walmart. Their presentation to Walmart had to include hard data that showed their marketing mix was already working well in other retail stores and evidence of their ability to supply the large quantities a retailer the size of Walmart would need.[25]

Decisions to add or drop lines or change buying policies may be handled by a *buying committee.* The seller still calls on and gives a pitch to a buyer—but the buyer does not have final responsibility. Instead, the buyer prepares forms summarizing proposals for new products and passes them on to the committee for evaluation. The seller may not get to present her story to the buying committee in person. This rational, almost cold-blooded, approach certainly reduces the impact of a persuasive salesperson. On the other hand, it may favor a firm that has hard data on how its whole marketing mix will help the retailer to attract and keep customers.

Buyers watch computer output closely

Most larger firms use sophisticated computerized inventory replenishment systems. Scanners at retail checkout counters keep track of what goes out the door—and computers use these data to update the records. Even small retailers and wholesalers use automated control systems that create daily reports showing sales of every product. Buyers with this kind of information know, in detail, the profitability of the different competing products. If a product isn't moving, the retailer isn't likely to be impressed by a salesperson's request for more in-store attention or added shelf space.

Reorders are straight rebuys

Retailers and wholesalers usually carry a large number of products. A drug wholesaler, for example, may carry up to 125,000 products. Because they deal with so many products, most intermediaries buy their products on a routine, automatic reorder basis—straight rebuys—once they make the initial decision to stock specific items. Automatic computer ordering is a natural outgrowth of computerized checkout systems. Sellers to these markets must understand the size of the buyer's job and have something useful to say and do when they call.

Retailers see themselves as buying agents for their target customers—but they also have to determine what they can profitably sell. Buyers are attracted to well-known brands like Dove. And Chiquita wants to remind convenience stores that selling bananas can bring profits.

The Government Market

Size and diversity

Some marketers ignore the government market because they think that government red tape is more trouble than it's worth. They probably don't realize how big the government market really is. Government is the largest customer group in many countries—including the United States. About 30 percent of the U.S. gross domestic product is spent by various government units. Different government units buy almost every kind of product. They run not only schools, police departments, and military organizations, but also supermarkets, public utilities, research laboratories, offices, hospitals, and even liquor stores. These huge government expenditures cannot be ignored by an aggressive marketing manager.

Competitive bids may be required

Government buyers in the United States are expected to spend money wisely—in the public interest—so their purchases are usually subject to much public review. To avoid charges of favoritism, most government customers buy by specification using a mandatory bidding procedure. Often the government buyer must accept the lowest bid that meets the specifications. You can see how important it is for the buyer to write precise and complete specifications. Otherwise, sellers may submit a bid that fits the specs but doesn't really match what is needed. By law, a government unit might have to accept the lowest bid—even for an unwanted product.

Writing specifications is not easy—and buyers usually appreciate the help of well-informed salespeople. Salespeople *want* to have input on the specifications so their product can be considered or even have an advantage. A contract can be landed without the lowest bid when lower bids don't meet minimum or requested specifications.

The approved supplier list

Specification and bidding difficulties aren't problems in all government orders. Items that are bought frequently—or for which there are widely accepted standards—are purchased routinely. The government unit simply places an order at a previously approved price. To share in this business, a supplier must be on the list of approved suppliers and agree on a price that will stay the same for a specific period—perhaps a year.[26]

Learning what government wants

In the United States, there are more than 89,527 local government units (school districts, cities, counties, and states) as well as many federal agencies that make purchases. Some firms sell directly to government agencies; others work with prime contractors that resell to the government. Both are good opportunities for many businesses. Often small

The City of San Jose worked with a number of suppliers when it built the Lake Cunningham Regional Skate Park. *California Skateparks* of Upland, California used 800 cubic yards of a special spray concrete mixture to create the park's bowls, halfpipes and walls. To light the park evenly, without shadows, the city turned to *Musco Lighting* from Oskaloosa, Iowa. It lit the park with 10 50-foot poles, each bearing three 1500-watt fixtures. To give the park's 50,000 annual visitors a shady place to rest, *Robert A. Bothman,* Inc. from San Jose, California created five planters that were filled with wildflowers, native grasses, and palms.

and medium-size businesses find it easier to sell to prime contractors rather than win a contract with a large government agency. Potential suppliers should focus on the government units or prime contractors they want to cater to and learn the bidding methods of those units. Then, they should monitor websites where government contracts are advertised. Target marketing can make a big contribution here—making sure the marketing mixes are well matched with the different bid procedures.

Because government agencies want to promote competition for their business, marketers are provided with a lot of information—in print form and online. The U.S. government has a central source and USA.gov is a great place to start. There are also resources at FedBizOpps.gov (www.fbo.gov), including videos, publications, and a search tool to find opportunities to fit a firm's strategy. The General Services Administration handles vendor contracts for off-the-shelf goods and services; information for vendors is available at www.gsa.gov. Every federal government agency has a separate office devoted to small businesses with direct links to prime contractors (osdbu.gov/offices.html). Various state and local governments also offer guidance, as do government units in other countries.

Dealing with foreign governments

Foreign governments offer a good opportunity for some organizations. But sellers should recognize that selling to government units in foreign countries can be a real challenge, one that should be approached with caution. In many cases, a firm must get permission from the government in its own country to sell to a foreign government. Moreover, most government contracts favor domestic suppliers if they are available. Even if such favoritism is not explicit, public sentiment may make it very difficult for a foreign competitor to get a contract. Or the government bureaucracy may simply bury a foreign supplier in so much red tape that there's no way to win.

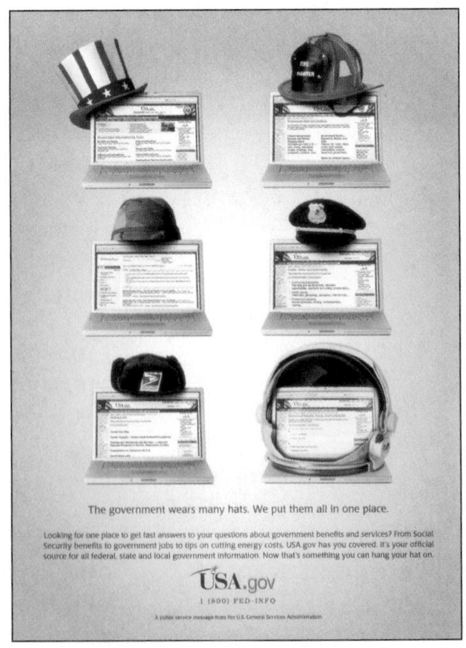

Is it unethical to "buy help"?

In some countries, government officials expect small payments (grease money) just to speed up processing of routine paperwork, inspections, or decisions from the local bureaucracy. Outright influence peddling—where government officials or their friends request bribe money to sway a purchase decision—is common in some markets. In the past, marketers from some countries have looked at such bribes as a cost of doing business. However, the **Foreign Corrupt Practices Act,** passed by the U.S. Congress in 1977, prohibits U.S. firms from paying bribes to foreign officials. A person who pays bribes, or authorizes an agent to pay them, can face stiff penalties. However, the law was amended in 1988 to allow small grease money payments if they are customary in a local culture. Since 1998, the law applies to foreign firms or foreign individuals who accept payments while in the United States. In recent years, prosecutions under this statute have increased thanks to more rigorous enforcement and greater cooperation with foreign governments. For example, in 2012 more than 80 firms were under investigation for violating the Foreign Corrupt Practices Act. This included Walmart Stores, which was alleged to have bribed officials in Mexico to quickly obtain permits to open stores. The Sarbanes-Oxley Act of 2002 makes individual executives responsible for their company's financial disclosures; and a bribe mischaracterized as a legitimate expense may violate the law. Managers need to be careful and up-front about such payments.[27]

CONCLUSION

In this chapter, we examined organizational buying and how it differs from final consumer buying. We saw that organizational buyers rely heavily on economic factors and cost–benefit analysis to make purchase decisions. This chapter showed how multiple influences are important in buying decisions—and how marketing managers must recognize and attend to the needs of all members of the buying center.

Buying behavior—and marketing opportunities—may change when there's a close relationship between a supplier and a customer. However, close relationships are not all or nothing. There are different ways that a supplier can build close relationships with its customers. We identified key dimensions of relationships and their benefits and limitations.

This chapter also showed how buying differs with the buying situation. The problem-solving modes used by final consumers and discussed in Chapter 5 also apply here—with some modification.

E-commerce plays a key role in organizational buying and B2B marketing. We discussed some of the different ways that these technologies are being used.

We saw that organizational buyers buy for resale or to produce other goods and services—and include manufacturers, farmers, distributors, retailers, government agencies, and nonprofit organizations. There are many similarities in how these organizations buy—but also differences. The chapter concludes by providing insights about buying practices particular to manufacturers, service firms, intermediaries, and governments.

Understanding how organizations buy can help marketing managers identify logical dimensions for segmenting markets and developing marketing mixes. But the nature of products being offered may require further adjustments in the mix. Different product classes are discussed in Chapter 8. Variations by product may provide additional segmenting dimensions to help a marketing manager fine-tune a marketing strategy.

KEY TERMS

LO 6.7

business and organizational customers, *144*
purchasing specifications, *147*
ISO 9000, *147*
purchasing managers, *147*
multiple buying influence, *148*
buying center, *149*
vendor analysis, *149*
requisition, *151*
new-task buying, *152*
straight rebuy, *152*
modified rebuy, *152*
competitive bid, *154*
just-in-time delivery, *157*
negotiated contract buying, *158*
outsource, *158*
North American Industry Classification System (NAICS) codes, *160*
Foreign Corrupt Practices Act, *164*

QUESTIONS AND PROBLEMS

1. In your own words, explain how buying behavior of business customers in different countries may have been a factor in speeding the spread of international marketing.
2. Compare and contrast the buying behavior of final consumers and organizational buyers. In what ways are they most similar and in what ways are they most different?

3. Briefly discuss why a marketing manager should think about who is likely to be involved in the buying center for a particular purchase. Is the buying center idea useful in consumer buying? Explain your answer.
4. If a nonprofit hospital were planning to buy expensive MRI scanning equipment (to detect tumors), who might be involved in the buying center? Explain your answer and describe the types of influence that different people might have.
5. Describe the situations that would lead to the use of the three different buying processes for a particular product—lightweight bumpers for a pickup truck.
6. Why would an organizational buyer want to get competitive bids? What are some of the situations when competitive bidding can't be used?
7. How likely would each of the following be to use competitive bids? (*a*) a small town that needed a road resurfaced, (*b*) a scouting organization that needed a printer to print its scouting handbook, (*c*) a hardware retailer that wants to add a new lawn mower line, (*d*) a grocery store chain that wants to install new checkout scanners, and (*e*) a sorority that wants to buy a computer to keep track of member dues. Explain your answers.
8. Discuss the advantages and disadvantages of just-in-time supply relationships from an organizational buyer's point of view. Are the advantages and disadvantages merely reversed from the seller's point of view?
9. Explain why a customer might be willing to work more cooperatively with a small number of suppliers rather than pitting suppliers in a competition against each other. Give an example that illustrates your points.
10. Would a tool manufacturer need a different marketing strategy for a big retail chain like Home Depot than for a single hardware store run by its owner? Discuss your answer.
11. How do you think a furniture manufacturer's buying habits and practices would be affected by the specific type of product to be purchased? Consider fabric for upholstered furniture, a lathe for the production line, cardboard for shipping cartons, and lubricants for production machinery.
12. Discuss the importance of target marketing when analyzing organizational markets. How easy is it to isolate homogeneous market segments in these markets?
13. Explain how NAICS codes might be helpful in evaluating and understanding business markets. Give an example.
14. Considering the nature of retail buying, outline the basic ingredients of promotion to retail buyers. Does it make any difference what kinds of products are involved? Are any other factors relevant?
15. The government market is obviously an extremely large one, yet it is often slighted or even ignored by many firms. Red tape is certainly one reason, but there are others. Discuss the situation and be sure to include the possibility of segmenting in your analysis.
16. Some critics argue that the Foreign Corrupt Practices Act puts U.S. businesses at a disadvantage when competing in foreign markets with suppliers from other countries that do not have similar laws. Do you think that this is a reasonable criticism? Explain your answer.

CREATING MARKETING PLANS

The Marketing Plan Coach software on the text website includes a sample marketing plan for Hillside Veterinary Clinic. Hillside decided to focus on final consumers and their pets rather than include organizational customers who might need veterinary care for animals. Such customers might range from dog breeders and farmers to animal protection shelters and law enforcement agencies who work with dogs. Would it be easy or hard for Hillside to expand its focus to serve customers who are not final consumers? Explain your thinking.

SUGGESTED CASES

5. Polystyrene Solutions   6. Applied Steel

COMPUTER-AIDED PROBLEM

6. VENDOR ANALYSIS

CompuTech, Inc., makes circuit boards for microcomputers. It is evaluating two possible suppliers of electronic memory chips.

The chips do the same job. Although manufacturing quality has been improving, some chips are always defective. Both suppliers will replace defective chips. But the only practical way to test for a defective chip is to assemble a circuit board and "burn it in"—run it and see if it works. When one chip on a board is defective at that point, it costs $2.00 for the extra labor time to replace it. Supplier 1 guarantees a chip failure rate of not more than 1 per 100 (that is, a defect rate of 1 percent). The second supplier's 2 percent defective rate is higher, but its price is lower.

Supplier 1 has been able to improve its quality because it uses a heavier plastic case to hold the chip. The only disadvantage of the heavier case is that it requires CompuTech to use a connector that is somewhat more expensive.

Transportation costs are added to the price quoted by either supplier, but Supplier 2 is further away so transportation costs are higher. And because of the distance, delays in supplies reaching CompuTech are sometimes a problem. To ensure that a sufficient supply is on hand to keep production going, CompuTech must maintain a backup inventory—and this increases inventory costs. CompuTech figures inventory costs—the expenses of finance and storage—as a percentage of the total order cost.

To make its vendor analysis easier, CompuTech's purchasing agent has entered data about the two suppliers on a spreadsheet. He based his estimates on the quantity he thinks he will need over a full year.

a. Based on the results shown in the initial spreadsheet, which supplier do you think CompuTech should select? Why?

b. CompuTech estimates it will need 100,000 chips a year if sales go as expected. But if sales are slow, fewer chips will be needed. This isn't an issue with Supplier 2; its price is the same at any quantity. However, Supplier 1's price per chip will be $1.95 if CompuTech buys less than 90,000 during the year. If CompuTech only needs 84,500 chips, which supplier would be more economical? Why?

c. If the actual purchase quantity will be 84,500 and Supplier 1's price is $1.95, what is the highest price at which Supplier 2 will still be the lower-cost vendor for CompuTech? (Hint: You can enter various prices for Supplier 2 in the spreadsheet—or use the analysis feature to vary Supplier 2's price and display the total costs for both vendors.)

7

CHAPTER SEVEN

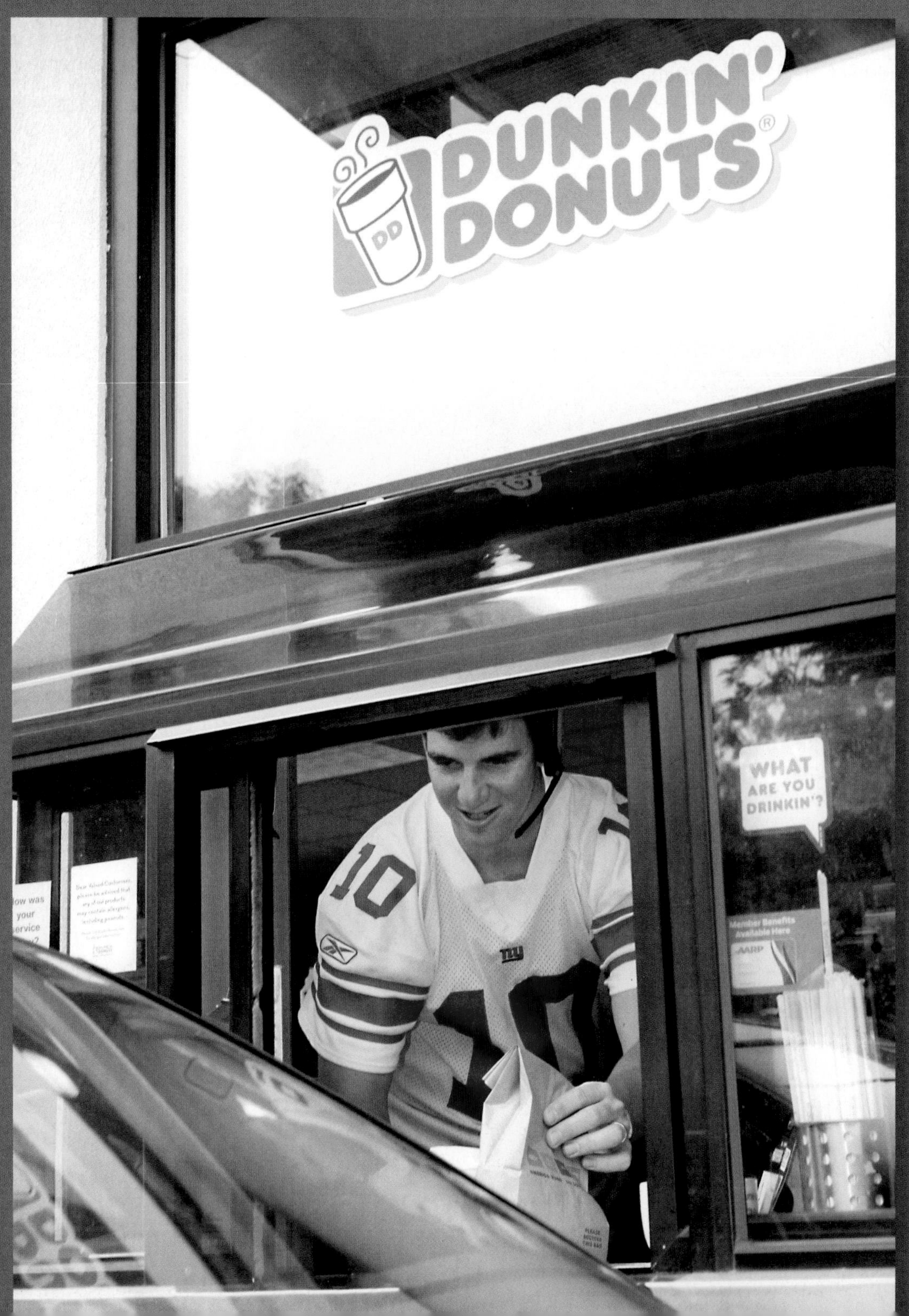

Improving Decisions with Marketing Information

In 1946 Bill Rosenberg launched Industrial Luncheon Services, delivering meals, snacks, and coffee to factory workers in the Boston area. From his daily sales totals Rosenberg knew his working class customers loved his coffee and doughnuts. Rosenberg thought a sit-down restaurant with these two menu items could be a success, and a few years later Dunkin' Donuts was born. Back then Dunkin' charged just $.05 for one of its 52 varieties of doughnuts. Dunkin's $.10 cup of coffee sounds like a bargain today, but it was double the going rate. Nevertheless, customers saw its higher quality coffee—that was always served fast and hot—as a good value.

By 2005 Dunkin' had about 5,000 franchised locations in the U.S. and 1,000 more in 29 other countries—and management wanted to triple in size in the next 10 years. Coffee represented almost two thirds of its sales, while doughnuts and sandwiches each accounted for about 17 percent. Dunkin's flavored coffees, lattes, Chai, iced coffee, and other beverages put it in direct competition with Starbucks, the heavy hitter in the coffee market. With 90 percent of its stores in the northeastern United States, it saw a big opportunity for growth. Yet Dunkin's marketing managers wondered if they should change its marketing strategy to better fit evolving customer behavior, changing competition, and new target markets.

Dunkin' managers knew they had many options: for example, adding new sandwiches, offering catering and delivery services, and providing cozier seating were just some of the choices. Copernicus Marketing conducted research and designed Dunkin's "store of the future." Product design software evaluated more than two billion combinations by varying portion sizes, exterior store design, interior music selection, and more. Using data from a nationally representative sample of more than 1,000 customers and prospects, sales and costs were forecast for each combination and the most profitable options identified. This research guided the construction of experimental prototype stores—which emphasized Dunkin's quality coffee and its speed of service at the counter and drive-through windows. Dunkin' didn't need to conduct marketing research to know its New York customers would enjoy having Eli Manning serve them at the drive-through window, but his day job as quarterback of the New York Giants kept this from happening on a regular basis. When the new stores exceeded sales and profit targets, its managers knew they had a future direction.

Marketing managers also wanted to better understand Dunkin's loyal coffee drinkers—and those of rival Starbucks. So, the company paid dozens of its loyal customers to buy coffee at Starbucks—while simultaneously paying a similar number of Starbucks loyalists to come to Dunkin' Donuts. After debriefing, the two groups were found to be so different that Dunkin' researchers dubbed them "tribes."

What each tribe detested about its rival's store was exactly what made it love its usual outlet. For example, Starbucks regulars found Dunkin' outlets boring, austere, and unoriginal. They also didn't like that workers dumped standard amounts of milk and sugar in their drinks—they didn't feel special at Dunkin' Donuts. While Dunkin' tribe members wanted newer looking stores, the Starbucks experience turned them off. All those laptop users made it hard to find a seat—and they wondered why coffee shops needed couches. They complained about Starbucks' higher prices and the slower speed of service. They didn't like Starbucks' "tall," "grande," and "venti" lingo; just give us "small," "medium," and "large" please! This exercise convinced Dunkin' that there were customers out there who wanted an alternative to Starbucks—and it could fine-tune a marketing strategy to provide it.

A psychographic survey offered further insight on the attitudes, values, and interests of Dunkin' tribe members. They're busy, love routine, prefer simple with no frills, and see themselves as down-to-earth folks without pretentions. One third of Americans fit this profile, but these people are more common in the Midwest and South than in the Northeast. So Dunkin' quickly targeted cities in Ohio, Tennessee, and Florida. This research also guided the "America Runs on Dunkin'" advertising campaign featuring office and construction workers getting through their days with the chain's help.

Dunkin' Donuts also wanted to refine its menu. Dunkin' knew that many busy customers were turning to snacks versus meals and using drive-through windows to get food on-the-go. So Dunkin' chefs created and tested a new line of hearty snacks. Focus groups liked the smoothies and hot flatbreads, but the tiny stuffed pinwheels did not satisfy their hunger. They liked it better when Dunkin' came back with larger size "bites" filled with pork and other ingredients.

Dunkin' encourages customer feedback and listens closely for ideas to fine-tune its marketing strategy. A group of its best customers serve on the Dunkin' Advisory Panel where they regularly complete online surveys and participate in online focus groups. The company also closely monitors its website and social media efforts—reading what Facebook fans and Twitter followers write and using analytical software that collects and analyzes buzz on the Internet and how people come to its website.

This feedback led Dunkin' to drop plans for a stuffed melt sandwich after customers commented that it sounded messy. When new stores were painted in coffee color hues, customers again complained, and Dunkin' responded by splashing on more of the traditional bright pink and orange. In addition, when customers requested music in its stores, Dunkin' created a distinctly non-Starbucks sound that was upbeat but not annoying.

Dunkin' is still growing, with more than 10,000 stores in 32 countries, though a tough economy moved the "triple in size" goal back to 2020. To achieve that goal Dunkin' Donuts marketing managers will keep relying on continuous information to aid their marketing strategy planning and its implementation and control.[1]

Learning Objectives

The Dunkin' Donuts case shows that successful marketing strategies require information about potential target markets and their likely responses to marketing mixes—as well as information about competitors and other market environment variables. Managers also need information for implementation and control. Without good information, managers are left to guess—and in today's fast-changing markets, that invites failure. In this chapter, we discuss how marketing managers get the information that they need.

When you finish this chapter you should be able to:

1 discuss marketing information systems.

2 understand the scientific approach to marketing research.

3 cite methods for collecting secondary and primary data.

4 understand the role of observing, questioning, and using experimental methods in marketing research.

5 understand the challenges to interpreting marketing research data.

6 recognize how market research information aids marketing planning in international markets.

7 understand important new terms (shown in red).

Effective Marketing Requires Good Information

LO 7.1

Information is a bridge to the market

To make good marketing decisions, managers need accurate information about what is happening in the market. They usually can't get all of the information they'd like, but part of their job is to find cost-effective ways to get the information that they really must have.

In this chapter, we'll focus on the two sources that marketing managers utilize for information to help them make better decisions. One source is **marketing research**—procedures that develop and analyze new information about a market. Marketing research involves a wide range of techniques including Internet searches, customer surveys, experiments, direct observation of customers, and many more. Marketing managers often find that one-at-a-time marketing research projects can be too costly or take too long to get the desired information. So, in many companies, marketing managers also routinely get help from a **marketing information system (MIS)**—which is an organized way of continually gathering, accessing, and analyzing information that marketing managers need to make ongoing decisions.

Marketing managers may need marketing research, an MIS, or a combination of both to get the information they need to make decisions during any step in the marketing strategy planning process—or to improve implementation and control. See Exhibit 7-1. In this

Exhibit 7–1 Marketing Information Inputs to Marketing Strategy Planning Decisions

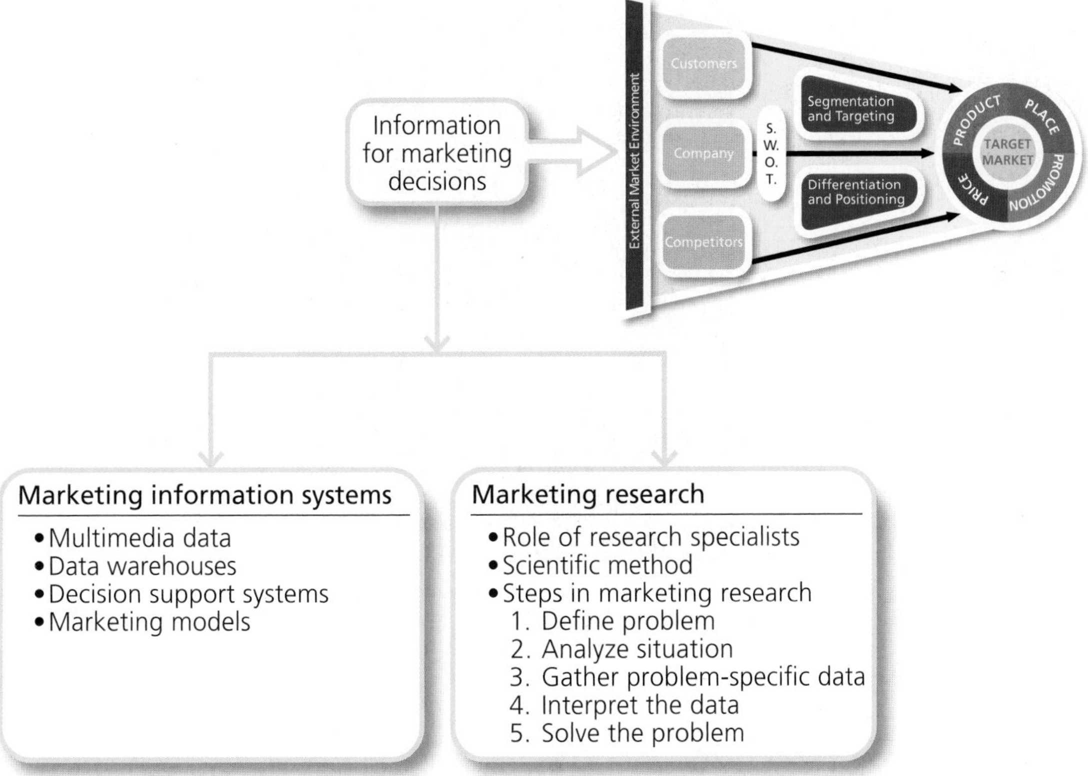

chapter, we'll discuss ways to make marketing research and an MIS more useful, and the key issues that marketing managers face in using them.

Success requires cooperation with specialists

Most large companies have a separate marketing research department to plan and manage research projects. People in these departments usually rely on outside specialists to carry out the work on particular projects. Further, they may call in specialized marketing consultants and marketing research organizations to take charge of a whole project.

Smaller companies usually don't have separate marketing research departments. They depend on their salespeople or managers to conduct what research they do. Nonprofit organizations rarely did market research in the past, but more have begun to see its value and often use outside specialists.

When it comes to setting up an MIS, a company usually turns to information technology (IT) experts. Sometimes this expertise resides in an organization's IT department. Even small firms may have a person who handles most of the technical work on its computer systems. Many small and large firms look to outside consultants and service providers for help with increasingly complex information systems.

Whether these activities are conducted inside the company or out, it is very important that marketing managers be closely involved in the design of marketing research or an MIS. Specialists in research and IT can make sure that the technical aspects are handled correctly, but marketing managers need to make sure they can access information to guide marketing strategy planning or implementation and control.

Changes Are Under Way in Marketing Information Systems

Marketing managers for some companies make decisions based almost totally on their own judgment—with very little hard data. The manager may not even know that he or she is about to make the same mistake that the previous person in that job already made! When it's time to make a decision, they may wish they had more information. But by then it's too late, so they do without.

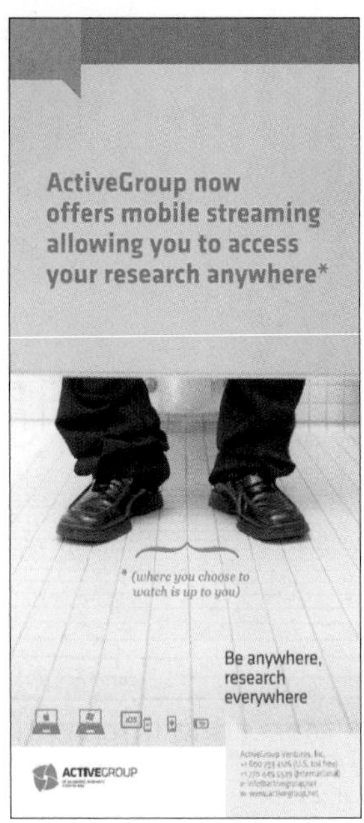

Development of powerful intranets, computer software, and mobile devices like tablet computers and smartphones, make it easier and less expensive for companies to gather, analyze, and access marketing information.

MIS makes information available and accessible

Many firms realize that it doesn't pay to wait until you have important questions you can't answer. They anticipate the information they will need. They work to develop a continual flow of information that is available and quickly accessible from an MIS when it's needed.

We won't cover all of the technical details of planning for an MIS. But you should understand what an MIS is so you know some of the possibilities. We'll be discussing the elements of a complete MIS as shown in Exhibit 7-2. As part of that review, we'll highlight how new sources of data and technology are changing MIS use.

Exhibit 7–2 Elements of a Complete Marketing Information System

The big data explosion

Many of today's businesses are awash in data. It has been estimated that organizations today process 1000 times as much data as they did in the year 2000. The explosion of data comes as organizations collect and store more information from internal sources (for example, e-mails, spreadsheets, documents, financial reports, and clickstreams—which track customers as they move through a company's website), external sources (for example, from government sources like the U.S. Census, social media websites like Facebook and LinkedIn, and digital sensors which can be found on industrial equipment, automobiles, and shopping crates) and market research studies (for example, previously conducted surveys, experiments, or other reports). The amount of data that organizations collect doubles every two years—so more and more data will continue to be available to marketing managers. This explosion is often referred to as **big data**—or data sets too large and complex to work with typical database management tools. Along with the growth of big data come new tools to analyze and sort these data. For example, machine learning systems are taught how to "read" and interpret messages and photos on social media websites.

An MIS organizes all of this incoming data and information into a **data warehouse**—a place where databases are stored so that they are available when needed. You can think of a data warehouse as an electronic library, where all of the information is indexed. With big data, firms have had to build larger data warehouses and find new ways to store, index, and access a wide variety of data.[2]

From data to information, knowledge, and wisdom

All that *data* in its raw form is not useful to a marketing manager. So an MIS includes software programs that convert the data to information that is useful to managers. Sales data becomes *information* when it provides answers to questions of "who," "what," "where," "how much," and "when." So for example, sales data might be presented in a table that shows the sales of different products over time and in different parts of the country. Photos of in-store displays (data) become information when combined with data that compares the sales increases generated by each display.

Information becomes *knowledge* when it helps a marketing manager answer "how" and "why" questions. Marketing managers can combine their experience in a market with information to generate knowledge. Or, the marketing manager might use the information to design a new marketing research project to generate knowledge. For example, a marketing manager at Frito Lay might have information that customers in the northeast United States are not satisfied with a recently launched snack food. This might cause the marketing manager to engage in a marketing research project to find out the reasons (why) for the dissatisfaction. As a marketing manager gains experience and understanding of why things happened in the past, they can put that together to build *wisdom* and better estimates about what will happen in the future. This helps them to better evaluate possible marketing strategy decisions.[3]

Get more accurate information faster and easier

Accessing all the information in an MIS is not easy—especially with the wide variety of different types of data and information. Fortunately, advances in information technology have ushered in improvements in marketing information systems. With good search software, much of the information is instantly available, often just a mouse click away. Many firms, even small ones, have their own **intranet**—a system for linking computers within a company. An intranet works like the Internet. However, to maintain security, access to websites or data on an intranet is usually limited to employees. Even so, information can be searched and available on demand. Further, it's a simple matter to "publish" new information to a website as soon as it becomes available.

Decision support systems can convert information to knowledge

With so much information available, marketing managers look to software programs for aid in interpreting what they find in the MIS. It can be helpful to have a **decision support system (DSS)**—a computer program that makes it easy for a marketing manager to get and use information. These types of programs help marketing managers convert information into knowledge that allows them to make informed marketing strategy decisions. Let's look at a couple of types of decision support systems.

Marketing dashboards monitor the market

One way to interface with a data warehouse and DSS is through a **marketing dashboard**, which displays up-to-the-minute marketing data in an easy-to-read format—much like a car's dashboard shows the speedometer and fuel gauge. Marketing dashboards are usually customized to a manager's areas of responsibility. For example, a dashboard for a customer service manager at Verizon Wireless might show the percentage of customer calls dropped by cell towers, the location of repair trucks in the field, and the number of callers "on hold" waiting for customer service help. With early warning about potential problems, the manager can quickly make corrections. For example, a manager might call in extra customer service help if too many customers are "on hold."[4]

Marketing managers want the ability to monitor the market and success of marketing strategies anywhere and anytime with marketing dashboards.

Information for planning, implementation, and control

Some decision support systems go even further—helping a marketing manager improve all aspects of their planning—blending individual Ps, combining the four Ps into mixes, and developing and selecting plans. Further, they can monitor the implementation of current plans, comparing results against plans and making necessary changes more quickly. Drawing on data showing how a marketing strategy worked in the past, a DSS can make sales estimates using a marketing model. A **marketing model** is a statement of relationships among marketing variables. It enables a manager to look at the sales (and costs) expected with different types of promotion and select the marketing mix that is best for a particular target market.[5]

For example, optical retailer LensCrafters, with 965 North American stores, carries a very large selection of frame styles, lenses, and sunglasses tailored not only to the age, gender, and ethnic makeup of the local market but also to what is selling at that particular

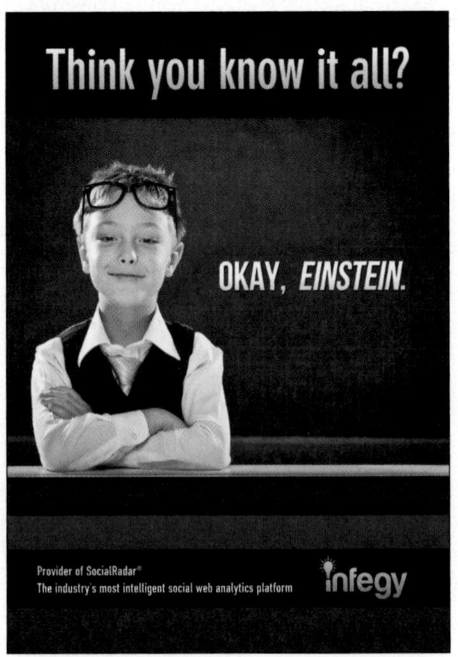

Marketing managers often use software and marketing models to plan, implement, and control marketing strategies.

Big data. Big opportunity.

Advances in technology are fueling a revolution in marketing research around big data. We are witnessing an explosion in the availability of a wide range of different types of data. Each time you buy something with a credit card, surf the web, watch a video on YouTube, or post a picture on Facebook, you create "data exhaust." Purchases tie into your name, age, and home address, and the web records where you go on the Internet and what you do there. Now firms are sucking up that exhaust from a variety of sources to learn more about you. While more data is being produced, it is also becoming much cheaper (practically free) to store and process. Finally, advances in machine learning allow computers to comb through all this data—videos, Instagram pictures, Facebook status updates, online reviews and more—to better predict customers' wants and needs. Together, these trends allow marketing managers access to more information and knowledge more quickly than ever before. Let's look at how some organizations are using this data in marketing strategy planning.

Online dating service Match.com uses big data to improve the quality of the algorithm it uses to match people seeking love at the site. Match.com scours the data posted by its customers to see which matches are working and why; this feedback improves the success of future matches.

When a customer shops for a camera at Amazon, the site takes into account which cameras are clicked on along with the amount of time spent on each page. Then Amazon analyzes its website logs to see what similar customers looked at and purchased. All this happens in an instant, because Amazon then suggests other possible cameras. After someone buys the camera, Amazon also wants to know if that customer tells friends about the purchase (on Facebook or Twitter) so it can predict if the model is poised to be the next hit.

Google examined billions of flu-related web searches over a five year period and found that it could predict where flu outbreaks were occurring two weeks before published reports from the Centers for Disease Control and Prevention. Google Flu Trends allows anyone to access this information. Marketing managers for Vicks Behind Ear Thermometer saw an opportunity to leverage Google's big data. Vicks managers targeted mothers. So they placed ads in apps like Pandora, which have basic data from users, including their gender and whether they have kids. Vicks further segmented moms by delivering ads in areas of the country experiencing flu outbreaks with the message: "Flu levels in your area are high. Be prepared with Vicks revolutionary Behind Ear Thermometer." Tapping the ad would direct the mom to the nearest store that sold the thermometer—"Buy at Walgreens .5 miles away."

Big data allowed Vicks to narrowly segment the market and deliver relevant messages that moms were happy to receive.

As big data continues to get bigger, smart marketing managers are leveraging it to create big opportunities for their customers.[6]

store. Shifts in eyewear fashions can come fast. So managers at LensCrafters routinely analyze sales data in the firm's marketing information system. Using a marketing model, they break down sales by product, store, and time period, and compare them to past results to help spot buying trends early and plan for them. In China, where LensCrafters has used different types of promotion over the years, a different marketing model identifies the best promotions to use when opening a new store. For example, scratch-off cards that give various levels of discounts are popular in some areas with price-sensitive Chinese families.[7]

Many firms resist adding an MIS

Of course not every organization has a useful MIS. The challenge and cost of setting up an MIS has been prohibitive for some firms. Some marketing managers just aren't comfortable with data and don't push for an MIS. But falling data storage costs, and low-cost, easy-to-use analytical tools are changing things quickly. For example, the free program Google Analytics allows a firm to gather and analyze data about visitors to its website. Marketing managers can find out which sites bring traffic to their own site, which pages are most popular, how long visitors spend on each page, and much, much more.

The Scientific Method and Marketing Research

LO 7.2

Marketing research—combined with the strategy planning framework we discussed in Chapter 2—can also help marketing managers make better decisions.

Marketing research is guided by the **scientific method**, a decision-making approach that focuses on being objective and orderly in *testing* ideas before accepting them. With the scientific method, managers don't just *assume* that their intuition is correct. Instead, they use their intuition and observations to develop **hypotheses**—educated guesses about the relationships between things or about what will happen in the future. Then they test their hypotheses before making final decisions.

A manager who relies only on intuition might introduce a new product without testing consumer response. But a manager who uses the scientific method might say, "I think (hypothesize) that consumers currently using the most popular brand will prefer our new product. Let's run some consumer tests. If at least 60 percent of the consumers prefer our product, we can introduce it in a regional test market. If it doesn't pass the consumer test there, we can make some changes and try again." With this approach, decisions are based on evidence, not just hunches.

The scientific method forces an orderly research process. Some managers don't carefully specify what information they need. They blindly move ahead—hoping that research will provide "the answer." Other managers may have a clearly defined problem or question but lose their way after that. These hit-or-miss approaches waste both time and money.

Five-Step Approach to Marketing Research

The **marketing research process** is a five-step application of the scientific method that includes:

1. Defining the problem
2. Analyzing the situation
3. Getting problem-specific data
4. Interpreting the data
5. Solving the problem

Exhibit 7-3 shows the five steps in the process. Note that the process may lead to a solution before all of the steps are completed. Or as the feedback arrows show, researchers may return to an earlier step if needed. For example, the interpreting step may point to a new question—or reveal the need for additional information—before a final decision can be made.

Exhibit 7–3 Five-Step Scientific Approach to Marketing Research Process

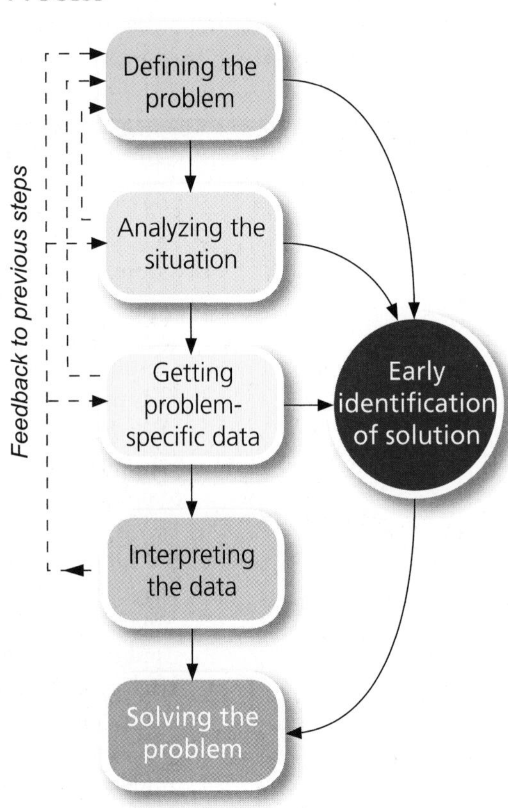

Effective research usually requires cooperation

Good marketing research requires cooperation between researchers and marketing managers. Researchers must be sure their research focuses on real problems.

Marketing managers must be able to explain what their problems are and what kinds of information they need. They should be able to communicate with specialists in the specialists' language. Marketing managers may only be "consumers" of research. But they should be informed consumers—able to explain exactly what they want from the research. They should also know about some of the basic decisions made during the research process so they know the limitations of the findings.

For this reason, our discussion of marketing research won't emphasize mechanics but rather how to plan and evaluate the work of marketing researchers.[8]

Defining the Problem—Step 1

Defining the problem is often the most difficult step in the marketing research process. But it's important for the objectives of the research to be clearly defined. The best research job on the wrong problem is wasted effort.

Pinpointing and identifying the problem is half the battle

Our strategy planning framework is useful for guiding the problem definition step. It can help the researcher identify the real problem area and what information is needed. Do we really know enough about our target markets to work out all of the four Ps? Before deciding how to position our product, do we understand our competitor's strengths and weaknesses? Do we know enough to decide what celebrity to use in an ad or how to handle the price war in New York City or Tokyo? If not, we may want to do research rather than rely on intuition.

Don't confuse problems with symptoms

The problem definition step sounds simple—and that's the danger. It's easy to confuse problems with symptoms. Marketers for Kiwi shoe polish encountered this situation. Kiwi's palm-size tin, embossed with the image of a Kiwi bird, is already the market leader in many countries. So, to get more growth, Kiwi managers did a number of consumer studies focused on the problem of how to improve the polish. Yet none of the new product ideas clicked with consumers. Things changed when a new CEO realized that the lack of interest in new polish products was just a symptom of the fact that today's footwear is made less from leather and more from synthetic materials. Further, Kiwi had traditionally targeted men rather than women, who tend to toss out worn shoes rather than work to keep them in good condition. So the CEO changed the focus of research to another problem—figuring out what feet- and footwear-related needs were not currently being met. That research showed that having comfortable, fresh-smelling shoes was the top priority for women. Further research focusing on how to solve that problem led to the development of several new products, including Kiwi Fresh'ins, which are lightly scented disposable and ultrathin shoe inserts that keep feet feeling fresh and comfortable all day.[9]

Setting research objectives may require more understanding

Sometimes the research objectives are very clear. A manager wants to know if the targeted households have tried a new product and what percent of them bought it a second time. But research objectives aren't always so simple. The manager might also want to know *why* some didn't buy or whether they had even heard of the product. Companies rarely have enough time and money to study everything. A manager must narrow the research objectives. One good way is to develop a list of research questions that includes all the possible problem areas. Then the manager can consider the items on the list more completely—in the situation analysis step—before narrowing down to final research objectives.

Analyzing the Situation—Step 2

LO 7.3

What information do we already have?

When the marketing manager thinks the real problem has begun to surface, a situation analysis is useful. A **situation analysis** is an informal study of what information is already available in the problem area. It can help define the problem and specify what additional information, if any, is needed.

The situation analysis may begin with quick research—perhaps an Internet search; a closer look at information in an MIS; and phone calls or informal talks with people familiar with the industry, problem, or situation.

Let's consider a situation facing the marketing manager for the Hershey's candy company. She reviews last month's sales and finds that sales in the Chicago region are down by 5 percent, which concerns her. She could begin a situation analysis by digging deeper into the MIS, and discover that sales of Hershey chocolate bars at one large grocery store chain are down by 25 percent. Otherwise sales in this region are up. Her next step might be an e-mail or phone call to the salesperson who calls on this grocery store chain. A phone call might reveal that last month the store had a big promotion going with a competitor's candy bars. Through this type of situation analysis, you can see that the marketing manager turned data into information and knowledge—she now knows why sales are down. This type of analysis might lead to an early solution—perhaps talking with the salesperson about how to set up a future promotion to try to gain back lost sales.

Situation analysis helps educate a researcher

The situation analysis is especially important if the marketing manager is dealing with unfamiliar areas or if the researcher is a specialist who doesn't know much about the management decisions to be made. They *both* must be sure they understand the problem area—including the nature of the target market, the marketing mix, competition, and other external factors. Otherwise, the researcher may rush ahead and make costly mistakes or simply discover facts that management already knows. The following case illustrates this danger.

A marketing manager at the home office of a large retail chain hired a research firm to do in-store interviews to learn what customers liked most, and least, about some of its stores in other cities. Interviewers diligently filled out their questionnaires. When the results came in, it was apparent that neither the marketing manager nor the researcher had done their homework. No one had even talked with the local store managers! Several of the stores were in the middle of some messy remodeling—so all the customers' responses concerned the noise and dust from the construction. The research was a waste of money.

Secondary data may provide the answers—or some background

The situation analysis should also find relevant **secondary data**—information that has been collected or published already. Later, in Step 3, we will cover **primary data**—information specifically collected to solve a current problem. Too often researchers rush to gather primary data when much relevant secondary information is already available—at little or no cost! See Exhibit 7-4.

Much secondary data are available

Ideally, much secondary data are already available from the firm's MIS. Data that have not been organized in an MIS may be available from the company's files and reports. Secondary data also are available from libraries, trade associations, government agencies, and private research organizations; increasingly, these organizations put their information online. So one of the first places a researcher should look for secondary data is on the Internet.

Search the web better

Marketing managers can find a treasure trove of useful information on the Internet. It's all readily accessible from a computer, tablet, or smartphone. But available is not the same as reliable. Anyone can post anything on the Internet. So, as with any other research source, you should carefully evaluate the accuracy of Internet sources.

The key to the Internet is finding what's needed. If you have a pretty clear idea about what you are seeking, search engines like Google are a good place to start. If you are looking for general information about a broader topic area, search directories like Yahoo's (dir.yahoo.com) may be more helpful. A major problem is that searches often identify too many irrelevant sources. There are techniques to getting better search results. If you have not had formal training on Internet search, you might look for an online tutorial to sharpen your search skills. We recommend "A short and easy search engine tutorial" by Pandia (www.pandia.com/goalgetter/). You can learn valuable tips in just 15–20 minutes.

Exhibit 7–4 Sources of Secondary and Primary Data

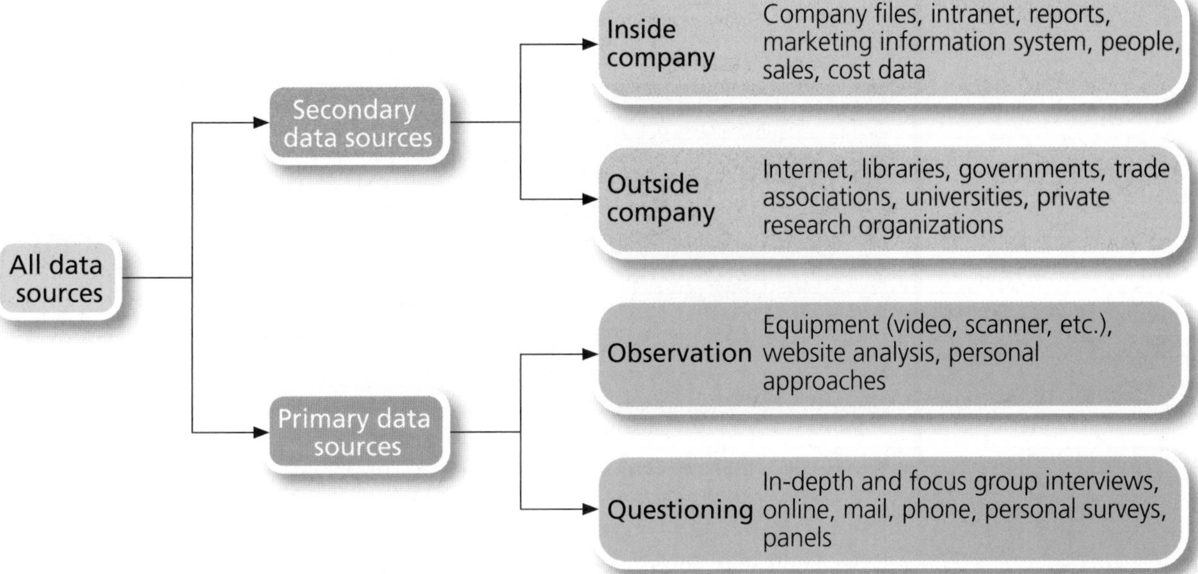

Search engines miss important databases

Many managers don't realize that much of the information stored on the Internet is in database formats that standard website search engines can't find. To search for information in those databases you must first locate the website with the relevant database and then use software at the site to search inside the database. Directories that describe database sites help with the first step. Complete Planet (www.completeplanet.com), for example, provides an organized listing of more than 70,000 searchable databases.

Monitor chatter on the web

Sometimes it can be useful to review or monitor what others are saying about your company or its products. There are useful tools that allow a marketing manager to quickly access what is being said online. For example, a marketing manager can simply enter a brand name at search.twitter.com or socialmention.com to find tweets, blog posts, comments, and other online mentions of that brand. By scanning these online posts, a marketing manager can get a sense of how customers feel about the brand. Social Mention takes this a step further and aggregates all kinds of content from users—bookmarks, blog posts, Twitter, Facebook, and many more. Social Mention's software automatically analyzes all of these sources and performs a *sentiment analysis* that categorizes each mention as positive, negative, or neutral.

These monitoring tools are alluring; they generate a lot of information very quickly and many are free. Yet this information is selective—choosing Internet users who choose to be vocal—and may not accurately reflect the sentiment of the target market. When Skittles launched a new website, its marketing managers were alarmed by early criticism of the site in social media outlets including blogs, Facebook, and Twitter. When Skittles managers tapped a broader set of customers, they found little need for concern.

However, online monitoring may provide a "head's up" about consumer attitudes or problems. If Kryptonite had monitored the web, it might have responded more quickly to YouTube videos showing how easy it was to pick its bicycle locks. When the videos went viral, the company's reputation was badly damaged.[10]

Internet Exercise

Marketing managers like to know what is being said online about their brand—and their competitors. Social Mention is a service that searches social media and aggregates the content it finds. Go to **www.socialmention.com** and compare three tablet computers. Conduct three separate searches using "Apple iPad," "Kindle Fire," and "Microsoft Surface"—for each search in "All." Which tablet has the most positive sentiment? Negative sentiment? What is the ratio of positive to negative sentiment for each tablet? Click on "negative" for each to learn the reasons for negative comments. Look at the measures of strength, sentiment, passion, and reach (hover over each to learn what it means) for each brand. How could this information be used by a marketing manager for the Microsoft Surface tablet computer?

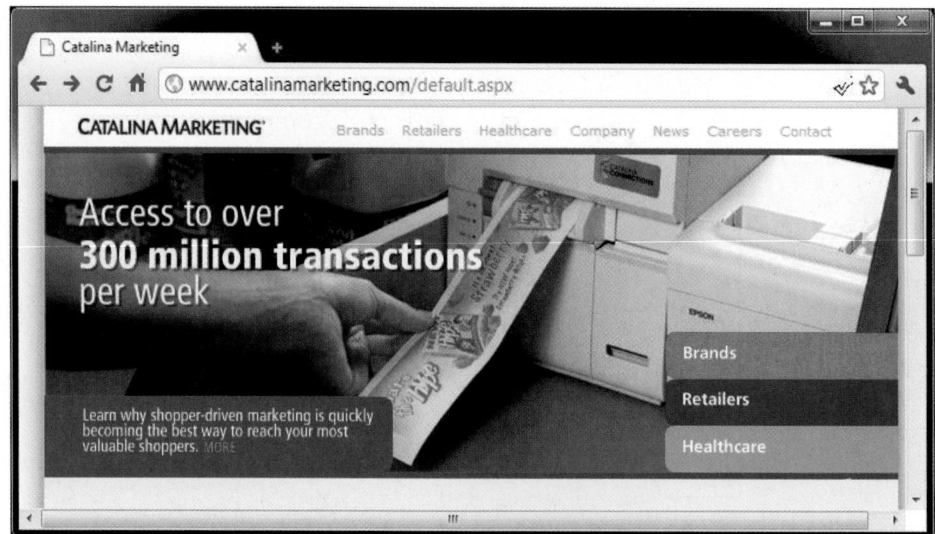

Some companies analyze data on their customers' past purchases to better predict their needs and interests.

Government data are inexpensive

Federal and state governments publish data on many subjects. Government data are often useful in estimating the size of markets. In Chapters 3 and 5 we gave a number of examples of the different types of data that are available. Almost all government data are immediately usable in inexpensive print and digital publications, on websites, and in downloads ready for further analysis.

Sometimes it's more practical to use summary publications with links or references that lead to more detailed reports. For the U.S. market, one of the most useful summary references is the *Statistical Abstract of the United States,* which provides a summary of statistics on the social, political, and economic organization of the United States. It is issued annually and can also be accessed online (www.census.gov/compendia/statab/). Similarly, the *United Nations Statistical Yearbook* is one of the best summaries of worldwide data; it can be downloaded in PDF format (http://unstats.un.org/unsd/syb/).

Secondary data are very limited on some international markets. However, most countries with advanced economies have government agencies that help researchers get the data they need. For example, *Statistics Canada* (www.statcan.gc.ca/) compiles a great deal of information on the Canadian market. *Eurostat* (http://epp.eurostat.ec.europa.eu/), the statistical office for the European Union countries, offers many publications packed with data on Europe, and data.australia.gov.au is an online source for the Australian government's public information datasets. In the United States, data.gov is an initiative to make a wide variety of government data more readily accessible. Some city and state governments have similar agencies for local data.

Situation analysis yields a lot—for very little

The virtue of a good situation analysis is that it can be very informative and takes little time. It's also inexpensive compared with more formal research efforts—like a large-scale survey. A phone, access to the Internet, and time might be all a marketing manager needs to gather a lot of insight. Situation analysis can help focus further research or even eliminate the need for it entirely. The situation analyst is really trying to determine the exact nature of the situation and the problem. This can lead the researcher back to step 1, defining the problem, to an early identification of the solution, or to identifying problem-specific data needs.

Determine what else is needed

At the end of the situation analysis, you can see which research questions—from the list developed during the problem definition step—remain unanswered. Then you have to decide exactly what information you need to answer those questions and how to get it. This may require discussion between technical experts and the marketing manager. Often companies use a written **research proposal**—a plan that specifies what information will be obtained and how—to be sure no misunderstandings occur later. The research plan may include information about costs, what data will be collected, how it will be collected, who will analyze it and how, and how long the process will take.

Getting Problem-Specific Data—Step 3

LO 7.4

Gathering primary data

There are different methods for collecting primary data. Which approach to use depends on the nature of the problem and how much time and money are available.

In most primary data collection, the researcher tries to learn what customers think about some topic or how they behave under some conditions. There are two basic methods for obtaining information about customers: *questioning* and *observing*. Questioning can be qualitative or quantitative; observing can take many forms.

Qualitative questioning—open-ended with a hidden purpose

Qualitative research seeks in-depth, open-ended responses, not yes or no answers. The researcher tries to get people to share their thoughts on a topic—without giving them many directions or guidelines about what to say.

One qualitative research method uses *non-directive interviews,* where an interviewer asks questions that encourage the interviewee to provide details. For example, a researcher might ask "Please tell me about your last grocery shopping trip." While some respondents talk about their preparation for the trip (preparing a list), another might talk about characteristics of the store, and another about prices and selection. Follow-up questions might just ask the respondent to elaborate. The real advantage of this approach is *depth.* Each person can be asked follow-up questions so the researcher really understands what *that* respondent is thinking. The depth of the qualitative approach gets at the details—even if the researcher needs a lot of judgment to summarize it all.

Focus groups stimulate discussion

One widely used form of qualitative questioning in marketing research is the **focus group interview**, which involves simultaneously interviewing 6 to 10 people in an informal group setting. A focus group also uses open-ended questions, but here an interviewer seeks group interaction—to stimulate thinking and get immediate reactions. Focus groups can be conducted in-person or online.

MOD-PAC, a large printing company, faced a problem: business from its traditional large customers was drying up. MOD-PAC managers wanted to know if there were niche markets willing to buy printing services over the Internet. So they conducted online focus groups, each with prospects from a different target market. The focus groups helped MOD-PAC managers see that each group had different needs and used different terms to discuss its problems. Each focus group also indicated that there was interest in buying printing services online. In response, MOD-PAC developed its "Print Lizard" website; the home page uses tabs to route customers from different segments to the part of the site that caters to their specific needs.[11]

Online focus groups help offset some of the limitations of traditional face-to-face focus groups. Participants who meet online usually feel freer to express their honest thoughts—and an aggressive individual is less likely to dominate the group. Regardless of how a focus group is conducted, conclusions reached from a session usually vary depending on who watches it. A typical problem—and serious limitation—with qualitative research is that it's hard to measure the results objectively. The results seem to depend largely on the viewpoint of the researcher. In addition, people willing to participate in a focus group—especially those who talk the most—may not be representative of the broader target market.

Focus groups can be conducted quickly and at relatively low cost—on average about $4,000 each. This is part of their appeal. But focus groups are probably being overused. It's easy to fall into the trap of treating an idea arising from a focus group as a "fact" that applies to a broad target market. To avoid this trap, some researchers use qualitative research to prepare for quantitative research. Qualitative research can provide good ideas—hypotheses. But we often need other approaches—based on more representative samples and objective measures—to test the hypotheses.

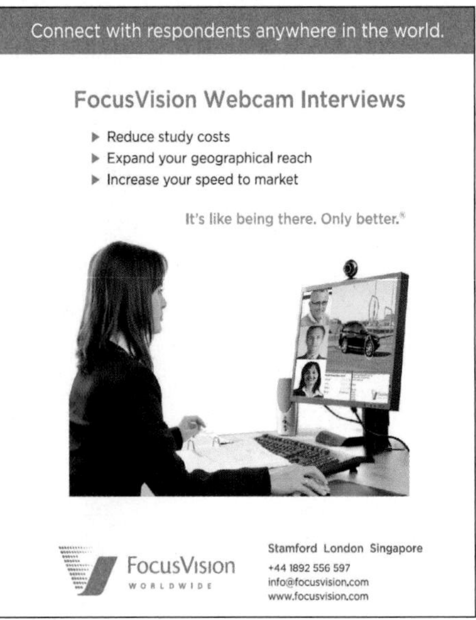

Online communities and panels as well as webcam interviews may be used to conduct qualitative or quantitative research.

Structured questioning gives more objective results

When researchers use identical questions and response alternatives, they can summarize the information quantitatively. Samples can be larger and more representative, and various statistics can be used to draw conclusions. For these reasons, most survey research is **quantitative research**—which seeks structured responses that can be summarized in numbers, like percentages, averages, or other statistics. For example, a marketing researcher might calculate what percentage of respondents have tried a new product and then figure an average score for how satisfied they were.

Fixed responses speed answering and analysis

Survey questionnaires usually provide fixed responses to questions to simplify analysis of the replies. This multiple-choice approach also makes it easier and faster for respondents to reply. Simple fill-in-a-number questions are also widely used in quantitative research. Fixed responses are also more convenient for computer analysis, which is how most surveys are analyzed.

Surveys come in many forms

Decisions about what specific questions to ask and how to ask them usually depend on how respondents will be contacted—by mail, e-mail, on the phone, or in person. What question and response approach is used may also affect the survey. There are many possibilities. For example, whether the survey is self administered or handled by an interviewer, the questionnaire may be on paper or online. The computerized or online survey can be programmed to skip certain questions, depending on answers given. Online surveys also allow the research to show pictures or play audio/video clips (for example, to get reactions to an advertising jingle). In an automated telephone interview, questions may be prerecorded and a subject responds by pushing touch-tone buttons on a phone.

Internet Exercise

Survey Monkey is one of several websites that host and help you create an online survey. Go to Survey Monkey's website (**www.surveymonkey.com**) and click on the "Take a Tour" link. Click through the tour to learn more about how the product works. What are some advantages of using Survey Monkey versus hiring an outside firm to develop a survey? What are some disadvantages? What types of research problems might be addressed with this type of survey?

Mail and online surveys are common and convenient

A questionnaire distributed by mail, e-mail, or online is useful when extensive questioning is necessary. Respondents can complete the questions at their convenience. They may be more willing to provide personal information—since a questionnaire can be completed anonymously. But the questions must be simple and easy to follow since no interviewer is there to help. If the respondent is likely to be a computer user, a questionnaire on a website can include a help feature with additional directions for people who need them.

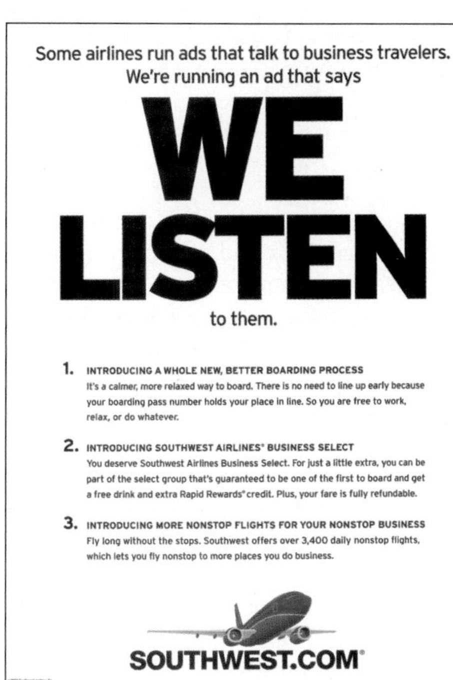

Southwest uses surveys and other types of research to "listen" to customer inputs. It also has a blog at www.blogsouthwest.com where it encourages customers and employees to share their opinions. For example, when Southwest changed how its frequent flyer loyalty program worked, the blog allowed customers to ask questions and comment on the change.

A big problem with questionnaires is that many people don't complete them. The **response rate**—the percentage of people contacted who complete the questionnaire—is often low and respondents may not be representative. Mail, e-mail, and online surveys are economical if a large number of people respond. But they may be quite expensive if the response rate is low. Worse, the results may be misleading if the respondents are not representative. For example, people who complete online questionnaires tend to be younger, better educated, or different in other ways that impact how they answer.

Distributing questionnaires by e-mail, or at a website, is popular. It is quick, and the responses come back in computer form. Surveys sent by regular mail usually take a lot longer.

Regardless of how quickly a questionnaire is distributed, it often takes a month or more to get the data back. That is too slow for some decisions. Moreover, it is difficult to get respondents to expand on particular points. In markets where illiteracy is a problem, it may not be possible to get any response. In spite of these limitations, the convenience and economy of self-administered surveys makes them popular.

Telephone surveys—fast and effective

Telephone interviews are also popular. They are effective for getting quick answers to simple questions. Telephone interviews allow the interviewer to probe and really learn what the respondent is thinking. In addition, with computer-aided telephone interviewing, answers are immediately recorded on a computer, resulting in fast data analysis. On the other hand, many consumers find calls intrusive—and about a third refuse to answer any questions. Moreover, respondents can't be certain who is calling or how personal information might be used.

Personal interview surveys—can be in-depth

A personal interview survey is usually much more expensive per interview than e-mail, mail, or telephone surveys. But it's easier to get and keep the respondent's attention when the interviewer is right there. The interviewer can also help explain complicated directions and perhaps get better responses. For these reasons, personal interviews are commonly used for research on business customers. To reduce the cost of locating consumer respondents, interviews are sometimes done at a store or shopping mall. This is called a mall intercept interview because the interviewer stops a shopper and asks for responses to the survey.

Researchers have to be careful that having an interviewer involved doesn't affect the respondent's answers. Sometimes people won't give an answer they consider embarrassing.

Or they may try to impress or please the interviewer. Further, in some cultures people don't want to give any information. For example, many people in Africa, Latin America, and Eastern Europe are reluctant to be interviewed. This is also a problem in many low-income, inner-city areas in the United States; even Census Bureau interviewers have trouble getting cooperation.[12]

Market research online communities combine qualitative and quantitative research methods

The Internet enables firms to explore and use a variety of research techniques. One technique combines qualitative and quantitative approaches in private online communities. A **market research online community (MROC)** is an online group of participants who are joined together by a common interest, and who participate in ongoing research. Online communities are recruited to fit a desired psychographic, lifestyle, or demographic profile and may be comprised of 50 to several hundred members. Members spend months, possibly years, online together brainstorming ideas and conversing with other customers and the firm's marketing managers. Communities often include online focus groups and question-and-answer sessions, as well as quantitative approaches like polls and surveys.

Hallmark Cards is one of the pioneers in this area. In the "Hallmark Idea Exchange," an online group of 200 mothers of young children are asked about everything from Hallmark's merchandising strategy to its pricing. Participants meet for at least a half hour each week and discuss their wants, needs, and preferences. Hallmark marketing managers stimulate discussion of relevant topics by posting questions. Sometimes they take polls to get a wider range of opinions on what it thinks are some of the best ideas. Hallmark Idea Exchange generates at least 10 to 15 concrete ideas each month.

Marketing managers need to be cautious when gathering data online. "Tricia," that 41-year-old mother from Wisconsin, may actually be "Jake," a 24-year-old bartender in Oregon who is just looking to score a few free gift cards or some extra cash by joining an online community. Nevertheless, with careful monitoring online communities can provide valuable insights.[13]

Questioning has limitations

Questioning—whether qualitative or quantitative—has its limitations. Respondents sometimes give answers that they think the questioner wants to hear, or they may not accurately recall past events. When that is the case, observing may be more accurate or economical.

Observing—what you see is what you get

Observing—as a method of collecting data—focuses on a well-defined problem. Here we are not talking about the casual observations that may stimulate ideas in the early steps of a research project. With the observation method, researchers try to see or record what the subject does naturally. They don't want the observing to *influence* the subject's behavior.

For example, marketing managers for Heinz Ketchup knew they had an opportunity if they could make it easier to eat French fries while driving. To learn more, marketing managers sat behind a one-way mirror and watched consumers sitting in minivans put ketchup on fries, burgers, and chicken nuggets during a simulated driving experience. They saw some people tear the corners off packets with their teeth and others squirt ketchup in their mouth before adding fries. Insights from this research fueled development of Heinz "Dip and Squeeze" ketchup packets, which can be squeezed from one end like the traditional foil pouch or a peel back lid can expose ketchup for dipping. Consumers like the new packaging and fast-food restaurants are selling more French fries out of the drive-through window.[14]

Ethnographic research looks at customers in their own environment

Ethnographic research has its roots in anthropology, which studies different cultures by observing participants in their natural habitat. In marketing research, ethnography involves studying customers in their homes or at work. Procter & Gamble managers used ethnography to learn about consumer needs in very poor parts of the world, places where people live on $2 a day or less. By spending time with these consumers, P&G found that these women value beauty and appreciate products that help them look good. So P&G doesn't want to simply dilute higher-end products to bring down costs; it wants to address these customers' particular needs. For example, in parts of rural China, water is very scarce—a woman may have only a few cups of water to rinse hair that extends to the middle of her back, or a cup of water to wash with. So P&G developed a leave-in hair conditioner and face soaps and hair dyes that require little or no water.[15]

Because today's consumers use TV, radio, and other media differently than in the past, advertisers want to follow those consumers in-home, at work, in a car—or anywhere they go. Arbitron's Portable People Meter (PPM) technology enables advertisers to do that.

Video cameras can be useful for ethnography because subjects often don't know their behavior is being recorded. Some researchers use this technique to study the routes consumers follow through a store or how they select products. A dog food manufacturer put video cameras on the pet food aisle in supermarkets to learn more about how people choose dog food and treats. The videos showed that kids often picked the treats, but that the kids' parents chose the food. The videos also revealed that kids couldn't reach treats when they were on higher shelves. Sales increased when the treats were moved to lower shelves.[16]

Walk a mile in the customer's shoes

Sometimes the best way to observe a customer is for a marketing manager to become a customer. By calling his firm's own customer service number and pretending to be a customer, a marketing manager can discover how long it takes someone to answer the phone—or the ability of a customer service rep to politely and efficiently solve a problem.

Marketing managers at Walgreens drugstores wanted to better understand the challenges facing senior citizens—an important and growing target market. So they donned glasses that blurred vision and wore large rubber gloves that simulated arthritic hands. After experiencing firsthand the difficulties facing seniors, Walgreens managers began to use larger print in the weekly circular and installed call buttons near heavy items like bottled water and laundry detergent.[17]

Observing is common in advertising research

Observation methods are common in advertising research. For example, Nielsen Media Research (www.nielsenmedia.com) uses a device called the "people meter" that adapts the observation method to television audience research. This device is attached to the TV set in the homes of selected families. It records when the set is on and what station is tuned in. Similarly, Arbitron developed its Portable People Meter (PPM) to automatically measure radio listening habits.[18]

Observing website visitors

Website analysis software allows marketing managers to observe customer behavior at a firm's website. For example, there are tools that help marketing managers understand how a customer came to a website—was it the keyword used in a Google search, a response to an e-mail promotion, or a link from an online review site? Reports show the series of clicks made by visitors and how long they stayed on each page. This information can help marketing managers make changes to the site so that it attracts the right customers and offers useful information so they stay and make purchases.

Online retailer Shipwreck Beads wanted to promote a summer sale of fire-polished beads, so it e-mailed 76,000 customers and placed banner ads on the websites for *BeadStyle* and *Bead and Button* magazines. Web analysis tools showed which promotions and which keywords generated the most leads. Because the answers were available very quickly, the firm revised the advertising copy to include more instances of the phrase "fire-polished beads." This simple change improved placement on search pages and, within a month, hits to its website increased fourfold.

Checkout scanners see a lot

Computerized scanners at retail checkout counters help researchers collect very specific, and useful, information. Often this type of data feeds directly into a firm's MIS. Managers of a large chain of stores can see exactly what products have sold each day and how much money each department in each store has earned. But the scanner also has wider applications for marketing research.

Information Resources, Inc. (www.infores.com), and ACNielsen (www.acnielsen.com) use **consumer panels**—a group of consumers who provide information on a continuing basis. Whenever a panel member shops for groceries, he or she gives an ID card to the clerk, who scans the number. Then the scanner records every purchase—including brands, sizes, prices, and any coupons used. In a variation of this approach, consumers use a handheld scanner to record purchases once they get home. Sometimes members of a panel answer questions and the answers are merged with the scanner data.

Analysis of panel data revealed that Ocean Spray was seeing sales slip to competitors. Households with kids are the heaviest purchasers of juice; yet they were purchasing Ocean Spray on a less frequent basis. Further research with these panel members revealed this was due to its "too tart" taste and tendency to stain. To combat this, the company focused its energies on developing White Cranberry Juice Drinks by harvesting the berries before they develop their traditional red color and pungent taste. An ad for the new product depicted a mom and her small son enjoying the taste of the new White Cranberry juice. When the boy accidentally spills it on the floor, it's also clear that it doesn't stain. Now that the "no stain" message has sunk in, Ocean Spray's ads put more emphasis on the idea that kids love the taste.[19]

Data captured by electronic scanners are equally important to e-commerce in business-to-business markets. Increasingly, firms mark their shipping cartons and packages with computer-readable bar codes that make it fast and easy to track inventory, shipments, orders, and the like. As information about product sales or shipments becomes available, it is instantly included in the MIS and accessible over the Internet.

Experimental method controls conditions

A marketing manager can get a different kind of information—with either questioning or observing—using the experimental method. With the **experimental method**, researchers compare the responses of two (or more) groups that are similar except on the characteristic being tested. The experimental method is sometimes called A/B testing, because it compares options labeled A and B. Researchers want to learn if the specific characteristic—which varies among groups—*causes* differences in some response among the groups. For example, a researcher might be interested in comparing responses of consumers who had seen an ad for a new product with consumers who had not seen the

Exhibit 7–5 Illustration of Experimental Method in Comparing Effectiveness of Two Ads

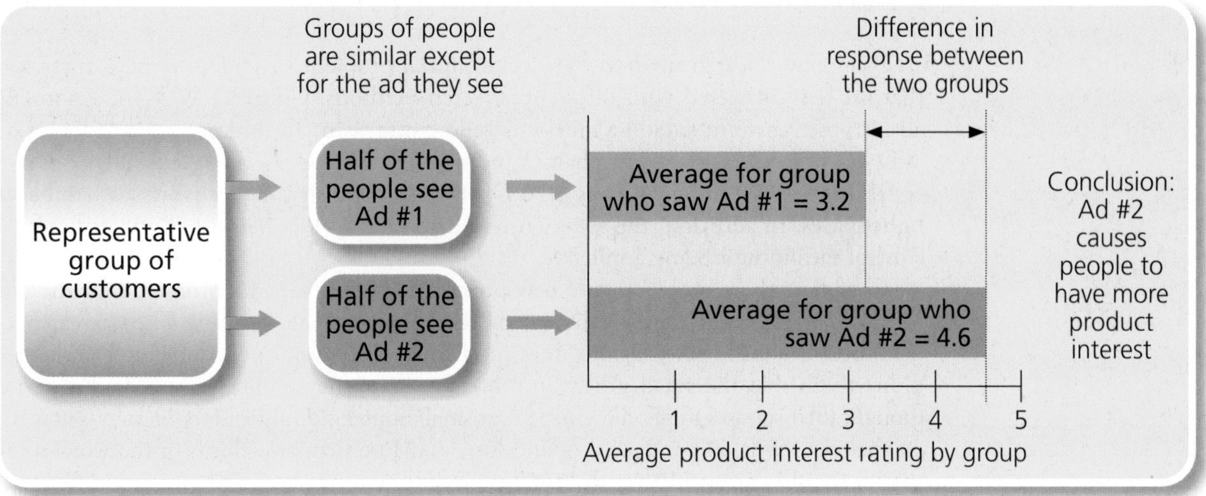

ad. The "response" might be an observed behavior—like the purchase of a product—or the answer to a specific question—like "How interested are you in this new product?" See Exhibit 7-5.

Marketing managers for Mars—the company that makes Snickers candy bars—used the experimental method to help solve a problem. They wanted to know if making their candy bar bigger would increase sales enough to offset the higher cost. To decide, they conducted a marketing experiment in which the company carefully varied the size of candy bars sold in *different* markets. Otherwise, the marketing mix stayed the same. Then researchers tracked sales in each market area to see the effect of the different sizes. They saw a big difference immediately; the added sales more than offset the cost of a bigger candy bar.

Online experiments can quickly generate knowledge

Online companies can conduct experiments and often get answers in just a few days. An online retailer might try two different versions of a web page and then see which one generates more sales. For example, online retailer Zappos thought that adding short product demonstration videos to each product page would increase sales (a hypothesis). Zappos knew that there would be some cost to creating so many videos, so it needed to know whether the videos would increase sales. Customers that linked on the tested products were randomly shown a product page with a video or an identical page without a video. Zappos found that purchases increased about 10 percent when pages included the video description. That experiment justified the production of more than 50,000 videos—and higher sales.

Test-marketing of new products is another type of marketing experiment. In a typical approach, a company tries variations on its planned marketing mix in a few geographic market areas. The results of the tests help to identify problems or refine the marketing mix—before the decision is made to go to broader distribution. However, alert competitors may disrupt such tests—perhaps by increasing promotion or offering retailers extra discounts.[20]

Syndicated research shares data collection costs

Some private research firms specialize in collecting data and then sell them to managers in many different client firms. Often the marketing manager subscribes to the research service and gets regular updates. About 40 percent of marketing research spending is for syndicated research, and this helps explain why it can be an economical approach when marketing managers from many different firms need the same type of data. For example, many different auto producers use J. D. Power's (www.jdpa.com) surveys of customer satisfaction—often as the basis for advertising claims. Subscription data services are available for many different industries—ranging from food services to prescription drugs to micro electronic devices.[21]

A combination of research methods may be needed

Using one research method to solve an initial problem may identify new questions that are best answered with different research methods. Consider WD-40, a popular all-purpose lubricant sold in a blue-and-yellow spray can. To find potential new uses of WD-40, researchers visited mechanics and watched them as they worked. These observers realized that even small cans of WD-40 were difficult for mechanics to handle in tight spaces. In addition, the spray created drips and messes because it was difficult to control the amount being applied.

To address these problems, the new-product team developed a prototype for the No Mess Pen, a small marker that delivers a precise amount of the lubricant. Then, researchers held focus groups to get reactions from mechanics. They weren't encouraging. Mechanics didn't think that the small unit would handle their large application needs. Yet many thought their spouses might like the pen for small household lubrication jobs. To follow up on this idea, WD-40 conducted online surveys. More than two-thirds of the women respondents said they would buy the product. To fine-tune targeting and promotion, WD-40 then conducted more than 40 in-home studies to learn how families actually used the No Mess Pen. This research confirmed that women were the primary target market, but that men used the pens as well. Moreover, the pen didn't replace the can of WD-40 already found in most households; rather, pens were stored in desk drawers, cars, and toolboxes so they'd be handy. WD-40 used different research methods to address different problems, but in combination they contributed to making the No Mess Pen a great success.[22]

Understand the costs and benefits of research

Whether collecting secondary data for a situation analysis or primary data from a focus group or survey, marketing research takes time and money. A good marketing manager knows that the value of additional information lies in the ability to design more effective marketing strategies. Similarly, different research methods provide different insights—and come at different costs. Marketing managers do not need to spend $100,000 to determine whether to spend $50,000 on advertising.

There are also benefits to getting information quickly—particularly in some markets. For example, competition and customer behavior can change quickly in high-technology markets. If a study takes six months to complete, the marketing manager may be developing a marketing strategy for a market that no longer exists—or, at best, looks quite different.

Small companies with limited budgets must be especially creative in identifying low-cost ways to get the information they need. Marketing managers can learn a lot by simply making sure they listen to what their firm's customers have to say. Even when doing informal research, marketers should have objectives for their questions. They can also learn a lot by studying competitors' websites and promotional materials or by shopping in their stores. When conducting formal research, they should be careful not to be too frugal. Skipping the pretesting of a questionnaire or using employees instead of real customers in a focus group may give managers a false sense of confidence—and worse, the wrong solution to a problem.[23]

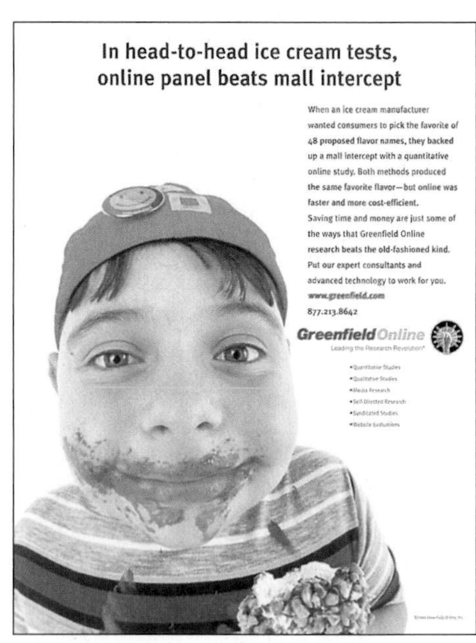

When marketing managers at an ice cream manufacturer wanted consumers to pick the favorite of 48 proposed flavor names, they backed up mall intercept interviews with a quantitative online survey. Both methods produced the same favorite flavor—but online was faster and more cost efficient.

Interpreting the Data—Step 4

LO 7.5

What does it really mean?

After someone collects the data, they have to be analyzed to decide what they all mean. In quantitative research, this step usually involves statistics. **Statistical packages**—easy-to-use computer programs that analyze data—have made this step easier. As we noted earlier, some firms provide *decision support systems* so managers can use a statistical package to interpret data themselves. More often, however, technical specialists are involved at the interpretation step.

Cross-tabulation is one of the most frequently used approaches for analyzing and interpreting marketing research data. It shows the relationship of answers to two different questions. Exhibit 7-6 is an example. The cross-tab analysis shows that households with higher incomes are much more likely to have broadband Internet service.

There are many other approaches for statistical analysis—the best one depends on the situation. The details of statistical analysis are beyond the scope of this book. But a good manager should know enough to understand what a research project can and can't do.[24]

Is your sample really representative?

It's usually impossible for marketing managers to collect all the information they want about everyone in a **population**—the total group they are interested in. Marketing researchers typically study only a **sample**, a part of the relevant population. How well a sample *represents* the total population affects the results. Results from a sample that is not representative may not give a true picture.

The manager of a retail store might want a phone survey to learn what consumers think about the store's hours. If interviewers make all of the calls during the day, consumers who work outside the home during the day won't be represented. Those interviewed might say the limited store hours are "satisfactory." Yet it would be a mistake to assume that *all* consumers are satisfied.

Research results are not exact

An estimate from a sample, even a representative one, usually varies somewhat from the true value for a total population. Managers sometimes forget this. They assume that survey results are exact. Instead, when interpreting sample estimates, managers should think of them as *suggesting* the approximate value.

If random selection is used to develop the sample, researchers can use statistical methods to help determine the likely accuracy of the sample value. This is done in terms of **confidence intervals**—the range on either side of an estimate that is likely to contain the true value for the whole population. Some managers are surprised to learn how wide that range can be.

Consider a wholesaler who has 2,000 retail customers and wants to learn how many of these retailers carry a product from a competing supplier. If the wholesaler randomly samples 100 retailers and 20 say yes, then the sample estimate is 20 percent. But with that information the wholesaler can only be 95 percent confident that the percentage of all

Exhibit 7–6 Cross-Tabulation Breakdown of Responses to an Internet Service Provider Consumer Survey

		What is your household income?				
		Less than $30,000	$30,000 to 50,000	$50,000 to $75,000	More than $75,000	Total Sample
Does your home have broadband Internet service?	Yes	23.7%	46.2%	52.3%	72.4%	47.1%
	No	76.3	53.8	47.7	27.6	52.9
	Total	100.0%	100.0%	100.0%	100.0%	100.0%

Interpretation: In the survey 47.1 percent of people said that they had broadband Internet service in their homes. However, the adoption of broadband Internet service was higher at higher income levels. For example, 72.4 percent of households with over $75,000 income have broadband but only 23.7 percent have it among homes with income less than $30,000.

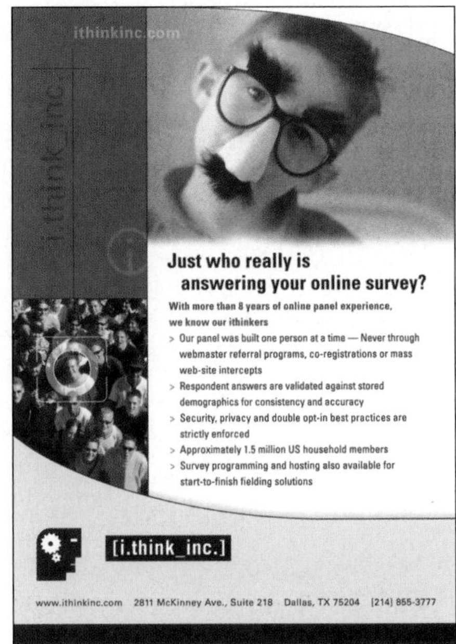

Survey Sampling and i.think_inc. help marketing researchers develop samples that are really representative of the target market.

retailers is in the confidence interval between 12 and 28 percent. The larger the sample size, the greater the accuracy of estimates from a random sample. With a larger sample, a few unusual responses are less likely to make a big difference.[25]

Validity problems can destroy research

Even if the sampling is carefully planned, it is also important to evaluate the quality of the research data itself.

Managers and researchers should be sure that research data really measure what they are supposed to measure. Many of the variables marketing managers are interested in are difficult to measure accurately. Questionnaires may let us assign numbers to consumer responses, but that still doesn't mean that the result is precise. An interviewer might ask, "How much did you spend on soft drinks last week?" A respondent may be perfectly willing to cooperate—and be part of the representative sample—but just not be able to remember.

Validity concerns the extent to which data measure what they are intended to measure. Validity problems are important in marketing research because many people will try to answer even when they don't know what they're talking about. Further, a poorly worded question can mean different things to different people and invalidate the results. Often, pretests of a research project are required to evaluate the quality of the questions and measures and to ensure that potential problems have been identified.

Interpretation balances analysis and judgment

Data and analysis are important inputs to decision making, but judgment is important, too. Research has found three distinct types of managers when it comes to the use of data and analytics. One group distrusts data and analytics while another completely trusts data, even over their own judgment. The study found that the most effective managers are comfortable with data and analytics, while also applying their own judgment when interpreting analytical findings. These managers actively seek input from a range of people and listen to opinions that differ from their own. With the growth of big data, there will be greater pressure to rely on data for decision making. While it is an important input, a manager's experience and judgment should also play a role.[26]

Ethics involved in interpreting and presenting results

Marketing managers want information they can trust when they make marketing decisions. But research often involves many hidden details. A person who wants to misuse research to pursue a personal agenda can often do so.

Put your foodservice research into some of the most experienced hands

... ours.

You may not know our name, but we bet you know our work. For more than 30 years, Restaurant Research Associates has partnered with some of the biggest names in foodservice. We know food research from every angle. And, it's not a part-time job - we live it, breathe it and even dream it, day in and day out.

365 days a year. Since 1979.

Restaurant Research Associates
A Leader in Foodservice Research
714.368.1890 • www.RestaurantResearchAssociates.com

Think so? Hope so? At Bravo we partner with our clients to develop insightful strategies and innovative plans that help them succeed in the Hispanic market. So, the next time your Hispanic prospect walks in, you can be sure your brand will shine, a sale will occur and your business will grow.

Hispanic marketing Experts since 1980
New York • Miami • Chicago • San Francisco
www.thinkbravo.com
bravo

Research firms sometimes specialize in particular markets. This might make it easier for them to interpret results.

Perhaps the most common ethical issues concern decisions to withhold certain information about the research. For example, a manager might selectively share only those results that support his or her viewpoint. Others involved in a decision might never know that they are getting only partial truths.[27]

Ethics Question

You're the new marketing manager for a small firm that offers computer repair services. The company's owner approves your proposal for a telephone survey to learn more about the needs of firms that are not current customers. You identify local firms for the sample and hire a researcher to call them. The interviewer tells respondents that their answers will be anonymous and used only for research purposes. About halfway through the data collection, the interviewer tells you that respondents are confused by one of the questions and that their answers to that question are probably useless. The question concerns the issue that is most important to your new boss. Do you admit the problem to others in your company? If the sales manager asks for the completed questionnaires, including all the names and responses, what would you say?

Solving the Problem—Step 5

The last step is solving the problem

In the problem solution step, managers use the research results to make marketing decisions.

Some researchers, and some managers, are fascinated by the interesting tidbits of information that come from the research process. They are excited if the research reveals something they didn't know before. But if research doesn't have action implications, it has little value and suggests poor planning by the researcher and the manager.

When the research process is finished, the marketing manager should be able to apply the findings in marketing strategy planning—the choice of a target market or the mix of the four Ps. If the research doesn't provide information to help guide these decisions, the company has wasted research time and money.

We emphasize this step because it is the reason for and logical conclusion to the whole research process. This final step must be anticipated at each of the earlier steps.

International Marketing Research

LO 7.6

Research contributes to international success

Marketing research on overseas markets is often a major contributor toward international marketing success. Conversely, export failures are often due to a lack of home office expertise concerning customer interests, needs, and other segmenting dimensions as well as environmental factors such as competitors' prices and products. Effective marketing research can help to overcome these problems.

Accurate data may be hard to find

In many countries, it is difficult—especially for a foreigner—to gather accurate information. Let's look at the challenge in China. Because the economy is growing so rapidly, secondary data that are out of date may be much more inaccurate than would be the case in a country with slow growth. Some important secondary data (such as the *China Statistical Yearbook*) are now available in an English language version, but that is often not the case. There are other problems, such as no explanation of the methods used to collect the data. That's important because the Chinese market is both large and complicated. Imagine how you would try to do a competitor analysis when there are over 1,000 Chinese firms that brew beer! Collecting primary data is difficult too. Western researchers feel that Chinese managers and consumers are not very receptive to direct questioning. Those who agree to cooperate may be hesitant to say anything negative about their own companies or anything favorable about competitors. So it takes experienced interviewers to carefully interpret responses.[28]

Avoid mistakes with local researchers

Whether a firm is small and entering overseas markets for the first time or already large and well established internationally, there are often advantages to working with local marketing research firms. They know the local situation and are less likely to make mistakes based on misunderstanding the customs, language, or circumstances of the customers they study.

Many large research firms have a network of local offices around the world to help with such efforts. Similarly, multinational or local advertising agencies and intermediaries can often provide leads on identifying the best research suppliers.

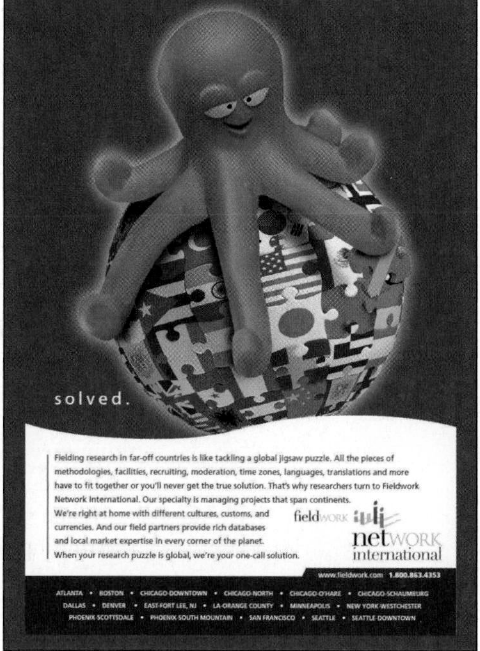

There are a large number of international marketing research firms that offer specialized services to marketing managers.

Some coordination and standardization makes sense

When a firm is doing similar research projects in different markets around the world, it makes sense for the marketing manager to coordinate the efforts. If the manager doesn't establish some basic guidelines at the outset, the different research projects may all vary so much that the results can't be compared from one market area to another. Such comparisons give a home office manager a better chance of understanding how the markets are similar and how they differ.[29]

CONCLUSION

Marketing managers face difficult decisions in selecting target markets and managing marketing mixes, but they rarely have all the information they would like to have before making those decisions. Even less information may be available in international markets. This doesn't mean that managers have to rely solely on intuition; they can usually obtain some good information that will improve the quality of their decisions. Both large and small firms can take advantage of Internet and intranet capabilities to develop marketing information systems (MIS) that help to ensure routinely needed data are available and quickly accessible.

Some questions can only be answered with marketing research. Marketing research should be guided by the scientific method. This approach to solving marketing problems involves five steps: (1) defining the problem, (2) analyzing the situation, (3) obtaining data, (4) interpreting data, and (5) developing and implementing a solution. This objective and organized approach helps to keep problem solving on task. It reduces the risk of doing costly and unnecessary research that doesn't achieve the desired end—solving the marketing problem.

Our strategy planning framework can be very helpful in evaluating marketing research. By finding and focusing on real problems, researchers and marketing managers may be able to move more quickly to a useful solution during the situation analysis stage—without the costs and risks of gathering primary data. With imagination, they may even be able to find answers in their MIS or in readily available secondary data. However, primary data from questioning, observing, or conducting experiments may be needed. Qualitative data often provide initial insights or hypotheses—which might be tested with more representative samples and quantitative approaches.

KEY TERMS

LO 7.7

marketing research, *170*
marketing information system (MIS), *170*
big data, *173*
data warehouse, *173*
intranet, *173*
decision support system (DSS), *173*
marketing dashboard, *174*
marketing model, *174*
scientific method, *176*
hypotheses, *176*
marketing research process, *176*
situation analysis, *177*
secondary data, *178*
primary data, *178*
research proposal, *180*
qualitative research, *181*
focus group interview, *181*
quantitative research, *182*
response rate, *183*
market research online community (MROC), *184*
consumer panels, *186*
experimental method, *186*
statistical packages, *189*
population, *189*
sample, *189*
confidence intervals, *189*
validity, *190*

QUESTIONS AND PROBLEMS

1. Discuss the concept of a marketing information system and why it is important for marketing managers to be involved in planning the system.
2. In your own words, explain why a decision support system (DSS) can add to the value of a marketing information system. Give an example of how a decision support system might help.
3. Discuss how output from a marketing information system (MIS) might differ from the output of a typical marketing research department.
4. Discuss some of the likely problems facing the marketing manager in a small firm who plans to search the Internet for information on competitors' marketing plans.

5. Explain the key characteristics of the scientific method and show why these are important to managers concerned with research.
6. How is the situation analysis different from the data collection step? Can both these steps be done at the same time to obtain answers sooner? Is this wise?
7. Distinguish between primary data and secondary data and illustrate your answer.
8. With so much secondary information now available free or at low cost over the Internet, why would a firm ever want to spend the money to do primary research?
9. If a firm were interested in estimating the distribution of income in the state of California, how could it proceed? Be specific.
10. If a firm were interested in estimating sand and clay production in Georgia, how could it proceed? Be specific.
11. Go to the library (or get on the Internet) and find (in some government publication or website) three marketing-oriented "facts" on international markets that you did not know existed or were available. Record on one page and show sources.
12. Explain why a company might want to do focus group interviews rather than individual interviews with the same people.
13. Distinguish between qualitative and quantitative approaches to research—and give some of the key advantages and limitations of each approach.
14. Define response rate and discuss why a marketing manager might be concerned about the response rate achieved in a particular survey. Give an example.
15. Prepare a table that summarizes some of the key advantages and limitations of mail, e-mail, telephone, and personal interview approaches for administering questionnaires.
16. Would a firm want to subscribe to a shared cost data service if the same data were going to be available to competitors? Discuss your reasoning.
17. Explain how you might use different types of research (focus groups, observation, survey, and experiment) to forecast market reaction to a new kind of disposable baby diaper, which is to receive no promotion other than what the retailer will give it. Further, assume that the new diaper's name will not be associated with other known products. The product will be offered at competitive prices.
18. Marketing research involves expense—sometimes considerable expense. Why does the text recommend the use of marketing research even though a highly experienced marketing executive is available?
19. A marketing manager is considering opportunities to export her firm's current consumer products to several different countries. She is interested in getting secondary data that will help her narrow down choices to countries that offer the best potential. The manager then plans to do more detailed primary research with consumers in those markets. What suggestions would you give her about how to proceed?
20. Discuss the concept that some information may be too expensive to obtain in relation to its value. Illustrate.

CREATING MARKETING PLANS

The Marketing Plan Coach software on the text website includes a sample marketing plan for Hillside Veterinary Clinic. Look through the "Customers" and "Competitors" sections in the Situation Analysis and consider the following questions.

a. What different types of marketing research were conducted to fill out these sections of the marketing plan?
b. What are the strengths of the research conducted? What are the weaknesses?
c. Keeping in mind probable cost and time to complete, what additional research would you recommend?

SUGGESTED CASES

3. NOCO United Soccer Academy
8. Besitti's Restaurant
9. Peaceful Rest Motor Lodge

COMPUTER-AIDED PROBLEM

7. MARKETING RESEARCH

Texmac, Inc., has an idea for a new type of weaving machine that could replace the machines now used by many textile manufacturers. Texmac has done a telephone survey to estimate how many of the old-style machines are now in use. Respondents using the present machines were also asked if they would buy the improved machine at a price of $10,000.

Texmac researchers identified a population of about 5,000 textile factories as potential customers. A sample of these were surveyed, and Texmac received 500 responses. Researchers think the total potential market is about 10 times larger than the sample of respondents. Two hundred twenty of the respondents indicated that their firms used old machines like the one the new machine was intended to replace. Forty percent of those firms said that they would be interested in buying the new Texmac machine.

Texmac thinks the sample respondents are representative of the total population, but the marketing manager realizes that estimates based on a sample may not be exact when applied to the whole population. He wants to see how sampling error would affect profit estimates. Data for this problem appear in the spreadsheet. Quantity estimates for the whole market are computed from the sample estimates. These quantity estimates are used in computing likely sales, costs, and profit contribution.

a. An article in a trade magazine reports that there are about 5,200 textile factories that use the old-style machine. If the total market is really 5,200 customers—not 5,000 as Texmac originally thought—how does that affect the total quantity estimate and profit contribution?

b. Some of the people who responded to the survey didn't know much about different types of machines. If the actual number of old machines in the market is really 200 per 500 firms—not 220 as estimated from survey responses—how much would this affect the expected profit contribution (for 5,200 factories)?

c. The marketing manager knows that the percentage of textile factories that would actually buy the new machine might be different from the 40 percent who said they would in the survey. He estimates that the proportion that will replace the old machine might be as low as 36 and as high as 44 percent—depending on business conditions. Use the analysis feature to prepare a table that shows how expected quantity and profit contribution change when the sample percent varies between a minimum of 36 and a maximum of 44 percent. What does this analysis suggest about the use of estimates from marketing research samples? (*Note:* Use 5,200 for the number of potential customers and use 220 as the estimate of the number of old machines in the sample.)

8 CHAPTER EIGHT

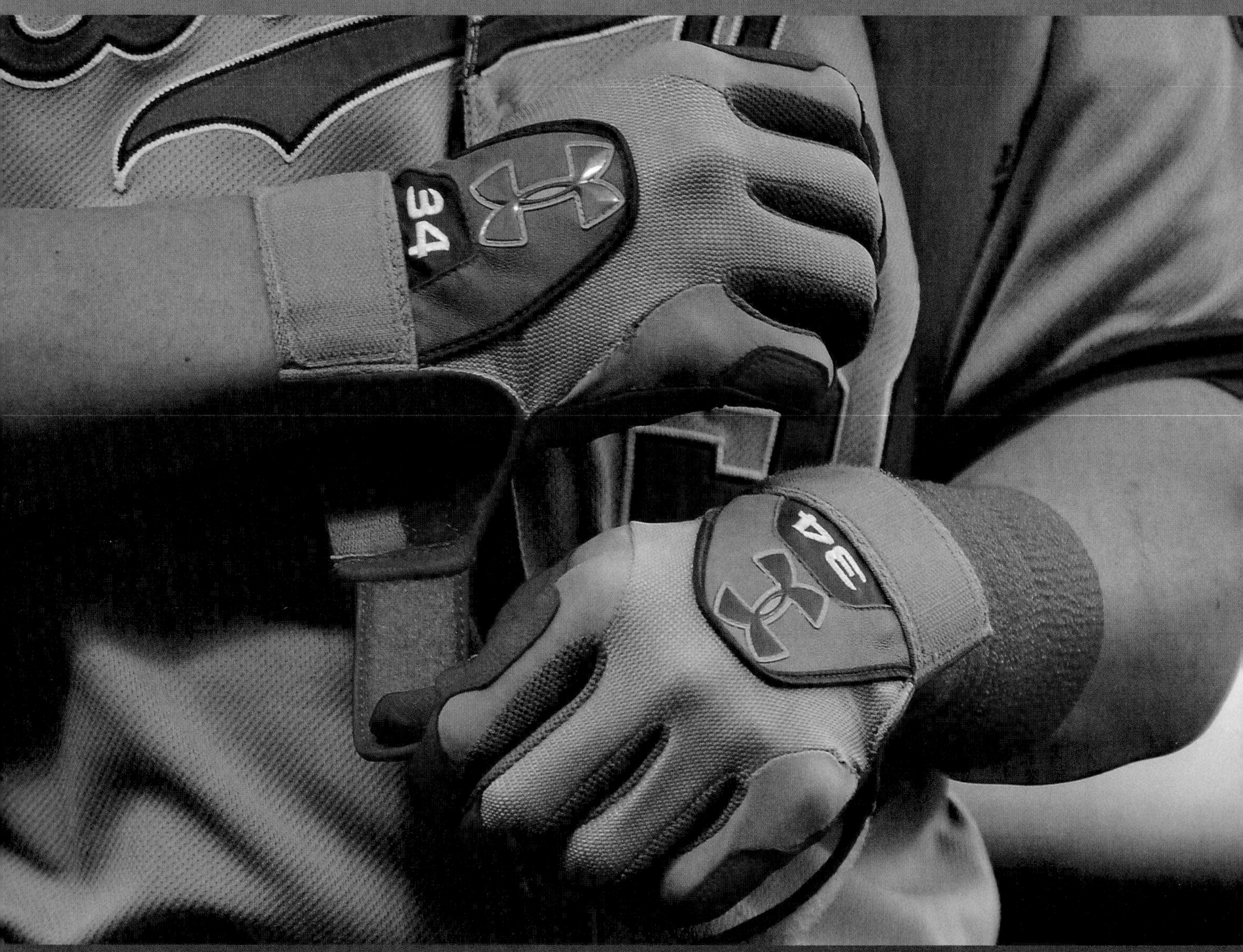

Elements of Product Planning for Goods and Services

Kevin Plank was a business major and football player at the University of Maryland when he spotted an opportunity. He and his teammates wore cotton T-shirts under their football pads, but the T-shirts quickly became sweat-soaked, heavy, and uncomfortable during practices and games. When Plank began looking for a product that would perform better than a T-shirt, he learned about new types of fabrics and performance clothing for bicyclists and hikers.

In New York City's garment district, Plank learned about a polyester-Lycra-blend fabric that didn't trap moisture. He worked with a tailor to develop several prototype shirts and then asked friends who were players in the National Football League to try them. The players really liked the skintight compression shirts. They fit comfortably under football gear and wicked away sweat—keeping the players cooler, drier, and lighter. When Plank's friends clamored for more shirts, he knew he was on to something. However, he couldn't afford a big ad campaign to tout the benefits of his product, and he didn't have relationships with retailers who could help build demand with final consumers. So Plank moved to commercialize his shirts with a focus on a target market he knew: college football teams.

Plank went back to New York and ordered 500 shirts, the first products with the Under Armour brand name and the start of what became the Heat-Gear warm weather product line. Then he loaded his shirts in his SUV and traveled to colleges across the Southeast. He tried to persuade coaches, players, and equipment managers about the benefits of his unique shirts. Many were not initially convinced of the value—especially since the price was three to five times the price of a T-shirt. But its advantage was clear after a player would try one for a football practice—and praise for the product spread quickly.

Success with college and professional athletes helped the company build credibility. It also led to relationships with specialty-sports retailers who could reach the larger and more profitable consumer market. Under Armour's well-known brand helped it gain exclusive display space in sports retailers like Dick's Sporting Goods. The "store within a store" highlights the Under Armour brand—and draws customers who buy other high-margin Under Armour products.

Under Armour's success attracted Nike and Adidas—and later dealer brands like Kohl's Tek Gear and J.C. Penney's Simply for Sports—to the performance clothing market. To fight back, Under Armour put more emphasis on creative promotion to build customer preference for the Under Armour brand. For example, Under Armour ran TV and print ads featuring professional athletes like Dallas Cowboy (and former Plank teammate) Eric Ogbogu. When the muscular Ogbogu barked the firm's tag line, "Protect This House," it instantly became a part of popular sports culture and a rallying cry of players and fans in football stadiums across the country.

Under Armour continues to look for growth from new product ideas. It isn't an easy decision to add new product lines, but Under Armour did when it moved into footwear. It started with baseball cleats, followed a year later by football cleats. It's tough to quickly steal away a large share of customers in a mature product-market, but that is just what Under Armour accomplished with its new design for football cleats. The new-product development team researched playing surfaces, player movements, and body types to design cleats that were more durable, lighter, and more breathable. Developers relied on 3-D design software to build virtual versions of shoes—and then rapidly prototyped models to be tested. Player feedback led to more refinements. Of course, it also took an innovative ad campaign and point-of-purchase promotion for the cleats to capture a 25 percent share of sales in this highly competitive market. Having NFL stars Tom Brady and Cam Newton on your team makes winning easier, too.

These results motivated moves into cross-trainer and running shoes—where similar success has been harder to achieve. A Super Bowl ad announced its entry into the new market. To attract attention and highlight its new technology, Under Armour's cross-trainer shoes use a box with a see-through top. Inside the box, a point-of-purchase display helps customers decide which of three models is best for them. In spite of some good shoes, creative advertising and clever packaging, Under Armour's cross-trainer and running shoes have struggled against entrenched competition. But this race isn't over yet, and new products like the $120 Charge RC running shoe show that Under Armour is not giving up.

Under Armour continues to seek out new opportunities. It recently signed a deal to sponsor the fast-growing Tough Mudder event series. Tough Mudder events are one-day endurance competitions over obstacle courses that range from 12–15 miles. The sponsorship gives Under Armour branding on all Tough Mudder T-shirts and the UA logo is prominently displayed at events across the U.S., Europe, and Australia. The international exposure will help, as Under Armour sets its sights on Europe and Asia. Under Armour sees big opportunities abroad; while Nike has more than 60 percent of its sales outside the U.S., international business accounts for less than 10 percent of Under Armour sales.

In less than 20 years, Under Armour went from a start-up in Plank's grandmother's basement to a firm with more than $1.5 billion in annual sales. Of course, growth in the performance clothing market is slowing, and competition from Nike, Adidas, and a growing number of dealer brands is increasing. But Kevin Plank is used to taking on bigger competitors. Once during his college football days, the 5-foot 11-inch, 229-pound Plank was assigned to block his 6-foot 4-inch, 269-pound buddy Ogbogu, and the bigger man ended up on his back with a concussion. Watch out Nike![1]

Learning Objectives

Developing a marketing mix that provides superior customer value for target customers is ultimately the focus of the marketing strategy planning process. To develop a successful marketing mix requires that each of the four Ps is carefully planned and works well with all the others. Many important strategy decisions are required. This chapter focuses on key ideas related to strategy planning for Product.

When you finish this chapter you should be able to:

1. understand what "Product" really means.
2. know the key differences between goods and services.
3. understand what branding is and how to use it in strategy planning.
4. understand the importance of packaging in strategy planning.
5. understand the role of warranties in strategy planning.
6. know the differences among various consumer and business product classes.
7. understand how product classes can help a marketing manager plan marketing strategies.
8. understand important new terms (shown in red).

The Product Area Involves Many Strategy Decisions

The Under Armour case highlights some of the important topics and strategy decision areas that we'll discuss in this chapter and in Chapter 9. As shown in Exhibit 8-1, there are many strategy decisions in the Product area. They're the focus of this chapter. Then, in Chapter 9, we'll take a "how to" look at developing new products and also explain how strategy usually changes as products move through their life in the market.

We'll start here by looking at Product through the eyes of the customer. This focuses attention on the total benefits provided by the Product—regardless of whether it is a physical good, a service, or both. Then we'll review strategy decisions for three important Product areas: branding, packaging, and warranties. We'll conclude by considering product classes, which are based on how customers think about and shop for products. They help show how strategy decisions for Product relate to decisions for Place, Promotion, and Price.

What is a Product?

LO 8.1

Customers buy satisfaction

When Jif sells its peanut butter, is it just selling roasted peanuts, sugar, salt, and oil?

When Air Jamaica sells a ticket for a flight to the Caribbean, is it just selling so much wear and tear on an airplane and so much pilot fatigue?

The answer to these questions is *no.* Instead, what these companies are really selling is the satisfaction, use, or benefit the customer wants.

Exhibit 8–1 Product Decisions for Marketing Strategy Planning

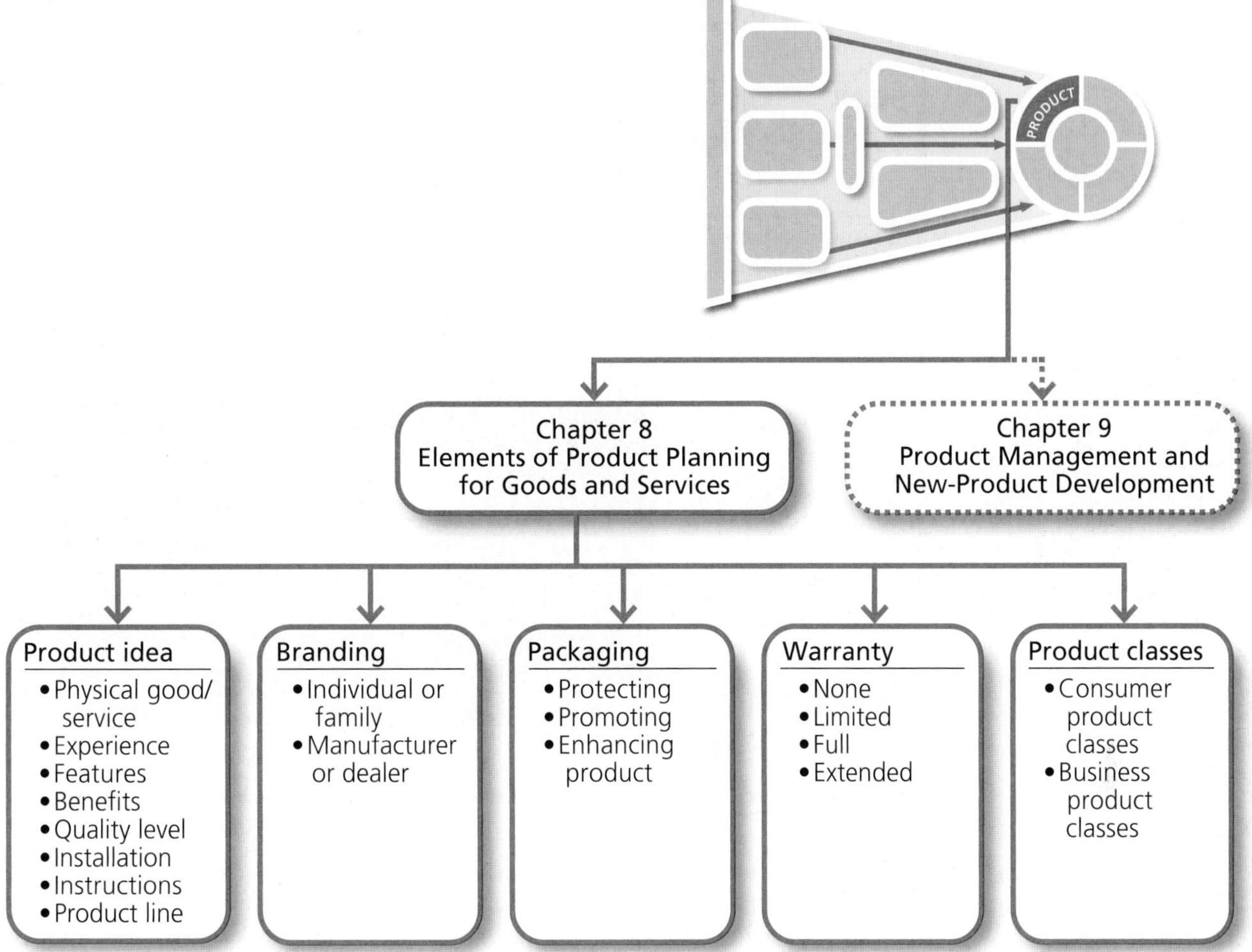

Consumers care that their Jif peanut butter tastes great, easily spreads on bread for a fast sandwich, and offers a source of protein in their diet. If they worry about too much fat or sugar in their diet they can buy Jif Reduced Fat or Simply Jif. Of course retailers who sell peanut butter are satisfied, because Jif tells customers about the brand in advertising and packages the peanut butter in bright eye-catching colors that help the brand sell.

Similarly, Air Jamaica's customers want a safe, comfortable on-time flight—but they also want easy online reservations, low prices, smooth check-in at the airport, and luggage that arrives undamaged and on time. In other words, purchases deliver the highest level of satisfaction when the customer's entire *experience* with the product meets or exceeds the customer's needs.

Product means the need-satisfying offering of a firm. The idea of "Product" as potential customer satisfaction or benefits is very important. Many business managers get wrapped up in the technical details involved in producing a product. But most customers think about a product in terms of the total satisfaction it provides. That satisfaction may require a "total" product offering that is really a combination of excellent service, a physical good with the right features, useful instructions, a convenient package, a trustworthy warranty, and perhaps even a familiar name that has satisfied the consumer in the past.

Product quality and customer needs

Product quality should also be determined by how customers view the product. From a marketing perspective, **quality** means a product's ability to satisfy a customer's needs or requirements. This definition focuses on the customer—and how the customer thinks a

When Volkswagen launched its environmentally friendly Bluemotion Technology cars, it wanted customers to know that it could be fun to do the right thing. A series of viral videos captured real people doing the right thing while having fun. For example, Volkswagen installed a musical staircase next to an escalator and soon people were taking the stairs more than the escalator. See the video for this example and more at www.thefuntheory.com.

product will fit some purpose. For example, the "best" satellite TV service may not be the one with the highest number of channels but the one that includes a local channel that a consumer wants to watch. Similarly, the best-quality clothing for casual wear on campus may be a pair of jeans, not a pair of dress slacks made of a higher-grade fabric.

Among different types of jeans, the one with the most durable fabric might be thought of as having the highest grade or *relative quality* for its product type. Marketing managers often focus on relative quality when comparing their products to competitors' offerings. However, a product with better features is not a higher-quality product if the features aren't what the target market wants.

In Chapter 9, we'll look at ways to manage product quality. For now, however, it is important to see that quality and satisfaction depend on the total product offering. If potato chips get stale on the shelf because of poor packaging, the consumer will be dissatisfied. A broken button on a shirt will disappoint the customer—even if the laundry did a nice job cleaning and pressing the collar.[2]

Ethics Question

Your construction firm was the low price bidder on a plan to build three new runways at an airport. After winning the contract, you assured the airport commissioner that your work would far exceed the minimum quality specs in the contract. However, a test of the batch of concrete for the second runway shows that it's not as strong as the concrete you've been using. It does exceed the specs in the contract, but barely. Throwing the concrete away would eat up most of the profit expected from the job and also delay the airport in using the runway. There are various options. You could proceed with the project and be quiet about it, or perhaps call the commissioner and ask for quick approval. Alternatively, you could proceed but later admit what happened. With or without approval, you could offer a special warranty. Explain what you would do. What, if anything, would you say to your employees about your decision?[3]

Exhibit 8–2 Examples of Possible Blends of Physical Goods and Services in a Product

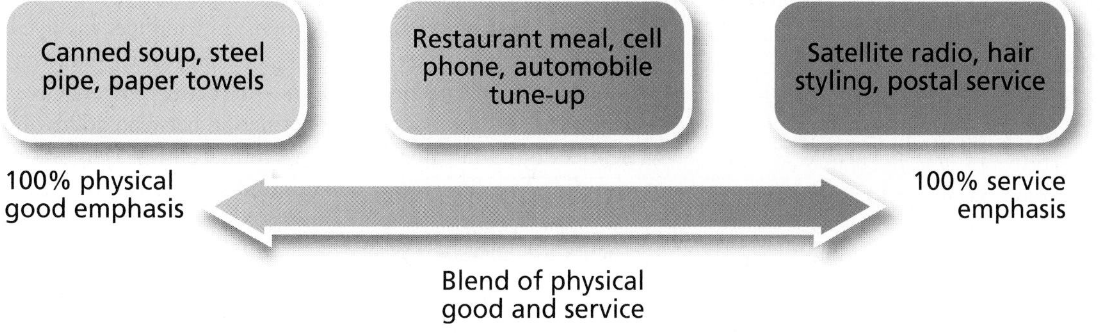

Goods and/or services are the product

A product may be a physical *good* or a *service,* or a *blend of both.* Exhibit 8-2 shows that a product can range from a 100 percent emphasis on a physical good—for a commodity like steel pipe—to a 100 percent emphasis on service—for a product like satellite radio from SiriusXM. Many products include a combination of goods and services. When you eat out, you are buying food (a physical good) that is prepared and served by a restaurant's staff (a service).

Differentiation with a combination of goods and services

When competitors focus only on physical goods, a firm may differentiate its offering by blending in a service valued by the target market. Many companies make high-quality HDTVs, but Panasonic's research revealed that some consumers worry about how to set up an HDTV when they got it home. So Panasonic added Plasma Concierge service to support its HDTV customers with well-trained advisors and priority in-home service. Software apps can offer services that add value to goods. Paint producer Benjamin Moore's "ben Color Capture" allows iPhone users to take a picture of any color and automatically match it to a Benjamin Moore paint color.

Some companies gather big data and, as a service, repackage the data to provide value to their customers. For example, Monsanto, which sells seeds to farmers, gathers extensive information about seeds, soil, and crop yields from computers installed in the cabs of farm equipment. Monsanto gathers this information from many farmers and uses it to provide advice to individual farmers about what, where, and when to plant.

This idea also works when the emphasis is on services, where goods in the offering provide differentiation. An overnight stay at a Westin Hotel has a service emphasis, but

IKEA furniture usually needs to be assembled after a buyer gets it home. To make customers aware of its assembly service, those who requested delivery service were sent a puzzle. When the puzzle was put together, they could see that the item was put together the wrong way, providing a gentle reminder that the customer could still request an Ikea assembly professional.

Internet Exercise

To support runners, Nike created a website and online services devoted specifically to them. Go to the website (**www.nikerunning.com**) and explore its contents. Be sure to learn about Nike+. What services are available? How do these services create value for runners? How does Nike gain value from the site?

Westin's ads highlight the Heavenly Bed—which includes a high-quality mattress, extra pillows, and luxury linens.

Regardless of the blend of goods and services involved, the marketing manager must consider most of the same elements in planning products and marketing mixes. Given this, we usually won't make a distinction between goods and services but will call all of them Products. However, understanding key differences in goods and services can help fine-tune marketing strategy planning. So let's look at some of these differences next.

Differences Between Goods and Services

LO 8.2

How tangible is the product?

Because a good is a physical thing, it can be seen and touched. You can try on a pair of Timberland shoes, smell Starbucks beans as they roast, and page through the latest issue of *People* magazine. A good is a *tangible* item. It's usually easy to know exactly what you will get before you decide to buy it. And once you've bought it, you own it.

In contrast, services are not physical—they are *intangible*. When you provide a customer with a service, the customer can't keep it. Rather, a service is experienced, used, or consumed. You go to a DreamWorks Pictures movie, but afterward all you have is a memory. You can buy a pass to ski at Vail and enjoy the experience, but you don't own the ski lift. Sometimes it's a challenge that customers can't see, feel, or smell a service before they buy it. For example, a person who wants advice from an accountant doesn't know in advance how good the advice will be.

To reduce this uncertainty, service customers often seek referrals from friends or advice from online reviews. They may also look for cues to help them judge the quality of a service before they buy. That's why some service providers emphasize physical evidence of quality. A lawyer is likely to have diplomas on the wall, shelves loaded with books, and furnishings that suggest success.

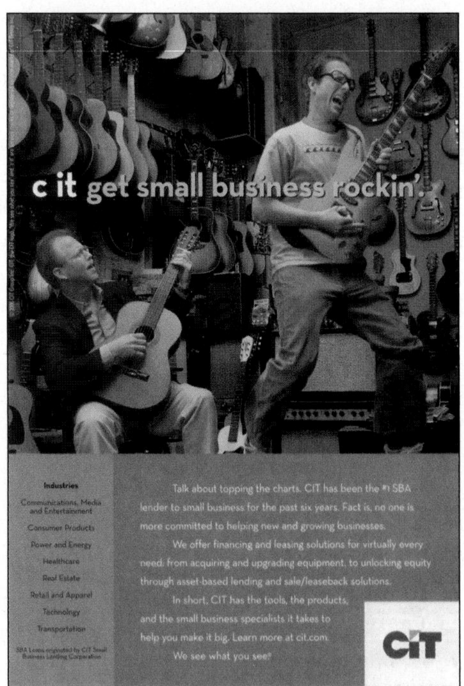

A consumer can't hold a service and look at it before purchasing, so service firms often use messages and images in their promotion that help make the benefits of the service experience more vivid.

Where the product is produced

Goods are typically mass-produced in a factory far away from the customer. A service is usually produced in person—where the customer is located—*after* the customer has committed to buy. It is often difficult to achieve economies of scale with personal services. One reason is that service suppliers often need duplicate equipment and staff at places where the service is actually provided. Merrill Lynch sells investment advice along with financial products worldwide. That advice could, perhaps, be produced more economically in a single building in New York City and made available only on its website. But Merrill Lynch has offices all over the world because many customers want a personal touch from their stockbroker.

Quality consistency

A worker in a factory that makes Whirlpool appliances can be in a bad mood and customers will never know. Even if there are production problems, quality controls

When an ad promotes several product lines, it can be difficult to allocate the correct portion of the cost to individual products.

are likely to catch defective goods before they leave the factory. Service quality often isn't that consistent; one reason is that it's hard to separate the service experience from the person who provides it. A rude teller in a bank can drive customers away. Service providers also vary in their ability, and problems with the service they deliver are usually obvious to customers. In addition, when many people must all work well together—as in a hospital or on a cruise ship—it's even more of a challenge to deliver consistent service quality.

Services cannot be stored

Services are perishable. They can't be produced and then stored to sell at some future time when more customers want to buy. This makes it difficult to balance supply and demand, especially if demand varies a lot. At Thanksgiving, Southwest Airlines has to turn away customers because most of its flights are fully booked; other airlines may get that business. Perhaps Southwest could buy more planes and hire more pilots, but most of the time that would result in costly excess capacity—planes flying with empty seats. The revenue that could have come from any empty seats is lost forever.

Because of problems like this, airlines, doctors, hotels, and other service firms sometimes charge fees to clients who don't show up when they say they will. Service organizations also use a variety of approaches to shift customer demand to less busy times. Movie tickets are cheaper for afternoon shows, restaurants offer early-bird specials, and hotels that cater to business travelers promote weekend getaways. Firms also try to reduce the dissatisfaction that customers may feel if they must wait for service. Golf courses provide practice greens, and some doctors' offices provide comfortable seating and magazines.[4]

Whole Product Lines Must Be Developed Too

A **product assortment** is the set of all product lines and individual products that a firm sells. A **product line** is a set of individual products that are closely related. The seller may see the products in a line as related because they're produced or operate in a similar way, sold to the same target market, sold through the same types of outlets, or priced at about the same level. Sara Lee, for example, has many product lines in its product assortment—including beverages, luncheon meats, desserts, insecticides, body care, air care, and shoe care. But Enterprise has one product line—different types of vehicles to rent. An **individual product** is a particular product within a product line. It usually is differentiated by brand, level of service offered, price, or some other characteristic. For example, each size and flavor of a brand of soap is an individual product. Intermediaries usually think of each separate product as a stock-keeping unit (SKU) and assign it a unique SKU number.

Product lines require strategy decisions

Marketing managers have several decisions to make about product lines. One strategy decision involves *product line length*—the number of individual products in a product line. Sometimes extending the length of the product line offers marketing managers new opportunities. Firms can add more colors, flavors, styles, and sizes to appeal to a wider range of customers. For example, Subway began to offer breakfast sandwiches to appeal to a new market segment. Coca-Cola in recent years has added Vanilla Coke, Cherry Coke, and Coke Zero to appeal to a wider range of customers.

Marketing managers should make product line length decisions with knowledge about the needs and wants of both end customers and intermediaries—as well as the company's own costs. Extending product line length can raise production and distribution costs and might confuse customers. Apple's narrow line of cell phones—just variations on the iPhone—have helped it keep costs low and consumer brand awareness high.

Each individual product and target market may require a separate strategy. For example, Clorox's strategy for selling Clorox Scented Bleach will differ from its strategy for selling Clorox Regular Bleach. In this book and the first marketing course, we'll focus mainly on developing one marketing strategy at a time. But remember that a marketing manager may have to plan *several* strategies to develop an effective marketing program for a product line or whole company.

Branding Is a Strategy Decision

LO 8.3

There are so many brands—and we're so used to seeing them—that we take them for granted. But branding is an important decision area, so we will treat it in some detail.

What is branding?

Branding means the use of a name, term, symbol, or design—or a combination of these—to identify a product. It includes the use of brand names, trademarks, and practically all other means of product identification.

Brand name has a narrower meaning. A **brand name** is a word, letter, or a group of words or letters. Examples include America Online (AOL), WD-40, 3M Post-its, and PT Cruiser.

Trademark is a legal term. A **trademark** includes only those words, symbols, or marks that are legally registered for use by a single company. A **service mark** is the same as a trademark except that it refers to a service offering.

The word *FedEx* can be used to explain these differences. The FedEx overnight delivery service is branded under the brand name FedEx (whether it's spoken or printed in any manner). When "FedEx" is printed in a certain typeface, however, it becomes a trademark. A trademark need not be attached to the product. It need not even be a word—it can be a symbol. Exhibit 8-3 shows some common trademarks.

Exhibit 8–3 Recognized Trademarks and Symbols Help in Promotion

These differences may seem technical. But they are very important to business firms that spend a lot of money to protect and promote their brands. Sometimes a firm's brand name is the only element in its marketing mix that a competitor can't copy.

Tropicana wanted to update the packaging for its orange juice. So it ditched the longtime Tropicana brand symbol of a colorful orange pierced by a straw for the package on the right showing a muted glass of orange juice. Sales fell as some loyal Tropicana customers failed to recognize their regular brand on store shelves. Soon the original package design was back in stores.

Brands meet needs

Well-recognized brands make shopping easier. Think of trying to buy groceries, for example, if you had to evaluate each of 25,000 items every time you went to a supermarket. Many customers are willing to buy new things—but having gambled and won, they like to buy a sure thing the next time. Brand names connect a product with the benefits a customer can expect. The connection may be learned from past consumer experience, from the firm's promotion, or in other ways. Customers *trust* the brand name if they consistently have a positive experience with the brand or they hear good things from the firm's promotion or other customers. If their marketing mixes work, customers trust that every time they eat *Certified Angus Beef* it will be "tender, high-quality meat" and that their oil changes at *Jiffy Lube* will always be "fast and convenient." If a brand consistently delivers on a promise that target customers consider important, those customers will pay a premium price for the certainty that comes with that brand name.

Brand promotion has other advantages for branders as well as customers. A good brand reduces the marketer's selling time and effort. Good brands can also improve the company's image—speeding acceptance of new products marketed under the same name. For example, many consumers quickly tried Listerine PocketPaks breath fresheners when they appeared because they already knew they trusted Listerine mouthwash.[5]

What conditions favor branding?

While branding helps customers make buying decisions, branding is not always easy to do. Building a well-respected brand name can be costly. It doesn't always make sense as part of a marketing strategy. In some industries, well-known brands are just not that common. Think about it. Can you recall a brand name for file folders, bed frames, electric extension cords, or nails? The following conditions are conditions that can make a market more favorable to successful branding:

1. The product is easy to label and identify by brand or trademark.
2. The product quality is easy to maintain and the best value for the price.
3. Dependable and widespread availability is possible. When customers start using a brand, they want to be able to continue using it.
4. Demand is strong enough that the market price can be high enough to make the branding effort profitable.
5. There are economies of scale. If the branding is really successful, costs should drop and profits should increase.
6. Favorable shelf locations or display space in stores will help. This is something retailers can control when they brand their own products.

In general, these conditions are less common in developing economies, and that may explain why efforts to build brands in emerging markets often fail. For example, one study found Chinese consumers willing to pay a premium of only 2 percent for branded products they regularly purchase—as compared to premiums of 20 percent or more in developed countries.[6]

Achieving Brand Familiarity Is Not Easy

Today, familiar brands exist for most product categories, ranging from crayons (Crayola) to real estate services (RE/MAX). Nevertheless, brand acceptance must be earned with a good product and regular promotion. **Brand familiarity** means how well customers recognize and accept a company's brand. The degree of brand familiarity affects the planning for the rest of the marketing mix—especially where the product should be offered and what promotion is needed.

Five levels of brand familiarity

Five levels of brand familiarity are useful for strategy planning: (1) rejection, (2) nonrecognition, (3) recognition, (4) preference, and (5) insistence.

Some brands have been tried and found wanting. **Brand rejection** means that potential customers won't buy a brand unless its image is changed—or if the customers have no other choice. Rejection may suggest a change in the product or perhaps only a shift to target customers who have a better image of the brand. Overcoming a negative image is difficult and can be very expensive. Sometimes customers have no other choice. Many music and sports fans would like to reject Ticketmaster, which sells tickets to sports and music events. But customers often have little choice when it comes time to buy tickets to see their favorite band or team perform live. Recently, comedian Louis C.K. sold tickets directly to his fans to avoid associating with Ticketmaster. This attitude has helped jump-start competitors for Ticketmaster, though the company is working hard to reverse that negative customer attitude.[7]

Brand rejection is a big concern for service-oriented businesses because it's hard to control the quality of service. A business traveler who gets a dirty room in a Hilton Hotel in Caracas, Venezuela, might not return to a Hilton anywhere. Yet it's difficult for Hilton to ensure that every maid does a good job every time.

Some products are seen as basically the same. **Brand nonrecognition** means final consumers don't recognize a brand at all—even though intermediaries may use the brand name for identification and inventory control. Examples include school supplies, inexpensive dinnerware, many of the items that you'd find in a hardware store, and thousands of dot-coms on the Internet.

Brand recognition means that customers remember the brand. This may not seem like much, but it can be a big advantage if there are many "nothing" brands on the market. Even if consumers can't recall the brand without help, they may be reminded when they see it in a store among other less familiar brands.

When customers buy new products, familiar brands convey trust. Customers may have past experience with the brand and expect the new product to be of similar quality. When Morton developed a line of snow and ice melters and Bissell added more products to clean up after pets, both relied on brand familiarity to gain retail distribution and customer trial.

Differentiation by design

Today, many companies are gaining a competitive advantage by bringing designers into decisions about product features and functions—rather than just having them there to finalize the look. Designers now help with decisions about what benefits a product will offer, including the right look and feel to achieve ease of use. Consider a few examples where attention to design differentiates products.

Office equipment and furniture manufacturer Herman Miller has redesigned many common products to appeal to customers who value sustainability. Its design for the Leaf personal desk lamp uses light-emitting diodes (LEDs) that allow the user to choose the color and intensity of the light. The LEDs last for 60,000 hours—much longer than the traditional fluorescent light bulbs they replace—yet use only 40 percent as much electricity. Leaf also contains 37 percent recycled materials. The sustainable features, combined with an artistic and functional design, differentiate the lamp and help it sell well, even at a price of $400.

Research by health care giant Kaiser Permanente revealed that its facilities were alienating many patients. Most patients already had health concerns when they arrived, so the stark waiting rooms made them anxious, the poor signage was confusing, and small exam rooms were lonely. Kaiser turned to designers for help. They expanded the exam rooms, added privacy curtains, and invited patients to have a friend wait with them. After the redesign, Kaiser's patients reported more satisfaction with the health care they received. The health care was actually the same, but the facilities were improved.

More than a decade ago, discount retailer Target relied on TV and magazine ads to try to build a cool image. But the products it carried were mostly the same stuff sold by rival Walmart. To differentiate itself, Target put more emphasis on products with affordable, attractive, and functional designs. Target recruited famous designers like Michael Graves to create new lines of housewares, office supplies, furniture, toys, and games—all of which helped to reposition Target's image. Today, Target's design-centered differentiation helps it reduce direct price competition.[8]

Most branders would like to win **brand preference**—which means that target customers usually choose the brand over other brands, perhaps because of habit or favorable past experience. **Brand insistence** means customers insist on a firm's branded product and are willing to search for it.

A brand is likely to have target customers at each level of brand familiarity. Ideally, customers move to higher levels of brand familiarity (brand preference and brand insistence) over time. Marketing strategies often aim to encourage this movement. Consider the café-bakery chain Panera Bread. It's possible that some target customers may reject the brand because of a bad previous experience. However, if Panera provides consistently excellent service and tries to recognize and compensate for (hopefully) rare instances of poor service, those who reject the brand should be a very small group. Other customers in the target market may not recognize the brand and need promotion that is directly aimed at them, possibly in the form of advertising. With successful promotion these customers will likely move to the brand recognition level. Because higher levels of brand familiarity will probably require first-hand experience, coupons or additional promotion efforts may encourage an actual visit to a café. If Panera delivers an enjoyable time (good food and service at a fair price), then more customers are likely to develop brand preference—and if customers are truly delighted, they may move to brand insistence.[9]

The right brand name can help

A good brand name can help build brand familiarity. It can help tell something important about the company or its product. Exhibit 8-4 lists some characteristics of a good brand name. Lululemon, Outback, Jelly Belly, Bonobos, and DieHard are examples of successful brand names that fit some of these criteria. Can you think of others?

Companies that compete in international markets face a special problem in selecting brand names. A name that conveys a positive image in one language may be meaningless in another. Or, worse, it may have unintended meanings. British food company

Exhibit 8–4
Characteristics of a Good Brand Name

• Short and simple	• Suggestive of product benefits
• Easy to spell and read	• Adaptable to packaging/labeling needs
• Easy to recognize and remember	• No undesirable imagery
• Easy to pronounce	• Always timely (does not go out of date)
• Can be pronounced in only one way	• Adaptable to any advertising medium
• Can be pronounced in all languages (for international markets)	• Legally available for use (not in use by another firm)

Sharwood discovered this after spending millions of dollars launching a curry sauce called *Bundh*. Unfortunately many Punjabi speakers, who were one of the target markets, thought the word sounded more like the Punjabi word for "backside." IKEA uses Swedish and Norwegian words as brand names, bringing a unique character to the brand. But when IKEA opened a store in Thailand, it discovered the *Redalen* bed and *Jättebra* plant pot sounded a lot like crude Thai terms related to sex.[10]

A respected name builds brand equity

Because it's costly to build brand recognition, some firms prefer to acquire established brands rather than try to build their own. The value of a brand to its current owner or to a firm that wants to buy it is sometimes called **brand equity**—the value of a brand's overall strength in the market. For example, brand equity is likely to be higher if many satisfied customers insist on buying the brand and if retailers are eager to stock it. That almost guarantees ongoing profits.

The financial value of the Coca-Cola brand illustrates brand equity. What is Coca-Cola but water, sugar, and flavoring? There is a unique flavor, but much of the value comes from associations people have with the brand name. In a research study, subjects' brains were scanned while they drank Coke and Pepsi in a taste test. When they drank the two soft drinks unlabeled (not knowing the brand) the subjects' preferences were evenly split. When the drinks were labeled, three-fourths chose Coke—and the brain scans suggested those favoring Coke used an area of the brain associated with memories. This suggested that Coke created pleasure because of people's experience with the brand. That type of association creates a competitive advantage that cannot be easily overcome. Many consumers have this positive association. Findings like these help explain the power of the Coca-Cola brand in building consumer preference and long-term profits. In 2012, the Coca-Cola brand was among the five most valuable in the world, estimated to be worth more than $70 billion.[11]

Protecting Brand Names and Trademarks

U.S. common law and civil law protect the rights of trademark and brand name owners. The **Lanham Act** (of 1946) spells out what kinds of marks (including brand names) can be protected and the exact method of protecting them. The law applies to goods shipped in interstate or foreign commerce.

The Lanham Act does not force registration. But registering under the Lanham Act is often a first step toward protecting a trademark to be used in international markets. That's because some nations require that a trademark be registered in its home country before they will register or protect it.

You must protect your own

A brand can be a real asset to a company. Each firm should try to see that its brand doesn't become a common descriptive term for its kind of product. When this happens, the brand name or trademark becomes public property—and the owner loses all rights to it. This happened with the names cellophane, aspirin, shredded wheat, and kerosene.[12]

Trademarks need to be protected around the globe

When introducing a new brand name, marketing managers must be sure to have rights to the trademark in all of its markets. Apple got into a dispute over the iPad trademark after the product was launched. Apple purchased rights to the name from a Taiwanese firm which held rights to the iPad name in several Asian countries—including, Apple believed, China. But when the iPad was launched, a Chinese firm claimed it still owned the rights to the iPad name. After battles in Chinese courts, Apple eventually settled by paying Proview Technology $60 million for the Chinese rights to the iPad name.

Counterfeiting is accepted in some cultures

Even when products are properly registered, counterfeiters may make unauthorized copies. Counterfeit products cause a brand to lose sales and jeopardize its reputation. Many well-known brands—ranging from Levi's jeans to Rolex watches to Zantax medicine—face this problem. International trade in counterfeit and pirated goods may exceed $500 billion annually. Counterfeiting continues to grow and is especially common in developing countries where regulation is weak or cultural values differ. In China for example, many DVDs, CDs, and software programs are bootleg copies. And counterfeiters are increasingly brazen. In Azerbaijan and Bulgaria, BP discovered counterfeit BP service stations—with low-quality fuel.[13]

What Kind of Brand to Use?

Keep it in the family

Branders of more than one product must decide whether they are going to use a **family brand**—the same brand name for several products—or individual brands for each product. Examples of family brands are Keebler snack food products and Sears Kenmore appliances.

The use of the same brand for many products makes sense if all are similar in type and quality. The main benefit is that the goodwill attached to one or two products may help the others. Money spent to promote the brand name benefits more than one product, which cuts promotion costs for each product.

A special kind of family brand is a **licensed brand**—a well-known brand that sellers pay a fee to use. For example, the familiar Sunkist brand name has been licensed to many companies for use on more than 400 products in 30 countries.[14]

Individual brands for outside and inside competition

A company uses **individual brands**—separate brand names for each product—when it's important for the products to each have a separate identity, as when products vary in quality or type.

If the products are really different, such as Elmer's glue and Borden's ice cream, individual brands can avoid confusion. Some firms use individual brands with similar products to make segmentation and positioning efforts easier. For example, when General Mills introduced a line of organic cereals, it used the Cascadian Farm name and the Big G logo was not on the box. The rationale was that consumers who try to avoid additives might not trust a big corporate brand.[15]

Internet Exercise

Go to the Procter & Gamble website (**www.pg.com**) and click on "Brands," then "Beauty & Grooming," and then select "Hair Care" from the category menu. Look at the different shampoos that P&G makes. Click through to each brand. How are the different brands positioned? To which target markets does each appeal?

Generic "brands"

Products that some consumers see as commodities may be difficult or expensive to brand. Some manufacturers and intermediaries have responded to this problem with **generic products**—products that have no brand at all other than identification of their contents and the manufacturer or intermediary. Generic products are usually offered in plain packages at lower prices. They are quite common in less-developed nations.[16]

Who Should Do the Branding?

Manufacturer brands versus dealer brands

Manufacturer brands are brands created by producers. These are sometimes called national brands because the brand is promoted all across the country or in large regions. Note, however, that many manufacturer brands are now distributed globally. Such brands include Nabisco, Colgate, Northwestern Mutual Life, Marriott, MasterCard, and McDonald's.

Dealer brands, also called **private brands**, (or private label) are brands created by intermediaries. Examples of dealer brands include Craftsman and Kenmore (Sears), Primo Taglio and Priority Pet (Safeway), Up & Up (Target), and Sam's Choice and Equate (Walmart). Traditionally dealer brands were knockoffs of manufacturer brands—often of lower quality with lower prices.

Del Monte wants retailers to remember that many consumers already know and trust its brand name. Establishing successful brand names in the produce section is no easy feat.

Who's winning the battle of the brands?

Manufacturer and dealer brands often sell in the same retail stores. The **battle of the brands**, the competition between dealer brands and manufacturer brands, is just a question of which brands will be more popular and who will be in control. At one time, manufacturer brands were much more popular than dealer brands. In some categories like soft drinks, they still are. But in categories like milk and cheese, dealer brands are very strong contenders. In the United States, almost 30 percent of grocery store purchases are now dealer brands, with percentages higher in many European countries. Over the past 30 years, dealer brands have been slowly gaining an upper hand. During the recent economic downturn, more consumers were motivated to try dealer brands—and many were pleasantly surprised by the quality and the variety they found.

There is plenty of motivation for intermediaries to develop dealer brands. The intermediary usually earns a better margin on the sale of a dealer brand. Strong dealer brands also give an intermediary leverage in negotiations with the manufacturer brand.

In the grocery trade, retailers are putting more attention behind new dealer brand products. Kroger and Safeway recently hired marketing managers with experience at major national brands. Recently, almost a third of all new product introductions were for dealer brands, up from less than 10 percent just a few years ago. Traditionally, dealer brands were knockoffs of manufacturer brands—often of lower quality with lower prices. Now some dealer brands sell premium products. Kroger's popular "Private Selection" line of frozen pizzas is priced the same as the national brand DiGiorno. Kroger conducts its own market research, which recently led to changes in the packaging of its Pet Pride pet food brand. It learned that dog owners like to see packages with dogs and owners playing together, while cat owners just want to see a happy cat. New packages reflect those changes.

Intermediaries have some advantages in this battle. With the number of large retail chains growing, they are better able to arrange reliable sources of supply at low cost. They can also give dealer brands special shelf position and promotion. Because manufacturer brands typically need to build strong brand preference or brand insistence through heavy promotion and quality ingredients—both of which raise costs and lead to higher prices—national brands' prices are about 30 percent higher on average. Still, national brands are not going to disappear. Intermediaries know that many customers are still attracted to Mountain Dew, Colgate, Tide, and Cheerios.[17]

General Mills owns the Cascadian Farm brand name, but uses the separate name to reinforce the positioning of its organic line of cereals. Both General Mills cereals and Cascadian Farm cereals may have to compete for shelf space—and consumer attention—against similar store (dealer) brands of cereal which often sell at lower prices.

Packaging Promotes, Protects, and Enhances

LO 8.4

Packaging involves promoting, protecting, and enhancing the product. Packaging can be important to both sellers and customers. See Exhibit 8-5. It can make a product more convenient to use or store. It can prevent spoiling or damage. Good packaging makes products easier to identify and promotes the brand at the point of purchase and even in use.

Packaging can enhance the product

A new package can make *the* important difference in a new marketing strategy—by meeting customers' needs better. Sometimes a new package makes the product easier or safer to use. For example, Aleve's new "Soft Grip Cap" makes it easier for aging customers with arthritis to open its bottle. And to ensure safety, most drug and food products now have special seals to prevent product tampering.

Exhibit 8–5 Some Ways Packaging Benefits Consumers and Marketers

Opportunity to Add Value	Some Decision Factors	Examples
Promoting	Link product to promotion	The bunny on the Energizer battery package is a reminder that it "keeps going and going."
	Branding at point of purchase or consumption	Coke's logo greets almost everyone each time the refrigerator is opened.
	Product information	Nabisco's nutrition label helps consumers decide which cookie to buy, and a UPC code reduces checkout time and errors.
Protecting	For shipping and storing	Sony's MP3 player is kept safe by Styrofoam inserts.
	From tampering	Tylenol's safety seal prevents tampering.
	From shoplifting	Cardboard hang-tag on Gillette razor blades is too large to hide in hand.
	From spoiling	Kraft's shredded cheese has a resealable zipper package to keep it fresh.
Enhancing product	The environment	Tide detergent bottle can be recycled.
	Convenience in use	The package for Better Oats brand oatmeal includes a built-in measuring cup pouch so consumers don't need a measuring cup.
	Added product functions	Plastic tub is useful for refrigerator leftovers after the Cool Whip is gone.

Packaging sends a message

Packaging can tie the product to the rest of the marketing strategy. Packaging for Energizer batteries features the pink bunny seen in attention-getting TV ads and reminds consumers that the batteries are durable. A good package sometimes gives a firm more promotional effect than it could get with advertising. Customers see the package in stores, when they're actually buying. A consumer who needs a new showerhead is likely to pick the brand and style by comparing alternatives at a retail store. Waterpik's package makes it easy for the consumer to see and evaluate the product and the curved design helps to focus attention on the flexible hose.

Packaging can lower distribution costs

Better protective packaging is very important to manufacturers and wholesalers. They sometimes have to pay the cost of goods damaged in shipment. Retailers need protective packaging too. It can reduce storing costs by cutting breakage, spoilage, and theft. Good packages also save space and weight so they are easier to transport, handle, and display—and better for the environment.[18]

Greener packaging creates value for buyers and sellers

U.S. shoppers generate much more trash per person than anywhere else on earth. Much of what is tossed out is packaging. It overloads landfills, litters streets, and pollutes the environment. For years plastic seemed to be the perfect packaging material because it is clean, light, and durable; consequences being that it's everywhere and lasts forever. Even colorful package graphics are troublesome. The ink to print them often has toxins that later creep into the soil and water. Firms should try to give consumers what they want, but in applying that logic to packaging many people have been short-sighted. Businesses and consumers alike have acted as if there was nothing an *individual* could do to reduce environmental problems. Now that attitude is changing.

Growing numbers of consumers are interested in making greener choices. Firms are making packaging choices that are better for the environment. For example, Timberland makes its shoe boxes with 100 percent recycled materials, soy-based inks, and water-based glues. Whole Foods Market uses salad bar containers made from sugar-cane waste that they safely turn into compost within about 90 days. It makes sense for firms to publicize such efforts to attract like-minded consumers. Publicity also calls attention to the idea that even small changes can add up to big improvements.

Frito-Lay made news when it packaged Sun Chips in the world's first 100% compostable chip package. Many consumers praised the eco-friendly packaging, but others were turned off by the bags' distinct crackling noise. In the U.S., Frito-Lay put all flavors except for "Original" back in standard packaging. In Canada, the packaging was retained—and Frito-Lay offered ear plugs to skeptical consumers who valued the sound of the package over its environmental benefits. Frito-Lay found truth in Kermit the Frog's song, "It's not easy being green."

Most sustainable packaging initiatives lower costs for producers too. For big brands, small changes can have huge impacts—on the environment and bottom line. Unilever has been a leader in this area. When it changed shipping cases for its Wishbone salad dressing, Unilever saved 21 metric tons of cardboard. A redesigned bottle and cap for Suave shampoo and conditioner is 15 percent lighter—reducing annual resin needed by 670 tons a year in the United States alone. Appliance manufacturers have eliminated cardboard in packaging, replacing it with foam blocks on corners. The foam is lighter and reduces shipping costs and damages that occur during loading, unloading, and transportation.[19]

Laws reduce confusion

The **Federal Fair Packaging and Labeling Act** (of 1966) requires that consumer goods be clearly labeled in easy-to-understand terms to give consumers more information. The law also calls on industry to try to reduce the confusing number of package sizes and make labels more useful. Since then, there have been further guidelines. The most far-reaching are based on the Nutrition Labeling and Education Act of 1990. It requires food manufacturers to use a uniform format that allows consumers to compare the nutritional value of different products. Recently there have been more changes, including requirements to clearly show the fat content of food and ingredients that trigger common food allergies.[20]

Ethical decisions remain

Although various laws provide guidance on many packaging issues, many areas still require marketing managers to make ethical choices. For example, some firms have been criticized for designing packages that conceal a downsized product, giving consumers less for their money. Similarly, some retailers design packages and labels for their private-label products that look just like, and are easily confused with, manufacturer brands. Are efforts such as these unethical, or are they simply an attempt to make packaging a more effective part of a marketing mix? Different people will answer differently.

Many critics think that labeling information is too often incomplete or misleading. For example, what does it really mean if a label says a food product is "organic" or "low fat"? How far should a marketing manager go in putting potentially negative information on a package? Should Häagen-Dazs affix a label that says "this product will clog your arteries"? That sounds extreme, but what type of information *is* appropriate?

Many consumers like the convenience that accompanies the myriad product and packaging choices available. Is it unethical for a marketing manager to give consumers with different preferences a choice? Some critics argue that it is. Others praise firms that give consumers choices.[21]

Warranty Policies Are a Part of Strategy Planning

LO 8.5

Warranty puts promises in writing

A **warranty** explains what the seller promises about its product. A marketing manager should decide whether to offer a specific warranty, and if so what the warranty will cover and how it will be communicated to target customers. This is an area where the legal environment—as well as customer needs and competitive offerings—must be considered.

U.S. common law says that producers must stand behind their products—even if they don't offer a specific warranty. A written warranty provided by the seller may promise more than the common law provides. However, it may actually *reduce* the responsibility a producer would have under common law.

The federal **Magnuson-Moss Act** (of 1975) says that producers must provide a clearly written warranty if they choose to offer any warranty. The warranty does not have to be strong. However, Federal Trade Commission (FTC) guidelines try to ensure that warranties are clear and definite and not deceptive or unfair. A warranty must also be available for inspection before the purchase.

A company has to make it clear whether it's offering a full or limited warranty—and the law defines what *full* means. Most firms offer a limited warranty if they offer one at all. In recent years, many firms have reduced the period of warranty coverage. Apple's popular iPod music player, for example, has a standard one-year warranty on hardware, but only a 90-day warranty on phone support. Apple sells a supplemental warranty to extend hardware and phone coverage for two years from date of purchase.

Warranty may improve the marketing mix

Some firms use warranties to improve the appeal of their marketing mix. They design more quality into their goods or services and offer refunds or replacement, not just repair, if there is a problem. Warranties reduce consumer risk. A strong warranty can send consumers a signal about brand quality. A few years ago, South Korean carmaker Hyundai significantly improved car quality. Yet among consumers its old reputation lingered. Consumers had more trust in Hyundai's quality claims after it put a 10-year warranty on its cars and used TV ads to tout it as "America's best warranty."

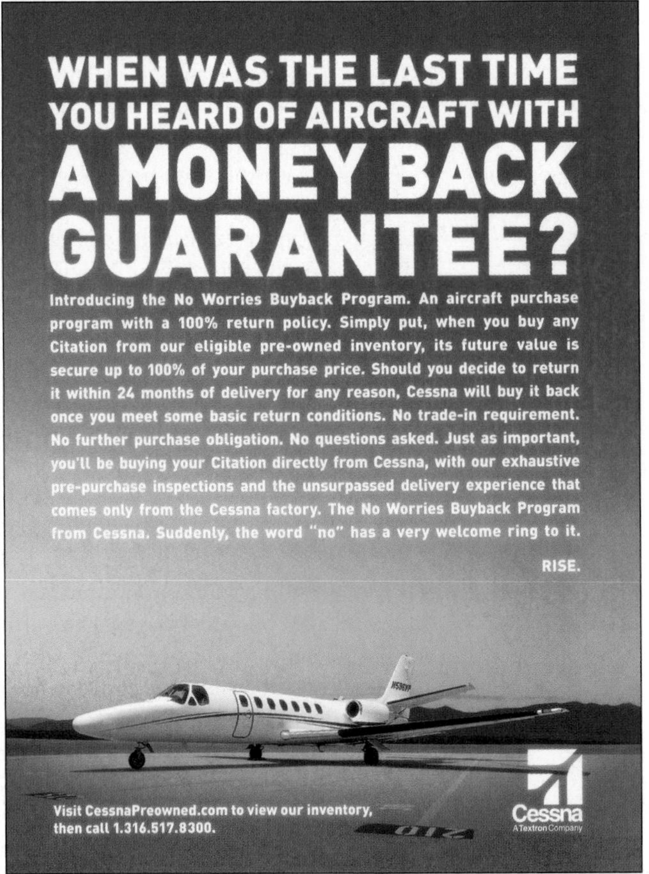

In a competitive market, a product's warranty or guarantee can be the critical difference in a firm's marketing mix.

Service guarantees

Service guarantees are becoming more common as a way to attract, and keep, customers. Some Pizza Hut locations guarantee a luncheon pizza in five minutes or it's free. General Motors set up a fast-oil-change guarantee to compete with fast-lube specialists who were taking customers away from dealers. If the dealer doesn't get the job done in 29 minutes or less, the next oil change is free.[22]

Product Classes Help Plan Marketing Strategies

LO 8.6

So far in this chapter, we've focused on key strategy decisions for Product (see Exhibit 8-1). Managers usually try to blend those decisions in a unique way to differentiate the firm's offering and create superior customer value. However, you don't have to treat *every* product as unique when planning strategies. Rather, some classes of products require similar marketing mixes. So now we'll introduce these product classes and show why they are a useful starting point for developing marketing mixes for new products and for evaluating present mixes.

Product classes start with type of customer

All products fit into one of two broad groups—based on the type of customer that will use them. **Consumer products** are products meant for the final consumer. **Business products** are products meant for use in producing other products.

The same product—like Bertolli Olive Oil—*might* be both a consumer product and a business product. Consumers buy it to use in their own kitchens, but food processing companies and restaurants buy it in large quantities as an ingredient in the products they sell. Selling the same product to both final consumers and business customers requires (at least) two different strategies.

There are product classes within each group. Consumer product classes are based on *how consumers think about and shop for products.* Business product classes are based on *how buyers think about products and how they'll be used.*

Consumer Product Classes

LO 8.7

Consumer product classes divide into four groups: (1) convenience, (2) shopping, (3) specialty, and (4) unsought. *Each class is based on the way people buy products.* See Exhibit 8-6 for a summary of how these product classes relate to marketing mixes.[23]

Convenience products—purchased quickly with little effort

Convenience products are products a consumer needs but isn't willing to spend much time or effort shopping for. These products are bought often, require little service or selling, don't cost much, and may even be bought by habit. A convenience product may be a staple, impulse product, or emergency product.

Staples are products that are bought often, routinely, and without much thought—like breakfast cereal, canned soup, and most other packaged foods used almost every day in almost every household.

Exhibit 8–6 Consumer Product Classes and Marketing Mix Planning

Consumer Product Class	Marketing Mix Considerations	Consumer Behavior
Convenience products		
Staples	Maximum exposure with widespread, low-cost distribution; mass selling by producer; usually low price; branding is important.	Routinized (habitual); low effort; frequent purchases; low involvement.
Impulse	Widespread distribution with display at point of purchase.	Unplanned purchases bought quickly.
Emergency	Need widespread distribution near probable point of need; price sensitivity low.	Purchase made with time pressure when a need is great.
Shopping products		
Homogeneous	Need enough exposure to facilitate price comparison; price sensitivity high.	Customers see little difference among alternatives and seek lowest price.
Heterogeneous	Need distribution near similar products; promotion (including personal selling) to highlight product advantages; less price sensitivity.	Extensive problem solving; consumer may need help in making a decision (salesperson, website, etc.).
Specialty products	Price sensitivity is likely to be low; limited distribution may be acceptable, but should be treated as a convenience or shopping product (in whichever category product would typically be included) to reach persons not yet sold on its specialty product status.	Willing to expend effort to get specific product, even if not necessary; strong preferences make it an important purchase; Internet becoming important information source.
Unsought products		
New unsought	Must be available in places where similar (or related) products are sought; needs attention-getting promotion.	Need for product not strongly felt; unaware of benefits or not yet gone through adoption process.
Regularly unsought	Requires very aggressive promotion, usually personal selling.	Aware of product but not interested; attitude toward product may even be negative.

Impulse products are products that are bought quickly—as *unplanned* purchases—because of a strongly felt need. True impulse products are items that the customer hadn't planned to buy, decides to buy on sight, may have bought the same way many times before, and wants right now. If the buyer doesn't see an impulse product at the right time, the sale may be lost.[24]

Emergency products are products that are purchased immediately when the need is great. The customer doesn't have time to shop around when a traffic accident occurs, a thunderstorm begins, or an impromptu party starts. The price of the ambulance service, raincoat, or ice cubes won't be important.

Shopping products—are compared

Shopping products are products that a customer feels are worth the time and effort to compare with competing products. Shopping products can be divided into two types, depending on what customers are comparing: (1) homogeneous or (2) heterogeneous shopping products.

Homogeneous shopping products are shopping products the customer sees as basically the same and wants at the lowest price. Some consumers feel that certain sizes and types of computers, television sets, washing machines, and even cars are very similar. So they shop for the best price. For some products, the Internet has become the fast way to do that.

Firms may try to emphasize and promote their product differences to avoid head-to-head price competition. For example, Rustoleum says that its spray paint goes on smoother and does a better job of preventing rust. But if consumers don't think the differences are real or important in terms of the value they seek, they'll just look at price.

Heterogeneous shopping products are shopping products the customer sees as different and wants to inspect for quality and suitability. Furniture, clothing, and membership in a spa are good examples. Often the consumer expects help from a knowledgeable salesperson. Quality and style matter more than price. In fact, once the customer finds the right product, price may not matter as long as it's reasonable. For example, you may have asked a friend to recommend a good dentist without even asking what the dentist charges.

Branding may be less important for heterogeneous shopping products. The more carefully consumers compare price and quality, the less they rely on brand names or labels. Some retailers carry competing brands so consumers won't go to a competitor to compare items.

Specialty products—no substitutes please!

Specialty products are consumer products that the customer really wants and makes a special effort to find. Shopping for a specialty product doesn't mean comparing—the buyer wants that special product and is willing to search for it. It's the customer's *willingness to search*—not the extent of searching—that makes it a specialty product.

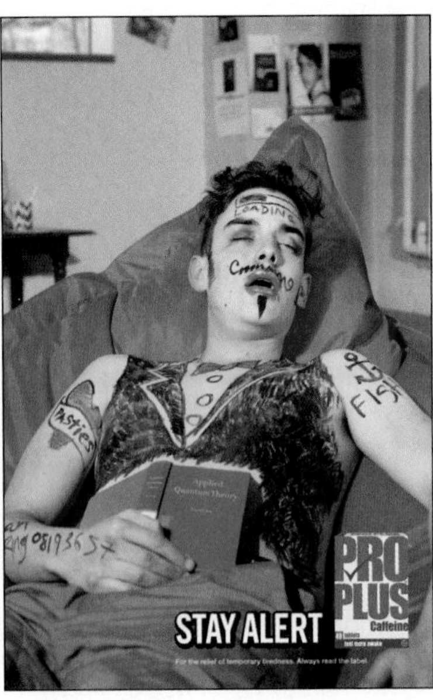

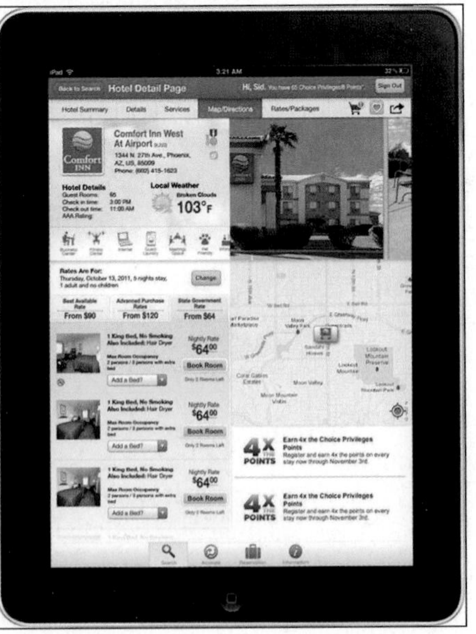

For some consumers a caffeine pill to help them stay awake is a convenience product. They may be purchased spontaneously so it is important they are displayed where easily seen by the target market. On the other hand, most consumers purchasing a few nights at a Choice Hotel view this as a shopping product and will invest time comparing competing products.

Any branded product that consumers insist on by name is a specialty product. Marketing managers want customers to see their products as specialty products and ask for them over and over again. Building that kind of relationship isn't easy. It means satisfying the customer every time. However, that's easier and a lot less costly than trying to win back dissatisfied customers or attract new customers who are not seeking the product at all.

Unsought products—need promotion

Unsought products are products that potential customers don't yet want or know they can buy. So they don't search for them at all. In fact, consumers probably won't buy these products if they see them—unless promotion can show their value.

There are two types of unsought products. **New unsought products** are products offering really new ideas that potential customers don't know about yet. Informative promotion can help convince customers to accept the product, ending its unsought status. Dannon's yogurt and Litton's microwave ovens are popular items now, but initially they were new unsought products.

Regularly unsought products are products—like gravestones, life insurance, and encyclopedias—that stay unsought but not unbought forever. There may be a need, but potential customers aren't motivated to satisfy it. For this kind of product, personal selling is *very* important.

Many nonprofit organizations try to "sell" their unsought products. For example, the Red Cross regularly holds blood drives to remind prospective donors of how important it is to give blood.

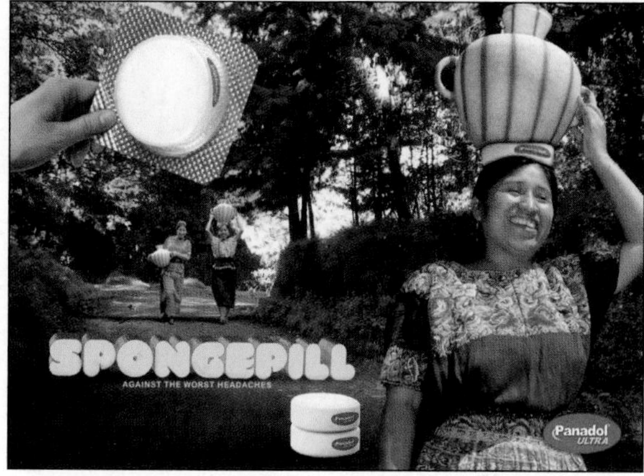

Brand managers for pain reliever Panadol Ultra faced two challenges in rural Guatemala: 1) a high level of illiteracy and 2) an unsought product because many in the target market didn't know about using pills for pain relief. Panadol created a sponge in the shape of the pill that local women could use as a cushion when carrying heavy items on their heads—a common practice. Soon women became a walking ad for the brand and sales increased by 45 percent among the target market.

One product may be seen in several ways

The same product might be seen in different ways by different target markets at the same time. For example, a product viewed as a staple by most consumers in the United States, Canada, or some similar affluent country might be seen as a heterogeneous shopping product by consumers in another country. The price might be much higher when considered as a proportion of the consumer's budget, and the available choices might be very different. Similarly, for some people salsa is seen as a staple; for others—who, for example, think it is worth tracking down W. B. Williams Georgia Style Peach Salsa on the Internet—it is a specialty product.

Business Products Are Different

Business product classes are different from consumer product classes—because they relate to how and why business firms make purchases. Thus, knowing the specific classes of business products helps in strategy planning. First, however, it's useful to note some important ways that the market for business products is different from the market for consumer products.

One demand derived from another

The big difference between the consumer products market and the business products market is **derived demand**—the demand for business products derives from the demand for final consumer products. For example, car manufacturers buy about one-fifth of all

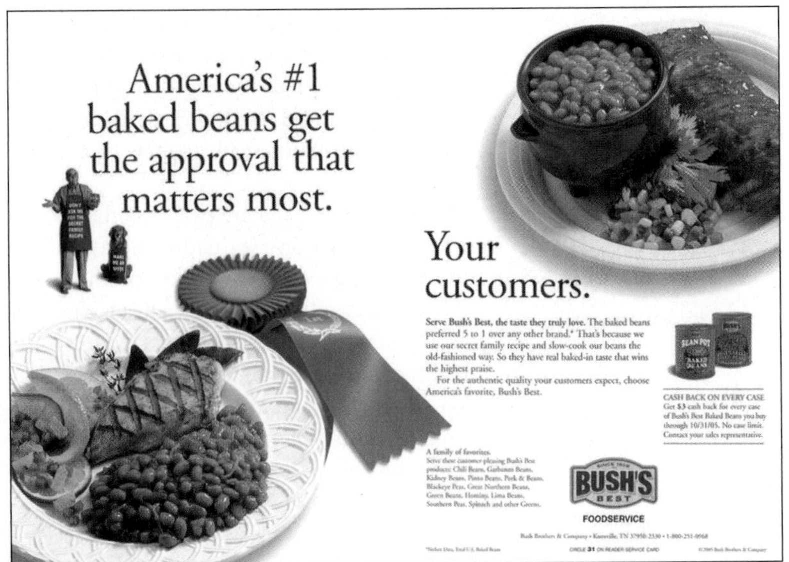

Many items in Bush's Best line of food products sell as both consumer and business products, and different marketing mixes are required to reach the different target markets.

steel products. But if demand for cars drops, they'll buy less steel. Then even the steel supplier with the best marketing mix is likely to lose sales.[25]

Price increases might not reduce quantity purchased

Total *industry* demand for business products is fairly inelastic. Business firms must buy what they need to produce their own products. Even if the cost of basic silicon doubles, for example, Intel needs it to make computer chips. However, sharp business buyers try to buy as economically as possible. So the demand facing *individual sellers* may be extremely elastic—if similar products are available at a lower price.

Tax treatment affects buying too

How a firm's accountants—and the tax laws—treat a purchase is also important to business customers. An **expense item** is a product whose total cost is treated as a business expense in the year it's purchased. A **capital item** is a long-lasting product that can be used and depreciated for many years. Often it's very expensive. Customers pay for the capital item when they buy it, but for tax purposes the cost is spread over a number of years. This may reduce the cash available for other purchases.

Business Product Classes—How They Are Defined

Business product classes are based on how buyers think about products and how the products will be used. The classes of business products are (1) installations, (2) accessories, (3) raw materials, (4) components, (5) supplies, and (6) professional services. Exhibit 8-7 relates these product classes to marketing mix planning.

Installations—a boom-or-bust business

Installations—such as buildings, land rights, and major equipment—are important capital items. One-of-a-kind installations—like office buildings and custom-made machines—generally require special negotiations for each sale. Negotiations often involve top management and can stretch over months or even years. Standardized major equipment is treated more routinely.

Installations are a boom-or-bust business. During growth periods, firms may buy installations to increase capacity. But during a downswing, sales fall off sharply.[26]

Specialized services are needed as part of the product

Suppliers sometimes include special services with an installation at no extra cost. A firm that sells (or leases) equipment to dentists, for example, may install it and help the dentist learn to use it.

Exhibit 8–7 Business Product Classes and Marketing Mix Planning

Business Product Classes	Marketing Mix Considerations	Buying Behavior
Installations	Usually requires skillful personal selling by producer, including technical contacts, or understanding of applications; leasing and specialized support services may be required.	Multiple buying influence (including top management) and new-task buying are common; infrequent purchase, long decision period, and boom-or-bust demand are typical.
Accessory equipment	Need fairly widespread distribution and numerous contacts by experienced and sometimes technically trained personnel; price competition is often intense, but quality is important.	Purchasing and operating personnel typically make decisions; shorter decision period than for installations; Internet sourcing.
Raw materials	Grading is important, and transportation and storing can be crucial because of seasonal production and/or perishable products; markets tend to be very competitive.	Long-term contract may be required to ensure supply; online auctions.
Component parts and materials	Product quality and delivery reliability are usually extremely important; negotiation and technical selling typical on less-standardized items; replacement after market may require different strategies.	Multiple buying influence is common; online competitive bids used to encourage competitive pricing.
Maintenance, repair, and operating (MRO) supplies	Typically require widespread distribution or fast delivery (repair items); arrangements with appropriate intermediaries may be crucial.	Often handled as straight rebuys, except important operating supplies may be treated much more seriously and involve multiple buying influence.
Professional services	Services customized to buyer's need; personal selling very important; inelastic demand often supports high prices.	Customer may compare outside service with what internal people could provide; needs may be very specialized.

Accessories—important but short-lived capital items

Accessories are short-lived capital items—tools and equipment used in production or office activities—like Canon's small copy machines, Rockwell's portable drills, and Steelcase's filing cabinets. Accessories are more standardized than installations and they're usually needed by more customers.

Since these products cost less and last a shorter time than installations, multiple buying influence is less important. Operating people and purchasing agents, rather than top managers, may make the purchase decision. As with installations, some customers may wish to lease or rent—to expense the cost.

Raw materials become part of a physical good

Raw materials are unprocessed expense items—such as logs, iron ore, and wheat—that are moved to the next production process with little handling. Unlike installations and accessories, *raw materials become part of a physical good and are expense items.*

There are two types of raw materials: (1) farm products and (2) natural products. **Farm products** are grown by farmers—examples are oranges, sugar cane, and cattle. **Natural products** are products that occur in nature—such as timber, iron ore, oil, and coal.

The need for grading is one of the important differences between raw materials and other business products. Nature produces what it will—and someone must sort and grade raw materials to satisfy various market segments.

Most buyers of raw materials want ample supplies in the right grades for specific uses—fresh vegetables for Green Giant's production lines or logs for Weyerhaeuser's paper mills. To ensure steady quantities, raw materials customers often sign long-term contracts, sometimes at guaranteed prices.

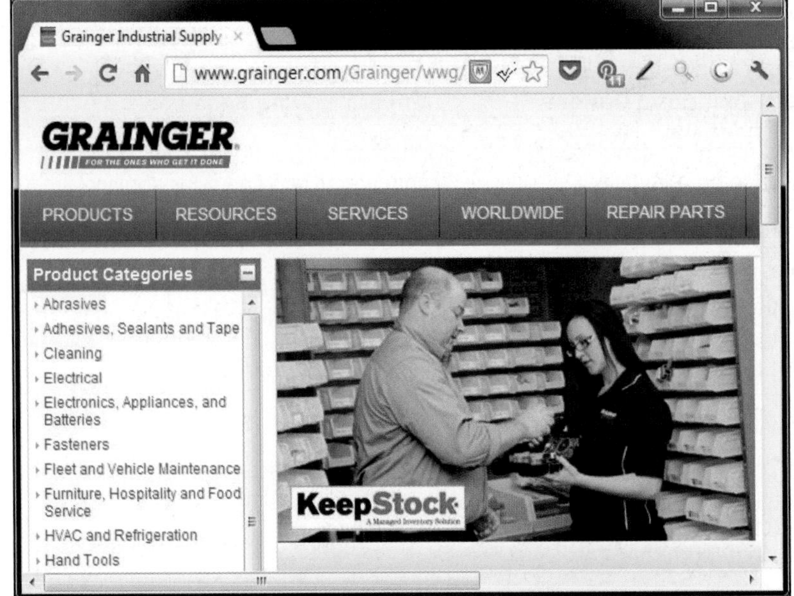

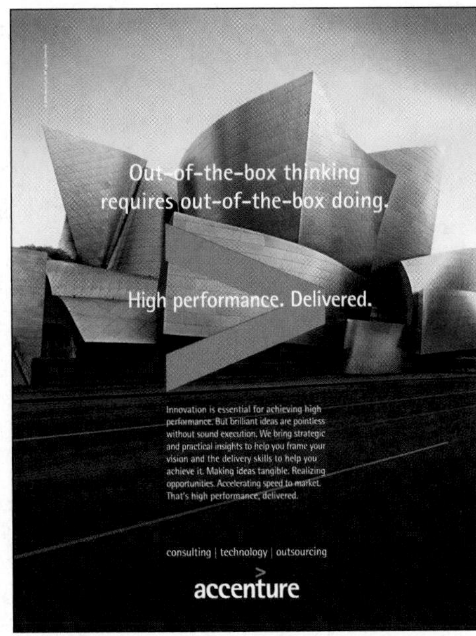

Business product classes are based on what buyers think about products and how the product will be used. Grainger is a wholesaler that offers a wide range of maintenance, repair, and operating supplies (often called MRO supplies). Accenture is a consulting firm that offers its professional services to a wide range of companies.

Component parts and materials must meet specifications

Components are processed expense items that become part of a finished product. Component *parts* are finished (or nearly finished) items that are ready for assembly into the final product. Intel's microprocessors included in personal computers and TRW's air bags in cars are examples. Component *materials* are items such as wire, plastic, or textiles. They have already been processed but must be processed further before becoming part of the final product. Quality is important with components because they become part of the firm's own product.

Some components are custom-made. Then teamwork between the buyer and seller may be needed to arrive at the right specifications. So a buyer may develop a close partnership with a dependable supplier. In contrast, standardized component materials are more likely to be purchased online using a competitive bidding system.

Since component parts go into finished products, a replacement market often develops. Car tires are components originally sold in the *OEM (original equipment market)* that become consumer products in the *aftermarket*.[27]

Supplies for maintenance, repair, and operations

Supplies are expense items that do not become part of a finished product. Supplies can be divided into three types: (1) maintenance, (2) repair, and (3) operating supplies—giving them their common name: MRO supplies.

Maintenance and small operating supplies are like convenience products. The item will be ordered because it is needed—but buyers won't spend much time on it. For such "nuisance" purchases branding is important, and so are breadth of assortment and the seller's dependability. Intermediaries usually handle the many supply items. They are often purchased via online catalog sites.[28]

Important operating supplies, like coal and fuel oil, receive special treatment. Usually there are several sources for such commodity products—and large volumes may be purchased at global exchanges on the Internet.

Professional services—pay to get it done

Professional services are specialized services that support a firm's operations. They are usually expense items. Management consulting services can improve the company's efficiency. Information technology services can maintain a company's networks and websites. Advertising agencies can help promote the firm's products. And food services can improve morale.

Managers compare the cost of buying professional services outside the firm (*outsourcing*) to the cost of having company people do them. Work that was previously done by an employee is now often purchased from an independent specialist. Clearly, the number of service specialists is growing in our complex economy.

CONCLUSION

In this chapter, we looked at Product broadly—which is the right vantage point for marketing strategy planning. We saw that a product may be a good or a service, or some combination of both. And we saw that a firm's Product is what it offers to *satisfy the needs of its target market*—which may include the customer's experience both before and after the purchase. We also described some key marketing differences between goods and services.

We reviewed the Product area strategy decisions required for branding and packaging—and saw how the right decisions can add value for customers and give a product a competitive edge. Customers view a brand as a guarantee of quality, which leads to repeat purchases, lower promotion costs, higher sales figures, and greater customer equity. Packaging offers promotional opportunities and informs customers. Variations in packaging can also help a product appeal to different segments of the market. And packaging can help protect the product anywhere in the channel of distribution. We also saw how warranties can play an important role in strategy planning—by reducing buying risk. Customers see warranties as a signal of quality.

The brand familiarity a product earns is a measure of the marketing manager's ability to carve out a separate market. Therefore, ultimately, brand familiarity affects Place, Price, and Promotion decisions. Strategy planning for the marketing mix will vary across product classes. We introduced both consumer product classes (based on *how consumers think about and shop for products*) and business product classes (based on *how buyers think about products and how they'll be used*). In addition, we showed how the product classes affect planning marketing mixes.

KEY TERMS

LO 8.8

product, *199*
quality, *199*
product assortment, *203*
product line, *203*
individual product, *203*
branding, *204*
brand name, *204*
trademark, *204*
service mark, *204*
brand familiarity, *206*
brand rejection, *206*
brand nonrecognition, *206*
brand recognition, *206*
brand preference, *207*
brand insistence, *207*
brand equity, *208*
Lanham Act, *208*
family brand, *209*
licensed brand, *209*
individual brands, *209*
generic products, *209*
manufacturer brands, *210*
dealer brands, *210*
private brands, *210*
battle of the brands, *210*
packaging, *211*
Federal Fair Packaging and Labeling Act, *212*
warranty, *213*
Magnuson-Moss Act, *214*
consumer products, *214*
business products, *215*
convenience products, *215*
staples, *215*
impulse products, *216*
emergency products, *216*
shopping products, *216*
homogeneous shopping products, *216*
heterogeneous shopping products, *216*
specialty products, *216*
unsought products, *217*
new unsought products, *217*
regularly unsought products, *217*
derived demand, *217*
expense item, *218*
capital item, *218*
installations, *218*
accessories, *219*
raw materials, *219*
farm products, *219*
natural products, *219*
components, *220*
supplies, *220*
professional services, *220*

QUESTIONS AND PROBLEMS

1. Define, in your own words, what a Product is.
2. Discuss several ways in which physical goods are different from pure services. Give an example of a good and then an example of a service that illustrates each of the differences.
3. What products are being offered by a shop that specializes in bicycles? By a travel agent? By a supermarket? By a new car dealer?
4. Consumer services tend to be intangible, and goods tend to be tangible. Use an example to explain how the lack of a physical good in a pure service might affect efforts to promote the service.
5. Explain some of the different aspects of the customer experience that could be managed to improve customer satisfaction if you were the marketing manager for: (*a*) an airport branch of a rental car agency, (*b*) a fast-food restaurant, (*c*) an online firm selling software directly to consumers from a website, and (*d*) a hardware store selling lawn mowers.
6. Is there any difference between a brand name and a trademark? If so, why is this difference important?
7. Is a well-known brand valuable only to the owner of the brand?
8. Suggest an example of a product and a competitive situation where it would not be profitable for a firm to spend large sums of money to establish a brand.
9. List five brand names and indicate what product is associated with the brand name. Evaluate the strengths and weaknesses of the brand name.
10. Explain family brands. Should Best Buy carry its own dealer brands to compete with some of the popular manufacturer brands it carries? Explain your reasons.
11. In the past, Sears emphasized its own dealer brands. Now it is carrying more well-known manufacturer brands. What are the benefits to Sears of carrying more manufacturer brands?
12. What does the degree of brand familiarity imply about previous and future promotion efforts? How does the degree of brand familiarity affect the Place and Price variables?
13. You operate a small hardware store with emphasis on manufacturer brands and have barely been breaking even. Evaluate the proposal of a large wholesaler that offers a full line of dealer-branded hardware items at substantially lower prices. Specify any assumptions necessary to obtain a definite answer.
14. Give an example where packaging costs probably (*a*) lower total distribution costs and (*b*) raise total distribution costs.
15. How would the marketing mix for a staple convenience product differ from the one for a homogeneous shopping product? How would the mix for a specialty product differ from the mix for a heterogeneous shopping product? Use examples.
16. Give an example of a product that is a *new* unsought product for most people. Briefly explain why it is an unsought product.
17. In what types of stores would you expect to find (*a*) convenience products, (*b*) shopping products, (*c*) specialty products, and (*d*) unsought products?
18. What kinds of consumer products are the following: (*a*) watches, (*b*) automobiles, and (*c*) toothpastes? Explain your reasoning.
19. Cite two examples of business products that require a substantial amount of service in order to be useful.
20. Explain why a new law office might want to lease furniture rather than buy it.
21. Would you expect to find any wholesalers selling the various types of business products? Are retail stores required (or something like retail stores)?
22. What kinds of business products are the following: (*a*) lubricating oil, (*b*) electric motors, and (*c*) a firm that provides landscaping and grass mowing for an apartment complex? Explain your reasoning.
23. How do raw materials differ from other business products? Do the differences have any impact on their marketing mixes? If so, what specifically?
24. For the kinds of business products described in this chapter, complete the following table (be brief, use one or a few well-chosen words).
    1. *Kind of distribution facility(ies) needed and functions they will provide.*
    2. *Caliber of salespeople required.*
    3. *Kind of advertising required.*

Products	1	2	3
Installations			
Buildings and land rights			
Major equipment			
Standard			
Custom-made			
Accessories			
Raw materials			
Farm products			
Natural products			
Components			
Supplies			
Maintenance and small operating supplies			
Important operating supplies			
Professional services			

CREATING MARKETING PLANS

The Marketing Plan Coach software on the text website includes a sample marketing plan for Hillside Veterinary Clinic. Look through the "Marketing Strategy" section.

a. What goods does Hillside Veterinary Clinic sell?
b. What services does Hillside Veterinary Clinic sell?
c. What consumer product classes are offered by Hillside Veterinary Clinic?
d. The discussion of product classes in this chapter indicates what marketing mix is typical for different classes of products. Does the marketing strategy recommended in the marketing plan fit with those considerations? Why or why not?

SUGGESTED CASES

1. McDonald's "Senior" Restaurant
3. NOCO United Soccer Academy
13. AAA Office World
31. Amato Home Health

Video Case 3. Toyota Prius
Video Case 7. Invacare

COMPUTER-AIDED PROBLEM

8. BRANDING DECISION

Wholesteen Dairy, Inc., produces and sells Wholesteen brand condensed milk to grocery retailers. The overall market for condensed milk is fairly flat, and there's sharp competition among dairies for retailers' business. Wholesteen's regular price to retailers is $8.88 a case (24 cans). FoodWorld—a fast-growing supermarket chain and Wholesteen's largest customer—buys 20,000 cases of Wholesteen's condensed milk a year. That's 20 percent of Wholesteen's total sales volume of 100,000 cases per year.

FoodWorld is proposing that Wholesteen produce private-label condensed milk to be sold with the FoodWorld brand name. FoodWorld proposes to buy the same total quantity as it does now, but it wants half (10,000 cases) with the Wholesteen brand and half with the FoodWorld brand. FoodWorld wants Wholesteen to reduce costs by using a lower-quality can for the FoodWorld brand. That change will cost Wholesteen $.01 less per can than it costs for the cans that Wholesteen uses for its own brand. FoodWorld will also provide preprinted labels with its brand name—which will save Wholesteen an additional $.02 a can.

Wholesteen spends $70,000 a year on promotion to increase familiarity with the Wholesteen brand. In addition, Wholesteen gives retailers an allowance of $.25 per case for their local advertising, which features the Wholesteen brand. FoodWorld has agreed to give up the advertising allowance for its own brand, but it is only willing to pay $7.40 a case for the milk that will be sold with the FoodWorld brand name. It will continue under the old terms for the rest of its purchases.

Sue Glick, Wholesteen's marketing manager, is considering the FoodWorld proposal. She has entered cost and revenue data on a spreadsheet—so she can see more clearly how the proposal might affect revenue and profits.

a. Based on the data in the initial spreadsheet, how will Wholesteen profits be affected if Glick accepts the Food-World proposal?
b. Glick is worried that FoodWorld will find another producer for the FoodWorld private label milk if Wholesteen rejects the proposal. This would immediately reduce Wholesteen's annual sales by 10,000 cases. FoodWorld might even stop buying from Wholesteen altogether. What would happen to profits in these two situations?
c. FoodWorld is rapidly opening new stores and sells milk in every store. The FoodWorld buyer says that next year's purchases could be up to 25,000 cases of Wholesteen's condensed milk. But Sue Glick knows that FoodWorld may stop buying the Wholesteen brand and want all 25,000 cases to carry the FoodWorld private label brand. How will this affect profit? (Hint: enter the new quantities in the "proposal" column of the spreadsheet.)
d. What should Wholesteen do? Why?

9 CHAPTER NINE

Product Management and New-Product Development

The founders of iRobot didn't know that their company would become the world leader in home robots. However, from the start they didn't intend to just imitate other firms' products. Instead they wanted to create totally new product concepts that would change society. That is where they're headed, with products that help consumers around the house—like Roomba, Scooba, and Looj—and products for business, government, and the military—like Seaglider and Packbot. The Seaglider monitored the Gulf of Mexico following an oil spill. The military used Packbot to clear roadside bombs in Iraq and search caves in Afghanistan.

When iRobot started, the company focused on just military and business products. One project with S. C. Johnson involved industrial cleaning robots. iRobot later entered the consumer market, developing concepts for robotic toys for Hasbro. Here they learned the importance of cost control; for two years, many toy ideas iRobot pitched to Hasbro were rejected. They were technically elegant but too expensive. These experiences helped iRobot focus on an idea for a low-priced robotic vacuum cleaner—later named the Roomba.

Roomba's new-product developers knew the importance of taking the customer's perspective. So early prototypes of the Roomba went home with iRobot employees, where their spouses, friends, and neighbors could test them. The developers gained valuable feedback and quickly learned that not everyone was technically savvy. So when design engineers talked about how best to train customers to use the Roomba, the team realized that was backwards. Instead of training customers, they designed Roomba's software to figure out what to do when a customer pushed the start button. The Roomba is so simple to use that the owner's manual is only a few pages long, and most people don't need it.

The original idea was for Roomba to just have sweeper brushes. However, in focus groups consumers said that the Roomba also needed a vacuum. Responding to this consumer input added extra expense late in the project, but iRobot was ready because of the cost-control lessons learned from working with Hasbro. With Roomba, developers had controlled every penny from the outset and were able to add the vacuum and value consumers wanted.

Before iRobot introduced the Roomba, the vacuum cleaner market was mature, with few breakthrough product ideas. Then came Roomba. It's a slick looking, 15-inch disk, less than 4 inches tall. It's a robot but requires no programming. You simply place it on the floor, press a button to turn it on, and Roomba scurries around the room doing its job. It can scoot under the sofa, avoid the furniture, and return to the battery charger when the job is done.

Marketing managers wanted to sell Roomba to a large market segment—people who hate to vacuum. But they were concerned the Roomba's appeal might be limited to a small market of gadget-loving techies. To offset consumer concerns about the complexity of the technology, introductory promotion described the Roomba as an intelligent vacuum cleaner. For the first three years, the word robot didn't even appear on the package (except in the iRobot company name).

For its launch, iRobot worked with specialty retailers like Sharper Image and Brookstone. These retailers were willing to show videos of Roomba in action and train their salespeople to explain and demonstrate Roomba in their stores. The extra promotion push was important because initially customers didn't know the brand name and were not looking for this sort of product. However, iRobot quickly generated publicity for the Roomba—with everything from appearances on the "Today" show and videos on YouTube, to reviews in magazines, newspapers, and at CNET.com. All of this media attention—and some traditional ads—propelled sales and quickly made Roomba a familiar brand. Soon iRobot expanded distribution to Bed Bath and Beyond, Target, and Amazon.com.

By controlling costs, iRobot initially priced Roomba at $200. A higher price might have been acceptable to some customers, but that low price helped fend off potential competitors, at least for a while. Soon other competitors, including Electrolux, P3, iTouchless, and Infinuvo jumped into the market. But Roomba's established brand kept it ahead of the pack.

Roomba sales grew quickly, and it is now a well-known brand with more than 6 million units sold. iRobot's product managers have responded with more specialized Roomba models for different target markets. Pet owners appreciate the special features of the Roomba Pet Series and small business owners buy the Professional Series Roomba to clean offices after workers have gone home for the night. The differentiation helps iRobot generate higher margins and better return on investment on all its Roomba models—which range in price from $200 to $700.

As the product life cycle for robotic vacuum cleaners moves through the market growth stage, iRobot is looking to create new product-markets. One idea being evaluated is called "Ava," a five-foot tall robot that can use an Android or Apple smartphone for a "brain." iRobot designed Ava so that independent developers can write apps and help "co-create" the next generation of service robots. While only a prototype now, iRobot sees opportunities for the flexible Ava in hospitals, retailers, and manufacturers.

iRobot's creative product development, along with the strategies designed to reach its target markets, have resulted in remarkable growth—with sales increasing from $54 million in 2003 to $465 million in 2011. iRobot has shown that it has the technical skills to create innovative and reliable new products while being guided by the voices of its customers. It may encounter some more bumps along the way—few firms can completely avoid problems with new products. Even so, iRobot is likely to enjoy more success as the product-market it pioneered experiences rapid growth in the next decade.[1]

Learning Objectives

Developing new products and managing them for profitable growth are keys to success for most firms. Yet many new products fail. Even products that succeed face new challenges as competition becomes more intense. So the marketing strategy that supported the product's initial success usually needs to change as the market evolves. This chapter will help you understand this evolution and how it relates to effective new-product development and creative strategy changes for existing products—both of which are crucial to attracting and retaining target customers.

When you finish this chapter you should be able to:

1. understand how product life cycles affect strategy planning.
2. know what is involved in designing new products and what "new products" really are.
3. understand the new-product development process.
4. appreciate the team effort that goes into new-product development.
5. understand the need for product or brand managers.
6. understand how total quality management can improve goods and services.
7. understand important new terms (shown in red).

Innovation and Market Changes Create Opportunities

Successful new products, like those in the iRobot case, are critical in driving profitable growth for both new and established companies. iRobot pioneered a fast-growing new product-market—and "computer-controlled cleaning tools" are meeting customer needs in new ways. Similarly, in Chapter 5, we looked at how the iPod and other innovations in digital media have changed personal entertainment. In fact, all around us there is a constant life-and-death struggle where old products are replaced by new products. Digital video recorders have pretty much made video-cassette recorders for TVs obsolete. Likewise, cell phones are replacing landline phones and phone booths, making it possible for people to communicate from places where it was previously impossible. Really new product ideas disrupt the old ways of doing things—not only for marketers, but also for customers.

These innovations show that products, customer behavior, and competition change over time. These changes create opportunities for marketing managers and pose challenges as well. Developing new products and managing existing products to meet changing conditions are important to the success of every firm. In Chapter 8 we looked at important strategy planning decisions that need to be made for new products and sometimes changed for existing products. In this chapter, we'll look at how successful new products are developed in the first place—and what marketing managers need to know and do to

Exhibit 9–1 The Role of Product Management and New-Product Development in Marketing Strategy

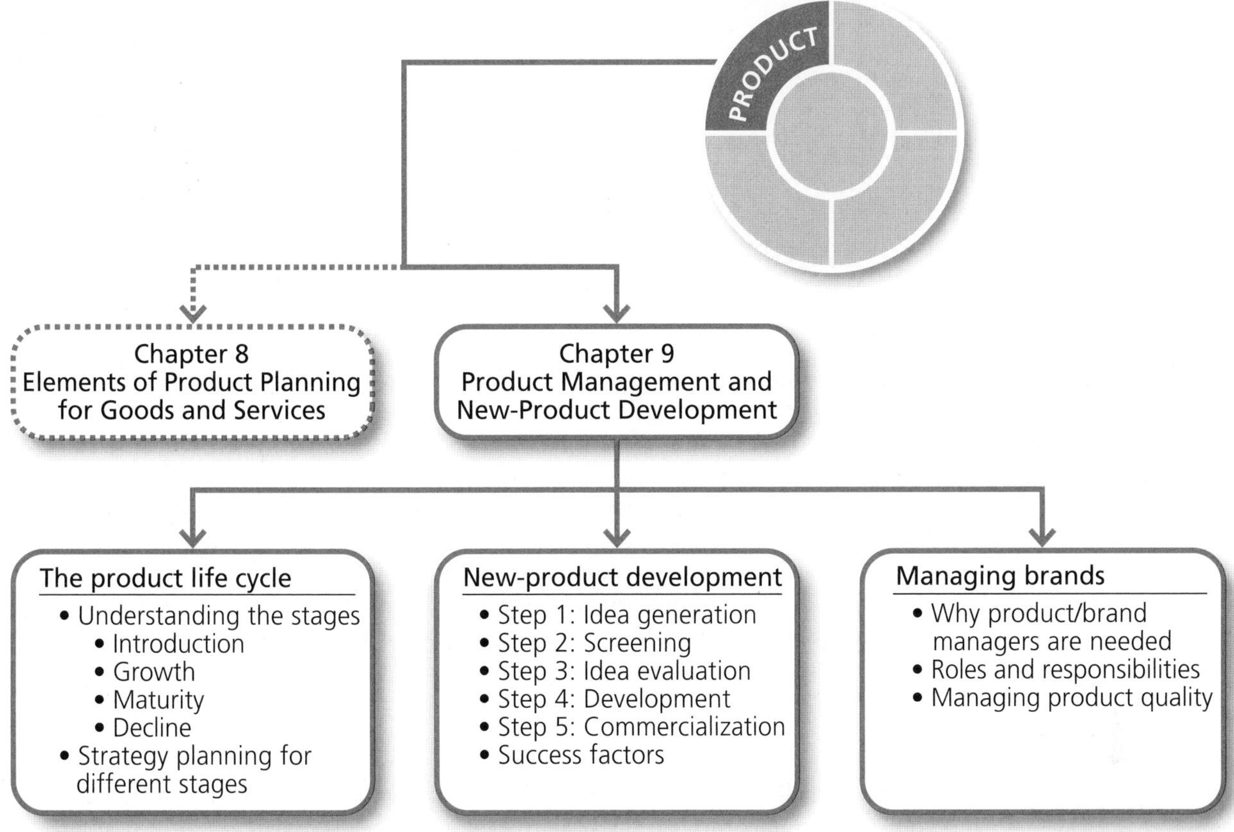

manage their growth. We'll start by explaining the cycle of growth and decline that new product innovations go through. When you understand the stages in this cycle, you can see *why* it is so critical for a firm to have an effective new-product development process—and why the challenges of managing a product change as it matures. See Exhibit 9-1.

Managing Products over Their Life Cycles

LO 9.1

Revolutionary products create new product-markets. But competitors are always developing and copying new ideas and products—making existing products out of date more quickly than ever. Products, like consumers, go through life cycles.

Product life cycle has four major stages

The **product life cycle** describes the stages a really new product idea goes through from beginning to end. The product life cycle is divided into four major stages: (1) market introduction, (2) market growth, (3) market maturity, and (4) sales decline. The product life cycle is concerned with new types (or categories) of products in the market, not just what happens to an individual brand.

A particular firm's marketing mix usually must change during the product life cycle. There are several reasons why customers' attitudes and needs may change over the product life cycle. The product may be aimed at entirely different target markets at different stages. And the nature of competition moves toward pure competition or oligopoly.

Further, total sales of the product—by all competitors in the industry—vary in each of its four stages. They move from very low in the market introduction stage to high at market maturity and then back to low in the sales decline stage. More important, the profit picture changes too. These general relationships can be seen in Exhibit 9-2. Note

Exhibit 9–2
Typical Life Cycle of a New Product Concept

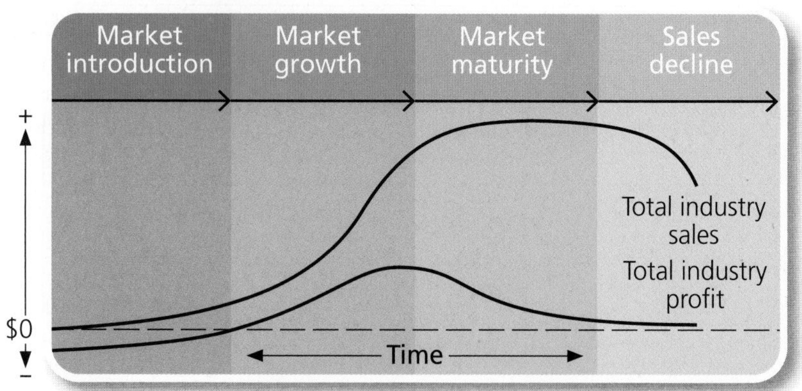

that sales and profits do not move together over time. *Industry profits decline while industry sales are still rising.*[2]

Market introduction—investing in the future

In the **market introduction** stage, sales are low as a new idea is first introduced to a market. Customers aren't looking for the product. Even if the product offers superior value, customers don't even know about it. Informative promotion is needed to tell potential customers about the advantages and uses of the new product concept.

Even though a firm promotes its new product, it takes time for customers to learn that the product is available. Most companies experience losses during the introduction stage because they spend so much money for Product, Place, and Promotion development. Of course, they invest the money in the hope of future profits.

Market growth—profits go up and down

In the **market growth** stage, industry sales grow fast—but industry profits rise and then start falling. The innovator begins to make big profits as more and more customers buy. But competitors see the opportunity and enter the market. After East African Breweries created a sensation in Nigeria with its non-alcoholic malt beverage Alvaro, Coca-Cola followed eight months later with its own malt drink Novida.[3] Some just copy the most successful product or try to improve it to compete better. Others try to refine their offerings to do a better job of appealing to some target markets. The new entries result in much product variety. So monopolistic competition—with down-sloping demand curves—is typical of the market growth stage.

This is the time of biggest profits *for the industry*. It is also a time of rapid sales and earnings growth for companies with effective strategies. *But it is toward the end of this stage when industry profits begin to decline* as competition and consumer price sensitivity increase. See Exhibit 9-2.

Market maturity—sales level off, profits continue down

The **market maturity** stage occurs when industry sales level off and competition gets tougher. Many aggressive competitors have entered the race for profits—except in oligopoly situations. Industry profits go down throughout the market maturity stage because promotion costs rise and some competitors cut prices to attract business. Less efficient firms can't compete with this pressure—and they drop out of the market. There is a long-run downward pressure on prices.

New firms may still enter the market at this stage—increasing competition even more. Note that late entries skip the early life-cycle stages, including the profitable market growth stage. And they must try to take a share of the saturated market from established firms, which is difficult and expensive. The market leaders have a lot at stake, so they fight hard to defend their share. Customers who are happy with their current relationship won't switch to a new brand. So late entrants usually have a tough battle.

Persuasive promotion becomes even more important during the market maturity stage. Products may differ only slightly. Most competitors have discovered effective appeals or just copied the leaders. As the various products become almost the same in the minds of potential consumers, price sensitivity is a real factor.[4]

In the United States, the markets for most cars, most household appliances, and many consumer packaged goods like breakfast cereal, carbonated soft drinks, and laundry detergent are in market maturity. This stage may continue for many years—until a basically new product idea comes along—even though individual brands or models come and go.

Sales decline—a time of replacement

During the **sales decline** stage, new products replace the old. Price competition from dying products becomes more vigorous—but firms with strong brands may make profits until the end because they have successfully differentiated their products.

As the new products go through their introduction stage, the old ones may keep some sales by appealing to their most loyal customers or those who are slow to try new ideas. These conservative buyers might switch later—smoothing the sales decline.

Product life cycles don't relate to individual products

Product life cycles describe *industry* sales and profits for a *product idea* within a particular product-market. The sales and profits of an individual brand may not, and often do not, follow the life-cycle pattern. They may vary up and down throughout the life cycle—sometimes moving in the opposite direction of industry sales and profits.

A firm may introduce or drop a specific product during *any* stage of the product life cycle. A "me-too" brand introduced during the market growth stage, for example, may never get sales at all and suffer a quick death. For example, Walmart tried to rent DVDs by mail after Netflix was already established as the market leader. When customers did not see Walmart's marketing mix as better, it failed to attract enough customers and closed operations.

Each market should be carefully defined

A product idea can also be in a different life-cycle stage in different markets. For example, in the United States, milk is in the market maturity stage. U.S. consumers drink 18 times more milk than Asian consumers—where milk is in the market introduction stage. Some firms in the dairy business are trying to grow the Asian market. To appeal to the Asian palate, they are selling milk with added flavors like ginger and honey.

Strategy planners who naïvely expect sales of an individual product to follow the general product life-cycle pattern are likely to be surprised. In fact, it might be more sensible to think in terms of "product-market life cycles" rather than product life cycles— but we will use the term *product life cycle* because it is commonly accepted and widely used.[5]

Evian wants to stand out in the mature and highly competitive bottled water market. The company's "Live Young" campaign focused on babies. The viral video of roller skating babies has been viewed more than 150 million times. See it at http://www.youtube.com/watch?v=XQcVllWpwGs.

Product Life Cycles Vary in Length

How long a whole product life cycle takes—and the length of each stage—varies wildly across products. The cycle may vary from 90 days—in the case of toys like the *Incredibles* movie line—to more than 100 years for gas-powered cars.

The product life-cycle concept does not tell a manager precisely *how long* the cycle will last. But a manager can often make a good guess based on the life cycle for similar products. Sometimes marketing research can help too. However, it is more important to expect and plan for the different stages than to know the precise length of each cycle.

Some products move quickly

A new-product idea will move through the early stages of the life cycle more quickly when it has certain characteristics. For example, the greater the *comparative advantage* of a new product over those already on the market, the more rapidly its sales will grow. Sales growth is also faster when the product is *easy to use* and if its advantages are *easy to communicate.* If the product *can be tried* on a limited basis—without a lot of risk to the customer—it can usually be introduced more quickly. Finally, if the product is *compatible* with the values and experiences of target customers, they are likely to buy it more quickly.

The fast adoption of DVD players is a good example. The idea of renting or buying movies to view at home was already *compatible* with consumer lifestyles, but many consumers hesitated before buying a DVD player. They also saw DVD rental as *compatible* when they went to a video rental store and saw video tapes and a growing number of DVDs to rent. A demo of a DVD movie at a store or a friend's house made for compelling *communication* of the *comparative advantage* of better picture and audio quality. Another advantage was highlighted in ads showing DVD extras such as deleted scenes and interviews with directors. Some consumers didn't see the value when DVD players were priced at several hundred dollars—but when prices dropped, these customers quickly bought DVD players.[6]

Product life cycles are getting shorter

Although the life of different products varies, in general product life cycles are getting shorter. This is partly due to rapidly changing technology. One new invention may make possible many new products that replace old ones. Tiny electronic microchips led to thousands of new products—from Texas Instruments calculators in the early days to microchip-controlled heart valves now.

Think about the product-market for listening to music. For many decades AM or FM radio and record albums were primary sources of music at home or on the road. Just over a decade ago MP3 players emerged. Then along came new radio formats via satellite and

New products that do a better job of meeting the needs of specific target customers are more likely to move quickly and successfully through the introductory stage of the product life cycle.

over-the-air high definition radio. This has been followed by Internet radio where listeners create their own stations on services like Pandora and Slacker. In less than a decade MP3 players are nearing market maturity, while the newer radio formats are early in the market growth stage.

Although life cycles keep moving in the developed economies, many advances bypass most consumers in less-developed economies. These consumers struggle at the subsistence level, without an effective macro-marketing system to stimulate innovation. However, some of the innovations and economies of scale made possible in the advanced societies do trickle down to benefit these consumers. Inexpensive antibiotics and drought-resistant plants, for example, are making a life-or-death difference.

Pioneer or follower—which strategy works best?

The product life cycle means that firms must be developing new products all the time. Further, they must try to use marketing mixes that will make the most of the market growth stage—when profits are highest. The question becomes, is it better to be the *pioneer*—the first to market with a new product idea—or a *follower*?

On average, pioneers tend to be less profitable over the long-run—in part because many do not survive. That said, there are some real success stories among pioneers. For example, FedEx invented overnight delivery and remains the market leader. More often, though, there is an advantage to being the *second-mover*—one that quickly follows the pioneer. Second-movers that have a strong customer focus and respond quickly with a superior marketing mix can build market share during the market growth stage.

There are many examples of successful second-movers. While many consider Apple to be an innovator, the iPod, iPhone, and iPad were not the first of their kind to market. Yet Apple responded quickly with a better marketing mix in each of these product categories. Likewise, Amazon wasn't the first online bookstore. Bookstacks launched the online books.com three years before Amazon. RC Cola had the first diet cola on the market—but Coke and Pepsi quickly copied the idea and took over the market. An observant second-mover can learn from the pioneer's mistakes and quickly come to market with a marketing mix that provides superior value.[7]

The short happy life of fashions and fads

The sales of some products are influenced by **fashion**—the currently accepted or popular style. Fashion-related products tend to have short life cycles. What is currently popular can shift rapidly. A certain color or style of clothing—baggy jeans, miniskirts, or four-inch-wide ties—may be in fashion one season and outdated the next. Marketing managers who work with fashions often have to make really fast product changes.

How fast is fast enough? Zara, a women's fashion retailer based in Spain, takes only about two weeks to go from a new fashion concept to having items on the racks of its stores. Zara quickly produces just enough of a new design to test the waters and then sends it out for overnight delivery to some of its stores around the world. At headquarters, sales managers sit at computers monitoring sales of the new design. When a garment is hot, more are produced and shipped—within weeks. Otherwise, it's dropped. Stores are stocked with new designs, not just new orders, about twice a week. Store managers use handheld computers that show how garments rank by sales, so clerks can reorder best-sellers in less than an hour. These orders arrive, together with new pieces, two days later.[8]

A **fad** is an idea that is fashionable only to certain groups who are enthusiastic about it. But these groups are so fickle that a fad is even more short lived than a regular fashion. Many toys—whether it's a Hasbro *Lord of the Rings* plastic figure or a Toymax Paintball pack—are fads but do well during a short-lived cycle.[9]

Planning for Different Stages of the Product Life Cycle

Length of cycle affects strategy planning

Where a product is in its life cycle—and how fast it's moving to the next stage—should affect marketing strategy planning. Marketing managers must make realistic plans for the later stages. Exhibit 9-3 shows the relationship of the product life cycle to the marketing mix variables. The technical terms in this figure are discussed later in the book.

Introducing new products

Exhibit 9-3 shows that a marketing manager has to do a lot of strategy planning to introduce a really new product. Money must be spent developing the new product. Even if the product is unique, this doesn't mean that everyone will immediately come running to the producer's door. The firm will have to build channels of distribution—perhaps offering special incentives to win cooperation. Promotion is needed to build demand *for the whole idea* not just to sell a specific brand. Because all this is expensive, it may lead the

Exhibit 9–3
Typical Changes in the Marketing Mix over the Product Life Cycle

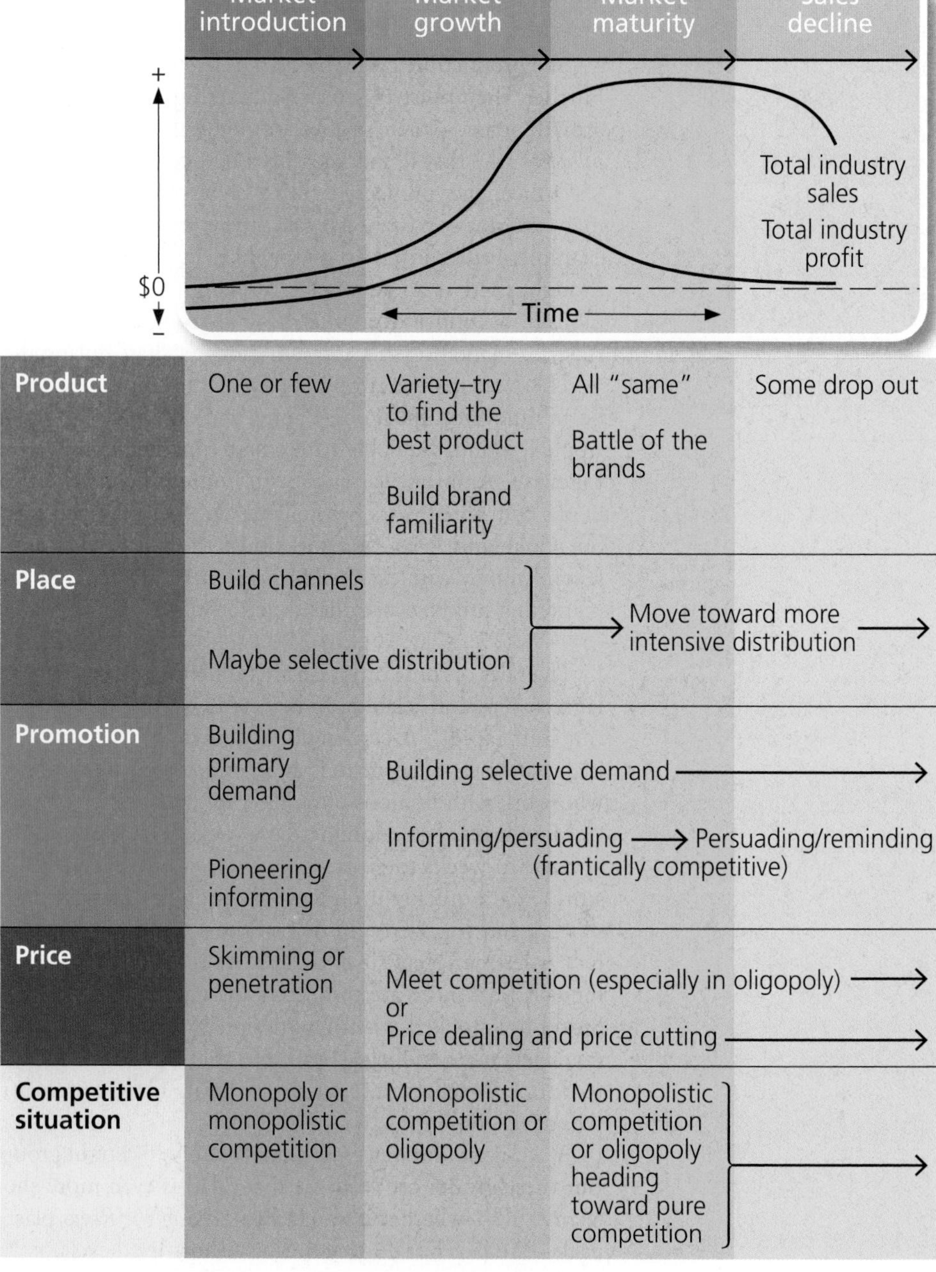

	Market introduction	Market growth	Market maturity	Sales decline
Product	One or few	Variety–try to find the best product Build brand familiarity	All "same" Battle of the brands	Some drop out
Place	Build channels Maybe selective distribution		Move toward more intensive distribution →	
Promotion	Building primary demand Pioneering/ informing	Building selective demand → Informing/persuading → Persuading/reminding (frantically competitive)		
Price	Skimming or penetration	Meet competition (especially in oligopoly) → or Price dealing and price cutting →		
Competitive situation	Monopoly or monopolistic competition	Monopolistic competition or oligopoly	Monopolistic competition or oligopoly heading toward pure competition →	

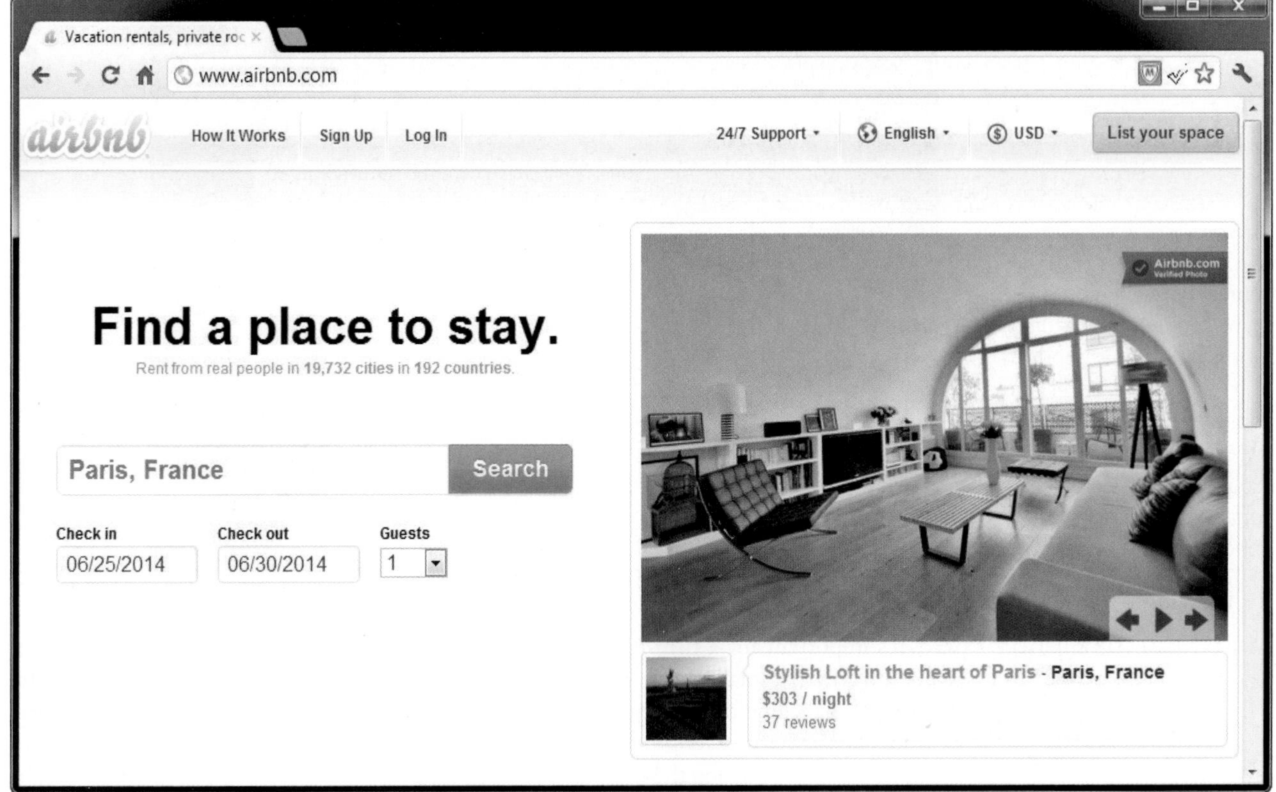

Airbnb is a community marketplace to discover, list, and book unique accommodations in over 25,000 cities around the world. Airbnb hosts list their extra space, be it a private island, a tree house, an igloo or a castle, and guests discover and book these spaces for short or long-term stays. Because this was a new idea to many of Airbnb's target customers, Airbnb had to build primary demand in the market introduction stage; it used promotion to tell its target market how the service works. E-mail campaigns, listings on Craigslist, publicity, and positive word-of-mouth have helped it rapidly grow in room nights booked.

marketing manager to try to "skim" the market—charging a relatively high price to help pay for the introductory costs.

The correct strategy, however, depends on how quickly the new idea will be accepted by customers—and how quickly competitors will follow with their own versions of the product. When the early stages of the cycle will be fast, a low initial (penetration) price may make sense to help develop loyal customers early and keep competitors out.

Be prepared to pivot to a new marketing mix

It can be difficult to predict customer response to a really new product. So marketing managers need to carefully monitor initial customer reactions and be prepared to *pivot*—or move to a new marketing mix. After all the effort planning a new product, this can be difficult for some marketing managers. Yet this is what the developers of "Game Neverending," a massively multiplayer online game did following the game's 2004 launch. The game did not catch on as the developers had hoped, but they noticed that a photo-sharing element of the game was a popular feature. Soon the game was gone, but a photo-sharing service called Flickr was born. Flickr became a great success—it now hosts more than 6 billion images—because of the developers' willingness to pivot to a different marketing mix.

Pioneers may need help

Sometimes, before an innovation can take off, a number of different companies need to come together. When Netflix first came out with video that would stream to your television, many of the top movies didn't allow their films to be distributed this way. Netflix also needed TVs or DVD players made by other firms to offer the Netflix service. Netflix's success was dependent on cooperation from the home electronics and movie industries. Along the same line, electric cars require charging stations—or drivers can't wander too far from home.

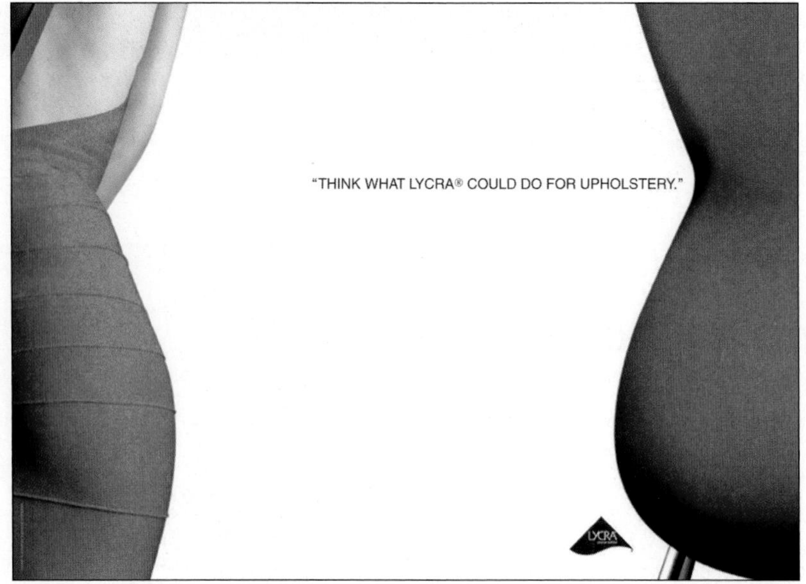

"THINK WHAT LYCRA® COULD DO FOR UPHOLSTERY."
LYCRA

Some companies continue to do well in market maturity by improving their products or by finding new uses and applications. DuPont International's Lycra has expanded from personal apparel to furniture upholstery.

Managing maturing products

It's important for a firm to have some competitive advantage as it moves into market maturity. Even a small advantage can make a big difference—and some firms do very well by carefully managing their maturing products. They are able to capitalize on a slightly better product or perhaps lower production or marketing costs. Or they are simply more successful at promotion—allowing them to differentiate their more or less homogeneous product from competitors. For example, graham crackers were competing in a mature market and sales were flat. Nabisco used the same ingredients to create bite-sized Teddy Grahams and then promoted them heavily. These changes captured new sales and profits for Nabisco.[10]

Industry profits are declining in market maturity. Top managers must see this, or they will expect the attractive profits that are no longer possible. If top managers don't understand the situation, they may place impossible burdens on the marketing department—causing marketing managers to think about deceptive advertising or some other desperate attempt to reach impossible objectives.

Product life cycles keep moving. But that doesn't mean a firm should just sit by as its sales decline. There are other choices. A firm can improve its product or develop an innovative new product for the same market. Or it can develop a new strategy targeted at a new market where the life cycle is not so far along. That approach is working for InSinkErator. It has an 80 percent share of all garbage disposals, but in the mature U.S. market, disposals are already in more than half of all homes. In contrast, garbage disposals are in only about 10 percent of homes in many areas of Europe. While many households there can afford a disposal, until recently most cities prohibited them on environmental grounds. When research showed that garbage disposals actually provide environmental benefits, InSinkErator adapted its strategy and sales in Europe have grown quickly.[11]

Improve the product or develop a new one

When a firm's product has won loyal customers, it can be successful for a long time—even in a mature or declining market. However, continued improvements may be needed as customers' needs shift. An outstanding example is Procter & Gamble's Tide. Introduced in 1947, Tide led to a whole new generation of powdered laundry products that cleaned better with fewer suds. But Tide continues to change because of new washing machines and fabrics. The Tide sold today has had at least 55 modifications!

Do product modifications—like those made with powdered Tide—create a wholly new product that should have its own product life cycle? Or are they technical adjustments of the original product idea? We will take the latter position—focusing on the product idea rather than changes in features. This means that some of these Tide changes were made in the market maturity stage. But this type of product improvement can help to extend the product life cycle.

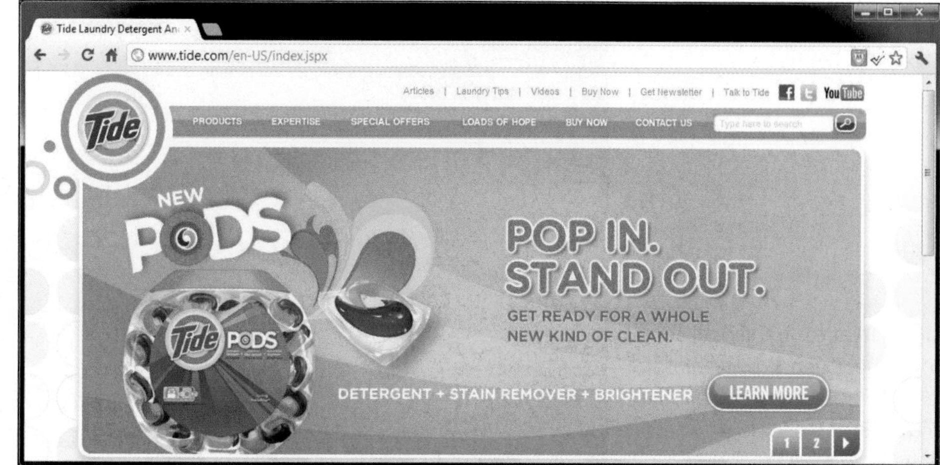

Tide laundry detergent has been improved many times over the years and currrently there are more than 30 different versions of Tide, including Tide Pods.

On the other hand, a firm that develops an innovative new product may move to a new product life cycle. For example, by 1985 new liquid detergents like Wisk were moving into the growth stage, and sales of powdered detergents were declining. To share in the growth-stage profits for liquid detergents and to offset the loss of customers from powdered Tide, Procter & Gamble introduced Liquid Tide.

Even though regular powdered detergents are in the decline stage, traditional powdered Tide continues to sell well because it still does the job for some consumers. But sales growth is likely to come from liquid detergents and the newer low-suds detergents.[12]

Develop new strategies for different markets

In a mature market, a firm may be fighting to keep or increase its market share. But if the firm finds a new use for the product, it may stimulate overall demand. DuPont's Teflon fluorocarbon resin is a good example. It was developed more than 50 years ago and has enjoyed sales growth as a nonstick coating for cookware and as a lining for chemically resistant equipment. But marketing managers for Teflon are not waiting to be stuck with declining profits in those mature markets. They are constantly developing strategies for new markets. For example, Teflon is now selling well as a special coating for the wires used in high-speed communications between computers and as a lightweight film that offers greater output power for photovoltaic solar panels.[13]

Stimulate growth with new uses

Marketing managers might also find new ways to use a product. Following years of slow growth, brand managers at Philadelphia Cream Cheese (Philly) looked more closely at the habits of the brand's most frequent buyers. They discovered these customers were using the product as an ingredient—not just as something to smear on bagels. European marketing managers launched an advertising campaign that promoted adding Philly to everything from spaghetti to Spanish tapas. Hoping to inspire creative home cooks, they persuaded Tesco, the U.K.'s leading grocer, to place Philly next to main-dish staples like salmon. Now the number of Philly customers in the U.K. using it as an ingredient is almost 40 percent—double the level before the campaign. And sales have grown more than 20 percent in a mature market.[14]

Phase out dying products

Not all strategies are exciting growth strategies. If prospects are poor in a product-market, a phase-out strategy may be needed. The need for phasing out becomes more obvious as the sales decline stage arrives. But even in market maturity, it may be clear that a particular product is not going to be profitable enough to reach the company's objectives. In any case, it is wise to remember that marketing plans are implemented as ongoing strategies. Salespeople make calls, inventory moves in the channel, advertising is scheduled for several months into the future, and so on. So the firm usually experiences losses if managers end a plan too abruptly. Because of this, it's sometimes better to phase out the product gradually.

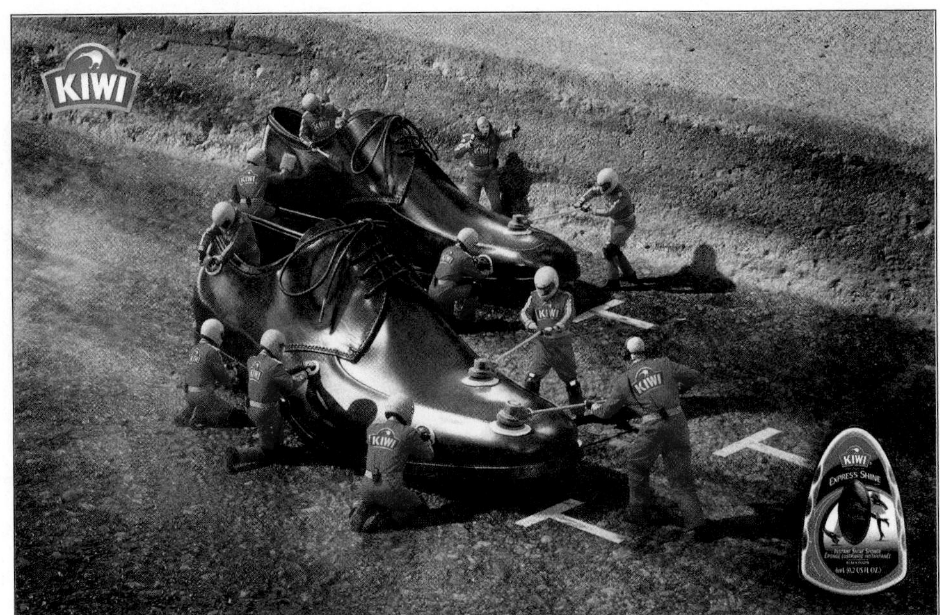

The market for traditional shoe polish has been in decline as leather shoes become less common and people have less time to polish their own shoes. Even in the sales decline stage, market leader Kiwi develops new products like Kiwi Express Shine.

Phasing out a product may involve some difficult implementation problems. But phase-out is also a *strategy*—and it must be market-oriented to cut losses. In fact, it is possible to milk a dying product for some time if competitors move out more quickly and there is ongoing (though declining) demand. Some customers are willing to pay attractive prices to get their old favorite.

New-Product Planning

LO 9.2

In most markets, progress marches on. So it is essential for a firm to develop new products or modify its current products to meet changing customer needs and competitors' actions. Not having an active new-product development process means that consciously, or subconsciously, the firm has decided to milk its current products and eventually go out of business. New-product planning is not an optional matter. It has to be done just to survive in today's dynamic markets.

What is a new product?

In discussing the introductory stage of product life cycles, we focused on the types of really new product innovations that tend to disrupt old ways of doing things. However, each year firms introduce many products that are basically refinements of existing products. So a **new product** is one that is new *in any way* for the company concerned. But customers don't see all new products in the same way.

Types of new products from the customer's point of view

Some new products are minor variations on existing products. These *continuous innovations* don't require customers to learn new behaviors. A new toothpaste flavor, a low-calorie iced tea, or a new style of earring would fit in this category. Promotion for this type of innovation focuses on awareness—often with packaging or advertising that touts the new feature.

Dynamically continuous innovations require minor changes in customer behavior. For example, 3M developed a Bluetooth-enabled stethoscope, which wirelessly records and stores the sounds of the heart, lung, and other body parts in a digital computer file. The sound files can be attached to computer records or sent to other doctors for help diagnosing and treating patients. Similarly, Lysol created a battery-operated hands-free soap dispenser for home use. Promotion for dynamically continuous innovations needs to clearly communicate the benefits of the innovation.

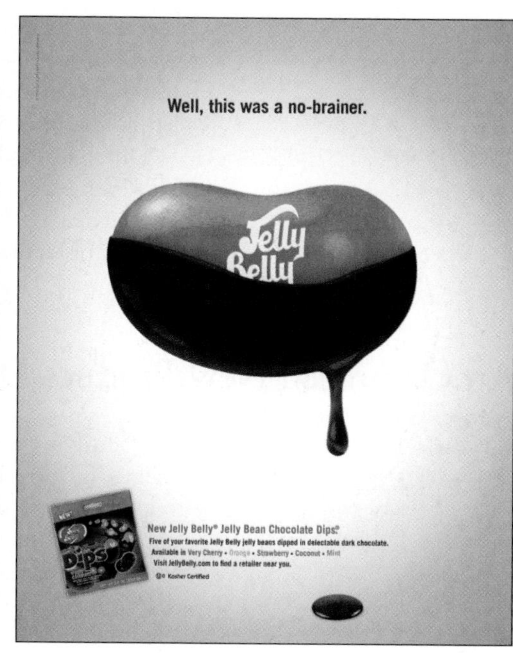

Some new products are refinements of existing products.

Internet Exercise

IDEO is a consulting firm that helps organizations with the innovation process. Click on IDEO's website (**www.ideo.com**) and choose "Work" and then "Social Innovation." Choose two of IDEO's key projects. What elements of the marketing strategy planning model do you see in action?

A *discontinuous innovation* requires customers adopting the innovation to significantly change their behavior. This type of innovation often results in a completely new product-market and new product life cycle. Appliance maker Godrej needed to think differently about refrigeration in rural India. In this part of the world, where most families make less than $5 a day and electricity is unreliable or unavailable, there is little demand for the major appliances Godrej produces. These consumers have basic needs—they just want to keep milk, vegetables, and fruit cool for a day or two. For this market, Godrej engineers created ChotuKool ("little cool" in Hindi), a portable cooler which runs on DC current or an external battery. The design minimizes heat loss and power usage. The innovation is life-altering for people in this part of the world and changes how they shop and cook. Promotion for discontinuous innovations usually requires personal selling and product demonstrations to educate customers about new behaviors.[15]

FTC says product is "new" only six months

A firm can call its product new for only a limited time. Six months is the limit according to the **Federal Trade Commission (FTC)**—the federal government agency that polices antimonopoly laws. To be called new, says the FTC, a product must be entirely new or changed in a "functionally significant or substantial respect."[16]

Ethical issues in new-product planning

New-product decisions—and decisions to abandon old products—often involve ethical considerations. For example, some firms (including firms that develop drugs) have been criticized for holding back important new-product innovations until patents run out, or sales slow down, on their existing products.

At the same time, others have been criticized for "planned obsolescence"—releasing new products that the company plans to soon replace with improved new versions. Similarly, wholesalers and retailers complain that producers too often keep their new-product introduction plans a secret and leave intermediaries with dated inventory that they can sell only at a loss.

Companies also face ethical dilemmas when they decide to stop supplying a product or the service and replacement parts to keep it useful. An old model of a Cuisinart food processor, for example, might be in perfect shape except for a crack in the plastic mixing bowl. It's sensible for the company to improve the design if the crack is a frequent problem, but if consumers can't get a replacement part for the model they already own, they're left holding the bag.

Different marketing managers might have very different reactions to such criticisms. However, product management decisions often have a significant effect on customers and intermediaries. A too-casual decision may lead to a negative backlash that affects the firm's strategy or reputation.[17]

An Organized New-Product Development Process Is Critical

LO 9.3

Identifying and developing new-product ideas—and effective strategies to go with them—is often the key to a firm's success and survival. But the costs of new-product development and the risks of failure are high. Experts estimate that consumer packaged-goods companies spend more than $20 million to introduce a new brand—and 80 to 95 percent of those new brands flop. That's a big expense—and a waste. In the service sector, the front-end cost of a failed effort may not be as high, but it can have a devastating long-term effect if dissatisfied consumers turn elsewhere for help.[18]

A new product may fail for many reasons. Most often, companies fail to offer a unique benefit or underestimate the competition. Sometimes the idea is good but the company has design problems—or the product costs much more to produce than was expected. Some companies rush to get a product on the market without developing a complete marketing plan.[19]

But moving too slowly can be a problem too. With the fast pace of change for many products, speedy entry into the market can be a key to competitive advantage. Marketing managers at Xerox learned this the hard way. Japanese competitors were taking market share with innovative new models of copiers. It turned out that the competitors were developing new models twice as fast as Xerox and at half the cost. For Xerox to compete, it had to slash its five-year product development cycle.[20]

The longer new-product development takes, the more likely it is that customer needs will be different when the product is actually introduced. Back in 2005, consumer interest

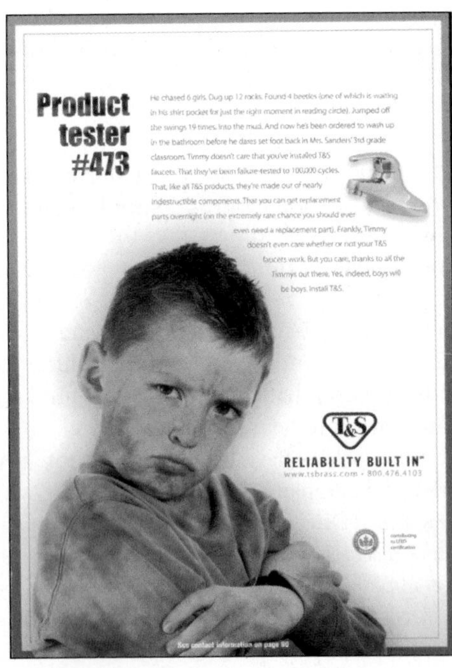

Generating innovative and profitable new products requires an understanding of customer needs—and an organized new-product development process.

It's a plant. It's an animal. It's a bug. And maybe it's a new product idea.

Over the last 3 billion years, nature has found ways to solve many problems. Biomimicry studies nature's best ideas and then emulates those designs to create new products. If we ask nature, it might offer ideas for new products.

How would nature create a flexible fastener? Perhaps the best known example of biomimicry is Velcro, which was invented in 1941 by a Swiss engineer who was curious why burrs stubbornly stuck to his dog's fur following a hike in the woods. Placing the burrs under a microscope, he saw the tiny hooks that grabbed tiny loops that could also be found in clothes, socks, or animal fur. This inspired the two-part Velcro fastener; one side with tiny hooks and the other with tiny loops.

How would nature create strong bonds? A professor at Oregon State University wondered how mussels keep such a tight grip on underwater rocks with waves pounding down on them. Subsequent research found that the mussels secrete proteins known as byssal threads. The threads create an adhesive with superior strength and flexibility. This finding inspired development of a soy-based adhesive used by Columbia Forest products to create its PureBond plywood. The adhesive replaces the environmentally harmful formaldehyde used in most plywood.

How would nature keep a building at a constant temperature? On the African savannas, temperatures can range from 35–110 degrees Fahrenheit. Termites there build and live in mounds stretching more than 15 feet high—and they maintain virtually constant temperatures inside. Looking closer at the termite mounds, scientists discovered the insects' secrets; they constantly open and close vents to draw in cool air at the base and ventilate hot air through chimneys. Drawing on these insights, architects designed Eastgate Center, a high-rise building in Zimbabwe, that consumes less than 10 percent of the energy used in similarly sized buildings.

Nature's problem-solving experience draws on millions of years of adaptation. For more ideas, you can ask questions—and see answers—at www.asknature.org. Today, more firms are turning to nature for new product ideas. When they ask how nature solves a problem, they are getting some pretty good answers.[21]

in trucks and SUVs was high. General Motors expected that popularity to continue when planning new models. But, by the time those vehicles were on the market in 2008, gasoline prices had skyrocketed—and consumer preferences were switching to smaller cars. In contrast, Toyota's new-product planning had focused on more fuel efficiency, and its new 2008 hybrid models were in hot demand.

To move quickly and also avoid expensive new-product failures, companies should follow an organized new-product development process. The following pages describe such a process, which moves logically through five steps: (1) idea generation, (2) screening, (3) idea evaluation, (4) development (of product and marketing mix), and (5) commercialization. See Exhibit 9-4.

The general process is similar for both consumer and business markets—and for both goods and services. There are some significant differences, but we will emphasize the similarities in the following discussion.

Process tries to kill new ideas—economically

An important element in the new-product development process is continued evaluation of a new idea's likely profitability and return on investment. The hypothesis tested is that the new idea will *not* be profitable. This puts the burden on the new idea—to prove itself or be rejected. Such a process may seem harsh, but experience shows that most new ideas have some flaw. Marketers try to discover those flaws early, and either find a remedy or reject the idea completely. Applying this process requires much analysis of the idea *before* the company spends money to develop and market a product. This is a major departure from the usual production-oriented approach—in which a company develops a product first and then asks sales to "get rid of it."

Exhibit 9–4 New-Product Development Process

Idea generation	Screening	Idea evaluation	Development	Commercialization
Ideas from: Customers and users Marketing research Competitors Other markets Company people Intermediaries, etc.	Strengths and weaknesses Fit with objectives Market trends Rough ROI estimate	Concept testing Reactions from customers Rough estimates of costs, sales, and profits	R&D Develop model or service prototype Test marketing mix Revise plans as needed ROI estimate	Finalize product and marketing plan Start production and marketing "Roll out" in select markets Final ROI estimate

Step 1: Idea generation

Finding new-product ideas can't be left to chance. Instead, firms need a formal procedure to generate a continuous flow of ideas. For some companies, a constant investment in research and development results in a flow of new technology with new product applications. But new ideas can come from a company's own sales or production staff, wholesalers or retailers, competitors, consumer surveys, or other sources such as trade associations, advertising agencies, or government agencies. By analyzing new and different views of the company's markets and studying present consumer behavior, a marketing manager can spot opportunities that have not yet occurred to competitors or even to potential customers. Let's look at some examples of how this works.

Ideas from customers

Customers can be a great source of new ideas—and if they suggest the idea, they are more likely to buy it. Companies like Rubbermaid and eBags comb through customer reviews for new product ideas. T-shirt maker Threadless takes this approach to another level. Threadless community members submit T-shirt designs as part of a contest. Winning designs are chosen based on ratings and comments from other members—a process called *crowdsourcing*. Threadless then produces the winners and sells them on its website—and because community members tell them which shirts to make, almost every product sells out.

Ideas from other companies and markets

No one firm can always be first with the best new ideas. So companies should pay attention to what competitors are doing. Some firms use what's called *reverse engineering*. For example, new-product specialists at Ford Motor Company buy other firms' cars as soon as they're available. Then they take the cars apart to look for new ideas or improvements. British Airways talks to travel agents to learn about new services offered by competitors.

Sometimes ideas from one product-market can be adapted for another—where it will be a *new* product. To get such ideas, some firms "shop" in international markets. For instance, food companies in Europe are experimenting with an innovation from Japan—a clear, odorless, natural film for wrapping food. Consumers don't have to unwrap it; when they put the product in boiling water or a microwave, the wrapper vanishes.[22]

Step 2: Screening

Screening involves evaluating the new ideas with the type of S.W.O.T analysis described in Chapter 2 and the product-market screening criteria described in Chapter 3. Recall that these criteria include the combined output of a resources (strengths and weaknesses) analysis, a long-run trends analysis, and a thorough understanding of the company's objectives. See Exhibit 2-9 and Exhibit 3-8. A "good" new idea should eventually lead to a product (and marketing mix) that will give the firm a competitive advantage—hopefully, a lasting one.

The life-cycle stage at which a firm's new product enters the market has a direct bearing on its prospects for growth. So screening should consider how the strategy for a new product will hold up over the whole product life cycle.

Safety must be considered

Real acceptance of the marketing concept prompts managers to screen new products on the basis of how safe they are. Safety is not a casual matter. The U.S. **Consumer Product Safety Act** (of 1972) set up the Consumer Product Safety Commission to encourage safety in product design and better quality control. The commission has a great deal of power. It can set safety standards for products. It can order costly repairs or the return of unsafe products. And it can back up its orders with fines and jail sentences. The Food and Drug Administration has similar powers for foods and drugs.

Product safety complicates strategy planning because not all customers—even those who want better safety features—are willing to pay more for safer products. Some features cost a lot to add and increase prices considerably. These safety concerns must be considered at the screening step because a firm can later be held liable for unsafe products.

Products can turn to liabilities

Product liability means the legal obligation of sellers to pay damages to individuals who are injured by defective or unsafe products. Product liability is a serious matter. Liability settlements may exceed not only a company's insurance coverage but its total assets!

Relative to most other countries, U.S. courts enforce a strict product liability standard. Sellers may be held responsible for injuries related to their products no matter how the items are used or how well they're designed. In one widely publicized judgment, McDonald's paid a huge settlement to a woman who was burned when her coffee spilled. The court concluded that there was not enough warning about how hot the coffee was.

Product liability is a serious ethical and legal matter. Many countries are attempting to change their laws so that they will be fair to both firms and consumers. But until product liability questions are resolved, marketing managers must be even more sensitive when screening new-product ideas.[23]

ROI is a crucial screening criterion

Getting by the initial screening criteria doesn't guarantee success for the new idea. But it does show that at least the new idea is in the right ballpark *for this firm.* If many ideas pass the screening criteria, a firm must set priorities to determine which ones go on to the next step in the process. This can be done by comparing the ROI (return on investment) for each idea—assuming the firm is ROI-oriented. The most attractive alternatives are pursued first.

Step 3: Idea evaluation

When an idea moves past the screening step, it is evaluated more carefully. This stage involves getting more reactions from customers, even though at this stage an actual product has yet to be developed. While this can make getting customer input more difficult, firms need extensive feedback before adding the expense of producing the product.

At this stage, marketing managers should describe and relate the assumptions they are making about each new idea. The product idea represents a hypothesis, or educated guess, about how to meet customer needs. For example, a law firm may assume its corporate clients care enough about convenience to pay a premium price for a new web-based document sharing service. By making assumptions—like the value customers place on convenience—explicit, marketing managers can conduct research to find out as quickly as possible if assumptions are true.

Initial evaluation may come from informal focus groups. Their reactions can be helpful—especially if they show that potential users are not excited about the new idea. A more formal method uses **concept testing**—getting reactions from customers about how well a new-product idea fits their needs. Concept testing uses market research—ranging from focus groups to surveys of potential customers. Some firms run concept tests online, which can lower costs and speed feedback. It can be fast and easy to show some photos or a video of a concept, along with possible prices, to a sample of target customers. Follow-up survey questions gauge consumer reactions.

Ideas that survive to the development stage receive more attention. An automaker might develop a scale model of a car or a full-fledged, operational prototype. Honda's Micro Commuter and BMW's i8 Spyder may be on the market if they survive continued scrutiny from customers and show signs of a positive ROI.

Product planners must think about wholesaler and retailer customers as well as final consumers. Intermediaries may have special concerns about handling a proposed product. A Utah ice-cream maker was considering a new line of ice-cream novelty products—and he had visions of a hot market in California. But he had to drop his idea when he learned that grocery store chains wanted payments of $20,000 each just to stock his frozen novelties in their freezers.[24]

Marketing research can also help identify the size of potential markets and that helps companies to estimate likely costs, revenue, and profitability. Together all this information helps marketing managers decide whether there is an opportunity, whether it fits with the firm's resources, *and* whether there is a basis for developing a competitive advantage. With such information, the firm can develop a more reliable estimate of ROI in various market segments and decide whether to continue the new-product development process.[25]

Step 4: Development

Product ideas that survive the screening and idea evaluation steps get further investment of time and money. Usually, this involves more research and development (R&D) to design and develop the physical part of the product. Or, in the case of a new service offering, the firm works out the details of what training, equipment, staff, and so on will be needed to deliver on the idea. Input from a firm's earlier efforts help guide this technical work.

With computer-aided design (CAD) software on their computers, designers can develop lifelike 3-D color drawings of packages and products. Changes can be made almost instantly. They can be sent by e-mail to managers all over the world for immediate review. They can even be put on a website for marketing research with customers.

Customers can react to prototypes

Passing that test often leads next to the creation of a **prototype**—an early sample or model built to test a concept. 3-D printing technology allows a CAD drawing to quickly be converted into a plastic replica, often at a relatively low cost. For example, automakers can "print" a life-size car fender, door, even an auto body. This allows for checking fit, finish and styling. A service firm may try to train a small group of service providers and test the service on real customers.

Customers may even be involved in a *co-creation process*—where customers react to prototypes and suggest improvements. This process often uses *rapid prototyping*, where customer input is received and quickly designed into a revision of the product—and then fed back to customers for further input. The repetitive process in rapid prototyping encourages innovations to "fail early and fail often" so the best ideas get to market more quickly.

Google uses this approach to test new features it wants to add to its family of online services (Google, Gmail, Google+ and others)—often incorporating feedback in less than 24 hours and then seeking additional feedback from a test group.[26]

With actual goods and services, potential customers can more realistically react to how well a product meets their needs. Focus groups, panels, and surveys provide feedback on features and the whole product idea. Sometimes that reaction kills the idea. For example, Coca-Cola Foods believed it had a great idea with Minute Maid Squeeze-Fresh, frozen orange juice concentrate in a squeeze bottle. In tests, however, Squeeze-Fresh bombed. Consumers loved the idea but hated the product. In real life it was messy to use, and no one knew how much concentrate to squeeze in the glass.[27]

Market testing uses real market conditions

Firms often use full-scale *market testing* to get customer reactions under real market conditions or to test variations in the marketing mix. For example, a firm may test alternative brand names, prices, or advertising copy in different test cities. Note that the firm tests the whole marketing mix, not just the product. For example, a hotel chain might test a new service offering at one location to see how it goes over. Running market tests is costly, but *not* testing is risky. Frito-Lay was so sure it understood consumers' snack preferences that it introduced a three-item cracker line without market testing. Even with network TV ad support, MaxSnax met with overwhelming consumer indifference. By the time Frito-Lay pulled the product from store shelves, it had lost $52 million.[28]

Step 5: Commercialization

A product idea that survives this far can finally be placed on the market. Putting a product on the market is expensive, and success usually requires cooperation of the whole company. Manufacturing or service facilities have to be set up. Goods have to be produced to fill the channels of distribution, or people must be hired and trained to provide services. Further, introductory promotion is costly—especially if the company is entering a very competitive market.

Because of the size of the job, some firms introduce their products city by city or region by region—in a gradual "rollout"—until they have complete market coverage. Rollouts also permit more market testing, but the main purpose is to do a good job implementing the marketing plan. Marketing managers also need to pay close attention to control—to ensure that the implementation effort is working and that the strategy is on target.

Steps should not be skipped

Because speed can be important, it's always tempting to skip needed steps when some part of the process seems to indicate that the company has a "really good idea." But the process moves in steps—gathering different kinds of information along the way. By skipping steps, a firm may miss an important aspect that could make a whole strategy less profitable or actually cause it to fail.

Ethics Question

You are the marketing manager for a company that creates video games. A big competitor has just released an action game that appeals to kids who own your best-selling game. Your competitor's release is a better game because it takes advantage of features available in a hot new video game box. Your firm's updated release won't be available for at least four months. One of your game developers suggests that you preannounce your game will be ready in two months—which is about as long as gamers are likely to wait. Should you announce that your new version is coming or just wait until you know more? If a reporter for a popular gaming magazine calls and asks for a statement about when your firm's release will be on the market, should you say two months, four months, or "we don't know yet"? If your product is preannounced but then not ready by that date, what should your firm communicate to customers? Explain your thinking.

New-Product Development: A Total Company Effort

LO 9.4

We've been discussing the steps in a logical, new-product development process. However, as shown in Exhibit 9-5, many factors can impact the success of the effort.[29]

Top-level support is vital

Companies that are particularly successful at developing new goods and services seem to have one key trait in common: enthusiastic top-management support for new-product development. New products tend to upset old routines that managers of established products often try in subtle but effective ways to maintain. So someone with top-level support, and authority to get things done, needs to be responsible for new-product development.

A culture of innovation

A culture that supports innovation can generate more ideas. For example, Google allows its employees the freedom to spend 20 percent of their time working on new ideas, even if the ideas are unrelated to their job description. When people don't see the incentive to push for new ideas, they are likely to get distracted by other priorities that seem more pressing. For many years 3M has had an objective that 30 percent of sales should come from products that didn't exist four years earlier. Consistent with that goal, 3M's innovative culture produced breakthrough products like Scotch Stretchy Tape, Post-it Note Cards, Scotch Brite Tub & Tile Scrubber, and Vikuiti brand films for video screens. However, when the company moved toward more emphasis on cost cutting, the new-product pipeline began to dry up. To regain its innovative edge, 3M is going back to a better balance of efficiency *and* innovation.[30]

Put someone in charge

Rather than leaving new-product development to someone in engineering, R&D, or sales who happens to be interested in taking the initiative, successful companies *put* someone in charge. It may be a person, department, or team. But it's not a casual thing. It's a major responsibility of the job.

A new-product development team with people from different departments helps ensure that new ideas are carefully evaluated and profitable ones are quickly brought to market. It's important to choose the right people for the job. Overly conservative managers may kill too many, or even all, new ideas. Or committees may create bureaucratic delays that make the difference between a product's success or failure.

Market needs guide R&D effort

From the idea generation stage to the commercialization stage, the R&D specialists, the operations people, and the marketing people must work together to evaluate the feasibility of new ideas. They may meet in person, or communicate with e-mail or

Exhibit 9–5 New-Product Development Success Factors

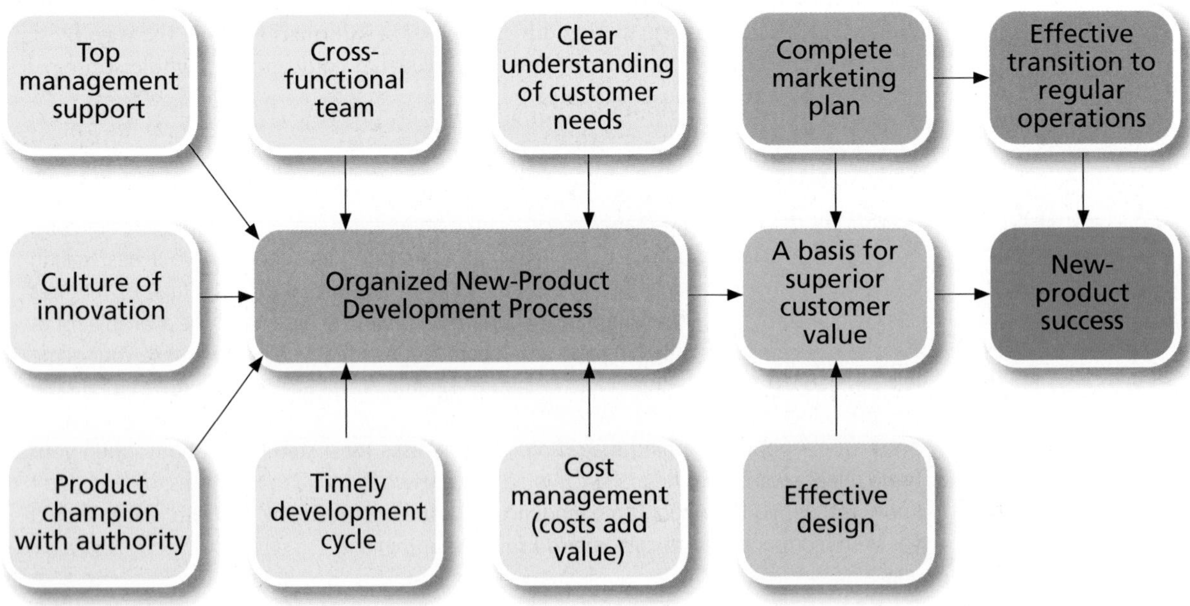

intranet sites, or perhaps via teleconferencing or some other technology. There are many ways to share ideas. So it isn't sensible for a marketing manager to develop elaborate marketing plans for goods or services that the firm simply can't produce—or produce profitably. It also doesn't make sense for R&D people to develop a technology or product that does not have potential for the firm and its markets. Clearly, a balancing act is involved here. But the critical point is the basic one we've been emphasizing throughout the whole book: Marketing-oriented firms seek to satisfy customer needs at a profit with an integrated, whole company effort.

Internet Exercise

A company called Quirky draws on an online community to move products through the new-product development process. Go to the Quirky website (**www.quirky.com**). Watch the short video overview and peruse the site. What advantages and disadvantages does Quirky have compared to a corporation or individual inventor? What would you do to improve the site?

Need for Product Managers

LO 9.5

Product variety leads to product managers

When a firm has only one or a few related products, everyone is interested in them. But when a firm has products in several different product categories, management may decide to put someone in charge of each category, or each brand, to be sure that attention to these products is not lost in the rush of everyday business. **Product managers** or **brand managers** manage specific products—often taking over the jobs formerly handled by an advertising manager. That gives a clue to what is often their major responsibility—Promotion—since the products have already been developed by the new-product people. However, some brand managers start at the new-product development stage and carry on from there.

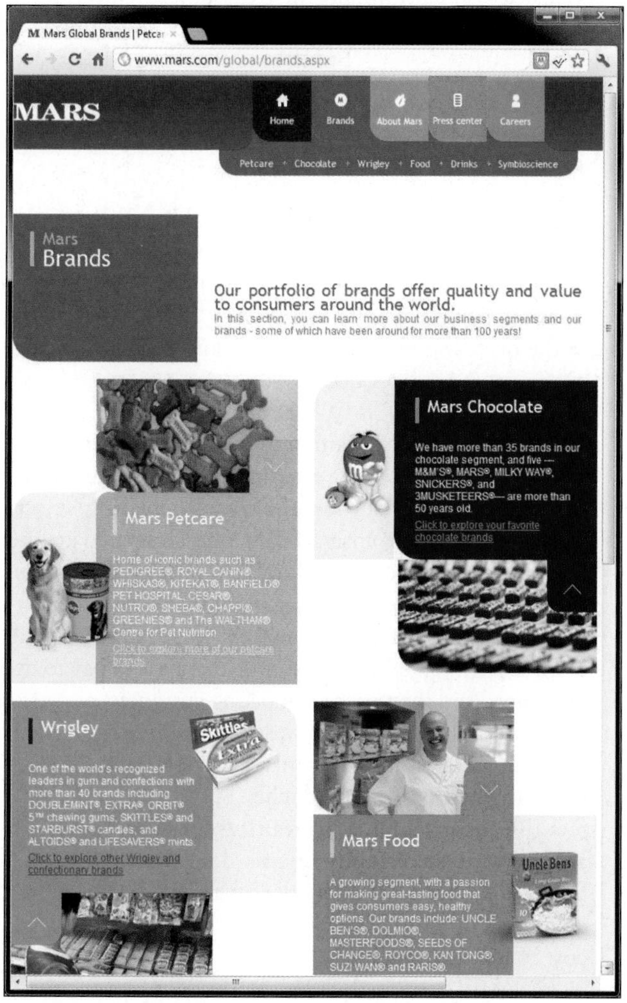

Product managers are especially common in large companies that produce many kinds of products. Several product managers may serve under a marketing manager. Sometimes these product managers are responsible for the profitable operation of a particular product's whole marketing effort. Then they have to coordinate their efforts with others, including

Mars has some of the world's best known brands: Pedigree and Whiskas in pet care; Snickers and M&Ms in chocolate; Altoids, Skittles, and Lifesavers in candy; and, believe it or not, Uncle Ben's rice. Each product or brand has a manager who primarily manages Promotion for each brand.

the sales manager, advertising agencies, production and research people, and even channel members. This is likely to lead to difficulties if product managers have no control over the marketing strategy for other related brands or authority over other functional areas whose efforts they are expected to direct and coordinate.

To avoid these problems, in some companies the product manager serves mainly as a "product champion"—concerned with planning and getting the promotion effort implemented. A higher-level marketing manager with more authority coordinates the efforts and integrates the marketing strategies for different products into an overall plan.

The activities of product managers vary a lot depending on their experience and aggressiveness and the company's organizational philosophy. Today, companies are emphasizing marketing *experience*—because this important job takes more than academic training and enthusiasm. But it is clear that someone must be responsible for developing and implementing product-related plans, especially when a company has many products.[31]

Adapting products for international markets

Product managers may work with managers in other countries to decide whether and how to adapt products for different markets. Some adaptations may be required and fairly simple—for example, many countries have different electrical voltages, necessitating different plugs for electrical products. Other adaptations demand more creativity. Nestlé adapted its Kit Kat chocolate candy bars for the Japanese palate with 19 unique flavors including soy sauce, miso, sweet potato, and blueberry. In Germany, Kit Kat lemon yogurt bars are popular; in the U.K., it's peanut butter. Nestlé adapts many of its other products to international preferences also. Whereas in the United States, fruit-flavored ice "popsicles" are a summertime treat all kids crave, in China, Nestlé created flavored milk ice on a stick to fit local preferences—the most popular flavor, banana.[32]

Managing Product Quality

LO 9.6

Total quality management meets customer requirements

In Chapter 8 we explained that product quality means the ability of a product to satisfy a customer's needs or requirements. Now we'll expand that idea and discuss some ways a manager can improve the quality of a firm's goods and services. We'll develop these ideas from the perspective of **total quality management (TQM)**, the philosophy that everyone in the organization is concerned about quality, throughout all of the firm's activities, to better serve customer needs.

The cost of poor quality is lost customers

Most of the early attention in quality management focused on reducing defects in goods produced in factories. At one time most firms assumed defects were an inevitable part of mass production. They saw the cost of replacing defective parts or goods as just a cost of doing business—an insignificant one compared to the advantages of mass production. However, many firms were forced to rethink this assumption when Japanese producers of cars, electronics, and cameras showed that defects weren't inevitable. Much to the surprise of some production-oriented managers, the Japanese experience showed that it is less expensive to do something right the first time than it is to pay to do it poorly and then pay again to fix problems. And their success in taking customers away from established competitors made it clear that the cost of defects wasn't just the cost of replacement!

From the customer's point of view, getting a defective product and having to complain about it is a big headache. The customer can't use the defective product and suffers the inconvenience of waiting for someone to fix the problem—*if* someone gets around to it. It certainly doesn't deliver superior value. Rather, it erodes goodwill and leaves customers dissatisfied, less trusting of the brand, and possibly spreading their dismay to others via word-of-mouth or the Internet. The big cost of poor quality is the cost of lost customers.

Firms that adopted TQM methods to reduce manufacturing defects soon used the same approaches to overcome many other problems. Their success brought attention to

A firm that understands the needs of its target customers can focus on the aspects of quality that are most important for developing superior customer value in its goods or services.

what is possible with TQM—whether the problem concerns poor customer service, flimsy packaging, or salespeople who can't answer customers' questions.

Getting a handle on doing things right the first time

The idea of identifying customer needs and doing things right the first time seems obvious, but it's easier said than done. Problems always come up, and it's not always clear what isn't being done as well as it could be. People tend to ignore problems that don't pose an immediate crisis. But firms that adopt TQM always look for ways to improve implementation with **continuous improvement**—a commitment to constantly make things better one step at a time. Once you accept the idea that there *may* be a better way to do something and you look for it, you may just find it!

Data drives quality improvement

In Chapter 7 we discussed big data and how firms now had access to more information about how customers behave and use their products. Firms are beginning to figure out how to evaluate this information to drive product improvements. For example, industrial equipment makers have added smart meters and digital sensors that can be constantly monitored to provide an early warning of failure. Parts can be replaced before they fail—and possibly be improved in future models.

Another example happens in publishing, where e-books have created opportunities for authors and publishers to learn more about just how their products are consumed. For example, data shows what lines users have highlighted, how long it takes them to read a book, what parts are read most quickly, how much they read in one sitting, and for those who fail to finish the book—when do they quit? Barnes and Noble shares this information with publishers to help them create books that might better hold people's attention.

Building quality into services

Services create particular quality management challenges. Most products involve some service component whether it is primarily a service, primarily a physical good, or a blend of both. Even a manufacturer of ball bearings isn't just providing wholesalers or producers with round pieces of steel. Customers need information about deliveries, they need orders filled properly, and they may have questions to ask the firm's accountant or engineers. Because almost every firm must manage the service it provides customers, let's focus on some of the special concerns of managing service quality.

Deliver quality at each touchpoint

Marketing managers must deliver quality throughout the entire customer experience. If they do not, even one problem can affect how the customer perceives the firm's quality. Think about how an otherwise great restaurant experience could be ruined by a rude waiter. The purchase and consumption process for many products involves multiple *touchpoints* or points where there is contact between the customer and the company. There are usually more touchpoints for services than for goods.

Consider everything that needs to go right for a customer getting an oil change at a Jiffy Lube. The experience might begin at the Jiffy Lube website, where a customer seeks information about the services offered, prices, hours of operation, and the phone number and address of a local Jiffy Lube. Is this information easy to find? A phone call to a local Jiffy Lube outlet should be promptly answered by a friendly knowledgeable person. Upon arrival, is the driveway well-marked? Is there a long queue for service? The attendant may have entered the license plate number and could already have the customer's details on his computer screen—or not. Is the check-in process quick? Is the attendant courteous? The waiting area should be clean and perhaps offer Wi-Fi. What happens if another customer has noisy young children—does that affect the quality of the oil change experience? The payment process should be fast—and offer the customer information about their car. The car should be clean when it is picked up. Finally, the car should not experience any service problems immediately following the oil change. Whew! That is a lot of things to get right, every time, if Jiffy Lube is to deliver high quality to its customers. Other types of products can have greater or fewer touchpoints, but a marketing manager should recognize that all of them contribute to the customer's perception of quality.

Train people and empower them to serve

A service provider usually deals directly with the customer, making it difficult to provide consistent service quality. People are just not as consistent in their actions as machines or computers. In addition, service quality often depends on a service provider interpreting each customer's needs. For example, a hair stylist has to ask good questions and successfully interpret the customer's responses before it's possible to provide the right cut. As a result, a person doing a specific service job may perform one specific task correctly but fail the customer in a host of other ways. Two keys to improving service quality are: (1) training and (2) empowerment.

All employees in contact with customers need training—many firms see 40 hours a year of training as a minimum. Good training usually includes role-playing on handling different types of customer requests and problems. A rental car attendant who is rude or inattentive when a customer is trying to turn in a car may leave the customer dissatisfied—even if the rental car was perfect.

Companies can't afford an army of managers to inspect how each employee implements a strategy—and such a system usually doesn't work anyway. Quality cannot be "inspected in." It must come from the people who do the service jobs. So firms that commit to service quality empower employees to figure out how to best satisfy customers' needs. **Empowerment** means giving employees the authority to correct a problem without first checking with management. At a hotel, for instance, an empowered room-service employee knows it's OK to run across the street to buy the specific brand of bottled water a guest requests.[33]

Managers lead the quality effort

To deliver high quality goods and services that satisfy customer needs, managers must show that they are committed to doing things right to satisfy customers and that quality is everyone's job. Without top-level support, some people won't get beyond their business-as-usual attitude—and TQM won't work.

Specify jobs and measure performance

Managers who develop successful quality programs clearly specify and write out exactly what tasks need to be done, how, and by whom. This may seem unnecessary. After all, most people know, in general, what they're supposed to do. However, if the tasks are clearly specified, it's easier to see what criteria should be used to measure performance.

Once criteria are established, there needs to be some basis on which to evaluate the job being done.

Getting a return on quality is important

While the cost of poor quality is lost customers, the type of quality efforts we've been discussing can also increase costs. It's easy to fall into the trap of running up unnecessary costs trying to improve some facet of quality that really isn't that important to customer satisfaction or customer retention. When that happens, customers may still be satisfied, but the firm can't make a profit because of the higher costs. In other words, there isn't a financial return on the money spent to improve quality. A manager should focus on quality efforts that really provide the customer with superior value—quality that costs no more to provide than customers will ultimately be willing to pay.[34]

CONCLUSION

This chapter introduced the product life-cycle concept and showed how life cycles affect marketing strategy planning. The product life-cycle concept shows why new products are so important to growth in markets and also helps to explain why different strategies—including strategies for new improved products—need to be developed over time. Innovators—or fast copiers—that successfully bring new products to market are usually the ones who achieve the greatest growth in customer equity.

In today's highly competitive marketplace it is no longer profitable to simply sell "me-too" products. Markets, competition, and product life cycles are changing at a fast pace. New products help a company appeal to new target markets by appealing to unmet needs. New products can also encourage current customers to purchase more. In addition, they can help retain customers by adapting to changing customer needs.

Just because a product is new to a company doesn't mean that it is a really new innovation and starts a new-product life cycle. However, from a marketing manager's perspective, a product is new to the firm if it is new in any way or to any target market. Firms don't just develop and introduce new products; they do so within the context of the whole marketing strategy.

Many new products fail. But we presented an organized new-product development process that helps to prevent that fate. The process makes it clear that new-product success isn't just the responsibility of people from R&D or marketing but rather requires a total company effort.

We also described product and brand management. To help a product or brand grow, managers in these positions usually recommend ways to adjust all of the elements of the marketing mix, but the emphasis is often on Promotion.

Poor product quality results in dissatisfied customers. So alert marketers look for ways to design better quality into new products and to improve the quality of ones they already have. Approaches developed in the total quality management (TQM) movement can be a big help in this regard. Ultimately, the challenge is for the manager to focus on aspects of quality that really matter to the target customer. Otherwise, the cost of the quality offered may be higher than what target customers are willing to pay.

In combination, this chapter and Chapter 8 introduce strategy decision areas for Product and important frameworks that help you see how Product fits within an overall strategy. These chapters also start you down the path to a deeper understanding of the 4Ps. In Chapter 10, we expand on that base by focusing on the role of Place in the marketing mix.

KEY TERMS

LO 9.7

product life cycle, *227*
market introduction, *228*
market growth, *228*
market maturity, *228*
sales decline, *229*
fashion, *231*
fad, *231*
new product, *236*
Federal Trade Commission (FTC), *237*
Consumer Product Safety Act, *241*
product liability, *241*
concept testing, *241*
prototype, *242*
product managers, *245*
brand managers, *245*
total quality management (TQM), *246*
continuous improvement, *247*
empowerment, *248*

QUESTIONS AND PROBLEMS

1. Explain how industry sales and industry profits behave over the product life cycle.
2. Cite two examples of products that you think are currently in each of the product life-cycle stages. Consider services as well as physical goods.
3. Explain how you might reach different conclusions about the correct product life-cycle stage(s) in the worldwide automobile market.
4. Explain why individual brands may not follow the product life-cycle pattern. Give an example of a new brand that is not entering the life cycle at the market introduction stage.
5. Discuss the life cycle of a product in terms of its probable impact on a manufacturer's marketing mix. Illustrate using personal computers.
6. What characteristics of a new product will help it to move through the early stages of the product life cycle more quickly? Briefly discuss each characteristic—illustrating with a product of your choice. Indicate how each characteristic might be viewed in some other country.
7. What is a new product? Illustrate your answer.
8. Explain the importance of an organized new-product development process and illustrate how it might be used for (*a*) a new hair care product, (*b*) a new children's toy, and (*c*) a new subscribers-only cable television channel.
9. Discuss how you might use the new-product development process if you were thinking about offering some kind of summer service to residents in a beach resort town.
10. Explain the role of product or brand managers. When would it make sense for one of a company's current brand managers to be in charge of the new-product development process? Explain your thinking.
11. If a firm offers one of its brands in a number of different countries, would it make sense for one brand manager to be in charge, or would each country require its own brand manager? Explain your thinking.
12. Discuss the social value of new-product development activities that seem to encourage people to discard products that are not all worn out. Is this an economic waste? How worn out is all worn out? Must a shirt have holes in it? How big?
13. What are the major advantages of total quality management as an approach for improving the quality of goods and services? What limitations can you think of?

CREATING MARKETING PLANS

The Marketing Plan Coach software on the text website includes a sample marketing plan for Hillside Veterinary Clinic. Look through the "Marketing Strategy" section.

a. Hillside offers many different products. Identify several of these products and indicate where you think each of them is in its product life cycle.
b. Exhibit 9-3 summarizes some marketing mix characteristics based on where a product fits in the product life cycle. Is Hillside's marketing plan consistent with what this exhibit suggests. Why or why not?

SUGGESTED CASES

6. Applied Steel
20. Blue Lagoon Marine & Camp
22. Brightlight Innovations: The Starlight Stove

Video Case 3. Toyota Prius
Video Case 8. Segway

COMPUTER-AIDED PROBLEM

9. GROWTH STAGE COMPETITION

AgriChem, Inc., has introduced an innovative new product—a combination fertilizer, weed killer, and insecticide that makes it much easier for soybean farmers to produce a profitable crop. The product introduction was quite successful, with 1 million units sold in the year of introduction. And AgriChem's profits are increasing. Total market demand is expected to grow at a rate of 200,000 units a year for the next five years. Even so, AgriChem's marketing managers are concerned about what will happen to sales and profits during this period.

Based on past experience with similar situations, they expect one new competitor to enter the market during each of the next five years. They think this competitive pressure will drive prices down about 6 percent a year. Further, although the total market is growing, they know that new competitors will chip away at AgriChem's market share—even with the 10 percent a year increase planned for the promotion budget. In spite of the competitive pressure, the marketing managers are sure that familiarity with AgriChem's brand will help it hold a large share of the total market and give AgriChem greater economies of scale than competitors. In fact, they expect that the ratio of profit to dollar sales for AgriChem should be about 10 percent higher than for competitors.

AgriChem's marketing managers have decided the best way to get a handle on the situation is to organize the data in a spreadsheet. They have set up the spreadsheet so they can change the "years in the future" value and see what is likely to happen to AgriChem and the rest of the industry. The starting spreadsheet shows the current situation with data from the first full year of production.

a. Compare AgriChem's market share and profit for this year with what is expected next year—given the marketing managers' current assumptions. What are they expecting? (Hint: Set number of years in the future to 1.)

b. Prepare a table showing AgriChem's expected profit, and the expected industry revenue and profit, for the current year and the next five years. Briefly explain what happens to industry sales and profits and why. (Hint: Do an analysis to vary the number of years in the future value in the spreadsheet from a minimum of 0—the current year—to a maximum of 5. Display the three values requested.)

c. If market demand grows faster than expected—say, at 280,000 units a year—what will happen to AgriChem's profits and the expected industry revenues and profits over the next five years? What are the implications of this analysis?

10

CHAPTER TEN

Place and Development of Channel Systems

In the 1970s the early "microcomputers" were very hard to set up and difficult to use—so few people wanted them. That also explains why there were no computer stores. Altair, one of the first brands, initially sold mainly at "electronics fairs." Most of these gatherings were in California; often buyers and sellers just met in an open market on Saturday mornings. Then Heath introduced its more powerful H89 computer through mail-order catalogs as a build-it-yourself kit. Heath added value with good telephone technical support.

Soon after that, Xerox used its competitive advantage in distribution to introduce its 820 model. Business customers liked buying computers from the same wholesalers that regularly handled their Xerox copiers. By 1980, Radio Shack's large retail store network helped the easy-to-use TRS-80 become the best-selling computer. Customers appreciated the accessibility of Radio Shack's in-store staff and tech support specialists.

As you read this, it probably occurs to you that most of the firms mentioned no longer sell computers. These early firms couldn't adjust quickly enough when IBM introduced its first PC. The pull of IBM's familiar brand gave more customers the confidence to buy. Sales of PCs surged as IBM established a chain of its own retail stores and worked closely with select dealers who promised to pay special attention to the IBM brand. Big-business customers bought in quantity directly from IBM's aggressive sales force. After IBM's design became an industry standard, firms like Compaq, HP, and Toshiba quickly jumped in with PC models of their own—often selling through independent computer dealers.

Soon after, Michael Dell, then just a freshman in college, started buying and reselling computers from his dorm room. Dell figured a target market of price-conscious customers would respond to a different marketing mix. He used direct-response advertising in computer magazines; customers called a toll-free number to order a computer with the exact features they wanted. Then Dell used UPS to ship directly to the customer. Prices were low, too, because the direct channel eliminated retailer markup and the build-to-order approach reduced inventory costs. Dell also built reliable machines and delivered superior customer service. It would have been tough to centralize all of this if he had been working with thousands of retailers.

Dell's advertising positioned the company in consumers' minds as an aggressive, value-oriented source of computers. At the same time, Dell added a direct-sales force to call on big government and corporate buyers—because they expected in-person selling and a relationship, not just a telephone contact. And when these important customers said they wanted Dell to offer high-power servers to run their corporate networks, Dell put money into R&D to create what they needed.

Dell also saw the prospect for international growth. Many computer firms had moved into Europe by exporting. But Dell made direct investments in the company's own operations there. Dell knew it would be tough to win over skeptical European buyers. They had never bought such big-ticket items as PCs over the phone. On the other hand, there were fewer big retail chains with low prices there, which gave Dell a significant price advantage. In less than five years, sales in Europe grew to 40 percent of Dell's total revenue.

Back home in the United States, HP and other firms tried to imitate Dell's successful direct-order approach. However, this move created conflict with the retailers already selling the bulk of HP's PCs; the retailers were not happy with competition from their own supplier! When these retailers responded by pushing other brands, HP limited the models sold online and added programs to support their dealers; for example, providing quick turnaround for retailers placing orders for custom-built computers.

Dell continued to adapt its marketing mix in response to evolving competition and customer needs. New advertising campaigns had mixed results, and some new product lines were unsuccessful (TVs and MP3 players) or late to market (small netbook and tablet computers). Dell also made changes to its supply chain and distribution. Dell was one of the first to utilize the Internet for distribution. The low-cost distribution channel fit with Dell's philosophy. Profits rose when Dell continued to find ways to increase efficiency and cut costs in its supply chain. Dell also saw an opportunity to target customers wanting to purchase "in person" from local stores, so it began selling through retailers like Walmart, Staples, and Best Buy. Using more channels of distribution exposed more customers to Dell's products. In the United States and Europe, many small business customers need technical support and training, so Dell also added wholesalers like Ingram Micro and Tech Data, which offer these services to its customers.

More recently Dell followed IBM, HP, and others into the fast-growing IT services market, where margins are higher than in the mature PC market. Many firms need to add and manage secure data storage as they collect and store increasing amounts of data. Dell works closely with customers at events like the Dell Storage Forum, where customers and channel partners interact with Dell executives and technical experts. One of Dell's strengths in this new product-market comes from its experience in developing computer hardware like servers, storage, and networking. On the other hand, Dell's forte has not been the delivery of solutions, services, and technical support—requiring Dell to hone its capabilities in this area.

To have continued success in both of these highly competitive markets, Dell will have to continue to pay close attention to strategy decisions for Place.[1]

Learning Objectives

This case shows that offering customers a good product at a reasonable price is not the whole story. Marketing managers must make decisions about how they will make goods and services available to a target customer's Place when the customer wants them. This chapter's learning objectives will help you understand the role of Place in marketing strategy.

When you finish this chapter you should be able to:

1 understand what product classes suggest about Place objectives.

2 understand why some firms use direct channel systems while others work with intermediaries and indirect systems.

3 understand how and why marketing specialists develop to make channel systems more effective.

4 understand how to develop cooperative relationships and avoid conflict in channel systems.

5 know how channel members in vertical marketing systems shift and share functions to meet customer needs.

6 understand the differences between intensive, selective, and exclusive distribution.

7 know how multichannel distribution and reverse channels operate.

8 know the main approaches firms use to reach customers in international markets.

9 understand important new terms (shown in red).

Marketing Strategy Planning Decisions for Place

Managers must think about **Place**—making goods and services available in the right quantities and locations, when customers want them. And when different target markets have different needs, a number of Place variations may be required. Our opening case makes it clear that new Place arrangements can dramatically change the competition in a product-market. This is especially important in business today because information technology, including websites and e-commerce, makes it easier for firms to work together more efficiently and also to reach customers directly.

In this chapter and the two that follow, we'll deal with the many important marketing strategy decisions that a marketing manager must make concerning Place. Exhibit 10-1 gives an overview. We'll start here with a discussion of Place objectives and how they relate to product classes and the product life cycle—ideas introduced in the Product chapters (8 and 9).

Exhibit 10–1 Marketing Strategy Planning Decisions for Place

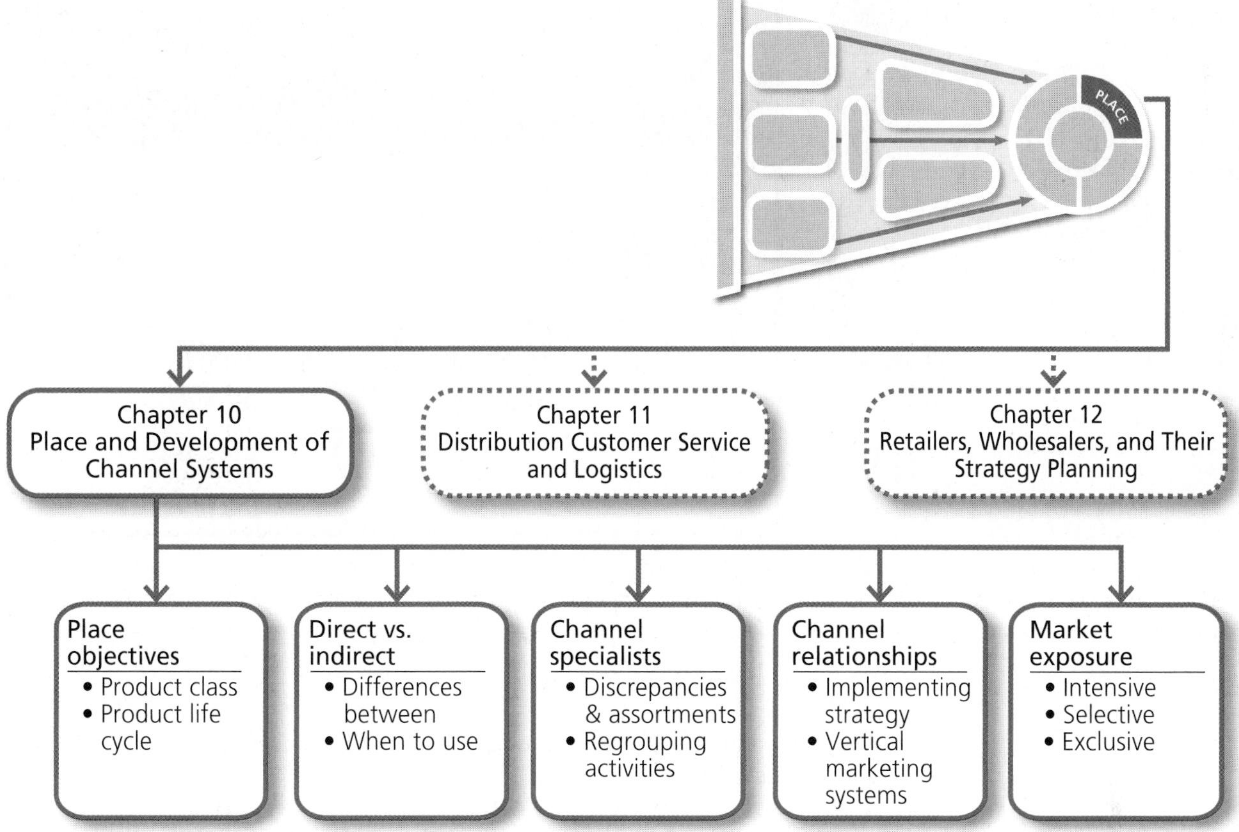

We'll then discuss the type of channel that most aptly meets customers' needs. We'll show why specialists are often involved and how they come together to form a **channel of distribution**—any series of firms or individuals who participate in the flow of products from producer to final user or consumer. We'll also consider how to manage relations among channel members to reduce conflict and improve cooperation. This chapter concludes by considering the desired level of market exposure (and how many channel outlets are needed) as well as approaches for reaching customers in international markets.

In Chapter 11, we'll expand the Place discussion to decisions that a marketing manager makes about physical distribution, including customer service level, transporting, and storing. Then, in Chapter 12, we'll take a closer look at the many different types of retailing and wholesaling firms. We'll consider their role in channels as well as the strategy decisions they make to satisfy their own customers.

Place Decisions Are Guided by "Ideal" Place Objectives

LO 10.1

All marketing managers want to be sure that their goods and services are available in the right quantities and locations—when customers want them. But customers may have different needs in these areas as they make different purchases.

Product classes suggest Place objectives

In Chapter 8 we introduced the product classes, which summarize consumers' urgency to have needs satisfied and willingness to seek information, shop, and compare. Now you should be able to use the product classes to handle Place decisions.

Exhibit 8-6 shows the relationship between consumer product classes and ideal Place objectives. Similarly, Exhibit 8-7 shows the business product classes and how they relate to customer needs. Study these exhibits carefully. They set the framework for making Place

For most target customers, the Iams brand of premium dog food is a staple or heterogeneous shopping product. So Iams distributes through supermarkets, pet superstores, and mass merchandisers, displaying it near competing products. On the other hand, iVet is likely to be perceived as a specialty product. Consequently it is sold only through veterinarians who give the product an extra push with their recommendation.

decisions. In particular, the product classes help us decide how much market exposure we'll need in each geographic area.

Place system is not automatic

Several different product classes may be involved if different market segments view a product in different ways. Thus, marketing managers may need to develop several strategies, each with its own Place arrangements. There may not be one Place arrangement that is best.

For example, many consumers view Tide laundry detergent as a staple for doing laundry at home. To meet their needs, it is widely distributed in grocery and discount stores. Customers who run out of detergent while doing wash at a Laundromat see Tide as an emergency product and want small boxes available in a vending machine. And some hotels look at Tide as an operating supply that the housekeeping department needs to provide guests with clean sheets and towels. For these hotels, Tide comes in large drums that are sold and delivered by wholesalers of housekeeping supplies.

Place decisions have long-run effects

The marketing manager must also consider Place objectives in relation to the product life cycle; see Exhibit 9-3. Place decisions often have long-run effects. They're usually harder to change than Product, Promotion, and Price decisions. Many firms that thought they could quickly establish effective websites for direct online sales, for example, found that it took several years and millions of dollars to work out the kinks. It can take even longer and cost more to develop effective working relationships with others in the channel. Legal contracts with channel partners may limit changes. And it's hard to move retail stores and wholesale facilities once they are set up. Yet as products mature, they typically need broader distribution to reach different target customers.

Channel System May Be Direct or Indirect

LO 10.2

One of the most basic Place decisions producers must make is whether to handle the whole distribution job themselves—perhaps by relying on direct-to-customer e-commerce selling or opening their own stores—or use wholesalers, retailers, and other specialists.

Many firms prefer to distribute directly to the final customer or consumer because they want to control the whole marketing job. They may think that they can serve target customers at a lower cost or do the work more effectively than intermediaries. While this can be true, marketing managers should carefully assess the value intermediaries add for end customers.

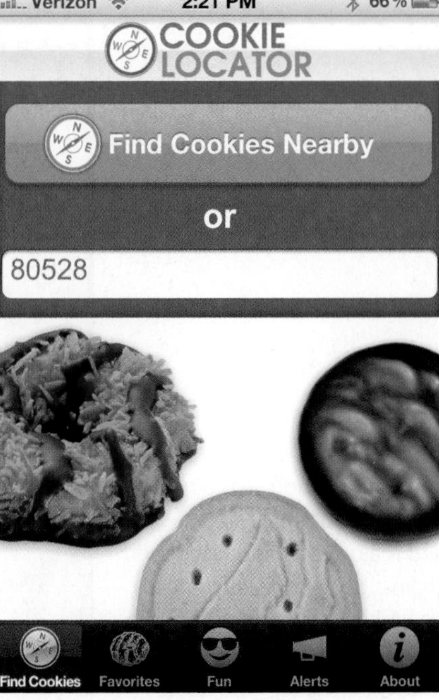

The Girls Scouts sell their cookies direct to customers. But you need to know when and where a girl scout will be selling the cookies. So they created the Cookie Locator app for the iPhone. Customers just enter their zip code and they will be directed to the nearest source of the tasty treats.

Direct distribution maintains control

Sometimes a producer utilizes direct distribution because they want to maintain control of the marketing mix. Wholesalers and retailers carry multiple products and will make decisions that are in their own best interest—and this may not always be aligned with the interests of an individual producer. For example, because Esurance sells insurance directly through a website or the phone, its own salespeople talk directly to customers. This allows Esurance tighter control of the marketing mix as compared to Progressive Insurance, which uses independent agents that sell more than one company's insurance products. The independent agents may not choose to promote Progressive if they don't know as much about its products or earn more when they sell a competitor's insurance products.

The Internet makes direct distribution easier

Website-based e-commerce systems and delivery services like UPS and FedEx give many firms direct access to customers whom it would have been impossible to reach in the past. Even small, specialized firms may be able to establish a web page and draw customers from all over the world.

Direct contact with customers

If a firm is in direct contact with its customers, it is more aware of changes in customer attitudes. It is in a better position to adjust its marketing mix quickly because there is no need to convince other channel members to help. If a product needs an aggressive selling effort or special technical service, the marketing manager can ensure that salespeople receive the necessary training and motivation.

Suitable intermediaries are not available

A firm may have to go direct if suitable intermediaries are not available or will not cooperate. Sometimes intermediaries that have the best contacts with the target market may be hesitant to add unproven vendors or new products. For example, when Glacéau began selling its now popular Vitaminwater, wholesale distributors had no interest in carrying it. So the owner of the company delivered the bottled water directly to small retailers in New York City. Once he proved his product would sell, distributor interest grew. On the other hand, to enter the California market, Glacéau gave distribution rights to just one distributor. As a result, it was in this distributor's interest to work closely with Glacéau to build the market. Eventually Coca-Cola purchased Glacéau; at that point Coke added many of its own distributors. Glacéau became a success by slowly building support from retailers and wholesalers, but many new products fail because the producer can't find willing channel partners and doesn't have the resources to handle direct distribution.[2]

In the United States, the Census Bureau publishes detailed data concerning wholesalers and retailers, including breakdowns by kind of business, product line, and geographic territory. Similar information is available for many other countries. It can be very valuable in

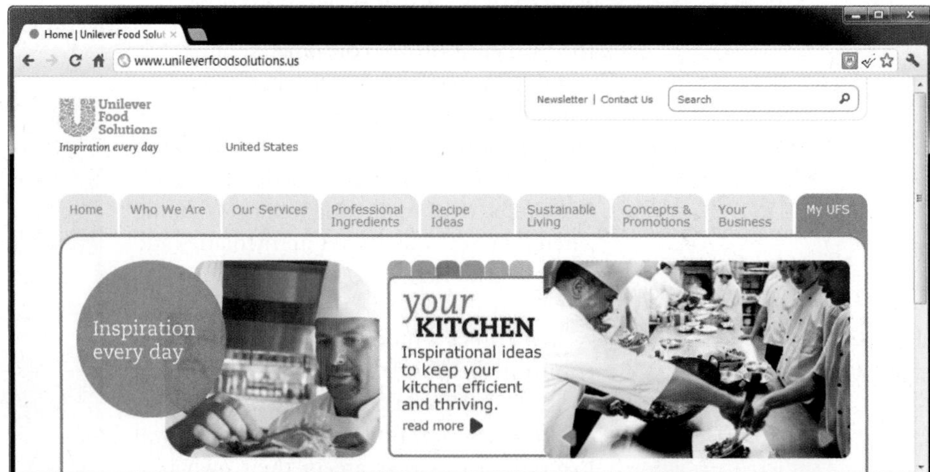

Even though the Unilever Food Solutions division sells direct to many restaurants, caterers, and major hotel and fast-food chains, Unilever relies primarily on indirect distribution through a variety of wholesalers and retailers in the United States and many other developed nations. However, in Spain it delivers frozen foods directly to consumers' homes, and in Vietnam a mobile store brings products to local consumers.

strategy planning—especially to learn whether potential channel members are serving a target market. You can also learn what sales volume current intermediaries are achieving.

Common with business customers and services

Many business products are sold direct-to-customer. Alcan sells aluminum to General Motors direct. Woodward produces products like pumps and fuel nozzles that it sells directly to aircraft makers like Boeing, Airbus, and Gulfstream. This is understandable since in business markets there are fewer transactions, orders are larger, and customers may be concentrated in one geographic area. Further, once relationships are established, e-commerce systems can efficiently handle orders.

Service firms often use direct channels. If the service must be produced in the presence of customers, there may be little need for intermediaries. An accounting firm like PricewaterhouseCoopers, for example, must deal directly with its customers.

Firms that produce physical goods turn to channel specialists to help provide the services customers expect. GE may hope that its authorized appliance dealers don't get many repair calls, but the service is available when customers need it. Here the intermediary produces the service.[3]

Some consumer products are sold direct

Many companies that produce consumer products have websites where a consumer can place a direct order. But for most consumer products this is still a small part of total sales. Most consumer products are sold through intermediaries.

Of course, some consumer products are sold direct to consumers where they live or work. Mary Kay and Avon cosmetics, Electrolux vacuum cleaners, Amway Global household products, and Tupperware are examples. These firms and many others are finding that this is a good way to crack open international markets ranging from India and China to Brazil and the U.K. Most of these firms rely on direct selling, which involves personal sales contact between a representative of the company and an individual

Park Seed Company uses both direct marketing—directly communicating to customers using a promotion method other than face-to-face personal selling—and direct distribution.

consumer. However, most of these "salespeople" are *not* company employees. Rather, they usually work independently and the companies that they sell for refer to them as *dealers, distributors, agents,* or some similar term. So in a strict technical sense, this is not really direct producer-to-consumer distribution.[4]

Don't be confused by the term *direct marketing*

Even though most consumer products are sold through intermediaries, an increasing number of firms rely on **direct marketing**—direct communication between a seller and an individual customer using a promotion method other than face-to-face personal selling. Sometimes direct marketing promotion is coupled with direct distribution from a producer to consumers. Park Seed Company, for example, sells the seeds it grows directly to consumers with a mail catalog and website.

However, many firms that use direct marketing promotion distribute their products through intermediaries. For example, Logitech, which produces personal computer peripherals, uses e-mails to communicate directly with customers who purchase Logitech products through retailers. So the term direct marketing is primarily concerned with the Promotion area, not Place decisions. We'll talk about direct marketing promotion in more detail in Chapter 13.[5]

When indirect channels are best

Even if a producer wants to handle the whole distribution job, sometimes it's simply not possible. Customers often have established buying patterns. For example, Square D, a producer of electrical supplies, might want to sell directly to electrical contractors. It can certainly set up a website for online orders or even open sales offices in key markets. But if contractors like to make all of their purchases in one convenient stop—at a local electrical wholesaler—the only practical way to reach them is through a wholesaler.

Similarly, consumers are spread throughout many geographic areas and often prefer to shop for certain products at specific places. Some consumers, for instance, see Sears as *the* place to shop for tires, so they'll only buy the brands that Sears carries. This is one reason most firms that produce consumer products rely so heavily on indirect channels (see Exhibit 2-6).[6]

Direct distribution usually requires a significant investment in facilities, people, and information technology. A company that has limited financial resources or that wants to retain flexibility may want to avoid that investment by working with established intermediaries.

Intermediaries may further reduce a producer's need for working capital by buying the producer's output and carrying it in inventory until it's sold. If customers want a good "right now," there must be inventory available to make the sale. And if customers are spread over a large area, it will probably be necessary to have widespread distribution.

Some wholesalers play a critical role by providing credit to customers at the end of the channel. A wholesaler who knows local customers can help reduce credit risks. As sales via the Internet grow, sellers are looking for faster and better ways to check the credit ratings of distant customers. It's an unhappy day when the marketing manager learns that a customer who was shipped goods based on an online order can't pay the invoice.

The most important reason for using an indirect channel of distribution is that an intermediary can often help producers serve customer needs better and at lower cost. Marketing managers should carefully evaluate each target market's needs and determine its customers' willingness to pay. A firm should also understand its capabilities and those of willing intermediaries. This will help the marketing manager determine whether to use intermediaries and, if so, which intermediaries would work best.

Some firms use direct and indirect channels

When a company serves multiple target markets, it may choose to sell direct and through intermediaries. For example, a company like Autolite uses direct channels to sell its spark plugs to automakers like Ford. Yet it also sells to consumers through intermediaries like Pep Boys. Traditionally, most firms targeting consumers relied on indirect channels, but that is changing. For example, while Bose electronics, Under Armour athletic gear, and Samsonite luggage sell through retail outlets, each also sells directly through its own outlet stores and online at the company's website.

Deciding whether to sell directly, indirectly, or both requires an understanding of discrepancies and separations (introduced briefly in Chapter 1). Now we'll go into more detail.

Channel Specialists May Reduce Discrepancies and Separations

LO 10.3

The assortment and quantity of products customers want may be different from the assortment and quantity of products companies produce. Producers are often located far from their customers and may not know how best to reach them. Customers in turn may not know about their choices. Specialists develop to adjust these discrepancies and separations.[7]

Intermediaries may supply needed information

Specialists often help provide information to bring buyers and sellers together. For example, most consumers don't know much about the wide variety of home and auto insurance policies available. A local independent insurance agent may help them decide which policy, and which insurance company, best fits their needs.

Because FedEx offers specialized services that facilitate exchange between producers and consumers, it helps to reduce discrepancies and separations.

Intermediaries who are close to their customers are often able to anticipate customer needs and forecast demand more accurately. This information can help reduce inventory costs in the whole channel—and it may help the producer smooth out production.

Most producers seek help from specialists when they first enter international markets. Specialists can provide crucial information about customer needs and insights into differences in the market environment.

Discrepancies of quantity and assortment

Discrepancy of quantity means the difference between the quantity of products it is economical for a producer to make and the quantity final users or consumers normally want. For example, most manufacturers of golf balls produce large quantities—perhaps 200,000 to 500,000 in a given time period. The average golfer, however, wants only a few balls at a time. Adjusting for this discrepancy usually requires intermediaries—wholesalers and retailers.

Producers typically specialize by product—and therefore another discrepancy develops. **Discrepancy of assortment** means the difference between the lines a typical producer makes and the assortment final consumers or users want. Most golfers, for example, need more than golf balls. They want golf shoes, gloves, clubs, a bag, and, of course, a golf course to play on. And they usually don't want to shop for each item separately. So, again, there is a need for wholesalers and retailers to adjust these discrepancies.

Channel specialists adjust discrepancies with regrouping activities

Regrouping activities adjust the quantities or assortments of products handled at each level in a channel of distribution. There are four regrouping activities: accumulating, bulk-breaking, sorting, and assorting. When one or more of these activities is needed, a marketing specialist may develop to fill this need.

Adjusting quantity discrepancies by accumulating and bulk-breaking

Accumulating involves collecting products from many small producers. Much of the coffee that comes from Colombia is grown on small farms in the mountains. Accumulating the small crops into larger quantities is a way of getting the lowest transporting rate and making it more convenient for distant food processing companies to buy and handle it. Accumulating is especially important in less-developed countries and in other situations, like agricultural markets, where there are many small producers.

Accumulating is also important with professional services because they often involve the combined work of a number of individuals, each of whom is a specialized producer. A hospital makes it easier for patients by accumulating the services of a number of health care specialists, many of whom may not actually work for the hospital.

Many wholesalers and retailers who operate from Internet websites focus on accumulating. Specialized sites for everything from Chinese art to Dutch flower bulbs bring together the output of many producers.

Bulk-breaking involves dividing larger quantities into smaller quantities as products get closer to the final market. The bulk-breaking may involve several levels in the channel. Wholesalers may sell smaller quantities to other wholesalers or directly to retailers. Retailers continue breaking bulk as they sell individual items to their customers.

Adjusting assortment discrepancies by sorting and assorting

Different types of specialists adjust assortment discrepancies. They perform two types of regrouping activities: sorting and assorting.

Sorting means separating products into grades and qualities desired by different target markets. For example, an investment firm might offer its customers shares in a mutual fund made up only of stocks for companies that pay regular dividends. Similarly, a wholesaler that specializes in serving convenience stores may focus on smaller packages of frequently used products.

Assorting means putting together a variety of products to give a target market what it wants. This usually is done by those closest to the final consumer or user—retailers or wholesalers who try to supply a wide assortment of products for the convenience of their customers. Thus, a wholesaler selling Yazoo tractors and mowers to golf courses might also carry Pennington grass seed and Scott fertilizer.

Bits and bytes need distribution, too

Many products, including music, television programs, movies, books, video games, and software, now exist in digital form. Distribution costs can be very low because there is often no physical good to distribute. Still, even without a physical form, distribution remains an important marketing strategy decision for firms with digital products.

Take video entertainment, for example. Traditionally, television programming allowed viewers to watch whatever happened to be on the few major networks at a particular time. But in today's marketplace, an explosion of networks, channels, and programming make it impossible to keep up with all the choices. Even the variety of programming shown on a single network like ESPN or HBO is a lot for most viewers to absorb. As a result, online intermediaries like Hulu are coming on the scene. Hulu collects programming from television networks and movie studios and streams it over the Internet to smartphones, computers, and TV sets.

As a channel specialist, Hulu reduces discrepancies and separations between consumers (viewers of video content) and producers (primarily creators of television programming and movies). Hulu matches the assortment and quantity of programming viewers want with the assortment and quantity of programming available. TV viewers face *discrepancies of quantity*—there are millions of hours of television programming produced, but most viewers only need a couple hours or less at a time. Viewers also face *discrepancies of assortment;* for instance, a viewer may enjoy watching nature programs, but that type of program is shown on Discovery Channel, National Geographic Channel, the Public Broadcasting Service, and MSNBC. So Hulu performs *regrouping* activities to better satisfy viewer needs. For example, by bringing together programming from multiple networks, Hulu *accumulates* content; this makes it easier for consumers to visit one site where they can search and find the desired programming. Hulu does *bulk-breaking;* it receives programming from networks in bulk—all the episodes of *Family Guy,* for example—and then offers them for viewing one episode at a time. By providing its viewers with features that tag and rate programs, Hulu also performs a *sorting* activity. The tagging system combines with other categories developed by Hulu to create an *assorting* activity that helps consumers view collections of programs that match their interests.[8]

As you can see from this short case, producers of digital products face many of the same challenges facing producers of physical goods. Keep that in mind as you consider the other topics in this chapter.

Adding or subtracting channels can add value and differentiate

Specialists develop to adjust separations and discrepancies if they need to be adjusted. Sometimes spotting such a need creates an opportunity. For example, many office workers in big cities don't have time to run out to a restaurant for lunch every day. The growth of food trucks in urban areas emerged as a new channel for some restaurants.

On the other hand, there is no point in having intermediaries just because that's the way it's always been done. Eliminating intermediaries might create other opportunities. Some manufacturers of business products now reach more customers in distant markets with a website than was previously possible for them to reach with independent manufacturers' reps who sold on commission (but otherwise left distribution to the firm). The website cost advantage can translate to lower prices and a marketing mix that is a better value for some target segments.[9]

Channel Relationship Must Be Managed

LO 10.4

Marketing manager must choose type of channel relationship

Intermediary specialists can help make a channel more efficient. But there may be problems getting the different firms in a channel to work together well. How well they work together depends on the type of relationship they have. This should be carefully considered since marketing managers usually have choices about what type of channel system to join or develop.

The whole channel should have a product-market commitment

Ideally, all of the members of a channel system should have a shared *product-market commitment*—with all members focusing on the same target market at the end of the channel and sharing the various marketing functions in appropriate ways. When members of a channel do this, they are better able to compete effectively for the customer's business. Unfortunately, many marketing managers overlook this idea because it's not the way their firms have traditionally handled channel relationships.

Traditional channel systems involve weak relationships

In **traditional channel systems**, the various channel members make little or no effort to cooperate with each other. They buy and sell from each other—and that's the extent of their relationship. Each channel member does only what it considers to be in its own best interest. It doesn't worry about other members of the channel. This is shortsighted, but it's easy to see how it can happen. The objectives of the various channel members may be different. For example, Cooper Industries wants a wholesaler of electrical building supplies to sell Cooper products. But a wholesaler who works with different producers may not care whose products get sold. The wholesaler just wants happy customers and a good profit margin.[10]

Conflict gets in the way

Specialization can make a channel more efficient—but not if the specialists are so independent that the channel doesn't work smoothly. Because members of traditional channel systems often have different objectives—and different ideas about how things should be done—conflict is common.

There are two basic types of conflict in channels of distribution. *Vertical conflicts* occur between firms at different levels in the channel of distribution. A vertical conflict may occur if a producer and a retailer disagree about how much promotion effort the retailer should give the producer's product. For example, when GameStop started selling used video games, game publishers were concerned the move would steal sales from new games. Not only would revenue from new games go down, but the game publishers would not earn any revenue on used game sales.[11]

Horizontal conflicts occur between firms at the same level in a distribution channel. For example, a bicycle store that keeps a complete line of bikes on display, has a knowledgeable sales staff, and lets customers take test rides isn't happy to find out that an online store with little inventory and no salespeople offers customers lower prices on the same models. The online retailer gets a free ride from the competing store's investments in inventory and sales staff.

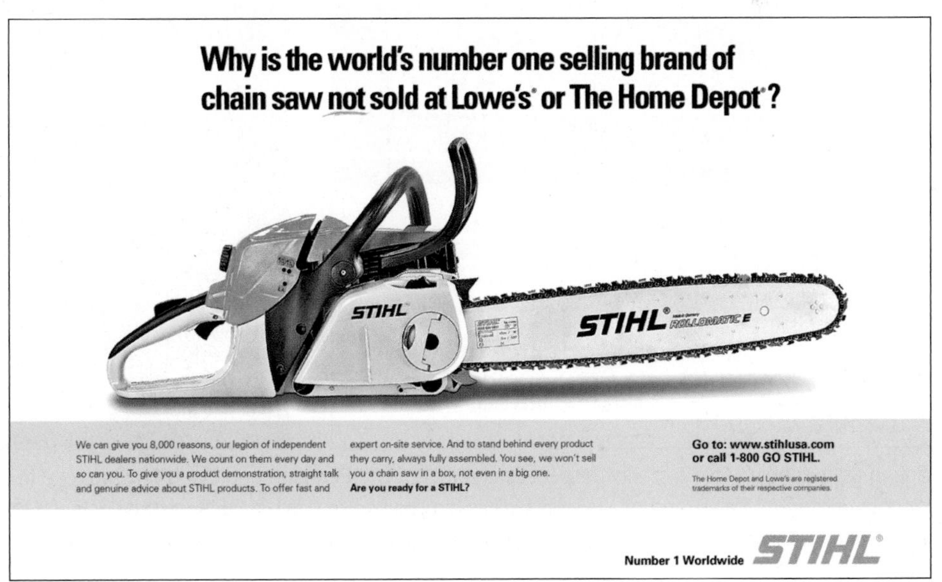

STIHL sells its high-quality chain saws through 8,000 independent STIHL dealers nationwide. These dealers provide product demonstrations, good advice, and expert on-site service, because STIHL limits horizontal conflict by not selling through home-improvement warehouses that put more emphasis on price competition and less on service.

Managing channel conflict

Some level of conflict may be inevitable—or even useful if that is what it takes for customers at the end of the channel to receive better value. However, most marketing managers try to avoid conflicts that harm relationships with channel partners. To appease channel partners, manufacturers often try to serve different market segments through each channel. For example, convenience stores like 7-11 and membership stores like Costco both sell Coke—but one offers it cold in individual servings and the other offers it warm and 24 cans at a time. Each offers a different marketing mix to a different target market.

Other firms manage conflict by offering different products through each channel. Gibson stopped selling guitars on its website after complaints from its traditional retailers and distributors. On the other hand, Gibson's website continued to sell a wide variety of accessories that most retailers did not want to stock. Another approach is to compensate participating channel members. When Allstate began to sell insurance products online direct to consumers, it mollified local agents by paying them a portion of their usual commission. In exchange, the agents provide personal service when local customers need it.

In general, treating channel partners fairly—even when one partner is more powerful—tends to build trust and reduce conflict. Trusting relationships lead to greater cooperation in the channel. As a consequence, channel members are better able to satisfy the needs of target customers at the end of the channel.[12]

Channel captain can guide channel relationships

While each channel system should act as a unit, some firms are in a better position to take the lead in the relationship and in coordinating the whole channel effort. This situation calls for a **channel captain**—a manager who helps direct the activities of a whole channel and tries to avoid or solve channel conflicts.

Acting as channel captains in their respective channels, both Peterson and Electrolux are able to get cooperation from many independent wholesalers and retailers (as well as big chains like Lowe's) because they develop marketing strategies that help the whole channel compete more effectively. This also helps everyone in the channel do a better job of meeting the needs of target customers at the end of the channel.

Can I download some popcorn with that movie?

The market for entertainment is changing rapidly—and Hollywood has responded with new channels of distribution. For a long time, movie studios carefully managed how their films proceeded through tightly controlled channels. Movies took years to trickle down from theaters to premium cable TV channels like HBO and eventually to network television. This approach maximized the studios' revenue from each channel—and kept channel conflict at a minimum. But those days are gone and movie studios are scrambling to get revenue faster from more channels of distribution.

Each new outlet for movies has provided more convenience or a different consumer experience. In the late 1970s, the first video stores started renting movies for $10 a day. Studios also began selling movies. Disney's animated classics were especially popular at first because kids would watch the same movie many times. However, sales did not really take off until prices dropped below $25. As sales grew, distribution became more intense and retailers like Walmart and Kmart were added to the mix. Blockbuster and other big rental chains also took off. Soon, Redbox vending machines appeared at the local McDonald's restaurant.

Now, if you don't feel like driving to pick up a flick, your cable channel or satellite television provider probably offers pay-per-view. Or, if you prefer, Netflix offers movie downloads or mails DVDs to your home and you can return them whenever you want. Illegal channels have developed, too. Pirates often post movies on the Internet before they're even available in theaters, and some consumers copy DVDs on home computers and pass them around. However, new movie download services that are legal are also coming online, and smaller digital file formats make movies portable with a video cell phone or laptop computer. You may not care about portability if you've got your own comfy home theater setup. And brick-and-mortar theaters, the traditional channel, are fighting to get customers back with stadium seating, bar and table service, and giant IMAX screens.

Concerns about movie piracy eroding sales have prompted movie studios to speed up the timing of movie distribution across channels. But this also increases competition and conflict across channels. Some studios are releasing movies to theaters and on DVD at the same time—or skipping the theater channel altogether.

So where will you watch your next movie? At an IMAX theater, in your home theater, or on your cell phone in a seat on a train—you can decide. These changes give you the power to choose—and movie studios hope all these channels get more people watching more movies.[13]

For example, when Harley-Davidson wanted to expand sales of fashion accessories, it was difficult for motorcycle dealers to devote enough space to all of the different styles. Harley considered selling the items directly from its own website, but that would take sales away from dealers who were working hard to help Harley sell both cycles and fashions. So Harley's president asked a group of dealers and Harley managers to work together to come up with a plan they all liked. The result was a website that sells Harley products through the dealer that is closest to the customer.[14]

The concept of a single channel captain is logical. But most traditional channels don't have a recognized captain. The various firms don't act as a coordinated system. Yet firms are interrelated, even if poorly, by their policies. So it makes sense to try to avoid channel conflicts by planning for channel relations. The channel captain arranges for the necessary functions to be performed in the most effective way.[15]

Some producers lead their channels

In the United States, producers frequently take the lead in channel relations. Intermediaries often wait to see what the producer intends to do and wants them to do. Then they decide whether their roles will be profitable and whether they want to join in the channel effort.

Exhibit 10-2A shows this type of producer-led channel system. Here the producer has selected the target market and developed the Product, set the Price structure, done some consumer and channel Promotion, and developed the Place setup. Intermediaries are then expected to finish the Promotion job in their respective places. Of course, in a retailer-dominated channel system, the marketing jobs would be handled in a different way.

Exhibit 10–2 How Channel Functions May Be Shifted and Shared in Different Channel Systems

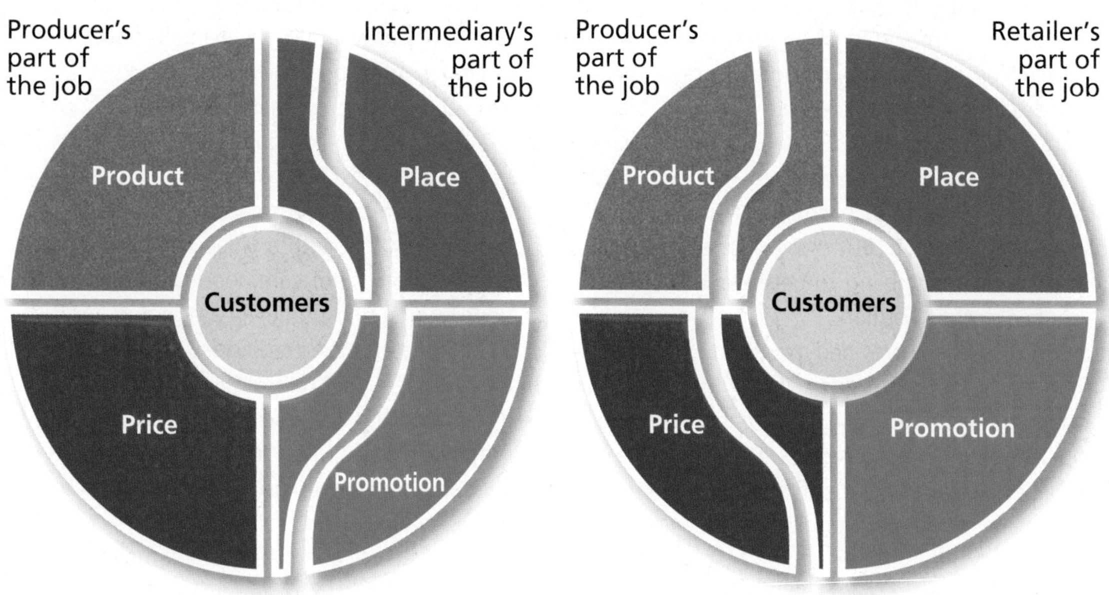

Some intermediaries are channel captains

Sometimes wholesalers or retailers do take the lead. They are closer to the final user or consumer and are in an ideal position to assume the channel captain role. Intermediaries that gather, analyze, and interpret big data often gain insights about their customers' needs and then seek out producers who can meet these needs with products at reasonable prices. With the growth of powerful chains like Walmart, Toys "R" Us, and Tesco, retailers now dominate the channel systems for many products in the United States, Asia, and Europe. Sometimes large retailers openly show their power. During a recent economic recession, the Belgian grocery chain Delhaize removed from its shelves about 300 Unilever products that it felt were priced too high. While no doubt harming the channel relationship, the grocer came across as a champion of the consumer and made its point with Unilever.[16]

Retailers like Sears and wholesalers like Ace Hardware who develop their own dealer brands in effect act like producers. They specify the whole marketing mix for a product and merely delegate production to a factory. Exhibit 10-2B shows how marketing strategy might be handled in this sort of retailer-led channel system.[17]

Vertical Marketing Systems Focus on Final Customers

LO 10.5

Many marketing managers accept the view that a coordinated channel system can help everyone in the channel. These managers are moving their firms away from traditional channel systems and instead developing or joining vertical marketing systems. **Vertical marketing systems** are channel systems in which the whole channel focuses on the same target market at the end of the channel. Such systems make sense, and are growing, because if the final customer doesn't buy the product, the whole channel suffers. There are three types of vertical marketing systems—corporate, administered, and contractual. Exhibit 10-3 summarizes some characteristics of these systems and compares them with traditional systems.

Corporate channel systems shorten channels

Some corporations develop their own vertical marketing systems by internal expansion or by buying other firms, or both. With **corporate channel systems**—corporate ownership all along the channel—we might say the firm is going "direct." But actually the firm

Exhibit 10–3 Characteristics of Traditional and Vertical Marketing Systems

	Type of Channel			
		Vertical Marketing Systems		
Characteristics	Traditional	Administered	Contractual	Corporate
Amount of cooperation	Little or none	Some to good	Fairly good to good	Complete
Control maintained by	None	Economic power and leadership	Contracts	Ownership by one company
Examples	Typical channel of "independents"	General Electric, Miller Beer, Scotts Miracle Grow	McDonald's, Holiday Inn, Ace Hardware, Super Valu, Coca-Cola, Chevrolet	Florsheim Shoes, Sherwin-Williams

may be handling manufacturing, wholesaling, *and* retailing—so it's more accurate to think of the firm as a vertical marketing system.

Corporate channel systems may develop by **vertical integration**—acquiring firms at different levels of channel activity. For example, in England, most of the quaint local pubs are now actually owned and operated by the large breweries.

Vertical integration has potential advantages—stable sources of supplies, better control of distribution and quality, greater buying power, and lower executive overhead. Provided that the discrepancies of quantity and assortment are not too great at each level in a channel, vertical integration can be profitable. However, many managers have found that it's hard to be really good at running manufacturing, wholesaling, and retailing businesses that are very different from each other. Instead, they try to be more efficient at what they do best and focus on ways to get cooperation in the channel for the other activities.[18]

Administered and contractual systems may work well

Firms can often gain the advantages of vertical integration without building a costly corporate channel. A manager can develop administered or contractual channel systems instead. In **administered channel systems**, the channel members informally agree to cooperate with each other. They can agree to routinize ordering, share inventory and sales information over computer networks, standardize accounting, and coordinate promotion efforts. In **contractual channel systems**, the channel members agree by contract to cooperate with each other. With both of these systems, the members retain some of the flexibility of a traditional channel system.

The opportunities to reduce costs and provide customers with superior value are growing in these systems because of help from information technology. For example, like many retailers, Costco has a system that it calls "vendor managed inventory" in which key suppliers take over responsibility for managing a set of products, often a whole product category. Costco uses this approach with Kimberly-Clark (KC), the firm that makes Huggies disposable diapers. Every day, an analyst at KC's headquarters reviews Costco's online data that details Huggies' sales and inventory at every Costco store. If inventory is getting low, a new order is placed and shipping is scheduled. This system reduces buying and selling costs, inventory management, lost sales from inventory stock-outs, and consumer frustration when products aren't available. Because KC does this job well, it makes more money and so does Costco.[19]

Internet Exercise

Franchising is a type of contractual channel. A franchisee buys into a business and agrees to contractual guidelines for operating the business, and the franchisor provides support and advice. Franchisees should extensively research the franchisor before signing a contract. One way to gather information is from online blogs. Imagine someone thinking about opening a Jimmy John's Gourmet Sandwiches shop. Go to Blue Mau Mau (**www.bluemaumau.org**) and the Franchise Pundit (**franchisepundit.com**) websites. Read about each blog site. Is each a credible source of information? Why or why not? Enter "Jimmy John's" in the search box and look at a few posts. What do you learn? With this new information, would you be more likely or less likely to open a Jimmy John's franchise? Explain your reasoning.

Vertical marketing systems—dominant force in the marketplace

Vertical systems in the consumer products area have a healthy majority of retail sales and should continue to increase their share in the future. Vertical marketing systems are becoming the major competitive units in the U.S. distribution system—and they are growing rapidly in other parts of the world as well.[20]

The Best Channel System Should Achieve Ideal Market Exposure

LO 10.6

You may think that all marketing managers want their products to have maximum exposure to potential customers. This isn't true. Some product classes require much less market exposure than others. **Ideal market exposure** makes a product available widely enough to satisfy target customers' needs but not exceed them. Too much exposure only increases the total cost of marketing.

Ideal exposure may be intensive, selective, or exclusive

Intensive distribution is selling a product through all responsible and suitable wholesalers or retailers who will stock or sell the product. **Selective distribution** is selling through only those intermediaries who will give the product special attention. **Exclusive distribution** is selling through only one intermediary in a particular geographic area. As we move from intensive to exclusive distribution, we give up exposure in return for some other advantage—including, but not limited to, lower cost.

Intensive distribution—sell it where they buy it

Intensive distribution is commonly needed for convenience products and business supplies—such as laser printer cartridges, ring binders, and copier paper—used by all offices. Customers want such products nearby. For example, Rayovac batteries were not selling well even though their performance was very similar to other batteries. Part of that was due to heavier advertising for Duracell and Energizer. But consumers usually don't go shopping for batteries. They're purchased on impulse 83 percent of the time. To get a larger share of purchases, Rayovac had to be in more stores. It offered retailers a marketing mix with less advertising and a lower price. In three years, the brand moved from being available in 36,000 stores to 82,000 stores—and that increase gave sales a big charge.[21]

Selective distribution—sell it where it sells best

Selective distribution covers the broad area of market exposure between intensive and exclusive distribution. It may be suitable for all categories of products. Only the better intermediaries are used here. Companies commonly use selective distribution to

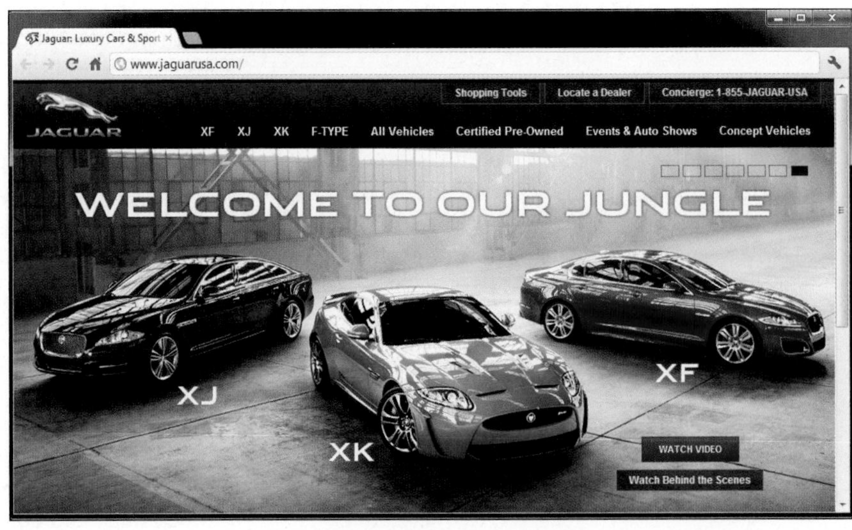

Starburst is a convenience product and is sold using intensive distribution. On the other hand, most members of Jaguar's target market view the car as a heterogeneous shopping or specialty product—so the carmaker uses exclusive distribution.

gain some of the advantages of exclusive distribution—while still achieving fairly widespread market coverage.

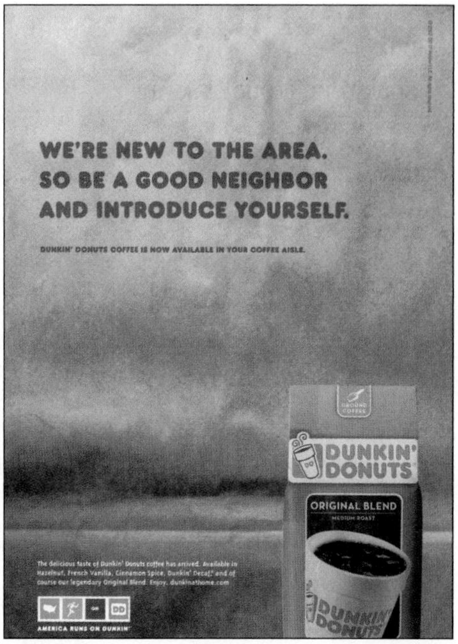

Reduce costs and get better partners

A selective policy might be used to avoid selling to wholesalers or retailers that (1) place orders that are too small to justify making calls, (2) make too many returns or request too much service, (3) have a poor credit rating, or (4) are not in a position to do a satisfactory job.

Selective distribution is becoming more popular than intensive distribution as firms see that they don't need 100 percent coverage of a market to support national advertising. Often the majority of sales come from relatively few customers—and the others buy too little compared to the cost of working with them. This is called the 80/20 rule—80 percent of a company's sales often come from only 20 percent of its customers *until it becomes more selective in choosing customers.*

Esprit—a producer of women's clothing—was selling through about 4,000 department stores and specialty shops in the United States. But Esprit's sales analysis showed that sales in Esprit's own stores were about four times better than sales in other outlets. Profits increased when Esprit cut back to about half as many outlets and opened more of its own stores and a website.[22]

As demand for premium coffee increased, Dunkin' Donuts took advantage of its brand reputation and the quality of its product to obtain distribution in supermarkets.

Get special effort from channel members

Selective distribution can produce greater profits not only for the producer but for all channel members. Wholesalers and retailers are more willing to promote products aggressively if they know they're going to obtain the majority of sales through their own efforts. They may carry wider lines, do more promotion, and provide more service—all of which lead to more sales.

Selective often moves to intensive as market grows

In the early part of the life cycle of a new unsought good, a producer may have to use selective distribution. Well-known wholesalers and retailers may have the power to get such a product introduced, but sometimes on their own terms. That often means limiting the number of competing wholesalers and retailers. The producer may be happy with such an arrangement at first but dislike it later when more retailers want to carry the product.

Exclusive distribution sometimes makes sense

Exclusive distribution is just an extreme case of selective distribution—the firm selects only one wholesaler or retailer in each geographic area. Besides the various advantages of selective distribution, producers may want to use exclusive distribution to help control prices and the service offered in a channel. Franchisors like McDonald's and 1-800-GOT-JUNK? offer franchisees exclusive territories.

Is limiting market exposure legal? It depends

Exclusive distribution is an area considered under U.S. antimonopoly laws. Courts currently focus on whether an exclusive distribution arrangement hurts competition.

Horizontal arrangements—among *competing* retailers, wholesalers, or producers— to limit sales by customer or territory have consistently been ruled illegal by the U.S. Supreme Court. Courts consider such arrangements obvious collusion that reduces competition and harms customers.

The legality of vertical arrangements—between producers and intermediaries—is not as clear-cut. A 1977 Supreme Court decision (involving Sylvania and the distribution of

TV sets) reversed an earlier ruling that it was always illegal to set up vertical relationships limiting territories or customers. Now courts can weigh the possible good effects against the possible restrictions on competition. They look at competition between whole channels rather than just focusing on competition at one level of distribution.

The Sylvania decision does not mean that all vertical arrangements are legal. Rather, it says that a firm has to be able to legally justify any exclusive arrangements.

Thus, firms should be extremely cautious about entering into *any* exclusive distribution arrangement. The courts can force a change in relationships that were expensive to develop. And even worse, the courts can award triple damages if they rule that competition has been hurt.

The same cautions apply to selective distribution. Here, however, less formal arrangements are typical—and the possible impact on competition is more remote. It is now more acceptable to carefully select channel members when building a channel system. Refusing to sell to some intermediaries, however, should be part of a logical plan with long-term benefits to consumers.[23]

Multichannel Distribution and Reverse Channels

LO 10.7

Trying to achieve the desired degree of market exposure can lead to complex channels of distribution. Firms may need different channels to reach different segments of a broad product-market or to be sure they reach each segment at different stages of the purchase process. Sometimes this results in competition and conflict between different channels. There are also issues when customers need to return or recycle products.

Many firms use more than one channel of distribution

Consider the different channels used by a company that publishes computer books. See Exhibit 10-4. This publisher sells through a general book wholesaler that in turn sells to Internet book retailers and independent book retailers. The publisher might also sell through a computer supplies wholesaler that serves electronics superstores like Best Buy. It may also sell some of its best sellers through a large chain or even to consumers who

Exhibit 10–4 An Example of Different Channels of Distribution Used by a Publisher of Computer Books

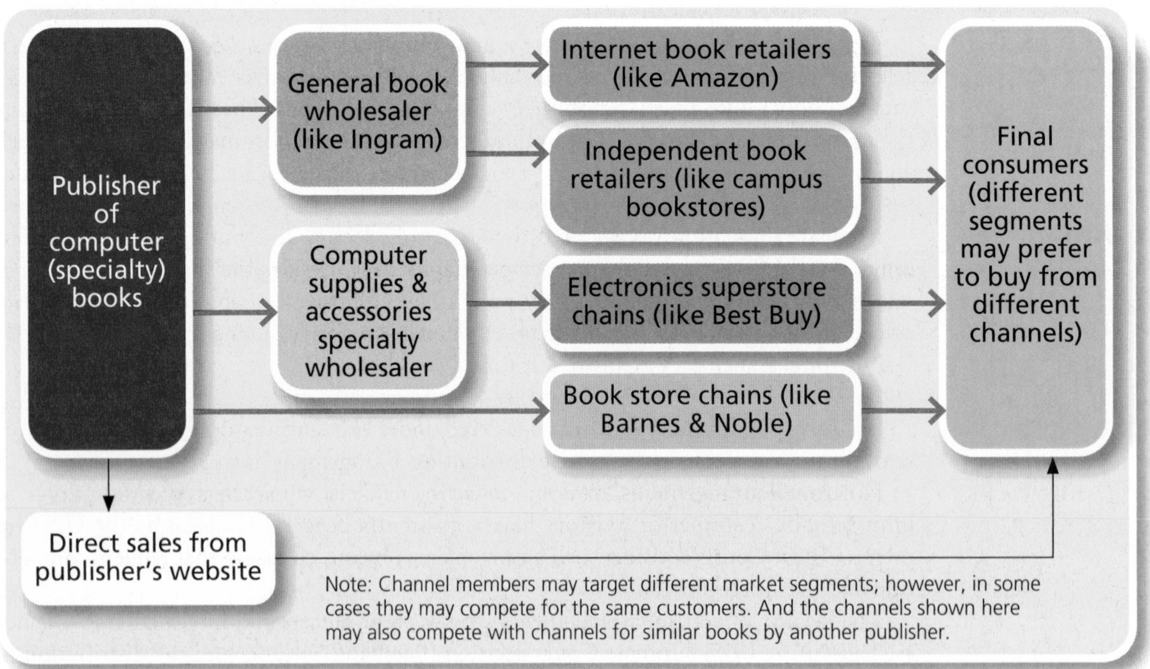

Note: Channel members may target different market segments; however, in some cases they may compete for the same customers. And the channels shown here may also compete with channels for similar books by another publisher.

The Guardian is a British daily newspaper. *The Guardian* has adapted to changing consumer behavior with a multichannel distribution approach—using print, a website, and apps for tablet computers and cell phones—to deliver the news. The multichannel format offers new services for consumers who can interact with the news in real time and watch video. To highlight those benefits, *The Guardian* created a short video that showed how *The Guardian* might cover the classic fairy tale, "The Three Little Pigs." The entertaining video has an unexpected conclusion which you can see at http://youtu.be/vDGrfhJH1P4.

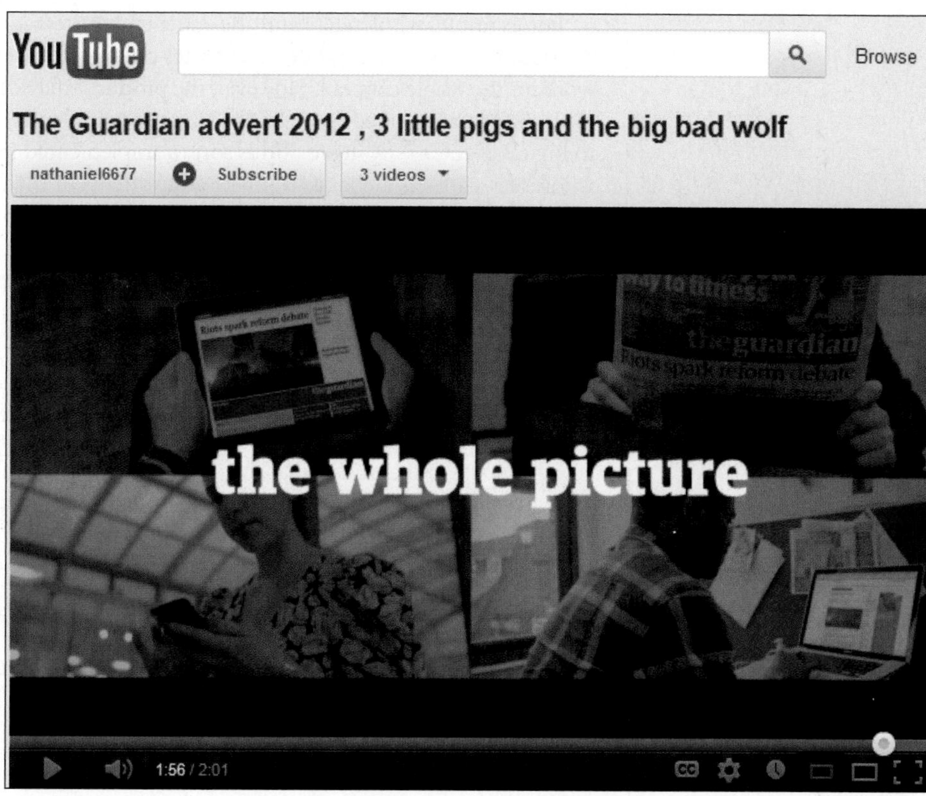

order directly from its website. An Internet retailer might offer books in print and as eBook downloads. All these channels can cause problems, because different wholesalers and retailers want different markups. It also increases competition, including price competition. And the competition among different intermediaries may lead to conflicts between the intermediaries and the publisher. Managers must consider the impact of conflict if they choose to increase market exposure by using more channels of distribution.

Multichannel distribution is becoming more common

Multichannel distribution occurs when a producer uses several competing channels to reach the same target market—perhaps using several intermediaries in addition to selling directly. Multichannel distribution is becoming more common. A single target market can buy a new Apple iPod at Apple's website, an Apple store, an online retailer, or a physical store like Target or a college bookstore. For another example, let's look at Zynga, which started out distributing its online games Farmville and Words with Friends through Facebook. Now Zynga offers the games through applications that can be downloaded to personal computers, tablets, and mobile phones. A partnership with Hasbro will bring the games to toy stores.

Sometimes producers use multichannel distribution because their present channels do a poor job or fail to reach some potential customers. For example, Reebok International had been relying on local sporting goods stores to sell its shoes to high school and college athletic teams. But Reebok wasn't getting much of the business. Sales jumped when it set up its own team-sales department to sell directly to the schools.[24]

The main reason for the growth of multichannel distribution is that it reflects how many customers want to shop. Customers may find that different channels are more effective at different stages in the purchase process. When customers search for information, evaluate products, and make purchases in different channels, they are multichannel shopping.

Ethical decisions may be required

If competition changes or customers' Place requirements shift, the current channel system may not be effective. The changes required to serve customer needs may hurt one or more members of the channel. Ethical dilemmas in the channels area arise in situations like this—because not everyone in the channel can win.

For example, wholesalers and the independent retailers that they serve in a channel of distribution may trust a producer channel-captain to develop marketing strategies that will work for the whole channel. However, the producer may decide that consumers, and its own business, are best served by a change (say, dropping current wholesalers and selling directly to big retail chains). A move of this sort, if implemented immediately, may not give current wholesaler-partners a chance to make adjustments of their own. The more dependent they are on the producer, the more severe the impact is likely to be. It's not easy to determine the best or most ethical solution in these situations. However, marketing managers must think carefully about the consequences of Place strategy changes for other channel members. In channels, as in any business dealing, relationships of trust must be treated with care.[25]

Ethics Question

Assume you are the sales manager for a small producer of hip-hop fashions. As you arrive at a trade show to promote your firm's new line, your assistant pulls you aside to warn you that some of the owners of shops that usually carry your line are looking for you—and several are hopping mad. They've heard rumors that a big retail chain will be carrying your new line in all of its stores. In the past, your firm has distributed its fashions only through these small, "independent" retail shops, and they see the big chains as threats. Although you have had some negotiations with a buyer for the big retail chain, no deal has been reached yet. What will you say to the owners of the small shops, many of whom helped your firm get started and have always supported your marketing plans? If you are certain that most of these small retailers will *not* place any orders if they think the big chain will be carrying the same line, will you respond differently? Explain your thinking.

Reverse channels are important too

Most firms focus on getting products to their customers. But some marketing managers must also plan for **reverse channels**—channels used to retrieve products that customers no longer want. The need for reverse channels may arise in a variety of different situations. Toy companies, automobile firms, drug companies, and others sometimes have to recall products because of safety problems. A firm that makes an error in completing an order may have to take returns. If a Viewsonic computer monitor breaks while it's still under warranty, someone needs to get it to the repair center. Soft-drink companies may need to recycle empty bottles. And, of course, consumers sometimes buy something in error and want to return it. This is common with online purchases where consumers can't see, touch, or try the product before purchasing it.[26]

New laws require reverse channels in some industries

Many firms have moved reluctantly to improve reverse channels—often doing so only when forced by new laws designed to help the environment. For example, some "take back" laws require manufacturers to recycle or reuse hazardous materials or products at the end of their useful life—at no additional cost to the customer. In Europe, automakers must take back and recycle or reuse 85 percent of any vehicle made after 2004, and the European Community's Waste Electrical and Electronic Equipment (WEEE) Directive has firms taking back products like computers and televisions. Similar laws are cropping up in the United States.

Reverse channels—sustainable and profitable

While reverse channels help the environment, many firms find them profitable, too. In rural China, for example, it's cheaper for Coke to reuse glass bottles than to rely on plastic packages or cans. Recycling has been even more important to Xerox. Customers responded well to Xerox's offer to dispose of old copy

Internet Exercise

Some websites are willing to buy your used electronics components. Go to My Bone Yard (**www.myboneyard.com**) and Gazelle (**www.gazelle.com**) and enter information about your cell phone or other electronic product. What were you offered? Would you be interested in using this type of service? What concerns do you think phone makers Motorola or Nokia might have?

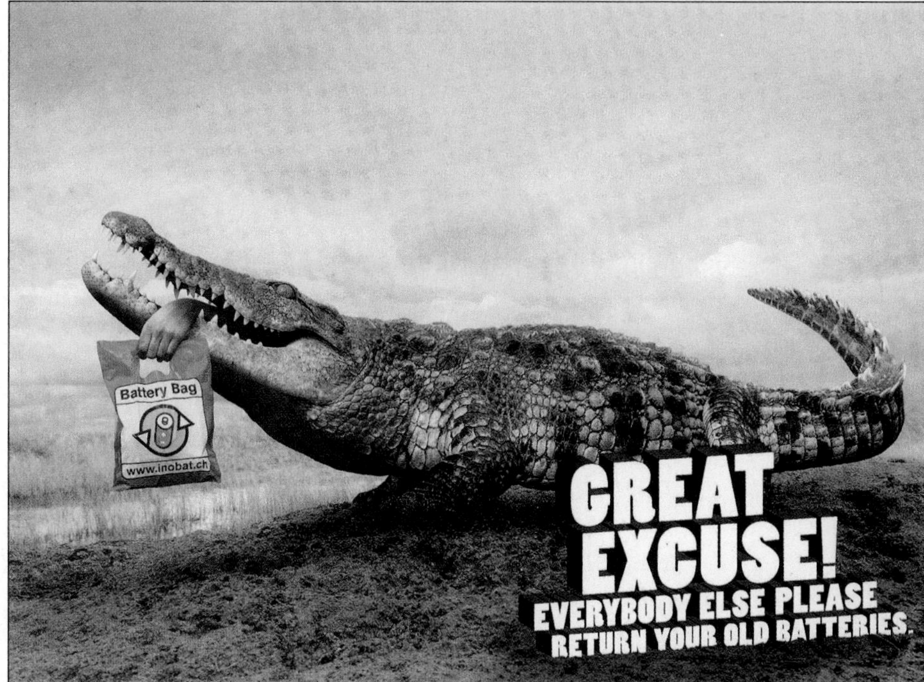

Disposing of batteries in the trash can be harmful to the environment. So the Swiss government created INOBAT, an organization that promotes recycling with creative promotion and an easy return bag.

machines with the purchase of new models. But in the first year of the program, Xerox saved $50 million by refurbishing and then reselling parts from the recycled models.

Reverse channels are also a way to give customers environmentally friendly choices. For example, new Ecoworx carpet tiles from Shaw Floors are manufactured using recycled carpets. Shaw also promises that when the time comes it will pick up and recycle the tiles at no cost to the customer. To make it easy for the customer to follow up, Shaw's telephone number is on the back of each tile. Firms like Sony, Office Depot, and Best Buy are seen as green corporate citizens as well because they help consumers recycle electronics.[27]

Plan for reverse channels

When marketing managers don't plan for reverse channels, the firm's customers may be left to solve "their" problem. That usually doesn't make sense. So a complete plan for Place may need to consider an efficient way to return products—with policies that different channel members agree on. It may also require specialists who were not involved in getting the product to the consumer. But if that's what it takes to satisfy customers, it should be part of marketing strategy planning.[28]

Entering International Markets

LO 10.8

All of the strategy decisions for Place (see Exhibit 10-1) apply whether a firm is just focused on its domestic market or is also trying to reach target customers in international markets. However, marketing managers typically face differences in international markets that require additional choices. In the external market environment, culture and laws are almost always different from those with which the marketing manager is familiar. Developing countries with less stable economies and political environments involve more risk. So we'll briefly discuss five basic ways to enter international markets. See Exhibit 10-5. As a rule, the approaches with greater risk and required investment offer the benefit of greater control over the marketing mix used.

Exporting often comes first

Some companies get into international marketing just by **exporting**—selling some of what the firm produces to foreign markets. Some firms start exporting just to take advantage of excess capacity—or even to get rid of surplus inventory. Some firms decide to

Exhibit 10–5 Basic Approaches for Entering International Markets

Exporting → Licensing → Management contracting → Joint venture → Direct investment

Generally increasing investment, risk, and control of marketing

change little if anything about the product, the label, or even the instructions. This explains why some early efforts at exporting are not very satisfactory. Other firms work closely with intermediaries who develop appropriate marketing mix changes and handle problems such as customs, import and export taxes, shipping, exchange rates, and recruiting or working with wholesalers and retailers in the foreign country.

Licensing is often an easy way

Licensing means selling the right to use some process, trademark, patent, or other right for a fee or royalty. The licensee in the foreign market takes most of the risk, because it must make some initial investment to get started. The licensee also does most of the marketing strategy planning for the markets it is licensed to serve. If good partners are available, this can be an effective way to enter a market. Gerber entered the Japanese baby food market this way, but exports to other countries.

Some firms tailor their websites to sell directly to export customers in foreign countries. Nike used this approach in Argentina.

Management contracting sells know-how

Management contracting means that the seller provides only management and marketing skills—others own the production and distribution facilities. Some mines and oil refineries are operated this way—and Hilton operates hotels all over the world for local owners using this method. This is another relatively low risk approach to international marketing. The low level of commitment to fixed facilities makes the approach attractive in developing nations or ones where the government is less stable.

Joint venturing increases involvement

In a **joint venture** a domestic firm enters into a partnership with a foreign firm. As with any partnership, there can be honest disagreements over objectives—for example, how much profit is desired and how fast it should be paid out—as well as operating policies. Where a close working relationship can be developed—perhaps based on one firm's technical and marketing know-how and the foreign partner's knowledge of the market and political connections—this approach can be very attractive to both parties. Typically the two partners must make significant investments and agree on the marketing strategy. Once a joint venture is formed, it can be difficult to end if things aren't working out. American investment bank J.P. Morgan used this approach to enter China, where stiff regulations prohibited a foreign firm from owning a controlling share of a Chinese investment bank or money management firm.

Direct investment involves ownership

When a foreign market looks really promising, a firm may want to take a bigger step with a direct investment. **Direct investment** means that a parent firm has a division (or owns a separate subsidiary firm) in a foreign market. This gives the parent firm complete control of marketing strategy planning. Direct investment is a big commitment and usually entails greater risks. If a local market has economic or political problems, the firm cannot easily leave. On the other hand, by providing local jobs, a company builds a strong presence in a new market. This helps the firm develop a good reputation with the government and customers in the host country. And the firm does not have to share profits with a partner.

Direct investment also helps a firm learn more about a new market. For example, U.S.-based quick-lube chain Grease Monkey entered the Chinese market by opening company-owned locations. It quickly discovered Chinese customers wanted a much broader range of services than was customary in the U.S. Grease Monkey added the services—and greater profits followed.[29]

CONCLUSION

In this chapter we discussed the role of Place in marketing strategy. Place decisions are especially important because they may be difficult and expensive to change. So marketing managers must make Place decisions very carefully.

We discussed how product classes and the product life cycle are related to Place objectives. This helps us determine how much a firm should rely on indirect channel systems with intermediaries or direct systems.

Marketing specialists and channel systems develop to adjust discrepancies of quantity and assortment. Their regrouping activities are basic in any economic system. And adjusting discrepancies provides opportunities for creative marketers.

Channels of distribution tend to work best when there is cooperation among the members of a channel—and conflict is avoided. So we discussed the importance of planning channel systems and the role of a channel captain. We stressed that channel systems compete with each other and that vertical marketing systems seem to be winning.

Channel planning also requires firms to decide on the degree of market exposure they want. The ideal level of exposure may be intensive, selective, or exclusive. We discussed the legal issues marketing managers must consider in developing channel systems. Finally, we examined different approaches for entering international markets.

KEY TERMS

LO 10.9

place, *254*
channel of distribution, *255*
direct marketing, *259*
discrepancy of quantity, *261*
discrepancy of assortment, *261*
regrouping activities, *261*
accumulating, *261*
bulk-breaking, *261*
sorting, *261*
assorting, *261*
traditional channel systems, *263*
channel captain, *264*
vertical marketing systems, *266*
corporate channel systems, *266*
vertical integration, *267*
administered channel systems, *267*
contractual channel systems, *267*
ideal market exposure, *268*
intensive distribution, *268*
selective distribution, *268*
exclusive distribution, *268*
multichannel distribution, *271*
reverse channels, *272*
exporting, *273*
licensing, *274*
management contracting, *274*
joint venture, *274*
direct investment, *275*

QUESTIONS AND PROBLEMS

1. Review the Dell case at the beginning of the chapter and then discuss the competitive advantages that Barnes & Noble would have over a small bookshop. What advantages does a small bookshop have?
2. Give two examples of service firms that work with other channel specialists to sell their products to final consumers. What marketing functions is the specialist providing in each case?

3. Discuss some reasons why a firm that produces installations might use direct distribution in its domestic market but use intermediaries to reach overseas customers.
4. Explain discrepancies of quantity and assortment using the clothing business as an example. How does the application of these concepts change when selling steel to the automobile industry? What impact does this have on the number and kinds of marketing specialists required?
5. Explain the four regrouping activities with an example from the building supply industry (nails, paint, flooring, plumbing fixtures, etc.). Do you think that many specialists develop in this industry, or do producers handle the job themselves? What kinds of marketing channels would you expect to find in this industry, and what functions would various channel members provide?
6. Insurance agents are intermediaries who help other members of the channel by providing information and handling the selling function. Does it make sense for an insurance agent to specialize and work exclusively with one insurance provider? Why or why not?
7. Discuss the Place objectives and distribution arrangements that are appropriate for the following products (indicate any special assumptions you have to make to obtain an answer):
   a. A postal scale for products weighing up to 2 pounds.
   b. Children's toys: (1) radio-controlled model airplanes costing $80 or more, (2) small rubber balls.
   c. Heavy-duty, rechargeable, battery-powered nut tighteners for factory production lines.
   d. Fiberglass fabric used in making roofing shingles.
8. Give an example of a producer that uses two or more different channels of distribution. Briefly discuss what problems this might cause.
9. Explain how a channel captain can help traditional independent firms compete with a corporate (integrated) channel system.
10. Find an example of vertical integration within your city. Are there any particular advantages to this vertical integration? If so, what are they? If there are no advantages, how do you explain the integration?
11. What would happen if retailer-organized channels (either formally integrated or administered) dominated consumer products marketing?
12. How does the nature of the product relate to the degree of market exposure desired?
13. Why would intermediaries want to be exclusive distributors for a product? Why would producers want exclusive distribution? Would intermediaries be equally anxious to get exclusive distribution for any type of product? Why or why not? Explain with reference to the following products: candy bars, batteries, golf clubs, golf balls, steak knives, televisions, and industrial woodworking machinery.
14. Explain the present legal status of exclusive distribution. Describe a situation where exclusive distribution is almost sure to be legal. Describe the nature and size of competitors and the industry, as well as the nature of the exclusive arrangement. Would this exclusive arrangement be of any value to the producer or intermediary?
15. Discuss the promotion a new grocery products producer would need in order to develop appropriate channels and move products through those channels. Would the nature of this job change for a new producer of dresses? How about for a new, small producer of installations?
16. Describe the advantages and disadvantages of the approaches to international market entry discussed in this chapter.

CREATING MARKETING PLANS

The Marketing Plan Coach software on the text website includes a sample marketing plan for Hillside Veterinary Clinic. Look through the "Marketing Strategy" section.

a. Why does Hillside sell its product directly instead of indirectly?

b. Hillside has a small selection of pet supplies that it sells to people who bring in their pets. What products does it resell at retail? What channel functions does it provide, and what channel functions are performed by its suppliers?

SUGGESTED CASES

13. AAA Office World
15. The Buckeye Group
16. J&J Lumber
32. Lever Ltd.
34. Chess Aluminum Worldwide

COMPUTER-AIDED PROBLEM

10. INTENSIVE VERSUS SELECTIVE DISTRIBUTION

Hydropump, Inc., produces and sells high-quality pumps to business customers. Its marketing research shows a growing market for a similar type of pump aimed at final consumers—for use with Jacuzzi-style tubs in home remodeling jobs. Hydropump will have to develop new channels of distribution to reach this target market because most consumers rely on a retailer for advice about the combination of tub, pump, heater, and related plumbing fixtures they need. Hydropump's marketing manager, Robert Black, is trying to decide between intensive and selective distribution. With intensive distribution, he would try to sell through all the plumbing supply, bathroom fixture, and hot-tub retailers who will carry the pump. He estimates that about 5,600 suitable retailers would be willing to carry a new pump. With selective distribution, he would focus on about 280 of the best hot-tub dealers (2 or 3 in the 100 largest metropolitan areas).

Intensive distribution would require Hydropump to do more mass selling—primarily advertising in home renovation magazines—to help stimulate consumer familiarity with the brand and convince retailers that Hydropump equipment will sell. The price to the retailer might have to be lower too (to permit a bigger markup) so they will be motivated to sell Hydropump rather than some other brand offering a smaller markup.

With intensive distribution, each Hydropump sales rep could probably handle about 300 retailers effectively. With selective distribution, each sales rep could handle only about 70 retailers because more merchandising help would be necessary. Managing the smaller sales force and fewer retailers, with the selective approach, would require less manager overhead cost.

Going to all suitable and available retailers would make the pump available through about 20 times as many retailers and have the potential of reaching more customers. However, many customers shop at more than one retailer before making a final choice—so selective distribution would reach almost as many potential customers. Further, if Hydropump is using selective distribution, it would get more in-store sales attention for its pump and a larger share of pump purchases at each retailer.

Black has decided to use a spreadsheet to analyze the benefits and costs of intensive versus selective distribution.

a. Based on the initial spreadsheet, which approach seems to be the most sensible for Hydropump? Why?

b. A consultant points out that even selective distribution needs national promotion. If Black has to increase advertising and spend a total of $100,000 on mass selling to be able to recruit the retailers he wants for selective distribution, would selective or intensive distribution be more profitable?

c. With intensive distribution, how large a share (percent) of the retailers' total unit sales would Hydropump have to capture to sell enough pumps to earn $200,000 profit?

11 CHAPTER ELEVEN

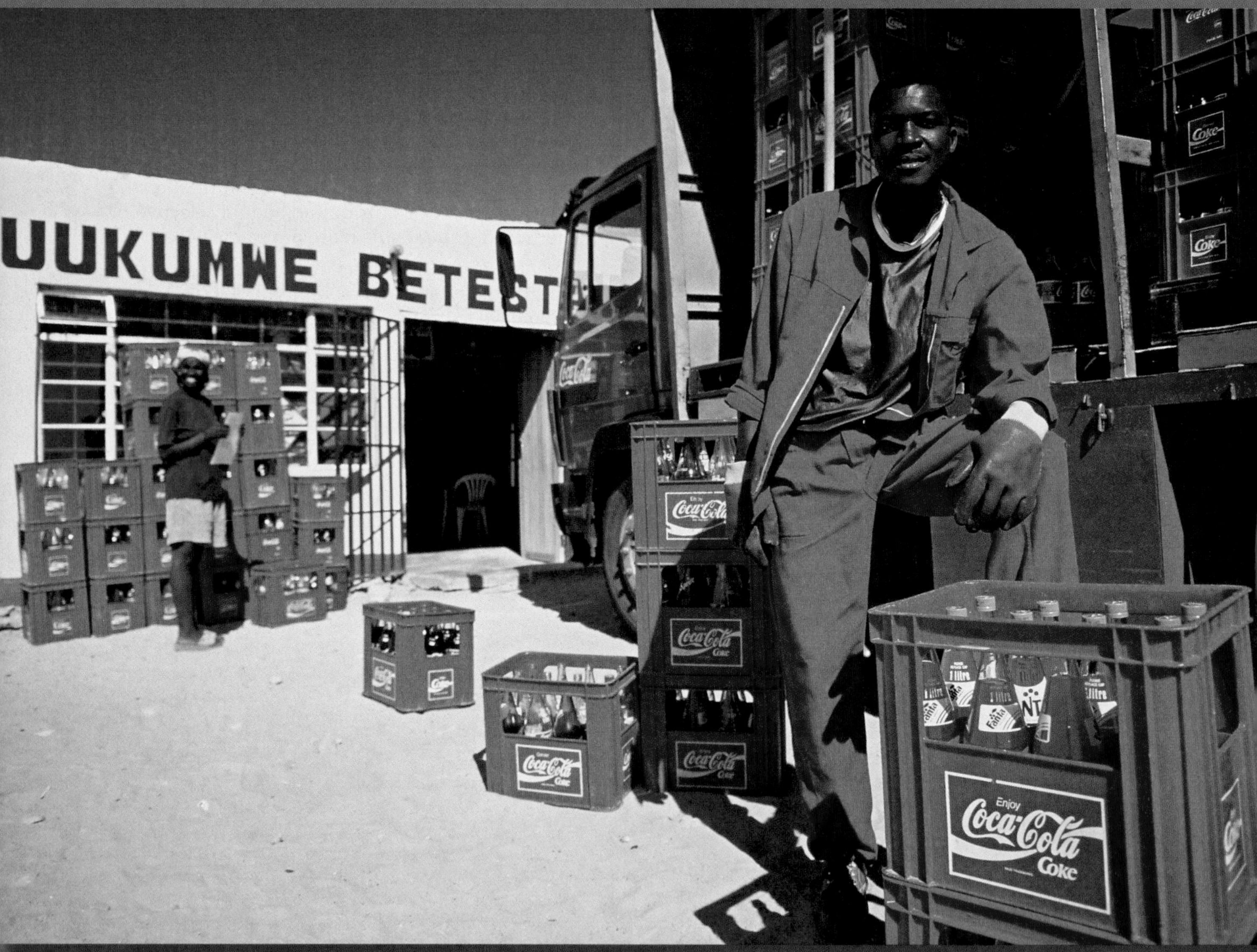

Distribution Customer Service and Logistics

If you want a Coca-Cola, there's usually one close by—no matter where you might be in the world. And that's no accident. An executive for the best-known brand name in the world stated the goal simply: "Make Coca-Cola available within an arm's reach of desire." To achieve that objective, Coke works with many different channels of distribution. But that's just the start. Think about what it takes for a bottle, can, or cup of Coke to be there whenever you're thirsty. In warehouses and distribution centers, on trucks, in restaurants and sports arenas, and thousands of other retail outlets, Coke handles, stores, and transports more than 400 billion servings of the soft drink a year. Getting all that product to consumers could be a logistical nightmare, but Coke does it effectively and at a low cost.

Fast information about what the market needs helps keep Coke's distribution on target. Coke uses an Internet-based data system that links about one million retailers and other sellers to Coke and its bottlers. The system lets Coke bottlers and retailers exchange orders, invoices, and pricing information online. Orders are processed instantly—so sales to consumers at the end of the channel aren't lost because of stock-outs. Similarly, computer systems show Coke managers exactly what's selling in each market; they can even estimate the effects of seasonal changes and promotions as they plan inventories and deliveries. Coke products move efficiently through the channel. In Cincinnati, for example, Coke built the beverage industry's first fully automated distribution center. And when Coke's truck drivers get to the retail store, they knowingly stock the shelves with the correct mix of products.

Coke's strategies in international markets rely on many of the same ideas. But the stage of market development varies in different countries, so Coke's emphasis varies as well. To increase sales in France, for example, Coke installed thousands of soft-drink coolers in French supermarkets. In Great Britain, Coke emphasizes multipacks because it wants to have more inventory at the point of consumption—in consumers' homes. In Japan, by contrast, Coke relies heavily on an army of truck drivers to constantly restock 1 million Coke vending machines, more per capita than anywhere else in the world. Japanese customers can even use their cell phone to buy a Coke from one of these vending machines.

In less developed areas, the focus may be on different challenges—especially if the limitations of the Place system can make Coke products hard to find or costly. In Africa, where per capita consumption of Coke products is one-tenth of that in the United States, Coca-Cola wants its products to be cold and available everywhere—even in the lowest income areas. So for example, in Kabira, a Kenyan slum, a local distributor uses three shipping containers as a portable warehouse. Dirt and gravel roads make it easier to deliver by hand, so delivery personnel stack a couple dozen crates onto two wheel carts and fan out to 345 small shops delivering Coke, Fanta, and Stoney Ginger Beer. Deliveries might occur once or twice a day because the small shops hold so little inventory. Coke provides shops with plenty of "red"—Coke signage, tablecloths, and refrigerated coolers. Returnable glass bottles help keep costs down and at prices of less than 25 cents (U.S.), Coke becomes a treat on hot days.

Fortune magazine recently put the spotlight on Coca-Cola's commitment to sustainability, and decisions in the logistics area can have big environmental effects. For example, Coca-Cola helped develop vending machines that are HFC-free and 40 to 50 percent more energy efficient than conventional beverage equipment. Similarly, in the U.S. and Canada, Coca-Cola's gas-electric hybrid delivery trucks cut emissions and fuel consumption by a third; in Uruguay, Coca-Cola's Montevideo Refrescos subsidiary uses electric trucks for deliveries in congested urban areas. In spite of positive steps like these, Coca-Cola still faces some challenges concerning sustainability and logistics. For example, critics argue that in a society where there is already a safe supply of tap water it doesn't make sense to bottle water (Coke's brand is Dasani), transport it in trucks that consume fuel and contribute to pollution, and then add worry about how best to dispose of the empty bottles and bottle tops.

With a 70 percent market share, Coca-Cola dominates the fountain channel for soft drinks. Building on that strength, Coca-Cola developed an innovative self-serve fountain dispenser that delivers custom-flavored soft drinks to customers and big data to Coca-Cola managers. The Coca-Cola Freestyle allows customers to pour up to 125 different flavors of soda—how about Grape Sprite or Peach Diet Coke? Flavors can be mixed in an almost infinite number of combinations. Freestyle also gives something back to Coca-Cola—lots of useful data. For example, Freestyle wirelessly communicates when any of the 30 flavor cartridges start to run low. It also uploads data to Coke's headquarters showing which flavors and combinations are most popular and how that varies by time of day and part of the country. Fast-food outlets and Coke's marketing managers use this data to suggest when and where to launch new products and to guide promotion efforts.

Of course, Pepsi has long been a tough competitor and isn't taking all of this sitting down. It has added more non-cola products, developed creative advertising and social media-driven promotion, and aggressively targeted international markets. Smaller players like Red Bull Energy Drink and Hansen's Natural Sodas also compete for distributors' attention and retail shelf space. Coke is pushing new products as well. Who wins customers and profits in this broader competition will depend on overall marketing programs—but clearly Place has an important role to play.[1]

Learning Objectives

Choosing the right distribution channels is crucial in getting products to the target market's Place. But, as the Coca-Cola case shows, that alone doesn't ensure that products are placed "within an arm's reach of desire"—when, where, in the quantities that customers want them, and at a price they're willing to pay. In this chapter we discuss how marketing managers ensure that they also have physical distribution systems that meet their customers' needs—at both an acceptable service level and an affordable cost.

When you finish this chapter you should be able to:

1 understand why logistics (physical distribution) is such an important part of Place and marketing strategy planning.

2 understand why the physical distribution customer service level is a key marketing strategy variable.

3 understand the physical distribution concept and why the coordination of storing, transporting, and related activities is so important.

4 see how firms can cooperate and share logistics activities that will provide added value to their customers.

5 know about the advantages and disadvantages of various transportation methods.

6 know how inventory and storage decisions affect marketing strategy.

7 understand the distribution center concept.

8 understand important new terms (shown in red).

Physical Distribution Gets It to Customers

LO 11.1

Whenever Product includes a physical good, Place requires logistics decisions. **Logistics** is the transporting, storing, and handling of goods in ways that match target customers' needs with a firm's marketing mix—both within individual firms and along a channel of distribution. **Physical distribution (PD)** is another common name for logistics.

There are many different combinations of logistics decisions. Each combination can result in a different level of distribution service and different costs. So companies must determine the best way to provide the level of distribution service that customers want and are willing to pay for. We start this chapter by considering these critical logistics decisions. See Exhibit 11-1. Next, we describe the choice among different modes of transportation: Each has its own costs and benefits. We conclude with decisions about inventory and the use of distribution centers.

Exhibit 11–1 The Role of Logistics and Physical Distribution Customer Service in Marketing Strategy

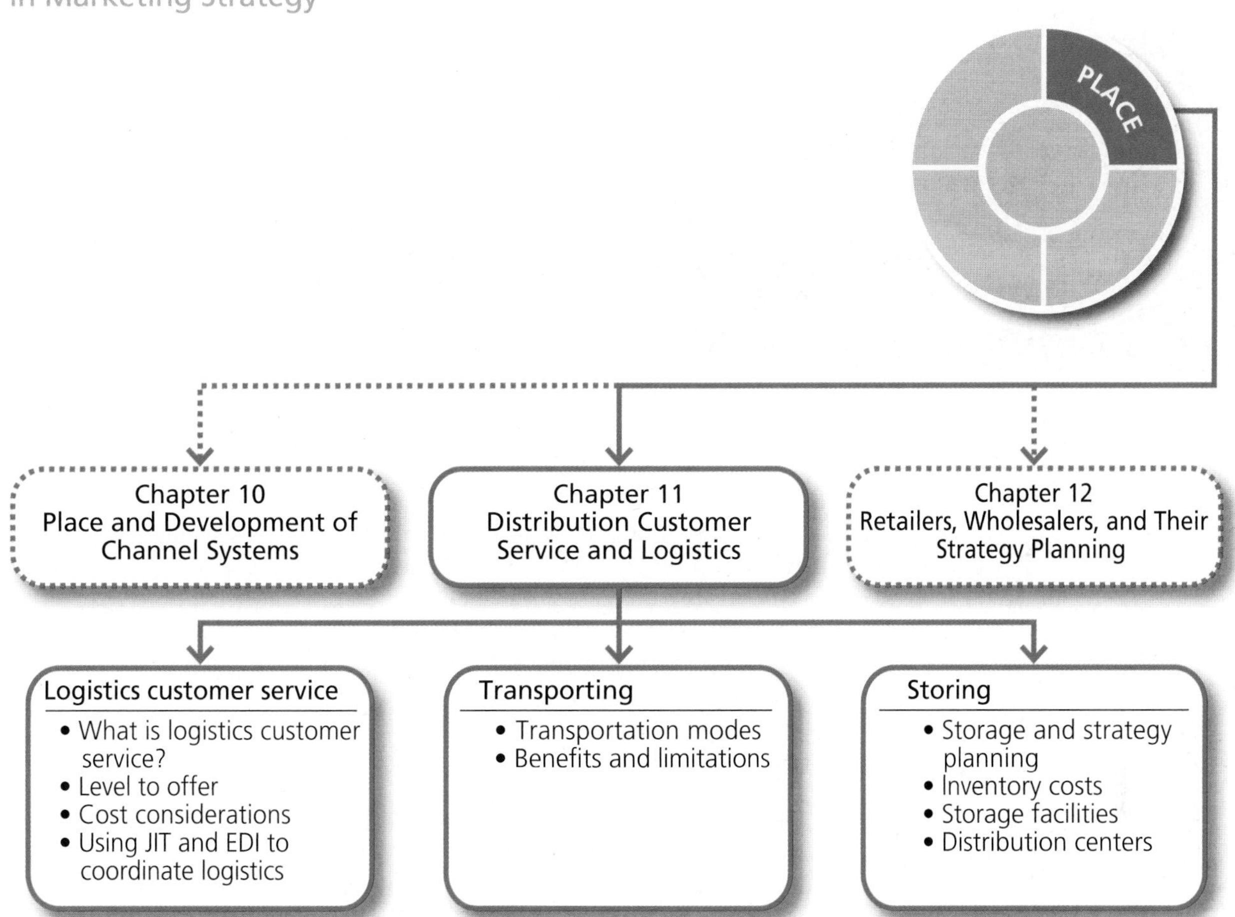

Logistics costs are very important to both companies and consumers. These costs vary from firm to firm and, from a macro-marketing perspective, from country to country. For some products, a company may spend half or more of its total marketing dollars on physical distribution activities. As lawmakers debate the high cost of health care, logistics costs represent more than one-third the expense attached to hospital supplies. While this is down from about 50 percent a few decades ago, there's still room for improvement.

Differences in logistics costs across countries can be substantial. Developed economies in the United States and Europe spend about 9 to 15 percent of GDP on logistics related costs—while in the developing economies of Latin America and Africa costs are 30 percent or more. Marketing managers must carefully consider these costs when entering new markets.[2]

Physical Distribution Customer Service

LO 11.2

From the beginning, we've emphasized that marketing strategy planning is based on meeting customers' needs. Planning for logistics and Place is no exception. So let's start by looking at logistics through a customer's eyes.

Customers want products, not excuses

Customers don't care how a product was moved or stored or what some channel member had to do to provide it. Rather, customers think in terms of the physical distribution **customer service level**—how rapidly and dependably a firm can deliver what they, the customers, want.

The best shipping method for any given product is usually a balancing act between service and cost.

What does this really mean? It means that Toyota wants to have enough windshields delivered to make cars *that* day—not late so production stops *or* early so there are a lot of extras to move around or store. It means that business executives who rent cars from Hertz want them to be ready when they get off their planes. It means that when you order a blue shirt at the Lands' End website you receive blue, not pink. It means you want your Tostitos to be whole when you buy a bag at the snack bar—not crushed into crumbs from rough handling in a warehouse.

Physical distribution is invisible to most consumers

PD is, and should be, a part of marketing that is "invisible" to most consumers. It only gets their attention when something goes wrong. At that point, it may be too late to do anything that will keep them happy.

In countries where physical distribution systems are inefficient, consumers face shortages of the products they need. By contrast, most consumers in the United States and Canada don't think much about physical distribution. This probably means that these market-directed macro-marketing systems work pretty well—that a lot of individual marketing managers have made good decisions in this area. But it doesn't mean that the decisions are always clear-cut or simple. In fact, many trade-offs may be required.

Trade-offs of costs, service, and sales

Most customers would prefer very good service at a very low price. But that combination is hard to provide because it usually costs more to provide higher levels of service. So most physical distribution decisions involve trade-offs between costs, the customer service level, and sales.

If you want a new HP computer and the Best Buy store where you would like to buy it doesn't have it on hand, you're likely to buy it elsewhere; or if that model HP is hard to get, you might just switch to some other brand. Perhaps the Best Buy store could keep your business by guaranteeing two-day delivery of your computer—by using airfreight from HP's factory. In this case, the manager is trading the cost of storing inventory for the extra cost of speedy delivery—assuming that the computer is available in inventory *somewhere* in the channel. In this example, missing one sale may not seem that important, but it all adds up. A few years ago a computer company lost over $500 million in sales because its computers weren't available when and where customers were ready to buy them.

Exhibit 11-2 illustrates trade-off relationships like those highlighted in the HP example. For instance, faster but more expensive transportation may reduce the need for a costly inventory of computers. If the service level is too low, customers will buy elsewhere and sales will be lost. Alternatively, the supplier may hope that a higher service level will attract more customers. But if the service level is higher than customers want or are willing to pay for, sales will be lost to competitors.

Exhibit 11–2
Trade-Offs among Physical Distribution Costs, Customer Service Level, and Sales

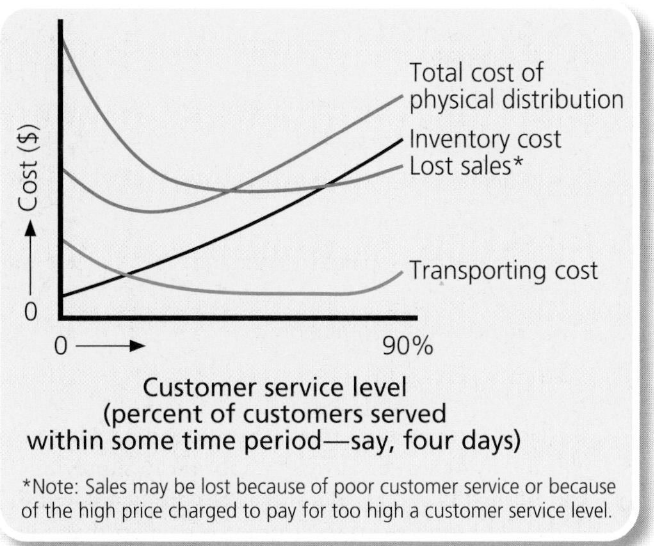

The trade-offs that must be made in the PD area can be complicated. The lowest-cost approach may not be best—if customers aren't satisfied. If different target markets want different customer service levels, several different strategies may be needed.[3]

Many firms are trying to address these complications with e-commerce. Information technology can sometimes improve service levels *and* cut costs at the same time. Better information flows make it easier to coordinate activities, improve efficiency, and add value for the customer.

Physical Distribution Concept Focuses on the Whole Distribution System

LO 11.3

The physical distribution concept

The **physical distribution (PD) concept** says that all transporting, storing, and product-handling activities of a business and a whole channel system should be coordinated as one system that seeks to minimize the cost of distribution for a given customer service level. Both lower costs and better service help to increase customer value. This seems like common sense, but until recently most companies treated physical distribution functions as separate and unrelated activities.

Traditionally, responsibility for different logistics activities was spread among various departments in a firm—production, shipping, sales, warehousing, purchasing, and others. No one person was responsible for coordinating storing and shipping decisions or customer service levels. It was even rarer for different firms in the channel to collaborate. Each just did its own thing. Unfortunately, in too many firms these old-fashioned ways persist—with a focus on individual functional activities rather than the whole physical distribution system.[4]

Decide what service level to offer

With broader adoption of the physical distribution concept, this is changing. Firms work together to decide what aspects of service are most important to customers at the end of the channel. Then they focus on finding the least expensive way to achieve the target level of service.

Exhibit 11-3 shows a variety of factors that may influence the customer service level (at each level in the channel). The most important aspects of customer service depend on target market needs. Xerox might focus on how long it takes to deliver copy machine repair parts once it receives an order. When a copier breaks down, customers want the repair "yesterday." The service level might be stated as "we will deliver 90 percent of all emergency repair parts within 24 hours." This might require that commonly needed parts be

Exhibit 11–3
Examples of Factors That Affect PD Service Levels

- Advance information on product availability
- Time to enter and process orders
- Backorder procedures
- Where inventory is stored
- Accuracy in filling orders
- Damage in shipping, storing, and handling
- Online status information
- Advance information on delays
- Time needed to deliver an order
- Reliability in meeting delivery date
- Complying with customer's instructions
- Defect-free deliveries
- How needed adjustments are handled
- Procedures for handling returns

available on the service truck, that order processing be very fast, and that parts not available locally be sent by airfreight. Obviously, supplying this service level will affect the total cost of the PD system. But it may also beat competitors.

Fast PD service can be critical for retailers that appeal to consumers who are eager to get a new product that is in hot demand—the latest CD or DVD release, a bestselling book, or a popular toy or video game.

Increasing service levels may also be very profitable in highly competitive situations where the firm has little else to differentiate its marketing mix. Marketing managers at Clorox, for example, must do everything they can to develop and keep strong partnerships with intermediaries. Many other firms sell products with precisely the same ingredients and are constantly trying to steal customers. Yet Clorox's high standards for customer service help it obtain a competitive advantage. For example, when the bleach buyer for a major retail chain went on vacation, the chain's central distribution center almost ran out of Clorox liquid bleach. But Clorox people identified the problem themselves—because of a computer system that allowed Clorox to access the chain's inventory records and sales data for Clorox products. Clorox rearranged production to get a shipment out fast enough to prevent the chain, and Clorox, from losing sales. In the future when another bleach supplier tells buyers for the chain that "bleach is bleach," they'll remember the distribution service Clorox provides.[5]

Find the lowest total cost for the right service level

In selecting a PD system, the **total cost approach** involves evaluating each possible PD system and identifying *all* of the costs of each alternative. This approach uses the tools of cost accounting and economics. Costs that otherwise might be ignored—like inventory carrying costs—are considered. The possible costs of lost sales due to a lower customer service level may also be considered.

For example, Vegpro Kenya compared different PD systems for shipping ready-to-eat fresh produce from fields in Kenya to grocery stores in major European cities. The analysis showed that the costs of airfreight transportation were significantly higher than using trucks and ships. But the firm also found that costs of spoilage and inventory could be much lower when airfreight is used. The faster airfreight-based PD system brought customers fresher produce at about the same total cost. So Vegpro cleans, chops,

Sauder tries to help customer firms do a better job of tracking the status of orders and making certain that products are where they are needed at the right time.

Disaster relief is no logistics picnic

Hurricanes, tsunamis, and earthquakes create immediate needs for emergency relief supplies. And the logistics involved in delivering them include many of the same activities found in the physical delivery of other goods. However, in a disaster situation, life and death often hinge upon the speed with which food, water, and medical supplies can be delivered. Yet, when bridges, roads, and airports are destroyed, local transportation can be complicated, if not impossible. And, even worse, there is no advance warning when or where aid will be needed. Imagine what it would be like for one business to be instantly ready to distribute millions of products to a target market that usually doesn't exist, moves around the world, and then without notice pops up somewhere with insatiable needs.

People in advanced societies have high expectations that help will be immediate when disaster strikes. Yet, it's nearly impossible for relief agencies to meet those expectations. Still, improved performance is on the way from both disaster relief agencies and private businesses, which have learned from recent efforts. For example, instead of stockpiling drugs, tents, and blankets, agencies are learning to rely on outsourcing. Agencies arrange open orders with suppliers who must be prepared to instantly ship supplies whenever and wherever they are needed.

Organizations with logistics expertise also lend a helping hand. Immediately following disasters in all parts of the world, transportation giants like FedEx, DHL, and China Southern Airlines have responded quickly with planes and trucks that facilitate delivery of needed supplies. Similarly, the Fritz Institute analyzes past relief efforts and consults with agencies to help them better prepare for future responses.

When chaos hits, coordination of relief efforts is possible only if there is good information. Agencies need to know what supplies are available, where they're located, what needs are greatest, and where and how quickly deliveries can be made. Having one central communication hub—to collect and share this type of information—and IT systems specifically dedicated to the task, are key. A new system called Suma allows relief workers to manage incoming donations, put them in the right storage places, and establish shipping priorities.

Other physical distribution solutions are decidedly low-tech, but equally important. For example, boxes need to be color coded so it's obvious which ones contain critical medical supplies and perishable food. And donated goods must be packed in cartons light enough to be carried manually in locations that have damaged roads and no power or equipment.[6]

and packages vegetables in its 27,000 square-foot air-conditioned facility at the Nairobi airport—using low-cost African labor. And the next day, fresh beans, baby carrots, and other vegetables are on store shelves in Madrid, London, and Paris.[7]

Coordinating Logistics Activities Among Firms

LO 11.4

Functions can be shifted and shared in the channel

As a marketing manager develops the Place part of a strategy, it is important to decide how physical distribution functions can and should be divided within the channel. Who will store, handle, and transport the goods—and who will pay for these services? Who will coordinate all of the PD activities?

There is no right sharing arrangement. Physical distribution can be varied endlessly in a marketing mix and in a channel system. And competitors may share these functions in different ways—with different costs and results.

How PD is shared affects the rest of a strategy

How the PD functions are shared affects the other three Ps—especially Price. The sharing arrangement can also make (or break) a strategy. Consider Channel Master, a firm that wanted to take advantage of the growing market for the dishlike antennas used to receive TV signals from satellites. The product looked like it could be a big success, but the small company didn't have the money to invest in a large inventory. So Channel Master decided to work only with wholesalers who were willing to buy (and pay for) several units—to be used for demonstrations and to ensure that buyers got immediate delivery.

In the first few months Channel Master earned $2 million in revenues—just by providing inventory for the channel. And the wholesalers paid the interest cost of carrying inventory—over $300,000 the first year. Here the wholesalers helped share the risk of the new venture, but it was a good decision for them, too. They won many sales from a competing channel whose customers had to wait several months for delivery. And by getting off to a strong start, Channel Master became a market leader.

JIT requires a coordinated effort

If firms in the channel do not plan and coordinate how they will share PD activities, PD is likely to be a source of conflict rather than a basis for competitive advantage. Let's consider this point by taking a closer look at just-in-time (JIT) delivery systems (which we introduced in Chapter 6).

A key advantage of JIT for business customers is that it reduces their PD costs—especially storing and handling costs. However, if the customer doesn't have any backup inventory, there's no security blanket if a supplier's delivery truck gets stuck in traffic, there's an error in what's shipped, or there are any quality problems. Thus, a JIT system requires that a supplier have extremely high quality control in every PD activity.

A JIT system usually requires that a supplier respond to very short order lead times and the customer's production schedule. Thus, e-commerce order systems and information sharing over computer networks are often required. JIT suppliers often locate their facilities close to important customers. Trucks may make smaller and more frequent deliveries—perhaps even several times a day.

A JIT system shifts greater responsibility for PD activities backward in the channel. If the supplier can be more efficient than the customer could be in controlling PD costs—and still provide the customer with the service level required—this approach can work well for everyone in the channel. However, JIT is not always the best approach. It may be better for a supplier to produce and ship in larger, more economical quantities—if the savings offset the distribution system's total inventory and handling costs.[8]

Supply chain may involve even more firms

In our discussion, we have taken the point of view of a marketing manager. This focuses on how logistics should be coordinated to meet the needs of customers at the end of the channel of distribution. Now, however, we should broaden the picture somewhat because the relationships within the distribution channel are sometimes part of a broader network of relationships in the **supply chain**—the complete set of firms and facilities and logistics activities that are involved in procuring materials, transforming them into intermediate or finished products, and distributing them to customers.

For example, Manitowoc is one of the world's largest manufacturers of cranes. Its huge mobile cranes are used at construction sites all around the world. Robert Ward, who is in charge of purchasing for Manitowoc, must ensure an unbroken flow of parts and materials so that Manitowoc can keep its promises to customers regarding crane delivery dates. This is difficult because each crane has component parts from many suppliers around the globe. Further, any supplier may be held up by problems with its own suppliers. In one case, Manitowoc's German factory was having trouble getting key chassis parts from two suppliers in Poland. Ward traced the problem back to a Scandinavian steel mill that was

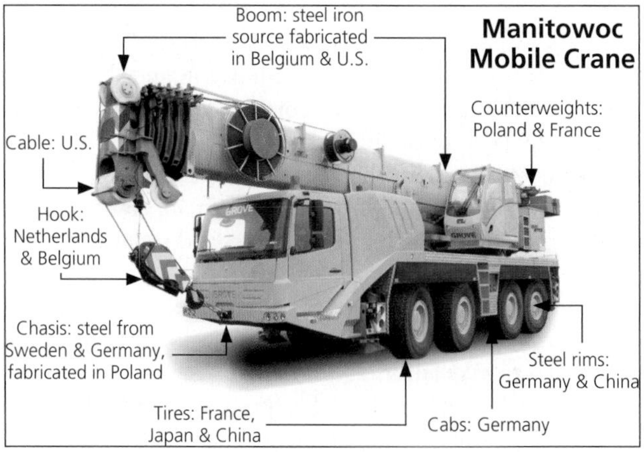

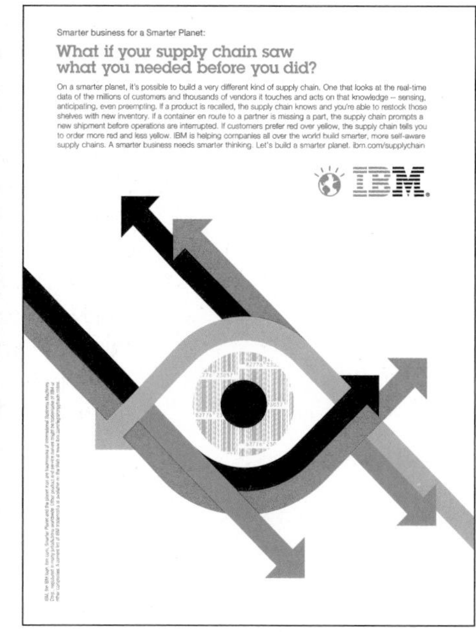

Companies like Marsh and IBM provide consulting services and software to help firms manage complex supply chains.

behind on shipments to the Polish firms. Manitowoc buys a lot of steel and has a lot of leverage with steel distributors, so Ward scoured Europe for distributors who had extra inventory of steel plate. The steel he found was more expensive than buying the steel directly from the mill, but the mill couldn't keep supplies flowing and the distributors could. By helping to coordinate the whole supply chain, Manitowoc was able to keep its promises and deliver cranes to its customers on schedule.[9]

Ideally, all of the firms in the supply chain should work together to meet the needs of the customer at the very end of the chain. That way, at each link along the chain the shifting and sharing of logistics functions and costs are handled to result in the most value for the final customer. This makes a supply chain more efficient and effective—giving it a competitive advantage against other supply chains competing to serve the same target market.[10]

Internet Exercise

Managers who are members of the Council of Supply Chain Management Professionals usually have responsibilities in purchasing, logistics, or materials management. The website of their organization (**www.cscmp.org**) provides many useful resources to both members and nonmembers. Review some of the resources shown. How would this site be useful to these managers? How is it useful to students interested in a career in a supply chain area?

Better information helps coordinate PD

Coordinating all of the elements of PD has always been a challenge—even in a single firm. Trying to coordinate orders, inventory, and transportation throughout the whole supply chain is even tougher. But information shared over the Internet and at websites has been important in finding solutions to these challenges. Physical distribution decisions will continue to improve as more firms are able to have their computers "talk to each other" directly and as websites help managers get access to up-to-date information whenever they need it.

Electronic data interchange sets a standard

Until recently, differences in computer systems from one firm to another hampered the flow of information. Many firms attacked this problem by adopting **electronic data interchange (EDI)**—an approach that puts information in a standardized format easily shared between different computer systems. In many firms, purchase orders, shipping reports, and other paper documents were replaced with computerized EDI. With EDI, a customer transmits its order information directly to the supplier's computer. The supplier's computer immediately processes the order and schedules production, order assembly, and transportation. Inventory information is automatically updated, and status reports are available instantly. The supplier might then use EDI to send the updated information to the transportation provider's computer. In fact, most international transportation firms rely on EDI links with their customers.[11]

Improved information flow and better coordination of PD activities is a key reason for the success of Pepperidge Farm's line of premium cookies. Most of the company's delivery truck drivers use handheld computers to record the inventory at each stop along their routes. They use a wireless Internet connection to instantly transmit the information into a computer at the bakeries, and cookies in short supply are produced. The right assortment of fresh cookies is quickly shipped to local markets, and delivery trucks are loaded with what retailers need that day. Pepperidge Farm moves cookies from its bakeries to store shelves in about three days; most cookie producers take about 10 days. That means fresher cookies for consumers and helps to support Pepperidge Farm's high-quality positioning and premium price.[12]

Ethical issues may arise

Some ethical issues that arise in the PD area concern communications about product availability. For example, some critics say that Internet sellers too often take orders for products that are not available or which they cannot deliver as quickly as customers expect. Yet a marketing manager can't always know precisely how long it will take before a product will be available. It doesn't make sense for the marketer to lose a customer if it appears that he or she can satisfy the customer's needs. But the customer may be inconvenienced or face added cost if the marketer's best guess isn't accurate. Similarly, some critics say that stores too often run out of products that they promote to attract consumers to the store. Yet it may not be possible for the marketer to predict demand, or to know when placing an ad that deliveries won't arrive. Different people have different views about how a firm should handle such situations. Some retailers just offer rain checks.

Ethics Question

Many major firms, ranging from Nike and Starbucks to Walmart and IKEA, have been criticized for selling products from overseas suppliers whose workers toil in bad conditions for long hours and at low pay. Defenders of the companies point out that overseas sourcing provides jobs that are better than what workers would have without it. Critics think that companies that sell products in wealthy countries have a social responsibility to see that suppliers in less-developed nations pay a fair wage and provide healthy working conditions. What do you think? Should U.S. firms be required to monitor the employment practices of suppliers in their supply chains? Should all suppliers be held to Western legal or moral standards? What solutions or compromises might be offered?[13]

The Transporting Function Adds Value to a Marketing Strategy

LO 11.5

Transporting aids economic development and exchange

Transporting is the marketing function of moving goods. Transportation makes products available when and where they need to be—at a cost. But the cost is less than the value added to products by moving them or there is little reason to ship in the first place.

Transporting can help achieve economies of scale in production. If production costs can be reduced by producing larger quantities in one location, these savings may more than offset the added cost of transporting the finished products to customers. Without low-cost transportation, both within countries and internationally, there would be no mass distribution as we know it today.

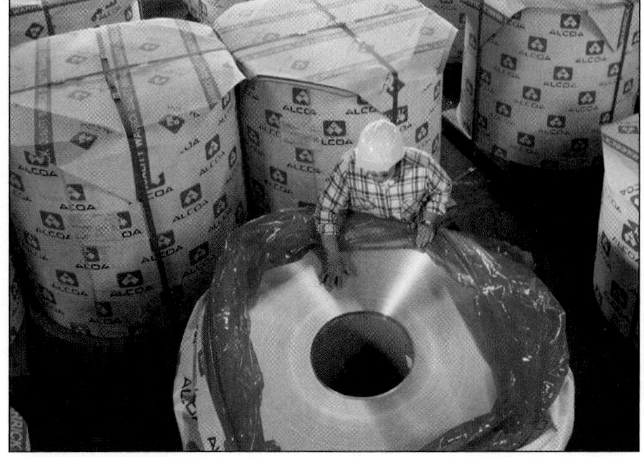

The cost of transportation adds little to the total cost of products like pharmaceutical drugs, which are already expensive relative to their size and weight. On the other hand, transporting costs can be a large part of the total cost for heavy products that are low in value like sheet aluminum.

Transporting can be costly

Transporting costs limit the target markets a marketing manager can serve. Shipping costs increase delivered cost—and that's what really interests customers. Transport costs add little to the cost of products that are already valuable relative to their size and weight. A case of medicine, for example, might be shipped to a drugstore at low cost. But transporting costs can be a large part of the total cost for heavy products of low value—like many minerals and raw materials. You can imagine that shipping a massive roll of aluminum to a producer of soft-drink cans is an expensive proposition. Exhibit 11-4 shows transporting costs as a percent of total sales dollars for several products.[14]

Governments may influence transportation

Government often plays an important role in the development of a country's transportation system, including its roads, harbors, railroads, and airports. And different countries regulate transportation differently, although regulation has in general been decreasing.

As regulations decreased in the United States, competition in the transportation industry increased. As a result, a marketing manager generally has many carriers in one or more modes competing for the firm's transporting business. Or a firm can do its own transporting. So knowing about the different modes is important.[15]

Exhibit 11–4
Transporting Costs as a Percent of Selling Price for Different Products

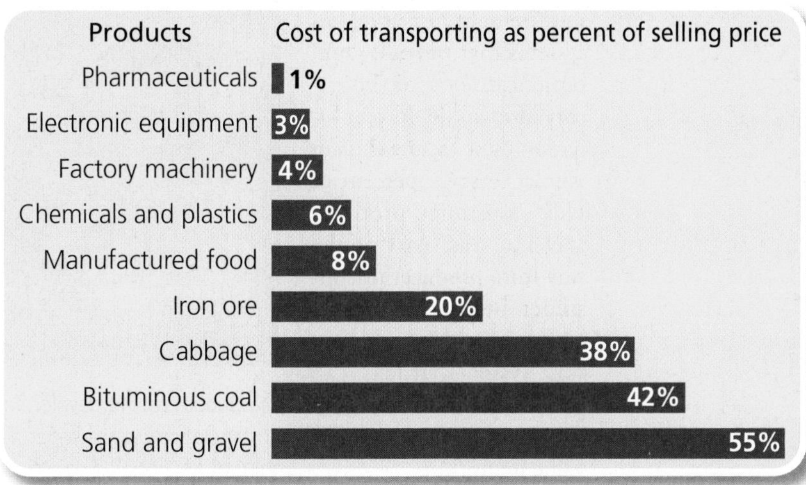

Exhibit 11–5 Benefits and Limitations of Different Transport Modes

	Transporting Features					
Mode	**Cost**	**Delivery Speed**	**Number of Locations Served**	**Ability to Handle a Variety of Goods**	**Frequency of Scheduled Shipments**	**Dependability in Meeting Schedules**
Truck	High	Fast	Very extensive	High	High	High
Rail	Medium	Average	Extensive	High	Low	Medium
Water	Very low	Very slow	Limited	Very high	Very low	Medium
Air	Very high	Very fast	Extensive	Limited	High	High
Pipeline	Low	Slow	Very limited	Very limited	Medium	High

Which Transporting Alternative Is Best?

Transporting function must fit the whole strategy

The transporting function should fit into the whole marketing strategy. But picking the best transporting alternative depends on the product, other physical distribution decisions, and what service level the company wants to offer. The best alternative should provide the level of service (for example, speed and dependability) required at as low a cost as possible. Exhibit 11-5 shows that different modes of transportation have different strengths and weaknesses. Low transporting cost is *not* the only criterion for selecting the best mode.[16]

Railroads—large loads moved at low cost

Railroads are still the workhorse of the U.S. transportation system. They carry more freight over more miles than any other mode. However, they account for less than 10 percent of transport revenues. They carry heavy and bulky goods—such as coal, steel, and chemicals—over long distances at relatively low cost. Because railroad freight usually moves more slowly than truck shipments, it is not as well suited for perishable items or those in urgent demand. Railroads are most efficient at handling full carloads of goods. Less-than-carload (LCL) shipments take a lot of handling, which means they usually move more slowly and at a higher price per pound than carload shipments.[17]

Trucks are more expensive, but flexible and essential

The flexibility and speed of trucks make them better at moving small quantities of goods for shorter distances. They can travel on almost any road. They go where the rails can't. They are also reliable in meeting delivery schedules, which is an essential requirement for logistics systems that provide rapid replenishment of inventory after a sale. In combination these factors explain why at least 75 percent of U.S. consumer products travel at least part of the way from producer to consumer by truck. And in countries with good highway systems, trucks can give extremely fast service. Trucks compete for high-value items.[18]

Low labor costs in developing countries can make transportation costs relatively low—especially for short distances. In Egypt one third of McDonalds' sales involve delivery.

Ship it overseas, but slowly

Water transportation is the slowest shipping mode, but it is usually the lowest-cost way of shipping heavy freight. Water transportation is very important for international shipments and often the only practical approach. This explains why port cities like Boston, New York City, Rotterdam, Osaka, and Singapore are important centers for international trade.

Internet Exercise

Shipping by sea can be a less costly mode of transportation. But with more than 100 carriers operating ships, it can be difficult to get a handle on all the options. OceanSchedules.com (**www.oceanschedules.com**) aims to change this. Go to the website and do a "port to port" search, with "Hong Kong" as the origin and "Vancouver, British Columbia" as the destination. Next select "by departure" and enter today's date and two weeks out. Finally, click "Get Schedules." How many different boats could take your shipment? Now change the longest transit time to four weeks and note the difference that makes in the number of available boats. What happens if you change the arrival date? How could this website be useful to a company shipping light fixtures from Hong Kong to Canada?

Inland waterways are important too

Inland waterways (such as the Mississippi River and Great Lakes in the United States and the Rhine and Danube in Europe) are also important, especially for bulky, nonperishable products such as iron ore, grain, and gravel. However, when winter ice closes freshwater harbors, alternate transportation must be used.

Pipelines move oil and gas

Pipelines are used primarily to move oil and natural gas. So pipelines are important both in the oil-producing and oil-consuming countries. Only a few major cities in the United States, Canada, Mexico, and Latin America are more than 200 miles from a major pipeline system. However, the majority of the pipelines in the United States are located in the Southwest, connecting oil fields and refineries.

Airfreight is expensive, but fast and growing

The most expensive cargo transporting mode is airplane—but it is fast! Airfreight rates are on average three times higher than trucking rates—but the greater speed may offset the added cost.

High-value, low-weight goods—like high-fashion clothing and parts for the electronics industry—are often shipped by air. Perishable products that previously could not be shipped are now being flown across continents and oceans. Flowers and bulbs from Holland, for example, now are jet-flown to points all over the world. And airfreight has become very important for small emergency deliveries, like repair parts.

But airplanes may cut the total cost of distribution

Using planes may reduce the cost of packing, unpacking, and preparing goods for sale and may help a firm reduce inventory costs by eliminating outlying warehouses. Valuable benefits of airfreight's speed are less spoilage, theft, and damage. Although the *transporting* cost of air shipments may be higher, the *total* cost of distribution may be lower. As more firms realize this, airfreight firms—like DHL Worldwide Express, FedEx, and Emery Air Freight—have enjoyed rapid growth.[19]

Put it in a container—and move between modes easily

Products often move by several different modes and carriers during their journey. This is especially common for international shipments. Japanese firms, like Sony, ship stereos to the United States, Canada, and Europe by boat. When they arrive at the dock, they are loaded on trains and sent across the country. Then the units are delivered to a wholesaler by truck or rail.

To better coordinate the flow of products between modes, transportation companies like CSX offer customers a complete choice of different transportation modes. Then CSX, not the customer, figures out the best and lowest-cost way to shift and share transporting functions between the modes.[20]

Loading and unloading goods several times used to be a real problem. Parts of a shipment would become separated, damaged, or even stolen. And handling the goods, perhaps many times, raised costs and slowed delivery. Many of these problems are reduced with **containerization**—grouping individual items into an economical shipping quantity and sealing them in protective containers for transit to the final destination. This protects the products and simplifies handling during shipping. Some containers are as large as truck bodies.

Piggyback—a ride on two or more modes

Piggyback service means loading truck trailers—or flatbed trailers carrying containers—on railcars to provide both speed and flexibility. Railroads now pick up truck trailers at the producer's location, load them onto specially designed rail flatcars, and haul them as close to the customer as rail lines run. The trailers are then hooked up to a truck tractor and delivered to the buyer's door. Similar services are offered on oceangoing ships—allowing door-to-door service between cities around the world.

Transportation in developing countries can cost more

Transportation choices are usually not so good in developing countries. Roads are often poor, rail systems may be limited, and ports may be undeveloped. Local firms that specialize in logistics services may not exist at all. Even so, firms that are willing to invest the effort can reap benefits and help their customers overcome the effects of these problems.

Metro AG, a firm based in Germany that has opened wholesale facilities in Bangalore and several other major cities in India, illustrates this point. Metro focuses on selling food products and other supplies to the thousands of restaurants, hotels, and other small businesses in the markets it serves. When Metro started in India, 40 percent of the fruits and vegetables it purchased from farmers were spoiled, damaged, or lost by the time they got to Metro. These problems piled up because the produce traveled from the fields over rough roads and was handled by as many as seven intermediaries along the way. To overcome these problems, Metro gave farmers crates to protect freshly picked crops from damage and to keep them away from dirt and bacteria that would shorten their shelf life. Further, crates were loaded and unloaded only once because Metro bought its own refrigerated trucks—to pick up produce and bring it directly to its outlets. Metro used the same ideas to speed fresh seafood from fishermen's boats. Many of Metro's restaurant customers previously bought what they needed from a variety of small suppliers, many of whom would run out of stock. Now the restaurant owners save time and money with one-stop shopping at Metro. Metro is growing fast in India because it has quality products that are in stock when they're needed, and it's bringing down food costs for its customers.[21]

Transportation choices have environmental costs too

Marketing managers must be sensitive to the environmental effects of transportation decisions. Trucks, trains, airplanes, and ships contribute to air pollution and global warming; estimates suggest that on average more than half of a firm's total carbon emissions come from transportation. There are other problems as well. For example, a damaged pipeline or oil tanker can spew thousands of gallons of oil before it can be repaired.

Many firms are taking steps to reduce such problems. FedEx and UPS are revamping their fleets to use more electric and alternative fuel vehicles. Rail is usually the cleanest way to move land freight a long distance, but General Electric's recently introduced Evolution locomotives have 5 percent better fuel economy and 40 percent lower emissions compared to previous models. GE is already working on a hybrid locomotive that will improve fuel economy another 10 percent. Truck manufacturers are also working to improve fuel efficiency and environmental impact. Peterbilt and International are among

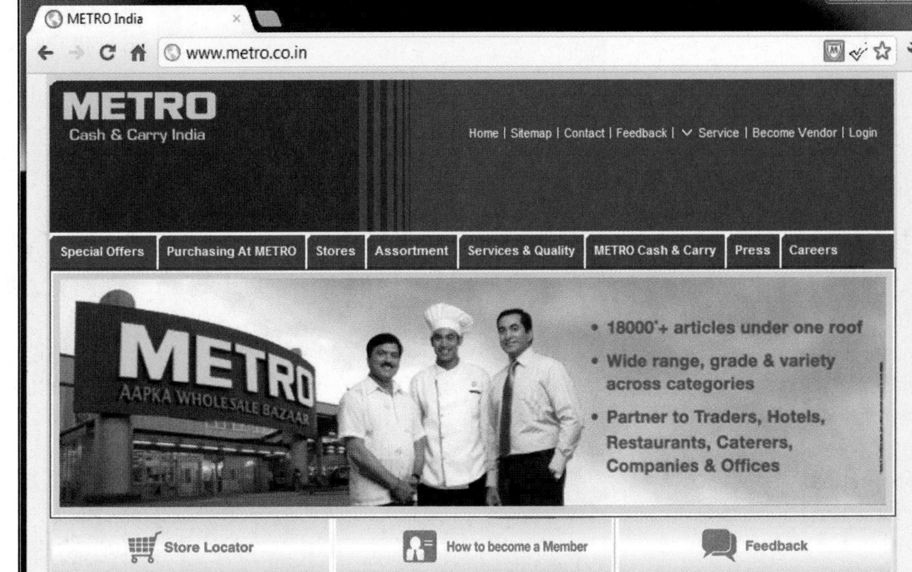

When Metro set up its cash-and-carry wholesale operations in India, it could not rely on the same logistics systems it used in Germany. Rather, Metro had to create its own fleet of refrigerated trucks to pick up produce directly from farmers. However, this reduced stock-outs and helped Metro offer customers better-quality produce at lower prices.

firms working to build diesel-hybrid 18-wheelers. The U.S. government supports these initiatives through the Environmental Protection Agency's SmartWay program (www.epa.gov/smartway/). It helps freight carriers, shippers, and logistics companies improve fuel efficiency and reduce environmental impact. Both trucking and railroad firms have procedures to ensure that transporting toxic cargo is safer. Today the public *expects* companies to manufacture, transport, sell, and dispose of products in an environmentally sound manner.[22]

Transportation analytics aid the environment and lower costs

Transportation companies routinely place sensors on trucks and train cars to monitor their movement. These sensors generate a lot of data. Managers use this to identify opportunities to more effectively manage the economic and environmental costs of transportation. For example, UPS uses global positioning data to learn and recommend routes for its drivers—routes that maximize service and minimize fuel consumption. Trucking company U.S. Xpress monitors the location and driving behavior of each of its 10,000 trucks; they know how many times a driver brakes hard, whether he sends a text message to a customer to let him know he's running late, and how long he takes for each rest stop. U.S. Xpress uses this data to show drivers how to improve service and save fuel. For instance, when a U.S. Xpress driver gets a 10-hour break, air conditioning lowers the cab temperature to 70 degrees for the first two hours, before kicking up to 78 degrees. This move alone saved the company $24 million in one year and also lowered U.S. Xpress's environmental impact.[23]

The Storing Function and Marketing Strategy

LO 11.6

Store it and smooth out sales, increase profits and consumer satisfaction

Storing is the marketing function of holding goods so they're available when they're needed. **Inventory** is the amount of goods being stored.

Storing is necessary when production of goods doesn't match consumption. This is common with mass production. Nippon Steel, for example, might produce thousands of steel bars of one size before changing the machines to produce another size. It's often cheaper to produce large quantities of one size, and store the unsold quantity, than to have shorter production runs. Thus, storing goods allows the producer to achieve economies of scale in production.

Menasha, a supplier of innovative packaging, wants its client firms to realize that its package designs can help to reduce both logistics costs and environmental impacts. The Environmental Protection Agency's voluntary SmartWay Transport Partnership is another approach to achieve environmental goals by reducing fuel costs as well as air pollution.

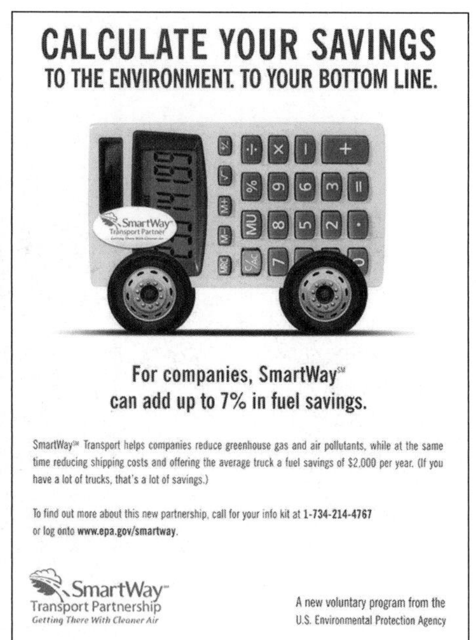

Storing varies the channel system

Storing allows producers and intermediaries to keep stocks at convenient locations, ready to meet customers' needs. In fact, storing is one of the major activities of some intermediaries.

Most channel members provide the storing function for some length of time. Even final consumers store some things for their future needs. Which channel members store the product, and for how long, affects the behavior of all channel members. For example, the producer of Snapper lawn mowers tries to get wholesalers to inventory a wide selection of its machines. That way, retailers can carry smaller inventories since they can be sure of dependable local supplies from wholesalers. And the retailers might decide to sell Snapper—rather than Toro or some other brand that they would have to store at their own expense.

If consumers "store" the product, more of it may be used or consumed. That's why Breyer's likes customers to buy its half-gallon packages. The "inventory" is right there in the freezer—and ready to be eaten—whenever the impulse hits.

Goods are stored at a cost

Storing can increase the value of goods, but *storing always involves costs* too. Different kinds of cost are involved. See Exhibit 11-6. Car dealers, for example, must store cars on their lots—waiting for the right customer. The interest expense of money tied up in the inventory is a major cost. In addition, if a new car on the lot is dented or scratched, there is a repair cost. If a car isn't sold before the new models come out, its value drops. There is also a risk of fire or theft—so the retailer must carry insurance. And, of course, dealers incur the cost of leasing or owning the display lot where they store the cars.

In today's competitive markets, most firms watch their inventories closely. They try to cut unnecessary inventory because it can make the difference between a profitable strategy and a loser. On the other hand, a marketing manager must be very careful in making the distinction between unnecessary inventory and inventory needed to provide the distribution service level customers expect.[24]

Rapid response cuts inventory costs

Many firms are finding that they can cut inventory costs and still provide the desired customer service level—if they can reduce the time it takes to replace items that are sold. This is one important reason that JIT has been widely adopted. The firms involved use EDI, the Internet, and similar computerized approaches to share information and speed up the order cycle and delivery process.

Exhibit 11–6 Many Expenses Contribute to Total Inventory Cost

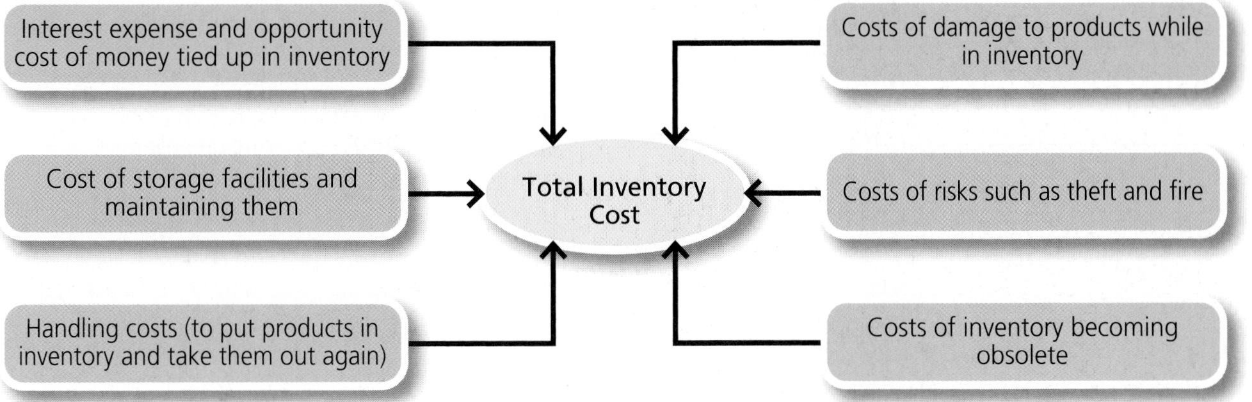

Specialized Storing Facilities May Be Required

New cars can be stored outside on the dealer's lot. Fuel oil can be stored in a specially designed tank. Coal and other raw materials can be stored in open pits. But most products must be stored inside protective buildings. Often, firms can choose among different types of specialized storing facilities. The right choice may reduce costs and serve customers better.

Private warehouses are common

Private warehouses are storing facilities owned or leased by companies for their own use. Most manufacturers, wholesalers, and retailers have some storing facilities either in their main buildings or in a separate location. A sales manager often is responsible for managing a manufacturer's finished-goods warehouse, especially if regional sales branches aren't near the factory.

Firms use private warehouses when a large volume of goods must be stored regularly. Yet private warehouses can be expensive. If the need changes, the extra space may be hard, or impossible, to rent to others.

Public warehouses fill special needs

Public warehouses are independent storing facilities. They can provide all the services that a company's own warehouse can provide. A company might choose a public warehouse if it doesn't have a regular need for space. For example, Tonka Toys uses public warehouses because its business is seasonal. Tonka pays for the space only when it is used. Public warehouses are also useful for manufacturers that must maintain stocks in many locations, including foreign countries. See Exhibit 11-7 for a comparison of private and public warehouses.[25]

Warehousing facilities cut handling costs too

The cost of physical handling is a major storing cost. Goods must be handled once when put into storage and again when removed to be sold. To reduce these costs, modern one-story buildings away from downtown traffic have replaced most old multistory warehouses. They eliminate the need for elevators and permit the use of power-operated lift trucks, battery-operated motor scooters, roller-skating order pickers, electric hoists for heavy items, and hydraulic ramps to speed loading and unloading. Bar codes, universal product code (UPC) numbers, and electronic radio frequency identification (RFID) tags make it easy for computers

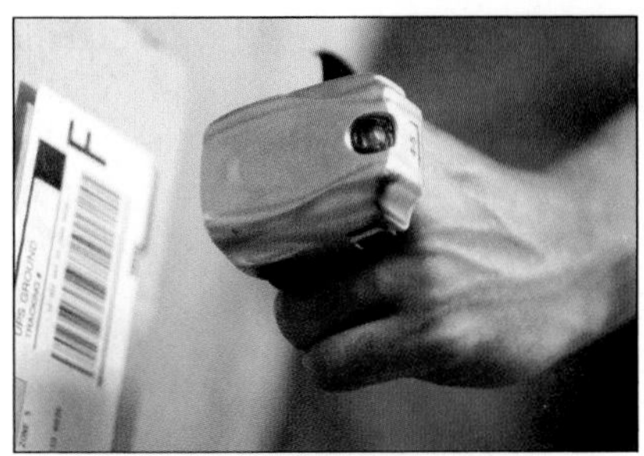

Exhibit 11–7
A Comparison of Private Warehouses and Public Warehouses

Characteristics	Type of Warehouse	
	Private	Public
Fixed investment	Very high	No fixed investment
Unit cost	High if volume is low Very low if volume is very high	Low: charges are made only for space needed
Control	High	Low managerial control
Adequacy for product line	Highly adequate	May not be convenient
Flexibility	Low: fixed costs have already been committed	High: easy to end arrangement

to monitor inventory, order needed stock, and track storing and shipping costs. For example, a warehouse worker may wear a tiny scanner ring when removing cartons from a shelf so that information in the bar codes can be instantly read and transmitted via a Bluetooth wireless network to the firm's information system. Similarly, RFID tags may transmit detailed information about the contents of a carton as it moves along a conveyor system. Some warehouses also have computer-controlled order-picking systems or conveyor belts that speed the process of locating and assembling the assortment required to fill an order.[26]

The Distribution Center—A Different Kind of Warehouse

LO 11.7

Is storing really needed?

Discrepancies of assortment or quantity between one channel level and another are often adjusted at the place where goods are stored. It reduces handling costs to regroup and store at the same place—*if both functions are required.* But sometimes regrouping is required when storing isn't.

Don't store it, distribute it

A **distribution center** is a special kind of warehouse designed to speed the flow of goods and avoid unnecessary storing costs. Today, the distribution center concept is widely used by firms at all channel levels. Many products buzz through a distribution center without ever tarrying on a shelf; workers and equipment immediately sort the products as they come in and then move them to an outgoing loading dock and the vehicle that will take them to their next stop. Technology is key to making distribution centers efficient.

Consider how food distributor Sysco addresses the challenge of shipping more than 21.5 million tons of fruit, vegetables, meats, and other food-related products each year. Sysco's customers include one in every three restaurants, school cafeterias, and other food service outlets in the United States and Canada. Because Sysco delivers so many products in so many different forms—from boxes of frozen French fries, crates of Granny Smith apples, and 80-pound tubs of flour to pots, pans, and utensils—its handling needs vary widely.

To move all these goods efficiently and quickly, Sysco relies on technology. It uses supply chain management software and an EDI system to automatically direct supplies from vendors like Kraft and Kellogg to one of two Sysco "redistribution centers." There, orders are quickly consolidated and moved to one of Sysco's 177 distribution centers. The 400,000+ square-foot distribution centers are organized by weight and temperature; heavier items—like cans weighing 40 to 50 pounds—are housed on one

Kiva Systems develops robots that handle order fulfillment in many warehouses. The orange Kivas get orders from a central computer that directs the robots to specific areas of a warehouse where they retrieve goods and bring them back to a central location for packaging.

side, and lighter items—like boxes of potato chips—on the other. To fill orders, custom software supplies fork-lift drivers with printouts telling them which items to pick first and how to stack them on a pallet based on the weight of the items, their location in the distribution center, and their ultimate destination. After calculating delivery routes that optimize time and fuel use, the software also provides instructions for loading the trucks.

Sysco delivers more than food to its customers; it offers recipes, insights on consumer trends, and food handling suggestions via the web at www.syscotabletop.com. Sysco also has more than 200 chefs who share their expertise and cost-saving tips with business customers. Together Sysco's combination of efficient operations, service and support, and quality products provide excellent value for its target market.[27]

Direct store delivery skips the distribution center

Some firms prefer to skip the distribution center altogether and ship products directly from where they are manufactured to retail stores. This may move products more quickly, but usually at a higher cost. Frito-Lay uses this approach. It handles more than 10,000 direct delivery routes to more than 200,000 small-store customers. The route drivers build close relationships with the many small retailers. That helps Frito-Lay better understand end consumers and adapt product mixes to particular stores. These extra services result in more shelf space and higher prices at the small stores.[28]

Managers must be innovative to provide customers with superior value

More competitive markets, improved technology, coordination among firms, and efficient new distribution centers are bringing big improvements to the PD area. Yet the biggest challenges may be more basic. As we've emphasized here, physical distribution activities transcend departmental, corporate, and even national boundaries. So taking advantage of ways to improve often requires cooperation all along the channel system. Too often, such cooperation doesn't exist—and changing ingrained ways of doing things is hard. But marketing managers who push for innovations in these areas are likely to win customers away from firms and whole channel systems that are stuck doing things in the old way.[29]

CONCLUSION

This chapter explained the major logistics activities and how they contribute to the value of products by getting them to the place that customers want or need them. *If* the distribution customer service level meets their needs and can be provided at a reasonable cost, customers may not even think about the logistics activities that occur behind the scenes. But if products are not available when and where they need to be, a strategy will fail. So decisions in these areas are an important part of Place and marketing strategy planning.

We emphasized the relation between customer service level, transporting, and storing. The physical distribution concept focuses on coordinating all the storing, transporting, and product-handling activities into a smoothly working system—to deliver the desired service level and customer value at the lowest total cost.

Marketing managers often want to improve service and may select a higher-cost alternative to improve their marketing mix. The total cost approach might reveal that it is possible both to reduce costs and to improve customer service—perhaps by working closely with other members of the supply chain.

We discussed various modes of transporting and their advantages and disadvantages. We also discussed ways to reduce inventory costs. For example, distribution centers are an important way to cut storing and handling costs, and computerized information links—within firms and among firms in the channel—are increasingly important in blending all of the logistics activities into a smooth-running system.

Effective marketing managers make important strategy decisions about physical distribution. Creative strategy decisions may result in lower PD costs while maintaining or improving the customer service level. And production-oriented competitors may not even understand what is happening.

KEY TERMS

LO 11.8

logistics, *280*
physical distribution (PD), *280*
customer service level, *281*
physical distribution (PD) concept, *283*
total cost approach, *284*
supply chain, *286*
electronic data interchange (EDI), *287*
transporting, *288*
containerization, *292*
piggyback service, *292*
storing, *293*
inventory, *293*
private warehouses, *295*
public warehouses, *295*
distribution center, *296*

QUESTIONS AND PROBLEMS

1. Explain how adjusting the customer service level could improve a marketing mix. Illustrate.
2. Briefly explain which aspects of customer service you think would be most important for a producer that sells fabric to a firm that manufactures furniture.
3. Briefly describe a purchase you made where the customer service level had an effect on the product you selected or where you purchased it.
4. Discuss the types of trade-offs involved in PD costs, service levels, and sales.
5. Give an example of why it is important for different firms in the supply chain to coordinate logistics activities.
6. Discuss some of the ways computers are being used to improve PD decisions.
7. Explain why a just-in-time delivery system would require a supplier to pay attention to quality control. Give an example to illustrate your points.
8. Discuss the problems a supplier might encounter in using a just-in-time delivery system with a customer in a foreign country.
9. Review the list of factors that affect PD service levels in Exhibit 11-3. Indicate which ones are most likely to be improved by EDI links between a supplier and its customers.
10. Explain the total cost approach and why it may cause conflicts in some firms. Give examples of how conflicts might occur between different departments.
11. Discuss the relative advantages and disadvantages of railroads, trucks, and airlines as transporting methods.
12. Discuss why economies of scale in transportation might encourage a producer to include a regional merchant wholesaler in the channel of distribution for its consumer product.
13. Discuss some of the ways that air transportation can change other aspects of a Place system.
14. Explain which transportation mode would probably be most suitable for shipping the following goods to a large Los Angeles department store:
    a. 300 pounds of Maine lobster.
    b. 15 pounds of screwdrivers from Ohio.

c. Three dining room tables from High Point, North Carolina.
d. 500 high-fashion dresses from the fashion district in Paris.
e. A 10,000-pound shipment of exercise equipment from Germany.
f. 600,000 pounds of various appliances from Evansville, Indiana.

15. Indicate the nearest location where you would expect to find large storage facilities. What kinds of products would be stored there? Why are they stored there instead of some other place?
16. When would a producer or intermediary find it desirable to use a public warehouse rather than a private warehouse? Illustrate, using a specific product or situation.
17. Discuss the distribution center concept. Is this likely to eliminate the storing function of conventional wholesalers? Is it applicable to all products? If not, cite several examples.
18. Clearly differentiate between a warehouse and a distribution center. Explain how a specific product would be handled differently by each.
19. If a retailer operates only from a website and ships all orders by UPS, is it freed from the logistics issues that face traditional retailers? Explain your thinking.

CREATING MARKETING PLANS

The Marketing Plan Coach software on the text website includes a sample marketing plan for Hillside Veterinary Clinic. Look through the "Marketing Strategy" section. To provide veterinary care to pets, Hillside needs to have a variety of medical supplies on hand. To handle that, it relies on deliveries from suppliers and its own inventory decisions. It also sells some retail pet products to customers, and that requires a separate set of decisions about how it will handle inventory.

a. What logistics issues related to medical supplies should Hillside consider? Can you think of ways in which delivery from its suppliers or its own inventory decisions will be important in its ability to help its patients?
b. With respect to the retail pet products that Hillside sells, what level of customer service should customers expect?
c. What issues are involved in storage of pet supplies?

SUGGESTED CASES

16. J&J Lumber 26. Abundant Harvest

COMPUTER-AIDED PROBLEM

11. TOTAL DISTRIBUTION COST

Proto Company has been producing various items made of plastic. It recently added a line of plain plastic cards that other firms (such as banks and retail stores) will imprint to produce credit cards. Proto offers its customers the plastic cards in different colors, but they all sell for $40 per box of 1,000. Tom Phillips, Proto's product manager for this line, is considering two possible physical distribution systems. He estimates that if Proto uses airfreight, transportation costs will be $7.50 a box, and its cost of carrying inventory will be 5 percent of total annual sales dollars. Alternatively, Proto could ship by rail for $2 a box. But rail transport will require renting space at four regional warehouses—at $26,000 a year each. Inventory carrying cost with this system will be 10 percent of total annual sales dollars. Phillips prepared a spreadsheet to compare the cost of the two alternative physical distribution systems.

a. If Proto Company expects to sell 20,000 boxes a year, what are the total physical distribution costs for each of the systems?
b. If Phillips can negotiate cheaper warehouse space for the rail option so that each warehouse costs only $20,000 per year, which physical distribution system has the lowest overall cost?
c. Proto's finance manager predicts that interest rates are likely to be lower during the next marketing plan year and suggests that Tom Phillips use inventory carrying costs of 4 percent for airfreight and 7.5 percent for railroads (with warehouse cost at $20,000 each). If interest rates are in fact lower, which alternative would you suggest? Why?

12 CHAPTER TWELVE

Retailers, Wholesalers, and Their Strategy Planning

From 1843 to 1855 Rowland Hussey Macy opened—and closed—four general stores that specialized in "dry goods," mainly textiles and ready-to-wear clothing. Learning from those early failures, Macy finally hit on a formula that worked with the R.H. Macy Dry Goods store he opened in New York City in 1858. Macy was soon adding departments with new product lines and moving into nearby buildings. Resembling a collection of specialty shops, Macy's became one of the world's first department stores. Innovative from the start, Macy's was the first to use the store Santa Claus and illuminated window displays to lure customers into its stores. In 1902 the original store moved uptown to Herald Square, where it remains today as the flagship in the 800+ store Macy's chain.

Department stores proved to be popular with American shoppers; the concept was in the growth stage of its life-cycle for more than a century before sales topped out in the 1970s. Department stores' large product assortment and attentive customer service appealed to many customers. Department stores typically located in city centers or regional malls and pulled customers from a wide geographic area. In the early 1900s, Sears and Marshall Fields branched out with mail-order catalogs and brought the department store to rural America. In the 1970s, department stores began to lose market share; first to mass-merchandisers and later to supercenters like Target and Walmart, which offered convenient neighborhood locations and lower prices. To compete, department stores pushed sale prices, but profits declined and customer service suffered. Many thought the arrival of Internet retailing in the late 1990s signaled the death knell for department stores. But some department stores successfully adapted their marketing mixes, making them relevant again. Macy's has been particularly successful.

Macy's revival stems from changes across its marketing strategy. Macy's started by clearly defining its target markets. Macy's saw an opportunity when research showed teens and the slightly older millennials (age 19–30) spend $60 billion dollars a year and 50 percent more per person than the average population. Macy's defined four distinct target markets: teen girls, teen boys, millennial women, and millennial men. Each segment has unique needs and shopping behaviors.

High-school-age teens want stylish clothes and spend a lot of time online. So Macy's connects with them through Tumblr, Pinterest, Facebook, text messages, and the mstylelab.com microsite. Macy's mstylelab.com features a mix of content that appeals to teens: videos with the latest fashion trends, online shopping, and m.mix, where teens can discover new bands, download music, and get tips on decorating a college dorm room. Macy's also developed exclusive clothing lines for this market, including Material Girl apparel from Madonna and a Glee-themed line based on the popular television program. In the store this group prefers to "self-serve," so Macy's trained its sales staff to be available but not pushy with teens.

The millennial market might be found in college, starting a career, or maybe having a family. These customers prefer to hear from Macy's via e-mail, catalog, or direct mail. Macy's created its Impulse Shop with products for this group. This target market favors fast-fashion retailers like Zara and H&M that produce a collection of clothes and get it into a store in just a couple of weeks. Macy's needed to do the same and geared up its supply chain to respond quickly to fashion trends. These customers appreciate suggestions and advice from Macy's salespeople. So in the Impulse Shop at Macys.com, a black handbag might be suggested to complement the black shoes a shopper puts into her shopping cart. And in the store, Macy's salespeople act friendlier and offer more suggestions to millennials.

Macy's further focuses on customers with the My Macy's program, which provides customers with more personalized shopping experiences. One element of this strategy involves analyzing data from 2.9 billion transactions to tailor product assortment to each store. To illustrate, you find more white leather couches in Miami, boys' formal wear in Utah, and swimsuits at stores near water parks.

My Macy's also mines customer data to adapt marketing communications to *individual* customers. Macy's customer relationship management database includes a great deal of insight about each customer: previous purchases, responses to e-mails, online shopping behavior, and other information collected over time. Macy's uses this data to customize promotions in e-mails and direct mail. For example, Macy's sent out 30,000 different versions of a direct mailing; the pieces varied from 32 to 76 pages long and featured merchandise designed to appeal to each customer. As a result, footwear fanatics saw more shoes and moms saw more kids' clothes.

Macy's recognizes that teens and millennials are multichannel shoppers, and Macy's wants to be in all those channels. Macy's developed its "omnichannel" strategy to create a seamless shopping experience across its mobile, online, and brick-and-mortar stores. So when the shoes a customer loves at the store are not in stock in their size, they are delivered to the customer's home two days later direct from Macys.com. Or when a customer finds the color of a comforter she ordered with the Macy's smartphone app doesn't match the drapes in her bedroom, she can return it to her local Macy's store.

Macy's has invested in software, RFID, and training to ensure accurate information on inventory in each warehouse and store. Macy's even uses some of its stores as satellite warehouses, delivering orders at Macys.com from a store closest to the customer. Macy's hopes this system will allow same-day delivery on orders from Macys.com.

In retail, not everything goes out the front door. Sometimes even Macy's One-Day Sale prices don't move the merchandise. When that happens, or when returns cannot be re-stocked, other channels of distribution are needed. Macy's Wholesale sells pallet loads of returned clothing and unsold merchandise to clearance centers or other countries.

Through a blend of online, mobile, and 800+ stores, an ability to transform big data into personalized shopping experiences, and a focus on the needs of its teen and millennial target markets, Macy's is leading a department store revival. Still, Macy's retail faces fierce competition from department stores like Nordstrom and Kohl's, specialty shops like Buckle and American Eagle, online stores like Zappos, and supercenters like Target. To keep growing, Macy's will have to continue adapting its marketing mix to meet its customers' needs.[1]

LEARNING OBJECTIVES

Retail and wholesale organizations exist as members of marketing channel systems. But they also do their own strategy planning as they compete for target customers. As the Macy's case shows, these firms make decisions about Product, Place, Promotion, and Price. This chapter overviews the strategy planning decisions of different types of retailers and wholesalers. The chapter shows how retailing and wholesaling are evolving—to give you a sense of how things may change in the future.

When you finish this chapter you should be able to:

1 understand how retailers plan their marketing strategies.

2 know about the many kinds of retailers that work with producers and wholesalers as members of channel systems.

3 understand how retailers evolve, including the roles of technology, scrambled merchandising, and the "wheel of retailing."

4 see why size or belonging to a chain can be important to a retailer.

5 understand some of the differences in retailing in different nations.

6 know what progressive wholesalers are doing to modernize their operations and marketing strategies.

7 know the various kinds of merchant and agent wholesalers and the strategies they use.

8 understand important new terms (shown in red).

Retailers and Wholesalers Plan Their Own Strategies

LO 12.1

In Chapter 10, we discussed the vital role that retailers and wholesalers perform in channel systems. Now we'll look at the decisions that retailers and wholesalers make in developing their own strategies. See Exhibit 12-1. The chapter begins with a discussion of strategy planning for retailers. Retailers must create a marketing mix that provides value for a target market. We also discuss how retailing has evolved and where it stands today, including some important international differences. Chapter 12 concludes by considering strategy planning by different types of wholesalers.

Exhibit 12–1 Marketing Strategy Planning for Retailers and Wholesalers

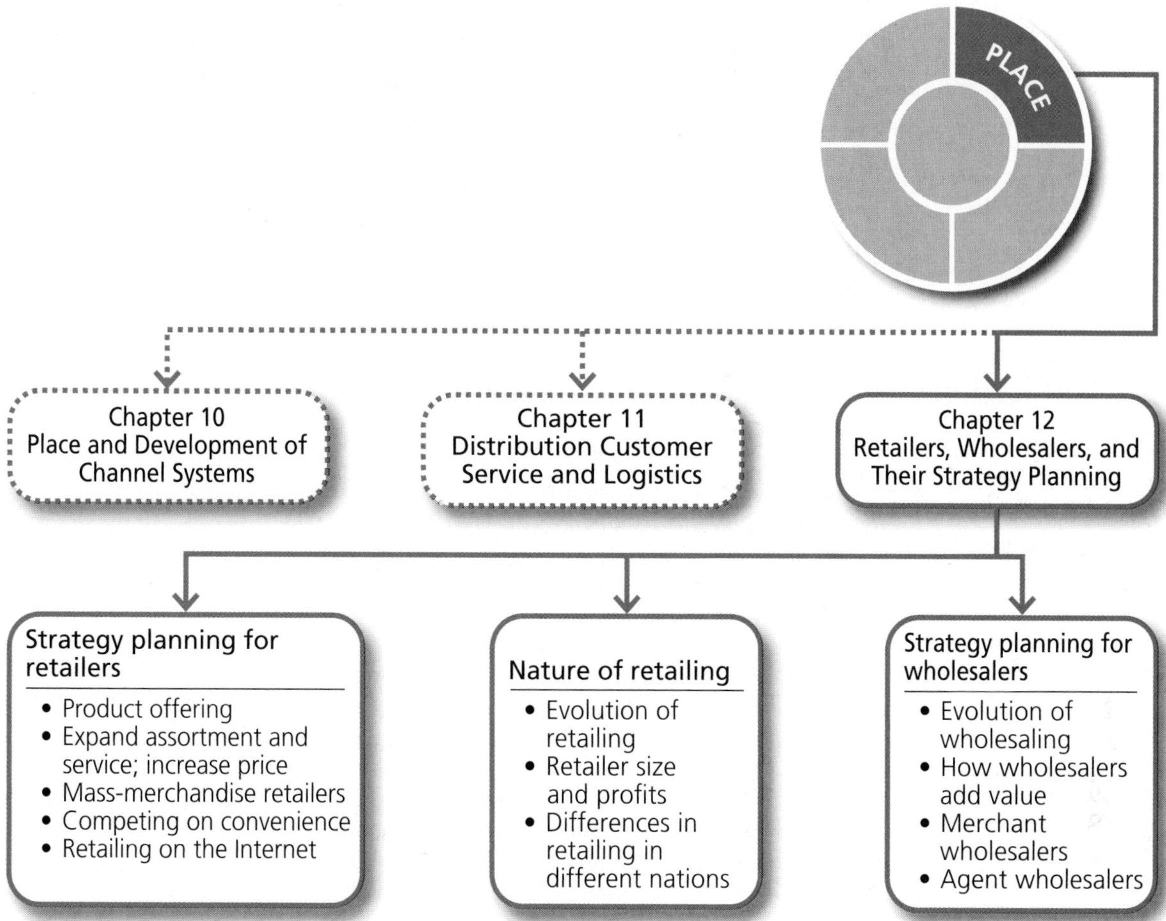

Understand how retailing and wholesaling are evolving

Understanding the how and why of past changes in retailing and wholesaling will help you know what to expect in the future. It will also make it clear that it is the whole strategy, not just one aspect of it, that ultimately is a success or failure. This may seem obvious, but it's a point that many people have ignored—at great cost.

Consider the dramatic changes prompted by the Internet. A few years ago many people were proclaiming that it would quickly change everything we thought about successful retailing. Yet many creative ideas for online retailing bombed precisely because managers of dot-coms failed to understand why retailing has evolved as it has. For many consumers and many types of purchases, it won't matter that an online retailer posts low prices for an incredible assortment if there's no way to get customer service, products are not actually available, or it's a hassle to return a green shirt that looked blue on the website.

So in this chapter we'll focus on decisions that apply to all retailers and wholesalers, while highlighting how their strategies are changing.

The Nature of Retailing

Retailing covers all of the activities involved in the sale of products to final consumers. Retailers range from large chains of specialized stores, like Toys "R" Us, to individual merchants like the woman who sells baskets from an open stall in the central market in Ibadan, Nigeria. Some retailers operate from stores and others operate without a store—by selling online, on TV, with a printed catalog, from vending machines, or even in consumers' homes. Most retailers sell physical goods produced by someone else. But in the case of service retailing—like dry cleaning, fast food, tourist attractions, online bank accounts, or one-hour photo processing—the retailer is also the producer. Because they serve individual consumers, even the largest retailers face the challenge of handling small transactions. And the total number of transactions with consumers is much greater than at other channel levels.

Retailing is crucial to consumers in every macro-marketing system. For example, consumers spend about \$4.5 *trillion* (that's \$4,500,000,000,000!) a year buying goods and services from U.S. retailers.

The nature of retailing and its rate of change are generally related to the stage and speed of a country's economic development. In the United States, retailing is more varied and dynamic than in most other countries. By studying the U.S. system, you will better understand where retailing is headed in other parts of the world.

Planning a Retailer's Strategy

Retailers interact directly with final consumers—so strategy planning is critical to their survival. If a retailer loses a customer to a competitor, the retailer is the one who suffers. Producers and wholesalers still make *their* sale regardless of which retailer sells the product.

Consumers have reasons for buying from particular retailers

Different consumers prefer different kinds of retailers. But many retailers either don't know or don't care why. All too often, beginning retailers just rent a store and assume customers will show up. As a result, in the United States about three-fourths of new retailing ventures fail during the first year. Even an established retailer will quickly lose if its customers find a better way to meet their needs. To avoid this fate, a retailer should carefully identify possible target markets and try to understand why these people buy where they do. In this way, the retailer can fine-tune its marketing mix to the needs of specific target markets.[2]

Retailers make decisions about the whole marketing mix

Like other organizations, retailers make marketing mix decisions about Product, Place, Promotion, and Price. See Exhibit 12-2. For retailers, some of the Product decisions include choices about what products to carry, how much assortment to offer, and which services to support. Place decisions include where stores will be located—online and/or brick-and-mortar, the number of stores, as well as store layout and design. Promotion involves letting customers know about the business and the goods and services offered through its in-store and out-of-store signage, advertising, salespeople, publicity (including social media), and other approaches. Price decisions are varied as well, and include, for

The Zappos product line originally included different shoes. It has since expanded its product assortment to include clothing and accessories. Online retailer Fab sends daily e-mails to its customers with samples of its ever-changing product assortment.

Exhibit 12–2 Examples of Marketing Strategy Decisions for Retailers

Product
- Product selection (width and depth of assortment, brands, quality)
- After-sale service
- Special services (special orders, entertainment, gift wrap)

Place
- Physical stores and/or sales over the Internet
- Number and location of stores
- Shopping atmosphere (comfort, safety)
- Store size, layout, and design
- Store hours

Price
- Credit cards—whether to offer a store card
- Discount policies
- Frequency and level of sales prices
- Charge (or not) for delivery or other services

Promotion
- Advertising
- Publicity (Facebook, Twitter, Pinterest)
- Salespeople (number and training)
- Helpful information (demonstrations, displays, online videos, online reviews)

example, whether to accept credit cards or charge for delivery, and how frequently to offer products at discounted sales prices.

Strategy requires carefully setting policies

In developing a strategy, a retailer should consciously make decisions that set policies on *all* of these marketing mix issues. Each of them can impact a customer's view of the costs and benefits of choosing that retailer. The combination of these marketing mix decisions differentiates one retailer's offering from another. These decisions affect its positioning in the market—how customers think about the retailer compared to others. A retailer must consider its target customers' economic, social, and emotional needs. If the combination doesn't provide superior value to some target market, the retailer will fail.

Consider the marketing strategies for two very different, yet successful, shoe retailers. Usually located in malls and shopping centers, Payless ShoeSource's primary target market is families looking for moderately priced shoes. While its shoes can be ordered online, most sales occur in one of its 4,500 brick-and-mortar stores. The stores have a self-service design that encourages customers to select and try on shoes without the help of a salesperson. Even though each store carries an average of 500 styles and 6,700 pairs of shoes—including dress, casual, boots, and athletic—for men, women, and children, Payless' product line is relatively narrow for a shoe retailer and includes mostly lesser-known brands. Payless' advertising in local newspapers emphasizes value and usually promotes its low prices. Further, Payless' Facebook page, with more than 600,000 "likes," keeps its most ardent fans informed of the next deal.[3]

Zappos.com offers a different marketing mix that appeals to a different target market. Zappos operates several online storefronts in addition to Zappos—including Zappos Couture with high fashion shoes and Zappos Running. While Zappos recently added clothing, handbags, housewares, and beauty supplies to its product assortment, its core product line remains shoes. Zappos' wide product line includes more than 150,000 styles and 1,400 brands—including many styles in well-known brands like Nike, Timberland, and Bandolino. Because shoppers are understandably reluctant to buy shoes without first trying them on, Zappos devotes a whole page to each shoe. There it provides eight or more photos from different angles, customer reviews, videos, and detailed descriptions. Zappos also offers free shipping and free returns—for up to 365 days after purchase! The retailer wins praise for its customer service, available 24/7 on the phone or the web. That service helps build positive word-of-mouth for Zappos and more than 75 percent of its customers are repeat buyers. It has a relatively small budget for its advertising on television, print, online, and the bottom of the plastic bins in airport security lines. A free monthly digital magazine for tablet computers, *Zappos Now,* keeps customers informed about fashion trends and offers tips about Zappos products. CEO and author Tony Hsieh's Twitter feed has more than 2.5 million followers. Zappos and Payless ShoeSource developed very different marketing mixes, but each keeps target customers coming back.[4]

Different types of retailers emphasize different strategies

Retailers have an almost unlimited number of ways in which to alter their offerings—their marketing mixes—to appeal to a target market. Because of all the variations, it's oversimplified to classify retailers and their strategies on the basis of a single characteristic—such as merchandise, services, sales volume, or even whether they operate in cyberspace. But a good place to start is by considering basic types of retailers and some differences in their strategies.

Conventional Retailers—Try to Avoid Price Competition

LO 12.2

Single-line, limited-line retailers specialize by product

About 150 years ago, **general stores**—which carried anything they could sell in reasonable volume—were the main retailers in the United States. But with the growing number of consumer products after the Civil War, general stores couldn't offer enough variety in all their traditional lines. So some stores began specializing in dry goods, apparel, furniture, or groceries.

Now most *conventional* retailers are **single-line** or **limited-line stores**—stores that specialize in certain lines of related products rather than a wide assortment. Many specialize not only in a single line, such as clothing, but also in a *limited line* within the broader line. Within the clothing line, a retailer might carry *only* shoes, formal wear, or even neckties but offer depth in that limited line.

Single-line, limited-line stores are being squeezed

The main advantage of limited-line retailers is that they can satisfy some target markets better. Perhaps some are just more conveniently located. But most adjust to suit specific customers. They build a relationship with their customers and earn a position as *the* place to shop for a certain type of product. But these retailers face the costly problem of having to stock some slow-moving items in order to satisfy their target markets. Many of these stores are small—with high expenses relative to sales. So they try to keep their prices up by avoiding competition on identical products.

Conventional retailers like this have been around for a long time and are still found in every community. They are a durable lot and clearly satisfy some people's needs. In fact, in

Exhibit 12–3 Types of Retailers and the Nature of Their Offerings (*with examples*)

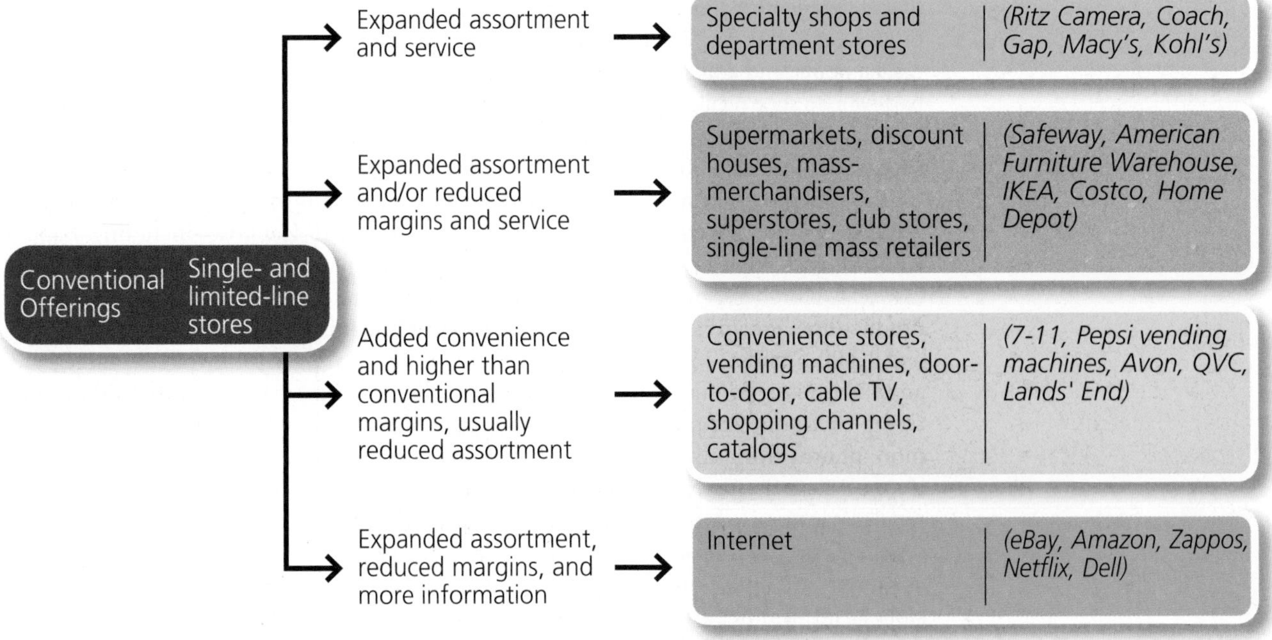

most countries conventional retailers still handle the vast majority of all retailing sales. However, this situation is changing fast. Nowhere is the change clearer than in the United States. Conventional retailers are being squeezed by retailers who modify their mixes in the various ways suggested in Exhibit 12-3. Let's look closer at some of these other types of retailers.

Expand Assortment and Service—To Compete at a High Price

Specialty shops usually sell shopping products

A **specialty shop**—a type of conventional limited-line store—is usually small and has a distinct "personality." Specialty shops sell special types of shopping products, such as high-quality sporting goods, exclusive clothing, baked goods, or even antiques. They aim at a carefully defined target market by offering a unique product assortment, knowledgeable salesclerks, and better service.

Catering to certain types of customers whom the management and salespeople know well simplifies buying, speeds turnover, and cuts costs due to obsolescence and style changes. Specialty shops probably will continue to be a part of the retailing scene as long as customers have varied tastes and the money to satisfy them.[5]

Department stores combine many limited-line stores and specialty shops

Department stores are larger stores that are organized into many separate departments and offer many product lines. Each department is like a separate limited-line store and handles a wide variety of shopping products, such as men's wear or housewares. They are usually strong in customer services, including credit, merchandise return, delivery, and sales help.

Department stores are still a major force in big cities. Although they have staged a bit of a comeback recently, in the United States, the number of department stores, the average sales per store, and their share of retail business has declined significantly since the 1970s. Well-run limited-line stores compete with good service and often carry the same brands. In the United States and many other countries, mass-merchandising retailers have posed an even bigger threat.[6]

Evolution of Mass-Merchandising Retailers

LO 12.3

Mass-merchandising is different from conventional retailing

The conventional retailers just discussed think that demand in their area is fixed—and they have a "buy low and sell high" philosophy. Many modern retailers reject these ideas. Instead, they accept the **mass-merchandising concept**—which says that retailers should offer low prices to get faster turnover and greater sales volumes—by appealing to larger markets. The mass-merchandising concept applies to many types of retailers, including both those that operate stores and those that sell online. But to understand mass-merchandising better, let's look at its evolution from the development of supermarkets and discounters to modern mass-merchandisers like Walmart in the United States, Tesco in the U.K., and Amazon.com on the Internet.

Supermarkets started the move to mass-merchandising

From a world view, most food stores are relatively small limited-line operations. Shopping for food is inconvenient and expensive. Many Italians, for example, still go to one shop for pasta, another for meat, and yet another for milk. This may seem outdated, but many of the world's consumers don't have access to **supermarkets**—large stores specializing in groceries with self-service and wide assortments.

The basic idea for supermarkets developed in the United States during the 1930s Depression. Some innovators introduced self-service to cut costs but provided a broad assortment in large bare-bones stores. Profits came from large-volume sales, not from high traditional markups.[7]

Modern supermarkets carry 47,000 product items and stores average around 47,000 square feet. To be called a supermarket, a store must have annual sales of at least $2 million, but the average supermarket sells about $17 million a year. In the United States, there are about 35,000 supermarkets, and in most areas they are at the saturation level and competition is intense. In many other countries, however, they are just becoming a force.[8]

Although U.S. supermarkets were the first mass-merchandisers, the mass-merchandising concept is now used by many retailers. Single-line mass-merchandisers like Office Depot offer selections and prices that make it difficult for conventional retailers to compete.

Supermarkets are planned for maximum efficiency. Scanners at checkout make it possible to carefully analyze the sales of each item and allocate more shelf space to faster-moving and higher-profit items. *Survival* depends on efficiency. Net profits in supermarkets usually run a thin 1 percent of sales *or less!*

Some supermarket operators have opened "super warehouse" stores. These 50,000-to 100,000-square-foot stores carry more items than supermarkets. These efficiently run, warehouse-like facilities can sell groceries at up to 25 percent less than the typical supermarket price.

Discount houses upset some conventional retailers

After World War II, some retailers started to focus on discount prices. These **discount houses** offered "hard goods" (cameras, TVs, and appliances) at substantial price cuts to customers who would go to the discounter's low-rent store, pay cash, and take care of any service or repair problems themselves. These retailers sold at 20 to 30 percent off the list price being charged by conventional retailers.

In the early 1950s, with war shortages finally over, manufacturer brands became more available. The discount houses were able to get any brands they wanted and to offer wider assortments. At this stage, many discounters turned respectable—moving to better locations and offering more services and guarantees. It was from these origins that today's mass-merchandisers developed.

Mass-merchandisers are more than discounters

Mass-merchandisers are large self-service stores with many departments that emphasize "soft goods" (housewares, clothing, and fabrics) and staples (like health and beauty aids) but still follow the discount house's emphasis on lower margins to get faster turnover. Mass-merchandisers, like Walmart and Target, have checkout counters in the front of the store and little sales help on the floor. Today, the average mass-merchandiser has nearly 60,000 square feet of floor space, but many new stores are 100,000 square feet or more. Mass-merchandisers grew rapidly—and they've become the primary place to shop for many frequently purchased consumer products.

By itself, Walmart handles 30 percent or more of the total national sales for whole categories of products. Even if you don't shop at Walmart, Sam Walton (who started the company)

has had a big impact on your life. He pioneered the use of high-tech systems to create electronic links with suppliers and take inefficiencies out of retailing logistics. That brought down costs *and* prices and attracted more customers, which gave Walmart even more clout in pressuring manufacturers to lower prices. Other retailers are still scrambling to catch up.[9]

Supercenters meet all routine needs

Some supermarkets and mass-merchandisers have moved toward becoming **supercenters (hypermarkets)**—very large stores that try to carry not only food and drug items but all goods and services that the consumer purchases *routinely.* These superstores look a lot like a combination of the supermarkets, drugstores, and mass-merchandisers from which they have evolved, but the concept is different. A supercenter is trying to meet *all* the customer's routine needs at a low price. Supercenter operators include Meijer, Fred Meyer, Target, and Walmart. In fact, Walmart's supercenters have turned it into the largest food retailer in the United States.

Supercenters average more than 150,000 square feet and carry about 50,000 items. Their assortment in one place is convenient, but many time-pressured consumers think that the crowds, lines, and "wandering around" time in the store are not. Some supercenters have responded by reducing product line depth. For example, Walmart recently decided that it didn't need to carry 24 tape measures, and now carries just four.[10]

New mass-merchandising formats keep coming

The warehouse club is another retailing format that quickly gained popularity. Sam's Club and Costco are two of the largest. Consumers usually pay an annual membership fee to shop in these large, no-frills facilities. Among the 3,500 items per store, they carry food, appliances, yard tools, tires, and other items that many consumers see as homogeneous shopping items and want at the lowest possible price. The growth of these clubs has also been fueled by sales to small-business customers. That's why some people refer to these outlets as wholesale clubs. However, when half or more of a firm's sales are to final consumers, it is classified as a retailer, not a wholesaler.[11]

Single-line mass-merchandisers are coming on strong

Since 1980, many retailers focusing on single product lines have adopted the mass-merchandisers' approach with great success. Toys "R" Us pioneered this trend. Similarly, IKEA (furniture), Home Depot (home improvements), Best Buy (electronics), and Staples (office supplies) attract large numbers of customers with their large assortment and low prices in a specific product category. These stores are called *category killers* because it's so hard for less specialized retailers to compete.[12]

Some Retailers Focus on Added Convenience

Convenience (food) stores must have the right assortment

Convenience (food) stores are a convenience-oriented variation of the conventional limited-line food stores. Instead of expanding their assortment, however, convenience stores limit their stock to pickup or fill-in items like bread, milk, beer, and eat-on-the-go snacks. Many also sell gas. Stores such as 7-Eleven and Stop-N-Go aim to fill consumers' needs between trips to a supermarket, and many of them are competing with fast-food outlets. They offer convenience, not assortment, and often charge prices 10 to 20 percent higher than nearby supermarkets. However, as many other retailers have expanded their hours, intense competition is driving down convenience store prices and profits.[13]

Vending machines are convenient

Automatic vending is selling and delivering products through vending machines. Vending machine sales account for only about 1.5 percent of total U.S. retail sales. Yet for some target markets this retailing method can't be ignored.

While vending machines can be costly to operate, consumers like their convenience. Traditionally, soft drinks, candy bars, and snack foods have been sold by vending machines. Now some higher-margin products are beginning to use this channel. In the United States, Standard Hotels use poolside vending machines to sell bathing suits.[14]

Stores come to the home—in person, on television, and in catalogs

In-home shopping in the United States started in the pioneer days with **door-to-door selling**—a salesperson going directly to the consumer's home. Variations on this approach are still important for firms like Amway Global and Mary Kay. It meets some consumers' need for convenient personal attention. While gaining popularity in some international markets like China, it now accounts for less than 1 percent of retail sales in the United States.

Customers can also shop at home by watching cable television channels dedicated to shopping, and then calling in their orders by phone. QVC and Home Shopping Network operate in the United States, Japan, and some European countries. Similarly, catalogs allow customers to page through merchandise and place orders on the phone or online. Deliveries will usually occur a few days later, handled by shippers UPS or FedEx. Both of these home shopping methods use a multichannel approach by adding a website.

Internet retailing has quickly become the most popular way to shop at home (and sometimes at work). Let's take a closer look at online retailing.[15]

Many firms have turned to automatic vending because target customers appreciate the convenience. U*tiques interactive touch sensitive vending machines offer luxury personal-care items. Redbox offers a wide range of movies.

Retailing on the Internet

Internet retail is growing rapidly

Internet retailing is still in the growth stage. In 1997, consumers spent about $2.7 billion on the Internet. To put that in perspective, it took about 3 percent of Walmart's stores to rack up the same sales. By 2015 that number will top $300 billion and grow to 9% of all retail sales in the U.S. In some categories, the share of online sales is even greater; more than half of all computer hardware and software and more than a quarter of all books are sold online. Owners of tablet computers like the iPad seem to especially enjoy online shopping. Online shopping and retailing are different, and it's useful to examine how online retailers are adapting their strategies.[16]

Online costs for retailers and customers—higher and lower

With no storefront and limited sales help, online retailers usually have lower operating costs than brick-and-mortar stores. Customers may not have to pay sales taxes either. These advantages lead many online stores to use low prices to attract customers. But because the Internet makes it easy to compare products and prices from different online sellers, price-sensitive shoppers usually choose the store with the lowest price. That puts constant price pressure on those Internet sellers who have not figured out how else to differentiate what they offer.

While customers can find low prices online, sometimes prices aren't what they seem. Many online retailers add high charges for handling and delivery. Returns and exchanges can create more expense and hassle. Customer concerns about fraud and security create hidden costs. Some customers worry about how an online retailer handles personal information like e-mail addresses and credit card numbers. Worse yet, a fly-by-night operator may take a customer's money and deliver inferior goods or not make a delivery at all.

The most successful online retailers have found ways to overcome these customer concerns. Many now offer free delivery. Some offer free exchanges or returns and pack bar-coded return labels with the original shipment to make returns easy. Other stores provide excellent customer service and build a good reputation, because word-of-mouth matters online. Organizations like TRUSTe place a seal of approval on sites that meet certain privacy standards. Together these efforts help lower the costs, worries, and hassles of online shopping.

Internet Exercise

Amazon Price Check for iPhone is a smartphone application that allows a shopper in a physical store to use an iPhone to scan a product's bar code and then check prices for the product at Amazon.com. Go to Amazon's website and read about this app (**http://tinyurl.com/4qdw9bt**). How will this type of application affect retailers and their marketing mix decisions? Which types of stores will see Price Check as a threat? How is this an opportunity for Amazon.com?

Online buying—more and less convenient

Traditional thinking about retail stores looked at shopping convenience from the perspective of product assortment and store location. On the Internet, by contrast, a consumer can get to a very wide assortment, perhaps from different sellers, or by clicking from one website to another. Product assortment on the Internet can be almost unlimited. Online stores are also open 24 hours a day, 7 days a week.

But the Internet makes shopping inconvenient in other ways. You have to plan ahead. When you buy something, you've actually just ordered it and you have to wait for delivery. Online retailers try to overcome these disadvantages with faster shipping. In some physical retail stores it can be difficult to get helpful buying information. Many stores don't have well-trained salespeople. With just the click of a mouse, an online shopper can access product descriptions and specifications, photos and videos, and reviews posted by other consumers. Some sites make virtual salesclerks available to chat—online or on the phone—at any time.

However, for some purchases the ultimate information comes from physically inspecting a product before purchase. To try to overcome this limitation, many online stores show photos and videos that demonstrate products. At eyeglass retailer EyeBuyDirect.com, customers can upload a photo of themselves and then see what they look like when they "try on" different eyeglass frames.

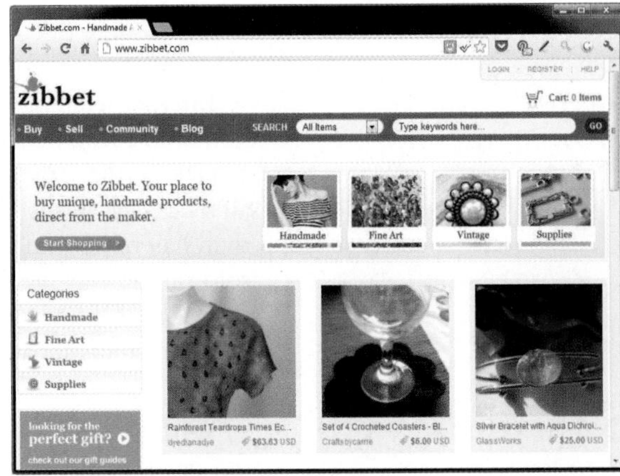

Like brick-and-mortar outlets, online retailers have different strategies. Woot! concentrates on a limited product line, selling only one product per day—usually a piece of computer hardware or an electronic gadget—at a discounted price. Zibbet is an online global marketplace that connects buyers and sellers of handmade goods, fine art, vintage items, and crafting supplies. The site operates like an online craft fair, where thousands of buyers operate their own storefront and buyers can search by various categories.

Showrooming brings channel conflict

Some Internet retail customers have found other ways to get around the challenge of physically inspecting products before buying online. These *multichannel shoppers* use different retailers as they move through the purchase process. For example, a multichannel shopper looking for a new tennis racquet might read consumer reviews of the Wilson Blade tennis racquet at The-Tennis-Store.com, go to a pro shop at a local tennis club to hit some balls with the Blade, and then ultimately purchase the tennis racquet at a steep discount from an online retailer. When consumers go to a brick-and-mortar store to inspect a product (a showroom) and then purchase from an online retailer with a lower price, this practice is called *showrooming*. Smartphone apps make the practice easy, allowing customers to scan products in a retail store and then see prices from across the web.

Battling against showrooming

Stores being used as showrooms don't like losing sales to online discounters. Producers worry that these stores will stop demonstrating their products if customers look but then buy elsewhere. Some target customers will not buy online.

So producers and retailers are working to prevent showrooming. Some manufacturers require all of their retail outlets to maintain a minimum price so customers can't find better deals online. Target asks its suppliers for exclusive products that cannot be found at other stores. Best Buy replaced standard bar codes with Best Buy-only bar codes to foil comparison apps. Unfortunately, these approaches fail to add value for customers and are not likely to be successful in the long run.

Other brick-and-mortar retailers are differentiating and creating value by blending online and offline stores. Some more closely *integrate* their online and brick-and-mortar stores. For example, AceHardware.com has found that more than three-fourths of its online shoppers pick up their orders in-store instead of waiting for shipment. Many Walmart.com shoppers want to pay in cash (maybe because they don't have or want to use a credit card), so they buy online and pick up in their local store. Other stores make returns more convenient by allowing online customers to drop off returns at their physical stores.

Kohl's uses its online presence to *supplement* its product assortment with more merchandise as compared to what customers find in the physical Kohl's location in their city. An in-store kiosk gives customers access to Kohl's more extensive online inventory and lets them place an order for home delivery.[17]

Where to go to buy an unpopular product

A local Borders bookstore that carries 100,000 book titles seems overwhelming. Yet at Amazon.com online shoppers can choose from over 7 million. A Walmart stocks about 4,000 best-selling CD titles, but the iTunes "jukebox" has more than 11 million songs for download. Does it really make sense for online stores to offer assortments that are so much larger?

Part of the answer to the assortment question relates to the cost of shelf space. Retailers with nice facilities and ample parking in high-traffic locations have a high cost per square foot of shelf space. Even if the retailer sells products at low prices, the store will draw customers from a limited geographic area; there would be little demand for less popular products. With high costs and limited demand it makes sense for the store to carry only the products that are the most in demand (popular) with the local target market. A larger store with more unpopular products would run up inventory carrying costs.

The cost to store inventory is usually a lot lower for an online retailer with a warehouse somewhere off the beaten path. Plus an online retailer can draw customers from across the country—or around the world—and added together they might be a large market for unpopular products. After all, when customers who want an "unpopular" choice can't find it at a local retail store, they are likely to look for it online. So, an online retailer's ability to offer a greater assortment is often a key source of competitive advantage. Many online retailers have found that sales of lots of unpopular products add up to big bucks. At Amazon.com more than 30 percent of total book sales come from books that are not among the 100,000 most popular titles, and over 25 percent of Netflix DVD rentals are titles outside the top 3,000 found at your local Blockbuster.

To get extra sales from the "unpopular" products, the trick for many online retailers is to help consumers find what they want among the endless "aisles" of choices. For example, ScannerWarehouse.com has more than 200 models of flatbed scanners, but for many customers that much choice is just confusing. To simplify their choice, the site offers customers an easy way to "filter" the list to show, for example, only the scanners that are priced under $100 and that have a document feeder.

In the early days of the Internet many people predicted that online stores would compete primarily on price. Certainly that is true of many. However, some successful online sellers attract customers with wide product selections, tools that help figure out the best choices, and service that encourages customer loyalty.[18]

Online retailers use big data to personalize shopping

Online retailers have access to extensive data about customer shopping behavior. For example, an online retailer can see just how customers move through its website, what information about each product is being consumed (do they watch videos or read reviews?), what competitive products are considered, and what (if anything) is ultimately purchased. Cookies (small data files placed on a customer's computer) can even tell a retailer what a shopper does at a competitor's site and pull information from a customer's Facebook page. All that data offers a retailer a great deal of insight into each of its customers.

The ability to collect and analyze big data in real time (while customers are shopping) gives retailers the opportunity to provide a more personalized shopping experience. So for example, a customer known to have shopped at a competitor's site might be seen as a "price-oriented shopper" and could receive a targeted discount. Knowing that a customer previously purchased a sweater from the store, an online retailer might show more sweaters of a similar style on the front page when the customer returns. When a customer shops for a DVD at Amazon.com, the site makes recommendations for other videos based on that customer's previous purchases and those of movie buyers with similar interests. That intimate knowledge might make such recommendations more relevant. All of these activities provide customers with a shopping experience tailored to their needs and interests.

Why Retailers Evolve and Change

Technology drives retail change

Technology has recently had a big influence on retail evolution. We have already seen how the Internet and the collection and analysis of customers' online activity are changing shopping and retailing, but physical stores are also leveraging technology to improve the in-store shopping experience. Customers' cell phone signals and in-store video cameras can be monitored to better understand how customers move through stores and how long and where they linger in each aisle. Even the video data analysis can be automated and analyzed to better understand how to lay out stores or better serve customers. At Kroger for example, cameras trained on checkout lanes automatically signal a manager when more than two customers are waiting in line. The store manager can then open additional checkout lanes—and the home office can evaluate service levels at every Kroger store.

Careful use of big data can be used to provide customers with more personalized shopping experiences. Stores' CRM databases combine purchase data from customer loyalty cards and credit cards, social information scraped from customers' Facebook pages, and demographic and lifestyle information purchased from outside vendors to develop detailed profiles of each customer. These profiles can be used to tailor relevant marketing messages for each customer. For example, Target stores know when a family is sending a child off to college, and it targets that family with a catalog filled with stuff for decorating a dorm room. A grocery store targets a loyal and valuable customer (and known ice cream lover) with a text message offering a $2 discount on a new flavor of Breyer's ice cream just as they push their cart through the frozen food section.[19]

The wheel of retailing keeps rolling

The **wheel of retailing theory** says that new types of retailers enter the market as low-status, low-margin, low-price operators and then, if successful, evolve into more conventional retailers offering more services with higher operating costs and higher prices. Then they're threatened by new low-status, low-margin, low-price retailers—and the wheel turns again. Department stores, supermarkets, and mass-merchandisers went through this cycle. Some Internet sellers are on this path.

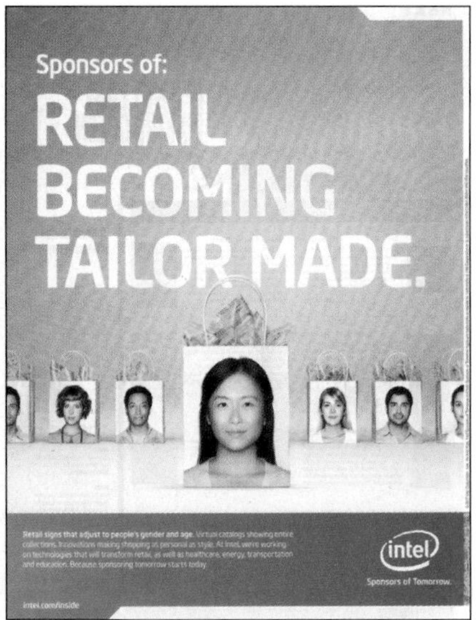

Many retailers use technology to enhance the customers' shopping experience. In South Korea, Homeplus wanted to expand its market share without the high cost of opening new stores. So Homeplus placed "virtual stores" in subway stations in Korean cities. The stores had no actual stock, only images with QR codes. On their way home from work, customers scanned the QR codes of items they wished to purchase. Shortly after they arrived home, their order was delivered. Intel is working on developing signage that recognize the age and gender of customers standing in front of the signs. The signs can then change to a message appropriate for that customer.

The wheel of retailing theory, however, doesn't explain all major retailing developments. Vending machines entered as high-cost, high-margin operations. Convenience food stores are high-priced. Suburban shopping centers don't emphasize low price.

The product assortment at a Publicis Drugstore includes more than medications and newspapers. The store sells jewelry and even caviar as well as other products.

Scrambled merchandising—mixing product lines for higher profits

Conventional retailers tend to specialize by product line. But many modern retailers are moving toward **scrambled merchandising**—carrying any product lines they think they can sell profitably. Supermarkets and drugstores sell anything they can move in volume—panty hose, phone cards, one-hour photo processing, motor oil, potted plants, and computer software. Mass-merchandisers don't just sell everyday items but also cell phones, computer printers, and jewelry.[20]

Product life-cycle concept applies to retailer types too

A retailer with a new idea may have big profits—for a while. But if it's a really good idea, the retailer can count on speedy imitation and a squeeze on profits. Other retailers will copy the new format or scramble their product mix to sell products that offer them higher margins or faster turnover. That puts pressure on the original firm to change or lose its market.

Some conventional retailers are in decline as these life and death cycles continue. Recent innovators, like the Internet merchants, are still in the market growth stage. See Exhibit 12-4. Some retailing formats that are mature in the United States are only now beginning to grow in other countries.

Exhibit 12–4
Retailer Life Cycles—Timing and Years to Market Maturity

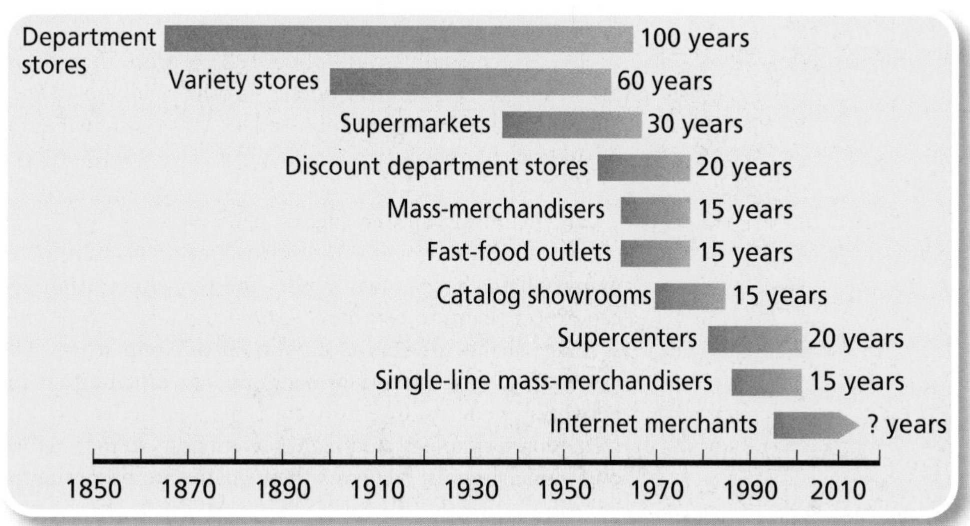

Ethical issues may arise

Most retailers face intense competitive pressure. The desperation that comes with such pressure has pushed some retailers toward questionable marketing practices.

Critics argue, for example, that retailers too often advertise special sale items to bring price-sensitive shoppers into the store or to a website but then don't stock enough to meet demand. Other retailers are criticized for pushing consumers to trade up to more expensive items. What is ethical and unethical in situations like these, however, is subject to debate. Retailers can't always anticipate demand perfectly, and deliveries may not arrive on time. Similarly, trading up may be a sensible part of a strategy—if it's done honestly.

Retailers are gathering and using information to offer customers a more personalized shopping experience, which appears consistent with the marketing concept. But is it ethical to monitor customers' shopping behavior without their knowledge? Do retailers need customers' permission? Does it depend on how this information is used?

The marketing concept should guide firms away from unethical treatment of customers. However, a retailer on the edge of going out of business may lose perspective on the need to satisfy customers in both the short and the long term.[21]

Ethics Question

Farmers in poor countries get very little money for crops—such as coffee, cocoa, and bananas—that they grow for export. Some consumers in prosperous nations are willing to pay retailers higher prices for "fair trade" goods so that the farmers receive greater compensation. But critics question whether fair trade works as it should. For example, Sainsbury's is a popular British food retailer. It was charging $2.74 per pound for "fair trade" bananas versus only $.69 per pound for regular bananas. Farmers, however, only got $.16 extra from that $2.05 price premium. Critics charge that Sainsbury's makes more from the "fair trade" promotion than the farmers it is supposed to help. Many retailers have similar programs. Do you think that Sainsbury's is acting ethically? What do you think Sainsbury's and other similar retailers should do? Why?[22]

Retailer Size and Profits

LO 12.4

A few big retailers do most of the business

The large number of retailers (1,128,112) might suggest that retailing is a field of small businesses. To some extent this is true. When the last census of retailers was published, just over half of all the retail stores in the United States had annual sales of less than $1 million. But that's only part of the story. Those same retailers accounted for less than 6 cents of every $1 in retail sales!

The larger retail stores—those selling more than $5 million annually—do most of the business. Less than 15 percent of the retail stores are this big, yet they account for almost 75 percent of all retail sales. Many small retailers are being squeezed out of business.[23]

Big chains are building market clout

The main way for a retailer to achieve economies of scale is with a corporate chain. A **corporate chain** is a firm that owns and manages more than one store—and often it's many. Chains have grown rapidly and now account for about half of all retail sales. You can expect chains to continue to grow and take business from independent stores.

Large chains use central buying for different stores. They take advantage of quantity discounts and develop their own efficient distribution centers. They can use computer networks to control inventory costs and stock-outs. They may also spread promotion, information technology, and management costs to many stores. Retail chains also have their own dealer brands. Many of these chains are becoming powerful members, or channel captains, in their channel systems. In fact, the most successful of these big chains, like Home Depot and Walmart, control access to so many consumers that they have the clout to dictate almost every detail of relationships with their suppliers.[24]

Independents form chains

Competitive pressure from corporate chains encouraged the development of both cooperative chains and voluntary chains. **Cooperative chains** are retailer-sponsored groups—formed by independent retailers—that run their own buying organizations and conduct joint promotion efforts. Cooperative chains face a tough battle. Some, like True Value Company, are still thriving as they exploit the weaknesses of corporate chains. For example, ads remind consumers that they can receive friendly expert advice at their True Value store.

Voluntary chains are wholesaler-sponsored groups that work with "independent" retailers. Some are linked by contracts stating common operating procedures and requiring the use of common storefront designs, store names, and joint promotion efforts. Examples include SuperValu in groceries and Ace in hardware.

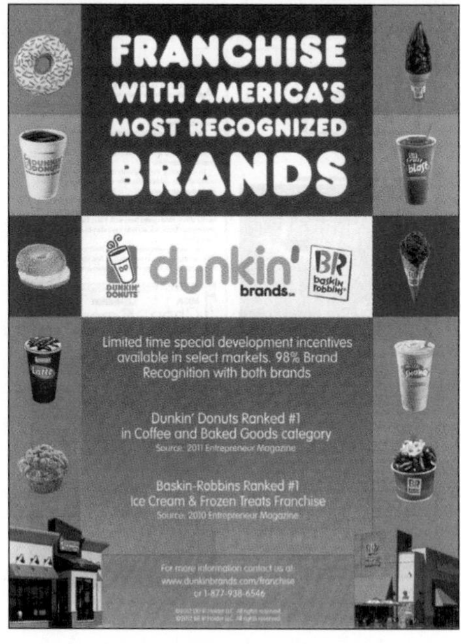

Some businesspeople like to open retail franchises with brand names consumers already know, like Dunkin' Donuts and Baskin Robbins.

Franchisors form chains

In a **franchise operation**, the franchisor develops a good marketing strategy, and the retail franchise holders carry out the strategy in their own units. Each franchise holder benefits from its relationship with the larger company and its experience, buying power, promotion, and image. In return, the franchise holder usually signs a contract to pay fees and commissions and to strictly follow franchise rules designed to continue the successful strategy.

Franchise holders' sales account for about a third of all retail sales. One reason is that franchising is especially popular with service retailers, a fast-growing sector of the economy.[25]

Differences in Retailing in Different Nations

LO 12.5

New ideas spread across countries

New retailing approaches that succeed in one part of the world are often quickly adapted to other countries. Self-service approaches that started with supermarkets in the United States are now found in retail operations worldwide. The supercenter concept, on the other hand, initially developed in Europe.

Mass-merchandising requires mass markets

The low prices, selections, and efficient operations offered by mass-merchandisers might be attractive to consumers everywhere. But consumers in less-developed nations often don't have the income to support mass distribution. The small shops that survive in these economies sell in very small quantities, often to a small number of consumers.

Retailers moving to international markets must adapt marketing strategies

Slow growth at home has prompted some large retail chains to move into international markets. They think that the competitive advantages that worked well in one market can provide a similar advantage in another country. But legal and cultural differences in international markets can make success difficult. Despite success in Latin America and Canada, Walmart has struggled in Germany and Japan. Similarly, French mass-merchandiser Carrefour expanded in Europe and South America, but its U.S. stores failed and it experienced legal problems in Indonesia.

Coca-Cola's desire to put its products "within an arm's reach of desire" anywhere in the world requires selling through a variety of different retail channels.

Other retailers, like California-based My Dollarstore, have seen quick international growth. My Dollarstore franchises the "dollar store" concept worldwide, and adapts its marketing strategy to local markets. In India, the price of each product is 99 rupees or about two dollars. Dollar stores in the United States target lower-income consumers, but in India the "Made in America" label attracts many higher-income consumers. Initially the merchandise in the Indian stores was the same as in U.S. stores. However, My Dollarstore quickly discovered what sold (Hershey's syrup is a hit) and what didn't (papaya and carrot juice). It also offered money-back guarantees, an unusual practice in India. Adaptations like these helped entice consumers into My Dollarstore's Indian franchises.[26]

Online retailing varies across nations

Online shopping behavior, and therefore online retailing, varies considerably across countries. For example, in the United Kingdom about half of all consumers regularly purchase online, while in emerging markets online sales are almost nonexistent. The most obvious prerequisite for online retailing is access to the Internet—in particular, broadband (fast) connections. In Chapter 3 we discussed the importance of technology and its uneven adoption around the globe. A reliable national postal system (lacking in many countries) is also needed for delivering online purchases.

Even when infrastructure is in place, cultural factors influence preferences for online shopping. For example, a European study of 20,000 clothing shoppers identified seven segments based on their shopping needs. One segment, "time-pressed optimizers," was particularly interested in online shopping. With very busy lives, this group had less time for in-store shopping so they sought the best possible product by doing research online. Yet only 3 percent of Italian shoppers and 6 percent of French shoppers fell into this segment—as compared to 16 percent of Brits and 18 percent of Germans. Another segment, "price-oriented bargain hunters," enjoyed going to many stores and rummaging to find bargain merchandise. This group was most common in Italy (31 percent of shoppers)—and helps to explain why only about 10 percent of Italians regularly purchased online.[27]

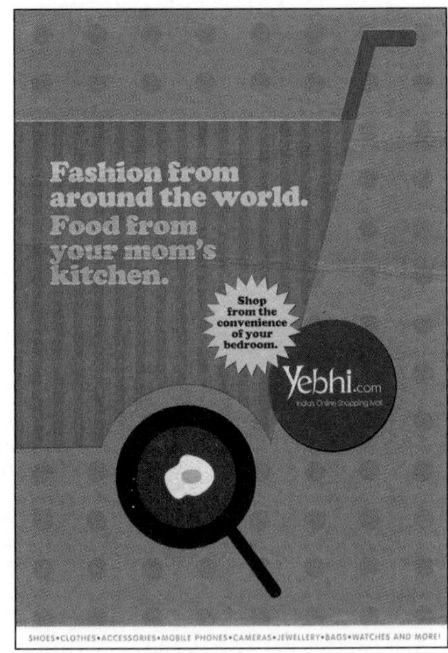

Yebhi is an online retailer that sells home, lifestyle, and fashion merchandise in India. Because online retailing is relatively new to India, Yebhi's advertising focuses on the benefits of online shopping.

What Is a Wholesaler?

LO 12.6

It's hard to define what a wholesaler is because there are so many different wholesalers doing different jobs. Some of their activities may even seem like manufacturing. As a result, some wholesalers describe themselves as "manufacturer and dealer." Some like to identify themselves with such general terms as *merchant, agent, dealer,* or *distributor.* And others just take the name commonly used in their trade—without really thinking about what it means.

To avoid a long technical discussion on the nature of wholesaling, we'll use the U.S. Census Bureau definition:

Wholesaling is concerned with the *activities* of those persons or establishments that sell to retailers and other merchants, or to industrial, institutional, and commercial users, but that do not sell in large amounts to final consumers. So **wholesalers** are firms whose main function is providing wholesaling activities. Wholesalers sell to all of the different types of organizational customers described in Chapter 6.

Wholesaling activities are just variations of the basic marketing functions—gathering and providing information, buying and selling, grading, storing, transporting, financing, and risk taking—we discussed in Chapter 1. You can understand wholesalers' strategies better if you look at them as members of channels. They add value by doing jobs for their customers and for their suppliers.

Wholesaling Is Changing with the Times

A hundred years ago wholesalers dominated distribution channels in the United States and most other countries. The many small producers and small retailers needed their services. This situation still exists in less-developed economies.

Wholesaling is in decline

However, in developed nations, as producers became larger many bypassed the wholesalers. Cost-conscious buyers at some large retail chains, including Walmart and Lowe's, even refuse to deal with some wholesalers who represent small producers. Efficient delivery services from UPS and FedEx also make it easier for many producers to ship directly to their customers, even those in foreign markets. The Internet also puts pressure on wholesalers whose primary role is providing information to bring buyers and sellers together. These factors have combined to decrease the number of wholesalers in the United States; there are about 435,000 wholesalers today—a decline of 16 percent in the last 15 years.

Opportunities remain for progressive wholesalers

Those that have survived are adapting their marketing strategies and finding new ways to add value in the channel. Progressive wholesalers are becoming more concerned with their customers and with channel systems. Many are using technology to offer better service. Some of the biggest B2B e-commerce sites on the Internet are wholesaler operations, and many wholesalers are enjoying significant growth. Others develop voluntary chains that bind them more closely to their customers.

Frieda's, Inc., is a good example; it is a wholesaler that each year supplies supermarkets and food-service distributors with $30 million worth of exotic fruits and vegetables. It was started by Frieda Caplan in 1962; today her daughters Karen and Jackie run the company. It is a sign of the marketing savvy of these women that artichokes, Chinese donut peaches, alfalfa sprouts, and spaghetti squash no longer seem very exotic. All of these crops were once viewed as unusual. Few farmers grew them, supermarkets didn't handle them, and consumers didn't know about them. Caplan helped to change all of that. She realized that some supermarkets wanted to attract less price-sensitive consumers who preferred more interesting choices in the hard-to-manage produce department. So she looked for products that would help her retailer-customers meet this need. For example, the funny looking kiwi fruit with its fuzzy brown skin was popular in New Zealand but virtually unknown to U.S. consumers. Caplan worked with small farmer-producers to ensure that she could provide her retailer-customers with a steady supply. She packaged kiwi with

interesting recipes and promoted it to consumers. Because of her efforts, demand has grown and most supermarkets now carry kiwi. That has attracted competition from larger wholesalers. But that doesn't bother the Caplans. When one of their specialty items becomes a commodity with low profit margins, another novel item replaces it. In a typical year, Frieda's introduces about 40 new products—like Asian pears, kiwano melons, sun-dried yellow tomatoes, and hot Asian chiles.

Frieda's also has an advantage because of the special services it provides. It was the first wholesaler to routinely use airfreight for orders and send produce managers a weekly "hot sheet" about the best sellers. The Caplans also use seminars and press releases to inform produce buyers about how to improve sales. For example, one attention-getting story about Frieda's "El Mercado de Frieda" line helped retailers do a better job serving Hispanic customers. Similarly, Frieda's website attracts final consumers with helpful tips and recipes. And now that more consumers are eating out, Frieda's has established a separate division to serve the special needs of food-service distributors.[28]

Wholesalers need to add value

Progressive wholesalers need to be efficient, but that doesn't mean they all have low costs. Some wholesalers' higher operating expenses result from the strategies they select, including the special services they offer to some customers. Let's look more closely at different types of wholesalers and the different ways they add value to channels of distribution.

Wholesalers Add Value in Different Ways

LO 12.7

Exhibit 12-5 compares the number, sales volume, and costs of some major types of wholesalers. The differences in operating costs suggest that each of these types performs, or does not perform, certain wholesaling functions. But which ones and why? And why do manufacturers use merchant wholesalers—costing 13.1 percent of sales—when agent wholesalers cost only 3.7 percent?

To answer these questions, we must understand what these wholesalers do and don't do. Exhibit 12-6 gives a big-picture view of the major types of wholesalers we'll be discussing. There are lots more specialized types, but our discussion will give you a sense of the diversity. Note that a major difference between merchant and agent wholesalers is whether they *own* the products they sell. Before discussing these wholesalers, we'll briefly consider producers who handle their own wholesaling activities.

Exhibit 12–5 U.S. Wholesale Trade by Type of Wholesale Operation

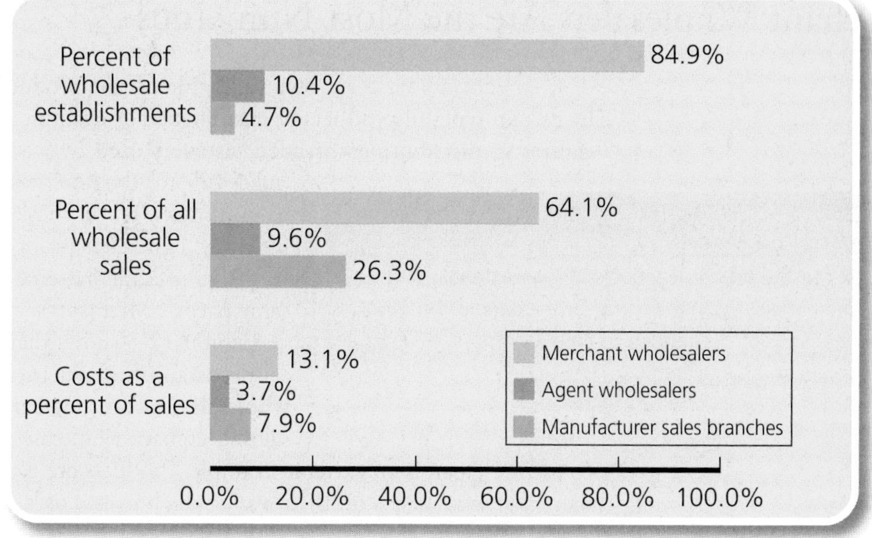

Manufacturers' sales branches are considered wholesalers

Manufacturers who just take over some wholesaling activities are not considered wholesalers. However, when they have **manufacturers' sales branches**—warehouses that producers set up at separate locations away from their factories—they're classified as wholesalers by the U.S. Census Bureau and by government agencies in many other countries.

In the United States, these manufacturer-owned branch operations account for about 4.7 percent of wholesale facilities—but they handle 26.3 percent of total wholesale sales. One reason sales per branch are so high is that the branches are usually placed in the best market areas. This also helps explain why their operating costs, as a percent of sales, are often lower. It's also easier for a manufacturer to coordinate information and logistics functions with its own branch operations than with independent wholesalers.[29]

Exhibit 12–6 Types of Wholesalers

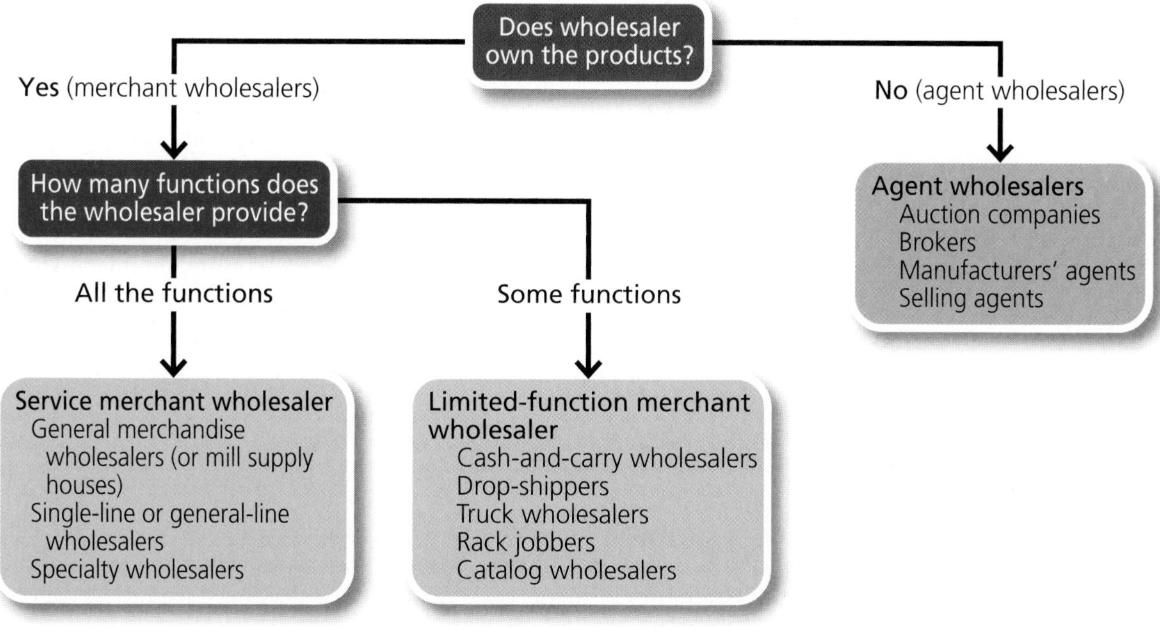

Merchant Wholesalers Are the Most Numerous

Merchant wholesalers own (take title to) the products they sell. They often specialize by certain types of products or customers. For example, Fastenal is a wholesaler that specializes in distributing threaded fasteners used by a variety of manufacturers. It owns (takes title to) the fasteners for some period before selling to its customers. If you think all merchant wholesalers are fading away, Fastenal is proof that they can serve a needed role. In the last decade Fastenal's profits have grown at about the same pace as Microsoft's.[30]

Internet Exercise

Check out the different aspects of the Fastenal website (**www.fastenal.com**). Give examples of ways that the website is intended to help Fastenal's customers and suppliers.

Exhibit 12-5 shows that almost 85 percent of the wholesaling establishments in the United States are merchant wholesalers—and they handle over 64 percent of wholesale sales. Merchant wholesalers are even more common in other countries. Japan is an extreme example. Products are often bought and sold by a series of merchant wholesalers on their way to the business user or retailer.[31]

Service wholesalers provide all the functions

Service wholesalers are merchant wholesalers that provide all the wholesaling functions. Within this basic group are three types: (1) general merchandise, (2) single-line, and (3) specialty.

General merchandise wholesalers are service wholesalers that carry a wide variety of nonperishable items such as hardware, electrical supplies, furniture, drugs, cosmetics, and automobile equipment. With their broad line of convenience and shopping products, they serve hardware stores, drugstores, and small department stores. *Mill supply houses* operate in a similar way, but they carry a broad variety of accessories and supplies to serve the needs of manufacturers.

Single-line (or general-line) wholesalers are service wholesalers that carry a narrower line of merchandise than general merchandise wholesalers. For example, they might carry only food, apparel, or certain types of industrial tools or supplies. In consumer products, they serve the single-and limited-line stores. In business products, they cover a wider geographic area and offer more specialized service.

Specialty wholesalers are service wholesalers that carry a very narrow range of products and offer more information and service than other service wholesalers. For example, a firm that produces specialized lights for vehicles might rely on specialty wholesalers to help reach automakers in different countries. A consumer products specialty wholesaler might carry only health foods instead of a full line of groceries. Some limited-line and specialty wholesalers are growing by helping independent retailer-customers compete with mass-merchandisers. But in general, many consumer-products wholesalers have been hit hard by the growth of retail chains that set up their own distribution centers and deal directly with producers.

A specialty wholesaler of business products might limit itself to fields requiring special technical knowledge or service. Richardson Electronics is an interesting example. It specializes in distributing replacement parts, such as electron tubes, for old equipment that many manufacturers still use on the factory floor. Richardson describes itself as "on the trailing edge of technology," but many of its customers operate in countries where new technologies are not yet common. Richardson gives them easy access to information from its website (www.rell.com) and makes its products available quickly by stocking them in locations around the world.[32]

Limited-function wholesalers provide some functions

Limited-function wholesalers provide only *some* wholesaling functions. In the following paragraphs, we briefly discuss the main features of these wholesalers. Although less numerous in some countries, these wholesalers are very important for some products.

Cash-and-carry wholesalers want cash

Cash-and-carry wholesalers operate like service wholesalers—except that the customer must pay cash. In the United States, big warehouse clubs have taken much of this business. But cash-and-carry operators are common in less-developed nations where very

Henry Schein is the largest distributor of health care products and services to office-based practitioners in North America. It also serves many international countries. It operates as a full-service wholesaler for medical, dental, and veterinary professionals.

small retailers handle the bulk of retail transactions. Full-service wholesalers often refuse to grant credit to small businesses that may have trouble paying their bills.

Drop-shippers do not handle the products

Drop-shippers own (take title to) the products they sell—but they do *not* actually handle, stock, or deliver them. These wholesalers are mainly involved in selling. They get orders and pass them on to producers. Then the producer ships the order directly to the customer. Drop-shippers commonly sell bulky products (like lumber) for which additional handling would be expensive and possibly damaging. Drop-shippers in the United States are already feeling the squeeze from buyers and sellers connecting directly via the Internet. But the progressive ones are fighting back by setting up their own websites and getting fees for referrals.

Truck wholesalers deliver—at a cost

Truck wholesalers specialize in delivering products that they stock in their own trucks. Their big advantage is that they promptly deliver perishable products that regular wholesalers prefer not to carry. A 7-Eleven store that runs out of potato chips on a busy Friday night doesn't want to be out of stock all weekend! They help retailers keep a tight rein on inventory, and they seem to meet a need.

Rack jobbers sell hard-to-handle assortments

Rack jobbers specialize in hard-to-handle assortments of products that a retailer doesn't want to manage—and rack jobbers usually display the products on their own wire racks. For example, a grocery store or mass-merchandiser might rely on a rack jobber to decide which paperback books or magazines it sells. The wholesaler knows which titles sell in the local area and applies that knowledge in many stores.

Catalog wholesalers reach outlying areas

Catalog wholesalers sell through catalogs that may be distributed widely to smaller industrial customers or to retailers that might not be called on by other wholesalers. Customers place orders at a website or by mail, e-mail, fax, or telephone. These wholesalers sell lines such as hardware, jewelry, sporting goods, and computers. For example, Inmac uses a catalog that is printed in six languages and a website (www.inmac.com) to sell a complete line of computer accessories. Many of its customers don't have a local wholesaler, but they can place orders from anywhere in the world. Most catalog wholesalers quickly adapted to the Internet. It fits what they were already doing and makes it easier. But they're facing more competition too; the Internet allows customers to compare prices from more sources of supply.[33]

Agents Are Strong on Selling

They don't own the products

Agent wholesalers are wholesalers who do *not* own the products they sell. Their main purpose is to help in buying and selling. Agent wholesalers normally specialize by customer type and by product or product line. But they usually provide even fewer functions than the limited-function wholesalers. They operate at relatively low cost—sometimes 2 to 6 percent of their selling price—or less in the case of website–based agents who simply bring buyers and sellers together. Worldwide, the role of agents is rapidly being transformed by the Internet. Those who didn't get on board this fast-moving train were left behind.

They are important in international trade

Agents are common in international trade. Many markets have only a few well-financed merchant wholesalers. The best many producers can do is get local representation through agents and then arrange financing through banks that specialize in international trade.

Agent wholesalers are usually experts on local business customs and regulations in their own countries. Sometimes a marketing manager can't work through a foreign government's red tape without the help of a local agent.

Manufacturers' agents—freewheeling sales reps

A **manufacturers' agent** sells similar products for several noncompeting producers—for a commission on what is actually sold. Such agents work almost as members of each company's sales force, but they're really independent wholesalers. More than half of all agent wholesalers are manufacturers' agents. Their big plus is that they already call on some customers and can add another product line at relatively low cost—and at no cost to the producer until something sells! If an area's sales potential is low, a company may use a manufacturers' agent because the agent can do the job at low cost. Small producers often use agents everywhere because their sales volume is too small to justify their own sales force.

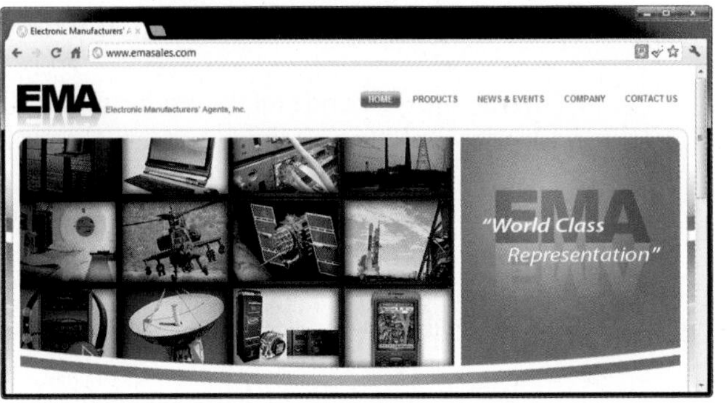

Electronic Manufacturers' Agents is a company of manufacturers' agents that represents 20 different suppliers of electronics parts. EMA reps make sales calls on customers in the southeastern United States.

Agents can be especially useful for introducing new products. For this service, they may earn 10 to 15 percent commission. (In contrast, their commission on large-volume established products may be quite low—perhaps only 2 percent.) A 10 to 15 percent commission rate may seem small for a new product with low sales. Once a product sells well, however, a producer may think the rate is high and begin using its own sales reps.

Export or import agents are basically manufacturers' agents who specialize in international trade. These agent wholesalers operate in every country and help international firms adjust to unfamiliar market conditions in foreign countries.

Manufacturers' reps will continue to play an important role in businesses that need an agent to perform order-getting tasks. But manufacturers' reps everywhere are feeling pressure when it comes to routine business contacts. More producers are turning to telephone selling, websites, e-mail, teleconferencing, and faxes to contact customers directly.[34]

Brokers provide information

Brokers bring buyers and sellers together. Brokers usually have a *temporary* relationship with the buyer and seller while a particular deal is negotiated. They are especially useful when buyers and sellers don't come into the market very often. The broker's product is information about what buyers need and what supplies are available. If the transaction is completed, they earn a commission from whichever party hired them. **Export and import brokers** operate like other brokers, but they specialize in bringing together buyers and sellers from different countries. Smart brokers quickly saw new opportunities to expand their reach by using the Internet. As the Internet causes consolidation, it will also provide more value. A smaller number of cyberbrokers will cut costs and dominate the business with larger databases of buyers and sellers.

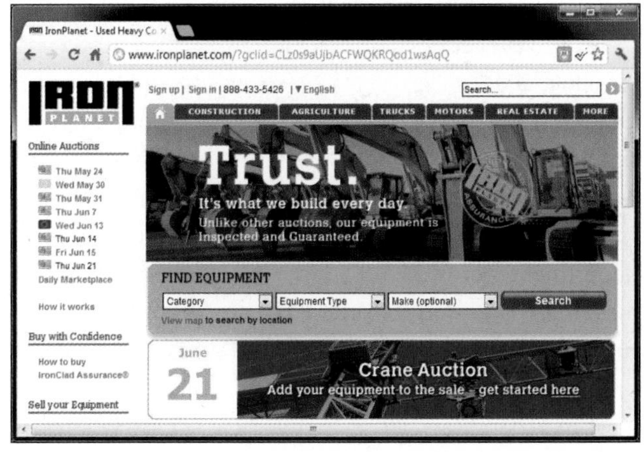

IronPlanet uses auctions to connect buyers and sellers of used heavy equipment like cranes, tractors, and trucks.

Selling agents—almost marketing managers

Selling agents take over the whole marketing job of producers—not just the selling function. A selling agent may handle the entire output of one or more producers, even competing producers, with almost complete control of pricing, selling, and advertising. In effect, the agent becomes each producer's marketing manager.

Financial trouble is one of the main reasons a producer calls in a selling agent. The selling agent may provide working capital and may also take over the affairs of the business. But selling agents also work internationally. A **combination export manager** is a blend of manufacturers' agent and selling agent—handling the entire export function for several producers of similar but noncompeting lines.

Auction companies speed up the sale

Auction companies provide a place where buyers and sellers can come together and bid to complete a transaction. Traditionally they were important in certain lines—such as livestock, fur, tobacco, and used cars—where demand and supply conditions change rapidly.

CONCLUSION

Modern retailing is scrambled—and we'll probably see more changes in the future. In such a dynamic environment, a producer's marketing manager must choose very carefully among the available kinds of retailers. And retailers must plan their marketing mixes with their target customers' needs in mind—while at the same time becoming part of an effective channel system.

In this chapter we described many different types of retailers, each offering different marketing mixes that appeal to different target customers. Lower margins and faster turnover are the modern philosophy for mass-merchandisers, but this is no guarantee of success as retailers' life cycles move on.

Retailing tends to evolve in predictable patterns—and we discussed the wheel of retailing theory to help understand this. But the growth of chains and scrambled merchandising will continue as retailing evolves to meet changing consumer demands. Important breakthroughs are possible—perhaps with the Internet—and consumers probably will continue to move away from conventional retailers.

Wholesalers can provide functions for those both above and below them in a channel of distribution. These services are closely related to the basic marketing functions. There are many types of wholesalers. Some provide all the wholesaling functions—while others specialize in only a few. Eliminating wholesalers does not eliminate the need for the functions they now provide, but technology is helping firms to perform these functions in more efficient ways.

Merchant wholesalers are the most numerous and account for the majority of wholesale sales. Their distinguishing characteristic is that they take title to (own) products. Agent wholesalers, on the other hand, act more like sales representatives for sellers or buyers—and they do not take title.

Despite dire predictions, wholesalers continue to exist. The more progressive ones are adapting to a changing environment. But some less-progressive wholesalers will fail. The Internet is already taking its toll. On the other hand, new types of intermediaries are evolving. Some are creating new ways of helping producers and their customers achieve their objectives by finding new ways to add value.

KEY TERMS

LO 12.8

retailing, *303*
general stores, *306*
single-line stores, *306*
limited-line stores, *306*
specialty shop, *307*
department stores, *307*
mass-merchandising concept, *307*
supermarkets, *307*
discount houses, *308*
mass-merchandisers, *308*
supercenters (hypermarkets), *309*
convenience (food) stores, *310*
automatic vending, *310*
door-to-door selling, *310*
wheel of retailing theory, *314*
scrambled merchandising, *315*
corporate chain, *316*
cooperative chains, *317*
voluntary chains, *317*
franchise operation, *317*
wholesaling, *319*
wholesalers, *319*
manufacturers' sales branches, *321*
merchant wholesalers, *322*
service wholesalers, *322*
general merchandise wholesalers, *322*
single-line (or general-line) wholesalers, *322*
specialty wholesalers, *322*
limited-function wholesalers, *322*
cash-and-carry wholesalers, *322*
drop-shippers, *323*
truck wholesalers, *323*
rack jobbers, *323*
catalog wholesalers, *323*
agent wholesalers, *324*
manufacturers' agent, *324*
export agents, *324*
import agents, *324*
brokers, *324*
export brokers, *324*
import brokers, *324*
selling agents, *325*
combination export manager, *325*
auction companies, *325*

QUESTIONS AND PROBLEMS

1. Compare and contrast the marketing mix and target market for a bike shop in your community with the online bicycle retailer Performance Bicycle (www.performancebike.com). Use your best judgment to identify each retailer's primary target market and some of its Product, Place, Promotion, and Price decisions.
2. What sort of a "product" are specialty shops offering? What are the prospects for organizing a chain of specialty shops?
3. Distinguish among discount houses, price-cutting by conventional retailers, and mass-merchandising. Forecast the future of low-price selling in food, clothing, and appliances. How will the Internet affect that future?
4. Discuss a few changes in the market environment that you think help to explain why telephone, mail-order, and Internet retailing have been growing so rapidly.
5. What are some advantages and disadvantages to using the Internet for shopping?
6. Apply the wheel of retailing theory to your local community. What changes seem likely? Will established retailers see the need for change, or will entirely new firms have to develop?
7. What advantages does a retail chain have over a retailer who operates with a single store? Does a small retailer have any advantages in competing against a chain? Explain your answer.
8. Many producers are now seeking new opportunities in international markets. Are the opportunities for international expansion equally good for retailers? Explain your answer.
9. Discuss how computer systems affect wholesalers' and retailers' operations.
10. Consider the evolution of wholesaling in relation to the evolution of retailing. List several changes that are similar, and several that are fundamentally different.
11. Do wholesalers and retailers need to worry about new-product planning just as a producer needs to have an organized new-product development process? Explain your answer.
12. How do you think a retailer of Maytag washing machines would react if Maytag set up a website, sold direct to consumers, and shipped direct from its distribution center? Explain your thinking.
13. What risks do merchant wholesalers assume by taking title to goods? Is the size of this risk about constant for all merchant wholesalers?
14. Why would a manufacturer set up its own sales branches if established wholesalers were already available?
15. What is an agent wholesaler's marketing mix?
16. Why do you think that many merchant wholesalers handle competing products from different producers, while manufacturers' agents usually handle only noncompeting products from different producers?
17. What alternatives does a producer have if it is trying to expand distribution in a foreign market and finds that the best existing merchant wholesalers won't handle imported products?
18. Discuss the future growth and nature of wholesaling if chains, scrambled merchandising, and the Internet continue to become more important. How will wholesalers have to adjust their mixes? Will wholesalers be eliminated? If not, what wholesaling functions will be most important? Are there any particular lines of trade where wholesalers may have increasing difficulty?

CREATING MARKETING PLANS

The Marketing Plan Coach software on the text website includes a sample marketing plan for Hillside Veterinary Clinic. Look through the "Marketing Strategy" section.

a. What kind of retail operation is the vet clinic? Does it fit any of the types described in this chapter?

b. How could Hillside make use of a website?

c. The marketing plan notes future plans to offer kennel (boarding) services and pet supplies. How will this change Hillside's current strategy? Does the marketing plan provide a good sense of what needs to be done? Do you have other recommendations for Hillside?

SUGGESTED CASES

11. Running Room
12. DrJane.com—Custom Vitamins
14. Showtime Media
15. The Buckeye Group
16. J&J Lumber Supply

Video Case 2. Bass Pro Shops
Video Case 5. Suburban Regional Shopping Malls

COMPUTER-AIDED PROBLEM

12. SELECTING CHANNEL INTERMEDIARIES

Art Glass Productions, a producer of decorative glass gift items, wants to expand into a new territory. Managers at Art Glass know that unit sales in the new territory will be affected by consumer response to the products. But sales will also be affected by which combination of wholesalers and retailers Art Glass selects. There is a choice between two wholesalers. One wholesaler, Giftware Distributing, is a merchant wholesaler that specializes in gift items; it sells to gift shops, department stores, and some mass-merchandisers. The other wholesaler, Margaret Degan & Associates, is a manufacturers' agent who calls on many of the gift shops in the territory.

Art Glass makes a variety of glass items, but the cost of making an item is usually about the same—$5.20 a unit. The items would sell to Giftware Distributing at $12.00 each—and in turn the merchant wholesaler's price to retailers would be $14.00—leaving Giftware with a $2.00 markup to cover costs and profit. Giftware Distributing is the only reputable merchant wholesaler in the territory, and it has agreed to carry the line only if Art Glass is willing to advertise in a trade magazine aimed at retail buyers for gift items. These ads will cost $8,000 a year.

As a manufacturers' agent, Margaret Degan would cover all of her own expenses and would earn 8 percent of the $14.00 price per unit charged the gift shops. Individual orders would be shipped directly to the retail gift shops by Art Glass, using United Parcel Service (UPS). Art Glass would pay the UPS charges at an average cost of $2.00 per item. In contrast, Giftware Distributing would anticipate demand and place larger orders in advance. This would reduce the shipping costs, which Art Glass would pay, to about $.60 a unit.

Art Glass' marketing manager thinks that Degan would only be able to sell about 75 percent as many items as Giftware Distributing—since she doesn't have time to call on all of the smaller shops and doesn't call on any department stores. On the other hand, the merchant wholesaler's demand for $8,000 worth of supporting advertising requires a significant outlay.

The marketing manager at Art Glass decided to use a spreadsheet to determine how large sales would have to be to make it more profitable to work with Giftware and to see how the different channel arrangements would contribute to profits at different sales levels.

a. Given the estimated unit sales and other values shown on the initial spreadsheet, which type of wholesaler would contribute the most profit to Art Glass Productions?

b. If sales in the new territory are slower than expected, so that the merchant wholesaler was able to sell only 3,000 units—or the agent 2,250 units—which wholesaler would contribute the most to Art Glass' profits? (*Note:* Assume that the merchant wholesaler only buys what it can sell; that is, it doesn't carry extra inventory beyond what is needed to meet demand.)

c. Prepare a table showing how the two wholesalers' contributions to profit compare as the quantity sold varies from 3,500 units to 4,500 units for the merchant wholesaler and 75 percent of these numbers for the manufacturers' agent. Discuss these results. (*Note:* Use the analysis feature to vary the quantity sold by the merchant wholesaler, and the program will compute 75 percent of that quantity as the estimate of what the agent will sell.)

13

CHAPTER THIRTEEN

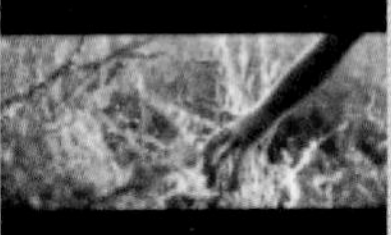

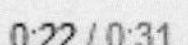

Promotion—Introduction to Integrated Marketing Communications

Back in the 1930s, in the depths of the Great Depression, Leo and Lillian Goodwin started the Government Employees Insurance Company—GEICO. GEICO kept operating costs low by only selling auto insurance to two low-risk target markets, federal employees and military personnel. GEICO passed the savings on in the form of lower premiums—and sales steadily grew for decades.

After becoming a wholly-owned subsidiary of Berkshire Hathaway in 1996, GEICO's management sought to accelerate earnings growth by targeting new markets. However, getting growth in the mature auto insurance market meant that GEICO would need to take customers away from better known competitors such as Allstate and State Farm. As if that wasn't difficult enough, many prospects didn't even know about GEICO. Ted Ward, GEICO's vice president of marketing, discussed this situation with the firm's ad agency, The Martin Agency of Richmond, Virginia. Together they decided that an aggressive advertising campaign could increase awareness of GEICO, bring in new customers, and result in profitable growth.

The GEICO campaign that emerged used an animated, talking lizard to help get attention and communicate the firm's message. In the first commercial, the charming reptile with the British accent stated, "I'm the Gecko, not to be confused with GEICO that can save you hundreds on car insurance. So please stop calling me." The humorous ads quickly generated awareness and interest among target customers, many of whom had never heard of GEICO. The original plan was for the Gecko campaign to run for a short time, but customers loved the Gecko, and he continues to be an important part of GEICO's image and promotions.

GEICO wants customers to know it offers good value—great car insurance at low prices. But to prove this, customers must get a price quote. It's quick and easy to get a quote at GEICO's website, so to spur the target audience to action, GEICO ads remind them that "15 minutes could save you 15 percent or more on your car insurance." Many people responded to the appeal of saving money, but others were hesitant, believing that requesting an online quote was too difficult.

To overcome this resistance, GEICO came up with a clever advertising campaign to convince people that getting a quote from the website is "so easy a caveman can do it." The print and TV ads feature refined cavemen living in the modern world who are offended that the ads imply they are not intelligent. The funny spots attract attention. While it is difficult to know just how effective each ad campaign has been, a recent study found that 93 percent of consumers recognized GEICO's ads—well ahead of the 82 percent who recognized competitor Progressive Insurance's "Flo" ads.

To communicate with many different target markets, GEICO relies on a variety of media and messages. For example, GEICO sponsors NASCAR driver Max Papis and the Miss GEICO powerboat and its racers Marc Granet and Scott Begovich. The Gecko icon appears on the cars, boats, and motorcycles that GEICO sponsors—and fans can learn more about all the teams at GEICOgarage.com. GEICO targets members of the armed forces with special services and communications like the HomeFront social media site that helps connects military personnel and their families. Of course GEICO has a Facebook page—but the Gecko has one, too, and with more likes.

While GEICO aims for its target market with advertising, it knows that that much of this advertising and promotion is seen by customers who are not currently looking to buy insurance. For highly targeted promotion, GEICO knows that when someone types "car insurance" into the search engine at Google or Bing, they are very likely to be looking for insurance. So a sponsored link to GEICO's website appears at the top of the search page. GEICO also collects and analyzes big data that shows websurfing behavior to help identify other target customers. This data helps GEICO place banner ads where they will be seen by customers in the market for insurance.

All this promotion helped make GEICO a familiar name, but many insurance buyers still want to talk to a real person before deciding what to do. These customers can visit with a GEICO salesperson at one of its local offices or call GEICO's toll-free number and talk on the phone with an inside sales rep. GEICO selects capable salespeople who are licensed insurance agents, and then trains them to develop an understanding of each customer's needs and concerns so that the agents can then explain GEICO's benefits to the customer in a persuasive way.

Of course, GEICO seeks to build an ongoing relationship with customers after they sign up for a policy. Regular contacts and updates are handled with promotional e-mails. Salespeople sometimes call customers to let them know about other GEICO products, such as less familiar umbrella insurance policies. Later, if a customer who purchases a policy has a problem, GEICO's highly rated customer service team works to resolve it quickly.

Among insurance companies, GEICO spends the most on advertising. Since 2000 GEICO has doubled its market share and is now the third largest insurer in the United States—and it doesn't want to stop there. To keep going, GEICO's integrated marketing communications program will continue to play a major role in acquiring and retaining customers.[1]

Learning Objectives

As the GEICO example shows, there are many decisions that a marketing manager must make concerning Promotion, and it is an important part of marketing strategy planning. Marketing managers usually blend a variety of different promotion methods to achieve promotion objectives because each method has its own strengths and limitations. In this chapter we introduce the major promotion options and how to integrate them into an effective whole.

When you finish this chapter you should be able to:

1. know the advantages and disadvantages of the promotion methods a marketing manager can use in strategy planning.
2. understand the integrated marketing communications concept and why firms use a blend of different promotion methods.
3. understand the importance of promotion objectives.
4. know how the traditional communication process affects promotion planning.
5. understand how customer-initiated interactive communication is different.
6. know how typical promotion plans are blended to get an extra push from wholesalers and retailers and help from customers in pulling products through the channel.
7. understand how promotion blends typically vary over the adoption curve and product life cycle.
8. understand how to determine how much to spend on promotion efforts.
9. understand important new terms (shown in red).

Promotion Communicates to Target Markets

LO 13.1

Promotion is communicating information between the seller and potential buyer or others in the channel to influence attitudes and behavior. The promotion part of the marketing mix involves telling target customers that the right Product is available at the right Place at the right Price. Just as Promotion must be fine-tuned for a specific target market, it must fit with the other variables of the marketing mix and reinforce the strategy's differentiation and positioning.

This is the first of three chapters that discuss issues important for Promotion. We begin with an overview of the major promotion methods. Marketing managers can choose from several basic types of promotion: personal selling, mass selling, and sales promotion (see Exhibit 13-1). Because these different methods have different strengths and limitations, a marketing manager typically uses them in combination to achieve specific objectives. We also discuss the specialists who are involved in managing different types of promotion and why it is important for them to work together as a team. This chapter also provides models that will help you understand how communication works. Finally, we look at some concepts that help marketing managers develop the best promotion blend.

Exhibit 13–1 Promotion and Marketing Strategy Planning

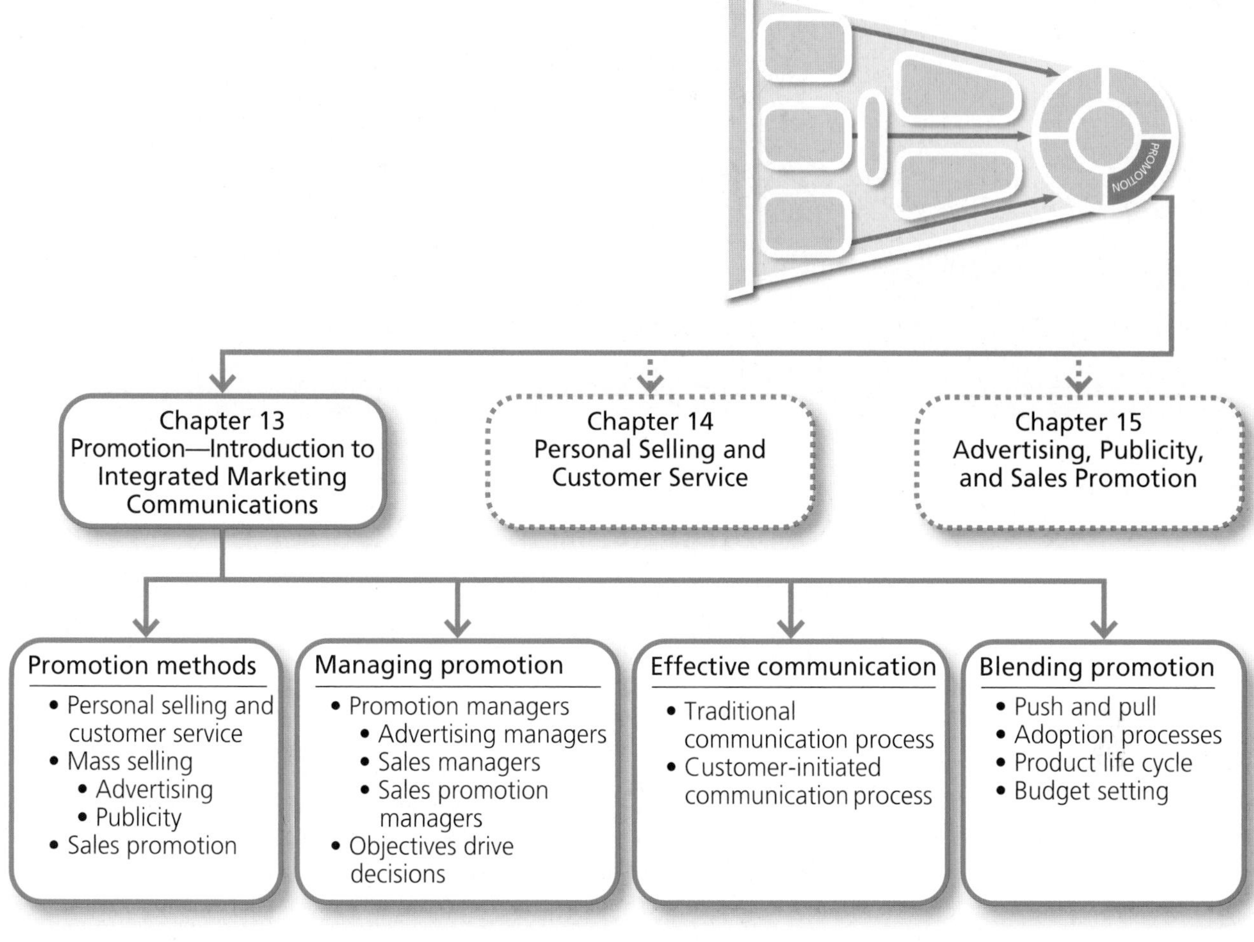

In Chapter 14, we take a closer look at the important promotion strategy decisions that marketing and sales managers make in personal selling and customer service. Chapter 15 provides a closer look at mass selling. It discusses the strategy planning decisions related to advertising, publicity, and sales promotion.

While we'll go into some detail about the different promotion methods, a key challenge for marketing managers is how best to blend them. So it's helpful to begin with a brief overview of the promotion methods available.

Several Promotion Methods are Available

Personal selling—flexibility is its strength

Personal selling involves direct spoken communication between sellers and potential customers. Customer service is a form of personal communication between a customer and seller to resolve a problem with a purchase. Salespeople get immediate feedback, which helps them to adapt. Although some personal selling is included in most marketing mixes, it can be very expensive. So it's often desirable to combine personal selling with mass selling and sales promotion.

Mass selling involves advertising and publicity

Mass selling is communicating with large numbers of potential customers at the same time. It's less flexible than personal selling, but when the target market is large and scattered, mass selling can be less expensive.

Advertising is the main form of mass selling. **Advertising** is any *paid* form of nonpersonal presentation of ideas, goods, or services by an identified sponsor. It includes the use

Everyone loves free snacks, so it's not surprising that many customers engaged with McDonald's outdoor ad. If customers could use their cell phone to snap a picture of a particular snack (on this day a sundae), they could bring the photo to the nearby McDonald's to claim their free snack.

of traditional media like magazines, newspapers, radio and TV, signs, and direct mail as well as new media such as the Internet. While advertising must be paid for, another form of mass selling—publicity—is "free."

Publicity avoids media costs

Publicity is any *unpaid* form of nonpersonal presentation of ideas, goods, or services. Of course, publicity people are paid. But they try to attract attention to the firm and its offerings *without having to pay media costs.* Some publicity involves getting favorable coverage in newspaper stories, magazines, or television. For example, movie studios try to get celebrities on TV talk shows because this generates a lot of interest and sells tickets to new movies without the studio paying for TV time. Publicity also involves creating and placing content on the Web for customers to find or pass on to others. For example, many companies create videos and post them on a company website or a service like YouTube, provide opportunities for customers to review products, or write blogs that include information of value for customers. When customers reach out for specific information to help solve a problem, many find publicity more useful than advertising. Companies need to plan for publicity in the promotion blend.

Sales promotion tries to spark immediate interest

Sales promotion refers to promotion activities—other than advertising, publicity, and personal selling—that stimulate interest, trial, or purchase by final customers or others in the channel. Sales promotion may be aimed at consumers, at intermediaries, or at a firm's own employees. Examples are listed in Exhibit 13-2. Relative to other promotion methods,

Exhibit 13–2
Example of Sales Promotion Activities

Aimed at final consumers or users	Aimed at wholesalers or retailers	Aimed at company's own sales force
Contests	Price deals	Contests
Coupons	Promotion allowances	Bonuses
Aisle displays	Sales contests	Meetings
Samples	Calendars	Portfolios
Trade shows	Gifts	Displays
Point-of-purchase materials	Trade shows	Sales aids
Banners and streamers	Meetings	Training materials
Frequent buyer programs	Catalogs	
Sponsored events	Merchandising aids	
	Videos	

sales promotion can usually be implemented quickly and get results sooner. In fact, most sales promotion efforts are designed to produce immediate results.

Less is spent on advertising than personal selling or sales promotion

Many people incorrectly think that promotion money gets spent primarily on advertising—because advertising is all around them. But all the special sales promotions—coupons, sweepstakes, trade shows, and the like—add up to even more money. Similarly, much personal selling goes on in the channels and in other business markets. In total, firms spend less money on advertising than on personal selling or sales promotion.

Someone Must Plan, Integrate, and Manage the Promotion Blend

LO 13.2

Each promotion method has its own strengths and weaknesses. In combination, they complement each other. Each method also involves its own distinct activities and requires different types of expertise. As a result, it's usually the responsibility of specialists—such as sales managers, advertising managers, and promotion managers—to develop and implement the detailed plans for the various parts of the overall promotion blend.

Sales managers manage salespeople

Sales managers are concerned with managing personal selling. Often the sales manager is responsible for building good distribution channels and implementing Place policies. In smaller companies, the sales manager may also act as the marketing manager and be responsible for advertising and sales promotion.

Advertising managers work with ads and agencies

Advertising managers manage their company's mass-selling effort—in television, newspapers, magazines, and other media. Their job is choosing the right media and developing the ads. Advertising departments within their own firms may help in these efforts—or they may use outside advertising agencies. The advertising manager may handle publicity too. Or it may be handled by an outside agency or by whoever handles **public relations**—communication with noncustomers, including labor, public interest groups, stockholders, and the government.

Sales promotion managers need many talents

Sales promotion managers manage their company's sales promotion effort. In some companies, a sales promotion manager has independent status and reports directly to the marketing manager. If a firm's sales promotion spending is substantial, it probably *should* have a specific sales promotion manager. Sometimes, however, the sales or advertising departments handle sales promotion efforts—or sales promotion is left as a responsibility of individual brand managers. Regardless of who the manager is, sales promotion activities vary so much that many firms use both inside and outside specialists.

Marketing manager talks to all, blends all

Although many specialists may be involved in planning for and implementing specific promotion methods, determining the blend of promotion methods is a strategy decision—and it is the responsibility of the marketing manager.

The various promotion specialists tend to focus on what they know best and their own areas of responsibility. A creative web page designer or advertising copywriter in New York may have no idea what a salesperson does during a call on a wholesaler. In addition, because of differences in outlook and experience, the advertising, sales, and sales promotion managers often have trouble working with each other as partners. Too often they just view other promotion methods as using up budget money they want.

The marketing manager must weigh the pros and cons of the various promotion methods and then devise an effective promotion blend—fitting in the various departments and personalities and coordinating their efforts. Then the advertising, sales, and sales promotion managers should develop the details consistent with what the marketing manager wants to accomplish.

Send a consistent and complete message with integrated marketing communications

Effective blending of all of the firm's promotion efforts should produce **integrated marketing communications**—the intentional coordination of every communication from a firm to a target customer to convey a consistent and complete message.

The GEICO case at the start of this chapter is a good example of integrated marketing communications. Different promotion methods handle different parts of the job. Yet the methods are coordinated so that the sum is greater than the parts. The separate messages are complementary, but also consistent.

It seems obvious that a firm's different communications to a target market should be consistent. However, when a number of different people are working on different promotion elements, they are likely to see the same big picture only if a marketing manager

In China, Pepsi depends on a blend of integrated marketing communications, including in-store sampling, outdoor advertising, and web-based publicity. The web page shown here promotes the "Pepsi Soccer Carnival" on Tencent, China's most popular social media site. Soccer fans can play online games, gamble, and use instant messaging to win prizes like virtual "cans" of Pepsi and phone calls from soccer stars like Jose Torres and Didier Drogba.

ensures that it happens. Getting consistency is harder when different firms handle different aspects of the promotion effort. For example, different firms in the channel may have conflicting objectives.

To get effective coordination, everyone involved with the promotion effort must clearly understand the plan for the overall marketing strategy. They all need to understand how each promotion method will contribute to achieve specific promotion objectives.[2]

Which Methods to Use Depends on Promotion Objectives

LO 13.3

Overall objective is to affect behavior

A marketing manager usually has to set priorities for the promotion objectives. The ultimate objective is to encourage customers to choose a *specific* product. However, which promotion objectives are of highest priority will depend on the market situation and target market. For example, as we saw in Chapters 5 and 6, customers often move along a step-by-step buying path—and the path may differ for different types of purchases. Sometimes customers are familiar with the product and sometimes it is completely new to them. Objectives should be guided by what we know about target customers. In this section, we discuss different types of promotion objectives and tie them to frameworks describing the purchase process.

Informing, persuading, and reminding are basic promotion objectives

Promotion objectives must be clearly defined—because the right promotion blend depends on what the firm wants to accomplish. It's helpful to think of three basic promotion objectives: *informing, persuading,* and *reminding* target customers about the company and its marketing mix. All try to affect buyer behavior by providing customers with information.

It's also useful to set more specific promotion objectives that state *exactly whom* you want to inform, persuade, or remind, and *why.* This is unique to each company's strategy—and specific objectives vary by promotion method. We'll talk about more specific promotion objectives in Chapters 14 and 15. Here we'll focus on the three basic promotion objectives and then link them to the adoption process and a new model.

Informing is educating

Potential customers must know something about a product if they are to buy it. A firm with a really new product may not have to do anything but inform consumers of the product's features and benefits. An *informing* objective can show that it meets consumer needs better than other products. Imagine a customer moving to a new town with an interest in joining a health club where he can work out. A health club might place brochures in local apartment complexes, or run ads in the newspaper to let target customers know about the features at its facility. A small business might want to have a service regularly clean its offices. The owner might begin by searching on the Internet. There she might find a local cleaning company's website with information about various services.

Persuading usually becomes necessary

When competitors offer similar products, the firm must not only inform customers that its product is available but also persuade them to buy it. A *persuading* objective means the firm will try to develop a favorable set of attitudes so customers will buy, and keep buying, its product. A persuading objective often tries to demonstrate how one brand is better than others. To convince consumers to buy Brawny paper towels, ads show Brawny as the towel that's best for tough cleanup jobs. A salesperson for Andersen Windows tries to convince homebuilders about the quality and affordability of Andersen Windows as compared to those of a competitor, so the builder chooses Andersen for future housing projects.

Reminding may be enough

If target customers already have positive attitudes about a firm's marketing mix—or a good relationship with a firm—a *reminding* objective might be suitable. Customers who have been attracted and sold once are still targets for competitors' appeals. Reminding them of their past satisfaction may keep them from shifting to a competitor. When Southwest Airlines' Ding! widget pops up on a computer desktop, it lets customers know of

Exhibit 13–3
Relation of Promotion Objectives, Adoption Process, and AIDA Model

Promotion Objectives	Adoption Process	AIDA Model
Informing	Awareness	Attention
	Interest	Interest
Persuading	Evaluation	Desire
	Trial	
Reminding	Decision	Action
	Confirmation	

lower fares to cities they want to visit. An accountant working for a small local firm might phone her customers once every few months to "check-in" and see if they have any questions. This serves as a reminder that the accountant is there and available.

Promotion objectives relate to adoption processes

In Chapter 5, we looked at consumer buying as a problem-solving process through which buyers go through steps on the way to adopting (or rejecting) an idea or product. The three basic promotion objectives relate to these steps. See the first two columns in Exhibit 13-3. *Informing* and *persuading* may be needed to affect the potential customer's knowledge and attitudes about a product and then bring about its adoption. Later, promotion can simply *remind* the customer about that favorable experience and confirm the adoption decision.

The AIDA model is a practical approach

The basic promotion objectives and adoption process fit very neatly with another action-oriented model—called AIDA—that we will use in this chapter and in Chapters 14 and 15 to guide some of our discussion. The **AIDA model** consists of four promotion jobs: (1) to get *Attention,* (2) to hold *Interest,* (3) to arouse *Desire,* and (4) to obtain *Action.*

The last two columns in Exhibit 13-3 show the relationship of the promotion objectives and adoption process to the AIDA jobs. Getting attention is necessary to make consumers aware of the company's offering. Holding interest gives the communication a chance to build the consumer's interest in the product. Arousing desire affects the evaluation process, perhaps building preference. And obtaining action includes gaining trial,

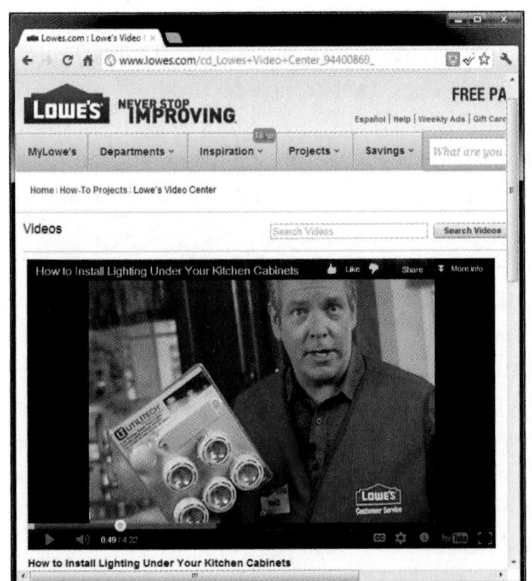

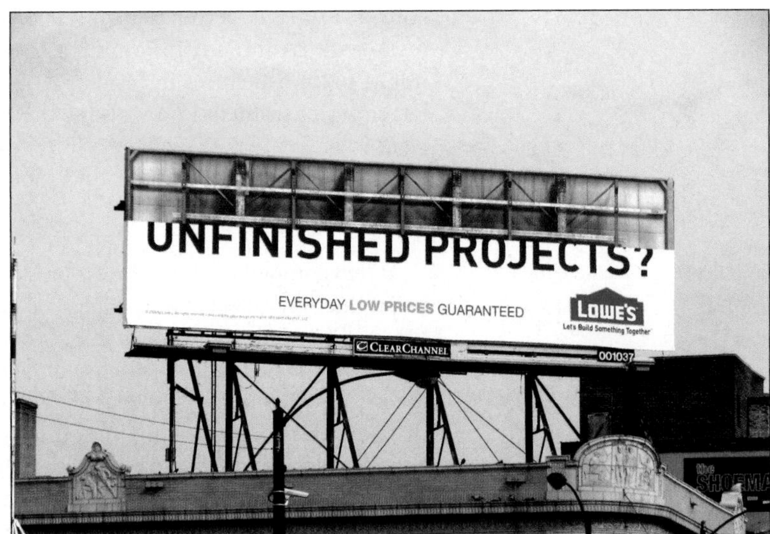

Lowe's, a home improvement retailer, places how-to videos on the lowes.com website to inform customers about do-it-yourself projects. Interested customers can learn about many topics, such as "How to Install Lighting Under Your Kitchen Cabinets." Each project includes a description of the materials necessary to complete it—all of which can conveniently be picked up at a local Lowes Home Improvement Center. When the promotion objective is reminding, Lowe's billboards employ a little humor to remind customers of projects they need to complete.

Exhibit 13–4 The Traditional Communication Process

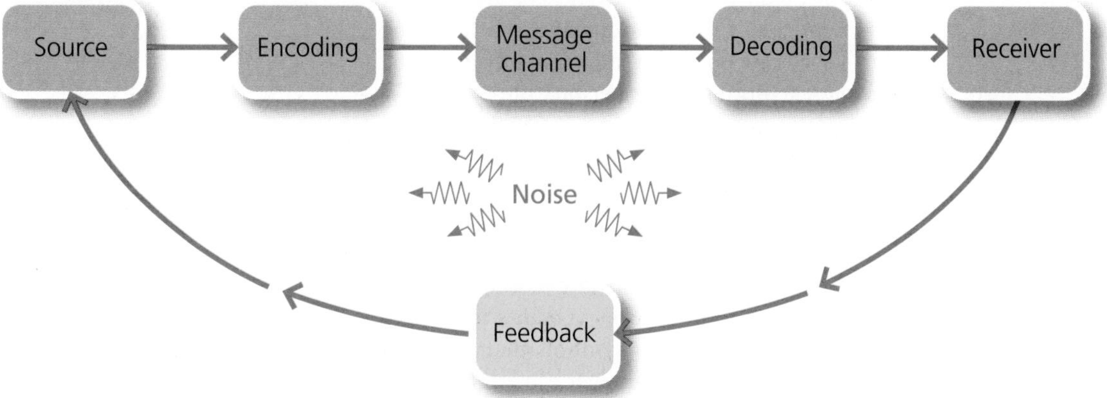

which may lead to a purchase decision. Continuing promotion is needed to confirm the decision and encourage an ongoing relationship and additional purchases.

British marketers for Pampers disposable diapers generated attention and interest with TV ads that showed the world from a baby's perspective. To encourage desire and action, they used creative in-store and point-of-purchase advertising. For example, on the doors of restrooms with baby-changing facilities, fake door knobs were placed unreachably high, with the message: "Babies have to stretch for things. That's why they like the extra stretchiness of Pampers Active fit." And on store shelves, in a play on babies' disobedient nature, pull-out Pampers information cards were marked "Do Not Pull."[3]

Promotion Requires Effective Communication

LO 13.4

Communication can break down

Promotion is wasted when it doesn't communicate effectively. There are many reasons why a promotion message can be misunderstood or not heard at all. To understand this, it's useful to think about a whole **communication process**—which means a source trying to reach a receiver with a message. Exhibit 13-4 shows the elements of the communication process. Here we see that a **source**—the sender of a message—is trying to deliver a message to a **receiver**—a potential customer. Customers evaluate both the message and the source of the message in terms of trustworthiness and credibility. For example, American Dental Association (ADA) studies show that Listerine mouthwash helps reduce plaque buildup on teeth. Listerine mentions the ADA endorsement in its promotion to help make the promotion message credible.

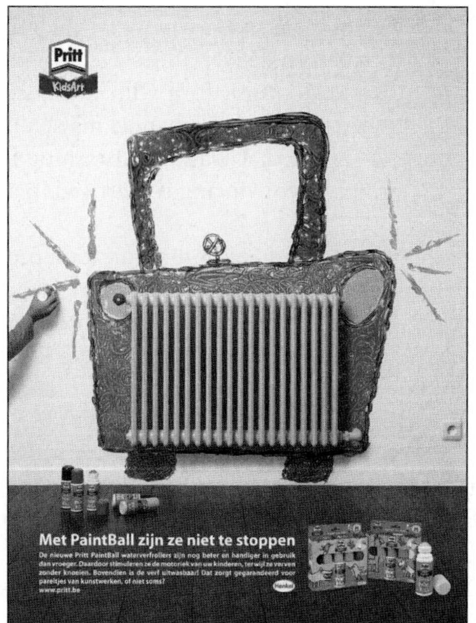

This German ad for an innovative rolling paint ball shows how a kid might decorate a wall. The target customer's frame of reference might be important in interpreting this ad. An uptight parent might see the ad and worry about kids making a mess of their bedroom walls. A different parent might see it as a way to stimulate a kid's artistic creativity.

A major advantage of personal selling is that the source—the seller—can get immediate feedback from the receiver. It's easier to judge how the message is being received and to change it if necessary. Mass sellers usually must depend on marketing research or total sales figures for feedback—and that can take too long. Many marketers include toll-free telephone numbers and website addresses as ways of building direct-response feedback from consumers into their mass-selling efforts.

The **noise**—shown in Exhibit 13-4—is any distraction that reduces the effectiveness of the communication process. Conversations and snack-getting during TV ads are noise. An industrial buyer reading a text message during a salesperson's presentation is noise. Advertisers who plan messages must recognize that many possible distractions—noise—can interfere with communications.

Exhibit 13–5
This Same Message May Be Interpreted Differently

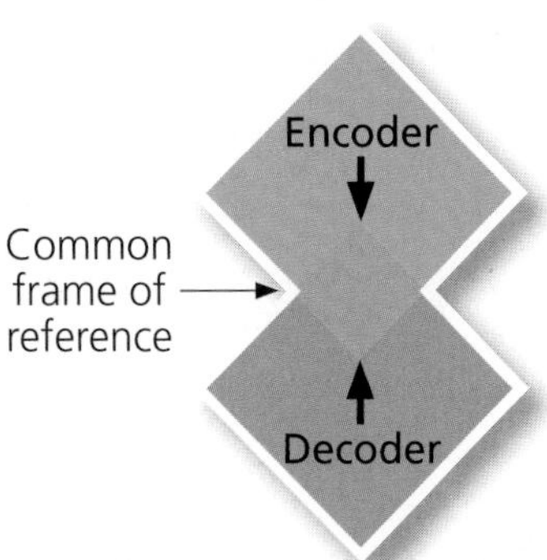

Encoding and decoding depend on a common frame of reference

The basic difficulty in the communication process occurs during encoding and decoding. **Encoding** is the source deciding what it wants to say and translating it into words or symbols that will have the same meaning to the receiver. **Decoding** is the receiver translating the message. This process can be very tricky. The meanings of various words and symbols may differ depending on the attitudes and experiences of the two groups. People need a common frame of reference to communicate effectively. See Exhibit 13-5. Maidenform encountered this problem with its promotion aimed at working women. The company ran a series of ads depicting women stockbrokers and doctors wearing Maidenform lingerie. The men in the ads were fully dressed. Maidenform was trying to show women in positions of authority, but some women felt the ads presented them as sex objects. In this case, the promotion people who encoded the message didn't understand the attitudes of the target market and how they would decode the message.[4]

The same message may be interpreted differently

Different audiences may interpret a message differently. Such differences are common in international marketing when cultural differences or translation are problems. In Taiwan, the translation of the Pepsi slogan "Come alive with the Pepsi Generation" came out as "Pepsi will bring your ancestors back from the dead." The Swedish brand, Samarin, thought it would avoid these problems with ads showing three simple drawings—and no words. The first picture shows a man holding his stomach in obvious pain, in the second he is drinking Samarin, and in the last he is smiling and happy. Worked great—except in the Middle East where people read from right to left. Uh oh! Many firms run into problems like this.[5]

Message channel is important too

The communication process is complicated even more because the message is coming from a source through some **message channel**—the carrier of the message. A source can use many message channels to deliver a message. The salesperson does it in person with voice and action. Advertising must do it with media such as magazines, TV, e-mail, or Internet websites. A particular message channel may enhance or detract from a message. A TV ad, for example, can *show* that Dawn dishwashing detergent "takes the grease away"; the same claim might not be convincing if it arrived in a consumer's e-mail.

Feedback takes many forms

The last element in the traditional communication process is *feedback*—communication from the receiver back to the source. Feedback may take many different forms: a customer may simply have a different attitude, seek more information, visit a store, or purchase the product. Objectives should state the desired feedback and marketing managers should measure whether the communication is having the anticipated response.

Integrated direct response seeks immediate feedback

Sometimes marketing managers want to get immediate feedback from *specific* customers. This prompts firms to turn to direct marketing—direct communication between a seller and an individual customer using a promotion method other than face-to-face personal selling. Most direct marketing communications are designed to prompt immediate feedback—a direct response—by customers. That's why this type of communication is often called *direct-response promotion.*

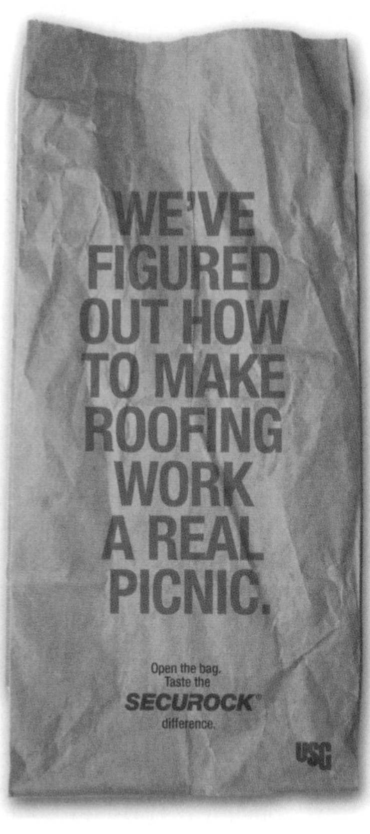

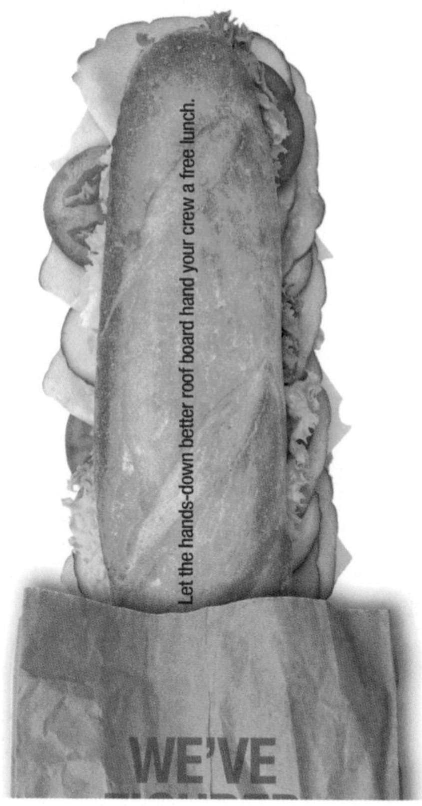

USG used a clever direct mailer to promote its Securock roofing material. On the outside is what looks like a brown-paper sandwich bag. The headline on the bag reads: "We've figured out how to make roofing work a real picnic." In the bag is a "sandwich" with the sentence: "Let the hands-down better roof board hand your crew a free lunch." The details on how to claim the free lunch are included. To get their meal, the roofers have to listen to a sales pitch, but this mailer has made it appetizing.

Direct mail and e-mail are two tools commonly used for direct-response promotion. A carefully selected mailing list—perhaps from the firm's customer relationship management (CRM) database—allows advertisers to reach customers with specific interests. For the best response, marketing managers carefully segment their customers and use mail or e-mail to deliver targeted messages. When target customers use e-mail, the approach offers benefits to buyers and sellers. Sellers like the relatively low cost compared to direct mail. E-mails give customers a chance to click through to photos and videos, media tools help them decide whether to make a donation or place an order.

Targeted direct-response promotion works best

Consider Clare Florist's efforts at direct-response promotion. The British flower retailer regularly sends e-mails to tell customers about special seasonal offers. (Mother's Day, Valentine's Day, etc.) Clare's used to send the same e-mail, featuring three different types of flowers at different prices, to all of the customers on its mailing list. About 6 percent of these e-mails were opened. With a little analysis, though, Clare's marketing manager found that 76 percent of repeat customers bought the same type of flowers on their next purchase; customers who bought roses last Mother's Day were very likely to buy roses again this Mother's Day. Then Clare Florist used its database to develop segmented promotions based on each customer's previous purchases. With precise knowledge of each customer's flower preferences, Clare promoted only one product to each customer. So last year's rose buyers received promotions for roses this year. A subject line indicated "Your Favorite Flowers" and included a personalized message for each customer—"We hope your mother enjoyed her roses last year." With this simple change, the open rate for the segmented e-mails doubled and sales quadrupled.[6]

Traditional communication process describes outbound Promotion

The traditional communication process describes an *outbound* model for Promotion. Marketing managers gather information about target markets to encode messages target customers will understand. They communicate through message channels target customers use. Marketing managers try to reach customers when they are most interested in receiving the messages and try to "listen" to feedback from customers, perhaps by conducting marketing research or monitoring the Internet to gauge customer reactions.

When Customers Initiate the Communication Process

LO 13.5

The traditional process in Exhibit 13-4 assumes that it's the seller ("source") who initiates communication. Let's look closer at another communication model, shown in Exhibit 13-6, where a customer ("receiver") initiates the communication process. For example, consumers look in the Yellow Pages for information or ask retail salespeople for help, and organizational buyers phone salespeople to ask questions or request bids. The growth of the Internet makes it much easier for customers to initiate the information gathering process, and more customers are doing just that. While this process has many of the same components as the traditional process we considered earlier, the differences and implications for Promotion are significant.

Customer initiates communication with a search process

In the process in Exhibit 13-6, a customer (*receiver*) initiates communication with a decision to *search* for information in a particular message channel. The most common and far-reaching *message channel* used for information searching is the Internet—usually queried through a search engine like Google or Bing and accessed by a personal computer, tablet, or cell phone. Sometimes a buyer immediately links to a particular seller's web page to seek out information. The message channel is still the carrier of the message, as was the case before, but searchable message channels usually feature an archive of existing messages on a number of topics. There may be many available topics—even millions.

Customer decides how much information to get

The receiver then reviews and screens the various options and decides which messages to pursue. A search engine returns a list of results that includes paid advertisements and free listings. A search can also occur at the website of a producer, retailer, or wholesaler. For example, a business customer may visit a distributor of janitorial supplies and search for industrial cleaning solutions—and then click on pricing information or perhaps the safety of the ingredients. Similarly, a consumer might visit Netflix and search for horror movies and then look for the director, actors, or the comments of people who have already seen the movie. The customer chooses the information of interest to them.

Marketers must grab attention to be selected

Because a customer now has so many options, it's important for a marketer to be among the first to grab that customer's attention. That means that an online retailer that sells golf gear wants to be near the top of the search results when someone searches for "Big Bertha golf," Callaway's popular line of golf clubs. In this case, the retailer can pay a search engine

Exhibit 13–6
A Model of Customer-Initiated Interactive Communication

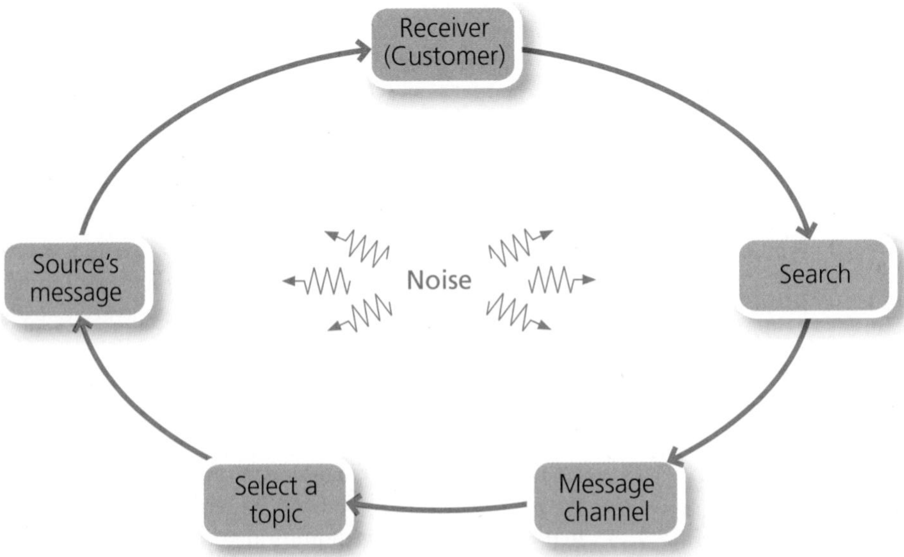

Many consumers turn to Internet search engines to gather information before making a purchase. When customers search, marketing managers want their products to be found. Some marketing managers try to understand how search engines work so that their sites show up high on the list of search results. Another approach is to pay a search engine firm for a sponsored link (ad). At the time of this search, a company would pay about $.75 each time a consumer clicked on the sponsored link to the right of the search results for "snowboards."

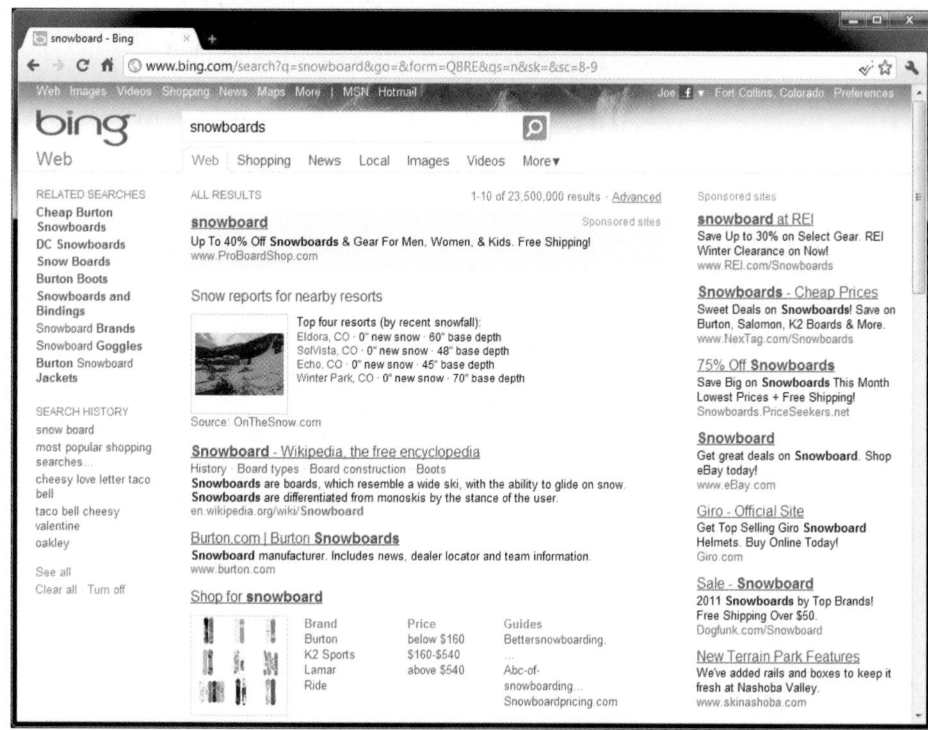

company to put a sponsored (advertising) link near the top of the list. There are also technical approaches that help a firm appear near the top of the organic search. Either way, the firm wants to be sure that when customers "look," its business is "seen"—or the firm's message won't be communicated. Search engine listings and ads only allow for brief messages—so this first message must interest the customer or it will not be selected.

When the receiver looks more closely at the information on screen, he decides whether to stay or leave the site. Usually more information is just a click away—and that click can be to dig deeper into the marketer's site or to click away to another website. Marketing managers need to make sure that page holds the receiver's interest or begins to arouse desire. Noise can still be a problem as well—and lead the searcher in a different direction. For example, a confusing website may make it difficult to figure out a retailer's return policy and discourage a customer from buying.

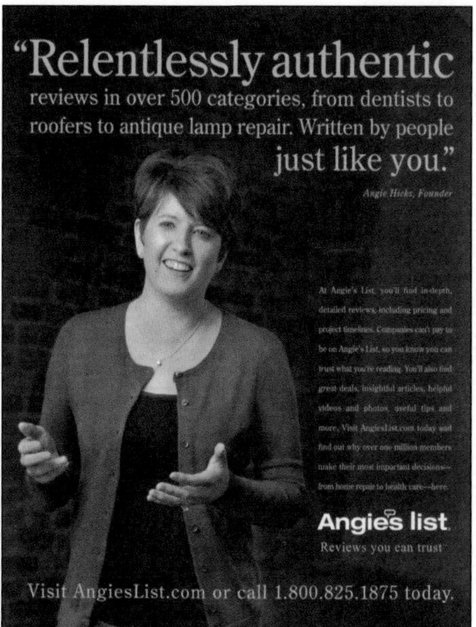

Angie's List is a website that offers its subscribers access to consumer reviews of service providers like plumbers, housekeepers, and family physicians.

Marketers don't control all the information

When customers search online, they often find messages outside the marketer's control. For example, a gadget lover might type "iPod dock" into a search engine. This might take her to CNET.com, where she reads professional reviews of several different docks with speakers for her iPod. The reviews help her identify two good alternatives. A couple of clicks later she is at online retailer Newegg.com, where she reads customer reviews of the dock/speaker. Finding a few reviews critical of one of the models, she looks more closely at the Logitech dock/speaker. She then clicks to the Logitech website where she can easily compare a couple of Logitech styles and colors. She was familiar with the Logitech name from its advertising. This helps her feel comfortable with the brand, and she buys the Logitech docking station. In this not uncommon purchase scenario, much of the information used by the customer to make a purchase was not produced or even influenced by a Logitech marketing manager.

This doesn't mean marketing managers should ignore the online information they don't create. Marketing managers need to know where customers are likely to search for information and should monitor what is being said there. While online compliments let the firm know what it is doing well, complaints can highlight unmet customer needs—and give managers a chance to turn things around. The owner of a California spa was horrified to learn her spa had only a two-and-a-half star rating (out of five) on the popular review site Yelp.com. To turn things around, she sent e-mails to try to make things right with the unhappy reviewers. She also encouraged her satisfied customers to post reviews. Soon the spa had an acceptable four-star rating at Yelp, and rather than scaring off prospects the review site was spurring them to action.[7]

Promotion timing and relevance have an impact

Communication that customers receive during the customer-initiated communication process is usually timely—it often occurs when a customer is actively gathering purchase information. Consequently, customers more readily pay attention and are more likely to be interested in promotional information. Think about a radio advertisement for an apartment rental. A customer with six months left on his apartment lease is unlikely to pay much attention to the ad and the advertiser wasted time targeting him. He may even be annoyed hearing the ad interrupt his music. On the other hand, a customer looking to move in the next few weeks would probably listen with great interest to this same radio ad. Customers pay attention when the promotion is timely and relevant to a problem they are trying to solve.

When customers surf the Internet, they often signal they are ready to make a purchase. For example, reading articles about different kinds of bicycles, visiting a couple of websites, and "liking" bike makers' the local bike shop on Facebook might all be indications of an impending bicycle purchase. There are companies that monitor and track consumers as they travel around the web. Customers often leave telltale signs that they might be interested in buying certain products. Marketing managers can identify target customers interested in buying their products and deliver timely and relevant online (and offline) advertising to these customers.

When customers initiate, communication is inbound

When customers have the power to decide where to click next, marketing managers need to create a different kind of promotion. When customers are *inbound* from a search, and have the choice about whether to stay at a company's website, promotion must address their needs at that moment. Customers are actively seeking information to help them make a better purchase decision—so marketing managers need promotion that meets those needs. Marketing managers also need to develop content that appears high on the list when customers use a search engine—and that interests customers enough to click through. And finally, promotion needs to keep them there to learn more about the seller's offering.

While the implications of inbound customers are greatest for advertising, publicity, and sales promotion as discussed in Chapter 15, let's look at one example here. The travel agency Discover Africa created content that attracted customers to its website. Discover Africa started by identifying nine different target markets (for example "Mr. Business," "The Campers," and "The Student/Backpacker"). Then Discover Africa created articles, videos, and travel guides designed to appeal to one or more target groups and posted them on its website. With a little outbound promotion of the discoverafrica.net website and its content, others started noticing and the site began to appear near the top of online searches related to travel in Africa. Discover Africa's positioning changed and it was soon viewed as an authority on African travel. Sales began to climb.[8]

Internet Exercise

Reputation.com offers services to help companies and individuals monitor and manage their online reputations. Go to the company's website (**www.reputation.com**) and view the services it offers for businesses. What types of companies might find this service useful? Why? Is there any ethical issue with managing your online reputation? Why or why not?

Ethical issues in marketing communications

Promotion is one of the most frequently criticized areas of marketing. Many criticisms focus on whether communications are honest and fair. Marketers must sometimes make ethical judgments in considering these charges and in planning their promotion.

For example, we often look to the source of a communication to decide whether we believe it is credible. When a TV news program broadcasts a video publicity release, consumers don't know it was prepared to achieve marketing objectives. They think the news staff is the source. That may make the message more credible, but is it fair? Many say yes—as long as the publicity information is truthful. Similar concerns are raised about the use of celebrities in advertisements. A person who plays the role of an honest and trustworthy person on a popular TV series may be a credible message source in an ad, but is using such a person misleading to consumers? Some critics believe it is. Others argue that consumers recognize advertising when they see it and know celebrities are paid for their endorsements.

The most common criticisms of promotion relate to exaggerated claims. If an advertisement or a salesperson claims that a product is the "best available," is that just a personal opinion or should every statement be backed up by proof? What type of proof should be required? Some promotions do misrepresent the benefits of a product. Customers look to online reviews for objective opinions. What about posting fake favorable reviews for your company or its products—or negative reviews about a competitor? Real reviews offer a way for consumers to see beyond potential exaggerated claims. But if consumers feel that at least some reviews are phony, they may distrust all reviews. Some people believe that the Internet will eventually expose dishonest players in the market.

There are also issues related to consumer privacy. Most consumers are unaware that their web-surfing habits are being tracked. While it offers them the potential benefit of more personalized communications, some consumers might want to remain anonymous.

Most marketing managers realize that the ultimate proof comes when the customer makes the purchase. Customers won't spread positive word-of-mouth or come back if the marketing mix doesn't deliver what the promotion promises. As a result, most marketing managers work to make promotion claims specific and believable.[9]

Ethics Question

A friend who recently took over his family's upscale Italian restaurant has complained that business has suddenly fallen off, except for the "regulars." His cook has heard that the owner of a competing restaurant has been pressuring his employees to post negative reviews on a local website about the food, service, and prices at your friend's restaurant. When you check the website, there are a number of unfavorable, anonymous reviews. You also notice that there are about 30 very upbeat reviews of the competing restaurant. Your friend wants you to help give the competitor "what he deserves" and write some negative reviews about that restaurant. Would you do what he asks? Why or why not? What else could you do?

How Typical Promotion Plans are Blended and Integrated

LO 13.6

There is no one right blend

There is no one *right* promotion blend for all situations. Each one must be developed as part of a marketing mix and should be designed to achieve the firm's promotion objectives in each marketing strategy. So let's take a closer look at typical promotion blends in different situations.

Get a push in the channel with promotion to intermediaries

When a channel of distribution involves intermediaries, their cooperation can be crucial to the success of the overall marketing strategy. **Pushing** (a product through a channel) means using normal promotion effort—personal selling, advertising, and sales promotion—to help sell the whole marketing mix to possible channel members. This

Green Mountain Coffee uses both push and pull to support its coffees. Green Mountain's website and membership program promote a "Deal of the Week" directly to consumers. The ad on the right targets purchasing agents at grocery stores, letting them know that Green Mountain's family of brands will bring volume and profits to their stores.

approach emphasizes the importance of securing the wholehearted cooperation of channel members to promote the product in the channel and to the final user.

Producers usually take on much of the responsibility for the pushing effort in the channel. However, wholesalers often handle at least some of the promotion to retailers. Similarly, retailers often handle promotion in their local markets. The overall effort is most likely to be effective when all of the individual messages are carefully integrated.

Promotion to intermediaries emphasizes personal selling

Salespeople handle most of the important communication with wholesalers and retailers. These clients don't want empty promises. They want to know what they can expect in return for their cooperation and help. A salesperson can answer questions about what promotion will be directed toward the final consumer, each channel member's part in marketing the product, and important details on pricing, markups, promotion assistance, and allowances. A salesperson can also help the firm determine when it should adjust its marketing mix from one intermediary to another.

When suppliers offer similar products and compete for attention and shelf space, intermediaries usually pay attention to the one with the best profit potential. So sales promotions targeted at intermediaries usually focus on short-term arrangements that will improve the intermediary's profits. For example, a soft-drink bottler might offer a convenience store a free case of drinks with each two cases it buys. The free case improves the store's profit margin on the whole purchase.

Firms run ads in trade magazines to recruit new intermediaries or to inform channel members about a new offering. Trade ads usually encourage intermediaries to contact the supplier for more information, and then a salesperson takes over.

Push within a firm—with promotion to employees

Some firms emphasize promotion to their own employees—especially salespeople or others in contact with customers. This type of *internal marketing* effort is basically a variation on the pushing approach. One objective of an annual sales meeting is to inform reps about important elements of the marketing strategy—so they'll work together as a team to implement it. Some firms use promotion to motivate employees to provide better customer service or achieve higher sales. This is typical in services where the quality of the employees'

Exhibit 13–7 Promotion May Encourage Pushing in the Channel, Pulling by Customers, or Both

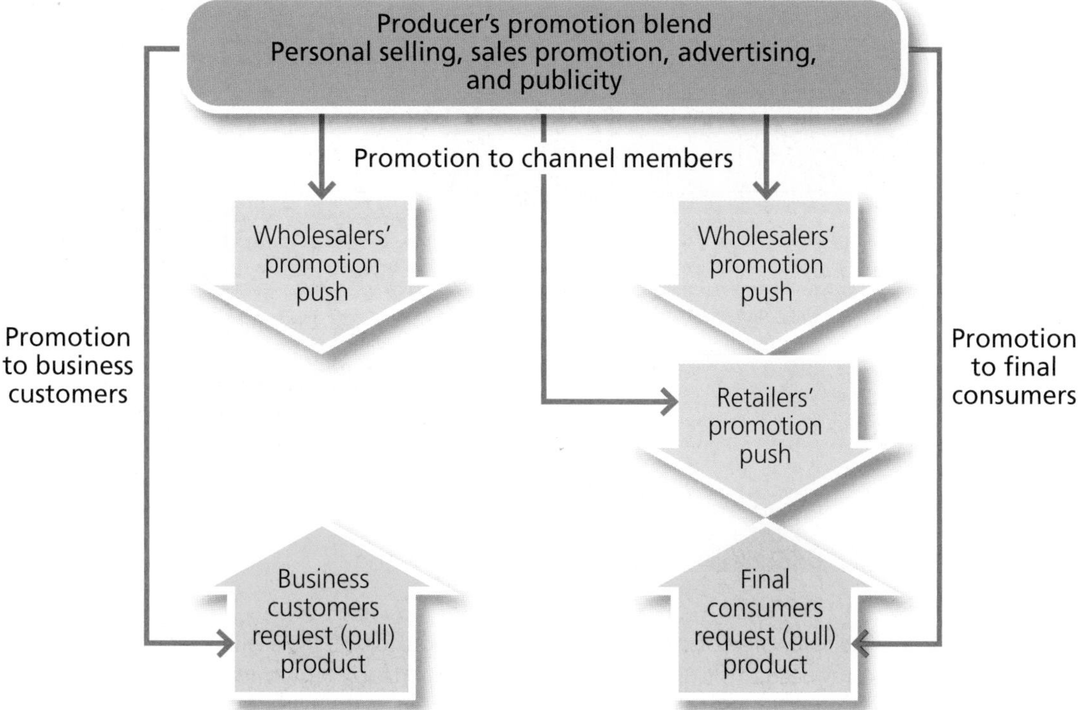

efforts is a big part of the product. For example, at one time, advertising for McDonald's used the theme "We love to see you smile." The ads communicate to customers, but also remind employees that the service they provide is crucial to customer satisfaction.

Pulling policy—customer demand pulls the product through the channel

Most producers focus a significant amount of promotion on customers at the end of the channel. This helps to stimulate demand and pull the product through the channel of distribution. **Pulling** means getting customers to ask intermediaries for the product.

Pulling and pushing are usually used in combination. See Exhibit 13-7. However, if intermediaries won't work with a producer—perhaps because they're already carrying a competing brand—a producer may try to use a pulling approach by itself. This involves highly aggressive promotion to final consumers or users—perhaps using coupons or samples—temporarily bypassing intermediaries. If the promotion works, the intermediaries are forced to carry the product to satisfy customer requests. However, this approach is risky. Customers may lose interest before reluctant intermediaries make the product available. At a minimum, intermediaries should be told about the planned pulling effort—so they can be ready if the promotion succeeds.

Who handles promotion to final customers at the end of the channel varies in different channel systems, depending on the mix of pushing and pulling. Further, the promotion blend typically varies depending on whether customers are final consumers or business users.[10]

Promotion to final consumers

The large number of consumers almost forces producers of consumer products and retailers to emphasize advertising, publicity, and sales promotion. Sales promotion—such as coupons, contests, or free samples—builds consumer interest and short-term sales of a product. An informative website that includes customer reviews and video demonstrations helps customers build favorable impressions of a company and its products. Effective mass selling may build enough brand familiarity so that little personal selling is needed, as in self-service and discount operations.[11]

Personal selling can be effective too. Aggressive personal selling to final consumers usually is found in channel systems for expensive products, such as those for financial services, furniture, consumer electronics, designer clothing, and automobiles.

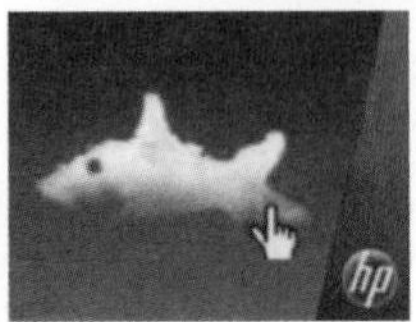

HP offers hardware, software, and consulting services to help firms with their information technology needs. As cloud computing grew in importance, HP wanted its customers to know HP could help them design a custom cloud computing solution. Ads and a direct mail brochure (complete with umbrella) drove customers to HP's website where they could find technical papers and sign up for HP Discovery Workshops and Cloud Roadmap services. The website also included an interactive feature that allowed users to literally create a cloud in any shape they wanted. HP's salespeople followed up on the leads in this integrated marketing comunications campaign.

Promotion to business customers

Producers and wholesalers that target business customers often emphasize personal selling. This is practical because there are fewer of these customers and their purchases are typically larger. Sales reps can be more flexible in adjusting their companies' appeals to suit each customer—and personal contact is usually required to close a sale. A salesperson is also able to call back later to follow up, resolve any problems, and nurture the relationship with the customer.

While personal selling dominates in business markets, mass selling is necessary too. A typical sales call on a business customer costs about $500. That's because salespeople spend less than half their time actually selling. The rest is consumed by such tasks as traveling, paperwork, sales meetings, and strictly service calls. So it's seldom practical for salespeople to carry the whole promotion load.

Business buyers often engage in Internet search to identify solutions for current needs. So it's important for a seller's website to appear near the top of the search results. Otherwise, it has no opportunity to draw buyers' attention and build interest for the firm's products. Ads in trade magazines or at a B2B e-commerce website, for instance, can inform potential customers that a product is available. Most trade ads give a toll-free telephone number and an e-mail or website address to stimulate direct inquiries. Domestic and international trade shows also help identify prospects. Even so, most sellers who target business customers spend only a small percentage of their promotion budget on mass selling and sales promotion.

Each market segment may need a unique blend

Knowing what type of promotion is typically emphasized with different targets is useful in planning the promotion blend. But each unique market segment may need a separate marketing mix and a different promotion blend. You should be careful not to slip into a shotgun approach (using a single promotion across market segments) when what you really need is a rifle approach (a specific mix for a particular target market). This can result from too much combining as discussed in Chapter 4.

Adoption Processes Can Guide Promotion Planning

LO 13.7

The AIDA and adoption processes look at individuals. This emphasis on individuals helps us understand how promotion affects the way that people behave. But it's also useful to look at markets as a whole. Different segments of customers within a market may behave differently—with some taking the lead in trying new products and, in turn, influencing others.

Promotion must vary for different adopter groups

Research on how markets accept new ideas has led to the adoption curve model. The **adoption curve** shows when different groups accept ideas. It emphasizes the relations among groups and shows that individuals in some groups act as leaders in accepting a new idea. Promotion efforts usually need to change over time to adjust to differences among the adopter groups.

Exhibit 13-8 shows the adoption curve for a typical successful product. Some of the important characteristics of each of these customer groups are discussed next. Which one are you? Does your group change for different products?

Innovators don't mind taking some risks

The **innovators** are the first to adopt. They are eager to try a new idea and willing to take risks. Innovators tend to be young and well educated. They are likely to be mobile and have many contacts outside their local social group and community. Business firms in the innovator group are often specialized and willing to take the risk of doing something new.

Innovators tend to rely on impersonal and scientific information sources, or other innovators, rather than salespeople. They often search for information on the Internet, read articles in technical publications, or look for informative ads in special-interest magazines.

Early adopters are often opinion leaders

Early adopters are well respected by their peers and often are opinion leaders. They tend to be younger, more mobile, and more creative than later adopters. But unlike innovators, they have fewer contacts outside their own social group or community. Business firms in this category also tend to be specialized.

Of all the groups, this one tends to have the greatest contact with salespeople. Mass media are important information sources too. Marketers should be very concerned with attracting and selling the early adopter group. Their acceptance is crucial. The next group, the early majority, look to the early adopters for guidance. The early adopters can help the promotion effort by spreading *word-of-mouth* information and advice among other consumers.

Exhibit 13–8 The Adoption Curve

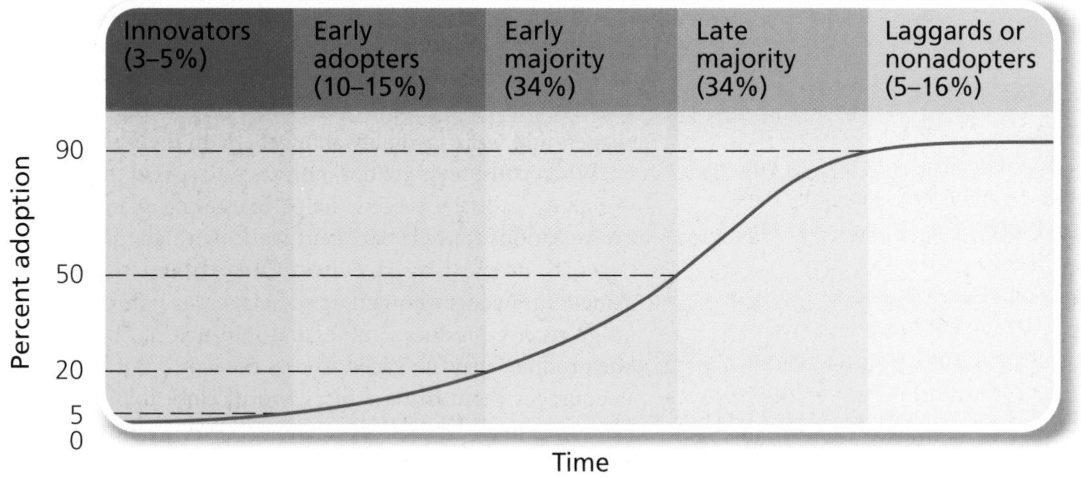

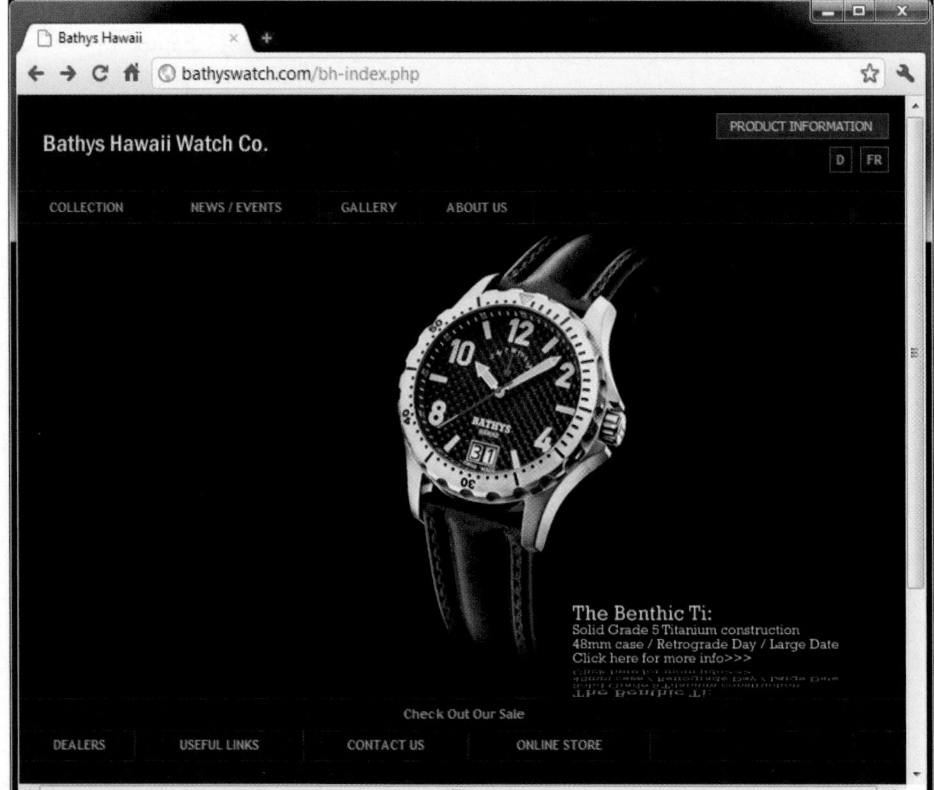

The website for Bathys Hawaii Watch Co. was getting about 60 hits a day until Gizmodo.com, a blog on new consumer technology that appeals to technology opinion leaders, wrote about the Bathys watch designed especially for surfers. After that, website hits jumped to 1,800 per day and sales increased by 300 percent.

Opinion leaders help spread the word

Marketers know the importance of personal recommendations by opinion leaders. For example, some movie fans like to be the first to see new flicks. If they like a movie, they quickly tell their friends and word-of-mouth publicity does the real selling job. When online grocer FreshDirect opened in New York City, positive word of mouth keyed its fast growth. However, consumers are even more likely to talk about a negative experience than a positive one. So, if early groups reject the product, it may never get off the ground. In a study of consumers, 64 percent said they would not shop at a store after being told about someone else's negative experience there.[12]

The popularity of blogs, online reviews, and similar web media gives power to "word of mouse." Some companies try to identify and work with online opinion leaders. There are a large number of so-called "mommy bloggers," stay-at-home moms who write blogs about child-rearing. With a loyal readership, these bloggers can influence many people. Kimberly-Clark recognized the importance of these influencers and sent samples of its new Huggies Pure & Natural premium diapers to 500 of them. Not to be left out, P&G flew a dozen mommy bloggers to its Cincinnati headquarters to show them how Pampers are developed. Both companies hope these opinion leaders will become fans of their diapers and write favorably about them on their blogs.[13]

When consumers are not motivated to spread the word, a company called BzzAgent helps marketing managers get conversations started. BzzAgent works with about 800,000 "agents" in the United States, Canada, and the United Kingdom. Agents who sign up to help with a particular campaign receive product samples and information. If they like the product, they are urged to pass the word. But BzzAgent encourages them to be ethical and disclose their status as "buzz agents." Kraft Foods, General Mills, and Dockers have run campaigns like this.[14]

Internet Exercise

BzzAgent has a code of conduct for its agents, but even so it has received some negative publicity that questions the ethics of its agents. Go to the BzzAgent site (**www.BzzAgent.com**) and click on "Join BzzAgent" and then on "Code of Conduct" to read through the code. If a BzzAgent follows the guidelines in the code, do you think the practice is ethical? In your opinion, what actions would make a BzzAgent's behavior unethical?

Blogging, Tweeting, and Pinning with Customers

Many marketers are adding new dimensions to their promotion blend by using blogs, Twitter, and Pinterest. A *blog,* short for *web log,* is a type of website that offers a running stream of messages, links, and videos in the form of regular posts. A blog also lets readers add comments to each entry. Blogs are usually created by an individual to express personal opinions about some topic; many companies encourage employees to write blogs about the company. As with other types of personal communication, including personal selling, blogs can help make a connection with customers and enhance the relationship with them.

Yogurt-maker Stonyfield Farm uses a blog to reinforce the healthy and wholesome positioning of its foods. Written by organic farmer Jonathan Gates, "The Bovine Bugle" reports on life at Gates' farm, which supplies milk used in Stonyfield Farm's yogurt. Fast-food chain McDonald's uses a blog to address criticisms it receives about contributing to obesity, trash, and other ills. Its Senior Director of Corporate Responsibility, Bob Langert, uses this format to reach out and interact with the company's customers and critics. Posts with titles such as "What's Best for Chickens—Controlled Atmospheric Stunning (CAS) or Electrical Stunning?" create an opportunity for McDonald's to deal directly with uncomfortable topics like the humane treatment of animals.

For bloggers with less to say, "microblogging" service Twitter allows users to send short (140 characters or less) "Tweets" to "followers." The Dell Outlet store uses Twitter to let more than 1.5 million followers know about its latest computer deals. In its first year, Twitter drove an additional $6.5 million worth of sales at Dell. The Xbox Tweet Fleet provides customer technical support for the popular video game. The team responds in 3–5 minutes to customer questions directed to @XboxSupport.

Pinterest takes a visual approach to connecting with customers. At Pinterest individuals and businesses can share images—their own photos or other images they find on the web—and organize them into theme-based collections. So for example, a young woman might have a board dedicated to "My Wedding," another with pictures of "Favorite Shoes," "Hairstyles," "Dogs," and "Sunsets." When people visit her Pinterest (everything is public), they can re-pin any images to their own board.

Businesses create Pinterest boards as a way to interact with their customers. Etsy, the online marketplace for vintage and handmade products, has dozens of boards showcasing products you can find at its site – as well as boards showing customers how to make stuff on their own. A visitor to the Etsy site could find a piece of pottery he likes, pin it to his "Things I want" board, and hope someone buys it for him when his birthday rolls around. Greek yogurt maker Chobani also maintains a couple dozen Pinterest boards that feature recipes using the yogurt or pictures of cool places to visit. Chobani hopes its fans feel better about the brand—and find more reasons to buy it.

Blogs, Twitter, and Pinterest create opportunities for marketers to update and interact *with* customers. These tools allow firms to communicate with customers in an informal, open, and honest manner that promotes trust in a way that advertising can't.[15]

Early majority group is deliberate

The **early majority** avoids risk and waits to consider a new idea after many early adopters have tried it—and liked it. Average-sized business firms that are less specialized often fit in this category. If successful companies in their industry adopt the new idea, they will too.

The early majority have a great deal of contact with mass media, salespeople, and early adopter opinion leaders. Members usually aren't opinion leaders themselves.

Late majority is cautious

The **late majority** is cautious about new ideas. Often they are older and more set in their ways, so they are less likely to follow early adopters. In fact, strong social pressure from their own peer group may be needed before they adopt a new product. Business firms in this group tend to be conservative, smaller-sized firms with little specialization.

The late majority makes little use of marketing sources of information—mass media and salespeople. They tend to be oriented more toward other late adopters rather than outside sources they don't trust.

Laggards or nonadopters hang on to tradition

Laggards or **nonadopters** prefer to do things the way they've been done in the past and are very suspicious of new ideas. They tend to be older and less well educated. The smallest businesses with the least specialization often fit this category. They cling to the status quo and think it's the safe way.

The main source of information for laggards is other laggards. This certainly is bad news for marketers. In fact, it may not pay to bother with this group.[16]

Promotion Blends Vary Over the Life Cycle

Stage of product in its life cycle

The adoption curve helps explain why a new product goes through the product life-cycle stages described in Chapter 9. Promotion blends usually have to change to achieve different promotion objectives at different life-cycle stages.

Market introduction stage—"this new idea is good"

During market introduction, the basic promotion objective is informing. If the product is a really new idea, the promotion must build **primary demand**—demand for the general product idea—not just for the company's own brand. Video phone service and "smart" appliances (that connect to the Internet) are good examples of product concepts where primary demand is just beginning to grow. There may be few potential innovators during the introduction stage, and personal selling can help find them. Firms also need salespeople to find good channel members and persuade them to carry the new product. Sales promotion may be targeted at salespeople or channel members to get them interested in selling the new product. And sales promotion may also encourage customers to try it.

Market growth stage—"our brand is best"

In the market growth stage, more competitors enter the market, and promotion emphasis shifts from building primary demand to stimulating **selective demand**—demand for a company's own brand. The main job is to persuade customers to buy, and keep buying, the company's product.

Now that there are more potential customers, mass selling becomes more economical. But salespeople and personal selling must still work in the channels, expanding the number of outlets and cementing relationships with channel members.

The evolution of promotion for Banquet Homestyle Bakes illustrates these first two stages. When ConAgra Foods introduced Homestyle Bakes, it was the first shelf-stable meal kit with the meat already in the package. ConAgra, also the producer of Armour processed meats, had the expertise to create a tasty product that a consumer could prepare in a few minutes and then just stick in the oven. When Homestyle Bakes came out, there

Compact fluorescent light bulbs are still in the market introduction stage, so this ad attempts to build primary demand by encouraging consumers to use this new technology. In contrast, the ad for Monster's Nitrous tells consumers why they should buy this particular brand of energy drink, building selective demand for Nitrous.

was no direct competition. The sales force used market research data to convince retailers to give the product shelf space, and ads used humor to highlight that the package was unusually heavy because it already included meat. However, over time new competition entered the market with similar offerings. So promotion shifted to emphasize why Homestyle Bakes were better, with a variety of new flavors and 10 percent more meat. Similarly, to keep customers interested in the Homestyle brand, the sales force shifted its efforts to get retailers to participate in Homestyle Bakes' "Super Meals/Super Moms" contests, which offered harried moms prizes such as a visit to a spa.[17]

Market maturity stage—"our brand is better, really"

In the market maturity stage, mass selling and sales promotion may dominate the promotion blends of consumer products firms. Business products may require more aggressive personal selling—perhaps supplemented by more advertising. The total dollars allocated to promotion may rise as competition increases.

If a firm already has high sales—relative to competitors—it may have a real advantage in promotion at this stage. For example, sales of Tylenol tablets are about four times the sales of Motrin competing tablets. If both Tylenol and Motrin spend the same percentage of sales (say 35 percent) on promotion, Tylenol will spend four times as much as its smaller competitor and will probably communicate to more people.

Firms that have differentiated their marketing mixes may favor mass selling because they have something to talk about. For instance, a firm with a strong brand may use reminder-type advertising or target frequent-buyer promotions at current customers to strengthen the relationship and keep customers loyal. This may be more effective than costly efforts to win customers away from competitors.

Special end-of-aisle displays, like this one for Wonder bread, and other point-of-purchase sales promotion materials are especially important for consumer staples in the highly competitive market maturity stage of the product life cycle.

However, as a market drifts toward pure competition, some companies resort to price-cutting. This may temporarily increase the number of units sold, but it is also likely to reduce total revenue and the money available for promotion. The temporary sales gains disappear and prices are dragged down even lower when competitors retaliate with their own short-term sales promotions, like price-off coupons. As cash flowing into the business declines, spending may have to be cut back.[18]

Sales decline stage—"let's tell those who still want our product"

During the sales decline stage, the total amount spent on promotion usually decreases as firms try to cut costs to remain profitable. Since some people may still want the product, firms need more targeted promotion to reach these customers.

On the other hand, some firms may increase promotion to try to slow the cycle, at least temporarily. Crayola had almost all of the market for children's crayons, but sales were slowly declining as new kinds of markers came along. Crayola increased ad spending to urge parents to buy their kids a "fresh box."

Setting the Promotion Budget

LO 13.8

Size of budget affects promotion efficiency and blend

There are some economies of scale in promotion. An ad on national TV might cost less *per person* reached than an ad on local TV. Similarly, citywide radio, TV, and newspapers may be cheaper than neighborhood newspapers or direct personal contact. But the *total cost* for some mass media may force small firms, or those with small promotion budgets, to use promotion alternatives that are more expensive per contact. For example, a small

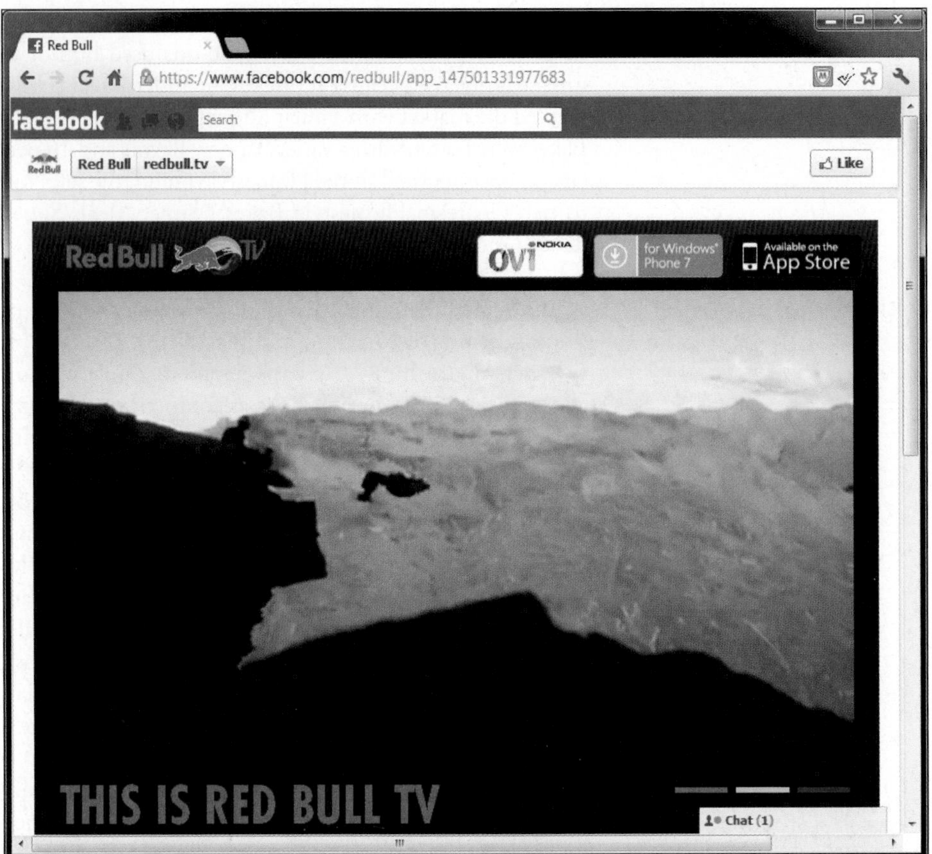

More than 25 million fans have "liked" Red Bull's Facebook page. Many of these fans come to see Red Bull's original "Adrenaline Series," which is entertaining and reinforces that Red Bull "gives wings to people who want to be mentally and physically active and have a zest for life." Marketing managers like that there is little cost to put promotional messages and videos on Facebook, because it can be expensive to create original programming like what is shown on Red Bull TV. Marketing managers must consider the cost to maintain a Facebook page when they add one to the promotion blend. The cost per person reached is probably low for Red Bull because of its large number of fans. But for every Facebook site with more than a million "likes," there are thousands with fewer than 100 "likes."

retailer might want to use local television but finds that there is only enough money for a web page, an ad in the Yellow Pages, and an occasional newspaper ad.

Find the task, budget for it

The most common method of budgeting for promotion expenditures is to compute a percentage of either past sales or sales expected in the future. The virtue of this method is its simplicity. However, just because this mechanical approach is common doesn't mean that it's smart. It leads to expanding marketing expenditures when business is good and cutting back when business is poor. When business is poor, this approach may just make the problem worse—if weak promotion is the reason for declining sales.

In the light of our continuing focus on planning marketing strategies to reach objectives, the most sensible approach to budgeting promotion expenditures is the **task method**—basing the budget on the job to be done. It helps a marketing manager to set priorities so that the money spent on promotion produces specific and desired results. In fact, this approach makes sense for *any* marketing expenditure, but here we'll focus on promotion.

A practical approach is to determine which promotion methods are most economical and effective for the tasks that need to be completed to achieve communication objectives. The costs of these tasks are then totaled to determine how much should be budgeted for promotion (just as money is allocated for other marketing activities required by the strategy). In other words, the firm can assemble its total promotion budget directly from detailed plans rather than by simply relying on historical patterns or ratios.

Of course this makes the process sound simpler than it really is. Some promotion activities and objectives can be readily measured. Setting a target of adding 10,000 new likes to Taco Bell's Facebook page and then offering discount coupons to each new like is pretty straightforward. Taco Bell can measure the cost of the promotion (coupons plus any advertising) and the number of new likes on the Facebook page. On the other hand, what if the objective is to change the level of brand familiarity of Bonobos pants for fashion-conscious men by running ads in select men's magazines? The results here can be more difficult to measure, but not impossible. Even when evaluation is difficult, marketing managers should still try to evaluate costs and returns to develop a realistic budget.[19]

CONCLUSION

Promotion is an important part of any marketing mix. Most consumers and intermediate customers can choose from among many products. To be successful, a producer must not only offer a good product at a reasonable price but also inform potential customers about the product and where they can buy it. Further, producers must tell wholesalers and retailers in the channel about their product and marketing mix. These intermediaries, in turn, must use promotion to reach their customers. And the promotion blend must fit with the rest of the marketing mix and the target market.

In this chapter, we introduced different promotion methods and we discussed the advantages and disadvantages of each method. We also discussed the integrated marketing communications concept and explained why most firms use a blend of different promotion methods. While the overall promotion objective is to affect buying behavior, the basic promotion objectives are informing, persuading, and reminding. These objectives help guide the marketing manager's decisions about the promotion blend.

Models from the behavioral sciences help us understand the communication process and how it can break down. These models recognize different ways to communicate. We discussed direct-response promotion for developing more targeted promotion blends. And we described an approach where customers initiate and interact with the marketer's communications. It provides new and different challenges for marketing managers.

This chapter also recognized other factors that influence decisions about promotion blends. Marketing managers must make decisions about how to split promotion that is directed at final consumers or business customers—and at channel members. Promotion blends are also influenced by the adoption curve and the product life-cycle stages. Finally, we described how promotion budgets are set and influence promotion decisions.

In this chapter, we considered some basic concepts that apply to all areas of promotion. In Chapters 14 and 15, we'll discuss personal selling, customer service, advertising, publicity, and sales promotion in more detail.

KEY TERMS

LO 13.9

promotion, *330*
personal selling, *331*
mass selling, *331*
advertising, *331*
publicity, *332*
sales promotion, *332*
sales managers, *333*
advertising managers, *333*
public relations, *333*
sales promotion managers, *333*
integrated marketing communications, *334*
AIDA model, *336*
communication process, *337*
source, *337*
receiver, *337*
noise, *338*
encoding, *338*
decoding, *338*
message channel, *338*
pushing, *343*
pulling, *345*
adoption curve, *347*
innovators, *347*
early adopters, *347*
early majority, *349*
late majority, *349*
laggards, *350*
nonadopters, *350*
primary demand, *350*
selective demand, *350*
task method, *352*

QUESTIONS AND PROBLEMS

1. Briefly explain the nature of the three basic promotion methods available to a marketing manager. What are the main strengths and limitations of each?
2. In your own words, discuss the integrated marketing communications concept. Explain what its emphasis on "consistent" and "complete" messages implies with respect to promotion blends.
3. Relate the three basic promotion objectives to the four jobs (AIDA) of promotion using a specific example.
4. Discuss the communication process in relation to a producer's promotion of an accessory product—say, a new electronic security system businesses use to limit access to areas where they store confidential records.
5. If a company wants its promotion to appeal to a new group of target customers in a foreign country, how can it protect against its communications being misinterpreted?
6. Promotion has been the target of considerable criticism. What specific types of promotion are probably the object of this criticism? Give a particular example that illustrates your thinking.
7. With direct-response promotion, customers provide feedback to marketing communications. How can a marketing manager use this feedback to improve the effectiveness of the overall promotion blend?
8. How can a promotion manager aim a message at a certain target market with electronic media (like the Internet) when the customer initiates the communication? Give an example.
9. What promotion blend would be most appropriate for producers of the following established products? Assume average- to large-sized firms in each case and support your answer.
   a. Chocolate candy bars.
   b. Car batteries.
   c. Panty hose.
   d. Castings for truck engines.
   e. A special computer used by manufacturers for control of production equipment.
   f. Inexpensive plastic rainhats.
   g. A digital tape recorder that has achieved specialty-product status.
10. A small company has developed an innovative new spray-on glass cleaner that prevents the buildup of electrostatic dust on computer screens and TVs. Give examples of some low-cost ways the firm might effectively promote its product. Be certain to consider both push and pull approaches.
11. Would promotion be successful in expanding the general demand for: (*a*) almonds, (*b*) air travel, (*c*) golf clubs, (*d*) walking shoes, (*e*) high-octane unleaded gasoline, (*f*) single-serving, frozen gourmet dinners, and (*g*) bricks? Explain why or why not in each case.
12. Explain how an understanding of the adoption process would help you develop a promotion blend for digital tape recorders, a new consumer electronics product that produces high-quality recordings. Explain why you might change the promotion blend during the course of the adoption process.
13. Explain how opinion leaders affect a firm's promotion planning.
14. Discuss how the adoption curve should be used to plan the promotion blend(s) for a new automobile accessory—an electronic radar system that alerts a driver if he or she is about to change lanes into the path of a car that is passing through a blind spot in the driver's mirrors.
15. If a marketing manager uses the task method to budget for marketing promotions, are competitors' promotion spending levels ignored? Explain your thinking and give an example that supports your point of view.
16. Discuss the potential conflict among the various promotion managers. How could this be reduced?

CREATING MARKETING PLANS

The Marketing Plan Coach software on the text website includes a sample marketing plan for Hillside Veterinary Clinic. Look through the "Marketing Strategy" section.

a. What are Hillside's promotion objectives? How do they differ for the various goods and services the company offers?
b. Do the promotion activities recommended in the plan fit with the promotion objectives? Create a table to compare them. Label the columns: good/service, promotion objective, and promotion activities.
c. Based on the situation analysis, target market, and intended positioning, recommend other (low-cost) promotion activities for Hillside.

SUGGESTED CASES

18. Whistler Township Volunteer Fire Department
19. MyPerfectWedding.com

COMPUTER-AIDED PROBLEM

13. SELECTING A COMMUNICATIONS CHANNEL

Helen Troy, owner of three Sound Haus stereo equipment stores, is deciding what message channel (advertising medium) to use to promote her newest store. Her current promotion blend includes direct-mail ads that are effective for reaching her current customers. She also has knowledgeable salespeople who work well with consumers once they're in the store. However, a key objective in opening a new store is to attract new customers. Her best prospects are professionals in the 25–44 age range with incomes over $38,000 a year. But only some of the people in this group are audiophiles who want the top-of-the-line brands she carries. Troy has decided to use local advertising to reach new customers.

Troy narrowed her choice to two advertising media: an FM radio station and a biweekly magazine that focuses on entertainment in her city. Many of the magazine's readers are out-of-town visitors interested in concerts, plays, and restaurants. They usually buy stereo equipment at home. But the magazine's audience research shows that many local professionals do subscribe to the magazine. Troy doesn't think that the objective can be achieved with a single ad. However, she believes that ads in six issues will generate good local awareness with her target market. In addition, the magazine's color format will let her present the prestige image she wants to convey in an ad. She thinks that will help convert aware prospects to buyers. Specialists at a local advertising agency will prepare a high-impact ad for $2,000, and then Troy will pay for the magazine space.

The FM radio station targets an audience similar to Troy's own target market. She knows repeated ads will be needed to be sure that most of her target audience is exposed to her ads. Troy thinks it will take daily ads for several months to create adequate awareness among her target market. The FM station will provide an announcer and prepare a tape of Troy's ad for a one-time fee of $200. All she has to do is tell the station what the message content for the ad should say.

Both the radio station and the magazine gave Troy reports summarizing recent audience research. She decides that comparing the two media in a spreadsheet will help her make a better decision.

a. Based on the data displayed on the initial spreadsheet, which message channel (advertising medium) would you recommend to Troy? Why?

b. The agency that offered to prepare Troy's magazine ad will prepare a fully produced radio ad—including a musical jingle—for $2,500. The agency claims that its musical ad will have much more impact than the ad the radio station will create. The agency says its ad should produce the same results as the station ad with 20 percent fewer insertions. If the agency claim is correct, would it be wise for Troy to pay the agency to produce the ad?

c. The agency will not guarantee that its custom-produced radio ad will reach Troy's objective—making 80 percent of the prospects aware of the new store. Troy wants to see how lower levels of awareness—between 50 percent and 70 percent—would affect the advertising cost per buyer and the cost per aware prospect. Use the analysis feature to vary the percent of prospects who become aware. Prepare a table showing the effect on the two kinds of costs. What are the implications of your analysis?

14

CHAPTER FOURTEEN

Personal Selling and Customer Service

As a student in the College of Business at the University of Illinois, Pooja Gupta wanted a job that would offer interesting challenges, give opportunities for professional growth, and value her enthusiasm. She found what she wanted with Ferguson. Ferguson was actively recruiting on college campuses to find the brightest and best candidates for its sales jobs—so, in a way, the job found her.

Gupta knew that motivated young people often find the best opportunities in fast-growing companies. She didn't expect, however, that her fast-growing company would be a wholesaler of plumbing supplies, pipes, valves, and fittings. To the contrary, she'd heard that many wholesalers were declining. But that didn't apply to Ferguson. For decades it has doubled in size about every five years—and now it's the largest U.S. distributor of plumbing products. And in a business that serves such a wide variety of customer types—large industrial firms, city waterworks, commercial builders and subcontractors, kitchen and bath dealers, and final consumers—you don't get that kind of growth without an effective sales force.

It's Ferguson's sales force that gets the initial orders with new customers, builds the relationships that instill customer loyalty, and provides the customer service support that Ferguson emphasizes. Its sales reps understand their customers' business problems and how Ferguson's products, e-commerce, and state-of-the-art logistics systems can help solve them. This expertise and focus on customer needs make Ferguson salespeople trusted partners. Because they're real experts on the company's products and how to cut customer costs, they've proved invaluable during the recent economic downturn when demand for Ferguson's core plumbing products plunged along with new home construction.

An effective sales force like the one at Ferguson doesn't just happen. Someone needs to figure out the promotion jobs that require personal selling and then get the right people on the job. That is why Ferguson's marketing managers work closely with sales managers.

Ferguson carries over a million products, provides service centers at 1,300 locations, and has divisions that specialize by different customer segments. It would be futile for sales reps to try to be experts in everything. Instead, sales managers carefully match each salesperson to particular territories, customers, and product lines. Gupta, for example, helps contractors in the Virginia market figure out how to satisfy the needs of final consumers for whom they are building or remodeling homes. She knows the current fashions for kitchen and bath renovations, how to reduce "behind-the-wall" plumbing installation costs for a big new apartment building, and the advantages and limitations of hundreds of brands from companies like Kohler, Elkay, Moen, and Jacuzzi.

Other Ferguson salespeople work with cities and huge waterworks contractors on infrastructure projects such as updating water purification facilities. And salespeople for Ferguson's Integrated Systems Division (ISD) are really selling a big business idea rather than "pipe." They show top executives at customer firms why they should invest millions of dollars in a full-service supply relationship where Ferguson does all of the purchasing and warehousing for entire manufacturing facilities. In stark contrast, the main sales job in one of Ferguson's new self-service Xpress outlets is to ring up sales when hurried plumbers need repair parts.

To recruit talented people for these varied jobs, Ferguson's sales managers use a wide variety of methods. For example, the careers section of Ferguson's website collects job applicant profiles on an ongoing basis. When a position opens up, qualified candidates are notified. And Ferguson actively recruits on college campuses, typically hiring about 700 graduates every year. After a pre-interview on campus, select candidates go to a regional office and meet a number of managers from that area.

After the best people are selected, Ferguson provides the sales training to make them even better. Of course, the training is different for different people. For example, most new college recruits work for a short time in a Ferguson warehouse, which helps them understand the company's logistics system, its products, and its industry as well as the company's "can-do" culture. Other training methods range from self-study online modules to role playing to working in the field with experienced managers who help them build professional problem-solving skills as well as technical knowledge.

Even experienced sales reps need ongoing training on new strategies or policies. When Ferguson's management saw an opportunity to enhance customer loyalty, a training program was developed and implemented with Ferguson's 19,000 associates. They participated in face-to-face and online courses covering topics like "the difference between customer satisfaction and loyalty" and "how to earn loyal customers." The return on investment for the training program was estimated at over 400 percent.

To be sure that each salesperson is highly motivated, Ferguson's sales managers make certain that sales compensation arrangements and benefits reward salespeople for producing needed results. For example, the evaluation considers how well individuals work within a team—because in the customer service culture at Ferguson, great teamwork is critical. Even in a slow economy, Ferguson continued to invest in the quality of its sales force. These efforts will pay off. As the economy and home-building pick up, its sales force will be busy helping contractors, builders, and home buyers choose the right supplies, fueling Ferguson's growth.[1]

Learning Objectives

Promotion is communicating with potential customers and others in the channel. As the Ferguson case suggests, personal selling is often the best way to do it. While face to face with prospects, salespeople can adjust what actions they take in response to the prospect's interests, needs, questions, and feedback. If, and when, the prospect is ready to buy, the salesperson is there to ask for the order. And afterward, the salesperson works to be certain that the customer is satisfied and will buy again in the future. In this chapter, you'll learn about the key strategy decisions related to personal selling that marketing managers and the sales managers who work with them make.

When you finish this chapter you should be able to:

1. understand the importance and nature of personal selling.
2. know the three basic sales tasks—order-getting, order-taking, and supporting—and what various kinds of salespeople can be expected to do.
3. understand why customer service presents different challenges than other personal selling tasks.
4. know the different ways sales managers can organize salespeople so that personal selling jobs are handled effectively.
5. know how sales technology affects the way sales tasks are performed.
6. know what the sales manager must do, including selecting, training, and organizing salespeople to carry out the personal selling job.
7. understand how the right compensation plan can help motivate and control salespeople.
8. understand when and where to use the three types of sales presentations.
9. understand important new terms (shown in red).

The Importance and Role of Personal Selling

LO 14.1

Personal selling requires strategy decisions

In this chapter, we'll discuss the importance and nature of personal selling and customer service so you'll understand the strategy decisions in this area. See Exhibit 14-1.

We'll also discuss a number of frameworks and how-to approaches that guide these strategy decisions. Because these approaches apply equally to domestic and international markets, we won't emphasize that distinction in this chapter. This does not mean, however, that personal selling techniques don't vary from one country to another. To the contrary, in dealing with *any* customer, the salesperson must adjust for cultural influences and other factors that might affect communication. For example, a Japanese customer and an Arab

Exhibit 14–1 Strategy Planning and Personal Selling

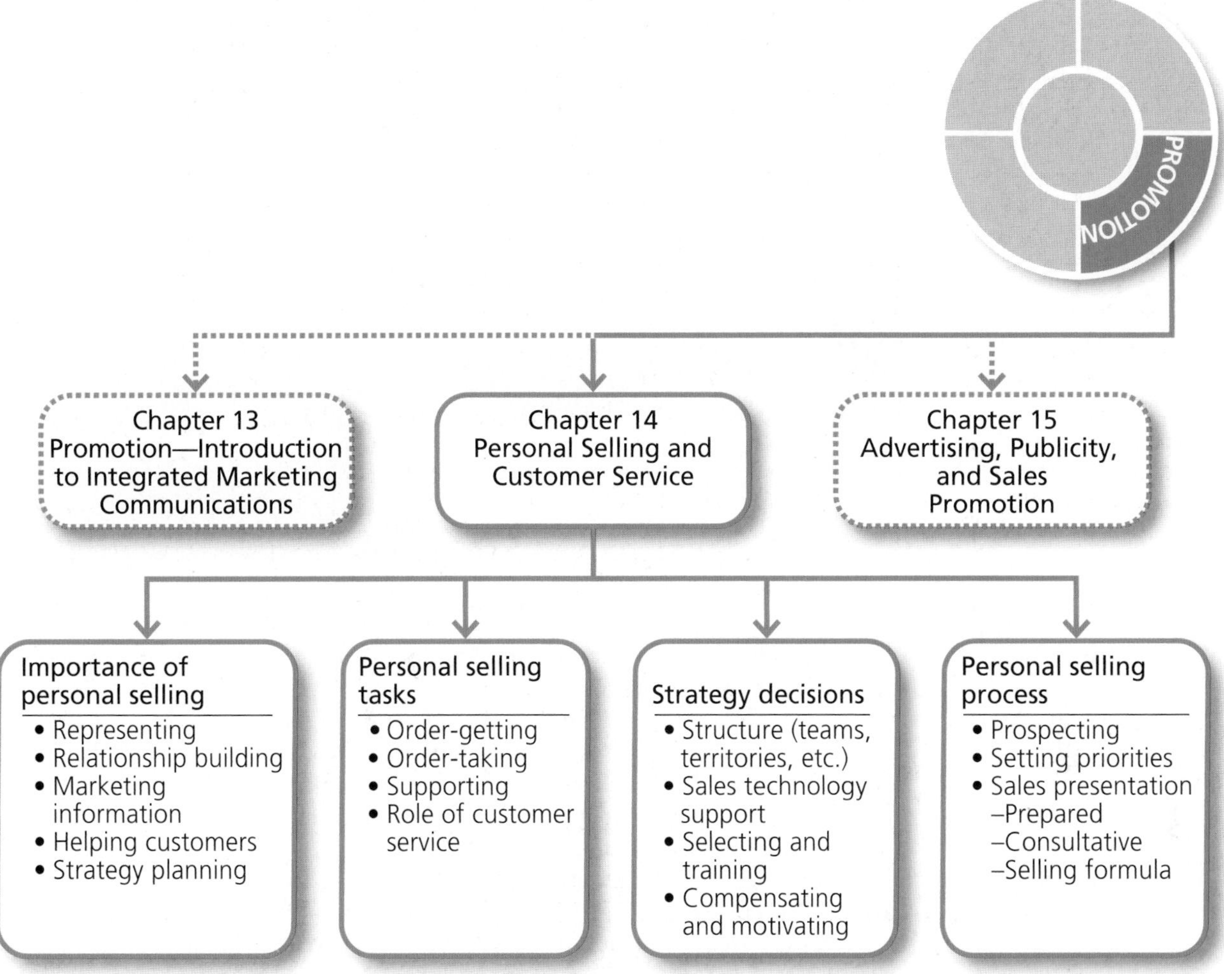

customer might respond differently to subtle aspects of a salesperson's behavior. The Arab customer might expect to be very close to a salesperson, perhaps only two feet away, while they talk. The Japanese customer might consider that distance rude. Similarly, what topics of discussion are considered sensitive, how messages are interpreted, and which negotiating styles are used vary from one country to another. A salesperson must know how to communicate effectively with each customer—wherever and whoever that customer is.[2]

Personal selling is important

Personal selling is absolutely essential in the promotion blends of some firms. Consider how you would feel if you regularly had to meet payrolls and somehow, almost miraculously, your salespeople kept coming in with orders just in time to keep the business profitable.

Personal selling is often a company's largest single operating expense. This is another reason why it is important to understand sales management decisions. Bad ones are costly in both lost sales and in actual out-of-pocket expenses.

Every economy needs and uses many salespeople. In the United States, one person out of every ten in the total labor force is involved in sales work. By comparison, that's about 20 times more people than are employed in advertising. Any occupation that employs so many people and is so important to the economy deserves study. Looking at what salespeople do is a good way to start.

Helping to buy is good selling

Good salespeople don't just try to *sell* the customer. Rather, they try to *help the customer buy*—by understanding the customer's needs and presenting the advantages and disadvantages of their products. Such helpfulness results in satisfied customers and

Good salespeople help customers find solutions to problems. Often that requires a trusting relationship that comes from carefully listening to a customer and learning how best to address their needs.

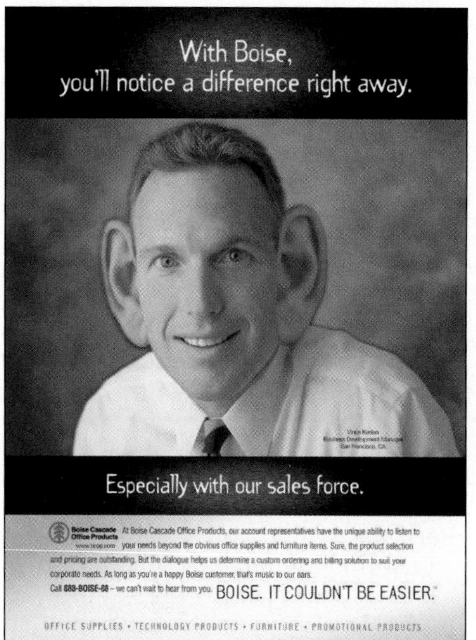

long-term relationships. And strong relationships often form the basis for a competitive advantage, especially in business markets.

Salespeople represent the whole company—and customers too

The salesperson is often a representative of the whole company—responsible for explaining its total effort to customers rather than just pushing products. The salesperson may provide information about products, explain company policies, and even negotiate prices or diagnose technical problems.

The sales rep is often the only link between the firm and its customers, especially if customers are far away. When a number of people from the firm work with the customer organization—which is common when suppliers and customers form close relationships—it is usually the sales rep who coordinates the relationship for his or her firm. See Exhibit 6-6.

The salesperson also represents the *customer* back inside the selling firm. Recall that feedback is an essential part of both the communication process *and* the basic management process of planning, implementing, and control. For example, it's likely to be the sales rep who explains to the production manager why a customer is unhappy with product quality.

As evidence of these changing responsibilities, some companies give their salespeople such titles as account representative, field manager, sales consultant, market specialist, or sales engineer.

Sales force aids in marketing information function as well

The sales force can aid in the marketing information function too. The sales rep may be the first to hear about a new competitor or a competitor's new strategy. And sales reps who are well attuned to customers' needs can be a key source of ideas for new products or new uses for existing products.

Material Sciences Corporation developed a product called Quiet Steel, two thin layers of steel bonded together to absorb vibration so that it doesn't rattle. A sales rep who worked with the Ford team developing the new F-150 truck probed to understand where Ford was trying to reduce noise and recommended how Quiet Steel could help. Feedback to Quiet Steel about Ford's most promising applications helped Quiet Steel reps who call on other car makers pursue similar applications. And the R&D department for Quiet Steel benefits from hearing from the sales reps about applications where the current product isn't quite right, but where there might be an opportunity for a new product.[3]

Salespeople can be strategy planners too

Some salespeople are expected to be marketing managers in their own territories. And some become marketing managers by default because top management hasn't provided detailed strategy guidelines. Either way, the salesperson may have choices about (1) which customers to target, (2) which particular products to emphasize, (3) which intermediaries to rely on or help, (4) what message to communicate and how to use promotion money, and (5) how to adjust prices. A salesperson who can put together profitable strategies and implement them well can rise very rapidly. The opportunity is there for those prepared and willing to work.[4]

What Kinds of Personal Selling are Needed?

LO 14.2

If a firm has too few salespeople, or the wrong kind, some important personal selling tasks may not be completed. And having too many salespeople wastes money. In addition, the balance that is right may change over time with other changes in strategy or the market environment. That's why many firms have to restructure their sales forces.

One of the difficulties of determining the right number and kind of salespeople is that every sales job is different. While an engineer or accountant can look forward to fairly specific duties, the salesperson's job changes constantly. However, there are three basic types of sales tasks. This gives us a starting point for understanding what sales tasks need to be done and how many people are needed to do them.

Personal selling is divided into three tasks

The three **basic sales tasks** are order-getting, order-taking, and supporting. For convenience, we'll describe salespeople by these terms—referring to their primary task—*although one person may do all three tasks in some situations.*

Order Getters Develop New Business Relationships

Order getters are concerned with establishing relationships with new customers and developing new business. **Order-getting** means seeking possible buyers with a well-organized sales presentation designed to sell a good, service, or idea.

Order getters must know what they're talking about, not just be personal contacts. Order-getting salespeople normally are well paid—many earn more than $100,000 a year!

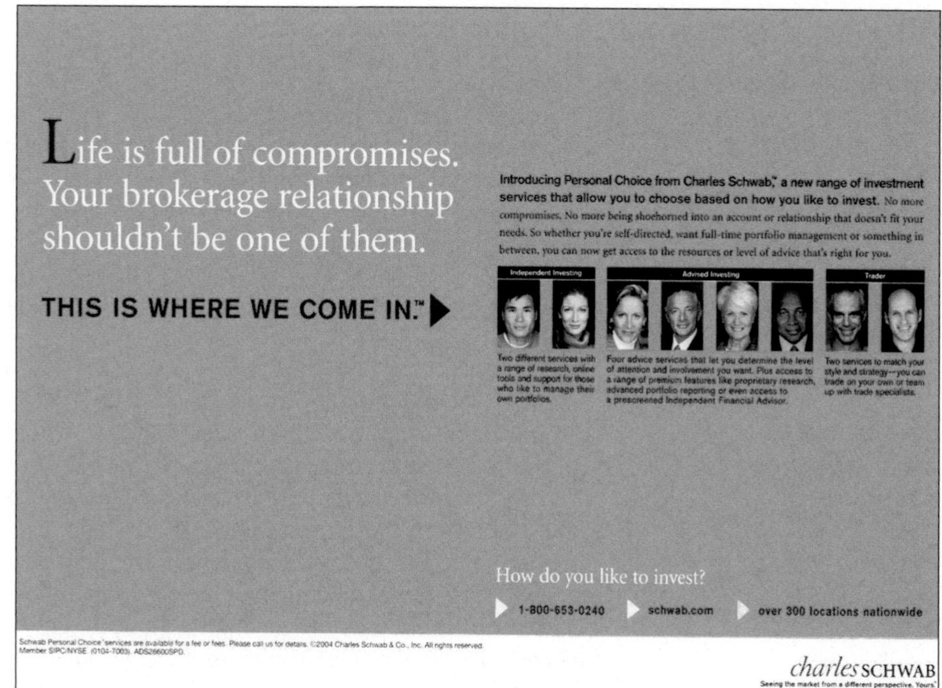

Life is full of compromises.
Your brokerage relationship shouldn't be one of them.
THIS IS WHERE WE COME IN.℠
Introducing Personal Choice from Charles Schwab,® a new range of investment services that allow you to choose based on how you like to invest. No more compromises. No more being shoehorned into an account or relationship that doesn't fit your needs. So whether you're self-directed, want full-time portfolio management or something in between, you can now get access to the resources or level of advice that's right for you.
Independent Investing
Advised Investing
Trader
Two different services with a range of research, online tools and support for those who like to manage their own portfolios.
Four advice services that let you determine the level of attention and involvement you want. Plus access to a range of premium features like proprietary research, advanced portfolio reporting or even access to a prescreened Independent Financial Advisor.
Two services to match your style and strategy—you can trade on your own or team up with trade specialists.
How do you like to invest?
1-800-653-0240
schwab.com
over 300 locations nationwide
Schwab Personal Choice services are available for a fee or fees. Please call us for details. ©2004 Charles Schwab & Co., Inc. All rights reserved. Member SIPC/NYSE. (0104-7003). ADS26600SPD.
charles SCHWAB
Seeing the market from a different perspective. Yours.

Customers who are making an important purchase decision want relationships with salespeople who understand their goals.

Producers' order getters—find new opportunities

Producers of all kinds of products, especially business products, have a great need for order getters. They use order getters to locate new prospects, open new accounts, see new opportunities, and help establish and build channel relationships.

Top-level customers are more interested in ways to save or make more money than in technical details. Good order getters cater to this interest. They help the customer identify ways to solve problems; then they sell concepts and ideas, not just physical products. The goods and services they supply are merely the means of achieving the customer's end.

To be effective at this sort of "solutions selling," an order getter often needs to understand a customer's whole business as well as technical details about the product and its applications. For example, a salesperson for automated manufacturing equipment must understand a prospect's production process as well as the technical details of converting to computer-controlled equipment.

Order getters for professional services—and other products where service is a crucial element of the marketing mix—face a special challenge. The customer usually can't inspect a service before deciding to buy. The order getter's communication and relationship with the customer may be the only basis for evaluating the quality of the supplier.

Wholesalers' order getters—almost hand it to the customer

Salespeople for agent wholesalers are often order getters—particularly the more aggressive manufacturers' agents and brokers. They face the same tasks as producers' order getters. But, unfortunately for them, once the order-getting is done and the customers become established and loyal, producers may try to eliminate the agents and save money with their own order takers.

Retail order getters influence consumer behavior

Convincing consumers about the value of products they haven't seriously considered takes a high level of personal selling ability. Order getters for unsought consumer products must help customers see how a new product can satisfy needs now being filled by something else. Without order getters, many common products—ranging from mutual funds to air conditioners—might have died in the market introduction stage. The order getter helps bring products out of the introduction stage into the market growth stage.

Order getters are also helpful for selling *heterogeneous* shopping products. Consumers shop for many of these items on the basis of suitability and value. They welcome useful information.

Order Takers Nurture Relationships to Keep the Business Coming

Order takers sell to the regular or established customers, complete most sales transactions, and maintain relationships with their customers. After a customer becomes interested in a firm's products through an order getter or supporting salesperson or through advertising or sales promotion, an order taker usually answers any final questions and completes the sale. **Order-taking** is the routine completion of sales made regularly to target customers. It usually requires ongoing follow-up to make certain that the customer is totally satisfied.

Producers' order takers—train, explain, and collaborate

Order takers work on improving the whole relationship with their accounts, not just on completing a single sale. Even in e-commerce, where customers place routine orders with computerized order systems, order takers do a variety of important jobs that are essential to the business relationship. Someone has to explain details, make adjustments, handle complaints, explain new prices or terms, place sales promotion materials, and keep customers informed of new developments. An order taker who fails to meet a customer's expectations on any of these activities might jeopardize the relationship and future sales.

Firms sometimes use order-taking jobs to train potential order getters and managers. Such jobs give them an opportunity to meet customers and better understand their needs. And, frequently, they run into some order-getting opportunities.

Order takers who are alert to order-getting possibilities can make the big difference in generating new sales. Some firms lose sales just because no one ever asks for the order. Banks try to avoid this problem. For example, when a customer walks into a First Bank branch to make a deposit, the teller's computer screen shows information about the customer's accounts. If the balance in a checking account is high and the customer does not use any of the bank's other investment services, the teller is trained to ask if the customer would be interested in learning about the bank's certificates of deposit. Some firms use more sophisticated customer relationship management (CRM) database systems that figure out which specific financial service would be best for the teller to recommend.[5]

Wholesalers' order takers—not getting orders but keeping them

While producers' order takers usually handle relatively few items, wholesalers' order takers often sell thousands of items. Sales reps who handle that many items may single out a few of the newer or more profitable items for special attention, but it's not possible to give aggressive sales effort to many. So the main job of wholesalers' order takers is to maintain close contact with customers, place orders, and check to be sure the company fills orders promptly. Order takers also handle any adjustments or complaints and generally act as liaisons between the company and its customers.

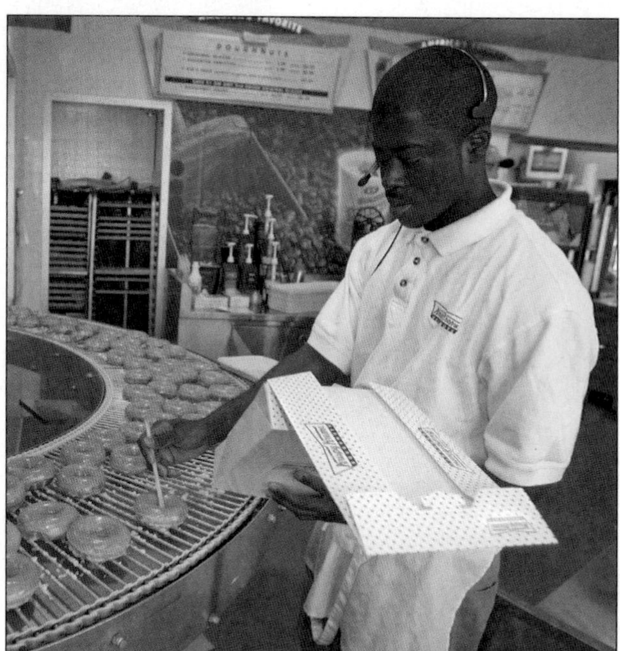

Friendly and capable retail order takers can play an important role in building good relations with customers.

Retail order takers—often they are poor salesclerks

Order-taking may be almost mechanical at the retail level—for example, at the supermarket checkout counter. Some retail clerks perform poorly because they aren't paid much—often only the minimum wage. Even so, retail order takers play a vital role in a retailer's marketing mix. Customers expect prompt and friendly service. They will find a new place to shop, or to do their banking or have their car serviced, rather than deal with a salesclerk who is rude or acts annoyed by having to complete a sale.

Supporting Sales Force Informs and Promotes in the Channel

Supporting salespeople help the order-oriented salespeople, but they don't try to get orders themselves. Their activities are aimed at enhancing the relationship with the customer and getting sales in the long run. For the short run, however, they are ambassadors of goodwill who may provide specialized services and information. There are three types of supporting salespeople: missionary salespeople, technical specialists, and customer service reps.

Missionary salespeople can increase sales

Missionary salespeople are supporting salespeople who work for producers—calling on intermediaries and their customers. They try to develop goodwill and stimulate demand, help intermediaries train their salespeople, and often take orders for delivery by intermediaries. Missionary salespeople are sometimes called *merchandisers* or *detailers.*

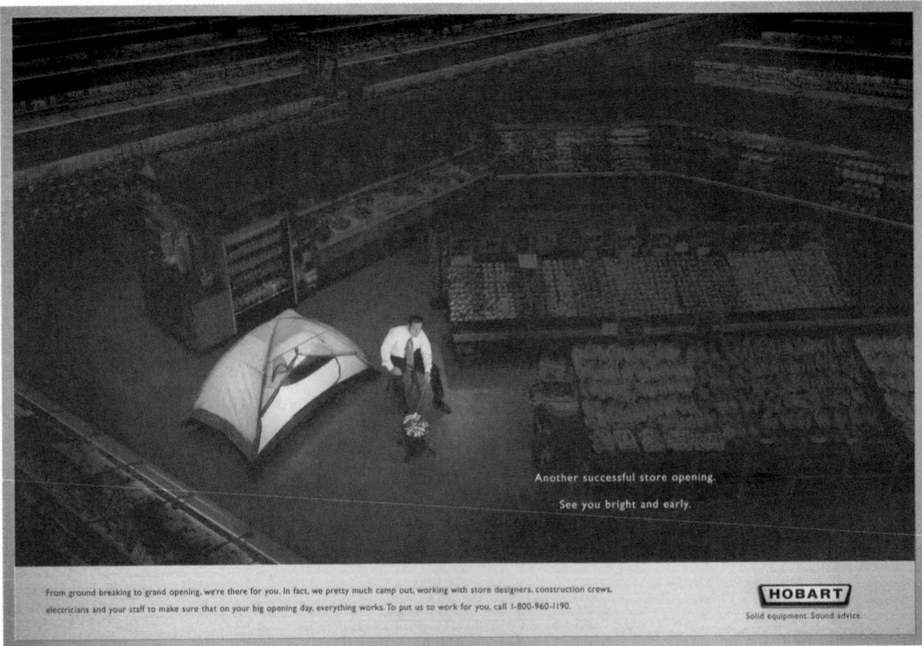

Another successful store opening.
See you bright and early.
From ground breaking to grand opening, we're there for you. In fact, we pretty much camp out, working with store designers, construction crews, electricians and your staff to make sure that on your big opening day, everything works. To put us to work for you, call 1-800-960-1190.
HOBART
Solid equipment. Sound advice.

When a customer firm, like a supermarket chain, buys Hobart equipment for a new store, Hobart people are there every step of the way to be certain that the customer's needs are met.

Producers who rely on merchant wholesalers or e-commerce to obtain widespread distribution often use missionary salespeople. The sales rep can give a promotion boost to a product that otherwise wouldn't get much attention because it's just one of many. A missionary salesperson for Vicks' cold remedy products, for example, might visit pharmacists during the cold season and encourage them to use a special end-of-aisle display for Vicks' cough syrup—and then help set it up. The wholesaler that supplies the drugstore would benefit from any increased sales but might not take the time to urge use of the special display.

An imaginative missionary salesperson can double or triple sales for a company. Naturally, this doesn't go unnoticed. Missionary sales jobs are often a route to order-oriented jobs.

La vida es móvil. Móvil es Vodafone.
Llegó la hora de llamar a Mi País por sólo 18 cént./min.
vodafone

In Spain, cell phone operator Vodafone has set up customer service hotlines with representatives who can communicate in 11 languages, from Arabic to Romanian. That's because Spain has one of Europe's fastest-growing immigrant populations, with more than 600,000 foreigners arriving annually, and Vodafone wants to increase its share of this fast-growing target market.

Technical specialists are experts who know product applications

Technical specialists are supporting salespeople who provide technical assistance to order-oriented salespeople. Technical specialists are often science or engineering graduates with the know-how to understand the customer's applications and explain the advantages of the company's product. They are usually more skilled in showing the technical details of their product than in trying to persuade customers to buy it. Before the specialist's visit, an order getter probably has stimulated interest. The technical specialist provides the details.

Customer service reps solve problems after a purchase

Customer service reps work with customers to resolve problems that arise with a purchase, usually after the purchase has been made. Unlike other supporting sales activities, which are needed only in certain selling situations, *every* marketing-oriented company needs good people to handle customer service. Customer service is important to both business customers and final consumers. There are times when a customer's problem simply can't be resolved without a personal touch.

In general, all types of personal selling help to win customers, but effective customer service is especially critical in keeping them. It is often the key to building repeat business. It's useful to think of customer service reps as *the salespeople who promote a customer's next purchase—by being sure that the customer is satisfied with a previous purchase.* In this chapter, you'll see that the strategy decisions for customer service reps are the same as for others involved in personal selling. In spite of this, some firms don't view customer service as a personal selling activity—or as part of the firm's integrated marketing communications. They manage it as a production operation where output consists of responses to questions from "problem customers." That approach is one reason that customer service is often a problem area for firms. So it's useful to take a closer look at why customer service activities are so important and why firms should manage them as part of the personal selling effort.

Customer Service Promotes the Next Purchase

LO 14.3

Customer service is not the product

People sometimes use the term *customer service* as a catch-all expression for anything that helps customers. Our focus here is on the service that is required *to solve a problem that a customer encounters with a purchase.* This highlights an important distinction in how customers look at their purchase experience. In that regard, it is useful to think about the difference between customer service and the service (or support) that is part of the product that a customer buys.

In Chapter 8, we discussed the idea that a firm's product is its need-satisfying offering, and that it may be a physical good, a service, or a combination of the two. See Exhibit 8-2. Wells Fargo offers consumers credit card services for a fee. Wolf Camera makes prints from customers' digital images. Dell sells computer hardware and software that is supported with telephone or website technical support for some period of time after the purchase. In all of these situations, customers see service as an important aspect of what they are purchasing.

However, from a customer's perspective, that kind of service is different from the customer service that is required to fix a problem when something doesn't work as the customer hopes or expects. For example, our customer doesn't expect the Wells Fargo ATM to eat her credit card when she's on a trip, doesn't want Wolf to charge more than the advertised price for her pictures, and isn't planning on Dell sending the wrong computer. These problems are breakdowns in the firms' marketing mixes. What the customer expected from the seller is not what the customer got.

When a customer service rep works to solve a customer's problem, it often involves taking steps to remedy what went wrong. But repairing a negative experience is fundamentally different from providing a positive experience in the first place. No matter how effective the customer service solution, the problem is an inconvenience or involves other types of

Dell's salespeople listen closely to customers before and after the sale. This helps Dell earn its customers' subsequent purchases.

costs to the customer. Thus, the customer value from the firm's marketing mix is lower than what the customer bargained for. Often it's also less than the value the firm *intended* to provide.

Why customer service is part of promotion

We mentioned before that customers weigh negative experiences more heavily than positive experiences when they decide whether to buy the same product (or from the same company) again. They are also more likely to tell other people about bad experiences with a company than about good ones. The practical matter is that customer service interactions arise because the customer is unhappy. So, if the firm doesn't have an effective way to provide customer service, it is, consciously or unconsciously, making a decision to kiss that customer good-bye. In today's highly competitive markets, that can be a big mistake, especially in situations where it's costly to acquire new customers or when the lifetime value of a customer is significant. Poor customer service reduces the firm's customer equity.

This is why firms should view customer service reps as a key part of personal selling. They are not just fixing the customer's problem, but rather fixing the company's problem, which is the risk of losing customers.

Customer service reps are customer advocates

A breakdown in any element of the marketing mix can result in a requirement for customer service. Ideally, a firm should deliver what it promises, but marketing is a human process and mistakes do happen. Consider, for example, a customer who decides to use Verizon cell phone service because its ad—or the salesperson at the Radio Shack who sold the phone—said that the first month of service would be free. If Verizon bills the customer for the first month, is it a pricing problem, a promotion problem, or a lack of coordination in the channel? From the customer's perspective, it really doesn't matter. What does matter is that expectations have been dashed. The customer doesn't need explanations or excuses but instead needs an advocate to make things right.

Sometimes the marketing mix is fine, but the customer makes a purchase that is a mistake. Or customers may simply change their minds. Either way, customers usually expect sellers to help fix purchasing errors. Firms need policies about how customer service reps should deal with customer errors. But most firms simply can't afford to alienate customers, even ones who have made an error, if they expect them to come back in the future. Sometimes the toughest sales job is figuring out how to keep a customer who is unhappy.

Regardless of whether the firm or customer causes the problem, customer service reps need to be effective communicators, have good judgment, and realize that they are advocates not only for their firm but also for its customers. As that implies, the rest of the company needs to be organized to provide the support reps need to fix problems.

The Right Structure Helps Assign Responsibility

LO 14.4

We have described three sales tasks—order-getting, order-taking, and supporting. A sales manager must organize the sales force so that all the necessary tasks are done well. In many situations, a particular salesperson might be given two, or all three, of these tasks. For example, 10 percent of a particular job may be order-getting, 80 percent order-taking, and the additional 10 percent customer service. On the other hand, organizations are often structured to have different salespeople specializing by different sales tasks and by the target markets they serve.

Sales tasks may be handled by a team

If different people handle different sales tasks, firms often rely on **team selling**—when different people work together on a specific account. Sometimes members of a sales team are not from the sales department at all. If improving the relationship with the customer calls for input from the quality control manager, then that person becomes a part of the

Assurant Solutions' Matchmaking Analytics Helps Retain Customers

Assurant Solutions sells credit insurance. Credit insurance pays the insured person's mortgage, car, or credit card payments if they lose their job or experience major medical problems. Customers often buy credit insurance as an add-on when making a large purchase like a home or car on credit. When customers make payments, they see an additional monthly fee for the credit insurance. After seeing the monthly fee, some customers second-guess their need for the insurance and decide they might be better off taking their chances. When that happens, they call Assurant's customer service team to cancel the policy.

Like many companies in the financial services industry, customer retention is very important to maintaining profitability. So the customer service team is the last chance for Assurant to keep customers looking to cancel an insurance policy. In the past, like most customer service operations, Assurant's customer service group was operationally optimized: staffing to assure 80 percent of customers waited less than 20 seconds to speak to a customer service representative (CSR), inbound phone calls were routed to CSRs with expertise in the product the customer owned, and computer screens displayed scripts that CSRs followed and offers they could make to try to keep a customer from following through on canceling their policy. With all those efforts, Assurant's CSRs retained just 16 percent of those calling to cancel—though that is above average for the industry. Still, with 5 of every 6 customers not convinced to keep their policy or buy a different product, Assurant figured there was an opportunity for improvement. So they turned to analytics.

Insurance companies are very data-driven, so it made sense for Assurant to take a more analytical approach to managing customer service. Assurant's customer service managers have access to lots of data, on customers, products, CSRs, and of course the outcome from each transaction for several years. Assurant also has plenty of statisticians and actuaries who know how to predict outcomes by mining data for insights. With some deep analysis of past transactions, they identified patterns that helped predict success (retaining a customer) and failure when customers call in to cancel a policy.

Assurant discovered that different CSRs were more successful dealing with certain kinds of customers and problems. So the analysts built computer models that predicted which CSRs would be most likely to retain different types of customers. Inbound calls can be analyzed in real-time, so each call can be routed to the CSR with the best chance of keeping the customer's business. If the best CSR for a specific customer is busy on another call, then it rolls to the next best CSR, and so on down the line. By matching customers with CSRs, Assurant's retention rate doubled. The new system also ensures that customers with the biggest premiums are assigned to the most successful customer service reps, so the dollars retained *tripled* as compared to before.

While the analytics don't tell *why* some reps outperform others, they're very accurate at matching customers and CSRs. Assurant's customer service managers attribute the success to rapport. The analytics know enough about each customer and each CSR to create matches where the possibility of connecting is greatest. Creating the right match makes it easier to build a foundation of trust, and persuasion and retention are likely to follow.[6]

team, at least temporarily. Producers of big-ticket items often use team selling. IBM uses team selling to sell information technology solutions for a whole business. Different specialists handle different parts of the job—but the whole team coordinates its efforts to achieve the desired result.

Different target markets need different sales tasks

Sales managers often divide sales force responsibilities based on the type of customer involved. For example, Bigelow—a company that makes quality carpet for homes and office buildings—divided its sales force into groups of specialists. Some Bigelow salespeople call only on architects to help them choose the best type of carpet for new office buildings. These reps know all the technical details, such as how well a certain carpet fiber will wear or its effectiveness in reducing noise from office equipment. Often no sale is involved because the architect only suggests specifications and doesn't actually

The Clorox sales team responsible for the launch of liquid bleach in the Brazilian market drew on people from R&D, marketing, and sales.

buy the carpet. Other Bigelow salespeople call on retail carpet stores. These reps encourage the store manager to keep a variety of Bigelow carpets in stock. They also introduce new products, help train the store's salespeople, and try to solve any problems that occur. Bigelow also has a group of customer service reps who are available via a toll-free number. They help final consumers who have purchased carpet but have a problem that the carpet store can't resolve.

Big accounts get special treatment

Very large customers often require special sales efforts—and relationships with them are treated differently. Moen, a maker of plumbing fixtures, has a regular sales force to call on building material wholesalers and an elite **major accounts sales force** that sells directly to large accounts—like Lowe's or other major retail chains that carry plumbing fixtures.

You can see why this sort of special attention is justified when you consider Procter & Gamble's relationship with Walmart. Walmart accounts for one-fourth or more of the total national sales in many of the product categories in which P&G competes. For instance, Walmart sells about one-third of the toothpaste in the United States. If P&G wants to grow its share of the toothpaste market, it has to make certain that it stimulates an effective sales effort with Walmart.

Some salespeople specialize in telephone selling

Some firms have a group of salespeople who specialize in **telemarketing**—using the telephone to "call" on customers or prospects. The National Do Not Call Registry in the United States and similar laws in other countries have largely eliminated telemarketing to consumers. Registered users cannot be called except by nonprofits and a few other select groups. However, the reception to telephone selling in business markets is often quite different.

In business markets, an "inside" sales force can often build profitable relationships with small or hard-to-reach customers the firm might otherwise have to ignore. Telephone selling is also used to extend personal selling efforts to new target markets or increase the frequency of contact with current customers. The big advantage of telephone selling by an inside sales group in these situations is that it saves time and money for the seller, and it gives customers a fast and easy way to solve a purchasing problem. For example, many firms use toll-free incoming telephone lines to make it convenient for customers to call the inside sales force for assistance or to place an order. Telephone contact may supplement a good website; the website provides standard information and an inside salesperson answers specific questions on the phone.

Companies that produce goods and services for final consumers also rely heavily on toll-free telephone lines to give final consumers easy access to customer service reps. In most cases, there is no other practical way for the producer to be sure that retailers are taking care of customers or their problems. A customer service call center provides a way for the producer to get direct feedback from customers—and perhaps find solutions to potential problems.[7]

Sales tasks are done in sales territories

Often companies organize selling tasks on the basis of a **sales territory**—a geographic area that is the responsibility of one salesperson or several working together. A territory might be a region of a country, a state, or part of a city, depending on the market potential. An airplane manufacturer like Boeing might consider a whole country as *part* of a sales territory for one salesperson.

Carefully set territories can reduce travel time and the cost of sales calls. Assigning territories can also help reduce confusion about who has responsibility for a set of sales tasks. Consider the Hyatt Hotel chain. At one time, each hotel had its own salespeople to get bookings for big conferences and business meetings. That meant that people who had responsibility for selecting meeting locations might be called on by sales reps from 20 or 30 different Hyatt hotels. Now, the Hyatt central office divides up responsibility for working with specific accounts; one rep calls on an account and then tries to sell space in the Hyatt facility that best meets the customer's needs.

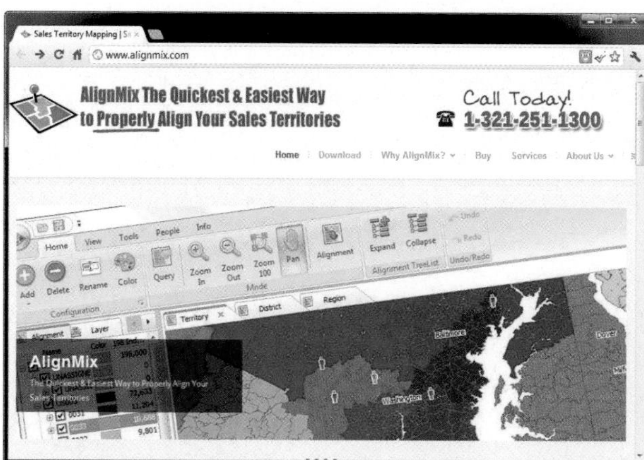

AlignMix software helps sales managers design sales territories to reduce travel time and costs while maximizing sales potential.

Sometimes simple geographic division isn't easy. A company may have different products that require very different knowledge or selling skills—even if products sell in the same territory or to the same customer. For example, DuPont makes special films for hospital X-ray departments as well as chemicals used in laboratory blood tests.

Size of sales force depends on workload

Once the important sales tasks are specified and the responsibilities divided, the sales manager must decide how many salespeople are needed. The first step is estimating how much work can be done by one person in some time period. Then the sales manager can make an educated guess about how many people are required in total, as the following example shows.

For many years, the Parker Jewelry Company was very successful selling its silver jewelry to department and jewelry stores in the southwestern region of the United States. But top managers wanted to expand into the big urban markets in the northeastern states. They realized that most of the work for the first few years would require order getters. They felt that a salesperson would need to call on each account at least once a month to get a share of this competitive business. They estimated that a salesperson could make only five calls a day on prospective buyers and still allow time for travel, waiting, and follow-up on orders that came in. This meant that a sales rep who made calls 20 days per month could handle about 100 stores (5/day × 20 days).

The managers purchased a database that included all of the telephone Yellow Pages listings for the country. Then they simply divided the total number of stores by 100 to estimate the number of salespeople needed. This also helped them set up territories—by defining areas that included about 100 stores for each salesperson. Obviously, managers might want to fine-tune this estimate for differences in territories—such as travel time. But the basic approach can be adapted to many different situations.[8]

Exhibit 14–2
Examples of Possible Personal Selling Emphasis

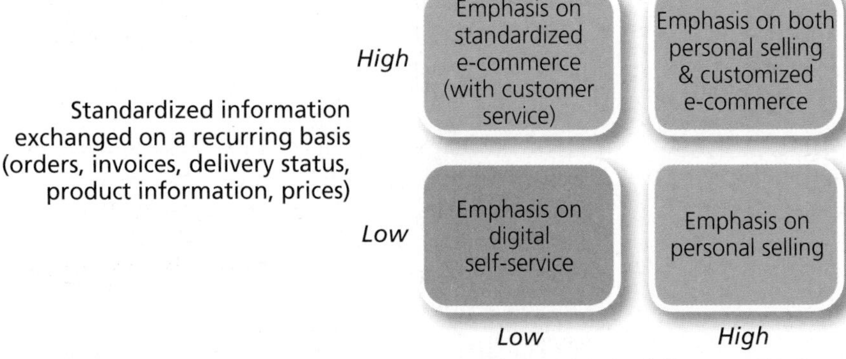

Some managers forget that over time the right number of salespeople may change as sales tasks change. Then when a problem becomes obvious, they try to change everything in a hurry—a big mistake. Consideration of what type of salespeople and how many should be ongoing. If the sales force needs to be reduced, it doesn't make sense to let a lot of people go all at once, especially when that could be avoided with some planning.

Sometimes technology can substitute for personal selling

Some sales tasks that have traditionally been handled by a person can now be handled effectively and at lower cost by an e-commerce system or other technology. The situation that the firm faces may influence which approach makes the most sense and how many salespeople are really needed. See Exhibit 14-2.

In important selling situations, a salesperson is needed to create and build relationships. Here the salesperson (or customer service rep) focuses on tasks like creative problem solving, persuading, coordinating among people who do different jobs, and finding new ways to support the customer. On the other hand, information technology is cost-effective for handling needs related to the recurring exchange of standardized information (such as inventory, orders, and delivery status). Similarly, details of product specifications and prices can be organized at a website. Of course, there should be some way to provide good customer service when needs arise. In a complex relationship, using technology for standard information frees the sales rep to spend time on value-added communication.

Digital self-service lowers costs

When relationship building by a salesperson is not required, a firm may be able to meet customers' needs best by providing digital self-service. This is the role of ATMs for banks. If the customer needs money at an airport in the middle of the night, the ATM provides better support than the customer could get with a real person at the bank. Many firms provide self-service at their websites. For example, at HPShopping.com customers configure computers to their own specs. When looking at options like "How much memory to buy," customers simply click on the "Help me decide" button for more information.

Delivering customer service

Because customers want problems resolved quickly, many firms rely on the Internet to deliver rapid and low-cost customer service. Websites can list FAQs (Frequently Asked Questions—with answers), provide copies of instructions, and show video demonstrations. Some firms even set up online communities where customers help each other with problems. The searchable communities make it easy to find someone else who has experienced the same problem—and see how it was fixed.

Consider Logitech, a maker of computer keyboards and mice, webcams, remote controls for television and home theater systems, and many other consumer electronics products. Most of Logitech's products work in conjunction with a non-Logitech product a consumer already owns. As a result, many customers have problems getting their new Logitech product to work perfectly out-of-the-box. Logitech's product support website lists a toll-free number and includes a FAQ section for each product. Logitech also set up a community support forum—where customers interact with each other (and Logitech experts). Many customers visit the forum to ask questions or to search for others with a similar problem; some visit just because they enjoy answering questions. Since Logitech monitors the forum to answer questions and discover any issues with its products, it can quickly add a new FAQ or a rewrite of the instructions included in a product's package. Because each question and subsequent responses live indefinitely in the searchable forums, the next customer seeing "blurry laggy video" with his new Logitech webcam can search and find the solution KachiWachi (a screen name) offered on July 10, 2008. Some customers prefer these quick and proven answers and Logitech likes the low cost.[9]

Internet Exercise

Go to the Logitech community support forum at **http://forums.logitech.com**. Scroll down the list to "Universal Remotes" and then choose the list of forums for "Harmony Remotes—Programming." Look through a few of the threads. Are customers getting their questions answered? How quickly do they get answers? How do you think this affects customer satisfaction for Logitech?

Big data and social media make for proactive customer service

We have portrayed customer service as a reactive form of communication—companies waiting for customers to phone in with a complaint. Many customers won't call the company to complain, they just voice their dissatisfaction online. Some companies have proactive customer service—they try to solve customers' problems even when the customers don't ask for help. They actively reach out to complaining customers to resolve problems.

Consider Comcast, which developed a well-earned reputation for poor customer service over the last couple decades. Now the company has begun to turn that reputation around—though turning a reputation around takes time. While Comcast continues to use inbound telemarketing to answer and respond to customer questions, another group inside the company trolls the Internet and accesses big data from Facebook, Twitter, blogs, and discussion forums to find anyone complaining about Comcast. Then Comcast reaches out to those customers to address their complaints. The new approach is beginning to turn Comcast's reputation around.[10]

We've focused on technology that substitutes for personal contact by a salesperson. But marketing managers also need to make decisions about providing sales technology support to help salespeople communicate more effectively.

Information Technology Provides Tools to Do the Job

LO 14.5

Changes in how sales tasks are handled

New sales technology tools are changing how sales tasks and responsibilities are planned and handled. It is usually the sales manager's job—perhaps with help from specialists in technology—to decide what types of tools are needed and how they will be used.

To get a sense of what is involved, consider a day in the life of a sales rep for a large consumer packaged goods firm. Over a hasty breakfast, she plans the day's sales calls on her laptop's organizer, checks a LinkedIn contact to learn more about a customer she will meet for the first time that afternoon, watches a 15-minute video presentation for a new product, and sorts through a dozen e-mail messages. One e-mail is from a buyer for a supermarket chain. Sales in the chain's paper towel category are off 10 percent, and he wants to know if the rep can help. The rep downloads sales trend data for the chain and its competitors from her firm's intranet. A spreadsheet analysis of the data reveals that the sales decline is due to new competition from warehouse clubs.

After a videoconference with a brand manager and a company sales promotion specialist to seek advice, she prepares a PowerPoint presentation, complete with a proposed shelf-space

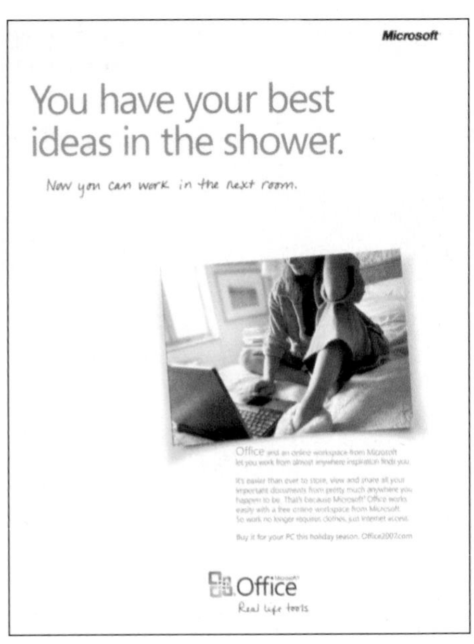

Information technology is making the modern sales force more efficient and giving salespeople new ways to meet the needs of their customers while achieving the objectives of their jobs.

plan that recommends the buyer promote larger-size packages of both her company's and competitors' brands. Before leaving home, the rep e-mails an advance copy of the report to the buyer and her manager. In her car, she calls the buyer to schedule an appointment.[11]

New software and hardware provide a competitive advantage

The sales rep in this example relies on support from an array of software and hardware, some of which wasn't even available a decade ago. Software for customer relationship management, spreadsheet sales analysis, digital presentations, time management, sales forecasting, customer contact, and shelf-space management is at the salesperson's fingertips—most of it available right online. Commonplace hardware includes everything from smartphones and tablet computers to personal videoconferencing systems. In many situations, these technologies give sales reps new ways to meet customers' needs while achieving the objectives of their jobs.

These tools change how well the job is done. Yet this is not simply a matter that is best left to individual sales reps. Use of these tools may be necessary just to compete effectively. For example, if a customer expects a sales rep to access data on past sales and provide an updated sales forecast, a sales organization that doesn't have this capability will be at a real disadvantage in keeping that customer's business.

On the other hand, these tools have costs. There is an obvious expense of buying the technology. But there is also the training cost of keeping everyone up-to-date. Often that is not an easy matter. Some salespeople who have done the sales job well for a long time "the old-fashioned way" resent being told that they have to change what they are doing, even if it's what customers expect. So if a firm expects salespeople to be able to use these technologies, that requirement needs to be included in selecting and training people for the job.[12]

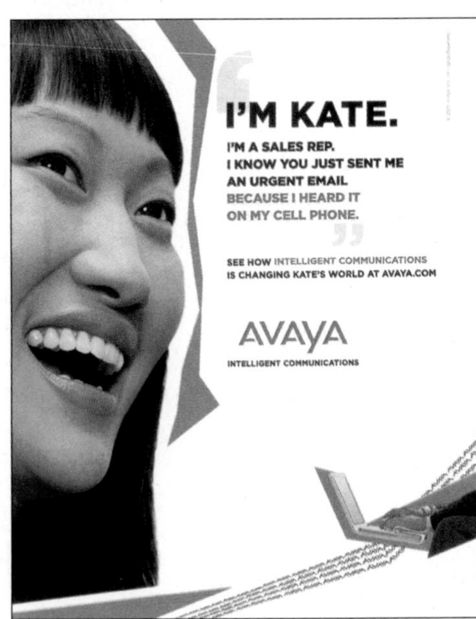

Firms like Avaya are always seeking new ways to help their sales reps stay in touch with customers, even when they are on the road.

Sound Selection and Training to Build a Sales Force

LO 14.6

Selecting good salespeople takes judgment, plus

It is important to hire *well-qualified* salespeople who will do a good job. But selection in many companies is done without serious thought about exactly what kind of person the firm needs. Managers may hire friends and relations, or whoever is available, because they feel that the only qualification for a sales job is a friendly personality. This approach leads to poor sales, lost customers, and costly sales force turnover.

Progressive companies are more careful. They constantly update a list of possible job candidates. They invite applications at the company's website. They schedule candidates for multiple interviews with various executives and do thorough background checks. Unfortunately, such techniques don't guarantee success. But a systematic approach based on several different inputs results in a better sales force.

One problem in selecting salespeople is that two different sales jobs with identical titles may involve very different selling or supporting tasks and require different skills. A carefully prepared job description helps avoid this problem.

Job descriptions should be in writing and specific

A **job description** is a written statement of what a salesperson is expected to do. It might list 10 to 20 specific tasks—as well as routine prospecting and sales report writing. Each company must write its own job specifications. And it should provide clear guidelines about what selling tasks the job involves. This is critical to determine the kind of salespeople who should be selected—and later it provides a basis for seeing how they should be trained, how well they are performing, and how they should be paid.

Good salespeople are trained, not born

The idea that good salespeople are born that way may have some truth—but it isn't the whole story. A salesperson needs to be taught about the company and its products, about giving effective sales presentations, and about building relationships with customers. But this isn't always done. Many salespeople do a poor job because they haven't had good training. Firms often hire new salespeople and immediately send them out on the road, or the retail selling floor, with no grounding in the basic selling steps and no information about the product or the customer. They just get a price list and a pat on the back. This isn't enough!

Customers who rent heavy construction equipment want to deal with a knowledgeable salesperson. So CAT selects salespeople who have experience with the applications for which the equipment will be used and gives them training on CAT products and new developments in the market.

All salespeople need some training

It's up to sales and marketing management to be sure that salespeople know what they're supposed to do and how to do it. Hewlett-Packard Co. recently faced this problem. For years the company was organized into divisions based on different product lines—printers, network servers, and the like. However, sales reps who specialized in the products of one division often couldn't compete well against firms that could offer customers total solutions to computing problems. When a new top executive came in and reorganized the company, all sales reps needed training in their new responsibilities, how they would be organized, and what they should say to their customers about the benefits of the reorganization.

Sales training should be modified based on the experience and skills of the group involved. But the company's sales training program should cover at least the following areas: (1) company policies and practices, (2) product information, (3) building relationships with customer firms, and (4) professional selling skills.

Selling skills can be learned

Many companies spend the bulk of their training time on product information and company policy. They neglect training in selling techniques because they think selling is something anyone can do. But training in selling skills can pay off. Estée Lauder, for example, has selling skills for the "beauty advisors" who sell its cosmetics down to a fine art—and its training manual and seminars cover every detail. Its advisors who take the training seriously immediately double their sales.[13] Training can also help salespeople learn how to be more effective in cold calls on new prospects, in listening carefully to identify a customer's real objections, in closing the sale, and in working with customers in difficult customer service situations.

Training often starts in the classroom with lectures, case studies, and videotaped trial presentations and demonstrations. But a complete training program adds on-the-job observation of effective salespeople and coaching from sales supervisors. Many companies also use web-based training, weekly sales meetings or work sessions, annual conventions, and regular e-mail messages and newsletters, as well as ongoing training sessions, to keep salespeople up-to-date.[14]

Internet Exercise

Sales managers need to think about what training their salespeople need, but sales reps also need to take the initiative and stay up-to-date on what is happening in the sales profession. *Selling Power* magazine maintains a website at **www.sellingpower.com**. Go to the website and identify several ideas that could be used by a salesperson to enhance his or her skills.

Compensating and Motivating Salespeople

LO 14.7

To recruit, motivate, and keep good salespeople, a firm has to develop an effective compensation plan. Ideally, sales reps should be paid in such a way that what they want to do—for personal interest and gain—is in the company's interest too. Most companies focus on financial motivation—but public recognition, sales contests, and simple personal recognition for a job well done can be highly effective in encouraging greater sales effort.[15] Our main emphasis here, however, will be on financial motivation.[16]

Two basic decisions must be made in developing a compensation plan: (1) the level of compensation and (2) the method of payment.

Compensation varies with job and needed skills

To build a competitive sales force, a company must pay at least the going market wage for different kinds of salespeople. To be sure it can afford a specific type of salesperson, the company should estimate—when the job description is written—how valuable such a salesperson will be. A good order getter may be worth $100,000 or more to one company but only $15,000 to $25,000 to another—just because the second firm doesn't have enough to sell! In such a case, the second company should rethink its job specifications, or completely change its promotion plans, because the going rate for order getters is much higher than $15,000 a year.

If a job requires extensive travel, aggressive pioneering, or customer service contacts with troublesome customers, the pay may have to be higher. But the salesperson's compensation level should compare, at least roughly, with the pay scale of the rest of the firm. Normally, salespeople earn more than the office or production force but less than top management.

Salespeople that meet certain sales targets may win fancy trips.

Payment methods vary

Given some competitive level of compensation, there are three basic methods of payment: (1) straight salary, (2) straight commission (incentive), or (3) a combination plan. A straight salary offers the most security for the salesperson. Commission pay, in contrast, offers the most incentive and is tied to results actually achieved. A commission is often based on a percentage of dollar sales, but it may be a financial incentive based on other outcomes—such as the number of new accounts, customer satisfaction ratings, or customer service problems resolved in some time period. Most salespeople want some security, and most companies want salespeople to have some incentive to do better work, so the most popular method is a combination plan that includes some salary and some commission. Bonuses, profit sharing, pensions, stock plans, insurance, and other fringe benefits may be included, too.

Salary gives control—if there is close supervision

A salesperson on straight salary earns the same amount regardless of how he or she spends time. So the salaried salesperson is expected to do what the sales manager asks—whether it is order-taking, supporting sales activities, solving customer service problems, or completing sales call reports. However, the sales manager maintains control *only* by close supervision. As a result, straight salary or a large salary element in the compensation plan increases the amount of sales supervision needed.

Commissions can both motivate and direct

If personal supervision would be difficult, a firm may get better control with a compensation plan that includes some commission, or even a straight commission plan, with built-in direction. One trucking company, for example, has a sales incentive plan that pays higher commissions on business needed to balance freight shipments—depending on how heavily traffic has been moving in one direction or another. Another company that wants to motivate its salespeople to devote more time to developing new accounts could pay higher commissions on shipments to a new customer. However, a salesperson on a straight commission tends to be his or her own boss. The sales manager is less likely to get help on sales activities that won't increase the salesperson's earnings.

An incentive compensation plan can help motivate salespeople, but incentives must be carefully aligned with the firm's objectives. For example, IBM at one time had a sales commission plan that resulted in IBM salespeople pushing customers to buy expensive computers that were more powerful than they needed. The sales reps got sales and increased their income, but later many customers were dissatisfied and switched to other suppliers. Now most IBM sales reps receive incentive pay that is in part based on satisfaction ratings they earn from their customers. Many firms use variations of this approach—because incentives that just focus on short-term sales objectives may not motivate sales reps to develop long-term, need-satisfying relationships with their customers.

Incentives should link efforts to results

The incentive portion of a sales rep's compensation should be large only if there is a direct relationship between the salesperson's efforts and results. Otherwise, a salesperson in a growing territory might have rapidly increasing earnings, while the sales rep in a poor

Exhibit 14–3 Relation between Total Selling Expenses and Sales Volume

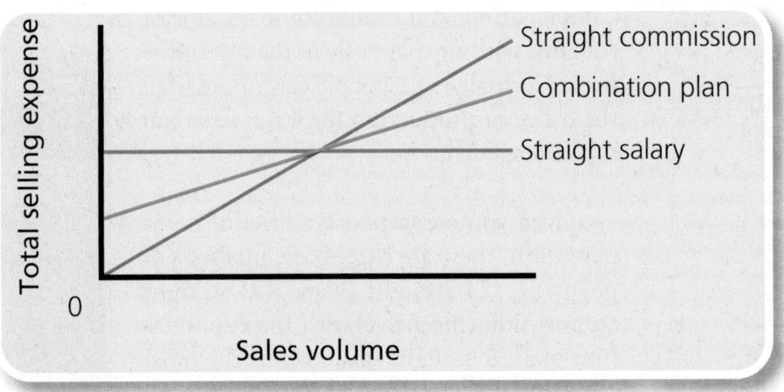

area will have little to show for the same amount of work. Such a situation isn't fair, and it can lead to high turnover and much dissatisfaction. A sales manager can take such differences into consideration when setting a salesperson's **sales quota**—the specific sales or profit objective a salesperson is expected to achieve. Often times a salesperson receives a bonus for meeting the sales quota.

Commissions reduce need for working capital

Small companies that have limited working capital or uncertain markets often prefer straight commission, or combination plans with a large commission element. When sales drop off, costs do too. Such flexibility is similar to using manufacturers' agents who get paid only if they deliver sales. This advantage often dominates in selecting a sales compensation method. Exhibit 14-3 shows the general relation between personal selling expense and sales volume for each of the basic compensation alternatives.

Compensation plans should be clear

Salespeople are likely to be dissatisfied if they can't see the relationship between the results they produce and their pay. A compensation plan that includes different commissions for different products or types of customers can become quite complicated. Simplicity is best achieved with straight salary. But in practice, it's usually better to sacrifice some simplicity to gain some incentive, flexibility, and control. The best combination of these factors depends on the job description and the company's objectives.

To make it easier for a sales rep to see the relationship between effort and compensation, some firms provide the rep with that information online. For example, sales reps at Oracle, a company that sells database systems, can check a website and see how they are doing. As new sales results come in, the report at the website is updated. Sales managers can also make changes quickly—for example, by putting a higher commission on a product or more weight on customer satisfaction scores.[17]

Sales managers must plan, implement, and control

Managers must regularly evaluate each salesperson's performance and be certain that all the needed tasks are being done well. The compensation plan may have to be changed if the pay and work are out of line. And by evaluating performance, firms can also identify areas that need more attention—by the salesperson or management. In Chapter 18 we'll talk more about controlling marketing activities.[18]

Personal Selling Techniques—Prospecting and Presenting

LO 14.8

We've stressed the importance of training in selling techniques. Now let's discuss these ideas in more detail so you understand the basic steps each salesperson should follow—including prospecting and selecting target customers, planning sales presentations, making sales presentations, and following up after the sale. Exhibit 14-4 shows the steps we'll consider. You can see that the salesperson is just carrying out a planned communication process, as we discussed in Chapter 13.[19]

Exhibit 14–4
Key Steps in the Personal Selling Process

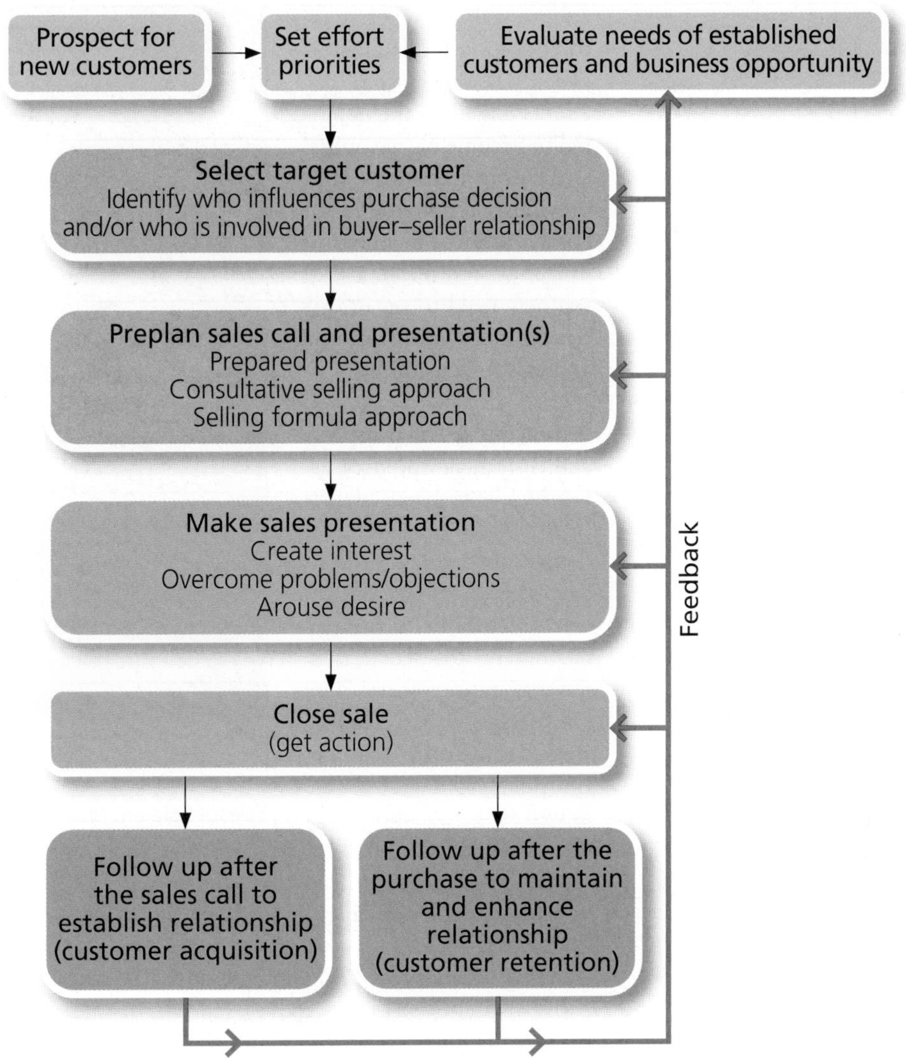

Prospecting—narrowing down to the right target

Narrowing the personal selling effort down to the right target requires constant, detailed analysis of markets and much prospecting. Basically, **prospecting** involves following all the leads in the target market to identify potential customers.

Finding live prospects who will help make the buying decision isn't as easy as it sounds. In business markets, for example, the salesperson may need to do some hard detective work to find the real purchase decision makers.

Some companies provide prospect lists or a customer relationship management (CRM) database to make this part of the selling job easier. The CRM database may be integrated with other marketing communication tools to help salespeople spend more time working on the best prospects. ThoughtLava, a website design firm, uses its CRM database to initially contact prospects by e-mail. It uses software that tracks which prospects open the e-mail, which click through to the firm's website, and even which pages they visit. Given this information, ThoughtLava's salespeople know in advance which of the firm's services interest each prospect, and that helps them decide which prospects to focus on.[20]

All customers are not equal

While prospecting focuses on identifying new customers, established customers require attention too. It's often time-consuming and expensive to establish a relationship with a customer, so once established it makes sense to keep the relationship healthy. That requires the rep to routinely review active accounts, rethink customers' needs, and reevaluate each customer's long-term business potential. Some small accounts may have the potential to become big accounts, and some accounts that previously required a lot of costly attention may no longer warrant it. So a sales rep may need to set priorities both for new prospects and existing customers.

Salespeople are constantly looking for ways to be more efficient in identifying sales leads and prospects.

How long to spend with whom?

Once a set of prospects and customers who need attention have been identified, the salesperson must decide how much time to spend with each one. A sales rep must qualify customers—to see if they deserve more effort. The salesperson usually makes these decisions by weighing the potential sales volume as well as the likelihood of a sale. This requires judgment. But well-organized salespeople usually develop some system because they have too many demands on their time.[21]

Many firms provide their reps with CRM systems to help with this process also. Most of them use some grading scheme. A sales rep might estimate how much each prospect is likely to purchase and the probability of getting and keeping the business given the competition. The computer then combines this information and grades each prospect. Attractive accounts may be labeled A—and the salesperson may plan to call on them weekly until the sale is made, the relationship is in good shape, or the customer is moved into a lower category. B customers might offer somewhat lower potential and be called on monthly. C accounts might be called on only once a year—unless they happen to contact the salesperson. And D accounts might be transferred to a telemarketing group.[22]

Three kinds of sales presentations may be useful

Once the salesperson selects a target customer, it's necessary to make a **sales presentation**—a salesperson's effort to make a sale or address a customer's problem. But someone has to plan what kind of sales presentation to make. This is a strategy decision. The kind of presentation should be set before the sales rep goes calling. And in situations where the customer comes to the salesperson—in a retail store, for instance—planners have to make sure that prospects are brought together with salespeople.

A marketing manager can choose two basically different approaches to making sales presentations: the prepared approach or the consultative selling approach. Another approach, the selling formula approach, is a combination of the two. Each of these has its place.

The prepared sales presentation

The **prepared sales presentation** approach uses a memorized presentation that is not adapted to each individual customer. This approach says that a customer faced with a particular stimulus will give the desired response—in this case, a yes answer to the salesperson's prepared statement, which includes a **close**, the salesperson's request for an order.

If one trial close doesn't work, the sales rep tries another prepared presentation and attempts another closing. This can go on for some time—until the salesperson runs out of material or the customer either buys or decides to leave. Exhibit 14-5 shows the relative participation of the salesperson and customer in the prepared approach. Note that the salesperson does most of the talking.

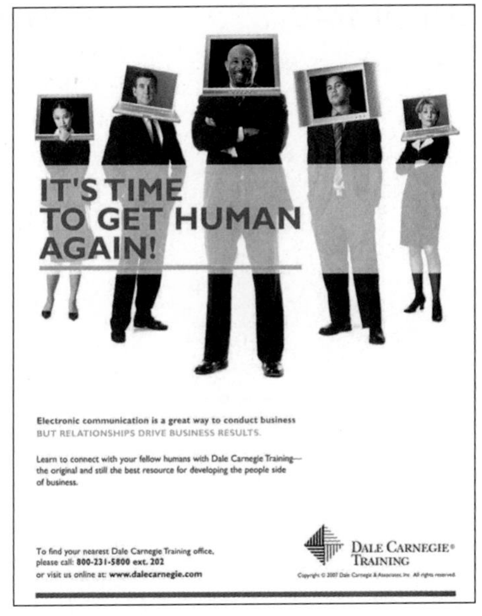

Many firms turn to outside training specialists, like Dale Carnegie Training, for programs that can help salespeople learn how to connect with customers.

Firms may rely on this canned approach when only a short presentation is practical. It's also sensible when salespeople aren't very skilled. The company can control what they say and in what order. For example, Novartis uses missionary salespeople to tell doctors about new drugs when they're introduced. Doctors are busy, so they only give the rep a minute or two. That's just enough time to give a short, prepared pitch and leave some samples. To get the most out of the presentation, Novartis refines it based on feedback from doctors whom it pays to participate in focus groups.[23]

But a canned approach has a weakness. It treats all potential customers alike. It may work for some and not for others. A prepared approach may be suitable for simple order-taking—but it is no longer considered good selling for complicated situations.

Consultative selling—builds on the marketing concept

The **consultative selling approach** involves developing a good understanding of the individual customer's needs before trying to close the sale. This name is used because the salesperson is almost acting as a consultant to help identify and solve the customer's problem. With this approach, the sales rep makes some general benefit statements to get the customer's attention and interest. Then the salesperson asks questions and *listens carefully* to understand the customer's needs. Once they agree on needs, the seller tries to show the customer how the product fills those needs and to close the sale. This is a problem-solving approach—in which the customer and salesperson work together to satisfy the customer's needs. That's why it's sometimes called the need-satisfaction approach. Exhibit 14-6 shows the participation of the customer and the salesperson during such a sales presentation.

The consultative selling approach takes skill and time. The salesperson must be able to analyze what motivates a particular customer and show how the company's offering would help the customer satisfy those needs. The sales rep may even conclude that the customer's problem is really better solved with someone else's product. That might result in one lost sale, but it also is likely to build real trust and more sales opportunities over the life of the relationship with the customer. That's why this kind of selling is typical in business markets when a salesperson already has established a close relationship with a customer.

Selling formula approach—some of both

The **selling formula approach** starts with a prepared presentation outline—much like the prepared approach—and leads the customer through some logical steps to a final close. The prepared steps are logical because we assume that we know something about the target customer's needs and attitudes.

Exhibit 14-7 shows the selling formula approach. The salesperson does most of the talking at the beginning of the presentation—to communicate key points early. This part of the presentation may even have been prepared as part of the marketing strategy. As the sales presentation moves along, however, the salesperson brings the customer into the discussion to help clarify just what needs this customer has. The salesperson's job is to

Exhibit 14–5
Prepared Approach to Sales Presentation

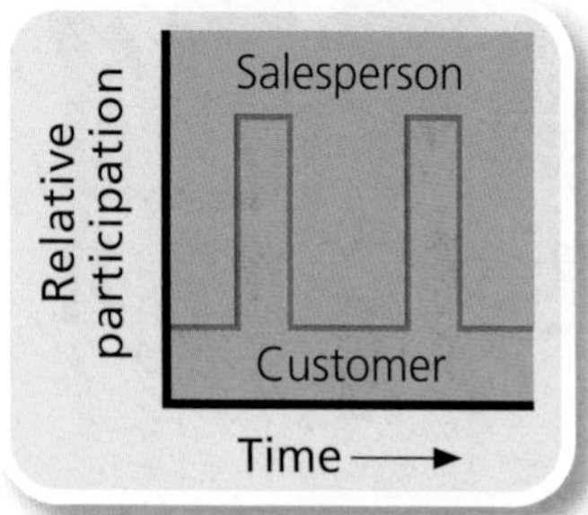

Exhibit 14–6
Consultative Selling Approach to Sales Presentation

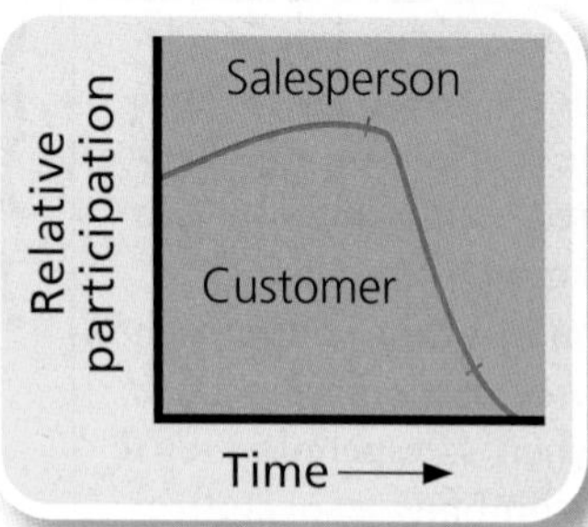

Exhibit 14–7
Selling Formula Approach to Sales Presentation

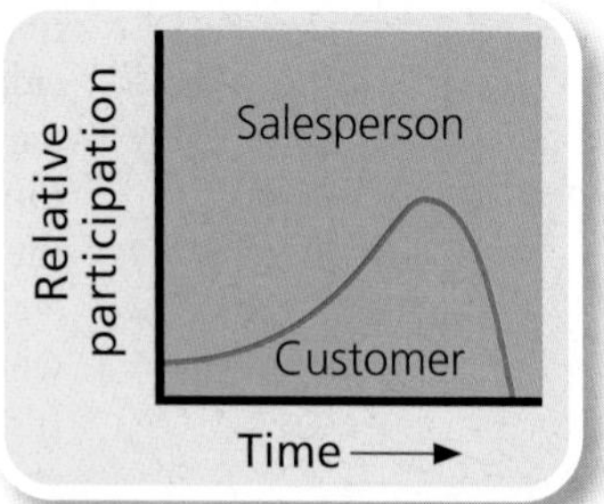

discover the needs of a particular customer to know how to proceed. Once it is clear what kind of customer this is, the salesperson comes back to show how the product satisfies this specific customer's needs and to close the sale.

AIDA helps plan sales presentations

AIDA—Attention, Interest, Desire, Action: Most sales presentations follow this AIDA sequence. The time a sales rep spends on each of the steps varies depending on the situation and the selling approach being used. But it is still necessary to begin a presentation by getting the prospect's *attention* and, hopefully, to move the customer to *action*.[24]

Ethical issues may arise

As in every other area of marketing communications, ethical issues arise in the personal selling area. The most basic issue, plain and simple, is whether a salesperson's presentation is honest and truthful. But addressing that issue is a no-brainer. No company is served well by a salesperson who lies or manipulates customers to get their business.

Ethics Question

Assume that you are a sales rep and sell costly electronic systems for use in automated factories. You made a sales presentation to a customer, but he didn't place an order—and then wouldn't take your calls when you tried to inform him that your company was coming out with a more reliable model at the same price. Months later, he faxes a purchase order for immediate delivery on the model you originally discussed. You have the old model in stock, and it will be difficult to sell once the new model arrives in two weeks. In fact, your company has doubled the usual commission rate to clear out the old model. Do you try to contact the customer again to tell him about the new model, or do you do what he has requested and immediately fill the order with the old model? Either way, if you make the sale, the commission will pay for your upcoming vacation to the Caribbean. Explain what you would do and why.

On the other hand, most sales reps sooner or later face a sales situation in which they must make more difficult ethical decisions about how to balance company interests, customer interests, and personal interests. Conflicts are less likely to arise if the firm's marketing mix really meets the needs of its target market. Similarly, they are less likely to occur when the firm sees the value of developing a longer-term relationship with the customer. Then the salesperson is arranging a happy marriage. By contrast, ethical conflicts are more likely when the sales rep's personal outcomes (such as commission income) or the selling firm's profits hinge on making sales to customers whose needs are only partially met by the firm's offering. A number of financial services firms, for example, have garnered bad publicity—and even legal problems—from situations like this.

Ideally, companies can avoid the whole problem by supporting their salespeople with a marketing mix that really offers target customers unique benefits. Moreover, top executives, marketing managers, and sales managers set the tone for the ethical climate in which a salesperson operates. If they set impossible goals or project a "do-what-you-need-to-do" attitude, a desperate salesperson may yield to the pressure of the moment. When a firm clearly advocates ethical selling behavior and makes it clear that manipulative selling techniques are not acceptable, the salesperson is not left trying to swim "against the flow."[25]

CONCLUSION

In this chapter, we discussed the importance and nature of personal selling. Selling is much more than just getting rid of the product. In fact, a salesperson who is not given strategy guidelines may have to become the strategy planner for the market he or she serves. Ideally, however, the sales manager and marketing manager work together to set some strategy guidelines: the kind and number of salespeople needed, what sales technology support will be provided, the kind of sales presentation desired, and selection, training, and motivation approaches.

We discussed the three basic sales tasks: (1) order-getting, (2) order-taking, and (3) supporting. Most sales jobs combine at least two of these three tasks. We also considered the role of customer service and why it is so important to a firm and its customers. Once a firm specifies the important tasks, it can decide on the structure of its sales organization and the number of salespeople it needs. The nature of the job and the level and method of compensation also depend on the blend of these tasks. Firms should develop a job description for each sales job. This, in turn, provides guidelines for selecting, training, and compensating salespeople.

Once the marketing manager agrees to the basic plan and sets the budget, the sales manager must implement the plan, including directing and controlling the sales force. This includes assigning sales territories and controlling performance. A sales manager is deeply involved with the basic management tasks of planning and control—as well as ongoing implementation of the personal selling effort.

We also reviewed some basic selling techniques and identified three kinds of sales presentations. Each has its place—but the consultative selling approach seems best for higher-level sales jobs. In these kinds of jobs, personal selling is achieving a new, professional status because of the competence and level of personal responsibility required of the salesperson. The day of the old-time glad-hander is passing in favor of the specialist who is creative, industrious, persuasive, knowledgeable, highly trained, and therefore able to help the buyer. This type of salesperson always has been, and probably always will be, in short supply. And the demand for high-level salespeople is growing.

KEY TERMS

LO 14.9

basic sales tasks, *361*
order getters, *361*
order-getting, *361*
order takers, *362*
order-taking, *362*
supporting salespeople, *363*
missionary salespeople, *363*
technical specialists, *364*
customer service reps, *364*
team selling, *366*
major accounts sales force, *368*
telemarketing, *368*
sales territory, *369*
job description, *373*
sales quota, *376*
prospecting, *377*
sales presentation, *378*
prepared sales presentation, *378*
close, *378*
consultative selling approach, *379*
selling formula approach, *379*

QUESTIONS AND PROBLEMS

1. What strategy decisions are needed in the personal selling area? Why should the marketing manager make these strategy decisions?
2. What kind of salesperson (or what blend of the basic sales tasks) is required to sell the following products? If there are several selling jobs in the channel

for each product, indicate the kinds of salespeople required. Specify any assumptions necessary to give definite answers.

a. Laundry detergent
b. Costume jewelry
c. Office furniture
d. Men's underwear
e. Mattresses
f. Corn
g. Life insurance

3. Distinguish among the jobs of producers', wholesalers', and retailers' order-getting salespeople. If one order getter is needed, must all the salespeople in a channel be order getters? Illustrate.
4. Discuss the role of the manufacturers' agent in a marketing manager's promotion plans. What kind of salesperson is a manufacturers' agent? What type of compensation plan is used for a manufacturers' agent?
5. Discuss the future of the specialty shop if producers place greater emphasis on mass selling because of the inadequacy of retail order-taking.
6. Compare and contrast missionary salespeople and technical specialists.
7. Think about a situation when you or a friend or family member encountered a problem with a purchase and tried to get help from a firm's customer service representative. Briefly describe the problem, how the firm handled it, and what you think about the firm's response. How could it have been improved?
8. Would it make sense for your school to have a person or group whose main job is to handle "customer service" problems? Explain your thinking.
9. A firm that produces mixes for cakes, cookies, and other baked items has an incoming toll-free line for customer service calls. The manager of the customer service reps has decided to base about a third of their pay on the number of calls they handle per month and on the average amount of time on the phone with each customer. What do you think are the benefits and limitations of this incentive pay system? What would you recommend to improve it?
10. Explain how a compensation plan could be developed to provide incentives for experienced salespeople and yet make some provision for trainees who have not yet learned the job.
11. Cite an actual local example of each of the three kinds of sales presentations discussed in the chapter. Explain for each situation whether a different type of presentation would have been better.
12. Are the benefits and limitations of a canned presentation any different if it is supported with a PowerPoint presentation or DVD than if it is just a person talking? Why or why not?
13. Describe a consultative selling sales presentation that you experienced recently. How could it have been improved by fuller use of the AIDA framework?
14. How would our economy operate if personal salespeople were outlawed? Could the economy work? If so, how? If not, what is the minimum personal selling effort necessary? Could this minimum personal selling effort be controlled by law?

CREATING MARKETING PLANS

The Marketing Plan Coach software on the text website includes a sample marketing plan for Hillside Veterinary Clinic. Look through the "Marketing Strategy" section.

a. What personal selling tasks are performed at Hillside Veterinary Clinic and who does them?
b. If Hillside wanted to put more emphasis on "order-getting" to promote growth, what ideas do you have for how to do it?
c. Based on the situation analysis, target market, and intended positioning, recommend some ways that Hillside could actively work to improve its reputation for customer service.

SUGGESTED CASES

12. DrJane.com—Custom Vitamins
21. Global Chemical, Inc.
23. Carson's Furniture
28. KCA Precision Tools

COMPUTER-AIDED PROBLEM

14. SALES COMPENSATION

Franco Welles, sales manager for Nanek, Inc., is trying to decide whether to pay a sales rep for a new territory with straight commission or a combination plan. He wants to evaluate possible plans—to compare the compensation costs and profitability of each. Welles knows that sales reps in similar jobs at other firms make about $36,000 a year.

The sales rep will sell two products. Welles is planning a higher commission for Product B—because he wants it to get extra effort. From experience with similar products, he has some rough estimates of expected sales volume under the different plans and various ideas about commission rates. The details are found in the spreadsheet. The program computes compensation and how much the sales rep will contribute to profit. "Profit contribution" is equal to the total revenue generated by the sales rep minus sales compensation costs and the costs of producing the units.

a. For the initial values shown in the spreadsheet, which plan—commission or combination—would give the rep the highest compensation, and which plan would give the greatest profit contribution to Nanek, Inc.?

b. Welles thinks a sales rep might be motivated to work harder and sell 1,100 units of Product B if the commission rate (under the commission plan) were increased to 10 percent. If Welles is right (and everything else stays the same), would the higher commission rate be a good deal for Nanek? Explain your thinking.

c. A sales rep interested in the job is worried about making payments on her new car. She asks if Welles would consider paying her with a combination plan but with more guaranteed income (an $18,000 base salary) in return for taking a 3 percent commission on Products B and A. If this arrangement results in the same unit sales as Welles originally estimated for the combination plan, would Nanek, Inc., be better off or worse off under this arrangement?

d. Do you think the rep's proposal will meet Welles' goals for Product B? Explain your thinking.

15 CHAPTER FIFTEEN

Advertising, Publicity, and Sales Promotion

In the summer of 1965, 17-year-old Fred DeLuca was trying to figure out how to pay for college. A family friend suggested that Fred open a sandwich shop—and then the friend invested $1,000 to help get it started. Within a month, they opened their first sandwich shop. From that humble start grew the Subway franchise chain, with more than 34,000 outlets in 97 countries.

Targeted advertising, timely publicity, and sales promotion have been important to Subway's growth. For more than 10 years, memorable Subway ads featured Jared Fogle, a college student who was overweight but lost 245 pounds by only eating Subway's low-fat sandwiches like the "Veggie Delite." Jared says it was a fluke that he ended up in Subway's ads. After all, he was recruited to do the ads because of good publicity that Subway got after national media picked up a story that Jared's friend wrote about him in a college newspaper. Subway's strategy at that time focused on its line of seven different sandwiches with under 6 grams of fat. The objective was to set Subway fare apart from other fast food, position it to appeal to health-conscious eaters, and spark new sales growth. Jared already knew he liked Subway sandwiches, but the "7 under 6" promotion inspired him to incorporate them into his diet.

As soon as Jared's ads began to run, word of his inspiring story spread, and consumer awareness of Subway and its healthy fare increased. It's always hard to isolate the exact impact of ads on sales, but sales grew more than 18 percent that year. The ads also attracted attention from potential franchisees. Many of them followed up by requesting the franchise brochure, which explains how Subway's strategy works and why Subway is a profitable small business opportunity. For instance, it describes how franchisees elect a group to help advertising managers at Subway headquarters with advertising and media buying decisions—so that Subway outlets get the most return from their advertising dollars.

Franchisees can develop their own promotions, too. A south Florida franchisee wanted to boost weekend sales at his two stores, so he offered footlong subs for $5 on Saturdays and Sundays. Business boomed—there were lines out the door. The down economy had made customers particularly price-sensitive, so the bargain had wide appeal. And the promotion was profitable because the increased volume of sandwiches made up for the lower margin on each footlong. Word got out and soon other franchisees were selling $5 footlongs. Then the franchisees' advertising group voted to take it nationwide for four weeks, later extending it indefinitely. Soon it was hard to find someone who didn't recognize the five-finger signs and catchy (and annoying) jingle from the campaign developed by the MMB ad agency. Awareness of the campaign reached 90 percent among 18–64-year-olds.

Subway tries to balance its menu and promotion to appeal to three segments: customers interested in low fat, those most concerned about taste, as well as those seeking a good value. The "eat fresh" theme and copy thrust of some of Subway's ads appeal to the first two target markets, while in-store signage promotes its "value meals." For those most concerned about taste, Subway counters high-end fare from Panera Bread and Quiznos Subs with its "Subway Selects" line of sandwiches. Subway reinforces its healthy positioning with spokespeople like NFL quarterback Robert Griffin III and Olympic gymnast Nastia Liukin. During college basketball's "March Madness," Subway generated publicity for a buy-one, get-one-free sub promotion by hooking Jared up with college basketball analyst Seth Davis. The two traveled to sub shops where they met customers and made sandwiches.

Subway recognizes that it needs to vary its creative approaches to get its message out to different target markets. For example, with so many younger people on smartphones, Subway created 30-second mobile video ads to promote its new avocado-inspired summer sandwiches. To taste the new sandwich, one tap provides directions to the nearest Subway. Subway includes many other elements in its promotion blend as well. For example, Subway's Facebook page promotes new products and short-term price specials while building relationships with customers. The SubwayFreshBuzz website provides tips on dieting and exercise as well as nutritional details about its sandwiches; these details help consumers who want all the health-related facts. The available information makes sense in light of the scrutiny the Federal Trade Commission gives to firms that make promotional claims related to weight loss and health.

To leverage its healthy fast-food positioning, Subway stepped up efforts to combat childhood obesity and increase sales to kids and teens. Its F.R.E.S.H. Steps promotion encourages kids and their parents to "Feel Responsible, Energized, Satisfied, and Happy." A television advertising campaign informs parents and kids how to make healthy eating choices and live a more active lifestyle. As a national sponsor of Little League Baseball and Softball, Subway advertises in *Little League* magazine and targets little leaguers and their parents via direct mail and with point-of-sale materials. It also teamed up with Discovery Kids cable TV to tell kids 6 to 12 years old to "play hard and fresh." This promotion included tie-ins with the network's *Endurance* show, where kids compete in outdoor activities.

Subway is in a very competitive, dynamic market. More change is sure to come. But, so far, Subway has achieved profitable growth with a targeted strategy that includes effective use of promotion.[1]

Learning Objectives

The Subway case shows that advertising, publicity, and sales promotion are often critical elements in the success or failure of a strategy. But many firms do a poor job with all three—so just copying how other firms handle these important strategy decisions is not "good enough." There is no sense in imitating bad practices. This chapter helps you understand important decisions that make effective use of advertising, publicity, and sales promotion.

When you finish this chapter you should be able to:

1 understand why a marketing manager sets specific objectives to guide the advertising effort.

2 understand when the various kinds of advertising are needed.

3 understand how to choose the "best" medium.

4 understand the main ways that digital advertising differs from advertising in other media.

5 understand how to plan the "best" message—that is, the copy thrust.

6 understand what advertising agencies do.

7 understand how to advertise legally.

8 understand the importance of and different types of publicity.

9 understand the importance and nature of sales promotion.

10 know the advantages and limitations of different types of sales promotion.

11 understand important new terms (shown in red).

Advertising, Publicity, Sales Promotion, and Marketing Strategy Planning

Advertising, publicity, and sales promotion can play a central role in the promotion blend. On a per-contact basis, these promotion methods provide a relatively low-cost way to inform, persuade, and activate customers. Advertising, publicity, and sales promotion can position a firm's marketing mix as the one that meets customer needs. They can help motivate channel members or a firm's own employees, as well as final customers.

Unfortunately the results that marketers *actually achieve* with advertising, publicity, and sales promotion are very uneven. It has been said that half of the money spent on these activities is wasted—but that most managers don't know which half. Mass selling can be exciting and involving, or it can be downright obnoxious. Sometimes it's based on careful research, yet much of it is based on someone's pet idea. A creative idea may produce great results or be a colossal waste of money. Ads may stir emotions or go unnoticed.

Exhibit 15–1 Marketing Strategy Planning, Advertising, Publicity, and Sales Promotion

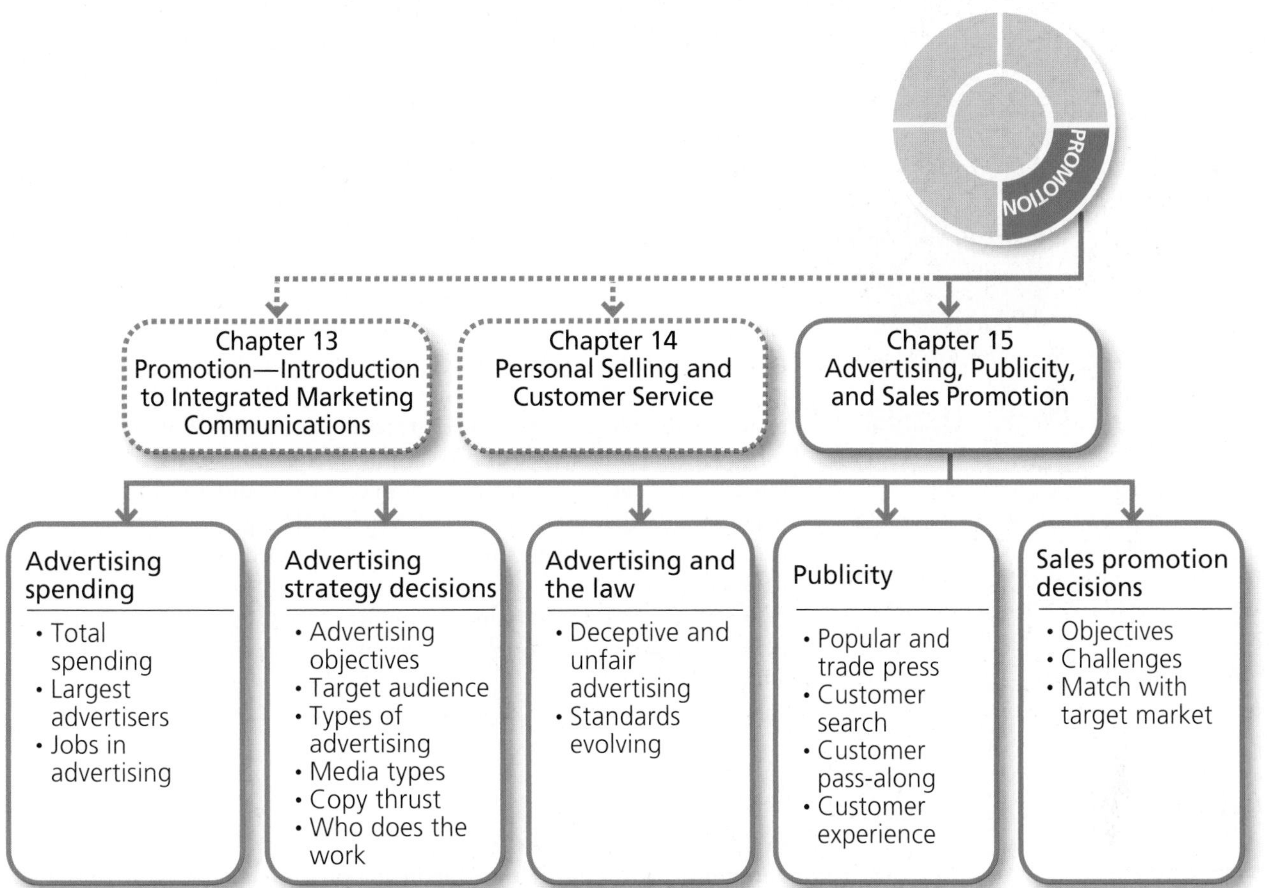

This chapter explains approaches to help you understand how successful advertising, publicity, and sales promotion works. See Exhibit 15-1. After a brief overview of the cost of advertising, we look at the different decisions marketing managers—and the advertising agencies they may work with—have to make: (1) what they want to achieve through advertising, (2) who the target audience is, (3) what kind of advertising to use, (4) which media to use to reach target customers, (5) what to say (the copy thrust), and (6) who will do the work—the firm's own marketing or advertising people or outside agencies. We also discuss legal issues in advertising.

Publicity involves unpaid media. The growth of the Internet and changes in consumer behavior have created many different types of publicity. For some promotion objectives, publicity offers a lower cost and more effective approach than advertising or sales promotion.

There are challenges in managing sales promotion, but it offers advantages over advertising for some objectives. So, this chapter also presents decisions that must be made with respect to different types of sales promotion for different targets.

International dimensions are important

The basic strategy planning decisions for advertising, publicity, and sales promotion are the same regardless of where in the world the target market is located. However, the look and feel can vary a lot in different countries. The choices available to a marketing manager within each of the decision areas may also vary dramatically from one country to another.

Commercial television may not be available. If it is, government rules may limit the type of advertising permitted or when ads can be shown. For example, privacy laws are stricter in Europe as compared to the U.S., making it more difficult to track consumers' online behavior and deliver highly targeted advertising. Radio broadcasts in a market area

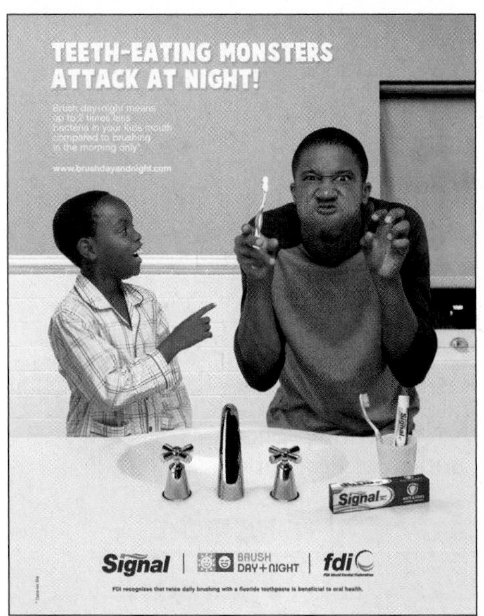

In Africa, there has not been a long tradition of brushing teeth, so Signal's advertising educates consumers on the importance of regular tooth-brushing.

may not be in the target market's language. The target audience may not be able to read. Access to interactive media like the Internet may be nonexistent. Cultural influences may limit ad messages. Ad agencies that already know a nation's unique advertising environment may not be available.

The trust that consumers place in publicity and online sources of information differs across countries. For example, many shoppers use online product reviews before making a purchase decision. A study by the Nielsen Company found that about 80 percent of Vietnamese and Italian Internet customers trusted online consumer opinions at review sites. On the other hand, only 46 percent of Internet users in Argentina and 50 percent in Finland trusted such information. As firms rely more on the Internet to get their messages out to wider audiences, they need to consider cultural differences.[2]

International dimensions also impact sales promotion. Trade promotion may be difficult, or even impossible, to manage. A typical Japanese grocery retailer with only 250 square feet of space, for example, doesn't have room for *any* special end-of-aisle displays. Consumer promotions may be affected, too. In some developing nations, samples can't be distributed through the mail, because they're routinely stolen before they get to target customers. And some countries ban consumer sweepstakes because they see them as a form of gambling.

In this chapter we'll consider a number of these international issues, but we'll focus on the array of choices available in the United States and other advanced economies.

Advertising is Big Business

Total spending is big—and growing internationally

As an economy grows, advertising becomes more important—because more consumers have income and advertising can get results. But good advertising results cost money. And spending on advertising is significant. In 1946, U.S. advertising spending was slightly more than $3 billion. By 2010, it was more than $200 billion. Ad spending dropped significantly with the recent downturn in the economy, but as the economy recovers ad spending will grow.[3]

Over the last decade, the rate of advertising spending has increased even more rapidly in other countries. Still, advertising in the United States accounts for about 35 percent of worldwide ad spending. Europe accounts for about 30 percent, and Asia about 24 percent (though spending in Asia is growing fast, especially in China). For most countries in other regions, advertising spending has traditionally been quite low.

The biggest marketers are investing ad dollars wherever they can find revenue or potential for growth—and increasingly, that's not the United States. China is getting a great deal of attention, and already five of the 100 largest advertisers invest more than 10 percent of their ad budgets in China. China will soon be the world's second-largest advertising market (replacing Japan as number two behind the United States). Long-term growth is now driven by emerging markets like Indonesia, Argentina, South Korea, Mexico, and Turkey.[4]

Most advertisers aren't really spending that much

While total spending on advertising seems high, U.S. corporations spend an average of only about 2.5 percent of their sales dollars on advertising. Worldwide, the percentage is even smaller. Exhibit 15-2 shows, however, that advertising spending as a percent of sales dollars varies significantly across product categories. Producers of consumer products generally spend a larger percent than firms that produce business products. For example, U.S. companies that make perfume and cosmetics spend about 20.3 percent. However, companies that sell plastics to manufacturers spend only about 1.7 percent on advertising. Some business products companies—those that depend on e-commerce or personal selling—may spend less than 1/10 of 1 percent.

Exhibit 15–2 Advertising Spending as Percent of Sales for Illustrative Product Categories

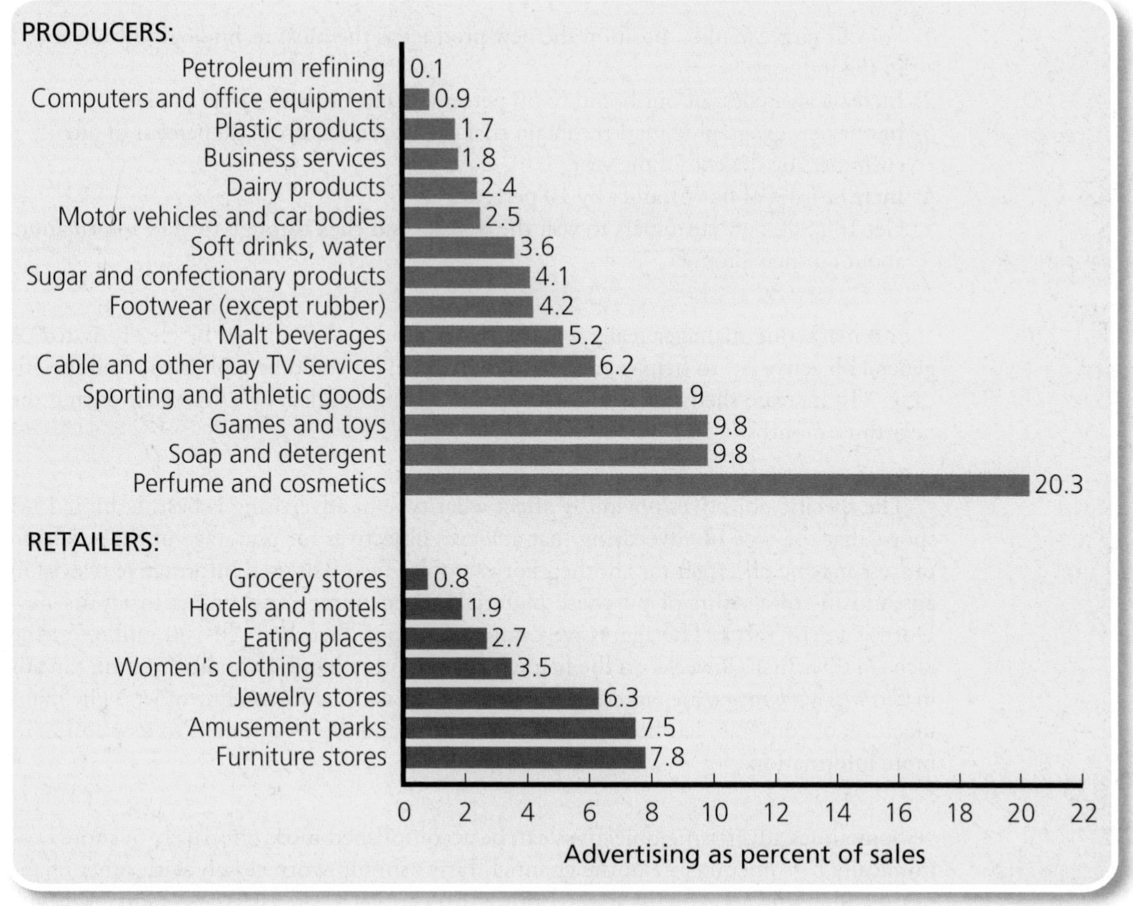

In general, the percent is smaller for retailers and wholesalers than for producers. While some large chains like Kohl's, Macy's, and JCPenney spend over 5 percent, other retailers and wholesalers spend 2 percent or less. Individual firms may spend more or less than others in the industry, depending on the role of advertising in their promotion blend.[5]

Advertising doesn't employ that many people

While total advertising expenditures are large, the advertising industry itself employs relatively few people. The major expense is for media time and space. Many students hope for a glamorous job in advertising, but there are fewer jobs in advertising than you might think. In the United States, only about 462,000 people work directly in the advertising industry. Advertising agencies employ only about half of all these people.[6]

Advertising Objectives Are a Strategy Decision

LO 15.1

Advertising objectives must be specific

Every ad and every advertising campaign should have clearly defined objectives. These should grow out of the firm's overall marketing strategy and the promotion jobs assigned to advertising. It isn't enough for the marketing manager to say, "Promote the product." The marketing manager must decide exactly what advertising should do.

Advertising objectives should be more specific than personal selling objectives. One of the advantages of personal selling is that a salesperson can shift the presentation for a specific customer. Each ad, however, must be effective not just for one customer but for thousands, or millions, of them.

The marketing manager sets the overall direction

Advertising objectives usually start with the marketing manager, who works with the advertising manager to develop the objectives and an appropriate budget to accomplish them. The following lists some potential advertising objectives:

1. For our target market, position the new product as the most technologically advanced in the industry.
2. Increase awareness of our brand to 50 percent in our primary target market.
3. In our new geographic market, obtain trial of our product from 20 percent of our customers by the end of the year.
4. Increase sales of our product by 10 percent.
5. Get 100,000 new customers to visit the website and click through to view information about our new product.

If you want half the market, say so!

If a marketing manager really wants specific results, they should be clearly stated. A general objective is "To help expand market share." This could be rephrased more specifically: "To increase shelf space in our cooperating retail outlets by 25 percent during the next three months."

Objectives guide implementation too

The specific objectives obviously affect what type of advertising is best. Exhibit 15-3 shows that the type of advertising that achieves objectives for one stage of the adoption process may be off target for another. For example, Taco Bell used informative television ads and in-store point-of-purchase materials to encourage consumers to try its new Doritos Locos Tacos. The aggressive campaign helped Taco Bell sell 100 million of the tacos in their first 10 weeks on the market. On the other hand, Dassault Aviation ran ads in *BusinessWeek* magazine targeting business leaders with its Falcon line of jets. The manufacturer of corporate jets hoped to raise awareness and drive customers to its website for more information.

Coordinating advertising across the channel to achieve objectives

Sometimes advertising objectives can be accomplished more effectively or more economically by someone else in the channel. Firms should work closely with other channel members to coordinate advertising efforts to get the best results. For example, a producer of office supplies like Avery Dennison may find that the most economical use of its advertising dollars is the weekly flyer of a retail chain like Office Depot. So Avery Dennison offers **advertising allowances**—price reductions to firms further along in the channel—encourage them to advertise or otherwise promote the firm's products locally.

Cooperative advertising involves producers sharing in the cost of ads with wholesalers or retailers. This helps the intermediaries compete in their local markets. It also helps the producer get more promotion for its advertising dollars because media usually give local advertisers lower rates than national or international firms. In addition, a retailer or wholesaler who is paying a share of the cost is more likely to follow through.[7]

Exhibit 15–3 Examples of Different Types of Advertising over Adoption Process Stages

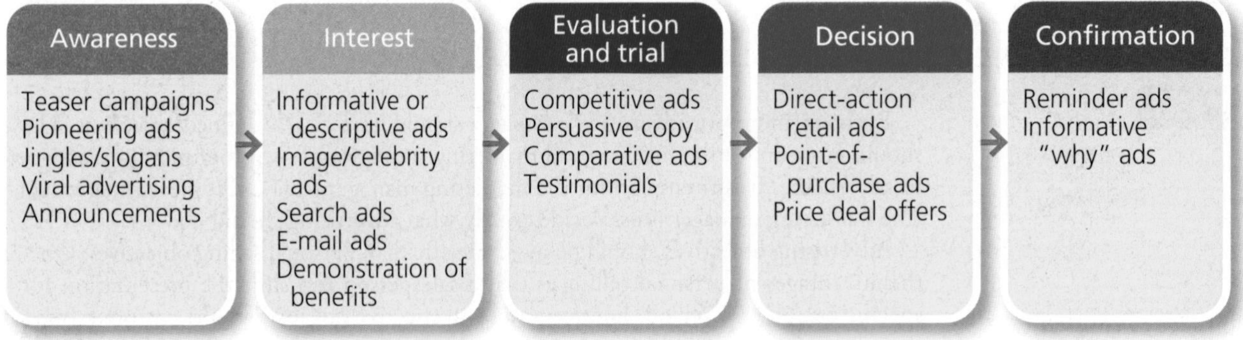

Exhibit 15–4
Types of Advertising

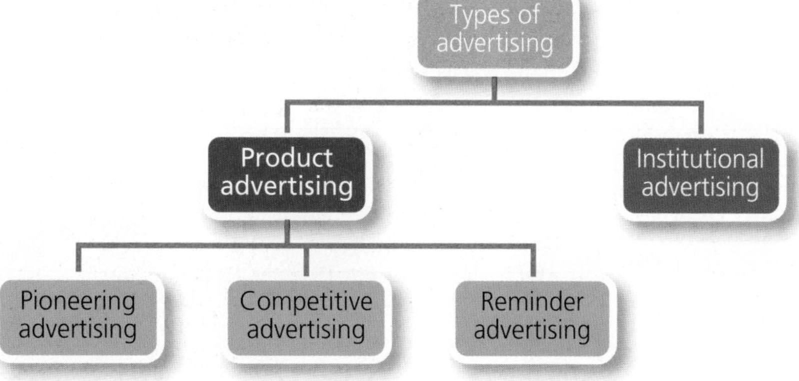

Objectives Determine the Kinds of Advertising Needed

LO 15.2

The chosen advertising objectives largely determine which of two basic types of advertising to use—product or institutional. See Exhibit 15-4. **Product advertising** tries to sell a product. We will discuss three categories of product advertising—pioneering, competitive, and reminder—which focus on getting consumers to know, like, and remember something. Then we will discuss **institutional advertising**, which promotes an organization's image, reputation, or ideas rather than a specific product.

Pioneering advertising builds primary demand

Pioneering advertising tries to develop primary demand for a product category rather than demand for a specific brand. Pioneering advertising is usually done in the early stages of the product life cycle; it informs potential customers about the new product and helps turn them into adopters. When digital cameras first came out, consumers didn't know their benefits or why they might want one—and at the same time they worried about how they could get printed pictures. So advertising for the early products in the market had to explain these basics and build primary demand.

Competitive advertising emphasizes selective demand

Competitive advertising tries to develop selective demand for a specific brand. A firm is forced into competitive advertising as the product life cycle moves along—to hold its own against competitors. For example, as digital cameras moved to the growth stage of the

Mini Cooper's Dutch advertising agency had multiple objectives when it left large empty boxes with torn ribbons and wrapping paper around Amsterdam shortly after Christmas. The boxes created awareness for the Mini Cooper and reinforced its positioning as small, different, and "fun"—like a toy.

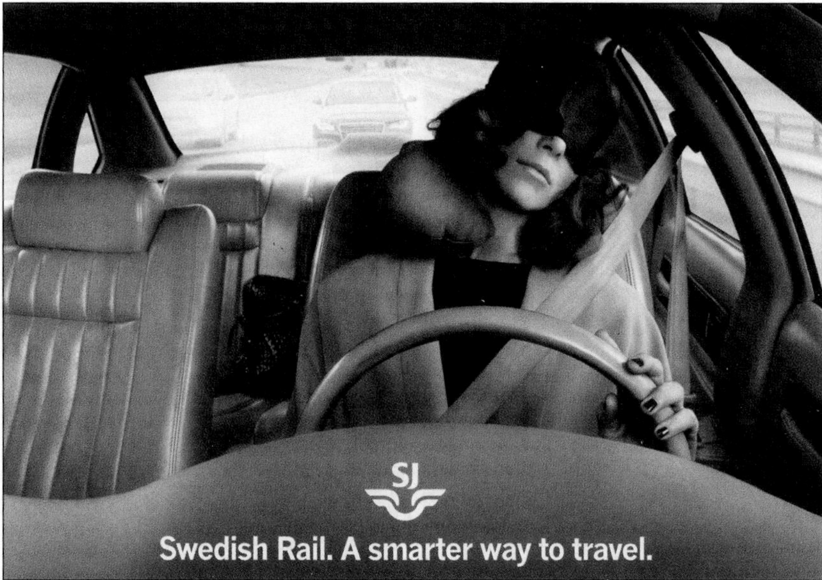

Purex Complete with Zout uses a direct type of competitive advertising; the ad offers a free sample to encourage immediate action. The indirect competitive ad for Swedish Rail points out advantages of taking the train (as compared to driving).

product life cycle, advertising emphasized features and benefits to persuade customers that they needed more megapixels, lower prices, or face recognition.

Competitive advertising may be either direct or indirect. The **direct type** aims for immediate buying action. The **indirect type** points out product advantages to affect future buying decisions.

Most of Delta Airlines' advertising is of the competitive variety. Much of it tries for immediate sales—so the ads are the direct type with prices, timetables, and phone numbers to call for reservations. Some of its ads are the indirect type. They focus on the quality of service and suggest you check Delta's website the next time you travel.

Comparative advertising is even rougher. **Comparative advertising** means making specific brand comparisons—using actual product names. Verizon touted its superior coverage with ads showing maps that highlighted its service as compared to AT&T. An Audi television ad shows a guy driving down the highway in his BMW. At full speed, he jumps out of his car and climbs onto a passing truck that is carrying a delivery of new Audi Q5s.

Pepsi used a fun image in this comparative ad with Coke.

Many countries forbid comparative advertising. But, in the United States, the Federal Trade Commission decided to encourage comparative ads because it thought they would increase competition and provide consumers with more useful information. Superiority claims are supposed to be supported by research evidence—but the guidelines aren't clear. When P&G's Dryel did not fare well in independent test comparisons with stain removal by professional dry cleaners, P&G changed its ad claims. However, some firms just keep running tests until they get the results they want. Others talk about minor differences that don't reflect a product's overall benefits. Comparative ads can also backfire by calling attention to competing products that consumers had not previously considered.

Reminder advertising reinforces a favorable relationship

Reminder advertising tries to keep the product's name before the public. It may be useful when the product has achieved brand preference or insistence, perhaps in the market maturity or sales decline stages. It is used primarily to reinforce previous promotion. Here the advertiser may use soft-sell ads that just mention or show the name—as a reminder. Hallmark, for example, often relies on reminder ads because most consumers already know the brand name and, after years of promotion, associate it with high-quality cards and gifts.

Institutional advertising—remember our name

Institutional advertising usually focuses on the name and prestige of an organization or industry. It may seek to inform, persuade, or remind. Its basic objective is to develop goodwill or improve an organization's relations with various groups—not only customers but also current and prospective channel members, suppliers, shareholders, employees, and the general public. The British government, for instance, uses institutional advertising to promote England as a place to do business. Many Japanese firms, like Hitachi, emphasize institutional advertising, in part because they often use the company name as a brand name.

Companies sometimes rely on institutional advertising to present the company in a favorable light, perhaps to overcome image problems. Other organizations use institutional advertising to advocate a specific cause or idea. Insurance companies and organizations like Mothers Against Drunk Driving, for example, use these advocacy ads to encourage people not to drink and drive.[8]

Choosing the "Best" Medium—How to Deliver the Message

LO 15.3

Advertising media are the various means by which the message is communicated to the target market. The first column of Exhibit 15-5 lists some of the most common kinds of media. Marketing managers seek the best medium, which varies with the situation. Effectiveness depends on how well the medium fits with the rest of a marketing strategy—that is, it depends on (1) your promotion objectives, (2) what target markets you want to reach, (3) the funds available for advertising, and (4) the nature of the media, including whom they *reach,* with what *frequency,* with what *impact,* and at what *cost.*

Exhibit 15-5 shows estimated ad spending, percent, and some pros and cons of major kinds of media. However, some of the advantages noted in this table may not apply in all markets. For example, direct mail may not be a flexible choice in a country with a weak postal system. Internet ads might be worthless if few target customers have access to the Internet. Similarly, TV audiences are often less selective and targeted, but a special-interest cable TV show may reach a very specific audience.[9]

Medium should fit promotion objectives

The medium should support the promotion objectives. If the objective requires demonstrating product benefits, TV or Internet with video may be the best alternative. If the objective is to inform, telling a detailed story and using precise pictures, then Internet advertising might be right. Newspapers work well for businesses operating in local markets. Alternatively, with a broad target market or when there is a need to show color, magazines may be better. For example, when Jockey wanted to show customers the variety of styles and colors in its men's underwear, it was concerned about showing men just wearing underwear on television. So Jockey switched its advertising to magazines, where it felt more comfortable showing those images.[10]

Match your market with the media

To guarantee good media selection, the advertiser first must *clearly* specify its target market. Then the advertiser can choose media that reach those target customers. Most media firms use marketing research to develop profiles of their audiences. Generally, this research focuses on demographic characteristics rather than the segmenting dimensions specific to the planning needs of *each* different advertiser.

Advertisers pay for the whole audience

The audience for media that *do* reach your target market may also include people who are *not* in the target group. But *advertisers pay for the whole audience the media delivers,* including those who aren't potential customers. For example, Delta Faucet, a faucet manufacturer that wanted its ads to reach plumbers, placed ads on ESPN's Saturday college

Exhibit 15–5 Estimated Ad Spending, Percent, Advantages, and Disadvantages of Major Media

Kinds of Media	2010 Ad Spending ($ billion)	2010 Percent (%) of total spending	Advantages	Disadvantages
Television	51.47	25.2	Demonstrations, image building, good attention, wide reach, cable can be selective	"Clutter"—ads compete for attention, expensive, technology can make it easy to skip ads
Direct mail	48.01	23.6	Highly targeted, flexible, message can be longer and more complex, can personalize	Relatively expensive per contact, poor image "junk mail," hard to retain attention
Newspaper	29.34	14.4	Flexible, timely, local market, ads can be saved by consumers, low cost	"Clutter"—ads compete for attention, poor photo reproduction, declining readership
Internet	23.42	11.5	Ads link to more detailed website, can contain video/animation and audio, can have direct feedback, some "pay for results," easier to track results	Hard to compare costs with other media, technology can make it easy to skip ads, only reaches computer users
Magazines	17.23	8.5	High reader involvement, high-quality images possible, very targeted, good detail, can convey complex messages	Inflexible, long lead times, cost can be high, declining readership
Radio	15.57	7.6	Wide reach, segmented audience, inexpensive, can target local market	Weak attention, many different rates, short exposure, no visual element, difficult to convey complex message
Yellow Pages & other directories	11.45	5.6	Reaches local customers ready to buy, relatively inexpensive, local	Many competitors listed in same place, hard to differentiate, new directories raise costs
Outdoor and cinema	7.37	3.6	Captive audience, can select geographic areas, low cost, high visibility	Outdoor—"glance" medium, must be a simple message, Cinema—primarily a younger audience

football telecasts. Research showed that many plumbers watched the ESPN games. Yet plumbers are only a very small portion of the total college football audience—and the size of the total audience determined the cost of the advertising time.[11]

Some media help zero in on specific target markets

Today, advertisers direct more attention to reaching smaller, more defined target markets. The most obvious evidence of this is in the growth of spending on direct-mail advertising to consumers in databases. For example, Germany's Otto Versand, the world's largest mail-order company, maintains CRM databases that track each customer's past purchases and responses to previous mailings. These data help the firm to accurately predict whether a customer will respond to a particular mailing. Such data also help mail-order firms segment customers, develop better messages, and increase the efficiency of their direct-mail campaigns.[12]

Even traditional media are becoming more targeted. TV is a good example. Cable TV channels—like CNN, Nickelodeon, ESPN, MTV and the Golf Channel—are taking advertisers away from the networks because they target specific audiences. The Golf Channel, for example, averages just over 100,000 viewers, but these upscale consumers are the target market for makers of golf clubs, balls, and accessories. Moreover, being specialized doesn't necessarily mean that the target market is small. MTV appeals most strongly to young viewers, but its programming is seen in about 400 million homes worldwide—more than any other programmer.

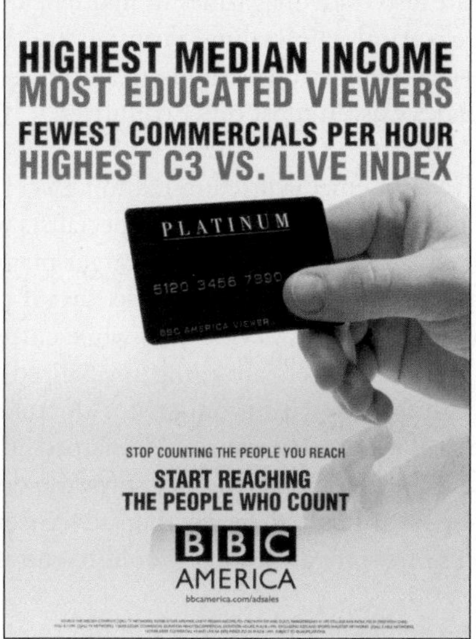

Radio and cable television can offer targeted messages to specific demographic, social, and cultural groups.

Radio has also become a more specialized medium. Some stations cater to particular ethnic and racial groups, such as Hispanics, African Americans, or French Canadians. Others aim at specific target markets with rock, country, or classical music. Satellite and Internet radio stations reach a larger number of consumers, so expect even more targeting.

A combination of cable television technology and big data are making television advertising more personalized and relevant to consumers. Some cable television operators can now show different television commercials to different households watching the same television show. Big data companies like Acxiom combine data from consumers' credit and loyalty cards, online activities, and other sources to give advertisers a detailed look at individual households. Cable TV companies use that information to match ads to specific households. The U.S. Army used the technology to send different ads to four target markets. For example, one market segment, called "family influencers," saw an ad showing a daughter discussing her enlistment decision with her parents. A second group, labeled "youth ethnic 1," featured African American men testing and repairing machinery. The other groups saw ads customized to their background. The approach demonstrates a convergence of different technologies to more narrowly target particular market segments.[13]

Many magazines serve only special-interest groups, such as cooks, new parents, and personal computer users. In fact, the most profitable magazines seem to be the ones aimed at clearly defined markets. Many specialty magazines also have international editions that help marketers reach consumers with similar interests in different parts of the world. Most magazines run companion websites and some have tablet versions. Both of these options allow for more interactive advertising as compared to standard print.

Advertising managers often look to grab attention with alternative media. The yellow stripes were already in part of the Swiss crosswalk and the red package was added for Zurifest, a well-attended event in Switzerland.

There are also trade magazines in many fields, such as chemical engineering, furniture retailing, electrical wholesaling, farming, and the aerospace market. *Standard Rate and Data* provides a guide to the thousands of magazines now available in the United States. Similar guides exist in most other countries.

Specialized media are small, but gaining

The advertising media listed in Exhibit 15-5 are attracting the vast majority of advertising media budgets. But advertising specialists always look for cost-effective new media that will help advertisers reach their target markets. For example, one company successfully sells space for signs on bike racks that it places in front of 7-Eleven stores. A new generation of ATMs shows video ads while customers wait to get their money.

Some B2B advertisers are using specialized media to target difficult-to-reach target markets. Companies with products for doctors and medical offices can be a particular challenge to reach. Practice Fusion developed ad-supported software that organizes medical records. In exchange for the free software, doctors get a daily dose of advertising. The doctors are so difficult to reach that advertisers pay 20 times as much to run ads on Practice Fusion's software as they would to run the same ad on Yahoo! or Facebook.[14]

Budget and "must buys" affect media blend

Selecting which media to use is still pretty much an art. The media buyer starts with a budgeted amount and tries to buy the best blend to reach the target audience. Often "must buys," like the Yellow Pages for a retailer in a small town, will use up much of an advertising budget.

For many firms, even national advertisers, the high cost of television may eliminate it from the media blend. The average cost just to produce a national TV ad is now about $400,000—and an ad with special effects can easily cost twice that. In the United States, it costs an average of about $200,000 to run a 30-second commercial during the prime evening time, but on hit shows the cost can be more. Prices can soar even higher for "big event" shows that attract the largest audiences. For example, 30 seconds of advertising on the 2013 Super Bowl cost sponsors about $3 million.[15]

Digital Advertising

LO 15.4

Customer viewing moves to new screens

Two new screens—the computer and the cell phone—are taking consumers' attention away from watching television and reading magazines and newspapers. Both screens allow consumers to access the Internet, where they socialize with friends, consume news and other information, enjoy entertainment like videos, and shop. This change in consumer behavior creates new challenges and opportunities for marketing managers as they try to target specific customers or segments through digital media (the Internet and mobile devices). These two media have some unique qualities, so we will look more closely at digital advertising. Later in this chapter we will examine how the Internet supports publicity.[16]

Most Internet ads seek a direct response

Advertising on the Internet has evolved quickly, as marketing managers find what works best—and technology creates new types of advertising. To get the attention of web surfers, Internet advertisers have created different types of ads. The most common type is a *banner ad*—which is a small rectangular box that usually includes text, graphics, and sometimes video to get attention and hold interest. These ads appear on many web pages and even social media sites like Facebook and Twitter. Variations include the annoying *pop-up ad* that opens in a new browser window (and blocks what the web user is trying to view—until it's closed). Most people find these ads annoying and many use software to block them. Yet some advertisers still use them because they get responses.

A sponsored search ad also seeks a direct response. Many consumers conduct searches to get information for buying decisions. As a result, Google, Yahoo!, and other search engines know customers' interests based on the keywords they enter into the search engine. Retailers, like REI, capitalize on this knowledge by paying a search engine firm for a sponsored search ad that appears above or next to the results of a search on "hiking boots."

Most advertisers pay only if ads deliver

Most websites use a *pay-per-click* advertising model, where advertisers pay only when a customer clicks on the ad and links to the advertiser's website. Pay-per-click advertising is a big shift from traditional media where firms pay for ads based on an estimate of how many people will see the ad. Many firms like this ability to directly track the cost of advertising and resulting sales. Consider Omaha Steaks, which sells frozen meat by mail order and uses Google search ads. Its ads appear when any of about 1,600 keywords, including *Omaha steaks* or *filet mignon,* are entered at Google. Omaha Steaks pays about 30–35 cents for each click-through. "Omaha Steaks" gets about 200–300 clicks per day.[17]

Click fraud raises ethical concerns

Advertisers don't mind paying when interested customers click on their ads. However, *click fraud* occurs when a person or software program automatically clicks on an ad without having any interest in the ad's subject. The intent is to defraud the advertiser and make money for an unscrupulous website. Consider Martin Fleischmann, for example. As owner of the insurance quote site MostChoice.com, he found that many of the click-throughs on his ads came from "customers" in Botswana, Mongolia, and Syria—where MostChoice did not do business. After investigating, Fleischmann discovered he was paying for clicks on sites with names like insurance1472.com—where uninterested people were being paid by the owners of these sites to simply click on the ads placed there by Google. Advertisers have been working to remedy this threat.[18]

Some ads know where customers have been on the web

Behavioral targeting delivers ads to consumers based on websites they have previously visited. Some websites place a small file called a cookie on the computer of people who visit their sites. These cookies give an advertiser some information about the consumer. For example, cookies show whether a web surfer has been to the company's website before, made a purchase on the last visit, or perhaps abandoned an online "shopping cart." A consumer who checks out a pair of red pumps at Nordstrom.com might find those same shoes appearing in ads at a wide range of sites for the next month. Perhaps you have felt like a product was stalking you online?

Based on other sites a customer has visited, it is sometimes possible to determine likely interest in an offering. A California theme park used this approach to increase vacation

The Internet offers some unique benefits for advertisers. The advertisement on the left appeared on the website for NBCNews.com after one of the authors made a purchase at the online clothing retailer Territory Ahead. The shirt featured in the ad was one the author considered but did not purchase. VW wants customers to understand that drivers can start the new Tiguan with their keys in their pocket, by simply pressing a button. To demonstrate this feature online, customers first click their cursor on the ad. Next, the customer is asked to touch their webcam—at which time the viewer hears the car start and sees it drive out of the ad.

package sales at its website. Special ads were delivered to web surfers whose computers had cookies to indicate that they lived in specific western states and who had also visited a travel site in the previous two weeks. While this proved to be a cost-effective way to target ads and boost online sales, some web surfers find the invasion of privacy a bit creepy.[19]

Big data tells advertisers even more about customers

Some advertisers are using new approaches to learn even more about customers before targeting them with online advertising. *Social targeting* delivers ads to consumers based on the conversations and behaviors they exhibit in social media and more generally surfing the web. Together this big data can be linked to individual consumers and give advertisers detailed insight about consumer wants and needs. Social targeting firms begin by identifying customers who have purchased a particular brand. These customers' online activities are then analyzed. The advertiser then looks all across the Internet to identify customers whose online behavior most closely matches the buyers—and those customers receive ads.

Let's look at how Ford Motor Company might use this approach to target potential buyers of the Ford Fiesta. Ford puts tracking cookies on tens of thousands of computers that it knows are used by buyers of the Ford Fiesta—perhaps they opened an e-mail sent to new owners and the e-mail installed the cookie. For a few weeks, Ford tracks those buyers—following their journeys around the web and social media activity. With this information Ford develops profiles that characterize Fiesta buyers. Then, from the hundreds of millions of customers already being tracked on the web (almost all the rest of us), Ford identifies the few million who have online profiles most similar to the recent Fiesta buyers. These customers then begin to receive ads for the Ford Fiesta.[20]

Ethics Question

A software company offers its useful program as a free download. Few downloaders ever read the license agreement, but it states that the program is paid for by advertising; specifically, it explains that when the program is installed, another "adware" program is also installed that helps advertisers serve up targeted ads. Assume that you own a small online flower business that is struggling to get started. A firm with an adware system like the one described above contacts you about buying Internet ads. You pay only when someone clicks-through to your site from an ad. You try the ads for a month and your online sales triple. But you also get complaints from many people who don't understand why your pop-up ads constantly appear in their browsers.[21] Would you continue to use this "contextual advertising"? Why or why not?

Text ads for those who ask

Among teens, texting is more popular than phone conversations—and the primary way many use their phones. Stores that target the teen demographic, including Charlotte Russe, Claire's, and Vans, have turned to text messages to communicate with this market. U.S. law requires cell phone users to sign up to receive the text messages. Consequently, many of these stores offer discounts as a way to get young people to sign up.[22]

Smartphones know customers' locations

Smartphones are becoming increasingly ubiquitous in many developed countries. Smartphones offer users anytime–anywhere access to the Internet. For many it is their primary or only avenue to the Internet. The smaller screen is one adaptation that advertisers need to recognize when placing online ads that might be viewed using a smartphone. An opportunity comes from the GPS located in the smartphone, which has the ability to tell advertisers where a customer is located. This works best for location based activities—retail stores, restaurants, and bars. For example, McDonald's placed ads on the "Hot Pics" section of *Us* magazine's mobile website. The ads promoted McDonald's new Blueberry Banana Nut Oatmeal. When customers tapped on the ad, they were taken to a site with more information about the new breakfast item. With one more click they could find the location and directions to the nearest McDonald's.

Some firms are even experimenting with ads that target customers based on the customer's location at a particular moment. Imagine walking down a city street on a hot day and suddenly getting a text-message offer for a discount on a cold Frappuccino at the Starbucks across the street. There are still some technical hurdles before this scene becomes common, but it illustrates the pinpoint targeting that will be possible.[23]

Planning the "Best" Message—What to Communicate

LO 15.5

Specifying the copy thrust

Once you decide *how* the messages will reach the target audience, you have to decide on the **copy thrust**—what the words and illustrations should communicate. Carrying out the copy thrust is the job of advertising specialists. But the advertising manager and the marketing manager need to understand the process to be sure that the job is done well.

Let AIDA help guide message planning

Basically, the overall marketing strategy should determine *what* the message should say. Then management judgment, perhaps aided by marketing research, can help decide how to encode this content so it will be decoded as intended.

As a guide to message planning, we can use the AIDA concept: getting Attention, holding Interest, arousing Desire, and obtaining Action.

Getting attention

Getting attention is an ad's first job. Many readers leaf through magazines without paying attention to any of the ads, and viewers get snacks during TV commercials. When watching a program on TiVo, they may zip past the commercial with a flick of a button. On the Internet, they may use a pop-up blocker or click on the next website before the ad message finishes loading onto the screen.

Many attention-getting devices are available. A large headline, computer animations, shocking statements, attractive models, animals, online games, special effects—anything different or eye-catching—may do the trick. However, the attention-getting device can't detract from, and hopefully should lead to, the next step, holding interest.

Holding interest

Holding interest is more difficult. A humorous ad, an unusual video effect, or a clever photo may get your attention—but once you've seen it, then what? If there is no relation between what got your attention and the marketing mix or the ad does not address your needs, you'll move on. To hold interest, the tone and language of the ad must fit with the experiences and attitudes of the target customers and their reference groups. As a result, many advertisers develop ads that relate to specific emotions. They hope that the good feeling about the ad will stick, even if its details are forgotten.

Arousing desire

Arousing desire to buy a particular product is one of an ad's most difficult jobs. The ad must convince customers that the product can meet their needs. Testimonials may persuade a consumer that other people with similar needs like the product. Product comparisons may highlight the advantages of a particular brand.

To arouse desire an ad should usually focus on a *unique selling proposition* that aims at an important unsatisfied need. This can help differentiate the firm's marketing mix and position its brand as offering superior value to the target market. Too many advertisers ignore the idea of a unique selling proposition. Rather than using an integrated blend of communications to

The copy thrust—both the text and the image—in this ad for Lurpak butter grabs attention and holds interest.

McDonald's created this 3-D billboard in Chicago, outside Wrigley Field, featuring an egg cracking open to showcase to customers that it uses fresh cracked eggs at breakfast to make the famous McMuffin breakfast sandwich. The egg cracked at dawn and stayed open until 10:30 a.m. (which is when McDonald's stops serving breakfast in its U.S. restaurants). The ad not only got attention, but also prompted passersby to think about its distinctive selling proposition.

tell the whole story, they cram too much into each ad—and then none of it has any impact.

Obtaining action

Getting action is the final requirement—and not an easy one. From communication research, we now know that prospective customers must be led beyond considering how the product *might* fit into their lives to actually trying it.

Direct-response ads can sometimes help promote action by encouraging interested consumers to do *something* even if they are not ready to make a purchase. For example, Fidelity Investments has run TV ads featuring colorful graphs, a sign with "Wow!" and the company's phone number and website address. And just in case viewers don't "get it," Blondie's song "Call Me" plays in the background. Fidelity wants to encourage interested consumers to make the first step in building a relationship.[24]

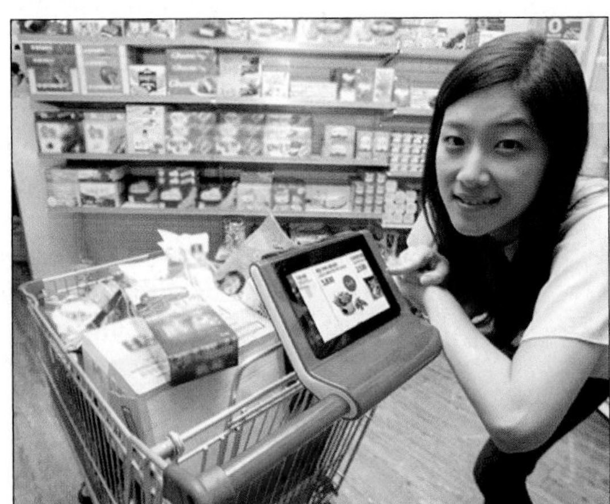

Grocery stores are testing different technology on grocery carts. The carts have the ability to sync with a shopper's cell phone and help them find things on their shopping list. The tablets can also serve up ads to customers based on their list and their location in the store.

Advertising Agencies Often Do the Work

LO 15.6

An advertising manager manages a company's advertising effort. Many advertising managers, especially those working for large retailers, have their own advertising departments that plan specific advertising campaigns and carry out the details. Others turn over much of the advertising work to specialists—the advertising agencies.

Ad agencies are specialists

Advertising agencies are specialists in planning and handling mass-selling details for advertisers. Agencies play a useful role. They are independent of the advertiser and have an outside viewpoint. They bring experience to an individual client's problems because they work for many other clients. They can often do the job more economically than a company's own department. And if an agency isn't doing a good job, the client can select

Does Advertising That's Everywhere Get Us Anywhere?

There's no holiday from advertising. You get to the beach, look down, and huge versions of the Skippy peanut butter logo are embossed in the sand. You roll your eyes in dismay and catch a view of a plane pulling a 100-foot-long banner ad with Catherine Zeta-Jones urging you to "Sign up for T-Mobile's free Friday minutes." You walk down the street and try to ignore the billboards and bus stop shelter ads. But it's hard not to notice trucks whose trailers are billboards—and there are even ads on the trucks' mud flaps. And is that a picture of Colonel Sanders on a fire hydrant—making your mouth water for KFC's "fiery" chicken wings? A bus drives by wrapped in an ad for McDonald's—and you see a cab with hubcaps advertising Taco Bell. You *are* getting hungry, but you packed a lunch and seek refuge in a nearby park. Not quite an escape from ads—the bench you sit on is an ad for a check-cashing service—and just for good measure the banana you pull out of your lunch bag has a sticker advertising Florida oranges. A couple of girls walk by wearing T-shirts emblazoned with "Abercrombie and Fitch" and "Old Navy." Then you hear a deep voice—but it's just a cell phone—the ring tone of the guy sitting next to you is promoting Stephen King's new movie with the author's voice. Then your cell phone displays a text message that offers you a discounted admission at a nearby club—how do they know where you are?

You need to get away from this commercial overload, so you head back to your condo to kick back, watch a movie, play computer games, and maybe read e-mail. But this is no escape! An ad and discount for the local Hard Rock Café are printed on the key to your rented condo. The "ad-free" pay-per-view movie—*National Treasure: Book of Secrets*—has product placements from Red Bull, Blackberry, MSN, and Mercedes. You pull out your laptop and load up Tony Hawk's American Wasteland video game—but you can't miss all the Jeep Wranglers, Cherokees, and Liberties driving around in the game—not a coincidence. So you close the game and check your e-mail. Getting onto a wireless Internet connection, your pop-up blocker stops many ads, but some still worm through. You sort through your e-mails—half of which are uninvited spam messages. You decide to just go read a book on your Amazon Kindle e-reader and then remember you bought the version with online ads—are you sure it was worth it to save $20 on the Kindle? Is there no place to hide?

There are certainly many cases where promotion benefits consumers and companies. After all, it is revenues from advertising that cover the cost of lots of great stuff consumers get for free. Yet sometimes you can't help but wish that you—and your wallet—were not the targets that so many companies are aiming at![25]

another. However, ending a relationship with an agency is a serious decision. Too many marketing managers just use their advertising agency as a scapegoat. Whenever anything goes wrong, they blame the agency.

Some full-service agencies handle any activity related to advertising, publicity, or sales promotion. They may even handle overall marketing strategy planning as well as marketing research, product and package development, and sales promotion. Other agencies are more specialized. For example, in recent years there has been rapid growth of digital agencies that specialize in developing Internet ads and online publicity and sales promotion.

The biggest agencies handle much of the advertising

The vast majority of advertising agencies are small, with 10 or fewer employees. But the largest agencies account for most of the billings. Over the past two decades many of the big agencies merged, creating mega-agencies with worldwide networks. Exhibit 15-6 shows a list of four of the largest agency networks and examples of some of their clients. Although their headquarters are located in different nations, they have offices worldwide. The move toward international marketing is a key reason behind the mergers and advertisers have responded as expected. For example, the "Big Four" now gets more than half of all advertising/media agency revenue.

The mega-agency can offer varied services, wherever in the world a marketing manager needs them. This may be especially important for managers in large corporations—like Toyota, Renault, Unilever, NEC, and PepsiCo—that advertise worldwide.[26]

Exhibit 15–6 "Big Four" Advertising Agency Supergroups

Organization	Largest Agency Networks	Headquarters Location	2011 Revenue ($ in billions)	Select Clients
WPP Group	Grey Group, JWT, Ogilvy & Mather, United Group, Wunderman, Young & Rubicam Brands	Dublin	15.59	Altria, American Express, Ford, GlaxoSmithKline, IBM, P&G
Omnicom Group	BBDO Worldwide, DDB Worldwide, TBWA Worldwide	New York	13.90	Apple, Bud, ExxonMobil, FedEx, GE, Pepsi, Visa
Publicis Groupe	Leo Burnett Worldwide, Publicis, Saatchi & Saatchi, Vivaki	Paris	7.12	British Airways, Coca-Cola, Disney, Kellogg, L'Oreal, McDonald's
Interpublic	DraftFCB, Lowe, McCann Worldgroup	New York	7.01	Freecreditreport.com, Geico, Microsoft, Yum Brands, Unilever, Verizon

The really big agencies are less interested in smaller accounts. Smaller agencies will continue to appeal to customers who want more personal attention and a close relationship that is more attuned to their marketing needs.

Ethical conflicts may arise

Ad agencies usually work closely with their clients, and they often have access to confidential information. This can create ethical conflicts if an agency is working with two or more competing clients. Most agencies are sensitive to the potential problems and keep people and information from competing accounts separated. Even so, that doesn't always happen. For example, PepsiCo got a restraining order to stop an ad agency from assigning four people who had worked on advertising for its Aquafina bottled water to the account for Coca-Cola's competing brand, Dasani. Coca-Cola, in turn, yanked the account away from the agency. Because of situations like this, many advertisers refuse to work with any agency that handles any competing accounts, even if they are handled in different offices.[27]

Measuring Advertising Effectiveness Is Not Easy

Success depends on the total marketing mix

It would be convenient if we could measure the results of advertising by looking at sales. Some breakthrough ads do have a very direct effect on a company's sales—and the advertising literature is filled with success stories that "prove" advertising increases sales. Similarly, market research firms like Information Resources can sometimes compare sales levels before and after the period of an ad campaign. Yet we usually can't measure advertising success just by looking at sales. Advertising managers should measure effectiveness against the advertising objectives. The total marketing mix—not just advertising—is responsible for the sales result. Sales results are also affected by what competitors do and by other changes in the external market environment.

Research and testing can improve the odds

Ideally, advertisers should pretest advertising before it runs rather than relying solely on their own guesses about how good an ad will be. The judgment of creative people or advertising experts may not help much. They often judge only on the basis of originality or cleverness of the copy and illustrations.

Many progressive advertisers now demand laboratory or market tests to evaluate an ad's effectiveness. For example, split runs on cable TV systems in test markets are an important approach for testing ads in a normal viewing environment. Scanner sales data from retailers in those test markets can provide an estimate of how an ad is likely to affect sales. This approach will become even more powerful in the future as more cable systems allow viewers to provide immediate feedback to an ad as it appears on TV or on the Internet.

The idea for Coke Zero came from research that showed that younger men wanted the taste of Coke without the calories, but didn't like the word "diet." Coke Zero has been very successful, but was it an aggressive advertising campaign, black packaging, a sampling program, or all of these efforts that drove sales?

Hindsight may lead to foresight

After ads run, researchers may try to measure how much consumers recall about specific products or ads. The response to radio or television commercials or magazine readership can be estimated using various survey methods to check the size and composition of audiences (the Nielsen and Starch reports are examples). Similarly, most Internet advertisers keep track of how many "hits" on the firm's website come from ads placed at other websites.[28]

How to Avoid Unfair Advertising

LO 15.7

Government agencies may say what is fair

In most countries, the government takes an active role in deciding what kinds of advertising are allowable, fair, and appropriate. For example, France and Japan limit the use of cartoon characters in advertising to children, and Canada bans *any* advertising targeted directly at children. In Switzerland, an advertiser cannot use an actor to represent a consumer. New Zealand limits political ads on TV. In the United States, print ads must be identified so they aren't confused with editorial matter; in other countries ads and editorial copy can be intermixed. Most countries limit the number and length of commercials on broadcast media.

What is seen as positioning in one country may be viewed as unfair or deceptive in another. For example, when Pepsi was advertising its cola as "the choice of the new generation" in most countries, Japan's Fair Trade Committee didn't allow it—because in Japan Pepsi was not "the choice."[29]

Differences in rules mean that a marketing manager may face very specific limits in different countries, and local experts may be required to ensure that a firm doesn't waste money developing ads that will never be shown or which consumers will think are deceptive.

FTC controls unfair practices in the United States

In the United States, the Federal Trade Commission (FTC) has the power to control unfair or deceptive business practices, including deceptive advertising. The FTC has been policing deceptive advertising for many years. And it may be getting results now that advertising agencies as well as advertisers must share equal responsibility for false, misleading, or unfair ads.

This is a serious matter. If the FTC decides that a particular practice is unfair or deceptive, it has the power to require affirmative disclosures—such as the health warnings on cigarettes—or **corrective advertising**—ads to correct deceptive advertising. Years ago the FTC forced Listerine to spend millions of dollars on advertising to "correct" earlier ads that claimed the mouthwash helped prevent colds. Advertisers still remember that lesson. The possibility of large financial penalties or the need to pay for corrective ads has caused more agencies and advertisers to stay well within the law.

However, sometimes ad claims seem to get out of hand anyway. The FTC has started to crack down on claims related to weight loss and health. For example, KFC quickly stopped running several of its TV ads after the FTC objected to the ads and opened an investigation. KFC's ads positioned fried chicken as a healthy choice in fast food, but there was also lots of small print at the bottom of the screen to qualify the claims. Skechers and Reebok claimed that their shoes would help customers lose weight and strengthen muscles. The FTC took issue with the unfounded claims and the two firms had to return millions of dollars to consumers.[30]

What is unfair or deceptive is changing

What constitutes unfair and deceptive advertising is a difficult question. The law provides some guidelines, but the marketing manager must make personal judgments as well. The social and political environment is changing worldwide. Practices considered acceptable some years ago are now questioned or considered deceptive. Saying or even implying that your product is best may be viewed as deceptive. And a 1988 revision of the Lanham Act protects firms whose brand names are unfairly tarnished in comparative ads.

Supporting ad claims is a fuzzy area

It's really not hard to figure out how to avoid criticisms of being unfair and deceptive. A little puffing is acceptable, and probably always will be. But marketing managers need to put a stop to the typical production-oriented approach of trying to use advertising to differentiate me-too products that are not different and don't offer customers better value.[31]

Customer Communication and Types of Publicity

LO 15.8

Publicity is any unpaid form of nonpersonal presentation of ideas, goods, or services. In recent years as consumers have become better at avoiding advertising, publicity has emerged as a more prominent promotion tool. As advertising becomes more costly and less effective at achieving many promotion objectives, publicity is gaining.

Publicity is closely related to advertising, and it may be managed by an advertising manager or public relations manager, often with the help of an outside advertising, public relations, or specialized digital agency. If separate groups handle advertising and publicity, they should work closely together to assure successfully integrated marketing communications.

What Promotion do customers trust?

As we discussed in Chapter 13, Promotion can influence buying decisions when customers trust the source and find the information credible. A recent study of 28,000 Internet consumers from 56 countries found that many of the most trusted sources for buying information are forms of publicity, not advertising. For example, 90 percent of customers trust recommendations from people they know, 70 percent trust online consumer opinions, and 58 percent trust brand websites. Various forms of advertising have lower levels of trust: less than half trust paid television, magazine, and newspaper ads (47 percent). Online ads fared even worse with trust in search engine ads, online video ads, and online banner ads trusted by just 41, 36, and 33 percent respectively. Sponsored ads on social network sites are only trusted by 36 percent and ads on mobile devices like smartphones by just 29 percent.[32]

Given their potential as a trusted communication source, let's take a closer look at how some of these publicity tools are being used today. Even though there is a wide variety of publicity tools, many of them are the result of advances in technology and changes in consumer behavior. Technology continues to create new possibilities, so marketing managers must be on the lookout for new tools that may work with the firm's promotion objectives.

Getting coverage in the press

Exhibit 15-7 organizes our discussion of publicity—let's start by looking at the left side of this exhibit. One message channel is the press, which includes newspapers, magazines, television, and trade magazines. For example, if a firm has a really new message, a published article may get more attention than advertising. Trade magazines carry articles featuring the newsworthy products of interest to people in a particular job or industry. Sometimes a firm's media relations people write the basic copy of an article and then try to convince magazine editors to print it. Both consumers and businesspeople tend to believe and pay more attention to articles than they do to advertising.

A public relations (PR) person or staff might provide information that makes it easy for the press to write stories about the company. PR develops press kits that include promotional materials designed for the media. To make it even easier for the press, most major companies also have a "Press" section, or "Media Room" on its corporate website that includes press releases and possibly photos or videos.

Exhibit 15–7 Types of Publicity

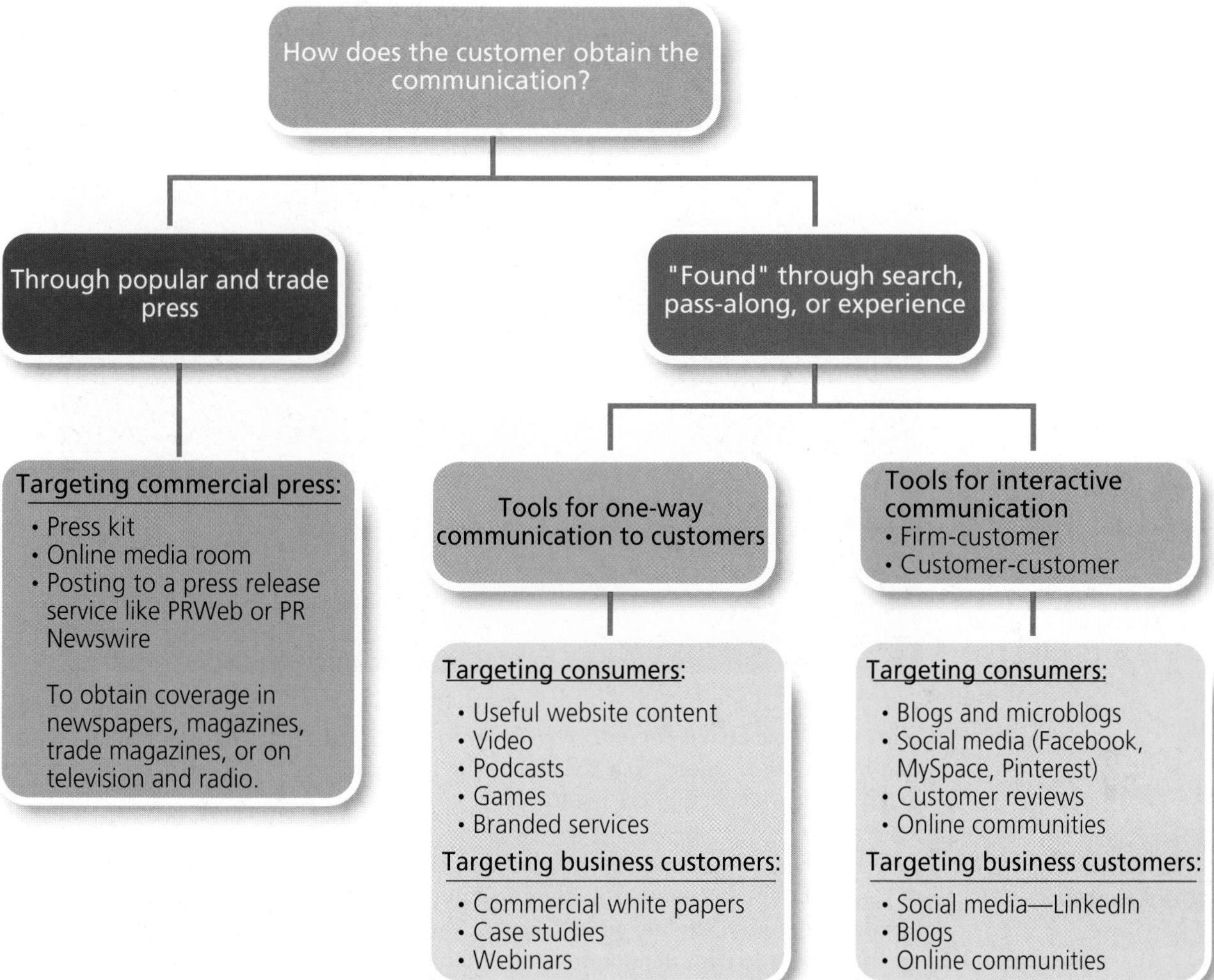

Southwest Airlines uses press releases to generate publicity in the popular press. When it wants to promote its special fares and new routes, its PR staff uses a targeted approach to get attention from news reporters. Since many reporters research story ideas on specialized search engines like PRWeb and Yahoo! News, the PR staff at Southwest writes press releases so they appear at the top of the reporters' search lists. Southwest's PR staff researches what keywords reporters use most frequently on these search engines—and then puts those words in press releases. For example, Southwest's press releases use the phrase "cheap airfare" because it is in four times as many search requests as "cheap airline tickets." Southwest also puts a hot link to its special promotion fare web page at the very start of each press release. The link allows Southwest PR staff to track which press releases work best; then it uses that information to fine-tune other messages. These extra efforts have paid off. In one case Southwest generated $1.5 million in online ticket sales with just four press releases.[33]

Marketers want to be "found" when customers "search"

Not all publicity relies on mass media message channels. Customers can also find publicity through search, pass-along, or experience. The right side of Exhibit 15-7 shows a variety of those types of publicity tools. We will look at a few of them in more detail, but first let's look at the consumer behavior behind search, pass-along, and experience.

In Chapter 13 we introduced the customer-initiated model of communication (see Exhibit 13-6). This model recognizes that customers are not passive receivers of communication; in fact, they often seek out and select information that meets their needs. We also noted that the Internet makes it easy for customers to conduct searches and find information. Because customers often search during the shopping process, marketing managers need to work hard to make sure that when customers search, their firm's website or

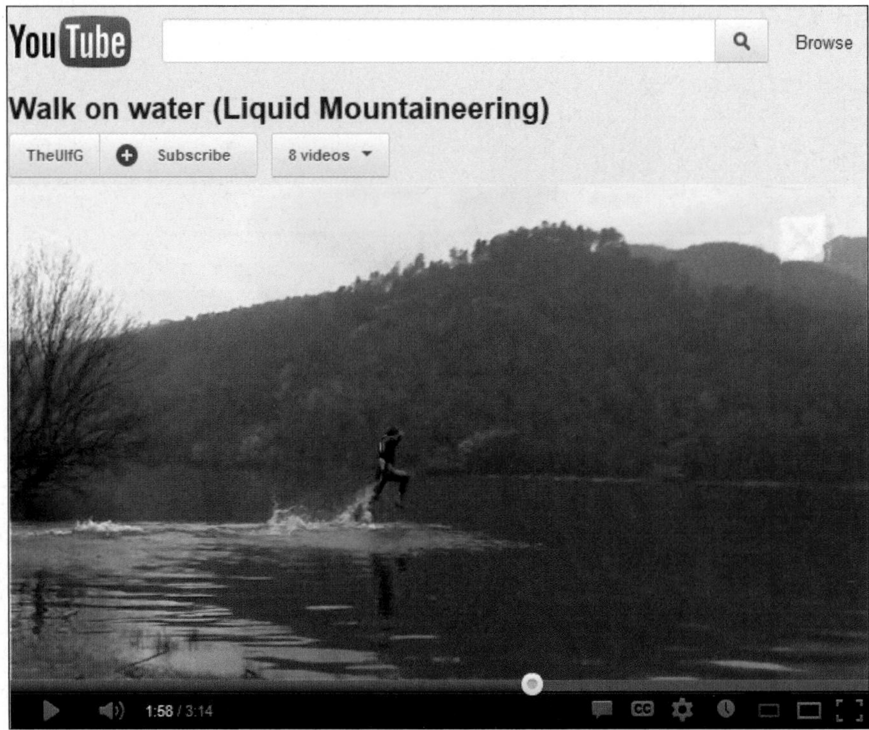

Footwear maker, Hi-Tec Sports, created a buzz when it launched a video showing a new extreme sport—liquid mountaineering—where participants run on water. While the sport wasn't exactly true, the video subtly promotes Hi-Tec's ion-mask waterproofing technology. Check out the video at http://youtu.be/Oe3St1GgoHQ.

other online material is "found." *Search engine optimization* refers to technical approaches that make websites more likely to come up high in search results. Some of the approaches described here will help those results.

Pass-along comes from trusted sources

While there are technical approaches that help a firm's website move closer to the top of the search results, another method is publicity with a customer pass-along element. *Pass-along* occurs when one person suggests that others read or watch something. People are more likely to pay attention to content recommended by a person they know.

Pass-along can go viral

While people have always been able to tell friends about an interesting ad, story, or product, the Internet enables a message to spread quickly—like a virus. As a result, some firms try to spark this sort of "viral" publicity. When Evian created its "Roller Skating Babies" video to promote its bottled water and posted it on YouTube, friends passed along the link in e-mails, with "You have to watch this!" in the subject line. The video—essentially an ad for Evian—has been viewed more than 100 million times.

Sometimes consumers create their own funny or clever videos and upload them to the web. This type of consumer-generated viral publicity can be helpful or harmful to a brand. So it's important for marketing managers to be prepared to manage it—as best they can. Consider the case of Mentos candy and Diet Coke. A combination of the two products is explosive—literally. When a Mentos candy is dropped in a bottle of Diet Coke, a geyser erupts. So two consumers created an elaborate fountain show which combined 200 liters of Diet Coke with 500 Mentos mints. They taped the performance and posted it online at their website (www.eepybird.com). It was an instant viral hit—eventually topping 10 million views.

What's interesting is how marketing managers at Diet Coke and Mentos responded to the video. At Diet Coke, marketing managers didn't think the video was a good fit with their brand and decided to distance the diet cola from the video. In contrast, Mentos' marketing managers saw the video as a perfect fit for their quirky, tongue-in-cheek positioning. They worked with the video's producers to create a contest and added a link from the Mentos website to the Eepybird site. The geyser video contest offered a prize of a year's supply of Mentos and 1,000 iTunes downloads and drew more than 100 entries and a million views. By riding the viral wave, Mentos achieved—at very little cost—greater awareness and stronger brand positioning among its target market of young people.[34]

Creating viral videos is not easy

Many marketing managers would be thrilled to get the low-cost exposure that Mentos and Evian received with their viral videos. Yet for every successful effort at creating the next viral hit, there are dozens of failures. Good viral videos need to be both entertaining and surprising. As with the Evian babies and the Diet Coke/Mentos videos, viewers must think they're doing their friends a favor by passing along the link. And of course the viral message should achieve a real promotion objective for the marketer.[35]

Customers experience branded services

Getting found doesn't always have to occur online. Sometimes it's a customer's experience with a brand that grabs attention—such as when brands offer everyday services that improve customers' lives. Consider consumer electronics maker Samsung, for example. When Samsung put charging stations (with a Samsung sign) in more than 100 major airports, it positioned itself as a "lifesaver" and built favorable attitudes with lucrative business travelers—who tend to buy a lot of consumer electronics. Now, Samsung is targeting another gadget-loving group—students—by putting its charging stations on college campuses.[36] Similarly, gadget-maker Apple has created beautiful must-see stores staffed with knowledgeable sales staff and experts at the Genius Bar. In doing so, it's able to "wow" its customers, showcase what's different about its products, and also provide immediate information and repair services. These branded services subtly communicate a positive message to target customers.

Communicating to customers—or with customers

To capture customer search, pass-along, or experience, firms may choose two different types of publicity tools: one-way communication tools or interactive communication tools. See the right side of Exhibit 15-7. No matter which approach and tools are used, they should be driven by the company's promotion objectives and should complement the rest of the promotion blend.

Customers want useful content

Let's start with a look at some one-way communication tools. Providing useful content on a company's website is one such tool. Valued content fills a customer need—often without requiring a customer to make a purchase. Online jeweler Blue Nile educates its customers. Before shelling out thousands of dollars for a new product, most people want to learn more about it. So Blue Nile created an extensive education section on its website to help customers learn the ins and outs of buying diamonds and other jewelry. Young men are a primary target for Blue Nile because, for most young men, a diamond engagement is a big purchase and not one they know much about. The "teacher" gets credit for its efforts; many "students" trust Blue Nile and buy their rings from the jeweler.

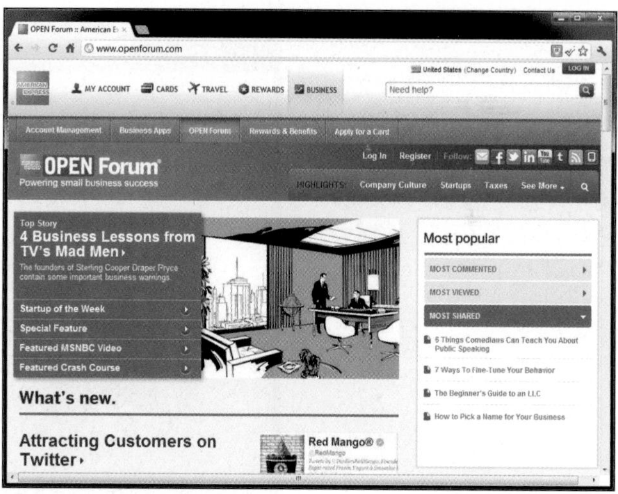

American Express helps its target market of small business owners to thrive with its Open Forum website. The site is filled with content on everything from leadership and compensation to advertising. An open community allows contributions from guest bloggers who offer advice, tips and tricks these customers appreciate. While visiting the site, these customers can easily link to all of American Express's business services. The site helps American Express build a closer relationship with its small business target market.

Business customers seek solutions online

The tools for providing one-way communication with business customers are different from those for final consumers. Because business customers often search the Internet for solutions to real business problems, they often turn to "thought leaders" in their industry first. But what publicity tools does a firm use to establish itself as a thought leader?

Consulting and technology companies often use

webinars, online seminars that may include PowerPoint presentations and video, usually with limited audience interaction. Another tool is the *white paper,* an authoritative report or guide that addresses important issues in an industry and offers solutions. Webinars and white papers are most successful when, in addition to describing a problem, they help the customer decide what to do about it without promoting a particular company's products. The more objective tone helps the provider build trust and credibility with potential customers. Business customers also like to read *case studies*—success stories about how a company helped another customer.

Consider the Canadian consulting firm Enquiro which helps websites rank higher in search results. The quality and objectivity of Enquiro's BuyerSphere reports lead many prominent B2B bloggers and reporters to link to the Enquiro website. These links serve as recommendations. At its website, Enquiro offers several case studies describing its work with previous customers—and the results. It has also recorded webinars that potential customers can watch. These efforts have helped position Enquiro in buyers' minds as a thought leader and a prime source for information in its industry.

Customers connect with companies and other customers

Another set of publicity tools may be used for interactive communication (connecting customers to a company or to other customers). In Chapter 13 we discussed blogs, Twitter, and Pinterest, all of which provide the opportunity for customers to converse with a firm. Blogs and Twitter can be used to communicate with consumers or business customers. Let's look more closely at other media which allow customers to post comments or provide feedback to a firm.

Facebook fans show their support

Social network websites are another publicity tool for interactive communication. They allow people with shared interests to interact. Facebook is a popular example; in the United States, it has more than 200 million visitors each day. Originally the site attracted mostly teens and young adults—but now the demographics are changing and the fastest-growing

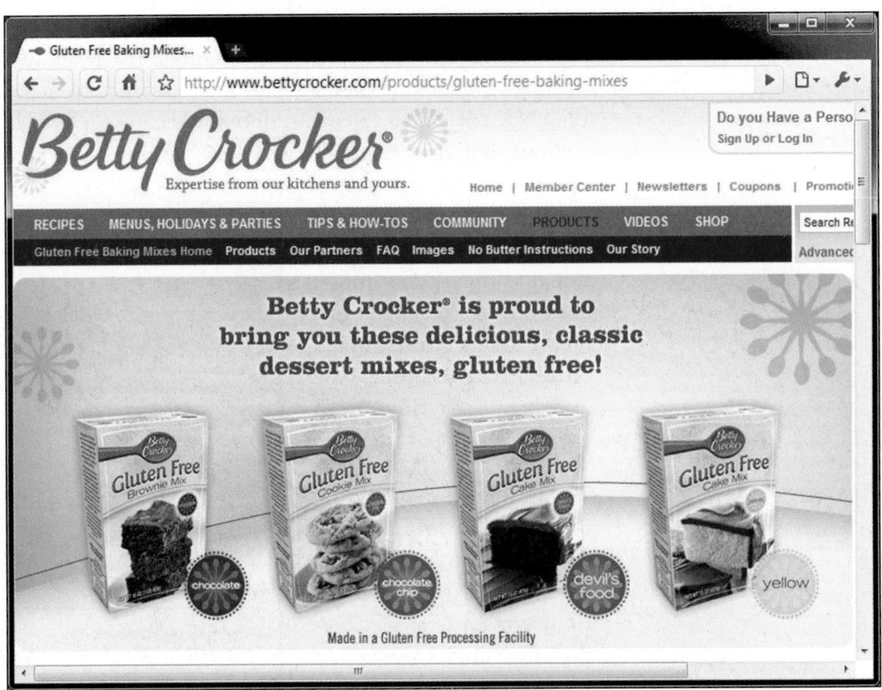

Customers who are interested in gluten-free products are a niche market—comprising the 2 percent of the population with Celiac disease (an intolerance for the glutens common in most baked products). This small target market wouldn't usually attract interest from a big company like General Mills and its Betty Crocker brand. However, when rumors of gluten free Betty Crocker baked goods spread across the Internet, its brand managers knew this group would have high interest. So it launched the products with very little advertising and created the Gluten Freely website. The site has useful content for those interested in a gluten-free lifestyle including recipes and links to the latest medical news on Celiac disease. The site also includes a community area where users can interact with each other and a store where consumers can buy General Mills gluten-free products.

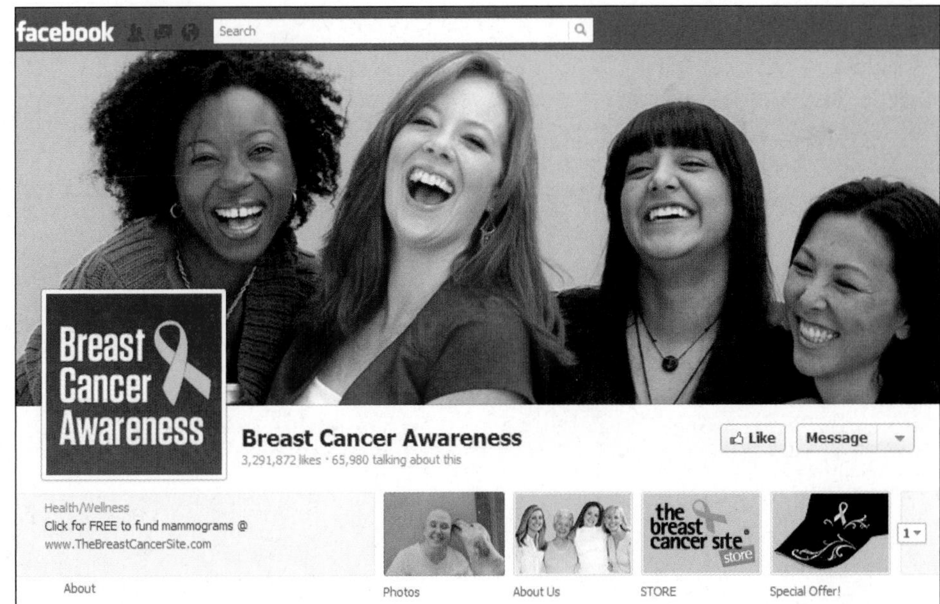

The Facebook page for The Breast Cancer Site has more than 3 million followers. The Facebook page allows the non-profit to build relationships with its most ardent supporters.

groups are over age 50. Different sites are popular in other countries. For example, Orkut has about 70 million users, with most living in Brazil or India. FourSquare is another social media site; it uses location information to show users where their friends are. FourSquare has the potential to target customers with promotions based on their location. For example, a customer out drinking with friends might receive a message about a dinner special from a nearby restaurant.

Because the most trusted source of information for customers is recommendations from people they know, Facebook provides an interesting opportunity for firms. When a Facebook user's news feed shows a friend "likes Coca-Cola" or "likes a new movie," this information registers. And when it happens over and over, brand equity increases—through referrals from friends. Because of social media's popularity, many companies are now trying to use these sites to promote their products. While social media users, in general, have resisted advertising efforts, they have supported company-sponsored pages. Tens of millions of Facebook users "like" the pages of Skittles candy, Coca-Cola, and MTV.[37]

Ratings and reviews let customers do the selling

Review sites also allow customers to sell to one another. Reviews can have a strong influence on customers because they're written by other people who have firsthand knowledge of the product. As a result, many marketing managers are adding rating and review capabilities to their companies' websites. Most major retailers use reviews because they increase sales. TripAdvisor, a travel services website, knows that recommendations carry more weight when the recommender is similar to the customer. So a traveler checking out The Mosser Hotel in San Francisco, for example, can go to the TripAdvisor website and screen reviews by "business travelers," "couples," or "family." Reviews can also be used offline; when Rubbermaid added star ratings and snippets from its online reviews to its print ads, coupon redemption jumped 10 percent.[38]

Internet Exercise

Go to eBags.com (**www.ebags.com**). Click on "Backpacks" and then "School Backpacks." Choose one of the "Best Sellers." Read a few of the reviews—both positive and negative. Look at pictures of your best seller choice and other information about it. Would you buy this bag? How was each source of information helpful in making a decision?

Business customers get social, too

Many of these social media tools can work for business customers as well. Some salespeople use the business social networking site LinkedIn to maintain relationships with customers and identify potential prospects. Similarly, online communities allow business customers to interact and share ideas. For example, tax and financial planning software company Intuit hosts an online community site where its QuickBooks customers can interact with each other about problems facing their small businesses.[39]

Exhibit 15–8 Examples of Different Types of Publicity and Different Promotion Objectives

Getting attention & holding interest	Developing a desired positioning
• Viral videos • Direct-to-consumer press releases • Articles in the press	• Viral videos • Games • Branded services • Commercial white papers

Arousing desire & obtaining action	Managing ongoing customer relationships
• Customer reviews • Case studies • Webinars	• Social media—Facebook, LinkedIn • Blogs • Online communities • Podcasts, webcasts, and webinars

Other advertising principles work for publicity, too

While publicity doesn't involve the use of paid media, most of the principles outlined earlier in the chapter with respect to advertising apply to publicity as well. A firm's promotion objectives should guide the choice of tools. Publicity can be used to help a firm sell more products, generate leads for the sales force, get contributions to a charitable cause, or encourage people to join an organization. Exhibit 15-8 suggests which types of publicity might work best with some common promotion objectives. As with advertising, measuring the effectiveness of publicity efforts can be challenging, but the best measures are tied to objectives.

Often publicity works in combination with other promotion tools—as part of an integrated marketing communications program with specific objectives. For example, Milwaukee Electric Tool Corp. wants its customers—which include retailers, contractors, and building professionals—to know about new models of its Sawzall electric saw, rotary hammer, and other tools. When the marketing manager looked at which pages of the website got the most attention, she found some customers especially liked to watch videos of the tools in action. So Milwaukee Electric Tool used its monthly e-mail newsletter "Heavy Duty News" to promote that feature of its website. Soon more than twice as many customers were watching videos at the company's website.[40]

When developing publicity, marketing managers must carefully consider copy thrust; websites, videos, blogs, and other publicity tools all utilize words and images to communicate with a target market. In addition, most laws covering advertising apply to most of the publicity approaches outlined here. Common sense, honesty, and fairness are important.

Ethics must guide publicity decisions

Companies need to be careful when treading in the new publicity space. For one thing, firms are often easily exposed when they engage in unethical practices. For example, a Honda manager went on the Facebook page for the Honda Crosstour and raved about the new car's design—when most other comments were negative. Some readers recognized the manager's name from articles in the automobile press and cried foul. Honda ended up embarrassed when the deception was reported on *Autoblog* and other sites. Sometimes TripAdvisor suspects some of the reviews on its site are fake—like when a hotel's employees post reviews that build up their facility and tear down a competitor. To prevent fake reviews from harming the credibility of its own site, TripAdvisor marks suspicious reviews with a red disclaimer.[41]

Publicity tools are evolving quickly

Publicity tools are evolving quickly. Just a few years ago customer ratings and reviews were rare, few people read blogs, and Facebook was only open to people with e-mail addresses ending in *.edu* to limit access to college students. Now these are prime message channels for publicity. By the time you read this there will be even newer tools—and newer ways to use current tools.

So how does a marketer keep up? Reading widely about these topics is essential. As a student, you can turn to our *Learn the 4 Ps* blog (www.learnthe4ps.com), Twitter feed (@Learn the 4 Ps), and the *Learn the 4 Ps* Facebook page—see the back cover of the book for more information. We post comments and link to articles and videos on this topic and other marketing issues to help keep you up-to-date.

Sales Promotion—Do Something Different to Stimulate Change

LO 15.9

The nature of sales promotion

Sales Promotion refers to those promotion activities—other than advertising, publicity, and personal selling—that stimulate interest, trial, or purchase by final customers or others in the channel. Exhibit 13-2 shows examples of typical sales promotions targeted at final customers, channel members, or a firm's own employees.

Sales promotion is generally used to complement the other promotion methods. While advertising campaigns and sales force strategy decisions tend to have longer-term effects, a particular sales promotion activity usually lasts for only a limited time period. But sales promotion can often be implemented quickly and get sales results sooner than advertising. Further, sales promotion objectives usually focus on prompting some short-term action. For an intermediary, such an action might be a decision to stock a product, provide a special display space, or give the product extra sales emphasis. For a consumer, the desired action might be to try a new product, switch from another brand, or buy more of a product. The desired action by an employee might be a special effort to satisfy customers.

Sales promotion objectives and situation should influence decision

There are many different types of sales promotion, but what type is appropriate depends on the situation and objectives. For example, Exhibit 15-9 shows some possible ways that a short-term promotion might affect sales. The sales pattern in the graph on the left might occur if Hellmann's issues coupons to help clear its excess mayonnaise inventory. Some consumers might buy earlier to take advantage of the coupon, but unless they use extra mayonnaise their next purchase will be delayed. In the center graph, kids might convince parents to eat more Big Macs while McDonald's has a Monopoly game promotion, but when it ends things go back to normal. The graph on the right shows a Burger King marketer's dream come true: Free samples of a new style of french fries quickly pull in new customers who like what they try and keep coming back after the promotion ends. From these examples, you can see that the situation and the objective of the promotion should determine what specific type is best.

Sales promotion spending has grown in mature markets

Sales promotion involves so many different types of activities that it is difficult to estimate accurately how much is spent in total. There is general consensus, however, that the total spending on sales promotion exceeds spending on advertising.[42]

Exhibit 15–9 Some Possible Effects of a Sales Promotion on Sales

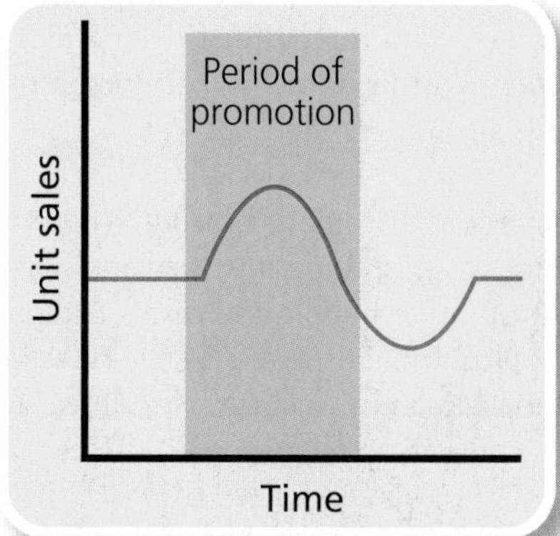

Sales temporarily increase, then decrease, then return to regular level

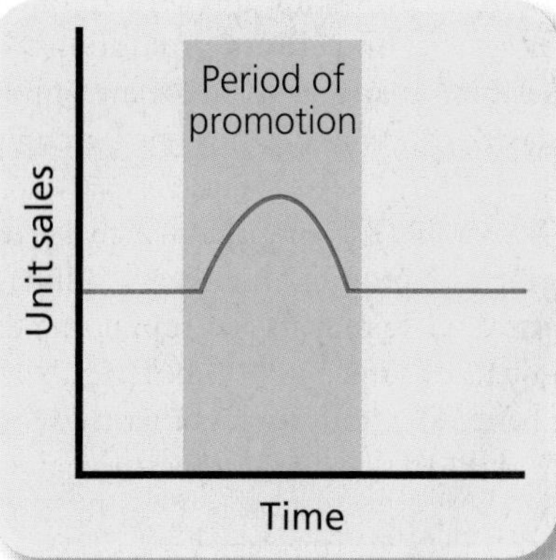

Sales temporarily increase and then return to regular level

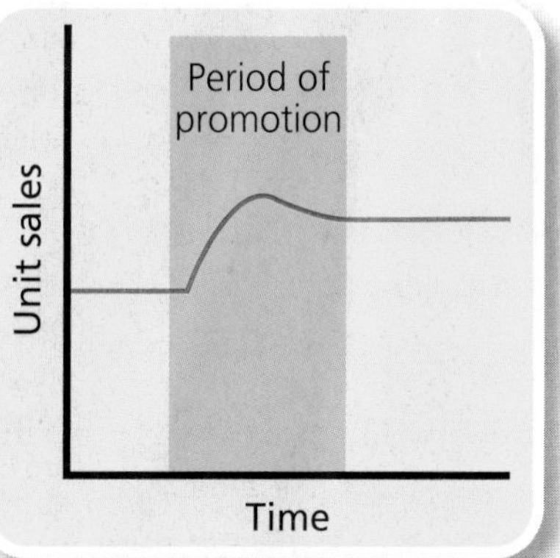

Sales increase and then remain at higher level

One reason for increased use of sales promotion by many consumer products firms is that they are generally competing in mature markets. There's only so much soap that consumers want to buy, regardless of how many brands there are vying for their dollars. There's also only so much shelf space that retailers will allocate to a particular product category.

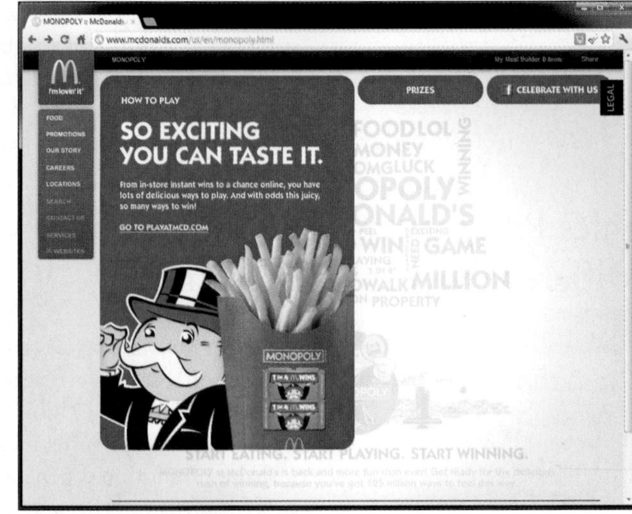

The McDonalds' Monopoly game promotion brings customers into restaurants to eat and to play the game.

The competitive situation is intensified by the growth of large, powerful retail chains. They have put more emphasis on their own dealer brands and also demanded more sales promotion support for the manufacturer brands they do carry.

Perhaps in part because of this competition, many consumers have become more price sensitive. Many sales promotions, like coupons, have the effect of lowering the prices consumers pay. So sales promotion has been used as a tool to overcome consumer price resistance creating a downward cycle of pricing and promotion.

The growth of sales promotion has also been fostered by the availability of more ad agencies and specialists who plan and implement sales promotion programs. Of course, the most basic reason for the growth of spending on sales promotion is that it can be very effective if it is done properly. But there are challenges in the sales promotion area.

Challenges in Managing Sales Promotion

Does sales promotion erode brand loyalty?

Some experts think that marketing managers—especially those who deal with consumer packaged goods—put too much emphasis on sales promotion. They argue that the effect of most sales promotion is temporary and that money spent on advertising and personal selling helps the firm more over the long term. When the market is not growing, sales promotion may just encourage "deal-prone" customers (and intermediaries) to switch back and forth among brands. Here, all the expense of the sales promotion simply contributes to lower profits. It also increases the prices that consumers pay because it increases selling costs.

However, once a marketing manager is in this situation there may be little choice other than to continue. In mature markets, frequent sales promotions may be needed just to offset the effects of competitors' promotions. One escape from this competitive rat race is for the marketing manager to seek new opportunities—with a strategy that doesn't rely solely on short-term sales promotions for competitive advantage.

There are alternatives

Procter & Gamble is a company that changed its strategy, and promotion blend, to decrease its reliance on sales promotion targeted at intermediaries. It is offering intermediaries lower prices on many of its products and supporting those products with more advertising and promotion to final consumers. P&G believes that this approach builds its brand equity, serves consumers better, and leads to smoother-running relationships in its channels. Not all retailers are happy with P&G's changes. However, many other producers are following P&G's lead.

Sales promotion is hard to manage

Another problem in the sales promotion area is that it is easy to make big, costly mistakes. Because sales promotion includes such a wide variety of activities, it's difficult for the typical company to develop skill in managing all of them. Even large firms and agencies that specialize in sales promotion run into difficulties because each promotion is typically

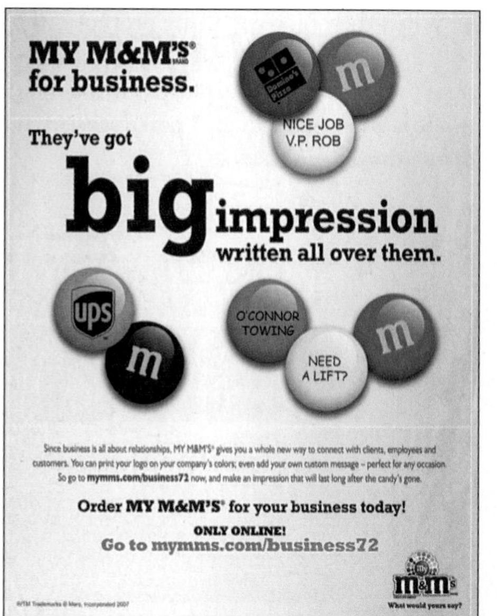

MY M&M'S®
for business.
They've got
big impression
written all over them.
NICE JOB
V.P. ROB
O'CONNOR
TOWING
NEED
A LIFT?
Order MY M&M'S® for your business today!
ONLY ONLINE!
Go to mymms.com/business72
What would yours say?

Most M&M's are sold as consumer products, but M&M's printed with special messages or brand logos are a sweet way to remind business customers about a firm.

custom-designed and then used only once. Yet mistakes caused by lack of experience can be costly or hurt relationships with customers.

In a promotion for Pampers diapers that was designed to reward loyal buyers and steal customers away from competing Huggies, marketing managers offered parents Fisher-Price toys if they collected points printed on Pampers' packages. At first the promotion seemed to be a big success because so many parents were collecting points. But that turned into a problem when Fisher-Price couldn't produce enough toys to redeem all the points. Pampers had to add 50 toll-free phone lines to handle all the complaints, and a lot of angry parents stopped buying Pampers for good. Problems like this are common.[43]

Not a sideline for amateurs

Sales promotion mistakes are likely to be worse when a company has no sales promotion manager. If the personal selling or advertising managers are responsible for sales promotion, they often give it less attention. They allocate money to sales promotion if there is any "left over" or if a crisis develops. This approach misuses a valuable element of the promotion blend.

Making sales promotion work is a learned skill, not a sideline for amateurs. That's why specialists in sales promotion have developed, both inside larger firms and as outside consultants. Some of these people are real experts. But it's the marketing manager's responsibility to set sales promotion objectives and policies that will fit in with the rest of each marketing strategy.[44]

Different Types of Sales Promotion for Different Targets

LO 15.10

Tie consumer sales promotions to objectives

Much of the sales promotion aimed at final consumers or users tries to increase demand, perhaps temporarily, or to speed up the time of purchase. Such promotion might involve developing materials to be displayed in retailers' stores, including banners, sample packages, calendars, and various point-of-purchase materials. It might include sweepstakes contests as well as coupons designed to get customers to buy a product by a certain date.

All of these sales promotion efforts are aimed at specific objectives. When customers already have a favorite brand, free samples can be used to get them to try something new. For example, Amazon.com's "Search Inside" feature allows a customer to view part of a book before buying. When Starbucks launched its new coffee-flavored ice creams, it offered coupons for a free pint to fans on its Facebook page. In this type of situation, sales of the product might start to pick up as soon as customers try the product and find that they like it. And sales will continue at the higher level after the promotion is over if satisfied customers make repeat purchases. Thus, the cost of the sales promotion in this situation might be viewed as a long-term investment.

Once a product is established, consumer sales promotion usually focuses on short-term sales increases. For example, after a price-off coupon for a soft drink is distributed, sales might temporarily pick up as customers take advantage of buying

Internet Exercise

ePrize.com is an agency that specializes in sales promotion. Go to **www.eprize.com** and click on "Our Work" to see samples of its work. Evaluate two promotions the agency has put together for different clients. For each, name the intended target market and indicate the objectives you think the client wanted to achieve with the promotion.

at a lower price. When the objective of the promotion is focused primarily on producing a short-term increase in sales, it's sensible for the marketing manager to evaluate the cost of the promotion relative to the extra sales expected. If the increase in sales won't at least cover the cost of the promotion, it probably doesn't make sense to do it. Otherwise, the firm is "buying sales" at the cost of reduced profit.

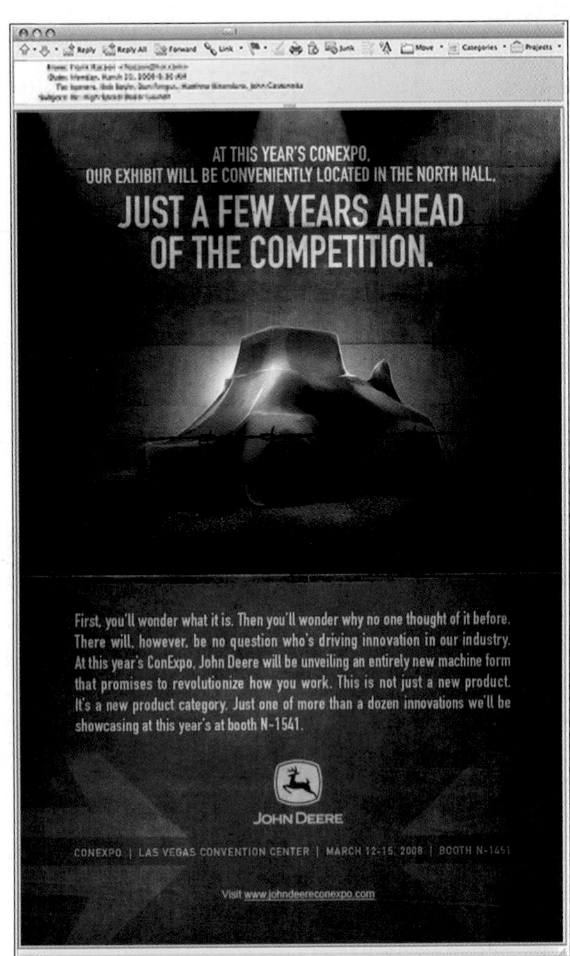

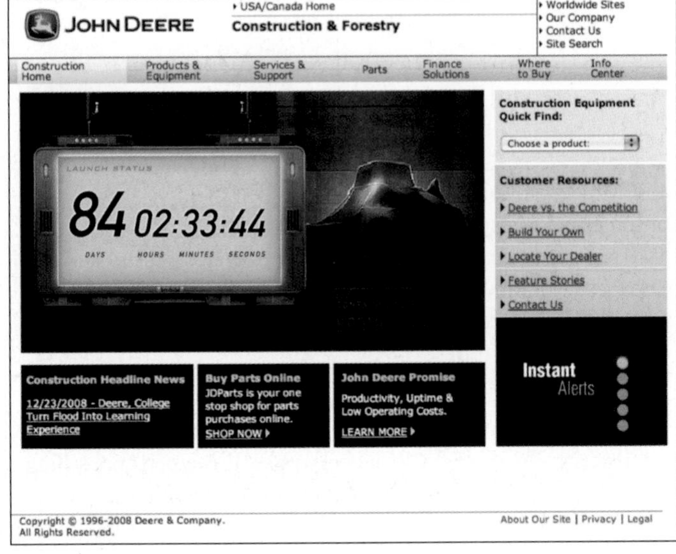

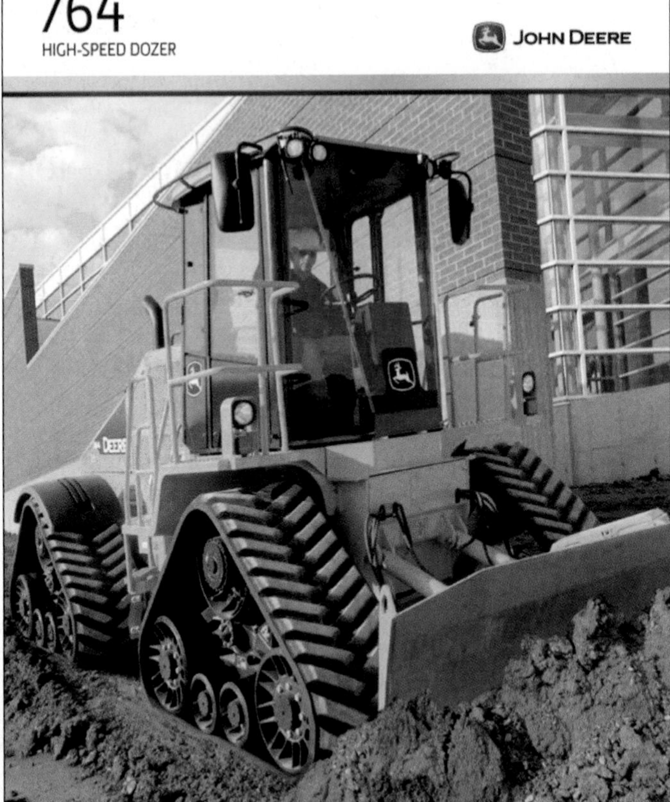

John Deere created buzz about its new 764 high-speed dozer (described as a cross between a tractor and a bulldozer) by launching it at the biggest trade show event of the year—the ConExpo show at the Las Vegas Convention Center. Promotion included e-mail, Internet, live CNBC broadcast, press conferences, electronic press kits, magazine articles, and various sales promotion items. All of this was intended to "whet the appetite of the marketplace so when the 764 hit the ground, people would line up to buy it." And it worked. Customers raised their hands and said, "I want one."

B2B promotions move products or generate leads

Sales promotion directed at industrial customers might use the same kinds of ideas. In addition, the sales promotion people might set up and staff trade show exhibits that generate attention and interest for a firm and its products. Trade shows usually occur in one city over a period of three to seven days. Customers attend to learn from industry experts. For example, the Consumer Electronics Show in Las Vegas each January lasts four days and attracts more than 2,500 electronics exhibitors and 140,000 attendees. After the show these customers become leads for the company's salespeople who try to convert customer interest to actual sales. Trade shows are big events that require significant planning.

Many customers would like to attend trade shows, but the cost in time or money make it difficult. So now many trade shows occur online. These virtual trade show "attendees" sit at their desks and choose which speakers to watch and which exhibits to visit. Virtual trade shows may be kept up year-round, making it convenient for customers to gather information when they are most interested in making a purchase.

Some sellers give promotion items—pen sets, watches, or clothing (perhaps with the firm's brand name on them)—to remind business customers of their products. This is common, but it can be a problem. Some companies do not allow buyers to accept any gifts.[44]

Sales promotion for intermediaries

Sales promotion aimed at intermediaries—sometimes called *trade promotion*—emphasizes price-related matters. The objective may be to encourage intermediaries to stock new items, buy in larger quantity, buy early, or stress a product in their own promotion efforts.

The tools used here include merchandise allowances, promotion allowances, and perhaps sales contests to encourage retailers or wholesalers to sell specific items or the company's whole line. Offering to send contest winners to Hawaii, for example, may increase sales.

About half of the sales promotion spending targeted at intermediaries has the effect of reducing the price that they pay for merchandise. So we'll go into more detail on different types of trade discounts and allowances in Chapter 16.

Sales promotion for own employees

Sales promotion aimed at the company's own sales force might try to encourage providing better service, getting new customers, selling a new product, or selling the company's whole line. Depending on the objectives, the tools might be contests, bonuses on sales or number of new accounts, and holding sales meetings at fancy resorts to raise everyone's spirits.

Ongoing sales promotion work might also be aimed at the sales force—to help sales management. Sales promotion might be responsible for preparing sales portfolios, digital videos, PowerPoint presentations, displays, and other sales aids, as well as sales training materials.

Service-oriented firms such as hotels and restaurants use sales promotions targeted at their employees. Some, for example, give a monthly cash prize for the employee who provides the "best service." And the employee's picture is displayed to give recognition.[45]

CONCLUSION

It may seem simple to develop an advertising campaign. Just pick the medium and develop a message. But it's not that easy.

This chapter discussed why marketing managers should set specific objectives to guide the entire advertising effort. Knowing what they want to achieve, marketing managers can determine what kind of advertising—product or institutional—to use. We also discussed three basic types of product advertising: pioneering, competitive (direct and indirect), and reminder.

Marketing managers must also choose from various media—so we discussed their advantages and disadvantages. Because the Internet offers new advertising opportunities and challenges, we discussed how it is similar to and different from other media. And, of course, marketing managers must determine the message—or copy thrust—that will appear in ads.

Many technical details are involved in mass selling. Advertising agencies often handle these jobs. But specific objectives must be set for agencies, or their advertising may have little direction and be almost impossible to evaluate. This chapter also discussed how to make sure that advertising is done legally.

Many of the lessons from advertising can also be applied to publicity. Yet publicity offers many new options for the marketing manager. Marketing managers can decide to target the press, hoping to get favorable articles or stories in newspapers, magazines, or on television. As customers engage in search activities to satisfy their needs, the key for marketers is to make sure they are "found." Publicity allows firms to engage directly with customers by placing valued content on the web or in public places. It also involves interacting with customers in online communities, with blogs, and on social media. This new space continues to evolve rapidly and offers many challenges and opportunities for marketers.

Sales promotion spending is big and growing. This approach is especially important in prompting action—by customers, intermediaries, or salespeople. There are many different types of sales promotion, and it is a problem area in many firms because it is difficult for a firm to develop expertise with all of the possibilities.

Advertising, publicity, and sales promotion are often important parts of a promotion blend, but in most blends personal selling also plays an important role. Further, promotion is only a part of the total marketing mix a marketing manager must develop to satisfy target customers. So to broaden your understanding of the four Ps and how they fit together, in Chapters 16 and 17 we'll go into more detail on the role of Price in strategy decisions.

KEY TERMS

LO 15.11

advertising allowances, *390*
cooperative advertising, *390*
product advertising, *391*
institutional advertising, *391*
pioneering advertising, *391*
competitive advertising, *391*
direct type advertising, *392*
indirect type advertising, *392*
comparative advertising, *392*
reminder advertising, *392*
copy thrust, *399*
advertising agencies, *400*
corrective advertising, *403*

QUESTIONS AND PROBLEMS

1. Identify the strategy decisions a marketing manager must make in the advertising arena.
2. Discuss the relation of advertising objectives to marketing strategy planning and the kinds of advertising actually needed. Illustrate.
3. List several media that might be effective for reaching consumers in a developing nation with low per capita income and a high level of illiteracy. Briefly discuss the limitations and advantages of each medium you suggest.
4. Give three examples where advertising to intermediaries might be necessary. What are the objective(s) of such advertising?
5. What does it mean to say that "money is invested in advertising"? Is all advertising an investment? Illustrate.
6. Find advertisements to final consumers that illustrate the following types of advertising: (*a*) institutional, (*b*) pioneering, (*c*) competitive, and (*d*) reminder. What objective(*s*) does each of these ads have? List the needs each ad addresses.
7. Describe the type of media that might be most suitable for promoting: (*a*) tomato soup, (*b*) greeting cards, (*c*) a business component material, and (*d*) playground equipment. Specify any assumptions necessary to obtain a definite answer.
8. Briefly discuss some of the pros and cons an advertising manager for a producer of sports equipment might want to think about in deciding whether to advertise on the Internet.
9. Discuss the use of testimonials in advertising. Which of the four AIDA steps might testimonials accomplish? Are they suitable for all types of products? If not, for which types are they most suitable?
10. Find a magazine ad that you think does a particularly good job of communicating to the target audience. Would the ad communicate well to an audience in another country? Explain your thinking.
11. Discuss the future of smaller advertising agencies now that many of the largest are merging to form mega-agencies.
12. Does advertising cost too much? How can this be measured?
13. Is it unfair to criticize a competitor's product in an ad? Explain your thinking.
14. Name two companies that you think would have success building a Facebook page. Why do you think they should choose to build a page? What type of content should each company place on its page?
15. What kinds of publicity would work best at a company that markets tractors, combines, and other farm equipment to farmers? Why would the publicity you suggest be effective?
16. How would your local newspaper be affected if local supermarkets switched their weekly advertising and instead used a service that delivered weekly free-standing ads directly to each home?
17. Explain why P&G and other consumer packaged goods firms are trying to cut back on some types of sales promotion like coupons for consumers and short-term trade promotions such as "buy a case and get a case free."

18. Discuss some ways that a firm can link its sales promotion activities to its advertising and personal selling efforts—so that all of its promotion efforts result in an integrated effort.
19. Indicate the type of sales promotion that a producer might use in each of the following situations and briefly explain your reasons:
    a. A firm has developed an improved razor blade and obtained distribution, but customers are not motivated to buy it.
    b. A competitor is about to do a test market for a new brand and wants to track sales in test market areas to fine-tune its marketing mix.
    c. A big grocery chain won't stock a firm's new popcorn-based snack product because it doesn't think there will be much consumer demand.
20. Why wouldn't a producer of toothpaste just lower the price of its product rather than offer consumers a price-off coupon?
21. If sales promotion spending continues to grow—often at the expense of media advertising—how do you think this might affect the rates charged by mass media for advertising time or space? How do you think it might affect advertising agencies?

CREATING MARKETING PLANS

The Marketing Plan Coach software on the text website includes a sample marketing plan for Hillside Veterinary Clinic. Look through the "Marketing Strategy" section.

a. What are Hillside's advertising objectives?
b. What types of advertising and media are being proposed? Why are these types used and not others?
c. What type of copy thrust is recommended? Why?
d. What sales promotion activities are being planned? What are the goals of sales promotion?

SUGGESTED CASES

18. Whistler Township Volunteer Fire Department
20. Blue Lagoon Marine and Camp
36. Skyline Homebuilders

COMPUTER-AIDED PROBLEM

15. SALES PROMOTION

As a community service, disc jockeys from radio station WMKT formed a basketball team to help raise money for local nonprofit organizations. The host organization finds or fields a competing team and charges $5 admission to the game. Money from ticket sales goes to the nonprofit organization.

Ticket sales were disappointing at recent games, averaging only about 300 people per game. When WMKT's marketing manager, Bruce Miller, heard about the problem, he suggested using sales promotion to improve ticket sales. The PTA for the local high school—the sponsor for the next game—is interested in the idea but is concerned that its budget doesn't include any promotion money. Miller tries to help them by reviewing his idea in more detail.

Specifically, he proposes that the PTA give a free T-shirt (printed with the school name and date of the game) to the first 500 ticket buyers. He thinks the T-shirt giveaway will create a lot of interest. In fact, he says he is almost certain the promotion would help the PTA sell 600 tickets, double the usual number. He speculates that the PTA might even have a sellout of all 900 seats in the school gym. Further, he notes that the T-shirts will more than pay for themselves if the PTA sells 600 tickets.

A local firm that specializes in sales promotion items agrees to supply the shirts and do the printing for $2.40 a shirt if the PTA places an order for at least 400 shirts. The PTA thinks the idea is interesting but wants to look at it more closely to see what will happen if the promotion doesn't increase ticket sales. To help the PTA evaluate the alternatives, Miller sets up a spreadsheet with the relevant information.

a. Based on the data from the initial spreadsheet, does the T-shirt promotion look like a good idea? Explain your thinking.
b. The PTA treasurer worries about the up-front cost of printing the T-shirts and wants to know where they would stand if they ordered the T-shirts and still sold only 300 tickets. He suggests it might be safer to order the minimum number of T-shirts (400). Evaluate his suggestion.
c. The president of the PTA thinks the T-shirt promotion will increase sales but wonders if it wouldn't be better just to lower the price. She suggests $2.60 a ticket, which she arrives at by subtracting the $2.40 T-shirt cost from the usual $5.00 ticket price. How many tickets would the PTA have to sell at the lower price to match the money it would make if it used the T-shirt promotion and actually sold 600 tickets? (Hint: Change the selling price in the spreadsheet and then vary the quantity using the analysis feature.)

16 CHAPTER SIXTEEN

Pricing Objectives and Policies

In a YouTube world, homemade videos are everywhere. But getting from the first "moving pictures" to widespread *home* movie-making took almost a century. The film for early movies was flammable and dangerous to handle—not exactly ideal for recording family memories. By 1960, safe film with good color and audio was readily available, but the prices for cameras, film, processing, and projectors limited home movie-making to the very wealthy. A turning point came in 1983 when Sony's Betamovie videotape combination camera-recorder-player hit the consumer market. It eliminated film and processing and used a regular TV screen to show movies. Still, its $1,500 sticker was high for the average consumer so adoption was slow. Before long, RCA, Panasonic, and other competitors brought down prices and prompted market growth.

By 2000, new competitors had jumped in, prices fell further, and home videos of special events—like kids' soccer games, birthday parties, and choir performances—were more common. Yet movie-making was complicated by a new generation of camcorders with many advanced features that consumers didn't know how to use. And once a movie was recorded, it was a big challenge to edit it—or show it to others. Making home movies seemed hard, so many families left their camcorder in a closet.

A startup company, Pure Digital Technologies (PDT), saw opportunities in this market situation. PDT's first products were one-time-use digital cameras for retailers like Ritz Camera and Walgreen's. The retailers sold the cameras for $10.99 and printed the 25 pictures for another $10.99, offering retailers good profit margins. Prompted by this, the CVS drugstore chain asked PDT for a one-time-use video camcorder. Unfortunately, not many CVS customers saw value in paying $29.95 for a camcorder and $12.99 more to transfer video clips to a DVD, so sales were slow.

But PDT's marketing managers noticed the CVS camcorder generated plenty of online buzz. Users liked its portability and simplicity—some even "hacked" the camcorders to make them reusable. PDT's marketing managers saw a new opportunity with a different marketing mix. They designed a camcorder that was small (40 × 2.50 × 10), ran on two AA batteries, included a 1.5-inch color playback screen, had built-in memory to hold 30 minutes of video, and needed just a few buttons to operate. Its flip-out USB connector made it easy to download videos to a computer and the included software made it easy to edit, save, organize, and e-mail videos. To keep costs low, manufacturing was outsourced to China.

In May 2006, PDT's Point and Shoot Video Camcorder launched at Target Stores. Later it was available at Amazon.com, Walmart, and other retailers. PDT knew economies of scale would lower production costs, and it feared new competitors would quickly enter the market and shorten the product life cycle for its innovation. So it chose a low manufacturer's suggested retail price of $129.99, and sales and market share climbed rapidly. To help differentiate the camcorder, PDT changed the brand name to Flip.

PDT soon added the Flip Ultra to the product line. For only $30 more than Flip, Flip Ultra offered better quality sound and video and five different colors. FlipShare software was built right into the Flip Ultra so it was even easier to upload movies to YouTube or other video-sharing websites.

While gadget lovers were the earliest adopters, Flip appealed primarily to two target markets. Moms tossed the camera into their handbags so it was convenient for capturing spontaneous family memories—and they loved how easy it was to send video clips to relatives. And teenagers enjoyed posting videos of themselves and their friends to YouTube, MySpace, and Facebook.

With a limited budget for promotion, Flip relied heavily on publicity to get the word out. Favorable reviews from influential technology writers drew attention to Flip. Positive customer reviews of Flip posted at Amazon.com touted how easy it was to take and share videos. It generated even more buzz when stars like Oprah Winfrey, Jessica Alba, and Ellen DeGeneres were photographed with a Flip or publicly sang its praises.

Sales continued to climb and before long Flip was the best-selling video camera on the market. As expected, new competitors like Kodak, Sony, and Creative jumped in. To stay ahead, PDT introduced the Flip Mino ("min-now") and high-definition Flip Mino*HD*. The new models were 40 percent smaller, sleeker in design, and included a rechargeable battery. Most retailers sold them for $20–30 less than the manufacturer suggested retail prices of $179.99 and $229.99.

By 2010, the product-market for small portable video cameras was showing signs of maturing, as sales began to level off and price competition intensified. In response, PDT added the Flip Slide*HD*, with an improved 4-hour recording time and a 3-inch wide touch screen for viewing and controlling the camera. When sales were slow at the initial price of $280, Flip dropped the price to $230, significantly cutting its margins. New competition from smartphones and still cameras with built-in video capability reduced sales and margins further. Many customers see more value in these multi-function devices than a separate video camera. So, instead of competing on price and accepting the low margins associated with the decline stage of the product life cycle, Flip exited the market in 2011.[1]

Learning Objectives

The Flip case demonstrates the importance of Price and how it interacts with the other marketing mix variables to create value and influence customer behavior. This chapter will help you better understand pricing objectives and policies that influence how firms make pricing decisions.

When you finish this chapter you should be able to:

1 understand how pricing objectives should guide strategy planning for pricing decisions.

2 understand choices marketing managers must make about price flexibility.

3 know what a marketing manager should consider when setting the price level for a product in the early stages of the product life cycle.

4 understand the many possible variations of a price structure, including discounts, allowances, and who pays transportation costs.

5 understand the value pricing concept and its role in obtaining a competitive advantage and offering target customers superior value.

6 understand the legality of price level and price flexibility policies.

7 understand important new terms (shown in red).

Price Has Many Strategy Dimensions

Price is one of the four major strategy decision variables that a marketing manager controls. Pricing decisions affect both the number of sales a firm makes and how much money it earns. Price is what a customer must give up to get the benefits offered by the rest of a firm's marketing mix, so it plays a direct role in shaping customer value.

Guided by the company's objectives, marketing managers develop specific pricing objectives. These objectives drive decisions about key pricing policies: (1) how flexible prices will be, (2) the level of prices over the product life cycle, (3) to whom and when discounts and allowances will be given, and (4) how transportation costs will be handled. See Exhibit 16-1. After we've looked at these specific areas, we will discuss how they combine to impact customer value as well as laws that are relevant. In Chapter 17, we will discuss how prices are set.

It's not easy to define price in real-life situations because price reflects many dimensions. People who don't realize this can make big mistakes.

Suppose you've been saving to buy a new car and you see in an ad that, after a $1,000 rebate, the base price for the new-year model is $16,494—5 percent lower than the previous year. At first this might seem like a real bargain. However, your view of this deal might change if you found out you also had to pay a $400 transportation charge and an extra $480 for an extended service warranty. The price might look even less attractive if you discovered that the navigation system, side air bags, and moonroof that were standard the previous year are now options that cost $1,900. The cost of the higher interest rate on the car loan and the

Exhibit 16–1 Strategy Planning and Pricing Objectives and Policies

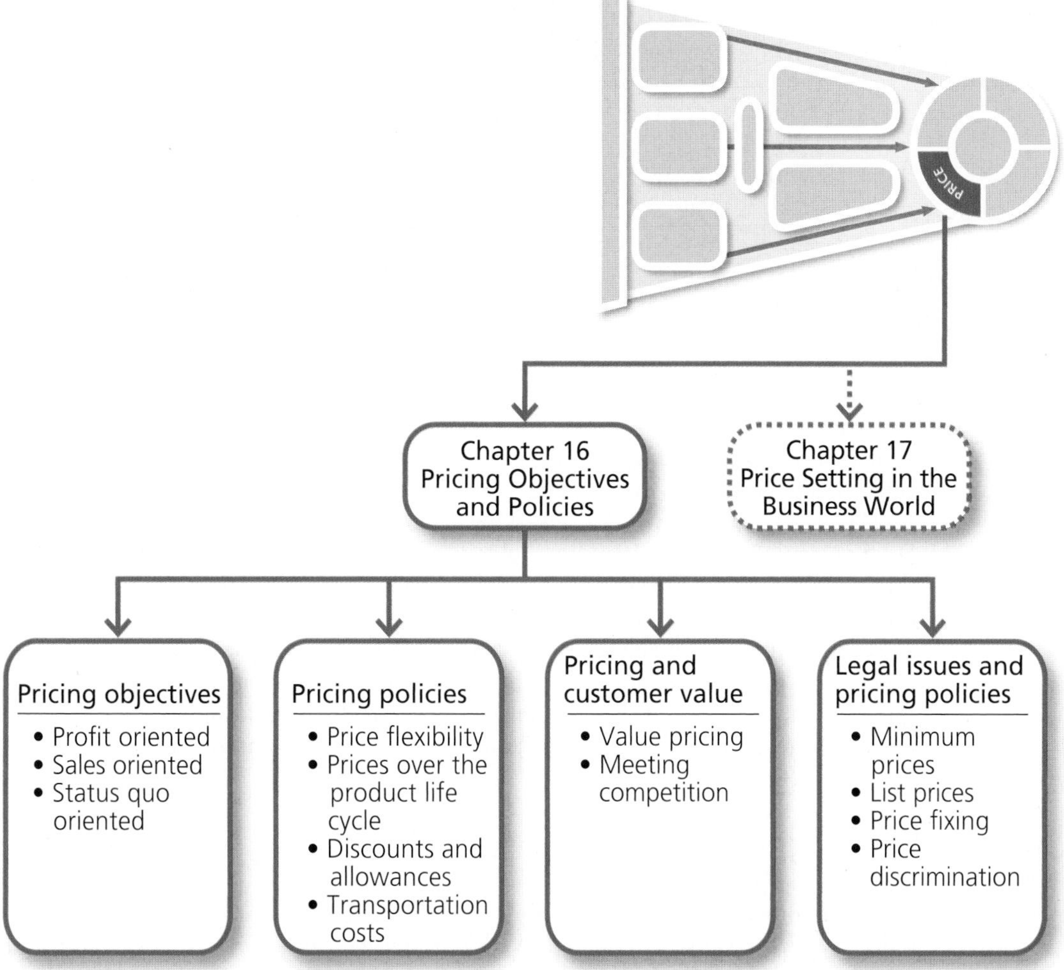

sales tax on all of this might come as an unpleasant surprise too. Further, how would you feel if you bought the car anyway and then learned that a friend who just bought the exact same model got a much lower price from the dealer by using a broker he found on the Internet?[2]

The price equation: Price equals something of value

This example emphasizes that when a seller quotes a price, it is related to *some* assortment of goods and services. So **Price** is the amount of money that is charged for "something" of value. Of course, price may be called different things in different settings. Colleges charge tuition. Landlords collect rent. Motels post a room rate. Country clubs get dues. Banks ask for interest when they loan money. Airlines have fares. Doctors set fees. Employees want a wage. People may call it different things, but *almost every business transaction in our modern economy involves an exchange of money—the Price—for something.*

The something can be a physical product in various stages of completion,

IKEA's clever—and carefully located—promotional signs remind customers that its price is a good value compared to what they pay for other everyday goods and services.

Exhibit 16–2 Price Exchanged for Something of Value (as seen by consumers or users)

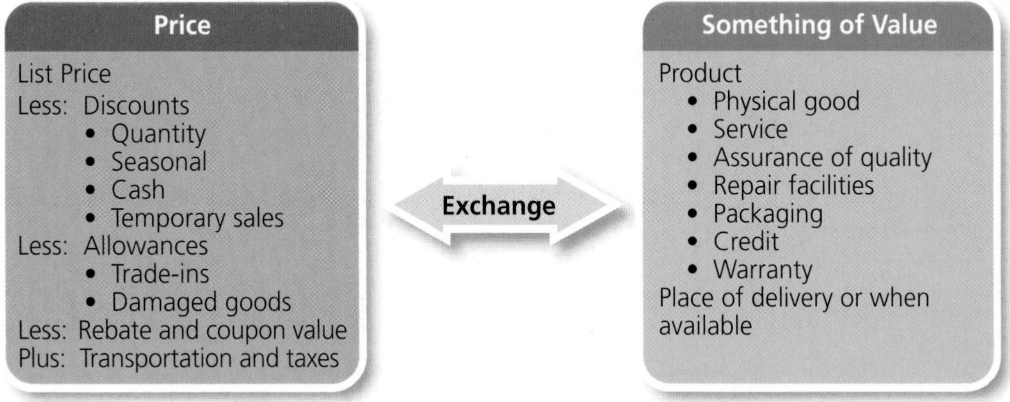

with or without supporting services, with or without quality guarantees, and so on. Or it could be a pure service—dry cleaning, a lawyer's advice, or insurance on your car.

The nature and extent of this something determines the amount of money exchanged. Some customers pay list price. Others obtain large discounts or allowances because something is *not* provided. Exhibit 16-2 summarizes some possible variations for consumers or users, and Exhibit 16-3 does the same for channel members. These variations are discussed more fully below, and then we'll consider the customer value concept more fully—in terms of competitive advantage. But here it should be clear that Price has many dimensions. How each of these dimensions is handled affects customer value. If a customer sees greater value in spending money in some other way, no exchange will occur.

Objectives Should Guide Strategy Planning for Price

LO 16.1

Pricing objectives should flow from, and fit within, company-level and marketing objectives. Pricing objectives should be *explicitly stated* because they have a direct effect on pricing policies as well as the methods used to set prices. Exhibit 16-4 shows the various types of pricing objectives we'll discuss.

Exhibit 16–3 Price Exchanged for Something of Value (as seen by channel members)

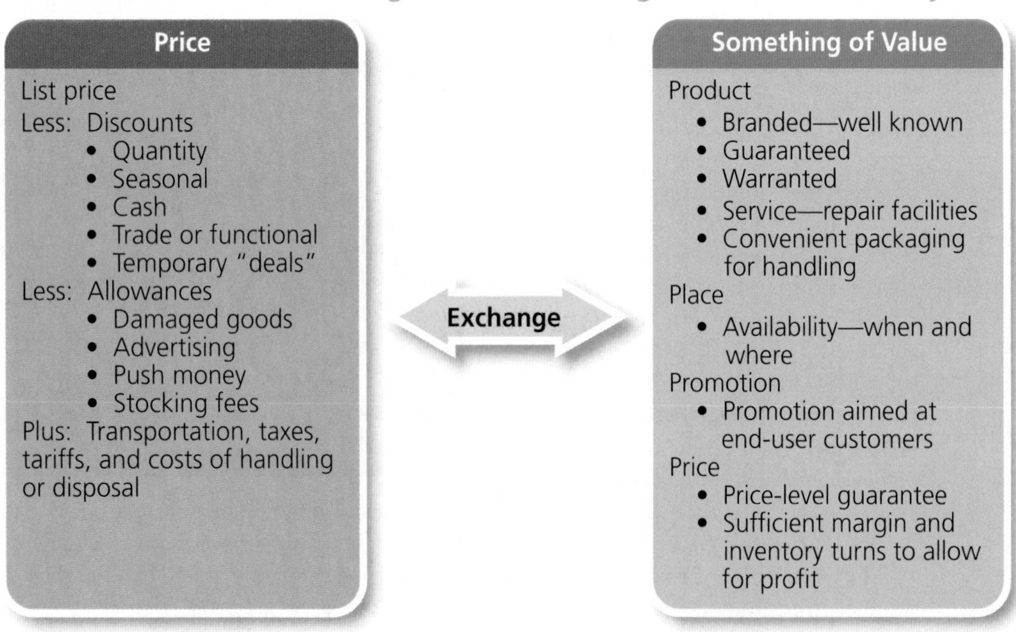

Exhibit 16–4
Possible Pricing Objectives

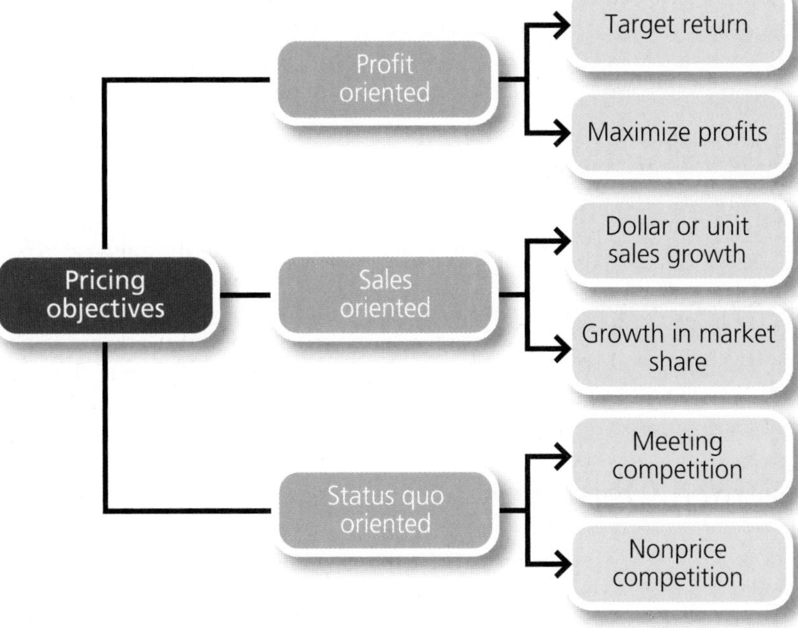

Profit-Oriented Objectives

Target returns provide specific guidelines

Over the long term, and often over the short term, marketing managers should set objectives oriented toward making a profit. A **target return objective** sets a specific level of profit as an objective. Often this amount is stated as a percentage of sales or of capital investment. A large manufacturer like Motorola might aim for a 15 percent return on investment. The target for Safeway and other supermarket chains might be a 1 percent return on sales.

A target return objective has administrative advantages in a large company. Performance can be compared against the target. Some companies eliminate divisions, or drop products, that aren't yielding the target rate of return. For example, General Electric sold its small appliance division to Black & Decker because it felt it could earn higher returns in other product-markets.

Some products have no direct competitors, but if customers value those products, then firms will have more flexibility in choosing prices to maximize profits. After arriving at a theater, a moviegoer has no snack options beyond the theater's snack bar.

Some just want satisfactory profits

Some managers aim for only satisfactory returns. They just want returns that ensure the firm's survival and convince stockholders they're doing a good job. Similarly, some small family-run businesses aim for a profit that will provide a comfortable lifestyle.[3]

Many private and public nonprofit organizations set a price level that will just recover costs. In other words, their target return figure is zero. For example, a government agency may charge motorists a toll for using a bridge but then drop the toll when the cost of the bridge is paid.

Similarly, firms that provide critical public services—including many utilities, insurance companies, and defense contractors—sometimes pursue only satisfactory long-run targets. They are well aware that the public expects them to set prices that are in the public interest. They may also have to face public or government agencies that review and approve prices.[4]

Profit maximization can be socially responsible

A **profit maximization objective** seeks to get as much profit as possible. It might be stated as a desire to earn a rapid return on investment—or, more bluntly, to charge all the traffic will bear.

Pricing to achieve profit maximization doesn't always lead to high prices. Low prices may expand the size of the market and result in greater sales and profits. For example, when prices of cell phones were very high, only businesses and wealthy people bought them. When producers lowered prices, nearly everyone bought one.

If a firm is earning a very large profit, other firms will try to copy or improve on what the company offers. Frequently, this leads to lower prices.

Sales-Oriented Objectives

A **sales-oriented objective** seeks some level of unit sales, dollar sales, or share of market—*without referring to profit.*

Sales growth doesn't necessarily mean big profits

Some managers are more concerned about sales growth than profits. They think sales growth always leads to more profits. This sometimes makes sense over the short term. For example, many Procter & Gamble brands in product categories like shampoo, soap, and diapers lost market share during the recent recession. When the economy began to recover, P&G kept prices low and sacrificed profits in order to grow with the recovering economy. It might also work well when products are in the introductory or early growth stages of the product life cycle. However, over the long term this kind of thinking causes problems when a firm's costs are growing faster than sales. While some firms have periods of declining profits in spite of growth in sales, business managers should usually pay more attention to profits, not just sales.

Some nonprofit organizations set prices to increase market share—precisely because they are *not* trying to earn a profit. For example, many cities set low fares to fill up their buses, reduce traffic, and help the environment. Buses cost the same to run empty or full, and there's more benefit when they're full even if the total revenue is no greater.

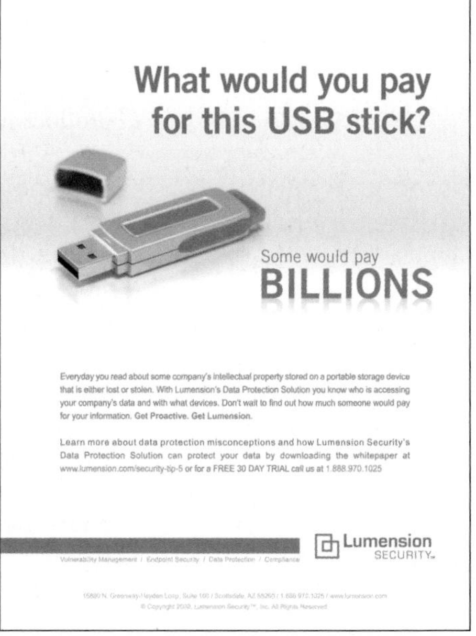

Michelin wants its customers to know that its more efficient tires make them a good value. Lumension Security reminds customers of the high cost of lax computer security.

Market share objectives are popular

Many firms seek to gain a specified share (percent) of a market. If a company has a large market share, it may have better economies of scale than its competitors. In addition, it's usually easier to measure a firm's market share than to determine if profits are being maximized.

A company with a longer-run view may aim for increased market share when the market is growing. The hope is that future volume will justify sacrificing some profit in the short run. HP, Dell, and Acer have waged pricing battles in an effort to gain market share in the personal computer market. High market share offers economies of scale and negotiating power with suppliers. Companies as diverse as 3M and Coca-Cola look at opportunities in Eastern Europe and Southeast Asia this way.

Of course, market share objectives have the same limitations as straight sales growth objectives. A larger market share, if gained at too low a price, may lead to profitless "success."

Status Quo Pricing Objectives

Don't-rock-the-boat objectives

Managers satisfied with their current market share and profits sometimes adopt **status quo objectives**—don't-rock-the-*pricing*-boat objectives. Managers may say that they want to stabilize prices, or meet competition, or even avoid competition. This don't-rock-the-boat thinking is most common when the total market is not growing.

Or stress nonprice competition instead

A status quo pricing objective may be part of an aggressive overall marketing strategy focusing on **nonprice competition**—aggressive action on one or more of the Ps other than Price. Some companies that sell through the Internet originally thought that they'd compete with low prices and still earn high profits from volume. However, when they didn't get the sales volume they hoped for, they realized that there were also some nonprice ways to compete. For example, Zappos.com offers free shipping and guarantees that it will meet local shoe store prices. But it wins customers with its enormous selection of shoes, a website that makes it easy for customers to find what they want, and excellent customer service before and after the sale.

Most Firms Set Specific Pricing Policies—To Reach Objectives

Administered prices help achieve objectives

Price policies usually lead to **administered prices**—consciously set prices. In other words, instead of letting daily market forces (or auctions) decide their prices, most firms set their own prices. They may hold prices steady for long periods of time or change them more frequently if that's what's required to meet objectives.

If a firm doesn't sell directly to final customers, it usually wants to administer both the price it receives from intermediaries and the price final customers pay. After all, the price final customers pay will ultimately affect the quantity it sells.

Yet it is often difficult to administer prices throughout the channel. Other channel members may also wish to administer prices to achieve their own objectives. This is what happened to Alcoa, one of the largest aluminum producers. To reduce its excess inventory, Alcoa offered its wholesalers a 30 percent discount off its normal price. Alcoa expected the wholesalers to pass most of the discount along to their customers to stimulate sales throughout the channel. Instead, wholesalers bought *their* aluminum at the lower price but passed on only a small discount to customers. As a result, the quantity Alcoa sold didn't increase much, and it still had excess inventory, while the wholesalers made much more profit on the aluminum they did sell.[5]

Some firms don't even try to administer prices. They just meet competition—or worse, mark up their costs with little thought to demand. They act as if they have no choice in selecting a price policy.

Remember that Price has many dimensions. Managers usually *do* have many choices. They *should* administer their prices. And they should do it carefully because, ultimately, customers must be willing to pay these prices before a whole marketing mix succeeds. In the rest of this chapter, we'll talk about policies a marketing manager must set to do an effective job of administering Price.[6]

Price Flexibility Policies

LO 16.2

One-price policy—the same price for everyone

One of the first decisions a marketing manager has to make is whether to use a one-price or a flexible-price policy. A **one-price policy** means offering the same price to all customers who purchase products under essentially the same conditions and in the same quantities. The majority of U.S. firms use a one-price policy—mainly for administrative convenience and to maintain goodwill among customers. But that is changing thanks to technology and the ability to identify different customer segments to which a firm wishes to charge higher or lower prices.

A one-price policy makes pricing easier. But a marketing manager must be careful to avoid a rigid one-price policy. This can amount to broadcasting a price that competitors can undercut, especially if the price is somewhat high. One reason for the growth of mass-merchandisers is that conventional retailers rigidly applied traditional margins and stuck to them.

Flexible-price policy—different prices for different customers

A **flexible-price policy** means offering the same product and quantities to different customers at different prices. When computers are used to implement flexible pricing, the decisions focus more on what type of customer will get a price break.

Pricing databases make flexible pricing easier

Various forms of flexible pricing are more common now that most prices are maintained in a central computer database. Frequent changes are easier. You see this when supermarket chains give loyalty club cardholders reduced prices on weekly specials. The checkout scanner reads the code on the package, and then the computer looks up the club price or the regular price depending on whether a club card has been scanned.

Some marketing managers set up relationships with Internet companies whose ads invite customers to "set your own price." For example, at www.priceline.com, visitors specify the desired schedule for a hotel. Hotels that use the site offer rooms that don't appear to have high demand at deeply discounted prices. So for example, if a hotel is only expected to be half full next weekend, the hotel offers big discounts through Priceline. Even at a discount, the hotel rooms can be profitable. It may appear that these marketing managers have given up on administering prices. Just the opposite is true. They are carefully administering a flexible price. They adapt the price based on supply and demand—offering few discounts if the hotel is close to capacity and more discounts when demand is low.

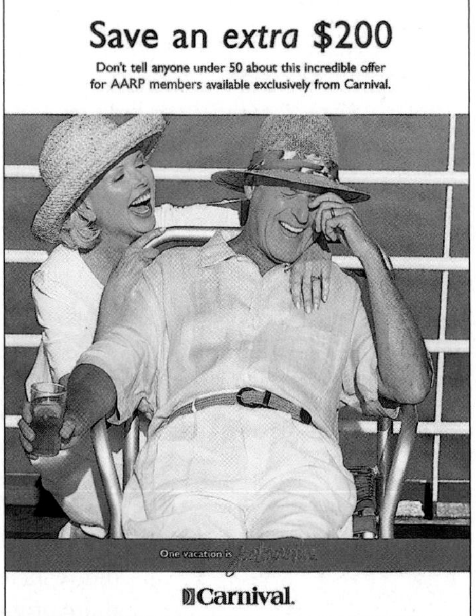

Carnival's marketing managers use flexible pricing, including discounts for members of the AARP who are over age 50.

Big data helps managers make the most of flexible pricing

Many firms use big data to more accurately identify target customers and offer them particular prices depending on the firm's marketing strategy. Many sources of big data can be read in real-time, so pricing "experiments" can be run. For example, an online retailer can cut prices for a day or even a few hours to see whether it stimulates demand and raises profits. Even brick-and-mortar retailers will use knowledge of individual customers to offer targeted price discounts to certain customers. For example, a grocery store can identify a customer as they shop the store—using their cell phone signal, for example. The store can then offer discounts to new or infrequent shoppers to encourage greater loyalty. On the other hand, the retailer may prefer to offer discounts to reward its best customers—and further cement loyalty. Retailers can then follow those customers' future purchases to determine whether targeting one or both groups with discounts yields more profits.

Dynamic pricing offers products at a price that changes according to the level of demand, the type of customer, or the state of the weather. Big data can be used to more accurately predict future demand and adapt prices to maximize revenue and profit. So for example, airlines typically adjust prices over time. If United Airlines sees that early morning Tuesday flights from St. Louis to Miami are not selling well, the airline can lower the price to stimulate demand—perhaps encouraging some flyers to fly out on Tuesday morning instead of Monday night when there are fewer available seats. It is better to sell some seats at a discount than to have the flight leave with half the seats empty.

Sports teams are increasing ticket revenue by analyzing big data and implementing dynamic pricing. For example, the San Francisco Giants baseball team adjusts ticket prices to maximize attendance and revenue for each game. Ticket prices for each seat at each game can be adjusted after crunching numbers that examine past ticket sales, the day of the week, time of the game, the opposing teams record, the pitching match-up, the going price at ticket resale sites like StubHub, and even the weather forecast. The Giants were expecting an additional $5 million in revenue the first year using the system. Other teams are following the Giants lead.[7]

Salespeople can adjust prices to the situation

Flexible pricing is most common in the channels, in direct sales of business products, and at retail for expensive shopping products. Retail shopkeepers in less-developed economies typically use flexible pricing—shopkeepers start with high prices but bargain to try to make a sale at a price the customer will accept while still providing maximum profit to the seller. These situations usually involve personal selling, not mass selling. The advantage of flexible pricing is that the salesperson can adjust price—considering prices charged by competitors, the relationship with the customer, and the customer's bargaining ability. Flexible-price policies often specify a *range* in which the actual price charged must fall.[8]

Too much price-cutting erodes profits

Some sales reps let price-cutting become a habit. This can lead to a lower price level and lower profit. A small price cut may not seem like much; but keep in mind that all of the revenue that is lost would go to profit. If salespeople for a producer that usually earns profits equal to 20 percent of its sales cut prices by an average of about 10 percent, profits would drop by half! See Exhibit 16-5.

Disadvantages of flexible pricing

Flexible pricing does have disadvantages. A customer who finds that others paid lower prices for the same marketing mix will be unhappy. This can cause real conflict in channels. For example, the Winn-Dixie supermarket chain stopped carrying products of some suppliers who refused to give Winn-Dixie the same prices available to chains in other regions of the country. Similarly, companies that post different prices for different segments on a website that all can see often get complaints.

If buyers learn that negotiating is in their interest, the time needed for bargaining will increase. This can increase selling costs and reduce profits. It can also frustrate customers. For example, most auto dealers use flexible pricing and bargain for what they can get. Inexperienced consumers, reluctant to bargain, often pay hundreds of dollars more than the dealer is willing to accept. By contrast, CarMax has earned high customer-satisfaction ratings by offering haggle-weary consumers a one-price policy.[9]

Exhibit 16–5
Impact of Price Cut on Profit

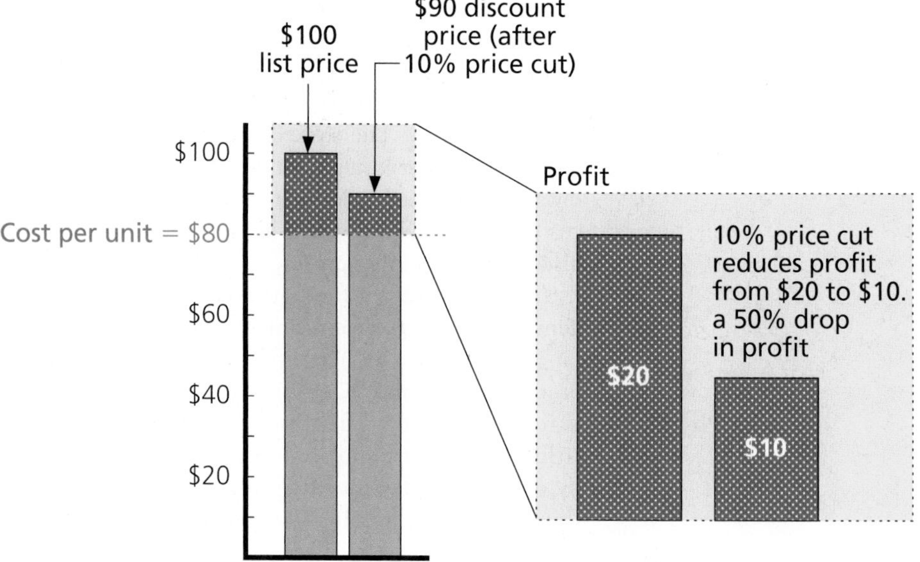

Price-Level Policies—Over the Product Life Cycle

LO 16.3

Marketing managers who administer prices must consciously set a price-level policy. As they enter the market, they have to set introductory prices that may have long-run effects. They must consider where the product life cycle is and how fast it's moving. And they must decide if their prices should be above, below, or somewhere in between relative to the market.

Let's look for a moment at a new product in the market introduction stage of its product life cycle. There are few (or no) direct substitute marketing mixes. So the price-level decision should focus first on the nature of market demand. A high price may lead to higher profit from each sale but also to fewer units sold. A lower price might appeal to more potential customers. With this in mind, should the firm set a high or low price?

Skimming pricing—feeling out demand at a high price

A **skimming price policy** tries to sell the top (skim the cream) of a market—the top of the demand curve—at a high price before aiming at more price-sensitive customers. Skimming may maximize profits in the market introduction stage for an innovation, especially if there are few substitutes or if some customers are not price sensitive. Skimming is also useful when you don't know very much about the shape of the demand curve. It's sometimes safer to start with a high price that can be reduced if customers balk.

Skimming has critics

Some critics argue that firms should not try to maximize profits by using a skimming policy on new products that have important social consequences—a patent-protected, life-saving drug or a technique that increases crop yields, for example. Many of those who need the product may not have the money to buy it. This is a serious concern. However, it's also a serious problem if firms don't have any incentive to take risks and develop new products.[10]

Price moves down the demand curve

A skimming policy usually involves a slow reduction in price over time. See Exhibit 16-6. Note that as price is reduced, new target markets are probably being sought. So as the price level steps down the demand curve, new Place, Product, and Promotion policies may be needed too.

When McCaw Cellular Communications—the firm that pioneered cellular phone service and was later bought out by AT&T—first came on the market, it set a high price. Each wireless minute cost about $1, and customers had to pay about $675 for a large, clunky phone. McCaw used dealers to sell the premium-priced packages because they

Exhibit 16–6 Alternative Introductory Pricing Policies

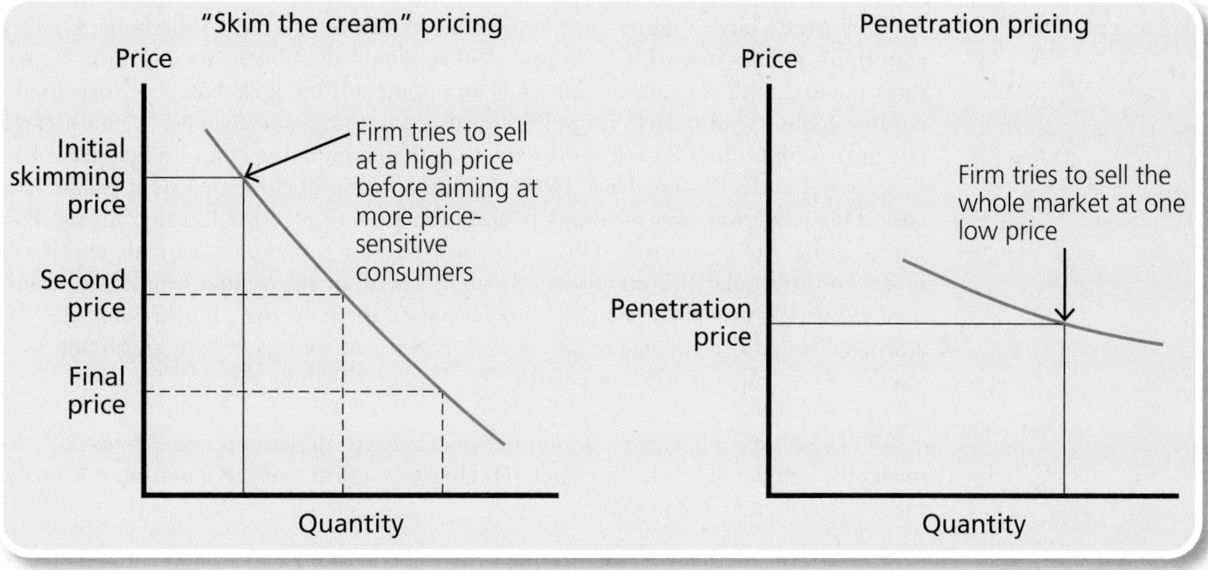

could explain the value of the system and get orders. They mainly targeted firms that gave phones to their on-the-go executives and salespeople. Many of these customers were not price sensitive because no good substitute was available. However, that changed as other cellular providers came into the market. To improve the value of its offering, McCaw bought large quantities of phones from Motorola at low cost and then packaged them with a service contract at a high discount. As the market grew, economies of scale kicked in and McCaw cut prices even more. McCaw also did more advertising and started to sell cellular services through a variety of retail outlets, including mass-merchandisers. These Promotion and Place changes cut selling costs and helped reach the growing number of families who wanted cell service. Free weekend and evening minutes for consumers when demand from business customers was low sweetened the deal. In addition, prices on phones had come down so much that retailers gave away a phone with a one-year service contract—and offered family plans where additional family members were added to a contract for about $10 each. By then, AT&T was relying more heavily on television advertising that encouraged customers to sign up at an AT&T store or at the AT&T website—which helped cut channel markups from the selling price. Promotion and discounting became even more aggressive as cell phone services merged, but AT&T was able to build its share because it was the exclusive service provider for Apple's hot iPhone. However, Sprint didn't just roll over and let AT&T win the competition for the growing number of smartphone users. Rather, it slashed the total costs of using smartphones with its "Simply Everything" plan. For $99 a month it offered customers unlimited talking, web browsing, text, picture and video messaging, music downloads, and even 150 radio stations. As this example suggests, as the skimming price in the market changes, it is often accompanied by a series of changes in marketing strategy, not just a stepping down of prices.[11]

Penetration pricing—get volume at a low price

A **penetration pricing policy** tries to sell the whole market at one low price. This approach might be wise when the elite market—those willing to pay a high price—is small. This is the case when the whole demand curve is fairly elastic. See Exhibit 16-6. A penetration policy is even more attractive if selling larger quantities results in lower costs because of economies of scale. Penetration pricing may be wise if the firm expects strong competition very soon after introduction.

Sony relied on penetration pricing when it battled with Toshiba to introduce a next-generation optical disc player. Sony's Blu-ray format and Toshiba's HD-DVD format were incompatible formats. Sony had to win market acceptance quickly. If Toshiba's HD-DVD format became the standard, Sony's investment to develop and promote Blu-ray would go down the drain.

To motivate buyers, Sony cut the price on its Blu-ray players to the bone. Getting adoptions quickly was critical because studios would distribute movies in the format most popular with consumers. Sony saw an opportunity to kick-start its efforts by including a Blu-ray disc drive in its PS3 third-generation game console. When it came out in late 2006, the PS3 was more expensive than competing consoles because it had more power and a Blu-ray drive. However, Sony priced it below its current production cost. This move was part of Sony's penetration pricing plan for Blu-ray. All the PS3 consoles that Sony sold that Christmas contributed to economies of scale and lower prices on the regular Blu-ray players. In addition, all of the excited people who clamored to buy PS3s for their favorite games also used them for their Blu-ray movies. This added to Sony's Blu-ray market share with consumers and gave it an advantage with studios. By spring of 2008, Sony had a clear lead and Toshiba threw in the towel on its HD-DVD format.[12]

Of course, even a low penetration price doesn't keep competitors out of a market permanently. Product life cycles do march on. However, a firm that gets a head start in a new market can often maintain its advantage.

Introductory price dealing—temporary price cuts

Low prices do attract customers. Therefore, marketers often use **introductory price dealing**—temporary price cuts—to speed new products into a market and get customers to try them. However, don't confuse these *temporary* price cuts with low penetration prices. The plan here is to raise prices as soon as the introductory offer is over. By then, hopefully, target customers will have decided it is worth buying again at the regular price. Introductory price dealing should be part of a larger marketing strategy. For example, some developers of software applications (or "apps") for smartphones, like those sold on Apple's iTunes, know that getting onto the store's list of "Top Apps" gets attention, which drives sales. So some app makers price the app low at launch to encourage sales, which moves it up the rankings. Then they raise prices to optimize profits.

Established competitors often choose not to meet introductory price dealing—as long as the introductory period is not too long or too successful. However, some competitors match introductory price deals with their own short-term sale prices to discourage customers from shopping around.

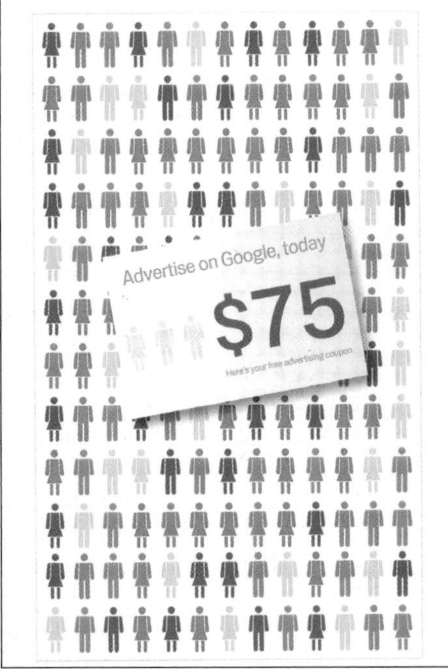

Marketers often use introductory price dealing—in the form of temporary price cuts, introductory coupons, or trade-in allowances—to speed new products into a market.

Exhibit 16–7
Exchange Rates for Various Currencies against the U.S. Dollar over Time

Base Currency	Number of Units of Base Currency per U.S. Dollar* 2002	2005	2008	2011
British pound	0.69	0.64	0.50	0.61
Thai baht	43.48	42.89	31.44	30.13
Japanese yen	131.19	120.04	101.40	83.30
Australian dollar	1.88	1.64	1.06	0.95
Canadian dollar	1.58	1.46	1.00	0.96
Euro	1.13	0.92	0.63	0.69

*Units shown are for April 16th in each year.

The price of money may affect the price level

We've been talking about the price level of a firm's product. But a nation's money also has a price level—what it is worth in some other currency. For example, on April 16, 2011, one U.S. dollar was worth 0.61 British pounds. In other words, the exchange rate for the British pound against the U.S. dollar was 0.61. Exhibit 16-7 lists exchange rates for money from several countries over a number of years. From this exhibit you can see that exchange rates change over time—and sometimes the changes are significant. For example, on April 16, 2005, a U.S. dollar was worth 42.89 Thai baht; just three years later the U.S. dollar was worth 27 percent less—only 31.44 Thai baht.

As the following example shows, exchange rate changes can have a significant effect on international trade and how a firm's price is viewed by customers in an overseas market. Jacquelyn Tran started BeautyEncounter.com, an online retail cosmetics website, in 1999. Before long, her domestic business was doing well and she was also attracting some sales from the United Kingdom, France, Germany, Japan, Canada, and Latin America. Her sales to international customers grew at an even faster rate after 2005 as the U.S. dollar weakened against other currencies (see Exhibit 16-7). You can see why this would happen by looking at the change in the exchange rate of the euro against the dollar. In April of 2005, the exchange rate for the euro against the dollar was 0.92, so a customer living in Europe paid 92 euros to purchase $100 worth of beauty supplies. Three years later, the exchange rate had dropped to 0.63, so at that point it cost the customer only 63 euros to purchase the same $100 worth of supplies. So, from the perspective of a European customer, the change in the exchange rate over that time period had the same effect as a price cut. Yet many of those customers didn't just buy the same beauty supplies and pocket the extra 29 euros. Instead, they continued to spend the same amount in their home currency (92 euros), which in 2008 was equal to $146. In effect, these customers increased the size of their orders from Beauty Encounter by 46 percent (from $100 to $146). The shift in exchange rates also made the firm's cosmetics cheaper relative to competing cosmetics retailers in Europe, and that attracted new overseas customers.

Beauty Encounter's export business benefited from exchange rates from 2005 to 2008. But by 2011 the exchange rate for the euro had climbed to 0.69. If a European customer continued to spend the same amount in 2011 as she did in 2008 (92 euros), then she would be purchasing just $133 worth of goods, not $146 as in 2008. The change in rates will likely have a negative impact on Beauty Encounter's sales because they amount to a price hike.[13]

Internet Exercise

There is a website (**www.x-rates.com**) that converts one country's currency to another. Go to the website, click on "Currency Calculator," and determine how much $100 U.S. is worth in Thai bahts, British pounds, and euros. How do those numbers compare with April 2011 (see Exhibit 16-7)?

Discount Policies—Reductions from List Prices

LO 16.4

Prices start with a list price

Most price structures are built around a base price schedule or list price. **Basic list prices** are the prices final customers or users are normally asked to pay for products. In this book, unless noted otherwise, list price refers to basic list price.

In Chapter 17, we discuss how firms set these list prices. For now, however, we'll consider variations from list price and why they are made.

Discounts are reductions from list price

Discounts are reductions from list price given by a seller to buyers who either give up some marketing function or provide the function themselves. Discounts can be useful in marketing strategy planning. In the following discussion, think about what function the buyers are giving up, or providing, when they get each of these discounts.

Quantity discounts encourage volume buying

Quantity discounts are discounts offered to encourage customers to buy in larger amounts. This lets a seller get more of a buyer's business, or shifts some of the storing function to the buyer, or reduces shipping and selling costs—or all of these. There are two kinds of quantity discounts: cumulative and noncumulative.

Cumulative quantity discounts apply to purchases over a given period—such as a year—and the discount usually increases as the amount purchased increases. Cumulative discounts encourage *repeat* buying by reducing the customer's cost for additional purchases. This is a way to develop loyalty and ongoing relationships with customers. For example, a Lowe's lumberyard might give a cumulative quantity discount to a building contractor who is not able to buy all of the needed materials at once. Lowe's wants to reward the contractor's patronage and discourage shopping around.

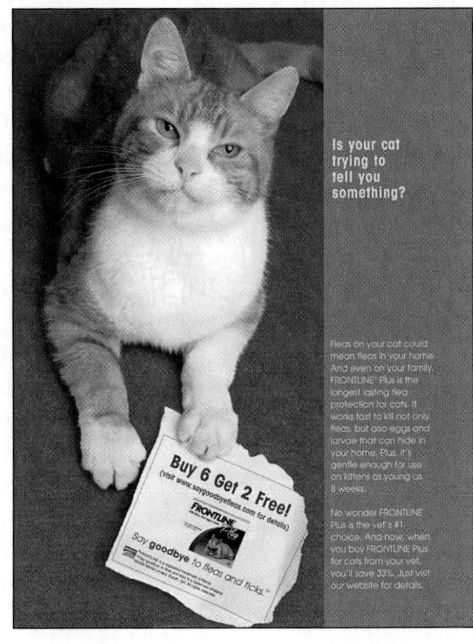

Customers who buy six applications of Frontline Plus flea protection get two more for free—essentially a quantity discount of 25 percent.

A cumulative quantity discount is often attractive to business customers who don't want to run up their inventory costs. They are rewarded for buying large quantities, even though individual orders may be smaller.

Noncumulative quantity discounts apply only to individual orders. Such discounts encourage larger orders but do not tie a buyer to the seller after that one purchase. Lowe's lumberyard may resell insulation products made by several competing producers. Owens-Corning might try to encourage Lowe's to stock larger quantities of its pink insulation by offering a noncumulative quantity discount.

Seasonal discounts—buy sooner

Seasonal discounts are discounts offered to encourage buyers to buy earlier than present demand requires. If used by a manufacturer, this discount tends to shift the storing function further along in the channel. It also tends to even out sales over the year. For example, Kyota offers wholesalers a lower price on its garden tillers if they buy in the fall, when sales are slow.

Service firms that face irregular demand or excess capacity often use seasonal discounts. For example, some tourist attractions, like ski resorts, offer lower weekday rates when attendance would otherwise be down.

Payment terms and cash discounts set payment dates

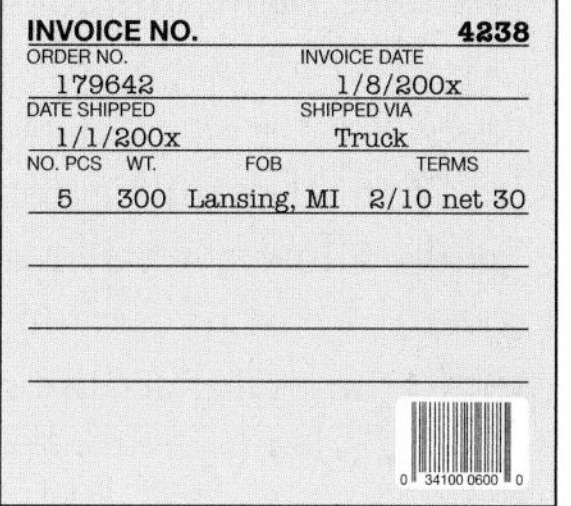

INVOICE NO. 4238

ORDER NO.	INVOICE DATE		
179642	1/8/200x		
DATE SHIPPED	SHIPPED VIA		
1/1/200x	Truck		
NO. PCS	WT.	FOB	TERMS
5	300	Lansing, MI	2/10 net 30

Most sales to businesses are made on credit. The seller sends a bill (invoice) by mail or electronically, and the buyer's accounting department processes it for payment. Some firms depend on their suppliers for temporary working capital (credit). Therefore, it is very important for both sides to clearly state the terms of payment—including the availability of cash discounts—and to understand the commonly used payment terms.

Net means that payment for the face value of the invoice is due immediately. These terms are sometimes changed to net 10 or net 30, which means payment is due within 10 or 30 days of the date on the invoice.

Cash discounts are reductions in price to encourage buyers to pay their bills quickly. The terms for a cash discount usually modify the net terms.

2/10, net 30 means the buyer can take a 2 percent discount off the face value of the invoice if the invoice is paid within 10 days. Otherwise, the full face value is due within 30 days. And it usually is stated or understood that an interest charge will be added after the 30-day free-credit period.

Why cash discounts are given and should be evaluated

Smart buyers carefully evaluate cash discounts. A discount of 2/10, net 30 may not look like much at first. But the buyer earns a 2 percent discount for paying the invoice just 20 days sooner than it should be paid anyway. By not taking the discount, the company in effect is borrowing at an annual rate of 36 percent. That is, assuming a 360-day year and dividing by 20 days, there are 18 periods during which the company could earn 2 percent—and 18 times 2 equals 36 percent a year.

Consumers say "charge it"

Credit sales are also important to retailers. Retailers usually accept credit cards from services such as Visa or MasterCard and pay a percent of the revenue from each credit sale for the service. Some retailers also have aggressive promotions to sign up customers for their own credit cards because customers that carry a store's credit card may spend more money at the store. Generous credit terms, such as "no interest or payments for one full year" do stimulate sales. However, credit that is too easy exposes retailers to the risk of losses when the economy turns down.

Buying on credit changes consumer behavior in developing countries

Making purchases with credit cards is a growing practice in many developing countries. This creates opportunities for producers of more expensive products. In Brazil, consumers are seeing offers to buy sneakers with four monthly payments, or a new stove for 10 monthly payments. Consumers often pay for the benefits of buying on credit with inflated prices. While offering credit can open new markets for many sellers, inexperienced consumers may find themselves in trouble down the road.[14]

Credit cards raise ethical and legal concerns

There are also ethical concerns about credit card companies and retailers that make it too easy for consumers to buy things they really can't afford. The problem becomes worse when an unpaid balance on a credit card carries a very high interest rate. This can significantly increase the price a consumer pays. Even worse, it leaves many low-income consumers trapped in debt.

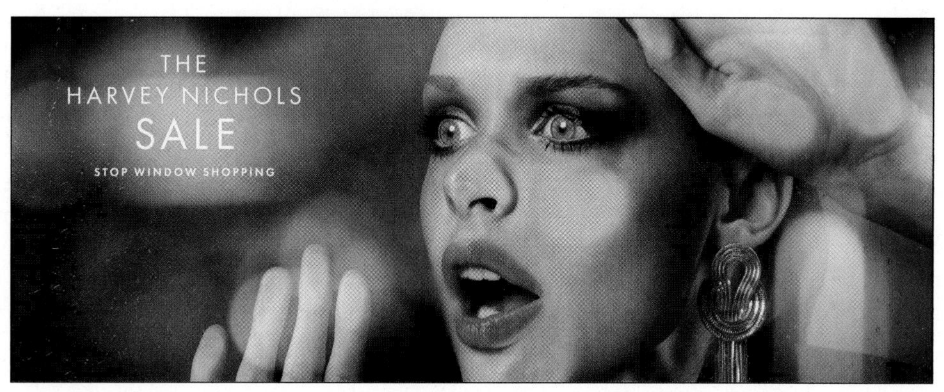

Sale prices encourage consumers to purchase products immediately. To get the sale price, customers give up the convenience of buying when they want to buy and instead buy when the seller wants to sell.

College students have traditionally been a target market for credit cards—in part because credit card issuers covet customers who don't have any previous card loyalties. Of course many students also arrive at college with no job, no income, few assets, and a sparse credit report. Wooed with free food or gifts, many sign up for cards and return home with significant debt. So the U.S. Congress passed the Credit CARD Act of 2009, which offers protections for college-age students. Anyone under 21 must now have a cosigner or prove they can repay any debt.[15]

Trade discounts are often set by tradition

A **trade (functional) discount** is a list price reduction given to channel members for the job they are going to do. A manufacturer, for example, might allow a retailer a 30 percent trade discount from the suggested retail list price to cover the cost of carrying inventory and providing knowledgeable salespeople to demonstrate the manufacturer's products. Similarly, the manufacturer might allow wholesalers a *chain* discount of 30 percent and 10 percent off the suggested retail price. In this case, the wholesalers would be expected to pass the 30 percent discount on to retailers.

Special sales reduce list prices—temporarily

A **sale price** is a temporary discount from the list price. Sale price discounts encourage immediate buying. In other words, to get the sale price, customers give up the convenience of buying when they want to buy and instead buy when the seller wants to sell.

Special sales provide a marketing manager with a quick way to respond to changing market conditions without changing the basic marketing strategy. For example, a retailer might use a sale to help clear extra inventory or to meet a competing store's price.

In recent years, sale prices and deals have become much more common. Some retailers have sales so often that consumers just wait to purchase when there's a sale. Others check out a website like www.fatwallet.com to figure out where the product they want is already on sale. At first it may seem that consumers benefit from all this. But prices that change constantly erode brand loyalty.

To avoid these problems, some firms that sell consumer convenience products offer **everyday low pricing**—setting a low list price rather than relying on frequent sales, discounts, or allowances. Some supermarkets use this approach.

Sale prices should be used carefully, consistent with well-thought-out pricing objectives and policies. A marketing manager who constantly uses temporary sales to adjust the price level probably has not done a good job setting the normal price or creating a marketing mix that offers sustainable competitive advantage.[16]

Internet Exercise

FatWallet (**www.fatwallet.com**) is one of many websites that can help consumers find good deals. To see how it works, assume that you are interested in buying a new printer for your personal computer. Start by selecting a specific model that you like at the HP website (**www.hpshopping.com**). Then, search at www.fatwallet.com to see what you can learn about buying that printer. For example, check for advice in the consumer forums and see if there are any coupons. Identify different retailers that sell the printer, and read the ratings of those retailers. Where would you buy the printer, and why did you choose that retailer?

Allowance Policies—Off List Prices

Allowances, like discounts, are given to final consumers, business customers, or channel members for doing something or accepting less of something.

Advertising allowances—something for something

Advertising allowances are price reductions given to firms in the channel to encourage them to advertise or otherwise promote the supplier's products locally. For example, Sony might give an allowance (3 percent of sales) to its retailers. They, in turn, are expected to spend the allowance on local advertising.

Stocking allowances—get attention and shelf space

Stocking allowances—sometimes called *slotting allowances*—are given to an intermediary to get shelf space for a product. For example, a producer might offer a retailer cash or free merchandise to stock a new item. Stocking allowances are used mainly to get supermarket chains to handle new products. Supermarkets are more willing to give space to a new product if the supplier will offset their handling costs and risks. With a big stocking allowance, the intermediary makes extra profit—even if a new product fails and the producer loses money.[17]

PMs—push for cash

Push money (or prize money) allowances—sometimes called *PMs* or *spiffs*—are given to retailers by manufacturers or wholesalers to pass on to the retailers' salesclerks for aggressively selling certain items. PM allowances are used for new items, slower-moving items, or higher-margin items. They are often used for pushing furniture, clothing, consumer electronics, and cosmetics. A salesclerk, for example, might earn an additional $5 for each new model Panasonic DVD player sold.

Bring in the old, ring up the new—with trade-ins

A **trade-in allowance** is a price reduction given for used products when similar new products are bought. Trade-ins give the marketing manager an easy way to lower the effective price without reducing list price. Proper handling of trade-ins is important when selling durable products.

Some Customers Get Something Extra

Coupons—more for less

Many producers and retailers offer discounts (or free items) through coupons distributed in packages, mailings, print ads, at the store, or online. By presenting a coupon to a retailer, the consumer is given a discount off list price. The fastest-growing distribution approach is online—where consumers can search for coupons and print them out, send them to their cell phone or directly add them to their store loyalty card. This is especially common in the consumer packaged goods business—but the use of price-off coupons is also growing in other lines of business.

Retailers are willing to redeem producers' coupons because it increases their sales and they usually are paid for the trouble of handling the coupons. For example, a retailer that redeems a 50 cents off coupon might be repaid 75 cents.[18]

"Deal-of-the-Day" sites give big discounts

Most coupons offer discounts of $.50 to $1.00—which isn't enough to move some customers to action. So "Deal-of-the-Day" websites like Groupon and Living Social offer customers real bargains—often half off or more. The bargain offers come from local businesses—usually retailers, restaurants, or service providers—and arrive in daily e-mails customers sign up to receive. Customers must purchase the deal that day—perhaps buying a certificate for $180 worth of auto detailing services for $90. Businesses offering these big discounts hope to attract new customers who will make future purchases at regular prices, or purchase more than the amount on the certificate. But marketers should be careful with such promotions; many deal-seekers are only loyal to the next deal—and not the business offering it.

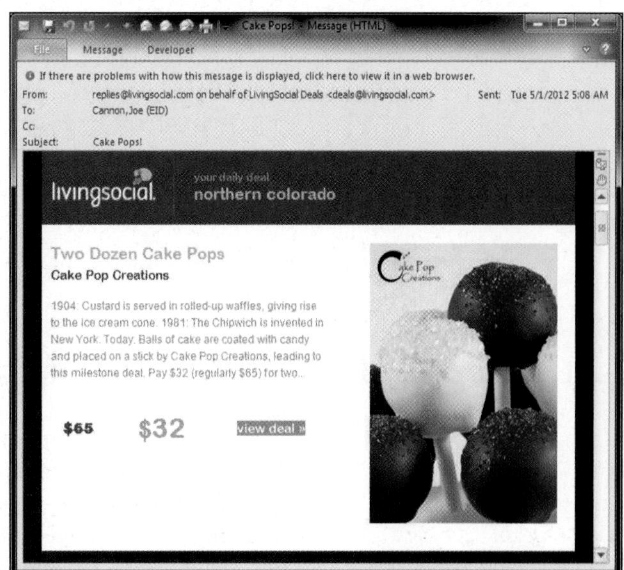

Rebates—cash back

Some firms offer **rebates**—refunds paid to consumers after a purchase. Sometimes the rebate is very large. Some automakers offer rebates of $500 to $6,000 to promote sales of slow-moving models. Rebates are also used on lower-priced items, ranging from Duracell batteries and Memorex CD-Rs to Logitech webcams and Paul Masson wines. Rebates give a producer a way to be certain that final consumers actually get the price reduction. If the rebate amount were just taken off the price charged intermediaries, they might not pass the savings along to consumers.

But rebates have their critics. While rebates prompt many consumers to make a purchase, many rebates—even high-value rebates—are never redeemed. A few years ago TiVo offered a $100 holiday season rebate, but half of the consumers eligible failed to even request their rebate. For many customers the paperwork and hassle deter them; others simply forget after they leave the store. The growing consumer backlash against rebates and the threat of government regulation have prompted many firms to drop rebates from their marketing strategies.[19]

Coupons, deals, and rebates can segment the market

Coupons, deals and rebates can help marketing managers attract new customers or move customers who are interested in a product to take action and buy. However, many marketing managers want to sell not only to customers looking for a bargain but also to customers willing to pay full price. But it's hard for a firm to appeal to both groups with the same price. For instance, if a firm persists in offering only higher prices, then sales are lost to the price-sensitive customer who wants only the lowest price. On the other hand, if a firm lowers its prices to appeal to the bargain hunters, then profits will be low from all customers—even those willing to pay a higher price.

To appeal to both groups and maximize profits, many firms now offer a variety of coupons, deals, and rebates. These discounts are an effective way to segment the market. For example, bargain hunters are willing to spend the time and energy necessary to find discounts—before purchasing the firm's products—and probably would not purchase without them. This makes the discounts a useful part of the price equation for these shoppers. But other customers will still pay full price because they value the whole marketing mix. They don't need the added incentive of a deal and won't look for the discounts. As a result, a marketing manager can increase total profits by segmenting the market and targeting each group separately.

Ethics Question

A pricing consultant has suggested that your firm set a premium price for the paper-shredding machines it sells through office equipment stores—but that there be a $20 mail-in rebate with each unit. The consultant says his research shows that, when an office shredder wears out, it's usually the administrative assistant who is sent to buy a replacement. The consultant says that many of these buyers will pick your firm's shredder, in spite of the higher price, so that they can pocket the rebate. At the end of his report he says, "This is an accepted way to motivate the decision maker. Think about all those executives who rack up frequent-flier miles on business trips and then use the free tickets they get for family vacations." Your boss has left the decision up to you. Would you follow the consultant's advice? Why or why not?

List Price May Depend on Geographic Pricing Policies

Retail list prices sometimes include free delivery. Or free delivery may be offered to some customers as an aid to closing the sale. But deciding who pays the freight charge is more important on sales to business customers than to final consumers because more money is involved. Purchase orders usually specify place, time, method of delivery, freight costs, insurance, handling, and other charges. There are many possible variations for an imaginative marketing manager, and some specialized terms have developed.

F.O.B. pricing is easy

A commonly used transportation term is **F.O.B.**—which means free on board some vehicle at some place. Typically, F.O.B. pricing names the place—often the location of the seller's factory or warehouse—as in F.O.B. Taiwan or F.O.B. mill. This means that the seller pays the cost of loading the products onto some vehicle; then title to the products passes to the buyer. The buyer pays the freight and takes responsibility for damage in transit.

If a firm wants to pay the freight for the convenience of customers, it can use F.O.B. delivered or F.O.B. buyer's factory. In this case, title does not pass until the products are delivered. If the seller wants title to pass immediately but is willing to prepay freight (and then include it in the invoice), F.O.B. seller's factory—freight prepaid can be used.

F.O.B. shipping point pricing simplifies the seller's pricing—but it may narrow the market. Since the delivered cost varies depending on the buyer's location, a customer located farther from the seller must pay more and might buy from closer suppliers.

Zone pricing smooths delivered prices

Zone pricing means making an average freight charge to all buyers within specific geographic areas. The seller pays the actual freight charges and bills each customer for an average charge. For example, a company in Canada might divide the United States into seven zones, then bill all customers in the same zone the same amount for freight even though actual shipping costs might vary.

Zone pricing reduces the wide variation in delivered prices that results from an F.O.B. shipping point pricing policy. It also simplifies transportation charges.

Uniform delivered pricing—one price to all

Uniform delivered pricing means making an average freight charge to all buyers. It is a kind of zone pricing—an entire country may be considered as one zone—that includes the average cost of delivery in the price. Uniform delivered pricing is most often used when (1) transportation costs are relatively low and (2) the seller wishes to sell in all geographic areas at one price, perhaps a nationally advertised price.

Freight-absorption pricing—competing on equal grounds in another territory

When all firms in an industry use F.O.B. shipping point pricing, a firm usually competes well near its shipping point but not farther away. As sales reps look for business farther away, delivered prices rise and the firm finds itself priced out of the market.

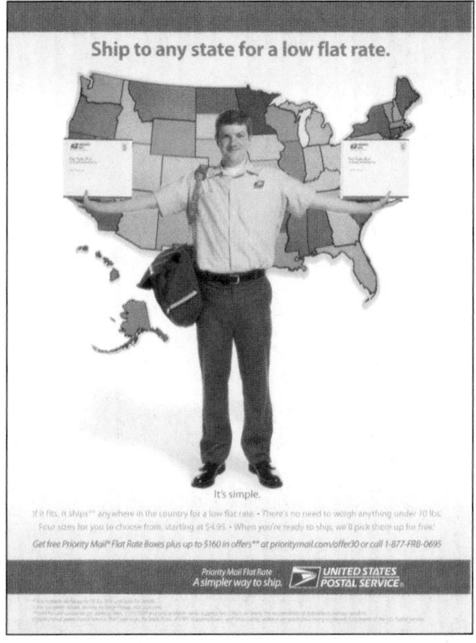

In today's competitive markets, a marketing manager must look for ways to enhance customer value from the firm's marketing mix. L.L. Bean uses free shipping and the U.S. Post Office offers the simplicity and convenience of shipping to any state for one low rate.

This problem can be reduced with **freight-absorption pricing**—which means absorbing freight cost so that a firm's delivered price meets that of the nearest competitor. This amounts to cutting list price to appeal to new market segments. Some firms look at international markets this way; they just figure that any profit from export sales is a bonus.

Pricing Policies Combine to Impact Customer Value

LO 16.5

Look at Price from the customer's viewpoint

We've discussed pricing policies separately so far, but from the customer's view they all combine to impact customer value. So when we talk about Price we are really talking about the whole set of price policies that define the real price level. On the other hand, superior value isn't just based on having a lower price than some competitor but rather on the whole marketing mix.

Value pricing leads to superior customer value

Smart marketers look for the combination of Price decisions that result in value pricing. **Value pricing** means setting a fair price level for a marketing mix that really gives the target market superior customer value.

Value pricing doesn't necessarily mean cheap if cheap means bare-bones or low-grade. It doesn't mean high prestige either if the prestige is not accompanied by the right quality goods and services. Rather, the focus is on the customer's requirements and how the whole marketing mix meets those needs.

Honda is a firm that has been effective with value pricing. It has different marketing mixes for different target markets. From the $15,000 Fit to the $36,000 S2000 Roadster and $40,000 four-wheel drive Pilot, Honda offers high quality at reasonable prices. Among fast-food restaurants, Wendy's was one of the first to create a Dollar Menu. This has helped to give it a reputation for value pricing.

Companies that use value pricing deliver on their promises. They try to give the consumer pleasant surprises—like an unexpected service—because it increases value and builds customer loyalty. They return the price if the customer isn't completely satisfied. They avoid unrealistic price levels—prices that are high only because consumers already know the brand name. They build relationships so customers will come back time and again.

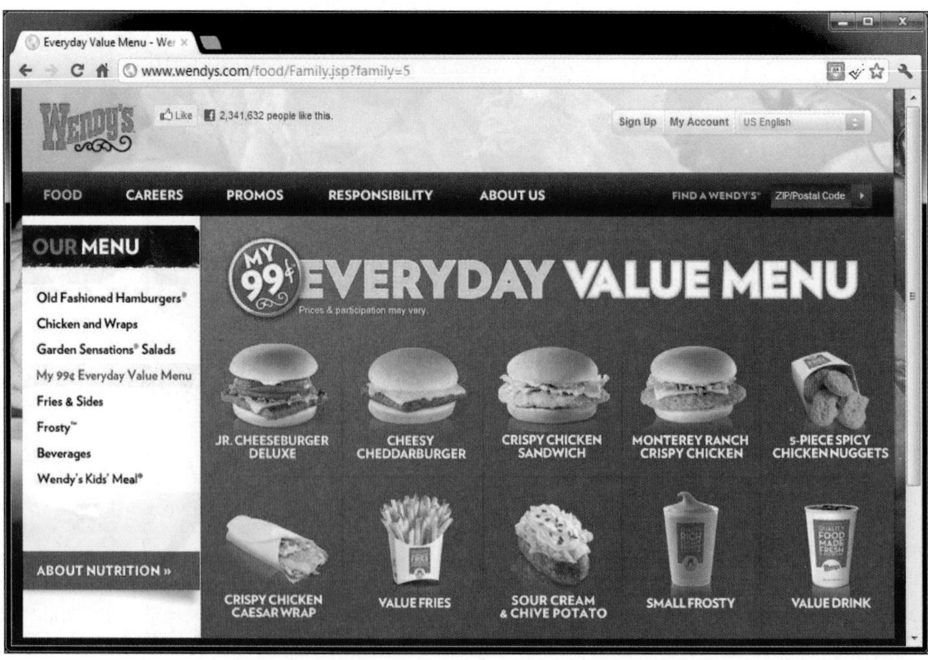

Wendy's $.99 Everyday Value Menu communicates value to its customers.

There are Price choices in most markets

Some marketing managers miss the advantages of value pricing. They've heard economists say that in perfect competition it's foolish to offer products above or below the market price. But most firms *don't* operate in perfect competition where what firms offer is exactly the same.

Most operate in monopolistic competition, where products and whole marketing mixes are *not* exactly the same. This means that there are pricing options. At one extreme, some firms are clearly above the market—they may even brag about it. Tiffany's is well known as one of the most expensive jewelry stores in the world. Other firms emphasize below-the-market prices in their marketing mixes. Prices offered by discounters and mass-merchandisers, such as Walmart and Tesco, illustrate this approach. They may even promote their pricing policy with catchy slogans like "guaranteed lowest prices."

Value pricers define the target market and the competition

In making price decisions and using value pricing, it is important to clearly define the *relevant target market* and *competitors* when making price comparisons.

Consider Walmart prices again from this view. Walmart may have lower prices on electronics products like flat-panel televisions, but it offers less expertise from the store's sales staff, less selection, and no help installing or setting up a new television. Walmart may appeal to budget-oriented shoppers who compare prices *and* value among different mass-merchandisers. But a specialty electronics store appeals to different customers and may not even be a direct competitor!

A producer of flat-panel televisions with this point of view may offer the specialty electronics store models that are not available to Walmart—to ensure that customers don't view price as the only difference between the two stores. Further, the specialty store needs to clearly communicate to its target market *how* it offers superior value. Walmart is certainly going to communicate that it offers low prices. If that's all customers hear, they will see no differences between retailers except for price. The specialty retailer must emphasize its expertise, selection, or the superior performance of its product line—so that target customers who value these differences know where to find them.

Meeting competitors' prices may be necessary

In a mature market there is downward pressure on both prices and profit margins. Moreover, differentiating the value a firm offers may not be easy when competitors can quickly copy new ideas. Extending our flat-panel example, if our speciality store is in a city with a number of similar stores with the same products, there may not be a way to convince consumers that one beats all of the others. In such circumstances there may be no real pricing choice other than to "meet the competition." With profit margins already thin, they would quickly disappear or turn into losses at a lower price. And a higher price would simply prompt competitors to promote their price advantage.[20]

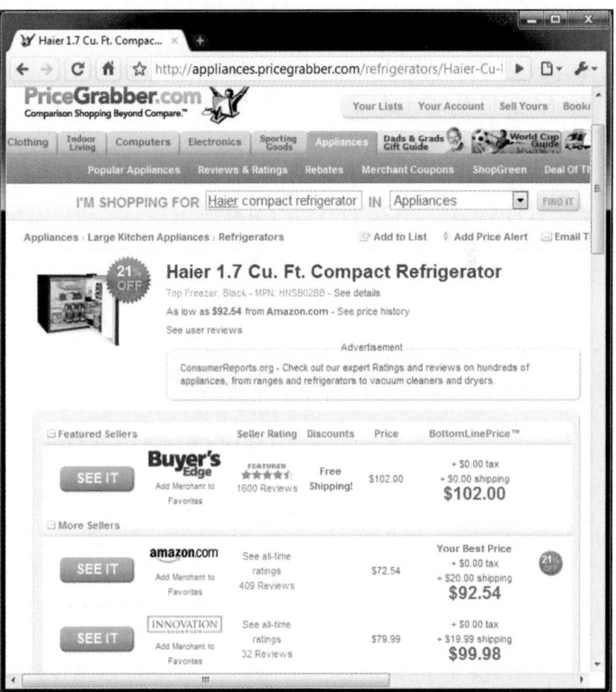

Consumers often use websites like PriceGrabber.com that search for the best prices on particular items. When it's easy for customers to compare prices, marketers must clearly communicate to the customer how the rest of the marketing mix is better and why it justifies a higher price.

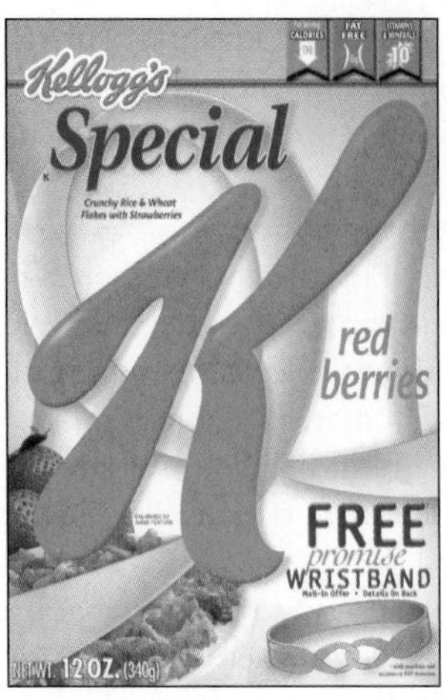

Even though competition can be intense, too many marketers give up too easily. They often can find a way to differentiate, even if it's something that competitors dismiss as less important. For example, Kellogg was facing soggy sales and tough competition in the dry cereal category. Dealer brands made price competition even tougher. However, when Kellogg added freeze-dried fruit to create Special K Red Berries, it attracted many customers away from competing brands. The berries did increase costs, but Kellogg's profits still improved. In Europe, where price sensitivity was greatest, Kellogg kept the price the same but reduced the size of the Red Berries box. In the United States, the size of the box is standard but the price was increased enough to provide profit margins. Even though General Mills later copied the idea, Kellogg had a head start and quickly came out with other fruit-added cereals. And both producers benefited by having a way to differentiate from the low-price store brands in their category.[21]

There may be little choice about Price in oligopoly situations. Pricing at the market—that is, meeting competition—may be the only sensible policy. To raise prices might lead to a large loss in sales, unless competitors adopt the higher price too. And cutting prices would probably lead to similar reductions by competitors—downward along an inelastic industry demand curve. This can only lead to a decrease in total revenue for the industry and probably for each firm. The major airlines faced these problems recently.

Value pricing fits with market-oriented strategy planning

There are times when the marketing manager's hands are tied and there is little that can be done to differentiate the marketing mix. However, most marketing managers do have choices—many choices. They can vary strategy decisions with respect to all of the marketing mix variables, not just Price, to offer target customers superior value. And when a marketer's hands are really tied, it's time to look for new opportunities that offer more promise.

Legality of Pricing Policies

LO 16.6

This chapter discusses the many pricing decisions that must be made. However, some pricing decisions are limited by government legislation. The first step to understanding pricing legislation is to know the thinking of legislators and the courts. Our focus will be on U.S. legislation but most countries have similar laws. Still, marketing managers may find that some countries have more restrictive laws. Intel was fined $1.45 billion by European regulators for price discounting practices that were used to keep competitors out of the market.[22]

Minimum prices are sometimes controlled

Unfair trade practice acts put a lower limit on prices, especially at the wholesale and retail levels. They have been passed in more than half the states in the United States. Selling below cost in these states is illegal. Wholesalers and retailers are usually required to take a certain minimum percentage markup over their merchandise-plus-transportation costs. The practical effect of these laws is to protect certain limited-line food retailers—such as dairy stores—from the kind of "ruinous" competition supermarkets might offer if they sold milk as a leader, offering it below cost for a long time.

The United States and most other countries control the minimum price of imported products with antidumping laws. **Dumping** is pricing a product sold in a foreign market below the cost of producing it or at a price lower than in its domestic market. These laws are usually designed to protect the country's domestic producers

A Brighter Way to Save

Compact fluorescent light (CFL) bulbs have quickly become a popular way for consumers to save money, energy, and planet Earth—if quickly means 35 years or so. General Electric (GE) invented the modern CFL in response to the 1973 oil crisis, but GE did not see CFL bulbs as a profitable opportunity and put the project on hold. A few years later its design leaked out and the first CFL bulbs came on the market in the 1980s. These early bulbs were bulky and didn't fit traditional light sockets; they also had an orange hue that made the light harsh. And in case customers were not bothered by these disadvantages, each bulb cost over $20. Needless to say, few consumers were beating down retailers' doors to buy CFLs.

Since then, the value equation has changed a lot. Current technology allows CFLs to screw into existing light fixtures—so consumers don't face extra costs and hassles to switch bulbs. The quality of the light is now very similar to that of the incandescent bulbs that CFL bulbs are designed to replace. Even so, consumers may still get sticker shock when they see the $3.00 price tag. That's about six times what they expect to pay for a traditional bulb. Yet, CFL bulbs are a better buy because they last 10 times longer. They also use a lot less electricity which can save a customer up to $40 on each bulb. Using less electricity also saves the planet; in one year each CFL bulb puts about 180 pounds less carbon dioxide emissions into the atmosphere.

There are still some drawbacks. Compared to incandescent bulbs, CFLs don't get to full brightness as quickly, don't dim as well, and contain small amounts of mercury—an environmental hazard that requires special handling. Yet most consumers who learn about the pros and cons of CFL bulbs see buying them as a no-brainer. Utility companies see them that way too. Because the bulbs reduce the overall demand for electricity, there's less need to build expensive new power plants. In light of that, some utilities subsidize half of the price that consumers pay for CFLs.

Environmentalists around the world salute efforts like these and are also pressing for new laws to support CFLs, limit incandescents, or spur new alternatives. More than a dozen countries, including the United States, Finland, and Pakistan, have passed such laws. U.S. regulations call for a phase out of incandescents between 2012 and 2020, but 20 percent of all incandescents have already been replaced with CFLs—and that percentage is growing rapidly as more people understand the value they get when they purchase them. Looking to the future, the U.S. Department of Energy ran a competition to spur lighting manufacturers to develop even better lighting solutions. Philips won the $10 million "L Prize" by developing a new bulb based on LED (light emitting diode) technology. The new bulb consumes just 10 watts of energy and produces more light than a standard 60 watt bulb—and they say will last 27.4 years if used 3 hours a day. At $60 each these new bulbs have not flown off store shelves. As economies of scale kick in, prices should fall and the value of LED bulbs will increase—making the new bulbs more convenient and better for the planet, too.[23]

and jobs. U.S. steelmakers have accused China of dumping and encouraged the U.S. government to take action.

Regulators can set prices

In some industries, often where there is little competition, a state government may control prices. For example, many utilities—like electric, gas, and cable television—have little or no competition to keep prices in check so states will usually have a board that governs the prices they charge. To assure all citizens have access to affordable auto insurance, most states control auto insurance rates as well. Sometimes a national government will impose temporary price controls, usually in an effort to control inflation. In countries with market-directed economies, these types of price controls are selective. Still, to maintain competition, there are several important regulations in the pricing area.

You can't lie about prices

Phony list prices are prices customers are shown to suggest that the price has been discounted from list. Some customers seem more interested in the supposed discount than in the actual price. Most businesses, trade associations, and government agencies consider the use of phony list prices unethical. In the United States, the FTC tries to stop such pricing—using the **Wheeler Lea Amendment**, which bans "unfair or deceptive acts in commerce."[24]

A few years ago, some electronics retailers were criticized on these grounds. They'd advertise a $300 discount on a computer when the customer signed up for an Internet service provider, but it might not be clear to the consumer that a three-year commitment—costing over $700—was required.

Price fixing is illegal—you can go to jail

Difficulties with pricing—and violations of pricing legislation—usually occur when competing marketing mixes are quite similar. When the success of an entire marketing strategy depends on price, there is pressure (and temptation) to make agreements with competitors (conspire). And **price fixing**—competitors getting together to raise, lower, or stabilize prices—is common and relatively easy. *But it is also completely illegal in the United States.* It is considered "conspiracy" under the Sherman Act and the Federal Trade Commission Act. To discourage price fixing, both companies and individual managers are held responsible. In a recent case, an executive at Archer Daniels Midland (ADM) Company was sentenced to three years in jail and the company was fined $100 million.[25]

Different countries have different rules concerning price fixing, and this has created problems in international trade. Japan, for example, allows price fixing, especially if it strengthens the position of Japanese producers in world markets.

Producers may set minimum retail prices

Manufacturers usually suggest a retail list price and then leave it up to retailers to decide what to charge in their local markets. In fact, until recently the courts prohibited manufacturers from imposing a minimum price at which their goods could be sold. This was viewed as a form of price fixing and a violation of the Sherman Antitrust Act. However, the ruling in a recent Supreme Court case changes that. The case involved Leegin Creative Leather Products and Kay's Kloset, a retailer that had been discounting Leegin's handbags. To prevent the discounting, Leegin stopped selling to Kay's Kloset. Kay's Kloset brought suit and said that retailers should be free to set their own prices—which, in turn, would keep prices lower for consumers. However, Leegin argued that its strategy focused on building the reputation of its brand with excellent service and advertising. Its retailers coudn't provide that level of service and promotion if they didn't charge a price that offered a sufficient profit margin. Leegin also argued that if one retailer ignored the strategy and cut its price on Leegin products, other retailers would follow suit—and soon the retailers wouldn't be able to provide the backing Leegin bags needed to compete. The court ruling, which supported Leegin, marks an important change because it gives manufacturers more power to control retail pricing.[26]

U.S. antimonopoly laws ban price discrimination unless . . .

Price level and price flexibility policies can lead to price discrimination. The **Robinson-Patman Act** (of 1936) makes illegal any **price discrimination**—selling the same products to different buyers at different prices—*if it injures competition.* The law does permit some price differences—but they must be based on (1) cost differences or (2) the need to meet competition. Both buyers and sellers are considered guilty if they know they're entering into discriminatory agreements.

What does "like grade and quality" mean?

Firms in businesses as varied as transportation services, book publishing, and auto parts have been charged with violations of the Robinson-Patman Act in recent, nationally publicized cases. Competitors who have been injured by a violation of the law have incentive to go to court because they can receive a settlement that is three times larger than the damage suffered.

The Robinson-Patman Act allows a marketing manager to charge different prices for similar products if they are *not* of "like grade and quality." But the FTC says that if the physical characteristics of a product are similar, then they are of like grade and quality. A landmark U.S. Supreme Court ruling against the Borden Company upheld the FTC's view that a well-known label *alone* does not make a product different from one with an unknown label. The company agreed that the canned milk it sold at different prices under different labels was basically the same.

But the FTC's victory in the Borden case was not complete. The U.S. Court of Appeals found no evidence of injury to competition and further noted that there could be no injury unless Borden's price differential exceeded the "recognized consumer appeal of the Borden label." How to measure "consumer appeal" was not spelled out, so producers who want to sell several brands—or dealer brands at lower prices than their main brand—probably should offer physical differences, and differences that are really useful.[27]

Can cost analysis justify price differences?

The Robinson-Patman Act allows price differences if there are cost differences—say, for larger quantity shipments or because intermediaries take over some of the physical distribution functions. But justifying cost differences is a difficult job. And the justification must be developed *before* different prices are set. The seller can't wait until a competitor, disgruntled customer, or the FTC brings a charge. At that point, it's too late.[28]

Can you legally meet price cuts?

Under the Robinson-Patman Act, meeting a competitor's price is permitted as a defense in price discrimination cases. A major objective of antimonopoly laws is to protect competition, not competitors. And "meeting competition in good faith" still seems to be legal.

Special promotion allowances might not be allowed

Some firms violate the Robinson-Patman Act by providing push money, advertising allowances, and other promotion aids to some customers and not others. The act prohibits such special allowances, *unless they are made available to all customers on "proportionately equal" terms.*[29]

How to avoid discriminating

Because price discrimination laws are complicated and penalties for violations heavy, many business managers follow the safest course by offering few or no quantity discounts and the same cost-based prices to *all* customers. This is *too* conservative a reaction. But when firms consider price differences, they may need a lawyer involved in the discussion!

CONCLUSION

The Price variable offers an alert marketing manager many possibilities for varying marketing mixes. This chapter began by discussing how a firm's pricing objectives may be oriented toward profit, sales, or maintaining the status quo. Clear pricing objectives help in making decisions about the firm's important pricing policies.

This chapter discussed the pros and cons of flexible pricing and some of the approaches that firms use to implement it. It also considered the initial price level decision—skim the cream or penetration—that the marketing manager must make with new products at the introductory stage of their life cycle. We also discussed a variety of ways that marketing managers adjust the basic list price under different circumstances—by using different types of discounts, allowances, and transportation costs. These policies need to be clearly defined by the marketing manager.

The chapter described how the different components of price are traded off against the other marketing mix variables to create something of value for the customer. We also discussed value pricing and how to create a competitive advantage by offering customers superior value—which isn't the same as just offering lower and lower prices.

Pricing comes under greater scrutiny from the law than some other marketing mix variables. So it is important to understand key legal constraints that influence pricing decisions.

This chapter provided a foundation for understanding the objectives and policies that guide pricing decisions. This information provides input into the price setting process, which we describe in greater detail in the following chapter when we look at both cost- and demand-oriented approaches to pricing.

KEY TERMS

LO 16.7

price, *421*
target return objective, *423*
profit maximization objective, *424*
sales-oriented objective, *424*
status quo objectives, *425*
nonprice competition, *425*
administered prices, *425*
one-price policy, *426*
flexible-price policy, *426*
skimming price policy, *428*
penetration pricing policy, *429*
introductory price dealing, *430*
basic list prices, *432*
discounts, *432*
quantity discounts, *432*
cumulative quantity discounts, *432*
noncumulative quantity discounts, *432*
seasonal discounts, *432*
net, *433*
cash discounts, *433*
2/10, net 30, *433*
trade (functional) discount, *434*
sale price, *434*
everyday low pricing, *434*
allowances, *434*
advertising allowances, *434*
stocking allowances, *435*
push money (or prize money) allowances, *437*
trade-in allowance, *435*
rebates, *436*
F.O.B, *437*
zone pricing, *437*
uniform delivered pricing, *437*
freight-absorption pricing, *438*
value pricing, *438*
unfair trade practice acts, *440*
dumping, *440*
phony list prices, *441*
Wheeler Lea Amendment, *441*
price fixing, *442*
Robinson-Patman Act, *442*
price discrimination, *442*

QUESTIONS AND PROBLEMS

1. Identify the strategy decisions a marketing manager must make in the Price area. Illustrate your answer for a local retailer.
2. How should the acceptance of a profit-oriented, a sales-oriented, or a status quo–oriented pricing objective affect the development of a company's marketing strategy? Illustrate for each.
3. Distinguish between one-price and flexible-price policies. Which is most appropriate for a hardware store? Why?
4. What pricing objective(*s*) is a skimming pricing policy most likely implementing? Is the same true for a penetration pricing policy? Which policy is probably most appropriate for each of the following products: (*a*) a new type of home lawn-sprinkling system, (*b*) a skin patch drug to help smokers quit, (*c*) a DVD of a best-selling movie, and (*d*) a new children's toy?
5. How would differences in exchange rates between different countries affect a firm's decisions concerning the use of flexible-price policies in different foreign markets?
6. Are seasonal discounts appropriate in agricultural businesses (which are certainly seasonal)?
7. What are the effective annual interest rates for the following cash discount terms: (*a*) 1/10, net 20; (*b*) 1/5, net 10; and (*c*) net 25?
8. Why would a manufacturer offer a rebate instead of lowering the suggested list price?
9. How can a marketing manager change a firm's F.O.B. terms to make an otherwise competitive marketing mix more attractive?
10. What type of geographic pricing policy is most appropriate for the following products (specify any assumptions necessary to obtain a definite answer): (*a*) a chemical by-product, (*b*) nationally advertised candy bars, (*c*) rebuilt auto parts, and (*d*) tricycles?
11. How would a ban on freight absorption (that is, requiring F.O.B. factory pricing) affect a producer with substantial economies of scale in production?
12. Give an example of a marketing mix that has a high price level but that you see as a good value. Briefly explain what makes it a good value.
13. Think about a business from which you regularly make purchases even though there are competing firms with similar prices. Explain what the firm offers that improves value and keeps you coming back.
14. Cite two examples of continuously selling above the market price. Describe the situations.
15. Explain the types of competitive situations that might lead to a meeting-competition pricing policy.
16. Would consumers be better off if all nations dropped their antidumping laws? Explain your thinking.
17. How would our marketing system change if manufacturers were required to set fixed prices on *all* products sold at retail and *all* retailers were required to use these prices? Would a manufacturer's marketing mix be easier to develop? What kind of an operation would retailing be in this situation? Would consumers receive more or less service?
18. Is price discrimination involved if a large oil company sells gasoline to taxicab associations for resale to individual taxicab operators for 2½ cents a gallon less than the price charged to retail service stations? What happens if the cab associations resell gasoline not only to taxicab operators but also to the general public?

CREATING MARKETING PLANS

The Marketing Plan Coach software on the text website includes a sample marketing plan for Hillside Veterinary Clinic. Look through the "Marketing Strategy" section.

a. A veterinary clinic located in another town gives its customers a 10 percent discount on their next vet bill if they refer a new pet owner to the clinic. Do you think that this would be a good idea for Hillside? Does it fit with Hillside's strategy?
b. The same clinic offered customers a sort of cumulative discount—an end-of-year refund if their total spending at the clinic exceeded a certain level. That clinic sees it as a way of being nice to people whose pets have had a lot of problems. Do you think that this is a good idea for Hillside? Why or why not?

SUGGESTED CASES

13. AAA Office World   25. Long Beach Plastics

COMPUTER-AIDED PROBLEM

16. CASH DISCOUNTS

Joe Tulkin owns Tulkin Wholesale Co. He sells paper, tape, file folders, and other office supplies to about 120 retailers in nearby cities. His average retailer-customer spends about $900 a month. When Tulkin started business in 1991, competing wholesalers were giving retailers invoice terms of 3/10, net 30. Tulkin never gave the issue much thought—he just used the same invoice terms when he billed customers. At that time, about half of his customers took the discount. Recently, he noticed a change in the way his customers were paying their bills. Checking his records, he found that 90 percent of the retailers were taking the cash discount. With so many retailers taking the cash discount, it seems to have become a price reduction. In addition, Tulkin learned that other wholesalers were changing their invoice terms.

Tulkin decides he should rethink his invoice terms. He knows he could change the percent rate on the cash discount, the number of days the discount is offered, or the number of days before the face amount is due. Changing any of these, or any combination, will change the interest rate at which a buyer is, in effect, borrowing money if he does not take the discount. Tulkin decides that it will be easier to evaluate the effect of different invoice terms if he sets up a spreadsheet to let him change the terms and quickly see the effective interest rate for each change.

a. With 90 percent of Tulkin's customers now taking the discount, what is the total monthly cash discount amount?
b. If Tulkin changes his invoice terms to 1/5, net 20, what interest rate is each buyer paying by not taking the cash discount? With these terms, would fewer buyers be likely to take the discount? Why?
c. Tulkin thinks 10 customers will switch to other wholesalers if he changes his invoice terms to 2/10, net 30, while 60 percent of the remaining customers will take the discount. What interest rate does a buyer pay by not taking this cash discount? For this situation, what will the total gross sales (total invoice) amount be? The total cash discount? The total net sales receipts after the total cash discount? Compare Tulkin's current situation with what will happen if he changes his invoice terms to 2/10, net 30.

17

CHAPTER SEVENTEEN

Price Setting in the Business World

Not long ago, Sony's strategy for its Bravia line of large-screen, flat-panel televisions seemed clear-cut. As with its other product lines, Sony's new-product teams coupled cutting-edge technology with stylish designs to give consumers a superior home entertainment experience. For each popular size of TV, Sony offered two or three models at different price points. The low-end model was a basic TV that was similar to other brands on the market, but with a few special features and a price premium that reflected Sony's reputation for reliability and picture clarity. Its strength, though, was at the high end, where it offered higher screen resolution with more contrast, more connections for different types of accessory equipment, and displays with richer color. Sony also trained retail salespeople to demonstrate why a Sony justified a higher price. While Sony's prices were often higher than competitors, retailers liked the high profit margins on Sony products, and Sony's promotion and brand name helped bring in customers.

For the past few years, however, Sony has scrambled to adjust its strategy. Let's look at how this market has evolved and how it has influenced Sony's strategy and pricing.

In 2001, the average price of flat-panel TVs was about $10,000. Demand was limited, so flat screens were distributed mainly by commercial audio-video suppliers who sold them to business customers. As prices came down over the next few years, consumer demand grew and Sony started to distribute its flat panels through electronics chains such as Best Buy and Circuit City. That helped to bring down selling costs, but an even larger factor in the rapid drop in prices was that economies of scale in production began to kick in.

Suppliers of LCD panels invested billions of dollars in new factories to make panels large enough for TVs. The LCD suppliers wanted to protect those investments and were concerned that competition and excess capacity would drive down prices too fast. So they met in secret to discuss and control prices and were later found guilty of price fixing. Even those efforts didn't keep prices of LCD panels from dropping as the suppliers tried to stimulate demand, though they probably fell slower than might have otherwise been expected in a perfectly competitive market.

By 2004, a 32-inch high-definition Sony LCD was about $3,999. At that price the size of the consumer market was limited, but retailers' profits looked good with the 30 percent margins they earned on large LCD TVs. Sony was holding its own against its traditional competitors—firms like Sharp and Panasonic.

Over the next couple of years, Sony suddenly experienced competition from almost 100 new upstart TV makers. Vizio has proved to be one of the most successful. It handled design and marketing itself, but left production to contract manufacturers in China. As a result, its overhead costs were less than 1 percent of sales; Sony's overhead costs were of 10 to 20 percent of sales. To gain market share, Vizio settled for slim profit margins of just 2 percent, much lower than Sony wanted. Vizio didn't try to offer a TV that had the most advanced video standards or technology. Rather it just tried to have a TV in its product line at each of the most popular sizes. This strategy gave Vizio a significant price advantage on the retail floor and helped it get distribution in discount stores like Walmart and Costco. Vizio did virtually no advertising. The promotion job was left to retailers who found they could easily draw in customers with Vizio's low prices.

Vizio's sales grew rapidly, but most of the upstart firms that offered undifferentiated no-name brands failed to get distribution through traditional electronics retailers and suffered a different fate. They struggled to get distribution. While these TVs were low-priced, few saw them as a good value. Even so, the focus on rock-bottom prices started a price war. The war increased unit sales, but it cut into retail margins and many retailers understandably didn't want to support products where they made few profits.

Retailers pressured TV makers, like Sony, to cut prices too. After the price war, the price of LCD flat screens continued to tumble and dropped 40 percent in less than a year. As Sony's premium prices disappeared, its profits were ravaged. Sony's strategy called for a high price, but there was simply too much supply relative to demand.

The ongoing focus on price in this market threatens to turn LCD TVs into a commodity. While Sony is cutting costs by better managing its inventory and supply chain, it continues to try to meaningfully differentiate its product line. To maintain its position as an innovator, Sony keeps adding new features it believes consumers want. For example, Sony believes that 3D TV may represent a new wave, but customer adoption has been slow because of limited availability of 3D content. Sony's new models fit with the growing digital lifestyles of its customers; Internet widgets connect its Bravia HDTVs with YouTube, Pandora, Flickr, and other online services. Sony was also the first manufacturer to run Google's Internet TV platform, which allows users to search the web for online videos to play on their TV screen.

Communicating the benefits of all these new features has been a challenge for Sony and others in this market. Sony continues to be attacked from the low end by firms like Vizio and from the high end by competitors like Samsung. Sony must keep adapting its whole marketing strategy to effectively communicate and deliver value to its target customers.[1]

Learning Objectives

Ultimately, the price that a firm charges must cover the costs of the whole marketing mix or the firm will not make a profit. So it's important for marketing managers to understand costs and how they relate to pricing. On the other hand, it doesn't make sense to set prices based just on costs because customers won't buy a product if they don't think that it represents a good value for their money. So setting prices is not an easy task and marketing managers must carefully balance costs, customer price sensitivity, and other factors. This chapter will help you better understand these issues and how to evaluate them in setting prices.

When you finish this chapter you should be able to:

1 understand how most wholesalers and retailers set their prices by using markups.

2 understand why turnover is so important in pricing.

3 understand the advantages and disadvantages of average-cost pricing.

4 know how to use break-even analysis to evaluate possible prices.

5 understand the advantages of marginal analysis and how to use it for price setting.

6 understand the various factors that influence customer price sensitivity.

7 know the many ways that price setters use demand estimates in their pricing.

8 understand how bid pricing and negotiated prices work.

9 understand important new terms (shown in red).

Price Setting Is a Key Strategy Decision

In Chapter 16 we discussed the idea that pricing objectives and policies should guide pricing decisions. We described different dimensions of the pricing decision and how they combine to create value for customers. This chapter builds on those concepts—all of which influence price setting—and gives you additional frameworks that will help you understand how marketing managers set prices. See Exhibit 17-1.

There are many ways to set prices. But, for simplicity, they can be reduced to two basic approaches—*cost-oriented* and *demand-oriented* price setting. We will discuss cost-oriented approaches first because they are most common. Also, understanding the problems of relying on a cost-oriented approach shows why a marketing manager must consider customer demand and price sensitivity to make good Price decisions. We conclude the chapter with a discussion of some special price setting issues—pricing full lines of products, bid pricing, and negotiated pricing.

Exhibit 17–1 Price Setting and Strategy Planning

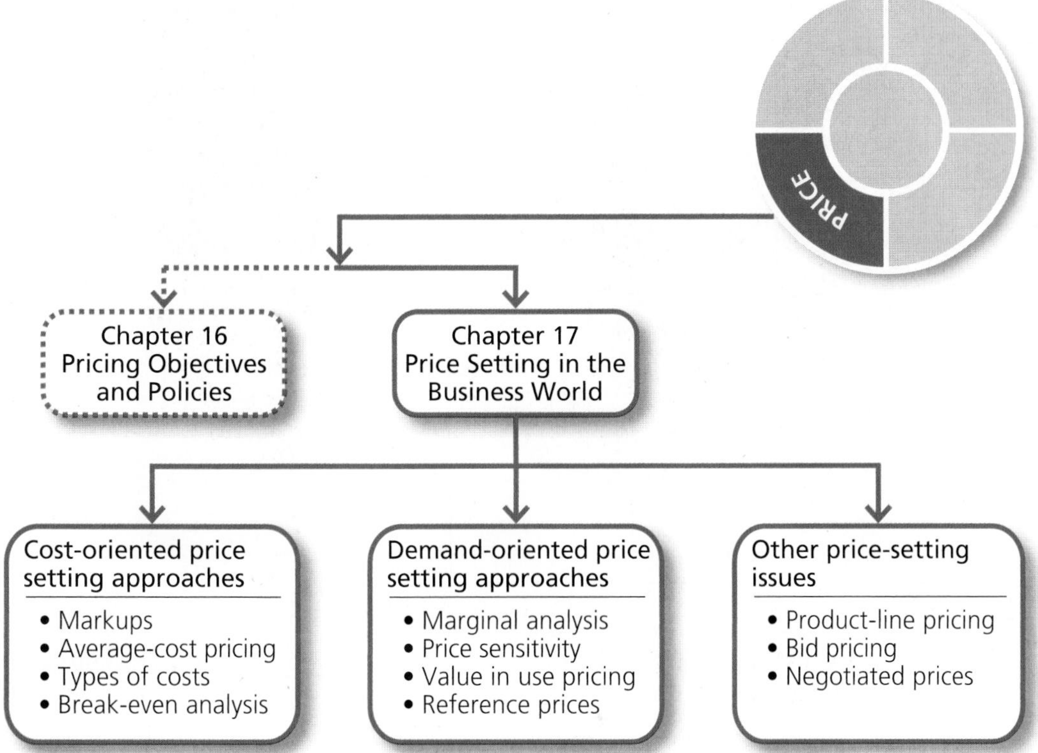

Some Firms Just Use Markups

LO 17.1

Markups guide pricing by intermediaries

Some firms, including most retailers and wholesalers, set prices by using a **markup**—a dollar amount added to the cost of products to get the selling price. For example, suppose that a CVS drugstore buys a bottle of Pert Plus shampoo and conditioner for $2.40. To make a profit, the drugstore obviously must sell Pert Plus for more than $2.40. If it adds $1.20 to cover operating expenses and provide a profit, we say that the store is marking up the item $1.20.

Markups, however, usually are stated as percentages rather than dollar amounts. And this is where confusion sometimes arises. Is a markup of $1.20 on a cost of $2.40 a markup of 50 percent? Or should the markup be figured as a percentage of the selling price—$3.60—and therefore be 33⅓ percent? A clear definition is necessary.

Markup percent is based on selling price—a convenient rule

Unless otherwise stated, **markup (percent)** means percentage of selling price that is added to the cost to get the selling price. So the $1.20 markup on the $3.60 selling price is a markup of 33⅓ percent. Markups are related to selling price for convenience.

There's nothing wrong with the idea of markup on cost. However, to avoid confusion, it's important to state clearly which markup percent you're using.

A manager may want to change a markup on selling price to one based on cost, or vice versa. The calculations used to do this are simple. (See the section on markup conversion in Appendix B on marketing arithmetic. The appendixes follow Chapter 20.)[2]

Many use a standard markup percent

Many intermediaries select a standard markup percent and then apply it to all their products. This makes pricing easier. When you think of the large number of items the average retailer and wholesaler carry—and the small sales volume of any one item—this approach may make sense. Spending the time to find the best price to charge on every item in stock (day to day or week to week) might not pay.

Moreover, different companies in the same line of business often use the same markup percent. There is a reason for this: Their operating expenses are usually similar. So they see

Many retailers have a standard markup on products like mouthwash and shampoo.

a standard markup as acceptable as long as it's large enough to cover the firm's operating expenses and provide a reasonable profit.

Markups are related to gross margins

How does a manager decide on a standard markup in the first place? A standard markup is often set close to the firm's *gross margin.* Managers regularly see gross margins on their operating (profit and loss) statements. The gross margin is the amount left—after subtracting the cost of sales (cost of goods sold) from net sales—to cover the expenses of selling products and operating the business. (See Appendix B on marketing arithmetic if you are unfamiliar with these ideas.) Our CVS manager knows that there won't be any profit if the gross margin is not large enough. For this reason, CVS might accept a markup percent on Pert Plus that is close to the store's usual gross margin percent.

Smart producers pay attention to the gross margins and standard markups of intermediaries in their channel. They usually allow discounts similar to the standard markups these intermediaries expect.

Markup chain may be used in channel pricing

Different firms in a channel often use different markups. A **markup chain**—the sequence of markups firms use at different levels in a channel—determines the price structure in the whole channel. The markup is figured on the *selling price* at each level of the channel.

For example, Black & Decker's selling price for a cordless electric drill becomes the cost the Ace Hardware wholesaler pays. The wholesaler's selling price becomes the hardware retailer's cost. And this cost plus a retail markup becomes the retail selling price. Each markup should cover the costs of running the business and leave a profit.

Exhibit 17-2 illustrates the markup chain for a cordless electric drill at each level of the channel system. The production (factory) cost of the drill is $43.20. In this case, the producer takes a 10 percent markup and sells the product for $48. The markup is 10 percent of $48 or $4.80. The producer's selling price now becomes the wholesaler's cost—$48. If the wholesaler is used to taking a 20 percent markup on selling price, the markup is $12—and the wholesaler's selling price becomes $60. The $60 now becomes the cost for the hardware retailer. And a retailer who is used to a 40 percent markup adds $40, and the retail selling price becomes $100.

Exhibit 17–2 Example of a Markup Chain and Channel Pricing

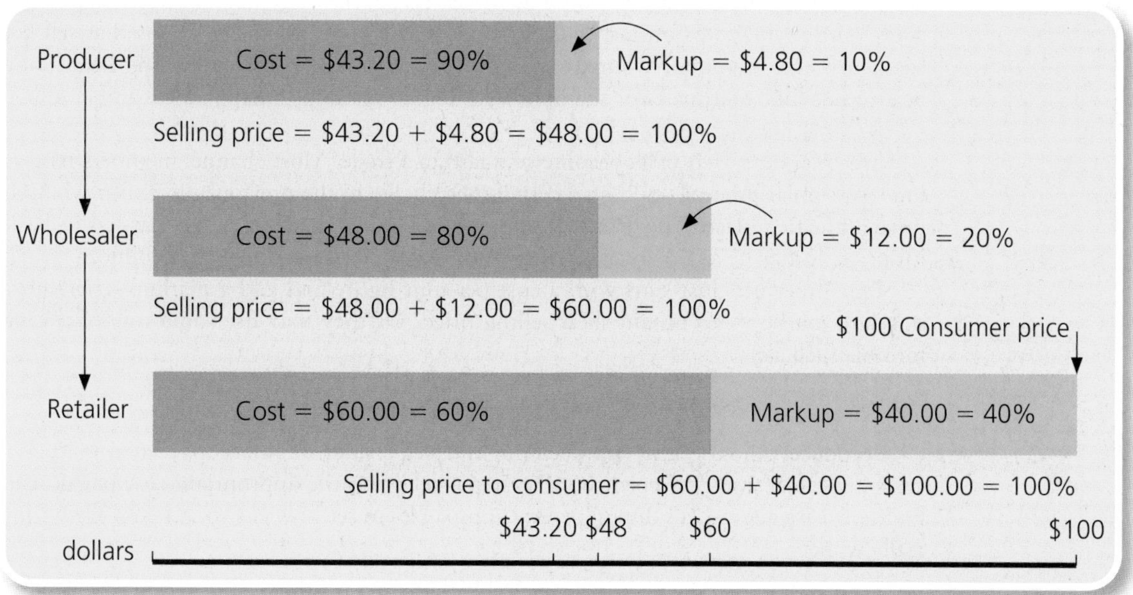

High markups don't always mean big profits

Some people, including many conventional retailers, think high markups mean big profits. Often this isn't true. A high markup may result in a price that's too high—a price at which few customers will buy. You can't earn much if you don't sell much, no matter how high your markup on a single item. So high markups may lead to low profits.

Lower markups can speed turnover and the stockturn rate

LO 17.2

Some retailers and wholesalers, however, try to speed turnover to increase profit—even if this means reducing their markups. They realize that a business runs up costs over time. If they can sell a much greater amount in the same time period, they may be able to take a lower markup and still earn higher profits at the end of the period.

An important idea here is the **stockturn rate**—the number of times the average inventory is sold in a year. Various methods of figuring stockturn rates can be used (see the section "Computing the Stockturn Rate" in Appendix B). A low stockturn rate may be bad for profits.

LOWER INVENTORY. INCREASED TURNS.
GREATER PROFITS.
• Shipment within 24 hours
• Industry-high 99%+ fill rate
• Error-free transactions
• No restocking fees
• No minimum orders
Guaranteed.
LEGEND VALVE
Downstream Thinking.

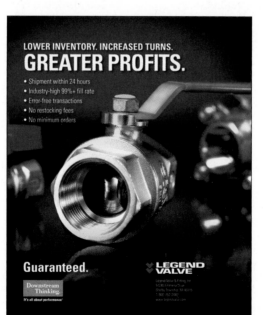

Legend Valve's 24-hour delivery and no minimum order policy allow wholesalers to carry less inventory and lower costs. Along with a higher stockturn rate, the wholesalers can make greater profits on Legend's product line.

At the very least, a low stockturn increases inventory carrying cost and ties up working capital. If a firm with a stockturn of 1 (once per year) sells products that cost it $100,000, it has that much tied up in inventory all the time. But a stockturn of 5 requires only $20,000 worth of inventory ($100,000 cost ÷ 5 turnovers a year). If annual inventory carrying cost is about 20 percent of the inventory value, that reduces costs by $16,000 a year. That's a big difference on $100,000 in sales!

Whether a stockturn rate is high or low depends on the industry and the product involved. An electrical parts wholesaler may expect an annual rate of 2—while a supermarket might expect 8 stockturns on average but 20 stockturns for soaps and 70 stockturns for fresh fruits and vegetables.

Mass-merchandisers run in fast company

Although some intermediaries use the same standard markup percent on all their products, this policy ignores the importance of fast turnover. Mass-merchandisers know this. They put low markups on fast-selling items and higher markups on items that sell less frequently. For example, Walmart may put a small markup on fast-selling health and beauty aids (like toothpaste or shampoo) but higher markups on appliances and clothing.

Where does the markup chain start?

Some markups eventually become standard in a trade. Most channel members tend to follow a similar process—adding a certain percentage to the previous price. But who sets price in the first place? The firm that brands a product is usually the one that sets its basic list price. It may be a large retailer, a large wholesaler, or most often, the producer.

Some producers just start with a cost per unit figure and add a markup—perhaps a standard markup—to obtain their selling price. Or they may use some rule-of-thumb formula such as:

$$\text{Selling price} = \text{Average production cost per unit} \times 3$$

A producer who uses this approach might develop rules and markups related to its own costs and objectives. Yet even the first step—selecting the appropriate cost per unit to build on—isn't easy. Let's discuss several approaches to see how cost-oriented price setting really works.

Average-Cost Pricing Is Common and Can Be Dangerous

LO 17.3

Average-cost pricing means adding a reasonable markup to the average cost of a product. A manager usually finds the average cost per unit by studying past records. Dividing the total cost for the last year by all the units produced and sold in that period gives an estimate of the average cost per unit for the next year. If the cost was $32,000 for all labor and materials and $30,000 for fixed overhead expenses—such as selling expenses, rent, and manager salaries—then the total cost is $62,000. See Exhibit 17-3A. If the company produced 40,000 items in that time period, the average cost is $62,000 divided by 40,000 units, or $1.55 per unit. To get the price, the producer decides how much profit per unit

Exhibit 17–3 Results of Average-Cost Pricing

A. Calculation of Planned Profit if 40,000 Items Are Sold		B. Calculation of Actual Profit if Only 20,000 Items Are Sold	
Calculation of Costs:		Calculation of Costs:	
Fixed overhead expenses	$30,000	Fixed overhead expenses	$30,000
Labor and materials ($.80 a unit)	32,000	Labor and materials ($.80 a unit)	16,000
Total costs	$62,000	Total costs	$46,000
"Planned" profit	18,000		
Total costs and planned profit	$80,000		
Calculation of Profit (or Loss):		Calculation of Profit (or Loss):	
Actual unit sales × price ($2.00*)	$80,000	Actual unit sales price × ($2.00*)	$40,000
Minus: total costs	62,000	Minus: total costs	46,000
Profit (loss)	$18,000	Profit (loss)	($6,000)
Result:		Result:	
Planned profit of $18,000 is earned if 40,000 items are sold at $2.00 each.		Planned profit of $18,000 is not earned. Instead, $6,000 loss results if 20,000 items are sold at $2.00 each.	

*Calculation of "reasonable" price: $\frac{\text{Expected total costs and planned profit}}{\text{Planned number of items to be sold}} = \frac{\$80{,}000}{40{,}000} = \$2.00$

to add to the average cost per unit. If the company considers 45 cents a reasonable profit for each unit, it sets the new price at $2.00. Exhibit 17-3A shows that this approach produces the desired profit if the company sells 40,000 units.

It does not make allowances for cost variations as output changes

It's always a useful input to pricing decisions to understand how costs operate at different levels of output. Further, average-cost pricing is simple. But it can also be dangerous. It's easy to lose money with average-cost pricing. To see why, let's follow this example further.

First, remember that the average price of $2.00 per unit was based on output of 40,000 units. But if the firm is only able to produce and sell 20,000 units in the next year, it may be in trouble. See Exhibit 17-3B. Twenty thousand units sold at $2.00 each ($1.55 cost plus 45 cents for expected profit) yield a total revenue of only $40,000. The overhead is still fixed at $30,000, and the variable material and labor cost drops by half to $16,000—for a total cost of $46,000. This means a loss of $6,000, or 30 cents a unit. The method that was supposed to allow a profit of 45 cents a unit actually causes a loss of 30 cents a unit!

When developing a new product, software companies and online services like GoToMyPC have high fixed overhead expenses relative to the variable cost for each additional user. This cost structure can make average-cost pricing especially dangerous.

The basic problem with the average-cost approach is that it doesn't consider cost variations at different levels of output. In a typical situation, costs are high with low output, and then economies of scale set in—the average cost per unit drops as the quantity produced increases. This is why mass production and mass distribution often make sense. It's also why it's important to develop a better understanding of the different types of costs a marketing manager should consider when setting a price.

Marketing Managers Must Consider Various Kinds of Costs

LO 17.4

Average-cost pricing may lead to losses because there are a variety of costs—and each changes in a *different* way as output changes. Any pricing method that uses cost must consider these changes. To understand why, we need to define six types of cost.

There are three kinds of total cost

1. **Total fixed cost** is the sum of those costs that are fixed in total—no matter how much is produced. Among these fixed costs are rent, depreciation, managers' salaries, property taxes, and insurance. Such costs stay the same even if production stops temporarily.
2. **Total variable cost**, on the other hand, is the sum of those changing expenses that are closely related to output—expenses for parts, wages, packaging materials, outgoing freight, and sales commissions.

At zero output, total variable cost is zero. As output increases, so do variable costs. If Levi's doubles its output of jeans in a year, its total cost for denim cloth also (roughly) doubles.

3. **Total cost** is the sum of total fixed and total variable costs. Changes in total cost depend on variations in total variable cost, since total fixed cost stays the same.

Exhibit 17–4 Cost Structure of a Firm

Quantity (Q)	Total Fixed Costs (TFC)	Average Fixed Costs (AFC)	Average Variable Costs (AVC)	Total Variable Costs (TVC)	Total Cost (TC)	Average Cost (AC)
0	$30,000	—	—	—	$ 30,000	—
10,000	30,000	$3.00	$0.80	$ 8,000	38,000	$3.80
20,000	30,000	1.50	0.80	16,000	46,000	2.30
30,000	30,000	1.00	0.80	24,000	54,000	1.80
40,000	**30,000**	**0.75**	**0.80**	**32,000**	**62,000**	**1.55**
50,000	30,000	0.60	0.80	40,000	70,000	1.40
60,000	30,000	0.50	0.80	48,000	78,000	1.30
70,000	30,000	0.43	0.80	56,000	86,000	1.23
80,000	30,000	0.38	0.80	64,000	94,000	1.18
90,000	30,000	0.33	0.80	72,000	102,000	1.13
100,000	30,000	0.30	0.80	80,000	110,000	1.10

$0.30 \text{(AFC)} = \frac{30{,}000 \text{ (TFC)}}{100{,}000 \text{ (Q)}}$

100,000 (Q)
×0.80 (AVC)
80,000 (TVC)

30,000 (TFC)
+80,000 (TVC)
110,000 (TC)

$1.10 \text{ (AC)} = \frac{110{,}000 \text{ (TC)}}{100{,}000 \text{ (Q)}}$

There are three kinds of average cost

The pricing manager usually is more interested in cost per unit than total cost because prices are usually quoted per unit.

1. **Average cost (per unit)** is obtained by dividing total cost by the related quantity (that is, the total quantity that causes the total cost).
2. **Average fixed cost (per unit)** is obtained by dividing total fixed cost by the related quantity.
3. **Average variable cost (per unit)** is obtained by dividing total variable cost by the related quantity.

An example shows cost relations

A good way to get a feel for these different types of costs is to extend our average-cost pricing example (Exhibit 17-3A). Exhibit 17-4 shows the six types of cost and how they vary at different levels of output. The line for 40,000 units is highlighted because that was the expected level of sales in our average-cost pricing example. For simplicity, we assume that average variable cost is the same for each unit. Notice, however, that total variable cost increases when quantity increases.

Exhibit 17-5 shows the three average cost curves from Exhibit 17-4. Notice that average fixed cost goes down steadily as the quantity increases. Although the average variable cost remains the same, average cost decreases continually too. This is because average fixed cost is decreasing. With these relations in mind, let's reconsider the problem with average-cost pricing.

Ignoring demand is the major weakness of average-cost pricing

Average-cost pricing works well if the firm actually sells the quantity it used to set the average-cost price. Losses may result, however, if actual sales are much lower than expected. On the other hand, if sales are much higher than expected, then profits may be very good. But this will only happen by luck—because the firm's demand is much larger than expected.

To use average-cost pricing, a marketing manager must make *some* estimate of the quantity to be sold in the coming period. Without a quantity estimate, it isn't possible to

Exhibit 17–5
Typical Shape of Cost (per unit) Curves When Average Variable Cost per Unit Is Constant

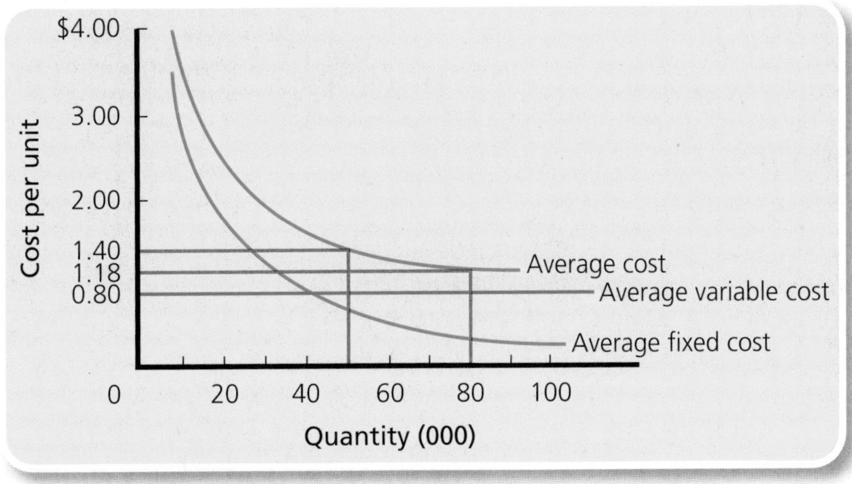

compute average cost. But unless this quantity is related to price—that is, unless the firm's demand curve is considered—the marketing manager may set a price that doesn't even cover a firm's total cost! You saw this happen in Exhibit 17-3B, when the firm's price of $2.00 resulted in demand for only 20,000 units and a loss of $6,000.

The demand curve is still important even if a manager has not taken time to think about it. For example, Exhibit 17-6 shows the demand curve for the firm we're discussing. This demand curve shows *why* the firm lost money when it tried to use average-cost pricing. At the $2.00 price, quantity demanded is only 20,000. With this demand curve and the costs in Exhibit 17-4, the firm will incur a loss whether management sets the price at a high $3 or a low $1.20. At $3, the firm will sell only 10,000 units for a total revenue of $30,000. But total cost will be $38,000—for a loss of $8,000. At the $1.20 price, it will sell 60,000 units—at a loss of $6,000. However, the curve suggests that at a price of $1.65 consumers will demand about 40,000 units, producing a profit of about $4,000.

In short, average-cost pricing is simple in theory but often fails in practice. In stable situations, prices set by this method may yield profits but not necessarily *maximum*

Exhibit 17–6
Evaluation of Various Prices along a Firm's Demand Curve

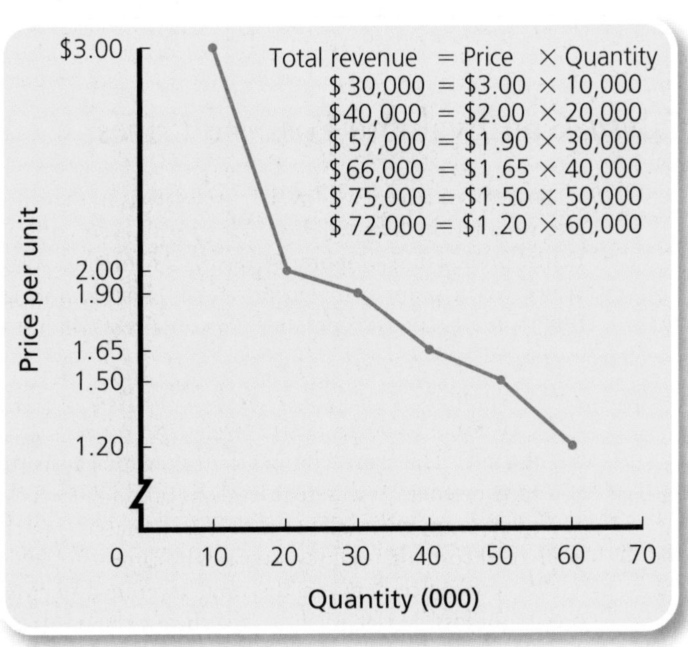

Exhibit 17–7
Summary of Relationships among Quantity, Cost, and Price Using Cost-Oriented Pricing

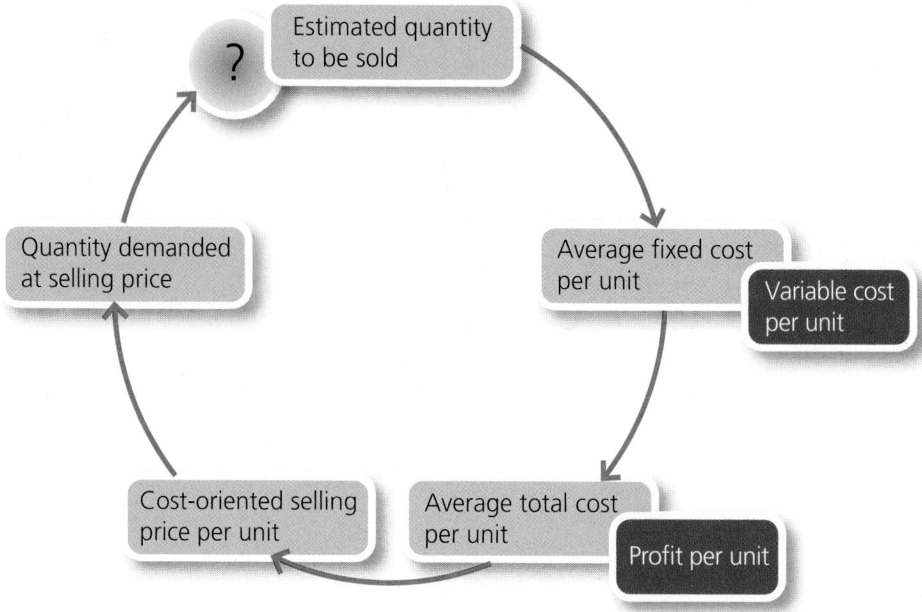

profits. And note that such cost-based prices may be higher than a price that would be more profitable for the firm, as shown in Exhibit 17-6. When demand conditions are changing, average-cost pricing is even more risky.

Exhibit 17-7 summarizes the relationships just discussed. Cost-oriented pricing requires an estimate of the total number of units to be sold. That estimate determines the *average* fixed cost per unit and thus the average total cost. Then the firm adds the desired profit per unit to the average total cost to get the cost-oriented selling price. How customers react to that price determines the actual quantity the firm will be able to sell. But that quantity may not be the quantity used to compute the average cost![3]

Don't ignore competitors' costs

Another danger of average-cost pricing is that it ignores competitors' costs and prices. Just as the price of a firm's own product influences demand, the price of available substitutes may impact demand. By finding ways to cut costs, a firm may be able to offer prices lower than competitors and still make an attractive profit.

Break-Even Analysis Can Evaluate Possible Prices

Some price setters use break-even analysis in their pricing. **Break-even analysis** evaluates whether the firm will be able to break even—that is, cover all its costs—with a particular price. This is important because a firm must cover all costs in the long run or there is not much point being in business. This method focuses on the **break-even point (BEP)**—the quantity where the firm's total cost will just equal its total revenue.

Break-even charts help find the BEP

To help understand how break-even analysis works, look at Exhibit 17-8, an example of the typical break-even chart. *The chart is based on a particular selling price*—in this case $1.20 a unit. The chart has lines that show total costs (total variable plus total fixed costs) and total revenues at different levels of production. The break-even point on the chart is at 75,000 units, where the total cost and total revenue lines intersect. At that production level, total cost and total revenue are the same—$90,000.

The difference between the total revenue and total cost at a given quantity is the profit—or loss! The chart shows that below the break-even point, total cost is higher than

Exhibit 17–8
Break-Even Chart for a Particular Situation

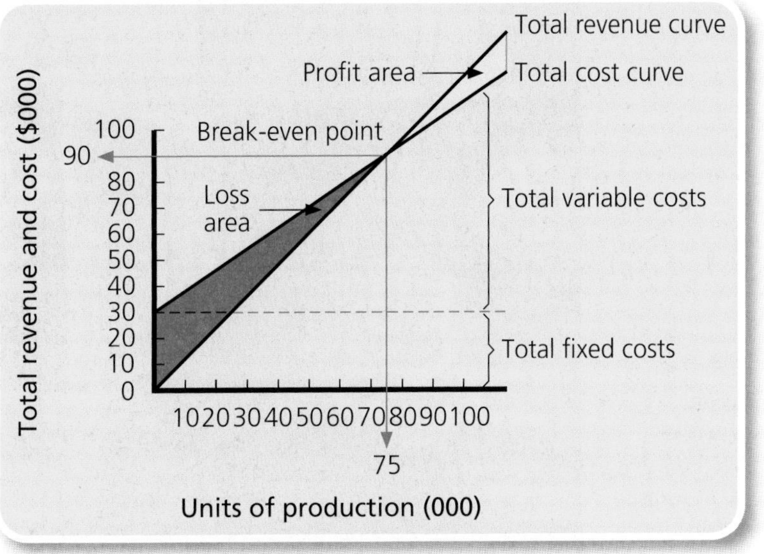

total revenue and the firm incurs a loss. The firm would make a profit above the break-even point. However, the firm would only reach the break-even point, or get beyond it into the profit area, *if* it could sell at least 75,000 units at the $1.20 price.

Break-even analysis can be helpful if used properly, so let's look at this approach more closely.

How to compute a break-even point

A break-even chart is an easy-to-understand visual aid, but it's also useful to be able to compute the break-even point.

The BEP, in units, can be found by dividing total fixed costs (TFC) by the **fixed-cost (FC) contribution per unit**—the assumed selling price per unit minus the variable cost per unit. This can be stated as a simple formula:

$$\text{BEP (in units)} = \frac{\text{Total fixed cost}}{\text{Fixed cost contribution per unit}}$$

This formula makes sense when we think about it. To break even, we must cover total fixed costs. Therefore, we must figure the contribution each unit will make to covering the total fixed costs (after paying for the variable costs to produce the item). When we divide this per-unit contribution into the total fixed costs that must be covered, we have the BEP (in units).

To illustrate the formula, let's use the cost and price information in Exhibit 17-8. The price per unit is $1.20. The average variable cost per unit is 80 cents. So the FC contribution per unit is 40 cents ($1.20 − 80 cents). The total fixed cost is $30,000 (see Exhibit 17-8). Substituting in the formula:

$$\text{BEP} = \frac{\$30{,}000}{.40} = 75{,}000 \text{ units}$$

From this you can see that if this firm sells 75,000 units, it will exactly cover all its fixed and variable costs. If it sells even one more unit, it will begin to show a profit—in this case, 40 cents per unit. Note that once the fixed costs are covered, the part of revenue formerly going to cover fixed costs is now *all profit.*

BEP can be stated in dollars too

The BEP can also be figured in dollars. The easiest way is to compute the BEP in units and then multiply by the assumed per-unit price. If you multiply the selling price ($1.20) by the BEP in units (75,000) you get $90,000—the BEP in dollars.

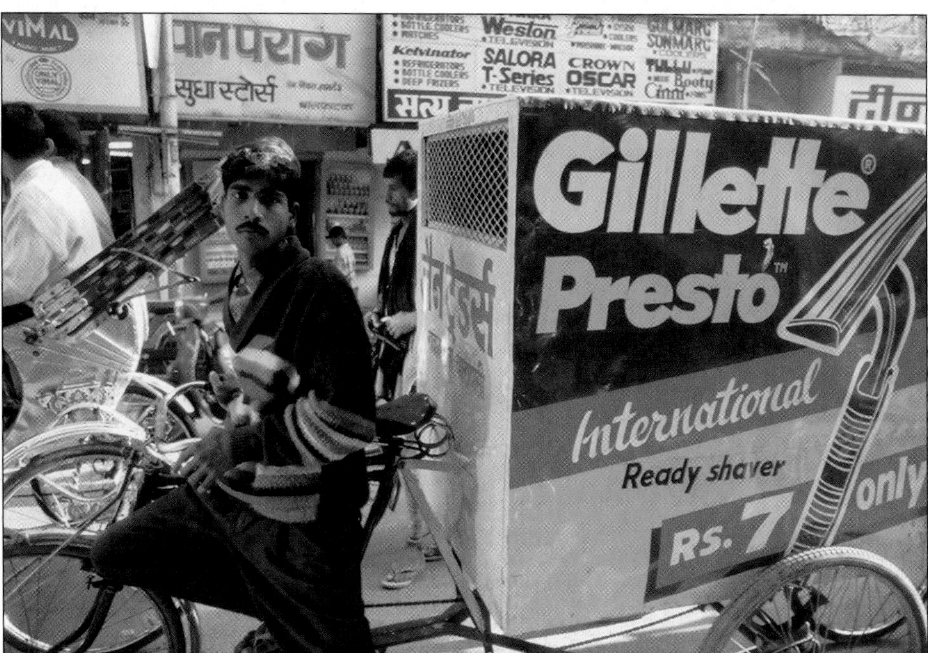

The money that a firm spends on marketing and other expenses must be covered, and then some, by a product's price if it is to make a profit. That's why Gillette enjoys big economies of scale by selling the same razors in many markets around the world.

Each possible price has its own break-even point

Often it's useful to compute the break-even point for each of several possible prices and then compare the BEP for each price to likely demand at that price. The marketing manager can quickly reject some price possibilities when the expected quantity demanded at a given price is way below the break-even point for that price.

Break-even analysis is helpful—but not a pricing solution

Break-even analysis is helpful for evaluating alternatives. It is also popular because it's easy to use. Yet break-even analysis is too often misunderstood. Beyond the BEP, profits seem to be growing continually. And the graph—with its straight-line total revenue curve—makes it seem that any quantity can be sold at the assumed price. But this usually isn't true. It is the same as assuming a perfectly horizontal demand curve at that price. In fact, most managers face down-sloping demand situations. And their total revenue curves do *not* keep going straight up.

Break-even analysis is a useful tool for analyzing costs and evaluating what might happen to profits in different market environments. But it is a cost-oriented approach. Like other cost-oriented approaches, it does not consider the effect of price on the quantity that consumers will want—that is, the demand curve. And from earlier in the chapter, we know that average-cost pricing does not accurately take into account cost variations at different levels of output.

So to really zero in on the most profitable price, marketers are better off estimating the demand curve by figuring out how much can be sold across a range of feasible prices. Total costs can then be estimated by combining variable and fixed costs across the same range. With better forecasts of sales and costs data, a marketing manager can more accurately estimate profits at different prices. Let's look more closely at this approach, called marginal analysis, next.[4]

Marginal Analysis Considers Both Costs and Demand

LO 17.5

Marginal analysis helps find the right price

The best pricing tool marketers have for looking at costs and revenue (demand) at the same time is marginal analysis. **Marginal analysis** focuses on the changes in total revenue and total cost from selling one more unit to find the most profitable price and quantity. Marginal analysis shows how costs, revenue, and profit change at different prices. The price that maximizes profit is the one that results in the greatest difference between total revenue and total cost.[5]

Demand estimates involve "if-then" thinking

Since the price determines what quantity will be sold, a manager needs an estimate of the demand curve to compute total revenue. A practical approach here is for managers to think about a price that appears to be too high and one that is too low. Then, for a number of prices between these two extremes, the manager estimates what quantity it might be possible to sell. You can think of this as a summary of the answers to a series of what-if questions—*What* quantity will be sold *if* a particular price is selected?

Profit is the difference between total revenue and total cost

The first two columns in Exhibit 17-9 give price and quantity combinations (demand) for an example firm. In this case, a manager estimates that sales will be zero at a price of $200; at a price of $175, one unit is predicted to sell; at a price of $160, two units, and so forth. Total revenue in column 3 of Exhibit 17-9 is equal to a price multiplied by its related quantity. Costs at the different quantities are also shown. The total variable costs are $60 per unit and fixed costs are $200 no matter how many units are sold. Column 6 shows the total cost by adding total variable cost and the fixed cost at each price and predicted quantity. The profit (column 7) at each quantity and price is the difference between total revenue and total cost. In this example, the best price is $115 (and a quantity of six units are expected to be sold) because that combination results in the highest profit ($130). Now let's look at this example in more detail.

Marginal revenue can be negative

This firm faces a demand curve that slopes down. That means that the marketer can expect to increase sales volume by lowering the price. Yet the lower price required to sell the larger quantity may reduce total revenue. Therefore, it's important to evaluate the likely effect of alternative prices on total revenue and profit. The way to do this is to look at marginal revenue.

Exhibit 17–9 Revenue, Cost, and Profit at Different Prices for a Firm

(1) Price (P)	(2) Quantity (Q)	(3) Total Revenue (TR = P × Q)	(4) Total Variable Cost (TVC)	(5) Fixed Cost (FC)	(6) Total Cost (TC = TVC + FC)	(7) Profit (Prf = TR − TC)	(8) Marginal Revenue (MR*)	(9) Marginal Cost (MC*)	(10) Marginal Profit (MP*)
$200	0	$0	$0	$200	$200	−$200			
175	1	175	60	200	260	−85	$175	$60	$115
160	2	320	120	200	320	0	145	60	85
145	3	435	180	200	380	55	115	60	55
135	4	540	240	200	440	100	105	60	45
125	5	625	300	200	500	125	85	60	25
115	**6**	**690**	**360**	**200**	**560**	**130**	**65**	**60**	**5**
105	7	735	420	200	620	115	45	60	−15
95	8	760	480	200	680	80	25	60	−35
85	9	765	540	200	740	25	5	60	−55
75	10	750	600	200	800	−50	−15	60	−75
65	11	715	660	200	860	−145	−35	60	−95
55	12	660	720	200	920	−260	−55	60	−115

*Marginal revenue refers to the change in revenue of selling one additional unit.
*Marginal cost refers to the change in cost of selling one additional unit.
*Marginal profit refers to the change in profit of selling one additional unit.

Marginal revenue is the change in total revenue that results from the sale of one more unit of a product. At a price of $135, the firm in this example can sell four units for total revenue of $540. By cutting the price to $125, it can sell five units for total revenue of $625. Thus, the marginal revenue for the fifth unit is $625 − 540, or $85 (see column 8). But will total revenue continue to rise if the firm sells more units at lower prices? Exhibit 17-9 shows that total revenue drops if prices are changed from $85 to $75. Note in the table that marginal revenue (column 8) is negative when total revenue decreases. The peak revenue is expected to occur when prices are $85 with sales of nine units. We will assume a profit maximizing pricing objective. Profit depends on both revenue and costs, so let's look at costs next.

The marginal cost of just one more can be important

Column 6 in Exhibit 17-9 shows the total cost increasing as quantity increases. Remember that total cost is the sum of fixed cost (in this example, $200) and total variable cost. The fixed cost does not change over the entire range of output. However, total variable costs increase by $60 with each additional unit produced. So it's the increases in variable cost that explain the increase in total cost.

There is another kind of cost that is vital to marginal analysis. **Marginal cost** is the change in total cost that results from producing one more unit. In Exhibit 17-9, you can see that it costs $440 to produce four units of a product and $500 to produce five units. Thus, the marginal cost for the fifth unit is $60 (see column 9). In other words, marginal cost is the additional cost of producing one more specific unit. By contrast, average cost is the average for all units (total cost divided by the number of units).

Profit is the largest when marginal revenue = marginal cost

To maximize profit, a manager generally wants to lower the price and sell more units as long as the marginal revenue from selling them is at least equal to the marginal cost of the extra units. From this we get the following **rule for maximizing profit**: The highest profit is earned at the price where marginal cost is just less than or equal to marginal revenue.*

You can see this rule operating in Exhibit 17-9. As the price is cut from $175 down to $115, the expected quantity sold increases from one to six units and the profit increases to its maximum level, $130. At that point, marginal revenue and marginal cost are about equal. However, beyond that point further price cuts result in revenue increases of less than the $60 increase in costs. This results in lower profits (or losses) starting with a price of $105. Column 7 in Exhibit 17-9 shows that when moving from a price of $115 to $105, profit actually falls by $15 (see column 10). Lower prices show further declines in profits.

At the point where marginal revenue (MR) equals marginal cost (MC), **marginal profit**—the extra profit on the last unit—is near zero. So when the firm is looking for the best price to charge, it should lower the price—to increase the quantity it will sell—as long as the last unit it sells will yield extra profit.

Profit maximization with total revenue and total cost curves

Exhibit 17-10 graphs the total revenue, total cost, and total profit relationships for the numbers we've been working with in Exhibit 17-9. The highest point on the total profit curve is at a quantity of six units. This is also the quantity where we find the greatest vertical distance between the total revenue curve and the total cost curve. Exhibit 17-9 shows that it is the $115 price that results in selling six units, so $115 is the price that leads to the highest profit. A price lower than $115 results in a higher sales volume, but you can see that the total profit curve declines beyond a quantity of six units. So a profit-maximizing marketing manager would not be interested in setting a lower price.

A profit range is reassuring

Marginal analysis focuses on the price that earns the highest profit. But a slight miss doesn't mean failure because demand estimates don't have to be exact. There is usually a

*This rule applies in typical situations where the curves are shaped similarly to those discussed here. As a technical matter, however, we should add the following to the rule for maximizing profit: The marginal cost must be increasing, or decreasing, at a lesser rate than marginal revenue.

Exhibit 17–10
Graphic Determination of the Price Giving the Greatest Total Profit for a Firm

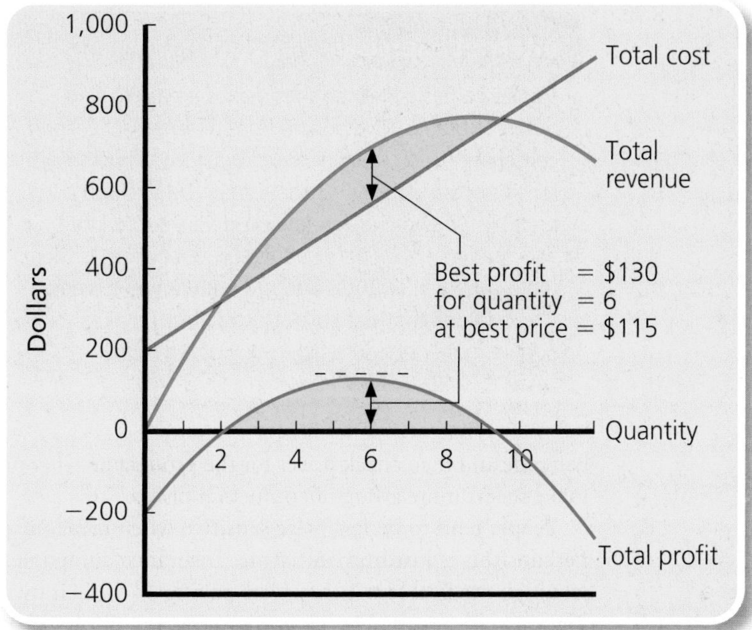

range of profitable prices. You can see this in Exhibit 17-9 and in the section of Exhibit 17-10 shown in yellow. Although the price that would result in the highest profit is $115, the firm's strategy would be profitable all the way from a price of $85 to $145. So the effort of trying to estimate demand will probably lead to being some place in the profitable range. In contrast, mechanical use of average-cost pricing could lead to a price that is much too high—or much too low.

A rough demand estimate is better than none

Some managers don't take advantage of marginal analysis because they think they can't determine the exact shape of the demand curve. But that view misses the point of marginal analysis. Marginal analysis encourages managers to think carefully about what they *do know* about costs and demand. Only rarely is either type of information exact. So, in practice, the focus of marginal analysis is not on finding the precise price that will maximize profit. Rather, the focus is on getting an estimate of how profit might vary across a *range of relevant prices.* Further, a number of practical demand-oriented approaches can help a marketing manager do a better job of understanding the likely shape of the demand curve for a target market. We'll discuss these approaches next.

Additional Demand-Oriented Approaches for Setting Prices

LO 17.6

Evaluating the customer's price sensitivity

A manager who knows what influences target customers' price sensitivity can do a better job estimating the demand curve that the firm faces. Marketing researchers have identified a number of factors that influence price sensitivity across many different market situations.

The first is the most basic. When customers have *substitute ways* of meeting a need, they are likely to be more price sensitive. A cook who wants a cappuccino maker to be able to serve something distinctive to guests at a dinner party may be willing to pay a high price. However, if different machines are available and our cook sees them as pretty similar, price sensitivity will be greater. It's important not to ignore dissimilar alternatives if the customer sees them as substitutes. If a machine for espresso were much less expensive than one for cappuccino, our cook might decide that an espresso machine would meet her needs just as well.

The impact of substitutes on price sensitivity is greatest when it is easy for customers to *compare prices.* For example, unit prices make it easier for our cook to compare the prices of

Internet Exercise

Bizrate.com is a website that makes it easy to find different brands of products from different sellers and compare prices. Go to **www.bizrate.com** and search for "popcorn popper." Review the products and prices listed and check a few of the links to related information. How useful is this sort of service? Is there more variety in features and prices than you expected? Do you think that this sort of comparison makes people more price sensitive? Why or why not?

espresso and cappuccino grinds on the grocery store shelf. Many people believe that the ease of comparing prices on the Internet increases price sensitivity and brings down prices. New smartphone technology makes comparisons possible while shopping in brick-and-mortar retail stores. Several smartphone software apps allow consumers to scan a product's bar code and then check prices for the product at other online stores. If nothing else, it may make sellers more aware of competing prices.

People tend to be less price sensitive when someone else pays the bill or *shares the cost.* Perhaps this is just human nature. Insurance companies think that consumers would reject high medical fees if they were paying all of their own bills. And executives might plan longer in advance to get better discounts on airline flights if their companies weren't footing the bills.

Customers tend to be more price sensitive the greater the *total expenditure.* Sometimes a big expenditure can be broken into smaller pieces. Mercedes knows this. When its ads focused on the cost of a monthly lease rather than the total price of the car, more consumers got interested in biting the bullet.

Customers are less price sensitive the greater the *significance of the end benefit* of the purchase. Computer makers will pay more to get Intel processors if they believe that having an "Intel inside" sells more machines. Positioning efforts often focus on emotional benefits of a purchase to increase the significance of a benefit. Ads for L'Oréal hair color, for example, show closeups of beautiful hair while popular celebrities tell women to buy it "because you're worth it." A consumer who cares about the price of a bottle of hair color might still have no question that she's worth the difference in price.

Customers are sometimes less price sensitive if there are *switching costs*—costs that a customer faces when buying a product that is different from what has been purchased or

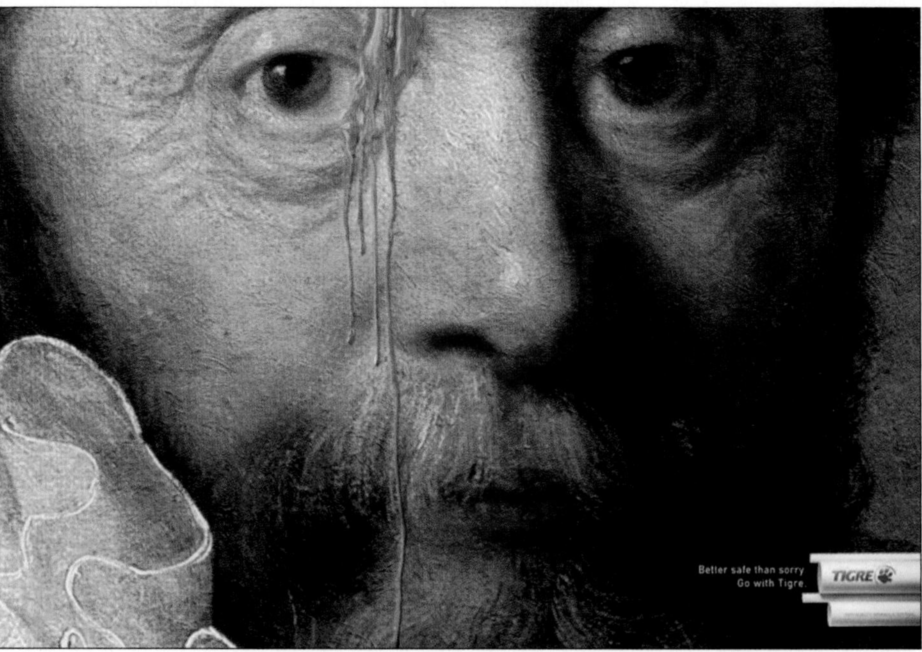

Business customers can be price sensitive unless given a reason to pay a higher price. Tigre sells pipes, fittings, and accessories for construction products—including an extensive line to prevent leaks. With this ad, "Better safe than sorry. Go with Tigre," Tigre wants to remind customers of the potential costs of a leaky pipe.

used in the past. Switching costs can be quite high for some business customers. For example, once a firm's employees know how to use Microsoft Excel, the company would not want to incur the financial cost and time it would take to train employees in a new spreadsheet software package. But switching costs can apply to final consumers as well. For example, if a hair salon raises its prices, many customers will not switch to a new salon. The hassles of looking for a new stylist—and the risk of ending up with a bad hair day—usually make it easier to simply pay the higher price.

These factors apply in many different purchase situations, so it makes sense for a marketing manager to consider each of them in refining estimates of how customers might respond at different prices.[6]

Ethics Question

You are a pricing specialist for a large grocery store chain that has always charged the same prices in all of its stores. However, average operating costs are higher for its inner-city stores. In addition, having the store nearby is very important to low-income, inner-city consumers who have to rely on public transportation. It's hard for them to shop around, and thus they are less price sensitive. Research indicates that these stores can charge prices that are 5 percent higher on average with little effect on sales volume. This would significantly increase profitability. Do you think the chain should charge higher prices at its inner-city stores? If the manager of the store decided to set higher prices on some products and leave others unchanged—to result in an overall average increase of 5 percent—what products would you recommend for higher prices? Why? If prices were increased and antipoverty activists got TV coverage by picketing the chain, how would you respond to a TV reporter covering the story?

Competitor analysis and price sensitivity

Customer demand depends on available alternatives. So a marketing manager can often improve pricing decisions and profitability by considering customer price sensitivity as part of a competitor analysis. The new CEO of Parker Hannifin (PH), a large industrial parts maker, realized this. Before he arrived, PH managers usually set the price for a part by summing all the costs that were involved in making it and then adding a 35 percent markup. Managers liked this approach; it was easy and also left some room for haggling. Yet the new CEO saw that they could improve what they were doing. First, he asked them to classify every product—and there were thousands—into

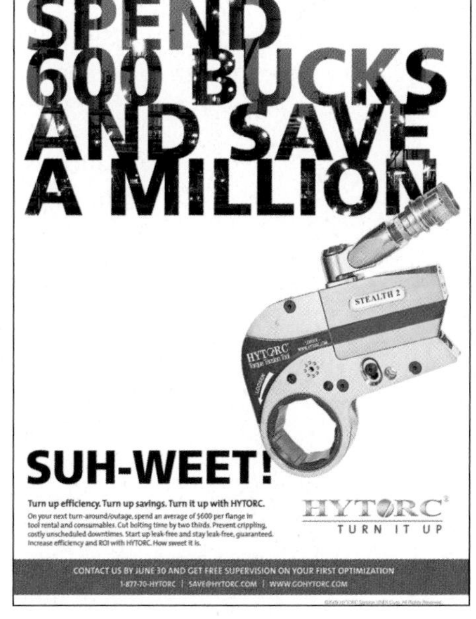

Value in use pricing considers what a customer will save by buying a product. Both ClimateMaster and Hytorc tout the savings realized by switching to their products.

categories. At one extreme, there was a new category for PH parts that were basically commodities and just like what competitors offered. At the other extreme, there was a category for PH parts that were important to customers and that were only available from PH. This category included a high-pressure valve that was used on airplane doors; no other supplier had a valve that worked as well for this critical application. Prices on parts in this category were raised by 5 percent or more—as long as the price still represented a good value. On commodity parts, prices were reduced by 5 percent to beat competitors. And, of course, there were a number of other levels of price adjustment for categories between the extremes. Fine-tuning PH prices to consider competition was simple, but it increased profits by 25 percent.[7]

Value in use pricing—how much will the customer save?

LO 17.7

Organizational buyers think about how a purchase will affect their total costs. Many marketers who aim at business markets keep this in mind when estimating demand and setting prices. They use **value in use pricing**—which means setting prices that will capture some of what customers will save by substituting the firm's product for the one currently being used.

For example, a producer of computer-controlled machines used to assemble cars knows that the machine doesn't just replace a standard machine. It also reduces labor costs, quality control costs, and—after the car is sold—costs of warranty repairs. The marketer can estimate what each auto producer will save by using the machine—and then set a price that makes it less expensive for the auto producer to buy the computerized machine than to stick with the old methods. The number of customers who have different levels of potential savings also provides some idea about the shape of the demand curve.

Creating a superior product that could save customers money doesn't guarantee that customers will be willing to pay a higher price. To capture the value created, the seller must convince buyers of the savings—and buyers are likely to be skeptical. A salesperson needs to be able to show proof of the claims.[8]

Auctions show what a customer will pay

Auctions have always been a way to determine exactly what some group of potential customers would pay, or not pay, for a product. However, the use of online auctions has dramatically broadened the use of this approach for both consumer and business products. Millions of auctions are on eBay each day. And some firms are setting up their own auctions, especially for products in short supply. The U.S. government is using online auctions as well. For example, the Federal Communications Commission (FCC) auctions rights to use airwaves for cell phones and other wireless devices. Count on more growth in online auctions.[9]

Some sellers use sequential price reductions

Some sellers are taking the auction approach and adapting it by using sequential price reductions over time. The basic idea is that the seller starts with a relatively high price and sells as much of the product as possible at that price, but plans from the start on a series of step-by-step price reductions until the product is sold out. This approach is most commonly used with products that have a short life or are in short supply, but which would just run up inventory costs if they are not sold. Retailers like TJ Maxx use this approach with women's fashions, and grocery stores use it with perishable food like fruits and vegetables. Cruise lines sell space this way; they don't want the ship to sail with empty cabins. Some people may think of this as a "clearance" sale. But the difference here is that the plan from the outset is to work down the demand curve in steps—appealing to segments who are least price sensitive first—until all of a product is sold. However, sellers hope that if they offer the right products they'll never get to price reductions (which earn lower margins). Rather, they prefer to be bringing in the next round of products to start the process over again.

Customers may have reference prices

Some people don't devote much thought to what they pay for the products they buy, including some frequently purchased goods and services. But consumers often have a **reference price**—the price they expect to pay—for many of the products they purchase. And different customers may have different reference prices for the same basic type of

Exhibit 17–11
How Customer's Reference Price Influences Perceived Value

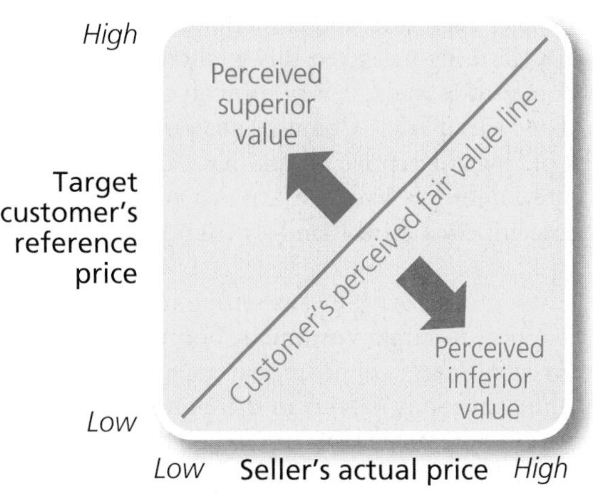

purchase. For example, a person who really enjoys reading might have a higher reference price for a popular paperback book than another person who is only an occasional reader.[10]

If a firm's price is lower than a customer's reference price, customers may view the product as a better value and demand may increase. See Exhibit 17-11. Sometimes a firm will try to position the benefits of its product in such a way that consumers compare it with a product that has a higher reference price. Public Broadcasting System TV stations do this when they ask viewers to make donations that match what they pay for "just one month of cable service." Insurance companies frame the price of premiums for homeowners' coverage in terms of the price to repair flood damage—and advertising makes the damage very vivid. Some retailers just want consumers to use the manufacturer's list price as the reference price, even if no one anywhere actually pays that list price.

Leader pricing—make it low to attract customers

Leader pricing means setting some very low prices—real bargains—to get customers into retail stores. The idea is not only to sell large quantities of the leader items but also to get customers into the store to buy other products. Certain products are picked for their promotion value and priced low but above cost. In food stores, the leader prices are the "specials" that are advertised regularly to give an image of low prices. Leader pricing is normally used with products for which consumers do have a specific reference price.

Leader pricing can backfire if customers buy only the low-priced leaders. To avoid hurting profits, managers often select leader items that aren't directly competitive with major lines—as when bargain-priced blank CDs are a leader for an electronics store.[11]

Grocery stores often use leader pricing on milk. The stores hope to attract customers who will purchase more than just milk when they visit.

Bait pricing—offer a steal, but sell under protest

Bait pricing is setting some very low prices to attract customers but trying to sell more expensive models or brands once the customer is in the store. For example, a furniture store may advertise a color TV for $199. But once bargain hunters come to the store, salespeople point out the disadvantages of the low-priced TV and try to convince them to trade up to a better, and more expensive, set. Bait pricing is something like leader pricing. But here the seller *doesn't* plan to sell many at the low price.

If bait pricing is successful, the demand for higher-quality products expands. This approach may be a sensible part of a strategy to trade up customers. And customers may be well served if—once in the store—they find a higher-priced product offers features better suited to their needs. But bait pricing is also criticized as unethical.

Is bait pricing ethical?

Extremely aggressive and sometimes dishonest bait-pricing advertising has given this method a bad reputation. Some stores make it very difficult to buy the bait item. The Federal Trade Commission considers this type of bait pricing a deceptive act and has banned its use in interstate commerce. Even well-known chains like Sears have been criticized for bait-and-switch pricing.

Exhibit 17–12
Demand Curve When Psychological Pricing Is Appropriate

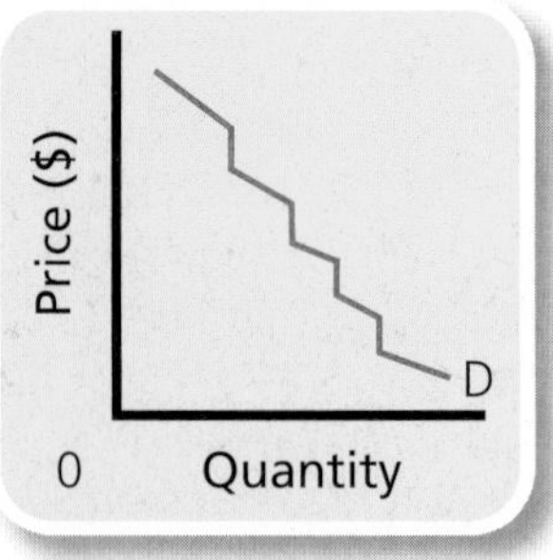

Psychological pricing—some prices just seem right

Psychological pricing means setting prices that have special appeal to target customers. Some people think there are whole ranges of prices that potential customers see as the same. So price cuts in these ranges do not increase the quantity sold. But just below this range, customers may buy more. Then, at even lower prices, the quantity demanded stays the same again—and so on. Exhibit 17-12 shows the kind of demand curve that leads to psychological pricing. Vertical drops mark the price ranges that customers see as the same. Pricing research shows that there *are* such demand curves.[12]

Odd-even pricing is setting prices that end in certain numbers. For example, products selling below $50 often end in the number 5 or the number 9—such as 49 cents or $24.95. Prices for higher-priced products are often $1 or $2 below the next even dollar figure—such as $99 rather than $100.

Some marketers use odd-even pricing because they think consumers react better to these prices—perhaps seeing them as "substantially" lower than the next highest even price. Marketers using these prices seem to assume that they have a rather jagged demand curve—that slightly higher prices will substantially reduce the quantity demanded. Long ago, some retailers used odd-even prices to force their clerks to make change. Then the clerks had to record the sale and could not pocket the money.[13]

Price lining—a few prices cover the field

Price lining is setting a few price levels for a product line and then marking all items at these prices. This approach assumes that customers have a certain reference price in mind that they expect to pay for a product. For example, many neckties are priced between $20 and $50. In price lining, there are only a few prices within this range. Ties will not be priced at $20, $21, $22, $23, and so on. They might be priced at four levels—$20, $30, $40, and $50.

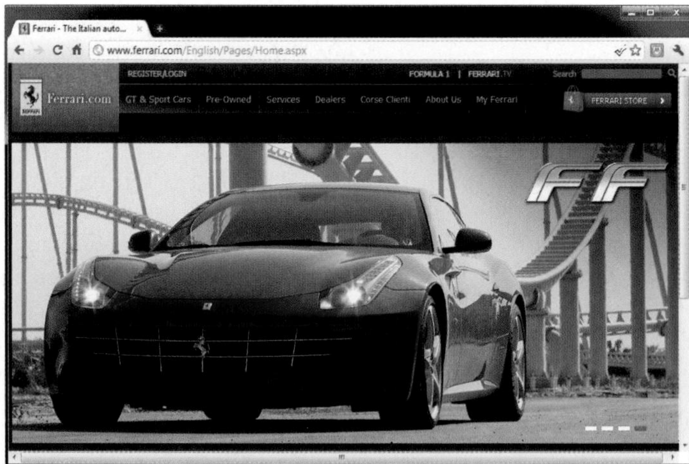

A restaurant may use demand-backward pricing to set a meal price that final consumers find attractive—while adjusting what food is included so that it's still profitable. Ferrari uses prestige pricing to signify the high quality and exclusivity of its sports cars.

How to make money by giving your product away

One way to generate customer demand is to give your product away. This not-so-new approach to pricing is gaining popularity. There are a few reasons for the resurgence of this tactic. First, technology, the Internet, and advances in manufacturing have significantly reduced the costs for many products. It costs close to nothing for Facebook to add another user or for one more customer to download Google's Picasa photo organizing and editing software. Second, offering something for free generates buzz and the promotional benefit often outweighs the costs. Further, in many product categories, consumers have come to expect things to be free. For example, most readers of online newspapers and magazines refuse to pay when publishers try to charge for subscriptions.

How do firms give something away and still make money? One approach relies on cross-subsidies, where a customer gets something for free but pays for something else. After King Gillette invented the safety razor in 1903, he had a hard time getting widespread adoption of his shaving innovation. But when he gave away the razors and sold replacement blades, sales and profits skyrocketed! Many banks will offer customers zero percent interest (a free loan) for a year when they transfer a credit card balance. This works best when customers need to experience the good value of the firm's offering to recognize the benefits.

Another approach counts on advertisers to provide the revenue. "Free" attracts customer eyeballs, and advertisers pay for access to eyeballs. For example, Japanese photocopy shop Tadacopy offers college students free photocopies—with advertising on the back of each page. Because *Time* magazine's website and Fox television are free, they draw a larger audience. The larger audience is attractive to advertisers who pay to place ads.

Some companies offer a basic product for free, while charging for more advanced features—a strategy called "freemium" (combining free and premium). For example, Flickr offers free online photo sharing, but some customers pay $24.95 a year to get the additional features of Flickr Pro. The revenue from paying customers allows Flickr to cover the freeloaders. The Brazilian band, Banda Calypso, uses a variation of this approach. It gives street vendors masters of its CDs and CD liner art at no charge. The street vendors' sales of high-quality, low-priced CDs bring in new fans, and Banda Calypso benefits when some of these fans pay for tickets to the band's live performances.

Once customers get something for free, they may be reluctant to pay for it later. So, before a firm offers something for nothing, it's important to think through what the firm will get in return—and how that relates to the firm's pricing objectives.[14]

Price lining has advantages other than just matching prices to what consumers expect to pay. The main advantage is simplicity—for both salespeople and customers. It is less confusing than having many prices. Some customers may consider items in only one price class. Their big decision, then, is which item(s) to choose at that price.

For retailers, price lining has several advantages. Sales may increase because (1) they can offer a bigger variety in each price class and (2) it's easier to get customers to make decisions within one price class. Stock planning is simpler because demand is larger at the relatively few prices. Price lining can also reduce costs because inventory needs are lower.

Demand-backward pricing and prestige pricing

Demand-backward pricing is setting an acceptable final consumer price and working backward to what a producer can charge. It is commonly used by producers of consumer products, especially shopping products such as women's clothing and appliances. It is also used with gift items for which customers will spend a specific amount—because they are seeking a $10 or a $15 gift. Many of Mexico's low-income consumers carry only 5 or 10 peso coins. So Ace laundry detergent developed a new version of its product that adjusted features and manufacturing costs to meet a 10 peso price point.[15]

Exhibit 17–13
Demand Curve Showing a Prestige Pricing Situation

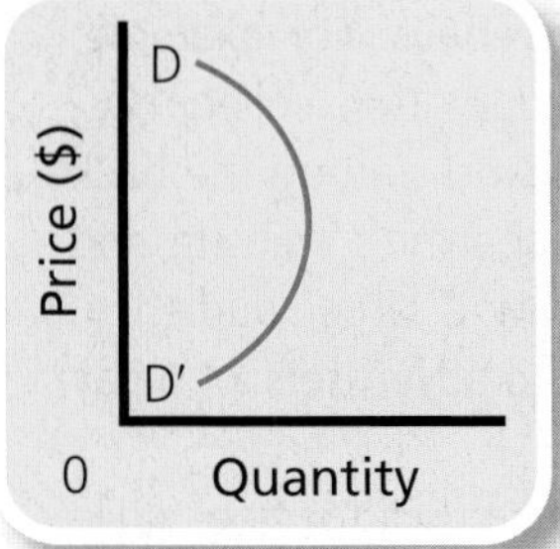

The producer starts with the retail (reference) price for a particular item and then works backward—subtracting the typical margins that channel members expect. This gives the approximate price the producer can charge. Then the average or planned marketing expenses can be subtracted from this price to find how much can be spent producing the item. Candy companies do this. They alter the size of the candy bar to keep the bar at the expected price.

Prestige pricing is setting a rather high price to suggest high quality or high status. Some target customers want the best, so they will buy at a high price. But if the price seems cheap, they worry about quality and don't buy. Prestige pricing is most common for luxury products such as furs, jewelry, and perfume.

It is also common in service industries, where the customer can't see the product in advance and relies on price to judge its quality. Target customers who respond to prestige pricing give the marketing manager an unusual demand curve. Instead of a normal down-sloping curve, the curve goes down for a while and then bends back to the left again.[16] See Exhibit 17-13.

Pricing a Full Line

Our emphasis has been, and will continue to be, on the problem of pricing an individual product mainly because this makes our discussion clearer. But most marketing managers are responsible for more than one product. In fact, their "product" may be the whole company line! So we'll discuss this matter briefly.

Full-line pricing—market- or firm-oriented

Full-line pricing is setting prices for a whole line of products. How to do this depends on which of two basic situations a firm is facing.

In one case, all products in the company's line are aimed at the same general target market, which makes it important for all prices and value to be logically related. This is a common approach with shopping products. A producer of TV sets might offer several models with different features at different prices to give its target customers some choice. The difference among the prices and benefits should appear reasonable when the target customers are evaluating them. Customer perceptions can be important here. A low-priced item, even one that is a good value at that price, may drag down the image of the higher end of the line. Alternatively, one item that consumers do not see as a good value may spill over to how they judge other products in the line. A marketing manager sometimes adds a higher-priced item to an existing product line to influence customer reference prices. The highest-priced product might not get many sales, but it makes the second-highest-product in the line appear less expensive by comparison.

Internet Exercise

Go to Best Buy's online site (**www.bestbuy.com**). Enter "Sony Bravia 46-inch TV" into the search bar. How many TVs come up? Scroll down and check the box marked "compare" underneath two or three of the 46-inch models and then click compare. Note: If you do not find at least two models, choose another size. What is the price of each model? What additional features are available on a more expensive model? Which model do you think will sell the best? Why?

In other cases, the different products in the line are aimed at entirely different target markets so there doesn't have to be any relation between the various prices. A chemical producer of a wide variety of products with several target markets, for example, probably should price each product separately.

Costs are complicated in full-line pricing

The marketing manager must try to recover all costs on the whole line—perhaps by pricing quite low on more competitive items and much higher on ones with unique benefits. However, estimating costs for each product is a challenge because there is no single right way to assign a company's fixed costs to each of the products. Regardless of how costs are allocated, any cost-oriented pricing method that doesn't consider demand can lead to very unrealistic prices. To avoid mistakes, the marketing manager should judge demand for the whole line as well as demand for each individual product in each target market.

Complementary product pricing

Complementary product pricing is setting prices on several products as a group. This may lead to one product being priced very low so that the profits from another product will increase, thus increasing the product group's total profits. When Gillette introduced the M3Power battery-powered wet-shaving system, the shaver, two blade cartridges, and a Duracell battery had a relatively low suggested retail price of $14.99. However, the blade refill cartridges, which must be replaced frequently, come in a package of four at a hefty price of $10.99.

Complementary product pricing differs from full-line pricing because different production facilities may be involved—so there's no cost allocation problem. Instead, the problem is really understanding the target market and the demand curves for each of the complementary products. Then various combinations of prices can be tried to see what set will be best for reaching the company's pricing objectives.[17]

Product-bundle pricing—one price for several products

A firm that offers its target market several different products may use **product-bundle pricing**—setting one price for a set of products. Firms that use product-bundle pricing usually set the overall price so that it's cheaper for the customer to buy the products at the same time than separately. A bank may offer a product-bundle price for a safe-deposit box, traveler's checks, and a savings account. AT&T bundles voice mail, caller ID, and call forwarding. Bundling encourages customers to spend more and buy products that they might not otherwise buy—because the added cost of the extras is not as high as it would normally be, so the value is better.

Most firms that use product-bundle pricing also set individual prices for the unbundled products. This may increase demand by attracting customers who want one item in a product assortment but don't want the extras. Many firms treat services this way. A software company may have a product-bundle price for its software and access to a toll-free telephone assistance service. However, customers who don't need help can pay a lower price and get just the software.[18]

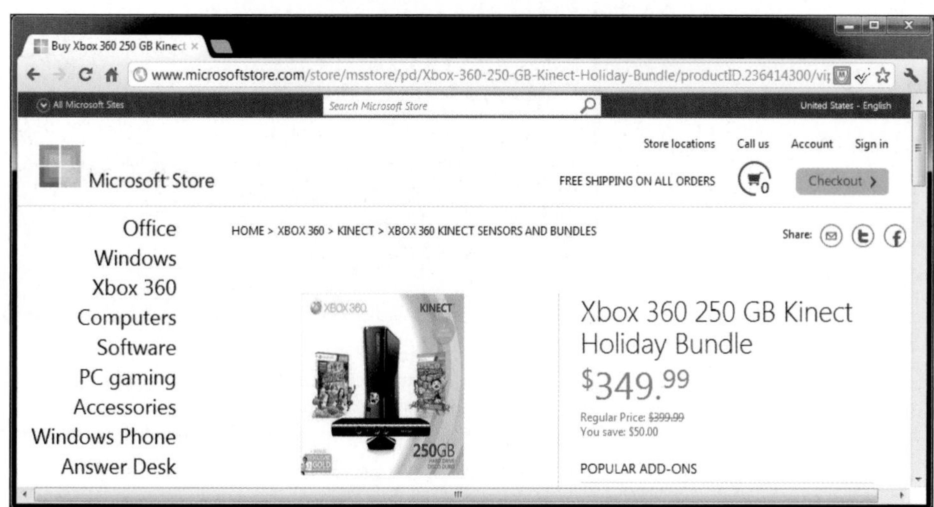

Microsoft offers a bundle that includes the Kinect game console and two games for a special price.

Bid Pricing and Negotiated Pricing Depend Heavily on Costs

LO 17.8

A new price for every job

We introduced the issue of competitive bidding in Chapter 6. But now let's take a closer look at bid pricing. **Bid pricing** means offering a specific price for each possible job rather than setting a price that applies for all customers. When submitting a bid price for a standardized product, the marketing manager may have to decide the firm's lowest acceptable price and how close to that price should be the bid. But in many situations bid pricing is more complicated. For example, building contractors and companies selling services (like cleaning or data processing) often bid on large projects with many variables.

A big problem in bid pricing on a complicated job is estimating all the costs that will apply. This may sound easy, but a complicated bid may involve thousands of cost components. Further, management must include an overhead charge and a charge for profit.

Because many firms use an e-mail distribution list or website to solicit bids, the process is fast and easy for the buyer. But a seller has to be geared up to set a price and respond quickly. However, this system does allow the seller to set a price based on the precise situation and what costs and revenue are involved.

Bids are usually based on purchase specifications provided by the customer. The specs may be sent by e-mail or posted on a website. Sometimes the seller can win the business, even with a higher bid price, by suggesting changes in the specs that save the customer money.

At times it isn't possible to figure out specs or costs in advance. This may lead to a negotiated contract where the customer agrees to pay the supplier's total cost plus an agreed-on profit figure (say, 10 percent of costs or a dollar amount)—after the job is finished.

Ethical issues in cost-plus bid pricing

Some unethical sellers give bid prices based on cost-plus contracts a bad reputation by faking their records to make costs seem higher than they really are. In other cases, there may be honest debate about what costs should be allowed. We've already considered, for instance, the difficulties in allocating fixed costs.

Demand must be considered too

Competition must be considered when adding in overhead and profit for a bid price. Usually, the customer will get several bids and accept the lowest one. So unthinking addition of typical overhead and profit rates should be avoided. Some bidders use the same overhead and profit rates on all jobs, regardless of competition, and then are surprised when they don't get some jobs.[19]

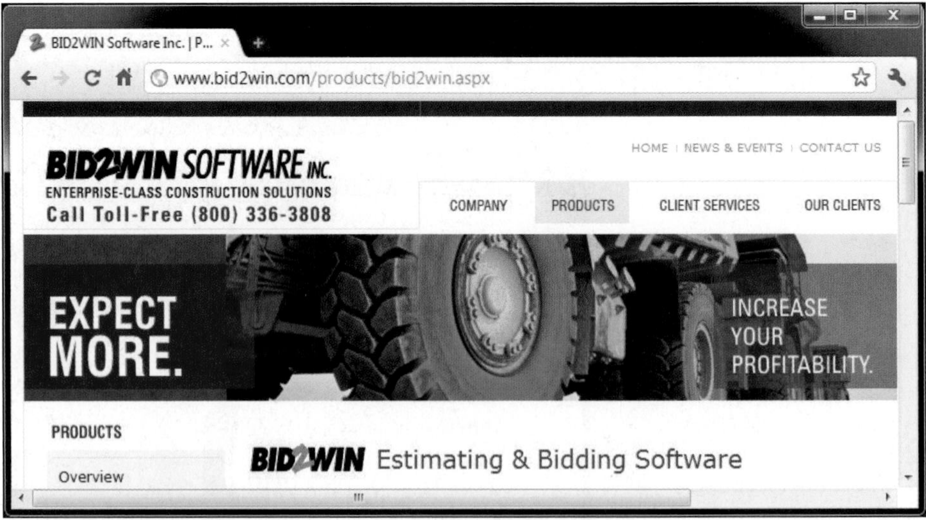

Many firms use software from companies like Bid2Win, to help manage the complex process of estimating costs and setting a bid price.

Negotiated prices—what will a specific customer pay?

Sometimes the customer asks for bids and then singles out the company that submits the *most attractive* bid, not necessarily the lowest, for further bargaining. What a customer will buy—if the customer buys at all—depends on the **negotiated price**, a price set based on bargaining between the buyer and seller. As with simple bid pricing, negotiated pricing is most common in situations where the marketing mix is adjusted for each customer—so bargaining may involve the whole marketing mix, not just the price level. Through the bargaining process, the seller tries to determine what aspects of the marketing mix are most important—and worth the most—to the customer.

Sellers must know their costs to negotiate prices effectively. However, negotiated pricing is a demand-oriented approach. Here the seller analyzes very carefully a particular customer's position on a demand curve, or on different possible demand curves based on different offerings, rather than the overall demand curve for a group of customers.

CONCLUSION

In this chapter, we discussed various approaches to price setting. Generally, retailers and wholesalers use markups. Some just use the same markups for all their items because it is simpler, but this is usually not the best approach. It's more effective to consider customer demand, competition, and how markups relate to turnover and profit.

It's important for marketing managers to understand costs; if customers are not willing to pay a price that is at least high enough to cover all of the costs of the marketing mix, the firm won't be profitable. So we describe the different types of cost that a marketing manager needs to understand and how average-cost pricing is used to set prices. But we note that this approach can fail because it ignores demand. We look at break-even analysis, which is a variation of the cost-oriented approach. It is useful for analyzing possible prices. However, managers must estimate demand to evaluate the chance of reaching these possible break-even points.

The major difficulty with demand-oriented pricing involves estimating the demand curve. But experienced managers, perhaps aided by marketing research, can estimate the nature of demand for their products. Even if estimates are not exact, they can help to get prices in the right ballpark . . . and there's usually a profitable range around the most profitable price. So marketers should consider demand when setting prices. We see this with value in use pricing, psychological pricing, odd-even pricing, full-line pricing, and even bid pricing. Understanding the factors that influence customer price sensitivity can make these approaches more effective.

While we do not recommend that cost-oriented approaches be used by themselves, they do help the marketing manager understand the firm's profitability. Pricing decisions should consider the cost of offering the whole marketing mix. But smart marketers do not accept cost as a given—target marketers always look for ways to be more efficient—to reduce costs while improving the value that they offer customers.

KEY TERMS

LO 17.9

markup, *449*
markup (percent), *449*
markup chain, *450*
stockturn rate, *451*
average-cost pricing, *452*
total fixed cost, *453*
total variable cost, *453*
total cost, *453*
average cost (per unit), *454*
average fixed cost (per unit), *454*
average variable cost (per unit), *454*
break-even analysis, *456*
break-even point (BEP), *456*
fixed-cost (FC) contribution per unit, *457*
marginal analysis, *458*
marginal revenue, *460*
marginal cost, *460*
rule for maximizing profit, *460*
marginal profit, *460*
value in use pricing, *464*
reference price, *464*
leader pricing, *465*
bait pricing, *465*
psychological pricing, *466*
odd-even pricing, *466*
price lining, *466*

demand-backward pricing, *467*
prestige pricing, *468*
full-line pricing, *468*
complementary product pricing, *469*
product-bundle pricing, *469*
bid pricing, *470*
negotiated price, *471*

QUESTIONS AND PROBLEMS

1. Why do many department stores seek a markup of about 30 percent when some discount houses operate on a 20 percent markup?
2. A producer distributed its riding lawn mowers through wholesalers and retailers. The retail selling price was $800, and the manufacturing cost to the company was $312. The retail markup was 35 percent and the wholesale markup 20 percent. What was the cost to the wholesaler? To the retailer? What percentage markup did the producer take?
3. Relate the concept of stock turnover to the growth of mass-merchandising. Use a simple example in your answer.
4. If total fixed costs are $200,000 and total variable costs are $100,000 at the output of 20,000 units, what are the probable total fixed costs and total variable costs at an output of 10,000 units? What are the average fixed costs, average variable costs, and average costs at these two output levels? Explain what additional information you would want to determine what price should be charged.
5. Construct an example showing that mechanical use of a very large or a very small markup might still lead to unprofitable operation while some intermediate price would be profitable. Draw a graph and show the break-even point(s).
6. The Davis Company's fixed costs for the year are estimated at $200,000. Its product sells for $250. The variable cost per unit is $200. Sales for the coming year are expected to reach $1,250,000. What is the break-even point? Expected profit? If sales are forecast at only $875,000, should the Davis Company shut down operations? Why?
7. Discuss the idea of drawing separate demand curves for different market segments. It seems logical because each target market should have its own marketing mix. But won't this lead to many demand curves and possible prices? And what will this mean with respect to discounts and varying prices in the marketplace? Will it be legal? Will it be practical?
8. Distinguish between leader pricing and bait pricing. What do they have in common? How can their use affect a marketing mix?
9. Cite a local example of psychological pricing and evaluate whether it makes sense.
10. Cite a local example of odd-even pricing and evaluate whether it makes sense.
11. How does a prestige pricing policy fit into a marketing mix? Would exclusive distribution be necessary?
12. Is a full-line pricing policy available only to producers? Cite local examples of full-line pricing. Why is full-line pricing important?

CREATING MARKETING PLANS

The Marketing Plan Coach software on the text website includes a sample marketing plan for Hillside Veterinary Clinic. Look through the "Marketing Strategy" section.

a. A veterinary clinic must have some system for dealing with emergencies that occur on weekends and at night when the clinic is closed. Individual vets usually rotate so that someone is always on call to handle emergencies. The price for emergency care is usually 50 percent higher than the price for care during normal hours. Do you think that Hillside should charge higher prices for emergency care? Does it fit with Hillside's strategy?
b. Some customers have expensive pedigree dogs and cats and are less price sensitive than others about fees for veterinary care. Do you think that it would be possible for Hillside to charge higher prices in caring for expensive pets? Why or why not?

SUGGESTED CASES

17. Simply Pure H2O4U, Inc.
24. WireWay
27. Advanced Molding, Inc.
35. Rizzuto's Pizzeria

COMPUTER-AIDED PROBLEM

17. BREAK-EVEN/PROFIT ANALYSIS

This problem lets you see the dynamics of break-even analysis. The starting values (costs, revenues, etc.) for this problem are from the break-even analysis example in this chapter (see Exhibit 17-8).

The first column computes a break-even point. You can change costs and prices to figure new break-even points (in units and dollars). The second column goes further. There you can specify target profit level, and the unit and dollar sales needed to achieve your target profit level will be computed. You can also estimate possible sales quantities, and the program will compute costs, sales, and profits. Use this spreadsheet to address the following issues:

a. Vary the selling price between $1.00 and $1.40. Prepare a table showing how the break-even point (in units and dollars) changes at the different price levels.

b. If you hope to earn a target profit of $15,000, how many units would you have to sell? What would total cost be? Total sales dollars? (*Note:* Use the right-hand ["profit analysis"] column in the spreadsheet.)

c. Using the "profit analysis" column (column 2), allow your estimate of the sales quantity to vary between 64,000 and 96,000. Prepare a table that shows, for each quantity level, what happens to average cost per unit and profit. Explain why average cost changes as it does over the different quantity values.

18
CHAPTER EIGHTEEN

Implementing and Controlling Marketing Plans: Evolution and Revolution

Ben & Jerry's brings its sweet-tooth "fans" (not "customers," if you please) a lot of pleasure—and sometimes raises their social conscience—with unique ice cream concoctions like "Imagine Whirled Peace." Royalties from sales of this flavor support charities that provide food and medical assistance for disadvantaged children. Ben & Jerry's hopes the attention it draws to poverty will help make it go away—but perhaps with a different spirit than the firm has had while making hundreds of flavors disappear.

When Ben & Jerry's adds a new flavor like Imagine Whirled Peace or Peanut Banana Greek Frozen Yogurt, it needs to drop other flavors to make room on store shelves and in scoop shop freezers. If your favorite flavor disappears from store shelves, you might find it at Ben & Jerry's website buried in the Flavor Graveyard with hundreds of other "dearly departed flavors." But the odds are the new flavor will be even more popular. That doesn't happen by chance; the proof is in the growth in sales that Ben & Jerry's has achieved over the years. Ben & Jerry's produces and distributes about 50 different flavors at a time, and its factory pumps out more than 200,000 pints of ice cream, sorbet, and fro-yo (frozen yogurt) each day. Tractor-trailer loads continuously flow into depots and from there are shipped to 600 scoop shops and 50,000 grocery stores in the United States and in 28 other countries.

Ben & Jerry's marketing managers use an information system that tracks every pint—from the ingredients that went into it to where it sells. They constantly study sales to see if Cherry Garcia is still in the number 1 sales spot or if Chunky Monkey is moving up or down the top-10 sellers list. And if sales of a flavor are not doing as well in Texas as in Pennsylvania, they alter the mix that goes to that region. If sales of a flavor start to slip in one channel of distribution, they watch to see if it's a onetime blip or if it's the start of a trend that spreads. And if it is a trend, they replace that flavor with a new one before the drop in sales turns into a problem.

Ben & Jerry's doesn't worry about inventory—but does keep track—when its ice cream cones are *virtual.* The company's marketing manager was pleased when Facebook users gave away 500,000 cones to each other. Ben & Jerry's also tracks how many fans download—and how they rate—the free iPhone app that lets them find local scoop shops, learn about ingredients for each flavor, and create a list of "favorites." While it's easy to track the costs of these programs, it's harder to measure the important benefits of loyalty and passion for the brand.

Everyone at Ben & Jerry's knows that customer loyalty starts with product quality. Each time a call or an e-mail with a comment or complaint arrives at the customer service department, they follow up and match it to the particular pint that prompted contact from the customer. Customer service determines when it was produced and where it was sold. They receive more than 200 calls and e-mails each week, scrutinizing all the inputs to see if they reveal undetected problems—whether it's the milk from a particular supplier, a specific production batch in the factory, or how the product is stored in the channel.

All this scrutiny sometimes reveals an implementation problem rather than a problem with product quality. In one such case, the customer service people were getting a lot of complaints from customers that their Cherry Garcia ice cream pops didn't have enough cherries. After service people matched the complaints with sales records, they concluded it wasn't a regional problem—complaints pointed to pints that were sold all over the country. There wasn't a quality problem with specific production batches either. Finally they discovered that the photo on the box was not of ice cream but of frozen yogurt treats—a product that contains more cherries. The difference wasn't great, but customers expected more cherries than they were getting. When Ben & Jerry's fixed the image on the box, the complaints melted away.

Information about costs and revenues are important for scoop shops, too. Ben & Jerry's scoop shops are typically run by entrepreneurs who operate as franchisees. Franchisees must carefully set plans for revenues, costs, and profits. New franchisees find this particularly challenging because they don't have past data to help them make estimates. So Ben & Jerry's provides franchisees with estimates that help them get started. For example, a franchisee usually has to spend $167,000 to $400,000 to open a 1,000-square-foot scoop shop—and then typically will need an additional $55,000 to cover operating expenses for the first three months. Ben & Jerry's breaks down the cost estimates into specific categories (like signage, inventory, and insurance). This helps the franchisee know if spending is on target or is over (or under) budget and on which items. On average, scoop shops bring in almost $400,000 a year in gross sales, but scoop shops are a seasonal business so both revenues and costs vary substantially over the year. A shop owner can monitor his or her own costs and revenues on a weekly or monthly basis and then compare them to the data from Ben & Jerry's. This helps the shop owner know if the store will meet targets or if adjustments to marketing strategy are needed.

In the United States, sales growth has also slowed at many scoop shop locations as competitors, like Cold Stone Creamery and Marble Slab, have grown in popularity. Similarly, sales of pints in retail stores face strong competition from Häagen-Dazs, Dreyer's, and other premium brands. Some consumers have cut back on any brand of premium ice cream because of the economy and increased concern about fat in their diets. That impacts the market, too. In spite of these changes, marketing managers at Ben & Jerry's have access to the data they need to get fast feedback—and that helps them to improve their strategy and how it is implemented.[1]

Learning Objectives

A carefully planned marketing strategy improves a firm's chances of success, but a plan that is not implemented well will not reach its potential—and may even fail. Timely control information helps a marketing manager improve both implementation and the basic strategy. Control can signal when plans need to be adapted—or changed completely—to adjust for new market conditions. This chapter will help you understand how to improve the implementation and control of marketing plans.

When you finish this chapter you should be able to:

1. understand how information technology speeds up feedback for better implementation and control.
2. know why effective implementation is critical to customer satisfaction and profits.
3. understand how sales analysis can aid marketing strategy planning.
4. understand the differences in sales analysis, performance analysis, and performance analysis using performance indexes.
5. understand the difference between the full-cost approach and the contribution-margin approach.
6. understand how planning and control can be combined to improve the marketing management process.
7. understand what a marketing audit is and when and where it should be used.
8. understand important new terms (shown in red).

Good Plans Set the Framework for Implementation and Control

Our primary emphasis in this book is on the strategy planning part of the marketing manager's job. There's a good reason for this focus. Effective strategy planning decisions set the firm on a course toward profitable opportunities. And when good strategies and plans are developed, everyone in the organization knows *what* needs to be done. Thus, good marketing plans set the framework for effective implementation and control.

Implementation puts plans into operation—and control provides feedback

Even so, successful marketing requires efficient implementation and control. See Exhibit 2-1. In fact, in today's competitive markets customer satisfaction often hinges on skillful implementation. Further, ongoing success usually depends on **control**—the feedback process that helps the marketing manager learn (1) how ongoing plans and implementation are working and (2) how to plan for the future.

Exhibit 18–1
Strategy Planning, Implementation, and Control

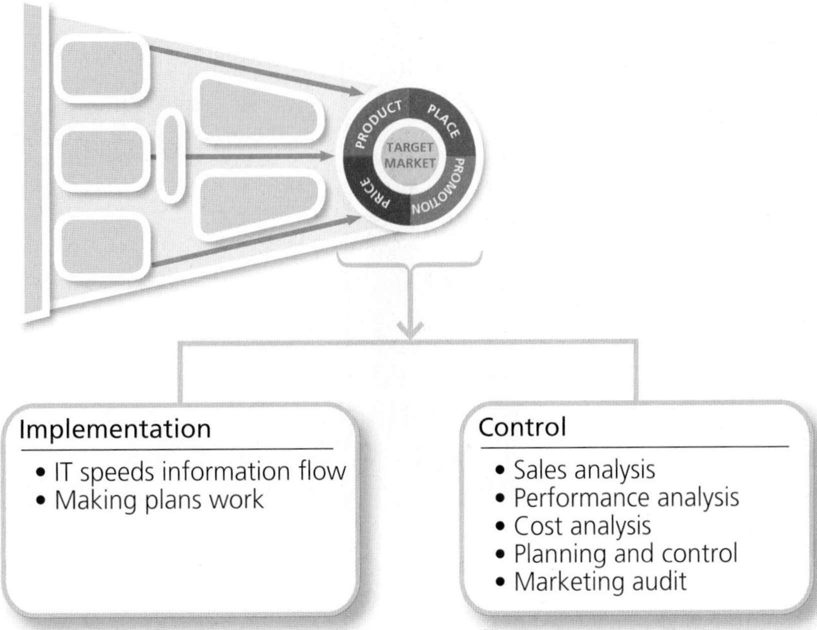

Implementation
- IT speeds information flow
- Making plans work

Control
- Sales analysis
- Performance analysis
- Cost analysis
- Planning and control
- Marketing audit

In this chapter, we'll go into more depth on concepts and how-to approaches for making implementation and control more effective. See Exhibit 18-1. We'll start with a discussion of how improvements in information technology and e-commerce have changed implementation and control. Next we'll highlight some approaches for improving implementation. Then we'll explain how marketing managers use control-related tools such as sales, performance, and cost analysis. Next, we'll combine these analyses to look at planning and control. We'll conclude with a discussion of what a marketing audit is, and why it is sometimes necessary.

Speed Up Information for Better Implementation and Control

LO 18.1

Feedback improves the marketing management process

Not long ago, marketing managers planned their strategies and put them into action—but then it usually took a long time to know if the strategy and implementation were really working as intended. For example, a marketing manager might not have much feedback on what was happening with sales, expenses, and profits until financial summaries were available—and that sometimes took months or even longer. Further, summary data often weren't very useful in pinpointing which specific aspects of the plan were working and which weren't.

That situation is dramatically different today. In Chapter 7, we discussed how firms are using intranets, databases, and marketing information systems to track sales and cost details day by day. For example, checkout scanner data can provide a retailer with immediate feedback on how well a new product is selling in each specific store. We also saw how many firms collect big data from a wide range of sources. For example, we saw how some companies track customers' movement around the Internet to better understand their wants, needs, and interests. Other companies place sensors in capital equipment that provide early detection of potential quality problems.

Fast feedback can be a competitive advantage

Marketing managers can use faster feedback to develop a competitive advantage. They can quickly fine-tune a smooth-running implementation to make it even better. If there are problems, they can spot them early and fix them. If there are opportunities, marketing managers can identify positive happenings and amplify the message. Marketing managers at Tide did that. Tide's brand managers use software to monitor social media—particularly as it relates to Tide and the laundry detergent market. Their software lit up after an incident at the nationally televised Daytona 500 stock car race. Workers were shown using

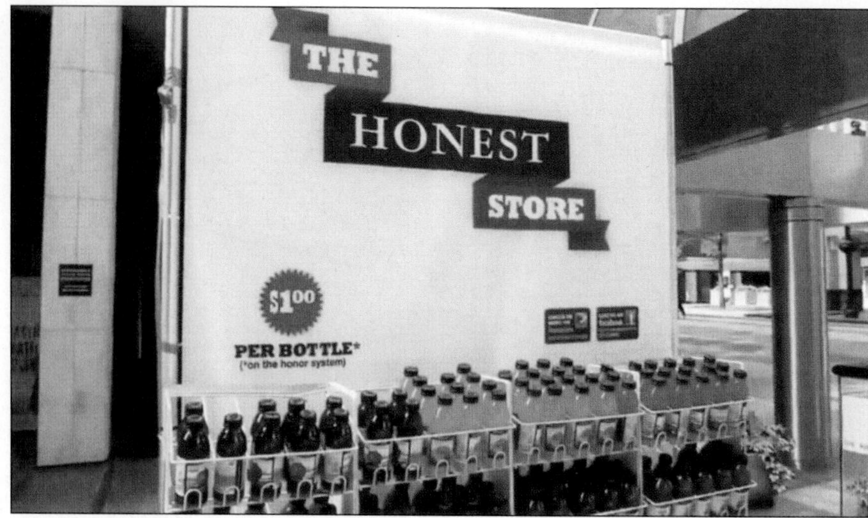

Honest Tea launched in 1997 when its founders saw an opportunity in the beverage market and filled it with less sweet versions of popular tea flavors, as well as some unique tea blends. The company sought to build healthy and honest relationships with its customers, suppliers, and the environment. With little money to spend for marketing, Honest Tea gradually expanded its product line and built distribution through health food stores and Whole Foods Market. Promotions included a partnership with Jamis bicycles and publicity from a social experiment it conducted. Honest Tea placed unmanned beverage kiosks in 12 U.S. cities—providing a box for people to make payment (clearly marked as $1 per bottle). A hidden camera recorded how many customers paid up. Chicago, with 99 percent of customers leaving a buck was the most honest city; while the least honest city was New York, where 86 percent left a dollar. The Honest Tea stores generated more than 160 press stories. See more at http://youtu.be/L8mbxsWKCAQ.

Tide to clean up the track following a crash and fuel spill. Tide's marketing managers saw an opportunity. A few days later Tide posted a new television commercial on YouTube. It showed the cleanup activity with a sportscaster narrating in the backround "...a new use for laundry detergent," as another message scrolled across the bottom of the screen: "You keep inventing stains. We'll keep inventing ways to get them out."[2]

The marketing manager must take charge

Fast feedback is not possible unless data are in a form that can be quickly sorted and analyzed by computer. Here the creative marketing manager plays a crucial role by insisting that necessary data be captured as they come in. It will be difficult, if not impossible, to get the information later. Sometimes the type of information to collect and monitor is not so obvious—so it helps to have a marketing manager in charge. For example, marketing managers at Kraft Foods, don't find that measuring whether there are more favorable or unfavorable comments about its Kraft Barbecue Sauce provides much insight. So they listen more generally to the way that consumers comment on social media about the barbecuing experience, related recipes, and favorite tricks. These comments give Kraft managers ideas about their target customers' wants and needs.

New information technologies offer speed and detail

Digital communication and e-commerce help solve these problems. Many companies use the Internet to immediately share data among locations. A sales manager with a notebook computer can pull data off the firm's intranet from anywhere in the world. Database applications that run on a website give similar access. Marketing managers working on different aspects of a strategy can use e-mail, messaging, social media, or online video conferencing to communicate.

With the electronic pipeline, a report summarizing sales by product, salesperson, or type of customer can be available whenever an online user wants it. Software can be programmed to flag results that indicate a problem or create graphs that are easy to interpret. Then the manager can allocate time to resolve whatever problems show up.

These approaches are becoming common. Marketing managers who don't adopt them are losing out to more nimble competitors who get information more quickly and adjust their implementation and strategies more often.[3]

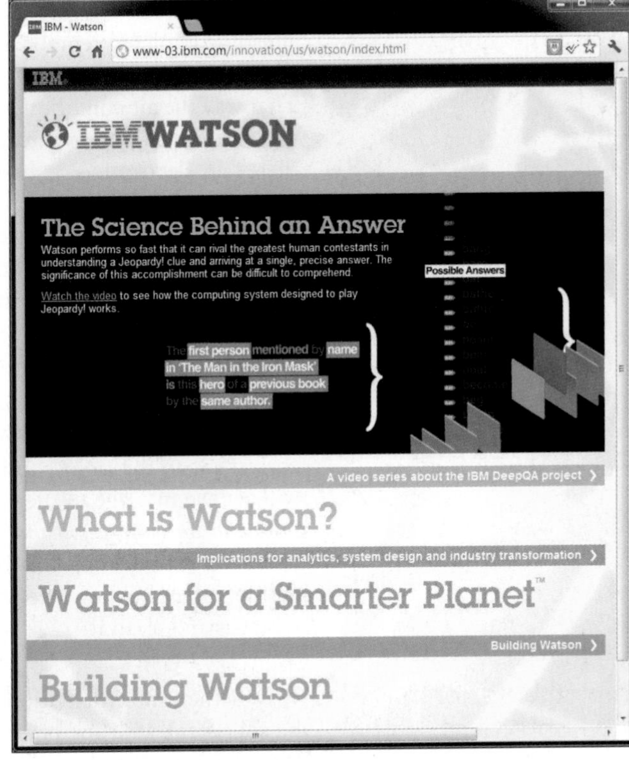

Advances in technology have the potential to help marketing managers make better decisions more quickly. Software programs from Sage can turn data into meaningful information. When IBM showed that a computer could beat champion Jeopardy (game show) players, it pointed to a future where artificial intelligence systems answer questions using natural language.

Effective Implementation Means That Plans Work as Intended

LO 18.2

A good marketing plan often involves the challenge of implementing hundreds of operational decisions and activities. In a small company, these may all be handled by a single person. In a large corporation, thousands of people may be involved in implementation, requiring careful coordination and communication. Either way, even a great plan can leave customers unhappy, and switching to someone else's offering, if implementation is poor.

Good implementation builds relationships with customers

Implementation is especially critical in mature and highly competitive markets. When several firms all follow basically the same strategy—quickly imitating competitors' ideas—customers are often won or lost based on the quality of implementation. Consider the rental car business. Hertz has a strategy that targets business travelers with a choice of quality cars, convenient online reservations, fast pick-up and drop-off, accessories like GPS, availability at most major airports, and a premium price. Hertz is successful with this strategy even though other companies can try the same approach. Hertz's success is due to implementation. Customers keep coming back because Hertz's service is reliable and pain-free.

When a Hertz #1 Club Gold customer calls to make a reservation, the company already has the standard information about that customer in a customer database. At the airport, the customer skips the line at the Hertz counter and instead just picks up an already-completed rental contract and goes straight to the Hertz bus. The driver gets the customer's name and radios ahead to have someone start the car that customer will drive. That way the air conditioner or heater is already doing its job when the bus driver delivers the customer right to the car. Customers are certain they're at the right place because there's an electronic sign beside each car with the customer's name on it. When the customer returns the car, an agent comes to the car, scans the customer's contract with a handheld computer, and prints the receipt.

It's all very smooth. Making this work—day in and day out, customer after customer—isn't easy. But Hertz has set up systems to make it all easier because that's what it takes to implement its plan and to keep customers loyal.

Implementation deals with internal or external matters

As the Hertz example illustrates, marketing implementation usually involves decisions and activities related to both internal and external matters. Figuring out how to get the correct car to the right parking slot, how the bus driver will contact the office, and who will get the message to the person who starts the car are all internal matters. They are *invisible to the customer if they work as planned.* On the other hand, some implementation issues are external and involve the customer. For example, the contract must be correct and in the right spot when the customer picks it up, and someone needs to fill the car with gas and clean it.

Implementation has its own objectives

Whether implementation decisions and activities are internal or external, they all must be consistent with the objectives of the overall strategy and with the other details of the plan. However, there are also three general objectives that apply to all implementation efforts. Other things equal, the manager wants to get each implementation job done:

Better, so customers really get superior value as planned.

Faster, to avoid delays that cause customers problems.

At lower cost, without wasting money on things that don't add value for the customer.

The ideal of doing things better, faster, and at lower cost is easy to accept. But in practice, implementation is often complicated by trade-offs among the three objectives. For example, doing a job better may take longer or cost more.

So just as a marketing manager should constantly look for new strategy opportunities, it's important to be creative in looking for better solutions to implementation problems. That may require finding ways to better coordinate the efforts of the different people involved, setting up standard operating procedures to deal with recurring problems, or juggling priorities to deal with the unexpected. When the Hertz bus driver is sick, someone still has to be there to pick up the customers and deliver them to their cars.

Customer complaints bring implementation problems to light

There are thousands of ways that a plan or its implementation can go astray. A consumer's box of laundry detergent may be missing the measuring scoop. A digital camera's instructions may be very clear about how to take a picture but not explain how to hook up the camera to a computer. Left unresolved, implementation glitches like these often result in dissatisfied customers. Smart marketers encourage customers to complain and make suggestions when there's a problem. Then it's possible

Internet Exercise

Companies handle customer complaints in different ways. Select three products that you use, and then, for each product, go to the website of either the firm that produces it or a retailer that sells it. How easy is it for you to register a complaint with each business? Does the company encourage phone calls? Or e-mails? Was it easy to find this information? Which of the three companies you visited does the best job with complaint management? Why?

to do something to correct it. In business markets complaints are usually handled by salespeople. But most firms that deal with large numbers of consumers have to rely on toll-free telephone lines, websites, and e-mail customer service support to help customers with questions and complaints.

Pillsbury's toll-free customer service telephone line is typical. Some calls involve a question or praise, but about a third are complaints. For example, soon after Pillsbury introduced Funfetti cake mix with bits of edible confetti, callers began complaining that the confetti packet was missing from their box. A check of the manufacturing line showed the confetti packets were too light to alert weight scales when they were missing from the boxes. After the firm changed to a heavier foil package, the complaints stopped.

Get ahead of customer complaints

We have mentioned the benefits of routinely monitoring the web. With real-time data collection and smart software that notifies managers of potential problems, marketing managers can get ahead of potential problems. Quick responses can help a company provide better customer service and manage its reputation—especially if it is likely to get blamed for something it didn't do. Consider how Comcast's customer service manager reacted when one evening he saw a spike in Twitter comments about Comcast and the National Hockey League. He very quickly discovered that Comcast's broadcast of a playoff game had disappeared from the screen. A couple of clicks later, the manager saw that DirectTV was having the same problem—so he knew the source of the problem was the channel originating the broadcast and not Comcast. He quickly relayed this information to Comcast's telephone customer service center so they could explain the situation to the deluge of complaining customers. The customer service team also recorded an explanation for customers placed on hold because of the sudden spike in call volume. It took 30 minutes to

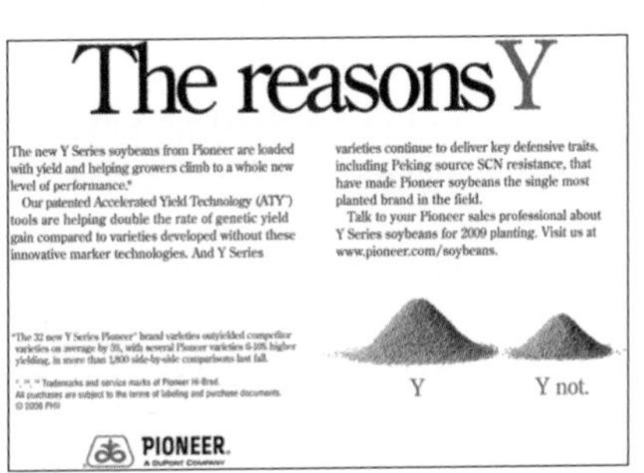

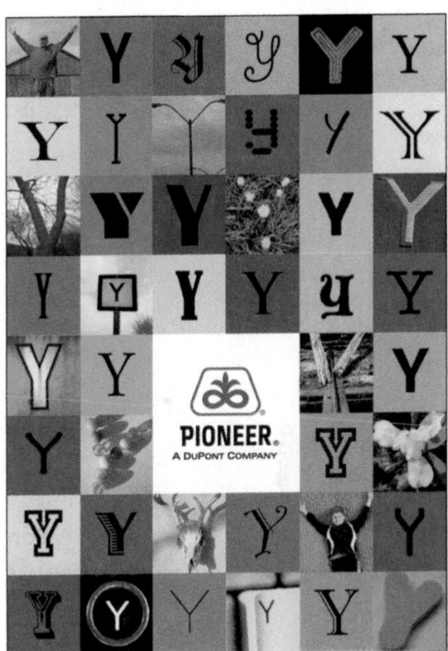

Soybean yields are going hYgher

This changes everYthing

Huge UpsYde

Better buY a bigger bin

New Y Series soybeans from PIONEER.

Changing customers' minds about a brand is not easy. You need a good product, and a good, well-implemented, campaign. While Pioneer Hi-Bred slowly gained market share in the soybean category, most farmers still thought of the brand as a corn supplier. So Pioneer shook things up a bit when it introduced its new Y-series high-yield soybeans. A multi-page insert in *Farm Journal* magazine attracted farmers' attention by telling "Y" the new soybeans would give "hYgher" yields. The campaign created plenty of interest and sales jumped 2.5 million units over the previous year.

Exhibit 18–2 Examples of Approaches to Overcome Specific Marketing Implementation Problems

Marketing Mix Decision Area	Operational Problem	Implementation Approach
Product	Develop design of a new product as rapidly as possible without errors.	Use 3-D computer-aided design software.
	Pretest consumer response to different versions of a label.	Prepare sample labels with graphics software and test them on the Internet.
Place	Coordinate inventory levels with intermediaries to avoid stock-outs.	Use bar code scanners, RFID (smart) tags, EDI, and inventory reorder software.
	Get franchisee's inputs and cooperation on ongoing activities.	Set up an online community.
Promotion	Quickly distribute TV ad to local stations in many different markets.	Distribute digital video version of the ad via satellite link.
	Answer final consumers' questions about how to use a product.	Put a toll-free telephone number and website address on product label.
Price	Identify frequent customers for a quantity discount.	Create a store loyalty card.
	Figure out if price sensitivity impacts demand for a product; make it easier for customers to compare prices.	Show unit prices (for example, per oz.) on shelf markers; set different prices in similar markets and track sales, including sales of competing products.

restore the broadcast, but Comcast gave the best customer service it could under the circumstances, and avoided blame for technical problems beyond its control.[4]

Complaints need a response

Toll-free customer service lines and e-mail features built into websites probably don't win many new customers. But they do help a firm keep its current customers—if complaints are handled well. Yet too many firms drop the ball in this area of implementation as well. The customer may be shuffled from one person to another with no one taking responsibility to solve the problem.

Firms that get feedback by e-mail need to have a system that ensures that there is follow-up on each complaint. Many firms handle the first step smoothly. There is someone who reads each message and forwards it to the department or person who seems right to handle the problem. However, there also should be a tracking system to be certain that the customer gets a response. This follow-up can be very important. One study found that callers who had their complaints resolved, on average, told five people about the help they got. The flip side is that those who weren't satisfied told twice as many people.[5]

Implementation requires innovation too

Sometimes implementation can be improved by approaching the task in a new way. Exhibit 18-2 shows some of the ways that firms are using information technology to improve specific implementation jobs. Note that some of the examples in Exhibit 18-2 focus on internal matters and some on external, customer-oriented matters.[6]

Control Provides Feedback to Improve Plans and Implementation

Keeping a firmer hand on the controls

Although information technology speeds up the flow of feedback and allows managers to improve plans and implementation continuously, the basic control questions that a marketing manager wants to answer are pretty similar to what they've always been.

A good manager wants to know which products' sales are highest and why, which products are profitable, what is selling where, and how much the marketing process is costing. Managers need to know what's happening, in detail, to improve the bottom line.

Unfortunately, traditional accounting reports are usually too general to be much help in answering these questions. A company may be showing a profit, while 80 percent of its business comes from only 20 percent of its products—or customers. The other 80 percent may be unprofitable. But without special analyses, managers won't know it. This 80/20 relationship is fairly common—and it is often referred to as the *80/20 rule.*

What happened at Allegiance Healthcare Corporation (AHC), which later became part of CardinalHealth, is a good example. As a major distributor of hospital supplies, AHC carried over 100,000 products—everything a hospital might need from scalpels and skin markers to gowns and bandages. The huge array of products was complicated, but AHC was doing well with its strategy of being a "single source" for hospitals. However, careful analysis of sales and costs by region and product line revealed that AHC's profitable level of sales was masking a problem: 57 percent of its products accounted for just 2 percent of sales. Further, these same products had larger than average costs. While waiting to be ordered, these products were sitting in warehouses all over the country, running up inventory costs. By analyzing sales within product categories, marketing managers were able to see where there was duplication and what they could drop. After all, they probably didn't need to give hospitals a choice among dozens of bedpans. Then they worked to make distribution of the products they kept more efficient. Products that hospitals order frequently—like needles and sutures—are stocked in the 68 regional distribution centers close to customers. Items that hospitals order infrequently—like odd sizes of surgical gloves—are shipped from a single distribution center. The changes allowed AHC to cut out 30 local warehouses and still offer hospitals just-in-time delivery by using its own trucks.[7]

As this example shows, it is possible for marketing managers to get detailed information about how marketing plans are working—but only if they ask for and analyze the

Zynga's FishVille is a Facebook-based game where players raise and feed cute baby fish, decorate their aquariums, and send gifts to friends who are also playing the game. Starting to play the game is free, but there are in-game purchases that provide revenue for Zynga. Zynga analyzes game player behavior to optimize users' experiences. For example, when it noticed that players purchased translucent angler fish at six times the rate of other imaginary sea creatures, Zynga had artists develop similar sea animals and sold them for $3–$4 each.

necessary data. In this section, we'll discuss the kinds of information that can be available and how to use it. The techniques are not really complicated. They basically require only simple arithmetic—and of course computers easily take care of that when a large volume of sorting, adding, and subtracting is required.

Sales Analysis Shows What's Happening

LO 18.3

Sales analysis looks at the details

Marketers are always interested in what sort of sales results they're achieving, but it's usually not enough to just know totals or summary information. Marketing executives need more detailed sales data to keep in touch with what's happening in the market. They get this detail by turning to **sales analysis**—a detailed breakdown of a company's sales records.

There is no one best way to break down or analyze sales data. Several breakdowns may be useful, depending on the nature of the company and product and what dimensions are relevant. Typical breakdowns include the following:

1. Product category, brand, package size, grade, or color
2. Geographic region—country, state, city, or sales rep's territory
3. Customer characteristics (new or existing account, frequency of purchases, etc.)
4. Channel of distribution (type of wholesaler or retailer involved, target markets served, store size, etc.)
5. Price or discount class
6. Method of sale—online, telephone, or sales rep
7. Financial arrangement—cash or charge
8. Order size

Sales analysis is easy to do, and usually it's inexpensive because the data for the analysis can easily be obtained as a by-product of basic billing and accounts receivable procedures. However, the manager must make sure the company captures identifying information on important dimensions such as territory, sales rep, product model, and customer in a database. Then the marketing information system can easily provide detailed sales analyses broken down by any variable (or combination of variables) in the database.

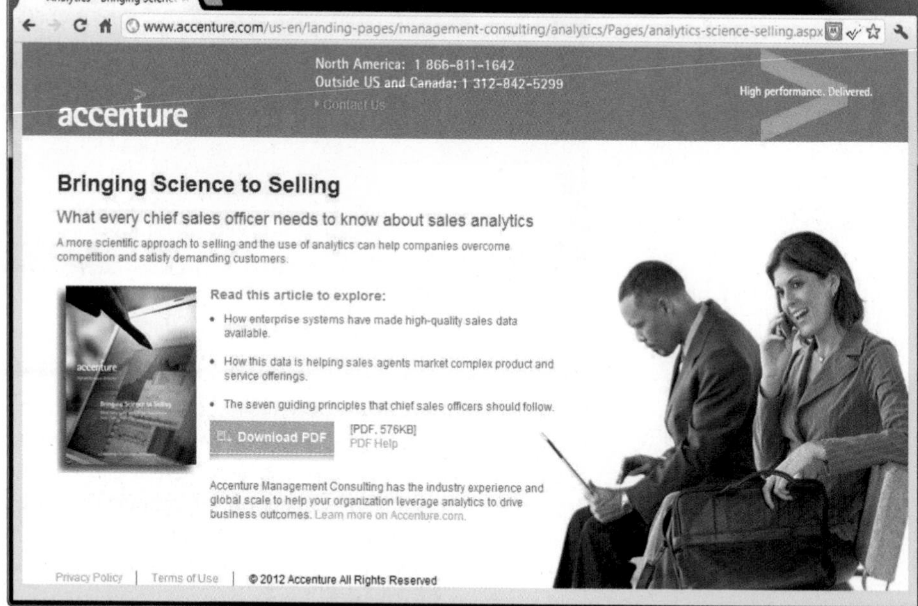

Accenture offers consulting services to help companies analyze sales data. To attract companies interested in its services, Accenture produced a white paper titled "Bringing Science to Selling: What every chief sales officer needs to know about sales analytics." Sales analysis helps companies to become more efficient and effective in their personal selling.

Sales analyses over time highlight trends

When sales analyses are routinely prepared over time (every day, week, month, or quarter), they show trends and help managers develop more accurate sales forecasts. A manager who ignores trends may not be able to spot shifts in the market that point to new opportunities or, alternatively, problems. This is critical because today's profit is no guarantee that you'll make money tomorrow.

A graph is worth a thousand numbers

While detailed and timely sales analysis can be very useful, information that is too detailed or complex can drown a manager. Information systems can spew out more data than a manager can absorb. Well-designed information systems provide managers with color graphs and charts that make it easy to see patterns that otherwise might be hidden scrolling through online tables with a browser. For example, a sales analysis breakdown of sales by product might show a bar graph for each product, where the height of the bar reflects the level of sales and where increases from the previous period are in green and decreases are in red.

While graphs can help a manager sort through raw sales data, another way to identify what data are most relevant and really need attention is *performance analysis*.

Performance Analysis Looks for Differences

LO 18.4

Numbers are compared

Performance analysis looks for exceptions or variations from planned performance. In simple sales analysis, the figures are merely listed or graphed—they aren't compared against standards. In performance analysis, managers make comparisons. They might compare one territory against another, against the same territory's performance last year, or against expected performance.

The purpose of performance analysis is to improve operations. The salesperson, territory, or other factors showing poor performance can be identified and singled out for detailed analysis and corrective action. Or outstanding performances can be analyzed to see if the successes can be explained and made the general rule.

Performance analysis doesn't have to be limited to sales. Other data can be analyzed too. These data may include the frequency of stock-outs, the number of sales calls made, the number of orders, customer satisfaction ratings, or the cost of various tasks.

A performance analysis can be quite revealing, as shown in the following example.

Straight performance analysis—an illustration

A manufacturer of business products sells to wholesalers through five sales reps, each serving a separate territory. Total net sales for the year amount to $4,772,000. Sales force compensation and expenses come to $396,000, yielding a direct-selling expense ratio of 8.3 percent—that is, $396,000 ÷ $4,772,000 × 100.

This information—taken from a profit and loss statement—is interesting, but it doesn't explain what's happening from one territory to another. To get a clearer picture, the manager compares the sales results with other data *from each territory.* See Exhibits 18-3 and 18-4. Keep in mind that exhibits like these and others that follow in this chapter are

Exhibit 18–3 Comparative Performance of Sales Reps

Sales Area	Total Calls	Total Orders	Order-Call Ratio	Sales by Sales Rep	Average Sales Rep Order	Total Customers
A	1,900	1,140	60.0%	$1,824,000	$1,600	195
B	1,500	1,000	66.7	1,440,000	1,440	160
C	1,400	700	50.0	1,120,000	1,600	140
D	1,030	279	27.1	264,000	956	60
E	820	165	20.1	124,000	748	50
Total	6,650	3,284	49.3%	$4,772,000	$1,269	605

Exhibit 18–4 Comparative Cost of Sales Reps

Sales Area	Annual Compensation	Expense Payments	Total Sales Rep Cost	Sales Produced	Cost-Sales Ratio
A	$ 45,600	$ 22,400	$ 68,000	$1,824,000	3.7%
B	43,200	28,800	72,000	1,440,000	5.0
C	40,800	23,200	64,000	1,120,000	5.7
D	38,400	49,600	88,000	264,000	33.3
E	40,000	64,000	104,000	124,000	83.9
Total	$208,000	$188,000	$396,000	$4,772,000	8.3%

easy to generate with programs like Microsoft Excel. Larger companies make such analysis available at a website so the manager can sort out whatever is needed.

The reps in sales areas D and E aren't doing well. Sales are low and marketing costs are high. Perhaps more aggressive sales reps could do a better job, but the number of customers suggests that sales potential might be low. Perhaps the whole plan needs revision.

The figures themselves, of course, don't provide the answers. But they do reveal the areas that need improvement. This is the main value of performance analysis. It's up to management to find the remedy, either by revising or changing the marketing plan.

Ethics Question

You are the marketing manager for a regional insurance company that specializes in auto insurance. You ask a summer intern to come up with a performance analysis to compare how profitable customers are based on where they live, the cost of their policies, and their past claims. It turns out that inner-city customers are the least profitable; the company actually loses money on many of them. Currently, telephone salespeople from your office are calling leads from a direct-mail ad campaign—and they are having success selling policies. Your bonus and the sales reps' commissions are based on sales of new policies, not on costs or customer profitability. What should you do in response to the information from the profitability analysis conducted by the summer intern? Should you change your marketing strategy? Should you tell salespeople not to call prospects from inner-city addresses? Explain your thinking.

Performance Indexes Simplify Human Analysis

Comparing against "what ought to have happened"

With a straight performance analysis, the marketing manager can evaluate the variations among sales reps to try to explain the "why." But this takes time. And poor performances are sometimes due to problems that bare sales figures don't reveal. Some uncontrollable factors in a particular territory—tougher competitors or ineffective channel members—may lower the sales potential. Or a territory just may not have much potential.

To get a better check on performance effectiveness, the marketing manager compares what did happen with what ought to have happened. This involves the use of performance indexes.

A performance index is like a batting average

When a manager sets standards—that is, quantitative measures of what ought to happen—it's relatively simple to compute a **performance index**—a number like a baseball batting average that shows the relation of one value to another.

Baseball batting averages are computed by dividing the actual number of hits by the number of times at bat (the possible number of times the batter could have had a hit) and then multiplying the result by 100 to get rid of decimal points. A sales performance index is computed the same way—by dividing actual sales by expected sales for the area (or sales rep, product, etc.) and then multiplying by 100. If a sales rep is batting 82 percent, the index is 82.

A simple example shows where the problem is

We show how to compute a performance index in the following example, which assumes that population is an effective measure of sales potential.

In Exhibit 18-5, the population of the United States is broken down by region as a percent of the total population. The regions are Northeastern, Southern, Midwestern, and Western. A firm already has $1 million in sales and now wants to evaluate performance in each region. Column 2 shows the actual sales of $1 million broken down in proportion to the population in the four regions. This is what sales *should* be if population were a good measure of future performance. Column 3 in Exhibit 19-5 shows the actual sales for the year for each region. Column 4 shows measures of performance (performance indexes)—Column 3 ÷ Column 2 × 100.

Internet Exercise

SPSS sells software that can be used for a variety of purposes, including analyses of sales, cost, and customer data. Browse the SPSS website (**www.spss.com**) and identify three ways that SPSS could make it easier for a manager to do a performance analysis.

The Western region isn't doing as well as expected. It has 20 percent of the total population—and expected sales (based on population) are $200,000. Actual sales, however, are only $120,000. This means that the Western region's performance index is only 60—(120,000 ÷ 200,000) × 100—because actual sales are much lower than expected on the basis of population. If population is a good basis for measuring expected sales (an important *if*), the poor sales performance should be analyzed further. Perhaps sales reps in the Western region aren't working as hard as they should. Perhaps promotion there isn't as effective as elsewhere. Or competitive products may have entered the market.

Whatever the cause, it's clear that performance analysis does not solve problems. Managers do that. But performance analysis does point out potential problems—and it does this well.

Exhibit 18–5 Development of a Measure of Sales Performances (by region)

Regions	(1) Population as Percent of United States	(2) Expected Distribution of Sales Based on Population	(3) Actual Sales	(4) Performance Index
Northeastern	20	$ 200,000	$ 210,000	105
Southern	25	250,000	250,000	100
Midwestern	35	350,000	420,000	120
Western	20	200,000	120,000	60
Total	100	$1,000,000	$1,000,000	

A Series of Performance Analyses May Find the Real Problem

Performance analysis helps a marketing manager see if the firm's marketing plans are working properly—and, if they aren't, it can lead to problem solving. But a marketing manager may need a series of performance analyses, as shown in the following example.

To get a feel for how performance analysis can be part of a problem-solving process, follow this example carefully—one exhibit at a time. Try to anticipate the marketing manager's decision.

The case of CarAudio, Inc.

CarAudio's sales manager finds that sales for the Pacific Coast region are $130,000 below the quota of $14,500,000 (that is, actual sales are $14,370,000) for the January through June period. The quota is based on forecast sales of the various types of replacement car audio equipment the company sells. Specifically, the quota is based on forecasts for each product type in each store in each sales rep's territory.

Pam Dexter, the sales manager, thinks this difference isn't too large (less than 1 percent) and is inclined to forget the matter—especially since forecasts usually err to some extent. But she thinks about sending an e-mail message to all sales reps and district supervisors in the region—a message aimed at stimulating sales effort.

Exhibit 18-6 shows the overall picture of CarAudio's sales on the Pacific Coast. What do you think the manager should do?

The Portland district has the poorest performance—but it isn't too bad. Before writing a "let's get with it" letter to Portland and then relaxing, the sales manager decides to analyze the performance of the four sales reps in the Portland district. Exhibit 18-7 shows a breakdown of the Portland figures by sales rep. What conclusion or action do you suggest now?

Since Shanna Smith previously was the top sales rep, the sales manager wonders if Smith is having trouble with some of her larger customers. Before making a drastic move, she does an analysis of Smith's sales to the five largest customers. See Exhibit 18-8. What action could the sales manager take now? Should Smith be fired?

Smith's sales in all the large stores are down significantly, although her sales in many small stores are holding up well. Smith's problem seems to be general. Perhaps she just isn't

Exhibit 18–6

Sales Performance—Pacific Coast Region, January–June ($000)

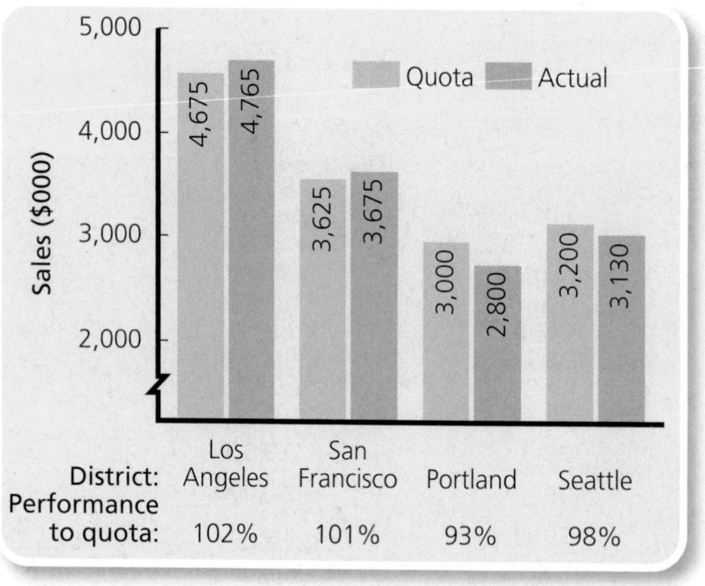

Exhibit 18–7
Sales Performance—Portland District, January–June ($000)

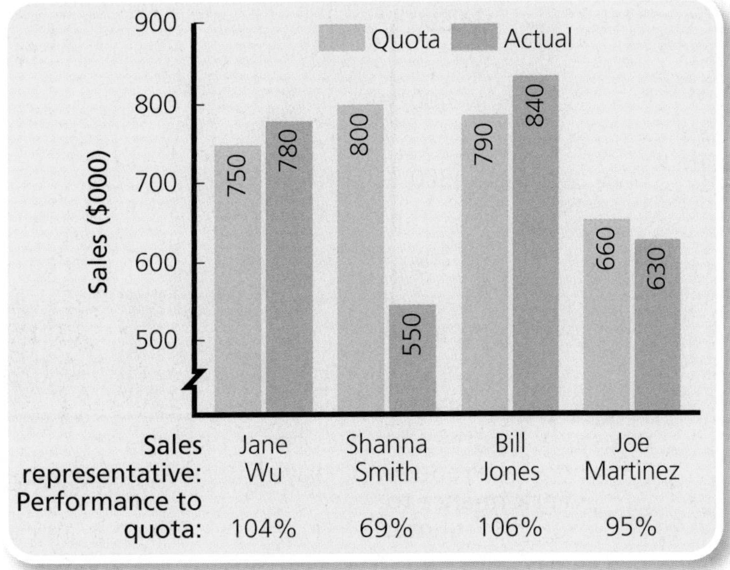

working. Before calling her, the sales manager decides to look at Smith's sales of the four major products. Exhibit 18-9 shows Smith's sales. What action is indicated now?

Smith is having real trouble with satellite radios. Was the problem Smith or the satellite radios?

Further analysis by product for the whole region shows that everyone on the Pacific Coast is having trouble with satellite radios because customers there are buying new removable satellite radios that come from another company. But higher sales on other products hid this fact. Since satellite radio sales are doing all right nationally, the problem is only now showing up. You can see that this is the *major* problem. If CarAudio doesn't offer a removable satellite radio, it will just slowly lose sales as more customers shift to units that will work in both their autos and their homes or offices.

Since overall company sales are fairly good, many sales managers wouldn't bother with this analysis. Some might trace the problem to Smith. But without detailed sales records and performance analysis, they might assume that Smith—rather than the missed opportunity to add a new product—is at fault. And Smith herself might not be able to pinpoint what's happening.

Exhibit 18–8
Sales Performance—Selected Stores of Shanna Smith in Portland District, January–June ($000)

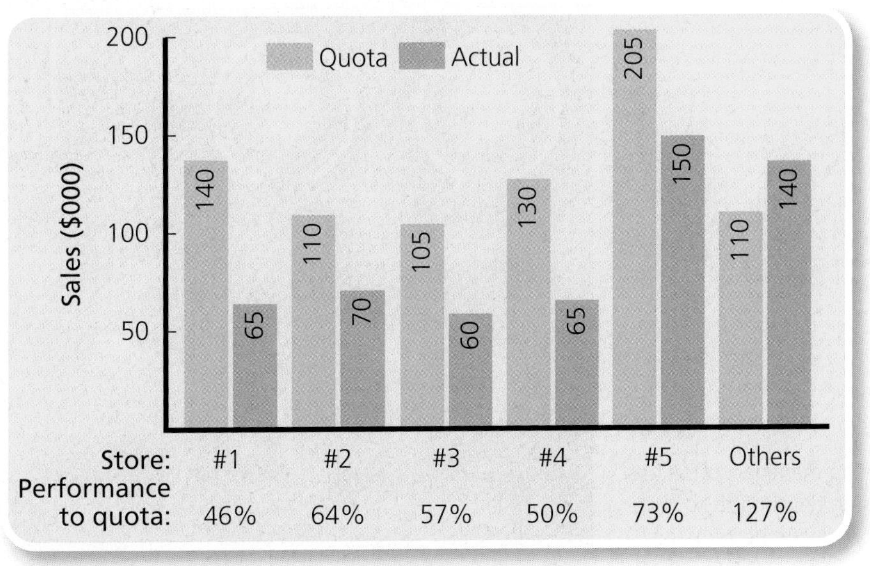

Exhibit 18–9
Sales Performance by Product for Shanna Smith in Portland District, January–June ($000)

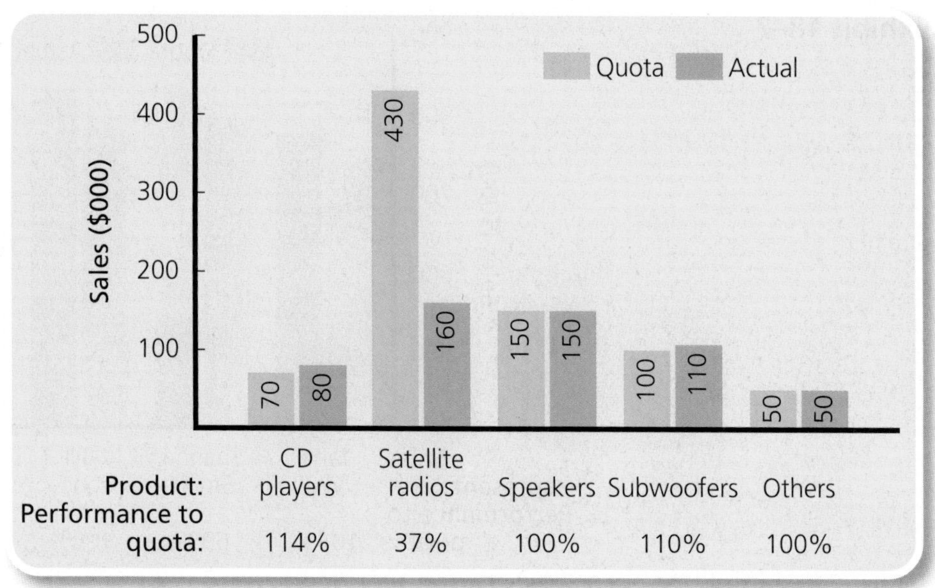

The iceberg principle—90 percent is below the surface

The CarAudio case illustrates the **iceberg principle**—much good information is hidden in summary data. Icebergs show only about 10 percent of their mass above water level. The other 90 percent is below water level, and not directly below either. The submerged portion almost seems to search out ships that come too near.

The same is true of much business and marketing data. Since total sales may be large and company activities varied, problems in one area may hide below the surface. Everything looks calm and peaceful. But closer analysis may reveal jagged edges that can severely damage or even sink the business. The 90:10 ratio—or the 80/20 rule we mentioned earlier—must not be ignored. Averaging and summarizing data are helpful, but be sure summaries don't hide more than they reveal. Marketing managers need facts to avoid rash judgments based on incomplete information. Some students want to fire Smith after they see the store-by-store data (Exhibit 18-8).

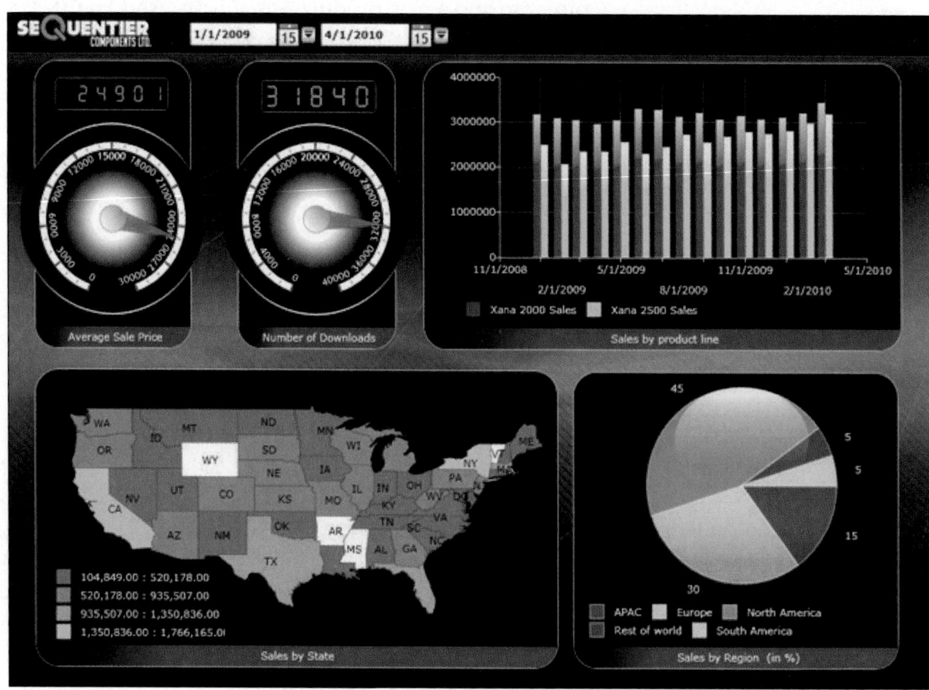

Marketing managers often use marketing dashboards to more easily conduct a performance analysis.

Marketing Cost Analysis—Controlling Costs Too

LO 18.5

So far we've emphasized sales analysis. But sales come at a cost. And costs can and should be analyzed and controlled too. You can see why in the case of Watanake Packaging, Ltd. (WPL). WPL developed a new strategy to target the packaging needs of producers of high-tech electronic equipment. WPL designed unique foam inserts to protect electronic equipment during shipping. It assigned order getters to develop new accounts and recruited agent wholesalers to develop overseas markets. WPL's marketing mix was well received and led to good profits. But over time as marketing managers at WPL analyzed costs, they realized their once-successful strategy was slipping. Personal selling expense as a percent of sales had doubled because it took longer to find and sell new accounts. It was costly to design special products for the many customers who purchased only small quantities. Profit margins were falling too because of increased price competition. In contrast, the analysis showed that online sales of ordinary shipping boxes for agricultural products made from recycled cardboard were very profitable. So WPL stopped calling on *small* electronics firms and developed a new plan to improve its website and build the firm's share of the less glamorous, but more profitable, cardboard box business.

Marketing costs have a purpose

Detailed cost analysis is very useful in understanding production costs—but much less is done with *marketing cost analysis.*[8] One reason is that many accountants show little interest in their firm's marketing process—or they don't understand the different marketing activities. They just treat marketing as overhead and forget about it.

In Chapter 19, when we discuss the relationship between marketing and accounting in more detail, we'll explain how some accountants and marketing managers are working together to address this problem. For now, however, you should see that careful analysis of most marketing costs shows that the money is spent for a specific purpose—for example, to develop or promote a particular product or to serve particular customers.

Let's reconsider Exhibit 18-4 from this perspective. It shows that the company's spending on sales compensation and sales expenses varies by salesperson and market area. By breaking out and comparing the costs of different sales reps, the marketing manager has a much better idea of what it costs to implement the strategy in each sales area. In this example, it's clear that the sales reps in sales areas D and especially E are not only falling short in sales, but also that their costs are high relative to other reps who are getting more results. The table shows that the difference isn't due to annual compensation; that's lower. Rather, these reps have expenses that are two or three times the average. The smaller number of total customers in these sales areas (Exhibit 18-3) might explain the lower levels of sales, but it probably doesn't explain the higher expenses. Perhaps the customers are more spread out and require more travel time to reach them. Here again, the cost analysis doesn't explain *why* the results are as they are—but it does direct the manager's attention to a specific area that needs improvement. A more detailed breakdown of costs may help pinpoint the specific cause.

When an ad promotes several product lines, it can be difficult to allocate the appropriate portion of the cost to individual products.

Allocate costs to specific customers and products

Because marketing costs have a purpose, it usually makes sense to allocate costs to specific market segments, or customers, or to specific products. In some situations, companies allocate costs directly to the various geographical market segments they serve. This may let managers directly analyze the profitability of the firm's target markets. In other cases, companies allocate costs to specific customers or specific products and then add these costs for market segments depending on how much of which products each customer buys.

Should all costs be allocated?

So far we've discussed general principles. But allocating costs is tricky. Some costs are likely to be fixed for the near future, regardless of what decision is made. And some costs are likely to be *common* to several products or customers, making allocation difficult.

There are two basic approaches to handling this allocating problem: the full-cost approach and the contribution-margin approach.

Full-cost approach—everything costs something

In the **full-cost approach**, all costs are allocated to products, customers, or other categories. Even fixed costs and common costs are allocated in some way. Because all costs are allocated, we can subtract costs from sales and find the profitability of various customers, products, and so on. This is of interest to some managers.

The full-cost approach requires that difficult-to-allocate costs be split on some basis. Here the managers assume that the work done for those costs is equally beneficial to customers, to products, or to whatever group they are allocated. Sometimes this allocation is done mechanically. But often logic can support the allocation—if we accept the idea that marketing costs are incurred for a purpose. For example, advertising costs not directly related to specific customers or products might be allocated to *all* customers based on their purchases—on the theory that advertising helps bring in the sales. We'll go into more detail on allocating costs in Chapter 19.

Contribution-margin—ignores some costs to get results

When we use the **contribution-margin approach**, all costs are not allocated in *all* situations. Why?

When we compare various alternatives, it may be more meaningful to consider only the costs directly related to specific alternatives. Variable costs are relevant here.

The contribution-margin approach focuses attention on variable costs rather than on total costs. Total costs may include some fixed costs that do not change in the short run and can safely be ignored or some common costs that are more difficult to allocate.[9]

The two approaches can lead to different decisions

The difference between the full-cost approach and the contribution-margin approach is important. The two approaches may suggest different decisions, as we'll see in the following example.

Full-cost example

Exhibit 18-10 shows a profit and loss statement, using the full-cost approach, for a department store with three operating departments. (These could be market segments or customers or products.)

Exhibit 18–10 Profit and Loss Statement by Department

	Totals	Dept. 1	Dept. 2	Dept. 3
Sales	$100,000	$50,000	$30,000	$20,000
Cost of sales	80,000	45,000	25,000	10,000
Gross margin	20,000	5,000	5,000	10,000
Other expenses:				
Selling expenses	5,000	2,500	1,500	1,000
Administrative expenses	6,000	3,000	1,800	1,200
Total other expenses	11,000	5,500	3,300	2,200
Net profit or (loss)	$ 9,000	$ (500)	$ 1,700	$ 7,800

Web analytics track online shoppers

It's useful for marketing managers to have an accurate idea of how customers will respond to a change in a marketing mix. One way to get this type of information is to carefully study what has happened in the past. This is one of the reasons that supermarket scanner data, which marketing managers have been using for several decades, are popular and useful. Analysis of scanner data reveals how consumers' purchasing behavior changes in response to strategy changes. For example, a manager might study how a brand's share of sales or total volume differs after a change in price or a change in the type or level of advertising or sales promotion.

Data for online purchases can be analyzed the same way, but it's also common for firms to use software to track and analyze what customers do when they visit the firm's website. This approach is referred to as web analytics. For example, a marketing manager might use web analytics to find out how a customer has come to the firm's website. It might be from clicking on a search engine link, in which case the manager can learn what search term was used. Or it may be from a link or an ad at another website. Or it may just be that the customer entered the site's address into a browser. Websites can also collect clickstream data—a record of the sequence of pages that a person sees while browsing a website—or a record of the information a person enters while there. This type of information can be helpful. For example, it may help identify which web pages encourage customers to stay at the site and which pages prompt them to exit, or what motivates a customer to add something to a "shopping cart" or checkout. It's also common to track actual sales that result from a particular ad or link at another website. Combining data on actual sales with data on the cost of the ad allows the marketing manager to evaluate the return on promotion spending.

The marketing manager at Personal Creations (www.personalcreations.com), an online retailer of personalized gifts, used web analytic tools to fine-tune implementation and increase profits. One analysis showed that the majority of people who visited the site only looked at the home page and never clicked to another page. The analysis also showed that most people who landed on the home page didn't even scroll down to the bottom of the page where it was possible to see other links. When the home page was redesigned so that more links and products were at the top of the page, single page visits were reduced by a third. Personal Creations' marketing manager also wanted to do a test to see if customers would abandon their shopping carts if a $1 personalization fee was added at checkout. The company tested the $1 fee for 15 days and compared the results to the 15 days before the fee was added. The fee did not affect customer checkouts, so it was added on a permanent basis.

NetSimplicity (www.netsimplicity.com), a firm that sells software from its website, relies on customer relationship management software that integrates web analytics. This allows the company to track the source of almost all of its leads and new sales. For example, the marketing manager can determine if a lead has come from a particular pay-per-click ad, an online search, an e-mail campaign, or a trade show. NetSimplicity can then adapt its promotion blend to make more effective use of the firm's integrated marketing communications budget.[10]

The administrative expenses, which are the only fixed costs in this case, have been allocated to departments based on the sales volume of each department. This is a typical method of allocation. In this case, some managers argued that Department 1 was clearly unprofitable and should be eliminated because it showed a net loss of $500. Were they right?

To find out, see Exhibit 18-11, which shows what would happen if Department 1 were eliminated.

Several facts become clear right away. The overall profit of the store would be reduced if Department 1 were dropped. Fixed administrative costs of $3,000, now being charged to Department 1, would have to be allocated to the other departments. This would reduce net profit by $2,500, since Department 1 previously covered $2,500 of the $3,000 in fixed costs. Such shifting of costs would then make Department 2 look unprofitable!

Exhibit 18–11 Profit and Loss Statement by Department if Department 1 Were Eliminated

	Totals	Dept. 2	Dept. 3
Sales	$50,000	$30,000	$20,000
Cost of sales	35,000	25,000	10,000
Gross margin	15,000	5,000	10,000
Other expenses:			
Selling expenses	2,500	1,500	1,000
Administrative expenses	6,000	3,600	2,400
Total other expenses	8,500	5,100	3,400
Net profit or (loss)	$ 6,500	$ (100)	$ 6,600

Contribution-margin example

Exhibit 18-12 shows a contribution-margin income statement for the same department store. Note that each department has a positive contribution margin. Here the Department 1 contribution of $2,500 stands out better. This actually is the amount that would be lost if Department 1 were dropped. (Our simple example assumes that the fixed administrative expenses are *truly* fixed—that none of them would be eliminated if this department were dropped.)

A contribution-margin income statement shows the contribution of each department more clearly, including its contribution to both fixed costs and profit. As long as a department has some contribution-margin, and as long as there is no better use for the resources it uses, the department should be retained.

Contribution-margin versus full-cost—choose your side

Using the full-cost approach often leads to arguments within a company. Any method of allocation can make some products or customers appear less profitable.

For example, it seems logical to assign all common advertising costs to customers based on their purchases. But this approach can be criticized on the grounds that it may make large-volume customers appear less profitable than they really are. Those in the company who want the smaller customers to look more profitable usually argue *for* this allocation method.

Exhibit 18–12 Contribution-Margin Statement by Departments

	Totals	Dept. 1	Dept. 2	Dept. 3
Sales	$100,000	$50,000	$30,000	$20,000
Variable costs:				
Cost of sales	80,000	45,000	25,000	10,000
Selling expenses	5,000	2,500	1,500	1,000
Total variable costs	85,000	47,500	26,500	11,000
Contribution margin	15,000	$ 2,500	$ 3,500	$ 9,000
Fixed costs				
Administrative expenses	6,000			
Net profit	$ 9,000			

Arguments over allocation methods can be deadly serious. The method used may reflect on the performance of various managers—and it may affect their salaries and bonuses. Product managers, for example, are especially interested in how the various fixed and common costs are allocated to their products. Each, in turn, might like to have costs shifted to others' products.

Arbitrary allocation of costs also may have a direct impact on sales reps' morale. If they see their variable costs loaded with additional common or fixed costs over which they have no control, they may ask, "What's the use?"

To avoid these problems, firms often use the contribution-margin approach. It's especially useful for evaluating alternatives and for showing operating managers and salespeople how they're doing. The contribution-margin approach shows what they've actually contributed to covering general overhead and profit.

Top management, on the other hand, often finds full-cost analysis more useful. In the long run, some products, departments, or customers must pay for the fixed costs. Full-cost analysis has its place too.

Planning and Control Combined

LO 18.6

We've been treating sales and cost analyses separately up to this point. But management often combines them to keep a running check on its activities—to be sure the plans are working—and to see when and where new strategies are needed.

Sales + Costs + Everybody helps = $163,000

Let's see how this works at Cindy's Fashions, a small-town apparel retailer. This firm netted $155,000 last year. Cindy Reve, the owner, expects no basic change in competition and slightly better local business conditions. So she sets this year's profit objective at $163,000—an increase of about 5 percent.

Next she develops tentative plans to show how she can make this higher profit. She estimates the sales volumes, gross margins, and expenses—broken down by months and by departments in her store—that she would need to net $163,000.

Exhibit 18-13 is a planning and control chart Reve developed to show the contribution each department should make each month. At the bottom of Exhibit 18-13, the plan for the year is summarized. Note that space is provided to insert the actual performance and a measure of variation. So this chart can be used to do both planning and control.

Exhibit 18-13 shows that Reve is focusing on the monthly contribution to overhead and profit by each department. The purpose of monthly estimates is to get more frequent feedback and allow faster adjustment of plans. Generally, the shorter the planning and control period, the easier it is to correct problems before they become emergencies.

In this example, Reve uses a modified contribution-margin approach—some of the fixed costs can be allocated logically to particular departments. On this chart, the balance left after direct fixed and variable costs are charged to departments is called Contribution to Store. The idea is that each department will contribute to covering *general* store expenses—such as top-management salaries and holiday decorations—and to net profits.

In Exhibit 18-13, we see that the whole operation is brought together when Reve computes the monthly operating profit. She totals the contribution from each of the four departments and then subtracts general store expenses to obtain the operating profit for each month.

As time passes, Reve can compare actual sales with what's projected. If actual sales were less than projected, corrective action could take either of two courses: improving implementation efforts or developing new, more realistic strategies.

Exhibit 18–13 Planning and Control Chart for Cindy's Fashions

	Contribution to Store							
	Dept. A	Dept. B	Dept. C	Dept. D*	Total	Store Expense	Operating Profit	Cumulative Operating Profit
January								
Planned	27,000	9,000	4,000	−1,000	39,000	24,000	15,000	15,000
Actual								
Variation								
February								
Planned	20,000	6,500	2,500	−1,000	28,000	24,000	4,000	19,000
Actual								
Variation								
November								
Planned	32,000	7,500	2,500	0	42,000	24,000	18,000	106,500
Actual								
Variation								
December								
Planned	63,000	12,500	4,000	9,000	88,500	32,000	56,500	163,000
Actual								
Variation								
Total								
Planned	316,000	70,000	69,000	−4,000	451,000	288,000	163,000	163,000
Actual								
Variation								

*The objective of minus $4,000 for this department was established on the same basis as the objectives for the other departments—that is, it represents the same percentage gain over last year when Department D's loss was $4,200. Plans call for discontinuance of the department unless it shows marked improvement by the end of the year.

The Marketing Audit

LO 18.7

While crises pop up, planning and control must go on

The analyses we've discussed so far are designed to help a firm plan and control its operations. They can help a marketing manager do a better job. Often, however, the control process focuses on short-run problems and adjustments.

To make sure that the whole marketing program is evaluated *regularly,* marketing specialists developed the marketing audit. A marketing audit is similar to an accounting audit or a personnel audit, which businesses have used for some time.

The **marketing audit** is a systematic, critical, and unbiased review and appraisal of the basic objectives and policies of the marketing function and of the organization, methods, procedures, and people employed to implement the policies.[11]

A marketing audit requires a detailed look at the company's current marketing plans to see if they are still the best plans the firm can offer. Customers' needs and attitudes change—and competitors continually develop new and better plans. Plans more than a year or two old may be out-of-date or even obsolete. Sometimes marketing managers are so close to the trees that they can't see the forest. An outsider can help the firm see whether it really focuses on some unsatisfied needs and offers appropriate marketing mixes. Basically, the auditor uses our strategy planning framework. But instead of developing plans, the auditor works backward and evaluates the plans being implemented. The consultant-auditor also evaluates the quality of the effort, looking at who is doing what and how well. This means interviewing customers, competitors, channel members, and employees. A marketing audit can be a big job. But if it helps ensure that the company's strategies are on the right track and being implemented properly, it can be well worth the effort.

An audit shouldn't be necessary—but often it is

A marketing audit takes a big view of the business—and it evaluates the whole marketing program. It might be done by a separate department within the company, perhaps by a marketing controller. But to get both expert and objective evaluation, it's probably better to use an outside organization such as a marketing consulting firm.

Ideally, a marketing audit should not be necessary. Good managers do their best in planning, implementing, and controlling—and they should continually evaluate the effectiveness of the operation. In practice, however, managers often become identified with certain strategies, and pursue them blindly, when other strategies might be more effective. Since an outside view can give needed perspective, marketing audits may be more common in the future.

CONCLUSION

In this chapter, we've focused on the important role of implementation and control in satisfying customers and ensuring the firm's ongoing success. We explained how improvements in information technology are playing a critical role in revolutionizing these areas. Managers should seek new and creative ways to improve implementation, which can often give a firm a competitive advantage in building stronger relationships with customers, even in highly competitive mature markets.

A marketing program must also be controlled. Good control helps the marketing manager locate and correct weak spots and at the same time find strengths that may be applied throughout the marketing program. Control works hand in hand with planning.

Simple sales analysis just gives a picture of what happened. But when sales forecasts or other data showing expected results are brought into the analysis, we can evaluate performance—using performance indexes.

Cost analysis also can be useful. There are two basic approaches to cost analysis—full-cost and contribution-margin. Using the full-cost approach, all costs are allocated in some way. Using the contribution-margin approach, only the variable costs are allocated. Both methods have their advantages and special uses.

Ideally, the marketing manager should arrange for a constant flow of data that can be analyzed routinely, preferably by computer, to help control present plans and develop new strategies. A marketing audit can help this ongoing effort. Either a separate department within the company or an outside organization may conduct this audit.

KEY TERMS

LO 18.8

control, *476*
sales analysis, *484*
performance analysis, *485*
performance index, *486*
iceberg principle, *490*
full-cost approach, *492*
contribution-margin approach, *492*
marketing audit, *496*

QUESTIONS AND PROBLEMS

1. Give an example of how a firm has used information technology to improve its marketing implementation and do a better job of meeting your needs.
2. Should marketing managers leave it to the accountants to develop reports that the marketing manager will use to improve implementation and control? Why or why not?
3. Give an example of a firm that has a competitive advantage because of the excellent job it does with implementation activities that directly impact customer satisfaction. Explain why you think your example is a good one.
4. Various breakdowns can be used for sales analysis depending on the nature of the company and its products. Describe a situation (one for each) where

each of the following breakdowns would yield useful information. Explain why.

a. By geographic region.
b. By product.
c. By customer.
d. By size of order.
e. By size of sales rep commission on each product or product group.

5. Distinguish between a sales analysis and a performance analysis.
6. Carefully explain what the iceberg principle should mean to the marketing manager.
7. Explain the meaning of the comparative performance and comparative cost data in Exhibits 18-3 and 18-4. Why does it appear that eliminating sales areas D and E would be profitable?
8. Most sales forecasting is subject to some error (perhaps 5 to 10 percent). Should we then expect variations in sales performance of 5 to 10 percent above or below quota? If so, how should we treat such variations in evaluating performance?
9. Why is there controversy between the advocates of the full-cost and the contribution-margin approaches to cost analysis?
10. The June profit and loss statement for the Browning Company is shown. If competitive conditions make price increases impossible and management has cut costs as much as possible, should the Browning Company stop selling to hospitals and schools? Why?

Browning Company Statement

	Retailers	Hospitals and Schools	Total
Sales:			
80,000 units at $0.70	$56,000		$56,000
20,000 units at $0.60		$12,000	12,000
Total	56,000	12,000	68,000
Cost of sales	40,000	10,000	50,000
Gross margin	16,000	2,000	18,000
Sales and administrative expenses:			
Variable	6,000	1,500	7,500
Fixed	5,600	900	6,500
Total	11,600	2,400	14,000
Net profit (loss)	$ 4,400	$ (400)	$ 4,000

11. Explain why a marketing audit might be desirable, even in a well-run company. Who or what kind of an organization would be best to conduct a marketing audit? Would a marketing research firm be good? Would the present CPA firms be most suitable? Why?

CREATING MARKETING PLANS

The Marketing Plan Coach software on the text website includes a sample marketing plan for Hillside Veterinary Clinic. Look through the "Implementation" section.

a. Does the plan say anything about how Hillside will handle complaints? What could Hillside do in this area?
b. How could Hillside break down its sales and performance analysis? What type of analysis would you recommend? How could this be used to provide control for the marketing plan?
c. What type of cost analysis should Hillside do? How could this be used to provide control of the marketing plan?

SUGGESTED CASES

12. DrJane.com—Custom Vitamins
33. Kennedy & Gaffney (K&G)
35. Rizzuto's Pizzeria
Video Case 6. Big Brothers and Big Sisters of America

COMPUTER-AIDED PROBLEM

18. MARKETING COST ANALYSIS

This problem emphasizes the differences between the full-cost approach and contribution-margin approach to marketing cost analysis.

Tapco, Inc., currently sells two products. Sales commissions and unit costs vary with the quantity of each product sold. With the full-cost approach, Tapco's administrative and advertising costs are allocated to each product based on its share of total sales dollars. Details of Tapco's costs and other data are given in the spreadsheet. The first column shows a cost analysis based on the full-cost approach. The second column shows an analysis based on the contribution-margin approach.

a. If the number of Product A units sold were to increase by 1,000 units, what would happen to the allocated administrative expense for Product A? How would the change in sales of Product A affect the allocated administrative expense for Product B? Briefly discuss why the changes you observe might cause conflict between the product managers of the two different products.

b. What would happen to total profits if Tapco stopped selling Product A but continued to sell 4,000 units of Product B? What happens to total profits if the firm stops selling Product B but continues to sell 5,000 units of Product A? (Hint: To stop selling a product means that the quantity sold would be zero.)

c. If the firm dropped Product B and increased the price of Product A by $2.00, what quantity of Product A would it have to sell to earn a total profit as large as it was originally earning with both products? (Hint: Change values in the spreadsheet to reflect the changes the firm is considering, and then use the What If analysis to vary the quantity of Product A sold and display what happens to total profit.)

19

CHAPTER NINETEEN

Managing Marketing's Link with Other Functional Areas

Going to one of the new blue and yellow U.S. IKEA stores is as much an adventure as it is a shopping trip. Perhaps any furniture store the size of six football fields would be an adventure. But let's face it, wandering through four or five complete model homes filled with stylish IKEA furnishings—all under one roof—is a bit different. For a store that size, there are relatively few salespeople; instead, there are information kiosks to provide advice on home décor. It is also distinctive that IKEA furniture is inexpensive. To keep costs low, it all breaks down into flat cartons that consumers can take home and assemble themselves.

These differences in strategy help explain how IKEA (of Swedish origin) has opened an average of 20 new stores per year over the last decade. By the end of 2012, there were almost 350 IKEA stores in more than 40 countries. While almost 80 percent of IKEA's sales are in Europe, the company is trying to change that. China is one of its fastest-growing markets, and IKEA is opening about two new stores per year there. Young adults in China like the casual, relaxed atmosphere and low prices they find in IKEA stores. An important part of IKEA's success is the care with which it coordinates its marketing strategy with appropriate information technology, production capabilities, human resources, and financial data.

Most of IKEA's growth has been financed from the cash flow generated by its profitable strategy. It is still a privately held company. One reason that IKEA has been able to grow so rapidly—without greater capital investments—is that it carefully manages its costs. This is particularly important because IKEA's customers have come to expect low prices. So IKEA's marketing managers often use demand-backward pricing to help select a specific factory. For example, they develop a plan for a stylish Poäng chair they know will sell for $149, and then they work to find the most cost-effective materials and production facilities before finalizing the design.

Two of IKEA's largest costs are manufacturing and transportation. These costs often involve trade-offs. Labor costs are low in China and Vietnam, but manufacturing there raises transportation costs to IKEA's largest markets in Europe and North America. So IKEA's Swedwood subsidiary manufactures much of IKEA's wood furniture products in 11 factories across Europe. It recently opened a U.S. factory in Danville, Virginia. In addition, IKEA outsources some production in the United States. Kitchen cabinets previously made in Eastern Europe are now produced by Sauder Woodworking in Ohio to supply IKEA stores in the United States. However, many IKEA products are still produced in Asia because the low manufacturing costs there often offset the higher transport costs.

IKEA knows that if it is going to produce its products in overseas factories it needs to pay attention to shipping costs. Because the furniture is designed to break down flat, shipping cartons are packed solid and that saves IKEA the expense of paying to ship "air." You can get a better idea of just how careful IKEA is in analyzing costs by considering how it has redesigned its popular fired-clay coffee mugs. With the original design, 864 mugs would fit on a shipping pallet. After IKEA refined the design to make the mug shorter and gave it a new handle, 2,024 would fit on a pallet. The mug's selling price has remained at $.50, but shipping costs have been reduced 60 percent. Production costs are also lower because more mugs will fit in the kiln at the factory. Given that IKEA sells 25 million of these mugs each year, this attention to detail adds up!

IKEA's marketing managers work closely with IT staff to develop creative promotions and to enhance the online shopping experience. The 2013 IKEA catalog features an augmented reality application. When customers wave a smartphone over pages with digital content, "X-ray" vision shows what's inside the cabinets. This cool feature shows more merchandise in the catalog and it has generated online buzz.

Pernille Spiers-Lopez, the president of IKEA North America, believes that addressing employees' concerns isn't just a nice thing to do; it's the best way to build a workforce committed to IKEA and its customers. On her watch, IKEA has given full benefits to the part-time employees who are crucial to IKEA's retail operations. Employees can also work flexible part-time hours and job-share to fill one full-time slot; this has proven especially helpful in recruiting women. The changes helped reduce annual sales-staff turnover by about 25 percent. Both *Fortune* and

Working Mother magazine have repeatedly recognized IKEA as one of the best companies for which to work.

Making IKEA's products available online offered new opportunities and challenges—requiring a true cross-functional effort. Operations assessed new approaches for inventory and delivery; accounting forecasted revenues and costs; finance examined capital investment in servers and assumed cash flows; IT made sure the site was user-friendly, could handle the projected number of visitors, and that customer data was secure; while the human resources department recruited people who could build and maintain the website. Marketing managers evaluated customer needs and competitive offerings and adapted the marketing mix for the new target market. Cross-functional cooperation will continue to drive profitable growth at IKEA.[1]

Learning Objectives

The success of IKEA's marketing strategy follows from close coordination of the company's finance, production, accounting, information systems, and human resources functions. Throughout the text we've emphasized that a marketing manager should try to develop a marketing strategy that will give the firm a competitive advantage in delivering value to target customers. Yet a strategy that would be the basis for competitive advantage by one firm might not fit well with another firm's resources. So, in this chapter, we'll take a closer look at how marketing strategy decisions are influenced by financial factors, the people available to implement a plan, and what the firm can effectively produce.

When you finish this chapter, you should be able to:

1 understand why turning a marketing plan into a profitable business requires money, information, people, and a way to get or produce goods and services.

2 understand the ways that marketing strategy decisions need to be adjusted in light of available financing.

3 understand how a firm can implement and expand a marketing plan using internally generated cash flow.

4 understand how different aspects of production capacity, flexibility, and the cost and location of production affect marketing strategy planning.

5 describe how marketing managers and accountants work together to analyze of the costs and profitability of specific products and customers.

6 understand how information systems enable marketing strategy.

7 know some of the human resource issues that a marketer should consider when planning a strategy and implementing a plan.

8 understand important new terms (shown in red).

Marketing in the Broader Context

LO 19.1

Cross-functional links affect strategy planning

In this chapter we'll consider some of the important ways that marketing links to other functional areas. Our emphasis is not on the technical details of other functional areas but rather on the most important ways that cross-functional links impact your ability to develop marketing strategies and plans that really work. See Exhibit 19-1.

Implementing a marketing plan usually requires a financial investment—so we'll consider money required both to start up a new plan and to meet ongoing expenses. Then we'll look at production and operations and review how available production capacity, production flexibility, and operating issues impact marketing planning. We'll also take a closer look at how accounting people and marketing managers work together to get a better handle on marketing costs. We'll conclude with a discussion of human resource issues—because it's people who put plans into action.

Exhibit 19–1 Marketing and Other Functional Areas Provide Company Resources for Strategy Planning and Implementation

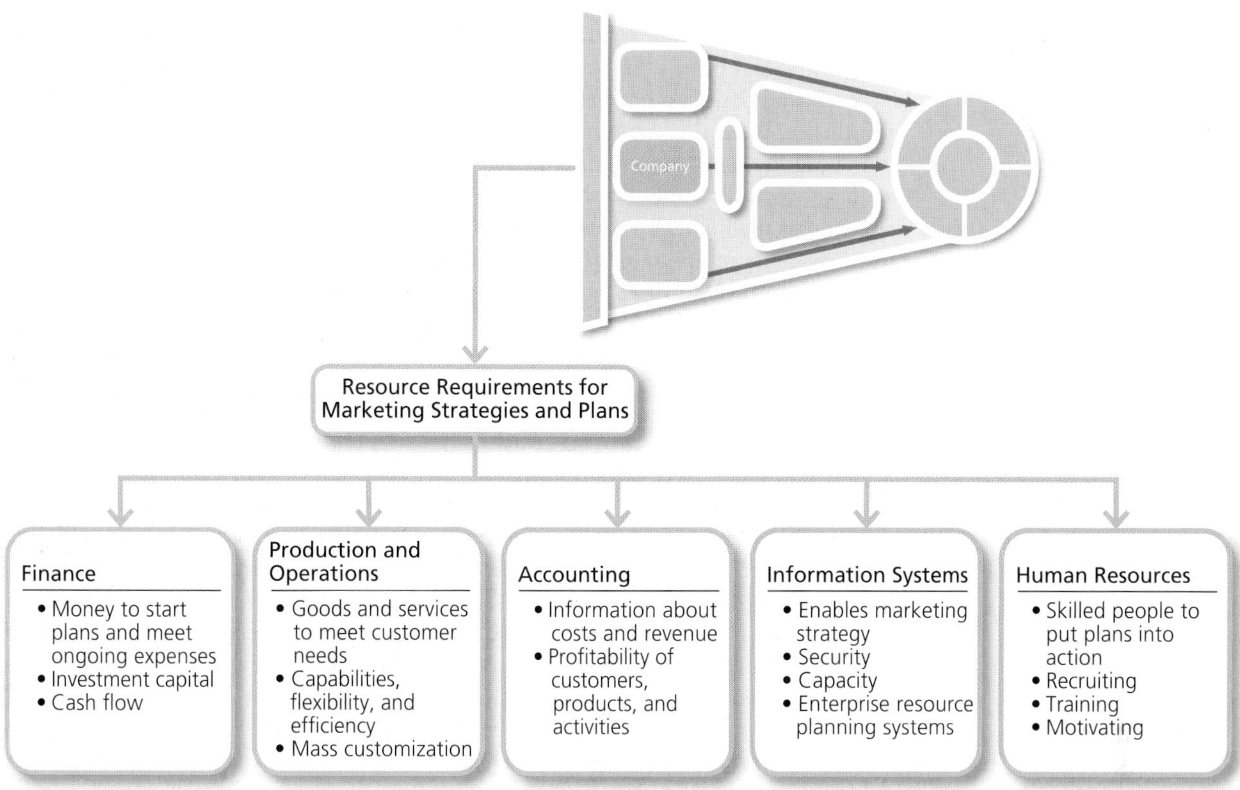

How important the linkages with production, finance, accounting, human resources, and information systems are for the marketing manager depends on the situation. In an entrepreneurial start-up, the same person may be making all of the decisions. In a big company, managing the linkages among many specialists may be much more complicated.

Cross-functional challenges are greatest with new efforts

Our emphasis will be on new efforts. When a new strategy involves only minor changes to a plan that the firm is already implementing, the specialists usually have a pretty good idea of how their activities link to other areas. However, when a potential strategy involves a more significant change—like the introduction of a totally new product idea—understanding the links between the different functional areas is usually much more critical.

The Finance Function: Money to Implement Marketing Plans

LO 19.2

Chief financial officer handles money matters

Bright marketing ideas for new ways to satisfy customer needs don't go very far if there isn't enough money to put a plan into operation. Finding and allocating **capital**—the money invested in a firm—is usually handled by a firm's chief financial officer. Entrepreneurs and others who own their own companies may handle this job themselves. In most firms, however, there is a separate financial manager who works with top management to make major finance decisions.

A firm's marketing manager and financial manager must work together to ensure that the firm can successfully implement its marketing plans with the money that is or will be available. Further, a successful strategy should ultimately generate profit. And the financial manager needs to know how much money to expect and when to expect it to be able to plan for how it will be used.

Opportunities compete for capital and budgets

In most firms, different possible opportunities compete for capital. There's usually not enough money to do everything, so strategies that are inconsistent with the firm's financial objectives and resources are not likely to be funded. That's why marketing managers use relevant financial measures as quantitative screening criteria when evaluating various alternatives in the first place. The best way to sell an idea to a financial manager is to explain the process and desired outcomes in quantitative terms.

Marketing plans that *are* funded usually must work within a budget constraint. Ideally, the marketing manager should have some inputs on what that budget is—to get the marketing tasks done. Further, strategy decisions may need to be adjusted to work within the available budget. For example, a marketing manager might prefer to have control over the selling effort for a new product by hiring new people for a separate sales force. However, if there isn't enough money available for salesperson salaries, then the best alternative might be to start with manufacturers' agents. They work for a commission and aren't paid until after they generate a sale and some sales revenue. Then after the market develops and the plan becomes profitable, the firm might expand its own sales force.

Working capital pays for short-term expenses

Financial managers usually think about two different uses of capital. First, capital may be required to pay for investments in facilities, equipment, computer networks, and other "fixed assets." These installations are usually purchased and then used, and depreciated, over a number of years. In addition, a firm needs **working capital**—money to pay for short-term expenses such as employee salaries, advertising, marketing research, inventory storing costs, and what the firm owes suppliers. A firm usually must pay for these ongoing expenses as they occur. As a result there is usually a continuing need for working capital.

Capital is usually a critical resource when a marketing plan calls for rapid growth, especially if the growth calls for expensive new facilities. Clearly, a plan to build a chain of 15 hotels requires more money for buildings and equipment, as well as more money for salaries, food, and supplies, than a plan for a single hotel. Such a plan might require that the firm borrow money from a commercial lender. In contrast, a plan that simply calls for improving the service in an existing hotel, perhaps by adding several people to handle room service, would require much less money. In fact, increased food sales from room service might quickly generate more than enough earnings to pay for the added people.

Capital comes from internal and external sources

As these examples imply, there are a number of different possible sources of capital. However, it's useful to boil them down to two categories: *external sources,* such as loans or sales of stocks or bonds, and *internal sources,* such as cash accumulated from the firm's profits. A firm usually seeks outside funding before it is needed to invest in a new strategy. Internally generated profits may be accumulated and used in the same way, but often internal money is used as it becomes available. In other words, with internally generated funding a firm's marketing program may be expected to "pay its own way."

The timing of when financing is available has an important effect on marketing strategy planning, so we'll look at this topic in more detail. We'll start by looking at external sources of funds.

External funding—investors expect a return

While a firm might like to fund its marketing program from rapid growth in its own profits, that is not always possible. New companies often don't have enough money to start that way. An established company may not have enough capital to make long-term investments and still pay for routine expenses. Getting started may also involve losses, perhaps for several years, before earnings come in. In these circumstances, the firm may need to turn to one of several sources of external capital.

A firm may be able to raise money by selling **stock**—a share in the ownership of the company. Stock sales may be public or private, and the buyers may be individuals, including a firm's own employees, or institutional investors (such as a pension fund or venture capital firm).

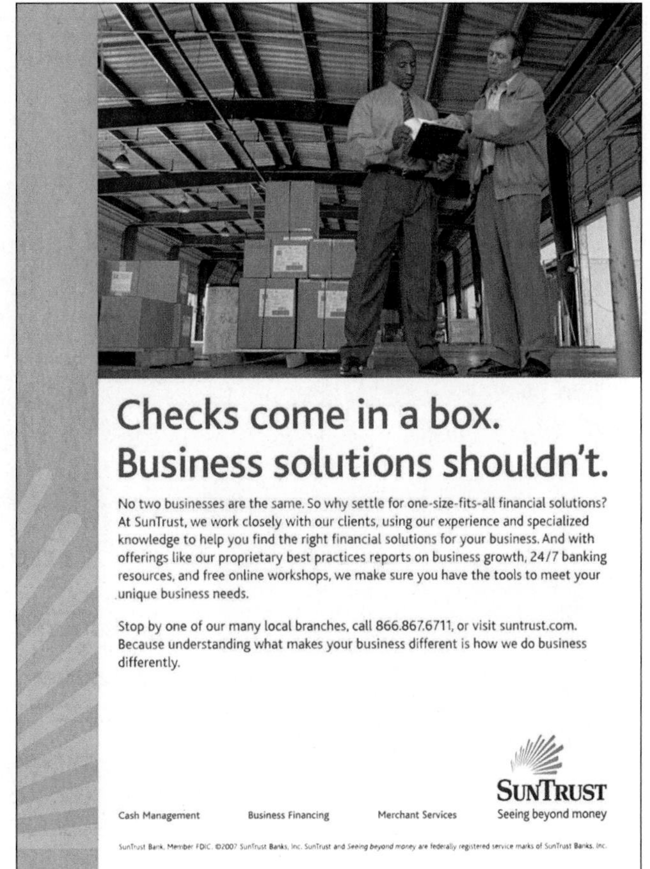

A firm that has a promising marketing plan will usually have more success in obtaining financial resources from external lenders or investors. SunTrust, for example, works with its client firms to find solutions to their financial challenges.

People who own stock in a firm want a good return on their investment. That can happen if the company pays owners of its stock a regular dividend. It also happens if the value of the stock goes up over time. Neither is likely if the firm isn't consistently earning profits. Further, the value of a firm's stock typically doesn't increase unless its profits are *growing.* This is one reason that marketing managers are always looking for profitable new growth opportunities. Profits can also improve by being more efficient—getting the marketing jobs done at lower cost, doing a better job of holding on to customers, and the like. Ultimately, a firm that doesn't have a successful or at least promising marketing strategy can't attract and keep investors.

On the other hand, it's a sad reality that a firm with a great strategy can't always attract investors. In a weak economy, many investors just have a wait-and-see attitude and won't invest in anything until overall business conditions seem more favorable. And, in a good economy, investors sometimes get caught up in the current fad—and then it seems that the only thing that will get their attention is a company in a "what's new" line of business.

Investors' time horizon is important

How quickly investors expect profit and growth is very important to the marketing manager. If investors are patient, a marketing manager may have the luxury of developing a plan that will be very profitable in the long run even if it racks up short-term losses. Many Japanese firms take this approach. However, most marketing managers face intense pressure to develop plans that will generate profits quickly; there's more risk for investors if potential profits are off in the future.

Sometimes it's a challenge to develop a plan that produces immediate profit but also positions the firm for long-run success. A low penetration price for a new product may help to prevent competition and to attract repeat purchasers long into the future. Yet a

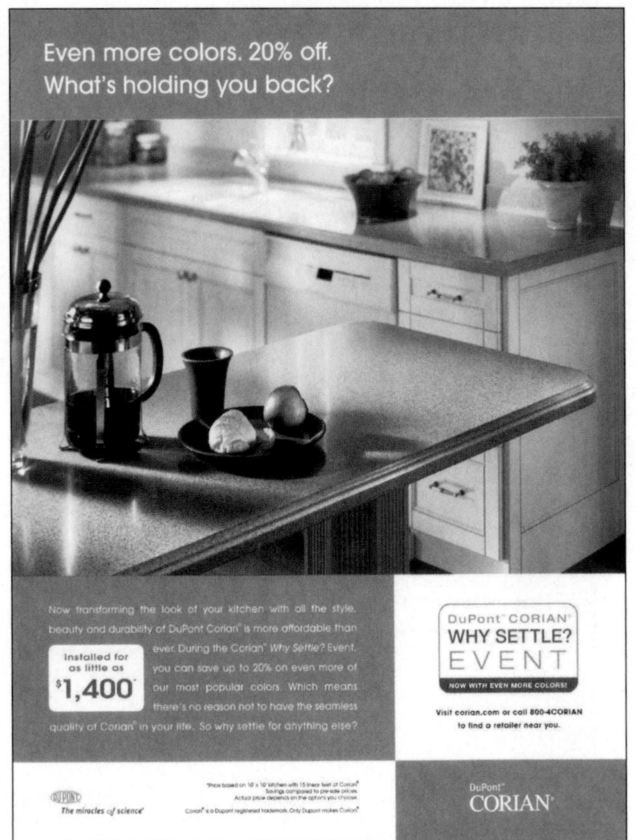

DuPont Corian, a solid countertop material, was costly to develop. When Corian was introduced, there was little direct competition and a premium price helped to recover development costs. Now that there is more competition, discounted prices are sometimes available.

skimming price may be better for profits in the short term. Even so, the marketing manager's plans must take the investors' time horizon into consideration. Unhappy investors can demand new management or put their money somewhere else.

Forecasts may become an ethical issue

Investors usually want detailed information about a firm's plans before they invest. The firm's financial people usually provide this information, but financial estimates don't mean much unless they're based on realistic estimates of demand, revenue, and marketing expenses from the marketing manager. An optimistic marketing manager may be hesitant to lay out the potential limitations of a plan or its forecasts, especially if the full story might scare off needed investors. However, this is an important ethical issue. While investors know that there is always some uncertainty in forecasts, they have a right to information that is as accurate as possible. Put another way, just as a marketing manager shouldn't mislead a buyer of the firm's products, it's not appropriate to mislead investors who are buying into the firm's marketing plan.

Debt financing involves an interest cost

Rather than sell stock, some firms prefer **debt financing**—borrowing money based on a promise to repay the loan, usually within a fixed time period and with a specific interest charge. This might involve a loan from a commercial bank or the use of corporate bonds. Entrepreneurs often borrow money from family and friends. People or institutions that loan the money typically do not get an ownership share in the company, and they are usually even less willing to take a risk than are investors who buy stock.

Most commercial banks are conservative. They usually won't loan money to a firm that doesn't have some valuable asset to put up as a guarantee that the lender will get its money. Investors who buy a firm's bonds are also very concerned about security—but they often don't have a legal right to some specific assets if the firm can't repay the borrowed money when it's due. In general, the greater the risk that the lender takes on to provide the loan, the greater the interest rate charge will be.

More bang for the buck—small loans in developing countries

Implementing a marketing plan takes money. But sometimes it doesn't take very much. Take entrepreneur Pakmogda Zarata, who owned a small restaurant in Burkina Faso, one of Africa's poorest countries. There's not much to her restaurant. A few rough logs prop up a ceiling made of thatch and dustbin liners. There are no walls. The menu is simple. "We serve only rice," she says, "but we do cook it." With a small loan from a specialized bank, she was able to start buying rice at wholesale instead of retail prices. With the cost savings, she repaid the loan, invested more in her restaurant, and increased profits. Now, she has seven employees and can afford to pay for her children's school and a secondhand motor scooter to get around.

Making small loans to help impoverished entrepreneurs start or grow a business is called *microfinancing.* Microloans help the poor to pull themselves out of poverty through enterprise rather than handouts. The power of microloans first came into focus in the 1970s when a young economics professor, Muhammad Yunus, loaned $27 to a group of craftsmen in Bangladesh. That success led to the development of the Grameen Bank. It has loaned almost $12 billion to more than 8 million borrowers.

Traditional banks want collateral to secure loans, so they're no help to the very poor. Grameen is different. Most of its loans go to women, and then Grameen relies on peer pressure from the women's friends to achieve high repayment rates. Typically, one of a group of rural women takes out a small loan, perhaps $25, to start a business. Other members of that woman's group can get a loan when she repays hers, so they encourage her. This works well and most of the loans are paid off.

Microloans foster marketing strategies for varied businesses—from rickshaw taxis and grain husking to sewing and tailoring services. What the businesses have in common is that they can grow. In Mongolia, a series of microloans helped a woman grow her small one-person, $100-a-year bakery business into a 37-employee, $75,000 operation. In Yugoslavia, Vahid Hujdar used $200 of his own money and a $1,500 microloan to set up a business repairing and reselling industrial sewing machines. Eight years and a few loans later, his business has 10 employees.

Yunus received the Nobel Peace Prize for his work at the Grameen Bank. That attention and Grameen's success in microlending has encouraged other lending innovations. For example, Kiva Microfunds set up a website (kiva.org) to directly connect individuals who want to lend a small amount of money—as little as $25—to a small business in a developing country. Anyone can go to the site, scroll through the list of projects, and select one to fund; an intermediary disperses the loan and collects payments. Traditional financial firms are involved as well. BlueOrchard Finance, set up with backing from Morgan Stanley and other large banks, loans to microfinance agencies because the investments generate good returns.[2]

Interest expense may impact prices

The cost of borrowing money can be a real financial burden. Just as a firm's selling price must cover all of the marketing expenses and the other costs of doing business before profits begin to accumulate, it must also cover the interest charge on borrowed money. The impact of interest charges on prices can be significant. For example, the spread between the prices charged by fast-growing, efficient supermarket chains and individual grocery stores would be even greater if the chains weren't paying interest on loans to fund new facilities.

While the cost of borrowing money can be high, it may still make sense if the money is used to implement a marketing plan that

Internet Exercise

Crowd funding site Kickstarter (**www.kickstarter.com**) matches people who want to support creative projects with projects that need funding. Go to the website and choose two projects in your area. You can enter your city or a major city nearby and potential projects will appear. Evaluate the projects. How well have they been funded? What type of people would be willing to support these projects?

earns an even greater return. In that way, the firm leverages the borrowed money to make a profit. Even so, there are often advantages if a firm can pay for its plans with internally generated capital.[3]

LO 19.3

Winning strategies generate capital

A company with a successful marketing strategy has its own internal funds—profits that become cash in the bank! For example, Apple reported a profit of about $2.45 billion on sales of about $19.3 billion in 2006. The company didn't pay any of that money to stockholders. Instead, Apple reinvested the money to research, develop, and bring to market new products like the iPad, and updated models of its iPhone, iPod, iMac, and MacBook, which helped 2012 fiscal sales swell to more than $148 billion and profits to grow to more than $43 billion! The value of the stock went from less than $15 a share in early 2003 to more than $600 a share nine years later—and investors also got two shares for each one they owned along the way.[4]

Reinvesting cash generated from operations is usually less expensive than borrowing money because no interest expense is involved. So internal financing often helps a firm earn more profit than a competitor that is operating on borrowed money—even if the internally financed company is selling at a lower price.

Expanding profits may support expanded plan

Firms that can't get a loan or that don't want the expense of borrowed money often start with a less costly strategy and a plan to expand it as quickly as is allowed by earnings. Consider the case of Sorrell Ridge, a small brand that wanted to compete with the jams and jellies of big competitors like Welch's and Smucker's. Sorrell Ridge started small with a strategy that focused on a better product—"spreadable fruit" with no sugar added—that was targeted at health-conscious consumers. After paying to update its production facilities, Sorrell Ridge didn't have much working capital to pay for promotion and other marketing expenses. So it turned to health-food wholesalers and retailers to give the product a promotion push in the channel. As profits from the health-food channel started to grow, Sorrell Ridge used some of the money for local TV and print ads in big cities in the Northeast. The ads increased consumer demand for Sorrell Ridge's spreads and helped get shelf space from supermarkets in that region. Success from selling through supermarkets in the Northeast generated more volume and profit, which provided Sorrell Ridge with the financial base to enter the big California market. The big supermarket chains there wouldn't consider carrying a new fruit spread without a lot of trade promotion, including hefty stocking allowances. Sorrell Ridge had the money to pay for a coupon program to stimulate consumer trial, but that didn't leave enough money for the stocking allowance. However, the marketing manager had a creative idea that involved giving retailers the stocking allowance in the form of a credit against future purchases rather than cash up front. With a plan for that blend of trade and consumer promotion in place, one of the best food brokers in California agreed to take on the line. And expanding into the new market resulted in profitable growth.[5]

Cash flow looks at when money will be available

A marketing manager who wants to plan strategies based on the expected flow of internal funding needs a good idea of how much cash will be available. A **cash flow statement** is a financial report that forecasts how much cash will be available after paying expenses. The amount that's available isn't always just the bottom line or net profit figure shown on the firm's operating statement. Some expenses, like depreciation of facilities, are subtracted from revenue for tax and accounting purposes but do not actually involve writing a check.

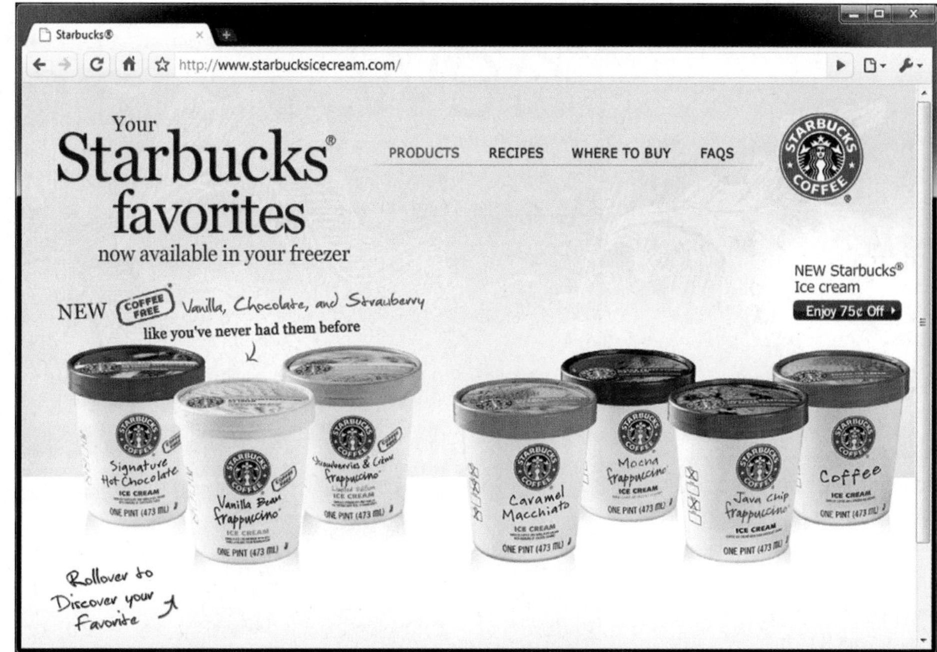

Starbucks took advantage of its brand reputation and the quality of its product to both expand its product line and obtain distribution in supermarkets.

So in determining cash flow, managers often look at a company's earnings *before* subtracting these noncash expenses.[6]

A slow economy makes it hard to find capital

Economic conditions have a big influence on the availability of capital. During the recent financial crisis, banks were reluctant to loan money, making it difficult for all businesses. At the same time, stock prices were depressed, so raising money through issuing more stock was costly. Any economic slowdown usually results in slower sales and uncertain cash flow. You can see why it is challenging for even a successful company to jump-start during a recession.

Improve return of current investment

When finances are tight, it's sensible to look for strategy alternatives that help get a better return on money that's already invested. A firm that sells diagnostic equipment to hospitals might look for another related product for its current salespeople to sell while calling on the same customers. Similarly, a firm that has a successful domestic product might look for new international markets. Any increase in profit contribution that the strategy generates—without increasing capital invested—increases the firm's return on investment.

Market mix decisions affect capital needed

Strategy decisions within each of the marketing mix areas often have different capital requirements. For example, offering more models of a product usually increases front-end capital needs.

Indirect distribution usually requires less investment capital than direct approaches. Intermediaries who pay for products when they purchase them and pay the costs of carrying inventory help a producer's cash flow. Public warehouses and transportation firms may reduce the capital needed for logistics facilities. Similarly, less capital is needed when intermediaries take on responsibility for promotion.

Production Must Be Coordinated with the Marketing Plan

LO 19.4

Production capacity takes many forms

If a firm is going to pursue an opportunity, there needs to be effective coordination between marketing planning and **production capacity**—the ability to produce a certain quantity and quality of specific goods or services.

Different aspects of production capacity have different impacts on marketing planning, so we'll consider this topic in more depth.[7]

Kikkoman was able to take advantage of both production capacity and production flexibility to introduce a new line of specialized condiments to appeal to additional market segments.

Use excess capacity to improve profits

If a firm has unused capacity, a marketing manager can try to identify new markets or new products that make more effective use of that investment. For example, a company that produces rubber floor mats for automobiles might be able to add a similar line of cargo-area mats for SUVs. Expanded production might result in lower costs because of economies of scale. Profit contribution from the new products could improve the return on investment the firm has already made. If a firm's production capacity is flexible, many different marketing opportunities might be possible. For example, there might be better growth and profits in static-electricity-free mats for Internet server equipment than for auto accessories.

Excess capacity may be a safety net, or a signal of problems

Excess capacity can be a safety net if demand suddenly picks up. For example, many firms that make products for the construction industry faced costly excess capacity in 2001. However, many of those firms were glad that they had that capacity when construction demand picked up again in 2003 and continued to grow for several years in the wake of heavy hurricane damage in the Southeast. A few years later mortgage and housing problems again resulted in excess capacity. This downturn hit the construction industry hard, and many construction firms went out of business or severely cut back capacity just to survive.

Excess capacity may exist because there is little demand for what a firm can produce or there's too much competition. In these situations, rather than struggling to improve capacity use, it might be better for the marketing manager to lead the firm toward other, more profitable alternatives.

Scarce supply wastes marketing effort

Another aspect of flexibility concerns how quickly and easily a firm can adjust the quantity of a product it produces. This can be especially important when demand is uncertain. If a new marketing mix is more successful than expected, demand can quickly outstrip supply. Promotion spending is wasted when this happens. Consider what happened when Frito-Lay introduced Tostitos Gold, a thicker version of Tostitos tortilla snack chips that was developed to work well with dips and salsa.

Marketing managers did not know if consumers would be willing to pay a premium price, normally reserved for low-fat or organic chips, for Tostitos Gold. To fuel demand, they ran a pair of celebrity ads on the New Year's Day Tostitos Fiesta Bowl national championship football game. In the ads, Jay Leno and Little Richard liven up parties with Tostitos Gold. The ads show how serving the chip "that's extra thick for hearty dips" can inject life into otherwise boring situations. The ads did a better job than expected in stirring interest, and chip lovers were so enthusiastic about Tostitos Gold that the chips were quickly out-of-stock at most supermarkets because the factory couldn't keep up with incoming orders. The stock-outs resulted in lost sales of about $500,000 a week.[8]

Staged distribution may match capacity

Problems of matching supply and demand often occur when a marketing plan calls for expansion into many market areas all at once. That's one reason a marketing manager may plan a regional rollout of a new product. Similarly, initial distribution may focus on certain channels—say, drugstores alone rather than drugstores and supermarkets. Experience with the initial distribution effort can help the marketing manager determine how much promotion is required to keep distribution channels full and avoid stock-outs.

Virtual corporations may not make anything at all

Many firms are finding that they can satisfy customers and build profits without doing any production in house. Instead, they look for capable suppliers to produce a product that meets the specs laid out in the firm's marketing plan. Nike has used this approach for decades.

Many firms now outsource manufacturing and basically act like a **virtual corporation**, where the firm is primarily a coordinator, with a good marketing concept. The opening case in Chapter 17 discusses flat-panel TV maker Vizio, which uses this approach.[9]

Outsourcing production can reduce costs and increase flexibility. However, it sometimes introduces problems. The reputation of a firm's brand often depends on the quality of the manufacturing behind it. Some firms find it difficult to control quality with outsourcing. When a Chinese manufacturer used dangerous lead paint in some Mattel toys, the toymaker recalled more than a million toys and its reputation took a hit. Another Chinese manufacturer decided on its own to leave out a safety feature when making tires for Firestone. When the treads began to separate from the tires, the ensuing recall hurt Firestone's brand equity.[10]

Outsourcing can also increase coordination and logistics problems. A company with a line of accessories for bicycle riders faced this problem when it decided to introduce a water bottle. Its other products were metal, so it turned to outside suppliers to produce the plastic bottles. However, getting the job done required three suppliers. One made the bottle, another printed the colorful designs on it, and the third attached a clip to hold the bottle to a bike. Moving the product from one specialist to another added costs, and whenever one supplier hit a snag, all of the others were affected. The firm was constantly struggling to fill orders on time, and too often it was losing the battle. To avoid these problems, the firm invested in its own production facilities.[11]

Where products are produced matters

It may make sense for a firm to produce where it can produce most economically, if the cost of transporting and storing products to match demand doesn't offset the savings. On the other hand, production in areas distant from customers can make the distribution job much more complicated. Consider the marketing implications of the decision to turn to offshore producers for many of Hanes men's underwear products. Mass-merchandiser chains put pressure on Hanes to find ways to cut prices—because they wanted to offer consumers low prices. So Hanes moved much of the sewing work to the Caribbean Islands where labor costs are low. However, the only practical way to transport the bulky and inexpensive finished products back to the U.S. market is by boat. Boats are slow and clearing customs adds further delays. At the port, the bulky cases of underwear must be handled again and broken down into quantities and assortments for shipping to the retailers' distribution centers. And, at the distribution centers, the cases need to be grouped with other products going to a specific store. All of these steps are necessary, but they also make it difficult to quickly adjust supply.[12]

In this German ad for the nonprofit UNICEF, a colorful athletic shoe is "decorated" with an image of a crying child working on a shoe. UNICEF wants consumers to remember that some products are inexpensive because they are produced in less-developed nations with low-cost child labor.

Moving production to low-cost countries

Many products—ranging from furniture and fashions to machinery and electronics—that in the recent past were manufactured in U.S. factories are now being produced on a contract basis in huge factories in China, Mexico, India, and other countries where wages and manufacturing costs are low.

Service firms are also finding ways to reduce the cost of some of their production work with **task transfer**—using telecommunications to move service operations to places where there are pools of skilled workers. For example, Bank of America puts its automatic teller machines and branch offices where they're convenient for customers, but many of the programmers who do its backroom computer work are in India.

Overseas production has critics

The trend toward outsourcing to where labor costs are low is resulting in the loss of thousands of manufacturing jobs in the United States. It's also sparking economic growth in some of the less-developed areas of the world and changing the balance of trade among nations. Some people think that workers in the United States will ultimately be able to shift to better jobs—where U.S. firms have a competitive advantage that doesn't rely on low-cost labor. But others worry that these shifts hurt the U.S. economy. Marketing managers must be aware of and sensitive to criticisms that may arise concerning overseas production.

Some of these concerns relate to nationalism. But other issues are sometimes at stake. Although overseas production may reduce prices for domestic consumers, some critics argue that the costs are lower because the work is handled in countries with no environmental protection rules, lower workplace safety standards, and fewer employee protections. Some firms have been boycotted for relying on suppliers who were accused of using child labor.

Marketing managers can't ignore such concerns. Just as a firm has a social responsibility in the country where it sells products, it also has a social responsibility to the people who produce its products. However, pay or safety standards that seem low in developed nations may make it possible for workers in an undeveloped nation to have a better, healthier life.[13]

Design flexibility into operations

Production flexibility can give a firm a competitive advantage in meeting a target market's needs better or faster. Without flexible operations, it can be difficult to provide business customers with just-in-time delivery or rapid response to orders placed by EDI or some other type of e-commerce reorder system.

Mass customization—serves individual needs

Automobile companies, producers of specialized machine tools, and other types of manufacturers, as well as many service firms, have been creating products based on specific orders from individual customers for a long time. However, a wide variety of companies are now looking for innovative ways to serve smaller segments of customers by using

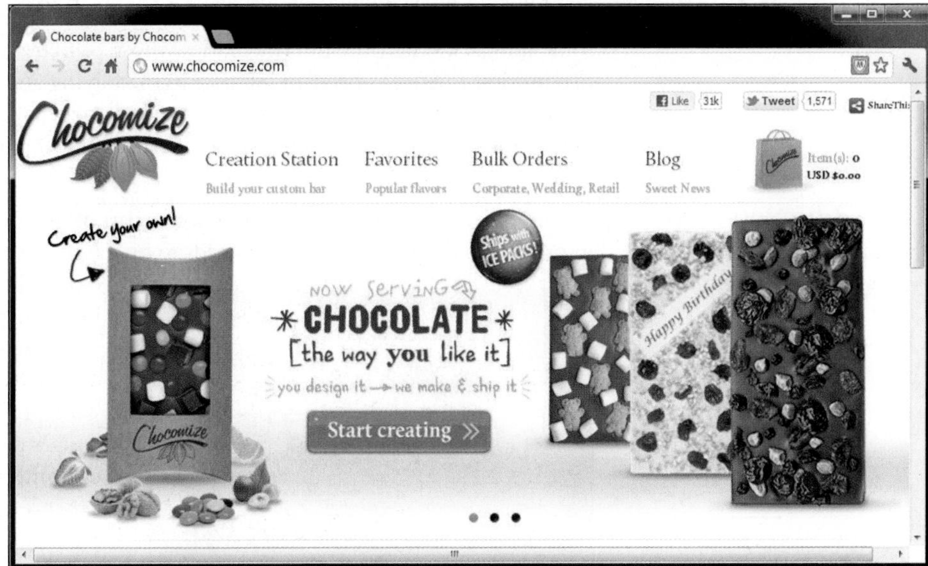

Chocomize allows its customers to create their own chocolate bars online. Handmade chocolate bars can be made from a range of chocolates and toppings. The finished confection is then packed with ice packs and shipped to its chocolate-loving customers.

mass customization—tailoring the principles of mass production to meet the unique needs of individual customers.

Note that using the principles of mass production is not the same thing as trying to appeal to everyone in some mass market. With the mass-customization approach, a firm may still focus on certain market segments within a broad product-market. However, in serving individuals within those target segments it tries to get a competitive advantage by finding a low-cost way to give each customer more or better choices.

A few years ago, there were predictions that thousands of companies would quickly begin to offer consumers better product choices based on mass customization. The widespread shift to mass customization has not occurred, mainly because many firms that experimented with it found that production costs were still high even if the Internet offered a low-cost way to get a lot of orders.

Some of the biggest successes in mass customization have been in business markets. For example, Andersen gives builders and architects software that they use to design custom windows by combining different types of glass, different sizes of frames, and a variety of hardware styles that Andersen already manufactures. Similarly, sales reps for ChemStation, a firm that produces industrial detergents, work closely with customers to understand their special cleaning needs—a car wash wants something very different from a metal-working plant. Then scientists at ChemStation develop just the right product, with the correct amount of foam, grease cutting agent, grit, and the like. After starting this program, ChemStation's profit margins doubled.[14]

Internet Exercise

Nike offers an online service called Nike ID through which customers can design their own shoes (or other Nike products). Go to the website (**www.nikeid.com**) and see how the Nike system works. Do you think that it's easy to design a product to your own preferences at the website? What do you think are the major strengths and weaknesses of this service?

Batched production requires inventories

If it is expensive for a firm to switch from producing one product (or product line) to another, there may be no alternative but to produce in large batches and maintain large inventories. Then it can supply demand from inventory while it is producing some other product. However, a firm that must pay the costs of carrying extra inventory to avoid stock-outs may not be able to compete with a firm that has more flexible production.

Excess inventory that a firm can't sell with its normal strategy can be a problem. In some industries there are intermediaries whose primary role is to buy and liquidate excess inventories. There has been an increase in the buying and selling of surplus inventory during the past few years, mainly because the Internet makes it possible for buyers to locate sellers. Excess inventory is often sold with an online auction.

Cut production costs that don't add value for customers

Production costs are usually an important part of the overall costs that must be considered in pricing, so a marketing manager needs to understand the costs associated with production, especially when product features called for in the marketing plan drive costs.

Marketing managers need to be aware of the costs associated with offering a marketing mix—and try to reduce or eliminate costs that do not add value for the customer. In the end, if a strategy's costs are more than what customers are willing to pay for the benefits, the strategy will not be profitable.

A well-informed marketing manager can play an important role in working with production people to decide which costs are necessary to add value that meets customer needs and which are just added expense with little real benefit. For example, a software firm was providing a very detailed instruction book along with a CD in its distribution package. The book was running up costs and causing delays because it needed to be changed and reprinted every time the firm came out with a new version of its software. The marketing manager realized that when users of the software had a problem, they didn't want to search for the book but instead wanted the information on their computer screen. Providing the updated information on just the CD was faster and cheaper, packaging costs were lower without the book, and customers were more satisfied with the online help. Looking back, this change seems obvious. However, for 20 years all software was sold with the other approach.

In a situation like this, it is easy to identify specific costs associated with the production job. However, often it's difficult to get a good handle on all of the costs associated with a product without help from the firm's accountants.

Accounting Data Can Help in Understanding Costs and Profit

LO 19.5

Accounting data that help managers track where costs and profit are coming from is an important aid for strategy decisions. Unfortunately, summary accounting statements that are prepared for tax purposes and for outside investors often aren't helpful for managers who need to make decisions about marketing strategy.

Understanding profitability depends on being able to identify the specific costs of different goods and services. You saw this in Chapter 18 when the full-cost approach and the contribution-margin approach to handling costs resulted in different views of profitability. Now let's look at how marketing managers and accountants can work together to allocate costs to products or customers. In recent years, accountants have devoted more attention to this problem and given it the name "activity-based accounting." In spite of the new name, the basic ideas behind marketing cost analysis were developed years ago by a marketing specialist.[15]

Marketing managers need to assign costs to specific products or customers to be able to understand the profitability of different possible strategies.

Marketing cost analysis usually requires a new way of classifying accounting data. Instead of using the type of accounts typically used for financial analysis, we have to use functional accounts.

Natural versus functional accounts—what is the purpose?

Natural accounts are the categories to which various costs are charged in the normal financial accounting cycle. These accounts include salaries, wages, supplies, raw materials, advertising, and others. These accounts are called natural because they have the names of their expense categories.

However, factories don't use this approach to cost analysis—and it's not the one we will use. In the factory, **functional accounts** show the *purpose* for which expenditures are made. Factory functional accounts include milling, grinding, maintenance, and so on. Factory cost accounting records are organized so that managers can determine the cost of particular products or jobs.

Marketing jobs are done for specific purposes too. With some planning, the costs of marketing can also be assigned to specific categories, such as customers and products. Then their profitability can be calculated.

First, get costs into functional accounts

The first step in marketing cost analysis is to reclassify all the dollar cost entries in the natural accounts into functional cost accounts. For example, the many cost items in the natural *salary* account may be allocated to functional accounts with the following names: storing, inventory control, order assembly, packing and shipping, transporting, selling, advertising, order entry, billing, credit extension, and accounts receivable. The same is true for rent, power, and other natural accounts.

The way natural account amounts are shifted to functional accounts depends on the firm's method of operation. It may require time studies, space measurements, actual counts, and managers' estimates.

Then reallocate to evaluate profitability of profit centers

The costs allocated to the functional accounts equal, in total, those in the natural accounts. But instead of being used only to show *total* company profits, the costs can now be used to calculate the profitability of territories, products, customers, salespeople, price classes, order sizes, distribution methods, sales methods, or any other breakdown desired. Each unit can be treated as a profit center.

Exhibit 19–2 Profit and Loss Statement, One Month

Sales		$17,000
Cost of sales		11,900
Gross margin		5,100
Expenses:		
Salaries	$2,500	
Rent	500	
Wrapping supplies	1,012	
Stationery and stamps	50	
Office equipment	100	
		4,162
Net profit		$ 938

Cost analysis helps track down the loser

The following example illustrates these ideas. This case is simplified, and the numbers are small, so you can follow each step. However, you can use the same basic approach in more complicated situations.

In this case, the usual financial accounting approach, with natural accounts, shows that the company made a profit of $938 last month (Exhibit 19-2). But this profit and loss statement doesn't show the profitability of the company's three customers. So the firm's managers decide to use marketing cost analysis because they want to know whether a change in the marketing mix will improve profit.

First, we distribute the costs in the five natural accounts to four functional accounts—sales, packaging, advertising, and billing and collection (see Exhibit 19-3)—according to the functional reason for the expenses. Specifically, $1,000 of the total salary cost is for sales reps who seldom even come into the office since their job is to call on customers; $900 of the salary cost is for packaging labor; and $600 is for office help. Assume that the office staff split their time about evenly between addressing advertising material and billing and collection. So we split the $600 evenly into these two functional accounts.

The $500 for rent is for the entire building. But the company uses 80 percent of its floor space for packaging and 20 percent for the office. Thus, $400 is allocated to the packaging account. We divide the remaining $100 evenly between the advertising and billing accounts because these functions use the office space about equally. Stationery, stamps, and office equipment charges are allocated equally to the latter two accounts for the same reason. Charges for wrapping supplies are allocated to the packaging account because these supplies are used in packaging. In another situation, different allocations and even different accounts may be sensible—but these work here.

Exhibit 19–3 Spreading Natural Accounts to Functional Accounts

		Functional Accounts			
Natural Accounts		Sales	Packaging	Advertising	Billing and Collection
Salaries	$2,500	$1,000	$ 900	$300	$300
Rent	500		400	50	50
Wrapping supplies	1,012		1,012		
Stationery and stamps	50			25	25
Office equipment	100			50	50
Total	$4,162	$ 1,000	$2,312	$425	$425

Exhibit 19–4 Basic Data for Cost and Profit Analysis Example

Product	Cost/Unit	Selling Price/Unit	Number of Units Sold in Period	Sales Volume in Period	Relative "Bulk" per Unit	Packaging "Units"
A	$ 7	$ 10	1,000	$10,000	1	1,000
B	35	50	100	5,000	3	300
C	140	200	10	2,000	6	60
			1,110	$17,000		1,360

Customers	Number of Sales Calls in Period	Number of Orders Placed in Period	Number of Each Product Ordered in Period		
			A	B	C
Rao	30	30	900	30	0
Mack	40	3	90	30	3
Davis	30	1	10	40	7
Total	100	34	1,000	100	10

Allocating functional cost to customers

Now we can calculate the profitability of the company's three customers. But we need more information before we can allocate these functional accounts to customers or products. It is presented in Exhibit 19-4.

Exhibit 19-4 shows that the company's three products vary in cost, selling price, and sales volume. The products also have different sizes, and the packaging costs aren't related to the selling price. So when packaging costs are allocated to products, size must be considered. We can do this by computing a new measure—a packaging unit—which is used to allocate the costs in the packaging account. Packaging units adjust for relative size and the number of each type of product sold. For example, Product C is six times larger than A. While the company sells only 10 units of Product C, it is bulky and requires 10 times 6, or 60 packaging units. So we must allocate more of the costs in the packaging account to each unit of Product C.

Exhibit 19-4 also shows that the three customers require different amounts of sales effort, place different numbers of orders, and buy different product combinations.

Mack seems to require more sales calls. Rao places many orders that must be processed in the office, with increased billing expense. Davis placed only one order—for 70 percent of the sales of highly valued Product C.

Exhibit 19-5 shows the calculations for allocating the functional amounts to the three customers. There were 100 sales calls in the period. Assuming that all calls took the same

Exhibit 19–5 Functional Cost Account Allocations

Sales calls	$1,000/100 calls	=	$10/call
Billing	$425/34 orders	=	$12.50/order
Packaging units costs	$2,312/1,360 packaging units	=	$1.70/packaging unit or $1.70 for Product A $5.10 for Product B $10.20 for Product C
Advertising	$425/10 units of C	=	$42.50/unit of C

amount of time, we can figure the average cost per call by dividing the $1,000 sales cost by 100 calls—giving an average cost of $10. We use similar reasoning to break down the billing and packaging account totals. Advertising during this period was for the benefit of Product C only—so we split this cost among the units of C sold.

Calculating profit and loss for each customer

Now we can compute a profit and loss statement for each customer. Exhibit 19-6 shows how each customer's purchases and costs are combined to prepare a statement for each customer. The sum of each of the four major components (sales, cost of sales, expenses, and profit) is the same as on the original statement (Exhibit 19-2)—all we've done is rearrange and rename the data.

For example, Rao bought 900 units of A at $10 each and 30 units of B at $50 each—for the respective sales totals ($9,000 and $1,500) shown in Exhibit 19-6. We compute cost of sales in the same way. Expenses require various calculations. Thirty sales calls cost $300—30 × $10 each. Rao placed 30 orders at an average cost of $12.50 each for a total ordering cost of $375. Total packaging costs amounted to $1,530 for A (900 units purchased × $1.70 per unit) and $153 for B (30 units purchased × $5.10 per unit). There were no packaging costs for C because Rao didn't buy any of Product C. Neither were any advertising costs charged to Rao—all advertising costs were spent promoting Product C, which Rao didn't buy.

Exhibit 19–6 Profitability of Individual Customers and Whole Company

	Rao		Mack		Davis		Whole Company
Sales							
Product A	$9,000		$ 900		$ 100		
Product B	1,500		1,500		2,000		
Product C			600		1,400		
Total sales		$10,500		$ 3,000		$ 3,500	$17,000
Cost of Sales							
Product A	6,300		630		70		
Product B	1,050		1,050		1,400		
Product C			420		980		
Total cost of sales		7,350		2,100		2,450	11,900
Gross margin		3,150		900		1,050	5,100
Expenses							
Sales calls ($10 each)	300		400.00		300.00		
Order costs ($12.50 each)	375		37.50		12.50		
Packaging costs							
Product A	1,530		153.00		17.00		
Product B	153		153.00		204.00		
Product C			30.60		71.40		
Advertising			127.50		297.50		
		2,358		901.60		902.40	4,162
Net profit (or loss)		$ 792		$ (1.60)		$147.60	$ 938

Analyzing the results

We now see that Rao was the most profitable customer, yielding over 75 percent of the net profit.

This analysis shows that Davis was profitable too—but not as profitable as Rao because Rao bought three times as much. Mack was unprofitable. Mack didn't buy very much and received one-third more sales calls.

The iceberg principle is operating here. Although the company as a whole is profitable, customer Mack is not. But before dropping Mack, the marketing manager should study the figures and the marketing plan very carefully. Perhaps Mack should be called on less frequently. Or maybe Mack will grow into a profitable account. Now the firm is at least covering some fixed costs by selling to Mack. Dropping this customer may only shift those fixed costs to the other two customers, making them look less attractive. (See the discussion on contribution margin in Chapter 18.)

The marketing manager may also want to analyze the advertising costs against results—since a heavy advertising expense is charged against each unit of Product C. Perhaps the whole marketing plan should be revised.

Ethics Question

Most banks grade their customers based on their assets, past banking behavior, and other personal information to decide how important or profitable the customers are. Bank employees use these grades in responding to a customer. For example, if a customer is charged a $25 fee for paying a credit card bill one day late and calls to request that the fee be waived, the customer service agent would immediately waive the fee for an A customer, firmly tell the C customer that the fee is a bank policy, and thoughtfully decide how to respond for the B customer. Similarly, the bank would assign an A customer a customer service phone number that is answered immediately by a capable rep, while the C customer would get a number where it's possible to wait on hold for several minutes—or longer. What do you think about banks segmenting customers based on profitability? Is this fair? Why or why not?[16]

Enabling Marketing Strategy with Information Technology

LO 19.6

Information technology aids marketing strategy planning

Most medium-size or larger organizations have a separate information technology management group. This group enables many activities in the marketing strategy process planning model. Consequently, the role of information technology (IT) has been covered in almost every chapter in the book. Marketing research utilizes software and hardware to collect and analyze customers. Customer databases, big data, different types of promotion, and almost anything to do with the Internet involve coordination among marketing managers and IT managers.

It has been suggested that it won't be long before marketing managers spend more money on information technology than IT managers. That just demonstrates marketing's reliance on IT; marketing managers need to work closely with those in the company directly involved with IT systems. There are a couple of important areas that don't fit neatly into previous chapters, so we cover them here.[17]

Customer information must be secure

As marketing managers do more promotion and selling over the Internet, it is critical that IT systems be robust from a security standpoint. As marketing managers seek to build closer relationships with customers, they gather, store, and maintain an increasing amount of personal information about customers in CRM databases. This might include purchase history, credit card numbers, or other personal data. Sony, LinkedIn, Citigroup, Best Buy, and Walgreens are just a few companies whose customer data—and reputation—were compromised by hackers. Sony for example, had over a dozen data breaches related to Sony PlayStation Network and Sony Pictures, among other sites. When a thief stole a desktop computer from Sutter Physicians Services, more than 3.3 million patients medical records were stolen, too. IT managers should take all measures to ensure customers' personal data is not compromised.

IT capacity must align with marketing strategy

Companies should also assure that online systems have the capacity to handle customer demands. This can be particularly problematic when marketing managers run a promotion that could spike demand. Southwest Airlines computers crashed under the weight of a one-day half-price ticket promotion. Worse yet, they billed some customers up to 10 times for the same ticket. These types of mistakes can result in lawsuits and harm a company's reputation.[18]

Enterprise resource planning systems tie the firm together

Many companies have turned to **enterprise resource planning (ERP) systems** which integrate internal and external information management across the entire organization. Such a system connects the rest of the firm with the marketing information system we discussed in Chapter 7. An ERP system facilitates the flow of information among all the business functions within the organization and connections to suppliers, customers, and other collaborators. Typically an ERP provides a central repository to collect and store all the information shared across functions—and a way to search and access it. Ready access to this information makes the marketing strategy planning process more efficient and effective.

People Put Plans into Action

LO 19.7

People are an important resource

A great marketing plan may fail if the right people aren't available to implement it. Large firms usually have a separate human resources department staffed by specialists who work with others in the firm to ensure that good people are available to do jobs that need to be done. A small firm may not have a separate department—but somebody (perhaps the owner or other managers) must deal with people-management matters, like recruiting and hiring new employees, deciding how people will be compensated, and what to do when a job is not being performed well or is no longer necessary. Human resource issues can be important both in a marketing manager's choice among different possible marketing opportunities and in the actual implementation of marketing plans—especially new plans that involve major change.

New strategies usually require people changes

New strategies often require changes that upset the status quo and vested interests. A production manager who has spent a career becoming an expert in fine wood furniture may not like the idea of switching to an assemble-it-yourself line—even if that's what

Marketing strategies require people with skills to carry them out. Both Brill and John Deere want customers to know that the knowledge and resourcefulness of their service people are an essential part of their marketing mixes.

customers want. And when the market maturity stage of the product life cycle hits, a financial manager who looked like a hero during the profitable growth stage may not see that the picnic is over, or that profit growth will resume only if the firm takes some risk and invests in a new product concept.

People affected by a new strategy may not be under the control of the marketing manager. And the marketing manager may not be able to change everyone into enthusiastic supporters of the plan. However, the marketing manager should think about how a new strategy will affect people—and how they will affect its success.

Communication helps promote change

Good communication is crucial. The marketing manager must find ways to explain the new strategy, what needs to happen, and why. You can't expect people to pull together in a companywide effort if they don't know what's going on. Communication might be handled in meetings, memos, casual discussions, newsletters, or any number of other ways. However, at a minimum, the marketing manager needs to have clear communication with other managers who will participate in preparing the firm's personnel for a change.

Rapid growth strains human resources

The success of a marketing plan often depends on how quickly the firm's personnel can get geared up for what needs to be done. Firms that grow rapidly may face challenges finding enough qualified people. A fast-growing retail chain like Lumber Liquidators that is opening many new stores needs new store managers, salespeople, customer service people, computer operators, and maintenance people. New employees have to learn about the company, its customers, and its products at the same time they are learning how to do their jobs well.

Allow time for training and other changes

Training takes time. A marketing manager who wants to reorganize the firm's sales force so that salespeople are assigned to specific customers rather than by product line may have a great idea, but it can't be implemented overnight. A salesperson who is supposed to be a specialist in meeting the needs of a certain customer won't be able to do a good job if all he or she knows about is the product line that was previously his or her specialty.

Each change may result in several others

A change in sales assignments is also likely to require changes in compensation. Someone needs to figure out the specifics of the new compensation system, and accountants need time to adjust their computer programs to make certain that the salespeople actually get paid. Similarly, the changes in the sales force are likely to require changes in whom they report to and the structure of sales management assignments. Our point with this example is that each change may require several others and that each change may take time.

Plan time for changes from the outset

A marketing manager who ignores the ripple effects of a change in strategy may later expect everyone to meet a schedule that won't work. Certainly there are cases of heroic efforts by people in organizations to turn someone's vision into a reality. Yet it's more typical for such a plan to fall behind schedule, to run up unnecessary costs, or to just plain fail.

Cutbacks need human resources plans too

Decisions to drop products, channels of distribution, or customers can be traumatic, especially if jobs will be cut. To the extent possible, it's important to plan a phase-out period so that people can make other plans. In fact, a carefully planned phase-out can sometimes work hand-in-hand with development of new strategies that will create exciting jobs for those who would otherwise be displaced.[19]

Investing in employees lowers costs

While this chapter emphasizes the need to manage costs in designing a marketing strategy, managers should be careful using low wages to manage costs. Experienced employees often cost more in dollars per hour, but save the firm money in other ways. Higher wages can help a firm attract and retain more competent employees. More experienced employees understand the business better, may be more productive, and deliver higher levels of customer service. A recent study of retailers found that the best performing retailers, including Costco, Trader Joe's and QuikTrip, pay above average wages while still charging the lowest prices in their industry. These stores operated more effectively and ultimately more efficiently than their competitors because they had motivated, competent, and well-trained personnel.[20]

Marketing pumps life into an organization

Marketing managers who create profitable marketing strategies and implement them well create a need for a firm's production workers, accountants, financial managers, and human resources people. In this chapter we've talked about marketing links with those other functions; but when you get down to brass tacks, organizations and the various departments within them consist of *individuals.* When the marketing manager makes good strategy decisions—ones that lead to satisfied customers and profits—each individual in the organization has a chance to prosper and grow.

CONCLUSION

Even when everyone in an entire company embraces the marketing concept, coordinating marketing strategies and plans with other functional areas is a challenge. Yet it's a challenge that marketing managers must address. It doesn't make sense to select a strategy that the firm can't implement. And implementing new plans usually requires money, people, and a way to produce goods or services the firm will sell.

Cooperation between the marketing manager and the finance people helps to ensure that there's enough money available for initial investments and to implement the marketing plan. If money comes from outside investors, the marketing manager may need to develop a strategy that satisfies them as well as customers. If funding is limited, the strategy may need to be scaled back, or the strategy may need to be phased in over time so that it generates enough cash flow to "pay its own way."

There also needs to be close coordination between a firm's production specialists and its marketing planners. The marketing manager needs to consider the firm's production capacity when evaluating alternative strategies. And flexibility in production may allow the firm to pursue different strategies at the same time or to switch strategies more easily when new opportunities develop.

Figuring out the profitability of a strategy, product, or customer often requires a real understanding of costs—production costs, marketing costs, and other costs that may accumulate. Traditional accounting reports are often not very useful in pinpointing these costs. However, marketing managers and accountants are now working together to get more accurate cost information—by developing functional accounts rather than just relying on natural accounts typically used for financial analysis.

Information systems aid the marketing strategy planning process and enable many of its actions. An ERP or similar system helps develop and adapt marketing strategies. Strong data security and sufficient IT capacity are critical to maintaining customer relationships and a firm's reputation.

Money, facilities, and information are all important in developing a successful strategy, but most strategies are implemented by people. So a marketing manager must also be concerned with the availability and skills of the firm's people—its human resources. New marketing strategies may upset established ways of doing things. Plans need to be clearly communicated so that everyone knows what to expect. Further, plans need to take into consideration the time and effort that will be required to get people up to speed on the new jobs they will be expected to do.

Making the strategic planning decisions that concern how a firm is going to use its overall resources—from marketing, production, finance, and other areas—is the responsibility of the chief executive officer, not the marketing manager. Further, the marketing manager usually can't dictate what a manager in some other department should do. However, it is sensible for the marketing manager to make recommendations on these matters. And marketing strategies and plans that the marketing manager recommends are more likely to be accepted, and then successfully implemented, if the links between marketing and other functional areas have been carefully considered from the outset.

KEY TERMS

LO 19.8

capital, *503*
working capital, *504*
stock, *504*
debt financing, *506*
cash flow statement, *508*
production capacity, *509*
virtual corporation, *511*
task transfer, *512*
mass customization, *513*
natural accounts, *515*
functional accounts, *515*
enterprise resource planning (ERP) systems, *520*

QUESTIONS AND PROBLEMS

1. Identify some of the ways that a firm can raise money to support a new marketing plan. Give the advantages and limitations—from a marketing manager's perspective—of each approach.
2. An entrepreneur who started a chain of auto service centers to do fast oil changes wants to quickly expand by building new facilities in new markets but doesn't have enough capital. His financial advisor suggested that he might be able to get around the financial constraint and still grow rapidly if he franchised his idea. That way the franchisees would invest to build their own centers, but fees from the franchise agreement would also provide cash flow to build more company-owned outlets. Do you think this is a good idea? Why or why not?
3. Explain, in your own words, why investors in a firm's stock might be interested in a firm's marketing manager developing a new growth-oriented strategy. Would it be just as good, from the investors' standpoint, for the manager to just maintain the same level of profits? Why or why not?
4. A woman with extensive experience in home health care and a good marketing plan has approached a bank for a loan, most of which she has explained she intends to "invest in advertising designed to recruit part-time nurses and to attract home-care patients for her firm's services." Other than the furniture in her leased office space, she has few assets. Is the bank likely to loan her the money? Why?
5. Could the idea of mass customization be used by a publisher of college textbooks to allow different instructors to order customized teaching materials—perhaps even unique books made up of chapters from a number of different existing books? What do you think would be the major advantages and disadvantages of this approach?
6. Give examples of two different ways that a firm's production capacity might influence a marketing manager's choice of a marketing strategy.
7. Is a small company's flexibility increased or decreased by turning to outside suppliers to produce the products it sells? Explain your thinking.
8. Explain how a marketing manager's sales forecast for a new marketing plan might be used by
   a. a financial manager;
   b. an accountant;
   c. a production manager; and
   d. a human resources manager.
9. Explain the difference between natural accounts and functional accounts.
10. Could the approaches to cost allocation that we discussed in this chapter apply to a firm, like a travel agency, that produces only services? Explain your thinking.
11. What types of human resource issues does a marketing manager face when planning to expand sales operations from a branch office in a new overseas market? Are the problems any different than they would be in a new domestic market?

CREATING MARKETING PLANS

The Marketing Plan Coach software on the text website includes a sample marketing plan for Hillside Veterinary Clinic. Think about the entire marketing plan—since you have been reviewing this all along. While there are not separate departments in a small business, there are different functions.

a. How can Hillside fund future growth plans?
b. Can Hillside calculate the profitability of individual customers? Should it try?
c. Has Hillside accounted for the local labor market in its growth plans?

SUGGESTED CASES

12. DrJane.com—Custom Vitamins
17. Simply Pure H2O4U, Inc.
22. Bright Light Innovations: The Starlight Stove
35. Rizzuto's Pizzeria

Video Case 6. Big Brothers & Big Sisters of America

CHAPTER TWENTY

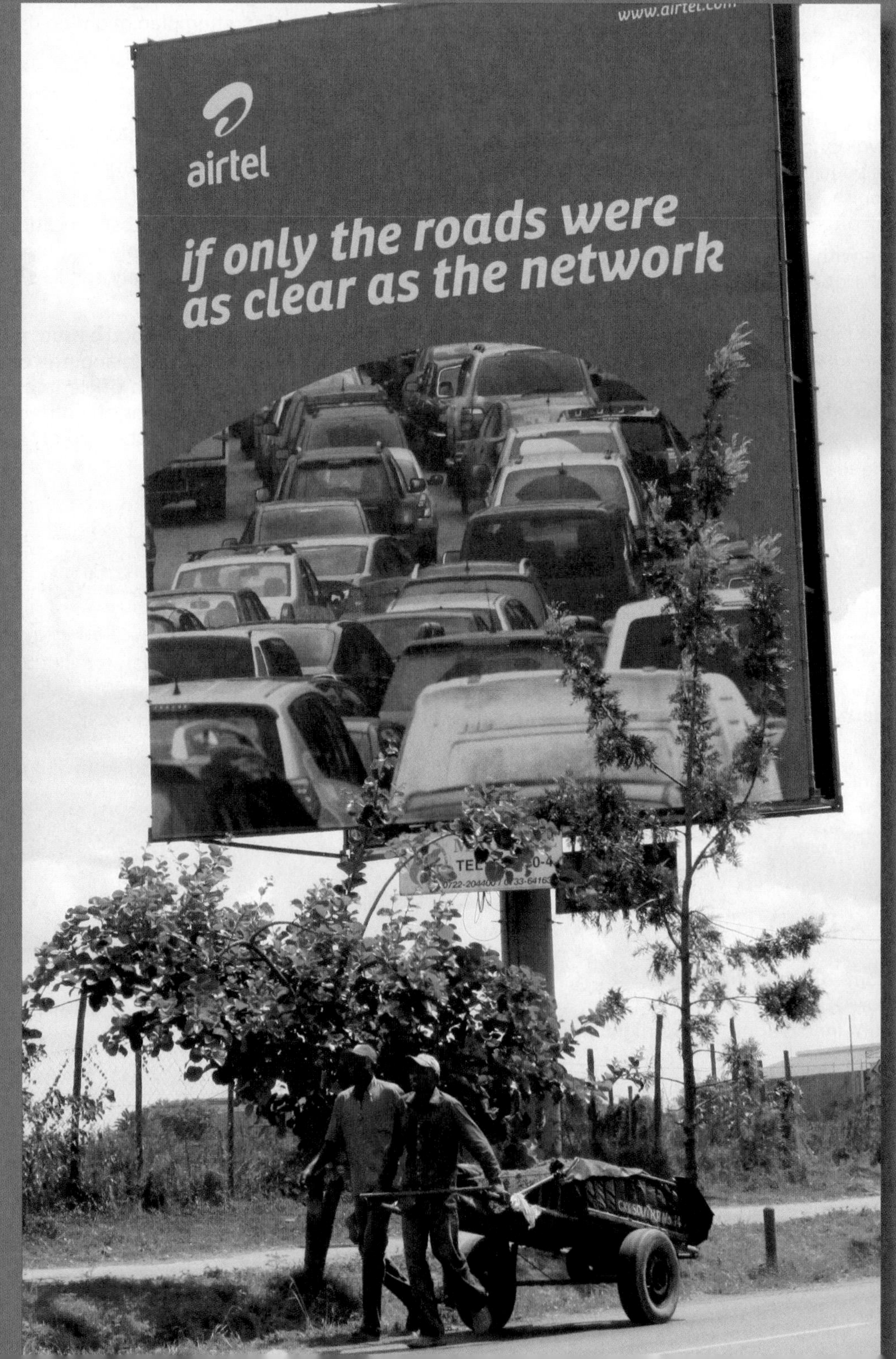

Ethical Marketing in a Consumer-Oriented World: Appraisal and Challenges

While consumers want marketplace choice, on a global scale we're not there yet. Someone in a village in Uganda may be able to get a glimpse of the quality of life that consumers in advanced Western economies enjoy, but for that person it doesn't seem real. What is real is the struggle of everyday life—living without electricity or running water—and, in fact, worrying about malnutrition, disease, and hunger. Cell phone carriers see growth opportunities in some of the world's poorest countries, yet average monthly billings are often less than $5. The vast majority of consumer-citizens in these societies can still only wonder if they'll ever have choices among a wide variety of goods and services—and the income to buy them—that most consumers take for granted in the United States, Canada, England, most countries in Western Europe, Australia, and a few other advanced economies.

Even in the face of a serious global economic downturn, the challenges faced by consumers, and marketing managers, in the advanced economies seem minor by contrast. In England, for example, some consumers who live in villages that are off the beaten path may worry, instead, that they are not included in the 96 percent of the British population served by Tesco delivery vans. Tesco, the largest supermarket chain in England, created its online shopping service for groceries (and hundreds of other products) just a few years ago, but now its fleet of vans make over 250,000 deliveries a week.

If online shopping for groceries has had a slower start in the United States, it just may be because many Americans are more interested in instant gratification. We expect the corner convenience store to have a nice selection of frozen gourmet dinners that we can prepare in minutes in a microwave oven. Or perhaps that's too much hassle. After all, Domino's will deliver a hot pizza in less than 30 minutes. And McDonald's has our Egg McMuffin ready when we pull up at the drive-thru at 7:00 in the morning. In a relative sense, few of the world's consumers can expect so much and get so much of what they expect.

But is it a good thing that firms give us what we want? Think about how automakers offered SUVs to appeal to consumers. SUVs do satisfy many of the needs of suburban lifestyles. But most are gas guzzlers and pollute our air. Some critics even charge that the United States has jumped into wars in the Middle East because of such overreliance on oil. On the other hand, as both gas prices and consumer environmental sensitivity have increased, producers have responded with hybrid technologies. Clean hydrogen vehicles may even be in our future. Of course, such adjustments take time.

Much national attention is now directed toward problems of obesity, especially among children. In the United States, more than a third of children and adolescents weigh too much. Actually, the surge of obesity among children is a global trend. Nutritionists say that in the United States and elsewhere, the key culprits are too much fat, starch, and sugar in diets. World Health Organization experts say that today's levels of childhood obesity will later lead to an explosion of illnesses (like heart disease, diabetes, and hypertension) that will drain economies, create enormous suffering, and cause premature deaths. Many nutritionists and public-health officials point the finger of blame at food processors and fast food. When a group of obese teenagers sued McDonald's, claiming that it made them fat, the widely publicized case was fodder for jokes on late-night TV shows. But fast-food companies are not laughing. The judge threw out the case but left open the door for future suits. Some legal experts say that this is just the beginning of legal actions—and they draw the parallel with suits against tobacco companies 30 years ago. Many fast-food companies are scrambling to add salads, fruit, and other low-fat fare to their menus. Do you think consumers should have the right to choose high-fat foods if that is what they want?

When you think about the contrast between problems of starvation and too much fast food, it's not hard to decide which consumers are better off. But is that just a straw man comparison? Is the situation in less-developed nations one extreme, with the system in the United States and similar societies just as extreme—only in a different way?

Would we be better off if we didn't put quite so much emphasis on marketing? Do we need so many brands of products? Does all the money spent on advertising really help consumers? Should we expect access to fast food any hour of the day—or to order groceries over the Internet and have a van deliver them to our front door? Conversely, do all of these choices just increase the prices consumers pay without really adding anything of value? More generally, does marketing serve society well?

These questions are what this chapter is about. Now that you have a better understanding of what marketing is all about, and how the marketing manager contributes to the macro-marketing process, you should be able to decide whether marketing costs too much.[1]

Learning Objectives

Throughout the text we've discussed ways that marketing can help customers while also meeting a firm's objectives. We've also considered many related ethical and societal questions. In this chapter, we evaluate the overall costs and benefits of marketing to society. This leads into an explanation of how to prepare a marketing plan—because the marketing plan integrates all of the decisions in the marketing strategy planning process and thus guides the firm toward more effective marketing.

When you finish this chapter, you should be able to:

1 understand why marketing must be evaluated differently at the micro and macro levels.

2 understand why this text argues that micro-marketing costs too much.

3 understand why this text argues that macro-marketing does not cost too much.

4 understand all of the elements of the marketing strategy planning process and strategy decisions for the four Ps.

5 know how to prepare a marketing plan and how it relates to the marketing strategy planning process.

6 know some of the challenges marketers face as they work to develop ethical marketing strategies that serve consumers' needs.

How Should Marketing Be Evaluated?

LO 20.1

We must evaluate at two levels

We've stressed the need for marketing to satisfy customers at a cost that customers consider a good value. So in this final chapter we'll focus on both customer satisfaction and the costs of marketing as we evaluate marketing's impact on society (see Exhibit 20-1). As we discussed in Chapter 1, it's useful to distinguish between two levels of marketing. Managerial (micro) marketing concerns the marketing activities of an individual firm, whereas macro-marketing concerns how the whole marketing system works. Some complaints against marketing are aimed at only one of these levels at a time. In other cases, the criticisms seem to be directed to one level but actually are aimed at the other. Some critics of specific ads, for example, probably would not be satisfied with any advertising. When evaluating marketing, we must treat each of these levels separately.

Nation's objectives affect evaluation

Different nations have different social and economic objectives. Dictatorships, for example, may be mainly concerned with satisfying the needs of society as seen by the political elite. In a socialist state, the objective might be to satisfy society's needs as defined by government planners. In some societies, the objectives are defined by religious leaders. In others, it's whoever controls the military.

Consumer satisfaction is the objective in the United States

In the United States, *the basic objective of our market-directed economic system has been to satisfy consumer needs as they, the consumers, see them.* This objective implies that political freedom and economic freedom go hand in hand and that citizens in a free society have the right to live as they choose. The majority of American consumers would be unwilling to give up the freedom of choice they now enjoy. The same can be said for Canada, Great

Exhibit 20–1 Ethical Marketing in a Consumer-Oriented World

External Market Environment
Customers
Company
Competitors
S.W.O.T.
Segmentation and Targeting
Differentiation and Positioning
PRODUCT PLACE PROMOTION PRICE
TARGET

Marketing's Impact on Society: Micro and Macro Views

Evaluating marketing
- Micro versus macro criteria
- Measuring consumer satisfaction
- Micro-marketing often costs too much
- Macro-marketing does not cost too much

Putting together innovative marketing plans
- Strategy planning process
- Understanding customers
- Blending marketing mix
- Content of the marketing plan

Challenges facing marketers
- Opportunities for improvement
- Marketing managers and social responsibility
- How far should the marketing concept go?

Britain, and most other countries in the European Union. However, for focus we will concentrate on marketing as it exists in American society.

Therefore, let's try to evaluate the operation of marketing in the American economy—where the present objective is to satisfy consumer needs *as consumers see them.* This is the essence of our system.

This upscale food store in Iran looks similar to those in Western economies, but prices of many consumer products have risen dramatically as the government has clashed with the West. The President of Iran pledged to use oil revenue to ease poverty, but so far that objective has not received much attention.

Can Consumer Satisfaction Be Measured?

Since consumer satisfaction is our objective, marketing's effectiveness must be measured by *how well* it satisfies consumers. There have been various efforts to measure overall consumer satisfaction not only in the United States but also in other countries. For example, a team of researchers at the University of Michigan has created the American Customer Satisfaction Index based on regular interviews with thousands of customers of about 200 companies in 39 industries. Similar studies are available for member countries of the European Union.

Satisfaction depends on individual aspirations

This sort of index makes it possible to track changes in consumer satisfaction measures over time and even allows comparison among countries. That's potentially useful. Yet there are limits to interpreting any measure of consumer satisfaction when we try to evaluate macro-marketing effectiveness in any absolute sense. One basic issue is that satisfaction depends on and is *relative to* your level of aspiration or expectation. Less prosperous consumers begin to expect more out of an economy as they see the higher living standards of others. Also, aspiration levels tend to rise with repeated successes and fall with failures. Products considered satisfactory one day may not be satisfactory the next day, or vice versa. Twenty-five years ago, most people were satisfied with a 21-inch color TV that pulled in three or four channels. But once you become accustomed to a large-screen HD model and enjoy all the options possible with a digital satellite receiver, on-demand programs, and a DVR, that old TV is never the same again.

In addition, consumer satisfaction is a highly personal concept. Thus, looking at the "average" satisfaction of a whole society does not provide a complete picture for evaluating macro-marketing effectiveness. At a minimum, some consumers are more satisfied than others. So, although efforts to measure satisfaction are useful, any evaluation of macro-marketing effectiveness has to be in part subjective.

Probably the supreme test is whether the macro-marketing system satisfies enough individual consumer-citizens so that they vote—in the ballot box—to keep it running. So far, we've done so in the United States.[2]

There are many measures of micro-marketing effectiveness

Measuring the marketing effectiveness of an individual firm is also difficult, but it can be done. Expectations may change just as other aspects of the market environment change—so firms have to do a good job of coping with the change. Individual business firms can and should try to measure how well their marketing mixes satisfy their customers (or why they fail). In fact, most large firms now have some type of ongoing effort to determine whether they're satisfying their target markets. For example, the J.D. Power and Associates marketing research firm is well known for its studies of consumer satisfaction with different makes of automobiles and computers. And the American Customer Satisfaction Index is also used to rate individual companies.

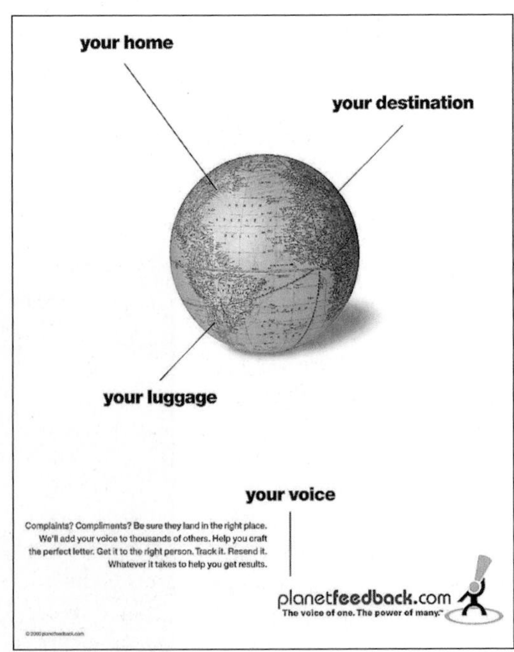

Planetfeedback.com makes it easy for consumers to give feedback to companies.

Many large and small firms measure customer satisfaction with attitude research studies. Other widely used

Internet Exercise

Let's take a closer look at the American Customer Satisfaction Index (ACSI). Go to the organization's website (**www.theacsi.org**). Click on "ACSI Results" and look at "Scores by Industry." In some industries, ACSI has been measuring customer satisfaction since 1994. What industries have shown the greatest improvement since that time? What industries have declined in customer satisfaction? Why do you think some industries have moved up, while others have moved down?

methods include comment cards, e-mail response features on websites, unsolicited consumer responses (usually complaints), opinions of intermediaries and salespeople, market test results, and profits. Of course, customers may be very satisfied about some aspects of what a firm is doing but dissatisfied about other dimensions of performance.[3]

In our market-directed system, it's up to each customer to decide how effectively individual firms satisfy his or her needs. Usually, customers will buy more of the products that satisfy them—and they'll do it repeatedly. That's why firms that develop really satisfying marketing mixes are able to develop profitable long-term relationships with the customers that they serve. Because efficient marketing plans can increase profits, profits can be used as a rough measure of a firm's efficiency in satisfying customers. Nonprofit organizations have a different bottom line, but they too will fail if they don't satisfy supporters and get the resources they need to continue to operate.

Evaluating marketing effectiveness is difficult, but not impossible

It's easy to see why opinions differ concerning the effectiveness of micro- and macro-marketing. If the objective of the economy is clearly defined, however—and the argument is stripped of emotion—the big questions about marketing effectiveness probably *can* be answered.

In this chapter, we argue that micro-marketing (how individual firms and channels operate) frequently *does* cost too much but that macro-marketing (how the whole marketing system operates) *does not* cost too much, *given the present objective of the American economy—consumer satisfaction.* Don't accept this position as *the* answer but rather as a point of view. In the end, you'll have to make your own judgment.[4]

Micro-Marketing Often Does Cost Too Much

LO 20.2

Throughout the text, we've explored what marketing managers could or should do to help their firms do a better job of satisfying customers—while achieving company objectives. Many firms implement highly successful marketing programs, but others are still too production-oriented and inefficient. For customers of these latter firms, micro-marketing often does cost too much.

Research shows that many consumers are not satisfied. But you know that already. All of us have had experiences when we weren't satisfied—when some firm didn't deliver on its promises. And the problem is much bigger than some marketers want to believe. Research suggests that the majority of consumer complaints are never reported. Worse, many complaints that are reported never get fully resolved.

Coke spent many millions of dollars to develop and promote Blak, a fusion of cola and coffee that was sold in the energy drink category. After more than a year of investments to build the brand, Coke finally abandoned the effort. Even companies with outstanding marketing talents sometimes make expensive marketing mistakes.

The failure rate is high

Further evidence that too many firms are too production-oriented—and not nearly as efficient as they could be—is the fact that so many new products fail. New and old businesses—even ones that in the past were leaders in their markets—fail regularly too.

Generally speaking, marketing inefficiencies are due to one or more of these reasons:

1. Lack of interest in or understanding of the sometimes fickle customer.
2. Improper blending of the four Ps—lack of understanding of or adjustment to the market environment, especially what competitors do.

Any of these problems can easily be a fatal flaw—the sort of thing that leads to business failures. A firm can't create value if it doesn't have a clue what customers think or say. Even if a firm listens to the "voice of the customer," there's no incentive for the customer to buy if the benefits of the marketing mix don't exceed the costs. And if the firm succeeds in coming up with a marketing mix with benefits greater than costs, it still won't be a superior value unless it's better than what competitors offer.

The high cost of missed opportunities

Another sign of failure is the inability of firms to identify new target markets and new opportunities. A new marketing mix that isn't offered doesn't fail—but the lost opportunity can be significant for both a firm and society. Too many managers seize on whatever strategy seems easiest rather than seeking really new ways to satisfy customers. Too many companies stifle really innovative thinking. Layers of bureaucracy and a "that's not the way we do things" mentality just snuff it out.

On the other hand, not every new idea is a good idea for every company. Many firms have lost millions of dollars with failed efforts to jump on the "what's new" bandwagon—without stopping to figure out how it is going to really satisfy the customer and result in profit for the firm. That is as much a ticket for failure as being too slow or bureaucratic.

Ethics Question

Your firm has a new strategy that will make its established product obsolete. However, it will take a year before you are ready to implement the new strategy. If you announce your plan in advance, profits will disappear because many customers and intermediaries will delay purchases until the new product is released. If you don't announce the new plan, customers and intermediaries will continue to buy the established product as their needs dictate, but some will be stuck owning the inferior product and won't do business with you again in the future. How would you decide what to do?

Micro-marketing does cost too much, but things are changing

For reasons like these, marketing does cost too much in many firms. Despite much publicity, the marketing concept is not applied in many places.

But not all firms and marketers deserve criticism. More of them *are* becoming customer-oriented. And many are paying more attention to market-oriented planning to carry out the marketing concept more effectively. Throughout the text, we've highlighted firms and strategies that are making a difference. The successes of innovative firms—like Nike, Cirque du Soleil, Amazon.com, Nintendo, Apple, iRobot, Best Buy, and GEICO—do not go unnoticed. Yes, they make some mistakes. That's human—and marketing is a human enterprise. But they have also shown the results that market-oriented strategy planning can produce.

Another encouraging sign is that more companies are recognizing that they need a diverse set of backgrounds and talents to meet the increasingly varied needs of their increasingly global customers. They're shedding "not-invented-here" biases and embracing new technologies, comparing what they do with the best practices of firms in totally different industries, and teaming up with outside specialists who can bring a fresh perspective.

Managers who adopt the marketing concept as a way of business life do a better job. They look for target market opportunities and carefully blend the elements of the marketing mix to meet their customers' needs. As more of these managers rise in business, we can look forward to much lower micro-marketing costs and strategies that do a better job of satisfying customer needs.

Macro-Marketing Does Not Cost Too Much

LO 20.3

Some critics of marketing take aim at the macro-marketing system. They typically argue that the macro-marketing system causes a poor use of resources and leads to an unfair distribution of income. Most of these complaints imply that some marketing activities by individual firms should not be permitted—and because they are, our macro-marketing system does a less-than-satisfactory job. Let's look at some of these positions to help you form your own opinion.

Micro-efforts help the economy grow

Some critics feel that marketing helps create a monopoly or at least monopolistic competition. Further, they think this leads to higher prices, restricted output, and reduction in national income and employment.

It's true that firms in a market-directed economy try to carve out separate monopolistic markets for themselves with new products. But consumers do have a choice. They don't *have* to buy the new product unless they think it's a better value. The old products are still available. In fact, to meet the new competition, prices of the old products usually drop. And that makes them even more affordable.

Over several years, the innovator's profits may rise—but rising profits also encourage further innovation by competitors. This leads to new investments, which contribute to economic growth and higher levels of national income and employment. Around the world, many countries failed to achieve their potential for economic growth under command systems because this type of profit incentive didn't exist.

Increased profits also attract competition. Profits and prices then begin to drop as new competitors enter the market and begin producing somewhat similar products. (Recall the rise and fall of industry profit during the product life cycle.)

Is advertising a waste of resources?

Advertising is the most criticized of all micro-marketing activities. Indeed, many ads *are* annoying, insulting, misleading, and downright ineffective. This is one reason why micro-marketing often does cost too much. However, advertising can also make both the micro- and macro-marketing processes work better.

Advertising is an economical way to inform large numbers of potential customers about a firm's products. Provided that a product satisfies customer needs, advertising can increase demand for the product—resulting in economies of scale in manufacturing, distribution, and sales. Because these economies may more than offset advertising costs, advertising can actually *lower* prices to the consumer.[5]

Consumers are not puppets

The idea that firms can manipulate consumers to buy anything the company chooses to produce simply isn't true. A consumer who buys a soft drink that tastes terrible won't

While many individual marketing efforts fail, others increase customer satisfaction. Shieldtox Naturgard uses natural ingredients to offer continuous control of flying insects including mosquitoes. Customers use Saridon as a pain reliever.

buy another can of that brand, regardless of how much it's advertised. In fact, many new products fail the test of the market. Not even large corporations are assured of success every time they launch a new product. Consider, for example, the dismal fate of Pets.com and eToys.com, Ford's Edsel, Sony's beta format VCRs, Xerox's personal computers, and half of the TV programs put on the air in recent years. And if powerful corporations know some way to get people to buy products against their will, would companies like Lucent, General Motors, and Eastern Airlines ever have gone through long periods losing hundreds of millions of dollars?

Gardenburger's ad takes a humorous approach, which might appeal to consumers who are cynical about advertiser's sales pitches. On the other hand, Hindu consumers (who would logically be potential consumers for Gardenburger products) might find it offensive that the ad pokes fun at Hindu religious beliefs.

Needs and wants change

Consumer needs and wants change constantly. Few of us would care to live the way our grandparents lived when they were our age. Marketing's job is not just to satisfy consumer wants as they exist at any particular point in time. Rather, marketing must keep looking for new *and* better ways to create value and serve consumers.[6]

Does marketing make people materialistic?

There is no doubt that marketing caters to materialistic values. However, people disagree as to whether marketing creates these values or simply appeals to values already there.

Even in the most primitive societies, people want to accumulate possessions. The tendency for ancient pharaohs to surround themselves with wealth and treasures can hardly be attributed to the persuasive powers of advertising agencies!

Products do improve the quality of life

Clearly, the quality of life can't be measured just in terms of quantities of material goods. But when we view products as the means to an end rather than the end itself, they *do* make it possible to satisfy higher-level needs. The Internet, for example, empowers people with information in ways that few of us could have even imagined a decade ago.

Marketing reflects our own values

Critics say that advertising elevates the wrong values—for example, by relying on sex appeal to get attention—and generally sending the signal that what really matters most is self-gratification. For example, GoDaddy.com sells Internet domain names and related services. Its stated objective for a Super Bowl ad was to create the most talked about ad ever, and it figured that a risqué ad was the way to go. The ad that it ultimately aired (after trying another dozen or so ideas that were rejected as inappropriate for TV) was a spoof on Janet Jackson's "wardrobe malfunction" during the Super Bowl halftime show the previous year. The sexy woman dancing around in the commercial doesn't have anything to do with GoDaddy.com, but she did get a lot of attention and GoDaddy's awareness levels went up significantly. A survey showed that it was one of the four most liked commercials during the Super Bowl and the year, but also one of the four most disliked. There are thousands of other ads that rely on something related to sex to get attention. But is it advertising that creates interest in sex or something else? Experts who study values seem to agree that, in the short run, marketing reflects social values, while in the long run it enhances and reinforces

them. Further, many companies work hard to figure out their customers' beliefs and values. Then they refuse to use ads that would be offensive to their target customers.[7]

Not all needs are met

Some critics argue that our macro-marketing system is flawed because it does not provide solutions to important problems, such as questions about how to help the homeless, the uneducated, dependent children, minorities who have suffered discrimination, the elderly poor, and the sick. Many of these people do live in dire circumstances. But is that the result of a market-directed system?

There is no doubt that many firms focus their effort on people who can pay for what they have to offer. But, as the forces of competition drive down prices, more people are able to afford more of what they need. And the matching of supply and demand stimulates economic growth, creates jobs, and spreads income among more people. In other words, a market-directed economy makes efficient use of resources. However, it can't guarantee that government aid programs are effective. It doesn't ensure that all voters and politicians agree on which problems should be solved first—or how taxes should be set and allocated. It can't eliminate the possibility of a child being ignored.

These are important societal issues. Consumer-citizens in a democratic society assign some responsibilities to business and some to government. Ultimately, consumer-citizens vote in the ballot box for how they want governments to deal with these concerns—just as they vote with their dollars for which firms to support. As more managers in the public sector understand and apply marketing concepts, we should be able to do a better job meeting the needs of all people.

Marketing Strategy Planning Process Requires Logic and Creativity

LO 20.4

We've said that our macro-marketing system *does not* cost too much, given that customer satisfaction is the present objective of our economy. But we admit that the performance of many business firms leaves a lot to be desired. This presents a challenge to serious-minded students and marketers—and raises the question: What needs to be done?

We hope that this book has convinced you that a large part of the answer to that question is that the *effectiveness and value of marketing efforts in individual firms is improved significantly when managers take the marketing concept seriously—and when they apply the marketing strategy planning process we've presented.* So let's briefly review these ideas and show how they can be integrated into a marketing plan.

Marketing strategy planning process brings focus to efforts

Developing a good marketing strategy and turning the strategy into a marketing plan requires creative blending of the ideas we've discussed throughout this text. Exhibit 20-2 provides a broad overview of the major areas we've been talking about. You first saw this exhibit in Chapter 2—before you learned what's really involved in each idea. Now we must integrate ideas about these different areas to narrow down to a specific target market and marketing mix that represents a real opportunity. This narrowing-down process requires a thorough understanding of the market. That understanding is enhanced by careful analysis of customers' needs, current or prospective competitors, and the firm's own objectives and resources. Similarly, trends in the external market environment may make a potential opportunity more or less attractive.

There are usually more different strategy possibilities than a firm can pursue. Each possible strategy usually has a number of different potential advantages and disadvantages. This can make it difficult to zero in on the best target market and marketing mix. However, as we discussed in Chapter 3, developing a set of specific qualitative and quantitative screening criteria—to define what business and market(s) the firm wants to compete in—can help eliminate potential strategies that are not well suited to the firm.

Careful analysis helps the manager focus on a strategy that takes advantage of the firm's strengths and opportunities while avoiding its weaknesses and threats to its success. These

Exhibit 20–2 Overview of Marketing Strategy Planning Process

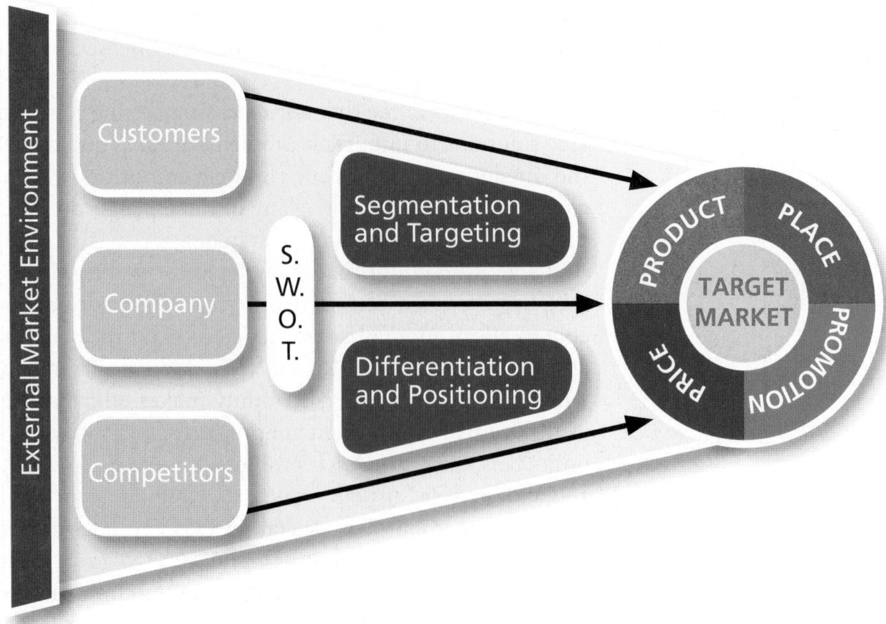

strengths and weaknesses can be compared with the pros and cons of strategies that are considered. For example, if a firm is considering a strategy that focuses on a target market that is already satisfied by a competitor's offering, finding a competitive advantage might require an innovative new product, improved distribution, more effective promotion, or a better price. Just offering a marketing mix that is like what is available from competitors usually doesn't provide any real basis for the firm to position or differentiate its marketing mix as offering superior customer value.

Marketing manager must blend the four Ps

Exhibit 20-3 reviews the major marketing strategy decision areas organized by the four Ps. Each of these requires careful decision making. Yet marketing planning involves much more than just independent decisions and assembling the parts into a marketing mix. The

Bolthouse Farms saw an opportunity to sell more baby carrots. Since teenagers were their target market, they knew that a "healthy snack" positioning was probably not the best approach. So they developed a creative marketing strategy to appeal to this target market—"Eat 'em like junk food." Creative packaging, fun promotion, and distribution in school lunchroom vending machines were just part of the strategy that helped grow a previously stagnant market for baby carrots.

Exhibit 20–3
Strategy Decision Areas Organized by the Four Ps

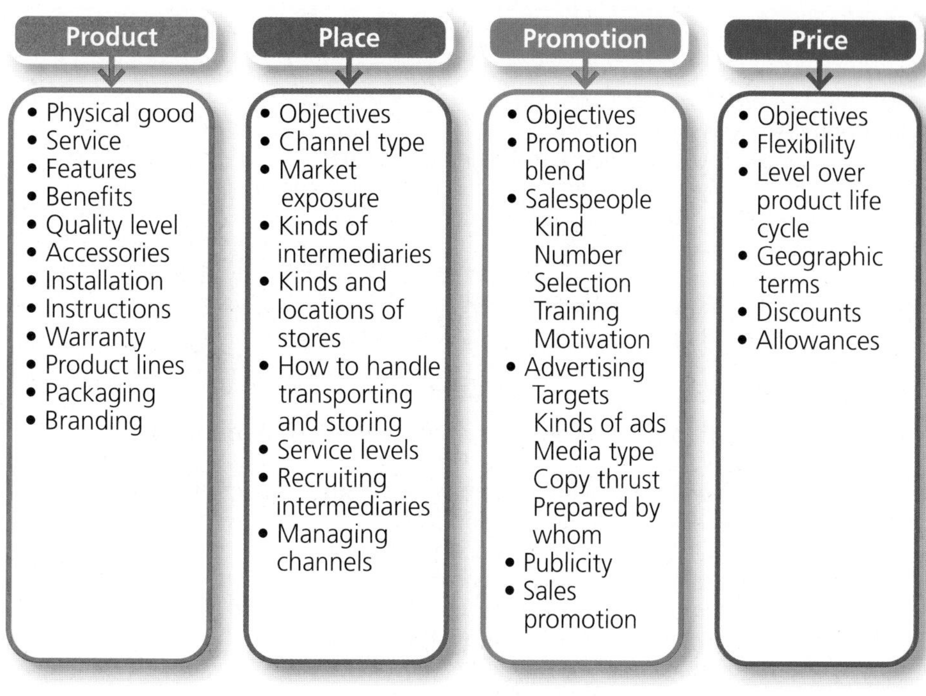

four Ps must be creatively *blended*—so the firm develops the best mix for its target market. In other words, each decision must work well with all of the others to make a logical whole.

Product
• Physical good
• Service
• Features
• Benefits
• Quality level
• Accessories
• Installation
• Instructions
• Warranty
• Product lines
• Packaging
• Branding
Place
• Objectives
• Channel type
• Market exposure
• Kinds of intermediaries
• Kinds and locations of stores
• How to handle transporting and storing
• Service levels
• Recruiting intermediaries
• Managing channels
Promotion
• Objectives
• Promotion blend
• Salespeople
Kind
Number
Selection
Training
Motivation
• Advertising
Targets
Kinds of ads
Media type
Copy thrust
Prepared by whom
• Publicity
• Sales promotion
Price
• Objectives
• Flexibility
• Level over product life cycle
• Geographic terms
• Discounts
• Allowances

In our discussion, we've given the job of integrating the four Ps strategy decisions to the marketing manager. Now you should see the need for this integrating role. It is easy for specialists to focus on their own areas and expect the rest of the company to work for or around them. This is especially true in larger firms where the size of the whole marketing job is too big for one person. Yet the ideas of the product manager, the advertising manager, the sales manager, the logistics manager, and whoever makes pricing decisions may have to be adjusted to improve the whole mix. It's critical that each marketing mix decision work well with all of the others. A breakdown in any one decision area may doom the whole strategy to failure.

The Marketing Plan Brings All the Details Together

LO 20.5

Marketing plan provides a blueprint for implementation

Once the manager has selected the target market, decided on the (integrated) marketing mix to meet that target market's needs, and developed estimates of the costs and revenues for that strategy, it's time to put it all together in the marketing plan. As we explained in Chapter 2, a marketing plan includes the time-related details—including costs and revenues—for a marketing strategy. Thus, the plan basically serves as a blueprint for what the firm will do.

Exhibit 20-4 provides a summary outline of the different sections of a complete marketing plan. You can see that this outline is basically an abridged overview of the topics we've covered throughout the text. Thus, you can flesh out your thinking for any portion of a marketing plan by reviewing the section of the book where that topic is discussed in more detail. Further, the Hillside Veterinary Clinic case in the Marketing Plan Coach on the text website gives you a real example of the types of thinking and detail that are included.

Marketing plan spells out the timing of the strategy

Some time schedule is implicit in any strategy. A marketing plan simply spells out this time period and the time-related details. Usually, we think in terms of some reasonable length of time—such as six months, a year, or a few years. But it might be only a month or two in some cases, especially when rapid changes in fashion or technology are important.

Exhibit 20–4 Summary Outline of Different Sections of Marketing Plan

<u>Situation Analysis</u>

Company Analysis

- Company objectives and overall marketing objectives
- Company resources (marketing, production, financial, human, etc.)
- Other marketing plans (marketing program)
- Previous marketing strategy
- Major screening criteria relevant to product-market opportunity selected
  - Quantitative (ROI, profitability, risk level, etc.)
  - Qualitative (nature of business preferred, social responsibility, environment, etc.)
- Major constraints
- Marketing collaborators (current and potential)

Customer Analysis (organizational customers and/or final consumers)

- Product-market
- Possible segmenting dimensions (customer needs, other characteristics)
  - Qualifying dimensions and determining dimensions
- Identify target market(s) (one or more specific segments)
  - Operational characteristics (demographics, geographic locations, etc.)
- Potential size (number of people, dollar purchase potential, etc.) and likely growth
- Key economic, psychological, and social influences on buying
- Type of buying situation
- Nature of relationship with customers

Competitor Analysis

- Nature of current/likely competition
- Current and prospective competitors (or rivals)
  - Current strategies and likely responses to plan
- Competitive barriers to overcome and sources of potential competitive advantage

Analysis of the Market Context—External Market Environment

- Economic environment
- Technological environment
- Political and legal environment
- Cultural and social environment

Key Factors from Situation Analysis

- S.W.O.T.: Strengths, weaknesses, opportunities, and threats from situation analysis

<u>Marketing Plan Objectives</u>

- Specific objectives to be achieved with the marketing strategy

<u>Differentiation and Positioning</u>

- How will marketing mix be differentiated from the competition?
- How will the market offering be positioned?
- Positioning statement

<u>Marketing Strategy</u>

Overview of the Marketing Strategy

- General direction for the marketing strategy
- Description of how the four Ps fit together

Target Market(s)

- Summary of characteristics of the target market(s) to be approached

Product

- Product class (type of consumer or business product)
- Current product life-cycle stage
- New-product development requirements (people, dollars, time, etc.)
- Product liability, safety, and social responsibility considerations
- Specification of core physical good or service
  - Features, quality, etc.
- Supporting service(s) needed
- Warranty (what is covered, timing, who will support, etc.)
- Branding (manufacturer versus dealer, family versus individual, etc.)

Packaging
Promotion and labeling needs
Protection needs
Cultural sensitivity of product
Fit with product line

Place
Objectives
Degree of market exposure required
Distribution customer service level required
Type of channel (direct, indirect)
Other channel members or collaborators required
Type/number of wholesalers (agent, merchant, etc.)
Type/number of retailers
How discrepancies and separations will be handled
How marketing functions will be shared
Coordination needed in company, channel, and supply chain
Information requirements (EDI, the Internet, e-mail, etc.)
Transportation requirements
Inventory product-handling requirements
Facilities required (warehousing, distribution centers, etc.)
Reverse channels (for returns, recalls, etc.)

Promotion
Objectives
Major message theme(s) (for integrated marketing communications/positioning)
Promotion blend
Advertising (type, media, copy thrust, etc.)
Personal selling (type and number of salespeople, compensation, effort allocation, etc.)
Publicity
Sales promotion (for customers, channel members, employees)
Interactive media
Mix of push and pull required
Who will do the work?

Price
Nature of demand (price sensitivity, price of substitutes)
Demand and cost analyses (marginal analysis)
Markup chain in channel
Price flexibility
Price level(s) (under what conditions) and impact on customer value
Adjustments to list price (geographic terms, discounts, allowances, etc.)

Marketing Information Requirements
Marketing research needs (with respect to customers, 4Ps, external environment, etc.)
Secondary and primary data needs
Marketing information system needs, models to be used, etc.

Implementation and Control

Special Implementation Problems to Overcome
People required
Manufacturing, financial, and other resources needed

Control
Marketing information systems and data needed
Criterion measures/comparison with objectives (customer satisfaction, sales, cost, performance analysis, etc.)

Budget, Sales Forecasts, and Estimates of Profit
Costs (all elements in plan, over time)
Sales (by market, over time, etc.)
Estimated operating statement (pro forma)

Timing
Specific sequence of activities and events, etc.
Likely changes over the product life cycle

Risk Factors and Contingency Plans

Or a strategy might be implemented over several years, perhaps the length of the early stages of the product's life.

Although the outline in Exhibit 20-4 does not explicitly show a place for the time frame for the plan or the specific costs for each decision area, these should be included in the plan—along with expected estimates of sales and profit—so that the plan can be compared with *actual performance* in the future. In other words, the plan not only makes it clear to everyone what is to be accomplished and how—it also provides a basis for the control process after the plan is implemented.[8]

A complete plan spells out the reasons for decisions

The plan outline shown in Exhibit 20-4 is quite complete. It doesn't just provide information about marketing mix decisions—it also includes information about customers (including segmenting dimensions), competitors' strategies, other aspects of the market environment, and the company's objectives and resources. This material provides important background information relevant to the "why" of the marketing mix and target market decisions.

Too often, managers do not include this information; their plans just lay out the details of the target market and the marketing mix strategy decisions. This shortcut approach is more common when the plan is really just an update of a strategy that has been in place for some time. However, that approach can be risky.

Managers too often make the mistake of casually updating plans in minor ways—perhaps just changing some costs or sales forecasts—but otherwise sticking with what was done in the past. A big problem with this approach is that it's easy to lose sight of why those strategy decisions were made in the first place. When the market situation changes, the original reasons may no longer apply. Yet if the logic for those strategy decisions is not retained, it's easy to miss changes taking place that should result in a plan being reconsidered. For example, a plan that was established in the growth stage of the product life cycle may have been very successful for a number of years. But a marketing manager can't be complacent and assume that success will continue forever. When market maturity hits, the firm may be in for big trouble—unless the basic strategy and plan are modified. If a plan spells out the details of the market analysis and logic for the marketing mix and target market selected, then it is a simple matter to routinely check and update it. Remember: The idea is for all of the analysis and strategy decisions to fit together as an integrated whole. Thus, as some of the elements of the plan or market environment change, the whole plan may need a fresh approach.

Challenges Facing Marketers

LO 20.6

Marketers face the challenge of preparing creative and innovative marketing plans, but that in itself will not improve the value of marketing to society. We need to face up to other basic challenges that require new ways of thinking.

Change is the only thing that's constant

We need better marketing performance at the firm level. Progressive firms pay attention to changes in the market—including trends in the market environment—and how marketing strategies need to be improved to consider these changes. Exhibit 20-5 lists some of the important trends and changes we've discussed throughout this text.

Most of the changes and trends summarized in Exhibit 20-5 are having a positive effect on how marketers serve society. And this ongoing improvement is self-directing. As consumers shift their support to firms that do meet their needs, laggard businesses are forced to either improve or get out of the way.

If it ain't broke, improve it

Marketing managers must constantly evaluate their strategies to be sure they're not being left in the dust by competitors who see new and better ways of doing things. It's crazy for a marketing manager to constantly change a strategy that's working well. But too many managers fail to see or plan for needed changes. They're afraid to do anything different and adhere to the idea that "if it ain't broke, don't fix it." But a firm can't always wait until a problem becomes completely obvious to do something about it. When customers move on

Exhibit 20–5 Some Important Changes and Trends Affecting Marketing Strategy Planning

Communication Technologies
The Internet and intranets
Satellite communications and Wi-Fi
E-mail and text messaging
Video conferencing and Internet telephony
Ubiquity of cell phones
Growing use of smartphones
Consumer online "search" shopping
More interactive communications with customers

Role of Computerization
E-commerce, websites
Spreadsheet analysis
Wireless networks
Scanners, bar codes, and RFID for tracking
Multimedia integration
"Cloud" computing

Marketing Research
Search engines and web analytics
Online research—surveys, focus groups, online communities
Growth of marketing information systems
Decision support systems
Single source data (and scanner panels)
Data warehouses and data mining
Customer relationship management (CRM) systems

Demographic Patterns
Technology usage around the globe
Explosion in senior and ethnic submarkets
Aging of the baby boomers
Population growth slowdown in U.S.
Geographic shifts in population
Slower real income growth in U.S.

Business and Organizational Customers
Closer relationships and single sourcing
Just-in-time inventory systems/EDI
Web portals and Internet sourcing
Interactive bidding and proposal requests
Internet as source of information
Shift to NAICS
ISO 9000
E-commerce and supply chain management

Product
More attention to "really new" products
Growth of dealer brands and private label
Faster new-product development
Computer-aided design (CAD)
R&D teams with market-driven focus
Role of customer experience
More attention to quality
More attention to service technologies
More attention to sustainable design
Category management

Channels and Logistics
Internet selling (wholesale and retail)
More vertical marketing systems
Clicks and bricks (multichannel)
More multichannel shopping
Larger, more powerful retail chains
More attention to distribution service
Real-time inventory replenishment
Radio frequency identification (RFID)
Automated warehousing and handling
Cross-docking at distribution centers
Logistics outsourcing
Growth of mass-merchandising

Sales Promotion
Database-directed promotion
Point-of-purchase promotion
Trade promotion becoming more sensible
Event sponsorships
Product placement
Better support from agencies
Customer loyalty programs
Customer acquisition cost analysis

Personal Selling
Post-sale customer service
Sales technology
Major accounts specialization
More telemarketing and team selling

Mass Selling
Interactive media (Internet ads, etc.)
Increasing role of publicity
More emphasis on "found" media
Role of customer reviews and ratings
Integrated marketing communications
Growth of more targeted media
Point-of-purchase
Growth of interactive agencies
Consolidation of global agencies
Consolidation of media companies
Changing agency compensation
Shrinking media budgets

Pricing
Electronic bid pricing and auctions
Value pricing
Overuse of sales and deals
Bigger differences in discounts
More attention to exchange rate effects
Lower markups on higher stockturn items
Use of "free" as a price

International Marketing
More international market development
Global competitors—at home and abroad
Global communication over Internet
New trade rules (NAFTA, WTO, EU, etc.)
More attention to exporting by small firms
International expansion by retailers
Impact of "pop" culture on traditional cultures
Tensions between "have" and "have-not" cultures
Growing income and population in emerging markets

General
Economic decline
S.W.O.T. analysis
Privacy issues
More attention to positioning and differentiation
Shift away from diversification
More attention to profitability, not just sales
Greater attention to superior value
Addressing environmental concerns

and profits disappear, it may be too late to fix the problem. Marketing managers who take the lead in finding innovative new markets and approaches get a competitive advantage.

We need to welcome international competition

Marketers can't afford to bury their heads in the sand and hope that international competition will go away. Rather, they must realize that it is part of today's market environment. It creates even more pressure on marketing managers to figure out what it takes to gain a competitive advantage—both at home and in foreign markets. But with the challenge comes opportunities. The forces of competition in and among market-directed economies will help speed the diffusion of marketing advances to consumers everywhere. As macro-marketing systems improve worldwide, more consumers will have income to buy products—from wherever in the world those products come.

We need to use technology wisely

We live in a time of dramatic new technologies. Many marketers hate the idea that what they've learned from years of on-the-job experience may no longer apply when a technology like the Internet comes along. Or they feel that it's the job of the technical specialist to figure out how a new technology can help the firm serve its customers. But marketers can't just pawn that responsibility off on "somebody else." If that means learning about new technologies, then that is just part of the marketing job.

At a broader level, firms face the challenge of determining what technologies are acceptable and which are not. For example, gene research has opened the door to life-saving medicines, genetically altered crops that resist drought or disease, and even cloning of human beings. Yet in all of these arenas there is intense conflict among different groups about what is appropriate. How should these decisions be made? There is no simple answer to this question, but it's clear that old production-oriented views are *not* the answer. Perhaps we will move toward developing answers if some of the marketing ideas that have been applied to understanding individual needs can be extended to better understand the needs of society as a whole.

Internet for consumers—sunny or partly cloudy

The Internet promised to create a more transparent business environment for customers. By shining "sunlight" on bad practices, the costs rise for firms producing a defective product or engaging in unethical behavior. In some ways this has proven to be the case. Early adopter customers review purchases on websites. Reports of a boring book, misleading product descriptions, poorly designed products, or bad customer service help

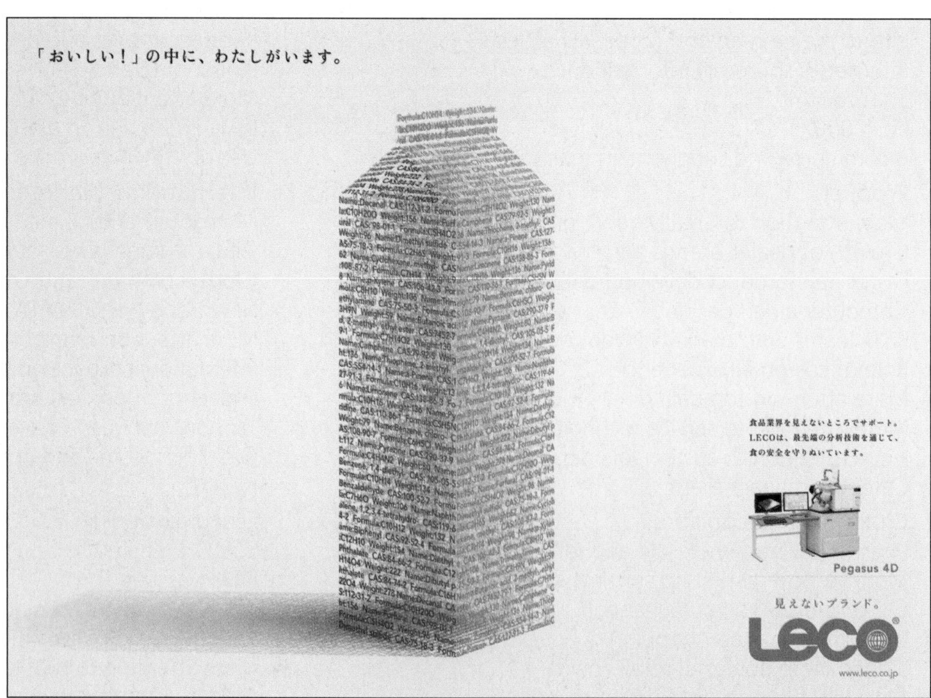

"I am inside your taste of goodness." Leco Japan produces instrumentation that helps protect food safety.

prospective customers make more informed choices. On the other hand, there are growing reports of companies gaming the review system with fake reviews—leading consumers to question this source of information.

Along the same lines, companies must work hard to bury negative information about their brands. Sometimes this is justified, as the web allows anyone with a gripe (valid or not) to post complaints. But now marketing managers have become much more clever about controlling their brand image online. It wasn't too long ago that when typing Nike into Google, the first page of the search returned several links questioning the company's ethics and practices. Now the same search turns up only positive messages. In part this is because Nike has responded to critics and actively engages in more sustainable and socially responsible practices. It is also because Nike is more aware of how to manage search results to effectively bury its critics.

In general, the Internet has helped to shine a light that helps consumers make more informed choices. The risk is that increasingly web-savvy brands find ways to clean up their image without cleaning up their practices.[9]

We must consider *long-run* consumer welfare

Throughout this book we have emphasized the importance of the marketing concept—satisfying customers through a total company effort at a profit. Unfortunately, some firms take too short-run a view. They satisfy customers in the near term and take their profits, without worrying about longer-term problems. For example, some banks, mortgage brokers, and credit card companies made credit too easy to get. Some customers enjoyed this for a while, but many purchased homes or built up credit card debt that they couldn't afford. While this helped companies earn high profits in the short term, many customers later defaulted on loans. Eventually, such activities harmed customers—and wreaked havoc on our global economy. Marketing managers must have a long-run view of customer satisfaction and recognize their social responsibility.

May need more social responsibility

Good business managers put themselves in the consumer's position. A useful rule to follow might be: Do unto others as you would have others do unto you. In practice, this means developing satisfying marketing mixes for specific target markets. It may mean building in more quality or more safety. The consumer's long-run satisfaction should be considered too. How will the product hold up in use? What about service guarantees? While trying to serve

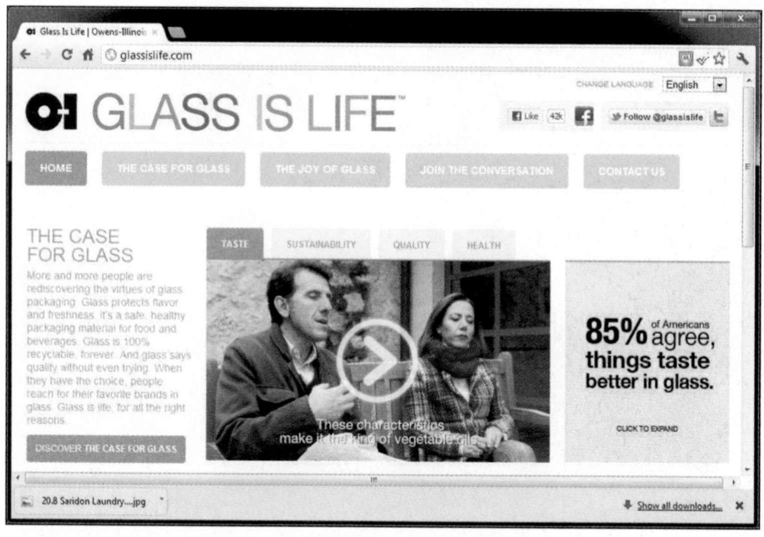

Companies that produce products with environmental benefits will find greater success when those products deliver other benefits as well. Owens Illinois developed a campaign that points out all the benefits of glass. Besides being endlessly recyclable, things taste better in glass. Products packaged in glass are also healthier and higher quality.

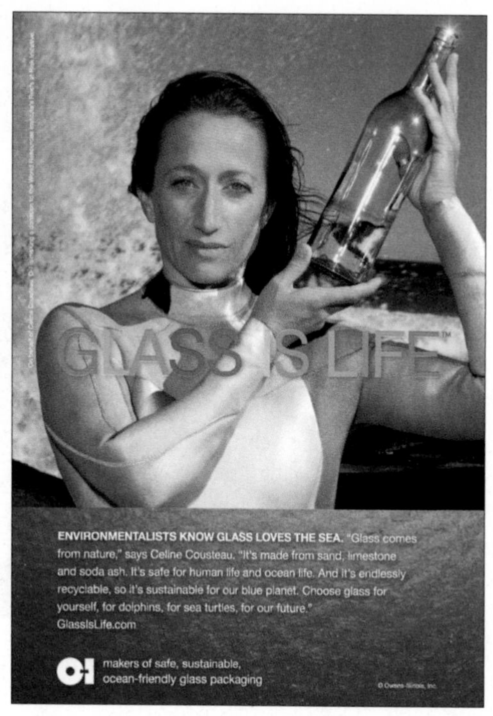

the needs of some target market, does the marketing strategy disregard the rights and needs of other consumers or create problems that will be left for future generations?[10]

We need the truth

Promotion provides powerful ways to communicate with customers. Yet too many firms lapse into telling only half the truth. This is most obvious when there is a shift in consumer interest. For example, a firm's ad may accurately proclaim that its food product has no "trans fat"—but do consumers think that means it's healthy, low calorie, or even low in fat? Today we're also seeing a lot of incomplete or misleading "greenwashing" claims about firms' environmental practices and eco-friendly products. It's good for a firm to create a biodegradable package and promote it, but the cleaning product in the package shouldn't contain chemicals that will be harmful once they're in the sewer system.

Growing consumer cynicism about promotion is also a problem. As it gets worse, both firms and consumers suffer. Regulations say that marketing communications shouldn't be false or misleading, but managers need to take seriously the responsibility to be truthful to their customers. Marketing communications should be helpful—not just legal. Managers who don't get this message are likely to learn a hard lesson—from activists who spread criticisms of their firms across the web and other media. The potential harm to a brand's reputation from this sort of negative publicity has many firms cautious about overstating their claims, including ones related to sustainability efforts.[11]

The environment is everyone's need

Marketers need to work harder and smarter at finding ways to satisfy consumer needs without sacrificing the environment. All consumers need the environment, whether they realize it yet or not. We are only beginning to understand the consequences of the environmental damage that's already been done. Acid rain, depletion of the ozone layer, global warming, and toxic waste in water supplies—to mention but a few current environmental problems—have catastrophic effects.

In the past, most firms didn't pass the cost of environmental damage on to consumers in the prices that they paid. Pollution was a hidden and unmeasured cost for most companies. That is changing rapidly. Firms are already paying billions of dollars to correct problems, including problems created years ago. The government isn't accepting the excuse that "nobody knew it was a big problem."[12]

Chemistry 101
You can learn a lot on the bus.
University of Utah students ride free with student I.D.
U T A

The Utah Transit Authority (UTA) thought that more university students would ride the bus long-term if they were motivated by personal benefit rather than environmental or social conscience. For most people, the pros and cons of riding the bus, like other product choices, are more a personal matter. So UTA decided it should offer an answer to the question, "What's in it for me?" The answer in this particular UTA ad is "social opportunities." Although public transit is not exactly a sexy product, the ad employs a "sex sells" approach. What do you think? Is this a good idea? Why?

Marketers use big data—cool or creepy

Throughout this book we describe big data. Individual social profiles are created from customers' clicks, conversations, Facebook likes, Twitter "tweets," cell phone activity, and credit card and loyalty card purchases. The social profiles allow marketing managers to deliver highly targeted, personalized (and presumably more appealing) marketing mixes. In exchange, customers give up some privacy.

Is this new practice cool? Or is it creepy? To better understand how the big data revolution affects customers let's take a closer look at how this might play out in real life by looking at two fictional college students, Nick and Shelby.

Nick often eats fast food and regularly receives e-mail coupons for fast food purchases. Saving money sounds cool. Data shows that Nick usually spends more than the coupon amount and analysis of Nick's photos and comments on Facebook suggest he is overweight. Soon Nick starts seeing ads for diets; he also receives a special introductory offer from a local health club. Cool or creepy? Nick's Facebook newsfeed and Twitter feed include "articles" from news sites on healthy eating with an emphasis on Kellogg's products and weight loss using South Beach Diet products. Cool or creepy? Some days as Nick walks home from school, he gets a text message with a picture of a bowl of ice cream (and $.50 off)—just a block before he passes the grocery store. Timely. Cool or creepy?

Shelby's friends know she works out regularly and eats healthy. Last week she was online reading articles about mountain bikes—now when she surfs, she sees ads for mountain bikes. Cool or creepy? As Shelby walks into her grocery store, a text message offers her a dollar off on Ben & Jerry's Greek Frozen Yogurt—she loves that stuff, but rarely eats it unless she's feeling down. Did the grocery store know she and her boyfriend just broke up? Yes, it did. It "saw" her Facebook status update. Cool or creepy? Shelby often receives direct-mail offers for low interest credit cards; Nick doesn't get those. Does the financial institution figure that healthier behavior is a sign of financial responsibility? Will insurance companies draw the same conclusions and adjust rates accordingly? Cool or creepy?

These examples are not the future—they happen today. Marketing managers use big data to customize advertising, promotion, pricing, and online content. Tracked by your cell phone's GPS, messages target your location. If a $.50 coupon motivates Nick to buy ice cream, but it takes $1.00 off to move Shelby, each gets a different coupon. The "articles" served to your news feed might be written by someone paid by a brand prominently featured in the article.

Cool or creepy? Probably depends on your values. As we move into a brave new world where customers surrender privacy (usually without their knowledge), you should have questions. Do you want to trade your privacy for personalized marketing mixes? What do you have to gain or lose? Who owns *your* data? Should governments regulate this—or should it be up to you? There are no easy answers.

Marketers need to consider the legal and ethical issues involved as well as their customers' attitudes and values. Consumers need to be more knowledgeable about their privacy. Is this cool? Creepy? A little of both?[13]

Consumer privacy needs to be protected

Marketers must also be sensitive to consumers' rights and privacy. Today, sophisticated marketing research methods, the Internet, and other technologies make it easier to abuse these rights. For example, credit card records—which reveal much about consumers' purchases and private lives—are routinely sold to anybody who pays for the computer file. Many people place loads of personal information on social networking websites, like Facebook, assuming they have some privacy. This is often not the case. For

Internet Exercise

Privacyscore provides a way to assess the privacy risk of using a particular website. At the site you can also see information about the relative privacy of various sites. For this exercise, go to the Privacyscore website (**www.privacyscore.com**). Read some of the FAQs and check out some of the sites listed as more and less private. How could using this site affect your browsing behavior? Should websites be required to report their use of online trackers?

example, a rogue marketer with an e-mail list can go to Facebook and quickly find a name, gender, friends, age, interests, job, location, and education level for each e-mail address.

Most consumers don't realize how much data about their personal lives—some of it incorrect but treated as fact—are collected and available. A simple computer billing error may land consumers on a bad-credit list without their knowledge. Worse, poor security can result in identity theft. Marketing managers should use technology responsibly to improve the quality of life, not disrupt it. If you don't think privacy is a serious matter, enter your social security number in an Internet search engine and see what pops up. You may be surprised.[14]

May need to change laws and how they are enforced

One of the advantages of a market-directed economic system is that it operates automatically. But in our version of this system, consumer-citizens provide certain constraints (laws), which can be modified at any time. Managers who ignore consumer attitudes must realize that their actions may cause new restraints.

Before piling on too many new rules, however, some of the ones we have may need to be revised—and others may need to be enforced more carefully. Antitrust laws, for example, are often applied to protect competitors from each other—but they were originally intended to encourage competition.

Specifically, U.S. antitrust laws were developed so that all firms in a market would compete on a level playing field. But in many markets, that level playing field no longer exists. In our global economy, individual U.S. firms now compete with foreign firms whose governments urge them to cooperate with each other. Such foreign firms don't see each other as competitors; rather they see U.S. firms, as a group, as the competitors.

Laws should affect top managers

Strict enforcement of present laws could have far-reaching results if more price fixers, fraudulent or deceptive advertisers, and others who violate existing laws—thus affecting the performance of the macro-marketing system—were sent to jail or given heavy fines. A quick change in attitudes might occur if unethical top managers—those who plan strategy—were prosecuted, instead of the salespeople or advertisers expected to deliver on weak or undifferentiated strategies.

Laws merely define minimal ethical standards

Whether a marketer is operating in his or her own country or in a foreign nation, the legal environment sets the *minimal* standards of ethical behavior as defined by a society. In addition, the American Marketing Association's Statement of Ethics (Exhibit 1-7) provides basic guidelines that a marketing manager should observe. But marketing managers constantly face ethical issues where there are no clearly defined answers. Every marketing manager should make a personal commitment to carefully evaluate the ethical consequences of marketing strategy decisions.

On the other hand, innovative new marketing strategies *do* sometimes cause problems for those who have a vested interest in the old ways. Some people try to portray anything that disrupts their own personal interest as unethical. But that is not an appropriate ethical standard. The basic ethical charge to marketers is to find new *and* better ways to serve society's needs.

Need socially responsible consumers

We've stressed that marketers should act responsibly—but consumers have responsibilities too. Some consumers abuse policies about returning goods, change price tags in self-service stores, and are downright abusive to salespeople. Others think nothing of ripping off businesses because "they're rich." Shoplifting is a major problem for most traditional retailers, averaging almost 2 percent of sales nationally. In supermarkets, losses to shoplifters are on average greater than profits. Online retailers, in turn, must fight the use of stolen or fraudulent credit cards. Honest consumers pay for the cost of this theft in higher prices.[15]

Americans tend to perform their dual role of consumer-citizens with a split personality. We often behave differently at the cash register than we do on our soap box. For example, we say that we want to protect the environment, but when it comes to making

Consumers also have to act in a socially responsible manner. Consumers must be cautious with their personal data and credit cards. Most identity thieves gather information from purses and wallets. Consumer demand for lower prices and willingness to purchase counterfeit products harms honest retailers and firms that produce legitimate products.

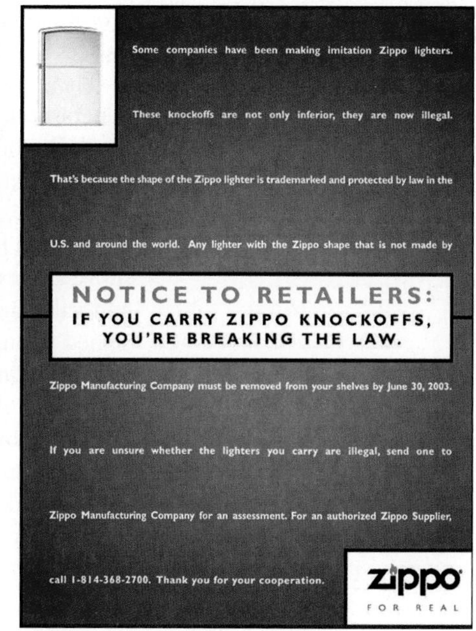

our own purchase decisions, we're likely to pick the product that is more convenient or lower priced rather than the one that is the sustainable choice. We protest sex and violence in the media, but some of the most profitable websites on the Internet are purveyors of pornography. Parents complain about advertising aimed at children but use TV as a Saturday morning babysitter.

> **Internet Exercise**
>
> The Consumerist (**www.consumerist.com**) is a widely read blog. It operates as a consumer watchdog and monitors corporate behavior. Go to this blog and read a posting critical of some firm's behavior—click through to the original source if necessary. What do you think of this story? Does it change your attitude toward the firm? How could sites like these influence consumers? How could they influence firms?

Unethical or illegal behavior is widespread. In a major survey of workers, managers, and executives from a wide range of industries, 48 percent admitted to taking unethical or illegal actions in the past year. Offenses included things like cheating on expense accounts, paying or accepting kickbacks, trading sex for sales, lying to customers, leaking company secrets, and looking the other way when environmental laws are violated. Think about it—we're talking about half of the workforce.[15]

As consumer-citizens, each of us shares the responsibility for preserving an effective macro-marketing system. And we should take this responsibility seriously. That even includes the responsibility to be smarter customers. Let's face it, a majority of consumers ignore most of the available information that could help them spend money (and guide the marketing process) more wisely. Consumerism has encouraged nutritional labeling, open dating, unit pricing, truth-in-lending, plain-language contracts and warranties, and so on. Many companies provide extensive information at their websites or in brochures. Government agencies publish many consumer buying guides on everything from tires to appliances, as do organizations such as Consumers Union. Most of this information is available from home, over the Internet. It makes sense to use it.

How Far Should the Marketing Concept Go?

Should marketing managers limit consumers' freedom of choice?

Achieving a better macro-marketing system is certainly a desirable objective. But what part should a marketer play in deciding what products to offer?

This is extremely important, because some marketing managers, especially those in large corporations, can have an impact far larger than they do in their roles as consumer-citizens. For example, should they refuse to produce hazardous products, like skis or motorcycles, even though such products are in strong demand? Should they install safety devices that increase costs and raise prices that customers don't want to pay?

These are difficult questions to answer. Some things marketing managers do clearly benefit both the firm and consumers because they lower costs or improve consumers' options. But other decisions may actually reduce consumer choice and conflict with a desire to improve the effectiveness of our macro-marketing system.

Consumer-citizens should vote on the changes

It seems fair to suggest, therefore, that marketing managers should be expected to improve and expand the range of goods and services they make available—always trying to add value and better satisfy consumers' needs and preferences. This is the job we've assigned to business.

If pursuing this objective makes excessive demands on scarce resources or has an unacceptable ecological effect, then consumer-citizens have the responsibility to vote for laws restricting individual firms that are trying to satisfy consumers' needs. This is the role that we, as consumers, have assigned to the government—to ensure that the macro-marketing system works effectively.

It is important to recognize that some *seemingly minor* modifications in our present system *might* result in very big, unintended problems. Allowing some government agency to prohibit the sale of products for seemingly good reasons could lead to major changes we never expected and could seriously reduce consumers' present rights to freedom of choice, including "bad" choices.

CONCLUSION

Macro-marketing does *not* cost too much. Consumers have assigned business the role of satisfying their needs. Customers find it satisfactory and even desirable to permit businesses to cater to them and even to stimulate wants. As long as consumers are satisfied, macro-marketing will not cost too much—and business firms will be permitted to continue as profit-making entities.

But business exists at the consumer's discretion. It's mainly by satisfying the consumer that a particular firm—and *our* economic system—can justify its existence and hope to keep operating.

In carrying out this role—granted by consumers—business firms are not always as effective as they could be. Many business managers don't understand the marketing concept or the role that marketing plays in our way of life. They seem to feel that business has a basic right to operate as it chooses. And they proceed in their typical production-oriented ways. Further, many managers have had little or no training in business management and are not as competent as they should be. Others fail to adjust to the changes taking place around them. And a few dishonest or unethical managers can do a great deal of damage before consumer-citizens take steps to stop them. As a result, marketing by individual firms often *does* cost too much. But the situation is improving. More business training is now available, and more competent people are being attracted to marketing and business generally. Clearly, *you* have a role to play in improving marketing activities in the future.

The marketing strategy planning process presented in this book provides a framework that will guide you to more effective marketing decisions—and marketing that really does deliver superior value to customers. It also benefits the firm, through profits and growth. It's truly a "win-win" situation. And in our competitive, market-driven economy, managers and firms that lead the way in creating these successes will not go unnoticed. As effective marketing management spreads to more companies, the whole macro-marketing system will be more efficient and effective.

To keep our system working effectively, individual firms should implement the marketing concept in a more efficient, ethical, and socially responsible way. At the same time, we—as consumers—should consume goods and services in an intelligent and socially responsible way. Further, we have the responsibility to vote and ensure that we get the kind of macro-marketing system we want. What kind do you want? What should you do to ensure that fellow consumer-citizens will vote for your system? Is your system likely to satisfy you as well as another macro-marketing system? You don't have to answer these questions right now—but your answers will affect the future you'll live in and how satisfied you'll be.

QUESTIONS AND PROBLEMS

1. Explain why marketing must be evaluated at two levels. What criteria should be used to evaluate each level of marketing? Defend your answer. Explain why your criteria are better than alternative criteria.
2. Discuss the merits of various economic system objectives. Is the objective of the American economic system sensible? Could it achieve more consumer satisfaction if sociologists or public officials determined how to satisfy the needs of lower-income or less-educated consumers? If so, what education or income level should be required before an individual is granted free choice?
3. Should the objective of our economy be maximum efficiency? If your answer is yes, efficiency in what? If not, what should the objective be?
4. Discuss the conflict of interests among production, finance, accounting, and marketing executives. How does this conflict affect the operation of an individual firm? The economic system? Why does this conflict exist?
5. Why does adoption of the marketing concept encourage a firm to operate more efficiently? Be specific about the impact of the marketing concept on the various departments of a firm.
6. In the short run, competition sometimes leads to inefficiency in the operation of our economic system. Many people argue for monopoly in order to eliminate this inefficiency. Discuss this solution.
7. How would officially granted monopolies affect the operation of our economic system? Consider the effect on allocation of resources, the level of income and employment, and the distribution of income. Is the effect any different if a firm obtains a monopoly by winning out in a competitive market?
8. Comment on the following statement: "Ultimately, the high cost of marketing is due only to consumers."
9. Distinguish clearly between a marketing strategy and a marketing plan. If a firm has a really good strategy, does it need to worry about developing a written plan?
10. How far should the marketing concept go? How should we decide this issue?
11. Should marketing managers, or business managers in general, refrain from producing profitable products that some target customers want but that may not be in their long-run best interest? Should firms be expected to produce "good" but less profitable products? What if such products break even? What if they are unprofitable but the company makes other profitable products—so on balance it still makes some profit? What criteria are you using for each of your answers?
12. Should a marketing manager or a business refuse to produce an "energy-gobbling" appliance that some consumers are demanding? Should a firm install an expensive safety device that will increase costs but that customers don't want? Are the same principles involved in both these questions? Explain.
13. Discuss how one or more of the trends or changes shown in Exhibit 20-5 are affecting marketing strategy planning for a specific firm that serves the market where you live.
14. Discuss how slower economic growth or no economic growth would affect your college community—in particular, its marketing institutions.

CREATING MARKETING PLANS

The Marketing Plan Coach software on the text website includes a sample marketing plan for Hillside Veterinary Clinic. Review the entire marketing plan.

a. How do the pieces fit together?
b. Does the marketing strategy logically follow from the target market dimensions?
c. Does the marketing strategy logically follow from the differentiation and positioning?
d. Does the plan appear reasonable given the stated objectives?

SUGGESTED CASES

17. Simply Pure H2O4U, Inc.
22. Bright Light Innovations: The Starlight Stove
27. Advanced Molding, Inc.
28. KCA Precision Tools
30. Walker-Winkle Mills
31. Amato Home Health
32. Lever Ltd.
34. Chess Aluminum Worldwide

Video Case 4. Potbelly Sandwich
Video Case 6. Big Brothers and Big Sisters of America

APPENDIX A

Economics Fundamentals

Learning Objectives

The economist's traditional analysis of supply and demand is a useful tool for analyzing markets. In particular, you should master the concepts of a demand curve and demand elasticity. A firm's demand curve shows how the target customers view the firm's Product—really its whole marketing mix. And the interaction of demand and supply curves helps set the size of a market and the market price. The interaction of supply and demand also determines the nature of the competitive environment, which has an important effect on strategy planning. The learning objectives and following sections of this appendix discuss these ideas more fully.

When you finish this appendix, you should be able to:

1. understand the "law of diminishing demand."
2. explain elasticity of demand and supply.
3. understand why demand elasticity can be affected by availability of substitutes.
4. understand demand and supply curves and how they set the size of a market and its price level.
5. know the different kinds of competitive situations and understand why they are important to marketing managers.
6. understand important new terms (shown in red).

Products and Markets as Seen by Customers and Potential Customers

Economists see individual customers choosing among alternatives

A basic idea from economics is that most customers have a limited income and simply cannot buy everything they want. They must balance their needs and the prices of various products. Economists usually assume that customers have a fairly definite set of preferences and that they evaluate alternatives in terms of whether the alternatives will make them feel better or in some way improve their situation.

But what exactly is the nature of a customer's desire for a particular product?

Usually economists answer this question in terms of the extra utility the customer can obtain by buying more of a particular product—or how much utility would be lost if the customer had less of the product. It is easier to understand the idea of utility if we look at what happens when the price of one of the customer's usual purchases changes.

The law of diminishing demand

LO A.1

Suppose that consumers buy potatoes in 10-pound bags at the same time they buy other foods such as bread and rice. If the consumers are mainly interested in buying a certain amount of food and the price of the potatoes drops, it seems reasonable to expect that they will switch some of their food money to potatoes and away from some other foods. But if the price of potatoes rises, you expect our consumers to buy fewer potatoes and more of other foods.

The general relationship between price and quantity demanded illustrated by this food example is called the **law of diminishing demand**—which says that if the price of a product is raised, a smaller quantity will be demanded and if the price of a product is lowered, a greater quantity will be demanded. Experience supports this relationship between price and total demand in a market, especially for broad product categories or commodities such as potatoes.

The relationship between price and quantity demanded in a market is what economists call a "demand schedule." An example is shown in Exhibit A-1. For each row in the table, column 2 shows the quantity consumers will want (demand) if they have to pay the price given in column 1. The third column shows that the total revenue (sales) in the potato market is equal to the quantity demanded at a given price times that price. Note that as prices drop, the total *unit* quantity increases, yet the total *revenue* decreases. Fill in the blank lines in the third column and observe the behavior of total revenue, an important number for the marketing manager. We will explain what you should have noticed, and why, a little later.

The demand curve—usually down-sloping

If your only interest is seeing at which price the company will earn the greatest total revenue, the demand schedule may be adequate. But a demand curve shows more. A **demand curve** is a graph of the relationship between price and quantity demanded in a market, assuming that all other things stay the same. Exhibit A-2 shows the demand curve for potatoes—really just a plotting of the demand schedule in Exhibit A-1. It shows how many potatoes potential customers will demand at various possible prices. This is a "down-sloping demand curve."

Most demand curves are down-sloping. This just means that if prices are decreased, the quantity customers demand will increase.

Exhibit A–1
Demand Schedule for Potatoes (10-pound bags)

Point	(1) Price of Potatoes per Bag (*P*)	(2) Quantity Demanded (bags per month) (*Q*)	(3) Total Revenue per Month (*P* × *Q* = TR)
A	$1.60	8,000,000	$12,800,000
B	1.30	9,000,000	________
C	1.00	11,000,000	11,000,000
D	0.70	14,000,000	________
E	0.40	19,000,000	________

Exhibit A–2
Demand Curve for Potatoes (10-pound bags)

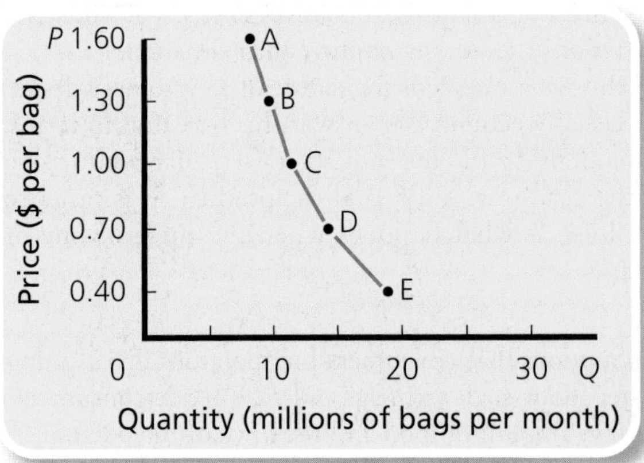

Demand curves always show the price on the vertical axis and the quantity demanded on the horizontal axis. In Exhibit A-2, we have shown the price in dollars. For consistency, we will use dollars in other examples. However, keep in mind that these same ideas hold regardless of what money unit (dollars, yen, francs, pounds, etc.) is used to represent price. Even at this early point, you should keep in mind that markets are not necessarily limited by national boundaries—or by one type of money.

Note that the demand curve only shows how customers will react to various possible prices. In a market, we see only one price at a time, not all of these prices. The curve, however, shows what quantities will be demanded, depending on what price is set.

Microwave oven demand curve looks different

To get a more complete picture of demand-curve analysis, let's consider another product that has a different demand schedule and curve. A demand schedule for standard 1-cubic-foot microwave ovens is shown in Exhibit A-3. Column (3) shows the total revenue that will be obtained at various possible prices and quantities. Again, as the price goes down, the quantity demanded goes up. But here, unlike the potato example, total revenue increases as prices go down—at least until the price drops to $150.

Every market has a demand curve, for some time period

These general demand relationships are typical for all products. But each product has its own demand schedule and curve in each potential market, no matter how small the market. In other words, a particular demand curve has meaning only for a particular market. We can think of demand curves for individuals, groups of individuals who form a target market, regions, and even countries. And the time period covered really should be specified, although this is often neglected because we usually think of monthly or yearly periods.

Exhibit A–3
Demand Schedule for 1-Cubic-Foot Microwave Ovens

Point	(1) Price per Microwave Oven (*P*)	(2) Quantity Demanded per Year (*Q*)	(3) Total Revenue (TR) per Year (*P* × *Q* = TR)
A	$300	20,000	$ 6,000,000
B	250	70,000	17,500,000
C	200	130,000	26,000,000
D	150	210,000	31,500,000
E	100	310,000	31,000,000

Exhibit A–4
Demand Curve for 1-Cubic-Foot Microwave Ovens

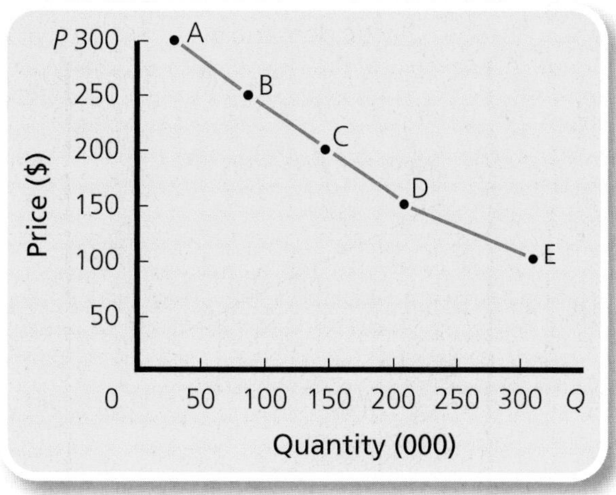

The difference between elastic and inelastic

LO A.2

The demand curve for microwave ovens (see Exhibit A-4) is down-sloping—but note that it is flatter than the curve for potatoes. It is important to understand what this flatness means.

We will consider the flatness in terms of total revenue, since this is what interests business managers.*

When you filled in the total revenue column for potatoes, you should have noticed that total revenue drops continually if the price is reduced. This looks undesirable for sellers and illustrates inelastic demand. **Inelastic demand** means that although the quantity demanded increases if the price is decreased, the quantity demanded will not "stretch" enough—that is, it is not elastic enough—to avoid a decrease in total revenue.

In contrast, **elastic demand** means that if prices are dropped, the quantity demanded will stretch (increase) enough to increase total revenue. The upper part of the microwave oven demand curve is an example of elastic demand.

But note that if the microwave oven price is dropped from $150 to $100, total revenue will decrease. We can say, therefore, that between $150 and $100, demand is inelastic—that is, total revenue will decrease if price is lowered from $150 to $100.

Thus, elasticity can be defined in terms of changes in total revenue. *If total revenue will increase if price is lowered, then demand is elastic. If total revenue will decrease if price is lowered, then demand is inelastic.* (Note: A special case known as "unitary elasticity of demand" occurs if total revenue stays the same when prices change.)

Total revenue may increase if price is raised

A point often missed in discussions of demand is what happens when prices are raised instead of lowered. With elastic demand, total revenue will *decrease* if the price is *raised.* With inelastic demand, however, total revenue will *increase* if the price is *raised.*

The possibility of raising price and increasing dollar sales (total revenue) at the same time is attractive to managers. This only occurs if the demand curve is inelastic. Here total revenue will increase if price is raised, but total costs probably will not increase—and may actually go down—with smaller quantities. Keep in mind that profit is equal to total revenue minus total costs. So when demand is inelastic, profit will increase as price is increased!

The ways total revenue changes as prices are raised are shown in Exhibit A-5. Here total revenue is the rectangular area formed by a price and its related quantity. The larger the rectangular area, the greater the total revenue.

*Strictly speaking, two curves should not be compared for flatness if the graph scales are different, but for our purposes now we will do so to illustrate the idea of "elasticity of demand." Actually, it would be more accurate to compare two curves for one product on the same graph. Then both the shape of the demand curve and its position on the graph would be important.

Exhibit A–5
Changes in Total Revenue as Prices Increase

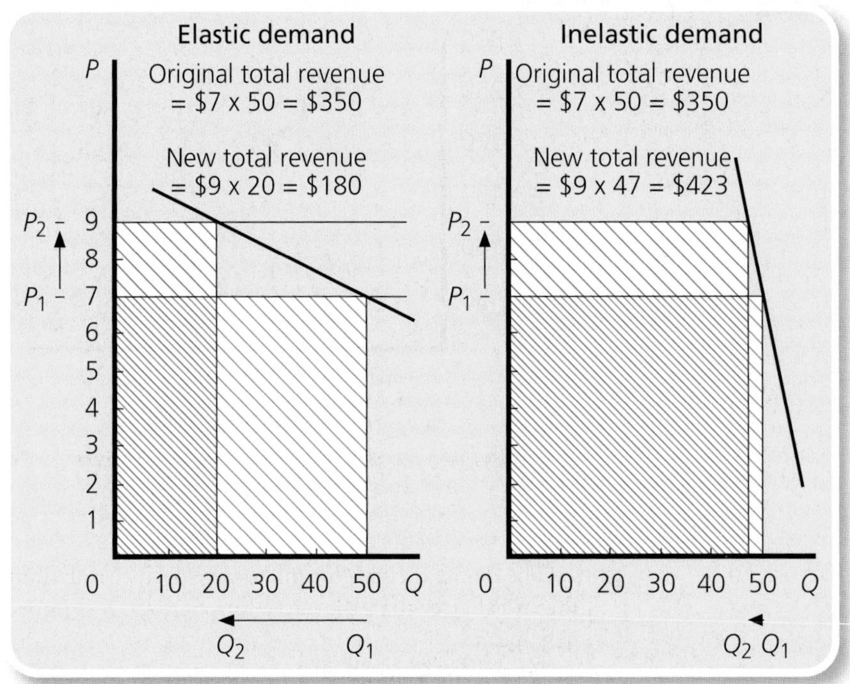

P_1 is the original price here, and the total potential revenue with this original price is shown by the area with blue shading. The area with red shading shows the total revenue with the new price, P_2. There is some overlap in the total revenue areas, so the important areas are those with only one color. Note that in the left-hand figure—where demand is elastic—the revenue added (the red-only area) when the price is increased is less than the revenue lost (the blue-only area). Now let's contrast this to the right-hand figure, when demand is inelastic. Only a small blue revenue area is given up for a much larger (red) one when price is raised.

An entire curve is not elastic or inelastic

It is important to see that it is *wrong to refer to a whole demand curve as elastic or inelastic.* Rather, elasticity for a particular demand curve refers to the change in total revenue between two points on the curve, not along the whole curve. You saw the change from elastic to inelastic in the microwave oven example. Generally, however, nearby points are either elastic or inelastic—so it is common to refer to a whole curve by the degree of elasticity in the price range that normally is of interest—the *relevant range.*

Demand elasticities affected by availability of substitutes and urgency of need

LO A.3

At first, it may be difficult to see why one product has an elastic demand and another an inelastic demand. Many factors affect elasticity, such as the availability of substitutes, the importance of the item in the customer's budget, and the urgency of the customer's need and its relation to other needs. By looking more closely at one of these factors—the availability of substitutes—you will better understand why demand elasticities vary.

Substitutes are products that offer the buyer a choice. For example, many consumers see grapefruit as a substitute for oranges and hot dogs as a substitute for hamburgers. The greater the number of "good" substitutes available, the greater will be the elasticity of demand. From the consumer's perspective, products are "good" substitutes if they are very similar (homogeneous). If consumers see products as extremely different, or heterogeneous, then a particular need cannot easily be satisfied by substitutes. And the demand for the most satisfactory product may be quite inelastic.

As an example, if the price of hamburger is lowered (and other prices stay the same), the quantity demanded will increase a lot, as will total revenue. The reason is that not only

Exhibit A–6
Demand Curve for Hamburger (a product with many substitutes)

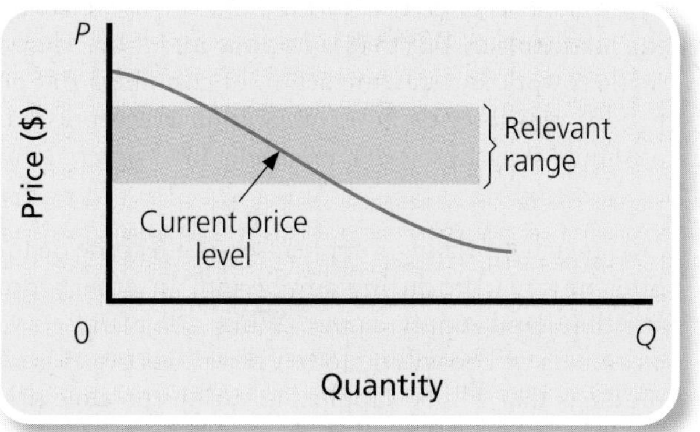

will regular hamburger users buy more hamburger, but some consumers who formerly bought hot dogs or steaks probably will buy hamburger too. But if the price of hamburger is raised, the quantity demanded will decrease, perhaps sharply. Still, consumers will buy some hamburger, depending on how much the price has risen, their individual tastes, and what their guests expect (see Exhibit A-6).

In contrast to a product with many "substitutes"—such as hamburger—consider a product with few or no substitutes. Its demand curve will tend to be inelastic. Motor oil is a good example. Motor oil is needed to keep cars running. Yet no one person or family uses great quantities of motor oil. So it is not likely that the quantity of motor oil purchased will change much as long as price changes are *within a reasonable range.* Of course, if the price is raised to a staggering figure, many people will buy less oil (change their oil less frequently). If the price is dropped to an extremely low level, manufacturers may buy more—say, as a lower-cost substitute for other chemicals typically used in making plastic (Exhibit A-7). But these extremes are outside the relevant range.

Demand curves are introduced here because the degree of elasticity of demand shows how potential customers feel about a product—and especially whether they see substitutes for the product. But to get a better understanding of markets, we must extend this economic analysis.

Markets as Seen by Suppliers

Customers may want some product—but if suppliers are not willing to supply it, then there is no market. So we'll study the economist's analysis of supply. And then we'll bring supply and demand together for a more complete understanding of markets.

Exhibit A–7
Demand Curve for Motor Oil (a product with few substitutes)

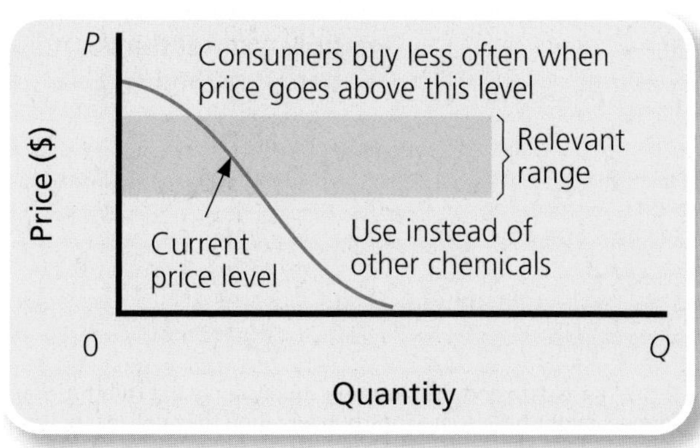

Economists often use the kind of analysis we are discussing here to explain pricing in the marketplace. But that is not our intention. Here we are interested in how and why markets work and the interaction of customers and potential suppliers. Later in this appendix we will review how competition affects prices, but how individual firms set prices, or should set prices, is discussed fully in Chapters 16 and 17.

Supply curves reflect supplier thinking

Generally speaking, suppliers' costs affect the quantity of products they are willing to offer in a market during any period. In other words, their costs affect their supply schedules and supply curves. While a demand curve shows the quantity of products customers will be willing to buy at various prices, a **supply curve** shows the quantity of products that will be supplied at various possible prices. Eventually, only one quantity will be offered and purchased. So a supply curve is really a hypothetical (what-if) description of what will be offered at various prices. It is, however, a very important curve. Together with a demand curve, it summarizes the attitudes and probable behavior of buyers and sellers about a particular product in a particular market—that is, in a product-market.

Some supply curves are vertical

We usually assume that supply curves tend to slope upward—that is, suppliers will be willing to offer greater quantities at higher prices. If a product's market price is very high, it seems only reasonable that producers will be anxious to produce more of the product and even put workers on overtime or perhaps hire more workers to increase the quantity they can offer. Going further, it seems likely that producers of other products will switch their resources (farms, factories, labor, or retail facilities) to the product that is in great demand.

On the other hand, if consumers are only willing to pay a very low price for a particular product, it's reasonable to expect that producers will switch to other products, thus reducing supply. A supply schedule (Exhibit A-8) and a supply curve (Exhibit A-9) for potatoes illustrate these ideas. This supply curve shows how many potatoes would be produced and offered for sale at each possible market price in a given month.

In the very short run (say, over a few hours, a day, or a week), a supplier may not be able to change the supply at all. In this situation, we would see a vertical supply curve. This situation is often relevant in the market for fresh produce. Fresh strawberries, for example, continue to ripen, and a supplier wants to sell them quickly—preferably at a higher price—but in any case, they must be sold.

If the product is a service, it may not be easy to expand the supply in the short run. Additional barbers or medical doctors are not quickly trained and licensed, and they only have so much time to give each day. Further, the prospect of much higher prices in the near future cannot easily expand the supply of many services. For example, a hit play or an "in" restaurant or nightclub is limited in the amount of product it can offer at a particular time.

Exhibit A–8
Supply Schedule for Potatoes (10-pound bags)

Point	Possible Market Price per 10-lb. Bag	Number of Bags Sellers Will Supply per Month at Each Possible Market Price
A	$1.60	17,000,000
B	1.30	14,000,000
C	1.00	11,000,000
D	0.70	8,000,000
E	0.40	3,000,000

Note: These data and the resulting supply curve in Exhibit A–9 are for a single month to emphasize that farmers might have some control over when they deliver their potatoes. There would be different data, and consequently a different curve, for each month.

Exhibit A–9
Supply Curve for Potatoes (10-pound bags)

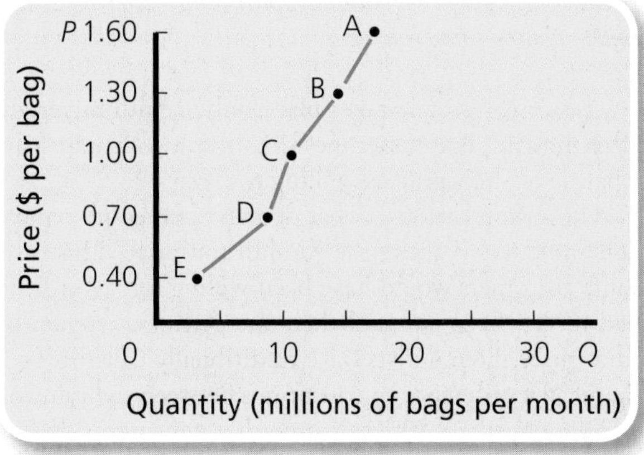

Elasticity of supply

The term *elasticity* also is used to describe supply curves. An extremely steep or almost vertical supply curve, often found in the short run, is called **inelastic supply** because the quantity supplied does not stretch much (if at all) if the price is raised. A flatter curve is called **elastic supply** because the quantity supplied does stretch more if the price is raised. A slightly up-sloping supply curve is typical in longer-run market situations. Given more time, suppliers have a chance to adjust their offerings, and competitors may enter or leave the market.

Demand and Supply Interact to Determine the Size of the Market and Price Level

LO A.4

We have treated market demand and supply forces separately. Now we must bring them together to show their interaction. The *intersection* of these two forces determines the size of the market and the market price—at which point (price and quantity) the market is said to be in *equilibrium.*

The intersection of demand and supply is shown for the potato data discussed earlier. In Exhibit A-10, the demand curve for potatoes is now graphed against the supply curve in Exhibit A-9.

In this potato market, demand is inelastic—the total revenue of all the potato producers would be greater at higher prices. But the market price is at the **equilibrium point**—where the quantity and the price sellers are willing to offer are equal to the quantity and price that buyers are willing to accept. The $1.00 equilibrium price for potatoes yields a smaller *total revenue* to potato producers than a higher price would. This lower equilibrium price comes about because the many producers are willing to supply enough potatoes

Exhibit A–10
Equilibrium of Supply and Demand for Potatoes (10-pound bags)

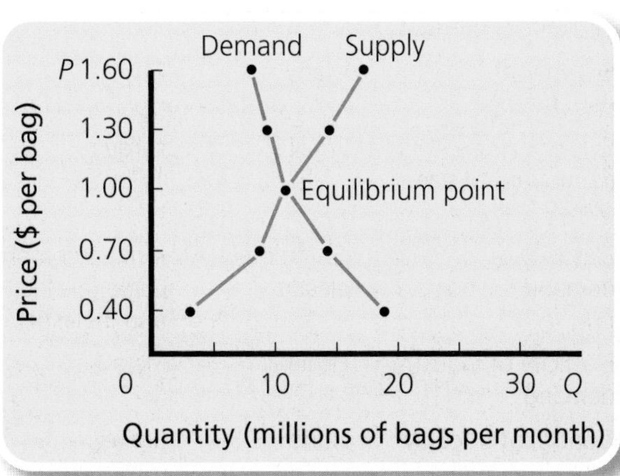

at the lower price. *Demand is not the only determiner of price level. Cost also must be considered—via the supply curve.*

Some consumers get a surplus

Presumably, a sale takes place only if both buyer and seller feel they will be better off after the sale. But sometimes the price a consumer pays in a sales transaction is less than what he or she would be willing to pay.

The reason for this is that demand curves are typically down-sloping, and some of the demand curve is above the equilibrium price. This is simply another way of showing that some customers would have been willing to pay more than the equilibrium price—if they had to. In effect, some of them are getting a bargain by being able to buy at the equilibrium price. Economists have traditionally called these bargains the **consumer surplus**—that is, the difference to consumers between the value of a purchase and the price they pay.

Some business critics assume that consumers do badly in any business transaction. In fact, sales take place only if consumers feel they are at least getting their money's worth. As we can see here, some are willing to pay much more than the market price.

Demand and Supply Help Us Understand the Nature of Competition

LO A.5

The elasticity of demand and supply curves and their interaction help predict the nature of competition a marketing manager is likely to face. For example, an extremely inelastic demand curve means that the manager will have much choice in strategy planning, especially price setting. Apparently customers like the product and see few substitutes. They are willing to pay higher prices before cutting back much on their purchases.

The elasticity of a firm's demand curve is not the only factor that affects the nature of competition. Other factors are the number and size of competitors and the uniqueness of each firm's marketing mix. Understanding these market situations is important because the freedom of a marketing manager, especially control over price, is greatly reduced in some situations.

A marketing manager operates in one of four kinds of market situations. We'll discuss three kinds: pure competition, oligopoly, and monopolistic competition. The fourth kind, monopoly, isn't found very often and is like monopolistic competition. The important dimensions of these situations are shown in Exhibit A-11.

Exhibit A–11
Some Important Dimensions Regarding Market Situations

	Types of Situations			
Important Dimensions	**Pure Competition**	**Oligopoly**	**Monopolistic Competition**	**Monopoly**
Uniqueness of each firm's product	None	None	Some	Unique
Number of competitors	Many	Few	Few to many	None
Size of competitors (compared to size of market)	Small	Large	Large to small	None
Elasticity of demand facing firm	Completely elastic	Kinked demand curve (elastic and inelastic)	Either	Either
Elasticity of industry demand	Either	Inelastic	Either	Either
Control of price by firm	None	Some (with care)	Some	Complete

When competition is pure

Many competitors offer about the same thing

Pure competition is a market situation that develops when a market has

1. Homogeneous (similar) products.
2. Many buyers and sellers who have full knowledge of the market.
3. Ease of entry for buyers and sellers; that is, new firms have little difficulty starting in business—and new customers can easily come into the market.

More or less pure competition is found in many agricultural markets. In the potato market, for example, there are thousands of small producers—and they are in pure competition. Let's look more closely at these producers.

Although the potato market as a whole has a down-sloping demand curve, each of the many small producers in the industry is in pure competition, and each of them faces a flat demand curve at the equilibrium price. This is shown in Exhibit A-12.

As shown at the right of Exhibit A-12, an individual producer can sell as many bags of potatoes as he chooses at $1—the market equilibrium price. The equilibrium price is determined by the quantity that all producers choose to sell given the demand curve they face.

But a small producer has little effect on overall supply (or on the equilibrium price). If this individual farmer raises 1/10,000th of the quantity offered in the market, for example, you can see that there will be little effect if the farmer goes out of business—or doubles production.

The reason an individual producer's demand curve is flat is that the farmer probably couldn't sell any potatoes above the market price. And there is no point in selling below the market price! So, in effect, the individual producer has no control over price.

Markets tend to become more competitive

Not many markets are *purely* competitive. But many are close enough so we can talk about "almost" pure competition situations—those in which the marketing manager has to accept the going price.

Such highly competitive situations aren't limited to agriculture. Wherever *many* competitors sell *homogeneous* products—such as textiles, lumber, coal, printing, and laundry services—the demand curve seen by *each producer* tends to be flat.

Markets tend to become more competitive, moving toward pure competition (except in oligopolies—see below). On the way to pure competition, prices and profits are pushed down until some competitors are forced out of business. Eventually, in long-run equilibrium,

Exhibit A–12 Interaction of Demand and Supply in the Potato Industry and the Resulting Demand Curve Facing Individual Potato Producers

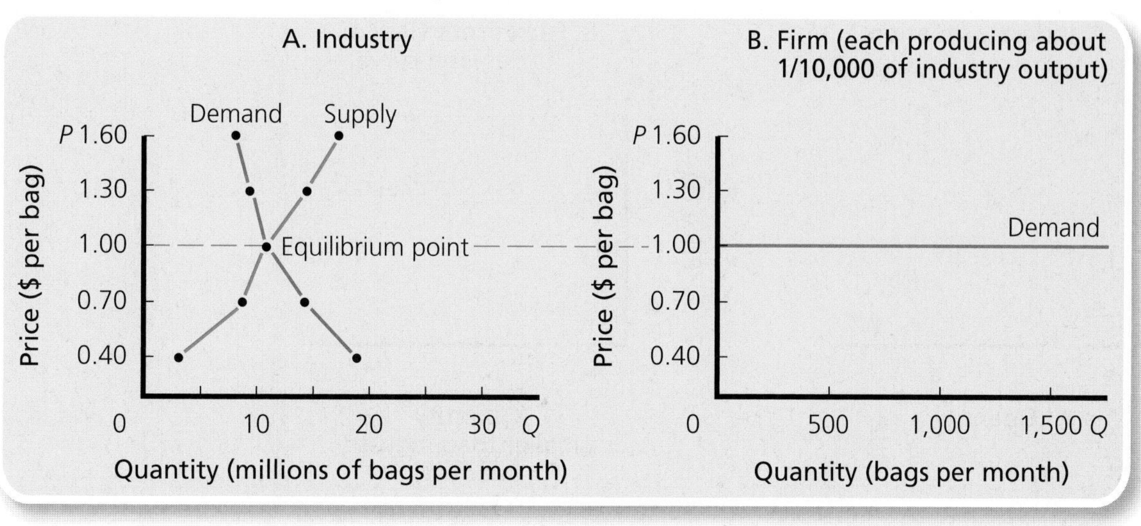

the price level is only high enough to keep the survivors in business. No one makes any profit—they just cover costs. It's tough to be a marketing manager in this situation!

When competition is oligopolistic

A few competitors offer similar things

Not all markets move toward pure competition. Some become oligopolies. **Oligopoly** situations are special market situations that develop when a market has

1. Essentially homogeneous products—such as basic industrial chemicals or gasoline.
2. Relatively few sellers—or a few large firms and many smaller ones who follow the lead of the larger ones.
3. Fairly inelastic industry demand curves.

The demand curve facing each firm is unusual in an oligopoly situation. Although the industry demand curve is inelastic throughout the relevant range, the demand curve facing each competitor looks "kinked." See Exhibit A-13. The current market price is at the kink.

There is a market price because the competing firms watch each other carefully—and they know it's wise to be at the kink. Each firm must expect that raising its own price above the market price will cause a big loss in sales. Few, if any, competitors will follow the price increase. So the firm's demand curve is relatively flat above the market price. If the firm lowers its price, it must expect competitors to follow. Given inelastic industry demand, the firm's own demand curve is inelastic at lower prices, assuming it keeps its share of this market at lower prices. Since lowering prices along such a curve will drop total revenue, the firm should leave its price at the kink—the market price.

Sometimes there are price fluctuations in oligopolistic markets. This can be caused by firms that don't understand the market situation and cut their prices to try to get business. In other cases, big increases in demand or supply change the basic nature of the situation and lead to price cutting. Price cuts can be drastic, such as Du Pont's price cut of 25 percent for Dacron. This happened when Du Pont decided that industry production capacity already exceeded demand, and more plants were due to start production.

It's important to keep in mind that oligopoly situations don't just apply to whole industries and national markets. Competitors who are focusing on the same local target market often face oligopoly situations. A suburban community might have several gas stations, all of which provide essentially the same product. In this case, the "industry" consists of the gas stations competing with each other in the local product-market.

Exhibit A–13 Oligopoly—Kinked Demand Curve—Situation

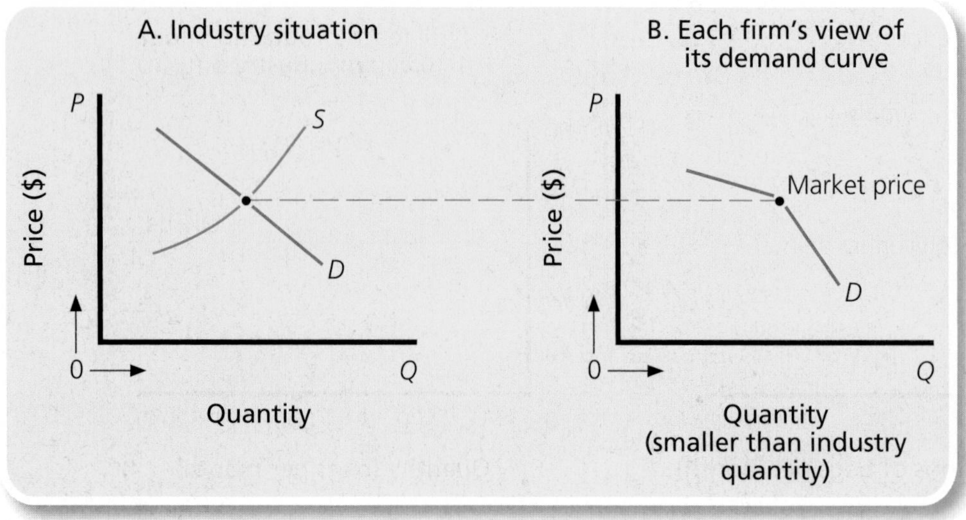

As in pure competition, oligopolists face a long-run trend toward an equilibrium level, with profits driven toward zero. This may not happen immediately—and a marketing manager may try to delay price competition by relying more on other elements in the marketing mix.

When competition is monopolistic

A price must be set

You can see why marketing managers want to avoid pure competition or oligopoly situations. They prefer a market in which they have more control. **Monopolistic competition** is a market situation that develops when a market has

1. Different (heterogeneous) products—in the eyes of some customers.
2. Sellers who feel they do have some competition in this market.

The word *monopolistic* means that each firm is trying to get control in its own little market. But the word *competition* means that there are still substitutes. The vigorous competition of a purely competitive market is reduced. Each firm has its own down-sloping demand curve. But the shape of the curve depends on the similarity of competitors' products and marketing mixes. Each monopolistic competitor has freedom—but not complete freedom—in its own market.

Judging elasticity will help set the price

Since a firm in monopolistic competition has its own down-sloping demand curve, it must make a decision about price level as part of its marketing strategy planning. Here, estimating the elasticity of the firm's own demand curve is helpful. If it is highly inelastic, the firm may decide to raise prices to increase total revenue. But if demand is highly elastic, this may mean there are many competitors with acceptable substitutes. Then the price may have to be set near that of the competition. And the marketing manager probably should try to develop a better marketing mix.

CONCLUSION

The economist's traditional demand and supply analysis provides a useful tool for analyzing the nature of demand and competition. It is especially important that you master the concepts of a demand curve and demand elasticity. How demand and supply interact helps determine the size of a market and its price level. The interaction of supply and demand also helps explain the nature of competition in different market situations. We discuss three competitive situations: pure competition, oligopoly, and monopolistic competition. The fourth kind, monopoly, isn't found very often and is like monopolistic competition.

The nature of supply and demand—and competition—is very important in marketing strategy planning. We discuss these topics more fully in Chapters 3 and 4 and then build on them throughout the text. This appendix provides a good foundation on these topics.

KEY TERMS

LO A.6

law of diminishing demand, *549*
demand curve, *549*
inelastic demand, *550*
elastic demand, *550*
substitutes, *552*
supply curve, *554*
inelastic supply, *555*
elastic supply, *555*
equilibrium point, *555*
consumer surplus, *556*
pure competition, *557*
oligopoly, *558*
monopolistic competition, *559*

QUESTIONS AND PROBLEMS

1. Explain in your own words how economists look at markets and arrive at the "law of diminishing demand."
2. Explain what a demand curve is and why it is usually down-sloping. Then give an example of a product for which the demand curve might not be down-sloping over some possible price ranges. Explain the reason for your choice.
3. What is the length of life of the typical demand curve? Illustrate your answer.
4. If the general market demand for men's shoes is fairly elastic, how does the demand for men's dress shoes compare to it? How does the demand curve for women's shoes compare to the demand curve for men's shoes?
5. If the demand for perfume is inelastic above and below the present price, should the price be raised? Why or why not?
6. If the demand for shrimp is highly elastic below the present price, should the price be lowered?
7. Discuss what factors lead to inelastic demand and supply curves. Are they likely to be found together in the same situation?
8. Why would a marketing manager prefer to sell a product that has no close substitutes? Are high profits almost guaranteed?
9. If a manufacturer's well-known product is sold at the same price by many retailers in the same community, is this an example of pure competition? When a community has many small grocery stores, are they in pure competition? What characteristics are needed to have a purely competitive market?
10. List three products that are sold in purely competitive markets and three that are sold in monopolistically competitive markets. Do any of these products have anything in common? Can any generalizations be made about competitive situations and marketing mix planning?
11. Cite a local example of an oligopoly, explaining why it is an oligopoly.

Marketing Arithmetic

APPENDIX B

Learning Objectives

Marketing students must become familiar with the essentials of the language of business. Businesspeople commonly use accounting terms when talking about costs, prices, and profit. And using accounting data is a practical tool in analyzing marketing problems. The objectives of this appendix and the sections that follow will help you understand these concepts and how they are used by marketing managers.

When you finish this appendix, you should be able to:

1. understand the components of an operating statement (profit and loss statement).
2. know how to compute the stockturn rate.
3. understand how operating ratios can help analyze a business.
4. understand how to calculate markups and markdowns.
5. understand how to calculate a return on investment (ROI) and return on assets (ROA).
6. understand the basic forecasting approaches and why they are used.
7. understand important new terms (shown in red).

The Operating Statement

LO B.1

An **operating statement** is a simple summary of the financial results of a company's operations over a specified period of time. Some beginning students may feel that the operating statement is complex, but as we'll soon see, this really isn't true. *The main purpose of the operating statement is determining the net profit figure and presenting data to support that figure.* This is why the operating statement is often referred to as the *profit and loss statement.*

Exhibit B-1 shows an operating statement for a wholesale or retail business. The statement is complete and detailed so you will see the framework throughout the discussion, but the amount of detail on an operating statement is *not* standardized. Many companies use financial statements with much less detail than this one. They emphasize clarity and readability rather than detail. To really understand an operating statement, however, you must know about its components.

Only three basic components

The basic components of an operating statement are *sales*—which come from the sale of goods and services; *costs*—which come from the producing and selling process; and the balance—called *profit or loss*—which is just the difference between sales and costs. So there are only three basic components in the statement: sales, costs, and profit (or loss). Other items on an operating statement are there only to provide supporting details.

Time period covered may vary

There is no one time period an operating statement covers. Rather, statements are prepared to satisfy the needs of a particular business. This may be at the end of each day or at the end of each week. Usually, however, an operating statement summarizes results for one month, three months, six months, or a full year. Since the time period does vary, this information is included in the heading of the statement as follows:

Perry Company
Operating Statement
For the (Period) Ended (Date)

Also see Exhibit B-1.

Management uses of operating statements

Before going on to a more detailed discussion of the components of our operating statement, let's think about some of the uses for such a statement. Exhibit B-1 shows that a lot of information is presented in a clear and concise manner. With this information, a manager can easily find the relation of net sales to the cost of sales, the gross margin, expenses, and net profit. Opening and closing inventory figures are available—as is the amount spent during the period for the purchase of goods for resale. Total expenses are listed to make it easier to compare them with previous statements and to help control these expenses.

All this information is important to a company's managers. Assume that a particular company prepares monthly operating statements. A series of these statements is a valuable tool for directing and controlling the business. By comparing results from one month to the next, managers can uncover unfavorable trends in the sales, costs, or profit areas of the business and take any needed action.

A skeleton statement gets down to essential details

Let's refer to Exhibit B-1 and begin to analyze this seemingly detailed statement to get first-hand knowledge of the components of the operating statement.

As a first step, suppose we take all the items that have dollar amounts extended to the third, or right-hand, column. Using these items only, the operating statement looks like this:

Gross sales	$540,000
Less: Returns and allowances	40,000
Net sales	500,000
Less: Cost of sales	300,000
Gross margin	200,000
Less: Total expenses	160,000
Net profit (loss)	$ 40,000

Exhibit B–1 An Operating Statement (profit and loss statement)

Perry Company Operating Statement For the Year Ended December 31, 201X			
Gross sales			$540,000
Less: Returns and allowances			40,000
Net sales			$500,000
Cost of sales:			
Beginning inventory at cost		$80,000	
Purchases at billed cost	$310,000		
Less: Purchase discounts	40,000		
Purchases at net cost	270,000		
Plus: freight-in	20,000		
Net cost of delivered purchases		290,000	
Cost of goods available for sale		370,000	
Less: Ending inventory at cost		70,000	
Cost of sales			300,000
Gross margin (gross profit)			200,000
Expenses:			
Selling expenses:			
Sales salaries	60,000		
Advertising expense	20,000		
Website updates	10,000		
Delivery expense	10,000		
Total selling expense		100,000	
Administrative expense:			
Office salaries	30,000		
Office supplies	10,000		
Miscellaneous administrative expense	5,000		
Total administrative expense		45,000	
General expense:			
Rent expense	10,000		
Miscellaneous general expenses	5,000		
Total general expense		15,000	
Total expenses			160,000
Net profit from operation			$ 40,000

Is this a complete operating statement? The answer is *yes*. This skeleton statement differs from Exhibit B-1 only in supporting detail. All the basic components are included. In fact, the only items we must list to have a complete operating statement are

Net sales	$500,000
Less: Costs	460,000
Net profit (loss)	$ 40,000

These three items are the essentials of an operating statement. All other subdivisions or details are just useful additions.

Meaning of sales

Now let's define the meaning of the terms in the skeleton statement.

The first item is sales. What do we mean by sales? The term **gross sales** is the total amount charged to all customers during some time period. However, there is always some customer dissatisfaction or just plain errors in ordering and shipping goods. This results in returns and allowances, which reduce gross sales.

A **return** occurs when a customer sends back purchased products. The company either refunds the purchase price or allows the customer dollar credit on other purchases.

An **allowance** usually occurs when a customer is not satisfied with a purchase for some reason. The company gives a price reduction on the original invoice (bill), but the customer keeps the goods and services.

These refunds and price reductions must be considered when the firm computes its net sales figure for the period. Really, we're only interested in the revenue the company manages to keep. This is **net sales**—the actual sales dollars the company receives. Therefore, all reductions, refunds, cancellations, and so forth made because of returns and allowances are deducted from the original total (gross sales) to get net sales. This is shown below.

Gross sales	$540,000
Less: Returns and allowances	40,000
Net sales	$500,000

Meaning of cost of sales

The next item in the operating statement—**cost of sales**—is the total value (at cost) of the sales during the period. We'll discuss this computation later. Meanwhile, note that after we obtain the cost of sales figure, we subtract it from the net sales figure to get the gross margin.

Meaning of gross margin and expenses

Gross margin (gross profit) is the money left to cover the expenses of selling the products and operating the business. Firms hope that a profit will be left after subtracting these expenses.

Selling expense is commonly the major expense below the gross margin. Note that in Exhibit B-1, **expenses** are all the remaining costs subtracted from the gross margin to get the net profit. The expenses in this case are the selling, administrative, and general expenses. (Note that the cost of purchases and cost of sales are not included in this total expense figure—they were subtracted from net sales earlier to get the gross margin. Note, also, that some accountants refer to cost of sales as cost of goods sold.)

Net profit—at the bottom of the statement—is what the company earned from its operations during a particular period. It is the amount left after the cost of sales and the expenses are subtracted from net sales. *Net sales and net profit are not the same.* Many firms have large sales and no profits—they may even have losses! That's why understanding costs, and controlling them, is important.

Detailed Analysis of Sections of the Operating Statement

Cost of sales for a wholesale or retail company

The cost of sales section includes details that are used to find the cost of sales ($300,000 in our example).

In Exhibit B-1, you can see that beginning and ending inventory, purchases, purchase discounts, and freight-in are all necessary to calculate cost of sales. If we pull the cost of sales section from the operating statement, it looks like this:

Cost of sales:			
Beginning inventory at cost.		$80,000	
Purchases at billed cost	$310,000		
Less: Purchase discounts	40,000		
Purchases at net cost	270,000		
Plus: freight-in.	20,000		
Net cost of delivered purchases		290,000	
Cost of goods available for sale.		370,000	
Less: Ending inventory at cost		70,000	
Cost of sales			$300,000

Cost of sales is the cost value of what is *sold,* not the cost of goods on hand at any given time.

Inventory figures merely show the cost of goods on hand at the beginning and end of the period the statement covers. These figures may be obtained by physically counting goods on hand on these dates or estimated from perpetual inventory records that show the inventory balance at any given time. The methods used to determine the inventory should be as accurate as possible because these figures affect the cost of sales during the period and net profit.

The net cost of delivered purchases must include freight charges and purchase discounts received since these items affect the money actually spent to buy goods and bring them to the place of business. A **purchase discount** is a reduction of the original invoice amount for some business reason. For example, a cash discount may be given for prompt payment of the amount due. We subtract the total of such discounts from the original invoice cost of purchases to get the *net* cost of purchases. To this figure we add the freight charges for bringing the goods to the place of business. This gives the net cost of *delivered* purchases. When we add the net cost of delivered purchases to the beginning inventory at cost, we have the total cost of goods available for sale during the period. If we now subtract the ending inventory at cost from the cost of the goods available for sale, we get the cost of sales.

One important point should be noted about cost of sales. The way the value of inventory is calculated varies from one company to another—and it can cause big differences in the cost of sales and the operating statement. (See any basic accounting textbook for how the various inventory valuation methods work.)

Exhibit B-1 shows the way the manager of a wholesale or retail business arrives at her cost of sales. Such a business *purchases* finished products and resells them. In a manufacturing company, the purchases section of this operating statement is replaced by a section called cost of production. This section includes purchases of raw materials and parts, direct and indirect labor costs, and factory overhead charges (such as heat, light, and power) that are necessary to produce finished products. The cost of production is added to the beginning finished products inventory to arrive at the cost of products available for sale. Often, a separate cost of production statement is prepared, and only the total cost of production is shown in the operating statement. See Exhibit B-2 for an illustration of the cost of sales section of an operating statement for a manufacturing company.

Expenses

Expenses go below the gross margin. They usually include the costs of selling and the costs of administering the business. They do not include the cost of sales, either purchased or produced.

There is no right method for classifying the expense accounts or arranging them on the operating statement. They can just as easily be arranged alphabetically or

Exhibit B–2
Cost of Sales Section of an Operating Statement for a Manufacturing Firm

Cost of sales:			
Finished products inventory (beginning)		$ 20,000	
Cost of production (Schedule 1)		100,000	
Total cost of finished products available for sale		120,000	
Less: Finished products inventory (ending) . . .		30,000	
Cost of sales			$ 90,000
Schedule 1, Schedule of cost of production			
Beginning work in process inventory.			15,000
Raw materials:			
Beginning raw materials inventory		10,000	
Net cost of delivered purchases.		80,000	
Total cost of materials available for use		90,000	
Less: Ending raw materials inventory		15,000	
Cost of materials placed in production		75,000	
Direct labor		20,000	
Manufacturing expenses:			
Indirect labor	$4,000		
Maintenance and repairs	3,000		
Factory supplies	1,000		
Heat, light, and power	2,000		
Total manufacturing expenses		10,000	
Total manufacturing costs.			105,000
Total work in process during period			120,000
Less: Ending work in process inventory			20,000
Cost of production			$100,000

according to amount, with the largest placed at the top and so on down the line. In a business of any size, though, it is clearer to group the expenses in some way and use subtotals by groups for analysis and control purposes. This was done in Exhibit B-1.

Summary on operating statements

The statement presented in Exhibit B-1 contains all the major categories in an operating statement—together with a normal amount of supporting detail. Further detail can be added to the statement under any of the major categories without changing the nature of the statement. The amount of detail normally is determined by how the statement will be used. A stockholder may be given a sketchy operating statement—while the one prepared for internal company use may have a lot of detail.

Computing the Stockturn Rate

LO B.2

A detailed operating statement can provide the data needed to compute the **stockturn rate**—a measure of the number of times the average inventory is sold during a year. Note that the stockturn rate is related to the *turnover during a year,* not the length of time covered by a particular operating statement.

The stockturn rate is a very important measure because it shows how rapidly the firm's inventory is moving. Some businesses typically have slower turnover than others. But a drop in turnover in a particular business can be very alarming. It may mean that the firm's assortment of products is no longer as attractive as it was. Also, it may mean that the firm will need more working capital to handle the same volume of sales. Most businesses pay a lot of attention to the stockturn rate, trying to get faster turnover (and lower inventory costs).

Three methods, all basically similar, can be used to compute the stockturn rate. Which method is used depends on the data available. These three methods, which usually give approximately the same results, are shown below.*

(1) $$\frac{\text{Cost of sales}}{\text{Average inventory at cost}}$$

(2) $$\frac{\text{Net sales}}{\text{Average inventory at selling price}}$$

(3) $$\frac{\text{Sales in units}}{\text{Average inventory in units}}$$

Computing the stockturn rate will be illustrated only for Formula 1, since all are similar. The only difference is that the cost figures used in Formula 1 are changed to a selling price or numerical count basis in Formulas 2 and 3. (*Note:* Regardless of the method used, you must have both the numerator and denominator of the formula in the same terms.)

If the inventory level varies a lot during the year, you may need detailed information about the inventory level at different times to compute the average inventory. If it stays at about the same level during the year, however, it's easy to get an estimate. For example, using Formula 1, the average inventory at cost is computed by adding the beginning and ending inventories at cost and dividing by 2. This average inventory figure is then divided into the cost of sales (in cost terms) to get the stockturn rate.

For example, suppose that the cost of sales for one year was $1,000,000. Beginning inventory was $250,000 and ending inventory $150,000. Adding the two inventory figures and dividing by 2, we get an average inventory of $200,000. We next divide the cost of sales by the average inventory ($1,000,000 ÷ $200,000) and get a stockturn rate of 5. The stockturn rate is covered further in Chapter 17.

Operating Ratios Help Analyze the Business

LO B.3

Many businesspeople use the operating statement to calculate **operating ratios**—the ratio of items on the operating statement to net sales—and to compare these ratios from one time period to another. They can also compare their own operating ratios with those of competitors. Such competitive data are often available through trade associations. Each firm may report its results to a trade association, which then distributes summary results to its members. These ratios help managers control their operations. If some expense ratios are rising, for example, those particular costs are singled out for special attention.

Operating ratios are computed by dividing net sales into the various operating statement items that appear below the net sales level in the operating statement. The net sales is used as the denominator in the operating ratio because it shows the sales the firm actually won.

We can see the relation of operating ratios to the operating statement if we think of there being another column to the right of the dollar figures in an operating statement.

*Differences occur because of varied markups and nonhomogeneous product assortments. In an assortment of tires, for example, those with low markups might have sold much better than those with high markups. But with Formula 3, all tires would be treated equally.

This column contains percentage figures, using net sales as 100 percent. This approach can be seen below.

Gross sales	$540,000	
Less: Returns and allowances	40,000	
Net sales	500,000	100%
Less: Cost of sales	300,000	60
Gross margin	200,000	40
Less: Total expenses	160,000	32
Net profit	$ 40,000	8%

The 40 percent ratio of gross margin to net sales in the preceding example shows that 40 percent of the net sales dollar is available to cover selling and administrative expenses and provide a profit. Note that the ratio of expenses to sales added to the ratio of profit to sales equals the 40 percent gross margin ratio. The net profit ratio of 8 percent shows that 8 percent of the net sales dollar is left for profit.

The value of percentage ratios should be obvious. The percentages are easily figured and much easier to compare than large dollar figures.

Note that because these operating statement categories are interrelated, only a few pieces of information are needed to figure the others. In this case, for example, knowing the gross margin percent and net profit percent makes it possible to figure the expenses and cost of sales percentages. Further, knowing just one dollar amount and the percentages lets you figure all the other dollar amounts.

Markups

LO B.4

A **markup** is the dollar amount added to the cost of sales to get the selling price. The markup usually is similar to the firm's gross margin because the markup amount added onto the unit cost of a product by a retailer or wholesaler is expected to cover the selling and administrative expenses and to provide a profit.

The markup approach to pricing is discussed in Chapter 17, so it will not be discussed at length here. But a simple example illustrates the idea. If a retailer buys an article that costs $1 when delivered to his store, he must sell it for more than this cost if he hopes to make a profit. So he might add 50 cents onto the cost of the article to cover his selling and other costs and, hopefully, to provide a profit. The 50 cents is the markup.

The 50 cents is also the gross margin or gross profit from that item *if* it is sold. But note that it is *not* the net profit. Selling expenses may amount to 35 cents, 45 cents, or even 55 cents. In other words, there is no guarantee the markup will cover costs. Further, there is no guarantee customers will buy at the marked-up price. This may require markdowns, which are discussed later in this appendix.

Markup conversions

Often it is convenient to use markups as percentages rather than focusing on the actual dollar amounts. But markups can be figured as a percent of cost or selling price. To have some agreement, *markup (percent)* will mean percentage of selling price unless stated otherwise. So the 50-cent markup on the $1.50 selling price is a markup of 33⅓ percent. On the other hand, the 50-cent markup is a 50 percent markup on cost.

Some retailers and wholesalers use markup conversion tables or spreadsheets to easily convert from cost to selling price, depending on the markup on selling price they want. To see the interrelation, look at the two formulas below. They can be used to convert either type of markup to the other.

$$\text{(4)} \qquad \begin{matrix}\text{Percent markup}\\ \text{on selling price}\end{matrix} = \frac{\text{Percent markup on cost}}{100\% + \text{Percent markup on cost}}$$

$$(5)\qquad \text{Percent markup on cost} = \frac{\text{Percent markup on selling price}}{100\% - \text{Percent markup on selling price}}$$

In the previous example, we had a cost of $1, a markup of 50 cents, and a selling price of $1.50. We saw that the markup on selling price was 33⅓ percent—and on cost, it was 50 percent. Let's substitute these percentage figures—in Formulas 4 and 5—to see how to convert from one basis to the other. Assume first of all that we only know the markup on selling price and want to convert to markup on cost. Using Formula 5, we get

$$\text{Percent markup on cost} = \frac{33^1/_3\%}{100\% - 33^1/_3\%} = \frac{33^1/_3\%}{66^2/_3\%} = 50\%$$

On the other hand, if we know only the percent markup on cost, we can convert to markup on selling price as follows:

$$\text{Percent markup on selling price} = \frac{50\%}{100\% + 50\%} = \frac{50\%}{150\%} = 33^1/_3\%$$

These results can be proved and summarized as follows:

Markup $0.50	=	50% of cost, or 33⅓% of selling price
+ Cost $1.00	=	100% of cost, or 66⅔% of selling price
Selling price $1.50	=	150% of cost, or 100% of selling price

Note that when the selling price ($1.50) is the base for a markup calculation, the markup percent (33⅓ percent = $.50/$1.50) must be less than 100 percent. As you can see, that's because the markup percent and the cost percent (66⅔ percent = $1.00/$1.50) sum to exactly 100 percent. So if you see a reference to a markup percent that is greater than 100 percent, it could not be based on the selling price and instead must be based on cost.

Markdown Ratios Help Control Retail Operations

The ratios we discussed above were concerned with figures on the operating statement. Another important ratio, the **markdown ratio**, is a tool many retailers use to measure the efficiency of various departments and their whole business. But note that it is *not directly related to the operating statement.* It requires special calculations.

A **markdown** is a retail price reduction required because customers won't buy some item at the originally marked-up price. This refusal to buy may be due to a variety of reasons—soiling, style changes, fading, damage caused by handling, or an original price that was too high. To get rid of these products, the retailer offers them at a lower price.

Markdowns are generally considered to be due to business errors, perhaps because of poor buying, original markups that are too high, and other reasons. (Note, however, that some retailers use markdowns as a way of doing business rather than a way to correct errors. For example, a store that buys overstocked fashions from other retailers may start by marking each item with a high price and then reduce the price each week until it sells.) Regardless of the reason, however, markdowns are reductions in the original price—and they are important to managers who want to measure the effectiveness of their operations.

Markdowns are similar to allowances because price reductions are made. Thus, in computing a markdown ratio, markdowns and allowances are usually added together and then divided by net sales. The markdown ratio is computed as follows:

$$\text{Markdown \%} = \frac{\$\text{ Markdowns} + \$\text{ Allowances}}{\$\text{ Net sales}} \times 100$$

The 100 is multiplied by the fraction to get rid of decimal points.

Returns are *not* included when figuring the markdown ratio. Returns are treated as consumer errors, not business errors, and therefore are not included in this measure of business efficiency.

Retailers who use markdown ratios usually keep a record of the amount of markdowns and allowances in each department and then divide the total by the net sales in each department. Over a period of time, these ratios give management one measure of the efficiency of buyers and salespeople in various departments.

It should be stressed again that the markdown ratio is not calculated directly from data on the operating statement since the markdowns take place before the products are sold. In fact, some products may be marked down and still not sold. Even if the marked-down items are not sold, the markdowns—that is, the reevaluations of their value—are included in the calculations in the time period when they are taken.

The markdown ratio is calculated for a whole department (or profit center), *not* individual items. What we are seeking is a measure of the effectiveness of a whole department, not how well the department did on individual items.

Return on Investment (ROI) Reflects Asset Use

LO B.5

Another off-the-operating-statement ratio is **return on investment (ROI)**—the ratio of net profit (after taxes) to the investment used to make the net profit, multiplied by 100 to get rid of decimals. Investment is not shown on the operating statement. But it is shown on the **balance sheet** (statement of financial condition), which is another accounting statement that shows a company's assets, liabilities, and net worth. It may take some digging or special analysis, however, to find the right investment number.

Investment means the dollar resources the firm has invested in a project or business. For example, a new product may require \$4 million in new money—for inventory, accounts receivable, promotion, and so on—and its attractiveness may be judged by its likely ROI. If the net profit (after taxes) for this new product is expected to be \$1 million in the first year, then the ROI is 25 percent—that is, (\$1 million ÷ \$4 million) × 100.

There are two ways to figure ROI. The *direct* way is

$$\text{ROI (in \%)} = \frac{\text{Net profit (after taxes)}}{\text{Investment}} \times 100$$

The *indirect* way is

$$\text{ROI (in \%)} = \frac{\text{Net profit (after taxes)}}{\text{Sales}} = \frac{\text{Sales}}{\text{Investment}} \times 100$$

This way is concerned with net profit margin and turnover—that is,

$$\text{ROI (in \%)} = \text{Net profit margin} \times \text{Turnover} \times 100$$

This indirect way makes it clearer how to *increase* ROI. There are three ways:

1. Increase profit margin (with lower costs or a higher price).
2. Increase sales.
3. Decrease investment.

Effective marketing strategy planning and implementation can increase profit margins or sales, or both. And careful asset management can decrease investment.

ROI is a revealing measure of how well managers are doing. Most companies have alternative uses for their funds. If the returns in a business aren't at least as high as outside uses, then the money probably should be shifted to the more profitable uses.

Some firms borrow more than others to make investments. In other words, they invest less of their own money to acquire assets—what we called *investments.* If ROI calculations use only the firm's own investment, this gives higher ROI figures to those who borrow a lot—which is called *leveraging.* To adjust for different borrowing proportions—to make comparisons among projects, departments, divisions, and companies easier—another ratio has come into use. **Return on assets (ROA)** is the ratio of net profit (after taxes) to the assets used to make the net profit—times 100. Both ROI and ROA measures are trying to get at the same thing—how effectively the company is using resources. These measures became increasingly popular as profit rates dropped and it became more obvious that increasing sales volume doesn't necessarily lead to higher profits—or ROI or ROA. Inflation and higher costs for borrowed funds also force more concern for ROI and ROA. Marketers must include these measures in their thinking or top managers are likely to ignore their plans and requests for financial resources.

Forecasting Target Market Potential and Sales

LO B.6

Effective strategy planning and developing a marketing plan require estimates of future sales, costs, and profits. Without such information, it's hard to know if a strategy is potentially profitable.

The marketing manager's estimates of sales, costs, and profits are usually based on a forecast (estimate) of target **market potential**—what a whole market segment might buy—and a **sales forecast**—an estimate of how much an industry or firm hopes to sell to a market segment. Usually we must first try to judge market potential before we can estimate what share a particular firm may be able to win with its particular marketing mix.

Three levels of forecasts are useful

We're interested in forecasting the potential in specific market segments. To do this, it helps to make three levels of forecasts.

Some economic conditions affect the entire global economy. Others may influence only one country or a particular industry. And some may affect only one company or one product's sales potential. For this reason, a common top-down approach to forecasting is to

1. Develop a *national income forecast* (for each country in which the firm operates) and use this to
2. Develop an *industry sales forecast,* which then is used to
3. Develop forecasts for a *specific company,* its *specific products,* and the *segments* it targets.

Generally, a marketing manager doesn't have to make forecasts for a national economy or the broad industry. This kind of forecasting—basically trend projecting—is a specialty in itself. Such forecasts are available in business and government publications, and large companies often have their own technical specialists. Managers can use just one source's forecast or combine several. Unfortunately, however, the more targeted the marketing manager's earlier segmenting efforts have been, the less likely that industry forecasts will match the firm's product-markets. So managers have to move directly to estimating potential for their own companies and for their specific products.

Two approaches to forecasting

Many methods are used to forecast market potential and sales, but they can all be grouped into two basic approaches: (1) extending past behavior and (2) predicting future behavior. The large number of methods may seem confusing at first, but this variety has an advantage. Forecasts are so important that managers often develop forecasts in two or three different ways and then compare the differences before preparing a final forecast.

Exhibit B–3
Straight-Line Trend Projection—Extends Past Sales into the Future

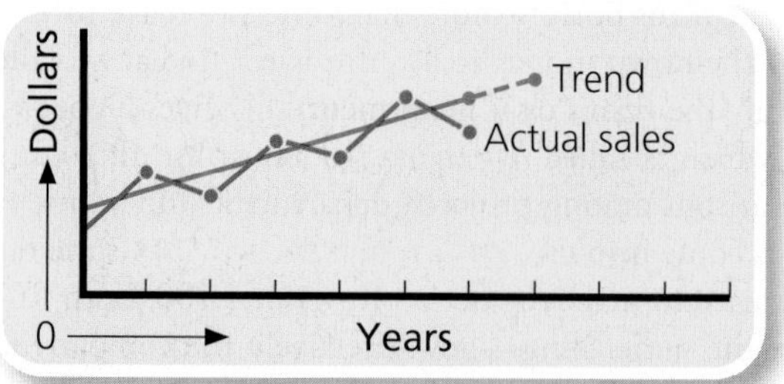

Extending past behavior can miss important turning points

When we forecast for existing products, we usually have some past data to go on. The basic approach, called **trend extension**, extends past experience into the future. With existing products, for example, the past trend of actual sales may be extended into the future. See Exhibit B-3.

Ideally, when extending past sales behavior, we should decide why sales vary. This is the difficult and time-consuming part of sales forecasting. Usually we can gather a lot of data about the product or market or about changes in the market environment. But unless we know the *reason* for past sales variations, it's hard to predict in what direction, and by how much, sales will move. Graphing the data and statistical techniques—including correlation and regression analysis—can be useful here. (These techniques, which are beyond our scope, are discussed in beginning statistics courses.)

Once we know why sales vary, we can usually develop a specific forecast. Sales may be moving directly up as population grows in a specific market segment, for example. So we can just estimate how population is expected to grow and project the impact on sales.

The weakness of the trend extension method is that it assumes past conditions will continue unchanged into the future. In fact, the future isn't always like the past. An agent wholesaler's business may have been on a steady path, but the development of the Internet may have added a totally new factor. The past trend for the agent's sales has changed because now the agent can quickly reach a broader market.

As another example, for years the trend in sales of disposable diapers moved closely with the number of new births. However, as the number of women in the workforce increased and as more women returned to jobs after babies were born, use of disposable diapers increased, and the trend changed. As in these examples, trend extension estimates will be wrong whenever big changes occur. For this reason—although they may extend past behavior for one estimate—most managers look for another way to help them forecast sharp market changes.

Predicting future behavior takes judgment

When we try to predict what will happen in the future, instead of just extending the past, we have to use other methods and add more judgment. Some of these methods (to be discussed later) include juries of executive opinion, salespeople's estimates, surveys, panels, and market tests.

Forecasting Company and Product Sales by Extending Past Behavior

Past sales can be extended

At the very least, a marketing manager ought to know what the firm's present markets look like and what it has sold to them in the past. A detailed sales analysis for products and geographic areas helps to project future results.

Just extending past sales into the future may not seem like much of a forecasting method. But it's better than just assuming that next year's total sales will be the same as this year's.

Factor method includes more than time

A simple extension of past sales gives one forecast. But it's usually desirable to tie future sales to something more than the passage of time.

The factor method tries to do this. The **factor method** tries to forecast sales by finding a relation between the company's sales and some other factor (or factors). The basic formula is: Something (past sales, industry sales, etc.) *times* some factor *equals* sales forecast. A **factor** is a variable that shows the relation of some other variable to the item being forecast. For instance, in the preceding example, both the birthrate and the number of working mothers are factors related to sales of disposable diapers.

A bread producer example

The following example, about a bread producer, shows how firms can make forecasts for many geographic market segments using the factor method and available data. This general approach can be useful for any firm—producer, wholesaler, or retailer.

Analysis of past sales relationships showed that the bread manufacturer regularly sold one-tenth of 1 percent (0.001) of the total retail food sales in its various target markets. This is a single factor. By using this single factor, a manager could estimate the producer's sales in a new market for the coming period by multiplying a forecast of expected retail food sales by 0.001.

Sales & Marketing Management magazine makes retail food sales estimates each year. Exhibit B-4 shows the kind of geographically detailed data available.

Let's carry this bread example further—using the data in Exhibit B-4 for the Denver, Colorado, metro area. Denver's food sales were $4,700,116,000 for the previous year. By simply accepting last year's food sales as an estimate of next year's sales and multiplying the food sales estimate for Denver by the 0.001 factor (the firm's usual share of food purchases in such markets), the manager would have an estimate of next year's bread sales in Denver. That is, last year's food sales estimate ($4,700,116,000) times 0.001 equals this year's bread sales estimate of $4,700,116.

Factor method can use several factors

The factor method is not limited to just one factor; several factors can be used together. For example, *Sales & Marketing Management* regularly gives a "buying power index" (BPI) as a measure of the potential in different geographic areas. See Exhibit B-4. This index considers (1) the population in a market, (2) the retail sales in that market, and (3) income in that market. The BPI for the Denver, Colorado, metro area, for example, is 0.9282—that is, Denver accounts for 0.9282 percent of the total U.S. buying power. This means that consumers who live in Denver have higher than average buying power. We know this because Denver accounts for about 0.77 percent of the U.S. population.

Using several factors rather than only one uses more information. And in the case of the BPI, it gives a single measure of a market's potential. Rather than falling back on using population only, or income only, or trying to develop a special index, the BPI can be used in the same way that we used the 0.001 factor in the bread example.

Predicting Future Behavior Calls for More Judgment and Some Opinions

These past-extending methods use quantitative data—projecting past experience into the future and assuming that the future will be like the past. But this is risky in competitive markets. Usually, it's desirable to add some judgment to other forecasts before making the final forecast yourself.

Jury of executive opinion adds judgment

One of the oldest and simplest methods of forecasting—the **jury of executive opinion**—combines the opinions of experienced executives, perhaps from marketing, production, finance, purchasing, and top management. Each executive estimates market potential and sales for the *coming years.* Then they try to work out a consensus.

The main advantage of the jury approach is that it can be done quickly and easily. On the other hand, the results may not be very good. There may be too much extending of the past. Some of the executives may have little contact with outside market influences. But their estimates could point to major shifts in customer demand or competition.

Exhibit B–4 Illustrative Page from *Sales & Marketing Management's* Survey of Buying Power: Metro and County Totals

COLORADO

METRO AREA County City	Population: Total Population (000s)	% Population by Age Group 18–24	25–34	35–49	50 +	House-holds (000s)	Retail Sales by Store Group ($000): Total Retail Sales	Food & Beverage Stores	Food Service & Drinking Establish-ments	General Merchan-dise	Furniture & Home Furnish. & Electron. & Appliances	Motor Vehicle & Parts Dealers	Effective Buying Income: Total EBI ($000)	Median Hsld. EBI	% of Hslds: by EBI Group: A $20,000–$34,999	B $35,000–$49,999	C $50,000 & Over	Buying Power Index
BOULDER-LONGMONT	**303.7**	**13.6**	**15.5**	**25.6**	**22.4**	**119.6**	**5,081,227**	**1,001,555**	**556,377**	**448,453**	**247,484**	**1,220,087**	**7,716,546**	**51,714**	**17.8**	**17.1**	**51.6**	**0.1360**
BOULDER	303.7	13.6	15.5	25.6	22.4	119.6	5,081,227	1,001,555	556,377	448,453	247,484	1,220,087	7,716,546	51,714	17.8	17.1	51.6	0.1360
• Boulder	97.1	26.4	18.8	20.0	20.1	40.7	2,147,663	439,133	267,970	121,357	117,520	447,464	2,480,204	43,427	21.5	15.8	43.1	0.0479
• Longmont	74.6	8.7	14.6	25.3	23.6	28.0	1,126,804	250,483	122,965	125,103	40,068	272,449	1,531,271	47,526	19.4	20.1	46.8	0.0290
COLORADO SPRINGS	**537.3**	**10.7**	**14.4**	**24.7**	**22.6**	**200.1**	**7,883,675**	**819,826**	**647,101**	**984,753**	**465,488**	**2,031,112**	**10,259,019**	**42,082**	**24.7**	**21.0**	**38.7**	**0.1994**
EL PASO	537.3	10.7	14.4	24.7	22.6	200.1	7,883,675	819,826	647,101	984,753	465,488	2,031,112	10,259,019	42,082	24.7	21.0	38.7	0.1994
• Colorado Springs	373.1	10.5	14.8	24.5	23.7	146.5	6,786,693	628,690	549,107	858,048	443,063	1,848,219	7,353,670	41,212	24.9	20.9	37.5	0.1515
DENVER	**2,199.5**	**9.2**	**16.2**	**25.0**	**23.8**	**858.0**	**33,750,880**	**4,700,116**	**3,232,590**	**3,615,646**	**2,518,616**	**9,368,057**	**52,585,220**	**49,109**	**18.8**	**19.0**	**48.9**	**0.9282**
ADAMS	382.9	10.5	16.7	23.3	21.1	134.3	4,558,882	670,017	371,810	416,956	385,657	1,466,781	6,459,840	42,802	22.5	22.4	38.7	0.1253
Thornton	87.3	9.7	17.5	24.9	18.0	30.6	707,386	152,812	68,679	122,478	40,099	150,769	1,594,293	48,053	19.4	22.4	46.8	0.0270
Westminster	105.4	9.9	17.1	26.0	20.3	40.1	1,052,771	153,993	114,177	292,678	100,304	88,416	2,368,971	51,512	17.0	21.6	51.9	0.0384
ARAPAHOE	505.4	8.8	15.1	25.7	23.9	197.5	9,846,119	1,160,676	872,314	963,885	595,477	4,049,257	13,314,002	52,887	18.2	18.6	53.1	0.2422
Aurora	286.8	10.4	17.2	24.0	21.0	109.0	3,889,713	531,245	378,269	566,166	225,882	1,236,463	5,874,943	47,398	20.7	21.5	46.0	0.1076
DENVER	568.5	11.1	19.9	22.1	25.1	243.7	9,287,630	1,235,129	1,270,413	730,810	755,362	1,701,220	13,899,851	42,540	21.6	18.4	41.0	0.2474
• Denver	568.5	11.1	19.9	22.1	25.1	243.7	9,275,551	1,224,988	1,269,426	730,810	755,362	1,700,815	13,899,851	42,540	21.6	18.4	41.0	0.2474
DOUGLAS	200.7	4.9	15.9	29.6	18.0	69.6	2,725,601	517,182	250,871	294,714	289,389	355,394	5,147,699	59,715	10.9	18.2	64.7	0.0851
JEFFERSON	542.0	8.3	13.2	26.8	26.5	212.9	7,332,648	1,117,112	467,182	1,209,281	492,731	1,795,405	13,763,828	54,470	16.4	18.6	55.1	0.2282
Arvada	104.0	8.0	11.9	25.9	28.1	40.0	1,007,245	224,707	79,597	133,524	60,181	74,965	2,332,241	51,557	18.1	19.3	51.8	0.0376
Lakewood	148.0	9.9	15.2	24.1	28.8	62.3	2,065,827	297,529	149,068	292,832	124,879	567,796	3,451,207	46,782	20.8	21.1	45.2	0.0599
DENVER-BOULDER-GREELEY **CONSOLIDATED AREA**	**2,695.8**	**10.0**	**15.9**	**24.9**	**23.6**	**1,044.7**	**40,882,936**	**5,939,206**	**3,929,714**	**4,267,775**	**2,809,610**	**11,246,398**	**63,170,157**	**48,397**	**19.2**	**19.0**	**47.9**	**1.1216**

Estimates from salespeople can help too

Using salespeople's estimates to forecast is like the jury approach. But salespeople are more likely than home office managers to be familiar with customer reactions and what competitors are doing. Their estimates are especially useful in some business markets where the few customers may be well known to the salespeople. But this approach can be useful in any type of market.

However, managers who use estimates from salespeople should be aware of the limitations. For example, new salespeople may not know much about their markets. Even experienced salespeople may not be aware of possible changes in the economic climate or the firm's other environments. And if salespeople think the manager is going to use the estimates to set sales quotas, the estimates may be low!

Surveys, panels, and market tests

Special surveys of final buyers, retailers, or wholesalers can show what's happening in different market segments. Some firms use panels of stores—or final consumers—to keep track of buying behavior and to decide when just extending past behavior isn't enough.

Surveys are sometimes combined with market tests when the company wants to estimate customers' reactions to possible changes in its marketing mix. A market test might show that a product increased its share of the market by 10 percent when its price was dropped 1 cent below competition. But this extra business might be quickly lost if the price were increased 1 cent above competition. Such market experiments help the marketing manager make good estimates of future sales when one or more of the four Ps is changed.

Accuracy depends on the marketing mix

Forecasting can help a marketing manager estimate the size of possible market opportunities. But the accuracy of any sales forecast depends on whether the firm selects and implements a marketing mix that turns these opportunities into sales and profits.

KEY TERMS

LO B.7

operating statement, *561*
gross sales, *564*
return, *564*
allowance, *564*
net sales, *564*
cost of sales, *564*
gross margin (gross profit), *564*
expenses, *564*
net profit, *564*
purchase discount, *565*
stockturn rate, *566*
operating ratios, *567*
markup, *568*
markdown ratio, *569*
markdown, *569*
return on investment (ROI), *570*
balance sheet, *570*
return on assets (ROA), *571*
market potential, *571*
sales forecast, *571*
trend extension, *572*
factor method, *573*
factor, *573*
jury of executive opinion, *573*

QUESTIONS AND PROBLEMS

1. Distinguish between the following pairs of items that appear on operating statements: (*a*) gross sales and net sales, and (*b*) purchases at billed cost and purchases at net cost.
2. How does gross margin differ from gross profit? From net profit?
3. Explain the similarity between markups and gross margin. What connection do markdowns have with the operating statement?
4. Compute the net profit for a company with the following data:

Beginning inventory (cost)	$ 150,000
Purchases at billed cost	330,000
Sales returns and allowances	250,000
Rent	60,000
Salaries	400,000
Heat and light	180,000
Ending inventory (cost)	250,000
Freight cost (inbound)	80,000
Gross sales	1,300,000

5. Construct an operating statement from the following data:

Returns and allowances	$ 150,000
Expenses	20%
Closing inventory at cost	600,000
Markdowns	2%
Inward transportation	30,000
Purchases	1,000,000
Net profit (5%)	300,000

6. Compute net sales and percent of markdowns for the following data:

Markdowns	$ 40,000
Gross sales	400,000
Returns	32,000
Allowances	48,000

7. (*a*) What percentage markups on cost are equivalent to the following percentage markups on selling price: 20, 37½, 50, and 66⅔? (*b*) What percentage markups on selling price are equivalent to the following percentage markups on cost: 33⅓, 20, 40, and 50?

8. What net sales volume is required to obtain a stockturn rate of 20 times a year on an average inventory at cost of $100,000 with a gross margin of 25 percent?

9. Explain how the general manager of a department store might use the markdown ratios computed for her various departments. Is this a fair measure? Of what?

10. Compare and contrast return on investment (ROI) and return on assets (ROA) measures. Which would be best for a retailer with no bank borrowing or other outside sources of funds (that is, the retailer has put up all the money that the business needs)?

11. Explain the difference between a forecast of market potential and a sales forecast.

12. Suggest a plausible explanation for sales fluctuations for (*a*) computers, (*b*) ice cream, (*c*) washing machines, (*d*) tennis rackets, (*e*) oats, (*f*) disposable diapers, and (*g*) latex for rubber-based paint.

13. Explain the factor method of forecasting. Illustrate your answer.

14. Based on data in Exhibit B-4, discuss the relative market potential of the city of Boulder, Colorado, and the city of Lakewood, Colorado, for (*a*) prepared cereals, (*b*) automobiles, and (*c*) furniture.

Career Planning in Marketing

APPENDIX C

Learning Objectives

One of the hardest decisions facing most college students is the choice of a career. Of course you are the best judge of your own objectives, interests, and abilities. Only you can decide what career you should pursue. However, you owe it to yourself to at least consider the possibility of a career in marketing. This chapter's objectives will help organize your thinking about a career and the marketing plan you could develop to help you achieve your career goals.

When you finish this appendix, you should be able to:

1 rest assured there is a job or career for you in marketing.

2 know that marketing jobs can be rewarding, pay well, and offer opportunities for growth.

3 understand how to conduct your own personal analysis for career planning.

4 evaluate the many marketing jobs from which you can choose.

5 prepare your own personal marketing plan.

There's a Place in Marketing for You

LO C.1

We're happy to tell you that many opportunities are available in marketing. There's a place in marketing for everyone, from a service provider in a fast-food restaurant to a vice president of marketing in a large company such as Microsoft or Procter & Gamble. The opportunities range widely, so it will help to be more specific. In the following pages, we'll discuss (1) the typical pay for different marketing jobs, (2) setting your own objectives and evaluating your interests and abilities, and (3) the kinds of jobs available in marketing. We'll also provide some ideas about using the Internet to get more information and perhaps apply for a job or post your own information; this material is in the box with the title "Getting Wired for a Career in Marketing."

There are Many Marketing Jobs, and They Can Pay Well

LO C.2

There are many interesting and challenging jobs for those with marketing training. You may not know it, but 60 percent of graduating college students take their initial job in a sales, marketing, or customer service position regardless of their stated major. So you'll have a head start because you've been studying marketing, and companies are always looking for people who already have skills in place. In terms of upward mobility, more CEOs have come from the sales and marketing side than all other fields combined. The sky is the limit for those who enter the sales and marketing profession prepared for the future!

Further, marketing jobs open to college-level students do pay well. According to the most recent salary surveys from the National Association of Colleges and Employers at the time this book went to press, marketing graduates were being offered starting salaries around $40,000, with a range from $25,000 to more than $60,000. Students with a master's in marketing averaged about $60,000; those with an MBA averaged about $75,000. Starting salaries can vary considerably, depending on your background, experience, and location.

Starting salaries in marketing compare favorably with many other fields. They are lower than those in such fields as computer science and electrical engineering where college graduates are currently in demand. But there is even better opportunity for personal growth, variety, and income in many marketing positions. The *American Almanac of Jobs and Salaries* ranks the median income of marketers number 10 in a list of 125 professions. Marketing also supplies about 50 percent of the people who achieve senior management ranks.

How far and fast your career and income rise above the starting level, however, depends on many factors, including your willingness to work, how well you get along with people, and your individual abilities. But most of all, it depends on *getting results*—individually and through other people. And this is where many marketing jobs offer the newcomer great opportunities. It is possible to show initiative, ability, creativity, and judgment in marketing jobs. And some young people move up very rapidly in marketing. Some even end up at the top in large companies or as owners of their own businesses.

Marketing is often the route to the top

Marketing is where the action is! In the final analysis, a firm's success or failure depends on the effectiveness of its marketing program. This doesn't mean the other functional areas aren't important. It merely reflects the fact that a firm won't have much need for accountants, finance people, production managers, and so on if it can't successfully meet customers' needs and sell its products.

Because marketing is so vital to a firm's survival, many companies look for people with training and experience in marketing when filling key executive positions. In general, chief executive officers for the nation's largest corporations are more likely to have backgrounds in marketing and distribution than in other fields such as production, finance, and engineering.

Develop Your Own Personal Marketing Strategy

Now that you know there are many opportunities in marketing, your problem is matching the opportunities to your own personal objectives and strengths. Basically the problem is a marketing problem: developing a marketing strategy to sell a product—yourself—to potential employers. Just as in planning strategies for products, developing your own strategy takes careful thought. Exhibit C-1 shows how you can organize your own strategy planning. This exhibit shows that you should evaluate yourself first—a personal analysis—and then analyze the environment for opportunities. This will help you sharpen your own long- and short-run objectives, which will lead to developing a strategy. Finally, you should start implementing your own personal marketing strategy. These ideas are explained more fully next.

Exhibit C–1
Organizing Your Own Personal Marketing Strategy Planning

Conduct Your Own Personal Analysis

LO C.3

You are the product you are going to include in your own marketing plan. So first you have to decide what your long-run objectives are—what you want to do, how hard you want to work, and how quickly you want to reach your objectives. Be honest with yourself—or you will eventually face frustration. Evaluate your own personal strengths and weaknesses—and decide what factors may become the key to your success. Finally, as part of your personal analysis, set some preliminary timetables to guide your strategy planning and implementation efforts. Let's spell this out in detail.

Set broad long-run objectives

Your strategy planning may require some trial-and-error decision making. But at the very beginning, you should make some tentative decisions about your own objectives—what you want out of a job and out of life. At the very least, you should decide whether you are just looking for a job or whether you want to build a career. Beyond this, do you want the position to be personally satisfying—or is the financial return enough? And just how much financial return do you need? Some people work only to support themselves (and their families) and their leisure-time activities. These people try to find job opportunities that provide adequate financial returns but aren't too demanding of their time or effort.

Other people look first for satisfaction in their job—and they seek opportunities for career advancement. Financial rewards may be important too, but these are used mainly as measures of success. In the extreme, the career-oriented individual may be willing to sacrifice a lot, including leisure and social activities, to achieve success in a career.

Once you've tentatively decided these matters, then you can get more serious about whether you should seek a job or a career in marketing. If you decide to pursue a career, you should set your broad long-run objectives to achieve it. For example, one long-run objective might be to pursue a career in marketing management (or marketing research). This might require more academic training than you planned, as well as a different kind of training. If your objective is to get a job that pays well, on the other hand, then this calls for a different kind of training and different kinds of job experiences before completing your academic work.

Evaluate personal strengths and weaknesses

What kind of a job is right for you?

Because of the great variety of marketing jobs, it's hard to generalize regarding the aptitudes you should have to pursue a career in marketing. Different jobs attract people with various interests and abilities. We'll give you some guidelines about what kinds of interests and abilities marketers should have. However, if you're completely lost about your own interests and abilities, see your campus career counselor and take some vocational aptitude and interest tests. These tests will help you to compare yourself with people who are now working in various career positions. They will *not* tell you what you should do, but they can help, especially in eliminating possibilities you are less interested in or less able to do well in.

Are you people-oriented or thing-oriented?

One useful approach is to decide whether you are basically "people-oriented" or "thing-oriented." This is a very important decision. A people-oriented person might be very unhappy in an inventory management job, for example, whereas a thing-oriented person might be miserable in a personal selling or retail management job that involves a lot of customer contact.

Marketing has both people-oriented and thing-oriented jobs. People-oriented jobs are primarily in the promotion area—where company representatives must make contact with potential customers. This may be direct personal selling or customer service activities—for example, in technical service or installation and repair. Thing-oriented jobs focus more on creative activities and analyzing data—as in advertising and marketing research—or on organizing and scheduling work—as in operating warehouses, transportation agencies, or the back-end of retailers.

People-oriented jobs tend to pay more, in part because such jobs are more likely to affect sales, the lifeblood of any business. Thing-oriented jobs, on the other hand, are often seen as cost generators rather than sales generators. Taking a big view of the whole company's operations, the thing-oriented jobs are certainly necessary—but without sales, no one is needed to do them.

Thing-oriented jobs are usually done at a company's facilities. Further, especially in lower-level jobs, the amount of work to be done and even the nature of the work may be spelled out quite clearly. The time it takes to design questionnaires and tabulate results, for example, can be estimated with reasonable accuracy. Similarly, running a warehouse, analyzing inventory reports, scheduling outgoing shipments, and so on are more like production operations. It's fairly easy to measure an employee's effectiveness and productivity in a thing-oriented job. At the least, time spent can be used to measure an employee's contribution.

A sales rep, on the other hand, might spend all weekend thinking and planning how to make a half-hour sales presentation on Monday. For what should the sales rep be compensated—the half-hour presentation, all of the planning and thinking that went into it, or the results? Typically, sales reps are rewarded for results—and this helps account for the sometimes extremely high salaries paid to effective order getters. At the same time, some people-oriented jobs can be routinized and are lower paid. For example, salespeople in some retail stores are paid at or near the minimum wage.

Managers needed for both kinds of jobs

Here we have oversimplified deliberately to emphasize the differences among types of jobs. Actually, of course, there are many variations between the two extremes. Some sales reps must do a great deal of analytical work before they make a presentation. Similarly, some marketing researchers must be extremely people-sensitive to get potential customers to reveal their true feelings. But the division is still useful because it focuses on the primary emphasis in different kinds of jobs.

Managers are needed for the people in both kinds of jobs. Managing others requires a blend of both people and analytical skills—but people skills may be the more important of the two. Therefore, people-oriented individuals are often promoted into managerial positions more quickly.

What will differentiate your product?

After deciding whether you're generally people-oriented or thing-oriented, you're ready for the next step—trying to identify your specific strengths (to be built on) and weaknesses (to be avoided or remedied). It is important to be as specific as possible so you can develop

Getting Wired for a Career in Marketing

The Internet is a great resource at every stage of career planning and job hunting. It can help you learn: how to do a self-assessment, the outlook for different industries and jobs, what firms have jobs open, how to improve a résumé and post it online for free, and just about anything else you can imagine. Here we'll highlight just a few ideas and websites that can help you get started. However, if you start with some of these suggestions, each website you visit will provide links to other relevant sites that will give you new ideas.

One good place to start is at Yahoo (www.yahoo.com). Select "HotJobs" and take a look at all of the information and services that are available when you select the "Career Tools" link. For example, you can browse résumé tools and salary information, look at job listings, and much more. You may also want to study the similar information at www.monster.com.

Another website to check is at www.marketing-jobs.com. It has listings of marketing jobs, links to a number of companies with openings, a résumé center with ideas for preparing a résumé and posting it on the Internet, and lists of helpful periodicals. You might also go to www.careerjournal.com. There are job listings, job-hunting advice, career articles from *The Wall Street Journal,* and more. You can create and post a résumé there as well. Professional associations are another great resource. For example, the American Marketing Association website is at www.marketingpower.com, and the Sales and Marketing Executives International website is at www.smei.org. The Council of Supply Chain Management Professionals website is at www.cscmp.org.

Another potentially useful website address is www.collegegrad.com. It has links for posting a résumé, information on writing cover letters and getting references, and ideas about how to find a company with job openings. To get a sample of what's possible in tracking down jobs, visit the website at www.thejobresource.com and experiment with its search engine, which lets you look at what's available by state. For example, you might want to search through job listings that mention terms such as *entry level, marketing, advertising,* and *sales.*

This should get you started. Remember, however, that in Chapter 7 we gave addresses for a number of websites with search engines. You can use one of them to help find more detail on any topic that interests you. For example, you might go to www.google.com and search on terms such as *marketing jobs, salary surveys, post a résumé,* or *entry level position.*

a better marketing plan. For example, if you decide you are more people-oriented, are you more skilled in verbal or written communication? Or if you are more thing-oriented, what specific analytical or technical skills do you have? Are you good at working with numbers, using a computer, solving complex problems, or coming to the root of a problem? Other possible strengths include past experience (career-related or otherwise), academic performance, an outgoing personality, enthusiasm, drive, and motivation.

It is important to see that your plan should build on your strengths. An employer will be hiring you to do something—so promote yourself as someone who is able to do something *well.* In other words, find your competitive advantage in your unique strengths—and then communicate these unique things about *you* and what you can do. Give an employer a reason to pick you over other candidates by showing that you'll add superior value to the company.

While trying to identify strengths, you also must realize that you may have some important weaknesses, depending on your objectives. If you are seeking a career that requires technical skills, for example, then you need to get those skills. Or if you are seeking a career that requires independence and self-confidence, then you should try to develop those characteristics in yourself—or change your objectives.

Set some timetables

At this point in your strategy planning process, set some timetables to organize your thinking and the rest of your planning. You need to make some decisions at this point to be sure you see where you're going. You might simply focus on getting your first job, or you might decide to work on two marketing plans: (1) a short-run plan to get your first job and (2) a longer-run plan—perhaps a five-year plan—to show how you're going to accomplish your long-run objectives. People who are basically job-oriented may get away with only a short-run plan, just drifting from one opportunity to another as their own objectives and opportunities change. But those interested in careers need a longer-run plan. Otherwise, they may find themselves pursuing attractive first-job opportunities that satisfy short-run objectives but quickly leave them frustrated when they realize that they can't achieve their long-run objectives without additional training or other experiences that require starting over again on a new career path.

Opportunities in Marketing

LO C.4

Strategy planning is a matching process. For your own strategy planning, this means matching yourself to career opportunities. So let's look at opportunities available in the market environment. (The same approach applies, of course, in the whole business area.) Exhibit C-2 shows some of the possibilities and salary ranges. The exhibit is assembled from salary data at www.salary.com. The salary ranges reflect the 25th percentile to the 75th percentile in the spring of 2010. For more information, look at Salary.com, where you can find job descriptions and data adjusted to different parts of the country. You can also find information about other career paths common to marketing majors—including logistics and purchasing/procurement management.

Keep in mind that the salary ranges in Exhibit C-2 are rough estimates. Salaries for a particular job often vary depending on a variety of factors, including company size, industry, and geographic area. People in some firms also get big bonuses that are not counted in their salary. There are many other sources of salary information. For example, *Advertising Age* publishes an annual survey of salary levels for different marketing and advertising jobs, with breakdowns by company size and other factors. Many trade associations, across a variety of different industries, also publish surveys, and the U.S. government's Bureau of Labor Statistics (www.bls.gov) includes salary data. If you use the search engine at www.google.com and do a search on *salary survey,* you will find hundreds of such surveys for a number of different industries.

Identifying current opportunities in marketing

Because of the wide range of opportunities in marketing, it's helpful to narrow your possibilities. After deciding on your own objectives, strengths, and weaknesses, think about where in the marketing system you might like to work. Would you like to work for manufacturers, or wholesalers, or retailers? Or does it really matter? Do you want to be involved with consumer products or business products? By analyzing your feelings about these possibilities, you can begin to zero in on the kind of job and the functional area that might interest you most.

One simple way to get a better idea of the kinds of jobs available in marketing is to review the chapters of this text—this time with an eye for job opportunities rather than new concepts. The following paragraphs contain brief descriptions of job areas that marketing graduates are often interested in with references to specific chapters in the text. Some, as noted, offer good starting opportunities, while others do not. While reading these paragraphs, keep your own objectives, interests, and strengths in mind.

Marketing manager (Chapter 2)

This is usually not an entry-level job, although aggressive students may move quickly into this role in smaller companies.

Customer or market analyst (Chapters 3 through 5)

Opportunities as consumer analysts and market analysts are commonly found in large companies, marketing research organizations, advertising agencies, and some consulting firms. Investment banking firms also hire entry-level analysts; they want to know what the market for a new business is like before investing. Beginning market analysts start in thing-oriented jobs until their judgment and people-oriented skills are tested. The job may involve collecting or analyzing secondary data or preparation of reports and plans.

Exhibit C–2 Some Career Paths and Compensation Ranges*

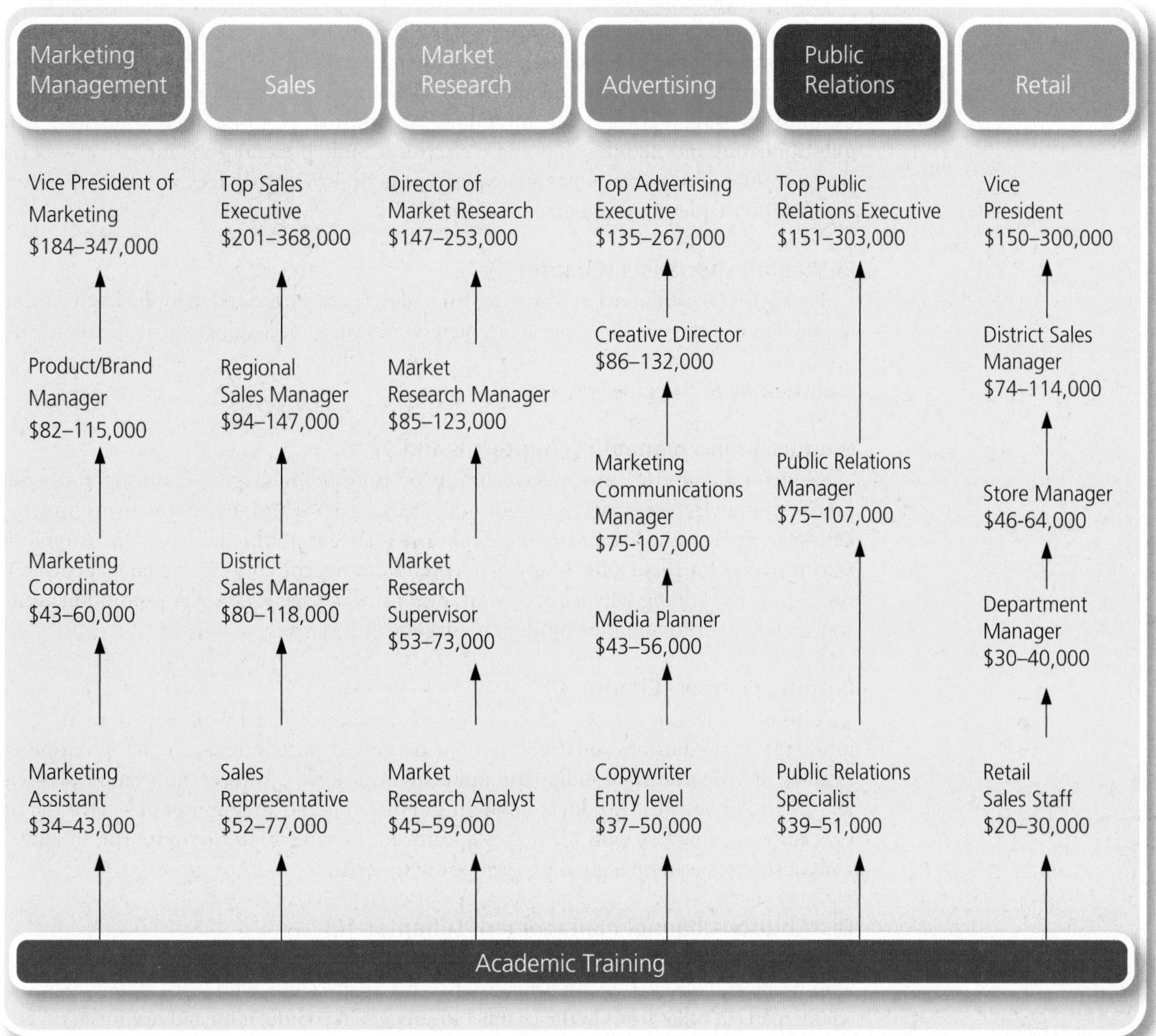

*Salaries are based on data from Salary.com and represent the range for a salary plus bonus from the 25th to the 75th percentile as of May 2010, rounded to the nearest 1,000. Salary for retail vice president was estimated.

Because knowledge of statistics, computer software, Internet search techniques, or behavioral sciences is very important, marketing graduates often find themselves competing with majors from statistics, sociology, computer science, and economics. Graduates who have courses in marketing *and* one or more of these areas may have the best opportunities.

Purchasing agent/buyer (Chapter 6)

Entry-level opportunities are commonly found in large companies, and there are often good opportunities in the procurement area. Many companies are looking for bright newcomers who can help them find new and better ways to work with suppliers. To get off on the right track, beginners usually start as trainees or assistant buyers under the supervision of experienced buyers. That's good preparation for a promotion to more responsibility.

Marketing research opportunities (Chapter 7)

There are entry-level opportunities at all levels in the channel (but especially in large firms where more formal marketing research is done in-house), in advertising agencies, and in marketing research firms. Some general management consulting firms also have marketing research groups. Quantitative and behavioral science skills are extremely important in marketing research, so some firms are more interested in business graduates who have studied statistics or psychology as electives. But there still are many opportunities in marketing research for marketing graduates, especially if they have some experience in working with computers and statistical software. A recent graduate might begin in a training program—conducting interviews or summarizing open-ended answers from questionnaires and helping to prepare electronic slide presentations for clients—before being promoted to a position as an analyst, assistant project manager, account representative, and subsequent management positions.

Packaging specialists (Chapter 8)

Packaging manufacturers tend to hire and train interested people from various backgrounds—there is little formal academic training in packaging. There are many sales opportunities in this field—and with training, interested people can become specialists fairly quickly in this growing area.

Product/brand manager (Chapters 8 and 9)

Many multiproduct firms have brand or product managers handling individual products—in effect, managing each product as a separate business. Some firms hire marketing graduates as assistant brand or product managers, although larger firms typically recruit MBAs for these jobs. Many firms prefer that recent college graduates spend some time in the field doing sales work or working with an ad agency or sales promotion agency before moving into brand or product management positions.

Product planner (Chapter 9)

This is usually not an entry-level position. Instead, people with experience on the technical side of the business or in sales might be moved onto a new-product development team as they demonstrate judgment and analytical skills. However, new employees with winning ideas for new products don't go unnoticed—and they sometimes have the opportunity to grow fast with ideas they spearhead. Having a job that puts you in contact with customers is often a good way to spot new needs.

Distribution channel management (Chapter 10)

This work is typically handled or directed by sales managers and therefore is not an entry-level position. However, many firms form teams of specialists who work closely with their counterparts in other firms in the channel to strengthen coordination and relationships. Such a team often includes new people in sales or purchasing because it gives them exposure to a different part of the firm's activities. It's also not unusual for people to start working in a particular industry and then take a different job at a different level in the channel. For example, a graduate who has trained to be a store manager for a chain of sporting goods stores might go to work for a manufacturers' representative that handles a variety of sports equipment.

Logistics opportunities (Chapter 11)

There are many sales opportunities with physical distribution specialists—but there are also many thing-oriented jobs involving traffic management, warehousing, and materials handling. Here training in accounting, finance, and computer methods could be very useful. These kinds of jobs are available at all levels in channels of distribution.

Retailing opportunities (Chapter 12)

Not long ago, most entry-level marketing positions in retailing involved some kind of sales work. That has changed rapidly in recent years because the number of large retail chains is expanding and they often recruit graduates for their management training programs. Retailing positions tend to offer lower-than-average starting salaries—but they often provide opportunities for very rapid advancement. In a fast-growing chain, results-oriented people can move up very quickly. Most retailers require new employees to have some selling experience before managing others—or buying. A typical marketing graduate can expect to work as an assistant manager or do some sales work and manage one or several departments before advancing to a store management position—or to a staff position that might involve buying, advertising, location analysis, and so on.

Wholesaling opportunities (Chapter 12)

Entry-level jobs with merchant wholesalers typically fall into one of two categories. The first is in the logistics area—working with transportation management, inventory control, distribution customer service, and related activities. The other category usually involves personal selling and customer support. Agent wholesalers typically focus on selling, and entry-level jobs often start out with order-taking responsibilities that grow into order-getting responsibilities. Many wholesalers are moving much of their information to the Internet, so marketing students with skills and knowledge in this arena may find especially interesting opportunities.

Personal selling opportunities (Chapter 14)

Because there are so many different types of sales jobs and so many people are employed in sales, there are many good entry-level opportunities in personal selling. This might be order-getting, order-taking, customer service, or missionary selling. Many sales jobs now rely on sales technology, so some of the most challenging opportunities will go to students who know how to prepare spreadsheets and presentation materials using software programs like Microsoft Office. Many students are reluctant to get into personal selling—but this field offers benefits that are hard to match in any other field. These include the opportunity to earn high salaries and commissions quickly, a chance to develop your self-confidence and resourcefulness, an opportunity to work with minimal supervision—almost to the point of being your own boss—and a chance to acquire product and customer knowledge that many firms consider necessary for a successful career in product/brand management, sales management, and marketing management. On the other hand, many salespeople prefer to spend their entire careers in selling. They like the freedom and earning potential that go with a sales job over the headaches and sometimes lower salaries of sales management positions.

Customer service opportunities (Chapter 14)

As this book points out, marketing managers are recognizing the growing importance in providing customers with service after the sale. There are a number of different opportunities in customer service. Many firms need qualified customer service representatives who work with customers to fulfill their needs and help ensure customer satisfaction. Customer service reps may interact with customers on the phone, by online chat, or via e-mail. But other service representatives help customers at their businesses with installations or equipment repair. While some of the entry level positions that require only high school education are being outsourced to other countries, positions requiring strong communication skills and a good education provide an opportunity for marketing majors. There are also management positions that develop customer service strategies, control costs, and focus on hiring, training, and retaining customer service reps and enhancing customer satisfaction.

Advertising opportunities (Chapters 13 and 15)

Job opportunities in this area are varied and highly competitive. And because the ability to communicate and a knowledge of the behavioral sciences are important, marketing and advertising graduates often find themselves competing with majors from fields such as English, communication, psychology, and sociology. There are thing-oriented jobs such as copywriting, media buying, art, computer graphics, and so on. Competition for these jobs is very strong—and they go to people with a track record. So the entry-level positions are as assistant to a copywriter, media buyer, or art director. There are also people-oriented positions involving work with clients, which are probably of more interest to marketing graduates. This is a glamorous but small and extremely competitive industry where young people can rise very rapidly—but they can also be as easily displaced by new bright young people. Entry-level salaries in advertising are typically low. There are sometimes good opportunities to get started in advertising with a retail chain that prepares its advertising internally. Another way to get more experience with advertising is to take a job with one of the media, perhaps in sales or as a customer consultant. Selling advertising space on a website or cable TV station or newspaper may not seem as glamorous as developing TV ads, but media salespeople help their customers solve promotion problems and get experience dealing with both the business and creative side of advertising.

Publicity and public relations opportunities (Chapters 13 and 15)

While the number of entry-level positions in publicity and public relations is expected to continue to grow rapidly, competition for jobs will be stiff. College graduates with degrees in journalism, public relations, communications, and marketing may qualify for these openings. Many are attracted to these high-profile jobs. In addition to the popular press, more firms are placing useful content on the Internet to inform and influence customers. To a large degree, the tools used in these fields rely on emerging technologies. This bodes well for recent college graduates who may be more comfortable using newer technologies than "old hands" in publicity and public relations. International experience and proficiency in a second language can sometimes help job candidates stand out.

Sales promotion opportunities (Chapters 13 and 15)

The number of entry-level positions in the sales promotion area is growing because the number of specialists in this area is growing. For example, specialists might help a company plan a special event for employees, figure out procedures to distribute free samples, or perhaps set up a database to send customers a newsletter. Because clients' needs are often different, creativity and judgment are required. It is usually difficult for an inexperienced person to show evidence of these skills right out of school, so entry-level people often work with a project manager until they learn the ropes. In companies that handle their own sales promotion work, a beginner usually starts by getting some experience in sales or advertising.

Pricing opportunities (Chapters 16 and 17)

Pricing decisions are usually handled by experienced executives. However, in some large companies and consulting firms there are opportunities as pricing analysts for marketing graduates who have quantitative skills. These people work as assistants to higher-level executives and collect and analyze information about competitors' prices and costs, as well as the firm's own costs. Thus, being able to work with accounting numbers and computer spreadsheets is often important in these jobs. However, sometimes the route to these jobs is through experience in marketing research or product management.

Credit management opportunities

Specialists in credit have a continuing need for employees who are interested in evaluating customers' credit ratings and ensuring that money gets collected. Both people skills and thing skills can be useful here. Entry-level positions normally involve a training program and then working under the supervision of others until your judgment and abilities are tested.

International marketing opportunities

Many marketing students are intrigued with the adventure and foreign travel promised by careers in international marketing. Some firms hire recent college graduates for positions in international marketing, but more often these positions go to MBA graduates. However, that is changing as more and more firms pursue international markets. It's an advantage in seeking an international marketing job to know a second language and to know about the culture of countries where you would like to work. Your college may have courses or international exchange programs that would help in these areas. Graduates aiming for a career in international marketing usually must spend time mastering the firm's domestic marketing operations before being sent abroad. So a good way to start is to focus on firms that are already involved in international marketing, or who are planning to move in that direction soon. On the other hand, there are many websites with listings of international jobs. For example, you might want to visit www.overseasjobs.com.

Customer relations/consumer affairs opportunities (Chapters 13 and 20)

Most firms are becoming more concerned about their relations with customers and the general public. Employees in this kind of work, however, usually have held various positions with the firm before doing customer relations.

Study trends that may affect your opportunities

A strategy planner should always be evaluating the future because it's easier to go along with trends than to buck them. This means you should watch for political, technical, or economic changes that might open, or close, career opportunities.

If you can spot a trend early, you may be able to prepare yourself to take advantage of it as part of your long-run strategy planning. Other trends might mean you should avoid certain career options. For example, technological changes in computers and communications, including the Internet, are leading to major changes in retailing and advertising, as well as in personal selling. Cable television, telephone selling, and direct-mail selling may reduce the need for routine order takers, while increasing the need for higher-level order getters. More targeted and imaginative sales presentations for delivery by mail, e-mail, phone, or Internet websites may be needed. The retailers that prosper will have a better understanding of their target markets. And they may need to be supported by wholesalers and manufacturers that can plan targeted promotions that make economic sense. This will require a better understanding of the production and physical distribution side of business, as well as the financial side. And this means better training in accounting, finance, inventory control, and so on. So plan your personal strategy with such trends in mind.

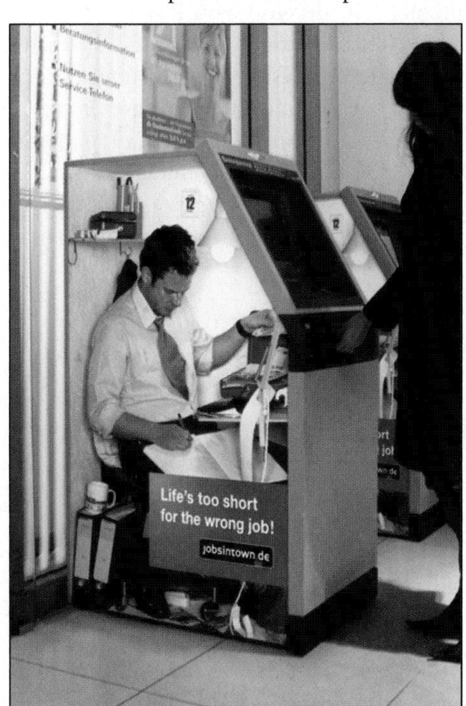

This humorous ad on the side of a vending machine says, "Life's too short for the wrong job!" Planning for the right job—like planning a marketing strategy—pays off.

One good way to get more detailed analysis is to go to the U.S. Bureau of Labor Statistics website at http://stats.bls.gov and use the search procedure to look for the term *occupational outlook.* The Bureau provides detailed comments about the outlook for employment and growth in different types of jobs, industries, and regions.

Evaluate business practices

Finally, you need to know how businesses really operate and the kind of training required for various jobs. We've already seen that there are many opportunities in marketing—but not all jobs are open to everyone, and not all jobs are entry-level jobs. Positions such as marketing manager, brand manager, and sales manager are higher rungs on the marketing career ladder. They become available only when you have a few years of experience and have shown leadership and judgment. Some positions require more education than others. So take a hard look at your long-run objectives—and then see what degree you may need for the kinds of opportunities you might like.

Develop Objectives

LO C.5

Once you've done a personal analysis and environment analysis—identifying your personal interests, your strengths and weaknesses, and the opportunities in the environment—define your short-run and long-run objectives more specifically.

Develop long-run objectives

Your long-run objectives should clearly state what you want to do and what you will do for potential employers. You might be as specific as indicating the exact career area you want to pursue over the next 5 to 10 years. For example, your long-run objective might be to apply a set of marketing research and marketing management tools to the food manufacturing industry, with the objective of becoming director of marketing research in a small food manufacturing company.

Your long-run objectives should be realistic and attainable. They should be objectives you have thought about and for which you think you have the necessary skills (or the capabilities to develop those skills) as well as the motivation to reach the objectives.

Develop short-run objectives

To achieve your long-run objective(s), you should develop one or more short-run objectives. These should spell out what is needed to reach your long-run objective(s). For example, you might need to develop a variety of marketing research skills *and* marketing management skills—because both are needed to reach the longer-run objective. Or you might need an entry-level position in marketing research for a large food manufacturer to gain experience and background. An even shorter-run objective might be to take the academic courses that are necessary to get that desired entry-level job. In this example, you would probably need a minimum of an undergraduate degree in marketing, with an emphasis on marketing research. (Note that, given the longer-run objective of managerial responsibility, a business degree would probably be better than a degree in statistics or psychology.)

Developing Your Marketing Plan

Now that you've developed your objectives, move on to developing your own personal marketing plan. This means zeroing in on likely opportunities and developing a specific marketing strategy for these opportunities. Let's talk about that now.

Identify likely opportunities

An important step in strategy planning is identifying potentially attractive opportunities. Depending on where you are in your academic training, this can vary all the way from preliminary exploration to making detailed lists of companies that offer the kinds of jobs that interest you. If you're just getting started, talk to your school's career counselors and placement officers about the kinds of jobs being offered to your school's graduates. Your marketing instructors can help you be realistic about ways you can match your training, abilities, and interests to job opportunities. Also, it helps to read business publications such as *BusinessWeek, Fortune, The Wall Street Journal,* and *Advertising Age.* If you are interested in opportunities in a particular industry, check at your library or on the Internet to see if there are trade publications or websites that can bring you up to speed on the marketing issues in that area. Your library or college may also have an online service to make it easier to search for articles about specific companies or industries. And many companies have their own websites that can be a very useful source of information.

Don't overlook the business sections of your local newspapers to keep in touch with marketing developments in your area. And take advantage of any opportunity to talk with marketers directly. Ask them what they're doing and what satisfactions they find in their jobs. Also, if your college has a marketing club, join it and participate actively in the club's programs. It will help you meet marketers and students with serious interest in the field. Some may have had interesting job experiences and can provide you with leads on part-time jobs or exciting career opportunities.

If you're far along in your present academic training, list companies that you know something about or are willing to investigate, trying to match your skills and interests with possible opportunities. Narrow your list to a few companies you might like to work for.

If you have trouble narrowing down to specific companies, make a list of your personal interest areas—sports, travel, reading, music, or whatever. Think about the companies that compete in markets related to these interests. Often your own knowledge about these areas and interest in them can give you a competitive advantage in getting a job. This helps you focus on companies that serve needs you think are important or interesting. A related approach is to do a search on the Internet for websites related to your areas of interest. Websites often display ads or links to firms that are involved in that specific interest area. Further, many companies post job openings on their own websites or at websites that specialize in promoting job searches by many companies.

Then do some research on these companies. Find out how they are organized, their product lines, and their overall strategies. Try to get clear job descriptions for the kinds of positions you're seeking. Match these job descriptions against your understanding of these jobs and your objectives. Jobs with similar titles may offer very different opportunities. By researching job positions and companies in depth, you should begin to have a feel for where you would be comfortable as an employee. This will help you narrow your target market of possible employers to perhaps five firms. For example, you may decide that your target market for an entry-level position consists of large corporations with (1) in-depth training programs, (2) a wide product line, and (3) a wide variety of marketing jobs that will enable you to get a range of experiences and responsibilities within the same company.

Planning your product

Just like any strategy planner, you must decide what product features are necessary to appeal to your target market. Identify which credentials are mandatory and which are optional. For example, is your present academic program enough, or will you need more training? Also, identify what technical skills are needed, such as computer programming or accounting. Further, are there any business experiences or extracurricular activities that might help make your product more attractive to employers? This might involve active participation in college organizations or work experience, either on the job or in internships.

Planning your promotion

Once you identify target companies and develop a product you hope will be attractive to them, you have to tell these potential customers about your product. You can write directly to prospective employers, sending a carefully developed résumé that reflects your strategy planning. Or you can visit them in person (with your résumé). Many colleges run well-organized interviewing services. Seek their advice early in your strategy planning effort.

Implementing Your Marketing Plan

When you complete your personal marketing plan, you have to implement it, starting with working to accomplish your short-run objectives. If, as part of your plan, you decide that you need specific outside experience, then arrange to get it. This may mean taking a low-paying job or even volunteering to work in political organizations or volunteer organizations where you can get that kind of experience. If you decide that you need skills you can learn in academic courses, plan to take these courses. Similarly, if you don't have a good understanding of your opportunities, then learn as much as you can about possible jobs by talking to professors, taking advanced courses, and talking to businesspeople. Of course, trends and opportunities can change—so continue to read business publications, talk with professionals in your areas of interest, and be sure that the planning you've done still makes sense.

Strategy planning must adapt to the environment. If the environment changes or your personal objectives change, you have to develop a new plan. This is an ongoing process—and you may never be completely satisfied with your strategy planning. But even trying will make you look much more impressive when you begin your job interviews. Remember, while all employers would like to hire a Superman or a Wonder Woman, they are also impressed with candidates who know what they want to do and are looking for a place where they can fit in and make a contribution. So planning a personal strategy and implementing it almost guarantee you'll do a better job of career planning, and this will help ensure that you reach your own objectives, whatever they are.

Whether or not you decide to pursue a marketing career, the authors wish you the best of luck in your search for a challenging and rewarding career, wherever your interests and abilities may take you.

Video Cases

Basic Marketing includes two different types of marketing cases: the 8 special video cases in this section and the 36 traditional cases in the next section. All of the cases offer you the opportunity to evaluate marketing concepts at work in a variety of real-world situations. However, the video cases add a multimedia dimension because we have produced a special video to accompany each of the written cases. The videos are available to professors who adopt *Basic Marketing* for use in their course. (These case-based videos are in addition to the teaching videos we have custom produced and made available to instructors for possible use with other parts of the text.)

The videos bring to life many of the issues considered in each case. However, you can read and analyze the written case descriptions even if there is no time or opportunity to view the video. Either way, you'll find the case interesting and closely tied to the important concepts you've studied in the text.

The set of questions at the end of each case will get you started in thinking about the marketing issues in the case. Further, we provide instructors with a number of suggestions on using the video cases—both for group discussion in class or individual assignments. Thus, as is also true with the traditional cases in the next section, the video cases can be used in many different ways and sequences. You can analyze all of the cases, or only a subset. In fact, the same case can be analyzed several times for different purposes. As your understanding of marketing deepens throughout the course, you'll "see" many more of the marketing issues considered in each case.

1. Chick-fil-A: "Eat Mor Chikin" (Except on Sunday)*

There aren't many companies like Chick-fil-A. Most U.S. companies struggle to balance ambitious financial objectives with the desire to be ethical in business dealings and demonstrate a social conscience. Chick-fil-A easily surpasses industry norms for financial performance and eagerly embraces and protects a corporate culture rich with religious values and charity. The contrast is striking to most observers. Yet the Chick-fil-A phenomenon is easily understood when you study its entrepreneurial heritage.

S. Truett Cathy, founder, chairman, and CEO of Chick-fil-A, started his restaurant career in 1946 when he and his brother Ben opened a restaurant in Atlanta called the Dwarf Grill (renamed the Dwarf House two years later). It was not until 1967 that Cathy opened the first Chick-fil-A restaurant in Atlanta's Greenbriar Shopping Center. He is credited with introducing the original boneless breast of chicken sandwich and pioneering the placement of fast-food restaurants in shopping malls. Today, Chick-fil-A is the second-largest quick-service chicken restaurant chain in the United States, based on sales ($1.975 billion in 2005). It operates more than 1,250 restaurants in 37 states and Washington, D.C.

Chick-fil-A's unique corporate culture derives from Cathy's Christian background and his desire to inspire and influence people. The company's official statement of corporate purpose is "to glorify God by being a faithful steward of all that is entrusted to us and to have a positive influence on all who come in contact with Chick-fil-A." This level of commitment to religious values is reflected in a number of ways. For example, all Chick-fil-A locations, in a mall or stand-alone, are closed on Sundays. Cathy has been quoted on numerous occasions as saying, "Our decision to close on Sunday (starting in 1946) was our way of honoring God and directing our attention to things more important than our business. If it took seven days to make a living with a restaurant, then we needed to be in some other line of work. Through the years, I have never wavered from that position."

Chick-fil-A also has an extensive corporate giving program. The company has helped thousands of restaurant employees, foster children, and other young people through the WinShape Foundation that Cathy established in 1984 to help "shape winners." The foundation sponsors WinShape Homes, which currently operates 14 homes in Georgia, Tennessee, Alabama, and Brazil. The WinShape College Program at Berry College in Rome, Georgia, is a co-op program offering joint four-year scholarship funding to incoming freshmen of up to $32,000. In addition to the WinShape scholarships, Chick-fil-A offers $1,000 college scholarships to its restaurant team members. Camp WinShape is a summer camp for boys and girls. WinShape Marriage provides development, education, and encouragement for married couples on the campus of WinShape Retreat, a multiuse conference and retreat facility located on the Mountain Campus of Berry College.

Chick-fil-A's unique corporate culture is matched by its equally unique marketing efforts, especially in the advertising and promotion areas. Its "Eat Mor Chikin" campaign is one of the longest-running advertising campaigns in the United States. Started in June 1995 when the first Chick-fil-A billboard was erected in Atlanta, the Eat Mor Chikin cows have become cult figures, convincing diners to stray from the herd of beef-burger eateries and to "eat mor chikin"—particularly in Chick-fil-A restaurants. In focus groups, respondents rate the cows as one of the three things they like best about the Chick-fil-A brand—the other two being the food and the company's policy of being closed on Sundays.

The Eat Mor Chikin theme, created by Dallas-based ad agency the Richards Group, was first introduced in 1995 as a three-dimensional billboard concept depicting a black-and-white cow sitting atop the back of another cow painting the words "Eat-Mor-Chikin" on the billboard. Since then, the theme has been used as the basis of an integrated marketing campaign, which encompasses billboards, in-store point-of-purchase materials, promotions, radio and TV advertising, clothing and merchandise (e.g., plush cows, bobble-head cows), and calendars. Introduced in 1998, Chick-fil-A's cow calendars have been a marketer's dream come true. The calendar is produced annually by the Richards Group. Sales have sharply increased—from 337,000 for the first printed calendar to 1.5 million for the 2006 renaissance-themed calendar entitled "Cows in Shining Armor," featuring "famous" medieval cows named Angus Kahn, Charbroilemagne, Boldhoof, Lady Guineveal, and Moolius Caesar. The calendars sell for $5 and contain Chick-fil-A food and beverage coupon offers.

Sponsorship of collegiate sports such as the Chick-fil-A Peach Bowl (renamed the Chick-fil-A Bowl in 2006) are another way in which Chick-fil-A builds its brand. A local promotion emphasis at the market and restaurant level completes Chick-fil-A's integrated marketing approach.

In 1998, the Eat Mor Chikin campaign won a national silver EFFIE award in the Fast Food/Restaurants category for creativity and effectiveness in advertising. The outdoor Advertising Association of America recognized Chick-fil-A and its renegade cows with the organization's OBIE Hall of Fame Award in 2006.

Chick-fil-A is growing rapidly through store openings and menu additions. Menu additions include Chick-fil-A Chick-n Strips in 1995, Chick-fil-A Cool Wraps in 2001, Chick-fil-A Southwest chargrilled salad in 2003, fruit cup in 2004, and a breakfast menu featuring Chick-fil-A Chick-n Minis, a chicken or sausage breakfast burrito, and a chicken, egg, and cheese bagel in 2004. The chain introduced the industry's first premium two-blend coffee line in 2005 with Café Blends and the complementary Cinnamon Cluster. Hand-Spun milkshakes were launched in 2006.

The company had sales of $1.975 billion in 2005 and forecasts sales of $3 billion by 2010. Also by 2010, the company looks to double its current size in terms of new locations, primarily through stand-alone restaurants and aggressive expansion into the western United States. Chick-fil-A also has licensed restaurants in nontraditional locations such as airports, corporate offices, hospitals, and college campuses.

Dan Cathy, the son of S. Truett Cathy and Chick-fil-A's current president and COO, takes restaurant openings seriously. The openings are not simple ribbon-cuttings. Cathy holds a dedication

*This case was prepared by Dr. J. B. Wilkinson, professor emeritus, Youngstown State University.

dinner during which he and other company leaders wait on newly hired employees. He also "camps out" the night before a store opening with Chick-fil-A raving fans and customers. Beginning in 2003, Chick-fil-A offered the first 100 customers in line at its new stores a free combo meal each week for a year. People lined up hours in advance, setting up tents and lawn chairs overnight in the parking lot to ensure a place in line. Observing this, Cathy decided to join them and since then, camping out with Chick-fil-A fans and customers at store openings has become a tradition for him.

Dan Cathy takes his role as a leader seriously and defines his role through his interaction with customers and employees. He frequently visits Chick-fil-A restaurants and often pitches in to help. Like his father, Dan Cathy is on a mission to meet customers, franchisees, and employees face to face and spread the Chick-fil-A business philosophy of "Second Mile" (making every extra effort) customer service, great food, and influencing others.

1. *What types of marketing strategies is Chick-fil-A following?*
2. *How would you describe Chick-fil-A's positioning strategy?*
3. *Is Sunday closing a competitive advantage for Chick-fil-A? Explain.*
4. *Should other retailers consider closing on Sunday? Why? Why not?*

2. Bass Pro Shops (Outdoor World)*

Have you ever seen an elk, an antelope, or a buffalo? What about a largemouth bass? Don't fret—you don't have to go to Montana to see what wildlife looks like! You can visit your nearest Bass Pro Shops Outdoor World and experience merchandising at its best, participate in workshops that teach outdoor skills (e.g., safe boating and hunting, beginning fishing, outdoor cooking, fly tying, nature photography, and GPS navigation), and take advantage of in-store amusements like an indoor trout stream, shooting arcades, or a live mermaid show (in the Las Vegas store). Better yet, you can visit the original Outdoor World store referred to as the "Grand Daddy," located in Springfield, Missouri, and spend your vacation at the largest hunting, boating, camping, and fishing outlet in the country—330,000 square feet of experiential retailing!

Bass Pro Shops are part of a larger trend in retailing called "destination development"—a trend in retail development that blends goods and services with theater and entertainment. Destination retailers offer shoppers more than just merchandise; each offers a unique environment in which customers enjoy a quality personal experience. The idea that a store is more than just a "big box filled with merchandise" has spawned a number of destination developments that function as open-air centers with exciting landscapes and architecture. Each store within the development operates as a stage for fresh and engaging experiences for shoppers (e.g., the Bass Pro Shops stock-car-racing simulations, snowboarding, or natural rock-climbing walls) and with unusual attractions, activities, learning opportunities, theme restaurants, and entertainment. These types of developments act as "tourism districts," attracting visitors from 200 to 300 miles away.

Bass Pro Shops have successfully implemented the concept of destination development. Operating about 50 large retail stores in the United States and one in Canada, Bass Pro Shops has become the nation's leading retailer of outdoor gear. Its stores rank among the top tourist destinations in their respective states. Over 100 million people visit its stores annually and spend an estimated $1.9 billion to experience one of the most exciting store environments in retailing today!

Industry analysts agree that Bass Pro stores are unlike any other in terms of customer service, awesome displays and visual imagery, exciting activities, and deep merchandise assortments in fishing, boating, hunting, outdoor gear, and camping. All stores have several common features including: taxidermy mounts, indoor water displays that showcase fish species, Outdoor Skills Workshops, artwork, and activity areas (e.g., archery and firing ranges, fishing tournaments). In addition, each store is uniquely designed to pick up the local flavor of the area's outdoor heritage and to include historical pictures, indigenous wildlife exhibits, and artifacts from local hunters and fishers. Several stores are spectacular in this regard. For example, the Denham Springs, Louisiana, store (near Baton Rouge) opened to crowds of shoppers (65,000 in the first four days). The store features an artistic replication of a Louisiana swamp complete with towering cypress trees draped in Spanish moss. Another example is the Bass Pro Shops Sportsman's Center in Miami, Florida. It is designed to make visitors feel like they are walking through a sunken ship, complete with barnacle-encrusted trusses. Suspended ceiling dioramas portray underwater scenes, and colorful fish appear to swim overhead. The Bass Pro Shops store located along the western shore of Lake Ray Hubbard (in Dallas, Texas) has a panoramic view of the lake through floor-to-ceiling windows that extend the entire Eastern exposure of the building. As shoppers progress toward this enticing feature, they have an equally panoramic view of a vast indoor boat showroom that can be reached by descending twin staircases that circle past waterfalls and around a swimming pool–size aquarium. The store also features a 365-seat World Famous Islamorada Fish Company Restaurant overlooking the lake. The recently opened Independence, Missouri, store features an indoor mill with a working wheel plus a 30-acre park complete with a lake stocked with bass and bluegill where customers can try out their new purchases.

Bass Pro stores have been difficult for competitors to emulate. They are large, expensive, and labor intensive. For example, the new 150,000-square-foot store in Rossford, Ohio (near Toledo) will employ 250 to 300 associates, many of whom are highly skilled in outdoor activities like fly-fishing, boating, and hunting. To make each Bass Pro store look different, an in-house group located in Nixa, Missouri, designs the interior and exterior of stores. An eclectic group of artisans and craftspeople—blacksmiths,

*This case was prepared by Dr. J. B. Wilkinson, professor emeritus, Youngstown State University.

metalworkers, welders, woodcarvers, and fabricators—handmake the chandeliers, lights, lanterns, wood carvings, ironwork, murals, mounted animals, displays, and special features that go into the stores. About 30 percent of each store's retail space is devoted to aquariums, waterfalls, murals, metalwork, museum-quality dioramas, and fireplaces. Bass Pro Shops' philosophy on merchandising also ups the ante. In-store displays aren't just fixtures—they are marketing tools designed to reflect local traditions and attract customers. For example, in the Lake Ray Hubbard store, canoes serve as shelving for apparel. In-store digital networks entertain and educate shoppers (how-to spots, technical features, PSAs for fishing, hunting, and conservation) and provide targeted advertising at the point of sale (vendor-sponsored ads and in-store promotions). The programming also includes vivid scenes of the outdoors and highlights of its NASCAR team. Six to seven 42-inch plasma-screen displays are located in key departments of each Bass Pro store. Some of the programming content is common across all stores, and some of it is customized to fit an individual store (targeted marketing). In addition, the level of customer service has become legendary. Bass Pro Shops has been recognized many times for its conservation efforts and outdoor education programs. The company supports a wide range of environmental, habitat conservation, and youth education programs through philanthropic efforts.

Bass Pro Shops can trace its roots to a small fishing department started by founder John Morris in 1972 to sell homemade bait and worms. Located in the back of his dad's liquor store in Springfield, Missouri (on the road to Table Rock Lake and Branson), the business was popular enough that Morris launched a catalog in 1974 to sell homemade bait. Soon, it became the world's largest mail-order sporting goods store. The flagship Springfield store has been improved over the years to become the tourist mecca that it is today. Along the way, other businesses were added: American Rod and Gun in 1975 (a wholesaling entity serving independently owned retailers), Tracker Marine in 1978 (a producer of recreational boats for Tracker dealerships and independent marine dealers under various brands, including Tracker Boats), Big Cedar Lodge in 1988 (a resort on Table Rock Lake), and the Islamorada Fish Company Restaurant chain. Other endeavors include Bass Pro Shops Outdoor World Television (on the Outdoor Channel), Bass Pro Shops Outdoor World Radio, Outdoor World Tips (written for newspapers and magazines), and Bass Pro Shops NASCAR participation. Beginning in 1995, the company began adding stores, beginning with the Bass Pro Shops Sportsman's Warehouse in Atlanta, Georgia. Since then, more than 48 stores have been added to the chain. Bass Pro Shops is regarded as the nation's leading retailer of outdoor gear, selling through massive stores, catalogs, and a website (www.basspro.com).

However, industry analysts have posed the question, "Are there limits to growth in the sporting and outdoor goods retail category?" Competition is intense. Competitors include large-format sporting goods stores, traditional and specialty sporting goods stores, mass-merchandisers, and catalog and Internet-based retailers. The most direct competitor to Bass Pro Shops is Cabela's—a chain of retail stores that has similar but less distinctive décor and merchandise. Other important competitors include Sports Authority, Dick's Sporting Goods, Academy Sports and Outdoors, Gander Mountain, Sportsman's Warehouse, and Walmart. All are growing rapidly despite the fact that the industry is declining in terms of active participants in outdoor activities like hunting, fishing, and camping. Some markets such as Denver, Kansas City, Dallas, and Milwaukee seem "overstuffed" with outdoor chains. But some experts are predicting renewed growth in outdoor sales as consumers experience Bass Pro's destination stores. They point to Home Depot's ability to "grow its customer base" (increasing the number of "do-it-yourself" consumers) through how-to clinics and quality construction materials and tools. In addition, U.S. demographics favor increased sales of outdoor goods as the baby-boom generation retires and takes up more leisure-time activities.

Pessimists argue that large-format stores are risky in economic downturns. To build a Bass Pro Shop Outdoor World requires a big initial investment. Once open, high overhead and low inventory turnover are common in some merchandise categories. As a consequence, break-even sales must draw customers from a large trading area. Recessions and adverse weather conditions may also hurt sales, especially in overstocked markets.

Despite concerns by industry experts, recent Bass Pro store openings have attracted hordes of customers. It's been estimated that the average customer travels two hours to reach the store and shops for more than three hours! Shoppers also seem blind to pricing differences for identical products between Bass Pro stores and discounters like Walmart. All of this suggests that destination retailing works and that the marriage between retailing and entertainment is here to stay!

1. *Prepare a S.W.O.T. analysis for Bass Pro Shops. What types of strategies do you recommend based on your analysis?*
2. *Can you think of retailers in other categories that might successfully emulate the format and execution of Bass Pro Shops?*

3. Toyota Prius: The Power of Excellence in Product Innovation and Marketing*

Prius (Latin for "to go before") was introduced to the Japanese market in 1997 amid much publicity and extravaganza. It was the world's first mass-produced car powered by a combination of gasoline and electricity. For the Toyota Motor Corporation, the Prius product launch represented a major strategic commitment and a long-term financial gamble.

The Prius story begins in the early 1990s when Toyota released its first Earth Charter, setting the goal of minimizing its overall environmental impact. In September 1993, the company began to plan for the development of a car for the next century.

*This case was prepared by Dr. J. B. Wilkinson, professor emeritus, Youngstown State University.

Called Globe 21st Century, or G21, the plan was to produce a car with better fuel economy and lower emissions than existing automobiles.

Alternative ideas were considered before deciding to press ahead with a gas-electric hybrid system; these included direct-injection diesel engines, electric motors, hydrogen-powered fuel cells, and solar-powered vehicles. Mass production of gasoline-electric hybrids was not possible until recently. Improved technology with respect to batteries and powerful control electronics to coordinate the two propulsion systems made the idea more attractive.

GM (as well as Ford, Honda, and Toyota) failed to successfully market electric cars in the 1990s. Although GM's EV1 was a technical triumph, consumers were scared off by its limited battery life. All three American carmakers developed diesel-electric hybrid cars in the 1990s, but none were deemed acceptable to the market. A diesel engine is more expensive than a gasoline engine, so a diesel hybrid required a higher price premium. Development of a hydrogen-powered fuel cell vehicle was simply not technically feasible within the time frame that Toyota had set for its goal.

The hybrid technology chosen to power the Prius combines a gasoline engine with an integrated electric-drive system. Like conventional cars and trucks, the hybrid system relies on a gasoline-fueled engine to generate power; the electric motor system provides a second power channel. These two complementary systems work together to create a more efficient powertrain.

At start-up, only the electric motor is used, and it powers the vehicle at low- to mid-range speeds. Under normal driving conditions, the gas engine is engaged and power is allocated between the two engines to maximize efficiency during operations such as acceleration, deceleration, coasting, and stopping. In the city, with its stop-and-go traffic, the Prius relies more on the electric engine, whereas for highway driving, the gas engine is the primary power producer. The benefits of this powertrain combination are greater fuel efficiency and low exhaust emissions. Compared to electric cars, the hybrid system offers a high level of convenience since the battery is recharged from surplus engine power.

The Prius development effort took four years. The biggest challenges Toyota engineers faced were handling the powerful voltage between the battery and the electric motor and determining how to fit the gas engine, the electric motor, and a jumbo battery into a compact car frame. Solving these problems involved adapting the heavy-duty transistors used in Japan's bullet trains and shrinking the parts through computer modeling. A prototype car was shown to the public in 1995 and in December 1997, the first production car rolled out of Toyota's Takaoka factory in Toyota City near Nagoya. For the next two years, Toyota sold Prius only in Japan. First-year sales were around 12,000 units due to limited production capability. Toyota elected to defer capital investment in manufacturing facilities and to produce the Prius on existing assembly lines: a "hedging" strategy in case the hybrid "flopped." The initial price was just $16,929, which industry analysts say was below the estimated cost of building a Prius. However, even at that price, buyers paid a premium of several thousand dollars for a Prius compared to similar-size conventional cars. Industry analysts speculated that Toyota would have to sell around 250,000 Priuses a year to make a profit.

Prius was introduced to the U.S. market in 2000. The Honda Insight, a two-seater gas-electric hybrid, had been in the U.S. market for a year with first-year sales of about 3,500. Toyota limited U.S. sales of the Prius to 17,000 units during the introductory year. Base price for the Prius was $19,995 (roughly the same as for a Honda Insight). Both the Prius and the Insight were priced below cost but several thousand dollars higher than similar-sized conventional cars. However, the higher price was partially offset by better gasoline mileage (52 m.p.g. in city driving for the first-generation Prius).

The advertising campaign that launched the Prius into the U.S. market used "Prius Genius" as its tagline and courted leading-edge buyers of the technological generation. Celebrity buyers like Cameron Diaz heightened Toyota's publicity efforts, which included an "Engine of Change" tour—a 15-city circuit where the Prius was shown to leaders in government, media, and environmental groups. In addition, the Prius was seen by millions of Academy Award viewers as an "alternative limo" used by environmentally friendly Hollywood celebrities.

Toyota enjoyed a dramatic jump in Prius sales after its U.S. debut. Sales were so strong that demand outstripped production capability. It was not uncommon for buyers to wait up to six months to receive their new Prius. By 2004, global sales totaled 250,000, and Toyota was earning a modest profit per vehicle. The second-generation Prius (Prius II) hit U.S. showrooms in October 2003. As other car manufacturers (Ford, GM) entered the market with hybrid vehicles and Honda increased its number of hybrid models (Civic), Toyota changed its marketing strategy to emphasize its Hybrid Synergy Drive in Prius II as the powertrain of choice—a classic selective demand-building strategy, suitable for the growth stage in a product's life cycle. The objective of this strategy was to differentiate Toyota's hybrid technology from other hybrid systems emerging in the market. Unlike competitive systems on the market in 2004, the new high-voltage/high-power Hybrid Synergy Drive powertrain was capable of operating in either gas or electric modes, as well as a mode in which both the gas engine and electric motor are in operation. Compared to the original Toyota Hybrid System (THS) in Prius I, the new Hybrid Synergy Drive system delivered significantly more power and performance, best-in-class fuel economy, and best-in-market emissions performance. Toyota also worked to reduce the cost of its hybrids. Because gasoline-electric hybrids employ two motors under the hood, hybrids are more expensive to produce than conventional gas-powered vehicles (about $3,000 more). Cost reductions would lead to price reductions, making Toyota's hybrid cars more affordable.

The 2004 second-generation Prius was designed to appeal to a broader market. It was larger, more powerful, with numerous technical improvements and aerodynamic styling (plus a four-door, lift-back configuration), and loaded with high-tech options like the Smart Entry/Smart Start, which allows the driver to open and start the vehicle without inserting a key. Other options included a hands-free cell phone system and a navigation system. Base price was held at $19,995, the same as the first Prius cost during its introductory year in the United States. This second-generation car won some of the industry's most prestigious awards and was named European Car of the Year 2005.

The success of the Prius has provided Toyota with numerous product opportunities, including hybrid technology extension and licensing strategies. Toyota introduced a hybrid Lexus

RX400h (2004) and Highlander (2005). A hybrid Camry and Lexus GS sedan were planned for 2006. Toyota expects that a quarter of its unit sales in the United States will use gasoline-electric technology by 2010. To achieve that goal, virtually all Toyota vehicles including trucks will offer hybrid power systems.

1. *In what stage of the product life cycle is the Toyota Prius? Explain.*
2. *Describe the marketing strategies being followed by Toyota for the Prius.*
3. *Do you think Toyota should convert all of its cars to hybrids? Why? Why not?*

4. Potbelly Sandwich Works Grows through "Quirky" Marketing*

Want an inexpensive gourmet sandwich served in a fun and funky place by friendly young people? Lots of people do, including celebrities Will Ferrell, Sandra Bullock, and Keanu Reaves. In fact, Potbelly Sandwich Works was ranked as one of the top fastest-growing chains in the restaurant industry.[1]

Chances are you have never eaten at a Potbelly, but you probably will in the near future. Under the leadership of Bryant Keil, chairman and CEO, Chicago-based Potbelly Sandwich Works is expanding rapidly (see Table 1). Keil bought the original Potbelly in 1996. Prior to that, it was a very successful neighborhood sandwich shop run by a couple who had originally started the business as an antique store in 1977. They added homemade sandwiches and desserts to bolster the business and soon the food became more popular than the antiques. As time went on, booths were added along with ovens for toasting the sandwiches and the antiques became "décor" rather than merchandise for sale. A prominently placed antique potbelly stove provided inspiration for the sandwich shop's name.

Although Potbelly has many sandwich shop rivals in the fierce quick-serve segment of the restaurant industry, Potbelly has more than held its own. Billed as "a unique and quirky sandwich joint," it has a unique appeal. Potbelly's core strategy elements include *product, place, promotion,* and *price.*

Product

According to Keil, "Anyone can sell a sandwich. You need to sell an experience." Industry observers point to several aspects of the Potbelly experience that make it the first choice for young professionals on a quick lunch break. First is the menu, which features made-to-order toasted sandwiches, soups, homemade desserts, malts, shakes, and yogurt smoothies. Toasting is part of what makes Potbelly's sandwiches distinctive. Quality ingredients, including a freshly baked Italian sub roll and freshly sliced meats and cheese also contribute to superior value. Friendly service and an upbeat atmosphere, live music, antique fixtures, real books for customers to read or borrow, and vintage memorabilia create a homey environment for customers. The idea behind Potbelly is simple: superior value, fun-filled atmosphere, warm, comfy décor, and quick, friendly service.

Place

Potbelly stores average 2,200 square feet but can top 4,000 square feet. Most units have indoor seating for more than 50 and outdoor seating during warmer months. Geographic locations are selected carefully. Keil looks for cities that are not saturated with sandwich chains and have an urban/suburban density of core customers—young professionals less than 35 years old. Locations must be convenient for them since Potbelly stores rely on high repeat business. All units are corporate owned and operated.

Promotion

Historically, Potbelly Sandwich Works has not had an ad budget. Promotions are keyed to events like store openings and National Sandwich Day. For example, on National Sandwich Day, Potbelly hosts a "Belly Buster" sandwich-eating contest at Potbelly stores. Prizes are awarded to winners and runners-up. Diners randomly receive free meals. Other event promotions raise money for local charities such as food banks, and community-based reading and music appreciation programs.

Price

Potbelly sandwiches sell for $3.79. Sheila's Dream Bar, made of oatmeal, caramel and chocolate, is $1.29, while homemade chocolate chip or sugar cookies go for only 99 cents. Checks average about $6.50. Pricing is an integral part of the value Potbelly offers customers and can be summed up as, "Just good food at good prices!"

Considered separately, any one of Potbelly's marketing strategy elements may not seem overly powerful as a competitive weapon, but combined and implemented with zeal, they are a significant competitive threat to national, regional, and local competitors. Brands like Subway, Quiznos, Cosi, Panera, Jimmy John's, and Schlotzsky's Deli are wary that Potbelly will become a major national competitor. The Potbelly experience appears to be difficult to duplicate. For example, Quiznos may have similar food quality but not similar atmosphere; Cosi may have the hangout ambience down but not the food! Subway is especially vulnerable since it has neither the food nor the warm and comfy store environment.

Yet Potbelly has a tough road ahead. It requires management to maintain the superior performance of current units while creating new Potbelly units in new markets. Each Potbelly is special in terms of location, décor, and staff. The unit must be tailored to its neighborhood and community. Attentive, enthusiastic workers

---

*This case was prepared by Dr. J. B. Wilkinson, professor emeritus, Youngstown State University.

[1]"Way to Grow: A Tight Real Estate Market Doesn't Deter Top Chains' Expansion Plans," *Restaurants and Institutions,* July 2005, p. 121.

Table 1 Potbelly Store Openings by Year and City, 1997–2005

Market	1997	1998	1999	2000	2001	2002	2003	2004	2005	Total
Chicago	1	1	1	2	3	8	11	9	11	48*
Washington, D.C.						8	3	4	3	18
Michigan							4	2	1	7
Minnesota							1	3	2	6
Wisconsin							2		2	4
Indiana								1	1	2
Texas								3	8	11
Ohio									6	6
Total	1	1	1	2	3	16	21	22	34	102

*Includes the original Potbelly opened in 1977 and bought by Keil in 1996.

must be found. Food quality and a fun atmosphere must become an integral part of the store culture. Not an easy task!

1. *Identify and describe Potbelly's strategy in terms of product (present or new) and market (present or new).*
2. *How would you describe Potbelly's positioning strategy?*
3. *What types of environmental opportunities and threats do you see in Potbelly's external environment? How might they affect Potbelly's current strategy?*

5. Suburban Regional Shopping Malls: Can the Magic Be Restored?*

The suburban regional shopping mall is regarded by many as the "crown jewel" of shopping experiences. In a single location, shoppers can visit over a hundred stores, go to a movie, eat, walk, and lounge for an entire day in a secure, pleasant atmosphere sheltered from undesirable weather and the demands of everyday life. Most Americans at one time or another have escaped for the day to such a mall and felt "uplifted" in spirit by the experience. So pervasive is the suburban regional shopping mall that William Kowinski in the *The Malling of America* (1985) claims that in the United States alone there are more enclosed malls than cities, four-year colleges, or television stations! Indeed, few of us can remember a time when shopping was a trip to "downtown," or the central business district (CBD) of a large city.

Many suburban regional shopping malls are over one million square feet in size, contain over a hundred stores, and offer shoppers free parking, restaurants, play facilities, lounge facilities, restrooms, and movie theaters. Some centers even provide amusement rides and other entertainment opportunities. One of the dominant features of these large shopping complexes is the presence of multiple department stores that "anchor" the extreme points of the mall's layout and "pull" shoppers to the mall from surrounding suburban areas. Department stores also encourage shoppers to walk through the mall. In fact, department stores were the driving force behind the original development of suburban regional shopping malls and have played a critical role in their continuing success.

*This case and the script for the accompanying video were prepared by Dr. J. B. Wilkinson, professor emeritus, Youngstown State University, and Dr. David J. Burns, Xavier University.

The movement of traditional department stores from CBD locations to the suburbs, complete with large "full-line" departments, contributed greatly to the explosive growth of suburban regional shopping malls during the post–World War II era. At its inception, the suburban regional shopping mall was designed to be a substitute, or even a replacement, for a city's CBD, but without the usual congestion or parking difficulties. This strategy was particularly attractive after the opening of Southdale Center in suburban Minneapolis in 1956 (www.southdale.com), which demonstrated the viability of a regional shopping mall with multiple anchors.

In 2002 there were a total of 46,336 shopping centers in the United States, of which about 1,200 could be considered regional or superregional malls (www.icsc.org). In addition to regional and superregional malls, numerous types of shopping centers have evolved since the 1950s. The International Council of Shopping Centers has defined eight principal shopping center types: neighborhood, community, regional, superregional, fashion/specialty, power, theme/festival, and outlet.

The suburban regional shopping malls and their department store anchors enjoyed great success for almost 50 years and seemed virtually invincible to threats until the final decade of the twentieth century. During that era, several chinks developed in the competitive armor of this type of retail institution, and the problems seem to be getting worse. Shopper activity is declining: the number of tenant vacancies is increasing; and the delinquency rate on mall mortgages is disturbing. Increasingly larger percentages of consumer discretionary income are being spent elsewhere. To make matters worse, many of the older malls need renovating to remain attractive to shoppers. Renovation of an older mall can cost tens of millions of dollars.

Changes in consumers and in their wants and needs appear to be the major factor that underlies the woes of suburban regional shopping malls. Since the first multi-anchor center opened in 1956, the lifestyles of American families have changed significantly. In 1950, for instance, only 24 percent of wives worked outside the home; today, that percentage exceeds 60 percent. Women between the ages of 18 and 45, the mainstay of mall shoppers, simply do not have the time to shop like they once had. As a result, shopping has become much more purpose-driven. Shopping statistics bear this out. Shoppers are visiting suburban regional shopping malls less frequently, visiting fewer stores when they do shop, and also spending less time at the mall when they shop. Mall visitors, however, are more likely to make a purchase when they shop. Yet the typical suburban regional shopping mall was designed for a "shop-all-day" or a "shop-'til-you drop" philosophy.

Another consumer trend that spells trouble for suburban regional shopping malls is increased shopper price sensitivity. A wider selection of shopping alternatives from which to choose and the desire to make the family income go further (which, in essence, is equal to a pay increase) have proven to be strong forces pushing shoppers to comparison shop between retail establishments—something that most malls are not designed to facilitate. Despite the large number of stores contained within a regional suburban shopping mall, comparison shopping between stores is not an easy task. Most malls are laid out to cater to a leisure-oriented shopper. Similar stores are located in different wings of the shopping mall to encourage shoppers to walk through the entire center. Shoppers may walk upwards to a quarter-mile in their quest to compare products! This is not consistent with the desire for shopping convenience and efficiency on the part of most consumers.

Competition also has played a role in the problems that plague suburban regional shopping malls. High levels of competition characterize most mature industries, and the shopping center industry is no exception. Regional malls have both direct and indirect competitors. Direct competitors are nearby shopping centers with either similar or dissimilar formats. Indirect competitors comprise other types of retail store sites like freestanding or clustered sites and nonstore retailing sites. Nonstore retailing includes online shopping, catalog shopping, home TV shopping, telemarketing, and other forms of direct marketing, all of which have made considerable inroads into retail store sales. Suburban regional shopping malls have been especially vulnerable to both forms of competition.

Many of the more successful retailers (e.g., Kohl's, Home Depot) are located on freestanding sites or in large open-air centers—locations that have greater appeal to time-pressed, purpose-driven shoppers than mall locations. Similarly, many outlet malls, which cater to price-sensitive shoppers, are typically open-air centers to facilitate store access. In addition, some of the newer small shopping centers cater to a focused lifestyle (teen or professional woman) or have an organizing theme (home decor, hobby) that satisfies the specific needs of a market niche by offering a more focused product assortment than what can be found in a suburban regional shopping mall.

Oversupply of retail space has posed considerable problems to all shopping centers. The United States has 20 square feet for every man, woman, and child, compared to 1.4 square feet per person in Great Britain. Sales per square foot of retail space is declining in the United States. In fact, revenue from retail sales is contracting. It grew an average of 2.5 percent in the 1970s; 1.3 percent in the 1980s; and only 0.8 percent in the 1990s, adjusted for inflation. The result has been retail consolidation, store closings, and bankruptcies, leaving shopping centers fighting for a shrinking base of retail tenants.

Finally, department stores, the primary traffic generators for suburban regional shopping malls, are experiencing serious competitive problems. Over the past two decades, department stores have lost half of their market share to discounters and specialty stores. They also have suffered a significant sales revenue decline, causing store closings and consolidation. Given the role department stores have played as traffic generators for shopping malls, the problems of department stores have added to the problems of suburban regional shopping malls. Quite simply, fewer department store shoppers have meant fewer shoppers in the mall. To make matters worse, an empty department store space in a mall gives shoppers less reason to visit that portion of the mall and often leads to the closure of nearby stores. Besides being unproductive, the resulting empty retail space is unsightly, projecting the same image that empty storefronts in the CBDs of cities do—decay and decline.

The predictable outcome of all these changes is that construction of new suburban regional shopping malls has virtually come to a halt. Furthermore, a significant number of existing centers are being "decommissioned"—converted into alternative uses such as office space, learning centers, and telemarketing call centers, or torn down to be replaced by other forms of retail centers. Over 300 malls have been decommissioned since the mid-1990s, a trend which is expected to continue.

The dim outlook for suburban regional shopping malls has stimulated much creative thought about turnaround strategies for those still in operation. One turnaround strategy that has been suggested deals with the way suburban regional shopping malls are traditionally configured and involves changing the way stores in the center are arranged with respect to one another. The traditional layout locates similar stores in different wings or corridors of the center to encourage shoppers to travel through the entire center in their quest to locate and compare products. This type of layout maximizes customer interchange between stores but does not address shopping efficiency. Zonal merchandising represents a different approach to a center's layout. Under zonal merchandising, similar tenants are located in close proximity to one another. This reduces shopping time for shoppers who come to the mall to purchase a specific product. It also creates opportunities for differentiating mall areas in terms of decor, music, amenities, and special events to suit the tastes of shoppers who are most likely to be visiting stores in those areas.

Zonal merchandising has been used most commonly for fast food. Called "food courts," these clusters of fast-food providers have been very successful. Food court tenants have experienced higher levels of sales than under traditional layouts. Food courts also have shown that they are able to draw shoppers from other locations in the mall, similar to the traffic-generating role of a traditional anchor store.

Based on the success of the food court, several attempts to implement zonal merchandising on a wider scale have been made. Beginning with Bridgewater Commons in New Jersey (www.bridgewatercommons.com), several new projects have incorporated zonal merchandising principles, including Rivertown Crossings in Grand Rapids, Michigan (www.rivertowncrossings.com), which has grouped some categories of stores by product line carried, and Park Meadows in Denver, Colorado (www.parkmeadows.com), which has grouped stores by customer lifestyle.

The results of these endeavors have been promising, and General Growth (www.generalgrowth.com), the developer of Rivertown Crossings, plans to implement some form of clustering at all of its future projects. Attempts to reconfigure existing centers around zonal merchandising ideas, such as the changes at Glendale Galleria in Glendale, California (www.glendalegalleria.com), seem to be successful as well.

An alternative strategy, which has been proposed for turning around traditional suburban regional shopping malls, is the incorporation of entertainment within the center. The idea behind this strategy is quite simple: Add value to the shopper's visit to a mall and give shoppers additional reasons to shop in the mall rather than at home. Entertainment can run the gamut from simple play areas or a carousel for children to video arcades and virtual golf courses to a full-scale amusement park, such as the Mall of America (www.mallofamerica.com). However, adding entertainment offerings to suburban regional shopping malls does not guarantee success. The entertainment must be something that will attract shoppers and keep their interest for a lengthy period of time—not something which shoppers tire of easily. Also the effect of the entertainment activities on a center's retailing activities must be considered. Entertainment centers in suburban regional malls often attract people with social goals instead of shopping goals, which does not benefit a center's merchandise-based stores.

Some industry analysts suggest that the key to revitalizing the suburban regional shopping mall is to make the shopping experience itself more exciting. Even at Mall of America, the home of the largest mall-based entertainment facility in the United States, the primary attraction of the center is the entertainment and excitement provided by the shopping experience itself; shoppers find stores and products which they cannot find elsewhere in the region.

Most suburban regional shopping malls are unexciting. They offer shoppers a relatively nondescript homogeneous shopping experience. They look alike, possess the same stores, and sell the same products. What has been forgotten by mall managers is that entertainment, in a mall sense, is not necessarily what activities can be added to the center, but what entertainment is provided by the shopping experience. Shoppers are searching for shopping experiences that are fresh, different, and fun. To provide this experience, suburban regional shopping malls need to attract stores and sell products that are unique, interesting, and ever-changing. The recent addition of the Build-a-Bear Workshop to several suburban regional shopping malls is one such example. The Build-a-Bear Workshop (www.buildabear.com) is a novel retail concept that provides a playful, creative environment. The challenge for mall managers is to find new and exciting retailing concepts like Build-a-Bear Workshop on a continual basis.

The Easton Town Center in Columbus, Ohio (www.eastontowncenter.com) is an example of a suburban regional shopping center that was explicitly designed to provide shoppers with a fun, exciting, entertaining place to shop. Easton Town Center was designed as an open-air center that mimics small-town America over 50 years ago. The center possesses an entertainment-oriented product mix with numerous restaurants, 30 movie theaters, spas, a comedy club, a cabaret, specialty stores, and Nordstrom and Lazarus as anchor department stores. The center has a "town square" and special event areas. It is considered to be one of the most successful retail centers in the region.

The challenge to mall developers and managers is clear. Since the opening of Southdale Center in 1956, changes in competition, retailing, and consumer shopping behavior have resulted in significant threats and opportunities. If suburban regional shopping malls are to enjoy continued success, they must creatively adapt to the new industry and shopping environment. Managers and owners of suburban regional shopping malls must determine the change strategy that is best for them. A number of considerations should guide their thinking—the competition, the needs of shoppers in their area, the opportunities available, and the center's resources. Just as one size does not fit all, the same turnaround strategy will not suit all suburban regional shopping malls.

1. *Imagine yourself as the manager of a struggling local suburban regional shopping mall. What do you think the mall should do to improve its performance?*
2. *What shopping trends do you foresee over the next 10 years? How might these trends affect suburban regional shopping malls?*
3. *What new retail concepts can you identify? How might you learn about more? What strategies do you suggest for learning* about *new retail concepts?*

6. Strategic Marketing Planning in Big Brothers Big Sisters of America*

For more than a century Big Brothers and Big Sisters of America (BBBSA) has helped children reach their potential through professionally supported one-on-one mentoring. With a network of about 400 agencies in all 50 states, BBBSA serves approximately 260,000 children between the ages of 6 and 18. A sister organization, BBBS International, has a global scope with agencies in 12 countries and similar plans to expand and improve international programs.

*This case was prepared by Dr. Jane S. Reid, Youngstown State University.

Programs

BBBSA has two core programs:

1. **Community-based mentoring** that requires a mentor ("big") to meet with a child ("little") at least one hour each week to engage in community activities.
2. **School-based mentoring** that encourages "bigs" to meet with their "littles" in schools, libraries, and community centers at least once a week to talk and play.

BBBSA "matches" between children ("littles") and mentors ("bigs") are carefully administered and supported by rigorous standards and trained personnel. Professional staff ensure that matches are safe and well-suited to the individuals involved. Each potential mentor ("big") is evaluated and trained before a match takes place. With each match, the intent is to provide a satisfying experience for both parties and to help the child develop positive outcomes.

BBBSA attempts to meet the needs of the most vulnerable children in a community. Because the demographics of these vulnerable children vary from community to community, BBBSA has developed different programs that consider these racial, ethnic, and social demographics. Each local affiliate launches a specific program that meets the needs of its community. The targets of these programs include:

1. **African American mentoring.** BBBSA recognizes that African American boys constitute one of the most at-risk populations in the United States. So it makes a concerted effort to recruit male African American "bigs" to serve this population by partnering with the Alpha Phi Alpha fraternity and United Methodist Men.
2. **Hispanic mentoring.** Given the huge increases in the Hispanic population, BBBSA also recognizes the many needs of Hispanic children in the U.S. It actively recruits Latino "bigs" by building collaborations within Hispanic communities.
3. **Native American mentoring.** With over 4 million Native Americans and Alaskan Natives living in the U.S. and more than a quarter of them living at or below poverty, BBBSA began a recruitment initiative in 2007 in Native American communities. The BBBSA program is run under the guidance of both formal and informal elders, members of Native American community programs, and American Indian/Alaska Native board members with 30 agencies participating in 16 states.
4. **Amachi Program (Mentoring Children of Promise).** BBBSA developed this program to serve children who have a parent in prison. Amachi is a Nigerian word of hope—"who knows but what God has brought us through this child." BBBSA focuses on recruiting "bigs" from local congregations.
5. **Military Children.** BBBSA established a partnership with the T. Boone Pickens Foundation to serve children with a parent in the military and to provide civic engagement for military personnel returning from deployment. A BBBSA Military Community Advisory Council has been set up for this program.

Organization

Like most national nonprofit organizations, BBBSA has two levels of operation. The national office in Philadelphia has an executive staff and national board of directors that provide strategic direction and support to local agencies across the U.S. Each local agency has an executive director, board of directors, and program staff who address the specific needs of children within its community. Each agency must operate under an affiliation agreement with BBBSA, which gives it the rights to:

1. Operate an organization using the BBBSA name.
2. Receive a designated service community area which is a specific geographical area in the U.S. The local agency is restricted to recruitment and fund-raising within that geographical area.
3. Associate with BBBSA long term, unless the affiliation is terminated by the local board or by the national office.
4. Collaborate with BBBSA and other member agencies.

Membership fees are paid quarterly and are based on the total expenditures of the agency. Four deductions are allowed: fees paid to BBBSA, capital purchases, depreciation, and fund-raising expenses. The fee is then calculated by taking 3.8 percent of the first $100,000; 2.25 percent of the next $100,000; 1 percent of the next $300,000; and 0.5 percent of the remaining expenditures. The affiliation fee is directly related to the size of the agency, with larger agencies paying more for the national affiliation than smaller agencies. Agencies are also given discounts if they pay their entire affiliation fee up front: 5 percent discount if paid by January 31, 4.5 percent discount if paid by February 28, or 4 percent discount if paid by March 31. Otherwise, affiliation fees are due on March 31, June 30, September 30, and December 31. In order to better manage its own annual budget, the national office encourages early payments from the affiliated agencies.

Local agencies benefit from their national affiliation with BBBSA. First and foremost, the national office provides strategic direction to local agencies. Second, BBBSA sets standards that local agencies must follow in order to use the BBBSA brand, but through networking, local agencies are able to share "best practices." Local agencies also have access to research that the national office conducts. In addition, the national office provides a management information system (MIS) which allows local agencies to process information about volunteers, children, families, and donors. Further, the MIS helps local agencies manage their efforts and measure outcomes. Last, and probably the most important from a marketing standpoint, local agencies benefit from a nationally recognized brand with high credibility, which helps them in recruiting "bigs" and "littles" and attracting donors. This is especially important during economic downturns when funding from foundations, the public sector, and individual donors decline. Agencies with proven programs and high brand recognition and credibility are more likely to survive. Moreover, BBBSA has a competitive advantage compared to other nonprofit organizations that provide programs for youth. It is the only national organization that focuses on one-on-one mentoring.

Strategic planning initiatives

In 2000, BBBSA launched its strategic-planning initiative by hiring Bridgespan Consulting (www.bridgespan.org). The Bridgespan Group helps nonprofit and philanthropic leaders to develop strategic plans and build organizations that inspire and accelerate social change. The use of a professional consulting service to develop a strategic planning process was made possible by the generous support of the Edna McConnell Clark Foundation (www.emcf.org), a foundation that seeks to improve the lives of people in poverty, especially low-income youth in the United States.

The first step was to establish a steering committee to work with the consulting firm. The steering committee consisted of four local agency leaders, one BBBSA board member who also served on a local BBBSA board, and five BBBSA leaders. One of the first activities of the committee was to collect information about the problems, practices, opinions, and attitudes of local agencies. The committee surveyed over 160 local agencies and received input from leaders at over 70 agencies, representing all of the different regions, sizes, and types of communities served by BBBSA.

As part of the process, Bridgespan Consulting guided BBBSA through a S.W.O.T. analysis that included examining its mission statement: "To help children reach their potential through professionally supported, one-to-one relationships with measurable impact." As a result of the analysis, the vision statement became: "Successful mentoring relationships for all children who need and want them, contributing to better schools, brighter futures, and stronger communities for all." BBBSA also included a promise statement as part of its guiding principles, which commits BBBSA to a culture of diversity and inclusion, partnership and collaboration, continuous learning, people development, and high performance.

In setting its organizational goals, BBBSA built on its past strengths of accountability for outcomes in three areas: (1) the number of children served; (2) how well those children are served; and (3) which children are served, with a focus on children who are most in need and most likely to benefit from BBBSA programs. From there, BBBSA developed four goals with specific outcomes:

1. Quality growth—to serve over 300,000 children by 2010 (a 25 percent increase over its 2006 level).
2. Positive outcomes for a higher percentage of children served—increasing the average match length from 10 to 13 months and increasing the six-month retention rate from 80 percent to 85 percent. The overall intent of this goal is to increase the strength of the relationship between "bigs" and "littles." During this planning period, BBBSA also committed to lead the development of new real-time outcome measures for local affiliates.
3. Increased intentionality about which children are served. Although each local agency serves a unique population, the overriding national goals would be
    a. Increase the percentage of boys served and the percentage of male volunteers (from 38 percent to 41 percent of all volunteers). The focus on males is to counteract the recent increase in the number of female matches and to better serve the large number of boys on the waiting lists.
    b. Increase the percentage of Hispanic youth served from 17 to 22 percent of all matches.
    c. Increase the percentage of African American and Hispanic youth served by same-ethnicity volunteers to at least 57 percent by increasing African American volunteers from 15 to 18 percent of all volunteers and by increasing Hispanic volunteers from 7 to 13 percent of all volunteers.
    d. Establish clear baseline data for measuring the percent of "littles" who are in moderate-to-high need.
4. Strengthen local agencies' capacity for sustainable, quality growth. The specific goals for making that happen include
    a. 10 percent annual total revenue growth to $385 million by 2010.
    b. 10 percent revenue growth by 50 percent of local agencies (up from 35 percent).
    c. 3 months' cash reserves by 65 percent of local agencies (up from 49 percent).
    d. $1 million in revenues by 80 percent of large market agencies (up from 67 percent).
    e. $500k in revenues by 40 percent of regional and smaller market agencies (up from 20 percent).
    f. Board and leadership development plans in 60 percent of agencies. In addition, each agency with $500k or more in revenue should have four key leadership positions: CEO, VP Program, Chief Development Officer, and VP Partnership/Recruitment.

The goals outlined above are detailed, measurable, and a "stretch" for both the local agencies and the national office. However, BBBSA outlined specific implications and expectations for the national office and agencies.

Agencies

- Sustained, quality growth should be at the core of each agency's effort.
- Each agency should work toward maximizing its impact and community support by being intentional about whom it serves.
- Both the Community-Based Mentoring and School-Based Mentoring programs should be strong and robust in terms of quality and growth.
- Resource development (funds and volunteer recruitment) should be a central leadership focus for all agencies.
- Agencies should ensure that their talent and organizational structures are strong enough to support the complex challenges of sustained quality growth.

National office

- Leadership on the definition of success (agreement on "what is achieved" versus "what is done").
- Increased direct support to agencies through financial grants.
- Maintenance of current level of support to agencies with a focus on technology, outcome data, and best practices sharing.
- Enhanced capacity in key central functions including marketing, corporate partnerships, and human resources.
- Emphasis on talent and leadership in the five key roles—board, executive director, vice president of program, chief development officer, and vice president of partnerships.

Research plays an important role within BBBSA. Its MIS is designed to measure the effectiveness of its programs. In a nationwide study, BBBSA found that "littles" were

- 46 percent less likely to begin using illegal drugs.
- 27 percent less likely to begin using alcohol.
- 52 percent less likely to skip school.
- 37 percent less likely to skip a class.

BBBSA has encouraged and supported similar strategic planning efforts in local agencies. Local agencies are encouraged to identify appropriate targets within their communities and to adapt national programs and strategies with measurable objectives. One example of how the national organization supports the marketing efforts of local agencies is public service announcements (PSAs). BBBSA has produced several PSAs that address the specific goals of recruiting male "bigs" and "littles" of both Hispanic and African American ethnicities. However, local agencies must decide which PSAs to use and then get local broadcast stations to run them—perhaps to coincide with major fund-raising events like Bowl for Kids' Sake. Local agencies also develop collateral material such as posters, flyers, and brochures.

Current and future strategic initiatives

BBBSA is committed to reviewing its strategic plan on a three-year cycle because it believes the key to an organization's survival is recognizing opportunities and threats and adjusting to them.

BBBSA has already begun its second planning cycle and it faces some specific challenges. The first is to achieve greater consistency in its brand image. Although local agencies are autonomous, BBBSA needs to have a consistent image across all communication efforts: ads, PSAs, events, web pages, etc.

Another key concern (identified in focus group research) is that BBBSA is now viewed as a "volunteer agency"—not an agency to which people would consider donating money. Consequently, this perception needs to be modified so that, when people think of BBBSA, they think of becoming donors as well as volunteers.

BBBSA recruitment is (and will continue to be) constrained by economic concerns and family demands. These constraints make it hard to attract not only volunteers, but also active and talented people to serve on boards of local agencies or to hire competent staff at modest salaries.

To address some of these concerns, BBBSA has initiated a repositioning campaign (Project: BigChange$) at the national level. It is working with Publicis Groupe on a pro-bono basis to redefine mentoring in a more powerful way and to establish itself as a donor-supported, as well as volunteer-supported, organization. To coordinate the campaign, the national office has provided local agencies with specific strategies for communicating to potential donors and volunteers. Some key points are

- Emphasizing BBBSA's commitment to measurable outcomes.
- Connecting donors to its program similar to the connection that volunteers feel.
- Describing services as donor-funded and not "free."
- Ensuring that each staff member understands his/her position is funded by a donor.
- Explaining to each potential "big" that donors make matches possible.
- Using adult "littles" (alumni) to demonstrate successes.
- Focusing on stewardship—the impact that the agency and the donors have on the community.

BBBSA is a strong nonprofit organization. It prides itself on being accountable to its stakeholders by providing meaningful and effective programs to children. Under a new president and CEO, BBBSA seems poised to be a significant influence during the next decade. It's focusing on its strengths and addressing its problems through strategic planning.

1. *Compare strategic planning by BBBSA with planning by for-profit organizations. What are the similarities? What are the differences?*
2. *Using the exhibit on the marketing strategy planning process in Chapter 2, identify the components of BBBSA's strategic planning process from the information presented in this case. Who are BBBSA's customers and competitors? How has BBBSA chosen to segment its market? Describe BBBSA's target markets. How does BBBSA differentiate itself from the "competition"? How would you describe the 4Ps of BBBSA's marketing strategy?*
3. *What are the benefits of a local nonprofit organization affiliating with a national nonprofit organization? Can you identify any disadvantages?*
4. *Refer to the BBBSA website (www.bbbs.org). What changes have occurred in the mission, vision, goals, and strategies? Has BBBSA successfully met the goals stated in this case? Has the organization successfully overcome the challenges of brand image and recruitment of volunteers?*

7. Invacare Says, "Yes, You Can!" to Customers Worldwide*

"On this vote the yeas are two hundred and nineteen, the nays are two hundred and twelve. The motion to concur in the Senate amendment is adopted." As he watched the U.S. House of Representatives pass Health Care Reform on March 23, 2010, Invacare Chairman and CEO Malachi "Mal" Mixon contemplated the impact of this landmark legislation on his company.

Company and industry history

Modern devices that provide mobility where it is needed can trace their history to the Fay Manufacturing Company in Elyria, Ohio, in the 1880s. Originally a bicycle and tricycle manufacturer, the company changed directions when Winslow Fay recognized the need for mobility among wounded veterans and children. He redesigned his tricycles to enable people considered "crippled" at that time to move about. After achieving nationwide distribution of these products, Fay sold out to the Worthington Manufacturing Company in the early 1890s. After a series of mergers and acquisitions, the company became Invacare and, in 1979, an entrepreneurial group led by Mal Mixon and J. B. Richey purchased the company.

Changes in the company paralleled changes in the wheelchair industry. Although wheelchair-like devices were used in ancient times, something akin to modern wheelchairs were not developed until the 16th century. However, since chronically ill or disabled people had short life spans, the need for wheelchairs was not perceived to be important. By the late 19th century, survival rates were higher, but most people needing a wheelchair were considered to be invalids—best kept at home or in an institution. Two world wars and a polio pandemic in the first half of the 20th century greatly increased the number of people with limited mobility, but attitudes about their care had not changed much.

When Franklin Delano Roosevelt, President of the United States from 1933 to 1945, became a victim of polio at the age of 39, perceptions started to change. Determined to lead an active

*This case was prepared by Dr. Douglas Hausknecht, The University of Akron. Using iron braces on his hips and legs, he also taught himself to walk a short distance by swiveling his torso while supporting himself with a cane. He funded and developed a hydrotherapy center for the treatment of polio patients in Warm Springs, Georgia, and after becoming president, helped to found the National Foundation for Infantile Paralysis (now known as the March of Dimes).

life, Roosevelt developed his own wheelchair—a lightweight chair on rollers that could pass through normal-sized doors.

In the 1970s, the Vietnam War produced large numbers of young wounded soldiers who wanted normal civilian lives. At the same time, there was greater awareness of the need to break down socioeconomic boundaries between groups, including the disabled. Heavy, bulky chairs were not suitable for people who wanted to work, participate in sports, dance, and travel with family and friends.

Other changes in the 1970s helped the medical devices industry grow and evolve. Up until that time, Everest & Jennings, then the major supplier of wheelchairs, set the standards for the rest of the industry through its contractual arrangements with the U.S. government. These government contracts determined styles and materials for the products that would be purchased directly—and indirectly influenced what would be acceptable for reimbursement under many insurance programs. This type of market power enabled Everest & Jennings to command a dominant market share without the necessity of adapting to the rapidly changing needs and wants of its target market.

The Medical Devices Act of 1976 changed the dynamics of the industry. The Bureau of Medical Devices was created within the Food and Drug Administration to oversee production of a vast array of devices from catheters to wheelchairs to MRI machines. This new agency took a fresh look at the needs and wants of individual users, as well as the needs of physicians and insurers. Change did not come immediately, but Invacare began to see new market opportunities.

Under its new leadership of Mixon and Richey, Invacare reexamined its strategy and found itself deficient in many areas. Product quality and delivery were poor; no new products were under development; production costs were high; competition from new producers in Asia was growing; and Invacare had done little to penetrate foreign markets. Moreover, the company had no real strategic plan.

Mixon addressed these issues by first working through the distributor network to improve product design, quality, and delivery times. Distributors were offered better financing support to offset high interest rates which were a problem at the time. New products, new product lines, and the acquisition of related companies followed. Invacare became a major player in the design, construction, and sale of therapeutic beds and oxygen concentrators, in addition to its traditional product lines. Invacare also entered the "prescription wheelchair" business. Prescription chairs are custom products, designed for individual users. Today, Invacare is known for its customized wheelchair products.

In a related change of strategy, Invacare brought new vitality to the self-powered wheelchair in 1981 with the introduction of a lighter, more capable model. The Rolls IV, as it was known, provided users with a much improved sense of independence and mobility. Wheelchair users began to recognize and communicate their needs and wants to distributors who conveyed this market information to Invacare's sales force. In turn, company engineers added desirable features and attributes, which improved products and increased customer satisfaction.

As a result, Invacare pioneered the idea of "One Stop Shopping" for medical devices. "One Stop Shopping" continues to define the company's product and distribution strategies to this day.

Current strategies and challenges

Today, Invacare is the world's leading manufacturer and distributor for medical equipment used in the home: power and manual wheelchairs, personal mobility, seating and positioning products, home care bed systems, and home oxygen systems. Vertical integration, Statistical Process Control, and total quality management (TQM) have all contributed to the success of Invacare's multiple product lines. In its modern manufacturing facilities in Ohio, Mexico, and elsewhere, the company produces and assembles many of the components for its products—whether standard or customized. Invacare also supplies the components necessary for service and repair of chairs, beds, oxygen concentrators, and other products. Its new-product development process includes representatives from marketing, quality, manufacturing, purchasing, finance, and design.

Because cost has become increasingly important in the medical devices industry, Invacare actively pursues a cost-containment strategy. While the need for specialized products has increased, the availability of insurance or government programs to pay for them has not. Prior to WWII, the cost of medical devices typically was borne by the family or community contributions. As medical insurance developed and evolved into an employee benefit, some of the costs were covered that way. Beginning in 1972, the federal government covered costs for the permanently disabled through Medicare, but because products were intended to be affordable, design took a back seat. Changes in government regulation, most notably the 1990 Americans with Disabilities Act (ADA), encouraged improvements in product design and extensions of existing product lines. Medicare policies were slow to change, however, and even in the 1980s insureds were only reimbursed for equipment necessary to "perform the activities of daily living within the four walls of the home." Customers were not permitted to upgrade from basic models unless they paid the entire cost themselves. Medicare rules at the time did not permit augmenting the basic cost with private funds.

Currently, a greater range of options in government support, insurance, and flexible spending plans—as well as private and foundation money—help to fund purchases of customized equipment. Invacare's domestic revenues are equally dependent on private insurance and Medicare: together contributing about 80 percent of its income. However, cost-containment language in the 2010 Health Care Reform Act may once again limit the availability of funds for high-end equipment.

Invacare sells its products to over 25,000 home health care and medical equipment providers, distributors, and government locations in the U.S., Australia, Canada, Europe, New Zealand, and Asia through its sales force, telesales associates, and various independent agent distributors. Distributors in individual markets work with medical care facilities, doctors, rehabilitation clinics, and retailers to identify potential new customers and current users. Invacare's sales force works with distributors to monitor and meet demand. Awareness of the available range of products is enhanced through a variety of means. Invacare has sponsored individual wheelchair races, a wheelchair racing circuit, and the Wounded Warrior Project. Team Invacare competes in racing, basketball, handcycling, and tennis. Special-purpose chairs encourage participation in sports as demanding as rugby—even to the extent of having specially-designed chairs for offense and defense. These sponsorships and participation in special events heighten awareness of customized equipment among potential customers and with the general public. Rather than featuring the attributes of specific pieces of equipment, Invacare's advertisements and promotional materials emphasize people enjoying life with its products.

As Mal Mixon considered Invacare's past strategies, he wondered about the future. How might the new environment for health care affect Invacare and its competitors? Everest & Jennings' sturdy and utilitarian chairs are still being manufactured under the umbrella of GF Health Products. They look the same as they always have. But other competitors have carved out positions in all-terrain accessibility (e.g., Permobil), lightweight portability (e.g., Lifecare Medical), niche uses (e.g., Colours in Motion), and increasingly low price (imports). Dean Kamen, inventor of the Segway, developed the IBOT—a pricey wheelchair that can climb stairs. Would future price pressures and regulatory changes allow all of these competitors to coexist?

Invacare is also a leader in the oxygen concentrator market. The HomeFill combines the efficiency of stationary oxygen concentrators with the convenience of pre-filled bottles to enable a greater range of travel for those who are dependent on supplementary oxygen. Will new regulations favor less costly "standard" products, such as those offered also by DeVilbiss and Respironics? Will pricing pressures allow for further innovation?

The Health Care Reform Act that was passed in 2010 broadly refers to changes in the managed care medical insurance system in the United States. It is expected to affect all Americans in some way and will impact all companies in the medical equipment, services, and insurance industries. In general, it requires all Americans to be covered by health insurance. Insurers are no longer allowed to deny coverage to individuals with pre-existing conditions, and young adults will be able to stay on their parents' plans until the age of 26. These changes are expected to be very costly, and some critics predict a shortage of primary care physicians. In addition, implementation of the bill will require cost reductions and savings that are likely to affect the availability of health care services and payments. However, some aspects of the act remain in flux. A sales tax on home medical devices was delayed. A provision that would reduce the ability to sell directly to the customer in favor of leasing arrangements has not been implemented. So the overall impact of the Health Care Reform Bill on Invacare is unknown. Will the promise of greater access to health care and life-improving treatment and devices create a larger domestic market, or will greater restrictions on prices and product design reverse decades of product innovation and improvements?

Markets outside the U.S. are a concern as well. As of 2010, Invacare produces components or complete products in several countries. It also distributes products in 80 countries worldwide (a range of coverage difficult for a company that prides itself on meeting the needs of its customers), but not all of the company's product lines are available in all markets. In addition, many of its products sold in foreign markets are still based in part on designs from acquired companies. So while quality, reliability, and service are emphasized throughout the global corporation, design has been allowed to fluctuate. This "globalization" of the company's strategy has led to nonstandard components and problems with "cataloging" the product line worldwide.

Further, in the global marketplace, cultural factors account for some differences in local markets. Take China, for example. Basic health care is provided by the government in China, but private health care and individual personal benefits (not available to everyone) are viewed negatively. In recent years, some of these attitudes have changed, but only slowly. Still, income and a willingness to spend on personal items is increasing among the middle-to-upper classes. At the same time, care of the elderly is becoming less reliant on immediate family. In addition, the "one child per household" policy and the preference for male children will continue to strain the ability of earning generations to support their parents. Invacare's competitors in China include the Jiangsu Yuyue Company with product lines very similar to its own. Invacare has some manufacturing and distribution in China now and is contemplating future strategy in light of the culture and competition.

Brazil is another example. It is a large emerging market, but the problems Invacare faces there are somewhat different from the ones in China. Brazil has a history of being a very protectionist economy. High tariffs and duties restrict the ability to import finished goods of many types, and there is a strong preference for locally manufactured products. Nevertheless, the country's abundant natural resources permit global corporations to compete through direct foreign investment in manufacturing and distribution. The downside is that direct investment requires duplication of production facilities and other corporate resources within the country. But Brazil is a major exporter to other South American markets and that could make it an attractive market for Invacare.

Mal Mixon believes in his company and its future. He thinks it has the resources and energy to grow and to serve a customer base that needs and appreciates its products. Invacare's motto of, "Yes, you can!" truly conveys the positive corporate attitude that underlies its mission: to remove real and perceived barriers that may restrict the lives of its customers. But Mal wonders how the company can best meet the challenges both within the U.S. and in foreign markets. How will the company grow and prosper in the next decade?

1. *How might the anticipated changes in U.S. health care coverage affect Invacare's current marketing strategies and demand for its products?*
2. *Conduct a S.W.O.T analysis for Invacare. What types of opportunities and threats do you see? What types of marketing strategies are suggested by your S.W.O.T. analysis?*
3. *What have been the "keys to success" for Invacare in the past? Are these likely to change in the future?*
4. *What do you think will be necessary for Invacare to conduct operations successfully in Brazil? What about China? Which of these two countries is a better "fit" for Invacare's business model?*

8. Segway Finds Niche Markets for Its Human Transporter Technology*

Amid heavy media coverage and much speculation, "Ginger" made its debut on ABC's *Good Morning America* on December 3, 2001. It thrilled some and disappointed others, but the technology was breathtaking to all.

Now known as the Segway Human Transporter (HT), Ginger was the brainchild of inventor and entrepreneur Dean Kamen, who is best known for his inventions in the medical field. While in college, Kamen invented the first wearable drug-infusion

*This case was prepared by Dr. J. B. Wilkinson, professor emeritus, Youngstown State University.

pump. In the following years, he invented the first portable insulin pump, the first portable dialysis machine, and an array of heart stents. This string of successes established Kamen's reputation and turned DEKA Research and Development Corp., the R&D lab he founded, into a premier company for medical-device design.

The inspiration for Ginger occurred during the development of the IBOT wheelchair at DEKA. Developed for and funded by Johnson & Johnson, the IBOT wheelchair is a gyro-stabilized, microprocessor-controlled wheelchair that gives disabled people the same kind of mobility the rest of us take for granted. Officially called the Independence IBOT mobility system, this six-wheel machine can go up and down curbs, cruise effortlessly through sand or gravel, climb stairs, and rise up on its wheels to lift its occupant to eye level while maintaining balance and maneuverability with such stability that it can't be knocked over. The IBOT wheelchair has been likened to a sophisticated robot.

As Kamen and his team at DEKA were working on the IBOT, it dawned on them that they could build a device using similar technology for pedestrians—one that could go farther, move more quickly, and carry more. The IBOT was also the source of the "Ginger" code name for the Segway HT during its development stage. Watching the IBOT "dance up the stairs," Kamen's team likened it to Fred Astaire—hence the name Ginger for its smaller partner with only two wheels!

Segway's breakthrough technology is based on dynamic stabilization. A self-balancing, electric-powered transport device, the Segway HT contains gyroscopes and sensors that monitor a user's center of gravity and respond to subtle shifts in weight. Lean forward, go forward; lean back, go back; lean back a bit more and you go in reverse; turn by twisting your wrist; arch your back a tad and you slow to a halt. Exactly how the Segway achieves this is difficult to explain, but in every Segway, there are gyroscopes that act like your inner ear, a computer that acts like your brain, motors that act like your muscles, and wheels that act like your feet. You step aboard and it "oscillates" for a few seconds, getting the feel of you, and then it's fully cruiseable at 6 mph in "learning mode," and 12.5 miles per hour "flat-out." It has a range of about 17 to 25 miles per battery charge and can support package weights of 80 pounds. It has no brakes, no engine, no throttle, no gearshift, no steering wheel, and gives off no emissions. It is much cleaner than a car and faster than a bike. It is more pedestrian-friendly than bikes or scooters and safer than a skateboard.

The commercial potential for Segway is enormous. For this reason, Kamen decided to move development and manufacturing of the Segway HT to a new company with the vision to develop highly efficient, zero-emission transportation solutions using dynamic stabilization technology. The new company, Segway LLC (changed to Segway, Inc., in 2005) is headquartered in Bedford, New Hampshire, and construction of a manufacturing and assembly plant was completed in 2001.

Kamen has openly stated that the Segway "will be to the car what the car was to the horse and buggy!" He imagines them everywhere: in parks, on battlefields, on factory floors, zipping around distribution centers, and especially on downtown sidewalks. But market acceptance and penetration has been slow for this engineering marvel.

The Segway HT was initially marketed to major corporations and government agencies. Kamen personally demonstrated the Segway to the postmaster general who was keen to put letter carriers on Segways and to the head of the National Park Service who wanted to do the same with park rangers. Both were among Segway's first customers. The Pentagon's research agency, DARPA, bought Segways to give to robotics labs. The objective was to use Segway bases in the development of robots to do menial tasks (cleaning, picking crops), specialized jobs (nurses aids), and dangerous missions (bomb removal or rescue work in earthquake debris). Amazon.com, GE Plastics, and Delphi Automotive Systems purchased Segways for use in warehouses and manufacturing plants. Police departments, cities, and airports bought Segways for use by foot patrols, security personnel, and meter readers. Customer studies by these early buyers showed double-digit productivity gains and reduced reliance on motorized transport. For postal workers, the Segway has increased their carrying capacity and delivery speed. Test studies with police officers and security personnel have shown faster response times and better sightlines from being higher in the air than pedestrians.

In 2002, Segways went on sale to the public for the first time on Amazon.com at a price of around $5,000. In 2003, the retail store Brookstone became the first retailer to sell the Segway HT. By January 2004, it was estimated by industry observers that about 6,000 Segways had been sold. Given Kamen's stated ambition of replacing automobiles and other forms of personal transport alternatives, initial consumer sales were disappointing.

However, the Segway HT is still in the early stages of its product life cycle. According to product life-cycle theories and related empirical studies on diffusion of innovations, products move through their life cycles in different ways and the length of any particular stage varies according to many factors. In general, the speed with which a product moves through its introduction and growth stages varies according to product characteristics, market characteristics, competition, and environmental factors. The initial marketing strategy for a product will also affect market acceptance (adoption). A product will move quickly through the introduction and growth stages when it has high relative advantage—cost and benefits—compared to alternative products and is highly compatible with a buyer's current attitudes, lifestyle, and usage situation. The more complex a product is to understand and use, the slower will be its rate of adoption. In addition, if the product can be tried in small amounts, potential buyers perceive less risk associated with initial trial and this will speed adoption. Communication of the new product will affect market acceptance since buyers must first learn about a new product before the buying process can be initiated. Thus, a company's communication strategies and the degree to which favorable word-of-mouth opinion occurs will impact sales. Finally, new products will have higher rates of market acceptance if market conditions, competition, and environmental trends are favorable.

Industrial and government applications for the Segway HT continue to be positive. It's ideally suited for use in large-scale manufacturing plants and warehousing operations, for use by the police and security personnel in certain types of situations, for meter reading, for corporate and university campus transportation, and for package and mail delivery. And it has found a number of new niches in recent years. For example, tour groups are using Segways to move tourists between attractions in cities where tour buses and cars have operational difficulties. For example, Bill and Emily Neuenschwander's tours use Segways equipped with a radio on the handlebars that provide a running commentary to guide customers through tours of the Minneapolis, Minnesota, riverfront and surrounding historic landmarks. Visitors to theme parks, museums, and islands (e.g., Amelia Island Plantation Resort) use them. Some lawyers use them between offices and courtrooms. Some medics use them to reach injured people faster.

However, in the consumer market, the Segway HT is still an unsought product for many people. Industry observers believe that the automobile is a preferred alternative for a number of reasons, including the infrastructure of cities, commuting distances, weather, and the American family lifestyle. Most people agree that the use of a Segway HT on highways and busy streets is dangerous. Also, many commuters live more than 5 miles from work. The need to recharge Segways raises the question of public sources of electricity. Issues related to public safety also have slowed consumer sales. Although the Segway HT is approved in most states for use on sidewalks, restrictions have been placed on speed, helmet use, minimum operating age, and use on streets and highways. At the local level, additional regulations apply. For example, San Francisco banned their use on city sidewalks, and they are outlawed in subways in Washington, D.C. Many see the mix of pedestrians, bicycles, skateboards, roller skates, ATVs, scooters, and Segways as a dangerous mix on sidewalks, hiking trails, and other public areas.

On the other hand, the Segway HT has obvious advantages to walking and other types of personal transport in situations where people need to get from one place to another rapidly and efficiently using a clean, quiet, and environment-friendly transport device. The market potential for the product has barely been tapped. Early consumer buyers were mostly "techies" who like to own new, high-tech products, and they have played an important role in communicating the benefits and fun of owning a Segway HT. They have established local clubs across America and have started a number of websites devoted to Segway. In 2003, owners and enthusiasts held the first SegwayFest to celebrate all things Segway. The Fest has been held every year since.

In 2004, Segway launched a repositioning campaign to change the image of the Segway HT from "staid," "high-tech," and "serious" to "fun, smart transportation." The new and more traditional marketing campaign included new customer materials, dealer displays, and cable TV advertising with the tagline "Get Moving." Segway also has been increasing the number of dealerships and distributors worldwide. The new distribution strategy allows potential buyers to see the different models and to try them out before buying. The dealer network increases the visibility of the product and lowers buyers' perceived risk associated with servicing. Publicity, media appearances, and product placement on television shows such as *Frasier, Arrested Development,* and *The Simpsons* continue to provide important market exposure.

The new positioning strategy emphasizes the leisure aspect of the Segway HT. New models aimed at the recreation market have been introduced. For example, the Segway GT is geared toward golf enthusiasts and includes a golf bag carrier. The Segway XT is the company's off-road vehicle which can perform well in a variety of environments. The Centaur is a four-wheeled ATV-like vehicle that can pick up its wheels to climb over obstacles or simply glide on two wheels at 25 mph.

To further develop the market for the Segway technology, the company has started to market Segway Smart Motion Technology through licensing and partnering with third parties to codevelop new products. Under this program, any number of specialized products could emerge.

The future for Segway is unlimited. America's commitment to end its dependence on petroleum and reduce harmful emissions is not likely to change. Segway 's technology supports this commitment. The consumer market for Segway has developed slowly, but the future is assured. For this "new-to-the-world" product, the life cycle will be long and classically configured. Its impact on all sectors of the economy will be profound. How we work, play, and get around will radically change in the 21st century. From the company's perspective, this is just dandy! Its ultimate goal is to "be to the car what the car was to the horse and buggy!"

1. *How might Segway, Inc. further develop the market for Segway technology? Hint: What types of marketing strategies are associated with sales growth?*
2. *What would be some advantages and disadvantages of using a Segway HT to get around on campus?*
3. *What types of applications and usage situations are there for Segway HTs in your area?*
4. *What kinds of problems would the use of Segway HTs create in your area? What are some possible solutions for these problems? Explain.*

Cases

Guide to the use of these cases

Cases can be used in many ways. And the same case can be analyzed several times for different purposes.

"Suggested cases" are listed at the end of most chapters, but these cases can also be used later in the text. The main criterion for the order of these cases is the amount of technical vocabulary—or text principles—that are needed to read the case meaningfully. The first cases are "easiest" in this regard. This is why an early case can easily be used two or three times—with different emphasis. Some early cases might require some consideration of Product and Price, for example, and might be used twice, perhaps regarding product planning and later pricing. In contrast, later cases, which focus more on Price, might be treated more effectively *after* the Price chapters are covered.

In some of the cases, we have disguised certain information—such as names or proprietary financial data—at the request of the people or firms involved in the case. However, such changes do not alter the basic substantive problems you will be analyzing in a case.

1. McDonald's "Seniors" Restaurant

Lisa Aham is manager of a McDonald's restaurant in a city with many "seniors." She has noticed that some senior citizens have become not just regular patrons—but patrons who come for breakfast and stay on until about 3 P.M. Many of these older customers were attracted initially by a monthly breakfast special for people aged 55 and older. The meal costs $1.99 and refills of coffee are free. Every fourth Monday, between 100 and 150 seniors jam Lisa's McDonald's for the special offer. But now almost as many of them are coming every day—turning the fast-food restaurant into a meeting place. They sit for hours with a cup of coffee, chatting with friends. On most days, as many as 100 will stay from one to four hours.

Lisa's employees have been very friendly to the seniors, calling them by their first names and visiting with them each day. In fact, Lisa's McDonald's is a happy place—with her employees developing close relationships with the seniors. Some employees have even visited customers who have been hospitalized. "You know," Lisa says, "I really get attached to the customers. They're like my family. I really care about these people." They are all "friends," and it is part of McDonald's corporate philosophy (as reflected in its website, www.mcdonalds.com) to be friendly with its customers and to give back to the communities it serves.

These older customers are an orderly group and very friendly to anyone who comes in. Further, they are neater than most customers and carefully clean up their tables before they leave. Nevertheless, Lisa is beginning to wonder if anything should be done about her growing "non-fast-food" clientele. There's no crowding problem yet, during the time when the seniors like to come. But if the size of the senior citizen group continues to grow, crowding could become a problem. Further, Lisa is concerned that her restaurant might come to be known as an "old people's" restaurant—which might discourage some younger customers. And if customers felt the restaurant was crowded, some might feel that they wouldn't get fast service. On the other hand, a place that seems busy might be seen as a "good place to go" and a "friendly place."

Lisa also worries about the image she is projecting. McDonald's is a fast-food restaurant (there are over 32,000 of them serving over 60 million people in over 100 countries every day), and normally customers are expected to eat and run. Will allowing people to stay and visit change the whole concept? In the extreme, Lisa's McDonald's might become more like a European-style restaurant where the customers are never rushed and feel very comfortable about lingering over coffee for an hour or two! Lisa knows that the amount her senior customers spend is similar to the average customer's purchase—but the seniors do use the facilities for a much longer time. However, most of the older customers leave McDonald's by 11:30, before the noon crowd comes in.

Lisa is also concerned about another possibility. If catering to seniors is OK, then should she do even more with this age group? In particular, she is considering offering bingo games during the slow morning hours—9 A.M. to 11 A.M. Bingo is popular with some seniors, and this could be a new revenue source—beyond the extra food and drink purchases that probably would result. She figures she could charge $5 per person for the two-hour period and run it with two underutilized employees. The prizes would be coupons for purchases at her store (to keep it legal) and would amount to about two-thirds of the bingo receipts (at retail prices). The party room area of her McDonald's would be perfect for this use and could hold up to 150 persons.

Evaluate Lisa Aham's current strategy regarding senior citizens. Does this strategy improve this McDonald's image? What should she do about the senior citizen market—that is, should she encourage, ignore, or discourage her seniors? What should she do about the bingo idea? Explain.

2. Golden Valley Foods, Inc.

It is 2012, and Neal Middleton, newly elected president of Golden Valley Foods, Inc., faces a severe decline in profits. Golden Valley Foods, Inc., is a 127-year-old California-based food processor. Its multiproduct lines are widely accepted under the Golden Valley Foods brand. The company and its subsidiaries prepare, package, and sell canned and frozen foods, including fruits, vegetables, pickles, and condiments. Golden Valley Foods, which operates more than 30 processing plants in the United States, is one of the larger U.S. food processors—with annual sales of about $650 million.

Until 2012, Golden Valley Foods was a subsidiary of a major Midwestern food processor, and many of the present managers came from the parent company. Golden Valley Foods' last president recently said:

> The influence of our old parent company is still with us. As long as new products look like they will increase the company's sales volume, they are introduced. Traditionally, there has been little, if any, attention paid to margins. We are well aware that profits will come through good products produced in large volume.

Alex May, a 25-year employee and now production manager, agrees with the multiproduct-line policy. As he puts it: "Volume comes from satisfying needs. We will can or freeze any vegetable or fruit we think consumers might want." May also admits that much of the expansion in product lines was encouraged by economics. The typical plants in the industry are not fully used. By adding new products to use this excess capacity, costs are spread over greater volume. So the production department is always looking for new ways to make more effective use of its present facilities.

Golden Valley Foods has a line-forcing policy, requiring any store that wants to carry its brand name to carry most of the 65 items in the Golden Valley Foods line. This policy, coupled with its wide expansion of product lines, has resulted in 88 percent of the firm's sales coming from major supermarket chain stores, such as Safeway, Kroger, and A&P.

Smaller stores are generally not willing to accept the Golden Valley Foods policy. May explains, "We know that only large stores can afford to stock all our products. But the large stores are the volume! We give consumers the choice of any Golden Valley

Foods product they want, and the result is maximum sales." Many small retailers have complained about Golden Valley Foods' policy, but they have been ignored because they are considered too small in potential sales volume per store to be of any significance.

In late 2012, a stockholders' revolt over low profits (in 2012, they were only $500,000) resulted in Golden Valley Foods' president and two of its five directors being removed. Neal Middleton, (introduced earlier), an accountant from the company's outside auditing firm, was brought in as president. One of the first things he focused on was the variable and low levels of profits in the past several years. A comparison of Golden Valley Foods' results with similar operations of some large competitors supported his concern. In the past 13 years, Golden Valley Foods' closest competitors had an average profit return on shareholders' investment of 5 to 9 percent, while Golden Valley Foods averaged only 1.5 percent. Further, Golden Valley Foods' sales volume has not increased much from the 1996 level (after adjusting for inflation)—while operating costs have soared upward. Profits for the firm were about $8 million in 1996. The closest Golden Valley Foods has come since then is about $6 million—in 2002. The outgoing president blamed his failure on an inefficient sales department. He said, "Our sales department has deteriorated. I can't exactly put my finger on it, but the overall quality of salespeople has dropped, and morale is bad. The team just didn't perform." When Middleton e-mailed Shelley Walton, the vice president of sales, with this charge, her reply was:

> It's not our fault. I think the company made a key mistake in the late '80s. It expanded horizontally—by increasing its number of product offerings—while major competitors were expanding vertically, growing their own raw materials and making all of their packing materials. They can control quality and make profits in manufacturing that can be used in promotion. I lost some of my best people from frustration. We just aren't competitive enough to reach the market the way we should with a comparable product and price.

In a lengthy e-mail from Shelley Walton, Middleton learned more about the nature of Golden Valley Foods' market. Although all the firms in the food-processing industry advertise heavily, the size of the market for most processed foods hasn't grown much for many years. Further, most consumers are pressed for time and aren't very selective. If they can't find the brand of food they are looking for, they'll pick up another brand rather than go to some other store. No company in the industry has much effect on the price at which its products are sold. Chain store buyers are very knowledgeable about prices and special promotions available from all the competing suppliers, and they are quick to play one supplier against another to keep the price low. Basically, they have a price they are willing to pay—and they won't exceed it. Then the chains will charge any price they wish on a given brand sold at retail. (That is, a 48- can case of beans might be purchased from any supplier for $23.10, no matter whose product it is. Generally, the shelf price for each is no more than a few pennies different, but chain stores occasionally attract customers by placing a well-known brand on sale.)

Besides insisting that processors meet price points, like for the canned beans, some chains require price allowances if special locations or displays are desired. They also carry non-advertised brands and/or their own brands at a lower price—to offer better value to their customers. And most willingly accept producers' cents-off coupons, which are offered by Golden Valley Foods as well as most of the other major producers of full lines.

At this point, Neal Middleton is trying to decide why Golden Valley Foods, Inc., isn't as profitable as it once was. And he is puzzled about why some competitors are putting products on the market with low potential sales volume. (For example, one major competitor recently introduced a line of exotic foreign vegetables with gourmet sauces.) And others have been offering frozen dinners or entrees with vegetables for several years. Apparently, Golden Valley Foods' managers considered trying such products several years ago but decided against it because of the small potential sales volumes and the likely high costs of new-product development and promotion.

Evaluate Golden Valley Foods' present situation. What would you advise Neal Middleton to do to improve Golden Valley Foods' profits? Explain why.

3. NOCO United Soccer Academy

Wesley Diekens came to the United States from the U.K. in 2002 on a soccer scholarship. Wesley grew up playing soccer on many competitive teams through high school and had a brief professional career in England. When St. Albans College recruited him to play soccer, he thought it would open his life to a grand adventure. That adventure changed his life.

While at St. Albans, Diekens met his future wife, Alyce Bilski, who also played soccer there. She graduated a year ahead of him and went to Fort Collins, Colorado, where she played on the semiprofessional Fort Collins Force women's soccer team. When Diekens finished college, he followed Bilski to northern Colorado. Bilski was captain of the Force and worked for the sports marketing company that owned the team.

Diekens got a job at a local meat packing plant, but soccer was his passion. He made the practice squad for the Colorado Rapids Major League Soccer team, but injuries cut his professional career short. Teaching soccer to kids became another passion for Diekens. He has a natural talent for coaching. Diekens is charismatic, kids enjoy his easygoing demeanor and British accent, and he really knows soccer and how to teach the game to youngsters.

In 2006, Diekens founded the NOCO United Soccer Academy (NOCO standing for NOrthern COlorado). At first he trained small groups of young players aged 7 to 14. He grouped them by age, gender, and skill and conducted training sessions for small groups of five to seven at a local park. The first kids he attracted came by word of mouth as they quickly told friends and teammates about "this British guy who teaches soccer and makes it fun." His small after-school camps quickly grew to include more than 50 kids. Word continued to get around, and by the following summer Diekens conducted 10 different camps—and quit his job at the meat packing plant. He also trained 11 different NOCO United 3v3 soccer teams that competed in tournaments across the state and nation during the summer. All of his players had bright blue jerseys with the NOCO United name across the front, and the success of these teams made the jerseys a great promotion vehicle. In 2008, four of his teams competed in the national 3v3 soccer tournament, with one winning a national championship.

To keep up with the rapid growth, Diekens brought a few friends over from England to assist with training. Will Bowman moved to the United States to become Diekens's assistant director of coaching. Diekens and Bowman planned to work year-round as trainers and hire a couple of local coaches to help them conduct training sessions. During the summer he added a couple of local college soccer players and a few former teammates from England. The summer season works well for his British mates, because that is the off-season for those still playing professionally. Diekens is confident he can hire and train more coaches if he needs them to handle future growth.

Youth soccer is big in Colorado and across much of the United States. It is the largest participation sport for kids. Fort Collins is a soccer hotbed, and this has helped Diekens's business grow. He now trains about 600 kids per year. But he has even greater ambitions. For example, he would like to build a training facility; the space he currently rents is not always well-suited to soccer. However, he figures he would need to double his business to justify the cost of the soccer complex he wants to build. So he is now wondering how to grow his business.

About 90 percent of his current customers live in Fort Collins, which has a population of about 125,000 people. Diekens believes awareness of his program is close to 100 percent among competitive soccer players ages 11 to 14—and is probably at about 40 percent among families with soccer-playing kids ages 6 to 10. Most of his customers are 10 to 13 years old and enroll in two to three NOCO United programs per year. He has also run a few camps in Boulder and Northglenn, which are about 50 miles from Fort Collins. These have been successful but are currently limited.

There are several small cities within 25 miles of Fort Collins. Loveland, a city of about 60,000, borders Fort Collins on the south. Greeley and Longmont, each with about 80,000 people, are about 25 miles away by interstate highway. These areas have very limited soccer training programs except for their competitive teams, and awareness of NOCO United is not very high. Those who have heard of his academy are often not familiar with its philosophy and programs. Diekens is not sure if parents in these communities would be willing to drive their kids to Fort Collins for training. If not, he would have to run his programs there.

Diekens knows that he wants to grow his business, but wonders how he can accomplish his goal. He currently sees a few options:

1. His current customer retention rate is pretty high: about 80 percent. However, when the kids reach 14 or 15 years old, other high school sports and activities make them less interested in extra soccer training. One option is to try to increase retention by developing programs targeted at kids over 14.
2. Another option is to develop a marketing strategy that would encourage his current customers to buy more. He wonders if they have other needs that he might be able to serve.
3. Diekens could try to grow the business by entering new markets and acquiring new customers. His market penetration with kids 6 to 9 years old is still quite modest. He might develop new programs to better meet this group's needs.
4. Another new market option would be to serve more kids from Loveland, Longmont, and Greeley.

Evaluate Diekens's different options for growing NOCO United's customer equity. Develop a set of marketing strategy ideas for each of the options. What could Diekens do for market research to better assess his options?

4. Hometown Tech

Wendy Woo is getting desperate about her new business. She's not sure she can make a go of it—and she really wants to stay in her hometown of Petoskey, Michigan, a beautiful summer resort area along the eastern shore of Lake Michigan. The area's permanent population of 10,000 more than triples in the summer months and doubles at times during the winter skiing and snowmobiling season.

Wendy spent four years in the Navy after college graduation, returning home in June 2011. When she couldn't find a good job in the Petoskey area, she decided to go into business for herself and set up Hometown Tech. Wendy's plan was to work by herself and basically serve as a "for hire" computer consultant and troubleshooter for her customers. She knew that many of the upscale summer residents relied on a home computer to keep in touch with business dealings and friends at home, and it seemed that someone was always asking her for computer advice. She was optimistic that she could keep busy with a variety of on-site services—setting up a customer's new computer, repairing hardware problems, installing software or upgrades, creating a wireless network, correcting problems created by viruses, and the like.

Wendy thought that her savings would allow her to start the business without borrowing any money. Her estimates of required expenditures were $7,000 for a used SUV; $1,125 for tools, diagnostic equipment, and reference books; $1,700 for a laptop computer, software, and accessories; $350 for an initial supply of fittings and cables; and $500 for insurance and other incidental expenses. This total of $10,675 still left Wendy with about $5,000 in savings to cover living expenses while getting started.

Wendy chose the technology services business because of her previous work experience. She worked at a computer "help desk" in college and spent her last year in the Navy troubleshooting computer network problems. In addition, from the time Wendy was 16 years old until she finished college, she had also worked during the summer for Eric Steele. Eric operates the only successful computer services company in Petoskey. (There was one other local computer store that also did some on-location service work when the customer bought equipment at the store, but that store recently went out of business.)

Eric prides himself on quality work and has been able to build up a good business with repeat customers. Specializing in services to residential, small business, and professional offices, Eric has built a strong customer franchise. For 20 years, Eric's major source of new business has been satisfied customers who tell friends or coworkers about his quality service. He is highly regarded as a capable person who always treats clients fairly and honestly. For example, seasonal residents often give Eric the keys to their vacation homes so that he can do upgrades or maintenance while they are away for months at a time. Eric's customers are so loyal, in fact, that Fix-A-Bug—a national computer service franchise—found it impossible to compete with him. Even price-cutting was not an effective weapon against Eric.

From having worked with Eric, Wendy thought that she knew the computer service business as well as he did; in fact, she had sometimes been able to solve technical problems that left him stumped. Wendy was anxious to reach her $70,000-per-year sales objective because she thought this would provide her with a comfortable living in Petoskey. While aware of opportunities to do computer consulting for larger businesses, Wendy felt that the sales opportunities for her services were limited because many firms had their own computer specialists or even IT departments. As Wendy saw it, her only attractive opportunity was direct competition with Eric.

To get started, Wendy spent $1,400 to advertise her business in the local newspaper and on an Internet website. With this money she bought two large announcement ads and 52 weeks of daily ads in the classified section, listed under "Miscellaneous Residential and Business Services." The website simply listed businesses in the Petoskey area and gave a telephone number, e-mail address, and brief description. She also listed her business under "Computer Services" at Craigslist for Northern Michigan—updating this notice and information once a month. She also built a small website with just a basic home page, a page with her picture and experience, and a third page that lists services she offers. She has thought about creating a Facebook page and blog, but hasn't done that yet. She put magnetic sign boards on her SUV and waited for business to take off.

Wendy had a few customers, but much of the time she wasn't busy and she was able to gross only about $200 a week. Of course, she had expected much more. Many of the people who did call were regular Eric customers who had some sort of crisis when he was already busy. While these people agreed that Wendy's work was of the same quality as Eric's, they preferred Eric's "quality-care" image and they liked the fact that they had an ongoing relationship with him.

Sometimes Wendy did get more work than she could handle. This happened during April and May, when seasonal businesses were preparing for summer openings and owners of summer homes and condos were ready to "open the cottage." The same rush occurred in September and October, as many of these places were being closed for the winter; those customers often wanted help backing up computer files or packing up computer equipment so they could take it with them. During these months, Wendy was able to gross about $150 to $200 a day.

Toward the end of her discouraging first year in business, Wendy Woo is thinking about quitting. While she hates to think about leaving Petoskey, she can't see any way of making a living there with her independent technology services business. Eric seems to dominate the market, except in the rush seasons and for people who need emergency help. And the resort market is not growing very rapidly, so there is little hope of a big influx of new businesses and homeowners to spur demand.

Evaluate Wendy Woo's strategy planning for her new business. Why isn't she able to reach her objective of $70,000? What should Wendy do now? Explain.

5. Polystyrene Solutions

Paige Chen, a chemist in Polystyrene Solutions' resins laboratory, is trying to decide how hard to fight for the new product she has developed. Chen's job is to find new, more profitable applications for the company's present resin products—and her current efforts are running into unexpected problems.

During the last four years, Chen has been under heavy pressure from her managers to come up with an idea that will open up new markets for the company's foamed polystyrene.

Two years ago, Chen developed the "foamed-dome concept"—a method of using foamed polystyrene to make dome-shaped roofs and other structures. She described the procedure for making domes as follows: The construction of a foamed dome involves the use of a specially designed machine that bends, places, and bonds pieces of plastic foam together into a predetermined dome shape. In forming a dome, the machine head is mounted on a boom, which swings around a pivot like the hands of a clock, laying and bonding layer upon layer of foam board in a rising spherical form.

According to Chen, polystyrene foamed boards have several advantages, such as:

1. Foam board is stiff—but can be formed or bonded to itself by heat alone.
2. Foam board is extremely lightweight and easy to handle. It has good structural rigidity.
3. Foam board has excellent and permanent insulating characteristics. (In fact, the major use for foam board is as an insulator.)
4. Foam board provides an excellent base on which to apply a variety of surface finishes, such as a readily available concrete-based stucco that is durable and inexpensive.

Using her good selling abilities, Chen easily convinced her managers that her idea had potential.

According to a preliminary study by the marketing research department, the following were areas of construction that could be served by the domes:

1. Bulk storage
2. Cold storage
3. Educational construction
4. Covers for industrial tanks
5. Light commercial construction
6. Planetariums
7. Recreational construction (such as a golf-course starter house)

The marketing research study focused on uses for existing dome structures. Most of the existing domes are made of cement-based materials. The study showed that large savings would result from using foam boards, due to the reduction of construction time.

Because of the new technology involved, the company decided to do its own contracting (at least for the first four to five years). Chen thought this was necessary to make sure that no mistakes were made by inexperienced contractor crews. (For example, if not applied properly, the plastic may burn.)

After building a few domes in the United States to demonstrate the concept, Chen contacted some leading U.S. architects. Reactions were as follows:

"It's very interesting, but we're not sure the fire marshal of Chicago would ever give his OK."

"Your tests show that foamed domes can be protected against fires, but there are no good tests for unconventional building materials as far as I am concerned."

"I like the idea, but foam board does not have the impact resistance of cement."

"We design a lot of recreational facilities, and kids will find a way to poke holes in the foam."

"Building codes in our area are written for wood and cement structures. Maybe we'd be interested if the codes change."

After this unexpected reaction, management didn't know what to do. Chen still thinks they should go ahead with the project. She wants to build several more demonstration projects in the United States and at least three each in Europe and Japan to expose the concept in the global market. She thinks architects outside the United States may be more receptive to really new ideas. Further, she says, it takes time for potential users to "see" and accept new ideas. She is sure that more exposure to more people will speed acceptance. And she is convinced that a few reports of well-constructed domes in leading trade papers and magazines will go a long way toward selling the idea. She is working on getting such reports right now. But her managers aren't sure they want to OK spending more money on "her" project. Her immediate boss is supportive, but the rest of the review board is less sure about more demonstration projects or going ahead at all—just in the United States or in global markets.

Evaluate how Polystyrene Solutions got into the present situation. What should Paige Chen do? What should Chen's managers do? Explain.

6. Applied Steel

Applied Steel is one of two major producers of wide-flange beams in the United States. The other producer is USX. A number of small firms also compete, but they tend to compete mainly on price in nearby markets where they can keep transport costs low. Typically, all interested competitors charge the same delivered price, which varies some depending on how far the customer is from either of the two major producers. In other words, local prices are higher in more remote geographic markets.

Wide-flange beams are one of the principal steel products used in construction. They are the modern version of what are commonly known as I-beams. USX rolls a full range of wide flanges from 6 to 36 inches. Applied Steel entered the field about 30 years ago, when it converted an existing mill to produce this product. Applied Steel's mill is limited to flanges up to 24 inches, however. At the time of the conversion, Applied Steel felt that customer usage of sizes over 24 inches was likely to be small. In recent years, however, there has been a definite trend toward the larger and heavier sections.

The beams produced by the various competitors are almost identical—since customers buy according to standard dimensional and physical-property specifications. In the smaller size range, there are a number of competitors. But above 14 inches, only USX and Applied Steel compete. Above 24 inches, USX has no competition.

All the steel companies sell these beams through their own sales forces. The customer for these beams is called a structural fabricator. This fabricator typically buys unshaped beams and other steel products from the mills and shapes them according to the specifications of each customer. The fabricator sells to the contractor or owner of the structure being built.

The structural fabricator usually must sell on a competitive-bid basis. The bidding is done on the plans and specifications prepared by an architectural or structural engineering firm and forwarded to the fabricator by the contractor who wants the bid. Although thousands of structural fabricators compete in the United States, relatively few account for the majority of wide-flange tonnage in the various geographical regions. Since the price is the same from all producers, they typically buy beams on the basis of availability (i.e., availability to meet production schedules) and performance (i.e., reliability in meeting the promised delivery schedule).

Several years ago, Applied Steel's production schedulers saw that they were going to have an excess of hot-rolled plate capacity in the near future. At the same time, development of a new production technology allowed Applied Steel to weld three plates together into a section with the same dimensional and physical properties and almost the same cross section as a rolled wide-flange beam. This development appeared to offer two key advantages to Applied Steel: (1) It would enable Applied Steel to use some of the excess plate capacity, and (2) larger sizes of wide-flange beams could be offered. Cost analysts showed that by using a fully depreciated plate mill and the new welding process it would be possible to produce and sell larger wide-flange beams at competitive prices—that is, at the same price charged by USX.

Applied Steel's managers were excited about the possibilities, because customers usually appreciate having a second source of supply. Also, the new approach would allow the production of up to a 60-inch flange. With a little imagination, these larger sizes might offer a significant breakthrough for the construction industry.

Applied Steel decided to go ahead with the new project. As the production capacity was converted, the salespeople were kept well informed of the progress. They, in turn, promoted this new capability to their customers, emphasizing that soon they would be able to offer a full range of beam products. Applied Steel sent several general information letters to a broad mailing list but did not advertise. The market development section of the sales department was very busy explaining the new possibilities of the process to fabricators at engineering trade associations and shows.

When the new production line was finally ready to go, the market reaction was disappointing. No orders came in and none were expected. In general, customers were wary of the new product. The structural fabricators felt they couldn't use it without the approval of their customers, because it would involve deviating from the specified rolled sections. And as long as they could still get the rolled section, why make the extra effort for something unfamiliar, especially with no price advantage. The salespeople were also bothered with a very common question: How can you take plate that you sell for about $460 per ton and make a product that you can sell for $470 per ton? This question came up frequently and tended to divert the whole discussion to the cost of production rather than to the way the new product might be used or its value in the construction process.

Evaluate Applied Steel's situation. What should Applied Steel do?

7. Omarama Mountain Lodge

Nestled in the high country of New Zealand's South Island is a getaway adventure playground aimed unashamedly at the world's very wealthy. Presidents, movie stars, and other such globe-trotters are the prime targets of this fledgling tourism business developed by Omarama Mountain Lodge. The lodge offers this exclusive niche the opportunity of a secluded holiday in a little-known paradise. Guests, commonly under public scrutiny in their everyday lives, can escape such pressures at a hunting retreat designed specifically with their needs in mind.

A chance meeting between a New Zealand Department of Conservation investigator and the son of the former Indonesian president marked the beginning of this specialty tourist operation. Recognizing that "filthy rich" public figures are constantly surrounded by security and seldom have the luxury of going anywhere incognito, the New Zealander, Peter Slater, suggested that he and his new friend purchase a high-country station and hunting-guide company that was for sale. Slater believed that the facilities, and their secluded and peaceful environment, would make an ideal holiday haven for this elite group. His Indonesian partner concurred.

Slater, who was by now the company's managing director, developed a carefully tailored package of goods and services for the property. Architecturally designed accommodations, including a game trophy room and eight guest rooms, were constructed using high-quality South Island furniture and fittings, to create the ambience necessary to attract and satisfy the demands of their special clientele.

Although New Zealand had an international reputation for being sparsely populated and green, Slater knew that rich travelers frequently complained that local accommodations were below overseas standards. Since the price (NZ$700 a night) was not a significant variable for this target market, sumptuous guest facilities were built. These were designed to be twice the normal size of most hotel rooms, with double-glazed windows that revealed breathtaking views. Ten full-time staff and two seasonal guides were recruited to ensure that visitors received superior customized service, in fitting with the restrained opulence of the lodge.

The 28,000 hectares of original farmland that made up the retreat and backed onto the South Island's Mount Cook National Park were converted into a big-game reserve. All merino sheep on the land were sold, and deer, elk, chamois, and wapiti were brought in and released. This was a carefully considered plan. Slater, the former conservationist, believed that financially and environmentally this was the correct decision. Not only do tourists, each staying for one week and taking part in safari shooting, inject as much cash into the business as the station's annual wool clip used to fetch, but the game does less harm to the environment than sheep. Cattle, however, once part of the original station, were left to graze on lower river-flat areas.

For those high-flying customers seeking less bloodthirsty leisure activities, Omarama Mountain developed photographic "safaris" and other product-line extensions. Horse-trekking, golfing on a nearby rural course (with no need for hordes of security forces), helicopter trips around nearby Lake Tekapo, nature walks, and other such activities formed part of the exclusive package.

While still in the early stages of operation, this retreat has already attracted a steady stream of visitors. To date, the manager has relied solely on positive word of mouth, publicity, and public relations to draw in new customers. Given the social and business circles in which his potential target market moves, Slater considers these to be the most appropriate forms of marketing communication. The only real concern for Omarama Mountain Lodge has been the criticism of at least one New Zealand lobby group that the company is yet another example of local land passing into "foreign" hands, and that New Zealanders are prevented from using the retreat and excluded from its financial returns. However, this unwelcome attention has been fairly short-lived.

Identify the likely characteristics of the market segment being targeted by the company. Why are most target customers likely to be foreigners rather than New Zealanders? Suggest what expectations target customers are likely to have regarding the quality, reliability, and range of services. What are the implications for Omarama Mountain Lodge? How difficult is it for Omarama Mountain Lodge to undertake market research? Elaborate.

8. Besitti's Restaurant

Rosa Besitti, the owner and manager of Besitti's Restaurant, is reviewing the slow growth of her restaurant. She's also thinking about the future and wondering if she should change her strategy. In particular, she is wondering if she should join a fast-food or family restaurant franchise chain. Several are located near her, but there are many franchisors without local restaurants. After doing some research on the Internet, she has learned that with help from the franchisors, some of these places gross $500,000 to $1 million a year. Of course, she would have to follow someone else's strategy and thereby lose her independence, which she doesn't like to think about. But those sales figures do sound good, and she has also heard that the return to the owner-manager (including salary) can be over $150,000 per year. She has also considered putting a web page for Besitti's Restaurant on the Internet but is not sure how that will help.

Besitti's Restaurant is a fairly large restaurant—about 3,000 square feet—located in the center of a small shopping center completed early in 2009. Besitti's sells mainly full-course "home-cooked" Italian-style dinners (no bar) at moderate prices. In addition to Besitti's restaurant, other businesses in the shopping center include a supermarket, a hair salon, a liquor store, a video rental store, and a vacant space that used to be a hardware store. The hardware store failed when a Home Depot located nearby. Rosa has learned that a pizzeria is considering locating there soon. She wonders how that competition will affect her. Ample parking space is available at the shopping center, which is located in a residential section of a growing suburb to the east, along a heavily traveled major traffic route.

Rosa graduated from a local high school and a nearby university and has lived in this town with her husband and two children for many years. She has been self-employed in the restaurant business since her graduation from college in 1994. Her most recent venture before opening Besitti's was a large restaurant that she operated successfully with her brother from 2000 to 2006. In 2006, Rosa sold out her share because of illness. Following her recovery, she was anxious for something to do and opened the present restaurant in April 2009. Rosa feels her plans for the business and her opening were well thought out. When she was ready to start her new restaurant, she looked at several possible locations before finally deciding on the present one. Rosa explained: "I looked everywhere, but here I particularly noticed the heavy traffic when I first looked at it. This is the crossroads for three major interstate highways. So obviously the potential is here."

Having decided on the location, Rosa signed a 10-year lease with option to renew for 10 more years, and then eagerly attacked the problem of outfitting the almost empty store space in the newly constructed building. She tiled the floor, put in walls of surfwood, installed plumbing and electrical fixtures and an extra washroom, and purchased the necessary restaurant equipment. All this cost $120,000—which came from her own cash savings. She then spent an additional $1,500 for glassware, $2,000 for an initial food stock, and $2,125 to advertise the opening of Besitti's Restaurant in the local newspaper. The paper serves the whole metro area, so the $2,125 bought only three quarter-page ads. These expenditures also came from her personal savings. Next she hired five waitresses at $275 a week and one chef at $550 a week. Then, with a $24,000 cash reserve for the business, she was ready to open. Reflecting her sound business sense, Rosa knew she would need a substantial cash reserve to fall back on until the business got on its feet. She expected this to take about one year. She had no expectations of getting rich overnight. (Her husband, a high school teacher, was willing to support the family until the restaurant caught on.)

The restaurant opened in April and by August had a weekly gross revenue of only $2,400. Rosa was a little discouraged with this, but she was still able to meet all her operating expenses without investing any new money in the business. She also got a few good customer reviews on Yelp. By September business was still slow, and Rosa had to invest an additional $3,000 in the business just to survive.

Business had not improved in November, and Rosa stepped up her advertising—hoping this would help. In December, she spent $1,200 of her cash reserve for radio advertising—10 late-evening spots on a news program at a station that aims at middle-income America. Rosa also spent $1,600 more during the next several weeks for some metro newspaper ads.

By April 2010, the situation had begun to improve, and by June her weekly gross was up to between $3,100 and $3,300. By March 2011, the weekly gross had risen to about $4,200. Rosa increased the working hours of her staff six to seven hours a week and added another cook to handle the increasing number of customers. Rosa was more optimistic for the future because she was finally doing a little better than breaking even. Her full-time involvement seemed to be paying off. She had not put any new money into the business since summer 2010 and expected business to continue to rise. She had not yet taken any salary for herself, even though she had built up a small surplus of about $9,000. Instead, she planned to put in a bigger air-conditioning system at a cost of $5,000 and was also planning to use what salary she might have taken for herself to hire two new waitresses to handle the growing volume of business. And she saw that if business increased much more she would have to add another cook.

Evaluate Rosa's past and present marketing strategy. What should she do now? Should she seriously consider joining some franchise chain?

9. Peaceful Rest Motor Lodge

Tristan Knaus is trying to decide whether he should make some minor changes in the way he operates his Peaceful Rest Motor Lodge motel or if he should join either the Days Inn or Holiday Inn motel chains. Some decision must be made soon because his present operation is losing money. But joining either of the chains will require fairly substantial changes, including new capital investment if he goes with Holiday Inn.

Tristan bought the recently completed 60-room motel two years ago after leaving a successful career as a production manager for a large producer of industrial machinery. He was looking for an interesting opportunity that would be less demanding than the production manager job. The Peaceful Rest Motor Lodge is located at the edge of a very small town near a rapidly expanding resort area and about one-half mile off an interstate highway. It is 10 miles from the tourist area, with several nationally franchised full-service resort motels suitable for "destination" vacations. There is a Best Western, a Ramada Inn, and a Hilton Inn, as well as many mom-and-pop and limited-service, lower-priced motels—and some quaint bed-and-breakfast facilities—in the tourist area. The interstate highway near the Peaceful Rest Motor Lodge carries a great deal of traffic, since the resort area is between several major metropolitan areas. No development has taken place around the turnoff from the interstate highway. The only promotion for the tourist area along the interstate highway is two large signs near the turnoffs. They show the popular name for the area and that the area is only 10 miles to the west. These signs are maintained by the tourist area's Tourist Bureau. In addition, the state transportation department maintains several small signs showing (by symbols) that near this turnoff one can find gas, food, and lodging. Tristan does not have any signs advertising Peaceful Rest Motor Lodge except the two on his property. He has been relying on people finding his motel as they go toward the resort area.

Initially, Tristan was very pleased with his purchase. He had traveled a lot himself and stayed in many different hotels and motels—so he had some definite ideas about what travelers wanted. He felt that a relatively plain but modern room with a comfortable bed, standard bath facilities, and free cable TV would appeal to most customers. Further, Tristan thought a swimming pool or any other nonrevenue-producing additions were not necessary. And he felt a restaurant would be a greater management problem than the benefits it would offer. However, after many customers commented about the lack of convenient breakfast facilities, Tristan served a free continental breakfast of coffee, juice, and rolls in a room next to the registration desk.

Day-to-day operations went fairly smoothly in the first two years, in part because Tristan and his wife handled registration and office duties as well as general management. During the first year of operation, occupancy began to stabilize around 55 percent of capacity. But according to industry figures, this was far below the average of 68 percent for his classification—motels without restaurants.

After two years of operation, Tristan was concerned because his occupancy rates continued to be below average. He decided to look for ways to increase both occupancy rate and profitability and still maintain his independence.

Tristan wanted to avoid direct competition with the full-service resort motels. He stressed a price appeal in his signs and brochures and was quite proud of the fact that he had been able to avoid all the "unnecessary expenses" of the full-service resort motels. As a result, Tristan was able to offer lodging at a very modest price—about 40 percent below the full-service hotels and comparable to the lowest-priced resort area motels. The customers who stayed at Peaceful Rest Motor Lodge said they found it quite acceptable. The hotels' online reviews at sites like TripAdvisor, while not numerous, were generally pretty positive. But he was troubled by what seemed to be a large number of people driving into his parking lot, looking around, and not coming in to register.

Tristan was particularly interested in the results of a recent study by the regional tourist bureau. This study revealed the following information about area vacationers:

1. 68 percent of the visitors to the area are young couples and older couples without children.
2. 40 percent of the visitors plan their vacations and reserve rooms more than 60 days in advance.
3. 66 percent of the visitors stay more than three days in the area and at the same location.
4. 78 percent of the visitors indicated that recreational facilities were important in their choice of accommodations.
5. 13 percent of the visitors had family incomes of less than $27,000 per year.
6. 38 percent of the visitors indicated that it was their first visit to the area.

After much thought, Tristan began to seriously consider affiliating with a national motel chain in hopes of attracting more customers and maybe protecting his motel from the increasing competition. There were constant rumors that more motels were being planned for the area. After some investigating, he focused on two national chain possibilities: Days Inn and Holiday Inn. Neither had affiliates in the area even though they each have about 2,000 units nationwide.

Days Inn of America, Inc., is an Atlanta-based chain of economy lodgings. It has been growing rapidly and is willing to take on new franchisees. A major advantage of Days Inn is that it would not require a major capital investment by Tristan. The firm is targeting people interested in lower-priced motels, in particular, senior citizens, the military, school sports teams, educators, and business travelers. In contrast, Holiday Inn would probably require Tristan to upgrade some of his facilities, including adding a swimming pool. The total new capital investment would be between $300,000 and $500,000, depending on how fancy he got. But then Tristan would be able to charge higher prices, perhaps $75 per day on the average rather than the $45 per day per room he's charging now.

The major advantages of going with either of these national chains would be their central reservation systems and their national names. Both companies offer nationwide, toll-free reservation lines, which produce about 40 percent of all bookings in affiliated motels. Both companies also offer websites (www.daysinn.com and www.holiday-inn.com) that help find a specific hotel by destination, rate, amenities, quality rating, and availability.

A major difference between the two national chains is their method of promotion. Days Inn uses little TV advertising and less print advertising than Holiday Inn. Instead, Days Inn emphasizes sales promotions. In one campaign, for example, Blue Bonnet margarine users could exchange proof-of-purchase seals for a free night at a Days Inn. This tie-in led to the Days Inn system *selling* an additional 10,000 rooms. Further, Days Inn operates a September Days Club for travelers 50 and over who receive such benefits as discount rates and a quarterly travel magazine.

Days Inn also has other membership programs, including its InnCentives loyalty club for frequent business and leisure travelers. Other programs targeted to business travelers include two Corporate Rate programs and its new Days Business Place hotels. Not to be outdone, Holiday Inn has a membership program called Priority Club Worldwide. Both firms charge 8 percent of gross room revenues for belonging to their chain—to cover the costs of the reservation service and national promotion. This amount is payable monthly. In addition, franchise members must agree to maintain their facilities and make repairs and improvements as required. Failure to maintain facilities can result in losing the franchise. Periodic inspections are conducted as part of supervising the whole chain and helping the members operate more effectively.

Evaluate Tristan Knaus's present strategy. What should he do? Explain.

10. Cooper's Ice Center

Claude Cooper, the manager of Cooper's Ice Center, is trying to decide what strategies to use to increase profits.

Cooper's Ice Center is an ice-skating rink with a conventional hockey rink surface (85 feet × 200 feet). It is the only indoor ice rink in a northern U.S. city of about 450,000. The city's recreation department operates some outdoor rinks in the winter, but they don't offer regular ice skating programs because of weather variability.

Claude runs a successful hockey program that is more than breaking even—but this is about all he can expect if he only offers hockey. To try to increase his profits, Claude is trying to expand and improve his public skating program. With such a program, he could have as many as 700 people in a public session at one time, instead of limiting the use of the ice to 12 to 24 hockey players per hour. While the receipts from hockey can be as high as $200 an hour (plus concession sales), the receipts from a two-hour public skating session—charging $5 per person—could yield up to $3,500 for a two-hour period (plus much higher concession sales). The potential revenue from such large public skating sessions could make Cooper's Ice Center a really profitable operation. But, unfortunately, just scheduling public sessions doesn't mean that a large number will come. In fact, only a few prime times seem likely: Friday and Saturday evenings and Saturday and Sunday afternoons.

Claude has included 14 public skating sessions in his ice schedule, but so far they haven't attracted as many people as he hoped. In total, they only generate a little more revenue than if the times were sold for hockey use. Offsetting this extra revenue are extra costs. More staff people are needed to handle a public skating session—guards, a ticket seller, skate rental, and more concession help. So the net revenue from either use is about the same. He could cancel some of the less attractive public sessions—like the noon-time daily sessions, which have very low attendance—and make the average attendance figures look a lot better. But he feels that if he is going to offer public skating he must have a reasonable selection of times. He does recognize, however, that the different public skating sessions do seem to attract different people and *really* different kinds of people.

The Saturday and Sunday afternoon public skating sessions have been the most successful, with an average of 200 people attending during the winter season. Typically, this is a "kid-sitting" session. More than half of the patrons are young children who have been dropped off by their parents for several hours, but there are also some family groups.

In general, the kids and the families have a good time—and a fairly loyal group comes every Saturday and/or Sunday during the winter season. In the spring and fall, however, attendance drops by about half, depending on how nice the weather is. (Claude schedules no public sessions in the summer, focusing instead on hockey clinics and figure skating.)

The Friday and Saturday evening public sessions are a big disappointment. The sessions run from 8 until 10, a time when he had hoped to attract teenagers and young adult couples. At $5 per person, plus $1.50 for skate rental, this would be an economical date. In fact, Claude has seen quite a few young couples—and some keep coming back. But he also sees a surprising number of 8- to 14-year-olds who have been dropped off by their parents. The younger kids tend to race around the rink playing tag. This affects the whole atmosphere, making it less appealing for dating couples and older patrons.

Claude has been hoping to develop a teenage and young-adult market for a "social activity," adapting the format used by roller-skating rinks. Their public skating sessions feature a variety of couples-only and group games as well as individual skating to dance music. Turning ice-skating sessions into such social activities is not common, however, although industry newsletters suggest that a few ice-rink operators have had success with the roller-skating format. Seemingly, the ice-skating sessions are viewed as active recreation, offering exercise or a sports experience.

Claude installed some soft lights to try to change the evening atmosphere. The music was selected to encourage people to skate to the beat and couples to skate together. Some people complained about the "old" music, but it was "danceable," and some skaters really liked it. For a few sessions, Claude even tried to have some couples-only skates. The couples liked it, but this format was strongly resisted by the young boys who felt that they had paid their money and there was no reason why they should be kicked off the ice. Claude also tried to attract more young people and especially couples by bringing in a local rock radio station disc jockey to broadcast from Cooper's Ice Center—playing music and advertising the Friday and Saturday evening public sessions. Cooper's son even set up Facebook and MySpace pages for Cooper's, but only a few people joined the groups. All of this appeared to have no effect on attendance, which varies from 50 to 100 per two-hour session during the winter.

Claude seriously considered the possibility of limiting the Friday and Saturday evening sessions to people age 14 and over—to try to change the environment. He knew it would take time to change people's attitudes. But when he counted the customers, he realized this would be risky. More than a quarter of his customers on an average weekend night appear to be 13 or under. This means that he would have to make a serious commitment to building the teen and young-adult market. And, so far, his efforts haven't been successful. He has already invested over $3,000 in lighting changes and over $9,000 promoting the sessions over the rock music radio station, with very disappointing results. Although the station's sales rep said the station reached teenagers all over town, an on-air offer for a free skating session did not get a single response!

Some days, Claude feels it's hopeless. Maybe he should accept that most public ice-skating sessions are a mixed bag. Or maybe he should just sell the time to hockey groups. Still he keeps hoping that something can be done to improve weekend evening public skating attendance, because the upside potential is so good. And the Saturday and Sunday afternoon sessions are pretty good money-makers.

Evaluate Cooper's Ice Center's situation. What should Claude Cooper do? Why?

11. Running Room

Raina Cisco, owner of Running Room, is trying to decide what she should do with her retail business and how committed she should be to her current target market.

Raina is 42 years old, and she started her Running Room retail store in 1994 when she was only 24 years old. She was a nationally ranked runner herself and felt that the growing interest in jogging offered real potential for a store that provided serious runners with the shoes and advice they needed. The jogging boom quickly turned Running Room into a profitable business selling high-end running shoes—and Raina made a very good return on her investment for the first 10 years. From 1994 until 2004, Raina emphasized Nike shoes, which were well accepted and seen as top quality. Nike's aggressive promotion and quality shoes resulted in a positive image that made it possible to get a \$5 to \$7 per pair premium for Nike shoes. Good volume and good margins resulted in attractive profits for Raina.

Committing so heavily to Nike seemed like a good idea when its marketing and engineering was the best available. In addition to running shoes, Nike had other athletic shoes Raina could sell. So even though they were not her primary focus, Raina did stock other Nike shoes, including walking shoes, shoes for aerobic exercise, basketball shoes, tennis shoes, and cross-trainers. She also added more sportswear to her store and put more emphasis on fashion rather than just function.

Even with this broadened product line, Raina's sales flattened out—and she wasn't sure what to do to get her business back in growth mode. She realized that she was growing older and so were many of her longer-term customers. Many of them were finding that jogging isn't just hard work—it's hard on the body, especially the knees. So many of her previously loyal runner-customers were switching to other, less demanding exercise programs. However, when she tried to orient her store and product line more toward these people, she wasn't as effective in serving the needs of serious runners—still an important source of sales for the store.

She was also facing more competition on all fronts. Many consumers who don't really do any serious exercise buy running shoes as their day-to-day casual shoes. As a result, many department stores, discount stores, and regular shoe stores have put more and more emphasis on athletic shoes in their product assortment. When Raina added other brands and put more emphasis on fashion, she found that she was in direct competition with a number of other stores, which put more pressure on her to lower prices and cut her profit margins. For example, in Raina's area there are a number of local and online retail chains offering lower-cost and lower-quality versions of similar shoes as well as related fashion apparel. Walmart also expanded its assortment of athletic shoes—and it offers rock-bottom prices. Other chains, like Foot Locker, have focused their promotion and product lines on specific target markets. Still, all of them (including Raina's Running Room, the local chains, Walmart, and Foot Locker) are scrambling to catch up with rival category killers whose selections are immense.

In the spring of 2010 Raina tried an experiment. She took on a line of high-performance athletic shoes that were made to order. The distinctive feature of these shoes was that the sole was molded to precisely fit the customer's foot. A pair of these custom-made shoes cost about \$170, so the market was not large. Further, Raina didn't put much promotional emphasis on this line. However, when a customer came in the store with a serious interest in high-performance shoes, Raina's sales clerks would tell them about the custom shoe alternative and show a sample. When a customer was interested, a mold of the customer's bare foot was made at the store, using an innovative material that hardened in just a few minutes without leaving a sticky mess. Raina sent the mold off to the manufacturer by UPS, and about two weeks later the finished shoes arrived. Customers who tried these shoes were delighted with the result. However, the company that offered them ran into financial trouble and went out of business.

Raina recently learned about another company that is offering a very similar custom shoe program. However, that company requires more promotion investment by retailers and in return provides exclusive sales territories. Another requirement is that the store establish a website promoting the shoes and providing more detail on how the order process works. Running Room had a pretty basic website, so Raina knew she would have to spend some money to make this happen. All of a retailer's salesclerks are also required to go through a special two-day training program so that they know how to present the benefits of the shoe and do the best job creating the molds. The training program is free, but Raina would have to pay travel, hotel, and food expenses for her salespeople. So before even getting started, the new program would cost her several thousand dollars.

Raina is uncertain about what to do. Although sales have dropped, she is still making a reasonable profit and has a relatively good base of repeat customers, with the serious runners still more than half of her sales and profits. She thinks that the custom shoe alternative is a way to differentiate her store from the mass-merchandisers and to sharpen her focus on the target market of serious runners. On the other hand, that doesn't really solve the problem that the "runners" market seems to be shrinking. It also doesn't address the question of how best to keep a lot of the aging customers she already serves who seem to be shifting away from an emphasis on running. She also worries that she'll lose the loyalty of her repeat customers if she shifts the store further away from her running niche and more toward fashionable athletic shoes or fashionable casual wear. Yet athletic wear—women's, in particular—has come a long way in recent years. Designers like Donna Karan, Calvin Klein, Georgio Armani, and Ralph Lauren are part of the fast-growing women's wear business.

So Raina is trying to decide if there is anything else she can do to better promote her current store and product line, or if she should think about changing her strategy in a more dramatic way. Any change from her current focus would involve retraining her current salespeople and perhaps hiring new salespeople. Adding and maintaining a website isn't an insurmountable challenge, but it is not an area where she has either previous experience or skill.

Clearly, a real shift in emphasis would require that Raina make some hard decisions about her target market and her whole marketing mix. She's got some flexibility—it's not like she's a manufacturer of shoes with a big investment in a factory that can't be changed. On the other hand, she's not certain she's ready for a big change, especially a change that would mean starting over again from scratch. She started Running Room because she was interested in running and felt she had something special to offer.

Now she worries that she's just grasping at straws without a real focus or any obvious competitive advantage. She also knows that she is already much more successful than she ever dreamed when she started her business—and in her heart she wonders if she wasn't just spoiled by growth that came fast and easy at the start.

Evaluate Raina Cisco's present strategy. Evaluate the alternative strategies she is considering. Is her primary problem her emphasis on running shoes, her emphasis on trying to hang on to her current customers, or is it something else? What should she do? Why?

12. DrJane.com—Custom Vitamins

Dr. Jane Chung has to decide how to handle a complaint letter from a customer. When she received the letter, she passed it along to Prince Zimbalist, the firm's customer service manager, to get his recommendation. Now Chung has a reply from Zimbalist, and she must decide how to respond to the customer and determine if changes are needed in her company's customer service operations.

Dr. Chung has a reputation as a health and nutrition guru. Her fame grew after she published two books—both of which were very popular and received a lot of attention in the press. Five years ago, Internet entrepreneur Tania Cox approached her with the idea of creating a website to sell custom vitamins under Dr. Jane's name.

Chung and Cox became partners, and the business enjoyed success in its first four years of operation. Cox handles the website technology, inventory, production, and shipping. Dr. Chung is the health expert, creates content provided on the website, and is in charge of marketing and customer service. The complaint letter and reply from Zimbalist follow:

Dear Dr. Chung,

I am a longtime fan of your books and like to visit your website for health tips. As a new grandmother, my health is even more important to me. I want to see my grandchildren graduate from high school, go to college, and have kids of their own.

You have made me a bit of a guru as well. I work out every day. People always ask me how I stay so fit and healthy. Having read both your books, I tell them they should exercise regularly and take vitamins and supplements for long-term health. I always recommend your DrJane.com website and especially the section on your custom vitamins. That is my favorite part of your website. I really like that you take information about me and my medical history—and then recommend custom vitamins and supplements. I also like how you send me packages that each contain a daily dose.

But after my recent experiences, my loyalty to you and your company is now in jeopardy. Here is my story.

Six months ago, I went to the website to reorder my vitamins and supplements. The home page announced a new and improved health survey and custom health program. So I went through the survey and filled out all the details—it would have been nice if you had saved some of them from my previous survey. At the end of the survey the website offered me a 90-day supply of a custom set of vitamins and supplements selected for my specific needs. The $212 price was about $50 more than my previous 90-day supply, but I trusted your advice so I placed the order.

About two-and-a-half months later, I phoned your 800 number for DrJane.com to place a refill order. The person on the phone was very nice and asked if I wanted to set up automatic refills. I said no because I hate those automatic programs. They remind me of those book clubs that automatically send you books you don't want if you do not reply fast enough. About a week later my order arrived—then two days later another identical order arrived. I did not understand this, but I figured I would eventually use them up and I kept everything (and I was billed for both orders—$424 on my credit card). I should mention there was no e-mail explaining this mystery delivery. I was a little annoyed and sent an e-mail to customer service seeking an explanation. I received an automated response, "Thank you for your inquiry; someone will get back to you within 24 hours." No one ever replied, but I forgot about it.

Then two weeks ago I received an e-mail from DrJane.com telling me my refill order had been shipped and would arrive in a few days. But I did not place a refill order! I did not even need more vitamins because I was still working off the two 90-day supplies that I received three months ago. So I replied by e-mail that I did not want the order and to cancel it. A reply e-mail (from Sally) told me that I had signed up for automatic refill six months ago. I replied that I certainly had not and that I would not pay for the order that was being sent.

A few days later I received a call from Prince Zimbalist, your director of customer service. He told me that I had originally signed up for automatic refill and that was why I received vitamins. I told him that was impossible, and he told me that unless I checked some box on my original order that this was done automatically, "for my convenience." He said there were also several warnings and that I must have missed those. *Basically, I think he told me this was my fault. I did not like that one bit!!!* Mr. Zimbalist told me the vitamins were on their way, but I could refuse delivery of them. He offered to let me have them for 20 percent off if I simply kept them. Unfortunately, the vitamins were on my doorstep when I arrived home that day. I had to take the vitamins to UPS to get them shipped back to you.

You guys are no longer very good at your business. You might have a great product, but I am now seeing other vitamin companies offering the same products. I have no doubt these other companies offer better customer service. If you want me back as a customer, I would expect a formal apology from Mr. Zimbalist and a free 90-day supply. Otherwise, I figure my business will be welcomed at one of your competitors. I will be sure all my friends know about my experience at DrJane.com, and I intend to post a bad review at resellerratings.com, too.

Sincerely,
Maxine Slezak

Next is the reply that Prince Zimbalist sent to Dr. Chung concerning Maxine Slezak's letter.

Dear Jane,

As per your request, I reviewed Mrs. Slezak's order history. Yes, she is a very good customer who spent almost $800 with us last year. And she is a member of our referral program—and we can count at least seven new customers she has directed to us in the last 18 months. But I want to clarify some of this particular situation.

- You might recall that our automatic refill program has been a big success. Since we instituted the program a year ago, our customer retention rate has jumped by 10 percent. There are occasional complaints, but given the large number of customers we serve, the complaints are really just a "drop in the bucket."
- When Mrs. Slezak placed her order six months ago, there were at least two different warnings about the automatic refill program—customers have to check a box at the bottom of the screen to "opt out" of the program. We all agreed that it was better to make them part of the program automatically, but to give them two chances to remove themselves from automatic delivery.
- I do not know if we replied to her e-mail asking for customer service help.
- I did not tell Mrs. Slezak that this was her fault, but I did tell her that when she signed up there were two chances for her to choose to not be part of the automatic refill program.
- Mrs. Slezak did not get an e-mail notifying her of the first refill order because that system was not yet in place. But this has now been fixed, and the e-mail notifying her when we ship shows that this works.
- I offered her 20 percent off, as is our standard policy when we make a mistake. Considering this was her mistake, I thought this was generous.
- If Mrs. Slezak had called and asked, I could have had UPS come out and pick up the package for return to us.

I do not recommend giving her a free 90-day supply. This may simply encourage her to complain again in the future. Besides, this was not our mistake. We may be better off without certain customers—and I think Mrs. Slezak falls into this category.

Feel free to call me if you have any more questions.

Prince

Assess the customer service operations at DrJane.com. What should Chung do about Mrs. Slezak? What changes, if any, should Chung make to customer service and ordering operations?

13. AAA Office World (AAA)*

Stasia Acosta, marketing manager for AAA Office World, must decide whether she should permit her largest customer to buy some of AAA's commonly used file folders under the customer's brand rather than AAA's own FILEX brand. She is afraid that if she refuses, this customer—Business Center, Inc.—will go to another file folder producer and AAA will lose this business.

Business Center, Inc., is a major distributor of office supplies and has already managed to put its own brand on more than 45 high-sales-volume office supply products. It distributes these products—as well as the branded products of many manufacturers—through its nationwide distribution network, which includes 150 retail stores. Now Lance Richardson, vice president of marketing for Business Center, is seeking a line of file folders similar in quality to AAA's FILEX brand, which now has over 60 percent of the market.

This is not the first time that Business Center has asked AAA to produce a file folder line for Business Center. On both previous occasions, Stasia turned down the requests and Business Center continued to buy. In fact, Business Center not only continued to buy the file folders but also the rest of AAA's product lines. And total sales continued to grow as Business Center built new stores. Business Center accounts for about 30 percent of Stasia Acosta's business. And FILEX brand file folders account for about 35 percent of this volume.

In the past AAA consistently refused such dealer-branding requests as a matter of corporate policy. This policy was set some years ago because of a desire (1) to avoid excessive dependence on any one customer and (2) to sell its own brands so that its success is dependent on the quality of its products rather than just a low price. The policy developed from a concern that if it started making products under other customers' brands, those customers could shop around for a low price and the business would be very fickle. At the time the policy was set, Stasia realized that it might cost AAA some business. But it was felt wise, nevertheless, to be better able to control the firm's future.

AAA has been in business 28 years and now has a sales volume of $40 million. Its primary products are file folders, file markers and labels, and a variety of indexing systems. AAA offers such a wide range of size, color, and type that no competitor can match it in its part of the market. About 40 percent of AAA's file folder business is in specialized lines such as files for oversized blueprint and engineer drawings; see-through files for medical markets; and greaseproof and waterproof files for marine, oil field, and other hazardous environmental markets. AAA's competitors are mostly small paper converters. But excess capacity in the industry is substantial, and these converters are always hungry for orders and willing to cut prices. Further, the raw materials for the FILEX line of file folders are readily available.

AAA's distribution system consists of 10 regional stationery suppliers (40 percent of total sales), Business Center, Inc. (30 percent), and more than 40 local stationers who have wholesale and retail operations (30 percent). The 10 regional stationers each have about six branches, while the local stationers each have one wholesale and three or four retail locations. The regional suppliers sell directly to large corporations and to some retailers. In contrast, Business Center's main volume comes from sales to local businesses and walk-in customers at its 150 retail stores.

Stasia has a real concern about the future of the local stationers' business. Some are seriously discussing the formation of buying groups to obtain volume discounts from vendors and thus compete more effectively with Business Center's 150 retail stores, the large regionals, and the superstore chains, which are spreading rapidly. These chains—for example, Staples, Office Max, and

*Adapted from a case by Professor Hardy, University of Western Ontario.

Office Depot—operate stores of 16,000 to 20,000 square feet (i.e., large stores compared to the usual office supply stores) and let customers wheel through high-stacked shelves to supermarket-like checkout counters. These chains stress convenience, wide selection, and much lower prices than the typical office supply retailers. They buy directly from manufacturers, such as AAA, bypassing wholesalers like Business Center. It is likely that the growing pressure from these chains is causing Business Center to renew its proposal to buy a file line with its own name. For example, Staples offers its own dealer brand of files and many other types of products.

None of Stasia's other accounts is nearly as effective in retailing as Business Center, which has developed a good reputation in every major city in the country. Business Center's profits have been the highest in the industry. Further, its brands are almost as well-known as those of some key producers—and its expansion plans are aggressive. And now, these plans are being pressured by the fast-growing superstores, which are already knocking out many local stationers.

Stasia is sure that AAA's brands are well entrenched in the market, despite the fact that most available money has been devoted to new-product development rather than promotion of existing brands. But Stasia is concerned that if Business Center brands its own file folders, it will sell them at a discount and may even bring the whole market price level down. Across all the lines of file folders, Stasia is averaging a 35 percent gross margin, but the commonly used file folders sought by Business Center are averaging only a 20 percent gross margin. And cutting this margin further does not look very attractive to Stasia.

Stasia is not sure whether Business Center will continue to sell AAA's FILEX brand of folders along with Business Center's own file folders if Business Center is able to find a source of supply. Business Center's history has been to sell its own brand and a major brand side by side, especially if the major brand offers high quality and has strong brand recognition.

Stasia is having a really hard time deciding what to do about the existing branding policy. AAA has excess capacity and could easily handle the Business Center business. And she fears that if she turns down this business, Business Center will just go elsewhere and its own brand will cut into AAA's existing sales at Business Center stores. Further, what makes Business Center's offer especially attractive is that AAA's variable manufacturing costs would be quite low in relation to any price charged to Business Center—that is, there are substantial economies of scale, so the extra business could be very profitable—if Stasia doesn't consider the possible impact on the FILEX line. This Business Center business will be easy to get, but it will require a major change in policy, which Stasia will have to sell to Ramon Torres, AAA's president. This may not be easy. Ramon is primarily interested in developing new and better products so the company can avoid the "commodity end of the business."

Evaluate AAA's current strategy. What should Stasia Acosta do about Business Center's offer? Explain.

14. Showtime Media

Bob Merita, manager of Showtime Media, is looking for ways to increase profits. But he's turning cautious after the poor results of his last effort during the previous Christmas season. Showtime Media is located along a busy cross-town street about two miles from the downtown of a metropolitan area of 1 million and near a large university. It sells a wide variety of products used for its different types of multimedia presentations. Its lines include high-quality video and digital cameras, color scanners for use with computers, flat-panel monitors, teleprompters and projection equipment, including video-beam overhead projectors, and electronic projectors that produce large-screen versions of computer output. Most of the sales of this specialized equipment are made to area school boards for classroom use, to industry for use in research and sales, and to the university for use in research and instruction.

Showtime Media also offers a good selection of production-quality video media, specialized supplies (such as the large-format acetates used with backlit signs), video and audio editing equipment, and a specialized video editing service. Instead of just duplicating videos on a mass production basis, Showtime Media gives each video editing job individual attention—to add an audio track or incorporate computer graphics as requested by a customer. This service is really appreciated by local firms that need help producing high-quality DVDs—for example, for training or sales applications.

To encourage the school and industrial trade, Showtime Media offers a graphics consultation service. If a customer wants to create a video or computerized presentation, professional advice is readily available. In support of this free service, Showtime Media carries a full line of computer software for multimedia presentations and graphics work. Showtime Media has four full-time store clerks and two outside sales reps. The sales reps call on business firms, attend trade shows, make presentations for schools, and help both current and potential customers in their use and choice of multimedia materials. Most purchases are delivered by the sales reps or the store's delivery truck. Many repeat orders come in by phone or mail, but e-mail and electronic file exchange have become common.

The people who make most of the over-the-counter purchases are (1) serious amateurs and (2) some professionals who prepare videos or computerized presentation materials on a fee basis. Showtime Media gives price discounts of up to 25 percent off the suggested retail price to customers who buy more than $2,000 worth of goods per year. Most regular customers qualify for the discount.

In recent years, many amateur photo buffs have purchased digital cameras to capture family pictures. Frequently, the buyer is a computer user who wants to use the computer as a digital darkroom—and the cameras now available make this easy. Showtime Media has not previously offered the lower-priced and lower-quality digital models such buyers commonly want. But Bob knew that lots of such digital cameras were bought and felt that there ought to be a good opportunity to expand sales during the Christmas gift-giving season. Therefore, he planned a special pre-Christmas sale of two of the most popular brands of digital cameras and discounted the prices to competitive discount store levels—about $129 for one and $189 for the other. To promote the sale, he posted large signs in the store windows, gave the sale a lot of space on the home page of Showtime's website, and ran ads in a Christmas gift-suggestion edition of the local newspaper. This edition appeared each Wednesday during the four weeks before Christmas. At these prices and with this promotion, Bob hoped to sell at least 100 cameras. However, when the Christmas returns were in, total sales were five cameras. Bob was extremely disappointed with these results—especially because trade experts suggested that sales of digital cameras in those price and quality ranges were up 300 percent over last year—during the Christmas selling season.

Evaluate what Showtime Media is doing and what happened with the special promotion. What should Bob Merita do to increase sales and profits?

15. The Buckeye Group

Theresa Campana, owner of The Buckeye Group, is deciding whether to take on a new line. She is very concerned because, although she wants more lines, she feels that something is wrong with her latest candidate.

Theresa graduated from a large Midwestern university in 2006 with a B.S. in business. She worked selling cell phones for a year. Then Theresa decided to go into business for herself and formed The Buckeye Group. Looking for opportunities, Theresa placed several ads in her local newspaper in Columbus, Ohio, announcing that she was interested in becoming a sales representative in the area. She was quite pleased to receive a number of responses. Eventually, she became the sales representative in the Columbus area for three local computer software producers: Accto Company, which produces accounting-related software; Saleco, Inc., a producer of sales management software; and Invo, Inc., a producer of inventory control software. All of these companies were relatively small and were represented in other areas by other sales representatives like Theresa. The companies often sent her leads when customers from her area expressed interest at a trade show or through the company's website.

Theresa's main job was to call on possible customers. Once she made a sale, she would fax the signed license agreement to the respective producer, who would then UPS the programs directly to the customer or, more often, provide a key code for a website download. The producer would bill the customer, and Theresa would receive a commission varying from 5 to 10 percent of the dollar value of the sale. Theresa was expected to pay her own expenses. And the producers would handle any user questions, either by using 800 numbers for out-of-town calls or by e-mail queries to a technical support group.

Theresa called on anyone in the Columbus area who might use the products she sold. At first, her job was relatively easy, and sales came quickly because she had little competition. Many national companies offer similar products, but at that time they were not well represented in the Columbus area. Most small businesses needed someone to demonstrate what the software could do.

In 2008, Theresa sold $250,000 worth of Accto software, earning a 10 percent commission; $100,000 worth of Saleco software, also earning a 10 percent commission; and $200,000 worth of Invo software, earning a 7 percent commission. She was encouraged with her progress and looked forward to expanding sales in the future. She was especially optimistic because she had achieved these sales volumes without overtaxing herself. In fact, she felt she was operating at about 60 percent of her capacity and could easily take on new lines. So she began looking for other products she could sell in the Columbus area.

A local software company has recently approached Theresa about selling its newly developed software, which is basically a network security product. It is designed to secretly track all of the keystrokes and mouse clicks of each employee as he or she uses the computer—so that an employer can identify inappropriate uses of its computers or confidential data. Theresa isn't too enthusiastic about this offer because the commission is only 2 percent on potential annual sales of about $150,000—and she also doesn't like the idea of selling a product that might undermine the privacy of employees who are not doing anything wrong.

Now Theresa is faced with another decision. The owner of the MetalCoat Company, also in Columbus, has made what looks like an attractive offer. She called on MetalCoat to see if the firm might be interested in buying her accounting software. The owner didn't want the software, but he was very impressed with Theresa. After two long discussions, he asked if she would like to help MetalCoat solve its current problem. MetalCoat is having trouble with marketing, and the owner would like Theresa to take over the whole marketing effort.

MetalCoat produces solvents used to make coatings for metal products. It sells mainly to industrial customers in the mid-Ohio area and faces many competitors selling essentially the same products and charging the same low prices.

MetalCoat is a small manufacturer. Last year's sales were $500,000. It could handle at least four times this sales volume with ease and is willing to expand to increase sales—its main objective in the short run. MetalCoat's owner is offering Theresa a 12 percent commission on all sales if she will take charge of its pricing, advertising, and sales efforts. Theresa is flattered by the offer, but she is a little worried because it is a different type of product and she would have to learn a lot about it. The job also might require a great deal more traveling than she is doing now. For one thing, she would have to call on new potential customers in mid-Ohio, and she might have to travel up to 200 miles around Columbus to expand the solvent business. Further, she realizes that she is being asked to do more than just sell. But she did have marketing courses in college and thinks the new opportunity might be challenging.

Evaluate Theresa Campana's current strategy and how the proposed solvent line fits in with what she is doing now. What should she do? Why?

16. J&J Lumber Supply

Jimmy Olson, owner of J&J Lumber Supply, feels his business is threatened by a tough new competitor. And now Jimmy must decide quickly about an offer that may save his business.

Jimmy has been a sales rep for lumber mills for about 20 years. He started selling in a clothing store but gave it up after two years to work in a lumberyard because the future looked much better in the building materials industry. After drifting from one job to another, Jimmy finally settled down and worked his way up to manager of a large wholesale building materials distribution warehouse in Richmond, Virginia. In 2000, he formed J&J Lumber Supply and went into business for himself, selling carload lots of lumber to lumberyards in southeastern Virginia.

Jimmy works with five large lumber mills on the West Coast. They notify him when a carload of lumber is available to be shipped, specifying the grade, condition, and number of each size board in the shipment. Jimmy isn't the only person selling for these mills—but he is the only one in his area. He isn't required to take any particular number of carloads per month—but once he tells a mill he wants a particular shipment, title passes to him and he has to sell it to someone. Jimmy's main function is to find a buyer, buy the lumber from the mill as it's being shipped, and have the railroad divert the car to the buyer.

Having been in this business for 20 years, Jimmy knows all of the lumberyard buyers in his area very well and is on good working terms with them. He does most of his business over the telephone or by e-mail from his small office, but he tries to see each of the buyers about once a month. He has been marking up the lumber between 4 and 6 percent—the standard markup, depending on the grades and mix in each carload—and has been able to make a good living for himself and his family. The going prices are widely publicized in trade publications and are listed on the Internet, so the buyers can easily check to be sure Jimmy's prices are competitive.

In the last few years, a number of Jimmy's lumberyard customers have gone out of business—and others have lost sales. The main problem is competition from several national home improvement chains that have moved into Jimmy's market area. These chains buy lumber in large quantities direct from a mill, and their low prices, available inventory, and one-stop shopping are taking some customers away from the traditional lumberyards. Some customers think the quality of the lumber is not quite as good at the big chains, and some contractors stick with the lumberyards out of loyalty or because they get better service, including rush deliveries when they're needed. Then came the mortgage crisis and the residential housing market really slowed down, though not as bad in Richmond as in other parts of the country. Fortunately for Jimmy, the commercial market remained pretty strong and he had good relationships there—or Jimmy's profits would have taken an even bigger hit.

Six months ago, though, things got even worse. An aggressive young salesman set up in the same business, covering about the same area but representing different lumber mills. This new salesman charges about the same prices as Jimmy but undersells him once or twice a week in order to get the sale. On several occasions he even set up what was basically an e-mail-based auction to quickly sell excess wood that was not moving fast enough. Many lumber buyers—feeling the price competition from the big chains and realizing that they are dealing with a homogeneous product—seem to be willing to buy from the lowest-cost source. This has hurt Jimmy financially and personally—because even some of his old friends are willing to buy from the new competitor if the price is lower. The near-term outlook seems dark, since Jimmy doubts that there is enough business to support two firms like his, especially if the markup gets shaved any closer. Now they seem to be splitting the shrinking business about equally, as the newcomer keeps shaving his markup.

A week ago, Jimmy was called on by Amy Balderas of Arbor Door and Window Co., a large manufacturer of windows, raised-panel doors, and accessories. Arbor doesn't sell to the big chains and instead distributes its quality line only through independent lumberyards. Amy knows that Jimmy is well acquainted with the local lumberyards and wants him to become Arbor's exclusive distributor (sales rep) of residential windows and accessories in his area. Amy gave Jimmy several brochures on Arbor's product lines. She also explained Arbor's new support program, which will help train and support Jimmy and interested lumberyards on how to sell the higher markup accessories. Later, in a lengthy e-mail, Amy explained how this program will help Jimmy and interested lumberyards differentiate themselves in this very competitive market.

Most residential windows of specified grades are basically "commodities" that are sold on the basis of price and availability, although some premium and very low end windows are sold also. The national home-improvement chains usually stock and sell only the standard sizes. Most independent lumberyards do not stock windows because there are so many possible sizes. Instead, the lumberyards custom order from the stock sizes each factory offers. Stock sizes are not set by industry standards; they vary from factory to factory, and some offer more sizes. Most factories can deliver these custom orders in two to six weeks, which is usually adequate to satisfy contractors who buy and install them according to architectural plans. This part of the residential window business is well established, and most lumberyards buy from several different window manufacturers—to ensure sources of supply in case of strikes, plant fires, and so on. How the business is split depends on price and the personality and persuasiveness of the sales reps. And given that prices are usually similar, the sales rep–customer relationship can be quite important.

Arbor gives more choice than just about any other supplier. It offers many variations in 1/8-inch increments—to cater to remodelers who must adjust to many situations. Arbor has even set up a special system on an Internet website. The lumberyard can connect to the website, enter the specs for a window online, and within seconds get a price quote and estimated delivery time.

One reason Amy has approached Jimmy is because of Jimmy's many years in the business. But the other reason is that Arbor is aggressively trying to expand—relying on its made-to-order windows, a full line of accessories, and a newly developed factory support system to help differentiate it from the many other window manufacturers. To give Jimmy a quick big picture of the opportunity she is offering, Amy explained the window market as follows:

1. For commercial construction, the usual building code ventilation requirements are satisfied with mechanical ventilation. So the windows do not have to operate to permit natural ventilation. They are usually made with heavygrade aluminum framing. Typically, a distributor furnishes and installs the windows. As part of its service, the distributor provides considerable technical support, including engineered drawings and diagrams to the owners, architects, and/or contractors.
2. For residential construction, on the other hand, windows must be operable to provide ventilation. Residential windows are usually made of wood, frequently with light-gauge aluminum or vinyl on the exterior. The national chains get some volume with standard-size windows, but lumberyards are the most common source of supply for contractors in Jimmy's

area. These lumberyards do not provide any technical support or engineered drawings. A few residential window manufacturers do have their own sales centers in selected geographic areas, which provide a full range of support and engineering services, but none are anywhere near Jimmy's area.

Arbor feels a big opportunity exists in the commercial building repair and rehabilitation market (sometimes called the retrofit market) for a crossover of residential windows to commercial applications—and it has designed some accessories and a factory support program to help lumberyards get this "commercial" business. For applications such as nursing homes and dormitories (which must meet commercial codes), the wood interior of a residential window is desired, but the owners and architects are accustomed to commercial grades and building systems. And in some older facilities, the windows may have to provide supplemental ventilation for a deficient mechanical system. So what is needed is a combination of the residential *operable* window with a heavy-gauge commercial exterior frame that is easy to specify and install. And this is what Arbor is offering with a combination of its basic windows and easily adjustable accessory frames. Two other residential window manufacturers offer a similar solution, but neither has pushed its products aggressively and neither offers technical support to lumberyards or trains sales reps like Jimmy to do the necessary job. Amy feels this could be a unique opportunity for Jimmy.

The sales commission on residential windows would be about 5 percent of sales. Arbor would do the billing and collecting. By getting just 20 to 30 percent of his lumberyards' residential window business, Jimmy could earn about a third of his current income. But the real upside would come in the long term by increasing his residential window share. Jimmy is confident that the housing market will turn around soon, and when it does he will be well-positioned for growth. To do this, he will have to help the lumberyards get a lot more (and more profitable) business by invading the commercial market with residential windows and the bigger markup accessories needed for this market. Jimmy will also earn a 20 percent commission on the accessories, adding to his profit potential.

Jimmy is somewhat excited about the opportunity because the retrofit market is growing. And owners and architects are seeking ways of reducing costs (which Arbor's approach does—over usual commercial approaches). He also likes the idea of developing a new line to offset the slow-growing market for new construction housing. But he is also concerned that a lot of sales effort will be needed to introduce this new idea. He is not afraid of work, but he is concerned about his financial survival.

Jimmy thinks he has three choices:

1. Take Amy's offer and sell both window and lumber products.
2. Take the offer and drop lumber sales.
3. Stay strictly with lumber and forget the offer.

Amy is expecting an answer within one week, so Jimmy has to decide soon.

Evaluate Jimmy Olson's current strategy and how the present offer fits in. What should he do now? Why?

17. Simply Pure H2O4U, Inc.

Morton Rinke established his company, Simply Pure H2O4U, Inc., to market a product designed to purify drinking water. The product, branded as the PURITY II Naturalizer Water Unit, is produced by Environmental Control, Inc., a corporation that focuses primarily on water purification and filtering products for industrial markets.

Simply Pure H2O4U is a small but growing business. Morton started the business with an initial capital of only $20,000, which came from his savings and loans from several relatives. Morton manages the company himself. He has a secretary and six full-time salespeople. In addition, he employs two college students part-time; they make telephone calls to prospect for customers and set up appointments for a salesperson to demonstrate the unit in the consumer's home. He has built a small website that primarily provides detailed information and allows customers to request a call from a salesperson. By holding spending to a minimum, Morton has kept the firm's monthly operating budget at only $4,500—and most of that goes for rent, his secretary's salary, and other necessities like computer supplies and telephone bills.

The PURITY II system uses a reverse osmosis purification process. Reverse osmosis is the most effective technology known for improving drinking water. The device is certified by the Environmental Protection Agency to reduce levels of most foreign substances, including fluoride, mercury, rust, sediment, arsenic, lead, phosphate, bacteria, and most insecticides.

Each PURITY II unit consists of a high-quality 1-micron sediment removal cartridge, a carbon filter, a sediment filter, a housing, a faucet, and mounting hardware. The compact system fits under a kitchen sink or a wet bar sink. A H2O4U salesperson can typically install the PURITY II in about a half hour. Installation involves attaching the unit to the cold water supply line, drilling a hole in the sink, and fastening the special faucet. It works equally well with water from a municipal system or well water, and it can purify up to 15 gallons daily. H2O4U sells the PURITY II to consumers for $395, which includes installation.

The system has no movable parts or electrical connections, and it has no internal metal parts that will corrode or rust. However, the system does use a set of filters that must be replaced after about two years. H2O4U sells the replacement filters for $80. Taking into consideration the cost of the filters, the system provides drinking water at a cost of approximately $.05 per gallon for the average family.

There are two major benefits from using the PURITY II system. First, water treated by this system tastes better. Blind taste tests confirm that most consumers can tell the difference between water treated with the PURITY II and ordinary tap water.

Consequently, the unit improves the taste of coffee, tea, frozen juices, ice cubes, mixed drinks, soup, and vegetables cooked in water. Perhaps more important, the PURITY II's ability to remove potentially harmful foreign matter makes the product of special interest to the growing number of people who are concerned about health and the safety of the water they consume. For example, there is growing controversy surrounding public fluoridation of drinking water—and many consumers are looking for filters that remove fluoride.

The number of people with health and safety concerns is growing. In spite of increased efforts to protect the environment and water supplies, there are still many problems. Hundreds of new chemical compounds—ranging from insecticides to industrial chemicals to commercial cleaning agents—are put into use each year. Some of the residue from chemicals and toxic waste eventually enters water supply sources. Further, floods and hurricanes have damaged or completely shut down water treatment facilities in some cities. Problems like these have led to rumors of possible epidemics of such dread diseases as cholera and typhoid—and more than one city has recently experienced near-panic buying of bottled water.

Given these problems and the need for pure water, Morton believes that the market potential for the PURITY II system is very large. Residences, both single-family homes and apartments, are one obvious target. The unit is also suitable for use in boats and recreational vehicles; in fact, the PURITY II is standard equipment on several upscale RVs. And it can be used in taverns and restaurants, in institutions such as schools and hospitals, and in commercial and industrial buildings.

There are several competing ways for customers to solve the problem of getting pure water. Some purchase bottled water. Companies such as Ozarka deliver water monthly for an average price of $.60 per gallon. The best type of bottled water is distilled water; it is absolutely pure because it is produced by the process of evaporation. However, it may be *too pure*. The distilling process removes needed elements such as calcium and phosphate—and there is some evidence that removing these trace elements contributes to heart disease. In fact, some health-action groups recommend that consumers not drink distilled water.

A second way to obtain pure water is to use some system to treat tap water. PURITY II is one such system. Another system uses an ion exchange process that replaces ions of harmful substances like iron and mercury with ions that are not harmful. Ion exchange is somewhat less expensive than the PURITY II process, but it is not well suited for residential use because bacteria can build up before the water is used. In addition, there are a number of other filtering and softening systems. In general, these are less expensive and less reliable than the PURITY II. For example, water softeners remove minerals but do not remove bacteria or germs.

Morton's first year with his young company has gone quite well. Customers who have purchased the system like it, and there appear to be several ways to expand the business and increase profits. For example, so far he has had little time to make sales calls on potential commercial and institutional users or residential builders. He also sees other possibilities such as expanding his promotion effort or targeting consumers in a broader geographic area.

At present, H2O4U distributes the PURITY II in the 13-county GULF COAST region of Texas. Because of the Robinson-Patman Act, the manufacturer cannot grant an exclusive distributorship. However, H2O4U is currently the only PURITY II distributor in this region. In addition, H2O4U has the right of first refusal to set up distributorships in other areas of Texas. The manufacturer has indicated that it might even give H2O4U distribution rights in a large section of northern Mexico.

The agreement with the manufacturer allows H2O4U to distribute the product to retailers, including hardware stores and plumbing supply dealers. Morton has not yet pursued this channel, but a PURITY II distributor in Florida reported some limited success selling the system to retailers at a wholesale price of $275. Retailers for this type of product typically expect a markup of about 33 percent of their selling price.

Environmental Control, Inc., ships the PURITY II units directly from its warehouse to the H2O4U office via UPS. The manufacturer's $200 per unit selling price includes the cost of shipping. H2O4U only needs to keep a few units on hand because the manufacturer accepts faxed orders and then ships immediately—so delivery never takes more than a few days. Further, the units are small enough to inventory in the back room of the H2O4U sales office. Several of the easy-to-handle units will fit in the trunk of a salesperson's car.

Morton is thinking about recruiting additional salespeople. Finding capable people has not been a problem so far. However, there has already been some turnover, and one of the current salespeople is complaining that the compensation is not high enough. Morton pays salespeople on a straight commission basis. A salesperson who develops his or her own prospects gets $100 per sale; the commission is $80 per unit on sales leads generated by the company's telemarketing people. For most salespeople, the mix of sales is about half and half. H2O4U pays the students who make the telephone contacts $4 per appointment set up and $10 per unit sold from an appointment. A growing number of leads are coming from the company's website, largely due to search ads placed on Google and Yahoo!

An average H2O4U salesperson easily sells 30 units per month. However, Morton believes that a really effective and well-prepared salesperson can sell much more, perhaps 50 units per month.

H2O4U and its salespeople get good promotion support from Environmental Control, Inc. For example, Environmental Control supplies sales training manuals and sales presentation flip charts. The materials are also well done, in part because Environmental Control's promotion manager previously worked for Electrolux vacuum cleaners, which are sold in a similar way. The company also supplies print copy for magazine and newspaper advertising and tapes of commercials for radio and television. Thus, all H2O4U has to do is buy media space or time. In addition, Environmental Control furnishes each salesperson with a portable demonstration unit, and the company recently gave H2O4U three units to be placed in models of condominium apartments.

Morton has worked long hours to get his company going, but he realizes that he has to find time to think about how his strategy is working and to plan for the future.

Evaluate Morton Rinke's current marketing strategy for Simply Pure H2O4U. How do you think he's doing so far, and what should he do next? Why?

18. Whistler Township Volunteer Fire Department (WTVFD)

Nolan Fenwick raced out the front door of the Target store where he worked as soon as his beeper sounded. In his pickup truck he heard the call on his special radio scanner, "Highway 18 Fire Department, there is a grass fire at the old McCullough place. That's a mile down the old dirt road just past the Wilson house." The directions might appear cryptic to someone who had not grown up around Whistler Township, but it was all Nolan needed to know. Upon arriving at the fire, Nolan quickly pulled on his fire-retardant bunker pants and boots. He left his Nomex hood, helmet, and fire pants in the back of his truck—he would not need them for this fire.

Less than 10 minutes from the time the call was placed, Nolan and 20 other members of the Whistler Township Volunteer Fire Department (WTVFD) had arrived at the old McCullough place. They were able to put out the fire in less than half an hour, but not before a football-field-size patch of grass was scorched. Their quick response saved the neighbor's barn and kept the fire from spreading to a nearby forest. A third straight year of drought has the crew on high alert.

Nolan threw his gear in the back of his truck and headed back to finish his shift at Target. He had worked there as a department manager for two years, ever since he graduated from the local state college with a marketing degree. As he drove, Nolan thought about what WTVFD Chief Fran Holland recently asked him to do. Over the last few years, the fire department had more to do but fewer people to do it with. So Chief Holland asked Nolan to draw up a marketing plan to recruit new volunteers.

Nolan had already started to gather information for the marketing plan. From an online search he found that WTVFD was one of an estimated 30,000 volunteer fire departments in the United States and that these departments had almost a million volunteers. Nolan was surprised that more than 75 percent of all U.S. firefighters were volunteers. Whistler Township, a small city of just over 100,000 and hours from a big city, only had volunteer firefighters.

There are 48 firefighters currently in the WTVFD—down from 55 five years ago. While there was a surge of interest in the year following the terrorist attacks in 2001, only a few of those volunteers remain. Over time, WTVFD has found that about half of new recruits quit before their three-year anniversary. Those who remain usually stay with the department until they can't keep up with the job's physical demands. Fran Holland has been chief for the last three years. She replaced long-time chief, Ken Reeb, who retired after being with WTVFD for more than 40 years—the last 10 as chief.

The current volunteers include 44 men and four women; more than half of the force is over 40 years old, and Nolan is one of only five members younger than 30. Almost all of them started volunteering while still in their 20s or early 30s. The crew represents all walks of life, and their ranks include a lawyer, a real estate salesperson, a college professor, a carpenter, a stay-at-home mom, and a few guys from the local factory. Many entered firefighting for the thrill of it or because they hoped the experience might help them land a paid firefighting job in a bigger city. But most of the crew stay with it because they feel good about giving back to their community, view it as a hobby, and enjoy the camaraderie with the other firefighters.

Being a volunteer firefighter is very much different than Nolan thought it would be when he started. Last year he counted 238 hours volunteering for WTVFD, but less than a third of that was actually responding to emergencies. And fewer than half of the emergencies were actual fires. He spent about a quarter of this time in required training and drills. He had to be trained for the many different possible calls, including car accidents, hazardous chemical spills, and terrorist attacks. Another 20 percent of his time was spent in meetings and a similar amount helping with fund-raising. Depending upon financial needs, WTVFD holds at least four fund-raising events a year—some years six or eight. These include annual activities like a chili cook-off, pancake breakfast, and booth at the county fair—and as-needed events like pie auctions, turkey shoots, and basketball tournaments.

The biggest requirement to be a volunteer firefighter is the willingness to make the time commitment. Nolan's time commitment and allocation of hours is typical of all the firefighters at WTVFD. Volunteers have to be able to attend at least 80 percent of the twice monthly drills—scheduled on the second and fourth Tuesdays of every month. Firefighters also have to live or work near the city of Whistler Township so they can quickly respond to an emergency. They also have to be at least 18 years old and have a valid driver's license. There is a physical ability test to make sure that firefighters can stand the rigors of the job. While one doesn't have to be a weightlifter, the job requires volunteers to be in good physical shape.

WTVFD has never really had a marketing strategy or any formal promotion efforts. Most of Nolan's fellow volunteers heard about WTVFD through word of mouth. People are always curious when a volunteer firefighter runs out the door from work or suddenly leaves a party. These occasions give volunteers a chance to tell others about what they do. Sometimes those questions bring someone out to see drills and to apply to become a volunteer. One of Nolan's high school friends was a volunteer and he encouraged Nolan to join up while Nolan was in his junior year of college. But still, awareness of volunteer firefighting in the Whistler Township area is very low. When Nolan tells friends about his volunteer work, most are surprised and think the town has full-time paid staff fighting fires.

Nolan thinks his marketing strategy should focus mostly on promotion. From his studies he remembers the AIDA model and integrated marketing communications. But he also wonders if his plan should focus only on gaining new recruits or if current volunteers might also be the target of new promotion. Nolan also considers how and what he should communicate to his target market. He knows he will have limited funding for his efforts. Should he consider starting a Facebook page or blog? Maybe a website would be better. What about advertising or information sessions? Who should be his target market?

Evaluate the promotion objectives Nolan Fenwick should include in his plan. What promotion methods should he use to achieve those objectives?

19. MyPerfectWedding.com

Jessica Eggleston is happy with her life but disappointed that the idea she had for starting her own business hasn't taken off as expected. Within a few weeks she either has to renew the contract for her Internet website or decide not to put any more time and money into her idea. She knows that it doesn't make sense to renew the contract if she can't come up with a plan to make her website–based business profitable—and she doesn't like to plan. She's a "doer," not a planner.

Jessica's business, MyPerfectWedding.com, started as an idea 18 months ago as she was planning her own wedding. She attended a bridal fair at the convention center in Raleigh, North Carolina, to get ideas for a wedding dress, check out catering companies and florists, and in general learn more about the various services available to newlyweds. While there, she and her fiancé went from one retailer's booth to another to sign up for their wedding gift registries. Almost every major retailer in the city—ranging from the Home Depot warehouse to the Belk's department store to the specialty shops that handle imported crystal glassware—offered a gift registry. Some had computers set up to provide access to their online registries. Being listed in all of the registries improved the odds that her wedding gifts would be items she wanted and could use—and it saved time and hassle for gift-givers. On the way back from the fair, Jessica and her fiancé discussed the idea that it would be a lot easier to register gift preferences once on a central Internet site than to provide lots of different stores with bits and pieces of information. A list at a website would also make it easier for gift-givers, at least those who were computer users.

When Jessica got home, she did an Internet search and found several sites that focused on weddings. The biggest seemed to be www.weddingchannel.com. It had features for couples who were getting married, including a national gift registry. The site featured products from a number of companies, especially large national retail chains; however, there was a search feature to locate people who provide wedding-related services in a local ZIP code area. Jessica thought that the sites she found looked quite good, but that they were not as helpful as a site could be with a more local focus.

The more Jessica and her fiancé discussed the idea of a website offering local wedding-related services, the more it looked like an interesting opportunity. Except for the annual bridal fair, there was no other obvious local place for consumers to get information about planning a wedding and buying wedding-related services. And for local retailers, florists, catering companies, insurance agents, home builders, and many other types of firms, there was no other central place to target promotion to newlyweds. Further, the amount of money spent on weddings and wedding gifts is substantial, and right before and after getting married many young couples make many important purchase decisions for everything from life insurance to pots and pans. Spending on the wedding itself can easily exceed the cost of a year of college.

Jessica was no stranger to the Internet. She worked as a website designer for a small firm whose only client was IBM. That IBM was the only client was intentional rather than accidental. A year earlier IBM had decided that it wanted to outsource certain aspects of its website development work and have it handled by an outside contractor. After negotiating a three-year contract to do IBM's work, several IBM employees quit their jobs and started the business. IBM was a good client, and all indications were that IBM could give the firm as much work as it could handle as it hired new people and prospected for additional accounts over the next few years. Jessica especially liked the creative aspects of designing the "look" of a website, and technical specialists handled a lot of the subtle details.

Before joining this new company, Jessica had several marketing-related jobs—but none had been the glamorous ad agency job she dreamed of in college as an advertising major. Her first job as a college graduate was with an ad agency, but she was in a backroom operation handling a lot of the arrangements for printing and mailing large-scale direct-mail promotions. In spite of promises that it was a path to other jobs at the agency, the pay was bad, the work was always pressured, and every aspect of what she had to do was boring. After six punishing months, she quit and went looking for something else.

When a number of job applications didn't turn up something quickly, she took a part-time job doing telemarketing calls for a mortgage refinance company. Jessica's boss told her that she was doing a great job reeling in prospects—but she hated disturbing people at night and just didn't like making sales pitches. Fortunately for her, that pain didn't last long. A neighbor in Jessica's apartment complex got Jessica an interview for a receptionist position at an ad agency. That, at least, got her foot in the door. Her job description wasn't very interesting, but in a small agency she had the opportunity to learn a lot about all aspects of the business—ranging from working on client proposals and media plans to creative sessions for new campaigns. In fact, it was from a technician at that agency that she learned to work with the graphics software used to create ad layouts and website pages. When the website design job came open at the new firm, her boss gave her a glowing recommendation, and in two days she was off on her new career.

Although Jessica's jobs had not been high-profile positions, they did give her some experience in sales promotion, personal selling, and advertising. Those skills were complemented by the technical computer skills of her fiancé (now husband), who made a living as a database programmer for a large software consulting firm. Taking everything as a whole, they thought that they could get a wedding-related website up and running and make it profitable.

There were several different facets to the original plan for MyPerfectWedding.com. One focused on recruiting local advertisers and "sponsors" who would pay to be listed at the website and be allocated a web page (which Jessica would design) describing their services, giving contact information, and links to their own websites. Another focused on services for people who were planning to be married. In addition to an online wedding gift registry, sections of the website provided information about typical wedding costs, planning checklists, details about how to get a required marriage license, and other helpful information (including a discussion forum with comments about the strengths and weaknesses of various local suppliers). Jessica also started a blog that helped foster more feedback from customers. A man and woman could sign up for the service online and could pay the modest $20 "membership" fee for a year by credit card. Friends, family, and invited guests could visit the website at no charge and get information about wedding preferences, local hotels, discounts on local car rentals, and even printable maps to all of the churches and synagogues in the area.

When Jessica told friends about her plan, they all thought it sounded like a great idea. In fact, each time she discussed it someone came up with another idea for a locally oriented feature to add to the website. Several friends said that they had tried national websites but that the information was often too general. But generating more new ideas was not the problem. The problem was generating revenue. Jessica had already contracted for space from an Internet service provider and created some of the initial content for the website, but she only had four paying sponsors, two of whom happened to be family friends.

Jessica started by creating a colorful flyer describing the website and sent it to most of the firms that had participated in the bridal fair. When no one sent back the reply coupon for more information, Jessica started to make calls (mainly during her lunch hour at her full-time job). Some stores seemed intrigued by the concept, but no one seemed ready to sign up. One reason was that they all seemed surprised at the cost to participate and get ad space at the website—$2,400 a year (about the same as a 1/16-page display ad in the Raleigh Yellow Pages). Another problem was that no one wanted to be the first to sign up. As one florist shop owner put it, "If you pull this off and other florists sign up, then come back and I will too."

Getting couples to sign up went slowly too. Jessica paid for four display ads in local Sunday newspapers in the society section, sent information sheets about the website to clergy in the area, listed the website with about 25 Internet search engines, and sent carefully crafted press releases announcing the service to almost every publication in the area. One article that resulted from a press release got some attention, and for a few weeks there was a flurry of e-mail inquiries about her web page. But after that it slowed to a trickle again. More recently she tried to use Google AdWords which placed ads next to Google search results when someone from the greater Raleigh area searched on the keyword *wedding*. She got a few more hits from this and wondered if she should increase the number of keywords—and wondered what the best keywords could be. She thought about creating a Facebook page but wondered how it would help. She knows that many brides are on Pinterest and wasn't sure if she should start her own page there.

Jessica's diagnosis of the problem was simple. Most people thought it was a great idea, but few couples knew where to look on the Internet for such a service. Similarly, potential advertisers—many of them small local businesses—were not accustomed to the idea of paying for Internet advertising. They didn't know if the cost was reasonable or if her site would be effective in generating business.

Jessica's life as a married person was going great and her job as a web page designer kept her very busy. Her free time outside of work was always in short supply because the young crowd at her office always had some scheme for how to keep entertained. So she wasn't about to quit her job to devote full time to her business idea. Further, she thought that once it got rolling she would only have to devote 10 hours a week to it to earn an extra $30,000 a year. She didn't have delusions of becoming a "dot-com millionaire." She just wanted a good locally oriented business.

However, it still wasn't clear how to get it rolling. After a year of trying on and off, she only had four paying ad sponsors, and one of them had already notified her that he didn't plan to sign up again because it wasn't clear that the website had generated any direct leads or sales. Further, it looked like anything she could do to attract more "members" would end up being expensive and inefficient.

Jessica thinks the idea has real potential, and she's willing to do the work. But she's not certain if she can make it pay off. She has to decide soon, however, because the bill for the Internet service provider is sitting on her desk.

What is Jessica's strategy? What should she do? If she were to move forward, what strategy would you recommend? Does her financial goal seem realistic? Why?

20. Blue Lagoon Marine & Camp

Jeffery Mauro, owner of Blue Lagoon Marine & Camp, is worried about his business' future. He has tried various strategies for two years now, and he's still barely breaking even.

Two years ago, Jeffery bought the inventory, supplies, equipment, and business of Blue Lagoon Marine & Camp, located on the edge of Minneapolis, Minnesota. The business is in an older building along a major highway leading out of town, several miles from any body of water. The previous owner had sales of about $500,000 a year but was just breaking even. For this reason—plus the desire to retire to Arizona—the owner sold to Jeffery for roughly the value of the inventory.

Blue Lagoon Marine & Camp had been selling two well-known brands of small pleasure boats, a leading outboard motor, two brands of snowmobiles and jet-skis, and a line of trailer and pickup-truck campers. The total inventory was valued at $250,000—and Jeffery used all of his own savings and borrowed some from two friends to buy the inventory and the business. At the same time, he took over the lease on the building—so he was able to begin operations immediately. Jeffery had never operated a business of his own before, but he was sure that he would be able to do well. He had worked in a variety of jobs—as a used-car salesman, an auto repairman, and a jack-of-all-trades in the maintenance departments of several local businesses.

Soon after starting his business, Jeffery hired his friend, Ginny Wooten. She had worked with Jeffery selling cars and had experience as a receptionist and in customer service. Together, they handle all selling and setup work on new sales and do maintenance work as needed. Sometimes the two are extremely busy—at the peaks of each sport season. Then both sales and maintenance keep them going up to 16 hours a day. At these times it's difficult to have both new and repaired equipment available as soon as customers want it. At other times, however, Jeffery and Ginny have almost nothing to do.

Jeffery usually charges the prices suggested by the various manufacturers, except at the end of a weather season when he is willing to make deals to clear the inventory. He is annoyed that some of his competitors sell mainly on a price basis—offering 10 to 30 percent off a manufacturer's suggested list prices—even at the beginning of a season! Jeffery doesn't want to get into that kind of business, however. He hopes to build a loyal following based on friendship and personal service. Further, he doesn't think he really has to cut prices because all of his lines are exclusive for his store. No stores within a five mile radius carry any of his brands, although nearby retailers offer many brands of similar products. Right now, the Internet does not provide much competition, but he fears future price competition from online boat shows.

To try to build a favorable image for his company, Jeffery occasionally places ads in local papers and buys some radio spots. The basic theme of this advertising is that Blue Lagoon Marine & Camp is a friendly, service-oriented place to buy the equipment needed for the current season. Sometimes he mentions the brand names he carries, but generally Jeffery tries to build an image for concerned, friendly service—both in new sales and repairs—stressing, "We do it right the first time." He chose this approach because, although he has exclusives on the brands he carries, there generally are 10 to 15 different manufacturers' products being sold in the area in each product category—and most of the products are quite similar. Jeffery feels that this similarity among competing products almost forces him to try to differentiate himself on the basis of his own store's services.

The first year's operation wasn't profitable. In fact, after paying minimal salaries to Ginny and himself, the business just about broke even. Jeffery made no return on his $250,000 investment.

In hopes of improving profitability, Jeffery jumped at a chance to add a line of lawn mowers, tractors, and trimmers as he was starting into his second year of business. This line was offered by a well-known equipment manufacturer that wanted to expand into the Minneapolis area. The equipment is similar to that offered by other lawn equipment manufacturers. The manufacturer's willingness to do some local advertising and to provide some point-of-purchase displays appealed to Jeffery. And he also liked the idea that customers probably would want this equipment sometime earlier than boats and other summer items. So he thought he could handle this business without interfering with his other peak selling seasons.

It's been two years since Jeffery bought Blue Lagoon Marine & Camp—and he's still only breaking even. Sales have increased a little, but costs have gone up too because he had to hire some part-time help. The lawn equipment helped to expand sales—as he had expected—unfortunately, it did not increase profits as he had hoped. Jeffery needed part-time helpers to handle this business—in part because the manufacturer's advertising had generated a lot of sales inquiries. Relatively few inquiries resulted in sales, however, because many people seemed to be shopping for deals. So Jeffery may have even lost money handling the new line. But he hesitates to give it up because he doesn't want to lose that sales volume, and the manufacturer's sales rep has been most encouraging, assuring Jeffery that things will get better and that his company will be glad to continue its promotion support during the coming year.

Jeffery is now considering the offer of a mountain bike producer that has not been represented in the area. The bikes have become very popular with students and serious bikers in the last several years. The manufacturer's sales rep says industry sales are still growing (but not as fast as in the past) and probably will grow for many more years. The sales rep has praised Jeffery's service orientation and says this could help him sell lots of bikes because many mountain bikers are serious about buying a quality bike and then keeping it serviced. He says Jeffery's business approach would be a natural fit with bike customers' needs and attitudes. As a special inducement to get Jeffery to take on the line, the sales rep says Jeffery will not have to pay for the initial inventory of bikes, accessories, and repair parts for 90 days. And, of course, the company will supply the usual promotion aids and a special advertising allowance of $10,000 to help introduce the line to Minneapolis.

Jeffery likes the idea of carrying mountain bikes because he has one himself and knows that they do require some service year-round. But he also knows that the proposed bikes are very similar in price and quality to the ones now being offered by the bike shops in town. These bike shops are service- rather than price-oriented, and Jeffery feels that they are doing a good job on service; consequently, he is concerned with how he can be "different."

Evaluate Jeffery Mauro's overall strategy(ies) and the mountain bike proposal. What should he do now?

21. Global Chemical, Inc. (GCI)

Global Chemical, Inc., (GCI) is a multinational producer of various chemicals and plastics with plants in the United States, England, France, and Germany. Its headquarters are in New Jersey.

Kenneth Shibata is marketing manager of GCI's plastics business. Kenneth is reconsidering his promotion approach. He is evaluating what kind of promotion—and how much—should be directed to car producers and to other major plastics customers worldwide. Currently, Kenneth has one salesperson who devotes most of his time to the car industry. This man is based in the Detroit area and focuses on GM, Ford, and Chrysler—as well as the various firms that mold plastics to produce parts to supply the car industry. This approach worked well when relatively little plastic was used in each car *and* the auto producers did all of the designing themselves and then sent out specifications for very price-oriented competitive bidding. But now the whole product planning and buying system is changing—and of course foreign producers with facilities in the United States are much more important.

How the present system works can be illustrated in terms of the team approach Ford used on its project to design the Flex, the full-size crossover introduced as a 2009 model. For the Flex, representatives from all the various functions—planning, design, engineering, purchasing, marketing, and manufacturing—work together. In fact, representatives from key suppliers were involved from the outset. The whole team takes final responsibility for a car. Because all of the departments are involved from the start, problems are resolved as the project moves on—before they cause a crisis. Manufacturing, for example, can suggest changes in design that will result in higher productivity or better quality, which is especially important at a time when Ford's initial quality ratings are beating those of Honda and Toyota.

The old approach was different. It involved a five-year process of creating a new vehicle in sequential steps. Under the old system, product planners would come up with a general concept and then expect the design team to give it artistic form. Next, engineering would develop the specifications and pass them on to manufacturing and suppliers. There was little communication between the groups and no overall project responsibility.

In the Flex project, Ford engineers followed the Japanese lead and did some reverse engineering of their own. They dismantled several competitors' cars, piece by piece, looking for ideas they could copy or improve. This helped them learn how the parts were assembled and how they were designed. Eventually, Ford incorporated or modified some of the best features into its design of the Flex. For example, the Flex uses a new design to seal the doors and eliminate wind noise.

In addition to reverse engineering, Ford researchers conducted a series of market studies. This led to positioning the Flex as an "anti-minivan." That positioning resulted in a decision to eliminate the sliding side doors and instead to use traditional hinged doors. That cut costs, but the savings were used for dress-up features, like 19-inch aluminum wheels and a special new seat design that reduces movement in the seat and gives the car an even smoother drive. The Flex's optional refrigerator/freezer is another example of a feature that did well in concept tests.

Ford also asked assembly-line workers for suggestions before the car was redesigned and then incorporated their ideas into the new car. Most bolts have the same-size head, for example, so workers don't have to switch from one wrench to another.

Finally, Ford included its best suppliers as part of the planning effort. Instead of turning to a supplier after the car's design was completed, Ford invited them to participate in product planning. For example, Microsoft's Sync system provides the Flex with voice control of the entertainment system.

Most other vehicles are now developed with an approach similar to this. GM, for example, used a very similar team approach to redesign its new Malibu. And major firms in many other industries are using similar approaches. A major outgrowth of this effort has been a trend by these producers to develop closer working relationships with a smaller number of suppliers. To some extent, this is a direct outgrowth of the decision to try to reduce unnecessary costs by using the same components for different vehicles. For example, the powertrain for the Flex is the same as the one used in Ford's Edge.

Many of the suppliers selected for the Flex project had not only the facilities, but also the technical and professional managerial staff who could understand—and become part of—the program management approach. Ford expected these major suppliers to join in its total quality management push and to be able to provide just-in-time delivery systems. Ford dropped suppliers whose primary sales technique was to entertain buyers and then submit bids on standard specifications.

Because many firms have moved to these team-oriented approaches and developed closer working relationships with a subset of their previous suppliers, Kenneth is trying to determine if GCI's present effort is still appropriate. Kenneth's strategy has focused primarily on responding to inquiries and bringing in GCI's technical people as the situation seems to require. Potential customers with technical questions are sometimes referred to other noncompeting customers already using the materials or to a GCI plant—to be sure that all questions are answered. But basically, all producer-customers are treated more or less alike. The sales reps make calls and try to find good business wherever they can.

Each GCI sales rep usually has a geographic area. If an area like Detroit needs more than one rep, each may specialize in one or several similar industries. But GCI uses the same basic approach—call on present users of plastic products and try to find opportunities for getting a share (or bigger share) of existing purchases or new applications. The sales reps are supposed to be primarily order getters rather than technical specialists. Technical help can be brought in when the customer wants it, or sometimes the sales rep simply sets up a conference call between GCI's technical experts, the buyer, and the users at the buyer's facility.

Kenneth sees that some of his major competitors are becoming more aggressive. They are seeking to affect specifications and product design from the start rather than after a product design is completed. This takes a lot more effort and resources, but Kenneth thinks it may get better results. A major problem he sees, however, is that he may have to drastically change the nature of GCI's promotion. Instead of focusing primarily on buyers and responding to questions, it may be necessary to try to contact *all* the multiple buying influences and not only answer their questions but help them understand what questions to raise—to find solutions. Such a process may even require more technically trained sales reps. In fact, it may require that people from GCI's other departments—engineering, design, manufacturing, R&D, and distribution—get actively involved in discussions with their counterparts in customer firms. Further, use of e-mail and a website might make ongoing contacts faster and easier.

While Kenneth doesn't want to miss the boat if changes are needed, he also doesn't want to go off the deep end. After all, many of the firm's customers don't seem to want GCI to do anything very different from what it's been doing. In fact, some say that they're very satisfied with their current supply arrangements and really have no interest in investing in a close relationship with a single supplier. Even with the Flex project, Ford wasn't 100 percent dedicated to the team approach. For example, when Ford's research showed that the target market viewed quiet and comfortable seats as an especially important factor in purchases, Ford didn't turn to a supplier for help but rather assigned a team of its own design engineers to develop and test them in-house. Now some of what was learned on the Flex project is going to be used in redesigning other models.

Contrast the previous approach to designing and producing cars to Flex's program management approach, especially as it might affect suppliers' promotion efforts. Given that many other major producers have moved in the program management direction, what promotion effort should Kenneth Shibata develop for Global ChemPlastics? Should every producer in every geographic area be treated alike, regardless of size? Explain.

22. Bright Light Innovations: The Starlight Stove*

The top management team of Bright Light Innovations is preparing to meet and review their market situation. The team is a combination of students and faculty from Colorado State University's (CSU) Colleges of Business and Engineering: Dr. Bryan Wilson, Paul Hudnut, Ajay Jha, Sachin Joshi, Katie Lucchesi, Dan Mastbergen, Ryan Palmer, and Chaun Sims. They are excited about the Starlight Stove product they have developed—and passionate about the opportunity that it provides to improve the quality of life for some of the world's poorest people. They know they have a great technology, but they need a marketing plan to bring this product to market.

Every day, over 2.4 billion people—more than one-third of the world's population—burn solid biomass fuel (wood, charcoal, dung, and coal) for cooking and heating. These fuels are usually burned indoors in open pits or traditional cook stoves. About two-thirds of the people using this fuel also have no electricity, so the open fires often burn into the night to provide light. These fires create indoor air pollution that is a leading contributor to respiratory diseases in these countries. U.N. Secretary General Kofi Annan has called for greater energy efficiency and noted that "indoor air pollution has become one of the top 10 causes of mortality and premature death." It is estimated that this source of pollution contributes each year to the deaths of 1 million children under the age of 5, and it is a leading cause of miscarriage and women's health problems.

Hoping to address these consumers' needs for safe cooking and electricity, CSU's Engines and Energy Conversion Laboratory developed the Starlight Stove. The Starlight Stove's improved technology requires 50 to 70 percent less biomass fuel than traditional stoves. It also has a thermoelectric generator that converts heat from the stove into electricity that can power a small lightbulb or be stored in a rechargeable battery for later use. The technology has been refined, and the team believes it is ready to go to market.

There are other competing enclosed cookstoves, but none produce electricity. Solar panels can provide electricity, but they are expensive—costing $360 each. Micro-hydropower allows households to convert the power from streams and rivers into electricity, but homes must be close to a river and water flow in many areas of the country is seasonal. These technologies—solar panels and hydropower—are understood by many consumers and are already in use in some areas. The Starlight Stove, on the other hand, offers a new technology, and that may slow its adoption.

The management team decided on Nepal as the initial target market for the Starlight Stove. Several factors made this market particularly attractive. The climate is relatively cold and only 11 percent of the households have access to electricity, so the heat and electricity production of the stove are particularly beneficial. Eighty-eight percent of the population uses firewood as their main source of energy. In addition, deforestation creates environmental problems in Nepal because it contributes to erosion and flooding. So the social benefits of the Starlight Stove will be particularly appealing to the Nepalese government and aid organizations.

There are approximately 9.2 million households in Nepal, but the gross national income per capita is only about $400, with most adults making between $1 and $3 per day. Nepal is largely rural, with only 17 percent of the population living in urban areas. The country is divided into 75 districts. Each district is further divided into about 60 village development committees (a sort of local government) consisting of about 450 households. The similar characteristics of northern India—immediately south of Nepal—make it a logical follow-up market.

The Starlight Stove offers several benefits to this population. For example, the longer hours with light—thanks to the electricity—and less time required to collect wood or other fuel could allow families to earn money by weaving, farming, or producing other crafts. Family productivity could increase 20 percent or more per day. Or the added hours with light might allow children to gain an education. If the product were manufactured locally, it could provide jobs for the population and help them learn the benefits of technology.

With obvious benefits for such a large number of people, the Bright Light Innovations team could look to donations to subsidize the Starlight Stove for the Nepalese people. But the team has concerns about this traditional form of aid. Financing in the form of grants, government relief, or donations is unreliable. If it is not renewed, projects wallow or die. Further, grants often fail to teach disadvantaged people skills and responsibility. So the team wants to create a sustainable venture that provides benefits for all—and has set up Bright Light Innovations as a for-profit business.

The management team has to make a number of marketing decisions. For example, it has to decide how to price the Starlight Stove. It estimates that the stove will cost about $60 to manufacture after setting up a plant in Nepal and expects that microfinancing organizations will provide loans for families. If units are sold for $80, the loan can be financed at 20 percent interest for three years with payments of $0.68 per week (microfinancing institutions typically collect on a weekly, or sometimes daily, basis). The team thinks that it will be easy to find a microfinancing institution to provide these loans. But the team is still unsure about whether this price will provide adequate margins for distributors.

The team also has to decide how to promote the stove to a population where less than half the adults can read. However, the team does have contacts with some business leaders, government officials, and nongovernmental organizations that may be able to provide advice and help.

What should be the marketing strategy of the Bright Light Innovations team for the Starlight Stove? Why?

23. Carson Furniture

Renee Carson, owner of Carson Furniture, is discouraged with her salespeople and is even thinking about hiring some new blood. Carson has been running Carson Furniture for 10 years and has slowly built the sales to $3.5 million a year. Her store is located on the outskirts of a growing city of 275,000 population. This is basically a factory city, and she has deliberately selected blue-collar workers as her target market. She carries some higher-priced furniture lines but emphasizes budget combinations and easy credit terms.

*This case is based on a business plan written by Ajay Jha, Sachin Joshi, Katie Lucchesi, Dan Mastbergen, Ryan Palmer, and Chaun Sims.

Table 1

In Shopping for Furniture I Found (Find) That	Demographic Groups			
	Group A	Group B	Group C	Group D
I looked at furniture in many stores before I made a purchase.	78%	72%	52%	50%
I went (am going) to only one store and bought (buy) what I found (find) there.	2	5	10	11
To make my purchase I went (am going) back to one of the stores I shopped in previously.	63	59	27	20
I looked (am looking) at furniture in no more than three stores and made (will make) my purchase in one of these.	20	25	40	45
I like a lot of help in selecting the right furniture.	27	33	62	69
I like a very friendly salesperson.	23	28	69	67

Carson is concerned that she may have reached the limit of her sales growth—her sales have not been increasing during the last two years even though total furniture sales have been increasing in the city as new people move in. Her local cable TV spots, newspaper advertising, and some ads on the local newspaper website seem to attract her target market, but many of these people come in, shop around, and leave. Some of them come back—but most do not. She thinks her product selections are very suitable for her target market and is concerned that her salespeople don't close more sales with potential customers. Several times, she has discussed this matter with her 10 salespeople. Her staff feels they should treat customers the way they personally want to be treated. They argue that their role is to answer questions and be helpful when asked—not to make suggestions or help customers make decisions. They think this would be too "hard sell."

Carson says their behavior is interpreted as indifference by the customers attracted to the store by her advertising. She has tried to convince her salespeople that customers must be treated on an individual basis and that some customers need more help in looking and deciding than others. Moreover, Carson is convinced that some customers would appreciate more help and suggestions than the salespeople themselves might want. To support her views, she showed her staff the data from a study of furniture store customers (see Tables 1 and 2) that she found on the Internet website for a furniture trade association. She tried to explain the differences in demographic groups and pointed out that her store was definitely trying to aim at specific people. She argued that they (the salespeople) should cater to the needs and attitudes of their customers and think less about how they would like to be treated themselves. Further, Carson announced that she is considering changing the sales compensation plan or hiring new blood if the present employees can't do a better job. Currently, the sales reps are paid $26,000 per year plus a 5 percent commission on sales.

Contrast Renee Carson's strategy and thoughts about her salespeople with their apparent view of her strategy and especially their role in it. What should she do now? Explain.

Table 2 The Sample Design

Demographic Status
Upper class (Group A); 13% of sample This group consists of managers, proprietors, or executives of large businesses; professionals, including doctors, lawyers, engineers, college professors, and school administrators; and research personnel and sales personnel, including managers, executives, and upper-income salespeople above level of clerks. *Family income over $60,000*
Middle class (Group B); 37% of sample Group B consists of white-collar workers, including clerical, secretarial, salesclerks, bookkeepers, etc. It also includes school teachers, social workers, semiprofessionals, proprietors or managers of small businesses, industrial foremen, and other supervisory personnel. *Family income between $35,000 and $70,000*
Lower middle class (Group C); 36% of sample Skilled workers and semiskilled technicians are in this category, along with custodians, elevator operators, telephone linemen, factory operatives, construction workers, and some domestic and personal service employees. *Family income between $20,000 and $45,000. No one in this group has above a high school education.*
Lower class (Group D); 14% of sample Nonskilled employees, day laborers. It also includes some factory operatives and domestic and service people. *Family income under $28,000.* *None has completed high school; some have only grade school education.*

24. Wireway

Shayla McGrorey, marketing manager of consumer products for Wireway, is trying to set a price for her most promising new product—a space-saving shoe rack suitable for small homes or apartments.

Wireway—located in Ft. Worth, Texas—is a custom producer of industrial wire products. The company has a lot of experience bending wire into many shapes and also can chrome- or gold-plate finished products. The company was started 16 years ago and has slowly built its sales volume to $3.6 million a year. Just one year ago, McGrorey was appointed marketing manager of the consumer products division. It is her responsibility to develop this division as a producer and marketer of the company's own branded products—as distinguished from custom orders, which the industrial division produces for others.

McGrorey has been working on a number of different product ideas for almost a year now and has developed several designs for DVD holders, racks for soft-drink cans, plate holders, doll stands, collapsible book ends, and other such products. Her most promising product is a shoe rack for crowded homes and apartments. The wire rack attaches to the inside of a closet door and holds eight pairs of shoes.

The rack is very similar to one the industrial division produced for a number of years for another company. That company sold the shoe rack and hundreds of other related items out of its "products for organizing and storing" mail-order catalog. Managers at Wireway were surprised by the high sales volume the catalog company achieved with the rack. In fact, that is what interested Wireway in the consumer market and led to the development of the separate consumer products division.

McGrorey has sold hundreds of the shoe racks to various local hardware, grocery and general merchandise stores, and wholesalers on a trial basis, but each time she has negotiated a price—and no firm policy has been set. Now she must determine what price to set on the shoe rack, which she plans to push aggressively wherever she can. Actually, she hasn't decided on exactly which channels of distribution to use. But trials in the local area have been encouraging, and as noted earlier, the experience in the industrial division suggests that there is a large market for this type of product. Further, she has noticed that a Walmart store in her local area is selling a similar rack made of plastic. When she talked casually about her product with the store manager, he suggested that she contact the chain's houseware buyers in the home office in Arkansas.

The manufacturing cost of her rack—when made in reasonable quantities—is approximately $2.80 if it is painted black and $3.60 if it is chromed. Similar products have been selling at retail in the $9.95 to $19.95 range. The sales and administrative overhead to be charged to the division will amount to $95,000 a year. This will include McGrorey's salary and some travel and office expenses. She expects that a number of other products will be developed in the near future. But for the coming year, she hopes the shoe rack will account for about half the consumer products division's sales volume.

Evaluate Shayla McGrorey's strategy planning so far. What should she do now? What price should she set for the shoe rack?

25. Long Beach Plastics

Simon Howe, the marketing manager of Long Beach Plastics, wants to increase sales by adding sales reps rather than "playing with price." That's how Simon describes what Judy Howe, his mother and Long Beach Plastics' president, is suggesting. Judy is not sure what to do, either. But she does want to increase sales, so something new is needed.

Long Beach Plastics—of Long Beach, California—is a leading producer in the plastic forming machinery industry. It has patents covering over 200 variations, but Long Beach Plastics' customers seldom buy more than 30 different types in a year. The machines are sold to plastic forming manufacturers to increase production capacity or replace old equipment.

Established in 1970, the company has enjoyed a steady growth to its present position with annual sales of $50 million. Judy took over as president 15 years ago, after her husband Charles, the founder of the company, died of a sudden heart attack. The first few years were tough, but Judy emerged as a strong executive who has steered the company well. She is well respected in the industry.

Twelve U.S. firms compete in the U.S. plastic forming machinery market. Several Japanese, German, and Swedish firms compete in the global market, but the Howes have not seen much of them on the West Coast. Apparently the foreign firms rely on manufacturers' agents who have not provided an ongoing presence. They are not good about following up on inquiries, and their record for service on the few sales they have made on the East Coast is not satisfactory. So the Howes are not worried about them right now.

Each of the 12 U.S. competitors is about the same size and manufactures basically similar machinery. Each has tended to specialize in its own geographic region. Six of the competitors are located in the East, four in the Midwest, and two—including Long Beach Plastics—on the West Coast. The other West Coast firm is in Tacoma, Washington. All of the competitors offer similar prices and sell F.O.B. from their factories. Demand has been fairly strong in recent years. As a result, all of the competitors have been satisfied to sell in their geographic areas and avoid price-cutting. In fact, price-cutting is not a popular idea in this industry. About 15 years ago, one firm tried to win more business and found that others immediately met the price cut—but industry sales (in units) did not increase at all. Within a few years, prices returned to their earlier level, and since then competition has tended to focus on promotion and avoid price.

Long Beach Plastics' promotion depends mainly on six company sales reps, who cover the West Coast. In total, these reps cost about $880,000 per year including salary, bonuses, supervision, travel, and entertaining. When the sales reps are close to making a sale, they are supported by two sales engineers—at a cost of about $130,000 per year per engineer. Long Beach Plastics does some advertising in trade journals—less than $100,000—and occasionally uses direct mailings and trade show exhibits. It also has a simple website on the Internet—the main content on the site consists of PDF files of all the company's sales brochures. But the main promotion emphasis is on personal selling. Any personal contact outside the West Coast market is handled by manufacturers' agents who are paid 4 percent on sales—but sales are very infrequent.

Judy is not satisfied with the present situation. Industry sales have leveled off and so have Long Beach Plastics' sales—although the firm continues to hold its share of the market. Judy would like to find a way to compete more effectively in the other regions because she sees great potential outside the West Coast.

Competitors and buyers agree that Long Beach Plastics is the top-quality producer in the industry. Its machines have generally been somewhat superior to others in terms of reliability, durability, and production capacity. The difference, however, usually has not been great enough to justify a higher price—because the others are able to do the necessary job—unless a Long Beach Plastics sales rep convinces the customer that the extra quality will improve the customer's product and lead to fewer production line breakdowns. The sales rep also tries to sell the advantages of Long Beach Plastics' better sales engineers and technical service people—and sometimes is successful. But if a buyer is mainly interested in comparing delivered prices for basic machines—the usual case—Long Beach Plastics' price must be competitive to get the business. In short, if such a buyer has a choice between Long Beach Plastics' and another machine *at the same price,* Long Beach Plastics will usually win the business in its part of the West Coast market. But it's clear that Long Beach Plastics' price has to be at least competitive in such cases.

The average plastic forming machine sells for about \$220,000, F.O.B. shipping point. Shipping costs within any of the three major regions average about \$4,000—but another \$3,000 must be added on shipments between the West Coast and the Midwest (either way) and another \$3,000 between the Midwest and the East.

Judy is thinking about expanding sales by absorbing the extra \$3,000 to \$6,000 in freight cost that occurs if a Midwestern or eastern customer buys from her West Coast location. By doing this, she would not actually be cutting price in those markets but rather reducing her net return. She thinks that her competitors would not see this as price competition and therefore would not resort to cutting prices themselves.

Simon disagrees. Simon thinks that the proposed freight absorption plan would stimulate price competition in the Midwest and East and perhaps on the West Coast. He proposes instead that Long Beach Plastics hire some sales reps to work the Midwest and Eastern regions—selling quality—rather than relying on the manufacturers' agents. He argues that two additional sales reps in each of these regions would not increase costs too much and might greatly increase the sales from these markets over that brought in by the agents. With this plan, there would be no need to absorb the freight and risk disrupting the status quo. Adding more of Long Beach Plastics' own sales reps is especially important, he argues, because competition in the Midwest and East is somewhat hotter than on the West Coast—due to the number of competitors (including foreign competitors) in those regions. A lot of expensive entertaining, for example, seems to be required just to be considered as a potential supplier. In contrast, the situation has been rather quiet in the West—because only two firms are sharing this market and each is working harder near its home base. The eastern and Midwestern competitors don't send any sales reps to the West Coast—and if they have any manufacturers' agents, they haven't gotten any business in recent years.

Judy agrees that her son has a point, but industry sales are leveling off and Judy wants to increase sales. Further, she thinks the competitive situation may change drastically in the near future anyway, as global competitors get more aggressive and some possible new production methods and machines become more competitive with existing ones. She would rather be a leader in anything that is likely to happen rather than a follower. But she is impressed with Simon's comments about the greater competitiveness in the other markets and therefore is unsure about what to do.

Evaluate Long Beach Plastics' current strategies. Given Judy Howe's sales objective, what should Long Beach Plastics Mfg. do? Explain.

26. Abundant Harvest

Chelsea Skye-Rice, president of Abundant Harvest, is not sure what she should propose to the board of directors. Her recent strategy change isn't working. And Don Bartley, Abundant Harvest's only sales rep (and a board member), is so frustrated that he refuses to continue his discouraging sales efforts. Don wants Chelsea to hire a sales force or do *something.*

Abundant Harvest is a long-time processor in the highly seasonal vegetable canning industry. Abundant Harvest packs and sells canned beans, peas, carrots, corn, peas and carrots mixed, and kidney beans. It sells mainly through food brokers to merchant wholesalers, supermarket chains (such as Kroger, Safeway, A&P, and Jewel), cooperatives, and other outlets, mostly in the Midwest. Of less importance, by volume, are sales to local institutions, grocery stores, and supermarkets—and sales of dented canned goods at low prices to walk-in customers.

Abundant Harvest is located in Wisconsin's beautiful Devil's Valley. The company has more than \$28 million in sales annually (exact sales data are not published by the closely held corporation). Plants are located in strategic places along the valley, with main offices in the valley also. The Abundant Harvest brand is used only on canned goods sold in the local market. Most of the goods are sold and shipped under a retailer's label or a broker's/wholesaler's label.

Abundant Harvest is well known for the consistent quality of its product offerings. And it's always willing to offer competitive prices. Strong channel relations were built by Robert Skye, Abundant Harvest's former chairman of the board and chief executive officer. Robert—who still owns controlling interest in the firm—worked the Chicago area as the company's sales rep in its earlier years, before he took over from his father as president in 1974. Robert was an ambitious and hard-working top manager—the firm prospered under his direction. He became well known within the canned food processing industry for technical/product innovations.

During the off-canning season, Robert traveled widely. In the course of his travels, he arranged several important business deals. His 1990 and 2001 trips resulted in the following two events: (1) inexpensive pineapple was imported from Taiwan and sold by

Abundant Harvest, primarily to expand the product line, and (2) a technically advanced continuous process cooker (65 feet high) was imported from England and installed at one of Abundant Harvest's plants. It was the first of its kind in the United States and cut processing time sharply while improving quality.

Robert retired in 2010 and named his daughter, 35-year-old Chelsea Skye-Rice, as his successor. Chelsea is intelligent and hardworking. She has been concerned primarily with the company's financial matters and only recently with marketing problems. During her seven years as financial director, the firm received its highest credit rating and was able to borrow working capital ($5 million to meet seasonal can and wage requirements) at the lowest rate ever.

The fact that the firm isn't unionized allows some competitive advantage. However, changes in minimum wage laws have increased costs. And these and other rising costs have squeezed profit margins. This led to the recent closing of two plants as they became less efficient to operate. Abundant Harvest expanded capacity of the remaining two plants (especially warehouse facilities) so they could operate more profitably with maximum use of existing processing equipment.

Shortly after Robert's retirement, Chelsea reviewed the company's situation with her managers. She pointed to narrowing profit margins, debts contracted for new plants and equipment, and an increasingly competitive environment. Even considering the temporary labor-saving competitive advantage of the new cooker system, there seemed to be no way to improve the status quo unless the firm could sell direct—as they do in the local market—thereby eliminating the food brokers' 5 percent commission on sales. This was the chosen plan, and Don Bartley was given the new sales job. An inside salesperson was retained to handle incoming orders and do some telemarketing to smaller accounts.

Don, the only full-time outside sales rep for the firm, lives in Devil's Valley. Other top managers do some selling but not much. Being a nephew of Robert, Don is also a member of the board of directors. He is well qualified in technical matters and has a college degree in food chemistry. Although Don formerly did call on some important customers with the brokers' sales reps, he is not well known in the industry or even by Abundant Harvest's usual customers.

It is now five months later. Don is not doing very well. He has made several selling trips, placed hundreds of telephone calls, and maintained constant e-mail contacts with prospective customers—all with discouraging results. He is unwilling to continue sales efforts on his own. There seems to be too many potential customers for one person to reach. And much negotiating, wining, and dining seems to be needed—certainly more than he can or wants to do.

Don insists that Abundant Harvest hire a sales force to continue the present way of operating. Sales are down in comparison both to expectations and to the previous year's results. Some regular supermarket chain customers have stopped buying—though basic consumer demand has not changed. Further, buyers for some supermarket chains that might be potential new customers have demanded quantity guarantees much larger than Abundant Harvest can supply. Expanding supply would be difficult in the short run—because the firm typically must contract with growers to ensure supplies of the type and quality they normally offer.

Robert, still the controlling stockholder, has asked for a special meeting of the board in two weeks to discuss the present situation.

Evaluate Abundant Harvest's past and current strategy planning. What should Chelsea Skye-Rice tell Robert Skye? What should Abundant Harvest do now?

27. Advanced Molding, Inc.

Anya Winrow is trying to decide whether to leave her present job to buy into another business and be part of top management.

Anya is now a sales rep for a plastics components manufacturer. She calls mostly on large industrial accounts—such as refrigerator manufacturers—who might need large quantities of custom-made products like door liners. She is on a straight salary of $55,000 per year, plus expenses and a company car. She expects some salary increases but doesn't see much long-run opportunity with this company.

As a result, she is seriously considering changing jobs and investing $60,000 in Advanced Molding, Inc., an established Chicago (Illinois) thermoplastic molder (manufacturer). Gary Beal, the present owner, is nearing retirement and has not trained anyone to take over the business. He has agreed to sell the business to Joseph O'Sullivan, a lawyer, who has invited Anya to invest and become the sales manager. Joseph has agreed to match Anya's current salary plus expenses, plus a bonus of 2 percent of profits. However, she must invest to become part of the new company. She will get a 5 percent interest in the business for the necessary $60,000 investment—all of her savings.

Advanced Molding, Inc., is well established and last year had sales of $3.2 million—but zero profits (after paying Gary a salary of $90,000). In terms of sales, cost of materials was 46 percent; direct labor, 13 percent; indirect factory labor, 15 percent; factory overhead, 13 percent; and sales overhead and general expenses, 13 percent. The company has not been making any profit for several years—but it has been continually adding new computer-controlled machines to replace those made obsolete by technological developments. The machinery is well maintained and modern, but most of it is similar to that used by its many competitors. Most of the machines in the industry are standard. Special products are made by using specially made dies with these machines.

Sales have been split about two-thirds custom-molded products (that is, made to the specification of other producers or merchandising concerns) and the balance proprietary items (such as housewares and game items, like poker chips).

The housewares are copies of items developed by others and indicate neither originality nor style. Gary is in charge of selling the proprietary items, which are distributed through any available wholesale channels. The custom-molded products are sold through two full-time sales reps—who receive a 10 percent commission on individual orders up to $30,000 and then 3 percent above that level—and also by three manufacturers' reps who get the same commissions.

The company seems to be in fairly good financial condition, at least as far as book value is concerned. The $60,000 investment will buy almost $88,000 in assets—and ongoing operations

Table 1 Advanced Molding, Inc., Statement of Financial Conditions, December 31, 2010

Assets			Liabilities and Net Worth	
Cash		$ 19,500	Liabilities:	
Accounts receivable . . .		82,500	Accounts payable	$ 105,000
Building	$337,500		Notes payable—7 years (machinery) . .	291,000
Less: depreciation . . .	112,500			
		225,000		
Machinery	2,100,000		Net worth:	
Less: depreciation . . .	675,000		Capital stock	1,350,000
		1,425,000	Retained earnings	6,000
Total assets.		$1,752,000	Total liabilities and net worth	$1,752,000

should pay off the seven-year note (see Table 1). Joseph thinks that with new management the company has a good chance to make big profits. He expects to make some economies in the production process—because he feels most production operations can be improved. He plans to keep custom-molding sales at approximately the present $2 million level. His new strategy will try to increase the proprietary sales volume from $1.2 million to $3 million a year. Anya is expected to be a big help here because of her sales experience. This will bring the firm up to about capacity level—but it will mean adding additional employees and costs. The major advantage of expanding sales will be spreading overhead.

Some of the products proposed by Joseph for expanding proprietary sales are listed below.

New products for consideration:
Safety helmets for cyclists
Water bottles for cyclists and in-line skaters
Waterproof cases for digital cameras
Toolboxes
Closet organizer/storage boxes for toys
Short legs for furniture
Step-on garbage cans without liners
Exterior house shutters and siding
Importing and distributing foreign housewares

Advanced Molding faces heavy competition from many other similar companies including firms that have outsourced production to China and Eastern Europe, where labor costs are much lower. Further, most retailers expect a wide margin, sometimes 50 to 60 percent of the retail selling price. Even so, manufacturing costs are low enough so that Advanced Molding can spend some money for promotion while still keeping the price competitive. Apparently, many customers are willing to pay for novel new products—if they see them in stores. And Anya isn't worried too much by tough competition. She sees plenty of that in her present job. And she does like the idea of being an "owner and sales manager."

Evaluate Advanced Molding's situation and Joseph O'Sullivan's strategy. What should Anya Winrow do? Why?

28. KCA Precision Tools (KCA)

Carlos Gonzalez, president and marketing manager of KCA Precision Tools, is deciding what strategy, or strategies, to pursue.

KCA Precision Tools (KCA) is a manufacturer of industrial cutting tools. These tools include such items as lathe blades, drill press bits, and various other cutting edges used in the operation of large metal cutting, boring, or stamping machines. Carlos takes great pride in the fact that his company—whose $5.7 million sales in 2010 is small by industry standards—is recognized as a producer of a top-quality line of cutting tools.

Competition in the cutting-tool industry is intense. KCA competes not only with the original machine manufacturers, but also with many other larger domestic and foreign manufacturers offering cutting tools as one of their many different product lines. This has had the effect, over the years, of standardizing the price, specifications, and, in turn, the quality of the competing products of all manufacturers. It has also led to fairly low prices on standard items.

About a year ago, Carlos was tiring of the financial pressure of competing with larger companies enjoying economies of scale. At the same time, he noted that more and more potential cutting-tool customers were turning to small tool-and-die shops that used computer-controlled equipment to meet specialized needs that could not be met by the mass production firms. Carlos thought perhaps he should consider some basic strategy changes. Although he was unwilling to become strictly a custom producer, he thought that the recent trend toward buying customized cutting edges suggested new markets might be developing—markets too small for the large, multi-product line companies to serve profitably but large enough to earn a good profit for a flexible company of KCA's size.

Carlos hired a marketing research company, MResearchPro, to study the feasibility of serving these markets. The initial results were encouraging. It was estimated that KCA might increase sales by 65 percent and profits by 90 percent by serving the emerging markets. The research showed that there are many large users of standard cutting tools who buy directly from large cutting-tool manufacturers (domestic or foreign) or wholesalers who represent these manufacturers. This is the bulk of the cutting-tool business (in terms of units sold and sales dollars). But there are also many smaller users all over the United States who buy in small but regular quantities. And some of these needs are becoming more specialized. That is, a special cutting tool may make a machine and/or worker much more productive, perhaps eliminating several steps with time-consuming setups. This is the area that the research company sees as potentially attractive.

Next, Carlos had the sales manager hire two technically oriented market researchers (at a total cost of $85,000 each per year, including travel expenses) to maintain continuous contact with potential cutting-tool customers. The researchers were supposed to identify any present or future needs that might exist in enough cases to make it possible to profitably produce a specialized product. The researchers were not to take orders or sell KCA's products to the potential customers. Carlos felt that only through this policy could these researchers talk to the right people.

The initial feedback from the market researchers was most encouraging. Many firms (large and small) had special needs—although it often was necessary to talk to the shop foreman or individual machine operators to find these needs. Most operators were making do with the tools available. Either they didn't know customizing was possible or doubted that their supervisors would do anything about it if they suggested that a more specialized tool could increase productivity. But these operators were encouraging because they said that it would be easier to persuade supervisors to order specialized tools if the tools were already produced and in stock than if they had to be custom made. So Carlos decided to continually add high-quality products to meet the ever-changing, specialized needs of users of cutting tools and edges.

KCA's potential customers for specialized tools are located all over the United States. The average sale per customer is likely to be less than $500, but the sale will be repeated several times within a year. Because of the widespread market and the small order size, Carlos doesn't think that selling direct—as is done by small custom shops—is practical. At the present time, KCA sells 90 percent of its regular output through a large industrial wholesaler—Superior Mill Supply—which serves the area east of the Mississippi River and carries a very complete line of industrial supplies (to "meet every industrial need"). Superior carries over 10,000 items. Some sales come from customers who know exactly what they want and just place orders directly by fax or at the firm's website. But most of the selling is by Superior's sales reps, who work from an electronic catalog on a laptop computer. Superior, although very large and well known, is having trouble moving cutting tools. It's losing sales of cutting tools in some cities to newer wholesalers specializing in the cutting tool industry. The new wholesalers are able to give more technical help to potential customers and therefore better service. Superior's president is convinced that the newer, less- experienced concerns will either realize that a substantial profit margin can't be maintained along with their aggressive strategies, or they will eventually go broke trying to overspecialize.

From Carlos's standpoint, the present wholesaler has a good reputation and has served KCA well in the past. Superior has been of great help in holding down Carlos's inventory costs—by increasing the inventory in Superior's 35 branch locations. Although Carlos has received several complaints about the lack of technical assistance given by Superior's sales reps—as well as their lack of knowledge about KCA's new special products—he feels that the present wholesaler is providing the best service it can. All its sales reps have been told about the new products at a special training session, and new pages have been added to the electronic catalog on their laptops. So regarding the complaints, Carlos says, "The usual things you hear when you're in business."

Carlos thinks there are more urgent problems than a few complaints. Profits are declining, and sales of the new cutting tools are not nearly as high as forecast—even though all research reports indicate that the company's new products meet the intended markets' needs perfectly. The high costs involved in producing small quantities of special products and in adding the market research team—together with lower than expected sales—have significantly reduced KCA's profits. Carlos is wondering whether it is wise to continue to try to cater to the needs of many specific target markets when the results are this discouraging. He also is considering increasing advertising expenditures including some search engine advertising in the hope that customers will pull the new products through the channel.

Evaluate KCA's situation and Carlos Gonzalez's present strategy. What should he do now?

29. Quality Iron Castings, Inc.

Mallory Rizocki, marketing manager for Quality Iron Castings, Inc., is trying to figure out how to explain to her boss why a proposed new product line doesn't make sense for them. Mallory is sure it's wrong for Quality Iron Castings, but isn't able to explain why.

Quality Iron Castings, Inc., is a producer of malleable iron castings for automobile and aircraft manufacturers and a variety of other users of castings. Last year's sales of castings amounted to over $70 million.

Quality Iron Castings also produces about 30 percent of all the original equipment bumper jacks installed in new U.S.-made automobiles each year. This is a very price-competitive business, but Quality Iron Castings has been able to obtain its large market share with frequent personal contact between the company's executives and its customers—supported by very close cooperation between the company's engineering department and its customers' buyers. This has been extremely important because the wide variety of models and model changes frequently requires alterations in the specifications of the bumper jacks. All of Quality Iron Castings' bumper jacks are sold directly to the automobile manufacturers. No attempt has been made to sell bumper jacks to final consumers through hardware and automotive channels—although they are available through the manufacturers' automobile dealers.

Tim Kingston, Quality Iron Castings' production manager, now wants to begin producing hydraulic garage jacks for sale through auto-parts wholesalers to auto-parts retailers. Tim saw a variety of hydraulic garage jacks at a recent automotive show and knew immediately that his plant could produce these products. This especially interested him because of the possibility of using excess capacity. Further, he says "jacks are jacks," and the company would merely be broadening its product line by introducing hydraulic garage jacks. (Note: Hydraulic garage jacks are larger than bumper jacks and are intended for use in or around a garage. They are too big to carry in a car's trunk.)

As Tim became more enthusiastic about the idea, he found that Quality Iron Castings' engineering department already had a patented design that appeared to be at least comparable to the products now offered on the market. Further, Tim says that the company would be able to produce a product that is better made than the competitive products (i.e., smoother castings)—although he agrees that most customers probably wouldn't notice the difference. The production department estimates that the cost of producing a hydraulic garage jack comparable to those currently offered by competitors would be about $48 per unit.

Mallory has just received an e-mail from Jesse Zachary, the company president, explaining the production department's enthusiasm for broadening Quality Iron Castings' present jack line into hydraulic jacks. Jesse seems enthusiastic about the idea too, noting that it would be a way to make fuller use of the company's resources and increase its sales. Jesse's e-mail asks for Mallory's reaction, but Jesse already seems sold on the idea.

Given Jesse's enthusiasm, Mallory isn't sure how to respond. She's trying to develop a good explanation of why she isn't excited about the proposal. The firm's six sales reps are already overworked with their current accounts. And Mallory couldn't possibly promote this new line herself—she's already helping other reps make calls and serving as sales manager. So it would be necessary to hire someone to promote the line. And this sales manager would probably have to recruit manufacturers' agents (who probably will want 10 to 15 percent commission on sales) to sell to automotive wholesalers who would stock the jack and sell to the auto-parts retailers. The wholesalers will probably expect trade discounts of about 20 percent, trade show exhibits, some national advertising, and sales promotion help (catalog sheets, mailers, and point-of-purchase displays). Further, Mallory sees that Quality Iron Castings' billing and collection system will have to be expanded because many more customers will be involved. It will also be necessary to keep track of agent commissions and accounts receivable.

Auto-parts retailers are currently selling similar hydraulic garage jacks for about $99. Mallory has learned that such retailers typically expect a trade discount of about 35 percent off of the suggested list price for their auto parts.

All things considered, Mallory feels that the proposed hydraulic jack line is not very closely related to the company's present emphasis. She has already indicated her lack of enthusiasm to Tim, but this made little difference in Tim's thinking. Now it's clear that Mallory will have to convince the president or she will soon be responsible for selling hydraulic jacks.

Contrast Quality Iron Castings, Inc.'s current strategy and the proposed strategy. What should Mallory Rizocki say to Jesse Zachary to persuade him to change his mind? Or should she just plan to sell hydraulic jacks? Explain.

30. Walker-Winkle Mills, Ltd.*

Valerie Boudreau, marketing manager of Walker-Winkle Mills, Ltd.—a Canadian company—is being urged to approve the creation of a separate marketing plan for Quebec. This would be a major policy change because Walker-Winkle Mills' international parent is trying to move toward a global strategy for the whole firm and Boudreau has been supporting Canada-wide planning.

Boudreau has been the marketing manager of Walker-Winkle Mills, Ltd., for the last four years—since she arrived from international headquarters in Minneapolis. Walker-Winkle Mills, Ltd., headquartered in Toronto, is a subsidiary of a large U.S.-based consumer packaged food company with worldwide sales of more than $2.8 billion in 2007. Its Canadian sales are just over $450 million, with the Quebec and Ontario markets accounting for 69 percent of the company's Canadian sales.

The company's product line includes such items as cake mixes, puddings, pie fillings, pancakes, prepared foods, and frozen dinners. The company has successfully introduced at least six new products every year for the last five years. Products from Walker-Winkle Mills are known for their high quality and enjoy much brand preference throughout Canada, including the Province of Quebec.

The company's sales have risen every year since Boudreau took over as marketing manager. In fact, the company's market share has increased steadily in each of the product categories in which it competes. The Quebec market has closely followed the national trend except that, in the past two years, total sales growth in that market began to lag.

According to Boudreau, a big advantage of Walker-Winkle Mills over its competitors is the ability to coordinate all phases of the food business from Toronto. For this reason, Boudreau meets at least once a month with her product managers—to discuss developments in local markets that might affect marketing plans. While each manager is free to make suggestions and even to suggest major changes, Boudreau has the responsibility of giving final approval for all plans.

One of the product managers, Jackie Provence, expressed great concern at the last monthly meeting about the poor performance of some of the company's products in the Quebec market. While a broad range of possible reasons—ranging from inflation and the threat of job losses to politics—were reviewed to try to explain the situation, Provence insisted that it was due to a basic lack of understanding of that market. She felt not enough managerial time and money had been spent on the Quebec market—in part because of the current emphasis on developing all-Canada plans on the way to having one global strategy.

Provence felt the current marketing approach to the Quebec market should be reevaluated because an inappropriate marketing

*This case was adapted from one written by Professor Roberta Tamilia, University of Windsor, Canada.

plan may be responsible for the sales slowdown. After all, she said, "80 percent of the market is French-speaking. It's in the best interest of the company to treat that market as being separate and distinct from the rest of Canada."

Provence supported her position by showing that Quebec's per capita consumption of many product categories (in which the firm competes) is above the national average (see Table 1). Research projects conducted by Walker-Winkle Mills also support the "separate and distinct" argument. Over the years, the firm has found many French–English differences in brand attitudes, lifestyles, usage rates, and so on.

Provence argued that the company should develop a unique Quebec marketing plan for some or all of its brands. She specifically suggested that the French-language advertising plan for a particular brand be developed independently of the plan for English Canada.

Currently, the Toronto agency assigned to the brand just translates its English-language ads for the French market. Boudreau pointed out that the present advertising approach assured Walker-Winkle Mills of a uniform brand image across Canada. Provence said she knew what the agency is doing, and that straight translation into Canadian-French may not communicate the same brand image. The discussion that followed suggested that a different brand image might be needed in the French market if the company wanted to stop the brand's decline in sales.

The managers also discussed the food distribution system in Quebec. The major supermarket chains have their lowest market share in that province. Independents are strongest there—the mom-and-pop food stores fast disappearing outside Quebec remain alive and well in the province. Traditionally, these stores have stocked a higher proportion (than supermarkets) of their shelf space with national brands, an advantage for Walker-Winkle Mills.

Finally, various issues related to discount policies, pricing structure, sales promotion, and cooperative advertising were discussed. All of these suggested that things were different in Quebec and that future marketing plans should reflect these differences to a greater extent than they do now. After the meeting, Boudreau stayed in her office to think about the situation. Although she agreed with the basic idea that the Quebec market was in many

Table 1 Per Capita Consumption Index, Province of Quebec (Canada = 100)*

Cake mixes	107	Soft drinks	126
Pancakes	87	Pie fillings	118
Puddings	114	Frozen dinners	79
Salad dressings	85	Prepared packaged foods	83
Molasses	132	Cookies	123

*An index shows the relative consumption as compared to a standard. In this table, the standard is all of Canada. The data shows that per capita consumption of cake mixes is 7% higher in Quebec and pancake consumption 13% lower compared to all of Canada.

ways different, she wasn't sure how far the company should go in recognizing this fact. She knew that regional differences in food tastes and brand purchases existed not only in Quebec but in other parts of Canada as well. But people are people, after all, with far more similarities than differences, so a Canadian and, eventually, a global strategy makes some sense too.

Boudreau was afraid that giving special status to one region might conflict with top management's objective of achieving standardization whenever possible—one global strategy for Canada, on the way to one worldwide global strategy. She was also worried about the long-term effect of such a policy change on costs, organizational structure, and brand image. Still, enough product managers had expressed their concern over the years about the Quebec market to make her wonder if she shouldn't modify the current approach. Perhaps they could experiment with a few brands—and just in Quebec. She could cite the language difference as the reason for trying Quebec rather than any of the other provinces. But Boudreau realizes that any change of policy could be seen as the beginning of more change, and what would Minneapolis think? Could she explain it successfully there?

Evaluate Walker-Winkle Mills, Ltd.'s present strategy. What should Valerie Boudreau do now? Explain.

31. Amato Home Health (AHH)

Maribeth Amato, executive director of Amato Home Health, is trying to clarify her strategies. She's sure some changes are needed, but she's less sure about how *much* change is needed and/or whether it can be handled by her people.

Amato Home Health (AHH), is a nonprofit organization that has been operating—with varying degrees of success—for 25 years, offering nursing services in clients' homes. Some of its funding comes from the local United Way—to provide emergency nursing services for those who can't afford to pay. The balance of the revenues—about 90 percent of the $2.2 million annual budget—comes from charges made directly to the client or to third-party payers, including insurance companies, health maintenance organizations (HMOs), and the federal government, for Medicare or Medicaid services.

Maribeth has been executive director of AHH for two years. She has developed a well-functioning organization able to meet most requests for service that come from local doctors and from the discharge officers at local hospitals. Some business also comes by self-referral—the client finds the AHH name in the Yellow Pages of the local phone directory.

The last two years have been a rebuilding time—because the previous director had personnel problems. This led to a weakening of the agency's image with the local referring agencies. Now the image is more positive. But Maribeth is not completely satisfied with the situation. By definition, Amato Home Health is a nonprofit organization. But it still must cover all its costs: payroll, rent payments, phone expenses, and so on, including Maribeth's own salary. She can see that while AHH is growing slightly and is now breaking even, it doesn't have much of a cash cushion to fall back on if (1) the demand for AHH nursing services declines, (2) the government changes its rules about paying for AHH's kind of nursing services, either cutting back what it will pay for or reducing the amount it will pay for specific services, or (3) new competitors enter the market. In fact, the last possibility concerns Maribeth greatly. Some hospitals, squeezed for revenue, are expanding into home health care—especially nursing services as patients are being released earlier from hospitals because of payment limits set by government guidelines. For-profit organizations (e.g., Kelly Home Care Services) are expanding around the country to provide a complete line of home health care services, including nursing services of the kind offered by AHH. These for-profit organizations appear to be efficiently run, offering good service at competitive and sometimes even lower prices than some nonprofit organizations. And they seem to be doing this at a profit, which suggests that it would be possible for these for-profit companies to lower their prices if nonprofit organizations try to compete on price.

Maribeth is considering whether she should ask her board of directors to let her offer a complete line of home health care services—that is, move beyond just nursing services into what she calls "care and comfort" services.

Currently, AHH is primarily concerned with providing professional nursing care in the home. But AHH nurses are much too expensive for routine home health care activities—helping fix meals, bathing and dressing patients, and other care and comfort activities. The full cost of a nurse to AHH, including benefits and overhead, is about $65 per hour. But a registered nurse is not needed for care and comfort services. All that is required is someone who is honest, can get along with all kinds of people, and is willing to do this kind of work. Generally, any mature person can be trained fairly quickly to do the job—following the instructions and under the general supervision of a physician, a nurse, or family members. The full cost of aides is $9 to $16 per hour for short visits and as low as $75 per 24 hours for a live-in aide who has room and board supplied by the client.

The demand for all kinds of home health care services seems to be growing. With more dual-career families and more single-parent households, there isn't anyone in the family to take over home health care when the need arises—due to emergencies or long-term disabilities. Further, hospitals send patients home earlier than in the past. And with people living longer, there are more single-survivor family situations where there is no one nearby to take care of the needs of these older people. But often some family members—or third-party payers such as the government or insurers—are willing to pay for some home health care services. Maribeth now occasionally recommends other agencies or suggests one or another of three women who have been doing care and comfort work on their own, part-time. But with growing demand, Maribeth wonders if AHH should get into this business, hiring aides as needed.

Maribeth is concerned that a new, full-service home health care organization may come into her market and be a single source for both nursing services *and* less-skilled home care and comfort services. This has happened already in two nearby but somewhat larger cities. Maribeth fears that this might be more appealing than AHH to the local hospitals and other referrers. In other words, she can see the possibility of losing nursing service business if AHH does not begin to offer a complete home health care service. This would cause real problems for AHH—because overhead costs are more or less fixed. A loss in revenue of as little as 10 percent would require some cutbacks—perhaps laying off some nurses or secretaries, giving up part of the office, and so on.

Another reason for expanding beyond nursing services—using paraprofessionals and relatively unskilled personnel—is to offer a better service to present customers *and* make more effective use of the computer systems and organization structure that she has developed over the last two years. Maribeth estimates that the administrative and office capabilities could handle twice as many clients without straining the system. It would be necessary to add some clerical help—if the expansion were quite large. But this increase in overhead would be minor compared to the present proportion of total revenue that goes to covering overhead. In other words, additional clients or more work for some current clients could increase revenue and ensure the survival of AHH, provide a cushion to cover the normal fluctuations in demand, and ensure more job security for the administrative personnel.

Further, Maribeth thinks that if AHH were successful in expanding its services—and therefore could generate some surplus—it could extend services to those who aren't now able to pay. Maribeth says one of the worst parts of her job is refusing service to clients whose third-party benefits have run out or for whatever reason can no longer afford to pay. She is uncomfortable about having to cut off service, but she must schedule her nurses to provide revenue-producing services if she's going to meet the payroll every two weeks. By expanding to provide more services, she might be able to keep serving more of these nonpaying clients. This possibility excites Maribeth because her nurse's training has instilled a deep desire to serve people in need, whether they can pay or not. This continual pressure to cut off service because people can't pay has been at the root of many disagreements and even arguments between the nurses serving the clients and Maribeth, as executive director and representative of the board of directors.

Maribeth knows that expanding into care and comfort services won't be easy. Some decisions would be needed about relative pay levels for nurses, paraprofessionals, and aides. AHH would also have to set prices for these different services and tell current customers and referral agencies about the expanded services.

These problems aren't bothering Maribeth too much, however—she thinks she can handle them. She is sure that care and comfort services are in demand and could be supplied at competitive prices.

Her primary concern is whether this is the right thing for Amato Home Health—basically a nursing organization—to do. AHH's whole history has been oriented to supplying *nurses' services.* Nurses are dedicated professionals who bring high standards to any job they undertake. The question is whether AHH should offer less-professional services. Inevitably, some of the aides will not be as dedicated as the nurses might like them to be. And this could reflect unfavorably on the nurse image. At a minimum, she would need to set up some sort of training program for the aides. As Maribeth worries about the future of AHH, and her own future, it seems that there are no easy answers.

Evaluate AHH's present strategy. What should Maribeth Amato do? Explain.

32. Lever, Ltd.*

Sung Wu is product manager for Guard Deodorant Soap. He was just transferred to Lever, Ltd., a Canadian subsidiary of Lever Group, Inc., from world headquarters in New York. Sung is anxious to make a good impression because he is hoping to transfer to Lever's London office. He is working on developing and securing management approval of next year's marketing plan for Guard. His first job is submitting a draft marketing plan to Sierra King, his recently appointed group product manager, who is responsible for several such plans from product managers like Sung.

Sung's marketing plan is the single most important document he will produce on this assignment. This annual marketing plan does three main things:

1. It reviews the brand's performance in the past year, assesses the competitive situation, and highlights problems and opportunities for the brand.
2. It spells out marketing strategies and the plan for the coming year.
3. Finally, and most importantly, the marketing plan sets out the brand's sales objectives and advertising/promotion budget requirements.

In preparing this marketing plan, Sung gathered the information in Table 1.

*Adapted from a case prepared by Daniel Aronchick, who at the time of its preparation was marketing manager at Thomas J. Lipton, Limited.

Sung was somewhat surprised at the significant regional differences in the bar soap market:

1. The underdevelopment of the deodorant bar segment in Quebec, with a corresponding overdevelopment of the beauty bar segment. But some past research suggested that this is due to cultural factors—English-speaking people have been more interested than others in cleaning, deodorizing, and disinfecting. A similar pattern is seen in most European countries, where the adoption of deodorant soaps has been slower than in North America. For similar reasons, the perfumed soap share is highest in French-speaking Quebec.
2. The overdevelopment of synthetic bars (Zest, Dial) in the Prairies (Manitoba/Saskatchewan and Alberta). These bars, primarily in the deodorant segment, lather better in the hard water of the Prairies. Nonsynthetic bars lather very poorly in hard-water areas and leave a soap film.
3. The overdevelopment of the "all-other" segment in Quebec. This segment, consisting of smaller brands, fares better in Quebec, where 43 percent of the grocery trade is done by independent stores. Conversely, large chain grocery stores dominate in Ontario and the Prairies.

Sung's brand, Guard, is a highly perfumed deodorant bar. His business is relatively weak in the key Ontario market. To confirm this share data, Sung calculated consumption of Guard per thousand people in each region (see Table 2).

Table 1 Past 12-Month Share of Bar Soap Market (percent)

	Maritimes	Quebec	Ontario	Manitoba/Saskatchewan	Alberta	British Columbia
Deodorant segment						
Zest	21.3%	14.2%	24.5%	31.2%	30.4%	25.5%
Dial	10.4	5.1	12.8	16.1	17.2	14.3
Lifebuoy	4.2	3.1	1.2	6.4	5.8	4.2
Guard	2.1	5.6	1.0	4.2	4.2	2.1
Beauty bar segment						
Camay	6.2	12.3	7.0	4.1	4.0	5.1
Lux	6.1	11.2	7.7	5.0	6.9	5.0
Dove	5.5	8.0	6.6	6.3	6.2	4.2
Lower-priced bars						
Ivory	11.2	6.5	12.4	5.3	5.2	9.0
Sunlight	6.1	3.2	8.2	4.2	4.1	8.0
All others (including stores' own brands)	26.9	30.8	18.6	17.2	16.0	22.6
Total bar soap market	100.0%	100.0%	100.0%	100.0%	100.0%	100.0%

Table 2 Standard Cases of 3-Ounce Bars Consumed per 1,000 People in 12 Months

	Maritimes	Quebec	Ontario	Manitoba/ Saskatchewan	Alberta	British Columbia
Guard	4.1	10.9	1.9	8.1	4.1	6.2
Sales index	66	175	31	131	131	100

These differences are especially interesting since per capita sales of all bar soap products are roughly equal in all provinces.

A consumer attitude and usage research study was conducted approximately a year ago. This study revealed that consumer "top-of-mind" awareness of the Guard brand differed greatly across Canada. This was true despite the even—by population—expenditure of advertising funds in past years. Also, trial of Guard was low in the Maritimes, Ontario, and British Columbia (see Table 3).

The attitude portion of the research revealed that consumers who had heard of Guard were aware that its deodorant protection came mainly from a high fragrance level. This was the main selling point in the copy, and it was well communicated by Guard's advertising. The other important finding was that consumers who had tried Guard were satisfied with the product. About 70 percent of those trying Guard had repurchased the product at least twice.

Sung has also discovered that bar soap competition is especially intense in Ontario. It is Canada's largest market, and many competitors want a share of it. The chain stores are also quite aggressive in promotion and pricing—offering specials, in-store coupons, and so on. They want to move goods. And because of this, two key Ontario chains have put Guard on their pending delisting sheets. These chains, which control about half the grocery volume in Ontario, are dissatisfied with how slowly Guard is moving off the shelves.

Now Sung feels he is ready to set a key part of the brand's marketing plan for next year: how to allocate the advertising/sales promotion budget by region.

Guard's present advertising/sales promotion budget is 20 percent of sales. With forecast sales of $4 million, this would amount to an $800,000 expenditure. Traditionally such funds have been allocated in proportion to population (see Table 4).

Sung feels he should spend more heavily in Ontario where the grocery chain delisting problem exists. Last year, 36 percent of Guard's budget was allocated to Ontario, which accounted for only 12 percent of Guard's sales. Sung wants to increase Ontario spending to 48 percent of the total budget by taking funds evenly from all other areas. Sung expects this will increase business in the key Ontario market, which has over a third of Canada's population, because it is a big increase and will help Guard "outshout" the many other competitors who are promoting heavily.

Sung presented this idea to King, his newly appointed group product manager. King strongly disagrees. She has also been reviewing Guard's business and feels that promotion funds have historically been misallocated. It is her strong belief that, to use her words, "A brand should spend where its business is." King believes that the first priority in allocating funds regionally is to support the areas of strength. She suggested to Sung that there may be more business to be had in the brand's strong areas, Quebec and the Prairies, than in chasing sales in Ontario. The needs and attitudes toward Guard, as well as competitive pressures, may vary a lot among the provinces. Therefore, King suggested that spending for Guard in the coming year be proportional to the brand's sales by region rather than to regional population.

Sung is convinced this is wrong, particularly in light of the Ontario situation. He asked King how the Ontario market should be handled. She said that the conservative way to build business in Ontario is to invest incremental promotion funds. However, before these incremental funds are invested, a test of this Ontario investment proposition should be conducted. King recommended that some of the Ontario money should be used to conduct an investment-spending market test in a small area or town in Ontario for 12 months. This will enable Sung to see if the incremental spending results in higher sales and profits—profits large enough to justify higher spending. In other words, an investment payout should be assured before spending any extra money in Ontario. Similarly, King would do the same kind of test in Quebec—to see if more money should go there.

After several e-mails back and forth, Sung feels this approach would be a waste of time and unduly cautious, given the importance of the Ontario market and the likely delistings in two key chains.

Evaluate the present strategy for Guard and Sung's and King's proposed strategies. How should the promotion money be allocated? Should investment-spending market tests be run first? Why? Explain.

Table 3 Usage Results (in percent)

	Maritimes	Quebec	Ontario	Manitoba/ Saskatchewan	Alberta	British Columbia
Respondents aware of Guard	20%	58%	28%	30%	32%	16%
Respondents ever trying Guard	3	18	2	8	6	4

Table 4 Allocation of Advertising/Sales Promotion Budget, by Population

	Maritimes	Quebec	Ontario	Manitoba/ Saskatchewan	Alberta	British Columbia	Canada
Percent of population	10%	27%	36%	8%	8%	11%	100%
Possible allocation of budget based on population (in 000s)	$80	$216	$288	$64	$64	$88	$800
Percent of Guard business at present	7%	51%	12%	11%	11%	8%	100%

33. Kennedy & Gaffney (K&G)

The partners of Kennedy & Gaffney are having a serious discussion about what the firm should do in the near future.

Kennedy & Gaffney (K&G) is a medium-size regional certified public accounting firm based in Grand Rapids, Michigan, with branch offices in Lansing and Detroit. Kennedy & Gaffney has nine partners and a professional staff of approximately 105 accountants. Gross service billings for the fiscal year ending June 30, 2010, were $6.9 million. See Table 1, which presents financial data for 2010, 2009 and 2008.

K&G's professional services include auditing, tax preparation, bookkeeping, and some general management consulting. Its client base includes municipal governments (cities, villages, and townships), manufacturing companies, professional organizations (attorneys, doctors, and dentists), and various other small businesses. A good share of revenue comes from the firm's municipal practice. Table 1 details K&G's gross revenue by service area and client industry for 2010, 2009, and 2008.

At the monthly partners' meeting held in July 2010, Robert Kennedy, the firm's managing partner (CEO), expressed concern about the future of the firm's municipal practice. Robert's presentation to his partners follows:

> Although our firm is considered to be a leader in municipal auditing in our geographic area, I am concerned that as municipals attempt to cut their operating costs, they will solicit competitive bids from other public accounting firms to perform their annual audits. Three of the four largest accounting firms in the world have local offices in our area. Because they concentrate their practice in the manufacturing industry—which typically has December 31 fiscal year-ends—they have "available" staff during the summer months.

Therefore, they can afford to low-ball competitive bids to keep their staffs busy and benefit from on-the-job training provided by municipal clientele. I am concerned that we may begin to lose clients in our most established and profitable practice area.*

Sherry Gaffney, a senior partner in the firm and the partner in charge of the firm's municipal practice, was the first to respond to Robert's concern.

> Robert, we all recognize the potential threat of being underbid for our municipal work by our large accounting competitors. However, K&G is a leader in municipal auditing in Michigan, and we have much more local experience than our competitors. Furthermore, it is a fact that we offer a superior

*Organizations with December fiscal year-ends require audit work to be performed during the fall and in January and February. Those with June 30 fiscal year-ends require auditing during the summer months.

Table 1 Fiscal Year Ending June 30

	2010	2009	2008
Gross billings	$6,900,000	$6,400,000	$5,800,000
Gross billings by service area:			
Auditing	3,100,000	3,200,000	2,750,000
Tax preparation	1,990,000	1,830,000	1,780,000
Bookkeeping	1,090,000	745,000	660,000
Other	720,000	625,000	610,000
Gross billings by client industry:			
Municipal	3,214,000	3,300,000	2,908,000
Manufacturing	2,089,000	1,880,000	1,706,000
Professional	1,355,000	1,140,000	1,108,000
Other	242,000	80,000	78,000

level of service to our clients—which goes beyond the services normally expected during an audit to include consulting on financial and other operating issues. Many of our less sophisticated clients depend on our nonaudit consulting assistance. Therefore, I believe, we have been successful in differentiating our services from our competitors. In many recent situations, K&G was selected over a field of as many as 10 competitors even though our proposed prices were much higher than those of our competitors.

The partners at the meeting agreed with Sherry's comments. Yet even though K&G had many success stories regarding their ability to retain their municipal clients—despite being underbid—they had lost three large municipal clients during the past year. Sherry was asked to comment on the loss of those clients. She explained that the lost clients are larger municipalities with a lot of in-house financial expertise and therefore less dependent on K&G's consulting assistance. As a result, K&G's service differentiation went largely unnoticed. Sherry explained that the larger, more sophisticated municipals regard audits as a necessary evil and usually select the low-cost reputable bidder.

Robert then requested ideas and discussion from the other partners at the meeting. One partner, Rosa Basilio, suggested that K&G should protect itself by diversifying. Specifically, she felt a substantial practice development effort should be directed toward manufacturing. She reasoned that since manufacturing work would occur during K&G's off-season, K&G could afford to price very low to gain new manufacturing clients. This strategy would also help to counter (and possibly discourage) low-ball pricing for municipals by the three large accounting firms mentioned earlier.

Another partner, Wade Huntoon, suggested that "if we have consulting skills, we ought to promote them more, instead of hoping that the clients will notice and come to appreciate us. Further, maybe we ought to be more aggressive in calling on smaller potential clients."

Another partner, Stan Walsh, agreed with Wade, but wanted to go further. He suggested that they recognize that there are at least two types of municipal customers and that two (at least) different strategies be implemented, including lower prices for auditing only for larger municipal customers and/or higher prices for smaller customers who are buying consulting too. This caused a big uproar from some who said this would lead to price cutting of professional services, and K&G didn't want to be price cutters: "One price for all is the professional way."

However, another partner, Isabel Ventura, agreed with Stan and suggested they go even further—pricing consulting services separately. In fact, she suggested that the partners consider setting up a separate department for consulting—like the large accounting firms have done. This can be a very profitable business. But it is a different kind of business and eventually may require different kinds of people and a different organization. For now, however, it may be desirable to appoint a manager for consulting services—with a budget—to be sure it gets proper attention. This suggestion too caused serious disagreement. Partners pointed out that having a separate consulting arm had led to major conflicts, especially in some larger accounting firms. The initial problems were internal. The consultants often brought in more profit than the auditors, but the auditors controlled the partnership and the successful consultants didn't always feel that they got their share of the rewards. There had also been serious external problems and charges of unethical behavior based on the concern that big accounting firms had a conflict of interest when they did audits on publicly traded companies that they in turn relied on for consulting income. Because of problems in this area, the Securities Exchange Commission created new guidelines that have changed how the big four accounting firms handle consulting. On the other hand, several partners argued that this was really an opportunity for K&G because their firm handled very few companies listed with the SEC, and the conflict of interest issues didn't even apply with municipal clients.

Robert thanked everyone for their comments and encouraged them to debate these issues in smaller groups and to share ideas by e-mail before coming to a one-day retreat (in two weeks) to continue this discussion and come to some conclusions.

Evaluate K&G's situation. What strategy(ies) should the partners select? Why?

34. Chess Aluminum Worldwide (CAW)*

Mickey Zhang, newly hired VP of marketing for Chess Aluminum Worldwide (CAW), is reviewing the firm's international distribution arrangements because they don't seem to be very well thought out. He is not sure if anything is wrong, but he feels that the company should follow a global strategy rather than continuing its current policies.

CAW is based in Atlanta, Georgia, and produces finished aluminum products, such as aluminum ladders, umbrella-type clothes racks, scaffolding, and patio tables and chairs that fold flat. Sales in 2010 reached $25 million, primarily to U.S. customers.

In 2006, CAW decided to try selling in select foreign markets. The sales manager, Jacqueline Windsor, believed the growing affluence of European workers would help the company's products gain market acceptance quickly.

Jacqueline's first step in investigating foreign markets was to join a trade mission to Europe, a tour organized by the U.S. Department of Commerce. This trade mission visited Italy, Germany, Denmark, Holland, France, and England. During this trip, Jacqueline was officially introduced to leading buyers for department store chains, import houses, wholesalers, and buying groups. The two-week trip convinced Jacqueline that there was ample buying power to make exporting a profitable opportunity.

On her return to Atlanta, Jacqueline's next step was to obtain credit references for the firms she considered potential distributors. To those who were judged creditworthy, she sent letters expressing interest and samples, brochures, prices, and other relevant information.

The first orders were from a French wholesaler. Sales in this market totaled $70,000 in 2007. Similar success was achieved in Germany and England. Italy, on the other hand, did not produce

*Adapted from a case written by Professor Hardy, University of Western Ontario, Canada.

any sales. Jacqueline felt the semi-luxury nature of the company's products and the lower incomes in Italy encouraged a "making do" attitude rather than purchase of goods and services that would make life easier.

In the United States, CAW distributes through fairly aggressive and well-organized merchant hardware distributors and buying groups, such as cooperative and voluntary hardware chains, which have taken over much of the strategy planning for cooperating producers and retailers. In its foreign markets, however, there is no recognizable pattern. Channel systems vary from country to country. To avoid channel conflict, CAW has only one account in each country. The chosen distributor is the exclusive distributor.

In France, CAW distributes through a wholesaler based in Paris. This wholesaler has five salespeople covering the country. The firm specializes in small housewares and has contacts with leading buying groups, wholesalers, and department stores. Jacqueline is impressed with the firm's aggressiveness and knowledge of merchandising techniques.

In Germany, CAW sells to a Hamburg-based buying group for hardware wholesalers throughout the country. Jacqueline felt this group would provide excellent coverage of the market because of its extensive distribution network.

In Denmark, CAW's line is sold to a buying group representing a chain of hardware retailers. This group recently expanded to include retailers in Sweden, Finland, and Norway. Together this group purchases goods for about 500 hardware retailers. The buying power of Scandinavians is quite high, and it is expected that CAW's products will prove very successful there.

In the United Kingdom, CAW uses an importer-distributor, who both buys on his own account and acts as a sales agent. The distributor approached CAW after finding the company from an online search. This firm sells to department stores and hardware wholesalers. This firm has not done very well overall, but it has done very well with CAW's line of patio tables and chairs.

Australia is handled by an importer that operates a chain of discount houses. It heard about CAW from a U.K. contact. After extensive e-mailing, this firm discovered it could land aluminum patio furniture in Melbourne at prices competitive with Chinese imports. So it started ordering because it wanted to cut prices in a high-priced garden furniture market.

The Argentina market is handled by an American who lives in Buenos Aires but came to the United States in search of new lines. CAW attributes success in Argentina to the efforts of this aggressive and capable agent. He has built a sizable trade in aluminum ladders.

In Trinidad and Jamaica, CAW's products are handled by traders who carry such diversified lines as insurance, apples, plums, and fish. They have been successful in selling aluminum ladders. This business grew out of inquiries sent to the U.S. Department of Commerce and in researching its website (www.commerce.gov), which Jacqueline followed up by phone.

Jacqueline's export policies for CAW are as follows:

1. *Product:* No product modifications will be made in selling to foreign customers. This may be considered later after a substantial sales volume develops.
2. *Place:* New distributors will be contacted through foreign trade shows. Jacqueline considers large distributors desirable. She feels, however, that they are not as receptive as smaller distributors to a new, unestablished product line. Therefore, she prefers to appoint small distributors. Larger distributors may be appointed after the company has gained a strong consumer franchise in a country.
3. *Promotion:* The firm does no advertising in foreign markets. Brochures and sales literature already being used in the United States are supplied to foreign distributors, who are encouraged to adapt them or create new materials as required. CAW will continue to promote its products by participating in overseas trade shows. These are handled by the sales manager. All inquiries are forwarded to the firm's distributor in that country.
4. *Price:* The company does not publish suggested list prices. Distributors add their own markup to their landed costs. Supply prices will be kept as low as possible. This is accomplished by (*a*) removing advertising expenses and other strictly domestic overhead charges from price calculations, (*b*) finding the most economical packages for shipping (smallest volume per unit), and (*c*) bargaining with carriers to obtain the lowest shipping rates possible.
5. *Financing:* CAW sees no need to provide financial help to distributors. The company views its major contribution as providing good products at the lowest possible prices.
6. *Marketing and planning assistance:* Jacqueline feels that foreign distributors know their own markets best. Therefore, they are best equipped to plan for themselves.
7. *Selection of foreign markets:* The evaluation of foreign market opportunities for the company's products is based primarily on disposable income and lifestyle patterns. For example, Jacqueline fails to see any market in North Africa for CAW's products, which she thinks are of a semi-luxury nature. She thinks that cheaper products such as wood ladders (often homemade) are preferred to prefabricated aluminum ladders in regions such as North Africa and Southern Europe. Argentina, on the other hand, she thinks is a more highly industrialized market with luxury tastes. Thus, Jacqueline sees CAW's products as better suited for more highly industrialized and affluent societies.

Evaluate CAW's present foreign markets strategies. Should it develop a global strategy? What strategy or strategies should Mickey Zhang (the new VP of marketing) develop? Explain.

35. Rizzuto's Pizzeria

Cassidy Newman manager of the Rizzuto's Pizzeria store in Flint, Michigan, is trying to develop a plan for the "sick" store she just took over.

Rizzuto's Pizzeria is an owner-managed pizza take-out and delivery business with three stores located in Ann Arbor, Southfield, and Flint, Michigan. Rizzuto's business comes from telephone, fax, or walk-in orders. Each Rizzuto's store prepares its own pizzas. In addition to pizzas, Rizzuto's also sells and delivers a limited selection of soft drinks.

Rizzuto's Ann Arbor store has been very successful. Much of the store's success may be due to being close to the University of Michigan campus. Most of these students live within 5 miles of Rizzuto's Ann Arbor store.

The Southfield store has been moderately successful. It serves mostly residential customers in the Southfield area, a largely residential suburb of Detroit. Recently, the store advertised—using direct-mail flyers—to several office buildings within 3 miles of the store. The flyers described Rizzuto's willingness and ability to cater large orders for office parties, business luncheons, and so on. The promotion was quite successful. With this new program and Rizzuto's solid residential base of customers in Southfield, improved profitability at the Southfield location seems assured.

Rizzuto's Flint location has had mixed results during the last three years. The Flint store has been obtaining only about half of its orders from residential delivery requests. The Flint store's new manager, Cassidy believes the problem with residential pizza delivery in Flint is due to the location of residential neighborhoods in the area. Flint has several large industrial plants (mostly auto industry related) located throughout the city. Small, mostly factory-worker neighborhoods are distributed in between the various plant sites. As a result, Rizzuto's store location can serve only two or three of these neighborhoods on one delivery run. Competition is also relevant. Rizzuto's has several aggressive competitors who advertise heavily, distribute cents-off coupons, and offer 2-for-1 deals. This aggressive competition is probably why Rizzuto's residential sales leveled off in the last year or so. And this competitive pressure seems likely to continue as some of this competition comes from aggressive national chains that are fighting for market share and squeezing little firms like Rizzuto's. For now, anyway, Cassidy feels she knows how to meet this competition and hold on to the present residential sales level.

Most of the Flint store's upside potential seems to be in serving the large industrial plants. Many of these plants work two or three shifts, five days a week. During each work shift, workers are allowed one half-hour lunch break—which usually occurs at 11 A.M., 8 P.M., or 2:30 A.M., depending on the shift.

Customers can order by phone, fax, e-mail, or at the Rizzuto's website. About 30 minutes before a scheduled lunch break Rizzuto's can expect an order for several (5 to 10) pizzas for a work group. Rizzuto's may receive many orders of this size from the same plant (i.e., from different groups of workers). The plant business is very profitable for several reasons. First, a large number of pizzas can be delivered at the same time to the same location, saving transportation costs.

Second, plant orders usually involve many different toppings (double cheese, pepperoni, mushrooms, hamburger) on each pizza. This results in $11 to $14 revenue per pizza. The delivery drivers also like delivering plant orders because the tips are usually $1 to $2 per pizza.

Despite the profitability of the plant orders, several factors make it difficult to serve the plant market. Rizzuto's store is located 5 to 8 minutes from most of the plant sites, so Rizzuto's staff must prepare the orders within 20 to 25 minutes after it receives the telephone order. Often, inadequate staff and/or oven capacity means it is impossible to get all the orders heated at the same time.

Generally, plant workers will wait as long as 10 minutes past the start of their lunch break before ordering from various vending trucks that arrive at the plant sites during lunch breaks. (Currently, no other pizza delivery stores are in good positions to serve the plant locations and have chosen not to compete.) But there have been a few instances when workers refused to pay for pizzas that were only five minutes late! Worse yet, if the same work group gets a couple of late orders, they are lost as future customers. Cassidy believes that the inconsistent profitability of the Flint store is partly the result of such lost customers.

In an effort to rebuild the plant delivery business, Cassidy is considering various methods to ensure prompt customer delivery. She thinks that potential demand during lunch breaks is significantly above Rizzuto's present capacity. Cassidy also knows that if she tries to satisfy all phone or fax orders on some peak days, she won't be able to provide prompt service and may lose more plant customers.

Cassidy has outlined three alternatives that may win back some of the plant business for the Flint store. She has developed

Table 1 Practical Capacities and Sales Potential of Current Equipment and Personnel

	11 A.M. Break	8 P.M. Break	2:30 A.M. Break	Daily Totals
Current capacity (pizzas)	48	48	48	144
Average selling price per unit	$ 12.50	$ 12.50	$ 12.50	$ 12.50
Sales potential	$600	$600	$600	$1,800
Variable cost (approximately 40 percent of selling price)*	240	240	240	720
Contribution margin of pizzas	360	360	360	1,080
Beverage sales (2 medium-sized beverages per pizza ordered at 75¢ a piece)†	72	72	72	216
Cost of beverages (30% per beverage)	22	22	22	66
Contribution margin of beverages	50	50	50	150
Total contribution of pizza and beverages	$410	$410	$ 410	$1,230

*The variable cost estimate of 40% of sales includes variable costs of delivery to plant locations.

†Amounts shown are not physical capacities (there is almost unlimited physical capacity), but potential sales volume is constrained by number of pizzas that can be sold.

Table 2 Capacity and Demand for Plant Customer Market

	Estimated Daily Demand	Current Daily Capacity	Proposed Daily Capacity
Pizza units (1 pizza)	320	144	300

these alternatives to discuss with Rizzuto's owner. Each alternative is briefly described below:

Alternative 1: Determine practical capacities during peak volume periods using existing equipment and personnel. Accept orders only up to that capacity and politely decline orders beyond. This approach will ensure prompt customer service and high product quality. It will also minimize losses resulting from customers' rejection of late deliveries. Financial analysis of this alternative—shown in Table 1—indicates that a potential daily contribution to profit of $1,230 could result if this alternative is implemented successfully. This would be profit before promotion costs, overhead, and net profit (or loss). *Note:* Any alternative will require several thousand dollars to reinform potential plant customers that Rizzuto's has improved its service and "wants your business."

Alternative 2: Buy additional equipment (one oven and one delivery car) and hire additional staff to handle peak loads. This approach would ensure timely customer delivery and high product quality as well as provide additional capacity to handle unmet demand. Table 2 is a conservative estimate of potential daily demand for plant orders compared to current capacity and proposed increased capacity. Table 3 gives the cost of acquiring the additional equipment and relevant information related to depreciation and fixed costs.

Using this alternative, the following additional pizza delivery and preparation personnel costs would be required:

	Hours Required	Cost per Hour	Total Additional Daily Cost
Delivery personnel	6	6	$36.00
Preparation personnel	8	6	48.00
			$84.00

The addition of even more equipment and personnel to handle all unmet demand was not considered in this alternative because the current store is not large enough.

Alternative 3: Add additional equipment and personnel as described in alternative 2, but move to a new location that would reduce delivery lead times to 2 to 5 minutes. This move would probably allow Rizzuto's to handle all unmet demand—because the reduction in delivery time will provide for additional oven time. In fact, Rizzuto's might have excess capacity using this approach.

A suitable store is available near about the same number of residential customers (including many of the store's current residential customers). The available store is slightly larger than needed. And the rent is higher. Relevant cost information on the proposed store follows:

Additional rental expense of proposed store over current store	$ 1,600 per year
Cost of moving to new store (one-time cost)	$16,000

Cassidy presented the three alternatives to Rizzuto's owner, Marcelo Rizzuto. Marcelo was pleased that Cassidy had done her homework. He decided that Cassidy should make the final decision on what to do (in part because she had a profit-sharing agreement with Marcelo) and offered the following comments and concerns:

1. Marcelo agreed that the plant market was extremely sensitive to delivery timing. Product quality and pricing, although important, were of less importance.
2. He agreed that plant demand estimates were conservative. "In fact, they may be 10 to 30 percent low."
3. Marcelo expressed concern that under alternative 2, and especially under alternative 3, much of the store's capacity would go unused over 80 percent of the time.
4. He was also concerned that Rizzuto's store had a bad reputation with plant customers because the prior store manager was not sensitive to timely plant delivery. So Marcelo suggested that Cassidy develop a promotion plan to improve Rizzuto's reputation in the plants and be sure that everyone knows that Rizzuto's has improved its delivery service.

Evaluate Cassidy possible strategies for the Flint store's plant market. What should Cassidy do? Why? Suggest possible promotion plans for your preferred strategy.

Table 3 Cost of Required Additional Assets

	Cost	Estimated Useful Life	Salvage Value	Annual Depreciation*	Daily Depreciation†
Delivery car (equipped with pizza warmer)	$11,000	5 years	$1,000	$2,000	$5.71
Pizza oven	$20,000	8 years	$2,000	$2,250	$6.43

*Annual depreciation is calculated on a straight-line basis.

†Daily depreciation assumes a 350-day (plant production) year. All variable expenses related to each piece of equipment (e.g., utilities, gas, oil) are included in the variable cost of a pizza.

36. Skyline Homebuilders*

Skip Patterson, who seven years ago founded Skyline Homebuilders in Asheville, North Carolina, is excited that he'll complete his first LEED-certified "green" home this month. The LEED (Leadership in Energy and Environmental Design) rating means that the home uses 30 percent less energy and 20 percent less water than a conventional house; construction waste going into landfills must also be reduced. The house will be the model home to showcase Skip's new development, which includes four more homes that he hopes to complete in the next six months.

Although Skip is excited, he is also nervous. Rising interest rates and an uncertain economy have reduced demand in the local housing market. People who do buy a home are more price-sensitive. That's a problem because building a green house usually increases construction costs—but customers are not always aware of the benefits that come with the higher price tag. So Skip has to figure out how to find home buyers that are willing to pay a premium for his "green" homes.

Prior to building this home, Skip tried to make environmentally responsible building choices that didn't increase his costs. However, two years ago while at the National Association of Home Builders' convention in Orlando, Florida, Skip visited a booth that described LEED Certification and it appealed to him. He also met a number of new suppliers who were offering sustainable building materials. When Skip returned from the convention in Orlando, Skyline Homebuilders salesperson Karen Toller told him that more home buyers were asking about environmental and energy-saving features. Skip thought the time was right to commit to building at least a few homes that met higher environmental standards.

Skip kept his eye out for a good piece of property for his project. Before long he found a 3-acre parcel of land about 15 minutes from downtown Asheville. The land had a nice mix of hardwood trees and a small stream, but lacked the panoramic mountain views expected by high-end home buyers in the area. Nevertheless, Skip thought the property would be ideal for a small neighborhood of moderate-size green homes. He purchased the land—and his first green project was under way.

Skip worked closely with a local architect, Katie Kelly, who had won several awards from the Green Building Council for her innovative designs. Katie proposed that each home follow a theme based on a classic Appalachian farmhouse design that would blend well with the rural surroundings and fit the concept of clustered development. Clustered development allows a builder to increase the number of home sites allowed if land is set aside for open space. For example, regulations usually required at least one acre for a rural home site. However, in a clustered development, the county would allow Skip to build five homes on 1.5 acres of his land if he dedicated the remaining 1.5 acres as open space controlled by a conservation easement.

Initially, Skip thought the additional two home sites and preservation of open space would be a huge benefit for his project. However, to get the development permit, he had to provide the county with a special land survey and biological inventory of the site. This extra survey work cost Skip $25,000 more than was normal.

Skip is behind schedule with construction because working with new types of materials has slowed him down. In some cases his workers even had to be trained by factory representatives on the proper installation of materials. In addition, many of the materials in a LEED home—such as low-E windows, blown foam insulation, a high-efficiency furnace and water heater, and Energy Star appliances—have premium prices. As a result, Skip's LEED-certified homes cost about 10 percent more than a conventionally built home of the same size.

However, LEED homes do offer buyers a number of benefits. Toxin-free building materials help combat indoor air pollution—and green homes are less likely to have problems with mold or mildew. Energy and water savings for the homes Skip is building should be $2,000 to $3,000 per year. Plus buyers can feel good that their homes produce fewer greenhouse gases, reduce dependence on fossil fuels, and send less construction waste to the local landfill.

Skip priced the five homes he is building at $250,000 to $300,000—about 10 percent more than similar non-LEED certified homes in the area. So far, the homes are getting a few looks, but none has sold and he hasn't had an offer. The feedback that Karen Toller hears is that people like the homes, but think that the price seems to be high; they like the general idea of owning a green home and saving money on energy, but they don't focus on the benefits. Perhaps that is because real estate agents in the area have little experience with green building and are used to talking about value in terms of "cost per square foot."

Karen Toller works full-time as a real estate agent—and Skyline Homebuilders is one of her clients. She receives a 1 percent sales commission for every Skyline home that is sold. She typically writes the listing that all real estate agents can read on the Multiple Listing Service (MLS) website and also handles the contract to complete a sale. However, with no movement on Skip's new houses and with prime spring selling season coming up fast, Skip has asked Karen to meet with him to discuss ways to spark more interest in his development. Skip wants a plan that will bring people out to see his new homes and development—and a way to ensure that they are aware of the benefits he is offering.

Skip wonders what needs to be done to tell customers about the benefits of green building. Some other builders are advertising in local media and developing brochures to leave in a rack outside of their homes—but Skip has not needed to do that before. He wonders if he might be able to generate some inexpensive publicity by working with the local newspaper; it has run several feature stories about the environment but none about green building. He also thinks he needs to do more to convince real estate agents about the benefits of green housing. One idea is to ask someone at the Green Building Council or possibly his architect to put on a seminar, but Skip doesn't know if real estate agents will show up. He also wonders if putting signs in his model home to point out the environmental benefits might be helpful.

When Skip started his project, he thought his green homes would sell themselves, but now he wonders if he isn't ahead of his time.

What do you think of Skip Patterson's marketing strategy so far? What promotion objectives should Skip set for his marketing strategy? What are the advantages and disadvantages of targeting communications at consumers as compared to real estate agents? What would you recommend as a promotion blend?

---

*Erik Hardy did the research for an earlier version of this case.

Computer-Aided Problems

Guide to the use of computer-aided problems

Computer-Aided Problem Solving

Marketing managers are problem solvers who must make many decisions. Solving problems and making good decisions usually involves analysis of marketing information. Such information is often expressed in numbers—like costs, revenues, prices, and number of customers or salespeople. Most marketing managers use a computer to keep track of the numbers and speed through calculations. The computer can also make it easier to look at a problem from many different angles—for example, to see how a change in the sales forecast might impact expected sales revenue, costs, and profit.

The computer can only take a manager so far. The manager is the one who puts it all together—and it still takes skill to decide what the information means. The computer-aided problems at the end of the chapters in this text were developed by the authors to help you develop this skill. To work on the problems, you use the computer-aided problem (CAP) software that is available at the text's online learning center.

The problems are short descriptions of decisions faced by marketing managers. Each description includes information to help make the decision. With each problem there are several questions for you to answer.

Although you will use the computer program to do an analysis, most problems ask you to indicate what decision you would make and why. Thus, in these problems—as in the marketing manager's job—the computer is just a tool to help you make better decisions.

Each problem focuses on one or more of the marketing decision areas discussed in the corresponding chapter. The earlier problems require less marketing knowledge and are simpler in terms of the analysis involved. The later problems build on the principles already covered in the text. The problems can be used in many ways. And the same problem can be analyzed several times for different purposes. Although it is not necessary to do all of the problems or to do them in a particular order, you will probably want to start with the first problem. This practice problem is simpler than the others. In fact, you could do the calculations quite easily without a computer. But this problem will help you see how the program works and how it can help you solve the more complicated problems that come later.

Spreadsheet Analysis of Marketing Problems

Marketing managers often use spreadsheet analysis to evaluate their alternatives—and the program for the computer-aided problems does computerized spreadsheet analysis. In spreadsheet analysis, costs, revenue, and other data related to a marketing problem are organized into a data table—a spreadsheet. The spreadsheet analysis allows you to change the value of one or more of the variables in the data table—to see how each change affects the value of other variables. This is possible because the relationships among the variables are already programmed into the computer. You do not need to do any programming. Let's look at an overly simple example.

You are a marketing manager interested in the total revenue that will result from a particular marketing strategy. You are considering selling your product at $10.00 per unit. You expect to sell 100 units. In our CAP analysis, this problem might be shown in a (very simple) spreadsheet that looks like this:

Variable	Value
Selling price	$10.00
Units sold	100
Total revenue	$1,000.00

There is only one basic relationship in this spreadsheet: Total revenue is equal to the selling price multiplied by the number of units sold. If that relationship has been programmed into the computer (as it is in these problems), you can change the selling price or the number of units you expect to sell, and the program will automatically compute the new value for total revenue.

Now you can ask questions like: What if I raise the price to $10.40 and still sell 100 units? What will happen to total revenue? To get the answer, all you have to do is enter the new price in the spreadsheet, and the program will compute the total revenue for you.

You may also want to do many "what-if" analyses—for example, to see how total revenue changes over a range of prices. Spreadsheet analysis allows you to do this quickly and easily. For instance, if you want to see what happens to total revenue as you vary the price between some minimum value (say, $8.00) and a maximum value (say, $12.00), the program will provide the results table for a what-if analysis showing total revenue for 11 different prices in the range from $8.00 to $12.00.

In problems like these—with easy numbers and simple relationships between the variables—the spreadsheet does not save you much work. You can do the calculations in your head. But with more complicated problems, the spreadsheet makes it very convenient to more carefully analyze different alternatives or situations.

Using the Program

You don't have to know about computers or using a spreadsheet to use the computer-aided problems program. It was designed to be easy to learn and use. The Help button will give you more detailed information if you need it. But it's best to just try things out to see how it works. A mistake won't hurt anything.

You're likely to find that it's quicker and easier to just use the program than it is to read the instructions. So you may want to go ahead and use the software at the online learning center to try the practice problem now. It takes just a few minutes and there's nothing to it.

The Spreadsheet Is Easy to Use

The spreadsheet software is very easy to use and specifically designed for the computer-aided problems. It is developed in Flash, so using this will be the same as using a browser to surf the Internet. However, if you want more general information, you can review the Help file.

As with other browser-based Flash programs, you typically use a mouse to move around in the program and select options. When you move the mouse, the cursor (which appears on your screen as an arrow) also moves. If you move the mouse so that the cursor is over one of the options on the screen and quickly press and release the left button on the mouse, the program will perform the action associated with that option. This process of using the mouse to position the cursor and then quickly pressing and releasing the left button is called "clicking" or "selecting." In these instructions, we'll refer to this often. For example, we'll say things like "click the Results button" or "select a problem from the list."

Let's use the first problem to illustrate how the program works.

Start by Selecting a Problem

When you go to the online learning center website, the first screen displayed is a home page with the title of the book and various options. Click on the label that says CAPs (short for computer-aided problems).

The computer-aided problem page will appear. Click the problem you want to work (in this case, select the first one, "Revenue, Cost, and Profit Relationships").

Note: When you first select a problem, be patient while the program loads. It may take a minute or so. Once the program has loaded, calculations are immediate.

Once you select a problem, the problem description window appears. This is simply a convenient reminder of the problem description found in this text. (The assignment questions for each problem are in this book, so it's useful to have your book with you at the computer when you're working on a problem.)

To the left of the box in which the problem description appears, you will see buttons labeled Description, Spreadsheet, Results, Graph, and Calculator. After you've reviewed the problem description, click the Spreadsheet button.

Each spreadsheet consists of one or two columns of numbers. Each column and row is labeled. Look at the row and column labels carefully to see what variable is represented by the value (number) in the spreadsheet. Study the layout of the spreadsheet, and get a feel for how it organizes the information from the problem description. The spreadsheet displays the starting values for the problem. Keep in mind that sometimes the problem description does not provide as much detail about the starting values as is provided in the spreadsheet.

You will see that some of the values in the spreadsheet appear in a highlighted edit box. These are usually values related to the decision variables in the problem you are solving. You can change any value (number) that appears in one of these boxes. When you make a change, the rest of the values (numbers) in that column are recalculated to show how a change in the value of that one variable affects the others. Think about how the numbers relate to each other.

Making changes in values is easy. When the spreadsheet first appears, your cursor appears as a free-floating arrow; however, when you pass the cursor over the box for the value that you want to change, the cursor changes to the shape of an I-beam. When you click on the value in that box, you can change it. Or to move the cursor to a value in a different box, just click on that box.

When you have selected the box with the value (number) you want to change, there are different ways to type in your new number. A good approach is to position the I-beam cursor before the first digit, and while depressing the mouse button, drag the cursor across all of the digits in the number. This will highlight the entire number. Then simply type in the new number and the old one will be replaced. Alternatively, you can use other keys to edit the number. For example, you can use the backspace key to erase digits to the left of the I-beam cursor; similarly, you can use the Del key to erase digits to the right of the cursor. Or you can use the arrow keys to move the cursor to the point where you want to change part of a number. Then you just type in your change. You may want to experiment to see which of these editing approaches you like the best.

When you have finished typing the new number, press the Enter key and the other values in the spreadsheet will be recalculated to show the effect of your new value.

When you are typing numbers into the edit boxes, you'll probably find it most convenient to type the numbers and the decimal point with the keys on the main part of the keyboard (rather than those on the cursor control pad). For example, a price of 1,000 dollars and 50 cents would be typed as 1000.50 or just 1000.5—using the number keys on the top row of the keyboard and the period key for the decimal point. *Do not type in the dollar sign or the commas to indicate thousands.* Be careful not to type the letters o or l (lowercase L) instead of the numbers 0 or 1.

Typing percent values is a possible point of confusion, since there are different ways to think about a percent. For example, "ten and a half" percent might be represented by 10.5 or .105. To avoid confusion, the program always expects you to enter percents using the first approach, which is the way percents are discussed in the problems. Thus, if you want to enter the value for ten and a half percent, you would type 10.5.

To help prevent errors, each problem is programmed with a set of permitted values for each boxed field. It may be useful to explain what we mean by "permitted values." For example, if you accidentally type a letter when the computer program expects a number, the entry will turn red and what you typed will not be accepted. Further, the program won't allow you to enter a new value for a variable that is outside of a permitted range of values.

For example, if you try to type −10.00 as the price of a product, the entry will turn red. (It doesn't make sense to set the price as a negative number!) If you make an error, check what range of values is permitted—and then retype a new number that is in the permitted range, and press the Enter key to recompute the spreadsheet. When you have entered a permitted value, the value will no longer appear in red.

Remember that a value on the spreadsheet stays changed until you change it again. Some of the questions that accompany the problems ask you to evaluate results associated with different sets of values. It's good practice to check that you have entered all the correct values on a spreadsheet before interpreting the results.

In addition to changing values (numbers) on the spreadsheet itself, there are other options on the spreadsheet menu bar. Click the Description button to go back and review the problem description—or you can use the drop-down list again to select another problem.

Adding Your Comments and Printing

After you have done an analysis, you may want to print a copy of your results (especially if you are expected to hand in your answers to the questions that accompany the computer-aided problem). In fact, the print feature gives you the opportunity to type your name and answers right on the sheet that is printed. To use this feature, just click the printer icon while the spreadsheet is displayed with the results you want to print. A new window will open with a printable version of your analysis. You will also see an edit box area where you can type in your comments. Each comment can be up to 300 characters, and that should be plenty of space for you to type your answers to a question. Sometimes you will want to print more than one spreadsheet (each with its own comments) to answer the different questions.

Once you are satisfied with any comments you have added, you are ready to print your results. Of course, to be able to print you will need to have a printer properly hooked up to your computer and configured for Windows. *Before you select the Print button, make sure that the printer is turned on and loaded with paper!*

Results of a What-if Analysis

The "Show what-if analysis" button makes it easy for you to study in more detail the effect of changing the value of a particular variable. It systematically changes the value of one variable (which you select) and displays the effect that variable has on two other variables. You could do the same thing manually on the spreadsheet—by entering a value for a variable, checking the effect on other variables, and then repeating the process over and over again. But the manual approach is time-consuming and requires you to keep track of the results after each change. A what-if analysis does all this very quickly and presents the results table summary; you can also print or graph the results table if you wish.

Now let's take a step-by-step look at how you can get the exact what-if analysis that you want. The first step is to decide what variable (value) you want to vary and what result values you want to see in the results table.

You select the variables for your analysis by simply clicking the circle ("radio button") beside the number of interest. Click the radio button beside the value of the variable in an edit box that you want to vary. The radio button for the selected value is filled in. You can only select one variable to vary at a time. So if you want to vary some other variable, simply click on your new selection.

When you select a value to vary, the program computes a default "suggested" minimum value and maximum value for the range over which that variable may vary. The minimum value is usually 20 percent smaller than the value shown on the spreadsheet, and the maximum value is 20 percent larger. These default values are used as the minimum and maximum values to compute the results table for a what-if analysis (when you click the Results button).

You can also select the two variables that you want to display in the results table of the what-if analysis. Typically, you will want to display the results (computed values) for variables that will be affected by the variable you select to vary. Remember the example we used earlier. If you had specified that price was going to vary, you might want to display total revenue—to see how it changes at different price levels.

You select a variable to display in the same way that you select the variable you are going to vary. Simply click on the radio button beside a number on the spreadsheet that is not in an edit box. Then use this approach to select a second variable to be displayed in the results table. If you change your mind, you can click on the radio button for another variable. When you have completed this step, you will see a solid radio button next to the variable you chose to vary and solid radio buttons next to the two variables that you want to display.

Now you can let the computer take over. Click the button to show the what-if analysis and it will appear. Each row in the first column of the results table will show a different value for the variable you wanted to vary. The minimum value will be in the first row. The maximum value will be in the bottom row. Evenly spaced values between the minimum and maximum will be in the middle rows. The other columns show the calculated results for the values you selected to display. Each column of values is labeled at the top to identify the column and row from the spreadsheet. The row portion of the label is a short version of the label from the spreadsheet. The results are based on the values that were in the spreadsheet when you selected the Results button, except for the value you selected to vary.

After the results table is displayed, you have the option to type in your own minimum value and maximum value in the edit boxes below the results table. To do that, just use the same approach you used to enter new values in the spreadsheet. When you enter a new minimum or maximum, the results table will be updated based on the new range of values between the minimum and maximum you entered.

At this point you will want to study the results of your analysis. You can also print a copy of the results table by clicking the Print button. The button bar also shows other possibilities. For example, if you select the Spreadsheet button, the spreadsheet will reappear. The radio buttons will still show the values you selected in the previous analysis. From there you can make additional changes in the values in the spreadsheet, check the results table for a new what-if analysis, or select another problem to work. Or you can look at (and print) a graph of values in the results table for the what-if analysis.

Viewing a Graph of Your Results

You can create a graph of values in the results table by clicking the Graph button. The horizontal axis for the graph will be the variable in the first column of the display. The vertical axis on the left side is based on the first variable you selected to display in the results table. The vertical axis on the right side of the graph is for the second variable. There will be a line on the graph that corresponds to each axis.

What to Do Next

The next section gives additional tips on the program. You will probably want to look through it after you have done some work with the practice problem. For now, however, you're probably tired of reading instructions. So work a problem or two. It's easier and faster to use the program than to read about it. Give it a try, and don't be afraid to experiment. If you have problems, remember that the Help button is available when you need it.

Some Tips on Using the CAP Program

Resetting the Spreadsheet to the Initial Values

The initial spreadsheet for each problem gives the "starting values" for the problem. While working a problem, you will often change one or more of the starting values to a new number. A changed value stays in effect, unless you change it again. This is a handy feature. But after you make several changes, you may not be able to remember the starting values. There is a simple solution—you can click the button to return to the home page, then click the CAPs label again, and reselect the problem you want. The spreadsheet will appear with the original set of starting values.

Checking the Computer's Calculations

Some values appear in the spreadsheet as whole numbers, and others appear with one or more digits to the right of a decimal point. For example, dollar values usually have two digits to the right of the decimal point, indicating how many cents are involved. A value indicating, say, number of customers, however, will appear as a whole number.

When you are doing arithmetic by hand, or with a calculator, you sometimes have to make decisions about how much detail is necessary. For example, if you divide 13 by 3 the answer is 4.33, 4.333, 4.3333, or perhaps 4.33333, depending on how important it is to be precise. Usually we round off the number to keep things manageable. Similarly, computers usually display results after rounding off the numbers. This has the potential to create confusion and seeming inaccuracy when many calculations are involved. If the computer uses a lot of detail in its calculations and then displays intermediate results after rounding off, the numbers may appear to be inconsistent. To illustrate this, let's extend the example. If you multiply 4.33 times 2640, you get 11431.20. But if you multiply 4.333 by 2640, you get 11439.12. To make it easier for you to check relationships between the values on a spreadsheet, the CAP software does not use a lot of hidden detail in calculations. If it rounds off a number to display it in the spreadsheet, the rounded number is used in subsequent calculations. It would be easy for the computer to keep track of all of the detail in its calculations—but that would make it harder for you to check the results yourself. If you check the results on a spreadsheet (perhaps with the calculator provided) and find that your numbers are close but do not match exactly, it is probably because you are making different decisions about rounding than were programmed into the spreadsheet.

The software was designed and tested to be easy to use and error free. In fact, it is programmed to help prevent the user from making typing errors. But it is impossible to anticipate every possible combination of numbers you might enter—and some combinations of numbers can cause problems. For example, a certain combination of numbers might result in an instruction for the computer to divide a number by zero, which is a mathematical impossibility. When a problem of this sort occurs, the word ERROR will appear in the spreadsheet (or in the results table for the what-if analysis) instead of a number. If this happens, you should recheck the numbers in the spreadsheet and redo the analysis—to make certain that the numbers you typed in were what you intended. That should straighten out the problem in almost every case. Yet with any computer program there can be a hidden bug that only surfaces in unusual situations or on certain computers. Thus, if you think you have found a bug, we would like to know so that we can track down the source of the difficulty.

Notes

CHAPTER 1

1. See www.nike.com; "Nike's new marketing mojo," *Fortune,* February 13, 2012; "Is Nike's Flyknit the Swoosh of the Future?" *Bloomberg Businessweek,* March 15, 2012; "In China, Nike Sets Out to Alter Sports Mindset," *Wall Street Journal,* October 12, 2011; "Nike's Sustainablility Report Takes Top Ceres-ACCA Award," *GreenBiz.com,* May 11, 2011, "How Nike Rules the World," *Fortune,* February 3, 2011; "Adidas' Brand Ambitions," *Portland Business Journal,* December 10, 2010; "Nike Releases Apparel Sustainability Software," *Waste and Recycling News,* December 6, 2010; "Nike, Inc.," *Datamonitor,* December 1, 2010; "Nike, Adidas readjust marketing strategy," *China Daily,* August 30, 2010; "Despite Its Way with Women, Underdog Reebok Fixates on Nike," *AdAge.com,* July 12, 2010; "Letter to Shareholders," July 1, 2010; "Nike Women's Biz Gets Pounded as Toning Footwear Kicks Butt," *AdAge.com,* June 7, 2010; "Nike Looks Beyond 'Swoosh' for Growth," *Wall Street Journal,* May 20, 2010; "Nike Launches GreenXchange for Corporate Idea-Sharing," *Fast Company,* February 2, 2010; "Li Ning and Ziba Design Want to Build China's First Truly Global Brand," *Fast Company,* October 1, 2009; "Best in Show: Nike's Scrappy Trash Talk Shoes," *Bloomberg Businessweek,* July 29, 2009; "Cool Runnings," *Time,* October 4, 2007.

2. See http://www.learnthe4ps.com/category/personal-marketing-plan/ for articles related to developing your own personal marketing plan.

3. Gregory D. Upah and Richard E. Wokutch, "Assessing Social Impacts of New Products: An Attempt to Operationalize the Macromarketing Concept," *Journal of Public Policy and Marketing,* #4 (1985).

4. An American Marketing Association committee recently defined marketing as "the activity, set of institutions, and processes for creating, communicating, delivering, and exchanging offerings that have value for customers, clients, partners, and society at large," The definition of marketing can be a source of debate; see "AMA's Definition of Marketing Stirs Debate," *B to B,* February 11, 2008; see also David Glen Mick, "The End(s) of Marketing and the Neglect of Moral Responsibility by the American Marketing Association," *Journal of Public Policy & Marketing,* Fall 2007; Debra Jones Ringold and Barton Weitz, "The American Marketing Association Definition of Marketing: Moving from Lagging to Leading Indicator," *Journal of Public Policy & Marketing,* Fall 2007; George M. Zinkhan and Brian C. Williams, "The New American Marketing Association Definition of Marketing: An Alternative Assessment," *Journal of Public Policy & Marketing,* Fall 2007; Gregory T. Gundlach, "The American Marketing Association's 2004 Definition of Marketing: Perspectives on Its Implications for Scholarship and the Role and Responsibility of Marketing in Society," *Journal of Public Policy & Marketing,* Fall 2007; Jagdish N. Sheth and Can Uslay, "Implications of the Revised Definition of Marketing: From Exchange to Value Creation," *Journal of Public Policy & Marketing,* Fall 2007; William L. Wilkie and Elizabeth S. Moore, "What Does the Definition of Marketing Tell Us About Ourselves?" *Journal of Public Policy & Marketing,* Fall 2007.

5. George Fisk, "Editor's Working Definition of Macromarketing," *Journal of Macromarketing* 2, #1 (1982); Shelby D. Hunt and John J. Burnett, "The Macromarketing/Micromarketing Dichotomy: A Taxonomical Model," *Journal of Marketing,* Summer 1982.

6. William McInnes, "A Conceptual Approach to Marketing," *Theory in Marketing,* second series, ed. Reavis Cox, Wroe Alderson, and Stanley J. Shapiro (Homewood, IL: Richard D. Irwin, 1964).

7. B. J. Calder, E. C. Malthouse, and U. Schaedel, "An Experimental Study of the Relationship between Online Engagement and Advertising Effectiveness," *Journal of Interactive Marketing* 23, #4, 2009; P. Gupta, M. S. Yadav, and R. Varadarajan, "How Task-Facilitative Interactive Tools Foster Buyers' Trust in Online Retailers: A Process View of Trust Development in the Electronic Marketplace," *Journal of Retailing* 85, #2, 2009; Roderick J. Brodie, Heidi Winklhofer, Nicole E. Coviello, and Wesley J. Johnston, "Is E-Marketing Coming of Age? An Examination of the Penetration of E-Marketing and Firm Performance," *Journal of Interactive Marketing,* Spring 2007.

8. Graham Hooley, Tony Cox, John Fahy, David Shipley, et al. "Market Orientation in the Transition Economies of Central Europe: Tests of the Narver and Slater Market Orientation Scales," *Journal of Business Research,* December 2000; Saeed Samiee, "Globalization, Privatization, and Free Market Economy," *Journal of the Academy of Marketing Science,* Summer 2001.

9. "Rustic Wisdom: Unilever to Take Project Shakti Global," *Economic Times,* January 19, 2009; "Strategic Innovation: Hindustan Lever Ltd.," *Fast Company,* December 19, 2007; "Shakti—Changing Lives in Rural India," http://hll.com/-citizen_lever/project_shakti.asp; P. Indu, Komal Chary, and Vivek Gupta, "Reviving Hindustan Lever Limited," ICFAI Center for Management Research, Case Study #306-410-1, 2006; V. Kasturi Rangan and Rhithari Rajan, "Unilever in India: Hindustan Lever's Project Shakti—Marketing FMCG to the Rural Consumer," Harvard Business School, Case #9-505-056; C. K. Prahalad, *The Fortune at the Bottom of the Pyramid* (Philadelphia: Wharton School Publishing, 2005).

10. Kevin D. Bradford, Gregory T. Gundlach, and William L. Wilkie, "Countermarketing in the Courts: The Case of Marketing Channels and Firearms Diversion," *Journal of Public Policy & Marketing,* Fall 2005; Marian Friestad and Peter Wright, "The Next Generation: Research for Twenty-First-Century Public Policy on Children and Advertising," *Journal of Public Policy & Marketing,* Fall 2005; Kathleen Seiders and Ross D. Petty, "Taming the Obesity Beast: Children, Marketing, and Public Policy Considerations," *Journal of Public Policy & Marketing,* Fall 2007; James M. Carman and Robert G. Harris, "Public Regulation of Marketing Activity, Part III: A Typology of Regulatory Failures and Implications for Marketing and Public Policy," *Journal of Macromarketing,* Spring 1986.

11. Elkington, John (1997) *Cannibals with Forks: the Triple Bottom Line of 21st Century Business,* Wiley: New York; "Triple Bottom Line," *The Economist,* November 17, 2009.

12. A. Grinstein, "The Effect of Market Orientation and Its Components on Innovation Consequences: A Meta-Analysis," *Journal of the Academy of Marketing Science* #2 2008; Ahmet H. Kirca, Satish Jayachandran, and William O. Bearden, "Market Orientation: A Meta-Analytic Review and Assessment of Its Antecedents and Impact on Performance," *Journal of Marketing,* April 2005; Jagdish N. Sheth, Rajendra S. Sisodia, and Arun Sharma, "The Antecedents and Consequences of Customer-Centric Marketing," *Journal of the Academy of Marketing Science,* Winter 2000; Stanley F. Slater and John C. Narver, "Market Orientation and the Learning Organization," *Journal of Marketing,* July 1995; R. W. Ruekert, "Developing a Market Orientation: An Organizational Strategy Perspective," *International Journal of Research in Marketing,* August 1992; Bernard J. Jaworski and Ajay K. Kohli, "Market Orientation: Antecedents and Consequences," *Journal of Marketing,* July 1993; Morgan, Neil, "Marketing and business performance," *Journal of the Academy of Marketing Science,* January, 2012; Lam, Son K., Florian Kraus, and Michael Ahearne, "The Diffusion of Market Orientation Throughout the Organization: A Social Learning Theory Perspective," *Journal of Marketing* 74, September, 2012; Kumar, V, Eli Jones, Rajkumar Venkatesan, and Robert P Leone, "Is Market Orientation a Source of Sustainable Competitive Advantage or Simply the Cost of Competing?" *Journal of Marketing* 75, January, 2010; Blocker, Christopher P., Daniel J. Flint, Matthew B. Myers, and Stanley F. Slater "Proactive customer orientation and its role for creating customer value in global markets," *Journal of the Academy of Marketing Science,* 2011.

13. A. F. Payne, K. Storbacka, and P. Frow, "Managing the Co-Creation of Value," *Journal of the Academy of Marketing Science* 36, #1, 2008; "Companies Strive Harder to Please Customers," *Wall Street Journal,* July 27, 2009; "Would You Recommend Us?" *BusinessWeek,* January 30, 2006; "Get Creative! How to Build Innovative Companies," *BusinessWeek,* August 1, 2005; Xie Chunyan, Richard P. Bagozzi, and Sigurd V. Troye, "Trying to Prosume: Toward a Theory of Consumers as Co-creators of Value," *Journal of the Academy of Marketing Science,* Spring 2008; Min Soonhong, John T. Mentzer, and Robert T. Ladd, "A Market Orientation in Supply Chain Management," *Journal of the Academy of Marketing Science,* Winter 2007; Wolfgang Ulaga and Andreas Eggert, "Value-Based Differentiation in Business Relationships: Gaining and Sustaining Key Supplier Status," *Journal of Marketing,* January 2006; Roger Baxter, Sheelagh Matear, James C. Anderson, James A. Narus, and Wouter van Rossum, "Customer Value Propositions in Business Markets," *Harvard Business Review,* March 2006; Ronald L. Hess, Jr., Shankar Ganesan, and Noreen M. Klein, "Service Failure and Recovery: the Impact of Relationship Factors on Customer Satisfaction," *Journal of the Academy of Marketing Science,* Spring 2003; Stanley F. Slater and John C. Narver, "Market Orientation, Customer Value, and Superior Performance," *Business Horizons,* March–April 1994; Sharon E. Beatty, "Keeping Customers," *Journal of Marketing,* April 1994.

14. See www.chipotle.com, "Fast Casual Nation," *Time,* April 23, 2012; "Chipotle aims to buck fast-food convention—while it still can," Advertising Age, March 3, 2012; "For Exploding All the Rule sof Fast Food," *Fast Company,* June, 2012; "Chipotle's Rise," *Fortune,* October 18, 2010; "The Great Casual Dining Upheaval," *Bloomberg Businessweek,* August 29–September 4, 2012; "Chipotle CMO Wants the Whole Enchilada," *Brandweek,* February 16, 2009; "Burrito Buzz—And So Few Ads," *BusinessWeek,* March 12, 2007.

15. "Nonprofits Tell Story on Social Networks," *Investor's Business Daily,* February 8, 2010; Stacy Landreth Grau and Judith Anne Garretson Folse, "Cause-Related Marketing (CRM)," *Journal of Advertising,* Winter 2007; "Uncle Sam Wants You in the Worst Way," *BusinessWeek,* August 11, 2005; "Modern Marketing Helps Sell Life as a Nun," *Wall Street Journal,* May 11, 1999; Glenn B. Voss and Zannie Giraud Voss, "Strategic Orientation and Firm Performance in an Artistic Environment," *Journal of Marketing,* January 2000; Dennis B. Arnett, Steve D. German, and Shelby D. Hunt, "The Identity Salience Model of Relationship Marketing Success: the Case of Nonprofit Marketing," *Journal of Marketing,* April 2003.

16. "NYC Promotes Free Water," *Brandweek,* July 9, 2007.

17. "Companies Try Keeping Ice Cream Frozen, Emissions Down," *Wall Street Journal,* May 4, 2005; "The Black Market vs. the Ozone," *BusinessWeek,* July 7, 1997; "CFC-Span: Refrigerant's Reign Nears an End," *USA Today,* August 22, 1994; "Air-Conditioner Firms Put Chill on Plans to Phase Out Use of Chlorofluorocarbons," *Wall Street Journal,* May 10, 1993. See also Xueming Luo and C. B. Bhattacharya, "Corporate Social Responsibility, Customer Satisfaction, and Market Value," *Journal of Marketing,* October 2006; Alan R. Andreasen, "Social Marketing: Its Definition and Domain," *Journal of Public Policy & Marketing,* Spring 1994.

18. Torelli, Carlos J., Alokparna Basu Monga, and Andrew M. Kaikati, "Doing Poorly by Doing Good: Corporate Social Responsibility and Brand Concepts," *Journal of Consumer Research,* 2012; Wilkie, William, and Elizabeth Moore, "Expanding our understanding of marketing in society," *Journal of the Academy of Marketing Science,* January 2012; C. B. Bhattacharya and Sankar Sen, "Doing Better at Doing Good: When, Why and How Customers Respond to Corporate Social Initiatives," *California Management Review,* Fall 2004.

19. Martin, Kelly, Jean Johnson, and Joseph French. 2011. "Institutional pressures and marketing ethics initiatives: the focal role of organizational identity," *Journal of the Academy of Marketing Science,* July; Agrawal, Nidhi, and Adam Duhachek. 2010; "Emotional Compatibility and the Effectiveness of Antidrinking Messages: A Defensive Processing Perspective on Shame and Guilt," *Journal of Marketing Research,* April; Andrew V. Abela and Patrick E. Murphy, "Marketing with Integrity: Ethics and the Service-Dominant Logic for Marketing," *Journal of the Academy of Marketing Science,* Spring 2008; Lawrence B. Chonko and Shelby D. Hunt, "Ethics and Marketing Management: a Retrospective and Prospective Commentary," *Journal of Business Research,* December 2000; Jeffrey G. Blodgett, Long-Chuan Lu, Gregory M. Rose, and Scott J. Vitell, "Ethical Sensitivity to Stakeholder Interests: A Cross-Cultural Comparison," *Journal of the Academy of Marketing Science,* Spring 2001; George G. Brenkert, "Ethical Challenges of Social Marketing," *Journal of Public Policy & Marketing,* Spring 2002.

20. "Too Much Corporate Power?" *BusinessWeek,* September 11, 2000; C. B. Bhattacharya and Daniel Korschun, "Stakeholder Marketing: Beyond The Four Ps and the Customer," *Journal of Public Policy & Marketing,* Spring 2008.

CHAPTER 2

1. See www.cirquedusoleil.com; "Cirque du Soleil Shows Big Brands How To Be Remarkable—And Magical," *Forbes,* February 27, 2012; "Viva Viva Elvis!" *Time,* February 22, 2010; "Cirque's Midlife Crisis," *Canadian Business,* May 10, 2010; "U.S. Casinos' Bet on Macau Pays Off," *USA Today,* January 12, 2010; "Stanley Ho's Last Laugh in Macao," *BusinessWeek,* May 11, 2009; "Big Top to Burlesque: A Circus Sampler," *Wall Street Journal,* January 24, 2008; "Talent Scouts for Cirque du Soleil Walk a Tightrope," *Wall Street Journal,* September 8, 2007; "CMO Strategy: Unleash Emotions for Business Growth," *Advertising Age,* March 12, 2007; "Super Pregame Show," *MiamiHerald*.com, January 10, 2007; "Cirque du Success," *U.S. News and World Report,* November 20, 2006; "The Onliness of Strong Brands," *BusinessWeek,* November 16, 2006; "Crazy for 'Delirium," Billboard, July 15, 2006; "The Disney of the New Age," *Maclean's,* June 26, 2006; "Cirque du Balancing Act," *Fortune,* June 12, 2006; "How Cirque du Soleil Uses Email to Sell Out Shows at Local Cities," *Marketing Sherpa,* June 1, 2006; W. Chan Kim and Renée Mauborgne, *Blue Ocean Strategy,* Boston: Harvard Business School Press, 2005; "Join the Circus," *Fast Company,* July 1, 2005; "Lord of the Rings," *Economist,* February 5, 2005; "Best Launch: Zumanity," *Marketing magazine,* November 11, 2004; "Big Top Television," *Marketing Magazine,* August 9–16, 2004; "Mario D'Amico—Cirque du Soleil," *Reveries,* July 2002.

2. Varadarajan, Rajan, "Strategic marketing and marketing strategy: domain, definition, fundamental issues and foundational premises," *Journal of the Academy of Marketing Science,* March 2012; J. Burnett, "Hidden in Plain Sight: How to Find and Execute Your Company's Next Big Growth Strategy," *Journal of Advertising Research* 48, #1, 2008; George S. Day, "Is It Real? Can We Win? Is It Worth Doing?" *Harvard Business Review,* December 2007; John G. Singer, "What Strategy Is Not," *Sloan Management Review,* Winter 2008; Rebecca J. Slotegraaf and Peter R. Dickson, "The Paradox of a Marketing Planning Capability," *Journal of the Academy of Marketing Science,* Fall 2004; Kwaku Atuahene-Gima and Janet Y. Murray, "Antecedents and Outcomes of Marketing Strategy Comprehensiveness," *Journal of Marketing,* October 2004; Gail J. McGovern, David Court, John A. Quelch, and Blair Crawford, "Bringing Customers into the Boardroom," *Harvard Business Review,* November 2004; George S. Day, "Marketing's Contribution to the Strategy Dialogue," *Journal of the Academy of Marketing Science,* Fall 1992; P. Rajan Varadarajan and Terry Clark, "Delineating the Scope of Corporate, Business, and Marketing Strategy," *Journal of Business Research,* October–November 1994.

3. See www.herbalessences.com/us/default.jsp; "The Issue: How P&G Brought Back Herbal Essences," *BusinessWeek,* June 17, 2008; "Herbal Essence Snags 2007 ReBrand 100 Global Award," *Marketing Daily,* July 11, 2007; "Nature Boy," *Brandweek,* September 7, 2008; Ram Charan and A. G. Lafley, *The Game Changer*, New York: Crown Business.

4. For information on Silverman's new business, see www.preschoolians.com. For more on Toddler University see "Genesco Names New Executive of Children's Footwear Division," Press Release, Genesco, July 15, 1994;

"Toddler University Ends Up in Westport," *Westport News,* March 8, 1991; "Whiz Kid," *Connecticut,* August 1989; "The Young and the Restless," *Children's Business,* May 1989.

5. Orville C. Walker, Jr., and Robert W. Ruekert, "Marketing's Role in the Implementation of Business Strategies: A Critical Review and Conceptual Framework," *Journal of Marketing,* July 1987; Thomas V. Bonoma, "A Model of Marketing Implementation," 1984 *AMA Educators' Proceedings,* Chicago: American Marketing Association, 1984.

6. Tarasi, Crina O, Ruth N Bolton, Michael D Hutt, and Beth A Walker. "Balancing Risk and Return in a Customer Portfolio," *Journal of Marketing,* May 2011; V. Kumar and Morris George, "Measuring and Maximizing Customer Equity: a Critical Analysis," *Journal of the Academy of Marketing Science,* Summer 2007; Thorsten Wiesel, Bernd Skiera, and Julin Villanueva, "Customer Equity: An Integral Part of Financial Reporting," *Journal of Marketing,* March 2008; Werner Reinartz, Jacquelyn S. Thomas, and Ganaël Bascoul, "Investigating Cross-Buying and Customer Loyalty," *Journal of Interactive Marketing,* Winter 2008; Robert P. Leone, Vithala R. Rao, Kevin Lane Keller, Anita Man Luo, Leigh McAlister, and Rajendra Srivastava, "Linking Brand Equity to Customer Equity," *Journal of Service Research,* May 2006; Roland T. Rust, Katherine N. Lemon, and Valarie A. Zeithaml, "Return on Marketing: Using Customer Equity to Focus Marketing Strategy," *Journal of Marketing,* January 2004; Jacquelyn S. Thomas, Werner Reinartz, and V. Kumar, "Getting the Most Out of All Your Customers," *Harvard Business Review,* July 2004; Michael D. Johnson, Andreas Herrmann, and Frank Huber, "The Evolution of Loyalty Intentions," *Journal of Marketing,* April 2006; Roland T. Rust, Valarie A. Zeithaml, and Katherine N. Lemon, "Customer-Centered Brand Management," *Harvard Business Review,* September 2004; Arnold, Todd J., Eric (Er) Fang, and Robert W. Palmatier, "The effects of customer acquisition and retention orientations on a firm's radical and incremental innovation performance," *Journal of the Academy of Marketing Science,* March 2011; Kumar, V., J. Andrew Petersen, and Robert P. Leone, "Driving Profitability by Encouraging Customer Referrals: Who, When, and How," *Journal of Marketing,* September 2010. "Putting the Service Profit Chain to Work," *Harvard Business Review,* July–August 2008; "What Customers Want," *Fortune,* July 7, 2003; "The Unprofitable Customers," *Wall Street Journal* Reports, October 28, 2002; Sunil Gupta, Dominique Hanssens, Bruce Hardie, William Kahn, V. Kumar, Nathaniel Lin, and Nalini Ravishanker S. Sriram, "Modeling Customer Lifetime Value," *Journal of Service Research,* May 2006; Edward C. Malthouse and Robert C. Blattberg, "Can We Predict Customer Lifetime Value?" *Journal of Interactive Marketing,* Winter 2004; Vikas Mittal, "Driving Customer Equity: How Customer Lifetime Value Is Reshaping Corporate Strategy," *Journal of Marketing,* April 2001.

7. See www.ford.com; "Ford Motor Company," at www.fundinguniverse.com/company-histories/Ford-Motor-Company-Company-History.html, March 10, 2010; www.fordvehicles.com/technology/sync/; "Why Ford Could Be the Next Media Company," *Advertising Age,* January 11, 2010; "Ford Voted 'Most Improved' in '09 in Consumer Poll," *Brandweek,* January 11, 2010; "Ford Gets into Twitter—omg!" *USA Today,* January 7, 2010; "How Ford Got Social Marketing Right," *Harvard Business Review blog,* Grant McCracken, January 7, 2010; "Ford Brings Wi-Fi to the Highway," *Wired.com,* January 6, 2010; "The Engine Finally Turns Over at Ford," *BusinessWeek,* November 16, 2009; "Ford's Fiesta to Party on—Without the Fiesta," *AdAge.com,* September 14, 2009; "Fixing Up Ford," *Fortune,* May 25, 2009; "Ford Is Counting on Army of 100 Bloggers to Launch New Fiesta," *AdAge.com,* April 20, 2009; "Ford Takes Online Gamble with New Fiesta," *Wall Street Journal,* April 8, 2009; "Cars Now Doing a Lot of Talking—and Safer Driving," *Investor's Business Daily,* January 14, 2009; "Ford's Sync Adds Interactive Features," *Wall Street Journal,* January 8, 2009; "Ford Escape Hybrid: OK but it's no Prius," *Automotive News,* March 3, 2006; Floyd Clymer, *Treasury of Early American Automobiles, 1877–1925* (McGraw-Hill, 1950); G. N. Georganao, *Cars: Early and Vintage, 1886–1930 (1985);* David Hounshell, *From the American System to Mass Production, 1800–1932* (Johns Hopkins University Press, 1984); Henry Ford, with Samuel Crowther, *My Life and Work* (Garden City Publishing Co., 1922).

8. Richard A. D'Aveni, "Mapping Your Competitive Position," *Harvard Business Review,* February 2008; George S. Day and Robin Wensley, "Assessing Advantage: A Framework for Diagnosing Competitive Superiority," *Journal of Marketing,* April 1988; Michael E. Porter, *Competitive Advantage—Creating and Sustaining Superior Performance* (New York: Free Press, MacMillan, 1986); Mark B. Houston, "Competing for the Future: Breakthrough Strategies for Seizing Control of Your Industry and Creating the Markets of Tomorrow," *Journal of the Academy of Marketing Science,* Winter 1996; Kevin P. Coyne, "Sustainable Competitive Advantage—What It Is, What It Isn't," *Business Horizons,* January–February 1986.

9. www.ikea.com; www.jetblue.com; www.in-n-out.com; Moon, Youngme (2010) *Different: Escaping the Competitive Herd,* New York: Crown Business; "Manland: Ikea's day-care for husbands," *The Week,* September 16, 2011.

10. Ruth N. Bolton, Katherine N. Lemon, and Peter C. Verhoef, "Expanding Business-to-Business Customer Relationships: Modeling the Customer's Upgrade Decision," *Journal of Marketing,* January 2008; Douglas W. Vorhies and Neil A. Morgan, "A Configuration Theory Assessment of Marketing Organization Fit with Business Strategy and Its Relationship with Marketing Performance," *Journal of Marketing,* January 2003.

11. For more on Coleman, see www.coleman.com; "The Grill of Their Dreams," *Business 2.0,* February 2002; "Growing to Match Its Brand Name," *Fortune,* June 13, 1994. See also Youjae Yi and Hoseong Jeon, "Effects of Loyalty Programs on Value Perception, Program Loyalty, and Brand Loyalty," *Journal of the Academy of Marketing Science,* Summer 2003.

12. For more on E-Z-Go, see www.ezgo.com; "Wanna Drag? Now Golf Carts Are in the Race," *Wall Street Journal,* March 6, 2007; "Off-Roading, Golf-Cart Style," *Wall Street Journal,* June 14, 2001. See also Michael S. Garver, "Best Practices in Identifying Customer-Driven Improvement Opportunities," *Industrial Marketing Management,* August 2003; John H. Roberts, "Developing New Rules for New Markets," *Journal of the Academy of Marketing Science,* Winter 2000.

13. For more on Campbell, see www.campbellsoup.com; "Campbell Soup Boosts Outlook as Net Rises," *Wall Street Journal,* November 24, 2009; "Campbell's: Not About to Let the Soup Cool," *BusinessWeek,* September 28, 2009; "Campbell's Lowering Sodium in Almost 50 Soups," *USA Today,* February 18, 2008. For more on ski resorts, see "Seeking Growth, Ski Areas Target Minorities," *Wall Street Journal,* December 22, 2004. For more on Nike, see 2009 Annual Report, Nike; "When Nike Met iPod," *Wall Street Journal,* May 24, 2006. See also Sarah J. Marsh and Gregory N. Stock, "Building Dynamic Capabilities in New Product Development Through Intertemporal Integration," *Journal of Product Innovation Management,* March 2003; George C. Kingston and Beebe Nelson, "Leading Product Innovation: Accelerating Growth in a Product-Based Business," *Journal of Product Innovation Management,* November 2001.

14. For more on McDonald's and its hotel diversification effort, see "Would You Like a Bed with Your Burger?" Ad Age Global, February 2001; "The Golden Arches: Burgers, Fries and 4-Star Rooms," *Wall Street Journal,* November 17, 2000.

15. For more on JLG, see www.jlg.com; "JLG Industries Acquisition Gives a Big Lift to Oshkosh Truck Sales," *Investor's Business Daily,* October 31, 2007; "The Secret of U.S. Exports: Great Products," *Fortune,* January 10, 2000.

16. For more on international marketing, see "Novelty of Mexican Food in India Is a Hit for Yum," *Wall Street Journal,* March 30, 2010; "Yum Brands Bet on India's Young for Growth," *Wall Street Journal,* December 17, 2009; "McDonald's Creates Asian-Inspired Versions of Food as Part of Olympics Blitz," *Wall Street Journal,* July 1, 2008; "In Vietnam, Fast Food Acts Global, Tastes Local," *Wall Street Journal,* March 12, 2008; "Foreign Distribution? Just Ask Mom (& Pop)," *Brandweek,* November 19, 2007; "Scrambling to Bring Crest to the Masses," *BusinessWeek,* June 25, 2007; Naresh K. Malhotra, Francis M. Ulgado, and James Agarwal, "Internationalization and Entry

Modes: A Multitheoretical Framework and Research Propositions," *Journal of International Marketing,* 2003; Shaoming Zou and S. Tamer Cavusgil, "The GMS: A Broad Conceptualization of Global Marketing Strategy and its Effect on Firm Performance," *Journal of Marketing,* October 2002; Susan P. Douglas, "Exploring New Worlds: the Challenge of Global Marketing," *Journal of Marketing,* January 2001.

CHAPTER 3

1. See www.amazon.com; *Amazon.com: the Hidden Empire,* faberNovel, May 2011; "No holiday cheer for Amazon.com," *Chicago Tribune,* November 27, 2011; "Amazon Pressured on Sales Tax," *New York Times,* March 13, 2011; "Retailers Struggle in Amazon's Jungle," *Wall Street Journal,* February 22, 2011; "Price Check for iPhone," *Wired,* November 23, 2010; "What's in Amazon's Box? Instant Gratification," *Bloomberg Businessweek,* November 23, 2010; "Wal-Mart Fires Shot in Toy War," *Wall Street Journal,* November 8, 2010; "Study: Amazon.com Is Most Trusted Brand in U.S," *CNET News,* February 22, 2010; "Now, It's Google Vs. . . . Amazon.com?" *Investor's Business Daily,* November 19, 2009; "Walmart Making Push Online, Where It's a Pygmy Vs. Amazon," *Investor's Business Daily,* October 20, 2009; "Walmart Strafes Amazon in Book War," *Wall Street Journal,* October 16, 2009; "Amazon Packages Green Site," *Investor's Business Daily,* February 25, 2009; "Amazon.com's Third-Party Sales Balloon," *Investor's Business Daily,* April 8, 2009; "When Service Means Survival: How Amazon Aims to Keep You Clicking," *BusinessWeek,* March 2, 2009; "The World's Most Innovative Companies," *Fast Company,* March 2009; For more on Kindle, see "Hachette Enters the E-Book Fray, Saying It, Too, Wants New Pricing," *Wall Street Journal,* February 5, 2010; "Trying to Avert a Digital Horror Story," *BusinessWeek,* January 11, 2010; "Sony E-Reader Opens New Chapters in Kindle Rivalry," *Wall Street Journal,* January 14, 2010; "More Makers Jump into the E-Reader Fray," *Wall Street Journal,* January 8, 2010; "Publishers Aren't Happy with Amazon's Pricing," *USA Today,* December 11, 2009; "IPod Touch, iPhone Join Kindle's Book Club," *USA Today,* March 4, 2009; "Amazon's Kindle 2 Improves the Good, Leaves Out the Bad," *Wall Street Journal,* February 26, 2009; "Kindle's New, but Price Is Old," *USA Today,* February 10, 2009.

2. www.redcross.org; Lance Leuthesser and Chiranjeev Kohli, "Corporate Identity: The Role of Mission Statements," *Business Horizons,* May–June 1997; Christopher K. Bart, "Sex, Lies, and Mission Statements," *Business Horizons,* November–December 1997. For more general discussions of marketing strategy see Peter F. Drucker, *Management: Tasks, Responsibilities, Practices, and Plans,* New York: Harper & Row, 1973; Sev K. Keil, "The Impact of Business Objectives and the Time Horizon of Performance Evaluation on Pricing Behavior," *International Journal of Research in Marketing,* June 2001; George S. Day and Christine Moorman, *Strategy from the Outside In,* 2010, McGraw-Hill.

3. www.usaa.com; "USAA's Battle Plan," *BusinessWeek,* February 18, 2010; "Customer Service Champs," *BusinessWeek,* March 5, 2007; "USAA Soldiering on in Insurance," *BusinessWeek,* March 5, 2007.

4. For more on Starbucks, see www.starbucks.com; "Starbucks Plans Big Expansion in China," *Wall Street Journal,* April 14, 2010; "Mature Coffee Brewer Finds New Ways to Stir Earnings Growth," *Investor's Business Daily,* January 6, 2010; "Starbucks Says Demand Perking Up," *Wall Street Journal,* November 6, 2009; "Starbucks Takes New Road with Instant Coffee," *Wall Street Journal,* September 29, 2009; "Howard Schultz versus Howard Schultz," *BusinessWeek,* August 17, 2009; "Starbucks Plays Common Joe," *Wall Street Journal,* February 9, 2009; "Starbucks' Dismal Quarter Leads to 'Value' Offerings," *Advertising Age,* January 28, 2009; "Starbucks' Surprise Success: Oatmeal," *AdvertisingAge,* October 13, 2008; "New Starbucks Brew Attracts Customers, Flak," *Wall Street Journal,* July 1, 2008.

5. For more on the BlackBerry patent case, see "In Blackberry Case, Big Winner Faces His Own Accusers," *Wall Street Journal,* August 23, 2006; "Blackberry Deal: Patently Absurd," *Newsweek,* March 13, 2006; "Pay Up—or You're Done For," *Fortune,* December 12, 2005. For more on patents, see "The Patent Epidemic," *BusinessWeek,* January 9, 2006; Patent Applications So Abundant That Examiners Can't Catch Up," *USA Today,* September 21, 2005.

6. Timothy B. Heath, Gangseog Ryu, Subimal Chatterjee, Michael S. McCarthy, "Asymmetric Competition in Choice and the Leveraging of Competitive Disadvantages," *Journal of Consumer Research,* December 2000; Kao, Cambridge, MA: Harvard Business School Press, 1984; Bruce R. Klemz, "Managerial Assessment of Potential Entrants: Processes and Pitfalls," *International Journal of Research in Marketing,* June 2001. For more on P&G's diaper competition in the United States see "Value Positioning Becomes a Priority," *Advertising Age,* February 23, 2004; "Rivals Take P&G to Court to Challenge Ads," *Wall Street Journal,* June 17, 2003; "Dueling Diapers," *Fortune,* February 17, 2003.

7. For more on corporate spying and competitive intelligence, see "Cybercrooks Stalk Small Businesses," *USA Today,* December 31, 2009; "Hounding the Hackers," *BusinessWeek,* September 14, 2009; "How Team of Geeks Cracked Spy Trade," *Wall Street Journal,* September 4, 2009; "Accusations of Snooping in Ink-Cartridge Dispute," *Wall Street Journal,* August 11, 2009; "Today's Spies Find Secrets in Plain Sight," *USA Today,* August 1, 2008; "Snooping on a Shoestring," *Business 2.0,* May 2003. See also Shaker A. Zahra, "Unethical Practices in Competitive Analysis: Patterns, Causes and Effects," *Journal of Business Ethics,* January 1994.

8. "Hyundai Smokes the Competition," *Fortune,* January 18, 2010; "A Year After Program, Under 100 Hyundais Returned," *NPR, All Things Considered,* January 8, 2010; "*Brandweek*'s Grand Marketer of the Year '09: Joel Ewanick of Hyundai," *Brandweek,* September 14, 2009; "Hyundai's Moment," *Brandweek,* April 6, 2009.

9. For more on economic environment, see Rajdeep Grewal, "Building Organizational Capabilities for Managing Economic Crisis: The Role of Market Orientation and Strategic Flexibility," *Journal of Marketing,* April 2001.

10. For more on technological environment, see Brian T. Ratchford, Debabrata Talukdar, and L. E. E. Myung-Soo, "The Impact of the Internet on Consumers' Use of Information Sources for Automobiles: A Re-Inquiry," *Journal of Consumer Research,* June 2007; Anand V. Bodapati, "Recommendation Systems with Purchase Data," *Journal of Marketing Research,* February 2008. For more on privacy, see Chapter 20.

11. "Chrysler's 'Imported from Detroit' Super Bowl Ad Inspires Political Debate," *CBSNews,* February 7, 2011; for other examples of nationalism, see "Coming Home: Appliance Maker Drops China to Produce in Texas," *Wall Street Journal,* August 24, 2009; "Buy American Clause Stirs Up Controversy," *USA Today,* February 4, 2009; "Which Is More American?" *USA Today,* March 22, 2007. See also Durairaj Maheswaran and Cathy Yi Chen, "Nation Equity: Incidental Emotions in Country-of-Origin Effects," *Journal of Consumer Research,* October 2006; George Balabanis and Adamantios Diamantopoulos, "Domestic Country Bias, Country-of-Origin Effects, and Consumer Ethnocentrism: a Multidimensional Unfolding Approach," *Journal of the Academy of Marketing Science,* Winter 2004; Zeynep Gurhan-Canli and Durairaj Maheswaran, "Determinants of Country-of-Origin Evaluations," *Journal of Consumer Research,* June 2000.

12. For other examples, see "German Shoppers May Get Sale Freedom," *Wall Street Journal,* January 23, 2002; "Border Crossings," *Wall Street Journal,* November 22, 1999. For another example, see "Corn Flakes Clash Shows the Glitches in European Union," *Wall Street Journal,* November 1, 2005. For more on EU, see "Euro Zone Debt Crisis Intensifies on Summit Eve," *Reuters,* March 10, 2011; "Hopes Raised, Punches Pulled," *The Economist,* February 10, 2011; "Squeezed by the Euro," *BusinessWeek,* June 6, 2005. See also Andrew Paddison, "Retailing in the European Union: Structures, Competition and Performance," *International Journal of Retail & Distribution Management,* #6 (2003).

13. For more on NAFTA, see www.nafta.org; "Central American Free Trade Agreement Faces Obstacles," *USA Today,* May 12, 2005; "Refighting NAFTA," *BusinessWeek,* March 31, 2008; "10 Years Ago, NAFTA Was Born," *USA Today,* December 31, 2003; "Was NAFTA Worth It? A Tale of What Free Trade Can and Cannot Do," *BusinessWeek,* December 22, 2003.

14. For more on Beech-Nut, see "What Led Beech-Nut Down the Road to Disgrace," *BusinessWeek*, February 22, 1988. See also Kersi D. Antia, Mark E. Bergen, Shantanu Dutta, and Robert J. Fisher, "How Does Enforcement Deter Gray Market Incidence?" *Journal of Marketing*, January 2006; Debra M. Desrochers, Gregory T. Gundlach, and Albert A. Foer, "Analysis of Antitrust Challenges to Category Captain Arrangements," *Journal of Public Policy & Marketing*, Fall 2003, "Europe: A Different Take on Antitrust," *BusinessWeek*, June 25, 2001; "In ArcherDaniels Saga, Now the Executives Face Trial," *Wall Street Journal*, July 9, 1998. See also Mary W. Sullivan, "The Role of Marketing in Antitrust," *Journal of Public Policy & Marketing*, Fall 2002; Jeff Langenderfer and Steven W. Kopp, "Which Way to the Revolution? The Consequences of Database Protection as a New Form of Intellectual Property," *Journal of Public Policy & Marketing*, Spring 2003. See also Louis W. Stern and Thomas L. Eovaldi, *Legal Aspects of Marketing Strategy: Antitrust and Consumer Protection Issues* (Englewood Cliffs, NJ: Prentice-Hall, 1984).

15. For more on auto safety, see "States Go After Texting Drivers: Safety Concerns Fuel New Legislation," *USA Today*, January 25, 2010; "The Number of Small-Car Owners Is Growing Even Though More Drivers Die in Small Cars," *USA Today*, August 20, 2007. For more on CPSC, see "More Paper Tiger than Watchdog?" *BusinessWeek*, September 3, 2007, p. 45; "Product-Safety Cops Handcuffed," *Wall Street Journal*, December 18, 2007. For an overview of the toy, food, and pet product recalls of 2007, see "The New China Price," *Fortune*, November 12, 2007; "Spate of Recalls Boosts Potency of User Reviews," *Advertising Age*, October 29, 2007; "China's Recall Woes Bad for Walmart," *Brandweek*, September 10, 2007.

16. "Time to Rethink Your Message: Now the Cart Belongs to Daddy," *Advertising Age*, January 17, 2011. For more on the changing role of women, see "The Rise of the Real Mom," *Advertising Age* White Paper, November 16, 2009; "Daisy Rock Amps Up Girl Power: Specially Designed Guitars Fit a Woman Just Right," *USA Today*, December 15, 2009; "Videogame Firms Make a Play for Women," *Wall Street Journal*, October 13, 2009; "Verizon Targets Women with Hub Phone," *Advertising Age*, March 9, 2009; "Pretty in Pink," CNN.com, October 5, 2007; "Meet Jane Geek," *BusinessWeek*, November 28, 2005.

17. Based on U.S. Census data including Statistical Abstract of the United States 2010 (Washington, DC: U.S. Government Printing Office, October 2009), Table 1296, pp. 818–20, available online at www.census.gov/statab; U.S. Census Bureau "International Data Base" available online at www.census.gov/ipc/www/idb/; Population Reference Bureau data, including 2009 World Pop Data Sheet, available online at www.prb.org/Publications/Datasheets/2009; World Bank data, available online at http://web.worldbank.org/WBSITE/EXTERNAL/DATASTATISTICS; CIA data, including CIA Factbook 2010, available online at https://www.cia.gov/library/publications/the-world-factbook; ICT Statistics Database, Mobile Cellular Subscriptions Per 100 People, 2008, International Telecommunications Union, available online at www.itu.int/ITU-D/icteye/Indicators/Indicators.aspx; and Internet World Stats, 2010, available online at www.internetworldstats.com/stats.htm; GlobalEDGE data from Michigan State University at http://globaledge.msu.edu. See also "Baby Bundle: Japan's Cash Incentive for Parenthood," *Wall Street Journal*, October 8, 2009; "China Inc. Looks Homeward as U.S. Shoppers Turn Frugal," *Wall Street Journal*, September 29, 2009; "Can Greed Save Africa?" *BusinessWeek*, December 10, 2007; "China's Grappling with One Helluva Problem," *USA Today*, September 18, 2007; "India Rising," *Newsweek*, March 6, 2006; "The Battle for the Face of China," *Fortune*, December 12, 2005; "The Rise of Central Europe," *BusinessWeek*, December 12, 2005; "India's Bumpy Ride," *Fortune*, October 31, 2005; "China & India," *BusinessWeek* (special issue), August 22, 2005; "Global Aging: Now, the Geezer Glut," *BusinessWeek*, January 31, 2005; "Tamer S. Cavusgil, "Measuring the Potential of Emerging Markets: An Indexing Approach," *Business Horizons*, January–February 1997. See also C. Riegner, "*Wired* China: The Power of the World's Largest Internet Population," *Journal of Advertising Research 48*, #4, 2008.

18. Based on World Bank GNI and GDP data and available online at http://web.worldbank.org/WBSITE/EXTERNAL/DATASTATISTICS.

19. Based on CIA data, including CIA Factbook 2010, available online at https://www.cia.gov/library/publications/the-world-factbook. See also Madhubalan Viswanathan, Jose Antonio Rosa, and James Edwin Harris, "Decision Making and Coping of Functionally Illiterate Consumers and Some Implications for Marketing Management," *Journal of Marketing*, January 2005; Natalie Ross Adkins, Julie L. Ozanne, Dawn Iacobucci, and Eric Arnould, "The Low Literate Consumer," *Journal of Consumer Research*, June 2005.

20. "In Kerala, Cell Phones Go Fishing," *Liberation*, October 2, 2006; "ITC eChoupal Initiative" *Harvard Business School Case #604016*, 2003.

21. A. M. Chircu and V. Mahajan, "Perspective: Revisiting the Digital Divide: An Analysis of Mobile Technology Depth and Service Breadth in the BRIC Countries," *Journal of Product Innovation Management* 26, #4, 2009.

22. Based on U.S. Census data including Statistical Abstract of the United States 2010, pp. 18 and 20, and available at www.census.gov/statab; "2010 America: What the 2010 Census Means for Marketing and Advertising," *Advertising Age* (White Paper), October 12, 2009; "No More Joe Consumer in America," *Advertising Age*, October 12, 2009. See also "For Florida, 'the End of an Era' of Growth," *USA Today*, September 1, 2009; "Is Florida Over?" *Wall Street Journal*, September 29, 2007; "The Coming Crunch," *Wall Street Journal*, October 13, 2006; "Fastest Growth Found in Red States," Also based on data from Population Reference Bureau at www.prb.org>www.prb.org.

23. Based on U.S. Census data including Statistical Abstract of the United States 2010, pp. 11–12, and available online at www.census.gov/statab. See also "Boomer$," *CNBC*, March 4, 2010; "The 15 Biggest Baby Boomer Brands," *Advertising Age*, March 1, 2010; "Clothing Stores Rediscover Boomers," *USA Today*, September 12, 2008; "Love Those Boomers," *BusinessWeek*, October 24, 2005; K. G. Gronbach, *The Age Curve: How to Profit from the Coming Demographic Storm*, 2008.; Charlene Li and Josh Bernoff, *Groundswell: Winning in a World Transformed by Social Technologies* (Cambridge: Harvard Business School Press, 2008).

24. "'iGeneration' Has No Off Switch," *USA Today*, February 10, 2010; Kit Yarrow and Jayne O'Donnell, *Gen BuY: How Tweens, Teens, and Twenty-Somethings Are Revolutionizing Retail* (Jossey-Bass, 2009); "Why 'Millennials' Are Impulse Shoppers," *Brandweek*, November 12, 2009; "Generation Y Forces Retailers to Keep Up with Technology, New Stuff," *Wall Street Journal*, September 14, 2009; "Trying to Connect with Generation Y," *Wall Street Journal*, October 13, 2005.

25. Frank R. Bacon, Jr., and Thomas W. Butler, Jr., *Planned Innovation*, rev. ed. (Ann Arbor: Institute of Science and Technology, University of Michigan, 1980).

26. "Ahead of the Pack," *Wall Street Journal*, March 24, 2008; "50 Ways to Green Your Business," *Fast Company*, December 19, 2007; www.greenbiz.com/news/.

27. Connelly, Brian, David Ketchen, and Stanley Slater, "Toward a 'theoretical toolbox' for sustainability research in marketing," *Journal of the Academy of Marketing Science*, January 2011; Cronin, J., Jeffery Smith, Mark Gleim, Edward Ramirez, and Jennifer Martinez, "Green marketing strategies: an examination of stakeholders and the opportunities they present," *Journal of the Academy of Marketing Science*, January 2011; Huang, Ming-Hui, and Roland Rust, "Sustainability and consumption," *Journal of the Academy of Marketing Science*, January 2011; Hunt, Shelby. "Sustainable marketing, equity, and economic growth: a resource-advantage, economic freedom approach," *Journal of the Academy of Marketing Science*, January 2011; Kronrod, Ann, Amir Grinstein, and Luc Wathieu, "Go Green!! Should Environmental Messages Be So Assertive??," *Journal of Marketing*, January 2012; Luchs, Michael G., Rebecca Walker Naylor, Julie R. Irwin, and Rajagopal Raghunathan, "The Sustainability Liability: Potential Negative Effects of Ethicality on Product Preference," *Journal of Marketing*, September 2010; Sheth, Jagdish, Nirmal Sethia, and Shanthi Srinivas, "Mindful consumption: a customer-centric approach to sustainability," *Journal of the Academy of Marketing Science*, January 2011; F. J. Montoro-Rios, T. Luque-Martinez, and M. A. Rodriguez-Molina, "How Green Should You Be: Can Environmental

Associations Enhance Brand Performance?" *Journal of Advertising Research* 48, #4, 2008; Jonathan Lash and Fred Wellington, "Competitive Advantage on a Warming Planet," *Harvard Business Review,* March 2007; "50 Ways to Green Your Business," *Fast Company,* December 19, 2007; "Business 3.0," *Fast Company,* December 19, 2007; "A Consumer's Guide to Going Green," *Wall Street Journal,* November 12, 2007; "Green Power," *CNNMoney,* September 26, 2007; "Sony Likes the Yield from Its Junk," *BusinessWeek,* September 17, 2007; "Where Computers Go When They Die," *Wall Street Journal,* April 11, 2007; "10 Ways to Go Green."

28. Paul F. Anderson, "Marketing, Strategic Planning and the Theory of the Firm," *Journal of Marketing,* Spring 1982; Ronnie Silverblatt and Pradeep Korgaonkar, "Strategic Market Planning in a Turbulent Business Environment," *Journal of Business Research,* August 1987.

29. Keith B. Murray and Edward T. Popper, "Competing under Regulatory Uncertainty: A U.S. Perspective on Advertising in the Emerging European Market," *Journal of Macromarketing,* Fall 1992; "Inside Russia—Business Most Unusual," *UPS International Update,* Spring 1994; "Freighted with Difficulties," *Wall Street Journal,* December 10, 1993; "Russia Snickers after Mars Invades," *Wall Street Journal,* July 13, 1993.

30. "Sensitive Export: Seeking New Markets for Tampons, P&G Faces Cultural Barriers," *Wall Street Journal,* December 8, 2000; "Pizza Queen of Japan Turns Web Auctioneer," *Wall Street Journal,* March 6, 2000; Kamran Kashani, "Beware the Pitfalls of Global Marketing," *Harvard Business Review,* September–October 1989.

CHAPTER 4

1 www.lego.com; "Innovation Almost Bankrupted LEGO—Until It Rebuilt with a Better Blueprint," *Knowledge@Wharton,* July 18, 2012; *The Brick* (Annual Magazine), 2010; *Company Profile: An Introduction to the LEGO Group, 2009;* Toymaker Grows by Listening to Customers, *Advertising Age,* November 9, 2009; "Innovating a Turnaround at LEGO," *Harvard Business Review,* September 2009; "LEGO Proves Itself a Blockbuster Once Again," *The Times,* February 24, 2009; Charlene Li and Josh Bernoff, *Groundswell* (Harvard Business School Press: Boston, 2008); "Innovation at the LEGO Group (A) and (B)" (case series), International Institute for Management Development, 2008; "Please Don't Touch Daddy's LEGO," *Maclean's,* October 6, 2008; "Lego Introduces WeDo package for Education," *Macworld,* June 30, 2008; "LEGO® Education WeDo™ Unveiled at 2008 National Educational Computing Conference," at Lego.com; "LEGO Learns a Lesson," *Change Agent,* June, 2008; "Geeks in Toyland," *Wired,* February 2006; Majken Schultz and Mary Jo Hatch, "The Cycles of Corporate Branding: The Case of LEGO Company," *California Management Review,* Fall 2003. See also H. J. Schau, A. M. Muniz, and E. J. Arnould, "How Brand Community Practices Create Value." *Journal of Marketing* 73, no. 5 (2009).

2. See www.hallmark.com.; 2011 Annual Report, Hallmark.

3. Glen L. Urban and John R. Hauser, "Listening In to Find and Explore New Combinations of Customer Needs," *Journal of Marketing,* April 2004; Terri C. Albert, "Need-Based Segmentation and Customized Communication Strategies in a Complex-Commodity Industry: a Supply Chain Study," *Industrial Marketing Management,* May 2003; Rajendra K. Srivastava, Mark I. Alpert, and Allan D. Shocker, "A Customer-Oriented Approach for Determining Market Structures," *Journal of Marketing,* Spring 1984.

4. "Life Stage: Its Impact on the Future of Traditional and Emerging Media," *e-Poll Market Research,* February 2010.

5. For more on Herman Miller, see www.hermanmiller.com; 2011 Annual Report, Herman Miller; "Herman Miller Is Sitting Pretty," *Fortune,* November 27, 2006; "A Cult Chair Gets a Makeover," *Wall Street Journal,* September 17, 2002.

6. Sally Dibb and Lyndon Simkin, "Market Segmentation: Diagnosing and Treating the Barriers," *Industrial Marketing Management,* November 2001; Terry Elrod and Russell S. Winer, "An Empirical Evaluation of Aggregation Approaches for Developing Market Segments," *Journal of Marketing,* Fall 1982; Frederick W. Winter, "A Cost-Benefit Approach to Market Segmentation," *Journal of Marketing,* Fall 1979.

7. See www.kaepa.com.; "Tapping into Cheerleading," *Adweek's Marketing Week,* March 2, 1992.

8. Thomas Reutterer, Andreas Mild, Martin Natter, and Alfred Taudes, "A Dynamic Segmentation Approach for Targeting and Customizing Direct Marketing Campaigns," *Journal of Interactive Marketing,* Summer 2006; S. Tamer Cavusgil, Tunga Kiyak, and Sengun Yeniyurt, "Complementary Approaches to Preliminary Foreign Market Opportunity Assessment: Country Clustering and Country Ranking," *Industrial Marketing Management,* October 2004; Malaika Brengman, Maggie Geuens, Bert Weijters, Scott M. Smith, and William R. Swinyard, "Segmenting Internet Shoppers Based on Their Web-Usage-Related Lifestyle: A Cross-Cultural Validation," *Journal of Business Research,* January 2005; Ruth N. Bolton and Matthew B. Myers, "Price-Based Global Market Segmentation for Services," *Journal of Marketing,* July 2003; Philip A. Dover, "Segmentation and Positioning for Strategic Marketing Decisions," *Journal of the Academy of Marketing Science,* Summer 2000.

9. "Ford offers free driver's ed in Vietnam," *USA Today,* August 5, 2010.

10. For more on ethics and segmentation, see "Just Say No . . . to Smarties? Faux Smoking Has Parents Fuming," *Wall Street Journal,* March 20, 2009; Marketers Find 'Tweens' Too Hot to Ignore," *USA Today,* July 10, 2001; "Yamada Card Gives Credit to Struggling Brazilians," *Wall Street Journal,* March 27, 2001; "Grown-Up Drinks for Tender Taste Buds," *BusinessWeek,* March 5, 2001; "Soda Pop That Packs a Punch," *Newsweek,* February 19, 2001; Dean M. Krugman, Margaret A. Morrison, and Yongjun Sung, "Cigarette Advertising in Popular Youth and Adult Magazines: A Ten-Year Perspective," *Journal of Public Policy & Marketing,* Fall 2006; Suzeanne Benet, Robert E. Pitts, and Michael LaTour, "The Appropriateness of Fear Appeal Use for Health Care Marketing to the Elderly: Is It OK to Scare Granny?" *Journal of Business Ethics,* January 1993; Richard W. Pollay, S. Siddarth, Michael Siegel, Anne Haddix, "The Last Straw? Cigarette Advertising and Realized Market Shares Among Youths and Adults, 1979–1993," *Journal of Marketing,* April 1996.

11. Elizabeth S. Moore and Victoria J. Rideout, "The Online Marketing of Food to Children: Is It Just Fun and Games?" *Journal of Public Policy and Marketing,* #2, 2007.

12. For more on new hotel features, see "Don't Use the R-Word: Hotels Find Trick to Business Bookings," *Wall Street Journal,* January 26, 2010; "Hotels Risk Losing Holiday Inn Brand," *Wall Street Journal,* November 13, 2009; "Marriott Gets a Wake-Up Call," *Fortune,* July 6, 2009; "The Heartbreak of High-Tech Hotels," *USA Today,* May 3, 2007; "Hotels Ditch Imposing Desks for Friendly 'Pods,'" *USA Today,* October 26, 2006; "A Room with a View—and More," *Fortune,* December 12, 2005; "At Holiday Inn Select, Gen X Marks the Spot," *Brandweek,* September 19, 2005; "An Xbox on Your Pillow," *Wall Street Journal,* August 17, 2005; "These Rooms Cater to the Kids," *USA Today,* July 22, 2005; "Hotels Pump Up Their Gyms to Lure Execs Seeking Pecs," *Wall Street Journal,* November 13, 2003; "New Concepts in Lodging," *Wall Street Journal,* October 8, 2003.

13. Stephen D. Ross, "Segmenting Sports Fans Using Brand Associations: A Cluster Analysis," *Sports Marketing Quarterly,* #1, 2007; Rajan Sambandam, "Cluster Analysis Gets Complicated," *Marketing Research,* Spring 2003; "Girish Punj and David W. Stewart, "Cluster Analysis in Marketing Research: Review and Suggestions for Application," *Journal of Marketing Research,* May 1983.

14. Timothy Bohling, Douglas Bowman, Steve Lavalle, Vikas Mittal, Das Narayandas, Girish Ramani, and Rajan Varadarajan, "CRM Implementation: Effectiveness Issues and Insights," *Journal of Service Research,* May 2006; H. Wilson, M. Clark, and B. Smith, "Justifying CRM Projects in a Business-to-Business Context: The Potential of the Benefits Dependency Network," *Industrial Marketing Management,* June 2007; Katherine N. Lemon, Tiffany Barnett White, and Russell S. Winer, "Dynamic Customer Relationship Management: Incorporating Future Considerations into the SeService Retention Decision," *Journal of Marketing,* January 2002.

15. "How Companies Learn Your Secrets," *New York Times,* February 16, 2012; Duhigg, Charles *The Power of Habit,* 2012, New York: Random

House; "Data Mining and Predictive Analytics," February 18, 2012; *Abbott Analytics;* "How Target Knew a High School Girl Was Pregnant Before Her Parents Did," *Time,* February 17, 2012.

16. Sonnier, Garrett, and Andrew Ainslie, "Estimating the Value of Brand-Image Associations: The Role of General and Specific Brand Image," *Journal of Marketing Research,* June, 2011; Kumar, V., and Denish Shah, "Uncovering Implicit Consumer Needs for Determining Explicit Product Positioning: Growing Prudential Annuities' Variable Annuity Sales," *Marketing Science,* #4, 2011; Park, Ji Kyung and Deborah Roedder John, "Got to Get You into My Life: Do Brand Personalities Rub off on Consumers?," *Journal of Consumer Research,* August, 2010; Charles Blankson, Stavros P. Kalafatis, Julian Ming-Sung Cheng, and Costas Hadjicharalambous, "Impact of Positioning Strategies on Corporate Performance," *Journal of Advertising Research,* March 2008; Girish Punj and Junyean Moon, "Positioning Options for Achieving Brand Association: a Psychological Categorization Framework," *Journal of Business Research,* April 2002; Kalpesh Kaushik Desai and S. Ratneshwar, "Consumer Perceptions of Product Variants Positioned on Atypical Attributes," *Journal of the Academy of Marketing Science,* Winter 2003; David A. Aaker and J. Gary Shansby, "Positioning Your Product," *Business Horizons,* May/June 1982; Al Ries and Jack Trout, *Positioning: The Battle for Your Mind* (New York: McGraw-Hill, 1981).

17. Douglas B. Holt, *How Brands Become Icons,* Cambridge, MA: Harvard Business Press, 2004, quote, slightly modified p. 63.

CHAPTER 5

1. "How Tim Cook is Changing Apple," *Fortune,* June 11, 2012; "How Long Can Apple Sustain Its Torrid Growth in China," *Advertising Age,* June 11, 2012; "Apple Navigates China Maze," *Wall Street Journal,* January 14, 2012; "Apple Macs Land on More Corporate Desks," *Wall Street Journal,* January 18, 2012; "Apple's Lower Prices Are All Part of the Plan," *New York Times,* October 24, 2011; "Secrets from Apple's Genius Bar: Full Loyalty, No Negativity," *Wall Street Journal,* June 15, 2011; Isaacson, Walter *Steve Jobs,* New York: Simon and Shuster; "iPad 2: Thin, Not Picture Perfect," *Wall Street Journal,* March 16, 2011; "iPad Storybook Apps and the Kids Who Love Them," *NPR.org,* February 7, 2011; "For iPad, Lines but No Shortage," *Wall Street Journal,* April 4, 2010; "Laptop Killer? Pretty Close: iPad is a Game Changer," *Wall Street Journal,* April 1, 2010; "App Developers Pump Up for iPad: It's a Winner," *USA Today,* April 1, 2010; "The iPad Changes Everything," *Fortune,* March 22, 2010; "Turning an iPad into an iMust-Have," *BusinessWeek,* February 15, 2010; "Apple Takes Big Gamble on New iPad," January 28, 2010; "AT&T Looks beyond the iPhone," *Wall Street Journal,* April 22, 2010; "Sales of iPhone Keep on Sizzling," *USA Today,* April 21, 2010; "Apple Vs. Google," *BusinessWeek,* January 25, 2010; "Apple Adds Second iPhone Seller in U.K.," *Wall Street Journal,* September 29, 2009; "The Next iPod Generation," *BusinessWeek,* August 10, 2009; "Apple's iPhone 3G S Offers Speed, Life; Old Model Now $99," *Investor's Business Daily,* June 9, 2009; "iPhone's Asian Disconnect," *BusinessWeek,* April 13, 2009; "New iPhone also Brings New Way of Mobile Marketing," *Advertising Age,* June 16, 2008; "All Eyes on Apple," *Fast Company,* December 2007; "Steve Jobs Offers Rare Apology, Credit for iPhone," *Wall Street Journal,* September 7, 2007; "From the Start, iPhone Is iFun," *USA Today,* June 27, 2007; "iPhone Mania Nears Fever Pitch," *USA Today,* June 20, 2007; "Apple Buffs Marketing Savvy to a High Shine," *USA Today,* March 9, 2007.

2. Based on U.S. Census data, including Statistical Abstract of the United States 2010, "Table F-1. Income Limits for Each Fifth and Top 5 Percent of Families (All Races): 1947 to 2008"; "Table F-2. Share of Aggregate Income Received by Each Fifth and Top 5 Percent of Families (All Races): 1947 to 2008"; and "Table F-7. Regions—Families (All Races) by Median and Mean Income: 1947 to 2008" (all three tables available at www.census.gov/hhes/income/hitinc); www.census.gov/hhes/www/income/histinc/incfamdet.html; and U.S. Census Bureau, Current Population Reports, P60-236, *Income, Poverty, and Health Insurance Coverage in the United States: 2008* (U.S. Government Printing Office, Washington, DC, 2009). For more on economic factors and consumer behavior see, Larson, Jeffrey S, and Ryan Hamilton, "When Budgeting Backfires: How Self-Imposed Price Restraints Can Increase Spending," *Journal of Marketing Research,* April 2012; R. Y. Du and W. A. Kamakura, "Where Did All That Money Go? Understanding How Consumers Allocate Their Consumption Budget," *Journal of Marketing,* #6, 2008; R. Saini and A. Monga, "How I Decide Depends on What I Spend: Use of Heuristics Is Greater for Time Than for Money," *Journal of Consumer Research,* #6, 2008; Ravindra Chitturi, Rajagopal Raghunathan, and Vijay Mahajan, "Delight by Design: The Role of Hedonic Versus Utilitarian Benefits," *Journal of Marketing,* June 2008.

3. Kristina D. Frankenberger, "Consumer Psychology for Marketing," *Journal of the Academy of Marketing Science,* Summer 1996, Maslow, A.H. *Motivation and Personality,* New York: Harper & Row 1970.

4. Bob Gilbreath, *The Next Evolution of Marketing* (New York: McGraw-Hill, 2010).

5. "Your Advertising Slogans Are Crummy. Can't You Do Better?" *Advertising Age,* January 14, 2008; "Who Said That? Buyers Don't Recognize Some Slogans," *USA Today,* October 1, 2003; "Super Tags, Still Believers," *Brandweek,* February 3, 2003. See also Claudiu V. Dimofte and Richard F. Yalch, "Consumer Response to Polysemous Brand Slogans," *Journal of Consumer Research,* December 2007.

6. See Billeter, Darron, Ajay Kalra, and George Loewenstein, "Underpredicting Learning after Initial Experience with a Product," *Journal of Consumer Research,* October 2011; Drèze, Xavier, and Joseph C Nunes, "Recurring Goals and Learning: The Impact of Successful Reward Attainment on Purchase Behavior," *Journal of Marketing Research,* April 2011; Marcus Cunha, Jr., Chris Janiszewski, and Juliano Laran, "Protection of Prior Learning in Complex Consumer Learning Environments," *Journal of Consumer Research,* April 2008; Les Carlson, Russell N. Laczniak, and Ann Walsh, "Socializing Children about Television: An Intergenerational Study," *Journal of the Academy of Marketing Science,* Summer 2001; Elizabeth S. Moore and Richard J. Lutz, "Children, Advertising, and Product Experiences: A Multimethod Inquiry," *Journal of Consumer Research,* June 2000; Thomas W. Gruen, Talai Osmonbekov, and Andrew J. Czaplewski, "eWOM: The Impact Of Customer-to-Customer Online Know-How Exchange on Customer Value and Loyalty," *Journal of Business Research,* April 2006; C. A. de Matos and C. A. V. Rossi, "Word-of-Mouth Communications in Marketing: A Meta-Analytic Review of the Antecedents and Moderators," *Journal of the Academy of Marketing Science,* #4, 2008.

7. Duhigg, Charles, *The Power of Habit,* 2012; Anna S. Mattila and Jochen Wirtz, "Congruency of Scent and Music as a Driver of In-Store Evaluations and Behavior," *Journal of Retailing,* Summer 2001.

8. "Sweet Success," *Brandweek,* May 12, 2003.

9. "Nike Makes Shoes from Trash, Nokia Envisions Remade Cell Phones," *Greenbiz,* February 15, 2008; "Nothing But Green Skies," *Inc.,* November 2007; "UPS: Getting Big Brown Machines to Go Green," *Investor's Business Daily,* November 26, 2007; "Subway's Diet: Less Oil, More Recycling," *Wall Street Journal,* November 21, 2007.

10. For examples, see "Will the British Warm Up to Iced Tea? Some Big Marketers Are Counting on It," *Wall Street Journal,* August 22, 1994 and "Starbucks Hits a Humorous Note in Pitching Iced Coffee to Brits," *Wall Street Journal,* September 1, 1999.

11. "My Days as a Zipster: It's Easy—and It Works," *Automotive News,* December 20, 2010; "Renting Cars by the Hour Is Becoming Big Business," *Economist,* September 4, 2010; "Car Sharing Grows," *Wall Street Journal,* March 24, 2010; "Zipcar Campus Car-Sharing Program Booms," *Design News,* December 2009; "Zipcar," *Advertising Age,* November 16, 2009; "An iPhone Gets Zipcar Drivers on Their Way," *USA Today,* September 30, 2009; "The Best New Idea in Business," *Fortune,* September 14, 2009; "Temporary Plates," *Brandweek,* July 12, 2007.

12. For more on wrinkle-free clothing, see "Botox for Broadcloth," *Wall Street Journal,* October 7, 2002; "'Wrinkle-Free' Shirts Don't Live Up to the Name," *Wall Street Journal,* May 11, 1994. For more on service quality, see Chapter 8. For more on service expectations, see "Can I Get a Smile with My Burger and Fries?" *Wall Street Journal,* September 23, 2003; "Service—with a Side of Sales,". See also Chezy Ofir and Itamar Simonson, "The Effect of Stating Expectations on Customer Satisfaction and Shopping Experience," *Journal of Marketing Research,* February 2007.

13. Schwartz, Janet, Mary Frances Luce, and Dan Ariely, "Are Consumers Too Trusting? The Effects of Relationships with Expert Advisers," *Journal of Marketing Research,* 2011; K. Grayson, D. Johnson, and D. F. R. Chen, "Is Firm Trust Essential in a Trusted Environment? How Trust in the Business Context Influences Customers," *Journal of Marketing Research,* #2, 2008; P. Gupta, M. S. Yadav, and R. Varadarajan, "How Task-Facilitative Interactive Tools Foster Buyers' Trust in Online Retailers: A Process View of Trust Development in the Electronic Marketplace," *Journal of Retailing,* #2, 2009.

14. "It's Mind Vending . . . in the World of Psychographics," *Time,* October 2003; "Lifestyles Help Shape Innovation," *DSN Retailing Today,* August 4, 2003; "Generation Next," *Advertising Age,* January 15, 2001; "Head Trips," *American Demographics,* October 2000; "Join the Club," *Brandweek,* February 15, 1999; "The Frontier of Psychographics," *American Demographics,* July 1996; W. D. Wells, "Psychographics: A Critical Review," *Journal of Marketing Research,* May 1975.

15. See www.strategicbusinessinsights.com/vals/; "Markets with Attitude," *American Demographics,* July 1994; Chernev, Alexander, Ryan Hamilton, and David Gal, "Competing for Consumer Identity: Limits to Self-Expression and the Perils of Lifestyle Branding," *Journal of Marketing,* May 2011; Lynn R. Kahle, Sharon E. Beatty, and Pamela Homer, "Alternative Measurement Approaches to Consumer Values: The List of Values (LOV) and Values and Life Styles (VALS)," *Journal of Consumer Research,* December 1986.

16. Patrick E. Murphy and William A. Staples, "A Modernized Family Life Cycle," *Journal of Consumer Research,* June 1979.

17. Based on U.S. Census data and "The American Consumer 2006," *Advertising Age,* January 2, 2006; "The State of Our Unions," *USA Today,* February 26, 2004; "Do Us Part," *American Demographics,* September 2002; "The Ex-Files," *American Demographics,* February 2001. See also James A. Roberts, Chris Manolis, and John F. Tanner, Jr., "Family Structure, Materialism, and Compulsive Buying: a Reinquiry and Extension," *Journal of the Academy of Marketing Science,* Summer 2003.

18. "Solo nation: American consumers stay single," *Fortune,* January 25, 2012.

19. Based on U.S. Census data and "Borders Aims to Capitalize on Teens with New Shops," *Wall Street Journal,* July 21, 2009; "It's Cooler Than Ever to Be a Tween," *USA Today,* February 4, 2009; "American Express Tries to Find Its Place with a Younger Crowd," *Wall Street Journal,* September 22, 2005.

20. Based on U.S. Census data and "The Older Audience is Looking Better Than Ever," *New York Times,* April 20, 2009; "Why Grown Kids Come Home," *USA Today,* January 11, 2005.

21. For more on kids' influence in purchase decisions, see A. M. Epp and L. L. Price, "Family Identity: A Framework of Identity Interplay in Consumption Practices," *Journal of Consumer Research,* #1, 2008; L. A. Flurry and Alvin C. Burns, "Children's Influence in Purchase Decisions: A Social Power Theory Approach," *Journal of Business Research,* May 2005; "Kiddies' *Wired* Wish Lists," *Wall Street Journal,* December 19, 2007; "Inconvenient Youths," *Wall Street Journal,* September 29, 2007; "This Is the Car We Want, Mommy," *Wall Street Journal,* November 9, 2006. See also Sharon E. Beatty and Salil Talpade, "Adolescent Influence in Family Decision Making: A Replication with Extension," *Journal of Consumer Research,* September 1994.

22. "Consumers Enjoy Lap of Luxury," *Investor's Business Daily,* October 27, 2003; "Downsized Luxury," *Wall Street Journal,* October 14, 2003. See also W. Amaldoss and S. Jain, "Trading Up: A Strategic Analysis of Reference Group Effects," *Marketing Science,* #5, 2008; Lan Nguyen Chaplin and Deborah Roedder John, "Growing Up in a Material World: Age Differences in Materialism in Children and Adolescents," *Journal of Consumer Research,* December 2007; Tamara F. Mangleburg, Patricia M. Doney, and Terry Bristol, "Shopping with Friends and Teens' Susceptibility to Peer Influence," *Journal of Retailing,* Summer 2004; Cornelia Pechmann and Susan J. Knight, "An Experimental Investigation of the Joint Effects of Advertising and Peers on Adolescents' Beliefs and Intentions about Cigarette Consumption," *Journal of Consumer Research,* June 2002; David B. Wooten and Americus Reed II, "Playing It Safe: Susceptibility to Normative Influence and Protective Self-Presentation," *Journal of Consumer Research,* December 2004.

23. For more on opinion leaders and word-of-mouth publicity, see Chapter 13. See also "Beware Social Media Snake Oil," *BusinessWeek,* December 3, 2009; "Why Brands Love Mommy Bloggers," *Adweek,* March 30, 2009. See also Dee T. Allsop, Bryce R. Bassett, and James A. Hoskins, "Word-of-Mouth Research: Principles and Applications," *Journal of Advertising Research,* December 2007; Ed Keller, "Unleashing the Power of Word of Mouth: Creating Brand Advocacy to Drive Growth," *Journal of Advertising Research,* December 2007; Girish N. Punj and Robert Moore, "Smart Versus Knowledgeable Online Recommendation Agents," *Journal of Interactive Marketing,* Fall 2007; Judith A. Chevalier and Dina Mayzlin, "The Effect of Word of Mouth on Sales: Online Book Reviews," *Journal of Marketing Research,* August 2006; Thomas W. Gruen, Talai Osmonbekov, and Andrew J. Czaplewski, "Customer-to-Customer Exchange: Its MOA Antecedents and Its Impact on Value Creation and Loyalty," *Journal of the Academy of Marketing Science,* Winter 2007.

24. "Art of Noise," *Brandweek,* November 1, 1999.

25. Hola: P&G Seeks Latino Shoppers," *Wall Street Journal,* September 11, 2011.

26. Statistics in this and previous section based on "2010 America," *Advertising Age* (White Paper), October 12, 2009; U.S. Census data including Current Population Survey 2009 Annual Social and Economic Supplement, "Table FINC-01. Selected Characteristics of Families by Total Money Income in 2008" and "Table FINC-02. Age of Reference Person, by Total Money Income in 2008, Type of Family, Race and Hispanic Origin of Reference Person" (see parts 1, 4, 6, 8, and 9 of both tables) and available online at www.census.gov/hhes/www/cpstables/032009/faminc; Current Population Reports, P60-236, *Income, Poverty, and Health Insurance Coverage in the United States: 2008;* Statistical Abstract of the United States 2010, pp. 16 and 51; and The Multicultural Economy 2004, America's Minority Buying Power, Selig Center for Economic Growth, University of Georgia. For an overview of ethnic populations in the United States, see "Brands Prepare for a More Diverse 'General Market," *Advertising Age,* November 30, 2009; "U.S. Allots $145 Million to Reach Out to Minorities," *Advertising Age,* October 26, 2009; "In Step with American Indians," *Investor's Business Daily,* February 6, 2008. For more on the African-American market, see U.S. Census data, including The Black Population in the United States: April 2003 at www.census.gov/population/www/socdemo/race; "Blacks Push for 'Unified' Census Tally," *USA Today,* January 12, 2010; "Report Shows A Shifting African-American Population," *Brandweek,* January 11, 2010; "Are Mattel's New Dolls Black Enough?" *Wall Street Journal,* December 3, 2009. For more on the Hispanic market, see U.S. Census data, including The Hispanic Population in the United States: www.census.gov/population/www/socdemo/race; Nitish Singh, Arun Pereira, Daniel W. Baack, and Donald Baack, "Culturally Customizing Websites for U.S. Hispanic Online Consumers," *Journal of Advertising Research* 48, #2, 2008; R. Villarreal and R. A. Peterson, "Hispanic Ethnicity and Media Behavior," *Journal of Advertising Research* 48, #2, 2008; "The Hispanic Market Is Set to Soar," *Adweek,* November 2, 2009; "Latin Flavor," *Next* (Supplement to *Brandweek*), November 2, 2009; "The Payoff from Targeting Hispanics," *BusinessWeek,* April 20, 2009; "Home Depot's New website Opens Door to Hispanics," *Wall Street Journal,* November 17, 2008. For more on the Asian-American market, see U.S. Census data, including The Asian and PI Population in the United States: March 2002 at www.census.gov/population/www/socdemo/race; "The Invisible Market," *Brandweek,* January 30, 2006; Sonya A. Grier, Anne M. Brumbaugh, and Corliss G. Thornton, "Crossover Dreams: Consumer Responses to Ethnic-Oriented Products," *Journal of Marketing,* April 2006; David Luna and Laura A. Peracchio, "Advertising to Bilingual Consumers: The Impact of Code Switching on Persuasion," *Journal of*

Consumer Research, March 2005; Shi Zhang and Bernd H. Schmitt, "Activating Sound and Meaning: The Role of Language Proficiency in Bilingual Consumer Environments," *Journal of Consumer Research,* June 2004; Ainsworth Anthony Bailey, "A Year in the Life of the African-American Male in Advertising: A Content Analysis," *Journal of Advertising,* Spring 2006; D. Anthony Platha and Thomas H. Stevenson, "Financial Services Consumption Behavior across Hispanic American Consumers," *Journal of Business Research,* August 2005.

27. "Women in Italy Like to Clean but Shun the Quick and Easy," *Wall Street Journal,* April 25, 2006. See also Üstuner, Tuba and Douglas B. Holt, "Toward a Theory of Status Consumption in Less Industrialized Countries," *Journal of Consumer Research,* February 2010; Eric J. Arnould and Craig J. Thompson, "Consumer Culture Theory (CCT): Twenty Years of Research," *Journal of Consumer Research,* March 2005; John L. Graham, "How Culture Works," *Journal of Marketing,* April 1996; Grant McCracken, "Culture and Consumption: A Theoretical Account of the Structure and Movement of the Cultural Meaning of Consumer Goods," *Journal of Consumer Research,* June 1986.

28. Weinberger, Michelle F. and Melanie Wallendorf, "Intracommunity Gifting at the Intersection of Contemporary Moral and Market Economies," *Journal of Consumer Research,* January 2012; Moreau, C. Page, Leff Bonney, and Kelly B Herd, "It's the Thought (and the Effort) That Counts: How Customizing for Others Differs from Customizing for Oneself," *Journal of Marketing,* September 2011; "Markus Giesler, "Consumer Gift Systems," *Journal of Consumer Research,* August 2006; Jennifer Chang Coupland, Dawn Iacobucci, and Eric Arnould, "Invisible Brands: An Ethnography of Households and the Brands in Their Kitchen Pantries," *Journal of Consumer Research,* June 2005; S. Christian Wheeler, Richard E. Petty, and George Y. Bizer, "Self-Schema Matching and Attitude Change: Situational and Dispositional Determinants of Message Elaboration," *Journal of Consumer Research,* March 2005; Russell W. Belk, "Situational Variables and Consumer Behavior," *Journal of Consumer Research,* #2 (1975); John F. Sherry, Jr., "Gift Giving in Anthropological Perspective," *Journal of Consumer Research,* September 1983.

29. Adapted and updated from James H. Myers and William H. Reynolds, *Consumer Behavior and Marketing Management* (Boston: Houghton Mifflin, 1967). See also Raquel Castaño, Mita Sujan, Manish Kacker, and Harish Sujan, "Managing Consumer Uncertainty in the Adoption of New Products: Temporal Distance and Mental Simulation," *Journal of Marketing Research,* #3, 2008; Anna Lund Jepsen, "Factors Affecting Consumer Use of the Internet for Information Search," *Journal of Interactive Marketing,* Summer 2007; Kineta H. Hung and Stella Yiyan Li, "The Influence of eWOM on Virtual Consumer Communities: Social Capital, Consumer Learning, and Behavioral Outcomes," *Journal of Advertising Research,* December 2007; "How and What Do Consumers Maximize?" *Psychology & Marketing,* September 2003; Ronald E. Goldsmith, "A Theory of Shopping," *Journal of the Academy of Marketing Science,* Fall 2000; Judith Lynne Zaichkowsky, "Consumer Behavior: Yesterday, Today, and Tomorrow," *Business Horizons,* May–June 1991; James R. Bettman, An Information Processing Theory of Consumer Choice (Reading, MA: Addison-Wesley Publishing, 1979); Richard W. Olshavsky and Donald H. Granbois, "Consumer Decision Making: Fact or Fiction?" *Journal of Consumer Research,* September 1979. Craig J. Thompson, "Consumer Risk Perceptions in a Community of Reflexive Doubt," *Journal of Consumer Research,* September 2005; Alice M. Tybout, Brian Sternthal, Prashant Malaviya, Georgios A. Bakamitsos, Se-Bum Park, Dawn Iacobucci, and Frank Kardes, "Information Accessibility as a Moderator of Judgments: The Role of Content versus Retrieval Ease," *Journal of Consumer Research,* June 2005; Laura L. Pingol and Anthony D. Miyazaki, "Information Source Usage and Purchase Satisfaction: Implications for Product-Focused Print Media," *Journal of Advertising Research,* March 2005; Stijn M. J. Van Osselaer, Joseph W. Alba, and Puneet Manchanda, "Irrelevant Information and Mediated Intertemporal Choice," *Journal of Consumer Psychology,* 2004; Judi Strebel, Tulin Erdem, and Joffre Swait, "Consumer Search in High Technology Markets: Exploring the Use of Traditional Information Channels," *Journal of Consumer Psychology,* #1 (2004); Ram D. Gopal, Bhavik Pathak, Arvind K. Tripathi, and Fang Yin, "From Fatwallet to eBay: An Investigation of Online Deal-Forums and Sales Promotions," *Journal of Retailing,* June 2006; Raj Arora, "Consumer Involvement—What It Offers to Advertising Strategy," *International Journal of Advertising* 4, #2 (1985); J. Brock Smith and Julia M. Bristor, "Uncertainty Orientation: Explaining Differences in Purchase Involvement and External Search," *Psychology & Marketing,* November/December 1994.

30. Jeffrey V. Rayport, "Demand-Side Innovation: Where IT Meets Marketing," *InformationWeek,* February 1, 2007; "Web Stores Tap Product Reviews," *Wall Street Journal,* September 11, 2007; Bell, David R, Daniel Corsten, and George Knox, "From Point of Purchase to Path to Purchase: How Preshopping Factors Drive Unplanned Buying," *Journal of Marketing,* January 2011; Boland, Wendy Attaya, Merrie Brucks, and Jesper H. Nielsen, "The Attribute Carryover Effect: What the "Runner-Up" Option Tells Us about Consumer Choice Processes," *Journal of Consumer Research*, October 2012; Khan, Uzma, Meng Zhu, and Ajay Kalra, "When Trade-offs Matter: The Effect of Choice Construal on Context Effects," *Journal of Marketing Research,* February 2011.

31. J. Jeffrey Inman and Marcel Zeelenberg, "Regret in Repeat Purchase versus Switching Decisions: the Attenuating Role of Decision Justifiability," *Journal of Consumer Research,* June 2002; Michael Tsiros and Vikas Mittal, "Regret: A Model of its Antecedents and Consequences in Consumer Decision Making," *Journal of Consumer Research,* March 2000; Thomas A. Burnham, Judy K. Frels, and Vijay Mahajan, "Consumer Switching Costs: a Typology, Antecedents, and Consequences," *Journal of the Academy of Marketing Science,* Spring 2003; Ziv Carmon, Klaus Wertenbroch, and Marcel Zeelenberg, "Option Attachment: When Deliberating Makes Choosing Feel Like Losing," *Journal of Consumer Research,* June 2003; Alan D. J. Cooke, Tom Meyvis, and Alan Schwartz, "Avoiding Future Regret in Purchase-Timing Decisions," *Journal of Consumer Research,* March 2001; Anna S. Mattila, "The Impact of Cognitive Inertia on Postconsumption Evaluation Processes," *Journal of the Academy of Marketing Science,* Summer 2003; William Cunnings and Mark Venkatesan, "Cognitive Dissonance and Consumer Behavior: A Review of the Evidence," *Journal of Marketing Research,* August 1976.

32. C. Aaron, E. Edwards, and X. Lanier, "Turning Blogs and User-Generated Content into Search Engine Results." *SES,* May 2009.

33. Adapted from E. M. Rogers, *Diffusion of Innovation* (New York: Free Press, 2003). See also Du, Rex Yuxing, and Wagner A Kamakura, "Measuring Contagion in the Diffusion of Consumer Packaged Goods," *Journal of Marketing Research,* February 2011; Donald Lehmann and Mercedes Esteban-Bravo, "When Giving Some Away Makes Sense to Jump-start the Diffusion Process," *Marketing Letters,* October 2006; Stephen J. Hoch, "Product Experience Is Seductive," *Journal of Consumer Research,* December 2002.

34. "Rethinking The Oreo For Chinese Consumers," *All Things Considered,* January 27, 2012; "Chasing China's Shoppers," *Wall Street Journal,* June 14, 2012.

35. "Fuel and Freebies," *Wall Street Journal,* June 10, 2002.Viswanathan, Madhu, José Antonio Rosa, and Julie A Ruth, "Exchanges in Marketing Systems: The Case of Subsistence Consumer–Merchants in Chennai, India," *Journal of Marketing,* May 2010; Martin, Kelly D., and Ronald Paul Hill, "Life Satisfaction, Self-Determination, and Consumption Adequacy at the Bottom of the Pyramid," *Journal of Consumer Research,* December 2011.

CHAPTER 6

1. See www.deere.com and www.metokote.com, 2011 Annual Report, Deere & Company; "Deere's Big Green Profit Machine," *Bloomberg Businessweek,* July 5, 2012; "Farmer's Prepare for the Data Harvest," *Wall Street Journal,* June 14, 2012; "Teaching Drones to Farm," *Wall Street Journal,* September 20, 2011; "American Farmers Venture into New Field: Social Media," *Technorati,* September 7, 2010; "John Deere India Introduces Two New Tractor Models," *Economic Times,* August 13, 2010; "Global Innovation: John Deere's Farm Team," *Fortune,* April 14, 2008; "John Deere's Big-Wheel Rally," *Investor's Business Daily,* September 24,

2007; "Why Deere Is Weeding Out Dealers Even as Farms Boom," *Wall Street Journal,* August 14, 2007; "Deere's Revolution on Wheels," *BusinessWeek,* July 2, 2007; "Deere," *Fortune,* April 30, 2007; "John Deere Cultivates Its Image," *Advertising Age,* July 25, 2005; "Metokote Develops Customized Systems for Applying High Tech Coatings; More than Just Painting a Part," *Diesel Progress,* April 2003; and "John Deere Golf & Turf One Source,"www.deere.com/en_US/golfturf/one_source_partners/; "Deere Uses E-Hubs to Build Relationships with Dealers," *BtoB,* September 9, 2002; "Outsourcing Is More Than Cost Cutting," *Fortune,* October 26, 1998.

2. "Expanding Abroad? Avoid Cultural Gaffes," *Wall Street Journal,* January 19, 2010. See also Chapter 14, endnote 2.

3. "Detroit to Suppliers: Quality or Else," *Fortune,* September 30, 1996. See also Thomas H. Stevenson and Frank C. Barnes, "What Industrial Marketers Need to Know Now about ISO 9000 Certification: a Review, Update, and Integration with Marketing," *Industrial Marketing Management,* November 2002; Roger Calantone and Gary Knight, "The Critical Role of Product Quality in the International Performance of Industrial Firms," *Industrial Marketing Management,* November 2000; Sime Curkovic and Robert Handfield, "Use of ISO 9000 and Baldrige Award Criteria in Supplier Quality Evaluation," *International Journal of Purchasing & Materials Management,* Spring 1996.

4. M. D. Steward, F. N. Morgan, L. A. Crosby, and A. Kumar, "Exploring Cross-National Differences in Organizational Buyers' Normative Expectations of Supplier Performance," *Journal of International Marketing,* #1, 2010; Kelly Hewett, R. Bruce Money, and Subhash Sharma, "An Exploration of the Moderating Role of Buyer Corporate Culture in Industrial Buyer-Seller Relationships," *Journal of the Academy of Marketing Science,* Summer 2002; Jae-Eun Chung, Brenda Sternquist, and Zhengyi Chen, "Retailer-Buyer Supplier Relationships: The Japanese Difference," *Journal of Retailing,* December 2006; Masaaki Kotabe and Janet Y. Murray, "Global Sourcing Strategy and Sustainable Competitive Advantage," *Industrial Marketing Management,* January 2004.

5. Gundlach, Gregory T., and Joseph P. Cannon, "Trust but verify"? The performance implications of verification strategies in trusting relationships," *Journal of the Academy of Marketing Science,* July 2010; E. Fang, R. Palmatier, L. K. Scheer, and N. Li, "Trust at Different Organizational Levels," *Journal of Marketing,* #2, 2008; Jeffrey E. Lewin and Naveen Donthu, "The Influence of Purchase Situation on Buying Center Structure and Involvement: A Select Meta-Analysis of Organizational Buying Behavior Research," *Journal of Business Research,* October 2005; Jae H. Pae, Namwoon Kim, Jim K. Han, and Leslie Yip, "Managing Intraorganizational Diffusion of Innovations: Impact of Buying Center Dynamics and Environments," *Industrial Marketing Management,* November 2002; R. Venkatesh, Ajay K. Kohli, and Gerald Zaltman, "Influence Strategies in Buying Centers," *Journal of Marketing,* October 1995.

6. Daniel J. Flint, Robert B. Woodruff, and Sarah Fisher Gardial, "Exploring the Phenomenon of Customers' Desired Value Change in a Business-to-Business Context," *Journal of Marketing,* October 2002; E. Stephen Grant, "Buyer-Approved Selling: Sales Strategies from the Buyers Side of the Desk," *Journal of the Academy of Marketing Science,* Winter 2004; Minette E. Drumwright, "Socially Responsible Organizational Buying: Environmental Concern As a Noneconomic Buying Criterion," *Journal of Marketing,* July 1994; Morgan P. Miles, Linda S. Munilla, and Gregory R. Russell, "Marketing and Environmental Registration/Certification: What Industrial Marketers Should Understand about ISO 14000," *Industrial Marketing Management,* July 1997.

7. "New Research: What Motivates Buyers to Receive and Engage with Vendor Email?" *Marketing Sherpa,* February 10, 2010.

8. "J&J Is Acccused of Kickbacks to Omnicare on Drug Sales," *Wall Street Journal,* January 16, 2010; "J&J Penalty May Total $2.2 Billion," *Wall Street Journal,* July 19, 2012; Richard F. Beltramini, "Exploring the Effectiveness of Business Gifts: Replication and Extension," *Journal of Advertising,* Summer 2000; Jeanette J. Arbuthnot, "Identifying Ethical Problems Confronting Small Retail Buyers During the Merchandise Buying Process," *Journal of Business Ethics,* May 1997; Gail K. McCracken and Thomas J. Callahan, "Is There Such a Thing as a Free Lunch?" *International Journal of Purchasing & Materials Management,* Winter 1996; Robert W. Cooper, Garry L. Frank, and Robert A. Kemp, "The Ethical Environment Facing the Profession of Purchasing and Materials Management," *International Journal of Purchasing & Materials Management,* Spring 1997; I. Fredrick Trawick, John E. Swan, Gail W. McGee, and David R. Rink, "Influence of Buyer Ethics and Salesperson Behavior on Intention to Choose a Supplier," *Journal of the Academy of Marketing Science,* Winter 1991; J. A. Badenhorst, "Unethical Behaviour in Procurement: A Perspective on Causes and Solutions," *Journal of Business Ethics,* September 1994.

9. Hoppner, Jessica J, and David A Griffith, "The Role of Reciprocity in Clarifying the Performance Payoff of Relational Behavior," *Journal of Marketing Research,* October 2011; Shachat, Jason, and Wei Lijia, "Procuring Commodities: First-Price Sealed-Bid or English Auctions?," *Marketing Science,* #2, 2012; S. Khan and B. Schroder, "Use of Rules in Decision-Making in Government Outsourcing," *Industrial Marketing Management,* #4, 2009; Neeraj Bharadwaj, "Investigating the Decision Criteria Used in Electronic Components Procurement," *Industrial Marketing Management,* May 2004; Jacques Verville and Alannah Halingten, "A Six-Stage Model of the Buying Process for ERP Software," *Industrial Marketing Management,* October 2003; Carol C. Bienstock, "Understanding Buyer Information Acquisition for the Purchase of Logistics Services," *International Journal of Physical Distribution & Logistics Management,* #8 (2002); David Tucker and Laurie Jones, "Leveraging the Power of the Internet for Optimal Supplier Sourcing," *International Journal of Physical Distribution & Logistics Management,* #3 (2000); H. L. Brossard, "Information Sources Used by an Organization During a Complex Decision Process: An Exploratory Study," *Industrial Marketing Management,* January 1998; Michele D. Bunn, "Taxonomy of Buying Decision Approaches," *Journal of Marketing,* January 1993; Mark A. Farrell and Bill Schroder, "Influence Strategies in Organizational Buying Decisions," *Industrial Marketing Management,* July 1996; Edward F. Fern and James R. Brown, "The Industrial/Consumer Marketing Dichotomy: A Case of Insufficient Justification," *Journal of Marketing,* Spring 1984.

10. Werner Delfmann, Sascha Albers, and Martin Gehring, "The Impact of Electronic Commerce on Logistics Service Providers," *International Journal of Physical Distribution & Logistics Management,* #3 (2002); Daniel Knudsen, "Aligning Corporate Strategy and E-procurement Tools," *International Journal of Physical Distribution & Logistics Management,* #8 (2003).

11. "The Role of Search in Business to Business Buying Decisions," Enquiro Search Solutions, October 27, 2004. See also "10 Great Websites," *B2B,* September 10, 2007; "Usability Problems Plague B-to-B Sites," *BtoBonline.com,* April 23, 2007; Goutam Chakraborty, Prashant Srivastava, and David L. Warren, "Understanding Corporate B2B websites' Effectiveness from North American and European Perspective," *Industrial Marketing Management,* July 2005; Samir Gupta, Jack Cadeaux, and Arch Woodside, "Mapping Network Champion Behavior in B2B Electronic Venturing," *Industrial Marketing Management,* July 2005; Cindy Claycomb, Karthik Iyer, and Richard Germain, "Predicting the Level of B2B E-Commerce in Industrial Organizations," *Industrial Marketing Management,* April 2005; D. Eric Boyd and Robert E. Spekman, "Internet Usage Within B2B Relationships and Its Impact on Value Creation: A Conceptual Model and Research Propositions," *Journal of Business-to-Business Marketing,* #1 (2004); B. Mahadevan, "Making Sense of Emerging Market Structures in B2B E-Commerce," *California Management Review,* Fall 2003.

12. See www.spiceworks.com; "Reaching Folks on Their Turf," *New York Times,* March 5, 2009.

13. "The New Golden Rule of Business," *Fortune,* February 21, 1994; Janet L. Hartley and Thomas Y. Choi, "Supplier Development: Customers as a Catalyst of Process Change," *Business Horizons,* July–August 1996.

14. "Green PC Push by Feds May Seed Wider Adoption," *Computerworld,* January 14, 2008; "Working with the Enemy," *Fast Company,* September 2007; "Eco Walmart Costs Marketers Green," *Advertising Age,* October 1, 2007; "Guide to the Business Case & Benefits of Sustainability

Purchasing," Sustainability Purchasing Network, March 2007; "The Mayor's Green Procurement Code," *Local Economy,* February 2007; "Innovation Wednesday: Walmart Surpasses Goal to Sell 100 Million Fluorescent Light Bulbs Three Months Early, *Fast Company,* October 3, 2007; "Home Depot to Display an Environmental Label," *New York Times,* April 17, 2007.

15. "Ford Seeks Big Savings by Overhauling Supply System," *Wall Street Journal,* September 29, 2005; Turning Vendors into Partners," *Inc.,* August 2005; "A 'China Price' for Toyota," *BusinessWeek,* February 21, 2005; "Ford to Suppliers: Let's Get Cozier," *BusinessWeek,* September 20, 2004; "How Would You Like Your Ford?" *BusinessWeek,* August 9, 2004; "Walmart's Low-Price Obsession Puts Suppliers through Wringer," *Investor's Business Daily,* January 30, 2004; "Push from Above," *Wall Street Journal,* May 23, 1996; Jan B. Heide, "Plural Governance in Industrial Purchasing," *Journal of Marketing,* October 2003; Shibin Sheng, James R. Brown, Carolyn Y. Nicholson, and Laura Poppo, "Do Exchange Hazards Always Foster Relational Governance? An Empirical Test of the Role of Communication," *International Journal of Research in Marketing,* March 2006; Erin Anderson and Sandy D. Jap, "The Dark Side of Close Relationships," *Sloan Management Review,* Spring 2005.

16. Much of the discussion in this section is based on research reported in Joseph P. Cannon and William D. Perreault, Jr., "Buyer-Seller Relationships in Business Markets," *Journal of Marketing Research,* November 1999. See also Blocker, Christopher P., Mark B. Houston, and Daniel J. Flint, "Unpacking What a "Relationship" Means to Commercial Buyers: How the Relationship Metaphor Creates Tension and Obscures Experience," *Journal of Consumer Research* 38, October 2012; Ganesan, Shankar, Steven P Brown, Babu John Mariadoss, and Hillbun (Dixon) Ho, "Buffering and Amplifying Effects of Relationship Commitment in Business-to-Business Relationships," *Journal of Marketing Research,* April 2010; Kumar, Alok, Jan B Heide, and Kenneth H Wathne, "Performance Implications of Mismatched Governance Regimes Across External and Internal Relationships," *Journal of Marketing,* March 2011; Tuli, Kapil R, Sundar G Bharadwaj, and Ajay K Kohli, "Ties That Bind: The Impact of Multiple Types of Ties with a Customer on Sales Growth and Sales Volatility," *Journal of Marketing Research,* February 2010; Grewal, Rajdeep, Anindita Chakravarty, and Amit Saini, "Governance Mechanisms in Business-to-Business Electronic Markets," *Journal of Marketing,* July 2010; R.W. Palmatier, "Interfirm Relational Drivers of Customer Value," *Journal of Marketing,* #4, 2008; R. W. Palmatier, L. K. Scheer, K. R. Evans, and T. J. Arnold, "Achieving Relationship Marketing Effectiveness in Business-to-Business Exchanges," *Journal of the Academy of Marketing Science,* #2, 2008; R. N. Bolton, K. N. Lemon, and P. C. Verhoef, "Expanding Business-to-Business Customer Relationships: Modeling the Customer's Upgrade Decision," *Journal of Marketing,* #1, 2008; Jan B. Heide and Kenneth H. Wathne, "Friends, Businesspeople, and Relationship Roles: A Conceptual Framework and a Research Agenda," *Journal of Marketing,* July 2006; Robert W. Palmatier, Rajiv P. Dant, Dhruv Grewal, and Kenneth R. Evans, "Factors Influencing the Effectiveness of Relationship Marketing: A Meta-Analysis," *Journal of Marketing,* October 2006; Kapil R. Tuli, Ajay K. Kohli, and Sundar G. Bharadwaj, "Rethinking Customer Solutions: From Product Bundles to Relational Processes," *Journal of Marketing,* July 2007; Joseph P. Cannon and Christian Homburg, "Buyer-Supplier Relationships and Customer Firm Costs," *Journal of Marketing,* January 2001; Das Narayandas and V. Kasturi Rangan, "Building and Sustaining Buyer-Seller Relationships in Mature Industrial Markets," *Journal of Marketing,* July 2004.

17. "Purchasing's New Muscle," *Fortune,* February 20, 1995.

18. "Early Warnings in the Supply Chain," *Financial Times,* March 24, 2009; "United They'll Stand," *Wall Street Journal,* March 23, 2009.

19. Jeffrey K. Liker and Thomas Y. Choi, "Building Deep Supplier Relationships," *Harvard Business Review,* December 2004; see also G. L. Frazier, E. Maltz, K. D. Antia, and A. Rindfleisch, "Distributor Sharing of Strategic Information with Suppliers," *Journal of Marketing,* #4, 2009.

20. For more on outsourcing, see "Big Three's Outsourcing Plan: Make Parts Suppliers Do It," *Wall Street Journal,* June 10, 2004; See also M. Ahearne and P. Kothandaraman, "Impact of Outsourcing on Business-to-Business Marketing: An Agenda for Inquiry," *Industrial Marketing Management,* #4, 2009; "HP Will Direct More U.S. Customers to U.S. Call Centers," *Investor's Business Daily,* February 28, 2008; "The Future of Outsourcing," *BusinessWeek,* January 30, 2006; "Pulling the Plug," *Fortune,* August 8, 2005, pp. 96B-D; "Outsourcing with a Twist," *Wall Street Journal,* January 18, 2005.

21. "H-P Wields Its Clout to Undercut PC Rivals," *Wall Street Journal,* September 25, 2009. For other examples of big/small partnerships, see "A Fruitful Relationship," *BusinessWeek,* November 20, 2000, pp. EB94–EB96; "Automating an Automaker," *Inc.* Tech 2000, #4.

22. "Thai Floods Jolt PC Supply Chain," *Wall Street Journal,* October 18, 2011.

23. See U.S. Census data including "Industry Statistics for Subsectors and Industries by Employment Size: 2007" from *2007 Economic Census—Manufacturing, Summary Series, General Summary* (Washington, DC: U.S. Government Printing Office, 2010) and available online at www.census.gov. See also "Radical Shifts Take Hold in U.S. Manufacturing," *Wall Street Journal,* February 3, 2010; "Manufacturing Index Hits 5-Year High," *Investor's Business Daily,* February 2, 2010; "Growth Hits 6-Year High," *Wall Street Journal,* January 30, 2010; "Lean Manufacturing Helps Companies Survive," *USA Today,* November 2, 2009; "Can the Future Be Built in America?" *BusinessWeek,* September 21, 2009; "Not Every Nation Can Export Its Way to Recovery," *USA Today,* September 3, 2009 "Are We Engineering Ourselves Out of Manufacturing Jobs," Federal Reserve Bank of Cleveland, January 1, 2006; "If You Can Make It Here," *New York Times,* September 4, 2005.

24. See www.naics.com. See also "Classified Information," *American Demographics,* July 1999; "SIC: The System Explained," Sales and Marketing Management, April 22, 1985; "Enhancement of SIC System Being Developed," *Marketing News* Collegiate Edition, May 1988.

25. "The Long Road to Walmart," *Wall Street Journal,* September 19, 2005, See also Peter Kaufman, Satish Jayachandran, and Randall L. Rose, "The Role of Relational Embeddedness in Retail Buyers' Selection of New Products," *Journal of Marketing Research,* November 2006.

26. Based on U.S. Census data and "Eyes Wide Open," *Fortune,* September 19, 2005, pp. 316B-D; "How Bikers' Water Backpack Became Soldiers' Essential," *Wall Street Journal,* July 19, 2005; "Targeting the DHS," *Inc.,* May 2005; "Heavy Load Now Lighter with Bleex," *Investor's Business Daily,* December 29, 2004; "Pentagon Sales Give Powerful Jolt to Ultralife's Business," *Investor's Business Daily,* April 6, 2004; "Uncle Sam Is a Tough Customer," *Investor's Business Daily,* October 20, 2003; "Super Soldiers," *BusinessWeek,* July 28, 2003.

27. "Not just Wal-Mart: Dozens of U.S. companies face bribery suspicions," *Fortune,* April 26, 2012For a detailed discussion of business ethics in a number of countries, see *Journal of Business Ethics,* October 1997. See also John B. Ford, Michael S. LaTour, and Tony L. Henthorne, "Cognitive Moral Development and Japanese Procurement Executives: Implications for Industrial Marketers," *Industrial Marketing Management,* November 2000; "U.S., Other Nations Step Up Bribery Battle," *Wall Street Journal,* September 12, 2008; "How Can a U.S. Company Go International, Avoid the Economic Disaster of a Thai Baht . . . and Pay No Bribes?" *USA Today,* November 17, 1997; Larry R. Smeltzer and Marianne M. Jennings, "Why an International Code of Business Ethics Would Be Good for Business," *Journal of Business Ethics,* January 1998.

CHAPTER 7

1. See www.dunkinvip.com; telldunkin.com; dunkindonuts.com; "When It Comes to Ads in Games, These Guys Aren't Playing Around,"*Adweek,* June 19, 2012; Marketing Case Studies: Dunkin' Donuts," *Copernicus Marketing;* "Brand Transformation: Dunkin' Donuts," *Ivy Cohen, Marketing Coach;* "High Five! Dunkin' Donuts Is Number One in Customer Loyalty," *Press Release,* Dunkin' Donuts, February 16, 2011; "The Cold Hard Facts: New Dunkin' Donuts Survey Shows Popularity of Iced Coffee in the Winter Is Heating Up," *Press Release,* Dunkin' Donuts, January 18, 2011; "Singular Pursuit: Dunkin'

Donuts Tests Expansion in Home Market," *Boston.com,* October 9, 2010; "CareerBuilder and Dunkin' Donuts Survey Finds Which Professions Need Coffee the Most," *Press Release,* Dunkin' Donuts, September 27, 2010; "Getting a Grip," *Marketing Management,* Spring 2010; "Dunkin' Donuts Tests Facebook," *Social Media Optimization,* March 16, 2009; "Facebook Fans and Dunkin' Donuts," *eMarketer,* February 27, 2009; "It's Not About the Doughnuts," *Fast Company,* December 19, 2007; "Takeout-Breakfast War Reheats," *Wall Street Journal,* September 5, 2007; "Dunkin' Donuts Going Zero Grams Trans Fat," *MSNBC.com,* August 27, 2007; "Dunkin' Donuts Whips Up A Recipe for Expansion," *Wall Street Journal,* May 3, 2007; "Dunkin' Donuts Uses Business Intelligence in War Against Starbucks," *Information Week,* April 16, 2007; "Brand New Buzz," *Time,* March 9, 2007; "Dunkin' Begins New Push Into China," *Wall Street Journal,* January 17, 2007; "Dunkin' Donuts Cheap Chic," *BusinessWeek,* April 12, 2006; "Dunkin' Donuts Tries to Go Upscale, But Not Too Far," *Wall Street Journal,* April 8, 2006; *Time to Make the Donuts,* William Rosenberg, 2001.

2. "Age of Big Data," *New York Times,* February 12, 2012; "What is big data?" *O'Reilly.com,* January 11, 2012; "Big Bets on Big Data," *Forbes,* June 22, 2012; "Big Data and Its Myths," *Forbes,* June 21, 2012;

3. Gellinger, Gene, Durval Castro, and Anthony Mills, "Data, Information Knowledge and Wisdom," 2004, http://www.systems-thinking.org/dikw/dikw.htm; Rowley, Jennifer, "The wisdom hierarchy: representations of the DIKW hierarchy," *Journal of Information Science,* #2, 2007.

4. Netzer, Oded, Ronen Feldman, Jacob Goldenberg, and Moshe Fresko, "Mine Your Own Business: Market-Structure Surveillance Through Text Mining," *Marketing Science,* #3, 2012; M. Reimann, O. Schilke, and J. S. Thomas, "Customer Relationship Management and Firm Performance: The Mediating Role of Business Strategy," *Journal of the Academy of Marketing Science,* (3) 2010; Venkatesh Shankar and Russell S. Winer, "When Customer Relationship Management Meets Data Mining," *Journal of Interactive Marketing,* Summer 2006; Amy Miller and Jennifer Cioffi, "Measuring Marketing Effectiveness and Value: The Unisys Marketing Dashboard," *Journal of Advertising Research,* September 2004; "Making Marketing Measure Up," *BusinessWeek,* December 13, 2004; "How Verizon Flies by Wire," *CIO Magazine,* November 1, 2004; Reimann, Martin, Oliver Schilke, and Jacquelyn Thomas, "Customer relationship management and firm performance: the mediating role of business strategy," *Journal of the Academy of Marketing Science,* May 2010.

5. Gary L. Lilien, Arvind Rangaswamy, Gerrit H. van Bruggen, and Berend Wierenga, "Bridging the Marketing Theory-Practice Gap with Marketing Engineering," *Journal of Business Research,* February 2002; "Virtual Management," *BusinessWeek,* September 21, 1998; John T. Mentzer and Nimish Gandhi, "Expert Systems in Marketing: Guidelines for Development," *Journal of the Academy of Marketing Science,* Winter, 1992; William D. Perreault, Jr., "The Shifting Paradigm in Marketing Research," *Journal of the Academy of Marketing Science,* Fall 1992.

6. "Big data: The next frontier for innovation, competition, and productivity," *McKinsey Global Institute,* May 2011; "Data Analytics: Crunching the Future," *Bloomberg Businessweek,* September 8, 2011; "Clouds, big data, and smart assets: Ten tech-enabled business trends to watch," *McKinsey Quarterly,* August 2012; "Unlocking Hidden Profits With Big Data Analystics," *Forbes,* September 27, 2012; "Seizing the Potential of 'big data,'" *McKinsey Quarterly,* #4, 2011; "Are you ready for the era of 'big data'?" *McKinsey Quarterly,* #4, 2011; "How Intuit Uses Big Data for the Little Guy," Forbes, April 26, 2012; "Big Data Requires Complex Analysis, But Don't Be Scared Off," *Advertising Age,* May 8, 2012; Dzyabura, Daria, and John R. Hauser, "Active Machine Learning for Consideration Heuristics," *Marketing Science,* #5, 2011.

7. See www.lenscrafters.com; "LensCrafters Focuses on China," *Wall Street Journal,* February 6, 2008; "At LensCrafters, Selling Candor and Designer Frames," *New York Times,* April 14, 2006; "LensCrafters Hits One Billion in Sales," *Business Wire,* February 3, 1998; "LensCrafters Polishes Image with Style," *Chain Store Age Executive,* October 1996.

8. J. Rubinson, "The New Marketing Research Imperative: It's About Learning," *Journal of Advertising Research,* #1, 2009; Larry Selden and Ian C. MacMillan, "Manage Customer Centric Innovation Systematically," *Harvard Business Review,* April 2006; Bruce H. Clark, "Business Intelligence Using Smart Techniques," *Journal of the Academy of Marketing Science,* Fall 2003; Mark Peyrot, Nancy Childs, Doris Van Doren, and Kathleen Allen, "An Empirically Based Model of Competitor Intelligence Use," *Journal of Business Research,* September 2002; Stanley F. Slater and John C. Narver, "Intelligence Generation and Superior Customer Value," *Journal of the Academy of Marketing Science,* Winter 2000; Jim Bessen, "Riding the Marketing Information Wave," *Harvard Business Review,* September–October 1993; Lawrence B. Chonko, John F. Tanner, Jr., and Ellen Reid Smith, "The Sales Force's Role in International Marketing Research and Marketing Information Systems," *Journal of Personal Selling and Sales Management,* Winter, 1991; William Boulding, Richard Staelin, Michael Ehret, and Wesley J. Johnston, "A Customer Relationship Management Roadmap: What Is Known, Potential Pitfalls, and Where to Go," *Journal of Marketing,* October 2005; Satish Jayachandran, Subhash Sharma, Peter Kaufman, and Pushkala Raman, "The Role of Relational Information Processes and Technology Use in Customer Relationship Management," *Journal of Marketing,* October 2005; Yong Cao and Thomas S. Gruca, "Reducing Adverse Selection Through Customer Relationship Management," *Journal of Marketing,* October 2005; Darrell K. Rigby and Dianne Ledingham, "CRM Done Right," *Harvard Business Review,* November 2004; Peter M. Chisnall, "The Effective Use of Market Research: A Guide for Management to Grow the Business," *International Journal of Market Research,* 42, #2, (Summer 2000); Seymour Sudman and Edward Blair, Marketing Research: A Problem Solving Approach (Burr Ridge, IL: Irwin/McGraw-Hill, 1998). See also Christine Moorman, Rohit Deshpande, and Gerald Zaltman, "Factors Affecting Trust in Market Research Relationships," *Journal of Marketing,* January 1993.

9. See www.kiwifreshins.com and www.kiwishoeproducts.com; "Kiwi Goes beyond Shine in Effort to Step up Sales," *Wall Street Journal,* December 20, 2007.

10. Charlene Li and Josh Bernoff, *Groundswell,* Boston: Harvard Business Press, 2008.

11. For more on focus groups, see "Mucus to Maxi Pads: Marketing's Dirtiest Jobs," *Advertising Age,* February 16, 2009; "Hypnosis Brings Groups into Focus," *Brandweek,* March 24, 2008; "The Perils of Packaging: Nestlé Aims for Easier Openings," *Wall Street Journal,* November 17, 2005; "Puppet's Got a Brand-New Bag," *Business 2.0,* October 2005; "Focus Groups Should Be Abolished," *Advertising Age,* August 8, 2005; "Web Enhances Market Research," *Advertising Age,* June 18, 2001. See also William J. McDonald, "Focus Group Research Dynamics and Reporting: An Examination of Research Objectives and Moderator Influences," *Journal of the Academy of Marketing Science,* Spring 1993; Thomas Kiely, "*Wired* Focus Groups," *Harvard Business Review,* January–February 1998; see also James R. Stengel, Andrea L. Dixon, and Chris T. Allen, "Listening Begins at Home," *Harvard Business Review,* November 2003; Bahl, Salini and George R. Milne, "Talking to Ourselves: A Dialogical Exploration of Consumption Experiences," *Journal of Consumer Research,* February 2010. "How to Run an Online Focus Group to Discover What Business Prospects Really Want (Tips on Launching an E-Commerce Website)," *Marketing Sherpa,* September 28, 2005; "The New Focus Groups: Online Networks," *Wall Street Journal,* January 14, 2008; "Expand Your Brand Community Online," *Advertising Age,* January 7, 2008; "Design It before You Buy It," *Wall Street Journal,* August 2, 2007; "P&G Plunges into Social Networking," *Wall Street Journal,* January 8, 2007; "It Takes a Web Village," *BusinessWeek,* September 4, 2006; "Shoot the Focus Group," *BusinessWeek* Online, November 14, 2005; "Take Your Market Research Online," *Fortune Small Business,* May 29, 2005.

12. "Selling Sibelius Isn't Easy," *American Demographics,* The 1994 Directory; "Symphony Strikes a Note for Research as It Prepares to Launch a New Season," *Marketing News,* August 29, 1988. For more on surveys, see "Forget Phone and Mail: Online's the Best Place to Administer Surveys," *Advertising Age,* July 17, 2006; "Electrolux Cleans Up," *BusinessWeek,* February 27, 2006; "Chrysler's Made-Up Customers Get

Real Living Space at Agency," *Wall Street Journal,* January 4, 2006; "VW's American Road Trip," *Wall Street Journal,* January 4, 2006; "The Only Question That Matters," *Business 2.0,* September 2005; See also Pierre Chandon, Vicki G. Morwitz, and Werner J. Reinartz, "Do Intentions Really Predict Behavior? Self-Generated Validity Effects in Survey Research," *Journal of Marketing,* April 2005; Stanley E. Griffis, Thomas J. Goldsby, and Martha Cooper, "Web-Based and Mail Surveys: A Comparison of Response, Data, and Cost," *Journal of Business Logistics,* #2 (2003); Terry L. Childers and Steven J. Skinner, "Toward a Conceptualization of Mail Survey Response Behavior," *Psychology & Marketing,* March 1996; J. B. E. M. Steenkamp, M. G. De Jong, and H. Baumgartner, "Socially Desirable Response Tendencies in Survey Research," *Journal of Marketing Research,* #2, 2010.

13. "'Quantilitative' Research & Beyond: New Platforms for Customer Insights," *Marketing News,* March 1, 2008; "Communispace and Charles Schwab Win Social Technologies Award for Generation X Online Customer Community," *Business Wire,* October 12, 2007; "Build Community to Build Brand and Business," Econtent, November 2008; "Qual Research by the Numbers," *Marketing News,* September 1, 2008; Pete Comley, "Online Research Communities: A User Guide," *International Journal of Market Research* 50, #5; "Customer-Centric Approach Earns CDW Corporation a Prestigious Social Media Award," *Business Wire,* October 28, 2009; "Expand Your Brand Community Online," *Advertising Age,* January 7, 2008; S. A. Thompson and R. K. Sinha, "Brand Communities and New Product Adoption: The Influence and Limits of Oppositional Loyalty," *Journal of Marketing,* #6, 2008.

14. "Old Ketchup Packet Heads for Trash," *Wall Street Journal,* September 19, 2011.

15. "Can P&G make money in places where people earn $2 a day?" *Fortune,* January 6, 2011.

16. Paco Underhill, *Why We Buy* (New York: Simon and Shuster, 1999); see also N. Diamond, J. F. Sherry, A. M. Muniz, M. A. McGrath, R. V. Kozinets, and S. Borghini, "American Girl and the Brand Gestalt: Closing the Loop on Sociocultural Branding Research," *Journal of Marketing,* #3, 2009; Stephen R. Rosenthal and Mark Capper, "Ethnographies in the Front End: Designing for Enhanced Customer Experiences," *Journal of Product Innovation Management,* May 2006; Pierre Berthon, James Mac Hulbert, and Leyland Pitt, "Consuming Technology: Why Marketers Sometimes Get It Wrong," *California Management Review,* Fall 2005. See also "Why Are Tech Gizmos So Hard to Figure Out?" *USA Today,* November 2, 2005; "Poll: Many Like Tech Gizmos but Are Frustrated," *USA Today,* October 31, 2005; "The Fine Art of Usability Testing," *Dev Source,* March 2005.

17. "Seeing Store Shelves through Senior Eyes," *Wall Street Journal,* September 14, 2009; "They Feel Your Pain," *Brandweek,* June 16, 2008.

18. For more on Nielsen's people meters, see "Made to Measure," *Fortune,* March 3, 2008; "Couch to Supermarket: Connecting Dots," *Wall Street Journal,* February 11, 2008; "TNS Aims to Take Bite Out of Nielsen," *Wall Street Journal,* January 31, 2008; "Where's the Ratings, Dude?" *Wall Street Journal,* March 7, 2005; "Confessions of a Nielsen Household," *American Demographics,* May 2001. See also Peter J. Danaher and Terence W. Beed, "A Coincidental Survey of People Meter Panelists: Comparing What People Say with What They Do," *Journal of Advertising Research,* January–February 1993. "Are Retailers Going Too Far Tracking Our Web Habits?" *USA Today,* October 26, 2009; "The Web Knows What You Want," *BusinessWeek,* July 27, 2009; "Connect the Thoughts: The Analysis of Social Networking Data . . . ," *Adweek-Media,* June 29, 2009; "The Next: Companies May Soon Know Where Customers Are Likely to Be Every Minute . . . ," *BusinessWeek,* March 9, 2009; "Feel like Someone's Watching You?" *USA Today,* February 9, 2009; "We Know Where You Are," *Wall Street Journal,* September 29, 2008; "Websites Want You to Stick Around," *Wall Street Journal,* April 15, 2008.

19. "Red, White, and Blue," Beverage Industry, February 2002.

20. "Will Your Web Business Work? Take It for a Test Drive," Ecompany, May 2001; "Ads Awaken to Fathers' New Role in Family Life," *Advertising Age,* January 10, 1994; "AT&T's Secret MultiMedia Trials Offer Clues to Capturing Interactive Audiences," *Wall Street Journal,* July 28, 1993; "Experimenting in the U.K.: Phone, Cable Deals Let U.S. Test Future," *USA Today,* June 28, 1993. See also Raymond R. Burke, "Virtual Shopping: Breakthrough in Marketing Research," *Harvard Business Review,* March–April 1996; Glen L. Urban, Bruce D. Weinberg, and John R. Hauser, "Premarket Forecasting of Really-New Products," *Journal of Marketing,* January 1996.

21. For more on types of observation, see "How to Get People to Change," *Inc.,* February 2010; "At CBS Television City, Tube-Watching Is a Science," *Advertising Age,* January 18, 2010; "Meet Melissa, Your Recessionary Consumer," *Advertising Age,* September 7, 2009; "A Virtual View of the Store Aisle," *Wall Street Journal,* October 3, 2007; "Marketers Zooming In on Your Daily Routines," *USA Today,* April 30, 2007; "Seeing Through Buyers' Eyes," *Wall Street Journal,* January 29, 2007; See also Stephen J. Grove and Raymond P. Fisk, "Observational Data Collection Methods for Services Marketing: An Overview," *Journal of the Academy of Marketing Science,* Summer 1992; Lee, Thomas Y, and Eric T Bradlow, "Automated Marketing Research Using Online Customer Reviews," *Journal of Marketing Research,* October 2011.

22. "Pen Proving to Be Mighty for Brands, Consumers," *Brandweek,* May 7, 2007; "More than Squeaking by: WD-40 CEO Garry Ridge Repackages a Core Product," *Wall Street Journal,* May 23, 2006; "WD-40 Is Well-Oiled for Growth," *BusinessWeek,* April 18, 2006; "P&G Provides Product Launchpad, a Buzz Network of Moms," *Advertising Age,* March 20, 2006; "Loosening the Wheels of Innovation," *Quirk's Marketing Research Review,* March 2006.

23. "Marketing Research on a Shoestring," *Fortune,* May 29, 2005; "Listen Up: Your Customers Are Talking About You Online," *MarketingProfs.com,* May 24, 2005 "Why Market Research Matters," *Fortune,* August 31, 2004; "On Target," *Entrepreneur,* August 2004; "Borrowing from the Big Boys," *MarketingProfs.com,* June 17, 2003.

24. For more detail on data analysis techniques, see Joe Hair, Rolph Anderson, Ron Tatham, and William Black, *Multivariate Data Analysis* (New York: Prentice-Hall, 2005) or other marketing research texts. See also "Ice Cream Shop Gets Scoop on Locales," *Investor's Business Daily,* February 17, 2006; "Is Your Business in the Right Spot?" *Business 2.0,* May 2004; Michael D. Johnson and Elania J. Hudson, "On the Perceived Usefulness of Scaling Techniques in Market Analysis," *Psychology & Marketing,* October 1996; Milton D. Rosenau, "Graphing Statistics and Data: Creating Better Charts," *Journal of Product Innovation Management,* March 1997.

25. "Careful What You Ask For," *American Demographics,* July 1998. See also John G. Keane, "Questionable Statistics," *American Demographics,* June 1985. Detailed treatment of confidence intervals is beyond the scope of this text, but it is covered in most marketing research texts, such as Donald R. Lehmann and Russ Winer, *Analysis for Marketing Planning* (Burr Ridge, IL: Irwin/McGraw-Hill, 2005).

26. "Good Data Won't Guarantee Good Decisions," *Harvard Business Review,* April 2012.

27. For a discussion of ethical issues in marketing research, see "What Makes Tesco, Kroger More Than Just Rivals?" *Wall Street Journal,* December 24, 2007; "Intimate Shopping: Should Everyone Know What You Bought Today?" *New York Times,* December 23, 2007; "Ma Bell, the Web's New Gatekeeper?" *BusinessWeek,* November 19, 2007; "Firm Mines Offline Data to Target Online Ads," *Wall Street Journal,* October 17, 2007; "How 'Tactical Research' Muddied Diaper Debate: a Case," *Wall Street Journal,* May 17, 1994. See also Rita Marie Cain, "Supreme Court Expands Federal Power to Regulate the Availability and Use of Data," *Journal of the Academy of Marketing Science,* Fall 2001; Malcolm Kirkup and Marylyn Carrigan, "Video Surveillance Research in Retailing: Ethical Issues," *International Journal of Retail & Distribution Management,* #11 (2000); Eve M. Caudill and Patrick E. Murphy, "Consumer Online Privacy: Legal and Ethical Issues," *Journal of Public Policy & Marketing,* Spring 2000; John R. Sparks and Shelby D. Hunt, "Marketing Researcher Ethical Sensitivity: Conceptualization, Measurement, and Exploratory Investigation," *Journal of Marketing,* April 1998; Naresh K. Malhotra, and Gina L. Miller, "An Integrated Model for

Ethical Decisions in Marketing Research," *Journal of Business Ethics,* February 1998.

28. "China Market Research Strategies," *China Business Review,* May–June 2004.

29. "More Companies Are Offshoring R&D," *Investor's Business Daily,* November 21, 2005; "Chinese Puzzle: Spotty Consumer Data," *Wall Street Journal,* October 15, 2003. See also Thomas Tsu Wee Tan and Tan Jee Lui, "Globalization and Trends in International Marketing Research in Asia," *Journal of Business Research,* October 2002; Masaaki Kotabe, "Using Euromonitor Database in International Marketing Research," *Journal of the Academy of Marketing Science,* Spring 2002.

CHAPTER 8

1. See www.underarmour.com; "Under Armour's Founder on Learning to Leverage Celebrity Endorsements," *Harvard Business Review,* May 2012; "Under Armour Scores $1 Billion In Sales Through Laser Focus On Athletes," *Womens Wear Daily,* December 1, 2011; "Tough Mudder Bring In $25 Million, Sign Under Armour," *CNBC,* December 5, 2011; "Under Armour Gets Serious," *Fortune,* November 7, 2011; "Under Armour's Best Idea: A Shirt That Measures Heart Rate and G-Force," *The Atlantic,* November 10, 2011; "Under Armour Signs Groundbreaking Deal with Tough Mudder," *Forbes,* December 8, 2011; "Under Armour Expands Fitness Line Overseas," *Business Insider,* March 16, 2011; "Under Armour's Kevin Plank: Creating 'the Biggest, Baddest Brand on the Planet'" *Knowledge@Wharton,* January 5, 2011; "Under Armour's Daring Half-Court Shot," *Bloomberg Businessweek,* November 1, 2010; "Under Armour Can't Live Up to Own Hype," *Advertising Age,* November 2, 2009; "Under Armour Reboots," *Fortune,* February 2, 2009; "Under Armour Enters the Running Shoe Race," *CNBC.com,* February 1, 2009; "Under Armour Hopes to Outrun Nike," *Advertising Age,* April 28, 2008; "Do These Clothes Help You Work Out?" *BusinessWeek,* March 24, 2008; "True Confessions of a Super Bowl Ad Virgin," *Advertising Age,* February 4, 2008; "Nike Seeks to Undercut New Under Armour Line," *Brandweek,* January 28, 2008; "Even Rookie Advertisers Feel Big-Game Pressure," *Wall Street Journal,* January 15, 2008; "No Sugar and Spice Here," *Advertising Age,* June 18, 2007; "Under Armour May Be Overstretched," *BusinessWeek,* April 30, 2007; "Under Armour: Thrown for a Loss," *BusinessWeek,* February 1, 2007; "Under Armour," *Apparel Magazine,* February 2007; "Perspiration Inspiration," *BusinessWeek,* June 5, 2006; "Rag Trade Rivalry," *Forbes,* June 5, 2006; "Under Armour, A Brawny Tee House? No Sweat," *BusinessWeek* Online, May 25, 2006; "Hot and Cool," Government Executive, October 15, 2005; "Protect this House," *Fast Company,* August 2005; "Under Armour Shows Feminine Side," *Women's Wear Daily,* February 24, 2005; "Under Armour's Apparel Appeal," *Brandweek,* February 21, 2005; 2009 Annual Report, Under Armour; 2009 Annual Report, Army and Air Force Exchange Service; "Kevin Plank," *Brandweek,* April 12, 2004.

2. Golder, Peter N, Debanjan Mitra, and Christine Moorman, "What Is Quality? An Integrative Framework of Processes and States," *Journal of Marketing,* July 2012; Bertini, Marco, Luc Wathieu, and Sheena S Iyengar, "The Discriminating Consumer: Product Proliferation and Willingness to Pay for Quality," *Journal of Marketing Research,* February 2012; T. Erdem, M. P. Keane, and B. Sun, "A Dynamic Model of Brand Choice When Price and Advertising Signal Product Quality," *Marketing Science,* #6, 2008; Neil A. Morgan and Douglas W. Vorhies, "Product Quality Alignment and Business Unit Performance," The *Journal of Product Innovation Management,* November 2001.

3. This example was inspired by other case studies: Robert Solomon and Kathleen Higgins, Case Study: Cement for Sale, Center for the Study of Ethics, Utah Valley State College; C. B. Fledderman (1999), Denver Runway Concrete, Engineering Ethics, Prentice Hall.

4. For more on service quality, see "The Payoff for Trying Harder," *Business 2.0,* July 2002; "Avis to Try Even Harder with Ads Touting High Quality of Service," *Wall Street Journal,* February 18, 2000. For more on air service, see "Paved Paradise: The New Airport Parking Lots," *Wall Street Journal,* November 12, 2003; "Flat-Out Winners," *BusinessWeek,* October 27, 2003. See also Ulaga, Wolfgang, and Werner J Reinartz, "Hybrid offerings: How Manufacturing Firms Combine Goods and Services Successfully," *Journal of Marketing;* November 2011; Janakiraman, Narayan, Robert J Meyer, and Stephen J Hoch, "The Psychology of Decisions to Abandon Waits for Service," *Journal of Marketing Research,* November 2011; Chung, Jaihak, and Vithala R Rao, "A General Consumer Preference Model for Experience Products: Application to Internet Recommendation Services," *Journal of Marketing Research,* June 2012; Brady, Michael K, Clay M Voorhees, and Michael J Brusco, "Service Sweethearting: Its Antecedents and Customer Consequences," *Journal of Marketing,* March 2012; Brüggen, Elisabeth C, Bram Foubert, and Dwayne D Gremler, "Extreme Makeover: Short- and Long-Term Effects of a Remodeled Servicescape," *Journal of Marketing,* September 2011; Roland T. Rust and Chung Tuck Siong, "Marketing Models of Service and Relationships," Marketing Science, November–December 2006; Frances X. Frei, "The Four Things a Service Business Must Get Right," *Harvard Business Review,* April 2008; Paul P. Maglio and Jim Spohrer, "Fundamentals of Service Science," *Journal of the Academy of Marketing Science,* Spring 2008; James C. Anderson and James A. Narus, "Capturing the Value of Supplementary Services," *Harvard Business Review,* January–February 1995; Matthew L. Meuter, Mary Jo Bitner, Amy L. Ostrom, and Stephen W. Brown, "Choosing Among Alternative Service Delivery Modes: An Investigation of Customer Trial of Self-Service Technologies," *Journal of Marketing,* April 2005; D. Todd Donavan, Tom J. Brown, and John C. Mowen, "Internal Benefits of Service-Worker Customer Orientation: Job Satisfaction, Commitment, and Organizational Citizenship Behaviors," *Journal of Marketing,* January 2004; Stephen L. Vargo and Robert F. Lusch, "Evolving to a New Dominant Logic for Marketing," *Journal of Marketing,* January 2004; Ruth N. Bolton, George S. Day, John Deighton, Das Narayandas, Evert Gummesson, Shelby D. Hunt, C. K. Prahalad, Roland T. Rust, and Steven M. Shugan, "Invited Commentaries on "Evolving to a New Dominant Logic for Marketing," *Journal of Marketing,* January 2004; Leonard L. Berry, Venkatesh Shankar, Janet Turner Parish, Susan Cadwallader, and Thomas Dotzel, "Creating New Markets Through Service Innovation," *Sloan Management Review,* Winter 2006; P. C. Verhoef, K. N. Lemon, A. Parasuraman, A. Roggeveen, M. Tsiros, L. A. Schlesinger, "Customer Experience Creation: Determinants, Dynamics and Management Strategies," *Journal of Retailing,* #1, 2009.

5. For more on Listerine PocketPaks, see "The Strip Club," *Business 2.0,* June 2003; "Marketer of the Year: PocketPaks, a Breath of Minty Fresh Air," *Brandweek,* October 14, 2002, pp. M42–M46. For more on brand extensions, see "A Little Less Salt, a Lot More Sales: Campbell's Line Extension," *Advertising Age,* March 10, 2008; "Like Our Sunglasses? Try Our Vodka!" *Wall Street Journal,* November 8, 2007; "P&G Rekindles an Old Flame: New Febreze Candles," *Wall Street Journal,* June 5, 2007; Sood, Sanjay, and Kevin Lane Keller, "The Effects of Brand Name Structure on Brand Extension Evaluations and Parent Brand Dilution," *Journal of Marketing Research,* June 2012; Hamilton, Ryan, and Alexander Chernev, "The Impact of Product Line Extensions and Consumer Goals on the Formation of Price Image,"*Journal of Marketing Research,* February 2010; Meyvis, Tom, Kelly Goldsmith, and Ravi Dhar, "The Importance of the Context in Brand Extension: How Pictures and Comparisons Shift Consumers' Focus from Fit to Quality," *Journal of Marketing Research,* April 2012; Franziska Vlckner and Henrik Sattler, "Drivers of Brand Extension Success," *Journal of Marketing,* April 2006; Chris Pullig, Carolyn J. Simmons, and Richard G. Netemeyer, "Brand Dilution: When Do New Brands Hurt Existing Brands?" *Journal of Marketing,* April 2006; Thomas J. Madden, Frank Fehle, and Susan Fournier, "Brands Matter: An Empirical Demonstration of the Creation of Shareholder Value Through Branding," *Journal of the Academy of Marketing Science,* Spring 2006; Thomas J. Reynolds and Carol B. Phillips, "In Search of True Brand Equity Metrics: All Market Share Ain't Created Equal," *Journal of Advertising Research,* June 2005; For more on brand equity and brand value, see Stahl, Florian, Mark Heitmann, Donald R Lehmann, and Scott A Neslin, "The Impact of Brand Equity on Customer Acquisition, Retention, and Profit Margin," *Journal of Marketing,*

July 2012; Fischer, Marc, Franziska Völckner, and Henrik Sattler, "How Important Are Brands? A Cross-Category, Cross-Country Study," *Journal of Marketing Research*, October 2010; Batra, Rajeev, Aaron Ahuvia, and Richard P Bagozzi, "Brand Love," *Journal of Marketing*, March 2010; J. J. Brakus, B. H. Schmitt, and L. Zarantonello, "Brand Experience: What Is It? How Is It Measured? Does It Affect Loyalty?" *Journal of Marketing*, #3, 2009; D. E. Boyd and K. D. Bahn, "When Do Large Product Assortments Benefit Consumers? An Information-Processing Perspective," *Journal of Retailing*, #3, 2009; R. J. Slotegraaf and K. Pauwels, "The Impact of Brand Equity and Innovation on the Long-Term Effectiveness of Promotions," *Journal of Marketing Research*, (3) 2008; "Built for the Long Haul," *BusinessWeek*, January 30, 2006; "Ranking Corporate Reputations," *Wall Street Journal*, December 6, 2005; "Hershey's Trumps Donald, McDonald's, and Martha," *Brandweek*, November 28, 2005; "High Tech High Loyalty," *Brandweek*, October 31, 2005, pp. 22–24; "Welch's Juices Equity with Fresh-Fruit Line," *Brandweek*, August 22, 2005; "Tech Sector Ponders: What's in a Name?" *Advertising Age*, May 9, 2005; "The New Science of Naming," *Business 2.0*, December 2004. See also Arjun Chaudhuri and Morris B. Holbrook, "The Chain of Effects from Brand Trust and Brand Affect to Brand Performance: the Role of Brand Loyalty," *Journal of Marketing*, April 2001; Russell Casey, "Designing Brand Identity: A Complete Guide to Creating, Building, and Maintaining Strong Brands," *Journal of the Academy of Marketing Science*, Winter 2004; Subramanian Balachander and Sanjoy Ghose, "Reciprocal Spillover Effects: a Strategic Benefit of Brand Extensions," *Journal of Marketing*, January 2003; Elizabeth S. Moore, William L. Wilkie, and Richard J. Lutz, "Passing the Torch: Intergenerational Influences as a Source of Brand Equity," *Journal of Marketing*, April 2002.

6. "What's New with the Chinese Consumer," *McKinsey Quarterly*, October 2008; R. Ahluwalia, "How Far Can a Brand Stretch? Understanding the Role of Self-Construal," *Journal of Marketing Research* 3, 2008.

7. "Rocking the Most Hated Brand in America," *Fast Company*, July/August 2011.

8. See www.hermanmiller.com; "Health Care Takes the Stage," *Fast Company*, May 2010. See also Peter Lawrence and Leigh McAllister, "Marketing Meets Design: Core Necessities for Successful New Product Development," *Journal of Product Innovation Management*, March 2005; Helen Perks, Rachel Cooper, and Cassie Jones, "Characterizing the Role of Design in New Product Development: An Empirically Derived Taxonomy," *Journal of Product Innovation Management*, March 2005; K. Scott Swan, Masaaki Kotabe, and Brent B. Allred, "Exploring Robust Design Capabilities, Their Role in Creating Global Products, and Their Relationship to Firm Performance," *Journal of Product Innovation Management*, March 2005; Lan Luo; Kannan, Babak Besharati, and Shapour Azarm, "Design of Robust New Products under Variability: Marketing Meets Design," *Journal of Product Innovation Management*, March 2005; M. Antioco, R. K. Monaert, R. A. Feinberg, & M. G. M. Wetzels, "Integrating Service and Design: The Influences of Organizational and Communication Factors on Relative Product and Service Characteristics," *Journal of the Academy of Marketing Science*, #4, 2008.

9. "He Really Rolls in the Dough," *Investor's Business Daily*, January 26, 2010; "Rising Dough," *Fast Company*, October 2009; "Slicing the Bread but Not the Prices," *Wall Street Journal*, August 18, 2009; "Panera Bakes a Recipe for Success," *USA Today*, July 23, 2009.

10. Argo, Jennifer J., Monica Popa, and Malcolm C. Smith, "The Sound of Brands," *Journal of Marketing*, 74, 4; "IKEA's Products Make Shoppers Blush in Thailand," *Wall Street Journal*, June 5, 2012; "Lost in Translation," *Business 2.0*, August 2004; "Global Products Require Name-Finders," *Wall Street Journal*, April 11, 1996; Martin S. Roth, "Effects of Global Market Conditions on Brand Image Customization and Brand Performance," *Journal of Advertising*, Winter 1995.

11. Samuel M. McClure, Jian Li, Damon Tomlin, Kim S. Cypert, Latané M. Montague, and P. Read Montague (2004). "Neural Correlates of Behavioral Preference for Culturally Familiar Drinks," *Neuron* 44, 2.

12. "McCurry Wins Big McAttack in Malaysia," *Wall Street Journal*, September 9, 2009; "Hey, That Nutrasweet Looks Like Splenda," *Advertising Age*, May 19, 2008; "TiVo's Time Ticks Away, DirecTV Programs Attack," *Brandweek*, October 10, 2005; "Road to Foreign Franchises Is Paved with New Problems," *Wall Street Journal*, May 14, 2001; "Tiger Fight Sees Kellogg, ExxonMobil Clash in Court," *Ad Age Global*, November 2000; "Wrestling, Wildlife Fund Battle over WWF Site," *USA Today*, October 25, 2000; "More Firms Flash New Badge," *USA Today*, October 4, 2000; "Name Lawsuit Prompts AppleSoup to Become Flycode," *USA Today*, September 11, 2000. See also Karen Gantt, "Revisiting the Scope of Lanham Act Protection," *Journal of the Academy of Marketing Science*, Winter 2004; Maureen Morrin and Jacob Jacoby, "Trademark Dilution: Empirical Measures for an Elusive Concept," *Journal of Public Policy & Marketing*, Fall 2000; F. C. Hong, Anthony Pecotich, and Clifford J. Schultz II, "Brand Name Translation: Language Constraints, Product Attributes, and Consumer Perceptions in East and Southeast Asia," *Journal of International Marketing*, #2 (2002); Lee B. Burgunder, "Trademark Protection of Product Characteristics: A Predictive Model," *Journal of Public Policy & Marketing*, Fall 1997.

13. For more on piracy, see "Raids Crack Down on Fake Goods," *USA Today*, December 18, 2009; "HP Declares War on Counterfeiters," *BusinessWeek*, June 8, 2009; "EBay Fined Over Selling Counterfeits," *Wall Street Journal*, July 1, 2008; "The Economic Effect of Counterfeiting and Piracy," Executive Summary, Organization for Economic Co-Operation and Development, 2007; Ashutosh Prasad and Vijay Mahajan, "How Many Pirates Should a Software Firm Tolerate?: An Analysis of Piracy Protection on the Diffusion of Software," *International Journal of Research in Marketing*, December 2003;. See also K. H. Wilcox, M. Kim, and S. Sen, "Why Do Consumers Buy Counterfeit Luxury Brands?" *Journal of Marketing Research*, (2) 2009; Laurence Jacobs, A. Coskun Samli, and Tom Jedlik, "The Nightmare of International Product Piracy: Exploring Defensive Strategies," *Industrial Marketing Management*, August 2001; Janeen E. Olsen and Kent L. Granzin, "Using Channels Constructs to Explain Dealers' Willingness to Help Manufacturers Combat Counterfeiting," *Journal of Business Research*, June 1993.

14. For more on licensing, see "The Final Frontier for Licensors," *Brandweek*, June 9, 2008; "The Power Behind J. D. Power," *Investor's Business Daily*, July 17, 2007; "Licensing Life," *Brandweek*, June 11, 2007; "Food Marketers Hope Veggies Look Fun to Kids," *USA Today*, July 15, 2005; "Testing Limits of Licensing: SpongeBob-Motif Holiday Inn," *Wall Street Journal*, October 9, 2003; "Making Tracks beyond Tires," *Brandweek*, September 15, 2003; "Candy Cosmetics: Licensing's Sweet Spot," *DSN Retailing Today*, August 4, 2003; "The Creative License," *Brandweek*, June 9, 2003; "Procter & Gamble Deals License Several Brand Names," *USA Today*, April 18, 2003.

15. For more on branding organic products, see "When Buying Organic Makes Sense—and When It Doesn't," *Wall Street Journal*, January 26, 2006; "The Organic Myth," *BusinessWeek*, October 16, 2006; "Private Food Labels also Seeking Organic Growth," *Brandweek*, November 7, 2005; "Soap Can Proudly Display Certified 'Organic' Label," *USA Today*, August 25, 2005; "Health-Food Maker Hain Faces Rivals," *Wall Street Journal*, August 13, 2003; "Big Brand Logos Pop Up in Organic Aisle," *Wall Street Journal*, July 29, 2003; "USDA Enters Debate on Organic Label Law," *New York Times*, February 26, 2003; "Food Industry Gags at Proposed Label Rule for Trans Fat," *Wall Street Journal*, December 27, 2002; "Curbs Are Eased on Food Makers' Health Claims," *Wall Street Journal*, December 19, 2002; "In Natural Foods, a Big Name's No Big Help," *Wall Street Journal*, June 7, 2002. See also Amitabh Mungale, "Managing Product Families," *Journal of Product Innovation Management*, January 1998; Gloria Barczak, "Product Management," *Journal of Product Innovation Management*, September 1997.

16. S. Chan Choi and Anne T. Coughlan, "Private Label Positioning: Quality versus Feature Differentiation from the National Brand," *Journal of Retailing*, June 2006; David E. Sprott and Terence A. Shimp, "Using Product Sampling to Augment the Perceived Quality of Store Brands," *Journal of Retailing*, Winter 2004.

17. "Store Brands Step Up Their Game, and Prices," *Wall Street Journal*, January 31, 2012; "Why Grocers Are Boosting Private Labels," *Bloomberg Businessweek*, November 23, 2011; "Consumers Praise Store

Brands," *Brandweek,* April 8, 2010; "Safeway Cultivates Its Private Labels as Brands to Be Sold by Other Chains," *Wall Street Journal,* May 7, 2009; "P&G, Colgate Hit by Consumer Thrift," *Wall Street Journal,* May 1, 2009; "How P&G Plans to Clean Up," *BusinessWeek,* April 13, 2009; "Store Brands Squeeze Major Food Makers," *Wall Street Journal,* March 27, 2009; "Private Label Winning Battle of Brands," *Advertising Age,* February 23, 2009; "P&G, Others Are Confident Higher Prices Will Stick," *Wall Street Journal,* February 20, 2009; "Brand-Name Food Makers, Private Labels Share Stage," *Wall Street Journal,* February 18, 2009; "Store Brands Lift Grocers in Troubled Times," *New York Times,* December 13, 2008; "Rise of Private-Label Products Gives Retailers Clout," *Wall Street Journal,* December 3, 2008. See also Geyskens, Inge, Katrijn Gielens, and Els Gijsbrechts, "Proliferating Private-Label Portfolios: How Introducing Economy and Premium Private Labels Influences Brand Choice,"*Journal of Marketing Research,* October 2010; Jack (Xinlei), Chen, Om Narasimhan, George John, and Tirtha Dhar, "An Empirical Investigation of Private Label Supply by National Label Producers," *Marketing Science,* # 4, 2010; Erdem, Tülin, and Sue Chang, "A cross-category and cross-country analysis of umbrella branding for national and store brands," *Journal of the Academy of Marketing Science,* January 2012; Steenkamp, Jan-Benedict E.M, Harald J Van Heerde, and Inge Geyskens, "What Makes Consumers Willing to Pay a Price Premium for National Brands over Private Labels?,"*Journal of Marketing Research,* December 2010; Maureen Morrin, Jonathan Lee, and Greg M. Allenby, "Determinants of Trademark Dilution," *Journal of Consumer Research,* August 2006; Bart J. Bronnenberg, Sanjay K. Dhar, and Jean-Pierre Dub, "Consumer Packaged Goods in the United States: National Brands, Local Branding," *Journal of Marketing Research,* February 2007; Donna F. Davis, Susan L. Golicic, and Adam J. Marquardt, "Branding a B2B Service: Does a Brand Differentiate a Logistics Service Provider?" *Industrial Marketing Management,* February 2008.

18. "Coke, Pepsi, A-B Attracted to Metal," *Brandweek,* December 17, 2007; "Can Wine in a Sippy Box Lure Back French Drinkers," *Wall Street Journal,* August 24, 2007; "As Costs Rise, Whirlpool Makes a Dent in Dings," *Wall Street Journal,* July 30, 2007; See also Brian Wansink and Koert van Ittersum, "Bottoms Up! The Influence of Elongation on Pouring and Consumption Volume," *Journal of Consumer Research,* December 2003; U. R. Orth and K. Malkewitz, "Holistic Package Design and Consumer Brand Impressions," *Journal of Marketing,* #3, 2008.

19. "Green Packaging: Waste Not, Want Not," *Inbound Logistics,* July 2008.

20. For more on food labeling, see "The Whole Truth about Whole Grain," *Wall Street Journal,* February 16, 2006; "Major Changes Set for Food Labels," *Wall Street Journal,* December 28, 2005; "FDA Says Food Labels Can Tout Tomatoes' Benefits on Cancer," *Wall Street Journal,* November 10, 2005; "Read It and Weep? Big Mac Wrapper to Show Fat, Calories," *Wall Street Journal,* October 26, 2005; "FDA Re-examines 'Serving Sizes,' May Change Misleading Labels," *Wall Street Journal,* November 20, 2003; "A 'Fat-Free' Product That's 100% Fat: How Food Labels Legally Mislead," *Wall Street Journal,* July 15, 2003. See also Lauren G. Block and Laura A. Peracchio, "The Calcium Quandary: How Consumers Use Nutrition Labels," *Journal of Public Policy & Marketing,* Fall 2006; Siva K. Balasubramanian and Catherine Cole, "Consumers' Search and Use of Nutrition Information: the Challenge and Promise of the Nutrition Labeling and Education Act," *Journal of Marketing,* July 2002; Bruce A. Silverglade, "The Nutrition Labeling and Education Act—Progress to Date and Challenges for the Future," *Journal of Public Policy & Marketing,* Spring 1996; Sandra J. Burke, Sandra J. Milberg, and Wendy W. Moe, "Displaying Common but Previously Neglected Health Claims on Product Labels: Understanding Competitive Advantages, Deception, and Education," *Journal of Public Policy & Marketing,* Fall 1997; Christine Moorman, "A Quasi Experiment to Assess the Consumer and Informational Determinants of Nutrition Information Processing Activities: The Case of the Nutrition Labeling and Education Act," *Journal of Public Policy & Marketing,* Spring 1996.

21. For more on package volume, see "Products Shrink but Prices Don't," *USA Today,* June 12, 2008; "Pay the Same, Get Less as Package Volume Falls," *USA Today,* March 17, 2003; "Taking the Value Out of Value-Sized," *Wall Street Journal,* August 14, 2002; "Critics Call Cuts in Package Size Deceptive Move," *Wall Street Journal,* February 5, 1991. For more on food claims, see R. Brennan, B/Czarnecka, S. Dahl, L. Eagle & O. Mourouti, "Regulation of Nutrition and Health Claims in Advertising," *Journal of Advertising Research,* #1, 2008;; Paula Fitzgerald, Bone Corey, and Robert J. Corey, "Ethical Dilemmas in Packaging: Beliefs of Packaging Professionals," *Journal of Macromarketing,* Spring 1992.

22. For more on Hyundai warranty, see "BMW, Mercedes—and Hyundai?" *BusinessWeek,* December 5, 2005; "Hyundai Makes Safety a Primary Selling Point," *Advertising Age,* May 2, 2005; "Extended Warranty Heats Up Auto Sales," *Advertising Age,* November 1, 2004. For more on warranties and service guarantees, see Chu, Junhong, and Pradeep K Chintagunta, "An Empirical Test of Warranty Theories in the U.S. Computer Server and Automobile Markets," *Journal of Marketing,* March 2011; "Little Tikes Proves Durable with Low-Tech Plastic Toys," *USA Today,* December 15, 2005. See also Monika Kukar-Kinney, Rockney G. Walters, and Scott B. MacKenzie, "Consumer Responses to Characteristics of Price-Matching Guarantees: The Moderating Role of Price Consciousness," *Journal of Retailing,* June 2007; Jennifer Hamilton and Ross D. Petty, "The European Union's Consumer Guarantees Directive," *Journal of Public Policy & Marketing,* Fall 2001; X. L. Chen, G. John, J. M. Hays, A.V. Hill, and S. E. Geurs, "Learning from a Service Guarantee Quasi Experiment," *Journal of Marketing Research,* no 5, 2009.

23. Edward M. Tauber, "Why Do People Shop?" *Journal of Marketing,* October 1972; Christopher H. Lovelock, "Classifying Services to Gain Strategic Marketing Insights," *Journal of Marketing,* Summer 1983; Tom Boyt and Michael Harvey, "Classification of Industrial Services," *Industrial Marketing Management,* July 1997.

24. Dennis W. Rook, "The Buying Impulse," *Journal of Consumer Research,* September 1987; Cathy J. Cobb and Wayne D. Hoyer, "Planned versus Impulse Purchase Behavior," *Journal of Retailing,* Winter 1986.

25. For example, see "Russian Maneuvers Are Making Palladium Ever More Precious," *Wall Street Journal,* March 6, 2000. See also William S. Bishop, John L. Graham, and Michael H. Jones, "Volatility of Derived Demand in Industrial Markets and Its Management Implications," *Journal of Marketing,* Fall 1984.

26. William B. Wagner and Patricia K. Hall, "Equipment Lease Accounting in Industrial Marketing Strategy," *Industrial Marketing Management* 20, #4, *1991;* Robert S. Eckley, "Caterpillar's Ordeal: Foreign Competition in Capital Goods," *Business Horizons,* March–April 1989; M. Manley, "To Buy or Not to Buy," *Inc.,* November 1987.

27. P. Matthyssens and W. Faes, "OEM Buying Process for New Components: Purchasing and Marketing Implications," *Industrial Marketing Management,* August 1985; Paul A. Herbig and Frederick Palumbo, "Serving the Aftermarket in Japan and the United States," *Industrial Marketing Management,* November 1993.

28. Ruth H. Krieger and Jack R. Meredith, "Emergency and Routine MRO Part Buying," *Industrial Marketing Management,* November 1985; Warren A. French, et al., "MRO Parts Service in the Machine Tool Industry," *Industrial Marketing Management,* November 1985. See also "The Web's New Plumbers," *Ecompany,* March 2001.

CHAPTER 9

1. See www.irobot.com; "For iRobot the Future is Getting Closer," *New York Times,* March 3, 2012; "In the Afgan War, a Little Robot Can Be a Soldier's Best Friend," *Wall Street Journal,* June 13, 2012; "Exploring the oceans: Fleets of robot submarines will change oceanography," *Economist,* June 9, 2012; "Where Humans Fear to Tread," *Wall Street Journal,* April 18, 2011; "Service Robots: The Rise of Machines (Again)," March 3, 2011; "The Future is Automated," *Canadian Business,* March 14, 2011; "The *Wired* Interview: iRobot CEO Colin Angle," *Wired.com,* October 23, 2010; "TR50 2010: The World's Most Innovative Companies," *Technology Review,* February 10, 2010; "The Robot Revolution May Finally Be Here," *US News & World Report,* April 9, 2008; "2008

CRM Service Awards: Elite—iRobot," CRM Magazine, April 2008; "IRobot," *Fast Company,* March 2008; "IRobot Boots Up 2 New Models," *Investor's Business Daily,* September 28, 2007; "IRobot's Military Business on a Roll," *Investor's Business Daily,* August 22, 2007; "Maker Eyes Mainstream with Its Cleanup Robot," *Investor's Business Daily,* August 22, 2007; "Cleaning Up with Customer Evangelists," *BtoB,* August 13, 2007; "Keep Up with the Jetsons: iRobot's New Scooba," *Fortune,* February 20, 2006; "Robotic Orb Can Scrubba, Dub, Dub," *Raleigh News and Observer,* December 25, 2005; "What Can Scooba Do? Wash the Floor for You," *USA Today,* December 8, 2005; "A Robot That Could Hit the Wall," *BusinessWeek* Online, September 5, 2005; "Death to Cool . . . iRobot," *Inc.,* July 2005; "How the Roomba Was Realized," *BusinessWeek,* October 6, 2003.

2. Raquel Castaño, Mita Sujan, Manish Kacker, and Harish Sujan, "Managing Consumer Uncertainty in the Adoption of New Products: Temporal Distance and Mental Simulation," *Journal of Marketing Research,* #3, 2008; Rosanna Garcia, Fleura Bardhi, and Colette Friedrich, "Overcoming Consumer Resistance to Innovation," *Sloan Management Review,* Summer 2007; Shih Chuan-Fong and Alladi Venkatesh, "Beyond Adoption: Development and Application of a Use-Diffusion Model," *Journal of Marketing,* January 2004; Youngme Moon, "Break Free from the Product Life Cycle," *Harvard Business Review,* May 2005; Alina B. Sorescu, Rajesh K. Chandy, and Jaideep C. Prabhu, "Sources and Financial Consequences of Radical Innovation: Insights from Pharmaceuticals," *Journal of Marketing,* October 2003; Christopher M. McDermott and Gina Colarelli O'Connor, "Managing Radical Innovation: An Overview of Emergent Strategy Issues," *Journal of Product Innovation Management,* November 2002; Ronald W. Niedrich and Scott D. Swain, "The Influence of Pioneer Status and Experience Order on Consumer Brand Preference: A Mediated-Effects Model," *Journal of the Academy of Marketing Science,* Fall 2003; Rajesh K. Chandy and Gerard J. Tellis, "The Incumbent's Curse? Incumbency, Size, and Radical Product Innovation," *Journal of Marketing,* July 2000; George Day, "The Product Life Cycle: Analysis and Applications Issues," *Journal of Marketing,* Fall 1981; Igal Ayal, "International Product Life Cycle: A Reassessment and Product Policy Implications," *Journal of Marketing,* Fall 1981.

3. "Soft Drink War Rages in Kenya—But Not Over Cola," *Wall Street Journal,* June 4, 2009.

4. See Jorge Alberto Sousa De Vasconcellos, "Key Success Factors in Marketing Mature Products," *Industrial Marketing Management* 20, #4, *1991;* Paul C. N. Michell, Peter Quinn, and Edward Percival, "Marketing Strategies for Mature Industrial Products," *Industrial Marketing Management* 20, #3, *1991;* Peter N. Golder and Gerard J. Tellis, "Pioneer Advantage: Marketing Logic or Marketing Legend?" *Journal of Marketing Research,* May 1993.

5. "Milk Industry's Pitch in Asia: Try the Ginger or Rose Flavor," *Wall Street Journal,* August 9, 2005.

6. "Video Slips as DVD Market Matures," *USA Today,* January 4, 2006; "DVD's Success Steals the Show," *USA Today,* January 8, 2004; "DVD: It Pays to Spend a Little More," *USA Today,* December 3, 2003; "Backseat Movies: Car DVD Entertainment Systems . . . ," *BusinessWeek,* May 26, 2003; "High-Definition Discs Aim to Outshine DVDs," *Investor's Business Daily,* May 6, 2003.

7. For another example involving the portable digital music market, see "An iPod Casualty: The Rio Digital-Music Player," *Wall Street Journal,* September 1, 2005; "When Being First Doesn't Make You #1," *Wall Street Journal,* August 12, 2004. See also Sungwook Min, Manohar U. Kalwani, and William T. Robinson, "Market Pioneer and Early Follower Survival Risks: A Contingency Analysis of Really New versus Incrementally New Product-Markets," *Journal of Marketing,* January 2006; W. Boulding and M. Christen, "Disentangling Pioneering Cost Advantages and Disadvantages," *Marketing Science,* #4, 2008, see also footnotes 4 and 9 from this chapter.

8. For more on Zara, see www.zara.com, "Zara Is to Get Big Online Push," *Wall Street Journal,* September 17, 2009; "Zara Grows as Retail Rivals Struggle," *Wall Street Journal,* March 26, 2009; "Pace-Setting Zara Seeks More Speed to Fight Its Rising Cheap-Chic Rivals," *Wall Street Journal,* February 20, 2008; "The Old World's New Vigor," *BusinessWeek,* May 14, 2007; "Solid Foundation Braces Spain," *Wall Street Journal,* January 31, 2007; "Fashion Conquistador," *BusinessWeek,* September 4, 2006; "Respond to Trends Early or Miss the Opportunity," *Investor's Business Daily,* July 25, 2005; "At Gucci, Mr. Polet's New Design Upends Rules for High Fashion," *Wall Street Journal,* August 9, 2005; "Making Fashion Faster," *Wall Street Journal,* February 24, 2004; "Just-in-Time Fashion," *Wall Street Journal,* May 18, 2001; "Zara Has a Made-to-Order Plan for Success," *Fortune,* September 4, 2000.

9. "The Problem with Being a Trendsetter," *Wall Street Journal,* April 29, 2010; "Forget Fleece? Wool Makes a Comeback," *Wall Street Journal,* November 28, 2009; "Cheap and Trendy Gains as Luxury Fades in Japan," *Wall Street Journal,* November 10, 2009; "Life after Lasik: A Clear-Eyed Urge to Wear Glasses, Specs Are Looking Hot on Runway Models," *Wall Street Journal,* April 26, 2008; "Put a Patent on That Pleat," *BusinessWeek,* March 31, 2008; "Runway to Rack: Finding Looks that Will Sell," *Wall Street Journal,* March 6, 2008; "Work Wear: Designers Who Get It," *Wall Street Journal,* February 14, 2008; "How Fashion Makes Its Way from the Runway to the Rack," *Wall Street Journal,* February 8, 2007; "Men Say Bling It On," *Wall Street Journal,* November 30, 2005. See also Craig J. Thompson and Diana L. Haytko, "Speaking of Fashion: Consumers' Uses of Fashion Discourses and the Appropriation of Countervailing Cultural Meanings," *Journal of Consumer Research,* June 1997.

10. 2010 Annual Report, RJR Nabisco; "Oreo, Ritz Join Nabisco's Low-Fat Feast," *Advertising Age,* April 4, 1994; "They're Not Crying in Their Crackers at Nabisco," *BusinessWeek,* August 30, 1993; "Nabisco Unleashes a New Batch of Teddies," *Adweek*'s Marketing Week, September 24, 1990.

11. "Going Global by Going Green," *Wall Street Journal,* February 26, 2008.

12. For more on Tide, see 2012 Annual Report, Procter & Gamble; "Marketer of the Year: Team Tide," *Next,* September 14, 2009; "Tide Turns 'Basic' for P&G in Slump," *Wall Street Journal,* August 6, 2009; "Why We Will Remember Tide Thursday," *Advertising Age,* May 25, 2009; "Tide, Woolite Tout Their Fashion Sense," *Wall Street Journal,* March 11, 2009; "P&G's Chemistry Test," *Fast Company,* July/August 2008; "The Endurance Test," *Advertising Age,* November 14, 2005, pp. 3, 38–39; "Testing New-Style Stain Removers," *Wall Street Journal,* July 5, 2005; "Life on the Go Means Eating on the Run, and a Lot of Spilling," *Wall Street Journal,* June 7, 2005; "Detergent Tablets of the '70s Make a Comeback," *USA Today,* July 27, 2000.

13. "Making Old Brands New," *American Demographics,* December 1997; "At DuPont, Time to Both Sow and Reap," *BusinessWeek,* September 29, 1997; "A Boring Brand Can Be Beautiful," *Fortune,* November 18, 1991; "Teflon Is 50 Years Old, but DuPont Is Still Finding New Uses for Invention," *Wall Street Journal,* April 7, 1988; Stephen W. Miller, "Managing Imitation Strategies: How Later Entrants Seize Markets from Pioneers," *Journal of the Academy of Marketing Science,* Summer 1996.

14. "Philly Cream Cheese's Spreading Appeal," *Bloomberg Businessweek,* December 8, 2011.

15. C. Christenson, *The Innovator's Dilemma,* 1997; C. Christenson and M. Overdorf, "Meeting the Challenge of Disruptive Change," *Harvard Business Review,* March-April 2000; S. D. Anthony, M. W. Johnson, J.V Sinfield, and E. J. Altman, *Innovator's Giuide to Growth—Putting Disruptive Innovation to Work,* 2008. "Ten for '10: New Gadgets for Home and Away," *Wall Street Journal,* January 7, 2010; "The World's Most Inventive Companies," *BusinessWeek,* December 23, 2009; "Book of Tens," *Advertising Age,* December 14, 2009; for more on ChotuKool see "Clarifying Innovation for Success," *Bloomberg Businessweek,* October 6, 2010; "How can you enter an emerging market—and improve the lives of millions?" Innosight.com, "Cool products for small towns," *The Times of Bangalore,* June 1, 2010; "India's New Retailers," *OutlookBusiness,* July 11, 2009.

16. For more on new-product definition, see "Electronic Code of Federal Regulations: Title 16 (Commercial Practices), Part 502 (Introductory Offers) at http://ecfr.gpoaccess.gov/. For more about types of new products see G. A. Athaide and R. R. Klink, "Managing Seller-Buyer Relationships During New Product Development," *Journal of Product Innovation Management,* #5, 2009; K. Aboulnasr, O. Narashimhan, E. Blair, and R. Chandy, "Competitive Response to Radical Product Innovations," *Journal of Marketing,* #3, 2008; D. L. Alexander, J. G. Lynch, and Q. Wang, "As Time Goes By: Do Cold Feet Follow Warm Intentions for Really New Versus Incrementally New Products?" *Journal of Marketing Research,* #3, 2008.

17. "Reposition: Simplifying the Customer's Brandscape," *Brandweek,* October 2, 2000; "Consumers to GM: You Talking to Me?" *BusinessWeek,* June 19, 2000; "How Growth Destroys Differentiation," *Brandweek,* April 24, 2000; "P&G, Seeing Shoppers Were Being Confused, Overhauls Marketing," *Wall Street Journal,* January 15, 1997.

18. "Ignore the Consumer," *Point,* September 2005; "Too Many Choices," *Wall Street Journal,* April 20, 2001; "New Products," *Ad Age International,* April 13, 1998; "The Ghastliest Product Launches," *Fortune,* March 16, 1998; "Flops: Too Many New Products Fail. Here's Why—and How to Do Better," *BusinessWeek,* August 16, 1993; Brian D. Ottum and William L. Moore, "The Role of Market Information in New Product Success/Failure," *Journal of Product Innovation Management,* July 1997; E. Ofek and O. Turut, "To Innovate or Imitate? Entry Strategy and the Role of Market Research," *Journal of Marketing Research,* #5, 2008.

19. "Flavor Experiment for KitKat Leaves Nestle with a Bad Taste," *Wall Street Journal,* July 6, 2006; "Makers of Chicken Tonight Find Many Cooks Say, 'Not Tonight,'" *Wall Street Journal,* May 17, 1994; "Failure of Its Oven Lovin' Cookie Dough Shows Pillsbury Pitfalls of New Products," *Wall Street Journal,* June 17, 1993; Sharad Sarin and Gour M. Kapur, "Lessons from New Product Failures: Five Case Studies," *Industrial Marketing Management,* November 1990.

20. "Design Software Helps Give Life to ZMP's Robots," *Investor's Business Daily,* August 9, 2005; "This Is Not a BMW Plant," *Fortune,* April 18, 2005; "Helping Designers Go Digital," *Investor's Business Daily,* January 24, 2005. See also Muammer Ozer, "Process Implications of the Use of the Internet in New Product Development: a Conceptual Analysis," *Industrial Marketing Management,* August 2003; J. Daniel Sherman, William E. Souder, and Svenn A. Jenssen, "Differential Effects of the Primary Forms of Cross Functional Integration on Product Development Cycle Time," The *Journal of Product Innovation Management,* July 2000; Daniel J. Flint, "Compressing New Product Success-to-Success Cycle Time: Deep Customer Value Understanding and Idea Generation," *Industrial Marketing Management,* July 2002.

21. This box was inspired by a TEDxBozeman talk by Professor Jakki Mohr, "Biomimicry: Business Innovations Inspired by Nature," "Biomimicry," *Wikipedia,* (accessed July 2012);"15 Coolest Cases of Biomimicry," *Brainz,* For more on other forms of idea generation, see: "Pipe Up, People! Rounding Up Staff Ideas," *Inc.,* February 2010; "Twitter Serves Up New Ideas from Its Followers," *New York Times,* October 25, 2009; "Where Do the Best Ideas Come From? The Unlikeliest Sources," *Advertising Age,* July 14, 2008; "The Customer Is the Company: Threadless," *Inc.,* June 2008; "Breakthrough Thinking from Inside the Box," *Harvard Business Review,* December 2007; "Let Consumers Control More than Just Ads," *Advertising Age,* April 9, 2007; "Turn Customer Input into Innovation," *Harvard Business Review,* January 2002; Judy A. Siguaw, Penny M. Simpson, and Cathy A. Enz, "Conceptualizing Innovation Orientation: A Framework for Study and Integration of Innovation Research," *Journal of Product Innovation Management,* November 2006; V. Blazevic and A. Lievens, "Managing Innovation through Customer Coproduced Knowledge in Electronic Services: An Exploratory Study," *Journal of the Academy of Marketing Science,* #1, 2008.

22. Martin Schreier and Reinhard Prugl, "Extending Lead-User Theory: Antecedents and Consequences of Consumers' Lead Userness," *Journal of Product Innovation Management,* July 2008; Lance A. Bettencourt and Anthony W. Ulwick, "The Customer-Centered Innovation Map," *Harvard Business Review,* May 2008; "Mosh Pits of Creativity," *BusinessWeek,* November 7, 2005; "Employers See Gold Mining Employees for Ideas," *Brandweek,* October 10, 2005 "It Was a Hit in Buenos Aires—So Why Not Boise?" *BusinessWeek,* September 7, 1998. See also Rudy K. Moenaert, Filip Caeldries, Annouk Lievens, and Elke Wauters, "Communication Flows in International Product Innovation Teams," *Journal of Product Innovation Management,* September 2000; Vittorio Chiesa, "Global R&D Project Management and Organization: a Taxonomy," *Journal of Product Innovation Management,* September 2000; John J. Cristiano, Jeffrey K. Liker, and Chelsea C. White III, "Customer-Driven Product Development Through Quality Function Deployment in the U.S. and Japan," *Journal of Product Innovation Management,* July 2000; Lisa C. Troy, David M. Szymanskis, and P. Rajan Varadarajan, "Generating New Product Ideas: an Initial Investigation of the Role of Market Information and Organizational Characteristics," *Journal of the Academy of Marketing Science,* Winter 2001; X. M. Song and Mitzi M. Montoya-Weiss, "Critical Development Activities for Really New versus Incremental Products," *Journal of Product Innovation Management,* March 1998.

23. P. N. Bloom, G. T. Gundlach, and J. P. Cannon, "Slotting Allowances and Fees: Schools of Thought and the Views of Practicing Managers," *Journal of Marketing,* April 2000; "Shielding the Shield Makers," *Wall Street Journal,* November 26, 2003; "Gun Makers to Push Use of Gun Locks," *Wall Street Journal,* May 9, 2001; Jennifer J. Argo and Kelley J. Main, "MetaAnalyses of the Effectiveness of Warning Labels," *Journal of Public Policy & Marketing,* Fall 2004.

24. "Want Shelf Space at the Supermarket? Ante Up," *BusinessWeek,* August 7, 1989; "Grocer 'Fee' Hampers New-Product Launches," *Advertising Age,* August 3, 1987.

25. Susumu Ogawa and Frank T. Piller, "Reducing the Risks of New Product Development," *Sloan Management Review,* Winter 2006; Joseph M. Bonner, Robert W. Ruekert, and Orville C. Walker, Jr., "Upper Management Control of New Product Development Projects and Project Performance," *Journal of Product Innovation Management,* May 2002; Sundar Bharadwaj and Anil Menon, "Making Innovations Happen in Organizations: Individual Creativity Mechanisms, Organizational Creativity Mechanisms or Both?" *Journal of Product Innovation Management,* November 2000; Paul S. Adler, Avi Mandelbaum, Vien Nguyen, and Elizabeth Schwerer, "Getting the Most Out of Your Product Development Process," *Harvard Business Review,* March–April 1996.

26. C. K. Chua, K. F. Leong, and C. S. Lim, *Rapid Prototyping: Principles and Applications,* 2010; Lledtka, Jeanne, "Learning to use design thinking tools for successful innovation," *Strategy & Leadership,* #5, 2011; T. Brown, "Design Thinking," *Harvard Business Review,* June 2008; T. Brown, *Change by Design: How Design Thinking Transforms Organizations and Inspires Innovation,* 2009; see also www.ideo.com.

27. "Torture Testing," *Fortune,* October 2, 2000; "Industry's Amazing New Instant Prototypes," *Fortune,* January 12, 1998; "Secrets of Product Testing," *Fortune,* November 28, 1994; "A Smarter Way to Manufacture," *BusinessWeek,* April 30, 1990.

28. "Oops! Marketers Blunder Their Way Through the 'Herb Decade,'" *Advertising Age,* February 13, 1989.

29. Burroughs, James E, Darren W Dahl, C. Page Moreau, Amitava Chattopadhyay, and Gerald J Gorn, "Facilitating and Rewarding Creativity During New Product Development,"*Journal of Marketing,* November 2011; Hoffman, Donna L, Praveen K Kopalle, and Thomas P Novak, "The 'Right' Consumers for Better Concepts: Identifying Consumers High in Emergent Nature to Develop New Product Concepts,"*Journal of Marketing Research,* October 2010; Chan, Kimmy Wa, Chi Kin (Bennett) Yim, and Simon S.K Lam, "Is Customer Participation in Value Creation a Double-Edged Sword? Evidence from Professional Financial Services Across Cultures,"*Journal of Marketing;* May 2010; Joshi, Ashwin W, "Salesperson Influence on Product Development: Insights from a Study of Small Manufacturing Organizations,"*Journal of Marketing* 74, no. 1: 94-107; Slotegraaf, Rebecca J, and Kwaku Atuahene-Gima, "Product Development Team Stability and New Product Advantage: The Role of Decision-Making Processes,"*Journal of Marketing,* January 2011; Sethi, Rajesh, Zafar Iqbal, and Anju Sethi, "Developing New-to-the-Firm Products: The Role of Micropolitical Strategies,"*Journal of Marketing,* March 2012; Jhang, Ji

Hoon, Susan Jung Grant, and Margaret C Campbell, "Get It?? Got It. Good! Enhancing New Product Acceptance by Facilitating Resolution of Extreme Incongruity,"*Journal of Marketing Research,* April 2012; L. C. Troy, T. Hirunyawipada, and A. K. Paswan, "Cross-Functional Integration and New Product Success: An Empirical Investigation of the Findings," *Journal of Marketing,* #6, 2008; Albert L. Page and Gary R. Schirr, "Growth and Development of a Body of Knowledge: 16 Years of New Product Development Research, 1989–2004," *Journal of Product Innovation Management,* May 2008; Gloria Barczak, Kenneth B. Kahn, and Roberta Moss, "An Exploratory Investigation of NPD Practices in Nonprofit Organizations," *Journal of Product Innovation Management,* November 2006; Kwaku Atuahene-Gima and Janet Y. Murray, "Exploratory and Exploitative Learning in New Product Development: A Social Capital Perspective on New Technology Ventures in China," *Journal of International Marketing,* #2, 2007; Khaled Aboulnasr, Om Narasimhan, Edward Blair, and Rajesh Chandy, "Competitive Response to Radical Product Innovations," *Journal of Marketing,* May 2008; Stephen J. Carson, "When to Give Up Control of Outsourced New Product Development," *Journal of Marketing,* January 2007; Subin Im and John P. Workman, Jr., "Market Orientation, Creativity, and New Product Performance in High-Technology Firms," *Journal of Marketing,* April 2004; Steven C. Michael and Tracy Pun Palandjian, "Organizational Learning and New Product Introductions," *Journal of Product Innovation Management,* July 2004; John P. Workman, Jr., "Marketing's Limited Role in New Product Development in One Computer Systems Firm," *Journal of Marketing Research,* November 1993.

30. See www.3m.com; 2010 Annual Report, 3M; "Counterintuitive Discovery of the Month," CopernicusMarketing.com, March 2008; "Scrutinizing Six Sigma," *BusinessWeek,* July 2, 2007; "At 3M, a Struggle between Efficiency and Creativity," *BusinessWeek,* June 2007; "Pushing Past Post-Its by Allowing Top Scientists to Peek over Horizon . . . ," *Business 2.0,* November 2005.

31. "Care, Feeding, and Building of a Billion-Dollar Brand," *Advertising Age,* February 23, 2004; "Brands at Work," *Brandweek,* April 13, 1998; "Auto Marketing & Brand Management," *Advertising Age,* April 6, 1998; "P&G Redefines the Brand Manager," *Advertising Age,* October 13, 1997. See also Sanjay K. Dhar, Stephen J. Hoch, and Nanda Kumar, "Effective Category Management Depends on the Role of the Category," *Journal of Retailing,* Summer 2001; Don Frey, "Learning the Ropes: My Life as a Product Champion," *Harvard Business Review,* September–October 1991; Stephen K. Markham, "New Products Management," *Journal of Product Innovation Management,* July 1997.

32. "Soy Sauce Flavored Kit Kats? In Japan, They're #1," *AdAge.com,* March 4, 2010; "Flavor Experiment for KitKat Leaves Nestlé with a Bad Taste," *Wall Street Journal,* July 6, 2006.

33. See "Hotels Train Employees to Think Fast," *USA Today,* November 29, 2006; "Takin' Off the Ritz—a Tad," *Wall Street Journal,* June 23, 2006; "Hotels Take 'Know Your Customer' to New Level," *Wall Street Journal,* February 7, 2006; "Listener Runner-up: W Hotels," *Fast Company,* October 2005; "Companies Give Front-Line Employees More Power," *USA Today,* June 27, 2005; "Thinking Outside the Cereal Box," *BusinessWeek,* July 28, 2003; "Pentair Fixes Its Own Mess," *Fortune,* September 30, 2002; "Glass Act: How a Window Maker Rebuilt Itself," *Fortune,* November 13, 2000. See also Douglas W. Vorhies and Neil A. Morgan, "Benchmarking Marketing Capabilities for Sustainable Competitive Advantage," *Journal of Marketing,* January 2005; Roland T. Rust, Tim Ambler, Gregory S. Carpenter, V. Kumar, and Rajendra K. Srivastava, "Measuring Marketing Productivity: Current Knowledge and Future Directions," *Journal of Marketing,* October 2004; Roland T. Rust, Anthony J. Zahorik, and Timothy L. Keiningham, Return on Quality (Chicago: Probus, 1994); J. J. Cronin and Steven A. Taylor, "SERVPERF versus SERVQUAL: Reconciling Performance-Based and Perceptions-Minus-Expectations Measurement of Service Quality," *Journal of Marketing,* January 1994; Shirley Taylor, "Waiting for Service: The Relationship Between Delays and Evaluations of Service," *Journal of Marketing,* April 1994; Mary J. Bitner, Bernard H. Booms, and Lois A. Mohr, "Critical Service Encounters: The Employee's Viewpoint," *Journal of Marketing,* October 1994.

34. For more on quality management and control, see Roland T. Rust, Anthony J. Zahorik, and Timothy L. Keiningham, "Return on Quality (ROQ): Making Service Quality Financially Accountable," *Journal of Marketing,* April 1995. See also Mark R. Colgate and Peter J. Danaher, "Implementing a Customer Relationship Strategy: the Asymetric Impact of Poor versus Excellent Execution," *Journal of the Academy of Marketing Science,* Summer 2000; Simon J. Bell and Bulent Menguc, "The Employee-Organization Relationship, Organizational Citizenship Behaviors, and Superior Service Quality," *Journal of Retailing,* Summer 2002; Pratibha A. Dabholkar, C. David Shepherd, and Dayle I. Thorpe, "A Comprehensive Framework for Service Quality: an Investigation of Critical Conceptual and Measurement Issues Through a Longitudinal Study," *Journal of Retailing,* Summer 2000.

CHAPTER 10

1. See www.dell.com; 2011 Annual Report, Dell; "Dell's Reinvention Efforts Hold Promise," *Wall Street Journal,* February 21, 2012; "Dell Outlook Cloudy," *Wall Street Journal,* November 16, 2011; "PC Makers Ready iPad Rivals," *Wall Street Journal,* February 18, 2011; "Dell's Faith in Business Sales Pays Off," *Wall Street Journal,* February 16, 2011; "Dell Spurs Sales by Lending to Hard-Hit Small Businesses," *Wall Street Journal,* March 30, 2010; "Discounting Continues to Haunt Dell as its Turnaround Struggles," *Wall Street Journal,* February 19, 2010; "Direct Seller Dell Now Offers the Full Middleman Route," *Investor's Business Daily,* April 15, 2009; "Dell to Lift Its Data-Center Game," *Wall Street Journal,* March 25, 2009; "New Dell Notebook Fashion-Model Thin, Unfashionable Price," *Investor's Business Daily,* March 18, 2009; "Former Direct-Only Seller Dell Adds Best Buy," *Investor's Business Daily,* December 7, 2007; "Dell's U.S. Sales Fall, Profits Disappear," *USA Today,* November 30, 2007; "Where Dell Sells with Brick and Mortar," *BusinessWeek,* October 8, 2007; "Direct-Selling PC Specialist Dell Hooks Up with Retailer in China," *Investor's Business Daily,* September 25, 2007; "Dell Pushes Reset Button on Its Image," *Wall Street Journal,* July 10, 2007; "Hmm, Hell Can Freeze Over—Dell to Sell PCs at Retail," *Investor's Business Daily,* May 25, 2007; "Where Dell Went Wrong," *BusinessWeek,* February 19, 2007; "Grudge Match in China," *BusinessWeek,* April 2, 2007; "Can Dell Succeed in an Encore?" *Wall Street Journal,* February 5, 2007; "Consumer Demand and Growth in Laptops Leave Dell Behind," *Wall Street Journal,* August 30, 2006; "Dell May Have to Reboot in China," *BusinessWeek,* November 7, 2005; "Dell Finds Itself in Blog Hell," *BusinessWeek,* September 5, 2005; "The Education of Michael Dell," *Fortune,* March 7, 2005; "What You Don't Know about Dell," *BusinessWeek,* November 3, 2003.

2. For more on Glaceau, see "Are Sodas Losing Their Fizz?" *Investor's Business Daily,* November 19, 2007; "Coke Unit Adds Some Muscle to Water Line," *USA Today,* October 31, 2007; "Coke Plan Riles Glaceau's Old Network," *Wall Street Journal,* September 14, 2007; "Move Over, Coke: How a Small Beverage Maker Managed to Win Shelf Space . . . ," *Wall Street Journal* Reports, January 30, 2006; "Pepsi Picks Water Fight with Surging Glaceau," *Advertising Age,* October 17, 2005.

3. S. Chan Choi, "Expanding to Direct Channel: Market Coverages as Entry Barrier," *Journal of Interactive Marketing,* Winter 2003; David Shipley, Colin Egan, and Scott Edgett, "Meeting Source Selection Criteria: Direct versus Distributor Channels," *Industrial Marketing Management* 20, #4, *1991;* R. E. Bucklin, S. Siddarth, and J. M. Silva-Risso, "Distribution Intensity and New Car Choice," *Journal of Marketing Research,* (4) 2008.

4. For more on Avon, see "Direct Sellers Happy to Toe the Party Line," *Advertising Age,* November 3, 2008; "Lean Times Swell Avon's Sales Force," *Wall Street Journal,* October 15, 2008; "Avon's Calling, but China Opens Door Only a Crack," *Wall Street Journal,* February 26, 2007; "China's New Rules Open Door to Amway, Avon, Others," *USA Today,* December 1, 2005. For other examples of direct channels, see "Amway: Shining Up a Tarnished Name," *BusinessWeek,* August 11, 2008; "Party Time: Home Events See Sales," *USA Today,* October 5, 2005; "Catwalk to Coffee Table," *Wall Street Journal,* November 7, 2003;

"India's Retailing Makeover," *Wall Street Journal,* October 28, 2003. See also Ruud T. Frambach, Henk C. A. Roest, and Trichy V. Krishnan, "The Impact of Consumer Internet Experience on Channel Preference and Usage Intentions across the Different Stages of the Buying Process," *Journal of Interactive Marketing,* Spring 2007.

5. Bob Stone and Ron Jacobs, *Successful Direct Marketing Methods,* New York: McGraw-Hill, 2008.

6. For an example of Levi Strauss's new indirect channels via discount stores, see "Levi's Signature Spreads Its Wings," *DSN Retailing Today,* April 25, 2005; "In Bow to Retailers' New Clout, Levi Strauss Makes Alterations," *Wall Street Journal,* June 17, 2004. For two examples of unsuccessful attempts at indirect channels, see "Ovens Are Cooling at Krispy Kreme as Woes Multiply," *Wall Street Journal,* September 3, 2004; "A Deal with Target Put Lid on Revival at Tupperware," *Wall Street Journal,* February 14, 2004.

7. For a classic discussion of the discrepancy concepts, see Wroe Alderson, "Factors Governing the Development of Marketing Channels," in *Marketing Channels for Manufactured Goods,* ed. Richard M. Clewett (Homewood, IL: Richard D. Irwin, 1954).

8. See hulu.com, "The Future of TV," *Advertising Age,* November 30, 2009; "Searching for Life on Hulu," *AdweekMedia,* May 25, 2009; "Hulu," *Fast Company,* March 2009.

9. For some examples of how channels change to adjust discrepancies, see "Selling Literature Like Dog Food Gives Club Buyer Real Bite," *Wall Street Journal,* April 10, 2002. See also Robert Tamilia, Sylvain Senecal, and Gilles Corriveau, "Conventional Channels of Distribution and Electronic Intermediaries: a Functional Analysis," *Journal of Marketing* Channels, (3, 4) 2002; Robert A. Mittelstaedt and Robert E. Stassen, "Structural Changes in the Phonograph Record Industry and Its Channels of Distribution, 1946–1966," *Journal of Macromarketing,* Spring 1994; Arun Sharma and Luis V. Dominguez, "Channel Evolution: A Framework for Analysis," *Journal of the Academy of Marketing Science,* Winter 1992; A. Ansari, C. F. Mela, and S. A. Neslin, "Customer Channel Migration," *Journal of Marketing Research,* #1, 2008.

10. Arne Nygaard and Robert Dahlstrom, "Role Stress and Effectiveness in Horizontal Alliances," *Journal of Marketing,* April 2002; M. B. Sarkar, Raj Echambadi, S. Tamer Cavusgil, and Preet S. Aulakh, "The Influence of Complementarity, Compatibility, and Relationship Capital on Alliance Performance," *Journal of the Academy of Marketing Science,* Fall 2001; Jakki J. Mohr, Robert J. Fisher, and John R. Nevin, "Collaborative Communication in Interfirm Relationships: Moderating Effects of Integration and Control," *Journal of Marketing,* July 1996; S. Ganesan, M. George, S. Jap, R.W. Palmatier, and B. Weitz, "Supply Chain Management and Retailer Performance: Emerging Trends, Issues, and Implications for Research and Practice," *Journal of Retailing,* #1, 2009.

11. "Gamers Applaud Used Games and Trade-Ins: Paying Less for Their Habit," *Investor's Business Daily,* April 20, 2009; Ode to Joystick: Downloading Titles without Leaving the Sofa," *Wall Street Journal,* February 17, 2009; "Used Games Score Big for GameStop," *Wall Street Journal,* January 21, 2009.

12. Nirmalya Kumar, "Living with Channel Conflict," *CMO,* October 2004. See also Gregory M. Rose and Aviv Shoham, "Interorganizational Task and Emotional Conflict with International Channels of Distribution," *Journal of Business Research,* September 2004.

13. "Thinking Outside the Box: Web TVs Skirt Cable Giants," *Advertising Age,* January 18, 2010; "Honest, Hollywood, Netflix Is Your Friend," *BusinessWeek,* January 11, 2010; "Blockbuster Tries to Recast Itself as More than DVD-Rental Chain," *Wall Street Journal,* December 17, 2009; "Blockbuster Kiosks Take Aim at Redbox's Weak Spots," *Wall Street Journal,* December 1, 2009; "Squeezing Every Dime from DVDs," *BusinessWeek,* October 19, 2009; "Movie Studios Discuss Ways to Rent Films over YouTube," *Wall Street Journal,* September 3, 2009; "Box Tops: Why Redbox Is the Biggest Movie-Rental Company . . . ," *Fast Company,* July/August 2009; "Netflix Boss Plots Life after the DVD," *Wall Street Journal,* June 23, 2009; "Universal Pushes to Disrupt Redbox's Video-Kiosk Sales," *Wall Street Journal,* December 11, 2008; "Netflix Player by Roku Provides Steady Stream of Instant Gratification," *USA Today,* June 5, 2008; "Streaming Movies—from Netflix," *BusinessWeek,* June 2, 2008; LG, Netflix to Offer Downloaded Movies on TV," *Wall Street Journal,* January 3, 2008; "Curtain Falls on Movie Download 1.0," *Investor's Business Daily,* December 12, 2007; Mukherjee, Anirban, and Vrinda Kadiyali, "Modeling Multichannel Home Video Demand in the U.S. Motion Picture Industry," *Journal of Marketing Research,* December 2011.

14. "Get Great Results from Salespeople by Finding What Really Moves Them," *Investor's Business Daily,* July 2, 2001.

15. Shailendra Gajanan, Suman Basuroy, and Srinath Beldona, "Category Management, Product Assortment, and Consumer Welfare," *MarketingLetters,* July 2007; Kenneth H. Wathne and Jan B. Heide, "Relationship Governance in a Supply Chain Network," *Journal of Marketing,* January 2004; David I. Gilliland, "Designing Channel Incentives to Overcome Reseller Rejection," *Industrial Marketing Management,* February 2004; James R. Brown, Anthony T. Cobb and Robert F. Lusch, "The Roles Played by Interorganizational Contracts and Justice in Marketing Channel Relationships," *Journal of Business Research,* February 2006; Keysuk Kim and Changho Oh, "On Distributor Commitment in Marketing Channels for Industrial Products: Contrast Between the United States and Japan," *Journal of International Marketing,* #1 (2002).

16. "Big Grocer Pulls Unilever Items Over Pricing," *Advertising Age,* February 11, 2009; see also: Gooner, Richard A, Neil A Morgan, and William D Perreault, "Is Retail Category Management Worth the Effort (and Does a Category Captain Help or Hinder)?" *Journal of Marketing;* September 2011.

17. See Janice M. Payan and Richard G. McFarland, "Decomposing Influence Strategies: Argument Structure and Dependence as Determinants of the Effectiveness of Influence Strategies in Gaining Channel Member Compliance," *Journal of Marketing,* July 2005; G. Peter Dapiran and Sandra Hogarth-Scott, "Are Co-operation and Trust Being Confused with Power? An Analysis of Food Retailing in Australia and the UK," *International Journal of Retail & Distribution Management,* #4 (2003); David I. Gilliland and Daniel C. Bello, "Two Sides to Attitudinal Commitment: The Effect of Calculative and Loyalty Commitment on Enforcement Mechanisms in Distribution Channels," *Journal of the Academy of Marketing Science,* Winter 2002; Jan B. Heide, "Interorganizational Governance in Marketing Channels," *Journal of Marketing,* January 1994; Jean L. Johnson, et al., "The Exercise of Interfirm Power and Its Repercussions in U.S.-Japanese Channel Relationships," *Journal of Marketing,* April 1993.

18. For some examples of vertical integration, see "Moving On Up: Agricultural Firms Are Looking for New Growth Model . . . Vertical Integration," *Wall Street Journal* Reports, October 25, 2004.

19. "Kimberly-Clark Keeps Costco in Diapers, Absorbing Costs Itself," *Wall Street Journal,* September 7, 2000. For another example, see "Made to Measure: Invisible Supplier Has Penney's Shirts All Buttoned Up," *Wall Street Journal,* September 11, 2003.

20. Gu, Flora F., Namwoon Kim, David K. Tse, and Danny T. Wang, "Managing Distributors' Changing Motivations over the Course of a Joint Sales Program,"*Journal of Marketing,* September 2010; Gilliland, David I., Daniel C. Bello, and Gregory T. Gundlach, "Control-based channel governance and relative dependence,"*Journal of the Academy of Marketing Science,* July 2010; Kashyap, Vishal, Kersi D Antia, and Gary L Frazier, "Contracts, Extracontractual Incentives, and Ex Post Behavior in Franchise Channel Relationships,"*Journal of Marketing Research,* April 2012; Kim, Stephen K, Richard G McFarland, Soongi Kwon, Sanggi Son, and David A Griffith, "Understanding Governance Decisions in a Partially Integrated Channel: A Contingent Alignment Framework,"*Journal of Marketing Research,* May 2011; Kevin L. Webb, "Managing Channels of Distribution in the Age of Electronic Commerce," *Industrial Marketing Management,* February 2002; Charles A. Ingene and Mark E. Parry, "Is Channel Coordination All It Is Cracked up to Be?" *Journal of Retailing,* Winter 2000; Kenneth H. Wathne and Jan B. Heide, "Opportunism in Interfirm Relationships: Forms, Outcomes, and Solutions," *Journal of Marketing,* October 2000; Kersi D. Antia and Gary L. Frazier, "The Severity of Contract Enforcement in Interfirm Channel Relationships," *Journal of Marketing,* October 2001;

Aric Rindfleisch and Jan B. Heide, "Transaction Cost Analysis: Past, Present, and Future Applications," *Journal of Marketing,* October 1997.

21. "A Talk with the Man Who Got Rayovac All Charged Up," *BusinessWeek,* February 21, 2000.

22. See www.esprit.com; "Esprit, a 1980s Fashion Icon, Struggles to Find a U.S. Fit," *Wall Street Journal,* October 28, 2005; "Esprit in the Spirit for Retail Expansion," *Brandweek,* June 20, 2005; "Esprit Tries to Shed Its Youth Image," *Wall Street Journal,* September 3, 2004; "Can Esprit Be Hip Again?" *Wall Street Journal,* June 17, 2002. See also Carol J. Johnson, Robert E. Krapfel, Jr., and Curtis M. Grimm, "A Contingency Model of Supplier-Reseller Satisfaction Perceptions in Distribution Channels," *Journal of Marketing* Channels, (1, 2) 2001; Gary L. Frazier and Walfried M. Lassar, "Determinants of Distribution Intensity," *Journal of Marketing,* October 1996.

23. "Antitrust Issues and Marketing Channel Strategy" and "Case 1—Continental T.V., *Inc.,* et al. v. GTE Sylvania, *Inc.,*" in Louis W. Stern and Thomas L. Eovaldi, Legal Aspects of Marketing Strategy (Englewood Cliffs, NJ: Prentice-Hall, 1984). See also Debra M. Desrochers, Gregory T. Gundlach, and Albert A. Foer, "Analysis of Antitrust Challenges to Category Captain Arrangements," *Journal of Public Policy & Marketing,* Fall 2003. For some examples of exclusive deals, see "Blue Nile: Online Jewelry Seller Looks to Be a Cut Above the Competition," *Investor's Business Daily,* December 15, 2005; "When Exclusivity Means Illegality," *Wall Street Journal,* January 6, 2005; "Bringing Chic to Sheets," *Wall Street Journal,* September 8, 2004.

24. For more on Reebok, see 2010 Annual Report and www.reebok.com; Reebok; "Reebok's Direct Sales Spark a Retail Revolt," *Adweek's* Marketing Week, December 2, 1991. For more on multichannel distribution see Godfrey, Andrea, Kathleen Seiders, and Glenn B Voss, "Enough Is Enough! The Fine Line in Executing Multichannel Relational Communication,"*Journal of Marketing,* July 2011; U. Konus, P. C. Verhoef, and S. A. Neslin, "Multichannel Shopper Segments and Their Covariates," *Journal of Retailing,* #4, 2008; Rajkumar Venkatesan, V. Kumar, and Nalini Ravishanker, "Multichannel Shopping: Causes and Consequences," *Journal of Marketing,* April 2007; Scott A. Neslin, Dhruv Grewal, Robert Leghorn, Venkatesh Shankar, Marije L. Teerling, Jacquelyn S. Thomas, and Peter C. Verhoef, "Challenges and Opportunities in Multichannel Customer Management," *Journal of Service Research,* May 2006; Sertan Kabadayi, Nermin Eyuboglu, and Gloria P. Thomas, "The Performance Implications of Designing Multiple Channels to Fit with Strategy and Environment," *Journal of Marketing,* October 2007; Arun Sharma and Anuj Mehrotra, "Choosing an Optimal Channel Mix in Multichannel Environments," *Industrial Marketing Management,* January 2007; Bert Rosenbloom, "Multi-channel Strategy in Business-to-Business Markets: Prospects and Problems," *Industrial Marketing Management,* January 2007; Asim Ansari, Carl F. Mela, and Scott A. Neslin, "Customer Channel Migration," *Journal of Marketing Research,* February 2008; Jule B. Gassenheimer, Gary L. Hunter, and Judy A. Siguaw, "An Evolving Theory of Hybrid Distribution: Taming a Hostile Supply Network," *Industrial Marketing Management,* May 2007; Peter C. Verhoef, Scott A. Neslin, and Björn Vroomen, "Multichannel Customer Management: Understanding the Research-Shopper Phenomenon," *International Journal of Research in Marketing,* June 2007; Jacquelyn S. Thomas and Ursula Y. Sullivan, "Managing Marketing Communications with Multichannel Customers," *Journal of Marketing,* October 2005.

25. Gregory T. Gundlach and Patrick E. Murphy, "Ethical and Legal Foundations of Relational Marketing Exchanges," *Journal of Marketing,* October 1993; Craig B. Barkacs, "Multilevel Marketing and Antifraud Statutes: Legal Enterprises or Pyramid Schemes?" *Journal of the Academy of Marketing Science,* Spring 1997; Robert A. Robicheaux and James E. Coleman, "The Structure of Marketing Channel Relationships," *Journal of the Academy of Marketing Science,* Winter 1994; Brett A. Boyle and F. Robert Dwyer, "Power, Bureaucracy, Influence and Performance: Their Relationships in Industrial Distribution Channels," *Journal of Business Research,* March 1995.

26. Ofek, Elie, Zsolt Katona, and Miklos Sarvary, "Bricks and Clicks": The Impact of Product Returns on the Strategies of Multichannel Retailers,"*Marketing Science,* # 1, 2011; Shulman, Jeffrey D., Anne T. Coughlan, and R. Canan Savaskan, "Optimal Reverse Channel Structure for Consumer Product Returns,"*Marketing Science,* #6, 2010; J. A. Petersen and V. Kumar, "Are Product Returns a Necessary Evil? Antecedents and Consequences," *Journal of Marketing,* #3, 2009; R. Glenn Richey, Haozhe Chen, Stefan E. Genchev, and Patricia J. Daugherty, "Developing Effective Reverse Logistics Programs," *Industrial Marketing Management,* November 2005; Joseph D. Blackburn, V. Daniel R. Guide, Jr., Gilvan C. Souza, and Luk N. Van Wassenhove, "Reverse Supply Chains for Commercial Returns," *California Management Review,* Winter 2004.

27. "Hyper-Green Products Go Cradle to Cradle," MSNBC.com, October 12, 2007; "Can One Green Deliver the Other," *Harvard Business Review,* 2005; "HP Wants Your Old PCs Back," *BusinessWeek.com,* April 10, 2006.

28. See Rene B. M. de Koster, Marisa P. de Brito, and Masja A. van de Vendel, "Return Handling: An Exploratory Study with Nine Retailer Warehouses," *International Journal of Retail & Distribution Management,* #8 (2002); Chad W. Autry, Patricia J. Daugherty, and R. Glenn Richey, "The Challenge of Reverse Logistics in Catalog Retailing," *International Journal of Physical Distribution & Logistics Management,* #1 (2001); Dale S. Rogers and Ronald TibbenLembke, "An Examination of Reverse Logistics Practices," *Journal of Business Logistics,* #2 2001.

29. "Year of the Grease Monkey in China," Denver Post, April 26, 2009; "Danone Pulls Out of Disputed China Venture," *Wall Street Journal,* October 1, 2009; "Special Report: Gone Global, How to Get Ahead in China," *Inc.,* May 2008; Joseph Johnson and Gerard J. Tellis, "Drivers of Success for Market Entry into China and India," *Journal of Marketing,* May 2008; Morgan, Neil, Constantine Katsikeas, and Douglas Vorhies, "Export marketing strategy implementation, export marketing capabilities, and export venture performance," *Journal of the Academy of Marketing Science,* March 2012;

CHAPTER 11

1. "Drink Dispenser Analytics: Coca-Cola Goes Freestyle, With Help from SAP BI," Business Analytics, June 19, 2009; "What Do You Call a Soda Dispenser With Onboard Data Analytics," Spotfire, Trends and Outliers, October 7, 2010; "Africa: Coke's Last Frontier," *Bloomberg Businessweek,* October 28, 2010; "Eliminating Inefficiencies through Automation," *Beverage Industry,* January 2010; "Coca-Cola Expands Hybrid Electric Fleet in Canada," *Beverage Industry,* January 2010; "Coca-Cola Deal Is U.S. Strategy Shift," *Wall Street Journal,* February 26, 2010; "Coke Takes Juice Lead from Pepsi," *Advertising Age,* February 1, 2010; "Masters of Design," *Fast Company,* October 2009; "Coke: Buy 1 Rival, Get Our Brand Free," *Advertising Age,* March 9, 2009; "Sustainability and a Smile," *Advertising Age,* February 25, 2008; "Iran's Cola War," *Fortune,* February 6, 2008; "Coke Tries to Pop Back in Vital Japan Market," *Wall Street Journal,* July 11, 2006; "Coke Gets a Jolt," *Fortune,* May 15, 2006; "Thirsting for More Variety," *Investor's Business Daily,* April 24, 2006; "In the Newest Snack Packs, Less Is More," *USA Today,* April 13, 2006; "Afghan Coke a Taste of Things to Come," Financial Times, December 6, 2005; "EU Limits Coke's Sales Tactics in Settlement of Antitrust Case," *Wall Street Journal,* June 23, 2005; "To Pitch New Soda, Coke Wants the World to Sing—Again," *Wall Street Journal,* June 13, 2005; "How a Global Web of Activists Gives Coke Problems in India," *Wall Street Journal,* June 7, 2005; "The Soda with Buzz," *Forbes,* March 28, 2005; "Into the Fryer: How Coke Officials Beefed Up Results of Marketing Tests," *Wall Street Journal,* August 20, 2003; "Mooove Over, Milkman," *Wall Street Journal,* June 9, 2003; "Fountain Dispenses Problems," *USA Today,* May 28, 2003.

2. "U.S. Logistics Costs Drop for First Time in Six Years, Benchmark Report Says," *Supply Chain Management Review,* June 18, 2009; "2009 Annual Report on State of Logistics: Collaboration Time," *Logistics Management,* 2009; "Latin America: Addressing High Logistics Costs and Poor Infrastructure for Merchandise Transportation and Trade Facilitation," Working Paper, The World Bank, August 2007; "The Cost of Being Landlocked: Logistics Costs and Supply Chain Reliability," Policy Research Working Paper, The World Bank, June 1, 2007.

3. "Compaq Stumbles as PCs Weather New Blow," *Wall Street Journal,* March 9, 1998; See also Alexander E. Ellinger, Scott B. Keller and John D. Hansen, "Bridging the Divide Between Logistics and Marketing: Facilitating Collaborative Behavior," *Journal of Business Logistics,* #2, 2006; Kofi Q. Dadzie, Cristian Chelariu and Evelyn Winston, "Customer Service in the Internet-Enabled Logistics Supply Chain: Website Design Antecedents and Loyalty Effects," *Journal of Business Logistics,* January 2005; Elliot Rabinovich and Philip T. Evers, "Product Fulfillment in Supply Chains Supporting Internet-Retailing Operations," *Journal of Business Logistics,* January 2003; Daniel Corsten and Thomas Gruen, "Stock-Outs Cause Walkouts," *Harvard Business Review,* May 2004; William D. Perreault, Jr., and Frederick A. Russ, "Physical Distribution Service in Industrial Purchase Decisions," *Journal of Marketing,* April 1976.

4. "H-P Wields Its Clout to Undercut PC Rivals," *Wall Street Journal,* September 24, 2009; "Walmart's H-P Elves," *Wall Street Journal,* December 15, 2005; "A More Profitable Harvest," *Business 2.0,* May 2005; "Costs Too High? Bring in the Logistics Experts," *Fortune,* November 10, 1997. See also G. Tomas M. Hult, Kenneth K. Boyer, and David J. Ketchen, Jr., "Quality, Operational Logistics Strategy, and Repurchase Intentions: A Profile Deviation Analysis," *Journal of Business Logistics,* #2, 2007; Thierry Sauvage, "The Relationship Between Technology and Logistics Third Party Providers," *International Journal of Physical Distribution & Logistics Management,* #3, 2003; Donald J. Bowersox, David J. Closs, and Theodore P. Stank, "Ten Mega-Trends That Will Revolutionize Supply Chain Logistics," *Journal of Business Logistics,* #2 (2000); James R. Stock, "Marketing Myopia Revisited: Lessons for Logistics," *International Journal of Physical Distribution & Logistics Management,* #1, 2002; Mark Goh and Charlene Ling, "Logistics Development in China," *International Journal of Physical Distribution & Logistics Management,* #9 (2003); James H. Bookbinder and Chris S. Tan, "Comparison of Asian and European Logistics Systems," *International Journal of Physical Distribution & Logistics Management,* #1, 2003.

5. For more on Clorox, see www.clorox.com; 2010 Annual Report, Clorox; "The Web @ Work/Clorox Co.," *Wall Street Journal,* October 9, 2000. See also Forrest E. Harding, "Logistics Service Provider Quality: Private Measurement, Evaluation, and Improvement," *Journal of Business Logistics,* 1998; Carol C. Bienstock, John T. Mentzer, and Monroe M. Bird, "Measuring Physical Distribution Service Quality," *Journal of the Academy of Marketing Science,* Winter 1997.

6. For more on Haiti, see "Sharing in the USA: Social Websites, 'Apps' among Latest Conduits," *USA Today* (Special Report), April 13, 2010; "Aid Frustration: We're Racing against the Clock," *USA Today,* January 18, 2010; "Haitian Rescue Stymied Amid Chaos," *Wall Street Journal,* January 15, 2010; "Quake Severely Strains Telecom Services," *USA Today,* January 15, 2010; "Companies Efficiently Pour Out $16M to Help Haiti," *USA Today,* January 15, 2010. See also Ozlem Ergun, Pinar Keskiocak, and Julie Swann, "Humanitarian Relief Logistics," OR/MS Today, December 2007. For more on Katrina, see "Good Logistics Offer Better Relief," Financial Times, December 16, 2005; "Disasters Demand Supply Chain Software, Research Shows," eWeek, October 5, 2005; "The Only Lifeline Was the Walmart," *Fortune,* October 3, 2005; "For FedEx, It Was Time to Deliver," *Fortune,* October 3, 2005; "They Don't Teach This in B-School," *BusinessWeek,* September 19, 2005, pp. 46–48: "At Walmart, Emergency Plan Has Big Payoff," *Wall Street Journal,* September 12, 2005; "Walmart Praised for Hurricane Katrina Response Efforts," NewsMax.com, September 6, 2005; Logistics and the Effective Delivery of Humanitarian Relief (The Fritz Institute, 2005); "Emergency Relief Logistics—A Faster Way across the Global Divide," Logistics Quarterly, Summer 2001; Anisya Thomas and Lynn Fritz, "Disaster Relief, Inc," *Harvard Business Review,* November 2006.

7. "More Green from Green Beans," *Business 2.0,* August 2004. See also Mikko Karkkainen, Timo Ala-Risku, and Jan Holmstrom, "Increasing Customer Value and Decreasing Distribution Costs with Merge-In-Transit," *International Journal of Physical Distribution & Logistics Management,* #1 (2003); Marc J. Schniederjans and Qing Cao, "An Alternative Analysis of Inventory Costs of JIT and EOQ Purchasing," *International Journal of Physical Distribution & Logistics Management,* #2 (2001).

8. For more on JIT, see "Retailers Rely More on Fast Deliveries," *Wall Street Journal,* January 14, 2004; "Uncertain Economy Hinders Highly Precise Supply System," *New York Times,* March 15, 2003; "Port Tie-Up Shows Vulnerability," *USA Today,* October 9, 2002; "Deadline Scramble: A New Hazard for Recovery, Last-Minute Pace of Orders," *Wall Street Journal,* June 25, 2002; "Parts Shortages Hamper Electronics Makers," *Wall Street Journal,* July 7, 2000. See also Richard E. White and John N. Pearson, "JIT, System Integration and Customer Service," *International Journal of Physical Distribution & Logistics Management,* #5 2001.

9. "A New Industrial Revolution," *Wall Street Journal,* April 28, 2008; "Global Scramble for Goods Gives Corporate Buyers a Lift," *Wall Street Journal,* October 2, 2007.

10. See "Clarity Is Missing Link in Supply Chain," *Wall Street Journal,* May 18, 2009; Martin Christopher and John Gattorna, "Supply Chain Cost Management and Value-Based Pricing," *Industrial Marketing Management,* February 2005; G. Tomas M. Hult, "Global Supply Chain Management: An Integration of Scholarly Thoughts," *Industrial Marketing Management,* January 2004; Daniel J. Flint, "Strategic Marketing in Global Supply Chains: Four Challenges," *Industrial Marketing Management,* January 2004; Daniel C. Bello, Ritu Lohtia, and Vinita Sangtani, "An Institutional Analysis of Supply Chain Innovations in Global Marketing Channels," *Industrial Marketing Management,* January 2004; Brian J. Gibson, John T. Mentzer, and Robert L. Cook, "Supply Chain Management: the Pursuit of a Consensus Definition," *Journal of Business Logistics,* 2005; Theodore P. Stank, Beth R. Davis, and Brian S. Fugate, "A Strategic Framework for Supply Chain Oriented Logistics," *Journal of Business Logistics,* 2005; Terry L. Esper, Thomas D. Jensen, Fernanda L. Turnipseed, and Scot Burton, "The Last Mile: An Examination of Effects of Online Retail Delivery Strategies on Consumers," *Journal of Business Logistics,* 2003; Christopher R. Moberg and Thomas W. Speh, "Evaluating the Relationship Between Questionable Business Practices and the Strength of Supply Chain Relationships," *Journal of Business Logistics,* #2 (2003); Subroto Roy, K. Sivakumar, and Ian F. Wilkinson, "Innovation Generation in Supply Chain Relationships: A Conceptual Model and Research Propositions," *Journal of the Academy of Marketing Science,* Winter 2004; Rakesh Niraj, "Customer Profitability in a Supply Chain," *Journal of Marketing,* July 2001.

11. For an excellent example of EDI, see "To Sell Goods to WalMart, Get on the Net," *Wall Street Journal,* November 21, 2003. See also Cornelia Droge and Richard Germain, "The Relationship of Electronic Data Interchange with Inventory and Financial Performance," *Journal of Business Logistics,* #2 (2000).

12. "A Smart Cookie at Pepperidge," *Fortune,* December 22, 1986.

13. "A New Push Against Sweatshops," *Time,* October 7, 2005; "Cops of the Global Village, *Fortune,* June 27, 2005; "Stamping Out Sweatshops," *BusinessWeek* Online, May 23, 2005; "Nike Opens Its Books on Sweatshop Audits," *BusinessWeek* Online, April 27, 2000; "Nike Names Names," *BusinessWeek* Online, April 13, 2005; "Corporate Social Responsibility—Companies in the News Nike," see www.mallenbaker.net/csr/CSRfiles/nike.html.

14. David Grant, Douglas Lambert, James R. Stock, and Lisa M. Ellram, *Fundamentals of Logistics* Burr Ridge, IL: Irwin/McGraw-Hill, 2005.

15. For more on transportation security, see "Calif. Port Goes Tech in Security," *Investor's Business Daily,* February 11, 2009; "Technology Roots Out Cargo Risks," *Investor's Business Daily,* October 4, 2005; "Keeping Cargo Safe from Terror," *Wall Street Journal,* July 29, 2005; "Protecting America's Ports," *Fortune,* November 10, 2003.

16. For a more detailed comparison of mode characteristics, see Robert Dahlstrom, Kevin M. McNeilly, and Thomas W. Speh, "Buyer-Seller Relationships in the Procurement of Logistical Services," *Journal of the Academy of Marketing Science,* Spring 1996.

17. "Rail Renaissance," *BusinessWeek,* November 3, 2008; "New Rail-Building Era Dawns," *Wall Street Journal,* February 13, 2008; "Next Stop: The 21st Century," *Business 2.0,* September 2003; "Back on Track: Left for

Dead, Railroads Revive by Watching Clock," *Wall Street Journal,* July 25, 2003; "Trains: Industry Report," *Investor's Business Daily,* May 7, 2001.

18. "Truckers Question Traffic-Relief Efforts," *USA Today,* December 27, 2007; "Shipping Hubs Spring Up Inland," *USA Today,* December 17, 2007; "Waterways Could Be Key to Freeing Up Freeways," *USA Today,* October 11, 2007; "Costs of Trucking Seen Rising under New Safety Rules," *Wall Street Journal,* November 12, 2003; "Trucker Rewards Customers for Good Behavior," *Wall Street Journal,* September 9, 2003; "Trucking: Rig and Roll," *Wall Street Journal,* October 23, 2000; "Trucking Gets Sophisticated," *Fortune,* July 24, 2000.

19. For more on overnight carriers, see "UPS Battles Traffic Jams to Gain Ground in India," *Wall Street Journal,* January 25, 2008; "Why FedEx Is Gaining Ground," *Business 2.0,* October 2003; "FedEx Recasts Itself on the Ground," *Wall Street Journal,* September 4, 2003; "UPS, FedEx Wage Handheld Combat," *Investor's Business Daily,* May 19, 2003.

20. "Foldable Shipping Containers Try to Stack Up," *Wall Street Journal,* April 12, 2010; "The Mega Containers Invade," *Wall Street Journal,* January 26, 2009; K. Raguraman and Claire Chan, "The Development of SeaAir Intermodal Transportation: An Assessment of Global Trends," *Logistics and Transportation Review,* December 1994; "Yule Log Jam," *Fortune,* December 13, 2004; "Monsters of the High Seas," *BusinessWeek,* October 13, 2003.

21. "Western Grocer Modernizes Passage to Indian Markets," *Wall Street Journal,* November 28, 2007; "Widening Aisles for Indian Shoppers," *BusinessWeek,* April 30, 2007.

22. "DHL Completes More Eco-Friendly Ship Voyage as Industry Comes Under Fire," GreenBiz.com, February 15, 2008; State of Green Business 2008, Greener World Media, 2008, GreenBiz.com. See also 2009 Annual Report, Du Pont; 2009 Annual Report, Matlack; 2009 Annual Report, Shell; 2009 Annual Report, FedEx; 2009 Annual Report, UPS.

23. "Data Analytics: Crunching the Future," *BloombergBusinessweek,* September 8, 2011.

24. "Hospital Cost Cutters Push Use of Scanners to Track Inventories," *Wall Street Journal,* June 10, 1997. See also Charu Chandra and Sameer Kumar, "Taxonomy of Inventory Policies for Supply-Chain Effectiveness," *International Journal of Retail & Distribution Management,* #4 (2001); Matthew B. Myers, Patricia J. Daugherty, and Chad W. Autry, "The Effectiveness of Automatic Inventory Replenishment in Supply Chain Operations: Antecedents and Outcomes," *Journal of Retailing,* Winter 2000.

25. "The Supersizing of Warehouses," *New York Times,* February 4, 2004; "New Warehouses Take On a Luxe Look," *Wall Street Journal,* June 18, 2003; Chad W. Autry, Stanley E. Griffis, Thomas J. Goldsby, and L. Michelle Bobbitt, "Warehouse Management-Systems: Resource Commitment, Capabilities, and Organizational Performance," *Journal of Business Logistics,* 2005.

26. "IBM, Smart Tags Helping Toyota Customize Its Cars," *Investor's Business Daily,* August 15, 2005; "Who Made My Cheese? Tags Track Parmesan's Age, Origin," *Wall Street Journal,* July 7, 2005; "Frequency of the Future," *DSN Retailing Today,* (1Q) 2005; "Electronic Tags Should Help Drug Makers Identify Fakes," *Investor's Business Daily,* November 29, 2004.

27. "Veggie Tales," *Fortune,* June 8, 2009; "Sysco Hustles to Keep Restaurants Cooking," *BusinessWeek,* May 18, 2009; "Sysco Website Helps Its Customers Build Business," *Nation's Restaurant News,* May 18, 2009; "Sysco Corporation: Company Profile," *Datamonitor,* June 10, 2008.

28. "Frito-Lay," Short Cases from the CSCMP Toolbox, 2005.

29. "Whirlpool Cleans Up Its Delivery Act," *Wall Street Journal,* September 24, 2009; "Walmart's Need for Speed," *Wall Street Journal,* September 26, 2005.

CHAPTER 12

1. See Macys.com, Macy's Annual Report, 2011; "Macy's Regroups in Warehouse Wars," *Wall Street Journal,* May 14, 2012; "When CMOs Learn to Love Data, They'll Be VIPs in the C-Suite," *AdAge,* February 13, 2012; "Luring Online Shoppers Offline," *New York Times,* July 4, 2012; "The Goal: A Perfect First Time Fit," *Wall Street Journal,* March 23, 2012; "Macy's in China Internet Push," *Women's Wear Daily,* May 24, 2012; "Macy's Sets Tech Push to Propel Growth," *Women's Wear Daily,* May 21, 2012; "Supply Chain in Action," *Apparel Magazine,* April 2012; "Macy's Sets Strategy for Gen-Y Shoppers," *Women's Wear Daily,* March 22, 2012; "Macy's Expands Fashion Incubator Program," *Women's Wear Daily,* March 27, 2012; "Macy's 2.0 Strategy Puts the Pedal to the Metal," *Forbes,* May 21, 2012; "A Holiday to Remember for Prestige Retailers, *Women's Wear Daily,* January 6, 2012; "Retailers are striving to combine the advantages of physical shops with the benefits of online selling," *Economist,* February 5, 2012; "Macy's Plan: Boots, Bieber, *Wall Street Journal,* November 26, 2011; "How Department Stores Came Back Into Fashion," *Bloomber-Businessweek,* March 21, 2011; "At Macy's Big Brother Is Watching You," *Wall Street Journal,* March 18, 2011; "Macy's transformation," DM News, April 1, 2012; "How Macy's latest moves are paying off," *Business Courier,* November 25, 2011; "DunnhumbyUSA, Macy's forge exclusive client agreement," August 13, 2008; "Dowdy Department Stores Start Looking Cool Again," *Wall Street Journal,* August 4, 2011; "For the New Macy's All Marketing is Local," *Adweek,* June 7, 2010; "Going on Impulse: Macy's Plots Push In Contemporary With Exclusives," *Womens Wear Daily,* January 27, 2011; "Retailers on quest to rekindle the personal touch of a bygone era," Advertising Age, February 14, 2011; "Atlanta Hats? Seattle Socks? Macy's Goes Local," *New York Times,* October 1, 2010.

2. See www.census.gov/retail/mrts/www/benchmark/2009/html/annrev09.html; U.S. Census Bureau, Statistical Abstract of the United States 2010 (Washington, DC: U.S. Government Printing Office, 2009); 2007 Economic Census—Retail Trade, Subject Series, Establishment and Firm Size (Washington, DC: U.S. Government Printing Office, 2010); "Pop-Up Stores Fill Retail Space as Vacancies Hit Decade Highs," *Investor's Business Daily,* November 12, 2009; "Retailers Embrace Pop-Ups," *USA Today,* October 30, 2009; "The Hard Sell: How Retailers Are Fighting for the Hearts and Minds of the New Consumer," *BusinessWeek,* October 15, 2009; "Retail 2.0," *Brandweek,* December 17, 2007; Desai, Preyas S, OdedKoenigsberg, and DevavratPurohit, "Forward Buying by Retailers,"*Journal of Marketing Research,* February 2010; Diehl, Kristin, and CaitPoynor, "Great Expectations?! Assortment Size, Expectations, and Satisfaction,"*Journal of Marketing Research,* April 2010; Jerath, Kinshuk, and Z. John Zhang, "Store Within a Store,"*Journal of Marketing Research,* August 2010; Che, Hai, Xinlei (Jack) Chen, and Yuxin Chen, "Investigating Effects of Out-of-Stock on Consumer Stockkeeping Unit Choice,"*Journal of Marketing Research,* August 2012; Bell, Simon J., BülentMengüç, and Robert E. Widing II, "Salesperson learning, organizational learning, and retail store performance,"*Journal of the Academy of Marketing Science,* March 2010; Hughes, Douglas E, and Michael Ahearne, "Energizing the Reseller's Sales Force: The Power of Brand Identification,"*Journal of Marketing,* July 2010; Velitchka D. Kaltcheva and Barton A. Weitz, "When Should a Retailer Create an Exciting Store Environment?" *Journal of Marketing,* January 2006; Kathleen Seiders, Glenn B. Voss, Dhruv Grewal, and Andrea L. Godfrey, "Do Satisfied Customers Buy More? Examining Moderating Influences in a Retailing Context," *Journal of Marketing,* October 2005; Ruth N. Bolton and Venkatesh Shankar, "An Empirically Derived Taxonomy of Retailer Pricing and Promotion Strategies," *Journal of Retailing,* Winter 2003; Katherine B. Hartman and Rosann L. Spiro, "Recapturing Store Image in Customer-Based Store Equity: A Construct Conceptualization," *Journal of Business Research,* August 2005; Mark J. Arnold, Kristy E. Reynolds, Nicole Ponder, and Jason E. Lueg, "Customer Delight in a Retail Context: Investigating Delightful and Terrible Shopping Experiences," *Journal of Business Research,* August 2005.

3. "Payless ShoeSource, Inc. Company Profile," *Datamonitor,* November 2, 2009; "Payless ShoeSource: Putting Its Best Foot Forward," *The Journal of Commerce,* May 29, 2006.

4. "Zappos.com: Developing a Supply Chain to Deliver WOW!" Stanford Graduate School of Business Case #GS 65, February 13, 2009;

"Tireless Employees Get Their Tribute, Even if It's in Felt and Polyester," *New York Times,* March 4, 2010; "Why Everybody Loves Zappos," *Inc.,* May 2009; Zappos CEO: How to Build a Brand without Spending Big on Ads," *Brandweek,* December 22, 2008; "Zappos Touts More than Just Shoes," *Adweek,* February 23, 2009.

5. "Malls Race to Stay Relevant in Downturn," *Wall Street Journal,* February 26, 2009; "As Malls Think Small, Boutiques Get Their Big Chance," *Wall Street Journal,* June 24, 2005; "Urban Rarity: Stores Offering Spiffy Service," *Wall Street Journal,* July 25, 1996; "Airports: New Destination for Specialty Retailers," *USA Today,* January 11, 1996; Sharon E. Beatty, Morris Mayer, James E. Coleman, Kristy E. Reynolds, and Jungki Lee, "Customer-Sales Associate Retail Relationships," *Journal of Retailing,* Fall 1996.

6. See www.census.gov; U.S. Census Bureau, 2007 Economic Census Retail Trade, Subject Series, Establishment and Firm Size. For more on department stores, see "Big Retailers Seek Teens (and Parents)," *USA Today,* April 14, 2008; "The Department Store Rises Again," *Business 2.0,* August 2004.

7. David Appel, "The Supermarket: Early Development of an Institutional Innovation," *Journal of Retailing,* Spring 1972.

8. See www.census.gov and www.fmi.org/facts_figs/?fuseaction=superfact; "Do-It-Yourself Supermarket Checkout," *Wall Street Journal,* April 5, 2007. See also R. A. Briesch, P. K. Chintagunta, and E. J. Fox, "How Does Assortment Affect Grocery Store Choice?" *Journal of Marketing Research,* #2, 2009.

9. For more on Target as mass-merchandiser, see "Look Who's Stalking Walmart," *BusinessWeek,* November 25, 2009.

10. For more on supercenters, see Ailawadi, Kusum L, Jie Zhang, Aradhna Krishna, and Michael W Kruger, "When Wal-Mart Enters: How Incumbent Retailers React and How This Affects Their Sales Outcomes,"*Journal of Marketing Research*, August 2010; "Retailers Cut Back on Variety, Once the Spice of Marketing," *Wall Street Journal,* June 26, 2009; "Walmart, the Category King," *DSN Retailing Today,* June 9, 2003; "Price War in Aisle 3," *Wall Street Journal,* May 27, 2003.

11. For more on warehouse clubs, see "Club Stores Accepting Coupons," *Wall Street Journal,* August 20, 2009; "Sam's Club Tests the Big-Box Bodega," *Wall Street Journal,* August 10, 2009; "Thinking Outside the Big Box: Costco," *Fast Company,* November 2008; "Costco's Artful Discounts," *BusinessWeek,* October 20, 2008; "Costco's Well-Off Customers Still Shopping," *Investor's Business Daily,* April 8, 2008; "Why Costco Is So Damn Addictive," *Fortune,* October 30, 2006.

12. For more on category killers, see "Newcomers Challenge Office-Supply Stalwarts," *Wall Street Journal,* April 29, 2009; "Big Boxes Aim to Speed Up Shopping," *Wall Street Journal,* June 27, 2007.

13. For more on 7-Eleven, see "Know What Customers Want," *Inc.,* August 2005; "Can 7-Eleven Win over Hong Kong Foodies?" *Time,* October 1, 2009; "Convenience Stores Score in Japan," *Wall Street Journal,* August 19, 2008.

14. For more on vending and wireless, see "Soda? IPod? Vending Machines Diversity," *USA Today,* September 4, 2007; Self-Serve Movie Rental Kiosks a Surprise Hit with Consumers," *Investor's Business Daily,* May 31, 2007.

15. "In Digital Era, Marketers Still Prefer a Paper Trail," *Wall Street Journal,* October 16, 2009; "Cutting the Stack of Catalogs," *BusinessWeek,* December 31, 2007; "This Isn't the Holiday Catalog You Remember," *Advertising Age,* October 29, 2007.

16. "E-commerce 2007," *U.S. Census Bureau, E-Stats,* May 28, 2009; "Forrester Forecast: Online Retail Sales Will Grow to $250 Billion by 2014," *TechCrunch,* March 8, 2010; "Forrester Forecast: Online Retail Sales Will Grow to $250 Billion by 2014," *TechCrunch,* March 8, 2010.

17. "Truth about Showrooming," *Retail Info Systems News,* November 7, 2012; "Luring Online Shoppers Offline, *Wall Street Journal,* July 4, 2012; "Showrooming Mushrooms But Is It Really A Threat," *CMO.com,* June 20, 2012;

18. Chris Anderson, *The Long Tail* (New York: Hyperion, 2006); "The Long Tail," *Wired,* October 2004; Eri Brynjolfsson, Yu "Jeffrey" Hu, and Michael D. Smith, "From Niches to Riches: Anatomy of a Long Tail," *Sloan Management Review,* Summer 2006, p. 67.

19. "Big Brother is Watching You Shop," *Bloomberg Businessweek,* December 15, 2011; "Check Out the Future of Shopping," *Wall Street Journal,* May 18, 2011; for more generally on the effects of technology on retail, see "Retailers Reach Out on Cellphones," *Wall Street Journal,* April 21, 2010; "The Hard Sell," *BusinessWeek,* October 26, 2009; "Ring Up E-Commerce Gains with a True Multichannel Strategy," *Advertising Age,* March 10, 2008; "Retailing: What's Working Online," *The McKinsey Quarterly,* #3, 2005; Avery, Jill, Thomas J Steenburgh, John Deighton, and Mary Caravella, "Adding Bricks to Clicks: Predicting the Patterns of Cross-Channel Elasticities Over Time,"*Journal of Marketing,* May 2012; Jing, Xiaoqing, and Michael Lewis, "Stockouts in Online Retailing,"*Journal of Marketing Research,* April 2011; J. Ganesh, K. E. Reynolds, M. Luckett, and N. Pomirleanu, "Online Shopper Motivations, and E-Store Attributes: An Examination of Online Patronage Behavior and Shopper Typologies," *Journal of Retailing,* #1, 2010; P. Gupta, M. S. Yadav, and R. Varadarajan, "How Task-Facilitative Interactive Tools Foster Buyers' Trust in Online Retailers: A Process View of Trust Development in the Electronic Marketplace," *Journal of Retailing,* #2, 2009; W. S. Kwon, and S. J. Lennon, "Reciprocal Effects between Multichannel Retailers' Offline and Online Brand Images," *Journal of Retailing,* #3, 2009; Joel E. Collier and Carol C. Bienstock, "How Do Customers Judge Quality in an E-tailer?" *Sloan Management Review,* Fall 2006; A. E. Schlosser, T. B. White, S. M. Lloyd, "Converting website Visitors into Buyers: How website Investment Increases Consumer Trusting Beliefs and Online Purchase Intentions," *Journal of Marketing,* April 2006; Yakov Bart, Venkatesh Shankar, Fareena Sultan, and Glen L. Urban, "Are the Drivers and Role of Online Trust the Same for All websites and Consumers? A Large-Scale Exploratory Empirical Study," *Journal of Marketing,* October 2005; S.A. Neslin and V. Shankar, "Key Issues in Multichannel Customer Management: Current Knowledge and Future Directions," *Journal of Interactive Marketing,* #1 2009.

20. Chip E. Miller, "The Effects of Competition on Retail Structure: An Examination of Intratype, Intertype, and Intercategory Competition," *Journal of Marketing,* October 1999; "Aspirin, Q-Tips and a New You: Drug-stores Try to Sell Glamour, Offering Cosmetic Boutiques, Facials, Eyebrow Bars," *Wall Street Journal,* March 25, 2010; "Root Canal? Try Aisle Five," *BusinessWeek,* October 13, 2008; "Doing Whatever Gets Them in the Door," *BusinessWeek,* June 30, 2008; "New Options for Saving at the Pump," *Wall Street Journal,* August 16, 2005; Ronald Savitt, "The 'Wheel of Retailing' and Retail Product Management," *European Journal of Marketing* 18, #6/7 (1984).

21. "How Did Sears Blow This Gasket?" *BusinessWeek,* June 29, 1992; "An Open Letter to Sears Customers," *USA Today,* June 25, 1992. See also John Paul Fraedrich, "The Ethical Behavior of Retail Managers," *Journal of Business Ethics,* March 1993.

22. "What Price Virtue? At Some Retailers, 'Fair Trade' Carries a Very High Cost," *Wall Street Journal,* June 8, 2004.

23. See U.S. Census data including "Summary Statistics by Employment Size of Establishments for the U.S.: 2007" from *2007 Economic Census—Retail Trade, Subject Series, Establishment and Firm Size* (Washington, DC: U.S. Government Printing Office, 2010) and available online at www.census.gov. See also Kusum L. Ailawadi, "The Retail Power Performance Conundrum: What Have We Learned?" *Journal of Retailing,*Fall 2001; Dale D. Achabal, John M. Heineke, and Shelby H. McIntyre, "Issues and Perspectives on Retail Productivity," *Journal of Retailing,* Fall 1984; Charles A. Ingene, "Scale Economies in American Retailing: A Cross-Industry Comparison," *Journal of Macromarketing* 4, #2 (1984).

24. For an excellent example of AutoZone as successful chain, see "*Fortune* 500: In the Zone," *Fortune,* April 13, 2009; "AutoZone Smashes Views as Aging Cars Need Parts," *Investor's Business Daily,* March 4, 2009; "Rallying the Troops to Get Back in the Profit Zone," *DSN Retailing Today,* September 6, 2004; See also Gary K. Rhoads, William R. Swinyard, Michael D. Geurts, and William D. Price, "Retailing as a Career: A Comparative Study of Marketers," *Journal of Retailing,* Spring 2002.

25. "Burger King Franchisees Can't Have It Their Way," I, January 21, 2010; "Do You Have What It Takes? *Wall Street Journal* Reports, September 19, 2005; "How to Grow a Chain That's Already Everywhere,"

Business 2.0, March 2005; "When Franchisees Lose Part of Their Independence," *New York Times,* February 3, 2005. See also Surinder Tikoo, "Franchiser Influence Strategy Use and Franchisee Experience and Dependence," *Journal of Retailing,* Fall 2002; Patrick J. Kaufmann and Rajiv P. Dant, "The Pricing of Franchise Rights," *Journal of Retailing,* Winter 2001; Madhav Pappu and David Strutton, "Toward an Understanding of Strategic Inter-Organizational Relationships in Franchise Channels," *Journal of Marketing* Channels, #1, 2 (2001); Rajiv P. Dant and Patrick J. Kaufmann, "Structural and Strategic Dynamics in Franchising," *Journal of Retailing,* #2 (2003); A. K. Paswan and C. M. Wittmann, "Knowledge Management and Franchise Systems," *Industrial Marketing Management,* #2, 2009.

26. "A Dollar Store's Rich Allure in India," *Wall Street Journal,* January 23, 2007; "Retailers Still Expanding in China: Walmart, Carrefour, Tesco," *Wall Street Journal,* January 22, 2009; "Walmart: Looking Overseas for Growth," CNNMoney.com, October 24, 2007; "Walmart: Struggling in Germany," *BusinessWeek,* April 11, 2005; "Japan Isn't Buying The Walmart Idea," *BusinessWeek,* February 28, 2005.

27. "Understanding Online Shoppers in Europe," *McKinsey Quarterly,* May 2009; "Forrester Forecast: Online Retail Sales Will Grow to $250 Billion by 2014," *TechCrunch,* March 8, 2010; "Forester Forecast: Double-Digit Growth for Online Retail in the US and Western Europe," *Tekrati,* March 9, 2010.

28. See www.friedas.com; "How Lower-Tech Gear Beat Web 'Exchanges' at Their Own Game," *Wall Street Journal,* March 16, 2001; "Family Firms Confront Calamities of Transfer," *USA Today,* August 29, 2000; "Business, Too Close to Home," *Time,* July 17, 2000; "The Kiwi to My Success," Hemispheres, July 1999; "Searching for the Next Kiwi: Frieda's Branded Produce," *Brandweek,* May 2, 1994; "Strange Fruits," *Inc.,* November 1989; "The Produce Marketer," Savvy, June 1988.

29. See U.S. Census data including "Summary Statistics for the U.S.: 2007" from *2007 Economic Census—Wholesale Trade, Geographic Area Series, United States* (Washington, DC: U.S. Government Printing Office, 2010) and available online at www.census.gov.

30. See www.fastenal.com; "The *BusinessWeek* 50: Fastenal," *BusinessWeek,* April 6, 2009; "Fastenal: Need to Fix Up a Building? This Firm's Got Your One-Stop Shop," *Investor's Business Daily,* November 28, 2005; "Fastenal: In This Sluggish Market, You Gotta Have Faith," *Investor's Business Daily,* August 13, 2001.

31. "Revolution in Japanese Retailing," *Fortune,* February 7, 1994; Arieh Goldman, "Evaluating the Performance of the Japanese Distribution System," *Journal of Retailing,* Spring 1992; "Japan Begins to Open the Door to Foreigners, a Little," *Brandweek,* August 2, 1993.

32. See www.rell.com; "Richardson Electronics Ltd.: Maker of Ancient Tech Finds a Way to Prosper," *Investor's Business Daily,* June 27, 2000; 2009 Annual Report, Richardson Electronics.

33. See www.inmac.com and www.grainger.com.

34. For more on manufacturers' agents being squeezed, see "Philips to End Long Relations with North American Reps—Will Build Internal Sales Force Instead," EBN, November 10, 2003. See also Daniel C. Bello and Ritu Lohtia, "The Export Channel Design: The Use of Foreign Distributors and Agents," *Journal of the Academy of Marketing Science,* Spring 1995.

CHAPTER 13

1. See www.geico.com; "GEICO Advertising Soars to $1 Billion," *Media Post,* June 26, 2012; "Big Blue Makes Big Moves in Big Data," *Forbes,* May 8, 2012; "Customer service playing a bigger role as a marketing tool," *Advertising Age,* November 7, 2011; "GEICO Launches Social Media Platform for Military Personnel," *InsuranceTech,* July 5, 2011; "Consumers: Who's Who?" *Advertising Age,* February 21, 2011; "How the Insurance Industry Got into a $4 Billion Ad Brawl," *Advertising Age,* February 21, 2011; "Umbrella Coverage for Preventing Your Ruin," *New York Times,* March 18, 2008; "Clan of the Caveman," *Fast Company,* December 19, 2007; "Geico," *Advertising Age,* October 15, 2007; "Leapin' Lizards," *Brandweek,* October 8, 2007; "Cavemen (TV Series)," Wikipedia, April 21, 2007; "Will the Cavemen's Evolution Boost Geico? *Fortune,* April 2, 2007; "The Caveman: Evolution of a Character," *Adweek,* March 12, 2007; "Trio of TV Ad Campaigns Succeeds in Wooing Different Target Audience," Television Week, March 12, 2007; "How a Gecko Shook Up Insurance Ads," *Wall Street Journal,* January 2, 2007; "When Geckos Aren't Enough," *BusinessWeek,* October 16, 2006; "10 Breakaway Brands," *Fortune,* September 8, 2006; "Loving the Lizard," *Adweek,* October 24, 2005; "Buffet Wants to Know: Do Geico Ads Get Job Done?" *USA Today,* January 24, 2005.

2. P. J. Kitchen, I. Kim, and D. E. Schultz, "Integrated Marketing Communication: Practice Leads Theory," *Journal of Advertising Research,* #4, 2008; Kim Bartel Sheehan and Caitlin Doherty, "Re-Weaving the Web: Integrating Print and Online Communications," *Journal of Interactive Marketing,* Spring 2001.

3. "In a Shift, Marketers Beef Up Ad Spending Inside Stores," *Wall Street Journal,* September 21, 2005.

4 Barbara B. Stern, "A Revised Communication Model for Advertising: Multiple Dimensions of the Source, the Message, and the Recipient," *Journal of* Advertising, June, 1994; George S. Low and Jakki J. Mohr, "Factors Affecting the Use of Information in the Evaluation of Marketing Communications Productivity," *Journal of the Academy of Marketing Science,* Winter 2001; David I. Gilliland and Wesley J. Johnston, "Toward a Model of Business-to-Business Marketing Communications Effects," *Industrial Marketing Management,* January 1997.

5. "Don't Let Your Brand Get Lost in Translation," *Brandweek,* February 8, 2010; "Capturing a Piece of the Global Market," *Brandweek,* June 20, 2005; "Global Branding: Same, But Different," *Brandweek,* April 9, 2001; "Hey, #!@*% Amigo, Can You Translate the Word 'Gaffe'?" *Wall Street Journal,* July 8, 1996; "Lost in Translation: How to 'Empower Women' in Chinese," *Wall Street Journal,* September 13, 1994.

6. "Clare Florist's Segmentation Campaign," *Marketing Sherpa Email Awards,* 2012; See also *Inbound Marketing,* 2009, New York: Wiley; for more on direct response promotion see: "Direct-Response TV," *Advertising Age,* March 23, 2009; "Depending on Direct: Discipline Grows to $161B," *Advertising Age,* October 24, 2005; "Direct Gets Respect: Budgets Swell as Marketers Seek Accountability," *Advertising Age,* August 30, 2004, pp. 1, 21. See also Sally J. McMillan and Jang-Sun Hwang, "Measures of Perceived Interactivity: An Exploration of the Role of Direction of Communication, User Control, and Time in Shaping Perceptions of Interactivity," *Journal of Advertising,* Fall 2002; Carrie M. Heilman, Frederick Kaefer, and Samuel D. Ramenofsky, "Determining the Appropriate Amount of Data for Classifying Consumers for Direct Marketing Purposes," *Journal of Interactive Marketing,* Summer 2003.

7. "How Amazon Is Turning Opinions into Gold," *BusinessWeek,* October 26, 2009; "What Do You Think?" *Wall Street Journal,* October 12, 2009; "Global Advertising: Consumers Trust Real Friends and Virtual Strangers the Most," *Nielsenwire,* July 7, 2009; Köhler, Clemens F, Andrew J Rohm, Ko de Ruyter, and Martin Wetzels, "Return on Interactivity: The Impact of Online Agents on Newcomer Adjustment," *Journal of Marketing,* March 2011; Feng Zhu and Xiaoquan Zhang, "Impact of Online Consumer Reviews on Sales: The Moderating Role of Product and Consumer Characteristics," *Journal of Marketing,* #2, 2010; James C. Ward and Amy L. Ostrom, "Complaining to the Masses: The Role of Protest Framing in Customer-Created Complaint websites," *Journal of Consumer Research,* August 2006; Shahana Sen and Dawn Lerman, "Why Are You Telling Me This? An Examination into Negative Consumer Reviews on the Web," *Journal of Interactive Marketing,* Fall 2007; V. Kumar, J. Andrew Petersen and Robert P. Leone, "How Valuable Is Word of Mouth?" *Harvard Business Review,* October 2007; J. Goldenberg, S. Han, D. R. Lehmann, and J. W. Hong, "The Role of Hubs in the Adoption Process," *Journal of Marketing,* #2, 2009; P. Huang, N. H. Lurie, and S. Mitra, "Searching for Experience on the Web: An Empirical Examination of Consumer Behavior for Search and Experience Goods," *Journal of Marketing,* #2, 2009.

8. "Brands as Publishers: The Changing Rules of SEO," *Search Engine Watch,* July 11, 2012.

9. We cover word-of-mouth later in this chapter.

10. As an example of cooperation between direct and indirect communication channels see Wierenga, Berend, and Han Soethoudt, "Sales promotions and channel coordination," *Journal of the Academy of Marketing Science,* May 2010.

11. "The New B-to-B Fundamentals," *Target Marketing,* October 2003, at www.targetonline.com; "The Changing Face of B-to-B Sales & Marketing," October 20, 2003, http://news.thomasnet.com/IMT/archives/; G. Martin-Herran, S. P. Sigue, and G. Zaccour, "The Dilemma of Pull- and Push-Price Promotions," *Journal of Retailing,* #1, 2010.

12. Retail Customer Dissatisfaction Study—2006, Verde Group—Baker Retail Initiative at Wharton, 2006.

13. "How Marketers Use Online Influencers to Boost Branding Efforts," *Advertising Age,* December 21, 2009; "Big Diaper Makers Square Off," *Wall Street Journal,* April 13, 2009.

14. For more on BzzAgent, see "BzzAgent Seeks to Turn Word of Mouth into a Saleable Medium," *Advertising Age,* February 13, 2006; "Small Firms Turn to Marketing Buzz Agents," *Wall Street Journal,* December 27, 2005. For more on opinion leaders, word-of-mouth publicity, and buzz marketing, see Chapter 5 and: Berger, Jonah, and Eric M Schwartz, "What Drives Immediate and Ongoing Word of Mouth?," *Journal of Marketing Research,* October 2011; Moore, Sarah G, "Some Things Are Better Left Unsaid: How Word-of-Mouth Influences the Storyteller," *Journal of Consumer Research,* #6, 2012; Chen, Yubo, Qi Wang, and Jinhong Xie, "Online Social Interactions: A Natural Experiment on Word of Mouth Versus Observational Learning," *Journal of Marketing Research,* April 2011; Cheema, Amar, and Andrew M Kaikati, "The Effect of Need for Uniqueness on Word of Mouth," *Journal of Marketing Research,* June 2010; Bruce, Norris I, Natasha Zhang Foutz, and Ceren Kolsarici, "Dynamic Effectiveness of Advertising and Word of Mouth in Sequential Distribution of New Products," *Journal of Marketing Research,* August 2012; Trusov, Michael, Anand V Bodapati, and Randolph E Bucklin, "Determining Influential Users in Internet Social Networks," *Journal of Marketing Research,* August 2010; M. Trusov, R. E. Bucklin, and K. Pauwels, "Effects of Word-of-Mouth Versus Traditional Marketing: Findings from an Internet Social Networking Site," *Journal of Marketing,* #5, 2009; C. A. de Matos and C. A. V. Rossi, "Word-of-Mouth Communications in Marketing: A Meta-Analytic Review of the Antecedents and Moderators," *Journal of the Academy of Marketing Science,* #4, 2008; G. Ryu and J. K. Han, "Word-of-Mouth Transmission in Settings with Multiple Opinions: The Impact of Other Opinions on WOM Likelihood and Valence," *Journal of Consumer Psychology,* #3, 2009; D. Godes and D. Mayzlin, "Firm-Created Word-of-Mouth Communication: Evidence from a Field Test," Marketing Science, #4, 2009; De Liu, Xianjun Geng, and Andrew B. Whinston, "Optimal Design of Consumer Contests," *Journal of Marketing,* October 2007; Kelly D. Martin and N. Craig Smith, "Commercializing Social Interaction: The Ethics of Stealth Marketing," *Journal of Public Policy & Marketing,* Spring 2008; George R. Milne, Shalini Bahl, and Andrew Rohm, "Toward a Framework for Assessing Covert Marketing Practices," *Journal of Public Policy & Marketing,* Spring 2008; Aviv Shoham and Ayalla Ruvio, "Opinion Leaders and Followers: A Replication and Extension," *Psychology & Marketing,* March 2008.

15. Social Media Marketing: 5 Lessons from Business Leaders Who Get It," *Mashable,* November 17, 2011; "Twitter Really Works: Makes $6.5 Million in Sales for Dell," *Fast Company,* December 8, 2009; David Scott Meerman, 2009, The New Rules of Marketing and PR; "Blogs in Business," Marketing(UK), March 1, 2006, pp. 35–36; "The Blog in the Corporate Machine," Economist, February 11, 2006; "When Blogs Go Bad," Inc, November 2005;. See also Huang Chun-Yao, Shen Yong-Zheng, Lin Hong-Xiang, and Chang Shin-Shin, "Bloggers' Motivations and Behaviors: A Model," *Journal of Advertising Research,* December 2007.

16. For more on diffusion of innovation, see the classic work of Everett M. Rogers and F. Floyd Shoemaker, *Communication of Innovations: A Cross-Cultural Approach,* New York: Free Press, 1971. See also Hokey Min and William P. Galle, "E-Purchasing: Profiles of Adopters and Non-adopters," *Industrial Marketing Management,* April 2003; Yikuan Lee and Gina Colarelli O'Connor, "The Impact of Communication Strategy on Launching New Products: The Moderating Role of Product Innovativeness," *Journal of Product Innovation Management,* January 2003; Subin Im, Barry L. Bayus, and Charlotte H. Mason, "An Empirical Study of Innate Consumer Innovativeness, Personal Characteristics, and New-Product Adoption Behavior," *Journal of the Academy of Marketing Science,* Winter 2003; Robert J. Fisher and Linda L. Price, "An Investigation into the Social Context of Early Adoption Behavior," *Journal of Consumer Research,* December 1992.

17. "All-in-One Dinner Kits Gain Popularity," *Food Retailing Today,* May 5, 2003; "Marketers of the Year: This One's a Stove Topper," *Brandweek,* October 14, 2002.

18. Kusum L. Ailawadi, Paul W. Farris, and Mark E. Parry, "Share and Growth Are Not Good Predictors of the Advertising and Promotion/Sales Ratio," *Journal of Marketing,* January 1994.

19. Aravindakshan, Ashwin, Kay Peters, and Prasad A Naik, "Spatio-temporal Allocation of Advertising Budgets," *Journal of Marketing Research,* February 2012; Kissan Joseph and Vernon J. Richardson, "Free Cash Flow, Agency Costs, and the Affordability Method of Advertising Budgeting," *Journal of Marketing,* January 2002; Kim P. Corfman and Donald R. Lehmann, "The Prisoner's Dilemma and the Role of Information in Setting Advertising Budgets," *Journal of Advertising,* June 1994; C. L. Hung and Douglas West, "Advertising Budgeting Methods in Canada, the UK and the USA," *International Journal of Advertising* 10, #3, *1991;* Pierre Filiatrault and Jean-Charles Chebat, "How Service Firms Set Their Marketing Budgets," *Industrial Marketing Management,* February 1990.

CHAPTER 14

1. Based on author interviews with Ferguson salespeople and management. See also www.ferguson.com; *2011 Annual Report and Accounts,* Wolseley; "Customer Focused," US Business Review, May 2005; "Customer Loyalty Pays Off," T+D, February 2011; "PP-R Piping Shaves Six Figures at Florida Football Stadium," *Contractor,* February 2012; Wolsley plc, *Datamonitor report,* February 16, 2012; Wolseley Faces the Future," *bmj,* December 2011.

2. "Expanding Abroad? Avoid Cultural Gaffes," *Wall Street Journal,* January 19, 2010; "Cultural Training Has Global Appeal," *USA Today,* December 22, 2009; "Where Yellow's a Faux Pas and White Is Death," *Wall Street Journal,* December 6, 2007; "Doing Business Abroad? Simple Faux Pas Can Sink You," *USA Today,* August 24, 2007; "Why the Chinese Hate to Use Voice Mail," *Wall Street Journal,* December 1, 2005; "Mind Your Manners," *Inc.,* September 2005; Paul A. Herbig and Hugh E. Kramer, "Do's and Don'ts of Cross-Cultural Negotiations," *Industrial Marketing Management,* November 1992; Alan J. Dubinsky, et al., "Differences in Motivational Perceptions among U.S., Japanese, and Korean Sales Personnel," *Journal of Business Research,* June 1994; Carl R. Ruthstrom and Ken Matejka, "The Meanings of 'YES' in the Far East," *Industrial Marketing Management,* August 1990. See also Chapter 6, endnote 2.

3. "Shhh!" *Forbes,* November 24, 2003; "Deliver More Value to Earn Loyalty," Selling, May 2003; "Hush: Improving NVH through Improved Material," Automotive Design and Production, July 2003.

4. C. R. Plouffe, J. Hulland, and T. Wachner, "Customer-Directed Selling Behaviors and Performance: A Comparison of Existing Perspectives," *Journal of the Academy of Marketing Science,* #4, 2009; Andris A. Zoltners, Prabhakant Sinha, and Sally E. Lorimer, "Match Your Sales Force Structure to Your Business Life Cycle," *Harvard Business Review,* July–August 2006; George R. Franke and Jeong-Eun Park, "Salesperson Adaptive Selling Behavior and Customer Orientation: A Meta-Analysis," *Journal of Marketing Research,* November 2006; Diane Coutu, "Leveraging the Psychology of the Salesperson," *Harvard Business Review,* July–August 2006; David Mayer and Herbert M. Greenberg, "What Makes a Good Salesman," *Harvard Business Review,* July–August 2006; Christian Pfeil, Thorsten Posselt, and Nils Maschke, "Incentives for Sales Agents after the Advent of the Internet," *Marketing Letters,* January 2008; Dawn R. Deeter-Schmelz, Daniel J. Goebel, and Karen Norman, "What Are the Characteristics of an Effective Sales Manager? An Exploratory Study Comparing Salesperson and Sales Manager Perspectives," *Journal of Personal Selling & Sales Management,* Winter 2008; Jerome A. Colletti and Mary S. Fiss, "The Ultimately Accountable Job: Leading Today's Sales Organization," *Harvard Business Review,* July–August 2006; Robert

W. Palmatier, Lisa K. Scheer, and Jan-Benedict E. M. Steenkamp, "Customer Loyalty to Whom? Managing the Benefits and Risks of Salesperson-Owned Loyalty," *Journal of Marketing Research,* May 2007; Judy A. Siguaw, Sheryl E. Kimes, and Jule B. Gassenheimer, "B2B Sales Force Productivity: Applications of Revenue Management Strategies to Sales Management," *Industrial Marketing Management,* October 2003; William C. Moncrief, Greg W. Marshall, and Felicia G. Lassk, "A Contemporary Taxonomy of Sales Positions," *Journal of Personal Selling & Sales Management,* Winter 2006; Eli Jones, Steven P. Brown, Andris A. Zoltners, and Barton A. Weitz, "The Changing Environment of Selling and Sales Management," *Journal of Personal Selling & Sales Management,* Spring 2005.

5. "Delta Brings Back Red Coats," *USA Today,* June 25, 2009; "Bank of (Middle) America," *Fast Company,* March 2003; "A French Bank Hits the Road," *BusinessWeek,* November 17, 2003; "NationsBank Asks Tellers to Branch Out," *Raleigh News & Observer,* September 12, 1993. For more on frontline sales, Zablah, Alex R., George R. Franke, Tom J. Brown, and Darrell E. Bartholomew, "How and When Does Customer Orientation Influence Frontline Employee Job Outcomes? A Meta-Analytic Evaluation,"*Journal of Marketing,* May 2012. Badrinarayanan, Vishag, and Debra A. Laverie, "Brand Advocacy and Sales Effort by Retail Salespeople: Antecedents and Influence of Identification with Manufacturers' Brands,"*Journal of Personal Selling & Sales Management,* Spring 2011; Cadwallader, Susan, Cheryl Burke Jarvis, Mary Jo Bitner, and Amy L. Ostrom, "Frontline employee motivation to participate in service innovation implementation," *Journal of the Academy of Marketing Science,* March 2010.

6. "Matchmaking With Math: How Analytics Beats Intuition to Win Customers," *MIT Sloan Management Review,* Winter 2011.

7. For more about major account selling see Blocker, Christopher P., Joseph P. Cannon, Nikolaos G. Panagopoulos, and Jeffrey K. Sager, "The Role of the Sales Force in Value Creation and Appropriation: New Directions for Research,"*Journal of Personal Selling & Sales Management,* Winter 2011; Bradford, Kevin D., Goutam N. Challagalla, Gary K. Hunter, and William C. Moncrief, "Strategic Account Management: Conceptualizing, Integrating, and Extending the Domain from Fluid to Dedicated Accounts,"*Journal of Personal Selling & Sales Management,* Winter 2012; Steward, Michelle, Beth Walker, Michael Hutt, and Ajith Kumar, "The coordination strategies of high-performing salespeople: internal working relationships that drive success,"*Journal of the Academy of Marketing Science,* Septmber 2010; Ahearne, Michael, Scott B MacKenzie, Philip M Podsakoff, John E Mathieu, and Son K Lam, "The Role of Consensus in Sales Team Performance,"*Journal of Marketing Research,* June 2010; Ahearne, Michael, Son K Lam, John E Mathieu, and Willy Bolander, "Why Are Some Salespeople Better at Adapting to Organizational Change?,"*Journal of Marketing,* May 2010; George S. Yip and Audrey J. M. Bink, "Managing Global Accounts," *Harvard Business Review,* September 2007; Paolo Guenzi, Catherine Pardo, and Laurent Georges, "Relational selling strategy and key account managers' relational behaviors: An Exploratory Study," *Industrial Marketing Management,* January 2007; Eli Jones, Andrea L. Dixon, Lawrence B. Chonko, and Joseph P. Cannon, "Key Accounts and Team Selling: A Review, Framework, and Research Agenda," *Journal of Personal Selling & Sales Management,* Spring 2005; Michael G. Harvey, Milorad M. Novicevic, Thomas Hench, and Matthew Myers, "Global Account Management: A Supply-Side Managerial View," *Industrial Marketing Management,* October 2003; Sanjit Sengupta, Robert E. Krapfel, and Michael A. Pusateri, "An Empirical Investigation of Key Account Salesperson Effectiveness," The *Journal of Personal Selling & Sales Management,* Fall 2000; Mark A. Moon and Susan F. Gupta, "Examining the Formation of Selling Centers: A Conceptual Framework," *Journal of Personal Selling & Sales Management,* Spring 1997.

8. "How to Remake Your Sales Force," *Fortune,* May 4, 1992; "Apparel Makers Play Bigger Part on Sales Floor," *Wall Street Journal,* March 2, 1988.

9. Charlene Li and Josh Bernoff, *Groundswell,* Boston: Harvard Business Press, 2008.

10. "A Twitterati Calls Out Whirlpool," *Forbes,* September 2, 2009; "The Customer Strikes Back," *Brandweek,* April 26, 2008; "Hello, Houston . . . We Have a Customer Service Problem," *Investor's Business Daily,* March 31, 2008; "Customer Service Champs," *BusinessWeek,* March 3, 2008; "Consumer Vigilantes," *BusinessWeek,* February 21, 2008; "Comcast Takes Its Whacks on Service," *USA Today,* December 3, 2007; "Comcast Must Die," *Advertising Age,* November 19, 2007, p. 1; "One Tough Customer," *Brandweek,* March 19, 2007, pp. 18–24; "Customer Service Champs," *BusinessWeek,* March 5, 2007, pp. 52–64; "Price Points: Good Customer Service Costs Money," *Wall Street Journal,* October 30, 2006, p. R7; "The Customer Vigilante Files," Church of the Customer Blog, November 25, 2003.

11. "Cloud's Fast Rise Even Surprised Salesforce's CEO," *Investor's Business Daily,* January 13, 2010; "Pfizer Adds New Type of Tablet to Sales Calls," *Wall Street Journal,* December 15, 2009; "Videoconferencing Eyes Growth Spurt," *USA Today,* June 23, 2009; "Salesforce Hits Its Stride," *Fortune,* March 2, 2009; "An Early Adopter's New Idea," *Wall Street Journal,* January 22, 2008; Scott M. Widmier, Donald W. Jackson, Jr., and Deborah Brown McCabe, "Infusing Technology into Personal Selling," *Journal of Personal Selling & Sales Management,* November 2002.

12. S. Albers, M. Krafft, and M. Mantrala, "Special Section on Enhancing Sales Force Productivity," *International Journal of Research in Marketing,* #1, 2010; L. Ferrell, T. Gonzalez-Padron, and O. C. Ferrell, "An Assessments of the Use of Technology in the Direct Selling Industry," *Journal of Personal Selling & Sales Management,* #2, 2010; S. Sarin, T. Sego, A. Kohli, and G. Challagalla, "Characteristics That Enhance Training and Effectiveness in Implementing Technological Change in Sales Strategy: A Field-Based Exploratory Study," *Journal of Personal Selling & Sales Management,* #2, 2010; G. Wright, K. Fletcher, B. Donaldson, and J. H. Lee, "Sales Force Automation Systems: An Analysis of Factors Underpinning the Sophistication of Deployed Systems in the UK Financial Services Industry," *Industrial Marketing Management,* #8, 2008; V. Crittenden, R. Peterson, and G. Albaum, "Technology and Business-to-Consumer Selling: Contemplating Research and Practice," *Journal of Personal Selling & Sales Management,* #2, 2010; Michael Ahearne and Adam Rapp, "The Role of Technology at the Interface Between Salespeople and Consumers," *Journal of Personal Selling & Sales Management,* #2, 2010; Gary K. Hunter and William D. Perreault, "Making Sales Technology Effective," *Journal of Marketing,* January 2007; Michael Ahearne, Douglas E. Hughes, and Niels Schillewaert, "Why Sales Reps Should Welcome Information Technology: Measuring the Impact of CRM-Based IT on Sales Effectiveness," *International Journal of Research in Marketing,* December 2007; Earl D. Honeycutt, Jr., Tanya Thelen, Shawn T. Thelen, and Sharon K. Hodge, "Impediments to Sales Force Automation," *Industrial Marketing Management,* May 2005; Alan J. Bush, Jarvis B. Moore, and Rich Rocco, "Understanding Sales Force Automation Outcomes: A Managerial Perspective," *Industrial Marketing Management,* May 2005; Richard E. Buehrer, Sylvain Senecal, and Ellen Bolman Pullins, "Sales Force Technology Usage—Reasons, Barriers, and Support: An Exploratory Investigation," *Industrial Marketing Management,* May 2005; Leroy Robinson, Jr., Greg W. Marshall, and Miriam B. Stamps, "An Empirical Investigation of Technology Acceptance in a Field Sales Force Setting," *Industrial Marketing Management,* May 2005; Devon S. Johnson and Sundar Bharadwaj, "Digitization of Selling Activity and Sales Force Performance: An Empirical Investigation," *Journal of the Academy of Marketing Science,* Winter 2005; Thomas G. Brashear, Danny N. Bellenger, James S. Boles, and Hiram C. Barksdale, Jr., "An Exploratory Study of the Relative Effectiveness of Different Types of Sales Force Mentors," *Journal of Personal Selling & Sales Management,* Winter 2006; Gary L. Hunter, "Information Overload: Guidance for Identifying When Information Becomes Detrimental to Sales Force Performance," *Journal of Personal Selling & Sales Management,* Spring 2004; Cheri Speier and Viswanath Venkatesh, "The Hidden Minefields in the Adoption of Sales Force Automation Technologies," *Journal of Marketing,* July 2002.

13. "Selling Salesmanship," *Business 2.0,* December 2002; "The Art of the Sale," *Wall Street Journal,* January 11, 2001.

14. See www.achievement.com/sales; Powers, Thomas L., Thomas E. DeCarlo, and Gouri Gupte, "An Update on the Status of Sales

Management Training,"*Journal of Personal Selling & Sales Management,* Fall 2010; Lassk, Felicia G., Thomas N. Ingram, Florian Kraus, and Rita Di Mascio, "The Future of Sales Training: Challenges and Related Research Questions,"*Journal of Personal Selling & Sales Management,* Winter 2012; M. Asri Jantan, Earl D. Honeycutt, Shawn T. Thelen, and Ashraf M. Atria, "Managerial Perceptions of Sales Training and Performance," *Industrial Marketing Management,* October 2004; Karen E. Flaherty and James M. Pappas, "Job Selection Among Salespeople: A Bounded Rationality Perspective," *Industrial Marketing Management,* May 2004; Anand Krishnamoorthy, Sanjog Misra, and Ashutosh Prasad, "Scheduling Sales Force Training: Theory and Evidence," *International Journal of Research in Marketing,* December 2005; William L. Cron, Greg W. Marshall, Jagdip Singh, Rosann L. Spiro, and Harish Sujan, "Salesperson Selection, Training, and Development: Trends, Implications, and Research Opportunities," *Journal of Personal Selling & Sales Management,* Spring 2005; Brian P. Matthews and Tom Redman, "Recruiting the Wrong Salespeople: Are the Job Ads to Blame?" *Industrial Marketing Management,* October 2001.

15. William H. Murphy, Peter A. Dacin, and Neil M. Ford, "Sales Contest Effectiveness: An Examination of Sales Contest Design Preferences of Field Sales Forces," *Journal of the Academy of Marketing Science,* Spring 2004; Steven P. Brown, Kenneth R. Evans, Murali K. Mantrala, and Goutam Challagalla, "Adapting Motivation, Control, and Compensation Research to a New Environment," *Journal of Personal Selling & Sales Management,* Spring 2005; Charles H. Schwepker, Jr., and David J. Good, "Marketing Control and Sales Force Customer Orientation," *Journal of Personal Selling & Sales Management,* Summer 2004; Jeong Eun Park and George D. Deitz, "The Effect of Working Relationship Quality on Salesperson Performance and Job Satisfaction: Adaptive Selling Behavior in Korean Automobile Sales Representatives," *Journal of Business Research,* February 2006; J. K. Sager, H. D. Strutton, and D. A. Johnson, "Core Self-Evaluations and Salespeople," *Psychology & Marketing,* February 2006; Joseph O. Rentz, C. David Shepherd, Armen Tashchian, Pratibha A. Dabholkar, and Robert T. Ladd, "A Measure of Selling Skill: Scale Development and Validation," *Journal of Personal Selling & Sales Management,* Winter 2002.

16. Krafft, Manfred, Thomas E. DeCarlo, F. Juliet Poujol, and John F. Tanner, "Compensation and Control Systems: A New Application of Vertical Dyad Linkage Theory,"*Journal of Personal Selling & Sales Management,* Winter 2012; Ahearne, Michael, Adam Rapp, Douglas E Hughes, and Rupinder Jindal, "Managing Sales Force Product Perceptions and Control Systems in the Success of New Product Introductions,"*Journal of Marketing Research,* August 2010; Garrett, Jason, and Srinath Gopalakrishna, "Customer value impact of sales contests,"*Journal of the Academy of Marketing Science,* November 2010; Lo, Desmond (Ho-Fu), Mrinal Ghosh, and Francine Lafontaine, "The Incentive and Selection Roles of Sales Force Compensation Contracts,"*Journal of Marketing Research,* August 2011; Darmon, René Y., and Xavier C. Martin, "A New Conceptual Framework of Salesforce Control Systems,"*Journal of Personal Selling & Sales Management,* Summer 2011; Fu, Frank Q., Keith A. Richards, Douglas E. Hughes, and Eli Jones, "Motivating Salespeople to Sell New Products: The Relative Influence of Attitudes, Subjective Norms, and Self-Efficacy,"*Journal of Marketing,* November 2010; Sridhar N. Ramaswami and Jagdip Singh, "Antecedents and Consequences of Merit Pay Fairness for Industrial Salespeople," *Journal of Marketing,* October 2003.

17. "New Software's Payoff? Happier Salespeople," *Investor's Business Daily,* May 23, 2000.

18. Eric G. Harris, John C. Mowen, and Tom J. Brown, "Re-examining Salesperson Goal Orientations: Personal Influencers, Customer Orientation, and Work Satisfaction," *Journal of the Academy of Marketing Science,* Winter 2005; Dominique Rouziès, Erin Anderson, Ajay K. Kohli, Ronald E. Michaels, Barton A. Weitz, and Andris A. Zoltners, "Sales and Marketing Integration: A Proposed Framework," *Journal of Personal Selling & Sales Management,* Spring 2005; Eric Fang, Kenneth R. Evans, and Shaoming Zou, "The Moderating Effect of Goal-Setting Characteristics on the Sales Control Systems Job Performance Relationship," *Journal of Business Research,* September 2005; Kenneth B. Kahn, Richard C. Reizenstein, and Joseph O. Rentz, "Sales-Distribution Interfunctional Climate and Relationship Effectiveness," *Journal of Business Research,* October 2004; Rolph E. Anderson and Wen-yeh Huang, "Empowering Salespeople: Personal, Managerial, and Organizational Perspectives," *Psychology & Marketing,* February 2006; Thomas G. Brashear, James S. Boles, Danny N. Bellenger, and Charles M. Brooks, "An Empirical Test of Trust-Building Processes and Outcomes in Sales Manager–Salesperson Relationships," *Journal of the Academy of Marketing Science,* Spring 2003; Andrea L. Dixon, Rosann L. Spiro, and Lukas P. Forbes, "Attributions and Behavioral Intentions of Inexperienced Salespersons to Failure: An Empirical Investigation," *Journal of the Academy of Marketing Science,* Fall 2003; Douglas N. Behrman and William D. Perreault, Jr., "A Role Stress Model of the Performance and Satisfaction of Industrial Salespersons," *Journal of Marketing,* Fall 1984.

19. "Chief Executives Are Increasingly Chief Salesmen," *Wall Street Journal,* August 6, 1991; Joe F. Alexander, Patrick L. Schul, and Emin-Babakus, "Analyzing Interpersonal Communications in Industrial Marketing Negotiations," *Journal of the Academy of Marketing Science,* Spring 1991.

20. "Managing Technology: Selling Software," *Wall Street Journal,* March 19, 2007.

21. Homburg, Christian, Michael Müller, and Martin Klarmann, "When Should the Customer Really Be King? On the Optimum Level of Salesperson Customer Orientation in Sales Encounters,"*Journal of Marketing,* March 2011; Gonzalez, Gabriel R., K. Douglas Hoffman, Thomas N. Ingram, and Raymond W. LaForge, "Sales Organization Recovery Management and Relationship Selling: A Conceptual Model and Empirical Test,"*Journal of Personal Selling & Sales Management,* Summer 2010; Dennis B. Arnett, Barry A. Macy, and James B. Wilcox, "The Role of Core Selling Teams in Supplier-Buyer Relationships," *Journal of Personal Selling & Sales Management,* Winter 2005; Kirk Smith, Eli Jones, and Edward Blair, "Managing Salesperson Motivation in a Territory Realignment," *Journal of Personal Selling & Sales Management,* Fall 2000; Andris A. Zoltners, "Sales Territory Alignment: An Overlooked Productivity Tool," *Journal of Personal Selling & Sales Management,* Summer 2000; Ken Grant, "The Role of Satisfaction with Territory Design on the Motivation, Attitudes, and Work Outcomes of Salespeople," *Journal of the Academy of Marketing Science,* Spring 2001.

22. "How to Get Your Company Where You Want It," American Salesman, December 2003; "When Should I Give Up on a Sales Prospect?" *Inc.,* May 1998. See also Sean Dwyer, John Hill, and Warren Martin, "An Empirical Investigation of Critical Success Factors in the Personal Selling Process for Homogenous Goods," *Journal of Personal Selling & Sales Management,* Summer 2000; Doris C. Van Doren and Thomas A. Stickney, "How to Develop a Database for Sales Leads," *Industrial Marketing Management,* August 1990.

23. "Novartis' Marketing Doctor," *BusinessWeek,* March 5, 2001.

24. For more on sales presentation approaches, see "Three Strategies to Get Customers to Say Yes," *Wall Street Journal,* May 29, 2009; Richard G. McFarland, Goutam N. Challagalla, and Tasadduq A. Shervani, "Influence Tactics for Effective Adaptive Selling," *Journal of Marketing,* October 2006; "The 60-Second Sales Pitch," *Inc.,* October 1994. See also Daniel M. Eveleth and Linda Morris, "Adaptive Selling in a Call Center Environment: a Qualitative Investigation," *Journal of Interactive Marketing,* Winter 2002; Thomas W. Leigh and John O. Summers, "An Initial Evaluation of Industrial Buyers' Impressions of Salespersons' Nonverbal Cues," *Journal of Personal Selling & Sales Management,* Winter 2002; Kalyani Menon and Laurette Dube, "Ensuring Greater Satisfaction by Engineering Salesperson Response to Customer Emotions," *Journal of Retailing,* Fall 2000; Susan K. DelVecchio, James E. Zemanek, Roger P. McIntyre, and Reid P. Claxton, "Buyers' Perceptions of Salesperson Tactical Approaches," *Journal of Personal Selling & Sales Management,* Winter 2002–2003; Alfred M. Pelham, "An Exploratory Model and Initial Test of the Influence of Firm Level Consulting-Oriented Sales Force Programs on Sales Force Performance," *Journal of Personal Selling & Sales Management,* Spring 2002; Thomas E. DeCarlo, "The Effects of Sales Message and Suspicion of Ulterior Motives on Salesperson Evaluation," *Journal of*

Consumer Psychology, 2005; Amy Sallee and Karen Flaherty, "Enhancing Salesperson Trust: An Examination of Managerial Values, Empowerment, and the Moderating Influence of SBU Strategy," *Journal of Personal Selling & Sales Management,* Fall 2003.

25. J. Hansen and R. Riggle, "Ethical Salesperson Behavior in Sales Relationships," *Journal of Personal Selling & Sales Management,* #2, 2009; Thomas N. Ingram, Raymond W. LaForge, and Charles H. Schwepker, Jr., "Salesperson Ethical Decision Making: The Impact of Sales Leadership and Sales Management Control Strategy," *Journal of Personal Selling & Sales Management,* Fall 2007; Jay Prakash Mulki, Fernando Jaramillo, and William B. Locander, "Effects of Ethical Climate and Supervisory Trust on Salesperson's Job Attitudes and Intentions to Quit," *Journal of Personal Selling & Sales Management,* Winter 2006; Lawrence B. Chonko, Thomas R. Wotruba, and Terry W. Loe, "Direct Selling Ethics at the Top: An Industry Audit and Status Report," *Journal of Personal Selling & Sales Management,* Spring 2002.

CHAPTER 15

1. See www.subway.com; "Subway mixes video into summer campaign to up mobile advertising strategy," *Mobile Marketer,* June 5, 2012; "Subway Runs Past McDonald's Chain," *Wall Street Journal,* March 8, 2011; "How Subway Built a $4B Brand, Five Bucks at a Time," *Brandweek,* September 27, 2010; "Celeb Dieters: What Happens When the Pounds Creep Back?" *Advertising Age,* February 15, 2010; "The Accidental Hero," *BusinessWeek,* November 16, 2009; "Subway's $5 Foot-Long Becomes Yardstick for Fast-Food Meal Deals," *Advertising Age,* June 8, 2009; "Subway Seeks to Slice Domino's, Pizza Hut Pie," *Brandweek,* April 9, 2007; "Friday's, Subway Tailor Meals for Health-Conscious," *USA Today,* March 1, 2007; "Finding Just Enough of That Sticky Stuff," *Brandweek,* January 29, 2007; "Subway Corporate Grabs for Advertising Control: Franchisees Wary of Power Play," April 24, 2006, *AdAge.com*; "Subway Announces 3-Year Little League Baseball and Softball Sponsorship, Reflects Chain's Dual Focus on Good Nutrition and Physical Activity," *PR Newswire US,* August 20, 2005; "Subway Targets Teen Appetites," *Connecticut Post,* May 17, 2005; "Subway to Sell Kids Pak Meal that Focuses on Health," *USA Today,* September 26, 2003; "Subway Orders Weightier Campaign," *Wall Street Journal,* August 21, 2003; "Marketers of the Year: Subway, in Search of Fresh Ideas," *Brandweek,* October 15, 2001.

2. "Nielsen Trust and Advertising Global Report July 09," The Nielsen Company, posted on Slideshare.net; G. L. Urban, C. Amyx, and A. Lorenzon, "Online Trust: State of the Art, New Frontiers, and Research Potential," *Journal of Interactive Marketing,* #2, 2009.

3. See "Annual 2010," *Advertising Age,* December 28, 2009.

4. See "Global ad spending seen stronger in 2012–2014," *Reuters,* March 13, 2012; "Global Ad Market Has Stabilized; Prospects for 2010 and Beyond Improving" (press release) at www.zenithoptimedia.com; "Top 100 Global Advertisers Heap Their Spending Abroad," *Advertising Age* (Special Report), November 30, 2009; and "Annual 2010," *Advertising Age* (Special Issue), December 28, 2009. See also D. Burgos, "Use and Abuse of Cultural Elements in Multicultural Advertising," *Journal of Advertising Research,* #2, 2008; D. Lam, A. Lee, and R. Mizerski, "The Effects of Cultural Values in Word-of-Mouth Communication," *Journal of International Marketing,* #3, 2009; Manfred Schwaiger, Carsten Rennhak, Charles R. Taylor, and Hugh M. Cannon, "Can Comparative Advertising Be Effective in Germany? A Tale of Two Campaigns," *Journal of Advertising Research,* March 2007; Yong Zhang and Betsy D. Gelb, "Matching Advertising Appeals to Culture: The Influence of Products' Use Conditions," *Journal of Advertising,* Fall 1996.

5. For more on advertising to sales ratios, see AdAge datacenter "Advertising to sales ratios by industry."

6. Exact data on this industry are elusive, but see U.S. Census Bureau, Statistical Abstract of the United States 2010 (Washington, DC: U.S. Government Printing Office, 2009), p. 403.

7. For more on Got Milk campaign (and others), see "Got Milk? (Got Mess)," *Brandweek,* April 19, 2004. See also Ruiliang, Yan, "Cooperative advertising, pricing strategy and firm performance in the e-marketing age," *Journal of the Academy of Marketing Science,* July 2012; Steffen Jorgensen, Simon Pierre Sigue, and Georges Zaccour, "Dynamic Cooperative Advertising in a Channel," *Journal of Retailing,* Spring 2000.

8. For more information on the various kinds of advertising see: "So Sue Me: Why Big Brands Are Taking Claims to Court," *Advertising Age,* January 4, 2010; "AT&T Sues Verizon over 'There's a Map for That' Ads," *Engadget.com,* November 3, 2009; "Comparative Disadvantage," *Adweek-Media,* June 15, 2009. "Feature: Cause Marketing," *Advertising Age,* June 13, 2005; "The Selling of Breast Cancer," *Business 2.0,* February 2003. See also Peter J. Danaher, André Bonfrer, and Sanjay Dhar, "The Effect of Competitive Advertising Interference on Sales for Packaged Goods," *Journal of Marketing Research,* May 2008; Debora Viana Thompson and Rebecca W. Hamilton, "The Effects of Information Processing Mode on Consumers' Responses to Comparative Advertising," *Journal of Consumer Research,* March 2006; Robert D. Jewell, H. Rao Unnava, David Glen Mick, and Merrie L. Brucks, "When Competitive Interference Can Be Beneficial," *Journal of Consumer Research,* September 2003; Diana L. Haytko, "Great Advertising Campaigns: Goals and Accomplishments," *Journal of Marketing,* April 1995. Michael J. Barone, Anthony D. Miyazaki, and Kimberly A. Taylor, "The Influence of Cause-Related Marketing on Consumer Choice: Does One Good Turn Deserve Another?" *Journal of the Academy of Marketing Science,* Spring 2000; Minette E. Drumwright, "Company Advertising with a Social Dimension: The Role of Noneconomic Criteria," *Journal of Marketing,* October 1996; Amaldoss, Wilfred, and Chuan He, "Product Variety, Informative Advertising, and Price Competition," *Journal of Marketing Research,* February 2010.

9. For more on various media see: D. W. Baack, R. T. Wilson, and B. D. Till, "Creativity and Memory Effects Recall, Recognition, and an Exploration of Nontraditional Media," *Journal of Advertising,* #4, 2008; J. Rubinson, "Marketing in the Era of Long-Tail Media," *Journal of Advertising Research,* #3, 2008; "TV Commercials: Who Needs Them?" *BusinessWeek,* May 25, 2009; "Days Growing Darker for Media," *Advertising Age,* November 3, 2008; "Phone Giants Roll Out 'Three Screen' Strategy," *Wall Street Journal,* June 26, 2008; "Lend Me Your Ears: Advertisers Begin to Target Podcasts," *Investor's Business Daily,* June 23, 2008; "Attention-Deficit Advertising," *BusinessWeek,* May 5, 2008; "The Results Issue," *Brandweek,* July 23, 2007; "Brands in the 'Hood," Point, December 2005; "TV's New Parallel Universe," *BusinessWeek,* November 14, 2005. For more on videogame medium, see V. Cauberghe and P. De Pelsmacker, "Advergames the Impact of Brand Prominence and Game Repetition on Brand Responses," *Journal of Advertising,* #1, 2010; Victoria Mallinckrodt and Dick Mizerski, "The Effects of Playing an Advergame on Young Children's Perceptions, Preferences, and Requests," *Journal of Advertising,* Summer 2007; Mira Lee and Ronald J. Faber, "Effects of Product Placement in On-Line Games on Brand Memory," *Journal of Advertising,* Winter 2007. For more on cell phone medium, see V. Shankar and S. Balasubramanian, "Mobile Marketing: A Synthesis and Prognosis," *Journal of Interactive Marketing,* #2, 2009; R. Friedrich, F. Grone, K. Holbling, and M. Petersen, "The March of Mobile Marketing: New Chances for Consumer Companies, New Opportunities for Mobile Operators," *Journal of Advertising Research,* #1, 2009; Shintaro Okazaki, Akihiro Katsukura, and Mamoru Nishiyama, "How Mobile Advertising Works: The Role of Trust in Improving Attitudes and Recall," *Journal of Advertising Research,* June 2007; Mark Ferris, "Insights on Mobile Advertising, Promotion, and Research," *Journal of Advertising Research,* March 2007. For more on in-store medium, see "In a Shift, Marketers Beef Up Ad Spending Inside Stores," *Wall Street Journal,* September 21, 2005; P. Chandon, J. W. Hutchinson, E. T. Bradlow, and S. H. Young, "Does in-Store Marketing Work? Effects of the Number and Position of Shelf Facings on Brand Attention and Evaluation at the Point of Purchase," *Journal of Marketing,* #6, 2009. For more on the outdoor medium, see "Celebrating the Renaissance of Out-of-Home Advertising," *Advertising Age* (special report), June 22, 2009; "Neighbors Hope to Pull Plug on Signs," *USA Today,* September 5, 2007; "In Billboard War, Digital Signs Spark a Truce," *Wall Street Journal,* February 3, 2007. See also Charles R. Taylor, George R. Franke, and Bang Hae-Kyong, "Use and Effectiveness of Billboards," *Journal of Advertising,* Winter 2006; Charles R. Taylor and

John C. Taylor, "Regulatory Issues in Outdoor Advertising: A Content Analysis of Billboards," *Journal of Public Policy & Marketing,* Spring 1994. For more on the radio medium, see "The New Radio Revolution: From Satellite to Podcasts . . . ," *BusinessWeek,* March 14, 2005; Daniel M. Haygood, "A Status Report on Podcast Advertising," *Journal of Advertising Research,* December 2007. For more on the newspaper medium, see "Major Detroit Newspaper Takes Cues from Advertisers," *Wall Street Journal,* November 2, 2009; "Extra! Extra! Are Newspapers Dying?" *USA Today,* March 18, 2009;. For more on the magazine medium, see "Mags Grow Online but Still Dwarfed by Web Bigs," *Advertising Age,* March 3, 2008. For more on the television and cable medium, see Y. Hu, L. M. Lodish, A. M. Krieger, and B. Hayati, "An Update of Real-World TV Advertising Tests," *Journal of Advertising Research,* #2, 2009; Kenneth C. Wilbur, "How the Digital Video Recorder (DVR) Changes Traditional Television Advertising," *Journal of Advertising,* Spring 2008; Ye Hu, Leonard M. Lodish, and Abba M. Krieger, "An Analysis of Real World TV Advertising Tests: A 15-Year Update," *Journal of Advertising Research,* September 2007; S. A. Brasel and J. Gips, "Breaking through Fast-Forwarding: Brand Information and Visual Attention," *Journal of Marketing,* #6, 2008.

10. "Underwear Ads Caught in Bind Over Sex Appeal," *Advertising Age,* July 8, 1996.

11. "Looking for Mr. Plumber," MediaWeek, June 27, 1994; "Those Really Big Shows Are Often Disappointing to Those Who Advertise," *Wall Street Journal,* June 14, 1994.

12. V. Kumar, Rajkumar Venkatesan, and Werner Reinartz, "Knowing What to Sell, When, and to Whom," *Harvard Business Review,* March 2006; Jacquelyn S. Thomas, Werner Reinartz, and V. Kumar, "Getting the Most Out of All Your Customers," *Harvard Business Review,* July–August 2004.

13. "TV's Next Wave: Tuning In to You," *Wall Street Journal,* March 6, 2011.

14. "Coming Soon to Your Desktop at Work: Ads," *Bloomberg Businessweek,* April 19, 2012.

15. "Sunday Night Football Remains Costliest TV Show," *Advertising Age,* October 26, 2009, and available at http://adage.com/print?article_id=139923; "Why This $3 Mil Baby Is Back on the Super Bowl," *Advertising Age,* January 25, 2010, "Social Media Gains Yardage in Bowl XLIV Marketing," *Brandweek,* January 18, 2010; "Super Bowl Spots Mix Sex, Humor," *BtoB,* January 18, 2010; "$2 Million Average Production Cost 1 $3 Million Average Cost of a Commercial = Pressure; Can Companies Justify Ad-Spending Equation?" *USA Today,* January 30, 2009.

16. "Video Consumer Mapping Study," *The Council for Research Excellence,* March 2009; Google's Latest Bid to Boost Revenue: Interest-Based Ads," *Investor's Business Daily,* March 12, 2009; "Online Ads: Beyond Counting Clicks," *BusinessWeek,* March 9, 2009. See also Agarwal, Ashish, Kartik Hosanagar, and Michael D Smith, "Location, Location, Location: An Analysis of Profitability of Position in Online Advertising Markets,"*Journal of Marketing Research,* December 2011; Goldfarb, Avi, and Catherine Tucker, "Implications of "Online Display Advertising: Targeting and Obtrusiveness" *Marketing Science,* #3, 2011; Chan, Tat Y., Chunhua Wu, and Ying Xie, "Measuring the Lifetime Value of Customers Acquired from Google Search Advertising,"*Marketing Science,* #5 2011; Rutz, Oliver J., Michael Trusov, and Randolph E. Bucklin, "Modeling Indirect Effects of Paid Search Advertising: Which Keywords Lead to More Future Visits?,"*Marketing Science,* #4, 2011; G. M. Fulgoni and M. P. Morn, "Whither the Click? How Online Advertising Works," *Journal of Advertising Research,* #2, 2009; B. J. Calder, E. C. Malthouse, and U. Schaedel, "An Experimental Study of the Relationship between Online Engagement and Advertising Effectiveness," *Journal of Interactive Marketing,* #4, 2009; J. Q. Chen, D. Liu, and A. B. Whinston, "Auctioning Keywords in Online Search," *Journal of Marketing,* #4, 2009; Juran Kim and Sally J. McMillan, "Evaluation of Internet Advertising Research," *Journal of Advertising,* Spring 2008.

17. "SmartMoney Finds Using Fewer Ads Can Boost Click-Through," *Advertising Age,* March 2, 2009; "Average Search CPC Data by Category for March 2008," Search Engine Watch, April 7, 2008. See also "So Many Ads, So Few Clicks," *BusinessWeek,* November 12, 2007; "Competing for Clients, and Paying by the Click," *New York Times,* October 15, 2007; "The New Benefits of Web-Search Queries," *Wall Street Journal,* February 6, 2007; "Web Numbers: What's Real?" *BusinessWeek,* October 23, 2006. See also "Click Fraud: The Dark Side of Online Advertising," *BusinessWeek,* October 2, 2006.

18. "Kicking Cash to Nefarious Clickers," *New York Times,* April 11, 2010; "Google Faces the Slickest Click Fraud Yet," *Forbes,* January 12, 2010; "Click Fraud: The Dark Side of Online Advertising," *BusinessWeek,* October 2, 2006; "In Click Fraud, Web Outfits Have a Costly Problem," *Wall Street Journal,* April 6, 2005; K. C. Wilbur and Y. Zhu, "Click Fraud," *Marketing Science,* #2, 2009.

19. "How Advertisers Use Internet Cookies to Track You," *Teach the 4 Ps,* August 8, 2010; "Help! A Web Ad Is Stalking Me," *PCWorld,* June 20, 2011; "Are Retailers Going Too Far Tracking Our Web Habits?" *USA Today,* October 26, 2009; "The Web Knows What You Want," *BusinessWeek,* July 27, 2009; "Connect the Thoughts: The Analysis of Social Networking Data . . . ," *AdweekMedia,* June 29, 2009; "The Next: Companies May Soon Know Where Customers Are Likely to Be Every Minute . . . ," *BusinessWeek,* March 9, 2009; "Feel like Someone's Watching You?" *USA Today,* February 9, 2009; "We Know Where You Are," *Wall Street Journal,* September 29, 2008; "Agencies Know the Score on Web Tracking," *Wall Street Journal,* April 21, 2008; "Internet Firms Get Better at Targeting Ads," *Investor's Business Daily,* December 3, 2007; "Behavioral Targeting: The New Killer App for Research," *Advertising Age,* January 22, 2007; "Technology: Analyze This," *BusinessWeek,* Winter 2006.

20. "Media6Degrees Knows What You Want To Buy Even Before You Do," *Fast Company,* June 26, 2012; "Time for Brands to Play Moneyball, Too" *AdAge,* February 7, 2012.

21. Idea originally inspired by "Flowers That Pop," *Businessweek,* December 3, 2003.

22. "Teen Stores Try Texts as Gr8 Nu Way to Reach Out," *Wall Street Journal,* August 1, 2012.

23. "Top 10 mobile advertising campaigns of Q2," *Mobile Marketer,* June 5, 2012; "Cell Phone Ads That Consumers Love," Harvard Business School Working Knowledge, February 28, 2005; Rama Yelkur, Chuck Tomkovick, and Patty Traczyk, "Super Bowl Advertising Effectiveness: Hollywood finds the Games Golden," *Journal of Advertising Research,* March 2004. For information on apps and shopping; "Yes, There's an App for That, Too: How Mobile Is Changing Shopping," *Advertising Age,* March 1, 2010; "Brands Get a Boost by Opening Up APIs to Outside Developers," *Advertising Age,* November 30, 2009.

24. For more examples of creative campaigns, see "Edgy Advertising in a Tenuous Time," *BusinessWeek,* January 12, 2009; "Hey, No Whopper on the Menu?" *Wall Street Journal,* February 8, 2008; "Did Telling a Whopper Sell the Whopper?" *Advertising Age,* January 14, 2008; "From Admirable to Addlebrained," *USA Today,* December 31, 2007; "Marketers Get More Creative with TV Ads," *USA Today,* November 12, 2007;. For some creative and controversial ads, see "Burger Joints Pull Out Oldest Ad Trick in Book: Sex," *USA Today,* December 21, 2009; "Taste Strips Give Ads a New Flavor," *Advertising Age,* June 2, 2008. See also M. R. Brown, R. K. Bhadury, and N. K. L. Pope, "The Impact of Comedic Violence on Viral Advertising Effectiveness," *Journal of Advertising,* #1, 2010; Josephine L. C. M. Woltman Elpers, Ashesh Mukherjee, and Wayne D. Hoyer, "Humor in Television Advertising: A Moment-to-Moment Analysis," *Journal of Consumer Research,* December 2004; 2005, p. 7; Edward F. McQuarrie and Barbara J. Phillips, "Indirect Persuasion in Advertising," *Journal of Advertising,* Summer 2005 Elder, Ryan S., and Aradhna Krishna, "The "Visual Depiction Effect" in Advertising: Facilitating Embodied Mental Simulation through Product Orientation,"*Journal of Consumer Research,* #6, 2012; Noseworthy, Theodore J., June Cotte, and Seung Hwan (Mark) Lee, "The Effects of Ad Context and Gender on the Identification of Visually Incongruent Products,"*Journal of Consumer Research,* #2, 2011.

25. "Can't-Escape TV," *Fast Company,* July/August 2008; "Guerrilla Marketing 2007," *Brandweek,* November 26, 2007; "Ads Keep Spreading, but Are Consumers Immune?" *Advertising Age,* November 19, 2007;

"What's In-Store? Lots of TV Ads," *Brandweek,* November 19, 2007; EcoHangers: A Clean, Green Brand Strategy," *Brandweek,* October 8, 2007; "Caught in the Clutter Crossfire: Your Brand," *Advertising Age,* April 2, 2007; "The Newest Ad Frontier: Airport Security Lines," *Advertising Age,* March 5, 2007; "Trash Trucks: A New Hot Spot for Ads," *Advertising Age,* February 5, 2007; "How a Gecko Shook Up Insurance Ads," *Wall Street Journal,* January 2, 2007; "Want to Stand Out? Make a Splash with Mini Billboards," *Inc.,* December 2006; "Product Placement—You Can't Escape It," *USA Today,* October 11, 2006; "Sky's the Limit for Advertisers," *USA Today,* August 10, 2006; "Look—Up in the Sky! Product Placement!" *Wall Street Journal,* April 18, 2006; "With Ads Everywhere, U.S. Culture Is Reshaped," The Detroit News, May 8, 2005; www.detnews.com and www.keyad.com; "Advertising on Truck Mud Flaps Comes to an Interstate near You," PR Newswire, January 6, 2005; "Get Me Rewrite! Miller Calls the TV Shots," *Wall Street Journal,* October 13, 2004; "The Robot Wore Converses," *Wall Street Journal,* September 2, 2004; "Trump to Brands: You're Hired," *Wall Street Journal,* September 2, 2004; Ross D. Petty and J. Craig Andrews, "Covert Marketing Unmasked: A Legal and Regulatory Guide for Practices That Mask Marketing Messages," *Journal of Public Policy & Marketing,* Spring 2008; F. K. Beard, "How Products and Advertising Offend Consumers," *Journal of Advertising Research,* #1, 2008.

26. See "Agency Report," *Advertising Age* (Special Report), April 26, 2010. See also "Madison Ave. Lights Up," *Fortune,* December 12, 2005; "Ending Advertising's Spiral," *Business 2.0,* September 2005; "Agencies Are from Mars, Clients Are from Venus," Point, July 2005; "The Fall of a Madison Avenue Icon," *Adweek,* July 25, 2005.

27. "Auto Companies Struggle to Get Green Message Right," *Brandweek,* November 19, 2007; "Domino's Has No Problem Sharing an Agency with Burger King," *Advertising Age,* September 24, 2007. See also M. E. Drumwright and P. E. Murphy, "The Current State of Advertising Ethics Industry and Academic Perspectives," *Journal of Advertising,* #1, 2009.

28. "Paying for Viewers Who Pay Attention," *BusinessWeek,* May 18, 2009; "Guess Which Medium Is as Effective as Ever: TV," *Advertising Age,* February 23, 2009; "Web vs. TV: Research Aims to Gauge Ads," *Wall Street Journal,* March 19, 2008.

29. For more on international differences see, "Beauty Riskier than Booze on Spanish TV," *Advertising Age,* January 25, 2010; "Catching the Eye of China's Elite," *BusinessWeek,* February 11, 2008; "In Korea, Ads Become Must-See TV," *Wall Street Journal,* December 13, 2007; "For Reality Shows in China, Rules Have Never Been Tighter," *Advertising Age,* October 8, 2007;. See also Young Sook Moon and George R. Franke, "Cultural Influences on Agency Practitioners' Ethical Perceptions: A Comparison of Korea and the U.S.," *Journal of Advertising,* Spring 2000.

30. "Skechers Settles Deceptive Ad Case with FTC for $40M," *Adweek,* May 16, 2012. For more on KFC, see "Hey, Fast Food: We Love You Just the Way You Are," *Brandweek,* November 24, 2003; "FTC Examines Health Claims in KFC's Ads," *Wall Street Journal,* November 19, 2003; "Garfield's Ad Review: KFC Serves Big, Fat Bucket of Nonsense in 'Healthy' Spots," *Advertising Age,* November 3, 2003. See also "The Plug Stops Here," Next, November 2, 2009; "Cheerios First in FDA Firing Line. Who's Next?" *Advertising Age,* May 18, 2009; "Health Claims for Cheerios Break Rules, FDA Warns," *Wall Street Journal,* May 13, 2009; "FDA Makes Viagra Feel Blue about Online Ads," *Brandweek,* September 15, 2008.

31. For more on deceptive advertising see Craig, Adam W, Yuliya Komarova Loureiro, Stacy Wood, and Jennifer M.C Vendemia, "Suspicious Minds: Exploring Neural Processes During Exposure to Deceptive Advertising," *Journal of Marketing Research,* June 2012; Jing Xu, Alison, and Robert S. Wyer, Jr, "Puffery in Advertisements: The Effects of Media Context, Communication Norms, and Consumer Knowledge," *Journal of Consumer Research,* #2, 2010; For more on advertising to kids, see Chapter 20; G. R. Milne, A. Rohm, and S. Bahl, "If It's Legal, Is It Acceptable? Consumer Reactions to Online Covert Marketing," *Journal of Advertising,* no.4, 2009; Kathy R. Fitzpatrick, "The Legal Challenge of Integrated Marketing Communication (IMC)," *Journal of Advertising,* Winter 2005.

32. "Nielsen: Global Consumers' Trust in 'Earned' Advertising Grows in Importance," Nielsen.com, April 10, 2012; "Online Consumers Trust Branded Sites Ads Most, SMS Least," Marketing Charts, February 2012. For more on whether advertising works, Bronnenberg, Bart J, Jean-Pierre Dub, and Carl F Mela, "Do Digital Video Recorders Influence Sales?" *Journal of Marketing Research,* December 2010; Ghosh, Bikram, and Axel Stock, "Advertising Effectiveness, Digital Video Recorders, and Product Market Competition," *Marketing Science* 29, no. 4: 639–649; Sethuraman, Raj, Gerard J Tellis, and Richard A Briesch, "How Well Does Advertising Work? Generalizations from Meta-Analysis of Brand Advertising Elasticities," *Journal of Marketing Research,* June 2011; Eisend, Martin, and Franziska Küster, "The effectiveness of publicity versus advertising: a meta-analytic investigation of its moderators," *Journal of the Academy of Marketing Science,* November 2011.

33. "How Southwest Airlines Sold $1.5 Million in Tickets by Posting Four Press Releases Online," *Marketing Sherpa,* October 27, 2004.

34. David Meerman Scott, *The New Rules of Marketing and PR* (New York: John Wiley and Sons, 2009).

35. "Three Secrets to Make a Message Go Viral," *Fast Company,* May 2009; Berger, Jonah, and Katherine L Milkman, "What Makes Online Content Viral??" *Journal of Marketing Research,* April 2012; Hinz, Oliver, Bernd Skiera, Christian Barrot, and Jan U. Becker, "Seeding Strategies for Viral Marketing: An Empirical Comparison,"*Journal of Marketing,* November 2011.

36. Bob Gilbreath, *The Next Evolution of Marketing,* New York: McGraw-Hill, 2010; "Samsung Mobile Installs 77 Charging Stations at 18 U.S. Colleges and Universities during 2010 Spring Semester to Help Students and Faculty Stay Connected for Free," *Business Wire,* April 17, 2010.

37. "Facebook Page Leaderboard," AllFacebook.com, May 3, 2010.

38. See www.bazaarvoice.com; Charlene Li and Josh Bernoff, *Groundswell,* Boston: Harvard Business School Press, 2008; Moe, Wendy W, and Michael Trusov, "The Value of Social Dynamics in Online Product Ratings Forums,"*Journal of Marketing Research,* June 2011; Moe, Wendy W., and David A. Schweidel, "Online Product Opinions: Incidence, Evaluation, and Evolution,"*Marketing Science,* #3, 2012; Zhu, Feng, and Xiaoquan (Michael) Zhang, "Impact of Online Consumer Reviews on Sales: The Moderating Role of Product and Consumer Characteristics,"*Journal of Marketing,* March 2010.

39. Charlene Li and Josh Bernoff, *Groundswell.* Boston: Harvard Business School Press, 2008.

40. "Case Study: Driving Video Views with E-Mail," *BtoB,* March 25, 2010.

41. "TripAdvisor Warns of Hotels Posting Fake Reviews," *MSNBC.com,* July 15, 2009; "Honda Purges Select Comments from Crosstour Facebook Page," *Autoblog,* September 3, 2009. For academic research on reviews see A. M. Weiss, N. H. Lurie, and D. J. Macinnis, "Listening to Strangers: Whose Responses Are Valuable, How Valuable Are They, and Why?" *Journal of Marketing Research,* #4, 2008; V. Dhar and E. A. Chang, "Does Chatter Matter? The Impact of User-Generated Content on Music Sales," *Journal of Interactive Marketing,* #4, 2009; A. Finn, L. M. Wang, and T. Frank, "Attribute Perceptions, Customer Satisfaction and Intention to Recommend E-Services," *Journal of Interactive Marketing,* #3, 2009; E. Keller and B. Fay, "The Role of Advertising in Word of Mouth," *Journal of Advertising Research,* #2, 2009.

42. "The Goody-Bag Game," *Wall Street Journal,* December 7, 2005; "High Noon in Aisle Five," *Inc.,* January 2004; "P&G Breaks Out of Its Slump," *USA Today,* October 14, 2003; "Ads Mmm, Junk Mail," Newsweek, August 18, 2003; "Road Shows Take Brands to the People," *Wall Street Journal,* May 14, 2003; "Offbeat Marketing Sells," *Investor's Business Daily,* March 27, 2002. For academic research on sales promotion, see G. Martin-Herran, S. P. Sigue, and G. Zaccour, "The Dilemma of Pull- and Push-Price Promotions," *Journal of Retailing,* #1, 2010; K. L. Ailawadi, J. P. Beauchamp, N. Donthu, D. K. Gauri, and V. Shankar, "Communication and Promotion Decisions in Retailing: A Review and Directions for Future Research," *Journal of Retailing,* #1, 2009; M. Tsiros and D. M. Hardesty, "Ending a Price Promotion: Retracting It in One Step or Phasing It Out Gradually," *Journal of Marketing,* #1, 2010; S. P. Sigue, "Consumer and Retailer Promotions: Who Is Better Off?" *Journal of Retailing,* #4, 2008; R. J. Slotegraaf and K. Pauwels, "The Impact of

Brand Equity and Innovation on the Long-Term Effectiveness of Promotions," *Journal of Marketing Research,* #3, 2008; Page Moreau, Aradhna Krishna, and Bari Harlam, "The Manufacturer-Retailer-Consumer Triad: Differing Perceptions Regarding Price Promotions," *Journal of Retailing,* Winter 2001; Devon DelVecchio, David H. Henard, and Traci H. Freling, "The Effect of Sales Promotion on Post-Promotion Brand Preference: A Meta-Analysis," *Journal of Retailing,* September 2006; Kusum L. Ailawadi, Bari A. Harlam, Jacques César, and David Trounce, "Promotion Profitability for a Retailer: The Role of Promotion, Brand, Category, and Store Characteristics," *Journal of Marketing Research,* November 2006; Kusum L. Ailawadi, Karen Gedenk, Christian Lutzky, and Scott A. Neslin, "Decomposition of the Sales Impact of Promotion-Induced Stockpiling," *Journal of Marketing Research,* August 2007.

43. For more on Pampers example, see "P&G Promotion Is Too Successful, Angering Buyers," *Wall Street Journal,* April 2, 2002. For another example, see "Shopper Turns Lots of Pudding into Free Miles," *Wall Street Journal,* January 24, 2000; "The Pudding Guy Flies Again (and Again) Over Latin America," *Wall Street Journal,* March 16, 2000.

44. George E. Belch and Michael E. Belch, Advertising and Promotion, an Integrated Marketing Communication Perspective (Burr Ridge, IL: McGraw-Hill, 2012); Priya Raghubir, J. Jeffrey Inman, and Hans Grande, "The Three Faces of Consumer Promotions," *California Management Review,* Summer 2004.

45. "BtoB's Best 2009 Marketers & Creative," *BtoB* (Special Issue), Fall 2009; "CEBA Awards," *Brandweek* (Special Section), October 12, 2009; "The Show Goes On: Online Trade Shows," *Wall Street Journal* Reports, April 28, 2003; "The Cyber-Show Must Go On," *Trade Media,* May 7, 2001; "Getting the Most from a Trade Show Booth," *Investor's Business Daily,* April 25, 2000. See also Li Ling-yee, "Relationship Learning at Trade Shows: Its Antecedents and Consequences," *Industrial Marketing Management,* February 2006; Timothy M. Smith, Srinath Gopalakrishna, and Paul M. Smith, "The Complementary Effect of Trade Shows on Personal Selling," *International Journal of Research in Marketing,* March 2004; Marnik G. Dekimpe, Pierre Francois, Srinath-Gopalakrishna, Gary L. Lilien, and Christophe Van den Bulte, "Generalizing About Trade Show Effectiveness: A Cross-National Comparison," *Journal of Marketing,* October 1997; Scott Barlass "How to Get the Most Out of Trade Shows," *Journal of Product Innovation Management,* September 1997; Srinath Gopalakrishna, Gary L. Lilien, Jerome D. Williams, and Ian K. Sequeira, "Do Trade Shows Pay Off?" *Journal of Marketing,* July 1995; "Trade Promotion Rises," *Advertising Age,* April 3, 2000.

46. "Creating Incentives Down in Ranks: Marriott Ties Pay to Guest Replies," *Investor's Business Daily,* July 6, 2001; "Get Great Results from Salespeople by Finding What Really Moves Them," *Investor's Business Daily,* July 2, 2001.

CHAPTER 16

1. "Cisco's Flip Flop Prompts Consumer Complaint, but Wall Street Cheers," *Advertising Age,* April 12, 2011; "Latest Flip Is about Sharing," *NetworkWorld.com,* April 19, 2010; "Cisco Revels in Simplicity with Router, Camcorder," *USA Today,* April 15, 2010; "FlipShare TV Puts Flip Videos on the Big Screen in Your Living Room," *USA Today,* December 3, 2009; "Videos on TV with a Flip of a Channel," *Wall Street Journal,* December 2, 2009; "Cisco's Extreme Ambitions," *BusinessWeek,* November 19, 2009; "Cisco Makes a Play for Mainstream Market," *Advertising Age,* May 25, 2009; "Flip Video," Wikipedia, retrieved May 2, 2009; "Sony Turns Focus to Low-Cost Video Camera," *Wall Street Journal,* April 17, 2009; "Consumers Flip for Mini Camcorders," *Fortune,* January 27, 2009; "Gadget of the Stars," *Newsweek,* December 15, 2008; "The Lebowski Flip Mino: If You Will It, Dude, It Is No Dream," *CNET,* October 14, 2008; "Moving Pictures," *Economist,* September 6, 2008; "Flip Video's Mighty Mino," *CNET News,* June 3, 2008; "How the Flip—a Bare-Bones Digital Camcorder—Grew from a Simple Idea . . . ," *BusinessWeek,* April 28, 2008; "An Easier Way to Make and Share Videos," *Wall Street Journal,* September 12, 2007; "Smile—You're Always On Camera," *Forbes,* June 18, 2007; "A Sweet and Simple Camcorder," *BusinessWeek,* May 23, 2007; "The History of Home Movies," *Internet Video Magazine,* 2007; "The History of Video Cameras," *Internet Video Magazine,* 2006; "Single-Use Digital Video Cams Now Available in CVS," *Engadget.com,* June 6, 2005.

2. "Car Makers Cut Free Maintenance," *Wall Street Journal,* July 7, 2005; "Detroit's Latest Offer: Pay More, Get Less," *Wall Street Journal,* July 24, 2002; "Sticker Shock: Detroit's Hidden Price Hikes," *Wall Street Journal,* April 10, 2002;. For another example involving the car rental industry, see "Car-Rental Agencies Talk of Realistic Total Pricing," *New York Times,* February 10, 2004; See also Srabana Dasgupta, S. Siddarth, and Jorge Silva-Risso, "To Lease or to Buy? A Structural Model of a Consumer's Vehicle and Contract Choice Decisions," *Journal of Marketing Research,* August 2007.

3. David M. Szymanski, Sundar G. Bharadwaj, and P. Rajan Varadarajan, "An Analysis of the Market Share-Profitability Relationship," *Journal of Marketing,* July 1993.

4. "Decision on Lipitor Sets Express Scripts Apart from Its Field," *Investor's Business Daily,* November 7, 2005; "EU Court Backs Resale of Drugs," *Wall Street Journal,* April 2, 2004; "The Telecom Follies," *Wall Street Journal,* March 26, 2004; "It's Time to Look at Rx Pricing," *Modern Healthcare,* March 15, 2004; "The New Drug War," *Fortune,* March 8, 2004; "Rethinking Restructuring," *Public Utilities Fortnightly,* February 2004; "The Economy: Steel Prices Jump, Spurring Protests from Customers," *Wall Street Journal,* January 23, 2004.

5. "Aluminum Firms Offer Wider Discounts but Price Cuts Stop at Some Distributors," *Wall Street Journal,* November 16, 1984. For another example of administered pricing, see "Why a Grand Plan to Cut CD Prices Went off the Track," *Wall Street Journal,* June 4, 2004.

6. Moritz Fleischmann, Joseph M. Hall, and David F. Pyke, "Smart Pricing," *Sloan Management Review,* Winter 2004; ManMohan S. Sodhi and Navdeep S. Sodhi, "Six Sigma Pricing," *Harvard Business Review,* May 2005; Eric Anderson and Duncan Simester, "Mind Your Pricing Cues," *Harvard Business Review,* September 2003; Kissan Joseph, "On the Optimality of Delegating Pricing Authority to the Sales Force," *Journal of Marketing,* January 2001; Michael V. Marn and Robert L. Rosiello, "Managing Price, Gaining Profit," *Harvard Business Review,* September–October 1992; Peter R. Dickson and Joel E. Urbany, "Retailer Reactions to Competitive Price Changes," *Journal of Retailing,* Spring 1994.

7. "Dynamic Pricing: The Future of Ticket Pricing in Sports," *Forbes,* January 6, 2012; "How Dynamic Pricing Is Changing Sports Ticketing," CNBC, July 18, 2012; "Pricing Baseball Tickets Like Airline Seats," Bloomberg Businessweek, May 20, 2010. See also Sucharita Chandran and Vicki G. Morwitz, "Effects of Participative Pricing on Consumers' Cognitions and Actions: A Goal Theoretic Perspective," *Journal of Consumer Research,* September 2005; B. T. Ratchford, "Online Pricing: Review and Directions for Research," *Journal of Interactive Marketing,* #1, 2009.

8. For more on pricing in business markets see Markus Voeth and Uta Herbst, "Supply-Chain Pricing: A New Perspective on Pricing in Industrial Markets," *Industrial Marketing Management,* January 2006; Howard Forman and James M. Hunt, "Managing the Influence of Internal and External Determinants on International Industrial Pricing Strategies," *Industrial Marketing Management,* February 2005; Eric Matson, "Customizing Prices," *Harvard Business Review,* November–December 1995; Michael H. Morris, "Separate Prices as a Marketing Tool," *Industrial Marketing Management,* May 1987; P. Ronald Stephenson, William L. Cron, and Gary L. Frazier, "Delegating Pricing Authority to the Sales Force: The Effects on Sales and Profit Performance," *Journal of Marketing,* Spring 1979.

9. "Hagglers Thrive in New Economy," *USA Today,* March 16, 2009; "Haggling Starts to Go the Way of the Tail Fin," *BusinessWeek,* October 29, 2007; "Online Stores Charge Different Prices Based on Shoppers' Surfing Habits," *USA Today,* June 2, 2005. For more on Amazon offering different prices to different customers, see "Price? For You, $2; For the Rich Guy, $5," *Investor's Business Daily,* September 29, 2000.

10. "What's a Fair Price for Drugs?" *BusinessWeek,* April 30, 2001; "AIDS Gaffes in Africa Come Back to Haunt Drug Industry at Home,"

Wall Street Journal, April 23, 2001; "Vaccine's Price Drives a Debate about Its Use," *Wall Street Journal,* February 16, 2000. See also Richard A. Spinello, "Ethics, Pricing and the Pharmaceutical Industry," *Journal of Business Ethics,* August 1992; Nicholas H. Lurie and Joydeep Srivastava, "Price-Matching Guarantees and Consumer Evaluations of Price Information," *Journal of Consumer Psychology,* 2005; Bruce McWilliams and Eitan Gerstner, "Offering Low Price Guarantees to Improve Customer Retention," *Journal of Retailing,* June 2006; Sujay Dutta and Abhijit Biswas, "Effects of Low Price Guarantees on Consumer Post-Purchase Search Intention: The Moderating Roles of Value Consciousness and Penalty Level," *Journal of Retailing,* 4, 2005.

11. For information about pricing in the early years of cell phones, see "Mobile Warfare," *Time,* May 26, 1997; "Motorola Goes for the Hard Cell," *BusinessWeek,* September 23, 1996; "Why Motorola Has Nonworking Numbers," *BusinessWeek,* July 22, 1996; "Cell-Phone Service May Be Getting Cheaper," *Wall Street Journal,* January 11, 1996; see also Liu, Hongju, "Dynamics of Pricing in the Video Game Console Market: Skimming or Penetration?," *Journal of Marketing Research,* June 2010.

12. "New Features Coming for Blu-ray Format," *USA Today,* March 19, 2008; "Sony's PS3 Gets Boost from Its Blu-ray Drive," *Wall Street Journal,* March 12, 2008; "Getting Back into the Game," *Investor's Business Daily,* December 18, 2006.

13. Check out foreign exchange rates at www.imf.org and www.federalreserve.gov and www.x-rates.com. See also "Small U.S. Firms Make Big Global Sales," *USA Today,* April 7, 2008; "Trade Winds," *Inc.,* November 2003.

14. "Brazil's Middle Class Goes on a Buying Spree," *Bloomberg Businessweek,* May 12, 2011.

15. "New Rules Place Barriers between Students, Credit Card Issuers," *U.S. News & World Report,* February 19, 2010; "More Consumers Just Say No to Credit Cards," *USA Today,* February 8, 2010; "The Latest Credit-Card Tricks," *BusinessWeek,* December 28, 2009; "Anger at Overdraft Fees Gets Hotter, Bigger, and Louder," *USA Today,* September 29, 2009; see also Wilcox, Keith, Lauren G Block, and Eric M Eisenstein, "Leave Home Without It? The Effects of Credit Card Debt and Available Credit on Spending" *Journal of Marketing Research;* Chatterjee, Promothesh, and Randall L. Rose, "Do Payment Mechanisms Change the Way Consumers Perceive Products?," *Journal of Consumer Research,* #6, 2012.

16. "Sale Sale Sale, Today, Everyone Wants a Deal," *USA Today,* April 21, 2010. For more on P&G's everyday low pricing, see "P&G, Others Try New Uses for Coupon-Heavy Media," *Advertising Age,* September 22, 1997; "Move to Drop Coupons Puts Procter & Gamble in Sticky PR Situation," *Wall Street Journal,* April 17, 1997. See also Kusum L. Ailawadi, Donald R. Lehmann, and Scott A. Neslin, "Market Response to a Major Policy Change in the Marketing Mix: Learning from Procter & Gamble's Value Pricing Strategy," *Journal of Marketing,* January 2001; Monika Kukar-Kinney and Rockney G. Walters, "Consumer Perceptions of Refund Depth and Competitive Scope in Price-Matching Guarantees: Effects on Store Patronage," *Journal of Retailing,* Fall 2003; P. B. Ellickson and S. Misra, "Supermarket Pricing Strategies," *Marketing Science,* #5, 2008; J. W. Henke, S. Yeniyurt, and C. Zhang, "Supplier Price Concessions: A Longitudinal Empirical Study," *Marketing Letters,* #1, 2009; Ashok K. Lalwani and Kent B. Monroe, "A Reexamination of Frequency Depth Effects in Consumer Price Judgments," *Journal of Consumer Research,* December 2005; Chris Janiszewski and Marcus Cunha . . . , "The Influence of Price Discount Framing on the Evaluation of a Product Bundle," *Journal of Consumer Research,* March 2004; V. Kumar, Vibhas Madan, and Srini S. Srinivasan, "Price Discounts or Coupon Promotions: Does It Matter?" *Journal of Business Research,* September 2004; David Smagalla, "Does Promotional Pricing Grow Future Business?" *Sloan Management Review,* Summer 2004; Priya Raghubir and Joydeep Srivastava, "Effect of Face Value on Product Valuation in Foreign Currencies," *Journal of Consumer Research,* December 2002.

17. For more on slotting fees, see "Kraft Speeds New Product Launch Times," *Advertising Age,* November 18, 2002; "The Hidden Cost of Shelf Space," *Business Week,* April 15, 2002; See also Ramarao Desiraju, "New Product Introductions, Slotting Allowances, and Retailer Discretion," *Journal of Retailing,* Fall 2001; David Balto, "Recent Legal and Regulatory Developments in Slotting Allowances and Category Management," *Journal of Public Policy & Marketing,* Fall 2002; William L. Wilkie, Debra M. Desrochers and Gregory T. Gundlach, "Marketing Research and Public Policy: the Case of Slotting Fees," *Journal of Public Policy & Marketing,* Fall 2002.

18. For more on coupons, see "Sign In with Pals, Get Better Coupons," *USA Today,* May 14, 2010; "Safeway Delivers Facebook Users Exclusive Coupons," *SN Supermarket News,* October 9, 2009; "A Clip-and-Save Renaissance," *New York Times,* September 24, 2009; "Coupons Are Hot, Clipping Is Not," *Wall Street Journal,* February 25, 2009.

19. "The Real Problem with Rebates," *Primedia,* January 11, 2006; "The Great Rebate Runaround," *BusinessWeek,* December 5, 2005; "Would You Like Some E-Mail with That Pizza? Papa John's, Blackberry Tie-in," *Advertising Age,* July 11, 2005; "Many Consumers Never Cash in Rebates," *Newsday,* January 23, 2005.

20. "Yes, You Can Raise Prices," *Fortune,* March 2, 2009; "Sweetening a Sour Economy: Americans Reach for Small Luxuries . . . ," *USA Today,* February 24, 2009; "Marketers Try to Promote Value without Cheapening Image," *USA Today,* November 17, 2008.

21. "Freeze-Dried Berries Heat Up Cereal Duel," *Wall Street Journal,* May 15, 2003; "Garfield's Ad Review: A Few Spoons of Truth Tossed into Special K Red Berries Spot," *Advertising Age,* May 12, 2003.

22. "Intel Fine Jolts Tech Sector," *Wall Street Journal,* May 14, 2009. See also "Europe Inc. Takes Aim at Price-Fixers," *BusinessWeek,* November 2, 2009. For an excellent discussion of laws related to pricing, see Louis W. Stern and Thomas L. Eovaldi, *Legal Aspects of Marketing Strategy: Antitrust and Consumer Protection Issues* (Englewood Cliffs, NJ: Prentice-Hall, 1984). See also Joseph P. Guiltinan and Gregory T. Gundlach, "Aggressive and Predatory Pricing: A Framework for Analysis," *Journal of Marketing,* July 1996.

23. See www.lightingprize.org; "The Future of Light Is the LED," *Wired,* August 19, 2011; "Philips' L Prize bulb is efficient, expensive, and available," *Extreme Tech,* April 18, 2012; "The Light Bulb Goes Digital," *Fortune,* February 8, 2010; "America's On-Again, Off-Again Light Bulb Affair," *Wall Street Journal,* May 29, 2009; "Ban on Incandescent Lamps Discussed by Finnish Parliament," *Helsingin Sanomat,* retrieved May 5, 2008; "A New Twist for Light Bulbs that Conserve Energy," *USA Today,* April 22, 2008; "Tesco to Sell Energy Saving Bulbs for a Penny," *Supermarket & Retailer,* March 18, 2008; "Venture Capitalists Tout Green Lighting," *Wall Street Journal,* March 17, 2008; "The Right Light," *Electric Perspectives,* March–April 2008; "The Shape of Light to Come? Not Everyone's Buying It," *USA Today,* February 28, 2008; "Bye Bye, Light Bulb," *Wall Street Journal,* January 2, 2008; "The Next Big Idea," *Retailing Today,* December 2007–January 2008; "Father of the Compact Fluorescent Bulb Looks Back," *CNETNews.com,* August 16, 2007; "Building a Better Light Bulb: At $10 to $20 Each, Buyers May Balk at New Technology," *Washington Post,* June 2, 1992.

24. Patrick J. Kaufmann, N. Craig Smith, and Gwendolyn K. Ortmeyer, "Deception in Retailer High-Low Pricing: A 'Rule of Reason' Approach," *Journal of Retailing,* Summer 1994.

25. Hunter-Gault, Charlayne (October 15, 1996). "ADM: Who's Next?". *MacNeil/Lehrer Newshour (PBS).* Retrieved 2007-10-17.

26. "Century-Old Ban Lifted on Minimum Retail Pricing," *New York Times,* June 29, 2007.

27. Richard L. Pinkerton and Deborah J. Kemp, "The Industrial Buyer and the Robinson-Patman Act," *International Journal of Purchasing & Materials Management,* Winter 1996.

28. "Firms Must Prove Injury from Price Bias to Qualify for Damages, High Court Says," *Wall Street Journal,* May 19, 1981.

29. "Booksellers Say Five Publishers Play Favorites," *Wall Street Journal,* May 27, 1994; Joseph P. Vaccaro and Derek W. F. Coward, "Managerial and Legal Implications of Price Haggling: A Sales Manager's Dilemma," *Journal of Personal Selling & Sales Management,* Summer 1993; John R. Davidson, "FTC, Robinson-Patman and Cooperative Promotion Activities," *Journal of Marketing,* January 1968; L. X. Tarpey, Sr.,

"Buyer Liability under the Robinson-Patman Act: A Current Appraisal," *Journal of Marketing*, January 1972.

CHAPTER 17

1. "Seoul Fines Six LCD Manufacturers in Price-Fixing Case," *Wall Street Journal*, October 31, 2011; "How Faulty Marketing Has Stalled TV Sales," *Bloomberg Businessweek*, January 20, 2011; "Sony TV Unit Seeks Path to Profitability," *Wall Street Journal*, November 26, 2010; "Sony Pledges to Corral Inventory," *Wall Street Journal*, November 2, 2010; "Samsung Edges Out TV Rivals," *Wall Street Journal*, February 17, 2010; "Sony Swings Back to the Black," *Wall Street Journal*, February 5, 2010; "Sony Bravia Internet Video Brings Social Media to Your 3D TV," *Media Mentalism*, January 15, 2010; "Sony Pins Future on a 3-D-Revival," *Wall Street Journal*, January 7, 2010; "Sony's 3D TV Plans Become Clearer," *PC World*, November 29, 2009; "U.S. Upstart Takes on TV Giants in Price War," *Wall Street Journal*, April 15, 2008; "Sony Teams with Sharp in Flat-Panel LCD Plant," *Investor's Business Daily*, February 27, 2008; "TV Makers Aren't Turned Off by Slump," *Wall Street Journal*, January 29, 2008; "The Picture Gets Fuzzy for TV Deals," *Wall Street Journal*, December 6, 2007; "How Walmart's TV Prices Crushed Rivals," *BusinessWeek*, April 23, 2007; "Flat Panels, Thin Margins," *BusinessWeek*, February 26, 2007; "Hefty Discounting of Flat-Panel TVs Pinches Retailers," *Wall Street Journal*, December 12, 2006; "As Flat-Panel TV Sales Soar, Unlikely Retailers Step In," *Wall Street Journal*, September 21, 2006; "Cheaper Flat-Panel TVs—from PC Makers," *Wall Street Journal*, December 23, 2004; "Texas Instruments Inside?" *BusinessWeek*, December 6, 2004; "Flat TV Prices Are Falling, but . . . Not Low Enough . . . Blame Retailers' Margins," *Wall Street Journal*, November 3, 2004.

2. For more on margins see Kusum L. Ailawadi and Bari Harlam, "An Empirical Analysis of the Determinants of Retail Margins: The Role of Store-Brand Share," *Journal of Marketing*, January 2004; Ritu Lohtia, Ramesh Subramaniam, and Rati Lohtia, "Are Pricing Practices in Japanese Channels of Distribution Finally Changing?" *Journal of Marketing* Channels, nos. 1, 2 (2001); Marvin A. Jolson, "A Diagrammatic Model for Merchandising Calculations," *Journal of Retailing*, Summer 1975; C. Davis Fogg and Kent H. Kohnken, "Price-Cost Planning," *Journal of Marketing*, April 1978.

3. Douglas G. Brooks, "Cost Oriented Pricing: a Realistic Solution to a Complicated Problem," *Journal of Marketing*, April 1975; Stephen M. Shugan," Retail Product-Line Pricing Strategy When Costs and Products Change," *Journal of Retailing*, Spring 2001.

4. For more on breakeven analysis see G. Dean Kortge, "Inverted Breakeven Analysis for Profitable Marketing Decisions," *Industrial Marketing Management*, October 1984; Thomas L. Powers, "Breakeven Analysis with Semifixed Costs," *Industrial Marketing Management*, February 1987.

5. Approaches for estimating price-quantity relationships are reviewed in Kent B. Monroe, *Pricing: Making Profitable Decisions*, New York: McGraw-Hill, 2003. See also Michael F. Smith and Indrajit Sinha, "The Impact of Price and Extra Product Promotions on Store Preference," *International Journal of Retail & Distribution Management*, no.2 (2000); Michael H. Morris and Mary L. Joyce, "How Marketers Evaluate Price Sensitivity," *Industrial Marketing Management*, May 1988; David E. Griffith and Roland T. Rust, "The Price of Competitiveness in Competitive Pricing," *Journal of the Academy of Marketing Science*, Spring 1997; Robert J. Dolan, "How Do You Know When the Price Is Right?" *Harvard Business Review*, September–October 1995.

6. Carter, Robert, and David Curry, "Transparent pricing: theory, tests, and implications for marketing practice," *Journal of the Academy of Marketing Science*, November 2010; E. T. Anderson and D. I. Simester, "Does Demand Fall When Customers Perceive That Prices Are Unfair? The Case of Premium Pricing for Large Sizes," *Marketing Science*, #3, 2008; F. Volckner, "The Dual Role of Price: Decomposing Consumers' Reactions to Price," *Journal of the Academy of Marketing Science*, #3, 2008; J. H. Chu, P. Chintagunta, and J. Cebollada, "A Comparison of Within-Household Price Sensitivity across Online and Offline Channels," *Marketing Science*, #2, 2008; Bolton, Lisa E, Hean Tat Keh, and Joseph W Alba, "How Do Price Fairness Perceptions Differ Across Culture?" *Journal of Marketing Research*, June 2010; Lisa E. Bolton and Joseph W. Alba, "Price Fairness: Good and Service Differences and the Role of Vendor Costs," *Journal of Consumer Research*, August 2006; Lan Xia, Kent B. Monroe, and Jennifer L. Cox, "The Price Is Unfair! A Conceptual Framework of Price Fairness Perceptions," *Journal of Marketing*, October 2004; Narayan Janakiraman, Robert J. Meyer, and Andrea C. Morales, "Spillover Effects: How Consumers Respond to Unexpected Changes in Price and Quality," *Journal of Consumer Research*, October 2006; Shuba Srinivasan, Koen Pauwels, and Vincent Nijs, "Demand-Based Pricing versus Past-Price Dependence: A Cost-Benefit Analysis," *Journal of Marketing*, March 2008; Marc Vanhuele, Gilles Laurent, and Xavier Drèze, "Consumers' Immediate Memory for Prices," *Journal of Consumer Research*, August 2006; Manoj Thomas and Geeta Menon, "When Internal Reference Prices and Price Expectations Diverge: The Role of Confidence," *Journal of Marketing Research*, August 2007; Kirk L. Wakefield and J. Jeffrey Inman, "Situational Price Sensitivity: The Role of Consumption Occasion, Social Context and Income," *Journal of Retailing*, Winter 2003. For the ethics exercise see D. Talukdar, "Cost of Being Poor: Retail Price and Consumer Price Search Differences across Inner-City and Suburban Neighborhoods," *Journal of Consumer Research*, #3, 2008; for more on price sensitivity see Frederick, Shane. 2012. "Overestimating Others' Willingness to Pay," *Journal of Consumer Research* 39, no. 1: 1-21; Miller, Klaus M, Reto Hofstetter, Harley Krohmer, and Z. John Zhang, "How Should Consumers' Willingness to Pay Be Measured? An Empirical Comparison of State-of-the-Art Approaches," *Journal of Marketing Research*, February 2011; Yuan, Hong, and Song Han, "The Effects of Consumers' Price Expectations on Sellers' Dynamic Pricing Strategies," *Journal of Marketing Research*, February 2011; Adaval, Rashmi, and Robert S Wyer, "Conscious and Nonconscious Comparisons with Price Anchors: Effects on Willingness to Pay for Related and Unrelated Products," *Journal of Marketing Research*, April 2011; Cunha, Jr. Marcus, and Jeffrey D. Shulman, "Assimilation and Contrast in Price Evaluations," *Journal of Consumer Research*, #5, 2011; Melancon, Joanna Phillips, Stephanie M. Noble, and Charles H. Noble, "Managing rewards to enhance relational worth," *Journal of the Academy of Marketing Science*, May 2011.

7. "Seeking Perfect Prices, CEO Tears Up the Rules," *Wall Street Journal*, March 27, 2007.

8. Thomas T. Nagle and Reed R. Holder, *The Strategy and Tactics of Pricing* (Englewood Cliffs, NJ: Prentice-Hall, 2002); Andreas Hinterhuber, "Towards Value-Based Pricing—An Integrative Framework for Decision Making," *Industrial Marketing Management*, November 2004; Benson P. Shapiro and Barbara P. Jackson, "Industrial Pricing to Meet Customer Needs," *Harvard Business Review*, November–December 1978; "The Race to the $10 Light Bulb," *BusinessWeek*, May 19, 1980. See also Michael H. Morris and Donald A. Fuller, "Pricing an Industrial Service," *Industrial Marketing Management*, May 1989.

9. For more on auctions, see "Copart: Auctioneer's Web Move Puts It in Fast Lane," *Investor's Business Daily*, June 16, 2004; "Renaissance in Cyberspace," *Wall Street Journal*, November 20, 2003; "Sold! to Save the Farm," *Wall Street Journal*, August 29, 2003. See also Larry R. Smeltzer and Amelia S. Carr, "Electronic Reverse Auctions: Promises, Risks and Conditions for Success," *Industrial Marketing Management*, August 2003; Sandy D. Jap, "An Exploratory Study of the Introduction of Online Reverse Auctions," *Journal of Marketing*, July 2003.

10. "The Price Is Really Right," *BusinessWeek*, March 31, 2003; "New Software Manages Price Cuts," *Investor's Business Daily*, March 31, 2003; "The Power of Optimal Pricing," *Business 2.0*, September 2002; "Priced to Move: Retailers Try to Get Leg Up on Markdowns with New Software," *Wall Street Journal*, August 7, 2001; "The Price Is Right," *Inc.*, July 2001. See also Ashutosh Dixit, Thomas W. Whipple, George M. Zinkhan, and Edward Gailey, "A Taxonomy of Information Technology-Enhanced Pricing Strategies," *Journal of Business Research*, April 2008; Devon DelVecchio, H. Shanker Krishnan, and Daniel C. Smith, "Cents or Percent? The Effects of Promotion Framing on Price Expectations and Choice," *Journal of Marketing*, July 2007; Kelly L. Haws and William O.

Bearden, "Dynamic Pricing and Consumer Fairness Perceptions," *Journal of Consumer Research,* October 2006; Tridib Mazumdar, S. P. Raj, and Indrajit Sinha, "Reference Price Research: Review and Propositions," *Journal of Marketing,* October 2005; Michael J. Barone, Kenneth C. Manning, and Paul W. Miniard, "Consumer Response to Retailers' Use of Partially Comparative Pricing," *Journal of Marketing,* July 2004; Chezy Ofir, "Reexamining Latitude of Price Acceptability and Price Thresholds: Predicting Basic Consumer Reaction to Price," *Journal of Consumer Research,* March 2004; Aradhna Krishna, Mary Wagner, Carolyn Yoon, and Rashmi Adaval, "Effects of Extreme-Priced Products on Consumer Reservation Prices," *Journal of Consumer Psychology,* 2006; Sangkil Moon, Gary J. Russell, and Sri Devi Duvvuri, "Profiling the Reference Price Consumer," *Journal of Retailing,* March 2006; John T. Gourville and Youngme Moon, "Managing Price Expectations Through Product Overlap," *Journal of Retailing,* Spring 2004; Marc Vanhuele and Xavier Dreze, "Measuring the Price Knowledge Shoppers Bring to the Store," *Journal of Marketing,* October 2002; Rashmi Adaval and Kent B. Monroe, "Automatic Construction and Use of Contextual Information for Product and Price Evaluations," *Journal of Consumer Research,* March 2002; Joel E. Urbany, Peter R. Dickson, and Alan G. Sawyer, "Insights into Crossand Within-Store Price Search: Retailer Estimates vs. Consumer Self-Reports," *Journal of Retailing,* Summer 2000; Ronald W. Niedrich, Subhash Sharma, and Douglas H. Wedell, "Reference Price and Price Perceptions: A Comparison of Alternative Models," *Journal of Consumer Research,* December 2001; Erica Mina Okada, "Trade-Ins, Mental Accounting, and Product Replacement Decisions," *Journal of Consumer Research,* March 2001; Aradhna Krishna, Richard Briesch, Donald R. Lehmann, and Hong Yuan, "A Meta-Analysis of the Impact of Price Presentation on Perceived Savings," *Journal of Retailing,* Summer 2002; Valerie A. Taylor and William O. Bearden, "The Effects of Price on Brand Extension Evaluations: The Moderating Role of Extension Similarity," *Journal of the Academy of Marketing Science,* Spring 2002.

11. For a classic example applied to a high-price item, see "Sale of Mink Coats Strays a Fur Piece from the Expected," *Wall Street Journal,* March 21, 1980.

12. FranziskaVölckner and Julian Hofmann, "The Price-Perceived Quality Relationship: A Meta-Analytic Review and Assessment of Its Determinants," *Marketing Letters,* October 2007; K. Douglas Hoffman, L. W. Turley, and Scott W. Kelley, "Pricing Retail Services," *Journal of Business Research,* December 2002; Steven M. Shugan and Ramarao Desiraju, "Retail Product Line Pricing Strategy When Costs and Products Change," *Journal of Retailing,* Spring 2001; Tung-Zong Chang and Albert R. Wildt, "Impact of Product Information on the Use of Price as a Quality Cue," *Psychology & Marketing,* January 1996; B. P. Shapiro, "The Psychology of Pricing," *Harvard Business Review,* July–August 1968; Lutz Hildebrandt, "The Analysis of Price Competition Between Corporate Brands," *International Journal of Research in Marketing,* June 2001.

13. Kenneth C. Manning and David E. Sprott, "Price Endings, Left-Digit Effects, and Choice," *Journal of Consumer Research,* #2, 2009; Keith S. Coulter and Robin A. Coulter, "Distortion of Price Discount Perceptions: The Right Digit Effect," *Journal of Consumer Research,* August 2007; Lee C. Simmons and Robert M. Schindler, "Cultural Superstitions and the Price Endings Used in Chinese Advertising," *Journal of International Marketing,* #2 (2003); Robert M. Schindler and Thomas M. Kibarian, "Image Communicated by the Use of 99 Endings in Advertised Prices," *Journal of Advertising,* Winter 2001; Robert M. Schindler and Patrick N. Kirby, "Patterns of Rightmost Digits Used in Advertised Prices: Implications for Nine-Ending Effects," *Journal of Consumer Research,* September 1997.

14. "The High Cost of Free," *Fast Company,* October 2009; "The Economics of Giving It Away," *Wall Street Journal,* January 31, 2009; "Would You Pay Money to See Your Favorite Site Ad-Free?" *AdvertisingAge,* December 8, 2008; "Free! Why $0.00 Is the Future of Business," *Wired Magazine,* March 2008; "Free Love" *Trendwatching.com,* March 2008; "Danger of Free," *ReadWriteWeb,* January 16, 2008. See also J. Y. Kim, M. Natter, and M. Spann, "Pay What You Want: A New Participative Pricing Mechanism," *Journal of Marketing,* #1, 2009; K. Pauwels and A. Weiss, "Moving from Free to Fee: How Online Firms Market to Change Their Business Model Successfully," *Journal of Marketing,* #3, 2008; Papies, Dominik, Felix Eggers, and Nils Wlömert, "Music for free? How free ad-funded downloads affect consumer choice," *Journal of the Academy of Marketing Science,* September 2012.

15. "P&G's Global Target: Shelves of Tiny Stores," *Wall Street Journal,* July 16, 2007.

16. For examples see "For Landlords, Jewelry Stores Are Big Gems," *Wall Street Journal,* May 20, 2005; "Diamond Store in the Rough: Opening of De Beers Boutique . . . ," *Wall Street Journal,* May 20, 2005; "Reaching Out to Younger Crowd Works for Tiffany," *USA Today,* February 26, 2004; "Tiffany & Co. Branches Out under an Alias," *Wall Street Journal,* July 23, 2003; "The Cocoon Cracks Open," *Brandweek,* April 28, 2003; "Goodbye, Mr. Goodbar: Chocolate Gets Snob Appeal," *Wall Street Journal,* February 13, 2003. See also Xing Pan, Brian T. Ratchford, and Venkatesh Shankar, "Can Price Dispersion in Online Markets Be Explained by Differences in E-Tailer Service Quality?" *Journal of the Academy of Marketing Science,* Fall 2002; G. Dean Kortge and Patrick A. Okonkwo, "Perceived Value Approach to Pricing," *Industrial Marketing Management,* May 1993.

17. For more on Gillette's complementary pricing, see "Will Frugal Shoppers Still Pay $25 for Razor Blades?" *Wall Street Journal,* October 6, 2008; "How Many Blades Is Enough?" *Fortune,* October 31, 2005; "Gillette's Smooth Bet: Men, Will Pay More for Five-Blade Razor," *Wall Street Journal,* September 15, 2005; "Can Gillette Regain Its Edge?" *BusinessWeek,* January 26, 2004.

18. For more on bundling, see "Google, Sun Agree to Bundle Programs," *Investor's Business Daily,* October 5, 2005; "Adobe Turns Page with New Software Line," *Investor's Business Daily,* November 13, 2003; "The Allure of Bundling," *Wall Street Journal,* October 7, 2003; "Dining Out at 32,000 Feet," *Wall Street Journal,* June 3, 2003; "Food Flights," *USA Today,* January 17, 2003. See also Balachander, Subramanian, Bikram Ghosh, and Axel Stock, "Why Bundle Discounts Can Be a Profitable Alternative to Competing on Price Promotions," *Marketing Science,* #4, 2010; Chen, Haipeng (Allan), Howard Marmorstein, Michael Tsiros, and Akshay R Rao, "When More Is Less: The Impact of Base Value Neglect on Consumer Preferences for Bonus Packs over Price Discounts," *Journal of Marketing,* July 2012; Khan, Uzma, and Ravi Dhar, "Price-Framing Effects on the Purchase of Hedonic and Utilitarian Bundles," *Journal of Marketing Research,* December 2010; see also Barone, Michael J, and Tirthankar Roy, "Does Exclusivity Always Pay off? Exclusive Price Promotions and Consumer Response" *Journal of Marketing,* March 2010; Alexander Chernev, "Differentiation and Parity in Assortment Pricing," *Journal of Consumer Research,* August 2006; Bram Foubert and Els Gijsbrechts, "Shopper Response to Bundle Promotions for Packaged Goods," *Journal of Marketing Research,* November 2007; R. Venkatesh and RabikarChatterjee, "Bundling, Unbundling, and Pricing of Multiform Products: The Case of Magazine Content," *Journal of Interactive Marketing,* Spring 2006; Andrea Ovans, "Make a Bundle Bundling," *Harvard Business Review,* November–December 1997; Manjit S. Yadav and Kent B. Monroe, "How Buyers Perceive Savings in a Bundle Price: An Examination of a Bundle's Transaction Value," *Journal of Marketing Research,* August 1993; Dorothy Paun, "When to Bundle or Unbundle Products," *Industrial Marketing Management,* February 1993.

19. Mary Anne Raymond, John F. Tanner, Jr., and Jonghoon Kim, "Cost Complexity of Pricing Decisions for Exporters in Developing and Emerging Markets," *Journal of International Marketing,* #3, 2001; Peter E. Connor and Robert K. Hopkins, "Cost Plus What? The Importance of Accurate Profit Calculations in Cost-Plus Agreements," *International Journal of Purchasing & Materials Management,* Spring 1997; Daniel T. Ostas, "Ethics of Contract Pricing," *Journal of Business Ethics,* February 1992.

CHAPTER 18

1. See www.benjerrys.com; *2011 Annual Report,* Ben & Jerry's; "Edelman," *Adweek,* February 2, 2010; "Facebook's Land Grab in the Face of a Downturn," *BusinessWeek,* December 1, 2008; "Ben & Jerry's

Bitter Crunch," *Newsweek,* December 3, 2007; "Ben & Jerry's: A Green Pioneer," *Advertising Age,* June 11, 2007; *Ben & Jerry's 2006 Social & Environmental Assessment* at www.benjerrys.com; "Ben & Jerry's Returns to Social Issues," *USA Today,* October 17, 2005; "It Only Looks Easy," *Point,* March 2005; "Economic Crunch," *Fortune,* December 8, 2003; "Vermont's Latest," *Dairy Foods,* September 2003; "Ice Cream Rivals Prepare to Wage a New Cold War," *Wall Street Journal,* June 26, 2003; "Summer of the Smush-In: 31 Flavors—in a Single Cone," *Wall Street Journal,* May 8, 2003; "Looking for Intelligence in Ice Cream," *Fortune,* March 17, 2003; "A Sweet Marketing Campaign," *Sales & Marketing Management,* November 2001; "Ben & Jerry's Keeps Its Folksy Focus," *Advertising Age,* February 12, 2001; "Ben & Jerry's: Surviving the Big Squeeze," *Food Business,* May 6, 1991; "The Peace Pop Puzzle," *Inc.,* March 1990.

2. "First look: Tide looks to clean up on free Daytona exposure," *USA Today*, March 4, 2012.

3. "Managing Smarter," *BusinessWeek,* March 23, 2009; "Time to Aim Lower," *Fast Company,* March 2009. Alex R. Zablah, Danny N. Bellenger, and Wesley J. Johnston, "Customer Relationship Management Implementation Gaps," *Journal of Personal Selling & Sales Management,* Fall 2004; Clayton M. Christensen, "Making Strategy: Learning by Doing," *Harvard Business Review*.

4. Bernoff, Josh and Ted Schadler, *Empowered,* 2010, Boston: Harvard Business Review Press.

5. For more on call centers and complaints see "HP Will Direct More U.S. Customers to U.S. Call Centers," *Investor's Business Daily,* February 28, 2008; "Customer Service: Call Centers, India's Competition in the Caribbean," *BusinessWeek,* December 24, 2007; "Wooing Customers with Call Centers: Netflix Switches to Human-Only Customer Service," *Investor's Business Daily,* October 22, 2007. See also C. S. Orsingher, S. Valentini, and M. de Angelis, "A Meta-Analysis of Satisfaction with Complaint Handling in Services," *Journal of the Academy of Marketing Science,* #2, 2010; S. Cadwallader, C. B. Jarvis, M. J. Bitner, and A. L. Ostrom, "Frontline Employee Motivation to Participate in Service Innovation Implementation," *Journal of the Academy of Marketing Science,* #2, 2010; C. Homburg, A. Furst, and N. Koschate, "On the Importance of Complaint Handling Design: A Multi-Level Analysis of the Impact in Specific Complaint Situations," *Journal of the Academy of Marketing Science,* #3, 2010; Lance A. Bettencourt and Stephen W. Brown, "Role Stressors and Customer-Oriented Boundary-Spanning Behaviors in Service Organizations," *Journal of the Academy of Marketing Science,* Fall 2003.

6. Hemant C. Sashittal and Avan R. Jassawalla, "Marketing Implementation in Smaller Organizations: Definition, Framework, and Propositional Inventory," *Journal of the Academy of Marketing Science,* Winter 2001; Thomas W. Gruen and Reshma H. Shah, "Determinants and Outcomes of Plan Objectivity and Implementation in Category Management Relationships," *Journal of Retailing,* Winter 2000; Jagdish N. Sheth and Rajendra S. Sisodia, "Marketing Productivity: Issues and Analysis," *Journal of Business Research,* May 2002.

7. See www.cardinal.com/mps; "Baxter's Big Makeover in Logistics," *Fortune,* July 8, 1996. See also William C. Taylor, "Control in an Age of Chaos," *Harvard Business Review,* November–December 1994; Bernard J. Jaworski, Vlasis Stathakopoulos, and H. Shanker Krishnan, "Control Combinations in Marketing: Conceptual Framework and Empirical Evidence," *Journal of Marketing,* January 1993; Subhash Sharma and Dale D. Achabal, "STEMCOM: An Analytical Model for Marketing Control," *Journal of Marketing,* Spring 1982.

8. "The Numbers Game," *BusinessWeek,* May 14, 2001; "Accounting Gets Radical," *Fortune,* April 16, 2001; "Kmart's Bright Idea," *BusinessWeek,* April 9, 2001; "Manufacturing Masters Its ABCs," *BusinessWeek,* August 7, 2000. See also Vikas Mittal, Matthew Sarkees, and Feisal Murshed, "The Right Way to Manage Unprofitable Customers," *Harvard Business Review,* April 2008; Werner Reinartz and Wolfgang Ulaga, "How to Sell Services More Profitably," *Harvard Business Review,* May 2008; Joseph P. Cannon and Christian Homburg, "Buyers—Supplier Relationships and Customer Firm Costs," *Journal of Marketing,* January 2001; Robin Cooper and W. B. Chew, "Control Tomorrow's Costs Through Today's Designs," *Harvard Business Review,* January–February 1996; Robin Cooper and Robert S. Kaplan, "Profit Priorities from Activity-Based Costing," *Harvard Business Review,* May–June 1991.

9. Technically, a distinction should be made between variable and direct costs, but we will use these terms interchangeably. Similarly, not all costs that are common to several products are fixed costs, and vice versa. But the important point here is to recognize that some costs are fairly easy to allocate, and other costs are not. See Stewart A. Washburn, "Establishing Strategy and Determining Costs in the Pricing Decision," *Business Marketing,* July 1985.

10. "Marketers Discover Analytics' Power," *BtoB*, July 16, 2007; "Personal Creations Boosts Online Sales 31% with WebTrends," *www.webtrends.com*, retrieved May 10, 2008; "Web Site Success Metrics: Addressing the Duality of Goals," *Communications of the ACM,* December 2006; "Web Sites Want You to Stick Around," *Wall Street Journal,* April 15, 2008; "Solving the Mystery of Web Analytics," *Associations Now Supplement,* June 2007; Avinash Kaushik, *Web Analytics: An Hour a Day* (Indianapolis, IN: Wiley Publishing, 2007); Jason Burby and Shane Atchison, *Actionable Web Analytics* (Indianapolis, IN: Wiley Publishing, 2007). See also Wendy W. Moe, "An Empirical Two-Stage Choice Model with Varying Decision Rules Applied to Internet Clickstream Data," *Journal of Marketing Research,* November 2006.

11. Neil A. Morgan, Bruce H. Clark, and Rich Gooner, "Marketing Productivity, Marketing Audits, and Systems for Marketing Performance Assessment: Integrating Multiple Perspectives," *Journal of Business Research,* May 2002; James T. Rothe, Michael G. Harvey, and Candice E. Jackson, "The Marketing Audit: Five Decades Later," *Journal of Marketing Theory & Practice,* Summer 1997; Douglas Brownlie, "The Conduct of Marketing Audits," *Industrial Marketing Management,* January 1996.

CHAPTER 19

1. See IKEA.com, "Company Profile: Ikea Group," *Marketline,* April 30, 2012; "Web Series Shows a Bit of Quality Can Help Sell 'Crap,'" *Advertising Age,* January 11, 2010; "IKEA in Russia: Enough Is Enough," *BusinessWeek,* July 13, 2009; "Sales of SIM Cards Might Shuffle Deck in Wireless Services," *Investor's Business Daily,* September 18, 2008; "Ikea Thinks Global, Acts Local," *Modern Materials Handling,* February 2008; "Ikea Group, Company Profile," *Datamonitor*, February 10, 2008; "Ikea to Give Staff Free Energy-Saving Lights," *GreenBiz.com,* June 12, 2007; "Sauder to Make Ikea Kitchen Cabinet Components," *Furniture Today,* February 12, 2007; "Ikea's New Plan for Japan," *BusinessWeek Online,* April 26, 2006; "Spotlight: Ikea," *Advertising Age,* April 17, 2006; "Ikea Hits Home in China," *Wall Street Journal,* March 3, 2006; "It's an Ikea World after All," *Point,* December 2005; "IKEA: How the Swedish Retailer Became a Global Cult Brand," *BusinessWeek,* November 14, 2005; "IKEA Passes Critical Hurdle for Brooklyn Store," *DSN Retailing Today,* October 25, 2004; "Late-Blooming IKEA U.S.," *DSN Retailing Today,* September 6, 2004, pp. 6, 59; "Create IKEA, Make Billions, Take Bus," *Fortune,* May 3, 2004; "Ikea Courts Buyers with Offbeat Ideas," *Advertising Age,* April 12, 2004; "IKEA: Furnishing Good Employee Benefits Along with Dining Room Sets," *Leadership and Change Wharton,* April 7, 2004; "Ikea Makes Vietnam a Big Supplier," *Wall Street Journal,* September 24, 2003; "Ikea Promotes Kid Connections," *DSN Retailing Today,* August 4, 2003; "Ikea Expands Style and Square Footage," *DSN Retailing Today,* June 23, 2003; "Ikea Adds Third Unit to Metro New York Market," *DSN Retailing Today,* July 21, 2003; "How Ikea Designs Its Sexy Price Tags," *Business 2.0,* October 2002; "Ikea's New Game Plan," *BusinessWeek,* October 6, 1997.

2. Galak, Jeff, Deborah Small, and Andrew T Stephen, "Microfinance Decision Making: A Field Study of Prosocial Lending," *Journal of Marketing Research,* 2011; "As Microfinance Grows in India, So Do Its Rivals," *Wall Street Journal,* December 15, 2009; "A Global Surge in Tiny Loans Spurs Credit Bubble in a Slum," *Wall Street Journal,* August 13, 2009; "Microlenders Widen Their Client Base," *Wall Street Journal,* March 31, 2009; "Problems for Microfinancing in Mexico," *New York*

Times, April 5, 2008; "Microlending for Microbankers," *Wall Street Journal,* March 20, 2008; "When the Bottom Line Is Ending Poverty," *BusinessWeek,* March 10, 2008; "Subprime Lender," *Wall Street Journal,* March 1, 2008; "Taking Microfinance to the Next Level," *BusinessWeek,* February 26, 2008; "Upwardly Mobile in Africa," *BusinessWeek,* September 24, 2007; "Saving the World One Cup of Yogurt at a Time," *Fortune,* February 19, 2007; "Web-Based Microfinancing," *New York Times,* December 10, 2006; "Taking Tiny Loans to the Next Level," *BusinessWeek,* November 27, 2006; "Microcredit Missionary," *BusinessWeek,* December 26, 2005; "EBay's Founder Starts Giving," *Fortune,* November 28, 2005; "He's Donating $100 Million . . . She's the Kind of Entrepreneur . . . to Fund," *USA Today,* November 4, 2005; "A Real Angel Investor," *Business 2.0,* August 2005.

3. Douglas Reid, "Marketing-Related Motives in Mergers & Acquisitions: The Perspective of the U.S. Food Industry," *Journal of the Academy of Marketing Science,* Winter 2004; Natalie Mizik and Robert Jacobson, "Trading off Between Value Creation and Value Appropriation: The Financial Implications of Shifts in Strategic Emphasis," *Journal of Marketing,* January 2003; Elliot Maltz and Ajay K. Kohli, "Reducing Marketing's Conflict with Other Functions: The Differential Effects of Integrating Mechanisms," *Journal of the Academy of Marketing Science,* Fall 2000; George M. Zinkhan and James A. Verbrugge, "The Marketing/Finance Interface: Two Divergent and Complementary Views of the Firm," *Journal of Business Research,* November 2000. See also L. C. Troy, T. Hirunyawipada, and A. K. Paswan, "Cross-Functional Integration and New Product Success: An Empirical Investigation of the Findings," *Journal of Marketing,* #6, 2008; P. C. Verhoef and P. S. H. Leeflang, "Understanding the Marketing Department's Influence within the Firm," *Journal of Marketing,* #2, 2009; A. Krasnikov and S. Jayachandran, "The Relative Impact of Marketing, Research-and-Development, and Operations Capabilities on Firm Performance," *Journal of Marketing,* #4, 2008.

4. For more on Apple, see Chapter 5 opening scenario and chapter 5 endnote 1.

5. *Sorrell Ridge: Slotting Allowances* (Cambridge, MA: Harvard Business School Press, 1988).

6. Richard Lancioni, Hope Jensen Schau, and Michael F. Smith, "Intraorganizational Influences on Business-to-Business Pricing Strategies: A Political Economy Perspective," *Industrial Marketing Management,* February 2005; Vivienne Shaw, Christopher T. Shaw, and Margit Enke, "Conflict between Engineers and Marketers: The Experience of German Engineers," *Industrial Marketing Management,* August 2003; Michael R. Hyman and Ike Mathur, "Retrospective and Prospective Views on the Marketing/Finance Interface," *Journal of the Academy of Marketing Science,* Fall 2005; Jeremy J. Michalek, Fred M. Feinberg, and Panos Y. Papalambros, "Linking Marketing and Engineering Product Design Decisions via Analytical Target Cascading," *Journal of Product Innovation Management,* January 2005; Julie H. Hertenstein and Sharon M. McKinnon, "Solving the Puzzle of the Cash Flow Statement," *Business Horizons,* January–February 1997; Ramesh K. S. Rao and Neeraj Bharadwaj, "Marketing Initiatives, Expected Cash Flows, and Shareholders' Wealth," *Journal of Marketing,* January 2008.

7. For more on production flexibility, see "Garmin Finds the Perfect Spot," *Business 2.0,* December 2003; "The Flexible Factory," *BusinessWeek,* May 5, 2003; "A Big Maker of Tiny Batches," *Fortune,* May 27, 2002. See also Yoram Wind, "Marketing as an Engine of Business Growth: A Cross-Functional Perspective," *Journal of Business Research,* July 2005; Edward F. McDonough III, "Investigation of Factors Contributing to the Success of Cross-Functional Teams," *Journal of Product Innovation Management,* May 2000; X. M. Song, Mitzi M. Montoya-Weiss, and Jeffrey B. Schmidt, "Antecedents and Consequences of Cross-Functional Cooperation: A Comparison of R&D, Manufacturing, and Marketing Perspectives," *Journal of Product Innovation Management,* January 1997.

8. For more on Tostitos Gold example, see "Buyers Seek Hard-to-Find Tostitos Gold," *USA Today,* February 9, 2003; "Relevance Is Operative Word in Catfight or Chip-Dip Ads," *Advertising Age,* January 27, 2003; "Frito-Lay Leverages National Championship Game as Major Marketing Platform for New Tostitos Gold Tortilla Chips," *PR Newswire,* December 30, 2002. See also Edward U. Bond III, Beth A. Walker, Michael D. Hutt, and Peter H. Reingen, "Reputational Effectiveness in Cross-Functional Working Relationships," *Journal of Product Innovation Management,* January 2004.

9. L. Scott Flaig, "The 'Virtual Enterprise': Your New Model for Success," *Electronic Business,* March 30, 1992; William H. Davidow and Michael S. Malone, *The Virtual Corporation,* New York: Harper- Collins, 1992. For more on Vizio, see Chapter 17, endnote 1. See also "FTD: Florist Delivers a Bouquet of Financial Gains," *Investor's Business Daily,* March 31, 2003; "Factory Fight: A Sneaker Maker Says China Partner Became Its Rival," *Wall Street Journal,* December 19, 2002; "Sri Lanka Keeps Victoria's Secret," *Wall Street Journal,* July 13, 1999; "Remember When Companies Made Things?" *Wall Street Journal,* September 18, 1997; "Virtual Companies Leave the Manufacturing to Others," *New York Times,* July 17, 1994, Sect. 3.

10. "Getting Rid of Recalled Toys Can Be a Problem," *USA Today,* August 16, 2007; "Mattel Does Damage Control After New Recall," *Wall Street Journal,* August 15, 2007; "Lead Paint Prompts Mattel to Recall 967,000 Toys," *New York Times,* August 2, 2007; "Chinese Tires Are Ordered Recalled, *New York Times,* June 26, 2007. See also Chapter 3, endnote 18.

11. For more on outsourcing, see Chapter 7. See also Kotabe, Masaaki, Michael Mol, Janet Murray, and Ronaldo Parente, "Outsourcing and its implications for market success: negative curvilinearity, firm resources, and competition," *Journal of the Academy of Marketing Science,* # 2, 2012; M. Ahearne, M. and P. Kothandaraman, "Impact of Outsourcing on Business-to-Business Marketing: An Agenda for Inquiry," *Industrial Marketing Management,* #4, 2009; *Sara Lee: Rapid Response at Hanes Knitware* (Cambridge, MA: Harvard Business School Press, 1993); "HP Will Direct More U.S. Customers to U.S. Call Centers," *Investor's Business Daily,* February 28, 2008; "The Future of Outsourcing," *BusinessWeek,* January 30, 2006; "Pulling the Plug," *Fortune,* August 8, 2005, pp. 96B-D; "Outsourcing with a Twist," *Wall Street Journal,* January 18, 2005; "Call Centers Phone Home," *Wall Street Journal,* June 9, 2004.

12. See the "Sara Lee Knit Products" case study, 1995, University of North Carolina.

13. For more on Levi Strauss hiring foreign labor, see "Sweatshops: Finally, Airing the Dirty Linen," *BusinessWeek,* June 23, 2003; Martha Nichols, "Third-World Families at Work: Child Labor or Child Care?" *Harvard Business Review,* January–February 1993. For a recent tragic example, see "Bangladesh Fire: What Wal-Mart's Supplier Network Missed," *Wall Street Journal,* December 10, 2012.

14. For more examples of mass customization see, "Web Tailored to Clothes Designers—You," *Investor's Business Daily,* July 5, 2005; "Why 'Buy' Buttons Are Booming," *Business 2.0,* July 2005; "Cashing in on the New World of Me," *Fortune,* December 13, 2004; "Planar Boosts In-Store Customization," *DSN Retailing Today,* October 25, 2004. See also N. Franke, P. Keinz, and C. J. Steger, "Testing the Value of Customization: When Do Customers Really Prefer Products Tailored to Their Preferences?" *Journal of Marketing,* #5, 2009; K. Song and A. M. Fiore, "Tradition Meets Technology: Can Mass Customization Succeed in China?" *Journal of Advertising Research,* #4, 2008; Andreas M. Kaplan, Detlef Schoder, and Michael Haenlein, "Factors Influencing the Adoption of Mass Customization: The Impact of Base Category Consumption Frequency and Need Satisfaction," *Journal of Product Innovation Management,* March 2007; Taylor Randall, Christian Terwiesch and Karl T. Ulrich, "User Design of Customized Products," *Marketing Science,* March–April 2007; Itamar Simonson, "Determinants of Customers' Responses to Customized Offers: Conceptual Framework and Research Propositions," *Journal of Marketing,* January 2005; C. Page Moreau, Darren W. Dahl, Dawn Iacobucci, and Eugene Anderson, "Designing the Solution: The Impact of Constraints on Consumers' Creativity," *Journal of Consumer Research,* June 2005; Kevin P. Gwinner, Mary Jo Bitner, Stephen W. Brown, and Ajith Kumar, "Service Customization through Employee Adaptiveness," *Journal of Service Research,* November 2005; Jerry Wind and Arvid Rangaswamy, "Customerization: The NEXT Revolution in Mass

Customization," *Journal of Interactive Marketing,* Winter 2001; James H. Gilmore and B. Joseph Pine, "The Four Faces of Mass Customization," *Harvard Business Review,* January–February 1997; B. Joseph Pine, Bart Victor, and Andrew C. Boynton, "Making Mass Customization Work," *Harvard Business Review,* September–October 1993.

15. For more on this topic, see "The Numbers Game," *Business-Week,* May 14, 2001; "Accounting Gets Radical," *Fortune,* April 16, 2001; "Manufacturing Masters Its ABCs," *BusinessWeek,* August 7, 2000. See also Thomas H. Stevenson and David W. E. Cabell, "Integrating Transfer Pricing Policy and Activity-Based Costing," *Journal of International Marketing,* #4 (2002); Fred A. Jacobs, Wesley Johnston, and Natalia Kotchetova, "Customer Profitability: Prospective vs. Retrospective Approaches in a Business-to-Business Setting," *Industrial Marketing Management,* May 2001; Erik M. van Raaij, Maarten J. A. Vernooij, and Sander van Triest, "The Implementation of Customer Profitability Analysis: a Case Study," *Industrial Marketing Management,* October 2003; Victoria Dickinson and John C. Lere, "Problems Evaluating Sales Representative Performance? Try Activity-Based Costing," *Industrial Marketing Management,* May 2003; Binshan Lin, James Collins, and Robert K. Su, "Supply Chain Costing: An Activity-Based Perspective," *International Journal of Physical Distribution & Logistics Management,* #9 (2001); Joseph A. Ness and Thomas G. Cucuzza, "Tapping the Full Potential of ABC," *Harvard Business Review,* July–August 1995; Jae K. Shim and Joel G. Siegel, *Modern Cost Management and Analysis* (Hauppauge, NY: *Barrons,* 1992); John K. Shank and Vijay Govindarajan, *Strategic Cost Management: The New Tool for Competitive Advantage* (New York: The Free Press, 1993); Robin Cooper and Robert S. Kaplan, "Profit Priorities from Activity-Based Costing," *Harvard Business Review,* May–June 1991.

16. "Why Service Stinks," *BusinessWeek,* October 23, 2000; "Weblining," *BusinessWeek,* April 3, 2000.

17. "Five Years From Now, CMOs Will Spend More on IT Than CIOs Do," *Forbes,* February 8, 2012.

18. "Top 5 commercial data security and privacy issues in 2012," *Thomson Reuters News & Insight,* January 30, 2012.

19. "A Company's Recipe for Entry-Level Staff," *Investor's Business Daily,* September 8, 2009; "The Case for Unequal Perks," *BusinessWeek,* March 23, 2009; "Pop Culture: Before Pepsi Introduced Its New Logo to the World, It Made Sure Employees Were on Board," *Brandweek,* February 16, 2009; "Stores Count Seconds to Cut Labor Costs," *Wall Street Journal,* November 17, 2008; "The Employee Is Always Right," *BusinessWeek,* November 19, 2007; "When Employees Occupy the Top Spot at Work," *Investor's Business Daily,* November 5, 2007; "Netflix: Flex to the Max," *BusinessWeek,* September 24, 2007; "How to Make a Microserf Smile," *BusinessWeek,* September 10, 2007; "The Art of Catching More Fun at Work," *Investor's Business Daily,* August 6, 2007; "How Surveying Workers Can Pay Off," *Wall Street Journal,* June 18, 2007; "How Understanding the 'Why' of Decisions Matters," *Wall Street Journal,* March 19, 2007. See also Jacqueline Chimhanzi and Robert E. Morgan, "Explanations from the Marketing/Human Resources Dyad for Marketing Strategy Implementation Effectiveness in Service Firms," *Journal of Business Research,* June 2005; Christian Homburg, John P. Workman, Jr., and Ove Jensen, "Fundamental Changes in Marketing Organization: The Movement Toward a Customer-Focused Organizational Structure," *Journal of the Academy of Marketing Science,* Fall 2000; Dave Ulrich, "A New Mandate for Human Resources," *Harvard Business Review,* January–February 1998; Vincent A. Mabert and Roger W. Schmenner, "Assessing the Roller Coaster of Downsizing," *Business Horizons,* July–August 1997; Madhubalan Viswanathan and Eric M. Olson, "The Implementation of Business Strategies: Implications for the Sales Function," *Journal of Personal Selling & Sales Management,* Winter 1992; Jeanie Daniel Duck, "Managing Change: The Art of Balancing," *Harvard Business Review,* November–December 1993.

20. Ton, Zeynop, "Why 'Good Jobs' Are Good for Retailers," 2012, *Harvard Business Review,* January–February; Reicheld, Frederick F. and Tomas Teal, *The Loyalty Effect,* Harvard Business Review Press.

CHAPTER 20

1. For more on global cell phone adoption, see "Wireless Carriers Facing Hurdles in India, Brazil," *Investor's Business Daily,* February 24, 2010. For more on consumer choice, see Ross D. Petty, "Limiting Product Choice: Innovation, Market Evolution, and Antitrust," *Journal of Public Policy & Marketing,* Fall 2002; Terry Clark, "Moving Mountains to Market: Reflections on Restructuring the Russian Economy," *Business Horizons,* March–April 1994. For more on Tesco, see "Tesco Tries to Catch a U.S. Curveball," *Wall Street Journal,* March 2, 2009; "Tesco Broadens Discount Line as Retailers Fight for Shoppers," *Wall Street Journal,* February 13, 2009; "British Invasion Hits Grocery Stores," *USA Today,* April 7, 2008; "British Supermarket Giant Cooks Up Plans to Go Global," *Wall Street Journal,* July 5, 2001; For more on obesity concerns, see Ogden CL, Carroll MD, Curtin LR, Lamb MM, Flegal KM, "Prevalence of high body mass index in US children and adolescents, 2007–2008," *Journal of the American Medical Association* 2010;303(3); National Center for Health Statistics. Health, United States, 2010: With Special Features on Death and Dying. Hyattsville, MD; U.S. Department of Health and Human Services; 2011Mohr, Gina S, Donald R Lichtenstein, and Chris Janiszewski, "The Effect of Marketer-Suggested Serving Size on Consumer Responses: The Unintended Consequences of Consumer Attention to Calorie Information," *Journal of Marketing,* January 2012; Raju, Sekar, Priyali Rajagopal, and Timothy J Gilbride, "Marketing Healthful Eating to Children: The Effectiveness of Incentives, Pledges, and Competitions," *Journal of Marketing,* May 2010; Van Ittersum, Koert and Brian Wansink, "Plate Size and Color Suggestibility: The Delboeuf Illusion's Bias on Serving and Eating Behavior," *Journal of Consumer Research,* #2, 2012; Dhar, Tirtha, and Kathy Baylis, "Fast-Food Consumption and the Ban on advertising Targeting Children: The Quebec Experience," *Journal of Marketing Research,* October 2011; Argo, Jennifer J, and Katherine White, "When Do Consumers Eat More? The Role of Appearance Self-Esteem and Food Packaging Cues," *Journal of Marketing,* March 2012; Irmak, Caglar, Beth Vallen, and Stefanie Rosen Robinson. 2011. "The Impact of Product Name on Dieters' and Nondieters' Food Evaluations and Consumption," *Journal of Consumer Research,* #2, 2011; Campbell, Margaret C., and Gina S. Mohr, "Seeing Is Eating: How and When Activation of a Negative Stereotype Increases Stereotype-Conductive Behavior," *Journal of Consumer Research,* #3, 2011; "Pepsi Brings in the Health Police," *BusinessWeek,* January 25, 2010; "A Revolution in School Lunches Takes Hold," *USA Today,* December 2, 2009; "Taxing the Rich—Foods, That Is," *BusinessWeek,* February 23, 2009; "Obesity of China's Kids Stuns Officials," *USA Today,* January 9, 2007; Debra M. Desrochers and Debra J. Holt, "Children's Exposure to Television Advertising: Implications for Childhood Obesity," *Journal of Public Policy & Marketing,* Fall 2007; Elizabeth S. Moore and Victoria J. Rideout, "The Online Marketing of Food to Children: Is It Just Fun and Games?" *Journal of Public Policy & Marketing,* Fall 2007; Kathleen Seiders and Leonard L. Berry, "Should Business Care About Obesity?" *Sloan Management Review,* Winter 2007; Jaideep Sengupta and Rongrong Zhou, "Understanding Impulsive Eaters' Choice Behaviors: The Motivational Influences of Regulatory Focus," *Journal of Marketing Research,* May 2007; Kelly Geyskens, Mario Pandelaere, Siegfried Dewitte, and LukWarlop, "The Backdoor to Overconsumption: The Effect of Associating 'Low-Fat' Food with Health References," *Journal of Public Policy & Marketing,* Spring 2007; Pierre Chandon and Brian Wansink, "Is Obesity Caused by Calorie Underestimation? A Psychophysical Model of Meal Size Estimation," *Journal of Marketing Research,* February 2007; Melissa Grills Robinson, Paul N. Bloom, and Nicholas H. Lurie, "Combating Obesity in the Courts: Will Lawsuits Against McDonald's Work?" *Journal of Public Policy & Marketing,* Fall 2005; Kathleen Seiders and Ross D. Petty, "Obesity and the Role of Food Marketing: A Policy Analysis of Issues and Remedies," *Journal of Public Policy & Marketing,* Fall 2004; Brian Wansink and Mike Huckabee, "De-Marketing Obesity," *California Management Review,* Summer 2005.

2. The American Customer Satisfaction Index, www.theacsi.org, and "Now Are You Satisfied? The 1998 American Customer Satisfaction

Index," *Fortune,* February 16, 1998. See also "Would You Recommend Us?" *BusinessWeek,* January 30, 2006; X. M. Luo and C. Homburg, "Satisfaction, Complaint, and the Stock Value Gap," *Journal of Marketing,* #4, 2008; L. Aksoy, B. Cooil, C. Groening, T. L. Keiningham, and A. Yalcin, "The Long-Term Stock Market Valuation of Customer Satisfaction," *Journal of Marketing,* #4, 2008.

3. Orsingher, Chiara, Sara Valentini, and Matteo de Angelis, "A meta-analysis of satisfaction with complaint handling in services," *Journal of the Academy of Marketing Science,* March 2010; Judy Strauss and Donna J. Hill, "Consumer Complaints by E-Mail: An Exploratory Investigation of Corporate Responses and Customer Reactions," *Journal of Interactive Marketing,* Winter 2001; James G. Maxham III and Richard G. Netemeyer, "Modeling Customer Perceptions of Complaint Handling over Time: The Effects of Perceived Justice on Satisfaction and Intent," *Journal of Retailing,* Winter 2002; James G. Maxham III, and Richard G. Netemeyer, "A Longitudinal Study of Complaining Customers' Evaluations of Multiple Service Failures and Recovery Efforts," *Journal of Marketing,* October 2002; James G. Maxham III, and Richard G. Netemyer, "Firms Reap What They Sow: The Effects of Shared Values and Perceived Organizational Justice on Customers' Evaluations of Complaint Handling," *Journal of Marketing,* January 2003; Michael Brady, "Improving Your Measurement of Customer Satisfaction: A Guide to Creating, Conducting, Analyzing, and Reporting Customer Satisfaction Measurement Programs," *Journal of the Academy of Marketing Science,* Spring 2000; David M. Szymanski, "Customer Satisfaction: A Meta-Analysis of the Empirical Evidence," *Journal of the Academy of Marketing Science,* Winter 2001; Thorsten Hennig-Thurau and Alexander Klee, "The Impact of Customer Satisfaction and Relationship Quality on Customer Retention: A Critical Reassessment and Model Development," *Psychology & Marketing,* December 1997; Scott W. Hansen, Thomas L. Powers, and John E. Swan, "Modeling Industrial Buyer Complaints: Implications for Satisfying and Saving Customers," *Journal of Marketing* Theory & Practice, Fall 1997.

4. Luo, Xueming, Christian Homburg, and Jan Wieseke, "Customer Satisfaction, Analyst Stock Recommendations, and Firm Value," *Journal of Marketing Research,* December 2010; Mogilner, Casse, Jennifer Aaker, and Sepandar D. Kamvar, "How Happiness Affects Choice," *Journal of Consumer Research,* #2, 2012; Morgeson III, Forrest V., Sunil Mithas, Timothy L. Keiningham, and Lerzan Aksoy, "An investigation of the cross-national determinants of customer satisfaction," *Journal of the Academy of Marketing Science,* March 2011; Ngobo, Paul-Valentin, Jean-François Casta, and Olivier Ramond, "Is customer satisfaction a relevant metric for financial analysts?," *Journal of the Academy of Marketing Science;* May 2012; Fornell, Claes, Roland T Rust, and Marnik G Dekimpe, "The Effect of Customer Satisfaction on Consumer Spending Growth," *Journal of Marketing Research,* February 2010; Claes Fornell, Sunil Mithas, Forrest V. Morgeson III, and M. S. Krishnan, "Customer Satisfaction and Stock Prices: High Returns, Low Risk," *Journal of Marketing,* January 2006; Neil A. Morgan, Eugene W. Anderson, and Vikas Mittal, "Understanding Firms' Customer Satisfaction Information Usage," *Journal of Marketing,* July 2005; Eugene W. Anderson, Claes Fornell, and Sanal K. Mazvancheryl, "Customer Satisfaction and Shareholder Value," *Journal of Marketing,* October 2004; Michael Tsirod, Vikas Mittal, and William T. Ross, Jr., "The Role of Attributions in Customer Satisfaction: A Reexamination," *Journal of Consumer Research,* September 2004. For a classic discussion of the problem and mechanics of measuring the efficiency of marketing, see Reavis Cox, Distribution in a High-Level Economy (Englewood Cliffs, NJ: Prentice-Hall, 1965).

5. For more on criticisms of advertising, see David C. Vladeck, "Truth and Consequences: the Perils of Half-Truths and Unsubstantiated Health Claims for Dietary Supplements," *Journal of Public Policy & Marketing,* Spring 2000; Barbara J. Phillips, "In Defense of Advertising: A Social Perspective," *Journal of Business Ethics,* February 1997; Charles Trappey, "A Meta-Analysis of Consumer Choice and Subliminal Advertising," *Psychology & Marketing,* August 1996; Karl A. Boedecker, Fred W. Morgan, and Linda B. Wright, "The Evolution of First Amendment Protection for Commercial Speech," *Journal of Marketing,* January 1995; Thomas C. O'Guinn and L. J. Shrum, "The Role of Television in the Construction of Consumer Reality," *Journal of Consumer Research,* March 1997. See also Robert B. Archibald, Clyde A. Haulman, and Carlisle E. Moody, Jr., "Quality, Price, Advertising, and Published Quality Ratings," *Journal of Consumer Research,* March 1983; M. L. Capella, C. R. Taylor, and C. Webster, "The Effect of Cigarette Advertising Bans on Consumption—a Meta-Analysis," *Journal of Advertising,* #2, 2008.

6. Thomas O. Jones and W. E. Sasser, "Why Satisfied Customers Defect," *Harvard Business Review,* November–December 1995; "The Satisfaction Trap," *Harvard Business Review,* March–April 1996.

7. "Retouching Ruckus Leaves Dove Flailing," *Advertising Age,* May 12, 2008; "For Unilever, P&G, No Good Deed Is Going Unpunished," *Advertising Age,* May 5, 2008; James E. Burroughs and Aric Rindfleisch, "Materialism and Well-Being: A Conflicting Values Perspective," *Journal of Consumer Research,* December 2002; John Watson, Steven Lysonski, Tamara Gillan, and Leslie Raymore, "Cultural Values and Important Processions: A Cross-Cultural Analysis," *Journal of Business Research,* November 2002; Roy F. Baumeister, "Yielding to Temptation: Self-Control Failure, Impulsive Purchasing, and Consumer Behavior," *Journal of Consumer Research,* March 2002; Donald F. Dixon, "The Economics of Conspicuous Consumption: Theory and Thought Since 1700," *Journal of Macromarketing,* 21, #1, June 2001. See also Michael J. Barone, Randall L. Rose, Kenneth C. Manning, and Paul W. Miniard, "Another Look at the Impact of Reference Information on Consumer Impressions of Nutrition Information," *Journal of Public Policy & Marketing,* Spring 1996; Arnold J. Toynbee, *America and World Revolution,* New York: Oxford University Press, 1966; John Kenneth Galbraith, *Economics and the Public Purpose,* Boston: Houghton Mifflin, 1973.

8. Peter R. Dickson, Paul W. Farris, and Willem J. M. I. Verbeke, "Dynamic Strategic Thinking," *Journal of the Academy of Marketing Science,* Summer 2001; Gloria Barczak, "Analysis for Marketing Planning," *Journal of Product Innovation Management,* September 1997; William A. Sahlman, "How to Write a Great Business Plan," *Harvard Business Review,* July–August 1997; Rita G. McGrath and Ian C. MacMillan, "Discovery-Driven Planning," *Harvard Business Review,* July 1995–August 1995; Jeffrey Elton and Justin Roe, "Bringing Discipline to Project Management," *Harvard Business Review,* March–April 1998; Andrew Campbell and Marcus Alexander, "What's Wrong with Strategy?" *Harvard Business Review,* November–December 1997.

9. "Why Chick-fil-A and Other Brands Aren't Being Bullied," BusinessWeek, August 1, 2012.

10. For more on corporate social responsibility, see Chapter 1. See also CB Bhattacharya, Sankar Sen, and Daneil Korschun, *Leveraging Corporate Responsibility,* Cambridge: Cambridge University Press; "Tuning In," *Wall Street Journal Magazine,* May 2010; "Smaller, Smarter," *Wall Street Journal,* February 11, 2008; "Her Signal Is Loud and Clear," *Investor's Business Daily,* December 26, 2007; "Behind One Effort to Tap into India's Water Market," *Wall Street Journal,* August 14, 2007; J. Craig Andrews, Richard G. Netemeyer, Scot Burton, D. Paul Moberg, and Ann Christiansen, "Understanding Adolescent Intentions to Smoke: An Examination of Relationships Among Social Influence, Prior Trial Behavior, and Antitobacco Campaign Advertising," *Journal of Marketing,* July 2004; Jill Gabrielle Klein, N. Craig Smith, and Andrew John, "Why We Boycott: Consumer Motivations for Boycott Participation," *Journal of Marketing,* July 2004; Robert V. Kozinets and Jay M. Handelman, "Adversaries of Consumption: Consumer Movements, Activism, and Ideology," *Journal of Consumer Research,* December 2004; Eric J. Arnould and Jakki J. Mohr, "Dynamic Transformations for Base-of-the-Pyramid Market Clusters," *Journal of the Academy of Marketing Science,* Summer 2005; Jagdip Singh, Jean E. Kilgore, Rama K. Jayanti, Kokil Agarwal, and Ramadesikan R. Gandarvakottai, "What Goes Around Comes Around: Understanding Trust—Value Dilemmas of Market Relationships," *Journal of Public Policy & Marketing,* Spring 2005; Julie M. Donohue and Ernst R. Berndt, "Effects of Direct-to-Consumer Advertising on Medication Choice: The Case of Antidepressants," *Journal of Public Policy & Marketing,* Fall 2004; Ajit M. Menon, Aparna D. Deshpande, Matthew Perri III, and George M. Zinkhan, "Consumers' Attention to the Brief

Summary in Print Direct-to-Consumer Advertisements: Perceived Usefulness in Patient–Physician Discussions," *Journal of Public Policy & Marketing,* Fall 2003; Donald A. Fuller and Jacquelyn A. Ottman, "Moderating Unintended Pollution: The Role of Sustainable Product Design," *Journal of Business Research,* November 2004; Marie-Louise Fry and Michael Jay Polonsky, "Examining the Unintended Consequences of Marketing," *Journal of Business Research,* November 2004; Joann Peck and Barbara Loken, "When Will Larger-Sized Female Models in Advertisements Be Viewed Positively? The Moderating Effects of Instructional Frame, Gender, and Need for Cognition," *Psychology & Marketing,* June 2004; Renato J. Orsato, "Competitive Environmental Strategies: When Does It Pay to be Green?" *California Management Review,* Winter 2006; Jill Meredith Ginsberg and Paul N. Bloom, "Choosing the Right Green Marketing Strategy," *Sloan Management Review,* Fall 2004.

11. "Green Goods, Red Flags," *Wall Street Journal,* April 24, 2010; "Going Truly Green Might Require Detective Work," *USA Today,* April 22, 2010; "Milestones in Green Consuming," *Wall Street Journal,* April 17, 2010; "False 'Green' Ads Draw Global Scrutiny," *Wall Street Journal,* January 30, 2008; "The Six Sins of Greenwashing," TerraChoice Environmental Marketing, *Inc.,* November 2007, www.terrachoice.com; "Most Americans and Canadians Say 'Green' Labeling Just a Marketing Tactic," GreenBiz.com, October 2, 2007; Gregory C. Unruh, "The Biosphere Rules," *Harvard Business Review,* February 2008.

12. For other environmental issues, see "PepsiCo in Recycling Push," *Wall Street Journal,* April 22, 2010; "Best Buy Wants Your Junk," *Fortune,* December 7, 2009; "War on the Water Front," *Time,* December 19, 2005; "Whole Fuels," *Business 2.0,* December 2005; "Is It Too Easy Being Green?" *Wall Street Journal,* October 19, 2005; "Turning Waste into Watts," *Business 2.0,* October 2005; "Getting More Miles to the Gallon—Fast," *BusinessWeek,* September 26, 2005; "It's Easier Being Green," *BusinessWeek,* September 19, 2005; "Automakers Jack Up MPG PDG," *USA Today,* September 16, 2005; "New Incentives for Being Green," *Wall Street Journal,* August 4, 2005; "The Great Windfall," *Business 2.0,* August 2005; "China: Wasteful Ways," *BusinessWeek,* April 11, 2005; "Eco Trends," *BusinessWeek,* March 21, 2005; Anil Menon and Ajay Menon, "Enviropreneurial Marketing Strategy: The Emergence of Corporate Environmentalism as Market Strategy," *Journal of Marketing,* January 1997; William E. Kilbourne, "Green Advertising: Salvation or Oxymoron?" *Journal of Advertising,* Summer 1995.

13. While the scenarios described are fictional and the brands listed are not necessarily involved in these practices, the activities described are real. Turow, Joseph, *The Daily You,* 2011, New Haven: Yale University Press; Andrews, Lori, *I Know Who You Are and I Saw What You Did,* 2012, New York: Free Press; Negroponte, Nicolas, *Being Digital,* 1995, New York: Knopf.

14. For more on privacy, see "Facebook Draws Protests on Privacy Issue," *USA Today,* May 14, 2010; "Facebook Wants to Know More than Just Who Your Friends Are," *Wall Street Journal,* April 22, 2010; "Friends No More? For Some, Social Networking Has Become Too Much of a Good Thing," *USA Today,* February 10, 2010; "Rogue Marketers Can Mine Your Info on Facebook," *Wired,* January 2010; "Why Facebook Wants Your ID," *BusinessWeek,* December 28, 2009; "Cracking the Code," *USA Today,* April 23, 2009; "Anti-Virus Software Isn't Only Online Security Tool," *USA Today,* April 9, 2008.

15. For more on socially responsible and ethical behavior, see www.consumerist.com; "Ordering Ethics Rx for Bedeviled Execs," *Investor's Business Daily,* September 21, 2009; "FTC Criticizes College-Themed Cans in Anheuser-Busch Marketing Efforts," *Wall Street Journal,* August 25, 2009; "Team-Color Bud Cans Leave Colleges Flat," *Wall Street Journal,* August 21, 2009; "To Catch a Corporate Thief," *BusinessWeek,* February 16, 2009; "Consumers Have Allies on the Web, *New York Times,* February 3, 2007; "Alcohol Makers Tread Tricky Path in Marketing to College Students," *USA Today,* November 17, 2005; "The Debate over Doing Good," *BusinessWeek,* August 15, 2005; "Cops of the Global Village," *Fortune,* June 27, 2005; "At Some Retailers, 'Fair Trade' Carries a Very High Cost," *Wall Street Journal,* June 8, 2004; "Drug Ills? Follow the Money," *Brandweek,* February 7, 2005, pp. 24–28; "Car Seats for Eight-Year-Olds," *Wall Street Journal,* January 27, 2005; "Money and Morals at GE," *Fortune,* November 15, 2004; "Nestlé Markets Baby Formula to Hispanic Mothers in U.S.," *Wall Street Journal,* March 4, 2004; "Teaching the Wrong Lesson," *Business 2.0,* November 2003. See also John C. Kozup, Elizabeth H. Creyer, and Scot Burton, "Making Healthful Food Choices: the Influence of Health Claims and Nutrition Information on Consumers' Evaluations of Packaged Food Products and Restaurant Menu Items," *Journal of Marketing,* April 2003; Sankar Sen, Zeynep Gurhan-Canli, and Vicki Morwitz, "Withholding Consumption: a Social Dilemma Perspective on Consumer Boycotts," *Journal of Consumer Research,* December 2001; Steve Hoeffler and Kevin Lane Keller, "Building Brand Equity Through Corporate Societal Marketing," *Journal of Public Policy & Marketing,* Spring 2002; Dwane Hal Dean, "Associating the Cooperation with a Charitable Event Through Sponsorship: Measuring the Effects on Corporate Community Relations," *Journal of Advertising,* Winter 2002; Paul N. Bloom, George R. Milne, and Robert Adler, "Avoiding Misuse of New Information Technologies: Legal and Societal Considerations," *Journal of Marketing,* January 1994; James A. Muncy and Scott J. Vitell, "Consumer Ethics: An Investigation of the Ethical Beliefs of the Final Consumer," *Journal of Business Research,* June 1992; Gene R. Laczniak and Patrick E. Murphy, "Fostering Ethical Marketing Decisions," *Journal of Business Ethics,* April 1991.

Illustration Credits

CHAPTER 1

P. 2, ©Joseph P. Cannon Ph.D. P. 5, Courtesy Nationwide Mutual Insurance Company; Agency: TM Advertising/Dallas, TX. P. 6, Royalty-Free/CORBIS. P. 6, Royalty-Free/CORBIS. P. 6, Pixtal/AGE Fotostock. P. 7, Courtesy Help Remedies, Inc. P. 10, *Both photos:* Courtesy POM Wonderful LLC. P. 12, Courtesy Canada Post Corporation. P. 12, Courtesy GE Capital; Photographer: Markku Lahdesmaki. P. 14, Courtesy Ten Thousand Villages. P. 17, Courtesy of Bank of the Wichitas®. P. 21, Courtesy L.L.Bean. P. 23, New York City Department of Health/DCF Advertising. P. 24, Courtesy San Diego Zoo. P. 25, PRNewsFoto/TOMS Shoes/AP Photo.

Exhibits: Exhibit 1-1, adapted from William McInnes, "A Conceptual Approach to Marketing," in *Theory in Marketing,* 2d ser., ed. Reavis Cox, Wroe Alderson, and Stanley J. Shapiro (Homewood, IL: Richard D. Irwin, 1964), pp. 51–67; Exhibit 1-2, model suggested by Professor A. A. Brogowicz, Western Michigan University; Exhibit 1-4, adapted from R. F. Vizza, T. E. Chambers, and E. J. Cook, *Adoption of the Marketing Concept—Fact or Fiction* (New York: Sales Executive Club, Inc., 1967), pp. 13–15; Exhibit 1-5, this exhibit is different from, but stimulated by, a graph that appears on the Satisfaction Management Systems, Inc., website, www.satmansys.com; Exhibit 1-7, adapted from discussions of an American Marketing Association Strategic Planning Committee.

CHAPTER 2

P. 30, Photo by Kevin Winter/NBCUniversal/Getty Images. P. 34, ©The Procter & Gamble Company. Used by Permission. P. 37, Courtesy Lan Airlines, S.A. P. 37, Courtesy Lufthansa USA. P. 39, *Both images:* Courtesy Toddler University. P. 40, *All images:* Courtesy of Campbell Soup Company. P. 43, Courtesy Grey Hong Kong; Photo: Connie Hong. P. 44, Courtesy Ford Motor Company. P. 46, ©2006 KCWW Reprinted with Permission. P. 47, Courtesy Philippine Department of Tourism/Chicago. P. 47, Courtesy Bayer Health Care LLC. P. 50, ©William D. Perreault, Jr., Ph.D. P. 51, Courtesy McCann Erickson Advertising Ltd./London. P. 51, Courtesy Delta Faucet Co.; www.deltafaucet.com. P. 52, Courtesy Levi Strauss & Co.; Agency: Edelman/Singapore.

Exhibits: Exhibit 2-9, Igor Ansoff, *Corporate Strategy* (New York; McGraw-Hill, 1965).

CHAPTER 3

P. 56–57, ©1996–2011, Amazon.com Inc. P. 60, Courtesy 3M; Agency: Grey Worldwide Johannesburg. P. 62, ©2008 General Mills, Inc. P. 62, Courtesy Nucor Corporation. P. 63, Courtesy Delta Dental. P. 64, Agency: John St./Toronto; Art Director: Nellie Kim; Copywriter: Chris Hirsch; Photographer: Mark Zibert. P. 66, Courtesy Great Clips. P. 68, ©2006–2012 The Coca-Cola Company. P. 69, ©K. Rousonelos. P. 69, Courtesy IBM Corporation. P. 70, Courtesy Adero, Inc. P. 71, Mucinex® is a registered trademark of Adams Respiratory Operations, Inc. P. 73, Copyright © 1995–2012 eBay Inc. All Rights Reserved. P. 75, Kevin Lee/EcopixFotoagentur. P. 77, Courtesy of Toyota Motor Sales, U.S.A., Inc. P. 78, ©M. Hruby. P. 82, Con Agra Foods Specialty Potato Products; Agency: Strahan Advertising. P. 82, Courtesy Click 2 Asia.

Exhibits: Exhibit 3-5: table based on U.S. Census data including *Statistical Abstract of the United States 2010* (Washington, DC: U.S. Government Printing Office, October 2009), Table 1296, pp. 818–20, available online at www.census.gov/statab; U.S. Census Bureau "International Data Base" available online at www.census.gov/ipc/www/idb/; Population Reference Bureau data, including *2009 World Pop Data Sheet,* available online at www.prb.org/Publications/Datasheets/2009; World Bank data, available online at http://web.worldbank.org/WBSITE/EXTERNAL/DATASTATISTICS; CIA data, including *CIA Factbook 2010,* available online at https://www.cia.gov/library/publications/the-world-factbook; ICT Statistics Database, Mobile Cellular Subscriptions Per 100 People, 2008, International Telecommunications Union, available online at http://www.itu.int/ITU-D/icteye/Indicators/Indicators.aspx; Internet World Stats, 2010, available online at www.internetworldstats.com/stats.htm; Exhibit 3-6: map developed by the authors based on "2010 America: What the 2010 Census Means for Marketing and Advertising," Advertising Age (White Paper), October 12, 2009; and U.S. Census data including *Statistical Abstract of the United States 2010,* pp. 18 and 20, and available at www.census.gov/statab; Exhibit 3-10, adapted from M. G. Allen, "Strategic Problems Facing Today's Corporate Planner," speech given at the Academy of Management, 36th Annual Meeting, Kansas City, Missouri, 1976.

CHAPTER 4

P. 86–87, Courtesy LEGO Company. P. 90, Courtesy Evins Ltd. P. 90, Courtesy Woodman Labs, Inc. P. 90, Courtesy Fuji Film USA. P. 90, Courtesy Lytro, Inc. P. 91, Courtesy Nestlé S.A. P. 94, Both ads: ©2012 The Clorox Company. Reprinted with permission. P. 95, Courtesy GlaxoSmithKline. P. 95, ©2012 Colgate-Palmolive Company. All Rights Reserved. P. 95, Photo courtesy of Del Pharmaceuticals. P. 97, ©William D. Perreault, Jr., Ph.D. P. 99, Courtesy Playtex Products, Inc. P. 99, Creative Director/Copywriter: Emily Smeraldo; Art Director: Wayne Kan & Jonathan Lee; School: School of Visual Arts, New York; Instructors: Richard Pels & Paul Jarvis. P. 104, Courtesy Hilton Hospitality, Inc.; Photographer: Stephen Austin Welch. P. 104, Courtesy Hilton Worldwide. P. 108, ©Joseph P. Cannon Ph.D. P. 110, Courtesy Client: AT&T; Agency: BBDO/Atlanta.

Exhibits: Exhibit 4-11, Russell I. Haley, "Benefit Segmentation: A Decision-Oriented Research Tool," *Journal of Marketing,* July 1968, p. 33.

CHAPTER 5

P. 116–117, Courtesy of Apple. P. 120, Courtesy GEICO. P. 120, Courtesy of ConAgra Foods. P. 121, ©2010 Nissan. Nissan, Nissan model names and the Nissan logo are registered trademarks of Nissan. P. 122, Courtesy Leo Burnett Sp. zo.o/Warsaw. P. 124, Courtesy eiligheidNL; Agency: Lemz/Netherlands. P. 125, Courtesy Zipcar. P. 126, ©World Wildlife Fund. P. 129, Courtesy Hunt Adkins; Art Director: Mark Fairbanks; Copywriter: Rob Franks. P. 131, ©Matthew Staver. P. 132, Courtesy Andric, Syfy, A Division of NBCUniversal. P. 133, Courtesy Yelp, Inc. P. 133, Courtesy Goya Foods, Inc. P. 133, Courtesy National Footbal League. P. 134, Courtesy, BoConcept USA, Inc. P. 134, Courtesy Groupon Inc. P. 138, Courtesy Dropbox. P. 139, AP Photo/Mandatory Credit: Christopher Morris/VII. P. 139, AP Photo/Saleh Rifai.

Exhibits: Exhibit 5-3, adapted from C. Glenn Walters, *Consumer Behavior,* 3d ed. (Homewood, IL: Richard D. Irwin, 1979); Exhibit 5-6, Joseph T. Plummer, "The Concept and Application of Life-Style Segmentation," *Journal of Marketing,* January 1974, pp. 33–37.

CHAPTER 6

P. 142–143, Reuters Pictures. P. 146, Courtesy Kyocera Mita America, Inc. P. 146, Courtesy T3 Motion. P. 147, Courtesy BASF Corporation. P. 148, Both images: ©Roger Ball Photography. P. 149, Courtesy Honda Motor Co., Inc. P. 150, Courtesy Comcast Cable Communications, Inc. P. 150, Courtesy AirTran Airways, Agency: Cramer-Krasselt. P. 151, Courtesy Eastman Chemical. P. 154, Courtesy The California Department of Transportation. P. 155, Courtesy AFLAC, Inc. P. 157, Courtesy EmpordAigUA® Water Design & Technology. P. 160, All photos: Courtesy of Alcoa. P. 161, Courtesy Hertz Corporation. P. 163, DOVE® is a registered trademark of Mars, Incorporated. This trademark and advertisement are used with permission. Mars, Incorporated is not associated with McGraw-Hill Higher Education. P. 163, Courtesy Chiquita Brands International Inc. P. 164, ©Dave Lauridsen. P. 164, Courtesy USA.gov.

Exhibits: Exhibit 6-4, adapted and updated from Rowland T. Moriarty, Jr., and Robert E. Spekman, "An Empirical Investigation of the Information Sources Used during the Industrial Buying Process, *Journal of Marketing Research,* May 1984, pp. 137–47; Exhibit 6-6, graph developed by the authors based on U. S. Census data including and available online at www.census.gov; Exhibit 6-7, available online at http://www.naics.com.

CHAPTER 7

P. 168–169, AP Photo/Insider Images for Dunkin' Donuts, Stuart Ramson. P. 172, Courtesy Pitney Bowes, Inc. P. 172, Courtesy of MapInfo. P. 172, Courtesy ActiveGroup; Design: Christian Baratto. P. 174, Image courtesy of iDashboards. P. 174, Copyright ©2011. SAS Institue Inc. All rights reserved. Reproduced with permission of SAS Institute Inc., Cary, NC, USA. P. 174, Courtesy Infegy Inc./Gabriel Marketing. P. 180, Courtesy Catalina Marketing. P. 182, Courtesy FGI Research, Inc. P. 182, Courtesy Focus Vision Worldwide, ™Inc. P. 183, Both images: Courtesy Southwest Airlines. P. 184, ©Fortunato M. Ramin. P. 185, Courtesy Arbitron. P. 186, Courtesy Ocean Spray Cranberries, Inc.; Photo: ©Margaret Lampert. P. 188, Courtesy Greenfield Online. P. 190, Source: Survey Sampling International 2008. P. 190, Courtesy of i.think, inc. P. 191, Courtesy Restaurant Research Associates. P. 191, Courtesy Bravo Group. P. 192, Courtesy P. Robert & Partners. P. 192, Courtesy Fieldwork Network Int'l.

CHAPTER 8

P. 196–197, Photo by Thearon W. Henderson/Getty Images. P. 200, Courtesy Volkswagen; Agency: DDB Stockholm. P. 201, Courtesy IKEA; Agency: Grabarz & Partner/Hamburg. P. 202, Courtesy Cit Group, Inc. P. 203, Courtesy BWM/Sydney. P. 205, ©Joseph P. Cannon Ph.D. P. 206, Courtesy Morton Salt. P. 206, Courtesy BISSELL Home Care, Inc. P. 210, Courtesy Del Monte Fresh Produce N.A., Inc. P. 211, ©William D. Perreault, Jr., Ph.D. P. 212, ©William D. Perreault, Jr., Ph.D. P. 212, AP Photo P. 213, ©William D. Perreault, Jr., Ph.D. P. 214, © 2009 Hewlett-Packard Development Company, L.P. Reproduced with permission. The Requested Material may include content that is owned by other parties (for example, photographs owned by the photographers). HP does not warrant or represent that it owns the copyright in the Requested Material, or that it does not infringe the rights of any other person or entity. HP does not grant any right of publicity in any likeness of an individual that may be included in the Requested Material. This permission provides only that HP will not make a claim of trademark or copyright infringement against you, provided you comply with all the terms herein. P. 214, Courtesy Cessna Aircraft Company. P. 216, Courtesy ProPlus; Agency: J. Walter Thompson/London. P. 216, PRNewsFoto/Choice Hotels International, Inc/AP Images. P. 217, Courtesy Panadol Ultra; Agency: Saatchi & Saatchi/Guatemala. P. 218, Both ads: Courtesy Bush Brothers & Company. P. 220, Courtesy W.W. Grainger, Inc. P. 220, Courtesy Accenture.

Exhibits: Exhibit 8.3: P. 204, Courtesy Under Armour®. P. 204, Courtesy Cisco Systems, Inc. P. 204, Courtesy Pepsi-Cola Company. P. 204, Courtesy Volkswagen of America. P. 204, Courtesy Michelin North America. P. 204, Courtesy Intel Corporation. P. 204, Courtesy Boys & Girls Clubs of America. P. 204, Courtesy The Hertz Corporation. P. 204, Created by Larry Ewing and The Gimp. P. 204, Courtesy ESPN Communications. P. 204, Courtesy Twitter, Inc. P. 204, The American Red Cross name and logo are registered trademarks of the American Red Cross. Used with permission. P. 204, Courtesy Roll Global. P. 204, Courtesy Adidas America. P. 204, Courtesy Dole Food Company, Inc. P. 204, Courtesy PUMA. P. 204, ©2011 Google. P. 204, Courtesy Dunkin Donuts, Inc.

CHAPTER 9

P. 224–225, Courtesy iRobot Corporation. P. 229, *Both Images:* Courtesy Groupe Danone; Agency: BETC EURO RSG/Paris; Photographer: Nathan Goldberg. P. 230, Courtesy Kaz, Inc. P. 231, ©Richard Levine/Alamy. P. 233, Courtesy Airbnb.com. P. 234, Courtesy DuPont Textiles & Interiors' LYCRA®; Agency: Saatchi & Saatchi/Zurich. P. 235, ©The Procter & Gamble Company. Used by permission. P. 236, Courtesy S.C. Johnson. P. 237, Courtesy Johnson & Johnson. P. 237, Courtesy Jelly Belly Candy Company. P. 238, Courtesy TS Brass. P. 238, Courtesy Sauder Woodworking Company. P. 242, Courtesy Honda Patents & Technologies North America, LLC. P. 242, Courtesy BMW of North America, LLC. P. 245, Courtesy Mars, Inc. P. 24, Courtesy Hertz Corporation. P. 247, Courtesy Jersey Mike's Franchise Systems. P. 248, Photo by David McNew/ Getty Images.

Exhibits: Exhibit 9-4, adapted from Frank R. Bacon, Jr., and Thomas W. Butler, *Planned Innovation* (Ann Arbor: University of Michigan Institute of Science and Technology, 1980).

CHAPTER 10

P. 252–253, Courtesy of Dell, Inc. P. 256, ©The Procter & Gamble Company. Used by permission. P. 256, Courtesy iVet. P. 257, © Joseph P. Cannon Ph.D. P. 258, Reproduced with kind permission of Unilever PLC and group companies. P. 258, Reproduced with kind permission of Unilever PLC and group companies. P. 258, Reproduced with kind permission of Unilever, P.L.C. and group companies; Photographer: Bill Prentice. P. 259, Courtesy Park Seed® Company. P. 260, Photo by Jb Reed/Bloomberg via Getty Images. P. 263, Courtesy Stihl Incorporated. P. 264, Courtesy Peterson Manufacturing Company. P. 264, Courtesy Electrolux North America. P. 268, Wrigley, Starburst, Flavor Morph and all affiliated designs owned by and used courtesy of the Wm. Wrigley Jr. Company or its affiliates. P. 268, Courtesy Jaguar Cars. P. 269, Courtesy Dunkin Brands, Inc. P. 271, ©Guardian News & Media Ltd 2012. P. 273, Courtesy INOBAT. P. 274, Courtesy Nike, Inc.

Exhibits: Exhibit 10-2, adapted from D. J. Bowersox and E. J. McCarthy, "Strategic Development of Planned Vertical Marketing Systems," in Vertical Marketing Systems, ed. Louis Bucklin (Glenview, IL: Scott, Foresman, 1970).

CHAPTER 11

P. 278–279, Clemens Emmier/picture-alliance/DUMONT Bildar/ Newscom. P. 282, Kevin Phillips/Getty Images. P. 282, Courtesy DM9 DDB/São Paulo, Brazil. P. 284, Courtesy Sauder Woodworking Company. P. 286, Courtesy Manitowac Crane Group. P. 287, *Both ads:* Courtesy Marsh. P. 287, Courtesy IBM Corporation. P. 289, ©Allan

Hunter Shoemake Photography, Inc. P. 289, ©Steve Smith. P. 290, Photo by Peter Macdiarmid/Getty Images. P. 292, ©Olivier Lantzendörffer/iStockphoto. P. 293, Courtesy Metro AG. P. 294, Courtesy Menasha Corporation. P. 294, Courtesy U.S. Environmental Protection Agency. P. 295, Courtesy Frog Design. P. 297, Courtesy Kiva Systems.

Exhibits: Exhibit 11-4, adapted from B. J. LaLonde and P. H. Zinzer, *Customer Service: Meaning and Measurement* (Chicago: National Council of Physical Distribution Management, 1976); and D. Phillip Locklin, *Transportation for Management* (Homewood, IL: Richard D. Irwin, 1972); Exhibit 11-7, adapted from Louis W. Stern and Adel I. El-Ansary, *Marketing Channels* (Englewood Cliffs, NJ: Prentice Hall, 1977), p. 150.

CHAPTER 12

P. 300–301, Courtesy Macy's Inc. P. 304, ©2012 Zappos.com, Inc. P. 304, © Joseph P. Cannon Ph.D. P. 308–309, Courtesy of Office Depot. P. 310, Courtesy Utique, Inc. P. 310, ©Brent Jones. P. 312, © Woot, Inc. 2004–2012. All Rights Reserved. P. 312, © 2012 Zibbet Pty Ltd. P. 314, ©Cheil Worldwide. P. 314, ©Intel Corporation. Used with permission. P. 315 Courtesy Publicis Conseil/Paris. P. 317, Courtesy Dunkin Brands. P. 318, ©Joel Rafkin/PhotoEdit. P. 318, Photo by Marco Di Lauro/Getty Images. P. 318, AP Photo/Peter Morgan. P. 318, Courtesy Eleven Brandworks Agency Gurgaon India. P. 320, Photo: Karen Capland; Courtesy Frieda's, Inc. P. 323, Courtesy Henry Schein, Inc. P. 324, Photo courtesy of Joseph Sandusky/EMA. P. 325, Courtesy IronPlanet.

Exhibits: Exhibit 12-2, developed by coauthor, Joseph P. Cannon; Exhibit 12-5, graph developed by the authors based on U.S. Census data including, and available online at http://www.census.gov.; Exhibit 12-5, "Summary Statistics for the U.S.: 2007" from 2007 Economic Census—Wholesale Trade, Geographic Area Series, United States (Washington, DC: U.S. Government Printing Office, 2010)

CHAPTER 13

P. 328–329, Courtesy GEICO. P. 332, *All images:* Courtesy DDB Stockholm. P. 334, Photo by China Photos/Getty Images. P. 334, Photo by Adrian Bradshaw/Getty Images. P. 334, Courtesy Pepsi-Cola Company. P. 336, *Both images:* Courtesy Lowe's Companies, Inc. P. 337, Courtesy The Young Ones/Antwerp Belgium. P. 339, Courtesy USG Corporation. P. 341, ©2011 Microsoft. P. 341, Courtesy Angie's List, Inc. P. 344, *Both images:* The GREEN MOUNTAIN COFFEE® trademarks and advertisements are used with permission from Green Mountain Coffee Roasters, Inc. P. 346, *All images:* ©2011 Hewlett-Packard Development Company, L.P P. 348, ©2008 Bathys Hawaii. P. 350, Courtesy Y&R Dubai. P. 350, Courtesy Monster Beverage Company. P. 351, Protagon Display Inc. P. 352, Courtesy Red Bull North America, Inc.

CHAPTER 14

P. 356–357, ©William D. Perreault, Jr., Ph.D. P. 360, Courtesy Boise Cascade Office Products. P. 360, ©Copyright True-Value Company. All Rights Reserved. P. 361, Courtesy The Charles Schwab Corporation. P. 363, AP Photo/Chuck Burton. P. 364, Courtesy Hobart Corporation. P. 364, Courtesy Vodafone. P. 365, Courtesy Dell Inc. P. 368, CLOROX® is a registered trademark of The Clorox Company. Used with permission. ©2012 The Clorox Company. Reprinted with permission. P. 369, Courtesy Cozmix, Inc. P. 372, Courtesy Salesforce.com, Inc. P. 372, Courtesy Microsoft Corporation. P. 372, Courtesy Avaya, Inc. P. 373, Reprinted Courtesy of Caterpillar Inc. P. 375, Courtesy Royal Caribbean International. P. 378, Courtesy Capterra; Agency: RMR & Associates. P. 379, Courtesy LaForce & Stevens Agency/New York.

Exhibits: Exhibit 14-3, exhibit suggested by Professor A. A. Brogowicz, Western Michigan University.

CHAPTER 15

P. 384, Brian Lawdermilk/AP Images for Subway. P. 388, Reproduced with kind permission of Unilever PLC and group companies. P. 391, Courtesy Ubachswisbrun/JWT Amsterdam. P. 392, Courtesy Henkel Consumer Goods. P. 392, Courtesy King Stockholm. P. 392, Courtesy Pepsi-Cola Company. P. 393, Courtesy Volkswagen Group of America. P. 393, Courtesy E! Entertainment Television, Inc. P. 393, Courtesy BBC World Wide Americas, Inc. P. 393, Courtesy International Networks/AZN TELEVISION. P. 395, Courtesy McDonald's; Agency: TBWA/Zurich. P. 397, Courtesy The Territory Ahead. P. 397, Courtesy Volkswagen Group of America. P. 399, Courtesy Saatchi & Saatchi/London. P. 400, *All photos:* Used with permission from McDonald's Corporation. P. 400, Courtesy SKTelecom. P. 403, Courtesy The Coca-Cola Company. P. 406, Courtesy Hi-Tec Sports, Liquid Manufacturing. P. 407, Courtesy American Express Company. P. 408, ©2010 General Mills. P. 409, Courtesy The Greater Good. P. 412, Used with permission from McDonald's Corporation. P. 413, Courtesy Mars, Inc. P. 414, *All images:* Courtesy Deere & Company.

Exhibits: Exhibit 15-2, graph developed by the authors based on "Advertising as Percent of Sales in 2009," at http://adage.com/datacenter/datapopup.php?article_id=137681; Exhibit 15-5, table developed by the authors based on ZenithOptimedia data provided in "Annual 2010," *Advertising Age* (Special Issue), December 28, 2009, p. 11; Exhibit 15-6, table developed by the authors based on "Agency Report 2010," *Advertising Age,* April 26, 2010; "Annual 2010," *Advertising Age* (Special Issue), December 28, 2009, p. 30; "Agency Report," *Advertising Age* (Special Report), April 27, 2009, p. 12; available online at www.adage.com/agencyreport10 and www.adage.com/agencyreport09; Exhibit 15-7, developed by coauthor, Joseph P. Cannon; Exhibit 15-8, developed by coauthor, Joseph P. Cannon.

CHAPTER 16

P. 418–419, Photo by Kevin Winter/Getty Images for NCLR. P. 421, Courtesy IKEA. P. 423, Courtesy Just Born, Inc. P. 424, Courtesy Michelin North America, Inc. P. 424, Courtesy Lumension; Agency: Lois Paul & Partners/Woburn, MA. P. 426, Courtesy Carnival Corporation. P. 430, Courtesy 8 in 1 Pet Products, Inc. P. 430, Courtesy Google Inc. P. 432, Courtesy Merial Limited. P. 433, No credit. P. 433, Courtesy Adam & Eve DDB/London; Photographer: Marc Philbert. P. 435, Courtesy LivingSocial. P. 437, Courtesy L.L. Bean. P. 437, Courtesy United States Postal Service. P. 438, Courtesy Wendy's International, Inc. P. 439, Courtesy Pricegrabber.com. P. 440, ©William D. Perreault, Jr., Ph.d. P. 443, ©William D. Perreault, Jr., Ph.d.

Exhibits: Exhibit 16-7, exchange rate data is available from the Federal Reserve Bank; see also International Monetary Fund data available online at http://www.imf.org/external/np/tre/sdr/drates and Universal Currency Converter available online at http://www.x-rates.com.

CHAPTER 17

P. 446–447, Imaginechina via AP Images. P. 450, Courtesy Kevin Summers. P. 450, ©The Procter & Gamble Company. Used by permission. P. 450, ©William D. Perreault, Jr., Ph.d. P. 451, Courtesy Legend Valve and Fitting, Inc. P. 453, Courtesy Citrix Online. P. 458, ©Mark Henley/Impact Photos/Imagestate. P. 462, Courtesy Tigre S.A. P. 463, Courtesy

Climate Master, Inc. P. 463, Courtesy Unex Corporation; Agency: Stein Rogan & Partners, Chief Creative Officer: Tom Stein, Associate Creative Director/Copywriter: Michael Ruby, Senior Art Director: Annabella Martamendi P. 465, Used by Permission of Deutsch Inc. as Agent for National Fluid Milk Processor Promotion Board. P. 466, Courtesy Texas Roadhouse, Inc. P. 466, Courtesy Porsche Cars North America, Inc. P. 469, Used with permission from Microsoft. P. 470, Justin Heitmann Software Graphic Designer, BID2WIN Software, Inc.

Exhibits: Exhibit 17-11, this exhibit is different from, but stimulated by, a graph that appears on the Satisfaction Management Systems, Inc., website at http://www.satmansys.com.

CHAPTER 18

P. 474, ©William D. Perreault, Jr., Ph.d. P. 478, *Both images:* Courtesy Honest Tea. P. 479, Courtesy Sage Software, Inc. P. 479, Courtesy IBM Corporation. P. 479, ©2004 Hertz System, Inc. Hertz is a registered service mark and trademark of Hertz System, Inc. P. 481, Image courtesy of P8ioneer Hi-Bred, a DuPont Business. P. 483, Courtesy Zynga. P. 484, ©2012 Accenture. All Rights Reserved. Jan Van der Linden is a senior executive in Accenture's Sales Transformation practice. Also contributing is Naveen Jain, Global Lead, Accenture's Sales Transformation practice. P. 490, Courtesy Dundas Data Visualization Ltd. P. 491, Courtesy Con Agra Foods Inc.

Exhibits: Exhibit 18-5, adapted and updated from discussions of an American Marketing Association Strategic Planning Committee.

CHAPTER 19

P. 500, © Lou Linwei/Alamy. P. 505, Courtesy Sun Trust Banks, Inc. P. 506, Courtesy Dupont Surfaces. P. 508, Courtesy Apple Computer; Agency: TBWA Chiat Day. P. 509, ©2010 Starbucks Corporation. All rights reserved. P. 510, Courtesy Kikkoman Sales USA, Inc.; Marshall Gordon Photography. P. 510, ©William D. Perreault, Jr., Ph.d. P. 512, Courtesy Springer & Jacoby/Hamburg. P. 513, Courtesy www.Chocomize.com. P. 514, Courtesy Red Gold, Inc. P. 515, Courtesy SMART Technologies, Inc. P. 520, Courtesy H.C.Brill Company, Inc. P. 520, Courtesy Deere & Company.

CHAPTER 20

P. 524, AP Photo/Khalil Senosi. P. 527, AP Photo/Vahid Salemi. P. 528, Courtesy Planetfeedback. P. 529, ©William D. Perreault, Jr., Ph.d. P. 531, Courtesy Reckitt Benckiser Group plc; Agency: Euro RSCG Bangkok. P. 531, BBDO Guerrero/Proximity Philippines; Chief Executive Officer: David Guerrero; Executive Creative Director: Brandie Tan; Creative Director: Gary Amante' Creative Director: Rey Tiempo; Account Director: Cindy Evangelista; Senior Account Manager: Iking Uy; Print Producer: Al Salvador; Photographers: Paolo Gripo & Abet Bagay Retouchers: Oliver Brillantes & Vilma Magsino; Client: Bayer Philippines/Consumer Care; Brand Managers: Edward Go & Christian Galvez. P. 532, Courtesy Rubin Postaer & Assoc.; Photography: Stock. P. 532, Courtesy of GoDaddy.com, Inc. P. 534, *All images:* Courtesy HL Group/New York.. P. 540, Client: LECO Japan; Ad Agency: Saatchi & Saatchi Fallon Tokyo; Creative Director: Keiichi Vemura; Art Director: Tetsuro Tandai; Designer: Masashi Fujiyoshi; Copywriter: Hiroyuki Iwase; Computer Graphics: Takashi Taniai. P. 542, *Both images:* Courtesy Owens Illinois. P. 542, Photo by: Bob Wolter & Associates. P. 545, Courtesy Your Credit Card Companies. P. 545, Courtesy Zippo Manufacturing Company, Inc.

APPENDIX B

Exhibits: Exhibit B-4, "2003 Survey of Buying Power," *Sales & Marketing Management,* Supplement, 2003.

APPENDIX C

Photos/ads: P. 587, ©Matthias Spactgens/Scholz & Friends/Berlin.

Exhibits: Exhibit C-2, table developed by the authors based on data from Salary.com and represent the range for a salary plus bonus from the 25th to the 75th percentile as of May 2010, rounded to the nearest $1,000. Salary for retail vice president was estimated.

Name Index

C

D

E

F

I

J

K

L

M

N

O

P

Q

R

S

T

U

V

W

X

Y

Z

Company Index

D

E

F

G

H

I

J

K

L

M

N

O

U

V

W

X

Y

Z

Subject Index

D

E

F

G

H

I

J

K

L

M

N

O

Q

R

T

U

V

W

Y

Z

Glossary

Accessories Short-lived capital items—tools and equipment used in production or office activities.

Accumulating Collecting products from many small producers.

Administered channel systems Various channel members informally agree to cooperate with each other.

Administered prices Consciously set prices aimed at reaching the firm's objectives.

Adoption curve Shows when different groups accept ideas.

Adoption process The steps individuals go through on the way to accepting or rejecting a new idea.

Advertising Any *paid* form of nonpersonal presentation of ideas, goods, or services by an identified sponsor.

Advertising agencies Specialists in planning and handling mass-selling details for advertisers.

Advertising allowances Price reductions to firms in the channel to encourage them to advertise or otherwise promote the firm's products locally.

Advertising managers Managers of their company's mass-selling effort in television, newspapers, magazines, and other media.

Agent wholesalers Wholesalers who do not own (take title to) the products they sell.

AIDA model Consists of four promotion jobs: (1) to get *Attention,* (2) to hold *Interest,* (3) to arouse *Desire,* and (4) to obtain *Action.*

Allowance (accounting term) Occurs when a customer is not satisfied with a purchase for some reason and the seller gives a price reduction on the original invoice (bill), but the customer keeps the goods or services.

Allowances Reductions in price given to final consumers, customers, or channel members for doing something or accepting less of something.

Assorting Putting together a variety of products to give a target market what it wants.

Attitude A person's point of view toward something.

Auction companies Agent wholesalers that provide a place where buyers and sellers can come together and complete a transaction.

Automatic vending Selling and delivering products through vending machines.

Average cost (per unit) The total cost divided by the related quantity.

Average-cost pricing Adding a reasonable markup to the average cost of a product.

Average fixed cost (per unit) The total fixed cost divided by the related quantity.

Average variable cost (per unit) The total variable cost divided by the related quantity.

Baby boomers People born between 1946 and 1964.

Bait pricing Setting some very low prices to attract customers but trying to sell more expensive models or brands once the customer is in the store.

Balance sheet An accounting statement that shows a company's assets, liabilities, and net worth.

Basic list prices The prices that final customers or users are normally asked to pay for products.

Basic sales tasks *Order-getting, order-taking,* and *supporting.*

Battle of the brands The competition between dealer brands and manufacturer brands.

Belief A person's opinion about something.

Bid pricing Offering a specific price for each possible job rather than setting a price that applies for all customers.

Birthrate The number of babies per 1,000 people.

Big data Data sets too large and complex to work with typical database management tools.

Brand equity The value of a brand's overall strength in the market.

Brand familiarity How well customers recognize and accept a company's brand.

Brand insistence Customers insist on a firm's branded product and are willing to search for it.

Brand managers Manage specific products, often taking over the jobs formerly handled by an advertising manager—sometimes called *product managers.*

Brand name A word, letter, or a group of words or letters.

Brand nonrecognition Final customers don't recognize a brand at all—even though intermediaries may use the brand name for identification and inventory control.

Brand preference Target customers usually choose the brand over other brands, perhaps because of habit or favorable past experience.

Brand recognition Customers remember the brand.

Brand rejection Potential customers won't buy a brand—unless its image is changed.

Branding The use of a name, term, symbol, or design—or a combination of these—to identify a product.

Break-even analysis An approach to determine whether the firm will be able to break even—that is, cover all its costs—with a particular price.

Break-even point (BEP) The sales quantity where the firm's total cost will just equal its total revenue.

Breakthrough opportunities Opportunities that help innovators develop hard-to-copy marketing strategies that will be very profitable for a long time.

Brokers Agent wholesalers who specialize in bringing buyers and sellers together.

Bulk-breaking Dividing larger quantities into smaller quantities as products get closer to the final market.

Business and organizational customers Any buyers who buy for resale or to produce other goods and services.

Business products Products meant for use in producing other products.

Buying center All the people who participate in or influence a purchase.

Buying function Looking for and evaluating goods and services.

Capital The money invested in a firm.

Capital item A long-lasting product that can be used and depreciated for many years.

Cash-and-carry wholesalers Like service wholesalers, except that the customer must pay cash.

Cash discounts Reductions in the price to encourage buyers to pay their bills quickly.

Cash flow statement A financial report that forecasts how much cash will be available after paying expenses.

Catalog wholesalers Sell out of catalogs that may be distributed widely to smaller industrial customers or retailers that might not be called on by other wholesalers.

Channel captain A manager who helps direct the activities of a whole channel and tries to avoid, or solve, channel conflicts.

Channel of distribution Any series of firms or individuals who participate in the flow of products from producer to final user or consumer.

Close The salesperson's request for an order.

Clustering techniques Approaches used to try to find similar patterns within sets of data.

Collaborators Firms that provide one or more of the marketing functions other than buying or selling.

Combination export manager A blend of manufacturers' agent and selling agent—handling the entire export function for several producers of similar but noncompeting lines.

Combined target market approach Combining two or more submarkets into one larger target market as a basis for one strategy.

Combiners Firms that try to increase the size of their target markets by combining two or more segments.

Command economy Government officials decide what and how much is to be produced and distributed by whom, when, to whom, and why.

Communication process A source trying to reach a receiver with a message.

Comparative advertising Advertising that makes specific brand comparisons using actual product names.

Competitive advantage A firm has a marketing mix that the target market sees as better than a competitor's mix.

Competitive advertising Advertising that tries to develop selective demand for a specific brand rather than a product category.

Competitive bids Terms of sale offered by different suppliers in response to the buyer's purchase specifications.

Competitive environment The number and types of competitors the marketing manager must face, and how they may behave.

Competitive rivals A firm's closest competitors.

Competitor analysis An organized approach for evaluating the strengths and weaknesses of current or potential competitors' marketing strategies.

Complementary product pricing Setting prices on several related products as a group.

Components Processed expense items that become part of a finished product.

Concept testing Getting reactions from customers about how well a new product idea fits their needs.

Confidence intervals The range on either side of an estimate from a sample that is likely to contain the true value for the whole population.

Consultative selling approach A type of sales presentation in which the salesperson develops a good understanding of the individual customer's needs before trying to close the sale.

Consumer panel A group of consumers who provide information on a continuing basis.

Consumer Product Safety Act A 1972 law that set up the Consumer Product Safety Commission to encourage more awareness of safety in product design and better quality control.

Consumer products Products meant for the final consumer.

Consumer surplus The difference to consumers between the value of a purchase and the price they pay.

Containerization Grouping individual items into an economical shipping quantity and sealing them in protective containers for transit to the final destination.

Continuous improvement A commitment to constantly make things better one step at a time.

Contractual channel systems Various channel members agree by contract to cooperate with each other.

Contribution-margin approach A cost analysis approach in which all costs are not allocated in *all* situations.

Control The feedback process that helps the marketing manager learn (1) how ongoing plans and implementation are working and (2) how to plan for the future.

Convenience (food) stores A convenience-oriented variation of the conventional limited-line food stores.

Convenience products Products a consumer needs but isn't willing to spend much time or effort shopping for.

Cooperative advertising Producers sharing in the cost of ads with wholesalers or retailers.

Cooperative chains Retailer-sponsored groups, formed by independent retailers, to run their own buying organizations and conduct joint promotion efforts.

Copy thrust What the words and illustrations of an ad should communicate.

Corporate chain A firm that owns and manages more than one store—and often it's many.

Corporate channel systems Corporate ownership all along the channel.

Corrective advertising Ads to correct deceptive advertising.

Cost of sales Total value (at cost) of the sales during the period.

Cues Products, signs, ads, and other stimuli in the environment.

Cultural and social environment Affects how and why people live and behave as they do.

Culture The whole set of beliefs, attitudes, and ways of doing things of a reasonably homogeneous set of people.

Cumulative quantity discounts Reductions in price for larger purchases over a given period, such as a year.

Customer equity The expected earnings stream (profitability)of a firm's current and prospective customers over some period of time.

Customer lifetime value Total stream of purchases that a customer could contribute to the company over the length of the relationship.

Customer relationship management (CRM) An approach where the seller fine-tunes the marketing effort with information from a detailed customer database.

Customer satisfaction The extent to which a firm fulfills a consumer's needs, desires, and expectations.

Customer service A personal communication between a seller and a customer who wants the seller to resolve a problem with a purchase—is often the key to building repeat business.

Customer service level How rapidly and dependably a firm can deliver what customers want.

Customer service reps Supporting salespeople who work with customers to resolve problems that arise with a purchase, usually after the purchase has been made.

Customer value The difference between the benefits a customer sees from a market offering and the costs of obtaining those benefits.

Data warehouse A place where databases are stored so that they are available when needed.

Dealer brands Brands created by intermediaries—sometimes referred to as *private brands*.

Debt financing Borrowing money based on a promise to repay the loan, usually within a fixed time period and with a specific interest charge.

Decision support system (DSS) A computer program that makes it easy for marketing managers to get and use information *as they are making decisions*.

Decoding The receiver in the communication process translating the message.

Demand-backward pricing Setting an acceptable final consumer price and working backward to what a producer can charge.

Demand curve A graph of the relationship between price and quantity demanded in a market, assuming all other things stay the same.

Department stores Larger stores that are organized into many separate departments and offer many product lines.

Derived demand Demand for business products derives from the demand for final consumer products.

Determining dimensions The dimensions that actually affect the customer's purchase of a *specific* product or brand in a *product-market*.

Differentiation The marketing mix is distinct from and better than what's available from a competitor.

Direct investment A parent firm has a division (or owns a separate subsidiary firm) in a foreign market.

Direct marketing Direct communication between a seller and an individual customer using a promotion method other than face-to-face personal selling.

Direct type advertising Competitive advertising that aims for immediate buying action.

Discount houses Stores that sell hard goods (cameras, TVs, appliances) at substantial price cuts to customers who go to discounter's low-rent store, pay cash, and take care of any service or repair problems themselves.

Discounts Reductions from list price given by a seller to buyers, who either give up some marketing function or provide the function themselves.

Discrepancy of assortment The difference between the lines a typical producer makes and the assortment final consumers or users want.

Discrepancy of quantity The difference between the quantity of products it is economical for a producer to make and the quantity final users or consumers normally want.

Discretionary income What is left of disposable income after paying for necessities.

Disposable income Income that is left after taxes.

Dissonance Tension caused by uncertainty about the rightness of a decision.

Distribution center A special kind of warehouse designed to speed the flow of goods and avoid unnecessary storing costs.

Diversification Moving into totally different lines of business—perhaps entirely unfamiliar products, markets, or even levels in the production-marketing system.

Door-to-door selling Going directly to the consumer's home.

Drive A strong stimulus that encourages action to reduce a need.

Drop-shippers Wholesalers that own (take title to) the products they sell but do not actually handle, stock, or deliver them.

Dumping Pricing a product sold in a foreign market below the cost of producing it or at a price lower than in its domestic market.

Early adopters The second group in the adoption curve to adopt a new product; these people are usually well respected by their peers and often are opinion leaders.

Early majority A group in the adoption curve that avoids risk and waits to consider a new idea until many early adopters try it and like it.

E-commerce Exchanges between individuals or organizations—and activities that facilitate those exchanges—based on applications of information technology.

Economic environment Refers to macro-economic factors including national income, economic growth, and inflation that affect patterns of consumer and business spending.

Economic buyers People who know all the facts and logically compare choices to get the greatest satisfaction from spending their time and money.

Economic needs Needs concerned with making the best use of a consumer's time and money—as the consumer judges it.

Economic system The way an economy organizes to use scarce resources to produce goods and services and distribute them for consumption by various people and groups in the society.

Economies of scale As a company produces larger numbers of a particular product, the cost of each unit of the product goes down.

Elastic demand If prices are dropped, the quantity demanded will stretch enough to increase total revenue.

Elastic supply The quantity supplied does stretch more if the price is raised.

Electronic data interchange (EDI) An approach that puts information in a standardized format easily shared between different computer systems.

Emergency products Products that are purchased immediately when the need is great.

Empowerment Giving employees the authority to correct a problem without first checking with management.

Empty nesters People whose children are grown and who are now able to spend their money in other ways.

Encoding The source in the communication process deciding what it wants to say and translating it into words or symbols that will have the same meaning to the receiver.

Equilibrium point The quantity and the price sellers are willing to offer are equal to the quantity and price that buyers are willing to accept.

Everyday low pricing Setting a low list price rather than relying on frequent sales, discounts, or allowances.

Exclusive distribution Selling through only one intermediary in a particular geographic area.

Expectation An outcome or event that a person anticipates or looks forward to.

Expense item A product whose total cost is treated as a business expense in the period it's purchased.

Expenses All the remaining costs that are subtracted from the gross margin to get the net profit.

Experimental method A research approach in which researchers compare the responses of two or more groups that are similar except on the characteristic being tested.

Export agents Manufacturers' agents who specialize in export trade.

Export brokers Brokers who specialize in bringing together buyers and sellers from different countries.

Exporting Selling some of what the firm produces to foreign markets.

Extensive problem solving The type of problem solving consumers use for a completely new or important need—when they put much effort into deciding how to satisfy it.

Factor A variable that shows the relation of some other variable to the item being forecast.

Factor method An approach to forecast sales by finding a relation between the company's sales and some other factor (or factors).

Fad An idea that is fashionable only to certain groups who are enthusiastic about it—but these groups are so fickle that a fad is even more short-lived than a regular fashion.

Family brand A brand name that is used for several products.

Farm products Products grown by farmers, such as oranges, sugar cane, and cattle.

Fashion Currently accepted or popular style.

Federal Fair Packaging and Labeling Act A 1966 law requiring that consumer goods be clearly labeled in easy-to-understand terms.

Federal Trade Commission (FTC) Federal government agency that polices antimonopoly laws.

Financing Provides the necessary cash and credit to produce, transport, store, promote, sell, and buy products.

Fishbone diagram A visual aid that helps organize cause and effect relationships for "things gone wrong."

Fixed-cost (FC) contribution per unit The selling price per unit minus the variable cost per unit.

Flexible-price policy Offering the same product and quantities to different customers at different prices.

F.O.B. A transportation term meaning free on board some vehicle at some point.

Focus group interview An interview of 6 to 10 people in an informal group setting.

Foreign Corrupt Practices Act A law passed by the U.S. Congress in 1977 that prohibits U.S. firms from paying bribes to foreign officials.

Franchise operation A franchisor develops a good marketing strategy, and the retail franchise holders carry out the strategy in their own units.

Freight-absorption pricing Absorbing freight cost so that a firm's delivered price meets the nearest competitor's.

Full-cost approach All costs are allocated to products, customers, or other categories.

Full-line pricing Setting prices for a whole line of products.

Functional accounts The categories to which various costs are charged to show the *purpose* for which expenditures are made.

General merchandise wholesalers Service wholesalers that carry a wide variety of nonperishable items such as hardware, electrical supplies, furniture, drugs, cosmetics, and automobile equipment.

General stores Early retailers who carried anything they could sell in reasonable volume.

Generation X (Gen X) People born between 1965 and 1977.

Generation Y (Gen Y) People born between 1978 and 1994.

Generic market A market with *broadly* similar needs—and sellers offering various and *often diverse* ways of satisfying those needs.

Generic products Products that have no brand at all other than identification of their contents and the manufacturer or intermediary.

Gross domestic product (GDP) The total market value of all goods and services provided in a country's economy in a year by both residents and nonresidents of that country.

Gross margin (gross profit) The money left to cover the expenses of selling the products and operating the business.

Gross national income (GNI) A measure that is similar to GDP, but GNI does not include income earned by foreigners who own resources in that nation.

Gross sales The total amount charged to all customers during some time period.

Heterogeneous shopping products Shopping products the customer sees as different and wants to inspect for quality and suitability.

Homogeneous shopping products Shopping products the customer sees as basically the same and wants at the lowest price.

Hypermarkets Very large stores that try to carry not only food and drug items but all goods and services that the consumer purchases *routinely* (also called *supercenters*).

Hypotheses Educated guesses about the relationships between things or about what will happen in the future.

Iceberg principle Much good information is hidden in summary data.

Ideal market exposure When a product is available widely enough to satisfy target customers' needs but not exceed them.

Implementation Putting marketing plans into operation.

Import agents Manufacturers' agents who specialize in import trade.

Import brokers Brokers who specialize in bringing together buyers and sellers from different countries.

Impulse products Products that are bought quickly as *unplanned* purchases because of a strongly felt need.

Indirect type advertising Competitive advertising that points out product advantages—to affect future buying decisions.

Individual brands Separate brand names used for each product.

Individual product A particular product within a product line.

Inelastic demand Although the quantity demanded increases if the price is decreased, the quantity demanded will not stretch enough to avoid a decrease in total revenue.

Inelastic supply The quantity supplied does not stretch much (if at all) if the price is raised.

Innovation The development and spread of new ideas, goods, and services.

Innovators The first group to adopt new products.

Installations Important capital items such as buildings, land rights, and major equipment.

Institutional advertising Advertising that tries to promote an organization's image, reputation, or ideas rather than a specific product.

Integrated marketing communications The intentional coordination of every communication from a firm to a target customer to convey a consistent and complete message.

Intensive distribution Selling a product through all responsible and suitable wholesalers or retailers who will stock or sell the product.

Intermediary Someone who specializes in trade rather than production.

Internet A system for linking computers around the world.

Intranet A system for linking computers within a company.

Introductory price dealing Temporary price cuts to speed new products into a market and get customers to try them.

Inventory The amount of goods being stored.

ISO 9000 A way for a supplier to document its quality procedures according to internationally recognized standards.

Job description A written statement of what a salesperson is expected to do.

Joint venture In international marketing, a domestic firm entering into a partnership with a foreign firm.

Jury of executive opinion Forecasting by combining the opinions of experienced executives, perhaps from marketing, production, finance, purchasing, and top management.

Just-in-time delivery Reliably getting products there *just* before the customer needs them.

Laggards Prefer to do things the way they have been done in the past and are very suspicious of new ideas; sometimes called *nonadopters*—see *adoption curve.*

Lanham Act A 1946 law that spells out what kinds of marks (including brand names) can be protected and the exact method of protecting them.

Late majority A group of adopters who are cautious about new ideas—see *adoption curve.*

Law of diminishing demand If the price of a product is raised, a smaller quantity will be demanded—and if the price of a product is lowered, a greater quantity will be demanded.

Leader pricing Setting some very low prices—real bargains—to get customers into retail stores.

Learning A change in a person's thought processes caused by prior experience.

Licensed brand A well-known brand that sellers pay a fee to use.

Licensing Selling the right to use some process, trademark, patent, or other right for a fee or royalty.

Lifestyle analysis The analysis of a person's day-to-day pattern of living as expressed in that person's Activities, Interests, and Opinions—sometimes referred to as *AIOs* or *psychographics.*

Limited-function wholesalers Merchant wholesalers that provide only *some* wholesaling functions.

Limited-line stores Stores that specialize in certain lines of related products rather than a wide assortment—sometimes called *single-line stores.*

Limited problem solving When a consumer is willing to put *some* effort into deciding the best way to satisfy a need.

Logistics The transporting, storing, and handling of goods in ways that match target customers' needs with a firm's marketing mix—both within individual firms and along a channel of distribution (i.e., another name for *physical distribution*).

Low-involvement purchases Purchases that have little importance or relevance for the customer.

Macro-marketing A social process that directs an economy's flow of goods and services from producers to consumers in a way that effectively matches supply and demand and accomplishes the objectives of society.

Magnuson-Moss Act A 1975 law requiring that producers provide a clearly written warranty if they choose to offer any warranty.

Major accounts sales force Salespeople who sell directly to large accounts such as major retail chain stores.

Management contracting The seller provides only management skills—others own the production and distribution facilities.

Manufacturer brands Brands created by producers.

Manufacturers' agents Agent wholesalers who sell similar products for several noncompeting producers for a commission on what is actually sold.

Manufacturers' sales branches Separate warehouses that producers set up away from their factories.

Marginal analysis Evaluating the change in total revenue and total cost from selling one more unit to find the most profitable price and quantity.

Marginal cost The change in total cost that results from producing one more unit.

Marginal profit Profit on the last unit sold.

Marginal revenue The change in total revenue that results from the sale of one more unit of a product.

Markdown A retail price reduction that is required because customers won't buy some item at the originally marked-up price.

Markdown ratio A tool used by many retailers to measure the efficiency of various departments and their whole business.

Market A group of potential customers with similar needs who are willing to exchange something of value with sellers offering various goods or services—that is, ways of satisfying those needs.

Market development Trying to increase sales by selling present products in new markets.

Market-directed economy The individual decisions of the many producers and consumers make the macro-level decisions for the whole economy.

Market growth A stage of the product life cycle when industry sales grow fast—but industry profits rise and then start falling.

Market information function The collection, analysis, and distribution of all the information needed to plan, carry out, and control marketing activities.

Market introduction A stage of the product life cycle when sales are low as a new idea is first introduced to a market.

Market maturity A stage of the product life cycle when industry sales level off and competition gets tougher.

Market penetration Trying to increase sales of a firm's present products in its present markets—probably through a more aggressive marketing mix.

Market potential What a whole market segment might buy.

Market segment A relatively homogeneous group of customers who will respond to a marketing mix in a similar way.

Market segmentation A two-step process of (1) *naming* broad product-markets and (2) *segmenting* these broad product-markets in order to select target markets and develop suitable marketing mixes.

Marketing The performance of activities that seek to accomplish an organization's objectives by anticipating customer or client needs and directing a flow of need-satisfying goods and services from producer to customer or client.

Marketing audit A systematic, critical, and unbiased review and appraisal of the basic objectives and policies of the marketing function and of the organization, methods, procedures, and people employed to implement the policies.

Marketing company era A time when, in addition to short-run marketing planning, marketing people develop long-range plans—sometimes five or more years ahead—and the whole company effort is guided by the marketing concept.

Marketing concept The idea that an organization should aim *all* its efforts at satisfying its *customers*—at a *profit*.

Marketing dashboard Displaying up-to-the-minute marketing data in an easy-to-read format.

Marketing department era A time when all marketing activities are brought under the control of one department to improve short-run policy planning and to try to integrate the firm's activities.

Marketing ethics The moral standards that guide marketing decisions and actions.

Marketing information system (MIS) An organized way of continually gathering, accessing, and analyzing information that marketing managers need to make ongoing decisions.

Marketing management process The process of (1) *planning* marketing activities, (2) directing the *implementation* of the plans, and (3) *controlling* these plans.

Marketing mix The controllable variables that the company puts together to satisfy a target group.

Marketing model A statement of relationships among marketing variables.

Marketing orientation Trying to carry out the marketing concept.

Marketing plan A written statement of a marketing strategy *and* the time-related details for carrying out the strategy.

Marketing program Blends all of the firm's marketing plans into one big plan.

Marketing research Procedures to develop and analyze new information to help marketing managers make decisions.

Marketing research process A five-step application of the scientific method that includes (1) defining the problem, (2) analyzing the situation, (3) getting problem-specific data, (4) interpreting the data, and (5) solving the problem.

Marketing strategy Specifies a target market and a related marketing mix.

Markup A dollar amount added to the cost of products to get the selling price.

Markup chain The sequence of markups firms use at different levels in a channel—determining the price structure in the whole channel.

Markup (percent) The percentage of selling price that is added to the cost to get the selling price.

Market research online community (MROC) An online group of participants who are joined together by a common interest, and who participate in ongoing research.

Mass customization Tailoring the principles of mass production to meet the unique needs of individual customers.

Mass marketing The typical production-oriented approach that vaguely aims at everyone with the same marketing mix.

Mass-merchandisers Large, self-service stores with many departments that emphasize soft goods (housewares, clothing, and fabrics) and staples (like health and beauty aids) and selling on lower margins to get faster turnover.

Mass-merchandising concept The idea that retailers should offer low prices to get faster turnover and greater sales volume by appealing to larger numbers.

Mass selling Communicating with large numbers of potential customers at the same time.

Merchant wholesalers Wholesalers who own (take title to) the products they sell.

Message channel The carrier of the message.

Metropolitan Statistical Area (MSA) An integrated economic and social unit with a large population nucleus.

Micro-macro dilemma What is good for some producers and consumers may not be good for society as a whole.

Mission statement Sets out the organization's basic purpose for being.

Missionary salespeople Supporting salespeople who work for producers by calling on intermediaries and their customers.

Modified rebuy The in-between process where some review of the buying situation is done—though not as much as in new-task buying or as little as in straight rebuys.

Monopolistic competition A market situation that develops when a market has (1) different (heterogeneous) products and (2) sellers who feel they do have some competition in this market.

Multichannel distribution When a producer uses several competing channels to reach the same target market—perhaps using several intermediaries in addition to selling directly.

Multiple buying influence Several people share in making a purchase decision—perhaps even top management.

Multiple target market approach Segmenting the market and choosing two or more segments, then treating each as a separate target market needing a different marketing mix.

Nationalism An emphasis on a country's interests before everything else.

Natural accounts The categories to which various costs are charged in the normal financial accounting cycle.

Natural products Products that occur in nature—such as timber, iron ore, oil, and coal.

Needs The basic forces that motivate a person to do something.

Negotiated contract buying Agreeing to a contract that allows for changes in the purchase arrangements.

Negotiated price A price that is set based on bargaining between the buyer and seller.

Net An invoice term meaning that payment for the face value of the invoice is due immediately—also see *cash discounts*.

Net profit What the company earns from its operations during a particular period.

Net sales The actual sales dollars the company receives.

New product A product that is new *in any way* for the company concerned.

New-task buying When an organization has a new need and the buyer wants a great deal of information.

New unsought products Products offering really new ideas that potential customers don't know about yet.

Noise Any distraction that reduces the effectiveness of the communication process.

Nonadopters Prefer to do things the way they have been done in the past and are very suspicious of new ideas; sometimes called *laggards*—see *adoption curve*.

Noncumulative quantity discounts Reductions in price when a customer purchases a larger quantity on an *individual order*.

Nonprice competition Aggressive action on one or more of the Ps other than Price.

North American Free Trade Agreement (NAFTA) Lays out a plan to reshape the rules of trade among the United States, Canada, and Mexico.

North American Industry Classification System (NAICS) codes Codes used to identify groups of firms in similar lines of business.

Odd-even pricing Setting prices that end in certain numbers.

Oligopoly A special market situation that develops when a market has (1) essentially homogeneous products, (2) relatively few sellers, and (3) fairly inelastic industry demand curves.

One-price policy Offering the same price to all customers who purchase products under essentially the same conditions and in the same quantities.

Open to buy A buyer has budgeted funds that he can spend during the current time period.

Operating ratios Ratios of items on the operating statement to net sales.

Operating statement A simple summary of the financial results of a company's operations over a specified period of time.

Operational decisions Short-run decisions to help implement strategies.

Opinion leader A person who influences others.

Order getters Salespeople concerned with establishing relationships with new customers and developing new business.

Order-getting Seeking possible buyers with a well-organized sales presentation designed to sell a good, service, or idea.

Order takers Salespeople who sell to regular or established customers, complete most sales transactions, and maintain relationships with their customers.

Order-taking The routine completion of sales made regularly to target customers.

Outsource When the buying organization chooses to contract with an outside firm to produce goods or services rather than producing them internally.

Packaging Promoting, protecting, and enhancing the product.

Pareto chart A graph that shows the number of times a problem cause occurs, with problem causes ordered from most frequent to least frequent.

Penetration pricing policy Trying to sell the whole market at one low price.

Perception How we gather and interpret information from the world around us.

Performance analysis Analysis that looks for exceptions or variations from planned performance.

Performance index A number that shows the relation of one value to another.

Personal needs An individual's need for personal satisfaction unrelated to what others think or do.

Personal selling Direct spoken communication between sellers and potential customers, usually in person but sometimes over the telephone or even via a video conference over the Internet.

Phony list prices Misleading prices that customers are shown to suggest that the price they are to pay has been discounted from list.

Physical distribution (PD) The transporting, storing, and handling of goods in ways that match target customers' needs with a firm's marketing mix—both within individual firms and along a channel of distribution (i.e., another name for *logistics*).

Physical distribution (PD) concept All transporting, storing, and product-handling activities of a business and a whole channel system should be coordinated as one system that seeks to minimize the cost of distribution for a given customer service level.

Physiological needs Biological needs such as the need for food, drink, rest, and sex.

Piggyback service Loading truck trailers or flatbed trailers carrying containers on railcars to provide both speed and flexibility.

Pioneering advertising Advertising that tries to develop primary demand for a product category rather than demand for a specific brand.

Place Making goods and services available in the right quantities and locations—when customers want them.

Population In marketing research, the total group you are interested in.

Portfolio management Treats alternative products, divisions, or strategic business units (SBUs) as though they are stock investments to be bought and sold using financial criteria.

Positioning An approach that refers to how customers think about proposed or present brands in a market.

Prepared sales presentation A memorized presentation that is not adapted to each individual customer.

Prestige pricing Setting a rather high price to suggest high quality or high status.

Price The amount of money that is charged for "something" of value.

Price discrimination Injuring competition by selling the same products to different buyers at different prices.

Price fixing Competitors illegally getting together to raise, lower, or stabilize prices.

Price leader A seller who sets a price that all others in the industry follow.

Price lining Setting a few price levels for a product line and then marking all items at these prices.

Primary data Information specifically collected to solve a current problem.

Primary demand Demand for the general product idea, not just the company's own brand.

Private brands Brands created by intermediaries—sometimes referred to as *dealer brands*.

Private warehouses Storing facilities owned or leased by companies for their own use.

Product The need-satisfying offering of a firm.

Product advertising Advertising that tries to sell a specific product.

Product assortment The set of all product lines and individual products that a firm sells.

Product-bundle pricing Setting one price for a set of products.

Product development Offering new or improved products for present markets.

Product liability The legal obligation of sellers to pay damages to individuals who are injured by defective or unsafe products.

Product life cycle The stages a new product idea goes through from beginning to end.

Product line A set of individual products that are closely related.

Product managers Manage specific products, often taking over the jobs formerly handled by an advertising manager—sometimes called *brand managers*.

Product-market A market with very similar needs—and sellers offering various *close substitute* ways of satisfying those needs.

Production Actually *making* goods or *performing* services.

Production capacity The ability to produce a certain quantity and quality of specific goods or services.

Production era A time when a company focuses on production of a few specific products—perhaps because few of these products are available in the market.

Production orientation Making whatever products are easy to produce and *then* trying to sell them.

Professional services Specialized services that support a firm's operations.

Profit maximization objective An objective to get as much profit as possible.

Promotion Communicating information between seller and potential buyer or others in the channel to influence attitudes and behavior.

Prospecting Following all the leads in the target market to identify potential customers.

Prototype An early sample or model built to test a concept.

Psychographics The analysis of a person's day-to-day pattern of living as expressed in that person's *A*ctivities, *I*nterests, and *O*pinions—sometimes referred to as *AIOs* or *lifestyle analysis*.

Psychological pricing Setting prices that have special appeal to target customers.

Public relations Communication with noncustomers—including labor, public interest groups, stockholders, and the government.

Public warehouses Independent storing facilities.

Publicity Any *unpaid* form of nonpersonal presentation of ideas, goods, or services.

Pulling Using promotion to get consumers to ask intermediaries for the product.

Purchase discount A reduction of the original invoice amount for some business reason.

Purchasing managers Buying specialists for their employers.

Purchasing specifications A written (or electronic) description of what the firm wants to buy.

Pure competition A market situation that develops when a market has (1) homogeneous (similar) products, (2) many buyers and sellers who have full knowledge of the market, and (3) ease of entry for buyers and sellers.

Pure subsistence economy Each family unit produces everything it consumes.

Push money (or prize money) allowances Allowances (sometimes called *PMs* or *spiffs*) given to retailers by manufacturers or wholesalers to pass on to the retailers' salesclerks for aggressively selling certain items.

Pushing Using normal promotion effort—personal selling, advertising, and sales promotion—to help sell the whole marketing mix to possible channel members.

Qualifying dimensions The dimensions that are relevant to including a customer type in a product-market.

Qualitative research Seeks in-depth, open-ended responses, not yes or no answers.

Quality A product's ability to satisfy a customer's needs or requirements.

Quantitative research Seeks structured responses that can be summarized in numbers—like percentages, averages, or other statistics.

Quantity discounts Discounts offered to encourage customers to buy in larger amounts.

Rack jobbers Merchant wholesalers that specialize in hard-to-handle assortments of products that a retailer doesn't want to manage—and they often display the products on their own wire racks.

Raw materials Unprocessed expense items—such as logs, iron ore, and wheat—that are moved to the next production process with little handling.

Real income Income that is adjusted to take out the effects of inflation on purchasing power.

Rebates Refunds to consumers after a purchase.

Receiver The target of a message in the communication process, usually a potential customer.

Reference group The people to whom an individual looks when forming attitudes about a particular topic.

Reference price The price a consumer expects to pay.

Regrouping activities Adjusting the quantities or assortments of products handled at each level in a channel of distribution.

Regularly unsought products Products that stay unsought but not unbought forever.

Reinforcement Occurs in the learning process when the consumer's response is followed by satisfaction—that is, reduction in the drive.

Reminder advertising Advertising to keep the product's name before the public.

Requisition A request to buy something.

Research proposal A plan that specifies what marketing research information will be obtained and how.

Resident buyers Independent buying agents who work in central markets for several retailer or wholesaler customers based in outlying areas or other countries.

Response An effort to satisfy a drive.

Response rate The percent of people contacted in a research sample who complete the questionnaire.

Retailing All of the activities involved in the sale of products to final consumers.

Return When a customer sends back purchased products.

Return on assets (ROA) The ratio of net profit (after taxes) to the assets used to make the net profit—multiplied by 100 to get rid of decimals.

Return on investment (ROI) Ratio of net profit (after taxes) to the investment used to make the net profit—multiplied by 100 to get rid of decimals.

Reverse channels Channels used to retrieve products that customers no longer want.

Risk taking Bearing the uncertainties that are part of the marketing process.

Robinson-Patman Act A 1936 law that makes illegal any price discrimination if it injures competition.

Routinized response behavior When consumers regularly select a particular way of satisfying a need when it occurs.

Rule for maximizing profit The highest profit is earned at the price where marginal cost is just less than or equal to marginal revenue.

Safety needs Needs concerned with protection and physical well-being.

Sale price A temporary discount from the list price.

Sales analysis A detailed breakdown of a company's sales records.

Sales decline A stage of the product life cycle when new products replace the old.

Sales era A time when a company emphasizes selling because of increased competition.

Sales forecast An estimate of how much an industry or firm hopes to sell to a market segment.

Sales managers Managers concerned with managing personal selling.

Sales-oriented objective An objective to get some level of unit sales, dollar sales, or share of market—without referring to profit.

Sales presentation A salesperson's effort to make a sale or address a customer's problem.

Sales promotion Those promotion activities—other than advertising, publicity, and personal selling—that stimulate interest, trial, or purchase by final customers or others in the channel.

Sales promotion managers Managers of their company's sales promotion effort.

Sales quota The specific sales or profit objective a salesperson is expected to achieve.

Sales territory A geographic area that is the responsibility of one salesperson or several working together.

Sample A part of the relevant population.

Scientific method A decision-making approach that focuses on being objective and orderly in *testing* ideas before accepting them.

Scrambled merchandising Retailers carrying any product lines that they think they can sell profitably.

Search engine A computer program that helps a marketing manager find information that is needed.

Seasonal discounts Discounts offered to encourage buyers to buy earlier than present demand requires.

Secondary data Information that has been collected or published already.

Segmenters Aim at one or more homogeneous segments and try to develop a different marketing mix for each segment.

Segmenting An aggregating process that clusters people with similar needs into a market segment.

Selective demand Demand for a company's own brand rather than a product category.

Selective distribution Selling through only those intermediaries who will give the product special attention.

Selective exposure Our eyes and minds seek out and notice only information that interests us.

Selective perception People screen out or modify ideas, messages, and information that conflict with previously learned attitudes and beliefs.

Selective retention People remember only what they want to remember.

Selling agents Agent wholesalers who take over the whole marketing job of producers, not just the selling function.

Selling formula approach A sales presentation that starts with a prepared presentation outline—much like the prepared approach—and leads the customer through some logical steps to a final close.

Selling function Promoting the product.

Senior citizens People over 65.

Service mark Those words, symbols, or marks that are legally registered for use by a single company to refer to a service offering.

Service wholesalers Merchant wholesalers that provide all the wholesaling functions.

Shopping products Products that a customer feels are worth the time and effort to compare with competing products.

Simple trade era A time when families traded or sold their surplus output to local distributors.

Single-line (or general-line) wholesalers Service wholesalers that carry a narrower line of merchandise than general merchandise wholesalers.

Single-line stores Stores that specialize in certain lines of related products rather than a wide assortment—sometimes called *limited-line stores.*

Single target market approach Segmenting the market and picking one of the homogeneous segments as the firm's target market.

Situation analysis An informal study of what information is already available in the problem area.

Skimming price policy Trying to sell the top of the market—the top of the demand curve—at a high price before aiming at more price-sensitive customers.

Social class A group of people who have approximately equal social position as viewed by others in the society.

Social needs Needs concerned with love, friendship, status, and esteem—things that involve a person's interaction with others.

Social responsibility A firm's obligation to improve its positive effects on society and reduce its negative effects.

Sorting Separating products into grades and qualities desired by different target markets.

Source The sender of a message.

Specialty products Consumer products that the customer really wants and makes a special effort to find.

Specialty shop A type of conventional limited-line store—usually small and with a distinct personality.

Specialty wholesalers Service wholesalers that carry a very narrow range of products and offer more information and service than other service wholesalers.

Standardization and grading Sorting products according to size and quality.

Staples Products that are bought often, routinely, and without much thought.

Statistical packages Easy-to-use computer programs that analyze data.

Status quo objectives "Don't-rock-the-*pricing*-boat" objectives.

Stock A share in the ownership of a company.

Stocking allowances Allowances given to wholesalers or retailers to get shelf space for a product—sometimes called *slotting allowances.*

Stockturn rate The number of times the average inventory is sold during a year.

Storing The marketing function of holding goods.

Storing function Holding goods until customers need them.

Straight rebuy A routine repurchase that may have been made many times before.

Strategic (management) planning The managerial process of developing and maintaining a match between an organization's resources and its market opportunities.

Substitutes Products that offer the buyer a choice.

Supercenters Very large stores that try to carry not only food and drug items, but all goods and services that the consumer purchases routinely (also called *hypermarkets*).

Supermarkets Large stores specializing in groceries—with self-service and wide assortments.

Supplies Expense items that do not become part of a finished product.

Supply chain The complete set of firms and facilities and logistics activities that are involved in procuring materials, transforming them into intermediate and finished products, and distributing them to customers.

Supply curve The quantity of products that will be supplied at various possible prices.

Supporting salespeople Salespeople who help the order-oriented salespeople but don't try to get orders themselves.

Sustainable competitive advantage A marketing mix that customers see as better than a competitor's mix and cannot be quickly or easily copied.

Sustainability The idea that it's important to meet present needs without compromising the ability of future generations to meet their own needs.

S.W.O.T. analysis Identifies and lists the firm's strengths and weaknesses and its opportunities and threats.

Target market A fairly homogeneous (similar) group of customers to whom a company wishes to appeal.

Target marketing A marketing mix is tailored to fit some specific target customers.

Target return objective A specific level of profit as an objective.

Target return pricing Pricing to cover all costs and achieve a target return.

Task method An approach to developing a budget—basing the budget on the job to be done.

Task transfer Using telecommunications to move service operations to places where there are pools of skilled workers.

Team selling Different sales reps working together on a specific account.

Technical specialists Supporting salespeople who provide technical assistance to order-oriented salespeople.

Technology The application of science to convert an economy's resources to output.

Telemarketing Using the telephone to call on customers or prospects.

Total cost The sum of total fixed and total variable costs.

Total cost approach Evaluating each possible PD system and identifying all of the costs of each alternative.

Total fixed cost The sum of those costs that are fixed in total—no matter how much is produced.

Total quality management (TQM) The philosophy that everyone in the organization is concerned about quality, throughout all of the firm's activities, to better serve customer needs.

Total variable cost The sum of those changing expenses that are closely related to output—such as expenses for parts, wages, packaging materials, outgoing freight, and sales commissions.

Trade (functional) discount A list price reduction given to channel members for the job they are going to do.

Trade-in allowance A price reduction given for used products when similar new products are bought.

Trademark Those words, symbols, or marks that are legally registered for use by a single company.

Traditional channel systems A channel in which the various channel members make little or no effort to cooperate with each other.

Transporting The marketing function of moving goods.

Transporting function The movement of goods from one place to another.

Trend extension Extends past experience to predict the future.

Truck wholesalers Wholesalers that specialize in delivering products that they stock in their own trucks.

Trust The confidence a person has in the promises or actions of another person, brand, or company.

Triple bottom line A measure of long-term success that includes an organization's economic, social, and environmental outcomes.

2/10, net 30 Allows a 2 percent discount off the face value of the invoice if the invoice is paid within 10 days.

Unfair trade practice acts Put a lower limit on prices, especially at the wholesale and retail levels.

Uniform delivered pricing Making an average freight charge to all buyers.

Universal functions of marketing Buying, selling, transporting, storing, standardizing and grading, financing, risk taking, and market information.

Universal product code (UPC) Special identifying marks for each product readable by electronic scanners.

Unsought products Products that potential customers don't yet want or know they can buy.

Validity The extent to which data measure what they are intended to measure.

Value in use pricing Setting prices that will capture some of what customers will save by substituting the firm's product for the one currently being used.

Value pricing Setting a fair price level for a marketing mix that really gives the target market superior customer value.

Vendor analysis Formal rating of suppliers on all relevant areas of performance.

Vertical integration Acquiring firms at different levels of channel activity.

Vertical marketing systems Channel systems in which the whole channel focuses on the same target market at the end of the channel.

Virtual corporation The firm is primarily a coordinator-with a good marketing concept-instead of a producer.

Voluntary chains Wholesaler-sponsored groups that work with independent retailers.

Wants Needs that are learned during a person's life.

Warranty What the seller promises about its product.

Wheel of retailing theory New types of retailers enter the market as low-status, low-margin, low-price operators and then, if successful, evolve into more conventional retailers offering more services with higher operating costs and higher prices.

Wheeler Lea Amendment Law that bans unfair or deceptive acts in commerce.

Wholesalers Firms whose main function is providing *wholesaling activities*.

Wholesaling The *activities* of those persons or establishments that sell to retailers and other merchants, or to industrial, institutional, and commercial users, but who do not sell in large amounts to final consumers.

Working capital Money to pay for short-term expenses such as employee salaries, advertising, marketing research, inventory storing costs, and what the firm owes suppliers.

Zone pricing Making an average freight charge to all buyers within specific geographic areas.